Constitutional & Administrative Law

TENTH EDITION

Hilaire Barnett

Routledge
Taylor & Francis Group

LONDON AND NEW YORK

Tenth edition published 2013
by Routledge
2 Park Square, Milton Park, Abingdon, Oxon OX14 4RN

Simultaneously published in the USA and Canada
by Routledge
711 Third Avenue, New York, NY 10017

Routledge is an imprint of the Taylor & Francis Group, an informa business

First edition published by Cavendish Publishing 1995
Ninth edition published by Routledge 2011

British Library Cataloguing in Publication Data
A catalogue record for this book is available from the British Library

Library of Congress Cataloging in Publication Data
Barnett, Hilaire.
Constitutional and administrative law / Hilaire Barnett. – Tenth edition.
pages cm
ISBN 978-0-415-62364-3 (hbk) – ISBN 978-0-415-62365-0 (pbk)   1. Constitutional
law–Great Britain.   2. Administrative law–Great Britain.   I. Title.
KD3989.B374 2013
342.41–dc23
                                                              2013001631

ISBN: 978-0-415-62365-0 (pbk)
ISBN: 978-0-203-74389-8 (ebk)

Typeset in Joanna
by RefineCatch Limited, Bungay, Suffolk

Printed and bound by CPI Group (UK) Ltd, Croydon, CR0 4YY

For Matthew and Essie, George and Amy

Outline Contents

Detailed Contents

Preface

The United Kingdom's constitution, while of ancient origins, remains both dynamic and vibrant. As every public lawyer is only too aware, nowadays, the proper boundaries of constitutional and administrative law are both increasingly wide and subject to debate. In compiling any textbook on this subject, one of the principal preliminary tasks lies in defining the scope of material to be included and the approach to be adopted in relation to that material. The task of writing is made more problematic by the many and varied depths in which, and the means by which, the subject is taught both in the United Kingdom and overseas. Full-time students, part-time students, students on long-distance learning programmes and students combining both constitutional and administrative law within a one-year course, all have differing needs. The aim in this book has been to provide sufficient detail to meet all such needs in a user-friendly manner.

As emphasised in the introductory chapters, the study of the United Kingdom's constitutional and administrative law involves rather more than a learning of rules of law, and necessarily encompasses – over and above an understanding of legal rules – an understanding of history, government, politics and conventional practices which form the foundations of the contemporary constitution. As a result, any constitutional and administrative law textbook must incorporate sufficient information relating to such matters so as to enable students to view the constitution in its historical, political and conventional context. In this book, I have addressed the subject in this manner in order to provide a rounded, contextual explanation of the United Kingdom's constitution, which goes beyond pure law while also adequately covering the law.

As previously, the text is divided into seven main parts. Part 1 provides a general introduction to the scope of constitutional law, the sources of the constitution and the structure of the United Kingdom. In Part 2, the fundamental concepts of the constitution are considered: the rule of law, separation of powers, the royal prerogative and parliamentary sovereignty. In Part 3, the European Union is discussed. The material is divided into two chapters. Chapter 7 considers the evolution, aims and structure of the Union and the principal institutions and their respective powers. In Chapter 8, the sources of European Union law and the relationship between national and European Union law are discussed.

In Part 4, the structure of government is discussed, Chapter 9 considering the role of Prime Minister, Cabinet and the Civil Service, Chapter 10 discussing the concept of responsible government and ministerial responsibility and Chapter 11 the devolution of power to the Northern Ireland Assembly, Scottish Parliament and Welsh Assembly and local government.

Part 5 is devoted to the United Kingdom Parliament: Westminster. Chapter 12 discusses the electoral system, and Chapter 13 introduces the reader to the House of Commons. Chapters 14 and 15 are devoted to parliamentary procedures for the scrutiny of legislative proposals and scrutiny of government administration. The House of Lords, its role, functions and the current reform proposals are considered in Chapter 16. Parliamentary privilege is discussed in Chapter 17.

Part 6 focuses on the individual and the state, covering civil liberties, police powers and the protection of human rights. The subject of state security is discussed in Chapter 22. Part 7 introduces administrative law. Judicial review of administrative action comprises three chapters, the first dealing with the role and scope of judicial review and procedural matters; the second and third analysing the grounds for judicial review. The role, functions and powers of Commissioners for Administration (Ombudsmen) are considered in Chapter 26, and Tribunals and Inquiries are discussed in Chapter 27.

Revising the text for a new edition always presents challenges. As with previous editions this tenth edition is published in the shadow of ongoing constitutional reform. The 2010 General Election resulted in a 'hung Parliament', with no political party winning a clear majority of seats entitling it to form a government. The formation of a coalition government between the Conservative Party and Liberal Democrat Party, which together commanded a majority of 363 (of 650) seats in Parliament (see Chapters 10 and 12), was the eventual outcome. To bolster stability, the Conservative Prime Minister announced that the agreement was intended to last for the life of the incoming Parliament, which would be for an unprecedented fixed five-year term, with the next general election scheduled for 2015. The Fixed-term Parliament Act 2011 provides for five-year fixed-term Parliaments. Further reforms agreed under the Coalition Agreement included holding a referendum on changing the voting system for general elections: this was held in May 2011, the result being a firm rejection of the proposal. The organisation of the police has been reformed, with Police Authorities replaced by elected Police and Crime Commissioners and Crime Panels. Reform has also been undertaken in relation to the parliamentary oversight of the security services and to the law relating to terrorism. The government's plans to reform the House of Lords further and to reduce the number of parliamentary constituencies from 650 to 600 by 2015 were both abandoned.

As this edition goes to print, other reforms remain to be completed. The Justice and Security Bill 2012–13 had finalised its parliamentary stages and awaited the Royal Assent. The Defamation Bill, so long awaited, was held up in part by manoeuvring in the House of Lords and the inclusion at the last minute of amendments designed to give effect to the Leveson Inquiry's recommendations for regulation of the media. While those amendments were withdrawn, at the last minute the government inserted Leveson measures into the Crime and Courts Bill. In 2012 the government's controversial Communications Data Bill was withdrawn but it is expected that it will be reintroduced in 2013.

As previously, my thanks to Fiona Briden and the team at Routledge, to Mel Dyer of RefineCatch Ltd and copyeditor Ian Howe, with whom it has been a pleasure to work. I would also like to thank all the students, past and present – both at home and, particularly, in the Far East – who over the years have deepened my understanding of the difficulties they face in studying such a rich, varied and essentially protean subject as that of the constitution of the United Kingdom. Family and all friends are again owed a large and unquantifiable debt of gratitude, not just for all their support, but also for allowing me the necessary time and solitude in which to update the text.

Hilaire Barnett
March 2013

Guide to the Interactive eTextbook and Instructor eResource

Routledge Interactive

New for the 10th Edition, *Constitutional & Administrative Law* now includes access to an Interactive eTextbook!

The enhanced electronic edition of the text, complete with hyperlinks, exercises and interactive media, is included with the paperback. This means that the full text and companion materials are always within reach – whether you're online, offline or on the go, via a wide range of devices.

Activate your eTextbook by registering at RoutledgeInteractive.com with the code inside the front cover. The access lasts for 12 months.

We at Routledge understand that studying and teaching doesn't just happen in a book any more and these interactive materials allow us to better meet the needs of students and instructors.

Interactive Timeline

This bespoke timeline will help you understand how the constitution has developed historically and how each milestone relates to the present day.

Hyperlinked Cases and Legislation

Almost 1,000 hyperlinks provide one-click access to the cases on LexisNexis™ and the statutes on the government's legislation archive.

Interactive Exercises

Found at the end of each chapter of the eTextbook, these multiple choice questions have been written to test your knowledge and understanding of each subject in the book.

Updates

Keep on track with the latest subject developments with bi-annual text updates. These will go live in the Interactive eTextbook and can be downloaded from the Instructor eResource.

| *The Student Law Review* | Access to articles on constitutional and administrative law from the online archive. |

For Instructors

Visit RoutledgeInteractive.com/instructors to learn how to share notes with your class through the Interactive eTextbook and access teaching resources such as:

Lecture Slides	Chapter-by-chapter customisable PowerPoint™ slides which can be used in seminars or lectures.
MCQs	A comprehensive bank of multiple choice questions which can be customised and adapted for formative assessment.
Diagrams	All of the diagrams from the text, ready to be integrated with your teaching.
Weblinks from the author	Download these links to save typing out citations from the text.

Routledge Interactive

Searchable. Portable. Interactive.

Table of Cases

Table of Legislation UK and International Legislation

Table of Statutory Instruments

Table of Decisions, Directives, Regulations, Treaties and Conventions

Treaties and Conventions

Part 1

General Introduction

Chapter 1

Introduction: The Scope of Constitutional Law

Introduction

Constitutional law is concerned with the role and powers of the institutions within the state and with the relationship between the citizen and the state. The constitution is a living, dynamic organism which at any point in time will reflect the moral and political values of the people it governs, and accordingly, the law of the constitution must be appreciated within the socio-political context in which it operates.

The study of the constitution of the United Kingdom involves acquiring an understanding of a variety of historical, legal, philosophical and political factors which have, over the centuries, shaped the organisation of the state. The United Kingdom appears to be almost unique in not having a constitution which is conveniently set out in a single written document. Israel and New Zealand share this constitutional feature. However, not too much weight should be given to the 'unwritten' nature of the constitution. Under all constitutions, not all of the rules will be written, and still less will they be collected within a single document.

In the United Kingdom, by contrast with most other states, the constitution is the product of many centuries of continuous and, mostly, gradual, peaceful evolution. With the exception of the constitutional turmoils of the seventeenth century,[1] the United Kingdom's constitutional development has an unbroken history dating from 1066. Accordingly, historical origins form the background for the study of the contemporary constitution, and no meaningful appreciation of the present constitution can be acquired without understanding this historical backcloth which reveals the moral and political influences that have shaped the constitution as it exists today. That said, it must always be remembered that the principal emphasis of study is on the contemporary constitution of the United Kingdom rather than on the many centuries of development which underlie it. With that point in mind, it is necessary to draw on historical sources and events with a view to understanding the contribution made to an evaluation of the many constitutional issues which present themselves today.

It is particularly true of the United Kingdom's constitution, which is more the product of evolution than conscious rational thought, that it is difficult to see clearly the demarcation lines between constitutional law, history, philosophy and political science. In order, therefore, to study the United Kingdom's constitution successfully, it is necessary to gain an insight into the history, politics and political philosophy which underpin the constitution. This task is not easy, particularly as many students will come to constitutional law without a background in history, politics or political philosophy. It is, however, an essential component of constitutional study, without which the structure, law and policies of the state cannot be understood. More than any other area of legal study except jurisprudence, constitutional law in the United Kingdom involves far more than a learning of legal rules. Indeed, it may be said, without exaggeration, that the non-legal rules and practices within the constitution are at least as important – if not more important on many occasions – as the legal rules. For example, in analysing and evaluating the extent to which the individual citizen enjoys constitutional protection of individual rights, it is necessary to appreciate the timeless and tireless quest to ensure the legal protection of the rights of individuals. This study involves, *inter alia*, an appreciation of natural law and social contract theories[2] which underpin the constitutional limitations on government power in order that the rights of individuals are protected against the power of the state.

Also, by way of example, the study of the constitutional relationship between the government and the legislature – the United Kingdom Parliament today encompasses a knowledge of the political backcloth, the rules of parliamentary practice and the non-legal or conventional

---

1   See in particular Chapters 2, 5 and 6.
2   See Chapters 3 and 18.

rules which apply in a given situation. By way of further illustration, when studying the legislative supremacy of Parliament, it is of fundamental importance to grasp that, in terms of
classical constitutional legal theory, the power of Parliament – in the absence of a written
constitution – is omnipotent or sovereign.[3] However, the constitutional and legal fact that
Parliament has the ultimate law-making power within the state does not mean that there are
no restraints on what Parliament may do. The law-making powers of Parliament, while theoretically and legally unlimited, are in fact constrained by the electorate to which Parliament is
accountable, and by economic, moral and political necessities. In terms of accountability to
the electorate and the limits which this imposes on Parliament's powers, it is necessary to
appreciate the philosophical and historical foundations of democracy and the idea of
individual rights. Notwithstanding the lack of a codified constituent document, under the
constitution of the United Kingdom, the principles on which the government operates today
are precisely those which govern the relationship between the government and the people
under a written constitution. Here, an understanding of the idea of 'social contract'[4] makes
it possible to understand the complex relationship between 'sovereign power' and the
power of the people to determine who holds that sovereign power and the manner in which
it may – and may not – be exercised.

Nowadays, the 'supremacy' of Parliament in the United Kingdom must also be considered
against the United Kingdom's membership of the European Union,[5] which has significant
implications for the classical doctrine of sovereignty. Since 1972, when the United Kingdom
acceded to the European Community (now European Union),[6] the United Kingdom has in
many respects ceased to be an autonomous, independent state and has become a member of
an ever-expanding European political, economic and legal order, the impact of which reaches
to the heart of the constitution. In legal terms, it is undeniable that the United Kingdom
Parliament could decide to withdraw from the European Union. It is, however, arguable that,
in light of the non-legal restraints – political and economic – there exists little real power to
withdraw from the Union. The non-legal restraints are in fact more important in this regard
than the simple legal rule that Parliament is sovereign in its law making powers.

To illustrate further the distinction between absolute legal power and practical power, in
terms of law, the Crown has the right to appoint the Prime Minister of its choice, to summon
Parliament and to enter into Treaties. To know these rules, however, is not to know very much,
for the legal powers of the Crown are restricted – constrained – by non-legal, 'conventional'
rules which determine the conditions under which the Crown has a discretion to exercise its
powers. In order, therefore, to understand how the constitution works, it is necessary to understand the conventional rules which have developed over time and have taken on binding force.

The Concept of Constitutionalism[7]

'Constitutionalism' is the doctrine which governs the legitimacy of government action. By
constitutionalism is meant – in relation to constitutions written and unwritten – conformity
with the broad philosophical values within a state. Constitutionalism implies something far

---

3 See Chapter 6.
4 See Chapter 3.
5 See Chapters 7 and 8.
6 The European Community forms a major part of the European Union, which came into being under the Treaty on European
   Union 1992 (the Maastricht Treaty). Under the Reform Treaty 2007, the Union shall 'replace and succeed the European
   Community'.
7 See Bogdanor, 1988, 'Introduction'; McAuslan and McEldowney, 1985, pp 11 ff.

more important than the idea of 'legality' which requires official conduct to be in accordance with pre-fixed legal rules. A power may be exercised on legal authority; however, that fact is not necessarily determinative of whether or not the action was 'constitutional'. The doctrine of constitutionalism suggests, at least, the following:

(a) that the exercise of power is kept within the legal limits conferred by Parliament – the concept of *intra vires* – and that those who exercise power are accountable to law;

(b) that the exercise of power – irrespective of legal authority – must conform to the notion of respect for the individual and the individual citizen's rights;

(c) that the powers conferred on institutions within a state – whether legislative, executive or judicial – be sufficiently dispersed between the various institutions so as to avoid the abuse of power; and

(d) that the government, in formulating policy, and the legislature, in legitimating that policy, are accountable to the electorate on whose trust power is held.

In summary, constitutionalism suggests the limitation of power,[8] the separation of powers,[9] the doctrine of responsible accountable government and the protection of individual rights and freedoms. It is against these conceptual and practical requirements that the constitution of the United Kingdom must be studied and evaluated.

What is a Constitution?

In lay terms, a constitution is a set of rules which governs an organisation. Every organisation, whether social club, trade union or nation state, which has defined objectives and departments or offices established to accomplish those objectives, needs a constitution to define the powers, rights and duties of the organisation's members. This set of rules, in addition to regulating the internal working of the organisation, will also make provision for the manner in which the organisation relates to outside bodies. It can therefore be said that a constitution looks to both internal and external regulation of the body to which it relates.

In addition to the function of allocating powers and duties and determining the relationships between the institutions of the state, a constitution fulfils two related purposes – those of definition and evaluation. In its defining function, the constitution is both descriptive and prescriptive (or normative). Differently expressed, the constitution will both define the manner in which the rules in fact operate and dictate what ought to happen in a given situation. As such, the rule or normative statement in question sets a standard of conduct or behaviour which is regarded as correct and which is expected to be adhered to by those to whom the rules are addressed. These constitutional rules – whether written or unwritten – facilitate the stability and predictability of behaviour. Further, when such normative rules exist, they provide a standard against which actual conduct can be judged or evaluated. If the accusation is made that members of an organisation have acted 'unconstitutionally', the speaker is claiming that those accused have acted in a manner which breaches the required standards of behaviour as laid down in the body of generally accepted pre-determined normative rules. In this sense, a constitutional rule, in addition to being descriptive, normative and predictive, is evaluative and judgmental.

---

8 See Chapter 3.
9 See Chapter 4.

When examining the rules of any organisation, it becomes apparent that individual rules have differing levels of importance and, moreover, that rules may have differing degrees of specificity or generality. The manner in which the rules are expressed may also differ; some may be written down, whereas some may be discernible only through observation of actual conduct. And thus it is with the constitution of a state, and particularly that of the United Kingdom, in which the sources of constitutional law are varied. The legal sources are represented by a mixture of statute and judicial precedent, and these legal sources are supplemented by the binding, non-legal, conventional rules and practices. The rules of constitutional law will also reveal differences in the manner in which they may be changed to adapt to changing circumstances. Under a written constitution, the constitution will itself define the procedure for amendment and may provide for varying degrees of ease or difficulty in amendment in relation to particular rules. The rules regarded as the most important are characterised by the greatest degree of difficulty in the process of amendment. Under the United Kingdom's constitution, by way of contrast, the manner in which constitutional change is effected will be dependent not upon clearly defined written rules but, rather, by accepted constitutional practice which has evolved over time.

Defining Constitutions

Professor KC Wheare defines the constitution of a state as:

> . . . the whole system of government of a country, the collection of rules which establish and regulate or govern the government. [1966, p 1]

An older definition, that of Thomas Paine, reveals a more complex set of ideas:

> A constitution is not the act of a government, but of a people constituting a government, and a government without a constitution is power without right . . . A constitution is a thing antecedent to a government; and a government is only the creature of a constitution. [1792, Pt II, p 93]

From this second definition, it can be discerned that a constitution is something which is prior to government, or, as Paine expresses it, 'antecedent' to government, giving legitimacy to the government and defining the powers under which a government may act. As such, the constitution sets limits both to the powers which can be exercised and to the manner in which they may be exercised. Accordingly, the constitution defines the legality of power. This notion is particularly apposite in a country with a written constitution and a Supreme Court which is conferred with jurisdiction to rule on the legality of government action. Under such a constitutional arrangement, it can be said that everything which the government does is either lawful or unlawful depending upon whether the contested conduct is held to be 'constitutional' or not. Under a largely unwritten constitution, the position is less clear-cut, and it may often be the case that conduct will be adjudged to be 'unconstitutional' and yet not be 'unlawful'. This distinction will be returned to in a subsequent discussion of the legal and non-legal sources of the constitution. At this introductory stage, it need only be noted that the unwritten nature of the United Kingdom's constitution has given rise to argument as to whether or not a constitution – as generally understood in the majority of states – exists. Sir Ivor Jennings, author of The Law and the Constitution, offers a balanced evaluation of this apparent paradox:

See Chapter 2.

If a constitution means a written document, then obviously Great Britain has no constitution. In countries where such a document exists, the word has that meaning. But the document itself merely sets out rules determining the creation and operation of governmental institutions, and obviously Great Britain has such institutions and such rules. The phrase 'British constitution' is used to describe those rules.[10]

Classifying Constitutions

When looking for the salient characteristics of the constitution, it is helpful to bear in mind the range of possible classifications which can be applied to any constitution. Professor KC Wheare identifies the following classifications (1966, Chapter 1):

(a) written and unwritten;
(b) rigid and flexible;
(c) supreme and subordinate;
(d) federal and unitary;
(e) separated powers and fused powers; and
(f) republican and monarchical.

Written and unwritten constitutions

A written constitution is one contained within a single document or a series of documents, with or without amendments, defining the basic rules of the state. The origins of written constitutions lie in the American War of Independence (1775–83) and the French Revolution (1789). More recent written constitutions derive from the grant – or devolution – of legislative power from previously imperial powers to former colonies and dominions,[11] whether secured as a result of peaceful settlement or violent revolution.[12]

As noted above, the feature which characterises all states with a written constitution is that there has been a clear historical break with a previously pertaining constitutional arrangement, thus providing the opportunity for a fresh constitutional start. As Wheare explains:

> If we investigate the origins of modern constitutions, we find that, practically without exception, they were drawn up and adopted because people wished to make a fresh start, so far as the statement of their system of government was concerned . . . The circumstances in which a break with the past and the need for a fresh start come about vary from country to country, but in almost every case in modern times, countries have a constitution for the very simple and elementary reason that they wanted, for some reason, to begin again . . . This has been the practice certainly since 1787 when the American constitution was drafted, and as the years passed, no doubt imitation and the force of example have led all countries to think it necessary to have a constitution. [1966, p 4]

---

10 Jennings, 1959b, p 36. See also McIlwain, 1958; Ridley, 1988.
11 See eg the South Africa Act 1909, the British North America Act 1867 (now the Constitution Act 1867) and the Canada Act 1982.
12 See eg the Nigeria Independence Act 1960 and the Zimbabwe Act 1979. See also de Smith, 1964, Chapter 5.

The absence of any such break in continuity in British history, from 1066 to the current time,[13] more than any other factor, explains the mainly unwritten nature of the United Kingdom's constitution.

The characterisation of constitutions into 'written' and 'unwritten' is, however, too limited, for such classification tells neither the whole constitutional story nor necessarily makes the constitution accessible to those seeking to understand it. A written constitution will provide the basic rules, but, for an understanding of the whole constitutional picture, it is also necessary to examine subsequent interpretations of the constitution contained in case law and the political practices which reveal the actual operation of the constitution. At the heart of this matter lies one simple fact: all constitutions – howsoever defined and categorised – are dynamic organisms. They are dependent for much of their meaning and relevance on the societal framework which surrounds them. Nowhere is this more apparent than in relation to individual rights and liberties. The vast majority of states have adopted both written constitutions and Bills of Rights stipulating the inviolable rights of citizens – nevertheless, the political reality for many citizens' rights around the world is very different from the formally drafted constitution. Irrespective of whether or not a state has a written constitution and a Bill of Rights, it must be recognised that the actual protection of individual rights, as with so much of the constitution, is explained not solely by reference to written rules. Regardless of the form in which rights are protected, in any society, it will be the democratic political process, political practice and norms of acceptable governmental conduct that, while not having the force of law, provide constitutional standards which determine the respect accorded to individual rights.[14] These constitutional features also establish standards against which the probity of official conduct may be measured. It is for this reason that a true understanding of constitutions and the concept of constitutionalism requires a deeper understanding than that provided for by an analysis of the formal written rules.

Rigid and flexible constitutions

This classification rests primarily on the question whether or not constitutions can be amended with ease. The framers of a written constitution, endeavouring to provide a comprehensive legal framework for the state, will naturally seek to protect its constitutional provisions from subsequent repeal or amendment. Towards this end, all or many of the rules will be 'entrenched', that is to say the constitution will stipulate stringent procedures to be followed in any attempt to amend the provision in question. As will be seen later, entrenchment may take several forms, but its central characteristic is that it either prevents, or makes difficult, amendment or repeal. By way of example, the federal Commonwealth of Australia Constitution Act of 1900 specifies the procedure to be adopted for its own alteration. An amending Bill must pass through at least one House of Parliament by a specified majority and the proposed amendment must be endorsed in a referendum which approves the measure by an overall majority in at least four of the six states.[15] Between 1900 and 1990, 42 proposals for constitutional amendment had been put forward. Of these, only eight were approved by a majority of electors nationally and a majority of electors in a majority of states. In this regard, it has been observed that 'constitutionally speaking, Australia is a frozen continent'.[16] As a further example, under the United States' constitution, constitutional amendments may be proposed either by a two-thirds

---

13 With the exception of the seventeenth century constitutional upheavals (see Chapters 5 and 6).
14 See Bogdanor, 1988.
15 Commonwealth of Australia Constitution Act 1900 (UK), s 128.
16 Sawer, 1967, p 208. See Lee, 1988.

majority of both Houses of Congress or, following a request by the legislatures of two-thirds of the states, by the convention summoned by Congress. To be accepted, the proposed amendments must then be approved by the legislatures of three-quarters of the states, or by conventions in three-quarters of the states. Between 1813 and 1913, only three amendments had been accepted; between 1913 and 1933 six amendments; and by 1951, only one further amendment.[17]

The United Kingdom's constitution, by comparison with the constitutions of the United States and Australia, represents the height of flexibility. Under the doctrine of parliamentary sovereignty examined in Chapter 6, Parliament is the supreme law-making body and can pass any law, by a simple majority vote in Parliament, on any subject matter whatsoever. Moreover, no court may hold an Act of Parliament to be void.[18] Note for now, therefore, that under the United Kingdom's constitution, no legal constraints can − under the traditional doctrine of sovereignty − fetter Parliament's powers.[19] Of particular importance in this regard is the fact that no Parliament may lay down irreversible rules regulating future legislative procedures which must be followed. The constitutional importance of this lies in flexibility. It has been argued, controversially, and continues to be argued, that the legislative supremacy of Parliament is constrained by various constitutional devices and acts of constitutional importance. However, it is significant that none of these challenges has yet succeeded in limiting Parliament's theoretical power.

The issue of flexibility, however, should not be exaggerated. That there are no legal restraints on what Parliament does, does not mean that there are no non-legal constraints. In practical terms, such 'extra-legal' constraints may be as important as legal controls. By way of illustration of the distinction between legal and non-legal constraints, Sir Ivor Jennings offers the example of Parliament passing an Act which bans smoking in the streets of Paris. As he states, there is nothing in the constitution which prevents Parliament from doing precisely that: 'If it enacts that smoking in the streets of Paris is an offence, then it is an offence' (1959b, p 170). The relevant Act so passed would be valid and recognised by the English courts. However, the Act would be totally ineffective and ignored by the courts and everyone else in France. Equally, as Jennings states, 'if Parliament enacted that all men should be women, they would be women so far as the law is concerned'. Sir Leslie Stephens, writing in the nineteenth century,[20] asks what restrains Parliament from passing an Act providing that all blue-eyed babies be put to death? The response to this question is that in legal−theoretical terms, of course Parliament could pass such a law, but in political terms, it neither could nor would do so because, ultimately, Parliament is dependent upon the support of the people.

Supreme and subordinate constitutions

This constitutional category overlaps in many respects, although not totally, with the classification into federal and unitary states. A 'supreme' constitution refers to a state in which the legislative powers of the governing body are unlimited. Conversely, a subordinate constitution is one whose powers are limited by some higher authority.[21]

---

17 See Wheare, 1963, Chapters 4 and 12.
18 *Edinburgh and Dalkeith Railway v Wauchope* (1842); **Sillars v Smith** (1982).
19 Complications arise in relation to the European Union, to be examined in Chapters 7 and 8.
20 See *The Science of Ethics*, 1882
21 See Chapter 6 for discussion in relation to New South Wales (Australia) and South Africa.

Federal and unitary constitutions

In many states, for example, the United States of America, Canada, Australia and Malaysia, there exists a division of powers between central government and the individual states or provinces which make up the federation. The powers divided between the federal government and states or provinces will be clearly set down in the constituent document. Some powers will be reserved exclusively to the federal government (most notably, such matters as defence and state security); some powers will be allocated exclusively to the regional government (such as planning and the raising of local taxation); and others will be held on the basis of partnership, powers being given to each level of government with overriding power, perhaps, reserved for central government. The common feature of all federal states is the sharing of power between centre and region – each having an area of exclusive power, other powers being shared on some defined basis. Equally common to all federations is the idea that the written constitution is sovereign over government and legislature and that their respective powers are not only defined by the constitution but are also controlled by the constitution, which will be interpreted and upheld by a Supreme Court.

The constitution of the United Kingdom presents a very different arrangement from that outlined above. The state is unitary and there is no defining written constitution controlling the powers of central government or of the United Kingdom Parliament. Instead of a written constitution, there exists a sovereign legislative body, which represents the ultimate law-making power in the state. Power is given to the Northern Ireland, Scottish and Welsh legislatures and to local government, under Acts of the United Kingdom Parliament, to fulfil defined functions such as the provision of services and raising of local revenue to finance such services. However, no power is given to the nations or to local government other than that decreed by Parliament. Regional Parliaments and assemblies and local authorities are entirely creatures of Acts of Parliament, and any power given can subsequently – subject only to political acceptability to the electorate – be withdrawn. An illustration of this point can be seen in relation to the statutory abolition of the Greater London Council and other Metropolitan Borough Councils in 1985, under the Local Government Act of that year. An example on a larger scale can be seen in the grant of limited legislative authority to the Northern Ireland Assembly under the Government of Ireland Act 1920. The law-making power given in 1920 was later revoked by the United Kingdom Parliament by the Northern Ireland Constitution Act 1973. In 1998, however, devolution of power was again on the constitutional agenda. The Northern Ireland Act 1998, Scotland Act 1998 and Government of Wales Act 1998 each involved a decentralisation of power, although ultimate sovereign power remains with the Westminster (ie the United Kingdom) Parliament.[22]

However, although the United Kingdom Parliament is legally 'sovereign', the transfer of wide-ranging law-making powers to the Northern Ireland Assembly, Scottish Parliament and the National Assembly of Wales represents a significant dispersal or diffusion of power. It is for this reason that nowadays it is less realistic than formerly to label the United Kingdom constitution 'unitary'. It is better and more accurately described as 'multi-layered'.

Separated powers and fused powers

The separation of powers is a fundamental constitutional concept which will be discussed more fully in Chapter 4. With respect to the classification of constitutions, the concept here

---

22 The Northern Ireland Act 2000 temporarily suspended the operation of the Northern Ireland Assembly and Executive. See further Chapter 11.

requires outline consideration. The doctrine is of great antiquity, dating back at least to Aristotle.[23] John Locke, Viscount Bolingbroke and Baron Montesquieu gave further expression to the idea.[24]

The essence of the doctrine is that the powers vested in the principal institutions of the state – legislature, executive and judiciary – should not be concentrated in the hands of any one institution.[25] The object of such separation is to provide checks on the exercise of power by each institution and to prevent the potential for tyranny which might otherwise exist. A constitution with clearly defined boundaries to power, and provisions restraining one institution from exercising the power of another, is one in conformity with the doctrine of separation of powers. This arrangement is most readily achievable under a written constitution, although it is arguable whether, under any constitution, a pure separation of powers is possible, or indeed desirable, a point which will be returned to later. At the other end of the spectrum of constitutional arrangements from a nearly 'pure' separation of powers is a totalitarian state or a purely monarchical state. Under such a constitution will be found a single figure, or single body, possessed with the sole power to propose and enact law, to administer the state, and both to apply and to adjudicate upon the law.

Under the largely unwritten constitution of the United Kingdom, the separation of powers is difficult to ascertain and evaluate. There is undeniably a distinct legislative body, executive, and judiciary, each exercising differing powers. On further examination, however, it will be found that, in practice, there are so many exceptions to the 'pure' doctrine that the significance of separation of powers is called into question. Suffice to say at this introductory stage that it is a doctrine which is respected under the constitution, despite many apparent anomalies.

Republican and monarchical constitutions

A republic is a state having as its figurehead a (usually) democratically elected President, answerable to the electorate and to the constitution. Presidential office is both a symbol of statehood and the repository of many powers. In the name of the state, the President will enter into treaties, make declarations of war, and represent the state on formal international and domestic occasions. Additionally, as with the President of the United States of America, the President has responsibility for proposing legislation to give effect to the political programme which gave him the mandate of the people. The President, however, has no formal power to initiate legislation, and it is the Congress of the United States which will ultimately determine the acceptability of legislative proposals. It may well be that the elected President is from a different political party than that which dominates Congress.[26] When that political situation pertains, the prospect of successful implementation of Presidential election promises is weakened, and although the President has a veto power over legislation passed by Congress, that veto can be overridden by Congress voting with a two-thirds majority.

Looking at the United Kingdom as an example of a sophisticated Western democracy based on constitutional monarchy, the position of the head of state is very different.[27] Queen Elizabeth II is the head of state, and all acts of government are undertaken in the name of the

---

23 384–323 BC; see *The Politics*.
24 Locke, 'Second treatise of civil government', 1690, Chapter XII, para 143; Bolingbroke, 1748; Montesquieu, 1748, Bk XI.
25 See Vile, 1967, Chapter IV.
26 As was the position under President Clinton (Democrat) and Congress (Republican).
27 See Chapter 9.

Crown. This statement implies that great power is accorded to the Queen. In reality, however, and with the exception of important residual powers, this is not the case. As with the President of the United States of America, the Queen is the figurehead – the symbol of nationhood – on a domestic and international level. The Crown also represents the continuity of the state. From an historical constitutional viewpoint, it matters little which leader of which political party at any one time occupies the office of Prime Minister, or whether he or she is a Labour or Conservative Prime Minister, for he or she will be exercising all powers in the Queen's name. Unlike the position of the head of state under the United States' constitution, however, the Queen is, by definition, unelected and unaccountable to the electorate in any democratic sense. The Crown enjoys enormous legal–theoretical power but little practical power, save in exceptional circumstances.

The legal powers held by the Crown are, for the most part,[28] exercised in her name by the elected government of the day. The rules which restrict the monarch's powers are for the most part non-legal. The restrictions comprise the all-important conventional rules of constitutional practice which regulate so much of the United Kingdom's constitution. Thus, for example, the Crown has the legal power to withhold royal assent from Bills passed by Parliament but, by convention, this assent will never be withheld (and has not been withheld since 1708) unless so advised by the government.

In addition to representing the symbolic figurehead, the role of the Crown may be said to be protective. The Queen, it has been said, has the power to 'warn and advise' the Prime Minister of the day.[29] Queen Elizabeth II, since her accession in 1952, has seen many Prime Ministers, both Conservative and Labour, enter and leave office. Throughout her 60-year reign, the Queen has quietly influenced government,[30] and garnered vast experience in domestic, international and particularly Commonwealth affairs. That experience represents a wealth of knowledge at the disposal of the government in power. While the role of the monarchy is a matter for contemporary debate, the continuity and longevity of monarchy remains a distinguishing feature of the United Kingdom's constitution.

Conclusion

From the discussion of classification above, some conclusions can now be reached about the characteristics of the United Kingdom's constitution. In summary, it can be said that it:

(a)   is largely unwritten in character;
(b)   is flexible in nature;
(c)   is supreme;
(d)   is formally unitary in structure, but with powers devolved to Northern Ireland, Scotland and Wales and to local government;
(e)   exhibits mainly but not completely separated powers; and
(f)   is monarchical.

Each of these features will become clearer as we examine the constitution in more detail.

---

28 See, however, Chapter 5 for discussion of the circumstances under which this theoretical power may become real power.
29 Bagehot, 1867, Chapter II.
30 See Macmillan, 1961–63; Wilson, 1971.

The Constitution in Flux

The absence of a written constitution, allied to the doctrine of parliamentary sovereignty, enables constitutional change to be brought about within the United Kingdom with the minimum of constitutional formality. The constitution has evolved in a pragmatic and gradual manner over the centuries. At the current time, however, the constitution is undergoing more major change than in previous decades. The last and greatest constitutional change occurred in 1973 when the United Kingdom joined the European Communities (now the European Union). Joining the European Union involved not only entering into an agreement which affected the economic life of the country, but also joining a unique legal order under which rights and obligations in matters regulated by the treaties are ultimately defined and enforced by the European Court of Justice. Moreover, the Treaties on European Union mark new and significant developments within the European Union in relation to economic, monetary and political union and the evolution of common policies in relation to co-operation in judicial and policing matters, home affairs and security and foreign affairs policies.

It was the general election of 1997 which presaged further significant constitutional change. The incoming Labour government had committed itself to several constitutional reforms. Devolution of limited, but nonetheless wide-ranging, law making powers to Scotland and Wales was the first issue to be addressed by the government.[31] An elected 'strategic authority' for London was also on the agenda, as was regional devolution in England. Reform of the membership of the House of Lords, the 'upper House' of the United Kingdom's bicameral Parliament, has already been effected, although the ultimate role and powers of the Lords remains to be determined. The settlement reached in April 1998 with regard to Northern Ireland culminated in devolved powers to a new Northern Ireland Assembly. The government was also committed to the better protection of rights and freedoms, and in order to achieve this objective, the Human Rights Act 1998 'incorporated' rights protected under the European Convention on Human Rights into domestic law, thereby for the first time providing a 'code' of human rights which is enforceable in the domestic courts. The Human Rights Act marks a change in perception about freedoms and rights among the British people who, by contrast with citizens living under written constitutions and Bills of Rights, have hitherto been largely unaware of their rights and freedoms.

Further reform was effected by the Constitutional Reform Act 2005, which reformed the office of Lord Chancellor, established a new Supreme Court physically separated from Parliament and provided for the House of Lords to elect its own speaker, an office formerly held by the Lord Chancellor. The Act is discussed further in Chapters 2 and 4.[32]

See Chapter 5.

In 2009 it was revealed that a number of Members of Parliament had been abusing the system of parliamentary allowances and expenses. This prompted the rapid introduction of the Parliamentary Standards Act 2009 which, for the first time, established a body outside Parliament – the Parliamentary Standards Authority – to regulate the system of pay and allowances. The Constitutional Reform and Governance Act 2010 effected further constitutional reform. This wide-ranging Act covers a number of different areas including the introduction of a statutory basis for the management of the civil service and the introduction of a new procedure for the approval (ratification) of treaties.

---

31 On devolution to Northern Ireland, Scotland and Wales, see Chapter 11.
32 In 2007 the government announced further constitutional reforms designed to strengthen the accountability of Ministers to Parliament in part through transferring a number of powers now exercised by the government under the royal prerogative. See further Chapter 5.

In 2010 a coalition government (formed of the Conservative Party and Liberal Democrat Party) was established. Included in its plans for constitutional reform were the introduction of fixed-term Parliaments, abolition of the Crown's power to dissolve Parliament and reform of the voting system for general elections. The Fixed-Term Parliaments Act 2011 achieved the first two objectives. The issue of reform of the voting system for general elections, however, was subject to a referendum of the people, who rejected the proposal by a significant majority. Reform of the organisation of the police, of parliamentary oversight of the security services and reform of the law relating to terrorism have been effected. In 2012 the Scottish government announced that it plans to hold a referendum in 2014 on the question of Scottish independence, an issue which raises profound questions about the constitutional structure of the United Kingdom. Each of these issues will be discussed in the relevant chapter.

The structure of the United Kingdom

The United Kingdom comprises the four nations of England, Northern Ireland, Scotland and Wales. The United Kingdom has a population of over 60 million, of which approximately 84 per cent live in England, three per cent in Northern Ireland, eight per cent in Scotland and five per cent in Wales.[33]

The terms United Kingdom and Great Britain are often used interchangeably. In law, however, there is a distinction. The United Kingdom – formally the United Kingdom of Great Britain and Northern Ireland – comprises the four nations. Great Britain, however, refers to Scotland, England and Wales but not Northern Ireland. The term the British Islands refers to the United Kingdom, the Channel Islands and the Isle of Man (on which see further below).

The United Kingdom comprises England, Wales, Scotland (which together comprise Great Britain) and Northern Ireland.[34] The Channel Islands and the Isle of Man, while not forming part of the United Kingdom other than for the purposes of nationality law,[35] are represented by the United Kingdom government in international affairs.

While it is correct to speak of the constitution of the United Kingdom, it should not be assumed that there is a single legal system within the constitutionally defined area. The English legal system extends to England and Wales. Scotland has its own system of private law which is distinct from English law. Equally, in Northern Ireland there exists a quite distinct legal system. Nevertheless, it is the United Kingdom Parliament (otherwise referred to as the Westminster Parliament) which has hitherto legislated for each jurisdiction, and been supreme or 'sovereign'. As noted above, change came about in 1998, with devolution of law-making powers to a Scottish Parliament, a Northern Ireland Assembly and to a Welsh Assembly.[36] Each enjoys limited legislative powers, which must be considered alongside the legislative powers which remain with Westminster. The United Kingdom will remain in being: the object of devolution is to provide more representative and accountable regional government, and to strengthen rather than undermine the union with England.[37]

The devolution of law-making powers to Northern Ireland, Scotland and Wales raises the question of the governance of England, for England alone remains without its own central

---

33 Office for National Statistics, August 2006: www.statistics.gov.uk.
34 Interpretation Act 1978, Sched 1.
35 British Nationality Act 1981, s 50(1).
36 Legislative power is conferred under the Government of Wales Act 2006.
37 Devolution is discussed in Chapter 11.

legislative body. As will be seen from Chapter 11, London now has its own form of devolved government. Plans to introduce regional assemblies in England, however, failed to attract popular support.

The United Kingdom also has a system of local government. Local government is made up of democratically elected local authorities with wide-ranging powers and responsibilities, and represents the most localised form of democratic governance. Local government pre-dates central government by many centuries. Local authorities are entirely creatures of statute: accordingly, the only powers they have are those conferred by the sovereign Westminster Parliament. Increasingly, however, the law of the European Union requires action at local authority level.

The British Islands

The United Kingdom, the Channel Islands and the Isle of Man together comprise the British Islands.[38] Accordingly, while the islands are not part of the United Kingdom, they are part of Her Majesty's dominions. Citizens of the islands are treated as citizens of the United Kingdom for the purposes of the British Nationality Act 1981.

The Channel Islands[39]

The Channel Islands comprise the islands of Jersey, Guernsey, Alderney and Sark. Historically part of the Duchy of Normandy, the Channel Islands remained in allegiance to the King of England when Normandy was lost by the English in 1204. The islands are organised under two separate Bailiwicks: the Bailiwick of Jersey and the Bailiwick of Guernsey, which includes Alderney and Sark. Each Bailiwick enjoys its own legislature, court structure and system of law. Alderney and Sark, whilst part of the Guernsey Bailiwick, enjoy a large measure of independence, having their own legislative assemblies.

The States of Jersey comprises 52 elected members and five non-elected members. The States of Guernsey comprises 61 members. Official links between the Crown and the United Kingdom government are through the Lieutenant Governor of the Bailiwicks. The legislature – the States – is headed by the Bailiff and Deputy Bailiff.

The Isle of Man

The Isle of Man became formally linked with England in 1405. From that time until 1765, it was ruled by 'Kings' or 'Lords' of Man. Under Acts of Parliament of 1765[40] and 1825,[41] the Westminster Parliament assumed, in the name of the Crown, the rights of the Lords. In 1958, under the Isle of Man Act of that year, much control over the Isle was relinquished by Westminster. The Isle enjoys full powers of self-government and has its own system of courts and law. The head of the Executive, the Lieutenant Governor of the Isle of Man, is the formal link between the local administration and the Crown and United Kingdom government. The Parliament (the Court of Tynwald) has executive and legislative functions. It comprises the Lieutenant Governor, the Legislative Council and the House of Keys. The lower

---

38 Interpretation Act 1978, s 5 and Sched 1.
39 See, inter alia, Report of the Royal Commission on the Constitution, Cmnd 5460, 1973, London: HMSO, Vol 1, Pt XI.
40 Isle of Man Purchase Act 1765.
41 Duke of Atholl's Rights, Isle of Man, Act 1825.

House – the House of Keys – has 24 members elected on a constituency basis for a five-year term of office. The Legislative Council comprises the senior Bishop, the Attorney General, a judge and seven members elected by the House of Keys.

The constitutional relationship between the islands and the United Kingdom

> The constitutional position of the islands is thus unique. In some respects, they are like miniature States with wide powers of self-government . . .[42]

See Chapter 11.

The Crown has ultimate responsibility for the islands. Under international law, the United Kingdom government is responsible both for the islands' international relations and for their defence. Where legislative measures are to extend to the islands, these are effected through the Privy Council. Acts of Parliament extend to the islands only if the statute expressly so provides, or where the Act applies to all Her Majesty's dominions 'by necessary implication'.[43] The Bailiwicks of Jersey and Guernsey do not accept that either the United Kingdom Parliament or the Queen in Council have the power to legislate for them without the consent of the local legislatures and registration in the Royal Court. Contrary to the accepted doctrine of parliamentary supremacy, the Channel Islands deny that Acts of Parliament or prerogative acts, under Orders in Council, can take effect without local registration.

The Islands and Europe

The European Union

When the United Kingdom signed the Treaty of Rome, special arrangements had to be effected for the islands.[44] Under Article 227(4) of the Treaty of Rome, the Treaty extends to all territories for which Member States have responsibility for their international relations. Were the Treaty to extend automatically to the islands, it would confer power on the institutions of the European Community (as it then was known, now the European Union) to legislate for the islands in matters such as taxation – which the United Kingdom Parliament, consistent with the convention, would have no *de facto* power to legislate. Accordingly, the islands sought special terms in relation to membership of the Community. The resulting solution was that the United Kingdom government negotiated special status for the islands in relation to the Union: the islands are part of the Union for the purpose of free movement of industrial and agricultural goods but not for the purpose of free movement of persons or taxation provisions.

The European Convention on Human Rights

While the position of the Channel Islands and the Isle of Man vis à vis the European Union is the same, the position is different in relation to the Convention. Initially, the Convention on Human Rights extended to both the Channel Islands and the Isle of Man, and nowadays it continues to apply to the Channel Islands.[45] While the Convention initially applied to the Isle

---

42 *Report of the Royal Commission on the Constitution,* Cmnd 5460, 1973, London: HMSO, Vol 1, para 1360.
43 **Sodor and Man (Bishop) v Derby (Earl)** (1751).
44 See Simmonds, 1970, 1971.
45 See **Gillow v United Kingdom** (1986).

of Man, the case of **Tyrer v United Kingdom** (1978) brought about a change. In this case, the European Court of Human Rights held that judicial birching in the Isle of Man of a juvenile amounted to degrading punishment in violation of Article 3 of the Convention. As a result, the Isle of Man government requested that the right of individual petition under the Convention be withdrawn. The United Kingdom government acceded to the request.

The European Union

The United Kingdom's membership of the European Union represents perhaps the most significant challenge to the constitution. It is no longer possible, realistically, to view the United Kingdom as an isolated constitutional entity. Rather, it must be viewed as a distinctive nation (or union of distinctive nations) within the larger Union. The aims and institutions of the Union, its law-making powers and the relationship between the law of the United Kingdom and European law will be discussed in Chapters 7 and 8.

The United Kingdom and the Commonwealth[46]
From Empire to Commonwealth

In the sixteenth and seventeenth centuries, Britain embarked on empire building, although the original expansion of British interests overseas was essentially undertaken by private commercial companies. Where territory was taken over by conquest, it became the property of the Crown.[47] Legal authority over such territories vested in the Crown and political control lay with the Privy Council.

The earliest 'revolution' against colonisation came with the American Declaration of Independence in 1776 in which Britain was deprived of 13 North American colonies. By the end of the nineteenth century, vast swathes of the world's map were 'coloured pink' – that is to say, under British power and control. The relationship between Britain and its colonies may be characterised as the movement from full British sovereignty over the territories through to increasing self-government and independence. In 1865, the Colonial Laws Validity Act was passed by the British Parliament in order to clarify the relationship between British law and colonial law and the capacity of colonial legislatures for self-regulation. While the Act confirmed self-regulating legislative capacity, it also affirmed the principle that such devolved powers were subject to the overriding sovereignty of the imperial Parliament.

In 1867, Canada became the first self-governing Dominion (a status implying equality with rather than subordination to Britain), to be followed by Australia in 1900, New Zealand in 1907, South Africa in 1910 and the Irish Free State in 1921. The recognition that the Empire was being transformed into a Commonwealth of Nations came in 1884.

The desire for formal recognition and explication of the constitutional relationship between Britain and the Dominions led to four-yearly Prime Ministerial conferences, which commenced in 1887. The Imperial Conference of 1926 adopted the Balfour Report, which defined the Dominions as:

autonomous communities within the British Empire, equal in status, in no way subordinate one to another in any aspect of their domestic or external affairs, though

---

46 See, *inter alia*, Roberts-Wray, 1966; Dale, 1983; Wheare, 1960; de Smith, 1964.
47 *Calvin's Case* (1608).

united by common allegiance to the Crown, and freely associated as members of the British Commonwealth of Nations.

The Statute of Westminster 1931 gave formal recognition to this definition. Section 2 of the Act extended the powers of Dominion legislatures to amend or repeal Acts of the United Kingdom Parliament, although this power did not extend to going against the limits on the Dominion's legislative capacity as laid down in the Acts containing that country's constitution.[48]

By the end of the Second World War in 1945, much of the remaining British power had been repossessed by its rightful owners, either through direct resistance to British rule (as in India) or by way of negotiated constitutional settlements between the British Crown and the formerly dependent territory.[49] From this time, what remained of the British Empire was transformed into a loosely defined, voluntary Commonwealth of nations, of which the British monarch represents the formal Head.[50] While the Commonwealth was originally characterised by its members' allegiance to the British Crown, the movement towards republicanism forced a change in direction for the Commonwealth. It was Indian independence that represented the catalyst for change. India had remained a Dominion under the India Act of 1935, until independence in 1947. In 1949, India's desire to become a republic and yet remain within the Commonwealth posed a novel question concerning allegiance to the British Crown. The London Declaration of 1949 revised the position and enabled India to enter as the first republican member. Heads of government also agreed, however, that members would continue to recognise the Crown as the 'symbol of their free association and thus Head of the Commonwealth', the position which still pertains.

The Commonwealth today

Unlike the European Union, the Commonwealth is undefined by legal texts; it is not established or regulated by treaty; nor do formal legal procedures regulate its intergovernmental relations. Rather, the Commonwealth is characterised by 'bonds of common origin, history and legal traditions'. The Commonwealth is made up of 54 countries,[51] ranging from monarchies – either under Queen Elizabeth II or national monarchs – to republics.[52]

Nowadays, 32 members are republics and five have national monarchies of their own, while 16 are constitutional monarchies which recognise Queen Elizabeth II as Head of State. The shared history and traditions of Britain and other Commonwealth members, including legal traditions, provides the basis for this voluntary association of states, which spans six continents and five oceans, and which operates without a formal Charter or Constitution.

The Commonwealth was defined in 1971 at the Commonwealth Heads of Government Meeting (CHOGM) as:

---

48 See *Harris v Minister of the Interior* (1952); *British Coal Corporation v R* (1935); *Ndlwana v Hofmeyer* (1937); and, further, Chapter 6. The constitutional position in relation to Canada was defined by the British North America Act 1867, which contained no amendment provisions. Accordingly, it remained for the United Kingdom Parliament to amend the Canadian Constitution. This anomalous position was resolved in 1982 by the Canada Act which 'repatriated' the Canadian Constitution. For a challenge to the Act, see *Re Amendment of the Constitution of Canada* (1982), discussed in Chapter 2.

49 The constitutional relationship between the United Kingdom Parliament and Australia was finally resolved in 1986 under the Australia Act, which severed the legislative links with Westminster and terminated appeals from the Australian courts to the Privy Council.

50 See further Dale, 1983; Roberts-Wray, 1966.

51 Nigeria's membership of the Commonwealth was suspended in 1995, as was Zimbabwe's in 2002.

52 See Appendix III, pp 793–94, for a full list of Member States.

> . . . a voluntary association of independent sovereign States, each responsible for its own policies, consulting and cooperating in the common interests of their peoples and in the promotion of international understanding and world peace.[53]

Further, at the 1971 CHOGM held in Singapore, Heads of Government issued the Declaration of Commonwealth Principles. The principles include:

(a)   the commitment to international peace in order to ensure the security and prosperity of mankind;
(b)   commitments to the liberty of the individual, irrespective of race, colour, creed or political belief and the individual's democratic right to participate in democratic political processes;
(c)   a commitment to combating racial discrimination;
(d)   an opposition to all forms of colonial domination;
(e)   a commitment to removal of disparities in wealth between nations and to raising standards of living; and
(f)   a commitment to international co-operation.

These principles were reaffirmed and extended at the Harare Commonwealth Heads of Government Meeting (CHOGM) in 1991, which declared the Commonwealth's commitment to promoting democracy, good government, human rights, the rule of law and gender equality within the context of sustainable economic and social development (the 'Harare Declaration'). Commonwealth members provide assistance to other countries in their transition to democracy by drafting legislation and reviewing electoral procedures.

In 2012 Commonwealth foreign ministers agreed on a draft Charter of the Commonwealth which requires the approval of Commonwealth Heads of Government.

The Commonwealth Secretariat

The Commonwealth is headed by a Secretary General. Under his stewardship, the Commonwealth Secretariat has been refashioned to enable it better to achieve Commonwealth objectives. The Secretariat was formed in 1965 and now has 12 separate divisions. The operational arm of the Secretariat is the Commonwealth Fund for Technical Co-operation, established in 1971, which, at the request of Commonwealth governments, provides 'technical assistance and expert advice on all issues within the Commonwealth's agenda'.

A Commonwealth Ministerial Action Group (CMAG) was established in 1995 to deal with serious or persistent violations of the Harare Declaration. Its task is to assess the nature of alleged infringements and recommend measures for collective Commonwealth action. The CMAG has authority to suspend a member country.

Appeals from Commonwealth courts to the Privy Council

The Judicial Committee of the Privy Council has jurisdiction to hear appeals from 'dependencies of the Crown'. Deriving from the royal prerogative, the jurisdiction was given statutory force under the Judicial Committee Acts of 1833 and 1844. Appeals may be with special leave

---

53 Commonwealth Declaration, 22 January 1971. CHOGMs take place every two years.

of the Privy Council, or without leave. Appeals with special leave are predominantly criminal cases. Appeals against the death penalty represent the majority of appeals.[54]

While before independence colonies had no power to abolish appeals to the Privy Council, on independence, this power arose. As a result, a majority of Commonwealth countries have abolished the right of appeal. The jurisdiction of the Judicial Committee of the Privy Council is now exercised by The Supreme Court (on which see Chapter 4).

On citizen-
ship, see the
Website.

 Further Reading

Barendt, E. (1997) 'Is There a United Kingdom Constitution?', Oxford Journal of Legal Studies, 17(1): 137.
Beatson, J. (2010) 'Reforming an Unwritten Constitution', Law Quarterly Review, 126: 48.
Bogdanor, V. and Vogenauer, S. (2008) 'Enacting a British Constitution: Some Problems', Public Law: 38.
Eleftheriadis, P. (2010) 'On Rights and Responsibilities', Public Law.
LeSueur, A. (2008) 'Gordon Brown's New Constitutional Settlement', Public Law: 21.
Loughlin, M. (2005) 'Constitutional Theory: a 25th Anniversary Essay', Oxford Journal of Legal Studies, 25: 183.
McIlwain, C.H. (1947) *Constitutionalism Ancient and Modern*, London: Cornell UP, Chapter 1.
Munro, C.R. (1999) *Studies in Constitutional Law* (2nd edn), London: Butterworths, Chapter 1.
Oliver, D. (2003) *Constitutional Reform in the United Kingdom*, Oxford: OUP.
Poole, T. (2007) 'Tilting at Windmills? Truth and Illusion in "The Political Constitution" ', Modern Law Review 70(2): 250.
Walker, D. (2002) 'The Idea of Constitutional Pluralism', Modern Law Review, 65: 317.

---

54 See *Hector v Attorney General of Antigua* (1990); *Runyowa v R* (1967); *Ong Ah Chuan v Public Prosecutor* (1981); *Riley v Attorney General of Jamaica* (1994); *Pratt v Attorney General of Jamaica* (1994); *Reckley v Minister of Public Safety (No 2)* (1996).

Chapter 2

Sources of the Constitution

Introduction

As has been seen in Chapter 1, the United Kingdom's constitution is classified as 'unwritten' or 'uncodified'. It is the result of gradual evolutionary development over centuries rather than a consciously constructed document drafted to meet the needs and aspirations of a country at a particular time and intended to remain largely unaltered in the future. As a result of this, in order to understand its content and scope it is necessary to study the various legal 'sources' which make up the constitution.

These include:

- statutes (Acts of Parliament);
- the powers of the Crown (the royal prerogative);
- the law relating to the working of Parliament (the law and custom of Parliament); and
- judicial decisions.

In addition, there are numerous non-legal, but binding, conventional rules which surround and give meaning to the legal rules of the constitution. Basic principles also form a part of the constitution, and in addition to the formal sources it is necessary to understand the concepts of:

- the Rule of Law (Chapter 3);
- Separation of Powers (Chapter 4); and
- Parliamentary Sovereignty or Supremacy (Chapter 6).

This approach is very different from that which applies to studying a written constitution where the original document – the Constitution – represents the principal document for analysis, supplemented by the judicial decisions of a Supreme Court which (usually) has the final say over the interpretation of the Constitution.

One key feature of the British constitution which results from its evolution is its flexibility. Constitutional change can be achieved with the minimum of formality with the passage of an ordinary Act of Parliament, involving no special procedures. By contrast, a written constitution is essentially one which is inflexible, with special procedures laid down for its amendment which ensure that the constitution is only altered in exceptional circumstances.

Definitional Difficulties

Defining the scope of sources which are correctly labelled 'constitutional' under an unwritten constitution is an inherently difficult exercise. Were the United Kingdom to have a written constitution, all of the rules now contained within various sources would be contained within it. By this means, a clear picture would be obtained as to those rules which the framers of the constitution regarded as being of 'constitutional importance'. In the absence of such a document, matters are less clear-cut and doubt exists as to precisely which rules – statutory, common law or conventional – are correctly defined as 'constitutional' rules. As Geoffrey Marshall explains:

> [N]o easy logical limit can be set to the labour of the constitutional lawyers . . . any branch of the law, whether it deals prima facie with finance or crime or local government, may throw up constitutional questions. [1971, p 6]

The disadvantage of such a lack of precision may be illustrated in relation to the legal protection of civil liberties and human rights before the Human Rights Act 1998. Having neither a written constitution nor a comprehensive enforceable Code, or Bill of Rights, an individual seeking to discover precisely what legal rights he or she had was obliged to scrutinise the statute book, the text of the European Convention on Human Rights and case law, both domestic and European. Furthermore, because rights protected under the European Convention on Human Rights were not enforceable before the domestic courts, the aggrieved individual had to seek a remedy by applying to the Court of Human Rights in Strasbourg – a lengthy procedure. The Human Rights Act 1998 remedied this deficiency by conferring jurisdiction on domestic courts to rule on and protect Convention rights.

In the absence of a written constitution, it is also difficult for the individual citizen to decide what is and what is not a 'constitutional' issue. As Marshall observes, all legal issues in the United Kingdom are potentially capable of being interpreted as constitutional issues. That fact is not, however, reassuring to the student of the constitution who is trying to define its scope and limits.

To illustrate this definitional difficulty, questions as to the status of many and differing statutes may be briefly examined.

Employment law

Statutes regulating relations between workers and employers define the extent to which an employee is free to withdraw his or her labour, to act in support of a dispute between him or herself and his or her employer, and to act in support of other workers in support of a dispute with employers. Such matters raise the fundamental question of the individual's right to withdraw his or her labour and the conditions under which this is lawful. Are such statutes 'constitutional' in nature?

Pornography

Also by way of illustration, in the United Kingdom, the Obscene Publications Act 1959 (as amended), an ordinary Act of Parliament having no particular 'constitutional status', provides the legal rules relating to pornographic literature. In contrast, in the United States of America, legal challenges to the availability of and access to allegedly pornographic material fall under the First Amendment to the Constitution.[1] The subject of pornography in the United States may accordingly be classified as a clearly constitutional issue, being regarded as a question of 'freedom of speech'.

Abortion

In the United Kingdom, the right to abortion is defined under the Abortion Act 1967 (as amended). In the United States of America, by contrast, the right to abortion falls under the constitutional right to privacy provisions of the constitution. The constitution of the Republic of Ireland prohibits abortion under its right-to-life provisions, and a challenge to that prohibition was launched under the guise of restrictions on equal access to information and the right to free movement to receive services under the law of the European Community.[2]

These examples are not intended to lead to an analysis of the substantive legal and constitutional issues, but rather demonstrate a very real and important point of principle. That point is that under a written constitution, a particular issue may be defined as a 'constitutional' issue. Under an unwritten constitution, matters are far less certain. Pornography and abortion are clearly regarded as constitutional matters in some jurisdictions.

---

1   *Roth v US* (1957).
2   *The Society of the Unborn Children Ireland Ltd v Grogan* (1991). See Spalin, 1992.

There are obvious limitations to the utility of merely listing statutory and common law sources of the constitution. It is, however, important at an early stage of study to be familiar with the major statutory sources of the constitution.

Legal Sources

The Magna Carta

One starting point is the Magna Carta of 1215.[3] Historically, the Magna Carta represented a formal settlement between the Crown and the barons. The Charter represented settlement of the grievances of citizens and challenged the untrammelled powers of the King. The settlement provided for freedom of the Church, and the right of merchants to be free from exorbitant taxation. Today, the document's importance lies in its declaration of the confirmation of the liberties enjoyed by 'freemen of the realm' and their future protection, and in the protection to be given to the enjoyment of these liberties by the requirement for trial by jury:

> No freeman shall be taken or imprisoned, or be disseised of his freehold, or liber-
> ties, or free customs, or be outlawed, or exiled, or any other wise destroyed; nor will
> we pass upon him, nor condemn him, but by lawful judgment of his peers, or by the
> law of the land. We will sell to no man, we will not deny or defer to any man either
> justice or right. [Holt, 1965, Chapter XXIX]

While of little legal importance today – for much of the original Magna Carta has been repealed – the document has symbolic value as an early assertion of the limits of monarchical power and the rights of individuals.

The Petition of Right 1628

The Petition of Right 1628 arose as a result of **Darnel's Case** (the **Five Knights' Case**) (1627), where the defendants had been convicted and imprisoned for refusing to pay a loan imposed by King Charles I. The Petition forbade such loans, taxes and other monetary demands without the consent of Parliament. The Petition, while still in force, was superseded by the Bill of Rights 1689.

The Bill of Rights 1689

The background

The Bill of Rights 1689 is of greater contemporary constitutional importance than the Magna Carta and the Petition of Right. The source of the Bill of Rights lies, in large measure, in the tensions between Roman Catholicism and the state, originating with the conflict between the Holy See of Rome and Henry VIII (1509–47). The Succession Act, Act of Supremacy and the Treason Act 1534 had established the supremacy of the King as head of the Church of England and destroyed formal papal authority in England. Catholicism did not die out, but over the next 150 years, suspicion and fear of 'popery' remained high at a public level. The death of Charles II in 1685 heralded the succession of James II, an avowed Roman Catholic, who nevertheless publicly declared himself bound 'to preserve this government both in Church and state as it is now by law established'.[4] Despite such assurances, in subsequent years

---

3   Magna Carta, Statute 25 Edw I (1297). See Holt, 1965.
4   Quoted in Lockyer, 1985, p 351.

James II strove to remove discrimination against Catholics and to place Catholics in prominent public administrative offices at both central and local level. Prominent Anglicans, dismayed by James's promotion of Catholicism, entered into negotiations with William of Orange, the Protestant husband of James's daughter Mary, with a view to their seizing the throne. In the absence of a male heir, Mary was next in line to the English Crown. However, in 1688, James's wife gave birth to a son, thus providing a Catholic heir. In July of that year, James dissolved Parliament. William of Orange landed in England with his army on 5 November 1688 and James II fled the country, landing in France in December 1688.

William and Mary's accession was not to be unconditional.[5] The Declaration of Right sought to resolve the actual and potential tensions between Crown and Parliament, Church and state. The terms of the Bill of Rights marked a sharp alteration in the balance of power between Crown and Parliament – in Parliament's favour.[6]

The major provisions of the Bill of Rights

The principal provisions of contemporary importance are:

Article I the pretended power of suspending … or executing laws by the Crown without parliamentary consent is illegal;

Article IV the levying of money for use of the Crown under the prerogative without parliamentary consent is illegal;

Article VI the raising or keeping of an army in peacetime without parliamentary consent is illegal;

Article VIII elections of Members of Parliament ought to be free;

Article IX freedom of speech and debates in proceedings in Parliament ought not to be impeached or questioned in any court or place out of Parliament;

Article X excessive bail ought not to be required, nor excessive fines imposed, nor cruel and unusual punishments inflicted;

Article XI jury trial is available; and

Article XIII for the redress of grievances, Parliament ought to meet frequently.

Subsequent to the Bill of Rights – and to give effect to its provisions – the Crown and Parliament Recognition Act 1689 gave statutory force to the Bill of Rights, and the Meeting of Parliament Act 1694 provided that Parliament must be summoned to meet at least once in three years.

The Act of Settlement 1700

The Act of Settlement 1700 clarified the line of succession to the throne. The Act also provided for security of tenure for the judiciary 'during good behaviour',[7] thus ending the power of the Crown to dismiss judges at will. In relation to succession to the throne, the Act tied the succession to Protestant heirs, thus prohibiting accession to the throne by persons who are Roman Catholics, or who marry a Roman Catholic.

The Treaty of Union 1706

The Treaty of Union also has enduring constitutional effect. The Treaty united England and Scotland under a single Parliament of Great Britain. Prior to the Treaty, each country enjoyed

---

5   As had been that of Charles II in 1660.
6   In Scotland, the Claim of Right 1689.
7   On the independence of the judiciary, see Chapter 4.

independent sovereign status. Scotland had its own Parliament and its own system of private law. Decades earlier, James VI, King of Scotland and subsequently King of England (as James I (1603–25)), had attempted but failed to bring about a union between Scotland and England. By the late seventeenth century, negotiations were continuing with a view to ending the historical conflicts between the two countries,[8] and the Treaty of Union represented the culmination of this process. See further Chapter 6.

The major provisions of the Treaty of Union 1706

For current purposes, the most important provisions are as follows:

Article I	that the two kingdoms of England and Scotland shall be united in one kingdom by the name of Great Britain;
Article II	that succession to the united throne be according to the Act of Settlement 1700;
Article III	that there be a single Parliament;
Article XVIII	that no alteration be made in laws which concern Scottish private rights except for the evident utility of the subjects; and
Article XIX	that the Court of Session in Scotland remain 'in all time being as now constituted', and that lower courts remain subject to alteration in their powers by Parliament.

The European Communities Act 1972

The European Communities Act 1972, as amended, together with the European Treaties, regulates the United Kingdom's membership of the European Union and continues to have immense significance for the constitution of the United Kingdom (see Chapters 7 and 8 and, further, below). The law of the European Union (EU) represents an increasingly significant source of constitutional law. By acceding to the European Community (now the European Union), the United Kingdom has undertaken the obligation to accept the law of the Union. To understand the constitutional implications of membership of the European Union, it is necessary to understand the scope of the Treaties and the law-making institutions, and the manner in which laws are made and enter into force within the legal systems of the Member States. It is also necessary to understand clearly the relationship between European law and domestic law and the question of which law has supremacy should a conflict between them arise. Under the traditional doctrine of parliamentary sovereignty, the United Kingdom Parliament alone has sovereign law-making power. The perception of the European Court of Justice – the highest court of the European Union – is much different. As will be seen, the European Court has long asserted the supremacy of EU law[9] over the laws of Member States, thus providing a fertile source for constitutional speculation about Parliament's sovereignty.

Acts establishing devolution

The Acts establishing a Scottish Parliament and Welsh Assembly and re-establishing a Northern Ireland Assembly have decentralised the process of government and law making, giving greater national autonomy to Northern Ireland, Scotland and Wales.

---

8 For a succinct account of the history, see Maitland, 1908, pp 331–32.
9 *Costa v ENEL* (1964).

The Human Rights Act 1998

The Human Rights Act 1998, which incorporates the rights enshrined in the European Convention on Human Rights and Freedoms into domestic law, represents a fundamental change in the domestic protection of rights. The impact of the Human Rights Act 1998 has been felt across wide areas of domestic law and provides citizens for the first time with a code of rights which are enforceable in the domestic courts rather than in the European Court of Human Rights in Strasbourg.

The Constitutional Reform Act 2005

The Constitutional Reform Act 2005 introduced changes in three principal areas. The Act reformed the office of Lord Chancellor, transferring his powers as head of the judiciary to the Lord Chief Justice and providing for the House of Lords to elect its own speaker. In addition the Appellate Committee of the House of Lords – formerly the highest domestic court in the United Kingdom – has been replaced by a Supreme Court which is physically separate from Parliament.

Further illustrations

Further statutes of major constitutional importance – and the list is by no means exhaustive – include the following:

(a) Acts extending and regulating elections and the right to vote (the franchise);[10]

(b) the Statute of Westminster 1931 gave statutory force to the conventions regulating relations between the sovereign United Kingdom Parliament and legislatures of the Dominions;

(c) His Majesty's Declaration of Abdication Act 1936 varied the succession to the throne established under the Act of Settlement 1700;

(d) the Regency Acts 1937–53 provided that if the Sovereign is under the age of 18, regal powers shall be exercised through a Regent appointed under the Acts;

(e) the Royal Titles Act 1953, which founded a challenge from Scottish lawyers to its compatibility with the Act of Union,[11] provided that the Sovereign may by Proclamation adopt such a style and titles as she may think fit;

(f) the Treaty of Union with Ireland Act 1800, the Government of Ireland Act 1920, the Ireland Act 1949 and the Northern Ireland Constitution Act 1973 have all reflected the changing constitutional relationship between Ireland, Northern Ireland and the United Kingdom;

(g) the Representation of the People Acts from 1832 to the present date, setting out the right to vote and the law relating to elections;

(h) the Parliament Acts 1911 and 1949 restricting the powers of the House of Lords in relation to legislation. The House of Lords Act 1999 reforming the membership of the House of Lords;

(i) the Acts devolving power to national Assemblies: the Northern Ireland Act 1998, the Scotland Act 1998 and 2012, the Government of Wales Act 1998 and 2006;

(j) the Parliamentary Standards Act 2009, the Constitutional Reform and Governance Act 2010, the Parliamentary Voting System and Constituencies Act 2011 and the Fixed-term Parliaments Act 2011;

---

10 1832, 1867, 1884, 1918, 1928, 1948, 1969, 1983, 2000, 2006.
11 **MacCormick v Lord Advocate** (1953). See further Chapter 6.

(k)   the Equality Act 2010 consolidating the law relating to freedom from discrimination;
(l)   the Localism Act 2011 reforming the structure and powers of local government;
(m) the Police Reform and Social Responsibility Act 2011 introducing elected Police and
      Crime Commissioners.

The Royal Prerogative

The prerogative powers of the Crown are those powers which arise out of the common law
and which are unique to the Crown. Two definitions may be given by way of introduction. To
Dicey, the prerogative powers were 'the residue of arbitrary and discretionary powers legally
left in the hands of the Crown' which, being exercised by the government in the name of the
Crown, entails 'every act which the executive government can do without the authority of an
Act of Parliament' (1885, p 425).

Blackstone, in his *Commentaries*, offers a more limited definition:

> . . . that special pre-eminence which the King hath over and above all persons, and
> out of the ordinary course of the common law . . . And . . . only applied to those rights
> and capacities which the King enjoys in contradistinction to others.

The prerogative will be discussed in detail in Chapter 5.

Judicial decisions

Throughout history, the judiciary has, through case law, defined the relationship between the
institutions of the state – the Crown, the executive, Parliament and the judiciary – and defined the
relationship between the state and the individual. As with statutory sources of the constitution,
the study of constitutional and administrative law concerns the examination and analysis of judicial precedents. The judiciary today has no power to question the validity of an Act of Parliament.[12]
However, whilst Acts of Parliament are unchallengeable as to their validity, delegated or secondary
legislation is not immune from such review. Furthermore, the judges have the power to review
the legality of acts of persons and organisations acting under powers conferred by Act of Parliament
in order to ensure that they act within (*intra vires*) the powers conferred by Parliament.

The extent to which judges have been able to protect individual rights under the common
law – in the light of Parliament's supremacy – has been limited. Traditionally, the United
Kingdom had no Bill of Rights in so far as such a document provides a written source of
protection for certain fundamental rights and freedoms. In the absence of such guaranteed
protection – protection which would prevail even against an Act of Parliament – the citizen
remained dependent either upon ad hoc statutory provisions – such as the Habeas Corpus Acts
(1679, 1816, 1862), the Race Relations Act 1976 or the Sex Discrimination Act 1975 – or
upon judicial protection under the common law (see Chapters 18–21). By way of introductory illustration, the contrasting cases of **Entick v Carrington** (1765) and **Liversidge v Anderson**
(1942) may be cited. In the former case, the court ruled that a general warrant issued by a
Home Secretary for the entry into private property and seizure of allegedly seditious material
was contrary to law and amounted to a trespass to property. This bold assertion of judicial
power to rule on the legality of acts of the executive and to control such acts is in stark contrast
to the ruling in **Liversidge v Anderson**. Here, in the context of a challenge to the legality of

---

12 **Edinburgh and Dalkeith Railway v Wauchope** (1842); **Pickin v British Railways Board** (1974). But see Chapters 6 and 8 on the position in
   relation to the law of the European Union.

detention without warrant under the order of the Home Secretary, the House of Lords held that the courts could not, in times of emergency, review the Home Secretary's belief that detention was justified. Such conflicting outcomes demonstrate that reliance on judicial protection from executive action, under common law, is by no means certain, let alone guaranteed. The Human Rights Act 1998, however, now enables citizens to challenge the legality of government action against the provisions of the Convention. As will be discussed in Chapter 18, the Act does not empower the courts to challenge the validity of Acts of Parliament, but rather preserves Parliament's traditional sovereignty by empowering the courts to make declarations of incompatibility between a statute and Convention requirements. Thereafter, it is for the government and Parliament to change the law if it wishes to comply with the Convention requirements.

Non-Legal Sources of the Constitution

Constitutional conventions

> The short explanation of the constitutional conventions is that they provide the flesh which clothes the dry bones of the law; they make the legal constitution work; they keep it in touch with the growth of ideas.[13]

Constitutional conventions form the most significant class of non-legal constitutional rules.[14] A clear understanding of their nature, scope and manner of application is essential to the study of the United Kingdom's constitution. Conventions supplement the legal rules of the constitution and define the practices of the constitution. Conventions, as Jennings states, 'provide the flesh which clothes the dry bones of the law' and represent the 'unwritten maxims' of the constitution. Conventions apply to virtually all aspects of the constitution, and for this reason it is, in part, unrealistic and unsatisfactory to attempt adequately to consider their role in a 'vacuum'. Nevertheless, given their central importance, conventions must be considered at this early stage, while bearing in mind that many and varied further illustrations will emerge throughout the course of study.

Conventions defined

Conventions are defined by AV Dicey as:

> ... conventions, understandings, habits or practices which, though they may regulate the ... conduct of the several members of the sovereign power ... are not in reality laws at all since they are not enforced by the courts. [1885, p clii]

Marshall and Moodie offer an alternative definition:

> ... rules of constitutional behaviour which are considered to be binding by and upon those who operate the constitution but which are not enforced by the law courts ... nor by the presiding officers in the Houses of Parliament. [1971, pp 23–24]

A number of important questions arise concerning these non-legal rules, namely:

(a) what are the characteristics of a conventional rule?
(b) what is the source or origin of the rule?

---

13 Jennings, 1959a, pp 81–82.
14 See, *inter alia*, Dicey, 1885, Chapter 14; Jennings, 1959a, Chapter 3; Marshall and Moodie, 1971, Chapter 2; Marshall, 1984, esp Chapters 1 and 13; Munro, 1999, Chapter 3.

(c)   in what manner are conventions distinguishable from laws?
(d)   who is bound by the conventional rules?
(e)   what is the consequence of a breach of the rule?
(f)   does the distinction between law and convention really matter?
(g)   what is the attitude of the courts to conventional rules?
(h)   how do conventions change?
(i)   how best can these rules be analysed and understood?
(j)   should conventions be codified?

Each of these questions, many of which overlap, must be addressed and answered.

Conventions illustrated

Before turning attention to the task of further analysis, some examples of constitutional conventions will aid understanding. Each of these conventions will be discussed in greater detail later in this book.

(a)   Acts of Parliament are technically enacted by the Queen in Parliament – the Crown, Commons and Lords. The Queen has the legal right to refuse to give royal assent to Bills passed by the House of Commons and Lords. By convention, the Queen must assent to such Bills unless advised to the contrary by her government (Chapter 5).
(b)   The Queen will appoint as Prime Minister the leader of the political party with the majority of seats in the House of Commons (Chapter 5).
(c)   The Prime Minister must be a member of the House of Commons (Chapter 5).
(d)   The government must maintain the confidence of the House of Commons. If a 'vote of confidence' on a matter central to government policy is lost, the government must resign (Chapter 5).
(e)   Ministers of the Crown are individually and collectively responsible to Parliament (Chapter 10).
(f)   Ministers must be members of either the House of Commons or the House of Lords (Chapter 9).
(g)   Parliament must be summoned to meet at least once a year (Chapter 13).
(h)   Judges shall not play an active part in political life (Chapter 4).
(i)   Members of Parliament shall not criticise the judiciary (Chapter 4).
(j)   The opinion of the law officers of the Crown is confidential (Chapter 10).

This list is not intended to be exhaustive, but is sufficient to give a flavour of the nature and scope of constitutional conventions.

The binding nature of conventions

The characteristics of conventions are suggested both by Dicey and by Marshall and Moodie. The latter authors correctly introduce the concept of a 'rule', and it is this concept which is central to our understanding and which requires further analysis. What is a rule? A rule may be defined as a statement prescribing the conduct which is required in a given situation and which imposes an obligation on those who are regulated by the rule.[15] The idea of obligation is of prime importance here, for if a person is under an obligation which is recognised by observers of the constitution, and that person fails to act in accordance with the obligation,

---

15 Hart, 1961, pp 79–88.

then that failure will give rise to legitimate criticism which will invariably be phrased in terms of 'constitutionality'. To reiterate, the obligation imposes a standard of conduct which is expected to be followed. The obligation is 'normative' or 'prescriptive' – that is, it dictates the appropriate form of action in a particular situation. As Sir Ivor Jennings states, conventions 'not only are followed but have to be followed' (1959a, p 2).

Dicey's definition suggests that conventions are of the same quality as 'understandings, habits or practices'. This view is inaccurate in so far as none of these words conveys the idea of obligation – the normative (or prescriptive) – the idea of what ought to be done in particular circumstances.

Conventions distinguished from habits

Conventions are conceptually different from 'habits' or 'practices' in that these concepts do not prescribe or dictate what ought to happen but are merely descriptive of what in fact does happen. To offer a simple but possibly outdated example, consider the statement that 'the English drink tea in the afternoon'. Drinking tea is a habit: the statement is simply reflective of actual observable conduct. There is nothing in the statement which requires that conduct, or which states that it ought to happen. Accordingly, it is a descriptive and not a normative state-ment. If the English fail to drink tea in the afternoon, or drink coffee instead, that action is not going to give rise to any criticism because a mere habit imposes no obligation. The observation is a statement of what 'is', and not what 'ought to be'. There is no obligation imposed on the English to drink tea and hence no criticism will follow from failure to do so. It is very different with a breach of a constitutional convention, which will invariably give rise to adverse criti-cism. Conventions are thus distinguishable from habits.

Conventions distinguished from understandings

To what extent is Dicey correct in equating conventions with 'understandings'? Once more, it is helpful to resort to definitions. The word 'understanding' connotes a mutual agreement between relevant actors as to the pertinent subject matter, or the manner in which it is appro-priate to respond or react to a given situation. As such, any understanding rests on a meeting of minds, and is capable of being the subject of misunderstanding, as in cases where the actors, through a lack of understanding of the situation (or as a result of a differing interpretation of the situation), fail to be 'of one mind'. An 'understanding' may well be relied on by the parties, as are conventions. Understandings may also be brought about by some form of previous, or precedent, conduct or mutual recognition: but this is not a prerequisite for their existence or nature. Most importantly, an understanding, while imposing some weak form of moral obliga-tion will not, in the case of failure to comply with its terms, give rise to a sanction in the form of criticism of the same magnitude as that of a breach of a constitutional convention. The explanation for this lies in the fact that an understanding – as opposed to a convention – does not amount to a rule, and accordingly is not obligation-imposing to the same degree as a convention.

Conventions distinguished from practices

The concept of a practice remains for consideration. A practice may be defined as being 'a usual or customary action or proceeding'.[16] A practice, therefore, is the normal manner in which a person or body will react to a factual situation on the basis of some precedent form of conduct. In everyday life – whether in commercial offices or in the professions of medicine or law – it

---

16 Collins English Dictionary.

is a commonplace assertion that 'it is our practice to do . . .'. That statement conveys the message that past experience of doing something in a particular way is the correct way of proceeding, and that – unless there are justifiable reasons for not so doing – the practice will be adhered to. A practice, therefore, may be distinguished from a mere habit on the basis that it imports a notion of reflectiveness, the idea of the 'right' way of reacting to a situation. How, then, is a practice distinguishable from a convention? The borderline between the two is admittedly fine. It may be, however, that the correct dividing line is drawn on the basis of the concept of obligation and rule, and that it is legitimate to argue that whilst a practice imposes some form of weak obligation – and requires some justification for departure from the practice – the practice is no more than an emergent or potential convention and has not yet acquired the binding characteristic of a rule.

Conventions distinguished from laws

Conventions are distinguishable from laws in a number of important respects. First, the source of a legal rule is, for the most part, identifiable and certain. In searching for a legal rule, its source will normally be found within a judicial decision or within an Act of Parliament. Conventions are far less certain in their origins, and it may at times be difficult to see whether a particular form of conduct is, for example, one of practice or convention. Secondly, the core content of a legal rule will generally have a settled meaning.[17] Conventions, however, are again less certain and the obligations imposed by a convention may be varied – as illustrated by the discussion of collective ministerial responsibility below.

The foregoing discussion can be presented – albeit with recognition of overlaps between, and ambiguities in, the concepts – in the tabular form below:

	Habits	Understandings	Practices	Conventions	Laws
Regularity of Conduct	yes	not necessarily	yes	yes	yes
Reflectiveness	no	yes	yes	yes	yes
Degree of obligation imposed	none	weak	strong	theoretically absolute	absolute
Sanction attending breach	none	justification required	justification required	charge of unconstitutional conduct	unlawful conduct

Summary of the meaning of constitutional conventions

A constitutional convention is a non-legal rule which imposes an obligation on those bound by the convention, breach or violation of which will give rise to legitimate criticism; and that criticism will generally take the form of an accusation of 'unconstitutional conduct'.

The source of conventions

The question concerning the source of the constitutional convention is in part interwoven with the characteristics of the convention. A conventional rule may be said to exist when a

---

17 See the analysis of a rule in HLA Hart, *The Concept of Law*, Chapter 7.

traditional practice has been consciously adopted and recognised by those who operate the constitution as the correct manner in which to act in a given circumstance. A practice will be seen to have become a convention at the point at which failure to act in accordance with it gives rise to legitimate criticism.

Sir Ivor Jennings once suggested that three questions must be asked in order to determine whether a convention exists. First, are there any precedents for the convention? 'Mere practice,' he tells us, 'is not enough. The fact that an authority has always behaved in a certain way is no warrant for saying that it ought to behave in that way.' What more, then, is required? According to Jennings, that turns on the normativity of the practice:

> . . . if the authority itself and those connected with it believe that they ought to do so
> [behave in a certain way], then the convention does exist . . . Practice alone is not
> enough. It must be normative. [1959a, p 135]

Finally, Jennings argues that neither practice nor precedent is sufficient. In addition, there must be a reason for the rule: '. . . the creation of a convention must be due to the reason of the thing because it accords with the prevailing political philosophy.'

The effects of breaching constitutional conventions

The question of consequences that flow from a breach of a conventional rule constitutes both a simple and a complex issue. If – as a starting point for discussion – the consequence of breaking a rule of law is examined, two basic points must be recognised. The first point is that a breach of law normally, but not invariably, leads to enforcement of the rule by the courts. The second point is that when a rule of law is breached, the rule remains valid and in force, unless repealed by Parliament or overruled by the judges. With conventional rules, the situation is very different. Being non-legal rules, there is no question of a breach of convention being enforced by the courts: the courts do not have the jurisdiction to enforce conventional rules, although they may give recognition to them.[18] However, it is also the case, as Dicey argued, that breach of a convention may lead to a breach of law. The most often cited example offered is that if Parliament, in breach of convention, did not meet annually, the consequence would be that money granted on an annual basis by Parliament for the maintenance of the armed forces would not be forthcoming. Accordingly, maintenance of the army would become unlawful by virtue of Article VI of the Bill of Rights 1689, which provides that the raising and keeping of an army in peacetime, without Parliament's consent, is unlawful. Such consequences are the exception. For the most part, the consequence of violating a conventional rule is political rather than legal.

That said, it is not possible to offer a single consequence. Much will turn on the particular convention 'broken', the extent of the 'breach' and the political mood of the country at the time. Conventions are obeyed because of the potential political difficulties which would arise if a firmly established convention was departed from without constitutional justification.

Two introductory illustrations of the very differing effects of breaching conventional rules are provided by the doctrine of collective ministerial responsibility and the House of Lords.[19]

---

18 *Attorney General v Jonathan Cape Ltd* (1976); *Manuel v Attorney General* (1983).
19 Discussed more fully in Chapters 10 and 16, respectively.

Collective ministerial responsibility

The doctrine of collective ministerial responsibility provides an example of the uncertainties entailed in the scope and binding nature of conventional rules. The convention of collective ministerial responsibility has two main elements. The first is that when a decision has been reached in Cabinet (the highest decision-making body of government) that decision is binding on all government ministers who must – irrespective of their personal feelings about the matter – support the decision in public. The second rule is that Cabinet discussions are absolutely confidential and may never be disclosed without prime ministerial authority. In two situations the doctrine has been 'waived' in order to respond effectively to political circumstances. In 1932, a coalition government was in office.[20] Following Cabinet disagreements over economic policy, the government adopted an 'agreement to differ', whereby members of Cabinet were free to express their divergent views both in Parliament and in public. Within months, the dissident members resigned from the Cabinet and collective responsibility was reinstated. In 1975, the Labour government was divided as to the benefits of continued membership of the European Community. It was decided that the matter should be put to the electorate in a referendum. The Cabinet itself was deeply divided on the question and the Prime Minister decided to 'lift' the convention of collective responsibility in order to facilitate full and free public debate. Thus, a convention was set aside for a particular purpose, for a defined period of time and for a specific matter. A similar situation arose in 2010. The general election resulted in the first coalition government in nearly 70 years (between the Conservative Party and Liberal Democrat Party). Policy differences between the two parties have necessitated an agreement to differ over a range of issues, without which conflict in Cabinet would occur and the stability of government would be threatened. Above all, these situations demonstrate the point that conventions can be adjusted, under certain circumstances which are undefined, to suit the exigencies of a particular situation.

The House of Lords 1908–10

A very different consequence followed a breach of convention by the House of Lords between 1908 and 1910.[21] Prior to the Parliament Act 1911, one major conventional rule regulated the relationship between the House of Lords and the House of Commons in legislative matters and most particularly in financial matters: namely, that the Lords would ultimately give way to the will of the elected House. This convention broke down in 1908 when the House of Lords rejected the Finance Bill of the Commons. After a deadlock between the two Houses, and a threat by the King to 'flood' the House of Lords with sufficient new peers to secure a majority for the Bill, the government introduced the Parliament Bill 1911. The Parliament Act, which will be looked at in detail in Chapter 16, provided that the House of Lords would no longer enjoy equal powers to approve or reject legislative proposals and that its power would be restricted to a power to delay legislation subject to strict time limits.[22] It can be seen from this that where the breach of a convention is deemed to be sufficiently grave, Parliament can – in the exercise of its sovereign power – place a convention on a statutory basis.

See Chapters 10 and 16.

Further illustrations will present themselves throughout the course of this book: conventional rules are of such fundamental importance that they regulate virtually every aspect of constitutional law. The main point to be understood here is that breaches of conventions have no automatic or defined ramifications.

See Chapter 16.

---

20 See Marshall, 1984, Chapter 4; and see further Chapter 10.
21 See Jennings, 1969, Chapter 12.4.
22 Money Bills, one month; non-Money Bills, two years over three parliamentary sessions.

The differing importance of individual conventions

A related factor which should also be understood is that not all conventions are of equal certainty or importance, and it is in part for this reason that the consequences of a breach will vary. For example, in legal terms, the right to assent or to refuse to assent to Bills passed by Parliament rests with the Crown. However, by convention, the Crown must assent to Bills passed by Parliament whenever so advised by the Prime Minister. So settled is the convention that the Crown must assent to Bills passed by Parliament that it is difficult to foresee circumstances under which it would be broken.[23] Perhaps a political situation could present itself where a Bill had been duly passed by Parliament and where the government had a change of heart and, despite parliamentary opposition, refused to present the Bill for assent. Would this represent a breach of convention? Arguably not, for the convention requires that the monarch give assent on the advice of her government. A situation such as this would undoubtedly cause a political furore; but it is doubtful that it would represent unconstitutional conduct on the part of the government, and still less so by the Crown. It could also be asked, speculatively, what the position would be if a Bill was duly passed by Parliament, the Bill was presented for royal assent and was refused on the basis that public opinion was so firmly set against the Bill that to assent would amount to defeating the rights of the electorate. Such a situation raises some fundamental questions about democracy and the relationship between the electorate and the elected government. Geoffrey Marshall questions whether the power to refuse assent to legislation is 'now a dead letter', and states that, 'under present constitutional arrangements, it may well be so' (1984, p 22), while recognising that the issue is not closed.

At the other end of the spectrum of the certainty of conventions and their meaning is the doctrine of individual ministerial responsibility. In essence, individual ministerial responsibility requires that ministers of the Crown are accountable to Parliament, and through Parliament to the electorate, for their personal conduct and for the conduct of their departments.[24] The doctrine is expressed in practical terms at Parliamentary Question Time, in debates, and in committee proceedings, whereby Parliament ensures that ministers explain and, if necessary, defend their actions.[25] In theory, if a minister's personal conduct falls below the high standard required of public figures, he or she should resign. Equally, if the government department under a minister's authority is found to have misused or mismanaged its powers, it is the minister who takes the responsibility in Parliament. If the matter is of sufficient gravity and the minister loses the support of his party and Prime Minister, he or she may be forced to resign. But, as with responsibility for personal conduct, there are no hard and fast rules. There exist no fixed criteria from which it can be predicted in advance the consequence which will flow from a breach of convention. In terms of consequences, this convention is the most uncertain of all conventional rules.

See further
Chapter 10.

Evolution and change

Implicit in the above discussion lies the answer to a further question: how do conventions change? It has been seen that conventions come into being, unlike legal rules, when a habit or practice becomes so established that it imposes obligations on those to whom it applies, and takes on the characteristics of a rule. And so it is with changes in conventions. A convention may change with changing circumstances: individual ministerial responsibility is a prime example of this feature of conventions. Conventions may adapt to meet particular needs, as with collective responsibility in relation to the European Community (now European Union) in 1975, discussed

---

23 See Marshall, 1984, p 22.
24 See Chapter 9.
25 See Chapter 15.

above. Conventions may be breached and placed on a statutory basis, as with the House of Lords in 1911. A legal rule has a relatively fixed and certain quality while in existence. If a legal rule is changed, either by judicial decision or by Parliament, the previous rule will be superseded by the new: it will 'go out with a bang'. The same cannot be said of conventions. For the most part, they evolve, adapt in amoeba-like fashion to meet the constitutional needs of the time. It is for this reason that they present the student of the constitution with such a fascinating challenge.

The courts and conventions

Given that conventional rules are non-legal rules, the attitude of the courts towards constitutional conventions is inevitably different from their attitude to legal rules. The courts do not have jurisdiction to adjudicate upon conventions. This is not to say that a court must take no cognisance of conventional rules, but rather, as Dicey asserted, conventions are not 'court enforceable'. The courts will give recognition to conventions, although they are rarely called upon to do so. Two cases are illustrative. The first is that of **Attorney General v Jonathan Cape Ltd** (1976). In 1976, the executors of the late Richard Crossman, a former Cabinet minister, decided to proceed with publication of the diaries he had kept while in government. The diaries included records of Cabinet discussions which, under the doctrine of collective ministerial responsibility, may never be revealed other than under the conditions specified by law or on the authority of the Cabinet Secretary. The government sought an injunction to restrain publication on the basis that Cabinet meetings are, by convention, confidential and that the diaries, accordingly, represented a breach of confidentiality. The court ruled in favour of the government in relation to the doctrine of confidentiality. In the event, however, the court declined to suppress 'secrets' which were over ten years old. The court ruled that, unless national security was involved, an eight-to-ten-year embargo was the maximum period that such material would be protected.

In 1982, in the Canadian case of **Reference re Amendment of the Constitution of Canada**, the principal question for decision by the Supreme Court of Canada was whether, as a matter of law, the constitution of Canada could be amended without the consent of the Provinces. A second question was whether the consent of the Provinces was required as a matter of convention. The British North America (No 2) Act 1949 conferred substantial powers on the Canadian Federal Parliament relating to the distribution of power between the Federal and Provincial legislatures.[26] One of the accepted principles regulating constitutional amendments was that there had to be consultation with and the agreement of the Provinces. By a majority the Supreme Court ruled that as a matter of law the consent of the Provinces was not required. The Court also ruled, however, that as a matter of constitutional convention, consent was required. Recognising the distinction between convention and law the Court ruled that the convention was unenforceable. However, the Court emphasised the importance of conventions, stating that 'some conventions may be more important than some laws' and that 'constitutional conventions plus constitutional law equal the total constitution of the country'.

Should conventions be codified?

One question asked earlier was whether or not constitutional conventions should be codified. Again, no straightforward or simple answer to this question presents itself. Much

---

26 The British North America Act 1867 could be amended only by an Act of the United Kingdom Parliament. The Statute of Westminster 1931 provided, in part, that there should be no change to the 1867 Act which affected the competence of the federal or provincial legislatures.

will turn on the perception of the value of the status quo. Much also turns on the constitutional implications of attempting to provide a comprehensive, binding code of constitutional conventions.

The Australian experiment

In Australia, a constitutional crisis in 1975 contributed to the experiment in codification of conventions into an authoritative but non-legally binding text. The crisis involved the prerogative power of the Crown in the person of the Governor General to dismiss the Prime Minister and appoint a caretaker Prime Minister on the condition of ensuring the passage of financial legislation and the holding of a general election. One outcome of the crisis – in which the inherent vagueness of the conventional rules was revealed – was formal consideration of the 'codification' of conventions, albeit in a non-legal form. In 1983, a plenary session of the Constitutional Convention adopted a set of 34 practices which were to be 'recognised and declared' as conventions of the Australian constitution. Among those 'recognised' were the powers of the Crown in relation to the Governor General, and his powers in relation to the dismissal of ministers and powers over Parliament, and the relationship between the Prime Minister and the Governor General in relation to the dissolution of Parliament.[27]

Professor Charles Sampford analysed the merits and demerits of the codification of conventions. Among the many unanswered questions raised are the following. Under what authority did the Constitutional Convention act? What is the effect of the resolution? Is it merely declaratory of the existing rules? If there is a conflict with the restatement and actual practice, which should be authoritative? Professor Sampford contends that there exist three possibilities here. If the code is followed in preference to conventional practice, then the codification goes beyond clarification and becomes a source of the rules themselves. This raises the question 'why should the old rules and old sources give way to the new?' The second approach is that the 'declaration' has whatever force the constitutional actors accord to it: it would be absurd if the declaration were to have no authority. Thirdly, it could be argued that the declaration is merely evidence of the rule. This latter possibility, however, is unsatisfactory in so far as the declaration was intended to be 'sole and conclusive evidence for the existence of the recognised convention. This effectively makes the Constitutional Convention a new source for conventions'. Furthermore, what is the position where a convention was agreed to only by a small majority? What then happens to its authority? To what extent will the new conventions be observed? What is the status of those pre-existing conventions which were not 'recognised and declared'? As can be seen, codification is – even if desirable – by no means a simple matter.

It is clear from the analysis thus far that conventions comprise a set of binding rules, non-legal in nature, which supplement and inform the legal rules of the constitution and which can adapt to meet changing circumstances. Viewed in that light, their primary importance lies in their flexibility. On the other hand, it may be argued cogently that for rules of such importance to be ill-defined, uncertain in application and unenforceable by the courts is, at best, anomalous, and at worst, a threat to the principle of government according to law.

Further considerations intrude upon the discussion. It has been seen that conventions are flexible. In this feature lies much of their value, and it is to be doubted whether, in relation to such a dynamic organism as the constitution, it would be possible to identify, define and formalise conventions in such a manner both to provide a comprehensive code and to allow for subsequent constitutional development. It may prove to be the case that codification

---

27 A previous convention in 1983 had adopted resolutions relating to the conventions regulating the powers of the Queen and the Governor General.

would stultify the growth of the constitution. On the other hand, such codification would undoubtedly provide greater insight into the rules regulating government and thereby act as some check on the power of government. Professor SA de Smith[28] states that codification of conventions would purchase certainty at the expense of flexibility, and this point must carry great weight in evaluating the desirability of codification.

The relationship between the government and the courts must also be weighed in the balance in this regard. It has been seen that the courts give recognition to, but cannot enforce, conventions. If the effect of codification were to give jurisdiction to the courts, this would represent a very real and problematic shift in the balance of authority and power between the government and the courts. In Chapter 4, the doctrine of the separation of powers is considered in detail. Enough has been said by way of introduction for it to be apparent that if the courts were to be given jurisdiction to adjudicate upon and enforce, by way of legal sanction, the conventional rules of the constitution, this would impinge greatly upon the concept of the separation of powers.

For these reasons, the loss of flexibility and the separation of powers doctrine, it can be argued that conventions should not be codified.

Authoritative works

Finally and in brief, mention should be made of the writings of eminent jurists such as Blackstone, Dicey, Jennings and later commentators to whose works the actors on the constitutional stage, including the judges, may make reference for elucidation of matters of constitutional law.

Summary

In order to understand the United Kingdom's constitution, which is largely but not wholly unwritten, it is necessary to examine the various legal and non-legal sources. The legal sources include Acts of Parliament and judicial decisions regulating the relationship between institutions of the state and the state and individual citizen. They also include the Royal Prerogative: acts of government undertaken under the authority of the Crown without an Act of Parliament. The law of the European Union and case law under the European Convention on Human Rights are also important sources. The principal non-legal sources of the constitution are constitutional conventions which are binding on those who operate the constitution and give rise to the accusation of unconstitutional (but not unlawful) conduct if not observed.

Underpinning, or underlying these sources are the constitutional principles of democracy and responsible government, the separation of powers and the rule of law and the doctrine of parliamentary sovereignty or supremacy.

Further Reading

Barber, N.W. (2009) 'Laws and Constitutional Conventions', Law Quarterly Review, 125: 294.

Dicey, A.V. (1885) *Introduction to The Study of The Constitution*, 1959, London: Macmillan.

---

28 de Smith and Brazier, 1998, Chapter 2.

Hennessey, P. (1986) 'Helicopter Crashes into Cabinet: Prime Minister and constitution Hurt', Journal of Legal Studies, 13: 423.

Jaconelli, J. (1999) 'The Nature of Constitutional Conventions', Legal Studies, 19: 24.

Jaconelli, J. (2005) 'Do Constitutional Conventions Bind?', Cambridge Law Journal, 64: 149.

Jennings, Sir Ivor (1959) Cabinet Government (3rd edn), Cambridge: CUP.

Jennings, Sir Ivor (1959) The Law and the Constitution (5th edn), London: Hodder & Stoughton.

Munro, C.R. (1975) 'Laws and Conventions Distinguished', Law Quarterly Review, 91: 224.

Munro, C.R. (1999) Studies in Constitutional Law (2nd edn), London: Butterworths, Chapter 3.

White Paper, The Governance of Britain, Cm 7170, 2007.

Wilson, R. (2004) 'The Robustness of Conventions in a Time of Modernisation and Change', Public Law, 407.

Part **2**

Fundamental Constitutional Concepts

Chapter 3

The Rule of Law

Where laws do not rule, there is no constitution.

Aristotle, *The Politics*, Bk iv, para 1292a31

Chapter Contents

Introduction

The rule of law represents one of the most challenging concepts of the constitution. The rule of law is a concept which is capable of different interpretations by different people, and it is this feature which makes an understanding of the doctrine elusive. Of all constitutional concepts, the rule of law is also the most subjective and value laden. The apparent uncertainties in the rule of law and its variable nature should not cause concern, although, inevitably, it will cause some insecurity. In the study of the rule of law, it is more important to recognise and appreciate the many rich and varied interpretations which have been given to it, and to recognise the potential of the rule of law for ensuring limited governmental power and the protection of individual rights, than to be able to offer an authoritative, definitive explanation of the concept.

The rule of law may be interpreted either as a *philosophy* or *political theory* which lays down fundamental requirements for law, or as a *procedural device* by which those with power rule under the law. The essence of the rule of law is that of the sovereignty or supremacy of law over man. The rule of law insists that every person – irrespective of rank and status in society – be subject to the law. For the citizen, the rule of law is both *prescriptive* – dictating the conduct required by law – and *protective* of citizens – demanding that government acts according to law. This central theme recurs whether the doctrine is examined from the perspective of philosophy, or political theory, or from the more pragmatic vantage point of the rule of law as a procedural device. The rule of law underlies the entire constitution and, in one sense, all constitutional law is concerned with the rule of law. The concept is of great antiquity and continues to exercise legal and political philosophers today.

The rule of law cannot be viewed in isolation from political society. The emphasis on the rule of law as a yardstick for measuring both the extent to which government acts under the law and the extent to which individual rights are recognised and protected by law, is inextricably linked with Western democratic liberalism.[1] In this respect, it is only meaningful to speak of the rule of law in a society which exhibits the features of a democratically elected, responsible – and responsive – government and a separation of powers, which will result in a judiciary which is independent of government. In liberal democracies, therefore, the concept of the rule of law implies an acceptance that law itself represents a 'good'; that law and its governance is a demonstrable asset to society.

Contrasting Attitudes to the Rule of Law

It should not be assumed that this acceptance of law as a benevolent ruling force is universally accepted. In differing societies, subscribing to very different political philosophies, the insistence on the rule of law – in the Western liberal sense – has little application. For example, from a Marxist perspective (on which see below) the law serves not to restrict government and protect individual rights but rather to conceal the injustices inherent in the capitalist system. Accordingly, the concept of the rule of law – denoting some form of morality in law – represents no more than a false idealisation of law designed to reinforce the political structure and economic status quo in society. Echoes of this thesis dominate the more moderate socialist conceptions of the rule of law and the critique of liberalism. It can be argued – from the socialist perspective – that liberalism pays too little regard to true equality between persons and too great attention to the protection of property interests. The liberal domain thus becomes one which, again, masks true social and economic inequality while at the same time proclaiming equality and justice under the rule of law.[2]

---

1   See, *inter alia*, Fine, 1984; Hutchinson and Monahan, 1987; Neumann, 1986.
2   For a critical account of the liberal tradition see Lustgarten, 1988.

The rule of law, as understood in liberal democracies, also has little relevance in a totalitarian state. While it is true that such a state will be closely regulated by law, there will not be government under the law – as adjudicated upon by an independent judiciary – which is insisted upon under the liberal tradition.

In traditional Oriental society, the Western preference for law is an alien notion. By way of example, in relation to traditional Chinese society, David and Brierley write:

> For the Chinese, legislation was not the normal means of guaranteeing a harmonious and smooth-working society. Laws, abstract in nature, could not take into account the infinite variety of possible situations. Their strict application was apt to affect man's innate sense of justice. To enact laws was therefore considered a bad policy by traditional Chinese doctrine. The very exactitude which laws establish in social relations, and the way in which they fix the rights and obligations of each individual, were considered evils, according to the Chinese, not benefits. The idea of 'rights', an inevitable development of the laws themselves, ran counter to the natural order. Once individuals think of their 'rights' there is, it was thought, some form of social illness; the only true matter of concern is one's duty to society and one's fellow men.
>
> The enactment of laws is an evil, since individuals, once familiar with them, will conclude that they have rights and will then be inclined to assert them, thereby abandoning the traditional rules of propriety and morality which should be the only guides to conduct. Legal disputes become numerous, and a trial, by reason of its very existence, is a scandalous disturbance of the natural order which may then lead to further disturbances of the social order to the detriment of all society. [1966, p 442; and see 3rd edn, 1985, Title III, Chapter 1 for the persistence of traditional ideas]

In Japan, despite the nineteenth-century adoption of codes based on French and German models,[3] law, in the Western sense, remained largely irrelevant to traditional Japanese life:

> Still essential for the Japanese are the rules of behaviour (*giri-ninjo*) for each type of personal relation established by tradition and founded, at least in appearance, on the feelings of affection (*ninjo*) uniting those in such relationships. A person who does not observe these rules is seeking his own interest rather than obeying the nobler part of his nature; he brings scorn upon himself and his family. Apart from the contracts arising between important but depersonalised business and industrial concerns, one does not attempt to have one's rights enforced in a court of law even though this is permitted by the various codes . . . [David and Brierley, 1966, p 458; see 3rd edn, Title III, Chapter 2.]

As the notion of the rule of law is dependent upon the political foundations of a state, so, too, it is dependent – according to the approach adopted to the concept – upon a nation's economic resources. It may be that law, as a mere regulator of individual behaviour, is perfectly feasible in an impoverished state, and accordingly, a state which maintains law and order, and no more, can conform to a narrow interpretation of the rule of law which insists simply on a citizen's unquestioning compliance with rules of the law. However, if the rule of law implies more than mere regulation by law and is elevated to a theory guaranteeing freedom from hunger and homelessness

---

3   Penal Code and Code of Criminal Procedure enacted in 1882; Codes on Judicial Organisation and Civil Procedure 1890; Commercial Code 1899.

and entitlement to a basic decent standard of life, then economic conditions are of paramount importance to conformity with the rule of law. Such an approach is adopted by the International Commission of Jurists, which in the New Delhi Declaration of 1959 included – alongside traditional civil and political rights – the realisation of social, economic, cultural and educational standards under which the individual could enjoy a fuller life within the ambit of the rule of law. On the other hand, reasoning such as this is anathema to radical conservatives such as Friedrich von Hayek (1944), who viewed the correct role of government as being best confined to establishing clear, fixed rules of law which ensure maximum economic freedom for individuals, unimpeded either by planning controls or ideas of redistributive justice. From von Hayek's perspective, the rule of law requires no more than the existence of a stable set of minimum rules which are to be applied in a uniform, non-discretionary manner. A legal system is viewed as just – and in conformity with the rule of law – if it exhibits both these features and an absence of discretionary rules or practices.

Uncertainty in the Western Rule of Law

An understanding and appreciation of the rule of law is both politically and culturally dependent. Moreover, it is also clear that the rule of law has more than one meaning, even within the Western liberal tradition. To some theorists, the rule of law represents an aspirational philosophy; to others, no more than a device under which compliance with law – good or bad in content – is secured. It has been remarked that:

> It would not be very difficult to show that the phrase 'the rule of law' has become meaningless thanks to ideological abuse and general over-use.[4]

Partly as a result of such 'over-use', some writers have refuted the claim that the rule of law represents anything other than a purely procedural or formalistic device. By way of example, Raz writes that the rule of law:

> . . . says nothing about how the law is to be made: by tyrants, democratic majorities, or any other way. It says nothing about fundamental rights, about equality, or justice.[5]

Contrast such views with that expressed in the following statement:

> The rule of law is a rare and protean principle of our political tradition. Unlike other ideals, it has withstood the ravages of constitutional time and remains a contemporary clarion-call to political justice. Apparently transcending partisan concern, it is embraced and venerated by virtually all shades of political opinion. The rule of law's central core comprises the enduring values of regularity and restraint, embodied in the slogan of 'a government of laws, not . . . men'. [Hutchinson and Monahan, 1987, p ix]

In light of such divergent assessments, it must be recognised that any attempt to align the rule of law with a broad philosophical doctrine – or indeed with any other interpretation – is likely to meet with opposition from some quarters. Notwithstanding such criticisms, the rule of law retains a secure grasp on political and legal thinking: in the words of Raz (1979), it has 'enduring importance as a central artefact in our legal and political culture'.

---

4   Shklar, 'Political theory and the rule of law', in Hutchinson and Monahan, 1987, p 1.
5   See Raz, 1979, p 210. On Dicey's influence see below, pp 64 ff; de Smith and Brazier, 1998.

The Rule of Law as Philosophical Doctrine

The rule of law is an aspect of ancient and modern natural law thought.[6] In essence, the natural law tradition – of which there are many strands – insists that the authority of law derives not from the power of any political ruler, but from a higher source, either theological or secular. The laws of man must be evaluated against the dictates of this 'higher' form of law. It is impossible to provide more than a mere sketch of the rich history of natural law in Western philosophy and political thought and the legacy it gives to modern constitutions. Nevertheless, a basic understanding of its nature and evolution is instructive, for it reveals the manner in which the requirements of good law – morally worthwhile law – have been stipulated over centuries.

Natural Law in Ancient Greece and Rome

Aristotle stated in *The Politics* that 'the rule of law is preferable to that of any individual'. The appeal to law as a control over naked power has been apparent throughout history. At a philosophical level, the natural law tradition, whether theological or secular, instructs that the power of man is not absolute, but is rather controlled and limited by the requirements of a higher law. To the ancient Greeks, man was under the governance of the laws of nature – the natural forces which controlled the universe – although this view is more closely aligned to the 'law of nature' than 'natural law' as it came to be understood in later times. However, from the time of Socrates (470–399 BC), Plato (427–347 BC) and Aristotle (384–322 BC), the quest for virtue – or goodness or justice under the law – has been a recurrent theme. Socrates, teacher and philosopher, was accused, tried and convicted by the grand jury of Athens for corrupting youth with his teachings. Despite the possibility of escape, Socrates chose to accept the verdict of death which had been imposed upon him, in order to demonstrate his fidelity to law. When pressed by Crito to escape, Socrates considered the questions which would be put to him by the laws and constitution of Athens were he to succumb to the temptation to escape the penalty of the law:

> Can you deny that by this act [of escaping] which you are contemplating you intend, so far as you have the power, to destroy us, the laws, and the whole state as well? Do you imagine that a city can continue to exist and not be turned upside down, if the legal judgments which are pronounced in it have no force but are nullified and destroyed by private persons? [Crito, in Hamilton and Cairns, 1989, p 50b]

In submitting to death, Socrates was doing nothing other than giving recognition to the supremacy of law: to the rule of law. An early – and famous – formulation of the dictates of natural law was offered by Cicero (106–43 BC):

> True law is right reason in agreement with nature; it is of universal application, unchanging and everlasting; it summons to duty by its commands, and averts from wrongdoing by its prohibitions. And it does not lay its commands or prohibitions upon good men in vain, though neither have any effect on the wicked. It is a sin to try to alter this law, nor is it allowable to attempt to repeal any part of it, and it is impossible to abolish it entirely. We cannot be freed from its obligations by Senate or People, and we need not look outside ourselves for an expounder or interpreter of it. And there will not be different laws at Rome and at Athens, or different laws now and in the future, but one eternal and unchangeable law will be valid for all nations and for all

---

6 On natural law, see d'Entrèves, 1970; and Finnis, 1980.

times, and there will be one master and one ruler, that is, God, over us all, for He is
the author of this law, its promulgator, and its enforcing judge. [De Republica, cited
in d'Entrèves, 1970, p 25]

It is from ancient Greek philosophy that natural law enters into Roman law. From the Corpus
Iuris Civilis (AD 534) is derived ius civilis, ius gentium and ius naturale. Ius civilis denotes the law of the
state; ius gentium the law of nations; and ius naturale 'a law which expresses a higher and more
permanent standard'. It is the law of nature (ius naturale) which corresponds to 'that which is
always good and equitable' (d'Entrèves, 1970, p 24).

Christian Natural Law thought

The scriptures and gospel provided the basis for Christian natural law thought which developed in the Middle Ages. Natural law was perceived as God-given, communicated to man by
Revelation, and remaining absolutely binding upon man and unchanging in its content. As a
result, the dictates of natural law take precedence over man-made laws. If the demands of the
state conflict with the laws of God, the obligation to God must prevail. Undoubtedly, the most
powerful writing of the Middle Ages comes from St Thomas Aquinas (1225–74):

This rational guidance of created things on the part of God . . . we can call the
Eternal Law.

But, of all others, rational creatures are subject to divine Providence in a very special
way; being themselves made participators in Providence itself, in that they control
their own actions and the actions of others. So they have a share in the divine reason
itself, deriving therefrom a natural inclination to such actions and ends as are fitting.
This participation in the Eternal Law by rational creatures is called Natural Law.
[Summa Theologica, cited in d'Entrèves, 1970, p 43]

In the thirteenth century, Bracton proclaimed that 'the King himself ought not be subject to
man but subject to God and to the law, because the law makes him King' (1968–77, f5 b). In
1534, Thomas More (1478–1535) – at the cost of his life – refused to recognise Henry VIII as
head of the Church, thereby acknowledging the higher duty of obedience to God rather than
the rule of his temporal King.

Natural Law and International Law

On an international level, natural law thought played a significant role in establishing the
over-arching dictates of international law. Grotius (1583–1645), for example, maintained
that natural law was discernible by man by virtue of his rationality and that a system of
natural law would accordingly exist independently of theological perceptions and dictates.
In short, natural law would exist even if God did not exist. In addition to the insistence on
rationalism, the emphasis of natural law at this time started to focus on the individual,
and from this period is discerned the origins of assertions of the rights of man. AP
d'Entrèves writes:

. . . when we read the American or the French Declarations we know that we are
confronted with a complete architecture, about the style of which there can be no
mistake. It is a political philosophy based upon a particular notion of the individual,
of society and of their mutual relationship. [1970, p 57]

Natural Law and Common Law

In the West, the sovereignty of law became inextricably linked with the Christian faith. In England, the break with the Roman Catholic Church in 1535 established Henry VIII as head of the English Church. By assuming supreme power over both spiritual and secular matters, Henry VIII ostensibly broke the logical separation of duty towards God and the duty owed to the King: obedience to the sovereign now became a religious as well as a political duty. The execution of Sir Thomas More in 1535 is illustrative of the King's reaction to an individual refusal to recognise the absolute supremacy of the King. Nevertheless, natural law thought continued to permeate the common law of England before the settlement of 1688 and the rise of parliamentary sovereignty.

One of the classic exponents of the demand for the King to be subject to the law – rather than above it – was Sir Edward Coke (1552–1634), whose struggle with the King led to his dismissal as Chief Justice in 1616. James I[7] viewed himself as imbued with ultimate power, derived from God under the prerogative. To Coke, laws derived from Parliament, and the power of Parliament was subject to the common law, and accordingly Coke took the view that:

> . . . when an Act of Parliament is against the common right or repugnant or impossible to be performed the common law will control it and adjudge such Act to be void.[8]

When, in 1608, Coke told the King that the common law protected the King, the King regarded his speech as traitorous. Nevertheless, Coke's view expresses an idea which is central to natural law thought, namely that there is a higher authority – based on moral judgement – than the law of man. With the settlement of 1688 and the Bill of Rights 1689, the doctrine of parliamentary supremacy over the King, the prerogative and common law was established. Thereafter, there were to be no assertions of any overriding higher law. The judges bowed to the sovereignty of Parliament.

The Rule of Law as Political Theory

Social contract theory

It is from natural law principles that the theories of social contract and the rights of man derive. The writings of John Locke and Thomas Paine are infused with the doctrine of the inalienability of individual human rights – rights which transcend the law of the state, which cannot be overridden by the state, and which affirm the supremacy of the law of the state with the important proviso that the law of the state is in compliance with natural law.[9]

Thomas Hobbes[10] offered the most extreme version of the social contract theory, arguing that man by nature is incapable of regulating his life in peace and harmony with his fellow man. Hobbes's view of man in a society lacking a restraining all-powerful sovereign was inherently pessimistic, an attitude encapsulated in the often quoted phrase that life is 'solitary, poor, nasty, brutish and short'. In order for there to be civil order, it was necessary for each man to surrender to the state his own sovereignty in exchange for security. Such a surrender was revocable only if the state abused its trust. The requirement of obedience to law is strict; and yet there are limits:

See Chapter 6.

---

7 King of Scotland 1567–1625; King of England and Scotland 1603–25.
8 **Dr Bonham's Case** (1610). But see the contrary explanation offered by Thorne, 1938.
9 Locke, 1690; Paine, 1791, Pt I.
10 *The Leviathan*, 1651.

> If the Soveraign command a man (though justly condemned) to kill, wound, or mayme himselfe; or not to resist those that assault him; or to abstain from the use of food, ayre, medicine, or any other thing, without which he cannot live; yet hath that man the Liberty to disobey.

Further, Hobbes states that:

> The Obligation of Subjects to the Soveraign, is understood to last as long, and no longer, than the power lasteth, by which he is able to protect them. For the right men have by Nature to protect themselves, when none else can protect them, can by no Covenant be relinquished.

According to Jean-Jacques Rousseau,[11] the citizen enters into a 'contract' with the state, surrendering to the state individual rights in exchange for the protection of the state. The state, according to Rousseau, is thus embodied in the 'general will' of the people and becomes both the agent and ruler of the people in the people's name. Rousseau's vision of man differs markedly from that of Thomas Hobbes – far from living in a state of 'war' with one another, men in the 'natural state' of primitive society would have nothing to fight over and would be united in a community of endeavour to secure the essential provisions of life. Man comes together – from necessity – within civil society, and, through participation in the decision-making processes, produces a democratic society. Rousseau distinguishes between supreme power – sovereignty – and the government. Sovereignty lies with the people, and is absolute and inalienable. The government's power is less absolute, established to implement the will of the people and accountable to the people. The government is dependent upon the sovereign people for the continuation of its power, and the people retain the right to revoke the power devolved.

Thus, for Rousseau, sovereignty is a concept which entails moral approval and acceptance by the people whose 'collective will' sovereignty represents.[12] Indeed, for Rousseau:

> . . . the sovereign, being formed wholly of the individuals who compose it, neither has nor can have any interest contrary to theirs; and consequently the sovereign power need give no guarantee to its subjects, because it is impossible for the body to wish to hurt all its members. We shall also see later on that it cannot hurt any in particular. The sovereign, merely by virtue of what it is, is always what it should be. [p 177]

Thomas Paine advances a social contract theory in which the rights of the individual are given central importance.[13] Paine both influenced and was influenced by the French and American Revolutions. In *Rights of Man*, Paine argued that the citizen gives up his rights to the state, but on a conditional basis. The state is placed in the position of trustee of the rights of man, and should that trust be broken, the citizen has the ultimate – or sovereign – right to depose the government. Paine argues that man has natural rights, 'those which appertain to man in right of his existence'. These rights are both individualistic and civil. The former category includes:

> . . . all the intellectual rights, or rights of the mind, and also all those rights of acting as an individual for his own comfort and happiness, which are not injurious to the natural rights of others.

---

11 *The Social Contract and Discourses*, 176.
12 *Ibid*, Bk I, Chapter VII, and Bk II.
13 *Rights of Man*, 1791, Pt 1

By way of distinction:

> Civil rights are those which appertain to man in right of his being a member of society. Every civil right has for its foundation, some natural right pre-existing in the individual. [p 90]

These natural and civil rights are held by government on trust for the people, and should – under an ideal constitution – be protected from governmental abuse by a Bill of Rights. Such an approach is also taken by John Locke, who regards the people, as a collectivity, as holding the sovereign power which is in some sense delegated to the government on trust, and who may accordingly exert their sovereign power to remove the government if it violates its sacred trust.

In *Two Treatises of Government*, John Locke advances powerful arguments for the limits of governmental power and the ultimate political sovereignty of the people. In Book II,[14] Locke argues that men come together in civil society and tacitly consent to be ruled by government directed to 'the peace, safety, and public good of the people'. Hence, the power accorded to government is not absolute, but whilst in existence, the legislative power is the 'supreme power'. Nevertheless, Locke concludes that if the people:

> . . . have set limits to the duration of their legislative, and made this supreme power in any person or assembly only temporary, it is forfeited; upon the forfeiture of their rules, or at the determination of the time set, it reverts to the society, and the people have a right to act as supreme, and continue the legislative in themselves or place it in a new form, or new hands, as they think good. [p 242]

Sovereignty, then, is limited and conditional: government holds supreme power on trust for the people. On this view, the authority of the constitution will be dependent upon its conformity with a higher law. As KC Wheare explains:

> This view of government limited by the natural rights of man lies at the basis of the American Constitution and finds a place . . . in many modern constitutions. It provides a moral basis upon which a government's actions can be judged and, what is more, upon which the validity of a constitution can be tested. A constitution binds in so far as it is in accordance with natural law. Neither a government nor a citizen may disregard the authority of a constitution except in so far as the action can be justified by the law of nature. This is indeed a 'higher law' than a constitution. [1966, p 65]

Liberalism, conservatism and the rule of law

The rule of law has been subjected to analysis by political theorists of all persuasions. From the vantage point of the liberal democrat, the rule of law will ensure the minimum rules in society to enable man to fulfil his life plan according to law, but with the minimum interference of law.

AV Dicey's writing on the rule of law has had a lasting influence on constitutional thought. His writing will be considered in detail below. However, Dicey has been criticised by Sir Ivor Jennings for being motivated, in his writings, by his conservative views. Dicey, in expressing his preference for clear and stable rules and the minimum of discretion within the legal process, was, according to Jennings, revealing his conservative preference for certainty

---

14 'An essay concerning the true original extent and end of civil government.'

within law rather than concern for the law being directed towards social justice which neces-sarily entails much discretionary power in the application of broad rules. Jennings (1959b, p 311) writes that Dicey was 'concerned not with clearing up of the nasty industrial sections of the towns, but with the liberty of the subject'. For Jennings, Dicey's view that 'Englishmen are ruled by the law, and by the law alone' is 'not enough':

> The powers of Louis XIV, of Napoleon I, of Hitler, and of Mussolini were derived from the law, even though that law be only 'The Leader may do and order what he pleases'. The doctrine involves some considerable limitation on the powers of every political authority, except possibly (for this is open to dispute) those of a representative legis-lature. Indeed it contains, as we shall see, something more, though it is not capable of precise definition. It is an attitude, an expression of liberal and democratic princi-ples, in themselves vague when it is sought to analyse them, but clear enough in their results. [1959b, p 48]

For Jennings, the doctrine implies, first, that the state as a whole must be regulated by law; secondly, that the separation of powers is implied within the doctrine in order to prevent dictatorship or absolutism. Accordingly, there are incorporated certain basic requirements[15] of the law: equality before the law; clearly defined police powers; clear general rules adjudicated upon by the courts; non-retrospectivity in penal statutes; and the strict construction of penal statutes. Thirdly, the doctrine incorporates the principle of *equality*: a notion which Jennings concedes is as vague as that of the rule of law itself (1959b, p 49). Moreover, and of prime importance, the rule of law implies the notion of *liberty*.

Marxism and the rule of law

Arguments against a formalistic perception of the rule of law adopted by, *inter alia*, Dicey and von Hayek present a formidable target for attack from a Marxist perspective. Where liberalism insists that law is neutral as between persons and classes and favours maximum liberty for all under the law, Marxism insists that law represents the interests of the powerful within society. Law is an ideological device engaged by those with power to mask the reality of that power in society, and the correlative powerlessness of the ordinary citizen. The rule of law is thus portrayed as a means of subterfuge: it is a mere pretence which hides injustice. Marxism stands in opposition to liberalism and yet, paradoxically, seeks as its end result the complete liberty of man. Law, from a Marxist perspective, is the reflection of economic power within society, a power which is used to exploit the powerless. Thus it is that, under capitalism, the worker is not rewarded with the full value of his labour: rather, he receives a price for his labour to which is added production costs and profits and together these comprise the final price of a product. The laws which regulate factories and employment terms are all underpinned by the acceptance of the capitalist ideal. Laws which ameliorate the conditions of the poor do not represent – as appears at first sight – real social justice, but rather they represent a calculated means by which the poor are kept compliant within their powerlessness.[16] Accordingly, the welfare state is but a cynical mask for maintenance of the status quo which defeats the move-ment towards revolutionary economic and social change:

> Far from hastening the revolution, the welfare state undermines efforts to create working class solidarity. By preventing the fullest development of the material

---

15 Cf Raz, 1979, Chapter 11; and Fuller, 1964.
16 See Cain and Hunt, 1979.

degradation of the working class and by providing a limited immunity from the vicissitudes of economic crises, a welfare state delays the formation of class consciousness and thus prevents a revolutionary situation from arising . . . [Collins, 1982, pp 126–27]

Whether law serves to oppress or merely to uphold the economic status quo – and there exists dispute on this matter between Marxists themselves – law, from a Marxist perspective, does not serve the interests of all in society. The rule of law thus becomes a grand slogan under which is hidden the reality of oppression and absence of liberty. The capitalist's insistence on the rule of law is seen as a 'fetishism' which must be removed along with economic oppression (Cain, 1979, Chapter 5). Only when the capitalist system breaks down, and the law which serves it 'withers away', will society become truly free. When that occurs, there will be no need for law and man will achieve true freedom.

Professor Joseph Raz and the rule of law

Professor Joseph Raz approaches the rule of law from a morally neutral but conceptual standpoint, and asserts that:

> The rule of law is a political ideal which a legal system may lack or may possess to a greater or lesser degree. That much is common ground. It is also to be insisted that the rule of law is just one of the virtues which a legal system may possess and by which it is to be judged. It is not to be confused with democracy, justice, equality (before the law or otherwise), human rights of any kind or respect for persons or for the dignity of man. A non-democratic legal system, based on the denial of human rights, on extensive poverty, on racial segregation, sexual inequalities, and religious persecution may, in principle, conform to the requirements of the rule of law better than any of the legal systems of the more enlightened Western democracies. [1979, p 211]

Raz acknowledges that his claim will 'alarm many', but insists that it presents 'a coherent view of one important virtue which legal systems should possess'. In seeking to elucidate the ideal of the rule of law, Raz draws the analogy between the rule of law and a knife. One quality of a good knife is sharpness. However, the quality of sharpness says nothing as to the use to which the knife might be put: beneficial surgery or murder. Sharpness is morally neutral. And thus it is with the rule of law. However, the purpose of law is to enable citizens to live within the law. Accordingly, there are certain principles that must be respected if that goal is to be fulfilled. For the rule of law to exist in society, certain qualities must be present. The law must be clear if it is to be capable of being obeyed. In **Merkur Island Shipping Corporation v Laughton** (1983), for example, Lord Donaldson MR stated that:

> The efficacy and maintenance of the rule of law, which is the foundation of any parliamentary democracy, has at least two pre-requisites. First, people must understand that it is in their interests, as well as in that of the community as a whole, that they should live their lives in accordance with the rules and all the rules. Secondly, they must know what those rules are . . .

Lord Donaldson's view was endorsed by Lord Diplock in the House of Lords:

> Absence of clarity is destructive of the rule of law; it is unfair to those who wish to preserve the rule of law; it encourages those who wish to undermine it. [p 612]

The law must be publicised in order that citizens are aware of its demands; reasonably stable in order that citizens can plan their lives according to law; prospective so that the law does not require the impossible;[17] non-contradictory for the same reason, and, in addition, the courts must be accessible and staffed by an independent judiciary. Compliance with each of these requirements will indicate that a society respects the rule of law. To make such a statement is not to say that the legal system is one which is necessarily morally 'good'. As seen in Raz's illustration with the quality of sharpness in relation to the knife, the fact of sharpness does not dictate the morality of the purposes to which the knife will be put. It is possible, accordingly, for the rule of law to exist without the legal system necessarily pursuing morally good ends.

'Law and order' and the rule of law: the obligation to obey law

An alternative perception of the rule of law may be labelled the 'law and order' model.[18] This view emphasises the peaceful settlement of disputes without recourse to violence, armed force or terrorism. In legal philosophy, the idea of absolute obedience to law is compatible with the analytical, positivist school of thought which dominated much jurisprudential thought from the nineteenth century until after the Second World War. Positivism is the antithesis of natural law. The primary quest for positivists is to separate legal and moral issues: to distinguish between the 'is' (that which exists as fact) and the 'ought' (that which is desirable). Under positivist theory – which is primarily concerned to explain law as it exists in fact – where valid law exists, that is to say law which is accorded validity under the fundamental constitutional rule in a state, there is an obligation on each citizen to obey that law. Hans Kelsen and other legal positivists regard the duty to obey validly created norms as absolute.[19]

Taken to its logical conclusion, however, the 'law and order' view can lead to the suppression of freedom. By way of illustration, it is a common cry of politicians that a demonstration by, for example, trade union members or students, contravenes the 'rule of law'. In a strict sense, any action which involves protest will almost inevitably violate some legal rule – whether it is the rule protested against or otherwise.[20] Public protest, for example, will often involve breach of rules against obstruction of the highway, of the police in the execution of their duty, trespass, or criminal damage, even though those laws are not the object of the protest. It becomes necessary, therefore, to consider – albeit in outline – the nature of an individual's obligation to obey valid law. The fundamental question in this regard lies in the extent to which citizens should be coerced into obedience to 'unjust laws'. Is there an absolute obligation to obey, irrespective of the quality of the law? Is the duty only prima facie? Is there ever a duty to disobey the law in pursuit of a higher ideal? Each of these vast and timeless philosophical questions underpins the concept of the rule of law.

Is there a duty to obey law?

To be balanced against the arguments for absolute obedience to law is the legitimacy of protest within society. Since the time of Aristotle, it has been argued that the law must be tempered with equity, which dictates the standards of justice and rightness in society. Law derives its authority from the obedience of the people.[21] Laws must be directed to the 'good', not only to comply with the dictates of morality, but also for the more pragmatic reason of ensuring voluntary compliance with law. It may be argued that nowadays in a responsive, democratic

---

17 A principle endorsed in **Phillips v Eyre** (1870) and **Waddington v Miah** (1974). See, however, the War Damage Act 1965 and the War Crimes Act 1991 for illustrations of Parliament's power to legislate retrospectively.
18 See Bradley and Ewing, 1997, Chapter 6.
19 Kelsen, 1961, 1967.
20 On 'direct' and 'indirect' civil disobedience, see Rawls, 1973, Chapter 7.
21 Aristotle, The Politics, 1269a.

state, any dispute as to the rights of individuals and grievances against government action will be dealt with through the provided channels of complaint, for example through the individual's Member of Parliament or through an investigation by the Commissioners for Administration.[22] Alternatively, it may be argued that if many citizens are commonly aggrieved, the media can be employed to influence government and that, ultimately, at least once every five years,[23] the electorate can express its views through the ballot box. None of these avenues, however, may yield the desired result, particularly if the aggrieved individual or group is a minority without popular support.

Is there a right to disobey law?

The question that then arises is whether the individual has a 'right' to disobey the law.[24] A government true to democratic precepts of representativeness and fairness must be sensitive to demands for change. If it fails in that regard, it is at least arguable that demands for change, while entailing technical breaches of the law, should be accommodated within the constitutional framework.

In 1848, Henry Thoreau refused to pay taxes to support the slavery laws and declared: '. . . the place for a just man in such a community is in jail.'

In the same century, the suffragette movement resorted to unlawful behaviour in the ultimately successful pursuit of the right to enfranchisement – the right to vote.[25] Mahatma Gandhi's peaceful civil disobedience campaign led to the independence of India in 1947. The Civil Rights movement in the United States in the 1950s, led by Martin Luther King, resulted in reforms of the law concerning racial segregation.[26] The tide of protest over American involvement in the Vietnam war had a direct impact on government policy and further raised legal and political interest in civil disobedience. Major social changes of such magnitude would have been impossible without recognition that under certain limited conditions there exists a right of legitimate protest, however inconvenient and uncomfortable this is for governments. The 'law and order' model of the rule of law would fail to respect any such 'right', and the reaction may be one of repression.[27] However, it is not necessary to look to such major societal changes brought about by defiance of law in order to refute the 'law and order' model and proclaim some entitlement to dissent.

John Rawls concedes a right to disobedience in pursuit of changing a society's 'sense of justice', but confines civil disobedience to peaceful protest.[28] Rawls's thesis is founded on the notion of social contract. That concept, as has been seen above, involves the mutual recognition, inter alia, of the rights of citizens and the rights of the state. The extent to which citizens participate in the law-making process is critical to an understanding of the extent to which there exists an obligation to obey the law. Participation in the democratic process may, however, be used as a means to deny any right to disobey. That is to say, it may be argued that democratic participation implies the individual's acceptance of all laws within the state. Here we must consider what it is that citizens consent to when electing a government. It seems implausible to argue that we each consent to every action of government throughout a possible five-year term of office, irrespective of its merits. However, Professor Plamenatz states that when a vote is cast:

---

22 See Chapter 26.
23 Under the Parliament Act 1911, the maximum life of a Parliament is five years. See further Chapter 13.
24 See Rawls, 1973, Chapter 7.
25 See, inter alia, Kent, 1987.
26 **Brown v Board of Education of Topeka** (1954); and see King, 1963.
27 As in Tiananmen Square 1989.
28 Rawls, 1973, Chapter 6.

> . . . you put yourself by your vote under an obligation to obey whatever government
> comes legally to power under the system, and this can properly be called giving
> consent. For the purpose of an election is to give authority to the people who win it
> and if you vote, knowing what you are doing and without being compelled to do it, you
> voluntarily take part in the process, which gives authority to those people. [1963,
> Vol 1, p 239]

This argument surely is contentious and represents a very limited view of the requirement that
a government should have moral authority to govern. Richard Wasserstrom (1963), on the
other hand, argues that, by the participatory democratic process, a prima facie obligation to obey
law is imposed, but this prima facie duty can be overridden by the demands of conscience.

The appropriate response of the state to acts of civil disobedience is a difficult matter.
Professor Ronald Dworkin, for example, argues for official tolerance in the face of dissent and
law breaking which is undertaken in pursuit of rights – even where violence is employed.[29] In
Taking Rights Seriously, Dworkin argues that the state should act with caution in prosecuting civilly
disobedient acts. First, the state should respect the stand taken in the defence of rights, even if
that stand should prove misguided when the matter ultimately comes before the Supreme
Court for a ruling on the validity of the contentious legislation. The decision to prosecute
should be decided on the basis of utilitarianism.[30] As Dworkin states in *A Matter of Principle*:

> Utilitarianism may be a poor general theory of justice, but it states an excellent neces-
> sary condition for just punishment. Nobody should ever be punished unless punishing
> him will do some good on the whole in the long run all things considered. [1986, p 114]

By prosecuting disobedience to law, the state upholds the positive law and reinforces it. On the
other hand, in prosecuting, the state may reveal the defects in the law and may be seen to be
enforcing that for which there exists little or no popular support. By way of example, the
acquittal of Clive Ponting on charges of breaching section 2 of the Official Secrets Act 1911[31]
is illustrative: the jury refusing to convict despite a clear ruling by the judge as to the illegality
of Ponting's conduct.[32] It may also be argued that by rigid enforcement the state enhances the
moral claims advanced by the civilly disobedient. In part, this was the view adopted by Socrates
in submitting to his fate. He drank the hemlock to show respect to the law and constitution of
Athens, although he must have known that in so doing he would bring the positive law of the
state into disrepute. What he could not foresee was the timeless example that Athens, in
executing Socrates, set for humanity.[33]

Is there a duty to disobey?

The converse position must also be considered: if a state violates the requirements of the rule
of law, to what extent is it the duty of citizens to disobey the law? Furthermore, what justification, if any, is there for another state or the international community taking action against the
'guilty' state? The Nazi regime in Germany provides the most obvious – but not unique –
example. On individual duty, Professor Lon Fuller maintained that the citizen is under no
obligation to obey unjust law: 'A mere respect for constituted authority must not be confused
with fidelity to law.' Fuller goes further and asserts that an evil regime, which grossly violates

---

29 Dworkin, 1977, Chapters 7 and 8; and see MacGuigan, 'Obligation and obedience', in Pennock and Chapman, 1970.
30 The doctrine which assesses the justification for a particular action according to the overall increase in the sum of benefit to
    society as a whole.
31 Discussed in Chapter 22.
32 **R v Ponting** (1985); and see Barker, 1990, pp 183–84.
33 See Plato, 'Socrates' defence and 'Crito', in Hamilton and Cairns, 1989.

the basic precepts of morality, is incapable of creating law at all.[34] In HLA Hart's view, this represents confused thinking on Fuller's part. His preferred approach is to recognise the validity of Nazi laws – however abhorrent in moral terms – but also to recognise that moral obligations can outweigh the legal obligation to obey.[35] In addition to facilitating clarity about law, this approach enables the regime to be held to account for its actions. Simply to deny – as does Professor Fuller – that there was any law during Nazi rule is to remove the basis for international legal sanctions.

AV Dicey and the Rule of Law[36]

In *Introduction to the Study of the Law of the Constitution*, AV Dicey offered a prosaic description of the rule of law. Here, there are none of the ringing proclamations of the theological or political philosophers. Nevertheless, Dicey's views have continued to exert their influence, despite many challenges, and it is this influence which requires examination.

Dicey argued that the rule of law – in its practical manifestation – has three main aspects:

- no man is punishable or can be lawfully made to suffer in body or goods except for a distinct breach of law established in the ordinary legal manner before the ordinary courts of the land. In this sense, the rule of law is contrasted with every system of government based on the exercise by persons in authority of wide, arbitrary, or discretionary powers of constraint;
- no man is above the law; every man and woman, whatever be his or her rank or condition, is subject to the ordinary law of the realm and amenable to the jurisdiction of the ordinary tribunals; and
- the general principles of the constitution (as, for example, the right to personal liberty, or the right of public meeting) are, with us, the result of judicial decisions determining the rights of private persons in particular cases brought before the courts.[37]

Each of these points requires examination.

Lack of arbitrariness and retrospectivity

The first element of this analysis is self-explanatory. It requires that no one be punished except for conduct which represents a clear breach of law.[38] Designed to deny to governments any right to make secret or arbitrary laws, or retrospective penal laws, and to limit the discretionary powers of government, the rule protects the individual. In order to comply fully with this requirement, laws should be open and accessible, clear and certain. In part, this idea ties in with that of the 'social contract' and the reciprocal relationship between the state and the individual. Under social contract theories, the individual citizen transfers his autonomous individual rights to the government, to be held by that government on trust. To express the matter differently, the citizen owes allegiance to the Crown in return for which he is under the protection of the Crown.[39] The doctrine of allegiance incorporates the idea of obedience to law – both on the part of the citizen and on the part of government. Laws which are arbitrary or secret are

---

34 Fuller, 1958.
35 Hart, 1958, p 593 – a view echoing that of St Thomas Aquinas.
36 See Jennings, 1959b, p 54; Heuston, 'The rule of law', in 1964a, p 40.
37 Dicey, 1885, pp 188, 193, 195, respectively. And see Craig, 1990.
38 The principle of *nulla poena sine lege*.
39 See Chitty, 1820, discussed in Chapter 6.

incapable of justification on the basis of the mandate of the people and, accordingly, offend against the reciprocal relationship on which constitutional democracy depends. Where wide discretionary powers are conferred on the executive – whether they be in the form of granting power to a minister of the Crown to act 'as he thinks fit' or on civil servants administering the social welfare system – it will be impossible for the individual to know what rights he or she has. Moreover, the delegation of broad discretionary power – albeit on the authority of the sovereign Parliament – renders such power difficult, if not impossible, to challenge before a court of law or other adjudicatory tribunal.[40]

If retrospective penal liability is imposed, the individual is placed in the position where his conduct was lawful at the time of his action but, subsequently, he is held responsible as if his conduct was then unlawful. An examination and evaluation of the relevance of this first proposition entails drawing on relevant illustrations from both statute and case law. For example, the courts construe penal statutes narrowly and will be slow to find that Parliament intended to impose retrospective liability. So important is the concept of *mens rea* in the criminal law[41] that it will rarely be appropriate for a prosecution to succeed in its absence, and it is for this reason that the courts employ the presumption of statutory interpretation against retrospectivity:

> Perhaps no rule of construction is more firmly established than this – that a retrospective operation is not to be given to a statute so as to impair an existing right or obligation, otherwise than as regards matters of procedure, unless that effect cannot be avoided without doing violence to the language of the enactment. If the enactment is expressed in language which is fairly capable of either interpretation, it ought to be construed as prospective only.[42]

In *Waddington v Miah* (1974), the House of Lords interpreted the Immigration Act 1971 in a manner which denied retrospective effect in relation to criminal offences, using, as an aid to construction, Article 7 of the European Convention on Human Rights, which guarantees freedom from retrospectivity. Nonetheless, the presumption will not be available where Parliament expressly provides for retrospectivity, as, for example, in the War Damage Act 1965 and the War Crimes Act 1991.[43] In *Burmah Oil v Lord Advocate* (1965), where the House of Lords had awarded compensation for the destruction of oil installations in wartime, the government speedily introduced legislation nullifying the effect of the decision under the War Damage Act 1965. This case demonstrates clearly the subordination of the judiciary to parliamentary supremacy and the limits thereby imposed on the judges' capacity to uphold rights.

Notwithstanding the general prohibition against retrospectivity, there may be instances where a decision which imposes, for example, criminal liability may be upheld by the courts. For example, until 1990, there existed a time-honoured exemption from the law of rape for husbands who 'raped' their wives. In the case of *R v R* (1991), however, the House of Lords upheld the conviction of a husband for the rape of his wife, arguing that the rule against liability for rape within marriage was anachronistic. In a challenge to this decision under the European Convention on Human Rights, on the basis that it infringed Article 7 of the Convention, which makes retrospectivity unlawful, the Court of Human Rights ruled that the sweeping away of husbands' immunity from criminal prosecution and conviction for rape represented an evolution towards greater equality between the sexes and was consistent with that equality.[44]

---

40 See Smith, 1985.
41 *Sweet v Parsley* (1970).
42 Wright J in *Re Athlumney* (1898), pp 551–52.
43 See Chapter 6.
44 *SW v United Kingdom; C v United Kingdom* (1995).

Equality before the law: government under the law

Dicey's second limb emphasises the notion that government itself is subject to law and that everyone, irrespective of rank, whether official or individual, shall be subject to the law,[45] and subject to the same courts. Dicey viewed the French system of special courts to deal with complaints against government as abhorrent, fearing that specially constituted courts would unduly favour the government over the citizen. Dicey has often been interpreted as requiring that there be actual equality in terms of legal rights, powers and capacities. Such an interpretation is, however, misguided. The idea of equality before the law, irrespective of status, is subject to so many exceptions 'that the statement is of doubtful value'.[46] In so far as equal powers are concerned, it must be recognised that the police have powers over and above the citizen,[47] that ministers have power to enact delegated legislation (but subject to parliamentary approval), that the Crown enjoys immunities under the law, that the government acting in the name of the Crown may exercise prerogative powers which may defeat the rights of individuals, that Members of Parliament have immunity from the law of defamation under the privileges of Parliament,[48] and that diplomats enjoy immunities not available to citizens. And, as Sir Ivor Jennings points out, no two citizens are entirely equal:

> . . . pawnbrokers, money lenders, landlords, drivers of motor cars, married women, and indeed most other classes have special rights and duties. [1959b, Appendix II, p 11]

Against this catalogue, which is not exhaustive, must be set the extent to which government and public officials are subject to law in the sense of being accountable for their actions before the ordinary courts, for this, indeed, was Dicey's real argument. The doctrine acknowledges the need of a consistent application of the law irrespective of status. No one is immune from criminal prosecution (other than the monarch: 'Against the King law has no coercive power').[49]

Official accountability to law is one of the foundations of the rule of law. Following a detailed analysis of Dicey's writing, Professor Jeffrey Jowell concludes that:

> . . . its ghost has refused to rest. It rises still to haunt a minister who publishes 'guidelines' that cut across the powers of the statute under which he operates, the minister who penalises local authorities for overspending without giving them a fair hearing, a government department which decides in accordance with a secret code not available to the public, or a Prime Minister who seeks to deprive civil servants of their rights to remain members of a trade union. ['The rule of law and its underlying values', in Jowell and Oliver, 2011]

Sir Ivor Jennings criticises Dicey's emphasis on government according to law on the basis that it is too narrow an interpretation:

> . . . it is a small point upon which to base a doctrine called by the magnificent name of 'rule of law', particularly when it is generally used in a very different sense. [1959b, p 312]

---

45 See Zellick, 1985.
46 Jackson and Leonard, 2001.
47 Under common law and the Police and Criminal Evidence Act 1984.
48 See Chapter 17.
49 Maitland, 1908, p 100.

TRS Allan subjects Dicey's analysis to detailed scrutiny, focusing on Dicey's second principle: that of equality before the law.[50] Allan seeks a solution to the apparent paradox presented by Dicey's insistence that both parliamentary sovereignty and the rule of law comprise the fundamental doctrines of the constitution – given that the former concept is inherently capable of damaging the latter. Towards this end, Allan presents a wealth of evidence directed to establishing a middle way between the formalism of the 'principle of legality' and the vagueness of the 'broad political ideal'. In other words, what is sought is an explanation of the means by which the power of sovereignty is restrained or restricted without expounding a 'complete social philosophy' (1985a, p 114). The key to such an understanding, according to Allan, lies in the role of the judiciary and in an acceptance that it is the judges who – in applying the 'juristic principle' of the rule of law – limit the power of Parliament. To summarise, Allan draws on the principles of statutory interpretation (non-retrospectivity, clarity, *mens rea* in penal statutes, etc); on the independence of the judiciary as ensured by the separation of powers; on the right of access to the courts for all citizens; and on the judiciary's reluctance for the jurisdiction of judicial review to be limited. By these and other means, Allan seeks to demonstrate that:

> . . . the rule of law strengthens democracy by ensuring that government operates only within rules adopted or sanctioned by Parliament . . .

and that:

> The constitutional principle of the rule of law serves, however, to bridge the gap between the legal doctrine of parliamentary sovereignty and the political doctrine of the sovereignty of the people. In interpreting statutes in conformity, so far as possible, with general notions of fairness and justice – in seeking to apply those common standards of morality which are taken for granted in the community – the judge respects the natural expectations of the citizen.
>
> The rule of law therefore assists in preventing the subversion of the political sovereignty of the people by manipulation of the legal sovereignty of Parliament. [1985a, p 130]

In order to evaluate such contrasting views as those expressed above, consideration of some evidence becomes necessary.

Judicial review

The means by which, and grounds upon which, judicial review may be granted are considered in Chapters 23 to 25. It is sufficient for current purposes to note that judicial review is the means by which administrative authorities – whether ministers of the Crown, government departments, local authorities or others with law-making and administrative powers – are confined within the powers granted to them by Parliament by the courts. It is for a court to determine – following the granting of an application for judicial review – whether the body in question has acted *intra vires* or *ultra vires* (that is, inside or outside its powers).

Actions for judicial review of administrative action, employing concepts of *intra* and *ultra vires* and the rules of natural justice, ensure that the executive acts within the law. Judicial review – in its infancy in Dicey's time – represents the means by which the sovereignty of Parliament

---

50 Allan, 1985a; 1993, Chapter 2; 2001.

is upheld and the rule of law applied. Dicey, writing in 1915, analysed the significance of **Board of Education v Rice** (1911) and **Local Government Board v Arlidge** (1915), claiming that:

> . . . each case finally lays down, as far as the courts of England are concerned, a clear and distinct principle by which any department of the government, such for example as the Board of Education, must be guarded in the exercise of powers conferred upon it by statute.[51]

Judicial review is confined to matters of public, rather than private law. Thus, where a relationship between an aggrieved citizen and a body is based, for example, on the law of contract, judicial review will not lie.[52] It is also necessary – in the interests of good administration – that aggrieved individuals have 'sufficient interest' – or *locus standi* – in the matter to bring it to court.[53] There are numerous grounds on which judicial review may be sought. By way of illustration, a body may act *ultra vires* if it uses its powers for the wrong purpose,[54] or if it abuses its powers,[55] or if it adopts a policy which is so rigid that it fails to exercise a discretion with which it has been invested.[56] The law imposes standards of reasonableness upon administrative bodies, and failure to act in a reasonable manner may cause a body to act *ultra vires*.[57] A body may act *ultra vires* if it is conferred with delegated powers but delegates them further to another.[58]

Statute may require that administrators adopt particular procedures in the exercise of these powers: should they not do so, and the procedures are judicially deemed to be 'mandatory' (compulsory) rather than 'directory' (advisory), a body will be held to be acting *ultra vires*. If a public body under a duty to act fails to act at all, the court can order it to do so by a mandatory order. The rules of natural justice must also be observed in decision making: where an individual has a right or interest at stake because of an administrative decision, he is entitled to fair treatment.[59] All of these grounds for review were rationalised by the Judicial Committee of the House of Lords (now the Supreme Court) into three principal categories: irrationality, illegality and procedural impropriety.[60] These categories were not regarded as exhaustive, and it was recognised that the European concept of 'proportionality' might emerge as a distinctive category. This has happened, most particularly in relation to the Human Rights Act 1998, which enables rights protected under the European Convention on Human Rights to be enforced in the domestic courts. The essence of proportionality is that a public body must only do what is necessary to achieve a legitimate objective, and no more. An early (pre-Human Rights Act) example of proportionality being applied is **R v Barnsley Metropolitan Borough Council ex parte Hook** (1976). In this case a market stall holder had his licence revoked by the Council for urinating in public. Lord Denning MR quashed the decision, partly on the basis that the penalty was disproportionate to the 'offence'.

The powers of the court can only be exercised over a matter which it is competent to determine. This introduces the concept of justiciability, and it is this latter doctrine which most particularly undermines the concept of the rule of law. In **Council of Civil Service Unions v Minister for the Civil Service**, the House of Lords identified the categories of decision which would be immune from judicial review – that is to say non-justiciable. Amongst these – and the list is not exhaustive – are the making of treaties, the dissolution of Parliament, the appointment of

---

51 Dicey, 1885, Appendix 2, p 493.
52 See eg **R v City Panel on Takeovers and Mergers ex parte Datafin plc** (1987); **O'Reilly v Mackman** (1983).
53 See, *inter alia*, **Inland Revenue Commissioner v National Federation of Self-Employed and Small Businesses Ltd** (1982).
54 **Attorney General v Fulham Corporation** (1921).
55 **Webb v Minister of Housing and Local Government** (1965); **Westminster Bank v Minister of Housing and Local Government** (1971).
56 **Padfield v Minister of Agriculture Fisheries and Food** (1968).
57 **Associated Provincial Picture Houses Ltd v Wednesbury Corporation** (1948).
58 **Barnard v National Dock Labour Board** (1953); **Vine v National Dock Labour Board** (1957).
59 **R v IRC ex parte Preston** (1985); **Wheeler v Leicester City Council** (1985).
60 **Council of Civil Service Unions v Minister for the Civil Service** (1985).

ministers, declarations of war and peace, and matters relating to the granting of honours. What unites these categories is the fact that each involves matters of high policy which is most appropriately determined – in the eyes of the judiciary – not by the courts but by the executive. Where this applies, it may be said that the rule of law is undermined by respect for the doctrine of the separation of powers: an ironic consequence.

The doctrine of judicial review nevertheless represents a bedrock for the application of the rule of law, keeping those with law making and discretionary powers within the law. From **Entick v Carrington** (1765) to **R v Secretary of State for the Home Department ex parte Fire Brigades' Union** (1993), wherein Kenneth Baker, the Home Secretary, was held to be acting *ultra vires* when attempting to introduce a new tariff for compensation under the Criminal Injuries Compensation Scheme under the royal prerogative rather than under power conferred by statute, the principle is established and reiterated.

The legal process

For the rule of law to be respected and applied, the legal process – civil and criminal – must exhibit certain features. These features may be categorised as accessibility and procedural fairness.

Accessibility

The law must be accessible to all if rights are to be enforced. As Lord Phillips of Worth Matravers PSC stated: '[A]ccess to a court to protect one's rights is the foundation of the rule of law.'[61] Accordingly, there must not only exist a system of courts available locally but the cost of having recourse to the courts must be such that there is real – rather than symbolic – access to the courts. For the law to be attainable, adequate legal advice and assistance must be provided at a cost affordable by all.[62]

The right to a fair trial is protected under Article 6 of the European Convention on Human Rights, and includes the right of the citizen:

> . . . to defend himself in person or through legal assistance of his own choosing or, if he has not sufficient means to pay for legal assistance, to be given it free when the interests of justice so require.

In **Granger v United Kingdom** (1990), the defendant had been denied further legal aid to pursue an appeal against conviction. Granger, unable to afford legal representation, acted in person. Representing the Crown were senior government counsel. On an application under the Convention, Granger alleged that he had been denied the protection of law. The Court of Human Rights ruled that the denial of legal aid infringed Granger's rights.

Procedural fairness

Justice and the rule of law demand that, in the conduct of legal proceedings, procedural fairness be observed. Subsumed within this requirement are many subsidiary conditions. The judge must be impartial: *nemo iudex in sua causa*. Where jurors are involved, they, too, must be free from bias. In addition, jurors should be reasonably representative of the society they serve. Evidence gathered by the police must be acquired by lawful means. The evidence admitted into court must be both of an admissible nature and fairly presented. The proceedings should be conducted in such a manner as to be intelligible to the parties, witnesses and jurors.[63]

---

61 *A v HM Treasury* (2010), at para 146.
62 See, *inter alia*, Smith, Bailey and Gunn, 2002, Chapter 9; Zander, 2003, Chapters 6 and 9; Slapper and Kelly, 2004, Chapter 12.
63 See, *inter alia*, Kafka, 1956; and Keedy, 1951 for illustrations of breaches of this requirement.

The jury

The precise origins of trial by jury in its modern form are shrouded in mist.[64] It is thought that by the end of the fifteenth century, the jury, as triers of fact, was established in what today would be a recognisable form. Trial by jury for serious criminal offences, and in civil cases where defamation, malicious prosecution, false imprisonment and allegations of fraud are at issue,[65] is regarded as the 'bulwark of our liberties'.[66] The decision of the jury is regarded as conclusive and unimpeachable. Criticisms have long been made of the lack of representativeness of the jury. Several factors militate against representativeness: the accuracy of the electoral register from which jurors are selected; the relative lack of randomness in jury selection; the vetting of jurors;[67] and challenges to members of the jury. Moreover, a wide range of persons are either ineligible for jury service, or disqualified from sitting or may be excused from jury service. When a jury is summoned, the presence of a juror may be challenged 'for cause' – that is, where some fact relating to the juror is known and gives rise to a challenge. Little is known about the individual juror – only the names and addresses are given.[68] This relative anonymity of jurors contrasts starkly with the position in the United States of America, where the selection of a jury entails a prolonged inquiry into the lives and attitudes of prospective jurors. While the process is protracted,[69] it is designed to ensure that the jury ultimately selected will be one free from bias in relation to the defendant. In the United Kingdom, a person may be excused from service on the basis of personal knowledge of the case, bias, personal hardship or conscientious objection to jury service. A juror should not be excused on general grounds such as race, religion, political beliefs or occupation.[70]

Evidence

For the rule of law to be observed, it is of central importance that the evidence before the court be both complete and reliable. Contravention of this requirement undermines the concept of a fair trial. Subsumed within this question is the complex and controversial matter of the manner in which evidence is obtained and the question of admissibility. While the Police and Criminal Evidence Act 1984[71] went some way to improving the safeguards for the accused and was introduced, in part, to rectify deficiencies which had come to light,[72] the cases of the Birmingham Six,[73] the Guildford Four and the Maguire Seven[74] illustrated the deficiencies in the criminal justice system. In each of these cases, the defendants had served long terms of imprisonment for alleged Irish Republican Army (IRA) terrorist acts. In each case, the evidence relied upon was unreliable. Their convictions were quashed by the Court of Appeal following years of campaigning by relatives and friends for a review of their cases. In each case, a serious miscarriage of justice had occurred and as a result the integrity of the criminal justice system was tarnished.

At common law, a confession which is improperly obtained is inadmissible.[75] The Police and Criminal Evidence Act 1984 places this rule on a statutory basis, providing that if a confession

---

64 See Maitland, 1908, pp 115–30. See also Denning, 1982, Pt 2.
65 Supreme Court Act 1981, subject to the proviso in s 69(1) which permits the court to refuse trial by jury in cases of complexity or impracticality.
66 *Ward v James* (1966), p 295, *per* Lord Denning MR.
67 *R v Mason* (1980); *Attorney General's Guidelines on Jury Checks* (1988).
68 Prior to 1973, jurors' occupations were made known.
69 Jury selection for the trial of John de Lorean took five weeks.
70 *Practice Direction* (1988).
71 See, *inter alia*, Zander, 2003.
72 See McConville and Baldwin, 1980.
73 *R v McIlkenny* (1992).
74 See May, J, *Interim Report on the Maguire Case*, HC 556 (1990–91), London: HMSO
75 *Marks v Beyfus* (1890).

has been obtained 'by oppression', the court shall not allow the confession to be given in evidence unless satisfied beyond reasonable doubt that the confession – even if true – has not been obtained improperly (section 76).

Whereas the rules on the admissibility of improperly obtained confessions are relatively clear, the admissibility of other evidence obtained by either dubious or unlawful means has proved less clear and less satisfactory. Until 1979, the judges exercised their discretion as to whether or not evidence improperly acquired would be admissible.[76] However, in **R v Sang** (1979) the House of Lords ruled that no discretion existed to exclude evidence which had been obtained by unlawful or improper means. The only basis on which evidence could be excluded would be where the effect of admitting it would prove unduly 'prejudicial' to the defence or 'unfair' to admit it. The fact that the evidence was unlawfully acquired does not amount to 'unfairness' *per se*.[77] The admissibility of such evidence is now governed by section 78 of the Police and Criminal Evidence Act 1984, which provides that the court may refuse to allow evidence if:

> . . . it appears to the court that, having regard to all the circumstances, including the circumstances in which the evidence was obtained, the admission of the evidence would have such adverse effect on the fairness of the proceedings that the court ought not to admit it.

Another aspect of the rules of evidence falls under the common law principle of open justice which, among other things, requires that documents which have been placed before a judge and referred to in court proceedings should be accessible. Where there were objections to access to the documents, those objections would be considered by the court. The Court of Appeal so held in **R (Guardian News and Media Ltd) v City of Westminster Magistrates' Court and Another** (2012). In this case a journalist sought access to documents relating to extradition proceedings brought by the government of the United States of America against two British citizens. The Court accepted that the claimant had a serious journalistic purpose in stimulating public debate on a matter of public interest.

The protection of rights under common law?

The third limb of Dicey's description of the rule of law reveals his preference for common law protection of human rights over and above a specially formulated code of rights, thus demonstrating a faith in the judiciary which is not sustainable nowadays. Evaluation of this aspect of the definition must await analysis of the Human Rights Act 1998 in Chapter 18 and the scope of the protection which it gives to individual citizens.

The Human Rights Act 1998 'incorporated' rights protected under the European Convention on Human Rights into domestic law. Accordingly, citizens no longer have to undertake the lengthy process of applying to the Court of Human Rights in Strasbourg, but are able to seek a remedy in the domestic courts. The method of incorporation adopted, however, fell far short of enabling the judges to invalidate or set aside domestic legislation. Instead, the judges of the higher courts are empowered to make 'declarations of incompatibility' with Convention rights. Once such a declaration has been made, it remains for Parliament to approve an amendment to the law. As a result, the Human Rights Act, far from elevating individual rights proclaimed in the Convention to a higher status than statute, preserves Parliament's sovereign law-making and amending power, and also maintains the separation of powers.

---

76 **Kuruma Son of Kaniu v R** (1955); **Jeffrey v Black** (1978).
77 See Heydon, 1973; Ashworth, 1977.

Notwithstanding the Act's status, the rule of law is undoubtedly buttressed by the Act: every public body – by no means a simple concept[78] – is required to comply with Convention rights, and to fail to do so is to act unlawfully save where there is no available alternative form of action because of the requirements of primary legislation (section 6). To support rights further, the Act requires that judges interpret primary and secondary legislation 'so far as it is possible to do so in a manner compatible with Convention requirements' (section 3(1)). Coming into effect in Scotland in 1999 and in England in 2000, the impact of the Act has been significant and is having the effect of requiring all public bodies to scrutinise their procedures for Convention compliance, or face legal action.

Evaluation of Dicey's 'equality before the law'

The evidence for the notion of equality before the law is neither clear nor uncontentious. As with so much of the constitution, there remains room for doubt and argument. Nevertheless, it is submitted that there exists sufficient evidence to suggest that Dicey's approach remains a fruitful avenue for inquiry and exploration. To dismiss – as some writers do – this aspect of Dicey's exposition of the rule of law, is to deprive the student of the constitution of a valuable tool for analysis.

The rule of law in international dimension

The Universal Declaration of Human Rights of the United Nations, published in 1948, declares that:

It is essential, if man is not to be compelled to have recourse, as a last resort, to rebellion against tyranny and oppression, that human rights should be protected by the rule of law.

The European Convention also recognises the concept of the rule of law. The preamble states that:

The governments of European countries which are like-minded and have a common heritage of political traditions, ideals, freedom and the rule of law . . . have agreed as follows . . .

On an international level, the rule of law is also advanced by the International Commission of Jurists, which strives to uphold and improve the rule of law within the legal systems of its members. The Declaration of Delhi, issued under the auspices of the International Commission of Jurists, affirms the rule of law and its value in promoting the protection of civil and political rights and linked such rights with the development and protection of social and economic rights. The Congress of the International Commission of Jurists met in 1959 in order to 'clarify and formulate a supranational concept of the rule of law'.[79] The Declaration of Delhi 1959 recognised that:

---

78 For discussion see Chapter 18, but note here that s 6(3)(a) and (b) includes courts and tribunals, and 'any person certain of whose functions are functions of a public nature, but does not include either House of Parliament or a person exercising functions in connection with proceedings in Parliament'.

79 Marsh, 'The rule of law as a supranational concept', in Guest, 1961, p 240, and Marsh, 1959.

> ... the rule of law is a dynamic concept for the expansion and fulfilment of which jurists are primarily responsible and which should be employed not only to safeguard and advance the civil and political rights of the individual in a free society, but also to establish social, economic, educational and cultural conditions under which his legitimate aspirations and dignity may be realised ...

Such aspirational statements recognise the need for the economic foundations to be such that the dignity of man can be a reality in society. It is meaningless to speak of the rule of law as insisting on decent, or even minimal, standards of living within the context of poverty and disease. In order to secure any such standards, a sufficient level of economic wealth must be achieved. Even where such standards do exist, there will remain resistances to any formulation of social and economic rights as enforceable positive legal rights, for such formulations require the allocation of resources within society. Whereas governments may be willing – indeed obliged – to respect civil and political rights in a democracy, the protection of such rights generally will be effected without significant national resource implications. The protection of freedoms, such as freedom of speech and association, requires no more than a restraint on government. The protection of social and economic rights requires positive action, at a high cost.[80]

Summary

The rule of law – in its many guises – represents a challenge to state authority and power, demanding both that powers be granted legitimately and that their exercise is according to law. 'According to law' means both according to the legal rules and something over and above purely formal *legality* and imputes the concepts of *legitimacy* and constitutionality. In its turn, legitimacy implies *rightness* or *morality* of law. The law is not autonomous but rests on the support of those it governs. The law is the servant of the sense of rightness in the community, and whilst the rule of law places law above every individual – irrespective of rank and station – it remains, paradoxically, subject to the ultimate judgment of the people.

 Further Reading

Allan, T. (1999) 'The Rule of Law as the Rule of Reason: Consent and Constitutionalism', Law Quarterly Review, 115: 221.

Allan, T. (2001) *Constitutional Justice: a Liberal Theory of the Rule of Law*, OUP, Chapters 1–4.

Bingham, Lord (2007) 'The Rule of Law', Cambridge Law Journal, 66(1): 67.

Hutchinson, A.P. and Monahan, P. (eds) (1987) *The Rule of Law: Ideal or Ideology*, Toronto: Carswell.

Jowell, J. (2011) 'The Rule of Law and its Underlying Values' in J. Jowell and D. Oliver (eds) *The Changing Constitution* (7th edn), Oxford: OUP.

Raz, J. (1977) 'The Rule of Law and its Virtue', Law Quarterly Review, 93.

Raz, J. (1979) *The Authority of Law*, Oxford: OUP.

Steyn, Lord (2009) 'Civil Liberties in Modern Britain', Public Law, 228.

Wasserstrom, R. (1963) 'The Obligation to Obey the Law', California UL Rev 780.

---

80 See Aubert, 1983, Chapters 2 and 7.

Chapter 4

The Separation of Powers

Chapter Contents

Introduction

The separation of powers, together with the rule of law and parliamentary sovereignty, runs like a thread throughout the constitution of the United Kingdom. It is a doctrine which is fundamental to the organisation of a state – and to the concept of constitutionalism – in so far as it prescribes the appropriate allocation of powers, and the limits of those powers, to differing institutions. The concept has played a major role in the formation of constitutions. The extent to which powers can be, and should be, separate and distinct was a central feature in formulating, for example, both the American and French revolutionary constitutions. In any state, three essential bodies exist: the executive, the legislature and the judiciary. It is the relationship between these bodies which must be evaluated against the backcloth of the principle. The essence of the doctrine is that there should be, ideally, a clear demarcation of personnel and functions between the legislature, executive and judiciary in order that none should have excessive power and that there should be in place a system of checks and balances between the institutions. However, as will be seen, there are significant departures from the pure doctrine under the United Kingdom's constitution, and it must be conceded that, while the doctrine is accorded respect, it is by no means absolute.

In order to evaluate the extent to which the separation of powers applies – and the many exceptions to the pure doctrine – it is necessary firstly to define the major institutions of the state and evaluate the relationship between them. In order to do this the following relationships will be examined:

- the executive and the legislature;
- the legislature and the judiciary;
- the executive and the judiciary.

Historical Development

The identification of the three elements of the constitution derives from Aristotle (384–322 BC). In *The Politics*, Aristotle proclaimed that:

> There are three elements in each constitution in respect of which every serious lawgiver must look for what is advantageous to it; if these are well arranged, the constitution is bound to be well arranged, and the differences in constitutions are bound to correspond to the differences between each of these elements. The three are, first, the deliberative, which discusses everything of common importance; second, the officials; and third, the judicial element. [Bk iv, xiv, 1297b35]

The constitutional seeds of the doctrine were thus sown early, reflecting the need for government according to and under the law, a requirement encouraged by some degree of a separation of functions between the institutions of the state.

The constitutional historian FW Maitland traces the separation of powers in England to the reign of Edward I (1272–1307):

> In Edward's day all becomes definite – there is the Parliament of the three estates, there is the King's Council, there are the well known courts of law. [1908, p 20]

Viscount Henry St John Bolingbroke (1678–1751), in *Remarks on the History of England*, advanced the idea of separation of powers. Bolingbroke was concerned with the necessary balance of powers within a constitution, arguing that the protection of liberty and security within the state depended upon achieving and maintaining an equilibrium between the Crown, Parliament and the people. Addressing the respective powers of the King and Parliament, Bolingbroke observed that:

> Since this division of power, and these different privileges constitute and maintain our government, it follows that the confusion of them tends to destroy it. This proposition is therefore true; that, in a constitution like ours, the safety of the whole depends on the balance of the parts. [1748, pp 80–83]

Baron Montesquieu (1689–1755, living in England from 1729–31) stressed the importance of the independence of the judiciary in De l'Esprit des Lois (1748):

> When the legislative and executive powers are united in the same person, or in the same body of magistrates, there can be no liberty . . . Again, there is no liberty if the power of judging is not separated from the legislative and executive. If it were joined with the legislative, the life and liberty of the subject would be exposed to arbitrary control; for the judge would then be the legislator. If it were joined to the executive power, the judge might behave with violence and oppression. There would be an end to everything, if the same man, or the same body, whether of the nobles or the people, were to exercise those three powers, that of enacting laws, that of executing public affairs, and that of trying crimes or individual causes.

Here is the clearest expression of the demand for a separation of functions. It has been remarked that Montesquieu's observations on the English constitution were inaccurate at the time, representing more a description of an idealised state than reality.[1] Moreover, it should not be assumed that Montesquieu's preferred arrangement of a pure separation of powers is uncontroversial. Throughout history, there has been exhibited a tension between the doctrine of separation of powers and the need for balanced government – an arrangement depending more on checks and balances within the system (as emphasised by Bolingbroke) than on a formalistic separation of powers. Sir Ivor Jennings has interpreted Montesquieu's words to mean not that the legislature and the executive should have no influence over the other, but rather that neither should exercise the power of the other.[2] Sir William Blackstone, a disciple of Montesquieu, adopted and adapted Montesquieu's strict doctrine, reworking his central idea to incorporate the theory of mixed government. While it was of central importance to Blackstone that, for example, the executive and legislature should be sufficiently separate to avoid 'tyranny', he nevertheless viewed their total separation as potentially leading to dominance of the executive by the legislature.[3] Thus, partial separation of powers is required to achieve a mixed and balanced constitutional structure.

The Contemporary Doctrine

The separation of powers doctrine does not insist that there should be three institutions of government each operating in isolation from each other. Indeed, such an arrangement would be unworkable, particularly under a constitution dominated by the sovereignty of Parliament.

---

1   Vile, 1967, pp 84–85.
2   Jennings, 1959b, Appendix I.
3   Commentaries on the Laws of England (1765–69), Vol I.

Under such an arrangement, it is essential that there be a sufficient interplay between each institution of the state. For example, it is for the executive, for the most part, to propose legislation for Parliament's approval. Once passed into law, Acts of Parliament are upheld by the judiciary. A complete separation of the three institutions could result in legal and constitutional deadlock. Rather than a pure separation of powers, the concept insists that the primary functions of the state should be allocated clearly and that there should be checks to ensure that no institution encroaches significantly upon the functions of the other. If hypothetical constitutional arrangements within a state are considered, a range of possibilities exists:

(a)   absolute power residing in one person or body exercising executive, legislative and judicial powers: no separation of powers;

(b)   power being diffused between three separate bodies exercising separate functions with no overlaps in function or personnel: pure separation of powers; and

(c)   powers and personnel being largely – but not totally – separated with checks and balances in the system to prevent abuse: mixed government and weak separation of powers.

It is to this third category that the constitution of the United Kingdom most clearly subscribes.

Defining the Institutions

The executive

See Chapters 9–10.

The executive may be defined as that branch of the state which formulates policy and is responsible for its execution. In formal terms, the sovereign is the head of the executive. The Prime Minister, Cabinet and other ministers, for the most part, are elected Members of Parliament.[4] In addition, the Civil Service, local authorities, police and armed forces, constitute the executive in practical terms.

The legislature

See Chapters 13–16.

The Queen in Parliament is the sovereign law-making body within the United Kingdom. Formally expressed, Parliament comprises the Queen, House of Lords and House of Commons. All Bills[5] must be passed by each House and receive royal assent.

Parliament is bicameral, that is to say there are two chambers, each exercising a legislative role – although not having equal powers – and each playing a part in ensuring the accountability of the government. By way of introduction, it should be noted that membership of the House of Lords is not secured by election and is accordingly not accountable in any direct sense to the electorate.[6] The House of Commons is directly elected, and a parliamentary term is limited under the Parliament Act 1911 to a maximum of five years. Under the Fixed-term Parliaments Act 2011, each Parliament (with limited exceptions) lasts for five years.

---

4   Note that some ministers are drawn from the unelected House of Lords. See further Chapter 16.
5   With the exception provided by the Parliament Acts 1911–49.
6   But note that there are proposals under consideration for reforming the composition of the House of Lords.

The House is made up of the governing party: the political party which secures the highest number of seats at the election, and the opposition parties. The opposition parties comprise the remainder of the now 650 Members of Parliament. The official Opposition is the party which represents the second largest party in terms of elected members. In principle, the role of the official Opposition is to act as a government in waiting, ready at any time to take office should the government be forced out of office.[7] The General Election of 2010 produced an unusual result with no one political party having a sufficient majority of seats to form a government. A Coalition Government made up of the larger Conservative Party and the Liberal Democrat Party was formed, with the Labour Party forming the Official Opposition.

The judiciary

The judiciary is that branch of the state which adjudicates upon conflicts between state institutions, between state and individual, and between individuals. The judiciary is independent of both Parliament and the executive. Judicial independence is of prime importance both in relation to government according to law and in the protection of the rights and freedoms of the citizen against the executive. As Blackstone observed in his *Commentaries*:

> . . . in this distinct and separate existence of the judicial power in a peculiar body of men, nominated indeed, but not removable at pleasure by the Crown, consists one main preservative of the public liberty which cannot subsist long in any state unless the administration of common justice be in some degree separated both from the legislative and from the executive power. [Vol 1, p 204]

It is apparent, however, that, whilst a high degree of judicial independence is secured under the constitution, there are several aspects of the judicial function which reveal an overlap between the judiciary, Parliament and the executive.

Appointment

The Lord Chief Justice, Master of the Rolls, President of the Family Division, Vice Chancellor, Lord Justices of Appeal and Justices of the Supreme Court are appointed by the Queen.[8] For appointments to the High Court, the candidate must be a barrister of ten years' standing, or a solicitor with rights of audience in the High Court, or a circuit judge of two years' standing. For appointment to the Court of Appeal, the candidate must either be a barrister of ten years' standing, a solicitor with rights of audience in the High Court, or a current member of the High Court Bench.[9]

The Lord Chief Justice is the head of the judiciary assuming the additional title of President of the Courts of England and Wales and Head of the Judiciary of England and Wales. The Lord Chief Justice of England and Wales, the Lord Chief Justice of Northern Ireland and the Lord President of the Court of Session in Scotland may make written representations to Parliament on matters relating to the judiciary or the administration of justice.[10]

The socio-economic and educational background of the judiciary has been subjected to much research. In brief, the picture presented is one of a middle- and upper-class, middle-aged,

---

7   For consideration of the role of the Opposition, see Chapters 13–15.
8   Supreme Court Act 1981, s 10(1), (2).
9   Courts and Legal Services Act 1990, s 71.
10 In respect of Northern Ireland and Scotland the function is qualified by s 5(2) and (3) in order to respect the devolution settlements with those countries.

white, predominantly male judiciary dominated by people with a public-school and Oxford or Cambridge University education.[11] The Constitutional Reform Act 2005 established a Judicial Appointments Commission which has responsibility for the recruitment and selection of judges for the courts in England and Wales.[12]

Tenure

The Act of Settlement 1700 secured a senior[13] judge's tenure of office during 'good behaviour'. In relation to the Supreme Court, the Constitutional Reform Act 2005, section 33, now provides that:

> A judge of the Supreme Court holds that office during good behaviour, but may be removed from it on the address of both Houses of Parliament.

Senior judges cannot be dismissed for political reasons. They can be removed by compulsory retirement if they are incapacitated or unable to resign through incapacity.

'Misbehaviour' relates to the performance of a judge's official duties or the commission of a criminal offence. Not every judge convicted of an offence will be dismissed: six judges have been convicted for driving with an excess of alcohol in their blood but have continued in office. In 1830, Sir Jonah Barrington was removed from office in Ireland under the Address procedure for the embezzlement of monies paid into court. Theoretically, a judge can also be removed by 'impeachment' for 'high crimes and misdemeanours', although this procedure has not been used since 1805[14] and is thought to be obsolete.[15] In Scotland, judges can only be removed on the grounds of misconduct.[16]

The Constitutional Reform Act 2005 established the Office for Judicial Complaints. The Lord Chief Justice and the Lord Chancellor can refer a matter to the Office for investigation and report. Any decision relating to further action lies with the Lord Chief Justice.

The Judicial Pensions and Retirement Act 1993 introduced the retirement age of 70, which may be extended to 75 if in the public interest. From 1959, the retirement ages were set at 75 for a High Court judge and 72 for a circuit judge, although judges appointed before this date were permitted to remain in office.[17]

Salaries

In order to further to protect the judiciary from political debate, judicial salaries are charged on the Consolidated Fund.[18] Judicial salaries are relatively high, on the basis that it is in the national interest 'to ensure an adequate supply of candidates of sufficient calibre for appointment to judicial office'.[19]

---

11 See, inter alia, Griffith, 1997; Blom-Cooper and Drewry, 1972.
12 There is a Northern Ireland Judicial Appointments Commission. The CRA 2005 created a Northern Ireland Judicial Appointments Ombudsman.
13 Justices of Appeal, Justices of the High Court.
14 The trial of Lord Melville. The previous trial was that of Warren Hastings in 1788. Two Lord Chancellors, Bacon (1620) and Macclesfield (1725), have been removed by impeachment.
15 Impeachment is not obsolete in the United States of America where President Nixon was threatened with impeachment and resigned and President Clinton was acquitted in impeachment proceedings.
16 Claim of Right 1689, Article 13; *Mackay and Esslemont v Lord Advocate* (1937).
17 As did the late Lord Denning, who retired at the age of 83.
18 Supreme Court Act 1981, s 12(5). The Consolidated Fund provides payments under the Civil List, the salaries of the Speaker, the judiciary, the Comptroller and Auditor General and the Parliamentary Commissioner. The Consolidated Fund Bill is passed without parliamentary debate. See further Chapter 12.
19 HC Deb, Vol 23, Cols 257–61.

Disqualifications

Holders of full-time judicial appointments are barred from legal practice,[20] and may not hold paid appointments as directors or undertake any professional or business work. Judges are also disqualified from membership of the House of Commons.[21] Membership of the House of Commons does not, however, disqualify that person from appointment to the Bench.

Immunity from suit

All judges have immunity from legal action in the performance of their judicial functions. Provided that a judge acts within his jurisdiction, or honestly believes he is acting within his jurisdiction, no action for damages may lie. A judge is immune from the law of defamation and, even if 'actuated by envy, hatred and malice and all uncharitableness', he is protected.[22] In **Sirros v Moore** (1975), Lord Denning MR and Ormrod LJ ruled that every judge – irrespective of rank and including the lay magistracy – is protected from liability in respect of his judicial function provided that he honestly believed that the action taken was within his jurisdiction.[23] The Crown Proceedings Act 1947 also provides protection for the Crown from liability for conduct of any person discharging 'responsibilities of a judicial nature vested in him' or in executing the judicial process.[24]

Bias or personal interest

A judge is under a duty not to adjudicate on cases in which he has either an interest – whether personal or financial – or where he may be influenced by bias. A fundamental doctrine of natural justice is that 'no man should be judge in his own cause': *nemo iudex in sua causa*. Judicial impartiality – or freedom from bias – is discussed in detail in Chapter 25.

See Chapter 25.

The Office of Lord Chancellor[25]

The office of Lord Chancellor derives from the Norman Conquest when the King's secretary became known as the royal 'chancellor'. The first Chancellor is recorded in 1068. In the Middle Ages, the primary role of the Chancellor was to preside over Parliament. From the fourteenth century, his functions have been both parliamentary and judicial, in the latter role presiding over the Court of Chancery until 1875.

Prior to the Constitutional Reform Act 2005, the office of Lord Chancellor spanned all three institutions of the state – the executive, legislature and judiciary. The Lord Chancellor was a politically appointed member of the Cabinet, the speaker of the House of Lords and the head of the judiciary. Furthermore, as a senior judge the Lord Chancellor was entitled to participate in judicial proceedings, although by convention he would not adjudicate in cases which involved the government or were overtly political in nature. As head of the judiciary, with wide-ranging powers relating to the appointment of judges, the Lord Chancellor acted as the spokesperson for the judges and defended their independence from interference by the executive.

---

20 Courts and Legal Services Act 1990, s 75 and Sched 11.
21 House of Commons Disqualification Act 1975, s 1 and Sched 1.
22 **Sirros v Moore** (1975), p 132, *per* Lord Denning MR. See also **Fray v Blackburn** (1863); **Anderson v Gorrie** (1895). Jury verdicts are similarly protected (**Bushell's Case** (1670)), as are words spoken by participants in legal proceedings (**Munster v Lamb** (1883)). Barristers cannot be sued for negligence in the presentation of a client's case (**Rondel v Worsley** (1969)). For a recent consideration of the scope of immunity by the Court of Appeal see **Heath v Commissioner of Police for the Metropolis** (2004).
23 See Brazier, 1976.
24 Crown Proceedings Act 1947, s 2(5).
25 See, *inter alia*, Heuston, 1964b and 1987; Bradney, 1989; Drewry, 1972. The title Lord Chancellor is first recorded in 1461.

However, whatever perceived advantages flowed from the close relationship between the executive and Lord Chancellor these were outweighed by the criticism that the office of Lord Chancellor represented a major breach in the separation of powers, and could not withstand the allegation that the office raised doubts about the independence of the judiciary.[26] As discussed below, the Constitutional Reform Act 2005 reformed the office of Lord Chancellor in a manner which establishes a clearer separation of powers between the executive, legislature and judiciary. The office of Lord Chancellor is retained in name but the powers of the office are radically curtailed. The post is combined with that of the Secretary of State for Justice. The office holder must be 'qualified by experience'[27] but need not be a lawyer, and the Lord Chancellor no longer exercises any judicial functions or acts as Speaker of the House of Lords. Section 1 of the Act makes explicit reference to the rule of law, stating that the Act does not adversely affect that principle or the Lord Chancellor's existing role in protecting the rule of law. Section 3 imposes a statutory duty on the Lord Chancellor and other ministers of the Crown and those with responsibility for matters relating to the judiciary to uphold the continued independence of the judiciary.

The Supreme Court

One constitutional curiosity which represented a challenge to the separation of powers was the existence of the highest court in the United Kingdom, the Appellate Committee of the House of Lords, sitting in Parliament. Judges elevated to the highest court were made Life Peers under the Appellate Jurisdiction Act 1876, and known as Lords of Appeal in Ordinary, or Law Lords. The Court was physically located in committee rooms of the House of Lords, and judgments were delivered in the chamber of the House of Lords where its legislative work is carried out. The judges also contributed to the legislative work of the House of Lords, further blurring the line between the judiciary and the legislature. The arrangement can only be understood by reference to the constitutional convention which regulated the relationship between the judges sitting in their judicial capacity and the judges participating in the law-making work of the House of Lords. Convention dictated that – in order to protect their independence and impartiality – judges would not participate in party political debate.

The Constitutional Reform Act 2005 remedied this anomalous situation by creating a Supreme Court physically removed from the Houses of Parliament.[28] Situated in Middlesex Guildhall, opposite the Houses of Parliament, the Supreme Court represents an improved separation of powers between Parliament and the judiciary and complements the reformed office of Lord Chancellor. Although the name 'Supreme Court' was adopted, the Court was not given additional powers and is not comparable to a Supreme Court under a written constitution. Accordingly, it has the same powers as the Appellate Committee of the House of Lords, and – as previously – has no power to invalidate Acts of Parliament.

The Justices of the Supreme Court sit in panels of five, seven or nine Justices. Proceedings are open to the public.

---

26 The requirements of judicial independence were considered by the European Court of Human Rights in **Findlay v United Kingdom** (1997) and **McGonnell v United Kingdom** (2000): see further Chapter 18.

27 Section 2 provides that relevant experience may include experience as a minister, as a Member of either House of Parliament, as a practitioner, as a teacher of law in a university and any other experience that the Prime Minister considers relevant.

28 The Supreme Court commenced work on 1 October 2009.

The Relationship between Executive and Legislature; Legislature and Judiciary; Executive and Judiciary

In light of the doctrine of separation of powers, it is necessary to evaluate the manner in which, and the extent to which, separate functions are allocated between the differing bodies and kept separate. This task is most conveniently undertaken by examining the relationship between first, the executive and legislature, secondly, the legislature and judiciary and, thirdly, the executive and judiciary.

Executive and legislature

The personnel of government

Parliament provides the personnel of government. Ministers of the Crown, including the Prime Minister, must be members of either House of Parliament. By convention, the Prime Minister must be a member of the House of Commons. It is thus immediately apparent that the executive, far from being separated from the legislature, is drawn from within its ranks. It is for this reason that Walter Bagehot in *The English Constitution* denounced the theory of the separation of powers under the English constitution. For Bagehot, this feature of the constitution, however, far from being a dangerous divergence from an ideal separation of powers, had clear merits. To Bagehot, the close relationship between executive and Parliament represented 'the efficient secret of the English constitution' which:

> . . . may be described as the close union, the nearly complete fusion, of the executive and legislative powers. No doubt by the traditional theory, as it exists in all the books, the goodness of our constitution lies in the entire separation of the legislative and executive authorities, but in truth its merit consists in their singular approximation. The connecting link [between the executive and parliament] is the Cabinet. [Bagehot, 1867, pp 67–68]

There are, however, opposing views. Lord Hailsham, the Lord Chancellor in the 1979–87 Parliament, asserted[29] that the current electoral process which, generally, but not invariably, returns a government with a large majority of seats in Parliament, contributes to what he termed an 'elective dictatorship' – that is to say, a situation in which the executive controls the legislature. While Bagehot's view may have been tenable at the time in which he wrote, it is nowadays too simplistic and inaccurate a description of the working of the constitution.[30]

See Chapters 13–15.

Prima facie, this close union of executive and legislature would suggest that the potential for abuse against which Montesquieu warned exists at the heart of the constitution. This would be so if it were to be demonstrated that the executive controls Parliament. Judgment on that matter must be suspended until the working of Parliament has been examined in detail. There exist, however, tenable grounds for such an argument, but these must be set against the extent to which procedural mechanisms in Parliament avoid an actual or potential abuse of power by the executive. The constitutional principle entailed in this close union between executive and legislature, deriving from historical practice, is that of 'responsible government': that is to say

---

29 (1976) 120 SJ 693.
30 Richard Crossman (1993) states that Bagehot provides a correct description of Cabinet government as it was between 1832 and 1867; but see the opposing view expressed by Vile, 1967.

that the powers of government are scrutinised adequately by a democratically elected Parliament to whom every member of government is individually and collectively responsible.

Statutory limits on membership

There exist statutory limits on the extent to which the executive can dominate Parliament. The House of Commons Disqualification Act 1975 preserves the separation between the executive and legislature by providing that certain categories of people are disqualified from holding parliamentary office. Under section 2, holders of judicial office, civil servants, members of the armed forces and the police and members of foreign legislatures are debarred from office.

The Act also limits the number of government ministers in the House of Commons to 95 (section 2). Despite this limitation, 95 ministers, when considered together with their loyal Parliamentary Private Secretaries,[31] ensures that the government will generally enjoy the automatic support of some 120 Members of Parliament. Where the government has been elected with a strong majority of seats – as in 1983, when the Conservative Party had a majority of 144, and in 1997, when the electorate returned a Labour government with a majority of 179 – it must be conceded that the potential for dominance exists. An evaluation of this matter depends upon the adequacy of parliamentary procedures.

Political and procedural checks on government

The government, it must be recognised, irrespective of the size of its majority of seats in Parliament, is dependent upon Parliament for its continuance in office.[32] The loss of a vote of confidence on a matter of policy central to a government's programme will cause the government to fall, as occurred in 1979 when the Labour Prime Minister, James Callaghan, was forced to seek a dissolution of Parliament and call a general election. Furthermore, parliamentary procedures are devised to secure adequate scrutiny for legislative proposals, and it cannot merely be assumed that the government will always get its legislation through in the form which it envisaged. By way of example, in 1983–84, the Police and Criminal Evidence Bill was substantially amended following pressure from politicians of all parties, pressure groups, academics and lawyers. Furthermore, in 1986 the government – despite having a strong majority in Parliament – was forced to abandon its plans for legislation to deregulate Sunday trading due to parliamentary pressure. In 2012 the Coalition government was forced to modify its plans for reform of the House of Lords in light of opposition from Conservative Party MPs.

The Opposition

The role of the official Opposition must also be considered. Her Majesty's Loyal Opposition is, constitutionally speaking, a 'government in waiting'. Not only is it the function of the Opposition to question, challenge and oppose the government, but it also puts forward alternative policies and solutions to problems. In order to ensure that there is adequate opportunity for the Opposition to fulfil its constitutional role, 20 days per session are set aside for debate on subjects chosen by the Opposition.

Question Time, debates and select committees

Question Time and debates in Parliament ensure the accountability of government to Parliament. The administration of the state is scrutinised by a system of select committees in Parliament with wide powers of inquiry.

---

31 Who are elected Members of Parliament.
32 Note that this remains the case when fixed-term parliaments are introduced under the Fixed-term Parliaments Act 2011.

The House of Lords

In addition to checks within the House of Commons, the House of Lords may cause government to modify or abandon proposed legislation. The House of Lords has the power to amend and delay non-Money Bills for approximately a year before the Bill can receive royal assent under the Parliament Acts 1911 and 1949. Rather than risk the delay of legislation, the government may prefer to compromise its proposals and accept proposed amendments from the Lords.

See Chapter 16.

The electorate

Finally, the electorate, in addition to its role in a general election, can also express its displeasure with government policies during a parliamentary term at by-elections and local government elections. In the 1993 county council elections, the government lost control of many of the councils which had been its traditional supporters – clear evidence that no government can afford to ignore the views of the people. Subsequent by-elections confirmed the government's loss of electoral support, as did the general election on 1 May 1997, when the Conservative government suffered a humiliating defeat. In 2011 the Coalition government's plan to replace the Simple Majority voting system with the Alternative Vote system was abandoned after the people delivered a decisive 'No' vote in a referendum.

Delegated legislation and the separation of powers

Delegated – or secondary – legislation raises important questions relating to the separation of powers. Delegated legislation refers to laws, rules and regulations, made by government departments, local authorities and other public bodies, under the authority of an Act of Parliament: '. . . every exercise of a power to legislate conferred by or under an Act of Parliament.'[33]

The principal justification for the delegation of such law-making power is efficiency. By granting delegated power, Parliament is freed from scrutinising every technical detail of a Bill. Delegated power also enables ministers and others to 'fill in the details' after the parent Act has been passed. AV Dicey approved of delegated powers on this basis.[34] Delegated power has, however, been questioned. In 1929, Chief Justice Hewart[35] criticised delegated legislation as being an abuse of power. An Interdepartmental Committee of Inquiry on Ministers' Powers[36] exonerated ministers from this charge and defended both the necessity and desirability of delegated legislation.

In any parliamentary year, some 40 to 50 Acts of Parliament will be passed. The volume of delegated legislation, however, may amount to some 3,000 statutory instruments per year. While general Bills – public and private – are subjected to full parliamentary scrutiny, it will be seen in Chapter 14 that delegated legislation receives far more cursory examination by Parliament as a whole. The implication of delegated legislation in constitutional terms is that a legislative function is being exercised by the executive and not Parliament. The delegation of law-making power is a necessity given the heavy legislative programme and the modern complexity of legal regulation. Provided that parliamentary scrutiny is adequate, and that the courts are vigilant and effective in ensuring that delegated powers are exercised consistently with the law – intra vires – it may be concluded that this ostensible breach of the separation of powers is unavoidable, although whether it is subject to adequate scrutiny and control remains questionable.

---

33 Joint Committee on Delegated Legislation, HL 184, HC 475 (1971–72), London: HMSO, para 6. See further Chapter 14.
34 Dicey, 1885, p 52.
35 Hewart, 1929.
36 Donoughmore-Scott Committee, Cmnd 4046, 1932, London: HMSO.

In addition to the delegation of power to make secondary legislation, Acts of Parliament may on occasion confer on ministers the power to amend primary legislation. Such powers are known as Henry VIII powers and are discussed at page 324 below.

See Chapter 14.

Legislature and judiciary

It has been stated above that Parliament is sovereign and that the judiciary is subordinate to Parliament, but that the independence of the judiciary is protected. At the head of the judiciary is the Crown. The Crown appoints senior judges and represents the 'fountain of justice': all judicial acts are carried out in the name of the Crown.

Rules against criticism of the judiciary

To reinforce the independence of judges, convention dictates that there should be no criticism levelled at them from members of the executive – but not from other Members of Parliament. Parliamentary practice prohibits the criticism of judges other than under a motion expressing specific criticism or leading to an Address to the Crown for the removal of a judge. It was not, however, regarded as a breach of conventional rules when the then Prime Minister, Mrs Thatcher, in Parliament, criticised the light sentence imposed on a child molester.[37] There have, however, been other incidents where judges have been criticised in Parliament. The manner in which Members of Parliament are controlled in terms of what they may, or may not, say is through the powers of the Speaker of the House of Commons. These powers will be considered in Chapters 13 and 17.

The sub judice rule

Where proceedings are either before a court or awaiting trial, Members of Parliament are barred from raising them in debate. If the matter has not yet reached the courts, debate may be barred if the Speaker considers that there would result a real and substantial danger of prejudice to the trial arising as a consequence. No reference may be made to criminal proceedings from the time of the charge being made until the final appeal is determined.

Parliamentary supremacy and the judicial function

The doctrine of parliamentary supremacy entails the necessary constitutional subordination of judges to Parliament and has several implications. First, it is well established that the sovereign Parliament can overturn any court decision by way of legislation.[38] Secondly, the judiciary's primary role in relation to the interpretation of statutes is to give effect to the latest expression of the will of Parliament.[39]

See Chapter 6.

The Human Rights Act 1998 was consciously drafted in such a manner as to preserve the balance of power – and separation of power – between the judiciary and Parliament. As will be seen more fully in Chapter 18, this is accomplished by providing that primary (but not secondary) legislation remains immune from being declared invalid even where that legislation is ruled to be incompatible with Convention rights. Where judges in the higher courts make 'declarations of incompatibility', the matter is referred back to the executive to determine whether, and in what form, amending primary legislation should be enacted by Parliament.

---

37 HC Deb, Vol 34, Cols 123–25, 285–86.
38 Eg, the War Damage Act 1965.
39 *Vauxhall Estates Ltd v Liverpool Corporation* (1932); *Ellen Street Estates Ltd v Minister of Health* (1934).

Judges as legislators

One of the most debated aspects of the relationship between the legislature and the judges lies in the question: 'Do judges make law?' In constitutional terms, the issue is whether by making law – either by virtue of the doctrine of precedent or through the interpretation of statutes – the judges are usurping the legislative function or, in other words, violating the separation of powers.[40]

The role of judges as law-makers must be understood against the backdrop of the long history of the common law – the law common to the whole country, developed by the judges rather than by Act of Parliament. In terms of the volume of law, Parliament only became the principal law-maker in the nineteenth century when the effects of industrialisation required major programmes of legislation, much of it relating to safety at work and employment law, housing, health and relief from poverty. As discussed in Chapter 6, Acts of Parliament are supreme and may overturn the common law, as occurred for example in **Burmah Oil v Lord Advocate** (1965) in which the House of Lords awarded compensation for property loss and Parliament overruled the decision by enacting the War Damage Act 1965. However, when judges make law, Parliament may also 'tacitly' approve the decision by not interfering with it: when this occurs it can be said that the judges and Parliament are acting in a form of constitutional partnership. Parliament may also expressly endorse a judicial decision by incorporating it into statute, as occurred with the amendment to the statutory definition of rape following the House of Lords' decision in **R v R** (1991).[41]

The rules of precedent have been developed by the judges in order to ensure certainty and uniformity in decisions.[42] The need for certainty is expressed in the words *stare decisis*: 'stand by the decided cases'. In essence, decisions of the highest court – the Supreme Court – are binding on all the courts lower in the hierarchy. Furthermore, the Supreme Court is very slow to go against a previous decision of its own, although the House of Lords had the power to do so since 1966.[43] Decisions of the next highest court – the Court of Appeal – are binding on courts lower in the hierarchy, and the Court of Appeal may only depart from its own previous decisions under limited circumstances.[44] There is thus a structure in place by which the lower courts are controlled by the decisions of the higher courts.

It is of course essential that while the law is certain, it is also able to reflect changes in society. The requisite flexibility is provided within the rules that structure the extent to which judges may depart from previous decisions. It should be noted that not all aspects of a previous case will be binding on a new case before the court. What is 'binding' is the *ratio decidendi* of the precedent case, and the *ratio* may be defined as 'the rule of law upon which the decision is founded', or 'the material facts of the case plus the decision thereon'.[45] Other aspects of the precedent judgments are known as *obiter dicta*: things said 'by the way', which are not binding on future courts but may nevertheless prove to be highly influential in the future. The rules also include the technique of *distinguishing*: the reasoning process through which it can be said that the facts before the court in the instant case can be distinguished from those of a precedent case, thereby making its decision inapplicable. Taken together, the rules relating to being bound by the higher courts and to the *ratio* and distinguishing produce a high degree of stability, while also allowing for necessary flexibility.

40 This issue is complex. See, for detailed discussion, Slapper and Kelly, 2006. See also Reid, 1972.
41 See the Criminal Justice and Public Order Act 1994.
42 The detailed rules are outside the scope of this text. See Slapper and Kelly 2012.
43 See *Practice Statement* [1966] WLR 1234.
44 As defined in **Young v Bristol Aeroplane Ltd** (1944).
45 There are many complexities in the concept of the *ratio* and further reading is recommended: see Williams, 2003; Goodhart, 1931, p 1.

The rules of statutory interpretation, devised by the judges themselves, are designed to limit judicial creativity. Statutory interpretation is not straightforward, even though Acts of Parliament are couched in detailed language in order to maximise clarity and minimise vagueness or obscurity. Despite this attempt to achieve clarity in statutory language, it is artificial to deny that judges 'make law'. Every new meaning conferred on a word, every application of a rule to a new situation, whether by way of statutory interpretation or under common law, 'creates' new law. Judges have themselves abandoned the fiction of the 'declaratory theory' which asserts that they do not 'make' law but merely discover its true meaning. From the separation of powers perspective, judicial law-making should cause disquiet only if judges display overtly dynamic law making tendencies. By way of illustration, in **Magor and St Mellons Rural District Council v Newport Corporation** (1965), Lord Denning MR was accused by Lord Simonds in the House of Lords of 'naked usurpation of the legislative function'.

The traditional techniques of statutory interpretation contrast markedly with the European method of interpretation. Civil Codes are, for the most part, phrased in broad language which indicates the objective(s) being sought. The interpretative technique – the teleological or purposive approach – is accordingly designed to guide the judge towards the desired outcome and involves far less detailed construction of the statutory words than is customary within the English legal system. The scope for 'creative' interpretation has been enlarged by the Human Rights Act 1998, section 3 of which requires the judges to 'read and give effect to' primary and subordinate legislation 'in a way which is compatible with Convention rights.' Even here, however, Parliament has restricted this requirement by the preceding words 'so far as it is possible to do so', and as we shall see in Chapter 18, the judges recognise and respect this limitation.

The High Court of Parliament

Parliament has the sovereign power to regulate its own composition and procedure. Under parliamentary privilege – derived from the law and custom of Parliament and thus part of the common law – Parliament, and not the courts, has jurisdiction to rule on its own powers. Parliament cannot, however – other than by an Act of Parliament – extend its own privileges.[46]

The role of the judges in relation to privilege is to rule on its existence and extent. Once the court is satisfied that a particular matter falls within Parliament's domain, it will defer to Parliament. Accordingly, if, for example, a citizen is defamed by the absolute privilege of free speech in parliamentary proceedings,[47] there is no legal redress. Privilege will thus protect the Member of Parliament from the law of defamation and leave the aggrieved individual without a legal remedy.

Privilege also extends to regulating the legislative process. It is for Parliament alone to determine the procedure by which an Act of Parliament should come into being. It is clearly established that, in order to become an Act of Parliament, a Bill must pass its legislative stages in the Commons and Lords (except where the Parliament Acts apply) before receiving royal assent. Once that process is complete, it is not for the judiciary to inquire behind the parliamentary roll.[48]

---

46 *Stockdale v Hansard* (1839).
47 Bill of Rights 1689, Article IX.
48 **Pickin v British Railways Board** (1974).

Executive and judiciary

With regard to the relationship between the executive and the judiciary, several matters having implications for the separation of powers require examination: the attitude of the courts in matters entailing the exercise of the royal prerogative; parliamentary privilege; judicial review; the role of judges in non-judicial functions; and the role of the Law Officers of the Crown.[49]

The royal prerogative

Detailed consideration of the royal prerogative will be undertaken in Chapter 5. The royal prerogative has significant implications for the separation of powers. Being the residue of monarchical power, the prerogative is part of the common law and thus amenable to the jurisdiction of the courts. Today, the vast majority of prerogative powers are exercised by the government in the name of the Crown. As will be seen later, the substance of many prerogative powers is political, entailing matters of policy on which the judges are not competent to decide. In other words, matters which, if ruled on by the judges in a manner inconsistent with the interpretation of the executive, would place the judges in a sensitive constitutional position and leave them open to accusations of a violation of the separation of powers. That is not to suggest, however, that the courts have no role to play with respect to the royal prerogative. The traditional role of the courts is to rule on the existence and scope of the prerogative, but – having defined its existence and scope – to decline thereafter to rule on the exercise of the power. However, in **Council of Civil Service Unions v Minister of State for Civil Service** (1985) (the **GCHQ** case), the House of Lords made it clear that the courts have jurisdiction to review the exercise of executive power irrespective of whether the source of power is statutory or under the prerogative. Having seemingly extended the jurisdiction of the courts in relation to the prerogative, the House of Lords, nevertheless, proceeded to rule that there exists a wide range of 'nonjusticiable' matters which should be decided by the executive rather than the courts: a clear expression of the separation of powers.

Law Officers of the Crown

The Law Officers of the Crown – the Attorney General and the Solicitor General – are members of the government. The Attorney General may also be a member of Cabinet. The Attorney General is bound by conventions which serve to limit the overlap in functions. Thus, where his consent to prosecution is required, by convention the Attorney General must avoid party political considerations, and may not take orders from government. This is a particularly delicate matter when essentially political prosecutions are being contemplated.[50] The Law Officers are advisers to government and its ministers, and, by convention, this advice must never be disclosed. In 1986, this convention was breached when Leon Brittan, then Secretary of State for Trade and Industry, revealed advice given on the Westland Helicopter rescue plan.[51]

Two recent matters have renewed concern over the office of Attorney General. The first relates to the legal advice given to the government on the legality of the war in Iraq, and allegations that the Attorney General's initial advice differed from that which was eventually disclosed to Parliament in 2003, and – following controversy and leaks to the media – ultimately published in 2005.

The second issue relates to the legality of the decision by the Director of the Serious Fraud Office (for whom the Attorney General had constitutional responsibility) to discontinue a

---

49 On the Home Secretary's former powers to determine the length of prison sentences and judicial review of his decisions, see the 4th edition of this book, pp 893–96.
50 See **R v Ponting** (1985).
51 See further Chapter 15.

tradition and thought. Judicial assertions of the importance of the doctrine can be explained in light of the constitutional position of judges in relation to Parliament. The concept of separation of powers offers the judiciary a device both for the protection of the independence of the judiciary and against allegations of judicial intrusion into matters more appropriate to Parliament or the executive. The reluctance of judges to be drawn into such matters is reflected particularly strongly in relation to matters of the royal prerogative and parliamentary privilege.[63] Accordingly, to deny the relevance of some form of separation of powers would be to misconstrue the evidence. The separation of powers is a principle respected under the constitution which exerts its influence on each of the fundamental institutions of the state. While the separation of powers is ill defined, and is not accorded absolute respect, it ought not to 'be lightly dismissed'.[64]

SEPARATION OF POWERS: THE UK and USA COMPARED

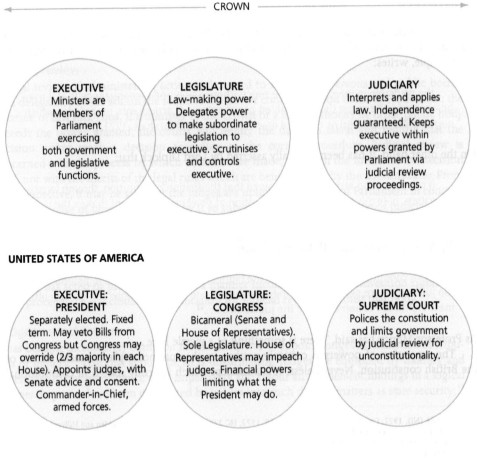

UNITED KINGDOM

CROWN

EXECUTIVE
Ministers are Members of Parliament exercising both government and legislative functions.

LEGISLATURE
Law-making power. Delegates power to make subordinate legislation to executive. Scrutinises and controls executive.

JUDICIARY
Interprets and applies law. Independence guaranteed. Keeps executive within powers granted by Parliament via judicial review proceedings.

UNITED STATES OF AMERICA

EXECUTIVE: PRESIDENT
Separately elected. Fixed term. May veto Bills from Congress but Congress may override (2/3 majority in each House). Appoints judges, with Senate advice and consent. Commander-in-Chief, armed forces.

LEGISLATURE: CONGRESS
Bicameral (Senate and House of Representatives). Sole Legislature. House of Representatives may impeach judges. Financial powers limiting what the President may do.

JUDICIARY: SUPREME COURT
Polices the constitution and limits government by judicial review for unconstitutionality.

---

63 See Chapters 5 and 17, respectively.
64 Munro, 1999, pp 195, 328–32.

SUMMARY OF THE UNITED KINGDOM'S SEPARATION OF POWERS

	The Executive	The Legislature	The Judiciary
Composition	Crown, Prime Minister, Cabinet and non-Cabinet ministers, civil service. Other institutions: devolved and local government, public bodies, police, armed forces, Revenue and Customs.	Crown, House of Commons, House of Lords. Other law-making bodies: the European Union; devolved legislatures (Northern Ireland, Scotland, Wales).	Judges and magistrates staffing courts and tribunals. The independence of the judiciary is guaranteed by the Act of Settlement 1700 which provides security of tenure for senior judges.
Functions and powers	• Government exercises royal prerogative powers on behalf of the Crown. • Makes policy. • Initiates legislation. • The civil service administers the law.	• Makes laws. • Scrutinises government policy and administration. • Holds government to account.	• Interprets and applies common law and statute. • Ensures the legality of the exercise of government powers through judicial review proceedings.
'Checks and balances'			
Composition	• By law civil servants, serving police officers and members of the armed forces cannot be members of either House of Parliament. • By convention Ministers must be members of either the House of Commons or House of Lords.	• By law the number of salaried government Ministers in the Commons is limited to 95.	

	The Executive	The Legislature	The Judiciary
Functions and powers	• Ministerial responsibility is the key concept in accountability of executive to Parliament. • A successful vote of 'No Confidence' in the House of Commons will lead to a government's resignation.	• The life of a Parliament is limited to five years. • Parliament's law-making powers are theoretically unlimited, in practice they are restricted by EU law, by devolution of law-making power to Northern Ireland, Scotland and Wales and by the political need to retain the support of the people. • The exercise of statutory powers may be reviewed by the courts in judicial review proceedings to ensure its compatibility with the power granted.	• Judges may not question the validity of Acts of Parliament. • The concept of justiciability restricts the role of judges to matters of law and prevents them ruling on matters of high policy. • By convention judges must be politically neutral. • Parliament scrutinises government and holds it to account: the government must maintain the confidence of the House of Commons on key areas of policy or resign.

Further Reading

Bradley, A.W. (2008) 'Relations between Executive, Judiciary and Parliament: an evolving saga?', Public Law, 470.

Cooke, Lord (2003) 'The Law Lords: An Endangered Heritage', Law Quarterly Review, 119: 49.

Hope of Craighead, Lord (2007) 'Voices from the Past – The Law Lords' Contribution to the Legislative Process', Law Quarterly Review, 123: 547.

Legal Studies (2004) Special Issue, Constitutional Innovation: The Creation of a Supreme Court for the United Kingdom; Domestic, Comparative and International Reflections, 2, 3, 5, 7, 8, 9, 10.

Munro, C. R. (1999) Studies in Constitutional Law (2nd edn), London: Butterworths, Chapter 9.

Reid, Lord (1972) 'The Judge as Law-Maker', JSPTL 22.

Steyn, Lord (2002) 'The Case for a Supreme Court', Law Quarterly Review, 118: 382.

Chapter 5

The Royal Prerogative

The King should not be over man, but under God and the law.

Bracton (1200–68)

Introduction

Under the constitution of the United Kingdom, all actions of government are undertaken in the name of the Crown. Any account of the prerogative is an account of power, and the prerogative, historically and contemporarily, concerns the power of the Crown.[1] The prerogative today represents one of the most intriguing aspects of the unwritten constitution. In order fully to appreciate the meaning of the term 'the Crown', an analysis of both who in fact exercises various powers in the name of the Crown, and the source of the power exercised, needs to be examined. The question to be asked is: is the power (to be exercised) a prerogative power or is it the outcome of statute? As will be seen, there is no certainty as to either the existing prerogative powers or the manner in which these may be extinguished. It is, however, clear that no new prerogative powers can be created.

The Prerogative Defined

Blackstone defines the prerogative in his *Commentaries* (1765–69) as:

> . . . that special pre-eminence which the King hath over and above all other persons, and out of the ordinary course of the common law, in right of his regal dignity. It signifies, in its etymology (from *prae* and *rogo*) something that is required or demanded before, or in preference to, all others.

Dicey, on the other hand, describes the prerogative in the following manner:

> . . . the residue of discretionary or arbitrary authority, which at any time is legally left in the hands of the Crown . . . Every act which the executive government can lawfully do without the authority of an Act of Parliament is done in virtue of this prerogative. [1885, p 424]

From these differing definitions, the following can be deduced:

(a) that these are powers which are inherent in, and peculiar to, the Crown;
(b) that the powers derive from common law;
(c) that the powers are residual;
(d) that the majority of the powers are exercised by the executive government in the name of the Crown; and,
(e) that no act of Parliament is necessary to confer authority on the exercise of such powers.

Joseph Chitty, whose work remains the most comprehensive account of the prerogative, explains the need for prerogative power in the following manner:

> The rights of sovereignty, or supreme power, are of a legislative and executive nature, and must, under any form of government, be vested exclusively in a body or bodies, distinct from the people at large. [1820, p 2]

In Chitty's analysis, the power of the King is but part of a reciprocal relationship between monarch and subject. To the King is owed a duty of allegiance on the part of all subjects; to the subjects is owed the duty of protection.

---

1 On the distinctions between the monarch and the Crown, see Marshall, 1971, pp 17–24.

The Prerogative before 1688

Before 1688, the King exercised powers relating to Parliament, law making and the administration of the courts, the regulation of trade, taxation and defence of the realm and miscellaneous other prerogatives. Principal among these powers were the following:

For further details, see the Website.

- The King would summon Parliament and prorogue it. The King could suspend Parliament's sittings and dissolve it. The absoluteness of the King's power came to a head in the reign of Charles I (1625–49) when Charles confronted Parliament over taxation to meet the cost of war, imprisoning over 70 people who refused to pay the forced loan, including the 'five knights'[2] who sought a writ of *habeas corpus* against the King. The conflict between the King and Parliament came to a head when in 1629 Charles dissolved Parliament and there commenced an 11-year period of personal monarchical rule. In 1641, under the leadership of Pym, the 'Grand Remonstrance' was drafted – listing the grievances of the country under the rule of prerogative. While the Commons was divided over the Remonstrance, it represented a starting point in history, one which was to lead to the Civil War, Charles's execution and the rule of Oliver Cromwell under the only Republican constitution Britain has ever experienced.[3]
- The King claimed the right to legislate by 'proclamation', thereby usurping Parliament's law making role. This power was challenged in the reign of James I (1603–25) in the **Case of Proclamations** (1611), in which Sir Edward Coke CJ declared that:

  > . . . the King by his proclamation or other ways cannot change any part of the common law, or statute law, or the customs of the realm . . . the King cannot create any offence by his prohibition or proclamation, which was not an offence before, for that was to change the law, and to make an offence which was not. . . . Also, . . . the King hath no prerogative but that which the law of the land allows him.

- The King's assent was needed for the enactment of statutes, but he also had the power to dispense with statutes and suspend their application.[4] The conflict between Crown and the courts in the seventeenth century is illustrated by the cases of **Thomas v Sorrell** (1674) and **Godden v Hales** (1686). In **Thomas v Sorrell**, it was declared that the King could not dispense with a penal law made for the good of the public. However, in **Godden v Hales**, the court accepted that the King could dispense with a penal law – under specific circumstances – where that law fell within his jurisdiction.
- It was within the King's prerogative to establish new courts of justice. The Court of Star Chamber, exercising extensive criminal jurisdiction with little of the formality of judicial proceedings and without the use of juries, was established either under the Statute of 1487 or under the Crown's inherent prerogative: doubt exists as to its source. Unlike the ordinary courts, the Court of Star Chamber used torture. It became one of the most feared and powerful weapons under the control of the Crown until its abolition in 1641.
- The King's claim to dispense justice in his own right and without the judges was dispelled in 1607. In **Prohibitions Del Roy (Case of Prohibitions)** (1607), the King sought to settle a dispute concerning land. In the Resolution of the Judges, Coke declared:

  > . . . that the King in his own person cannot adjudge any case, either criminal, as treason, felony, etc, or betwixt party and party, concerning his inheritance,

---

2 **Darnel's Case** (1627).
3 See Lockyer, 1985, Chapters 12–13.
4 **Case of Proclamations** (1611).

chattels, or goods, etc, but this ought to be determined and adjudged in some Court of Justice, according to the law and custom of England; and always judgments are given . . . so that the Court gives the judgment . . .

When, in 1617, the King ordered the Court of King's Bench to adjourn proceedings until he had been consulted, Chief Justice Coke refused, declaring that:

Obedience to His Majesty's command to stay proceedings would have been a delay of justice, contrary to the law, and contrary to oaths of the judges.[5]

Coke was dismissed from the Bench.

- The King claimed the power to detain a subject free from interference by the courts. Whether a writ of *habeas corpus* would lie against the King was determined in 1627. In **Darnel's Case** (the **Five Knights' Case**) (1627), it was held that, where the King detained a prisoner under special order, the court would not look behind the order. Thus, while the King could not determine cases, he could nevertheless hold a subject free from interference by the judges. The Petition of Right 1628 declared such power to be unlawful, and in 1640, the Habeas Corpus Act guaranteed that *habeas corpus* would lie against the Crown.
- Historically, much of the commerce and trade of the country was under the prerogative of the Crown, but such a power was effectively abolished by statute.
- The King had a duty to protect the realm, a duty which encompassed the powers to restrict imports of raw material of war and the right to erect ports and havens, beacons and lighthouses.
- The Crown's power of taxation is inextricably linked to the notion of the King as ultimate lord of all land. The King was the largest landowner in the Kingdom and exercised his right to collect revenues from the land. In addition, the King received profits from legal proceedings in the form of fees paid by litigants and fines. Pardons were also sold. The granting of supply to the King by Parliament from direct taxation had been established in 1215, from which time it was accepted that the King had no power to levy direct taxation without parliamentary consent.[6] The position of indirect taxation was, however, unclear. The power to regulate trade, including the power to establish, open and close ports, was within the royal prerogative. Accordingly, it could be argued that the correlative power to levy taxes on imports and exports was within the power of the Crown. Indirect taxation was in issue in the **Case of Ship Money (R v Hampden)** (1637). Hampden had refused to pay taxes levied by Charles I to raise money for the navy in times of emergency. The King argued that it was for the Crown to determine whether or not an emergency situation existed and that this determination was conclusive of his right to exercise his prerogative power to raise revenue. The courts upheld the power of the Crown. The Shipmoney Act of 1640 reversed the decision, and Article IV of the Bill of Rights 1689 declared it illegal for the Crown to raise money without parliamentary approval.

The Bill of Rights 1689, provided, *inter alia*, that there should be regular meetings of Parliament; that elections should be free; that the Crown's power to raise taxation[7] was subject to Parliament's approval, as was the power to maintain an army; that the powers of suspending or dispensing with laws by the Crown[8] were illegal; and, of the greatest significance, that the

---

5 **John Colt and Glover v Bishop of Coventry and Lichfield** (the **Commendam Case**) (1617).
6 In the reign of Edward I, 1271–1307.
7 **R v Hampden** (1637).
8 **Godden v Hales** (1686).

'freedom of speech and debates or proceedings in Parliament ought not to be impeached or questioned in any court or place out of parliament'.[9]

From this time, the supremacy of Parliament over the Crown was established and the prerogative powers of the Crown continued in existence or were abolished or curtailed as Parliament determined. No new prerogative powers may be claimed by the Crown: as Diplock LJ stated in **BBC v Johns** (1965): '. . . it is 350 years and a civil war too late for the Queen's courts to broaden the prerogative.'

Miscellaneous prerogatives included the right to raise revenue from the demesne lands of the Crown,[10] to the ownership of tidal riverbeds, and to the land beneath a non-tidal riverbed – provided that it had not become a dry riverbed, whereupon the soil is equally owned by the owners of the adjoining banks. Equally, the King, by virtue of his prerogative, was owner of the shores of seas and navigable rivers within his dominions. The ancient right of the King to wild creatures, to franchises of forest, 'free chase', park or free warren have been abolished[11] with the exception of the right to royal fish (sturgeon) and swans, which is expressly reserved by the 1971 Act. Additionally, the Crown had the right to treasure trove, now regulated under the Treasure Act 1996.[12]

The Prerogative Today

The constitutional questions requiring answer include those relating to the relationship between statute and prerogative and the control, judicial or political, of the prerogative. The most significant question which continues to intrigue and concern constitutional theorists today relates to the very existence and scope of the powers themselves, together with the constitutional implications of this ill-defined reservoir of power. As Maitland observed, and as remains true in the twenty-first century, examination of the prerogative is:

> . . . set about with difficulties, with prerogatives disused, with prerogatives of doubtful existence, with prerogatives which exist by sufferance, merely because no one has thought it worthwhile to abolish them. [1908, p 421]

Under the United Kingdom's constitutional monarchy, the Queen is part of the legislature: Parliament comprises the Crown, Lords and Commons. The Queen is the 'fountain of justice' – and while the Queen has no power to make laws or suspend laws or to act in a judicial capacity,[13] the entire administration of justice is conducted in the name of the Crown.[14] The Queen is Supreme Head of the Church of England.[15] The Queen is Head of State in relation to foreign affairs. The Queen is head of the executive, and all acts of government, whether domestic or foreign, are conducted in the name of the Crown. The right to summon Parliament remains a legal power vested in the Crown. The Queen is the Fountain of Honour, and all honours in the United Kingdom are conferred by the Crown.

---

9 Bill of Rights, 1689, Article IX, discussed in Chapter 17.
10 Chitty, 1820, p 206.
11 Wild Creatures and Forest Laws Act 1971.
12 See MacMillan, 1996, and **Attorney General of Duchy of Lancaster v GE Overton (Farms) Ltd** (1982). Treasure found must be reported within 14 days to the local coroner. Failure to do so will be a criminal offence. A Treasure Valuation Committee has been established which has the duty to value treasure and advise on *ex gratia* payments to the finder.
13 *Case of Proclamations* (1611); Bill of Rights 1689; *Case of Prohibitions* (1607), respectively.
14 See Blackburn, R (2004) 'Monarchy and the Personal Prerogatives' [2004] PL 546.
15 Act of Supremacy 1558. See Leigh, I (2004) 'By Law Established? The Crown, Constitutional Reform and the Church of England' [2004] PL 266.

While regal powers are exercised in the name of the Crown by the government of the day, the Crown nevertheless retains important residual powers which are discussed below. It must also be recognised that a few powers remain the personal prerogative of the Crown. Illustrations include the grant of honours such as the Order of Merit, and the Orders of the Garter and Thistle. More importantly, there still remains the prerogative notion that the Crown never dies and that the Crown is never an infant (thus ensuring continuity of monarchy), and that the Crown can 'do no wrong', thus placing the Queen outside the jurisdiction of the courts and guaranteeing immunity from prosecution in her own courts. Beyond these limited powers and immunities, the sovereign has, in the words of Bagehot (1867): '... under a constitutional monarchy such as ours, three rights – the right to be consulted, the right to encourage, the right to warn.' In legal theory, however, the position is much different. As Bagehot stated:

> Not to mention other things, she could disband the army (by law, she cannot engage more than a certain number of men, but she is not obliged to engage any men); she could dismiss all the officers, from the General Commander in Chief downwards; she could dismiss all the sailors too; she could sell off all our ships of war and all our naval stores; she could make a peace by the sacrifice of Cornwall, and begin a war for the conquest of Brittany. She could make every parish in the United Kingdom a 'university'; she could dismiss most of the civil servants; she could pardon all offenders. In a word, the Queen could by prerogative upset all the action of civil government within the government, could disgrace the nation by a bad war or peace, and could, by disbanding our forces, whether land or sea, leave us defenceless against foreign nations. [1867, 'Introduction' and pp 287–88]

In order to understand the power of the Crown, it is necessary to look beyond the superficial phrase 'in the name of the Crown'. The actual power which is exercisable by the Crown is limited in two ways. First, by convention, the majority of powers are exercised by Her Majesty's government or Her Majesty's judges in her name. Second, the existence and scope of a purported prerogative power is subjected to the scrutiny of the courts: 'The King has no power save that allowed by law.'[16] However, that should not be considered as equivalent to a power to control the prerogative.[17]

The Prerogative Illustrated

Before examining the nature, scope and constitutional significance of the prerogative, some examples are necessary to indicate the areas of power which fall under the prerogative. Under the United Kingdom's unwritten constitution, there exists no formal and agreed text as to the prerogative. In order, therefore, to ascertain the contents of the prerogative, an examination of the historical attributes of the Crown and the attitude of the courts to the prerogative is required. It is paradoxical – but undeniable – in a modern democracy that there is no comprehensive, authoritative 'catalogue' of prerogative powers.[18]

To make an analysis of prerogative powers manageable, they may be separated into two categories:[19] those relating to foreign affairs and those relating to domestic affairs. Under foreign affairs can be subsumed:

---

16 **Case of Proclamations** (1611)
17 See **Council of Civil Service Unions v Minister for Civil Service** (1985), discussed below, pp 103–104.
18 The most recent authoritative account remains that of Chitty, 1820.
19 As does Blackstone, in his *Commentaries*.

- the power to make declarations of war and peace;
- power to enter into treaties;
- the recognition of foreign states;
- diplomatic relations; and
- disposition of the armed forces overseas.

Within the domestic category falls:

- the summoning of Parliament;[20]
- appointment of ministers;
- royal assent to Bills;
- the granting of honours;
- defence of the realm;
- the keeping of the peace;
- the protective jurisdiction of the courts in relation to children: *parens patriae*;
- the power to stop criminal prosecutions – *nolle prosequi*;
- reduction of sentences;
- pardoning of offenders; and
- the right to royal fish and swans.

It can be seen from this list, which is by no means exhaustive, that the powers are wide and diverse.

The Prerogative and Domestic Affairs

The dissolution of Parliament

Prior to a general election being held, it is necessary to bring the life of the existing Parliament to an end. This is done through the dissolution of Parliament. Prior to the Fixed-term Parliaments Act 2011, the Crown dissolved Parliament under the royal prerogative at the request of the Prime Minister. This power gave rise to many doubts and criticisms. The main political criticism was that the Prime Minister could choose the date of a general election when it most favoured the re-election of the government. The Coalition government formed in 2010 introduced a fixed five-year parliamentary term. The Fixed-term Parliaments Act 2011 places the dissolution of Parliament on a statutory basis.

The rules relating to the dissolution of Parliament under the Fixed-term Parliaments Act 2011 are discussed in Chapter 13. Discussion of the Crown's former powers in relation to the dissolution of Parliament is on the companion website.

Appointment of Prime Minister

In constitutional theory, the Queen – under the royal prerogative – may appoint whomsoever she pleases to the office of Prime Minister.[21] In practice, the position is governed by convention and the Queen must appoint the person who can command a majority in the House of Commons; this, under normal circumstances, will be the leader of the political party which secures the greatest number of parliamentary seats at a general election. Several differing

---

20 Note that prior to the Fixed-term Parliaments Act 2011, the dissolution of Parliament was regulated under the royal prerogative.
21 See, *inter alia*, Jennings, 1959a; Marshall and Moodie, 1971; Laski, 1951; Brazier, 1990, Chapters 1 and 2; Marshall, 1984, Chapter II.

situations present themselves: the government of the day may be returned by the electorate with a majority and the Prime Minister will remain in office. Alternatively, the government may lose the election, and the incoming Prime Minister will be the leader of that political party which commands a majority of seats in the House of Commons. More difficult is the position where the election produces no outright winner, resulting in no one party having an overall majority. Here, the spectre of a 'hung parliament' arises (as in 2010). The situation may also arise where a Prime Minister resigns through old age or ill health during the course of his term of office – as was the case in 1935 (Ramsey MacDonald), 1955 (Winston Churchill) and 1957 (Anthony Eden) – or dies in office (Campbell-Bannerman, 1905–08). Finally, it may be the case that a Prime Minister chooses to retire, as occurred in 1937 (Stanley Baldwin), in 1976 (Harold Wilson) and most recently in 2007 when Tony Blair relinquished office.

Appointment of Prime Minister following a general election

In a general election the electoral system usually returns a single party with an overall majority of seats in the House of Commons, and no question arises as to whom the Queen should appoint as Prime Minister. It is not out of the question, however, for a different political scenario to present itself. Should the Queen send for the leader of the party having the largest number of seats, or the leader of the party which will hold the balance of power? There is much debate over this issue,[22] but once again no clear-cut answer.

In February 1974, the Conservative Party lost the general election by a small number of seats and could command no overall majority in the House of Commons. Following the election results, the Prime Minister, Edward Heath, did not tender his resignation immediately but rather entered into negotiations over the following weekend with the Liberal Party, with a view to forming a political pact which would ensure a majority over the opposition parties. When those negotiations broke down, Mr Heath immediately resigned, and the Queen invited the Leader of the Labour Party to become Prime Minister.[23]

A similar result occurred in 2010, with no political party winning a clear majority of seats. The Labour Party, which had been in office since 1997, won fewer seats than the Conservative Party. The incumbent Labour Prime Minister remained in post until an agreement was reached between the Conservatives and Liberal Democrats, resulting in a full Coalition government. Once that agreement was reached the Prime Minister resigned office and the Crown appointed the Leader of the Conservative Party, David Cameron, as Prime Minister, with the Leader of the Liberal Democrat Party being appointed Deputy Prime Minister.

See Chapter 10.

Appointment of Prime Minister following retirement of the incumbent

When the Prime Minister retires, the government still retains the mandate of the people and hence the choice of the new Prime Minister will be dictated by the wishes of the Party. It may be that there is a 'Prime Minister in waiting' who commands the support of the Party and will hence be appointed without delay.[24] Under such circumstances, it is unrealistic to speak of the Crown having any choice in the matter. Where no Party consensus as to a successor exists, the political process will come into play. Nowadays, each of the major political parties utilises a method of election of its leader, and it is that process which will determine the successor: again, the Queen has no practical 'say' in the matter. It was not always thus.

---

22 See, inter alia, Jennings, 1959a, Chapter II; Marshall, 1984, pp 29–35; Marshall and Moodie, 1971, pp 44–51; Brazier, 1982.
23 See, inter alia, Bogdanor, 1983, Chapters 5–8; Butler, 1983.
24 As in 2007 when the Chancellor of the Exchequer, Gordon Brown, succeeded Tony Blair as Prime Minister.

In 1957, Sir Anthony Eden resigned office, and there was no obvious successor – nor was there in place at that time an electoral process within the governing Conservative Party which would produce a successor. The Queen was thus left with a choice. The Queen consulted elder statesmen of the Conservative Party and acted upon their advice that Harold Macmillan be appointed. Had she not acted upon impartial advice, the Crown could have been damaged by charges of political decision-making. One consequence of the 1957 dilemma was that the Labour Party announced its intention to introduce a selection procedure for its leader: a move designed to remove any discretion from the Crown. The Conservative Party did not react in this manner until after the difficulties revealed in 1963. The resignation of Harold Macmillan fell at a time when there were several contenders for leadership of the Party. The matter was resolved by the appointment of Lord Home, a Conservative peer who relinquished his peerage and took a seat in the House of Commons as Sir Alec Douglas-Home. However, the saga emphasised the uncertainties in the choice of Party Leader and an electoral system for the leadership of the Party was subsequently introduced.

The Prerogative of Mercy

Nowadays, the prerogative of mercy entails two aspects: the power to grant pardons and the power to enter a *nolle prosequi*.

Pardons and commutation of sentence

A complete pardon is used to remove the 'pains, penalties and punishments' which flow from a conviction for a criminal offence, but does not eliminate the conviction itself.[25] The right of pardon does not extend to civil matters. The power is exercisable in England and Wales on the advice of the Secretary of State for the Home Department, who is accountable to Parliament. The Crown therefore has no personal involvement in its exercise. Commutation of sentence is a limited – or conditional – form of pardon. The sentence will be reduced on conditions: '. . . a condemned murderer is pardoned on condition of his going into penal servitude.' As Maitland comments (1908, p 480): 'It is a nice question whether he might not insist on being hanged.' Commutation is distinguishable from remission of sentence. The latter reduces the sentence imposed but does not alter its form.

The prerogative of mercy has traditionally been regarded as unreviewable by the courts. In 1976, in **De Freitas v Benny** (1976), Lord Diplock was to state that:

> At common law, this has always been a matter which lies solely in the discretion of the sovereign, who by constitutional convention exercises it in respect of England on the advice of the Home Secretary to whom Her Majesty delegates her discretion. Mercy is not the subject of legal rights. It begins where legal rights end.[26]

In **Council of Civil Service Unions v Minister for the Civil Service** (1985), Lord Roskill confirmed that the prerogative of mercy was not 'susceptible to judicial review'. However, the case of **Bentley** (1993) suggests a different approach. In 1952, Derek Bentley, aged 19, and with the mental age of an 11-year-old, was convicted of the murder of a policeman. At the time, the death penalty was the mandatory sentence for murder. Derek Bentley was hanged in 1953, a mere

---

25 **R v Foster** (1985).
26 At p 247. See also **R v Allen** (1862); **Hanratty v Lord Butler** (1971).

three months after the murder. His co-defendant, Christopher Craig, who fired the fatal shot at the police officer who died, was also convicted of murder, but escaped execution because he was aged only 16. Despite a recommendation by the jury that mercy be exercised, the Home Secretary decided not to exercise the prerogative. In an application for judicial review brought by Derek Bentley's family, the court considered the question whether the prerogative of mercy was amenable to judicial review.[27] The applicant sought a declaration that the Home Secretary had erred in law in declining to recommend a posthumous free pardon, and *mandamus* to require the Home Secretary to reconsider the matter.

Counsel for the Home Secretary argued that the exercise of the royal prerogative of mercy was not reviewable in the instant case, on the basis that the criteria upon which the pardon should be granted was a question of policy, which was not justiciable. The court ruled that the view that 'the formulation of the criteria for the exercise of the prerogative by the grant of a free pardon was entirely a matter of policy which is not justiciable' was 'probably right' (p 453). However, it ruled that the Home Secretary failed to recognise that the prerogative of mercy is 'capable of being exercised in many different circumstances and over a wide range', and should have considered the form of pardon which might be appropriate to the facts of the case.[28] This the Home Secretary did not do, and this failure was reviewable by the courts. The court expressed the view that the prerogative of mercy is now 'a constitutional safeguard against mistakes'. The court also ruled, however, that it had no power to direct the way in which the prerogative of mercy should be exercised, but that it had a role to play by way of judicial review. The court declined to make any formal order, but invited the Home Secretary to reconsider the matter 'in light of the now generally accepted view that this young man should have been reprieved' (p 455).

In 1998, the Court of Appeal, Criminal Division[29] quashed Derek Bentley's conviction for murder. The Court ruled that the conviction had been unsafe (**R v Bentley** (1998)). Thus, 45 years after the event, Bentley's name was cleared by the courts on the basis that his conviction had been unsafe, the royal prerogative of mercy in the hands of the politicians having failed to provide a remedy.

Nolle prosequi

On proceedings on indictment, the Attorney General, in the name of the Crown, can enter a *nolle prosequi*, the effect of which stops the legal proceedings. The power is not subject to the control of the courts: **R v Comptroller of Patents** (1899). The grant of a *nolle prosequi* does not amount to an acquittal, and accordingly, the accused may be brought before the court on the same charge. The effect of this would be to invite a further application for a *nolle prosequi*.

Power to Establish Non-Statutory Agencies

The Criminal Injuries Compensation Board was established under the prerogative in 1964. Its objective was to provide compensation for the victims of criminal offences[30] through *ex gratia* payments calculated on the same principles as compensation paid to victims of tort. The Board was reconstituted under statute in 1988,[31] although the provisions had not been brought into

27 **R v Secretary of State for the Home Department ex parte Bentley** (1993).
28 On the power to issue a pardon, see **R (Shields) v Secretary of State for Justice** (2008).
29 On a reference by the Criminal Cases Review Commission under section 9 of the Criminal Appeal Act 1995.
30 See Newburn, 1989, p 41
31 Criminal Justice Act 1988, ss 108–17 and Scheds 6–7.

force. Was the setting up of the Board in 1964 the exercise of a true prerogative? Reverting to Blackstone's definition, the answer must be negative. The power to establish such a scheme clearly fell within Parliament's jurisdiction, as the Criminal Justice Act 1988 proves. However, under Dicey's definition, the government is effectively given a choice in the manner of establishing such bodies: a surely questionable prerogative?

The Granting of Honours

Whilst legally still in the hands of the Crown, the effective control over the granting of the majority of honours lies with the executive. The Queen has the personal right to confer the Order of the Garter, the Order of the Thistle, the Royal Victorian Order and the Order of Merit. Otherwise, the conferment of honours is by the Queen, acting on the advice of the Prime Minister who is, in turn, advised by a Political Honours Scrutiny Committee comprising three Privy Counsellors.[32] The link between the granting of honours and the financing of political parties has been a matter of concern for decades. This issue is discussed in Chapter 12.

Regulation of the Civil Service[33]

Prior to the Constitutional Reform and Governance Act 2010, on which see below, the control of the Civil Service was vested in the Crown. Appointments were based on merit and permanent. A civil servant would not be dismissed other than for misconduct.[34] Civil servants had no contractual relationship with the Crown.[35] Salaries and other benefits were prescribed by statute, but for the most part, the Civil Service was governed under the prerogative.[36]

The government's 2007 Green Paper, *The Governance of Britain*, envisaged legislation 'enshrining the core values and principles of the Civil Service'. The Constitutional Reform and Governance Act 2010 places the Civil Service on a statutory basis for the first time. Section 2 provides for the establishment of the Civil Service Commission with functions relating to the appointment of Civil Servants. The management of the Civil Service remains with the Minister for the Civil Service (usually the Prime Minister), with the exception of the Diplomatic Service which remains under the control of the Foreign and Commonwealth Office. It also provides for a Code for Special Advisers (on whom see further Chapter 9), defines their role and provides an overall limit on the number of Special Advisers to be made by Order.

Section 1(2) of the Constitutional Reform and Governance Act 2010 provides that the Act does not apply to the Secret Intelligence Service, the Security Service, the Government Communications Headquarters, the Northern Ireland Civil Service or the Northern Ireland Court Service. The Act also does not apply to the appointment of civil servants outside the United Kingdom whose duties are carried out wholly outside the United Kingdom.

---

32 Cmnd 1789, 1922, London: HMSO; see *Parkinson v Royal College of Ambulance* (1925), which led to the passing of the Honours (Prevention of Abuses) Act 1925; and see Wagner and Squibb, 1973. It has been proposed that the Scrutiny Committee be merged with the Independent Appointments Commission to ensure greater scrutiny.

33 See further Chapter 9. The structure and conditions of employment are outside the scope of this work: see Jackson and Leonard, 2001, Chapter 17.

34 Fulton Committee Report, Cmnd 3638, 1971, London: HMSO.

35 *CCSU v Minister for the Civil Service* (1985), p 419.

36 For a detailed and critical analysis of the Civil Service, see Hennessy, 1990. On proposed reforms, see further Chapter 9.

Regulation of the Armed Forces

As with the Civil Service, members of the armed forces are regulated under the royal prerogative, and statutory protection of employment in, for example, the Employment Protection (Consolidation) Act 1978 does not apply to members of the armed forces.[37]

The sovereign is Commander in Chief of the armed forces. The Bill of Rights 1689 prohibits the maintenance of an army by the Crown in peacetime without the consent of Parliament. The control, organisation and disposition of the forces are within the prerogative and cannot be questioned in a court of law.[38]

The Prime Minister, acting in the name of the Crown, has the ultimate say in committing British troops to war. For example in 1939 (following months of an attempt to reach a peaceful agreement with Germany) when German troops invaded Poland on 1 September, the British Prime Minister declared that Britain was at war with Germany. More recently, in 2003 the British Prime Minister backed the United States' invasion of Iraq by committing British troops, without prior parliamentary approval. However, while the power to declare war is for the Crown, the conduct of war cannot be effected without Parliament's approval of finance for the war – accordingly Parliament must (albeit belatedly) approve the government's decision.

Reform

The wide-reaching power relating to war, exercised without Parliament's prior consent, is controversial. The government's 2007 Green Paper, *The Governance of Britain*, proposed that there should be a House of Commons' Resolution requiring the government to consult Parliament prior to declaring war. The Constitutional Reform and Governance Bill 2009–10 provided that in relation to war, international armed conflict and international peace-keeping activities, prior approval must be given by each House, by Resolution, except where the Prime Minister considers that exceptional considerations require immediate action. The provision, however, did not survive the passage of the Bill and accordingly the prerogative power relating to war remains in the hands of the government.

The Prerogative and Foreign Affairs
Acts of state[39]

An act of the executive as a matter of policy performed in the course of its relations with another state, including its relations with the subjects of that state, unless they are temporarily within the allegiance of the Crown.[40]

Acts of state in relation to foreign states

The recognition of foreign states, diplomatic relations – including the sending of diplomats and the reception of foreign diplomats, declarations of war (see above) and peace, and the annexation or cession of territory fall within this part of the definition.

---

37 For details of the organisation and control of the armed forces see Jackson and Leonard, 2001, Chapter 18.
38 **China Navigation Company Ltd v Attorney General** (1932); **Chandler v Director of Public Prosecutions** (1964). See also the Crown Proceedings Act 1947, s 11.
39 See Anson, 1933, Vol II, Pt I, Chapter 6.8.
40 Wade, ECS, 1934, p 103.

Recognition of foreign states

The recognition of foreign states is within the prerogative of the Crown. Several statutes regulate the privilege and immunities enjoyed by heads of foreign states[41] and their diplomatic representatives.[42]

Diplomatic relations

In 1708, the Diplomatic Privileges Act was passed after a Russian Ambassador had been arrested for debt. The Russian Czar, Peter the Great, regarded this action as a criminal offence. The Court of Queen's Bench was uncertain as to the legal position.[43] The Act of 1708 provided that no judicial proceedings could be brought against diplomats or their servants and that it was an offence to commence proceedings.

Under the Diplomatic Privileges Act 1964, diplomatic staff enjoy full immunity – both civil and criminal – whereas administrative and technical staff have immunity for actions taken in the course of their duties but are otherwise civilly – but not criminally – liable for other acts. Members of service staff are immune only in respect of official acts. Whether a particular member of diplomatic staff falls within a certain category is determined by the Foreign Secretary by means of a certificate. The court will determine whether the action performed is within – or without – the individual's official duties.[44]

Where an individual enjoys immunity from the courts, the only redress will be for the Foreign Secretary to request the diplomat's government to recall him as *persona non grata*.

Annexation and cession of territory

In 1955, the Crown exercised its prerogative power to take possession of the island of Rockall, which subsequently was incorporated into the United Kingdom as part of Scotland.[45] Once territory has been annexed, the Crown has a discretion as to the extent to which it will take over the liabilities of the former government of the state.[46]

The Crown also has the power to alter the limits of British territorial waters.[47] However, while this prerogative seems firmly established, there are doubts as to the power of the Crown – without parliamentary approval – to cede territory and thereby deprive British citizens of their nationality and other rights under United Kingdom law.[48] When the Crown sought to cede Heligoland to Germany in 1890, parliamentary approval was sought. While the law may be doubtful, there is at least a convention that Parliament's approval will be sought and granted.

The regulation of colonial territories

Colonies and dependent territories are regulated by Orders in Council made in the exercise of the prerogative powers of the Crown. The control of Crown power in relation to such territories – exercised by the government – has been considered by the courts.[49]

---

41 State Immunity Act 1978. On state immunity and its effect on the protection of human rights, see Chapter 18.

42 Diplomatic Privileges Act 1964. On immunities and privilege accorded to international and commonwealth organisations, see the International Organisations Acts 1968 and 1981; Diplomatic Immunities (Conferences with Commonwealth Countries and Republic of Ireland) Acts 1952 and 1961; International Headquarters and Defence Organisations Act 1964.

43 *Mattueof's Case* (1709).

44 In *Aziz v Aziz, Sultan of Brunei intervening* (2007), the Court of Appeal ruled that the head of a foreign state had no right to anonymity in court proceedings.

45 Island of Rockall Act 1972.

46 *West Rand Central Gold Mining Company v The King* (1905).

47 *R v Kent Justices ex parte Lye* (1967); *Post Office v Estuary Radio* (1968).

48 Anson, 1933, pp 137–42; Holdsworth, 1942. See further Chapter 23.

49 See in particular *R (Quark Fishing Ltd) v Secretary of State for Foreign and Commonwealth Affairs* (2005) and references therein.

In **R (Bancoult) v Secretary of State for Foreign and Commonwealth Affairs (No 2)** (2007), the Court of Appeal ruled that the use of Orders in Council to frustrate a ruling of the court was an unlawful abuse of power.[50] Under the British Indian Ocean Territory Ordinance No 1 of 1971, the inhabitants of the Chagos Islands were compulsorily removed from their home on the basis that, pursuant to a Treaty with Britain, the principal island was required for use by the United States of America as a military base. In 2000 the Divisional Court quashed the 1971 Immigration Ordinance on the ground that it fell outside the purpose of the British Indian Ocean Territory Order in Council.[51] However, Orders subsequently drafted declared that no person had the right of abode in the territory, or the right without authorisation to enter and remain there: these were declared unlawful.

One ground of appeal was that constitutionally and legally it was the Monarch and not the Minister who made a colonial order and that fact placed the matter outside the jurisdiction of the courts. This submission the Court rejected, Sedley LJ stating that: 'The present case concerned not a sovereign act of the Crown but a potentially justiciable act of executive government.'

The House of Lords, however, in **R (Bancoult) v Secretary of State for Foreign and Commonwealth Affairs** (2008) allowed the government's appeal, by a majority of three to two. Lord Hoffmann placed great emphasis on the practicalities of the situation. The islanders would be unable to exercise their 'right of abode' without financial support from the government, and the policy as to expenditure of public resources (and diplomatic interests of the Crown) were 'peculiarly within the competence of the executive'. It was impossible to say that the decision had been unreasonable or an abuse of power. Lords Rodger of Earlsferry and Lord Carswell agreed. Lord Rodger emphasised that there was here no breach of legitimate expectations: the government had not made any 'clear and unambiguous promise' to the islanders on which they could rely. Lord Carswell stated that where there was 'an overriding public interest' behind a change in policy there will 'not be an abuse of power'.[52] Lords Bingham of Cornhill and Lord Mance, however, dismissed the appeal. Lord Bingham stated that there was no prerogative power to make the Order in Council and that it was void on two grounds. First, it was irrational on the basis that there was no good reason for making it, and secondly the provision contradicted a representation made by the Secretary of State on which the islanders were entitled to think that their right to return was assured. The government 'could not lawfully resile from its representation without compelling reason, which was not shown'.[53] Lord Mance ruled that the order was *ultra vires*, that it was made without regard to relevant interests and that the decision was irrational.[54]

Issue of passports

Consistent with the Crown's power to regulate its boundaries and those who enter and leave is the power to issue passports: again, under Blackstone's definition, this is a questionable prerogative power, for the government is doing no more than what it is free to do under statute and the power has no legal effect as such. Nevertheless, the conventional classification of the right to issue and withhold passports is that of the prerogative. At common law, citizens

---

50 See also the earlier cases of **R v Secretary of State for Foreign and Commonwealth Affairs ex parte Bancoult** (2001); **Chagos Islanders v Attorney General** (2003).
51 SI 1965 No 1920.
52 See para 135.
53 At para 73.
54 See paras 183 to 186. Note that in December 2012 the Secretary of State for Foreign and Commonwealth Affairs announced that the government was reviewing its position and considering how the islanders could be returned to their former homeland.

have the right to enter and leave the realm. It is nevertheless extremely difficult in practice to travel without a passport, which is issued under the prerogative. In **R v Foreign Secretary ex parte Everett** (1989), the court for the first time held that the granting and withholding of passports was subject to review by the courts. The position in the United Kingdom – both uncertain and unsatisfactory – may be contrasted with that in the United States of America where the Supreme Court has held that freedom of travel is a basic constitutional liberty.[55]

The ancient right to issue the writ *ne exeat regno* – forbidding a person from leaving the realm – is declared by Jackson and Leonard (2001), relying on **Felton v Callis** (1969), to be 'obsolescent'. The doctrine of obsolescence has never been one accepted in English law. The rationale for such acceptance in relation to the writ *ne exeat regno*, and that of impressment into naval service, is that offered by Lord Simon of Glaisdale in **McKendrick v Sinclair** (1972) to the effect that:

> . . . a rule of English common law, once clearly established, does not become extinct merely by disuse . . . but may 'go into a cataleptic trance' . . . and revive in propitious circumstances . . . but not revive if it is 'grossly anomalous and anachronistic'.

That it is not obsolete is confirmed by two cases. In **Al Nahkel for Contracting Ltd v Lowe** (1986), the writ was used to prevent a defendant leaving the country to avoid a judgment of the court. In **Parsons v Burk** (1971), an unsuccessful attempt was made to prevent the New Zealand rugby team from leaving the country to play in South Africa.

Treaty-making powers

The power to enter into treaties under international law is a feature of the sovereignty of a state. In the United Kingdom, it is generally accepted that such power is an emanation of the prerogative. As such, the entry into treaties is regarded as a matter solely for the executive and not for Parliament. A treaty is defined as a written agreement between states governed by international law.[56] It will be seen in Chapter 6 that under the doctrine of parliamentary sovereignty, an Act of Parliament alone can alter domestic law. Accordingly, a treaty – being a creature of international law – cannot alter national law without being given effect by an Act of Parliament.[57] It is for this reason that, *inter alia*, the European Communities Act 1972 was enacted to provide for the entry and application of European Community law into the United Kingdom.

The treaty-making power of the executive was challenged in **R v Secretary of State for Foreign and Commonwealth Affairs ex parte Rees-Mogg** (1994). In February 1991, the Heads of Government of the Member States of the European Community signed the Treaty on European Union – the Maastricht Treaty (see Chapter 7). The Treaty was to come into effect on ratification by the Member States. In some countries, ratification was dependent upon the approval of the majority of the people voting in a referendum, as for example in France and Denmark. Under the constitution of the United States of America, treaties are ratified by the President with the advice and consent of two-thirds of the Senators present and voting.

In the United Kingdom, no such constitutional arrangements exist. Under constitutional practice, a treaty need only be approved by Parliament if it requires a change in legislation or the grant of public money. Under the Ponsonby Rule,[58] a constitutional convention, the

---

55 See, *inter alia*, **Aptheker v Secretary of State** (1964); **Kent v Dulles** (1958).
56 Vienna Convention on the Law of Treaties, Cmnd 4848, 1969, London: HMSO.
57 **Walker v Baird** (1982); *The Parlement Belge* (1879); **JH Rayner (Mincing Lane) Ltd v Department of Trade and Industry** (1990).
58 Under Secretary of State for Foreign Affairs 1924. See HC Deb Vol 171 Cols 2001–04.

government undertook to lay every treaty, when signed, for a 21-day period before ratification, and secondly to inform the House of all other 'international agreements and commitments which may bind the nation to specific action in certain circumstances'. The Ponsonby undertaking also included a commitment on the part of government to make time for debate on a treaty if there is a formal demand from the Opposition or other party. The issue raised in **Rees-Mogg** was whether the government had the power to ratify the Maastricht Treaty without the approval of the House of Commons. It was clear that there was substantial opposition to the Treaty on all sides of the House, and the government was not confident that any vote would approve the Treaty. As a result, or as a failsafe device, the Prime Minister announced that, if necessary, the Treaty would be ratified under the prerogative: thus avoiding the risk of parliamentary disapproval. The Queen's Bench Division refused to grant an application for judicial review: the matter was within the prerogative of the Crown. In the long run, the Bill bringing the Treaty into legal effect was passed by both Houses of Parliament.

Reform

The Labour government's 2007 Green Paper, *The Governance of Britain*, stated that the procedure for parliamentary scrutiny of treaties should be formalised. The Constitutional Reform and Governance Act 2010, section 20, provides that a treaty is not to be ratified unless a Minister has laid a copy of the treaty before Parliament and neither the House of Commons nor the House of Lords has resolved, in a period of 21 sitting days, that the treaty should not be ratified. If the House of Commons has resolved (whether or not the House of Lords has also resolved), the treaty may still be ratified if a Minister lays before Parliament a statement of reasons why the treaty should be ratified and a period of 21 sitting days has expired without the House of Commons resolving that it should not be ratified. If the House of Lords (but not the House of Commons) resolves that the treaty should not be ratified, the treaty may be ratified if a Minister has laid before Parliament a statement indicating, with reasons, that he or she is of the opinion that it should be ratified.

Judicial Control of the Prerogative

> . . . the King hath no prerogative, but that which the law of the land allows him.[59]

This bold statement by Sir Edward Coke above, however, did not entitle the courts at that time to question the *manner* in which the prerogative was exercised – rather its role was limited to enquiring whether a particular prerogative power existed, and its scope.

That limitation, as recognised by Lord Scarman in **Council for Civil Service Unions v Minister for the Civil Service** (1985),[60] had now gone, 'overwhelmed by the developing modern law of judicial review'. The courts' modern power to review the exercise of the prerogative was forcefully expressed by Lord Parker CJ in **R v Criminal Injuries Compensation Board ex parte Lain** (1967),[61] in which he stated that the fact that the Board had been established under the prerogative rather than statute did not make it immune from review. This approach is reflected in the dicta of Sedley LJ in **Bancoult** (2007):

---

59 **Case of Proclamations** (1611).
60 On which see further below.
61 A case described by Lord Scarman as a 'landmark case . . . comparable in its day to the *Proclamations Case*' of 1611.

... an Order in Council is an act of the executive and as such is amenable to any appropriate form of judicial review, whether anticipatory or retrospective. What determines the constitutional status of a measure – a statute, a judgment or an order – is not its formal authority, which is always that of the Crown,[62] but its source in the interlocking but unequal limbs of the state.[63]

Statute and the prerogative[64]

Although there is a degree of certainty as to the existence and scope of the prerogatives discussed above, the discussion of all prerogatives must be regarded as overlain with a degree of doubt. Consistent with the doctrine of parliamentary sovereignty, Parliament has the right and power to abolish, restrict or preserve prerogative powers.

Where an Act of Parliament seeks to regulate a matter previously falling under the prerogative but does not expressly abolish the prerogative, the statute will prevail. In **Attorney General v de Keyser's Royal Hotel Ltd** (1920), the court was faced with a claim for compensation by the owners of the hotel, under the Defence of the Realm Act 1914, for compensation due as a result of occupation by the armed forces in wartime. The government sought to rely on the prerogative under which a lesser, discretionary sum of compensation would be payable. The House of Lords rejected the government's right to rely on the prerogative, holding that, once a statute had been enacted, the prerogative power fell into 'abeyance', that is to say, it was set aside for the duration of the life of the statute. Should the statute be repealed, the prerogative would once more come into operation.

In **Laker Airways v Department of Trade** (1977), statute and prerogative were considered once again. The facts involved regulation of the transatlantic air route. Under the Bermuda Agreement of 1946, the United States and United Kingdom governments agreed that air carriers should be approved by both governments: the 'designation' requirement. In 1971, the Civil Aviation Act was passed by Parliament, providing for the licensing of airlines by the Civil Aviation Authority (the CAA). The Act provided that the Secretary of State could give 'guidance' to the CAA as to the policy to be followed in the consideration of licence applications. Mr Freddie Laker had both applied for designation under the Bermuda Treaty and been granted a licence under the Civil Aviation Act 1971.

A change in government led to a change in policy, and it was decided that British Airways should have a monopoly on the transatlantic route. Accordingly, the Secretary of State issued 'guidance' to the CAA to the effect that Mr Laker's licence should be withdrawn. The Secretary of State also requested that the United States government did not proceed to grant designation to Laker Airways under the Treaty. In an application for judicial review by Mr Laker, it was argued that the Secretary of State's 'guidance' was *ultra vires*. The court agreed, regarding the instruction given to the CAA as beyond the normal meaning of the word 'guidance'. The court also rejected the government's argument that it had the right, under the prerogative, to deny Laker Airways' right to fly the Atlantic route. The government could not, it was held, defeat a statutory right by use of a prerogative power.

In **Council of Civil Service Unions v Minister of State for Civil Service** (1985), the prerogative returned to the courts. The Prime Minister, as the Minister for the Civil Service, by a prerogative

---

62 On the distinction between the Crown and the Executive see **R (Quark Fishing Ltd) v Secretary of State for Foreign and Commonwealth Affairs** (2005).

63 At para 35.

64 Note that the Human Rights Act 1998 provides that prerogative orders (Orders in Council) are not subject to challenge by the judiciary. This appears to confuse s 15 and the distinctive status of Acts of Parliament with the prerogative. See further Chapter 18.

order (an Order in Council) terminated the right of workers at the Government Communications Headquarters (GCHQ) to belong to trade unions. The order followed industrial unrest which threatened to disrupt the interception of signals intelligence. The Unions challenged the order under judicial review proceedings, claiming that they had a legitimate expectation to be consulted prior to their rights to membership being withdrawn. The Unions won at first instance, but lost before both the Court of Appeal and the House of Lords.

The House of Lords accepted that the terms and conditions of employment of civil servants were within the prerogative powers of the Crown.[65] Their Lordships likewise accepted that the employees had a legitimate expectation to be consulted before their rights were adversely affected. Nevertheless, the government's plea of national security trumped the interests of the union members.[66]

The significance of the **GCHQ case** in relation to prerogative power is twofold. On the question of the reviewability of the royal prerogative, the House of Lords declared that the exercise of the prerogatives of the Crown were, in principle, as reviewable as powers exercised under statute. However, having boldly declared the principle, the court proceeded to qualify the approach by stating that a number of matters would not be subjected to review. Utilising the concept of 'justiciability', the court held that matters such as the appointment of ministers, dissolution of Parliament, grant of honours, treaties, and par excellence matters of national security were not appropriate subjects for review by the courts.[67] Each of these matters was regarded as involving matters of high policy which it should be for ministers to decide and, by implication, for Parliament to control.[68] It remains the case after GCHQ that many significant attributes of the prerogative remain immune from judicial review.[69]

The case of **R v Secretary of State for the Home Department ex parte Northumbria Police Authority** (1988) reveals a far less robust judicial attitude towards the control of the prerogative than did the **Laker Airways** case. Once again, the issue involved was the relationship between statute and the prerogative. The Police Act 1964 sets out the respective powers of the Home Secretary, the police authorities and the Chief Constables of police with regard to, inter alia, the supply of equipment to police forces (sections 4 and 5).

The Secretary of State, by way of a Circular, advised that the Secretary of State would be making available supplies of riot control equipment to police forces, irrespective of approval by the police authorities. The Northumbria Police Authority sought judicial review of the legality of the Circular. The Home Secretary argued that, as a matter of statutory interpretation, he had power to issue the equipment, and that, independent of the statutory power which he claimed, he had the power under the prerogative to issue the weapons. On the point of statutory interpretation, the Court of Appeal held that no monopoly was reserved to the Police Authority and that, accordingly, the Secretary of State had not acted ultra vires.

On the prerogative aspect, the court's reasoning was both surprising and interesting. First, the Court of Appeal accepted that the Police Act 1964 left unaffected the prerogative powers to keep the peace. Little evidence was adduced as to the existence of such a prerogative, but nevertheless, Croom-Johnson LJ felt able to hold that he had 'no doubt' that the Crown had such a prerogative. Nourse LJ stated that there was no historical or other basis for denying that

---

65 On HWR Wade's doubts concerning the accuracy of this classification, see Wade, 1985, p 180.
66 A Labour government subsequently reinstated the right of workers to join trade unions.
67 In **R v Jones (Margaret)** (2006) the House of Lords ruled that the legality of the Iraq war could not be pleaded in defence to various statutory charges.
68 See also **Patriotic Front – ZAPU v Minister of Justice, Legal and Parliamentary Affairs** (1986), discussed by Walker, 1987.
69 Note, however, that in **R v Ministry of Defence ex parte Smith** (1995), Simon Brown LJ stated, obiter, that the question of whether homosexuals were allowed to serve in the armed forces – a matter falling within the prerogative – was not immune from review. There were no operational considerations nor security implications: the courts were qualified to rule on the matter.

a prerogative to keep the peace could be viewed as a 'sister' prerogative to the power to declare war, without making any reference to Blackstone's division of prerogatives into 'foreign' and 'domestic' categories. Recalling that it had never been possible to identify all the prerogatives of the Crown and that their existence could be ascertained only by means of piecemeal decisions, Nourse LJ declared that there had never been 'a comparable occasion for investigating a prerogative of keeping the peace within the realm':

> The Crown's prerogative of making war and peace, the war prerogative, has never been doubted . . . it is natural to suppose that it was founded, at least in part, on the wider prerogative of protection . . .
>
> The wider prerogative must have extended as much to unlawful acts within the realm as to the menaces of a foreign power. There is no historical or other reason for denying to the war prerogative a sister prerogative of keeping the peace within the realm . . .

More surprisingly, the judge argued that the fact that no evidence existed was almost conclusive proof that it did exist. In the seminal case of **Entick v Carrington** (1765), Lord Camden had asserted that, if there existed authority for the lawful exercise of power, it would be found 'in the books'. It might be thought that in passing the Police Act, Parliament considered that it was providing comprehensive regulation of the terms and conditions under which each regulatory body could act. It cannot have been contemplated that, by plea of a previously unconsidered prerogative, the provisions of the Act could be circumvented. Nevertheless, Purchas LJ was clear that:

> . . . the prerogative powers to take all reasonable steps to preserve the Queen's peace remain unaffected by the Act and these include the supply of equipment to police forces which is reasonably required for the more efficient discharge of their duties.

The **Northumbria Police Authority** case is indicative of the fine line to be drawn between updating a prerogative and creating a new prerogative. Prerogatives, being a feature of monarchical power are, as Dicey stated, residual. Accordingly, for the judges to give recognition to an alleged prerogative, it must be shown that the prerogative claimed existed before 1688. In **BBC v Johns** (1965), Lord Diplock gave judicial expression to this in the statement '. . . it is 350 years and a civil war too late for the Queen's courts to broaden the prerogative'.

In **R v Secretary of State for the Home Department ex parte Fire Brigades' Union** (1995), the matter in issue was whether the Secretary of State, having failed to implement the statutory scheme provided in the Criminal Justice Act 1988, was free to implement a different scheme under the royal prerogative.[70] The scheme introduced a 'tariff' for compensation for injuries at a substantially lower rate than provided for under the statute.

The Master of the Rolls accepted that the Home Secretary had the power to invite Parliament to repeal the provisions or to seek enactment of the tariff provisions in statute, or, alternatively, to seek to have the statutory provisions abolished and then implement the tariff provisions under the royal prerogative. But:

> . . . what he could not do, so long as the 1988 provisions stood unrepealed as an enduring statement of Parliament's will, was to exercise prerogative powers to introduce a scheme radically different from what Parliament had approved . . .

---

70 As announced in the White Paper, *Compensating Victims of Violent Crime: Changes to the Criminal Injuries Compensation Scheme*, Cmnd 2434, 1993, London: HMSO. The scheme was implemented on 1 April 1994.

Accordingly, the Secretary of State could not avoid the requirements of the 1988 Act and introduce – by means of the prerogative – a different scheme.

The House of Lords ruled, by a majority (Lord Keith of Kinkel and Lord Mustill dissenting), that the decisions of the Secretary of State not to implement the statutory scheme, and to introduce an alternative scheme under the prerogative, were unlawful. The House of Lords refused, however, to rule that the Secretary of State was under a legally enforceable duty to bring the statutory scheme into effect at a particular date.

However, the Secretary of State did not enjoy an unfettered discretion as to whether to bring the scheme into effect, and he could not, through use of the prerogative, defeat the purpose of the statute. Lord Keith, dissenting, argued that the court should not become involved in a matter which was for Parliament to determine.

Here, within one case, are seen differing considerations weighing on the judges in the House of Lords. The majority decision rests squarely on the rule of law and the preference for statute over the prerogative. The minority view, however, leans far more clearly in favour of the doctrine of separation of powers and the supremacy of Parliament in regulating its own affairs and in calling ministers to account.[71]

Political Control of the Prerogative

Political control over the exercise of the prerogative, while preserving the separation of powers between the executive and judiciary, may in practice prove to be inadequate. In theory, the prerogative, as is the case with any other act of government, is capable of being subjected to the full range of parliamentary procedure.[72] Thus, Question Time, debates and select committees may be utilised in order to scrutinise prerogative acts. However, under parliamentary practice, there exist a number of issues on which ministers conventionally decline to provide information, and many of these matters are precisely those which fall within the scope of the prerogative. The grant of honours, for example, is a matter not for parliamentary discussion. On matters of the disposition of the armed forces, weaponry for the armed forces, government contracts, judicial appointments, and investigations by the Director of Public Prosecutions, the government will decline to answer questions. Aside from such specific matters, the government may plead such wide notions as national security, confidentiality or the public interest in order to avoid scrutiny.

The royal prerogative and the Human Rights Act 1998

The Human Rights Act 1998 – discussed in detail in Chapter 18 – enables the rights protected under the European Convention on Human Rights to be enforced before the domestic courts. Section 6(1) of the Act makes it unlawful for a public authority to act in a way which is incompatible with Convention rights, thereby extending protection to actions taken under the prerogative. However, section 21 of the Act protects the prerogative by raising the status of Orders in Council made under the prerogative to that of primary legislation. As a result, although the courts may make a declaration that an action is incompatible with Convention rights, the Orders in Council cannot be annulled by the courts and will remain valid in the same way as Acts of Parliament.

---

71 Note that, following the decision of the House of Lords, the Criminal Injuries Compensation Act 1995 repealed the Criminal Justice Act 1988, ss 108–17, and made provision for a scheme of payments of a standard amount of compensation calculated in accordance with a tariff prepared by the Secretary of State.
72 This is to be discussed in more detail in Chapters 14 and 15.

Reform of the Prerogative?

It has been seen from the above discussion that prerogative powers have been the subject of much discussion and proposals for reform, the latest of which are considered in *The Governance of Britain* 2007, and now governed by the Constitutional Reform and Governance Act 2010 which provides for parliamentary scrutiny of treaties, and a statutory basis for the civil service. The Fixed-term Parliaments Act 2011 brings the dissolution of Parliament under statutory authority, thereby removing the power of the Crown over the dissolution of Parliament.[73]

All reform of the prerogative, however, entails constitutional and legal challenges. Firstly, the extent to which placing the prerogative under statutory authority would clarify questions as to the scope of the power in question, and its control, is necessarily a matter for speculation. In relation to the scope of power, the case of the **Northumbria Police Authority** (1988), discussed above, illustrates the difficulty. It was seen there that the prerogative 'to keep the peace' was pleaded as an alternative to the existence of power under the Police Act 1964: seemingly a 'reserve power' claimed as insurance against the court finding that the minister had acted outside the power granted by the Act. That the Court of Appeal upheld the minister's claim was by no means a foregone conclusion, and to do so, in the virtual absence of authority and precedent, and with little analysis, was remarkable.

In terms of the control over the exercise of the prerogative, the limits of such control must be remembered. While an application for judicial review of the exercise of power may be granted, it has been seen in relation to the **GCHQ case** that the courts have developed a category of non-justiciable matters. The concept of non-justiciability protects the judges from encroaching on decisions which – in light of separation of powers – are within the proper sphere of decision of the democratically accountable executive. That protective concept is unlikely to change if and when such non-reviewable matters are placed under statutory authority. In light of that, the extent to which governments demonstrate their real commitment to openness and transparency and allow parliamentary scrutiny of their actions becomes all the more important. It is by no means certain that placing such powers under statutory authority, even if they were correctly identified and defined, would guarantee the degree of control which the rule of law requires.

Summary

Under all constitutions, written or unwritten, there will be a number of powers reserved to the executive, powers which are exercisable without the passage of legislation. Such powers may include entering into treaties, declarations of war and peace, and recognition of foreign states and diplomats. Such powers are referred to as 'inherent executive powers', or 'prerogative powers'.

Under the United Kingdom constitution, it may be concluded, quite reasonably, that parliamentary control over the exercise of prerogative power is less than adequate. Set alongside or juxtaposed with the excluded areas of judicial review under the concept of justiciability, it can be seen that there exists a reservoir of power, much of which is undefined or at best ill defined, which is not amenable to either judicial or parliamentary control.

---

73 The Act preserves the Crown's role in the summoning of Parliament.

 **Further Reading**

Blackburn, R. (2004) 'Monarchy and the Personal Prerogatives', Public Law, 546.

Blackburn, R. (2007) *King and Country: Monarchy and the future King Charles II*, London: Politico's.

Blackburn, R. (2009) 'The Prerogative Power of Dissolution of Parliament: Law, Practice and Reform', Public Law, 766.

Blom-Cooper, L. and Drabble, R. (2010) 'GCHQ Revisited', Public Law, 18.

Butler, D. (1976) 'The Australian Crisis of 1975', Parliamentary Affairs, 29: 201.

Chitty, J. (1820) *The Prerogatives of the Crown*, London: Butterworths.

Daly, P. (2010) 'Justiciability and the "Political Question" Doctrine', Public Law, 160.

Markesinis, B.A. (1972) *The Theory and Practice of Dissolution of Parliament*, Cambridge: CUP.

Munro, C. (1999) *Studies in Constitutional Law* (2nd edn), London: Butterworths, Chapter 8.

Sunkin, M. and Payne, S. (eds) (1999) *The Nature of the Crown: a Legal and Political Analysis*, Oxford: Clarendon Press.

Chapter 6

Parliamentary Sovereignty

Chapter Contents

Introduction

Under any constitution – whether written or unwritten – there must be a source of ultimate authority: one supreme power over and above all other power in the state. Under a written constitution the highest source of power is the constitution as interpreted by the Supreme Court. Under the British constitution, in theory if not in practice, the highest source of authority is the United Kingdom Parliament and Acts of Parliament are the highest form of law.

Writing in the late nineteenth century, AV Dicey took the view that the supremacy of Parliament is 'the dominant characteristic of our political institutions'.[1] However, the concept of sovereignty has long caused controversy and is one which assumes differing interpretations according to the perspective being adopted. For example, international lawyers are concerned with the attributes which identify a state as independent and sovereign within the international community. Political scientists on the other hand are concerned with the source of political power within a state. From the perspective of legal theorists and constitutional lawyers the focus is on the ultimate legal power within a state.

To categorise Britain as a sovereign independent state with the ultimate source of legal authority vesting in its Parliament was accurate in the nineteenth century. However, in today's world of increasing economic legal and political interdependence the traditional theory of sovereignty has an air of unreality about it. International relations and obligations, membership of the European Union, devolution of law-making powers away from Westminster to Northern Ireland, Scotland and Wales and other factors all restrict what Parliament can in fact do: theory and practice are increasingly separated. In this chapter we examine the various aspects of sovereignty, and the challenges posed to the orthodox view.

Legal and Political Sovereignty

Political sovereignty refers to the supreme political authority within a state. Legal sovereignty – from the standpoint of sovereignty within the state as opposed to sovereignty as understood in international law – refers to the supreme legal authority within a state.[2]

It is often difficult to distinguish clearly between legal and political sovereignty. The distinction is nevertheless one insisted upon by authorities such as Sir Edward Coke, Sir William Blackstone and AV Dicey. As with so much of the United Kingdom's constitutional law, contemporary thinking about sovereignty remains influenced by Dicey's legacy, which will be examined below. At this introductory stage, however, it is necessary to note that Dicey drew a strict separation between legal sovereignty and political sovereignty (as did Coke and Blackstone). In Dicey's view, the people hold political sovereignty whilst legal sovereignty rests with the 'Queen in Parliament'. In large measure, this clear demarcation between the political and the legal is explained by the unwritten nature of the United Kingdom's constitution. In the majority of states having a written constitution, the constitution defines the limits of governmental power. In the United Kingdom, by way of contrast, the powers of government – whilst ultimately dependent upon the electoral 'mandate' – remain unconstrained by any fundamental written document and subject only to Parliament's approval. All law-making power thus derives, not from a power conferring and power-delimiting constitutional document, endorsed by the people, but from the sovereignty of the legislature: Parliament.

See the
Website.

---

1 Dicey, 1885, p 39.
2 For a more elaborate categorisation, see Rees, 'The theory of sovereignty restated', in Laslett, 1975, Chapter IV.

Sovereignty and Written Constitutions

Where a written constitution exists, it will have come into being either by a grant of independence from a previously sovereign power or through a revolution – peaceful or otherwise. Where the constitution arises from the authority of the native people, it is 'autochthonous':

> . . . [the people] assert not the principle of autonomy only; they assert also a principle of something stronger, of self-sufficiency, of constitutional autarky . . . of being constitutionally rooted in their own soil. [Wheare, 1960, Chapter 4]

Where autochthony[3] exists, the authority for the constitution arises from the people. The phrase 'We the People' has powerful psychological – and legal – force, and the resultant document, the constitution, will be supreme. All power entrusted to government comes from the people: it is accordingly understandable that, under such a constitutional arrangement, there is a strongly held belief that government holds its power on 'trust' for the people. It may be said, as a result, that both law-making and executive powers are conditionally conferred on those who hold public office, subject to the doctrine of trust which will be enforced by the courts in the name of the people. All constitutions – written and unwritten – exist against the backcloth of historical, political and moral evolution: none exists in a vacuum. However, under a written constitution, this background has a particular significance. The constitution, being the expression of the political morality of its age – updated by the judiciary through interpretative methods – is a constant reflection and reminder of the will of the people and the restraints which that will imposes on government.

Chief Justice Marshall, in **Marbury v Madison** (1803), explained the power of the constitution:

> It is a proposition too plain to be contested that the constitution controls any legislative act repugnant to it; or, that the legislature may alter the constitution by an ordinary act. Between these two alternatives, there is no middle ground. The constitution is either a superior, paramount law, unchangeable by ordinary means, or it is on a level with ordinary legislative acts, and, like other acts, is alterable when the legislature shall please to alter it. If the former part of the alternative is true, then a legislative act contrary to the constitution is not law; if the latter part be true, then written constitutions are absurd attempts, on the part of the people, to limit a power in its own nature illimitable.

It is possible, accordingly, under such a constitutional arrangement, for the constitutional court[4] effectively to redefine the relationship between the governors and the governed, the state and its citizens. By this means, the constitution is renewed and reinvigorated. By way of example, the American Bill of Rights, enacted as amendments to the 1787 Constitution, provides that:

> All persons born or naturalized in the United States, and subject to the jurisdiction thereof, are citizens of the United States and of the state wherein they reside. No state may . . . deprive any person of life, liberty, or property, without due process of law; nor deny to any person within its jurisdiction the equal protection of the laws . . . [5]

---

3   See Marshall, 1971, Chapter III.4.
4   Howsoever labelled: in the United States of America, the Supreme Court; in Australia, the High Court.
5   Bill of Rights, Article XIV, s 1, ratified 9 July 1868.

This 'equal protection' clause has been the focus of the development of equal civil and political rights in the United States of America. In 1896, the Supreme Court was called upon to determine whether the policy of segregation of black and white citizens was lawful under the Constitution. The court ruled that 'separate but equal treatment' laws did not amount to a denial of the equal protection of law.[6] When, however, in 1954, the question of 'equal protection' came before the Supreme Court concerning segregation in the schools of the states of Kansas, South Carolina, Virginia and Delaware, the court was to rule that such 'treatment' violated the Fourteenth Amendment of the Constitution.[7]

The Source of Sovereignty in the United Kingdom

The sovereignty of Parliament is not itself laid down in statute: nor could it be, for the ultimate law maker cannot confer upon itself the ultimate power. As legal theorists[8] have demonstrated, when searching for ultimate legal power, there comes a point of inquiry beyond which one cannot logically move. In order to understand the ultimate authority of law the inquirer must move beyond the law itself. The key to understanding parliamentary sovereignty lies in its acceptance – but not necessarily moral approval – by the judges within the legal system. Sovereignty is therefore a fundamental rule of the common law, for it is the judges who uphold Parliament's sovereignty. For as long as the judges accept the sovereignty of Parliament, sovereignty will remain the ultimate rule of the constitution. As Salmond explains:

> All rules of law have historical sources. As a matter of fact and history they have their origin somewhere, though we may not know what it is. But not all of them have legal sources ... But whence comes the rule that Acts of Parliament have the force of law? This is legally ultimate; its source is historical only, not legal ... It is the law because it is the law, and for no other reason that it is possible for the law to take notice of. No statute can confer this power upon Parliament, for this would be to assume and act on the very power that is to be conferred.[9]

Accordingly, the rule that confers validity on legislation is 'logically superior to the sovereign'. The logical consequence of this is stated by HWR Wade:

> ... if no statute can establish the rule that the courts obey Acts of Parliament, similarly no statute can alter or abolish that rule. The rule is above and beyond the reach of statute ... because it is itself the source of the authority of statute.[10]

The sovereignty of Parliament will only be lost under two conditions. The first condition would be where Parliament decided – perhaps on the authority of the people, tested in a referendum – to abolish its sovereignty and to place its residual authority under that of a written constitution to be adjudicated upon by the judiciary. The second condition would be where the judiciary itself underwent a 'revolution' in attitude, and accepted that Parliament was no longer the sovereign law-making body and that the judges owed allegiance to an alternative – or different – sovereign power. These points will be returned to when considering challenges to the traditional Diceyan view of sovereignty.

---

6 **Plessey v Ferguson** (1896).
7 **Brown v Board of Education of Topeka** (1954). The ruling did not end segregation on other grounds. See King, 1964; see further the Civil Rights Acts 1964 and 1968.
8 See Kelsen, 1961, p 116; Hart, 1961, p 104. See also Kelsen, 'The function of a constitution', in Tur and Twining, 1986.
9 Williams (ed), *Jurisprudence*, 10th edn, p 155, cited by Wade, 1955, p 187.
10 Wade, 'Introduction', in Dicey, 1885, 1959 edn.

In the United Kingdom, in the absence of a written constitution which asserts the sovereignty of the people and the sovereignty of the constitution – as interpreted by the judiciary – over the legislature and executive, the vacuum is filled by the doctrine of parliamentary sovereignty, or supremacy. Under this doctrine, political sovereignty vests in the people: legal sovereignty vests with Parliament over which no legal controls are exerted, but which remains responsible to the electorate for the continued, and regularly renewed, grant of law making and executive authority. The constitution is renewed through the democratic process and the concept of a responsive responsible government, rather than through the means of a Supreme Court reinterpreting the constitution according to judicial perceptions of the mores in society. This is not to suggest that under a written constitution, there is no responsive, accountable and democratic government or that the evolution of the constitution lies solely within the domain of the judges. Rather, the point to be emphasised is that, under a written constitution, there is an additional element in effecting constitutional change. Depending upon the independence, integrity and motivation of the courts, acts of the executive and legislature can be subjected to the control of the constitution.

The origins of parliamentary sovereignty

In Chapter 5, the manner in which the near absolute powers of the Crown[11] were reduced by the courts and Parliament was discussed. With the reduction in the King's prerogative powers, there came about the correlative rise in the sovereignty of Parliament. From 1688, the supremacy of Parliament over the Crown was established. From this time, the prerogative powers of the Crown continued in existence or were abolished or curtailed as Parliament determined. No new prerogative powers may be claimed by the Crown, as Diplock LJ stated in **BBC v Johns** (1965).

Dicey and Sovereignty

The classical definition of sovereignty, offered from a constitutional law rather than a jurisprudential perspective, is that of AV Dicey (1885). Dicey insisted that it was essential to separate the political from the legal and to recognise that, as matters stand, legal sovereignty remains with the United Kingdom Parliament, although there may be political restraints which effectively inhibit the exercise of those powers. On sovereignty, Dicey stated:

> The principle of parliamentary sovereignty means neither more nor less than this: namely, that Parliament thus defined has, under the English constitution, the right to make or unmake any law whatever; and, further, that no person or body is recognised by the law of England as having a right to override or set aside the legislation of Parliament.

> A law may, for our present purpose, be defined as 'any rule which will be enforced by the courts'. The principle, then, of parliamentary sovereignty may, looked at from its positive side, be thus described: any Act of Parliament, or any part of an Act of Parliament, which makes a new law, or repeals or modifies an existing law, will be obeyed by the court. The same principle, looked at from its negative side, may be thus stated: there is no person or body of persons who can, under the English constitution, make rules which override or derogate from an Act of Parliament, or which [to

---

11 To make laws by proclamation, to rule under the prerogative without Parliament, and to participate in the judicial process.

express the same thing in other words) will be enforced by the courts in contravention of an Act of Parliament. [1885, p 39]

From this description can be deduced three basic rules:

(a)   Parliament is the supreme law-making body and may enact laws on any subject matter;
(b)   no Parliament may be bound by a predecessor or bind a successor;
(c)   no person or body – including a court of law – may question the validity of Parliament's
      enactments.

It is the correctness of this definition which must be tested and evaluated. Having considered
the concept of sovereignty in theoretical terms, examination of the manner in which this is
translated into a practical legal doctrine is required. Dicey's description of sovereignty will
provide the framework for discussion.

Parliament's unlimited law-making power

This aspect of sovereignty is the easiest both to explain and to understand: the rule means that
there is no limit on the subject matter on which Parliament may legislate. Thus Parliament may
legislate to alter its term of office. In 1716, the life of a Parliament was limited to three years
under the Act of 1694. Fearing the effects of an election, the government introduced, and
Parliament passed, the Septennial Act, extending the life of Parliament to seven years. The
consequence of this Act was to confer authority on the Commons to legislate without the
express consent of the electorate: thus usurping the rights of the people.[12] The Septennial Act,
under a written constitution such as that of the United States, would be legally invalid.
Nevertheless, as Dicey argued, 'Parliament made a legal though unprecedented use of its
powers' (1885, p 47). Parliament also extended its own life between 1910 and 1918, and the
Parliament elected in 1935 was to endure until 1945.[13] Parliament may also legislate to alter
the succession to the throne, as with the Act of Settlement 1700 and His Majesty's Declaration
of Abdication Act 1936. Parliament may 'abolish' itself and reconstitute itself as a different
body, as occurred with the Union with Scotland Act 1706. Parliament may also legislate to alter
its own powers, as with the Parliament Acts 1911 and 1949, whereby the powers of the House
of Lords in respect of legislation were curtailed. Parliament may grant independence to
dependent states, whether dominions or colonies, as with the Nigeria Independence Act 1960
and the Zimbabwe Independence Act 1979. Furthermore, Parliament may legislate to limit its
own powers in relation to dependent territories, as shown by the Colonial Laws Validity Act
1865 and the Statute of Westminster 1931.[14]

Parliament may also legislate with retrospective effect, as with the War Damage Act 1965.
The War Damage Act effectively overruled the decision of the House of Lords in **Burmah Oil
Company v Lord Advocate** (1965). In 1942, British troops had destroyed oil installations in
Rangoon, with the intention of preventing them from falling into the hands of the Japanese.
The British government made an *ex gratia* payment of some £4 million to the company. Burmah
Oil sued the government for some £31 million in compensation. The House of Lords held that
compensation was payable by the Crown for the destruction of property caused by the exercise
of the prerogative power in relation to war. The government immediately introduced into
Parliament the War Damage Bill to nullify the effect of the decision.

---

12 See Priestley, 1771, cited in Dicey, 1885, p 47.
13 Dicey, 1885, p 47.
14 Prolongation of Parliament Act 1944.

Parliament may legislate with extra-territorial effect; that is to say, it may enact laws affecting the rights and duties of citizens and non-citizens outside the territorial jurisdiction of the United Kingdom. For example, certain offences committed in a foreign state will be triable in this country. Thus, murder, manslaughter, treason, bigamy and tax offences committed abroad will not render the accused immune from prosecution in this country.[15] Parliament may expressly legislate for overseas territory, as in the Continental Shelf Act 1964, under which exploration and exploitation rights of the continental shelf vest in the Crown. However, it is a presumption of statutory interpretation that statutes will not be given extra-territorial effect other than where it is expressly or impliedly provided for under the Act.[16] Such statutes will normally be passed in order to give effect to obligations undertaken under an international treaty.[17] The Hijacking Act 1971, for example, gave legislative effect to the Convention for the Suppression on Unlawful Seizure of Aircraft. Section 1 of the Aviation Security Act 1982, which succeeded the Hijacking Act 1971, provides that the crime of hijacking is committed when a person on board an aircraft in flight unlawfully seizes control of the aircraft and exercises control over it by the use of force or by threats. The jurisdiction of the United Kingdom courts, with limited exceptions, extends to an act of hijacking, wherever it occurs, and irrespective of the nationality of the hijacker.[18] Similarly, the Terrorist Asset-Freezing Act 2010, section 33, provides that a criminal offence may be committed by British citizens or incorporated bodies, by act or omission wholly or partly outside the United Kingdom. The most often quoted and best remembered examples of Parliament's theoretically untrammelled legislative powers are those offered by Sir Ivor Jennings (1959): Parliament can legislate to ban smoking on the streets of Paris; Parliament can legally make a man into a woman; and Sir Leslie Stephens (1882): Parliament could legislate to have all blue eyed babies put to death. These extreme, hypothetical examples illustrate the distinction between what is theoretically possible and what is practically possible, or, to express it differently, the distinction between *validity* and *effectiveness* discussed above. The distinction is important and helps to explain the apparent paradox of unlimited legislative power.

An Act of Parliament will be valid if it has passed through the requisite parliamentary stages and received royal assent. The manner in which the judges deal with this 'enrolled Bill' rule is discussed further below. All that need be noted for now is that, provided an Act of Parliament is 'on the parliamentary roll', it will be held to be good law. That is not to say that every rule-making power exercised by Parliament results in an 'Act of Parliament' which alone can alter the law, and is thus 'sovereign'.

Acts of Parliament alone are supreme

Resolutions of Parliament

Resolutions of either House of Parliament – for example, decisions of the House of Commons – do not have the force of law and cannot alter the law of the land and thereby affect individual rights and duties.[19] For a resolution to have the force of law, it must be placed on a statutory basis.

Proclamations

Proclamations of the Crown, issued under the royal prerogative, do not have the force of law. To understand the status of proclamations, it is necessary to turn to the reign of Henry VIII. Under the Statute of Proclamations 1539, the King was given wide – though not

---

15 Law Com No 91, *Territorial and Extra-territorial Extent of Criminal Law*, 1978, London: HMSO.
16 *Treacy v DPP* (1971); *R v Kelly* (1982).
17 Parliament may, however, legislate contrary to the requirements of international law. See *Mortensen v Peters* (1906); *Cheney v Conn* (1968).
18 See also the Taking of Hostages Act 1982 giving effect to the International Convention Against the Taking of Hostages.
19 *Stockdale v Hansard* (1839); *Bowles v Bank of England* (1913).

unlimited – power to make law without Parliament's consent. The Act was repealed in 1547, although monarchs continued to 'legislate' by proclamation. The **Case of Proclamations** (1611) clarified the constitutional position. The most significant aspects of the case lay in the findings, first, that the King could not by proclamation create an offence previously unknown to law, and secondly, that the King had only such prerogative power as was granted under law.

Treaties

Treaties entered into under the royal prerogative cannot alter the law of the land. The courts have made it clear that treaties can take legal effect only under the authority of an Act of Parliament.[20] This point will be returned to when the constitutional relationship between the United Kingdom and the European Union is examined in Chapters 7 and 8. It is sufficient to note here that a treaty has no legal force under domestic law unless and until its provisions are incorporated into law by way of statute.

Resolutions, proclamations and treaties are but three species of 'law making' which are distinguishable from statute: and it is the statute alone which will be valid, provided that the required parliamentary procedures have been followed.

Intrinsic and extrinsic limits on Parliament's power

As seen above, the criterion of effectiveness underlies the supremacy of Parliament and represents one important – albeit extra-legal – constraint on Parliament's power. As Dicey says, sovereignty 'is limited on every side by the possibility of popular resistance' (1885, p 79). Leslie Stephens makes the same point and is quoted at length by Dicey:

> Lawyers are apt to speak as though the legislature were omnipotent, as they do not require to go beyond its decision. It is, of course, omnipotent in the sense that it can make whatever law it please, in as much as a law means any rule which has been made by the legislature. But, from the scientific point of view, the power of the legislature is of course strictly limited. It is limited, so to speak, both from within and from without; from within, because the legislature is the product of certain social conditions, and determined by whatever determines the society; and from without, because the power of imposing laws is dependent upon the instinct of subordination, which is itself limited. If a legislature decided that all blue eyed babies should be murdered, the preservation of blue eyed babies would be illegal; but legislators must go mad before they could pass such a law, and subjects be idiotic before they could submit to it. [p 81]

These views are indicative of the constitutional role of government today. In a representative democracy, the proper purpose of government is to serve the people. In former times, when government was conducted by the King in Council, this was not necessarily the case. But even then, there were limits on monarchical and aristocratic power: ultimately, law cannot be enforced against the will of the governed. Compliance – in the absence of a military or police state – depends for the most part on voluntary acquiescence, not on the application of power. Nowadays, with a more or less democratic House of Commons, the internal and external constraints discussed by Dicey and Stephens coalesce. As Dicey explains:

---

20 See, inter alia, The Parlement Belge (1879); **AG for Canada v AG for Ontario** (1937); **McWhirter v AG** (1972); **Blackburn v AG** (1971).

The aim and effect of such (representative) government is to produce a coincidence, or at any rate diminish the divergence, between the external and the internal limitations on the exercise of sovereign power.

Where a Parliament truly represents the people, the divergence between the external and the internal limit to the exercise of sovereign power can hardly arise, or if it arises, must soon disappear. [1885, pp 82–83]

No Parliament may be bound by its predecessor or bind its successor

The rationale for this aspect of Dicey's definition of sovereignty lies in the recognition that for a body to be sovereign it must be, in Austin's word, illimitable. For a sovereign body to be subordinate to another body would be a logical contradiction:

The logical reason why Parliament has failed in its endeavours to enact unchangeable enactments is that a sovereign power cannot, while retaining its sovereign character, restrict its own powers by any particular enactment . . . 'Limited sovereignty', in short, as in the case of a parliamentary as of every other sovereign, is a contradiction in terms. [1885, p 68]

It follows, therefore, that each Parliament must enjoy the same unlimited power as any Parliament before it. No Parliament can enact rules which limit future Parliaments.[21] It is this aspect of Dicey's definition which gives rise to the most argument and which requires the most careful analysis.

The doctrine of implied repeal

The doctrine of implied repeal provides the mechanism by which the judge gives effect to the rule against Parliament being bound by previous Parliaments or being able to bind subsequent Parliaments, and thereby guarantees contemporary sovereignty. Parliament may, of course, repeal any previous law by expressly declaring that law to be repealed. The position of the judiciary is then clear: they must give effect to the latest expression of sovereign will and judges are not free to apply the earlier statute. The position, however, may not always be so clear cut. Parliament may pass, perhaps through inadvertence, a statute which, while not expressly repealing an earlier Act, is inconsistent with it. When the judges are thus faced with two apparently conflicting statutes, the doctrine of implied repeal will come into play, the judges applying the latest statute in time and deeming the earlier provisions to be impliedly repealed.

Two cases which illustrate the principle in operation are **Vauxhall Estates Ltd v Liverpool Corporation** (1932) and **Ellen Street Estates Ltd v Minister of Health** (1934), each of which entailed similar facts. Section 7(1) of the Acquisition of Land (Assessment of Compensation) Act 1919 provided that:

The provisions of the Act or order by which the land is authorised to be acquired . . . shall . . . have effect subject to this Act and so far as inconsistent with this Act those provisions shall cease to have or shall not have effect . . .

The Housing Act 1925 provided for a less generous scheme for compensation on the compulsory acquisition of land than the 1919 Act. In both cases, the plaintiffs argued that section 7(1)

---

21 On the distinction between 'continuing' and 'self-embracing' sovereignty, see below, pp 133–135.

of the 1919 Act was binding on the courts and should be applied in preference to the Housing Act 1925. If that claim were to succeed, the constitutional position would be that the provisions of the 1919 Act were effectively 'entrenched' – that is to say, have a superior legal status to that of other Acts of Parliament and therefore binding – on a future Parliament. In the **Vauxhall Estates** case, the Divisional Court held that the 1925 Act impliedly repealed the conflicting provisions in the 1919 Act and, in the **Ellen Street Estates** case, the Court of Appeal again ruled that the 1919 Act must give way to the 1925 legislation. Maugham LJ stated that:

> The legislature cannot, according to our constitution, bind itself as to the form of subsequent legislation, and it is impossible for Parliament to enact that in a subsequent statute dealing with the same subject matter there can be no implied repeal. If, in a subsequent Act, Parliament chooses to make it plain that the earlier statute is being to some extent repealed, effect must be given to that intention just because it is the will of the legislature.[22]

While the implied repeal rule still applies in relation to most statutes, it has been regarded by some senior judges as inapplicable to statutes of major constitutional importance. This view has been expressed in relation to the European Communities Act 1972 and the Human Rights Act 1998: see below for further discussion.

With the doctrines of express and implied repeal firmly in mind, consideration must now be given to the special problems allegedly posed for legislative supremacy by grants of independence, the Acts of Union with Scotland and Ireland, 'manner and form' and 'redefinition' theories. The impact of membership of the European Community and Union also requires careful consideration, as does the recent devolution of power to the Scottish Parliament and the Northern Ireland and Welsh Assemblies, and the Human Rights Act 1998.

Grants of independence

The Statute of Westminster 1931 was enacted to give statutory force to the constitutional convention that the United Kingdom Parliament would not legislate for Dominions without their consent. Section 4 provides:

> No Act of Parliament of the United Kingdom passed after the commencement of this Act shall extend, or be deemed to extend, to a Dominion as part of the law of that Dominion unless it is expressly declared in that Act that that Dominion has requested, and consented to, the enactment thereof.

Where Parliament confers partial competence on a subordinate legislature, the question arises as to whether the United Kingdom Parliament can revoke that grant of power. The principle that Parliament cannot be bound by the acts of its predecessor has already been established. The issue here is the relationship between the sovereign Parliament and a Parliament dependent for

---

22 See, however, the earlier case of **Nairn v University of St Andrews** (1909), in which the House of Lords ruled that the Universities (Scotland) Act 1889, which empowered commissioners to make ordinances, *inter alia*, to enable universities to confer degrees on women, did not impliedly repeal the Representation of the People (Scotland) Act 1868, s 27, which provided the right to vote for, *inter alia*, 'every person whose name is for the time being on the register, . . . if of full age, and not subject to any legal incapacity'. In **Jex-Blake v Senatus of the University of Edinburgh** (1873), following **Chorlton v Lings** (1868), the court ruled that 'women' were not 'persons' within the meaning to be applied to the right to vote. The House of Lords in **Nairn** ruled that only Parliament, in the most express terms, could 'effect a constitutional change so momentous and far-reaching', and it could not be taken to have done so by 'so furtive a process' as this later Act ((1909), per Lord Loreburn LC). Given the date of this case, and its positioning in the continuing struggle for women's right to vote, which was so consistently obstructed by the courts, the decision is perhaps best understood within the political climate of the time rather than as an illustration of objective legal analysis.

its powers upon Westminster. This issue arose in **British Coal Corporation v The King** (1935). The Judicial Committee of the Privy Council had to determine whether or not the Canadian legislature had the power to regulate or prohibit appeals in criminal matters to the King in Council. A determination of that matter entailed consideration of the scope of legislative competence of the legislature. The relevant Acts were the British North America Act 1867, the Colonial Laws Validity Act 1865, the Statute of Westminster 1931 and the Canadian Criminal Code which prohibited appeal to the courts of the United Kingdom. The Statute of Westminster had removed any legislative incompetence from the Canadian legislature and accordingly the legislature had full power to enact the section in question. It was accepted by the Judicial Committee of the Privy Council that, whilst the power of the Imperial Parliament remained 'in theory unimpaired' and that, 'as a matter of abstract law', section 4 of the Statute of Westminster could be repealed by the Parliament of the United Kingdom, in practice it could not be: '. . . legal theory must march alongside practical reality.' **British Coal Corporation v The King** is, however, no more than a recognition of the extrinsic or practical limitations on the exercise of sovereignty, and not of any legal limitations on Parliament's supremacy.

In **Ndlwana v Hofmeyer** (1937),[23] the Appellate Division of the South African High Court adopted the view that such a restriction amounted to a fetter on Parliament's powers. Again, however, it is to be noted that such judicial utterances do no more than recognise the practical political restraints which are imposed on Parliament, not its legal powers. It is correct, therefore, to view such *obiter* as reflecting the distinction between legal and political sovereignty: a point emphasised by Dicey himself.

The question of the status and effect of section 4 of the Statute of Westminster arose once more in **Manuel v Attorney General** (1982). The issue was whether the Canada Act 1982, passed by the United Kingdom Parliament at the request and consent of Canada, was a valid enactment. The plaintiffs' argument was that the United Kingdom Parliament had no power to amend the Constitution of Canada to the detriment of the native population without their consent. It was argued that section 4 of the Statute of Westminster required not just the consent of the federal Parliament but also that of all the provincial legislatures and the native minority population. The application failed. The Statute of Westminster required only that the 1982 Act declared that Canada had requested and consented to the Act.

The Acts of Union with Scotland 1706/1707 and Ireland 1800[24]

The Acts of Union, their status and their effect on Parliament's sovereignty have provided a fertile source for academic debate which represents a powerful argument against the unlimited freedom of any Parliament at any time to legislate as it pleases. The whole debate centres on the notion that the new United Kingdom Parliament was, in the words of Professor JDB Mitchell,[25] 'born unfree'. The idea being conveyed here is that the Acts of Union have some form of 'higher law' status which binds and limits the powers of Parliament.

The union with Scotland

Prior to the accession to the throne of James I (James VI of Scotland), England and Scotland were both independent sovereign states, each having its own monarch and Parliament. With James's accession to the English throne in 1603, the two countries were united under one monarch but retained their sovereign Parliaments until 1706. The Treaty of Union 1706

---

23 See also **Ibralebbe v R** (1964); **Blackburn v AG** (1971).
24 The English Parliament's legislation was the Union with Scotland Act 1706; the Scottish Parliament's was the Union with England Act 1707.
25 Mitchell, 1963; and see Munro, 1999.

effected, conceptually, the abolition of both Parliaments and the birth of the Parliament of Great Britain.

Article I of the Act of Union provides:

> That the two kingdoms of England and Scotland shall upon the first day of May which shall be in the year one thousand seven hundred and seven and for ever after be united into one Kingdom by the name of Great Britain . . .

The sovereignty issue has been argued in three cases concerning the Act of Union with Scotland. In **MacCormick v Lord Advocate** (1953), MacCormick sought an injunction against the Lord Advocate, as representative of the Crown, preventing the use of the title Queen Elizabeth II of the United Kingdom of Great Britain. The objection to the use of the title was based on historical inaccuracy[26] and a contravention of Article I of the Treaty of Union which provided for the union of the two countries from 1707. The petition was dismissed, as was the subsequent appeal. Lord Cooper, the Lord President, however, proceeded to discuss the doctrine of sovereignty:

> The principle of the unlimited sovereignty of Parliament is a distinctively English principle which has no counterpart in Scottish constitutional law . . . Considering that the Union legislation extinguished the Parliaments of Scotland and England and replaced them by a new Parliament, I have difficulty in seeing why it should have been supposed that the new Parliament of Great Britain must inherit all the peculiar characteristics of the English Parliament but none of the Scottish Parliament, as if all that happened in 1707 was that Scottish representatives were admitted to the Parliament of England. That is not what was done. . .

> I have not found in the Union legislation any provision that the Parliament of Great Britain should be 'absolutely sovereign' in the sense that that Parliament should be free to alter the Treaty at will.

In **Gibson v The Lord Advocate** (1975), the issue tested was whether allowing fishermen of Member States of the European Community to fish in Scottish coastal waters infringed Article XVIII of the Act of Union. Article XVIII provides that:

> . . . no alteration be made in laws which concern private right except for the evident utility of the subjects within Scotland.

The claim was dismissed, Lord Keith ruling that the European Community Regulations did not confer rights or obligations on individual citizens and accordingly were matters of public and not private law and, accordingly, that Article XVIII could not be invoked. On the sovereignty question, Lord Keith, however, stated:

> Like Lord President Cooper, I prefer to reserve my opinion what the position would be if the United Kingdom Parliament passed an Act purporting to abolish the Court of Session or the Church of Scotland or to substitute English law for the whole body of Scots law. I am, however, of the opinion that the question whether a particular Act of the United Kingdom Parliament altering a particular aspect of Scots private law is

---

26 Queen Elizabeth I was Queen of England, not of Scotland.

or is not 'for the evident utility' of the subjects within Scotland is not a justiciable issue in this court. The making of decisions upon what must essentially be a political matter is no part of the function of the court, and it is highly undesirable that it should be.

In **Sillars v Smith** (1982), a similar challenge was lodged over the validity of the Criminal Justice (Scotland) Act 1980, on the basis that the United Kingdom Parliament, which had passed the Scotland Act 1978, which created a legislative Assembly for Scotland, had no power to repeal that Act – as had been done – and accordingly, Parliament, it was argued, had no power to pass the Criminal Justice (Scotland) Act. The claim was dismissed, the court adopting the classical view expressed in **Edinburgh and Dalkeith Railway Company v Wauchope** (1842) by Lord Campbell:

> All that a court of justice can look to is the parliamentary roll; they see that an Act has passed both Houses of Parliament, and that it has received the royal assent, and no court of justice can enquire into the manner in which it was introduced into Parliament, what was done previously to its being introduced, or what passed in Parliament during the various stages of its progress through both Houses of Parliament.

Despite the questioning *dicta* of Lords Cooper and Keith on sovereignty, the evidence to date goes clearly against the notion that the Act of Union is legally unalterable. To take but one example, the Protestant Religion and Presbyterian Church Act 1707 provision that 'the true Protestant religion and the worship, discipline and government' of the established church were 'to continue without any alteration to the people of this land in all succeeding generations' was incorporated into the Treaty of Union and declared to be 'a fundamental and essential condition of the . . . Union in all times coming'. The Act also required that teachers in universities and schools had to subscribe to the faith. Yet, in 1711, the Scottish Episcopalians Act and the Church Patronage (Scotland) Act were passed to reflect greater religious toleration, and by the Universities (Scotland) Act 1853 and the Parochial and Burgh Schoolmasters (Scotland) Act 1861, the requirement that teachers must subscribe to the Protestant faith was removed. Further changes in the organisation of the Church were made in the Church of Scotland Act 1921.

The union with Ireland

The Act of Union with Ireland 1800 has given rise to similar arguments, although these arguments are even less convincing than those addressed to the Act of Union with Scotland. The Act of Union was declared to 'last forever'. Article 5 provided for a United Church of England and Ireland that 'shall be and shall remain in full force for ever, and that this be deemed and taken to be an essential and fundamental part of the Union'. Nevertheless, in 1869 the Irish Church was disestablished under the Irish Church Act of that year. In **Ex parte Canon Selwyn** (1872), a clergyman sought an order of mandamus against the Lord President of the Council ordering him to petition the Queen for adjudication of the question of whether the giving of royal assent to the Irish Church Act 1869 was contrary to the coronation oath and the Act of Settlement. The coronation oath contained a commitment to maintain a unified and established Church of England and Ireland. The court dismissed the petition on the basis that the statute was supreme and could not be questioned in a court of law.

The Acts of Union[27] provided for the permanent union between Ireland and Great Britain. However, the Ireland Act 1949 recognised the republican status and independence of southern Ireland, thereby terminating the union. The 1949 Act also provided that Northern Ireland:

---

27 The Act of Union (Ireland) 1800; the Act of Union with Ireland 1800.

... remains part of His Majesty's dominions and of the United Kingdom and it is hereby affirmed that in no event will Northern Ireland or any part thereof cease to be part of His Majesty's dominions and of the United Kingdom without consent of the Parliament of Northern Ireland. [s 1(2)]

That commitment is reiterated in section 1 of the Northern Ireland Act 1998. However, such assurances, whilst morally and politically binding on the government, do not amount – under Diceyan theory – to a legal restriction on Parliament's powers. Parliament remains free, in legal theoretical terms, to legislate contrary to such undertakings, although the political implications of so doing guarantee that Parliament will not do so.

AV Dicey and the Acts of Union

AV Dicey had argued that the Acts of Union had no greater legal status than the Dentists Act 1878, or indeed any other unimportant Act.[28] Moreover, as has been seen, Dicey viewed the Acts of Union as being ordinary Acts of Parliament by which – in the case of the Union with Scotland – the English and Scottish Parliaments 'abolished' themselves, to be reconstituted as the Parliament of Great Britain, and in the case of the Act of Union with Ireland, were reconstituted as the Parliament of the United Kingdom.

Alternative interpretations of the Acts of Union

The power of Parliament to 'abolish itself' and be reconstituted as a 'new parliament' is one of the principal matters to which opponents to Diceyan theory address their arguments. Professor JDB Mitchell (1963), for example, questions Dicey's insistence on the equal legal status of Acts of Parliament, distinguishing between rules which create and represent the foundation of the state, and other derivative rules of law: '... the one set of rules creates or is the legal foundation of the state, the other is built upon that foundation.'

The Acts of Union of Scotland and England creating the unified Parliament of Great Britain represents a 'fresh starting point'. In Mitchell's view, the Acts of Union, being antecedent to the Parliament of Great Britain, imposed valid legal limitations on its powers. Conceding that many legislative changes have been made to the provisions of the Acts of Union, Mitchell nevertheless argues that the provisions, at least in relation to the Church of Scotland and the Court of Session, are essential limitations on Parliament's powers.

Professor Neil MacCormick also challenges Diceyan orthodoxy.[29] In MacCormick's view, the Acts of Union amounted to a rudimentary written constitution: the Anglo-Scottish Treaty of 1706 and the Union with Ireland 1800 represent the 'historically first constitution' of Great Britain and the United Kingdom respectively, and accordingly have a very special status in constitutional law. Harry Calvert (1968) specifically rejects Dicey's view of the effects of the Acts of Union as 'untenable'. Calvert adopts Professor RVF Heuston's arguments (1964a, pp 20–30) regarding the legal status of the Acts of Union and proceeds to argue that royal assent could be denied – in a departure from constitutional convention – to a Bill purporting to sever the union between Northern Ireland and the rest of the United Kingdom against the wishes of the people, the expression of which has been provided for by statute. Such a severance would, in Calvert's view, be unconstitutional. Accordingly, it would be for the Crown to defeat any attempt to act unconstitutionally:

[A]t all events, it cannot readily be conceded that a constitutional monarch has no constitutional power to resist being implicated in unconstitutionality by his ministers. The bounds of the British constitution are very widely drawn. There is very little

---

28 Dicey, 1885, p 145.
29 1978; see also 2001.

that a Prime Minister, supported by his Cabinet and a majority of the House of Commons, cannot do. But if there is nothing that he cannot do, there is no constitution at all. [1968, p 32]

These differing arguments about the status of the Acts of Union, and the future of the Union with Scotland in particular, are set to be re-ignited by the announcement by the First Minister of Scotland that there is to be a referendum on Scottish independence, to be held in 2014. On this issue, see further Chapter 11.

Manner and form and redefinition theories

Parliament, in the exercise of its sovereign power, may specify particular procedures which must be undertaken in order to enact legislation. It has been seen, for example, that the Northern Ireland Constitution (Amendment) Act 1973 provided that the six counties of Northern Ireland shall not cease to be part of the United Kingdom unless the proposed separation is approved by a majority of the electorate in a border poll (referendum). This may be interpreted to mean either that Parliament has specified the procedure – or manner and form – for enacting laws, or that Parliament has 'redefined' itself for the purposes of enacting laws, by including in the definition of Parliament the electorate of Northern Ireland. Any provision relating solely to procedure but not affecting the composition of Parliament may be termed a 'manner and form' provision; whereas when the actual composition of Parliament is altered, the appropriate term is 'redefinition'. The Northern Ireland Constitution (Amendment) Act straddles both theories.

The essential question to be asked is whether such provisions, however labelled, are capable of binding a future Parliament. If that were to be the case – and, as will be seen, there are supporters for that view – two possible conclusions would follow: first, that Parliament has unlimited power – exercisable only at one single point in time, for ever after to limit the sovereignty of future Parliaments; and, secondly, that future Parliaments would be less than sovereign – a contradiction in terms, for it would not then be correct to speak of Parliament having unlimited sovereignty.

A seminal case illustrating manner and form theory is that of **Attorney General for New South Wales v Trethowan** (1932). In 1929, the government of New South Wales, Australia, sought to prevent a subsequent government from abolishing the Legislative Council (the upper chamber). An Act of Parliament was passed, amending the Constitution Act 1902, providing that any Bill purporting to abolish the upper House must have the approval of both legislative chambers and of two-thirds of the members of each chamber. Further, there had to be popular electoral support for the abolition, to be determined in a referendum. In addition, to prevent a subsequent Parliament ignoring the provisions of the 1929 Act, it was provided that any Bill attempting to repeal the 1929 Act must follow the same procedure: a device known as 'double entrenchment'. In 1930, following an election, the incoming government decided to abolish the upper chamber and to do so by ignoring the provisions of the 1929 Act. Members of the Legislative Council sought an injunction restraining the grant of royal assent to the Bill, and a declaration that such a grant of assent would be unlawful, being *ultra vires* the lower House. The High Court of Australia ruled that the provisions of the 1929 Act could not be avoided, and that royal assent could not be given to the Bill. The matter was referred to the Privy Council, which affirmed the judgment of the High Court of Australia.

The constitutional reason underlying the court's rejection of the government's claim that the 1932 Bill could lawfully receive royal assent was that the Parliament in New South Wales was a legislative body having subordinate and not supreme power. Such powers as the legislature enjoyed were derived from the sovereign United Kingdom Parliament under the Constitution Acts 1902–29 and the Colonial Laws Validity Act 1865. The Colonial Laws Validity Act 1865 represented a landmark in the clarification of powers between the sovereign United Kingdom Parliament and subordinate colonial legislatures. The Act gave statutory affirmation to the non-legal conventional rule that laws enacted in the colony which were contradictory to statute or the common law of the United Kingdom would not be held to be invalid by the courts of the United Kingdom. The Act further clarified the extent to which the colonial legislature had power to amend its own composition and procedure. Section 5 is the all-important provision for current purposes. It provides that:

> . . . every representative legislature shall . . . have and be deemed at all times to have had, full power to make laws respecting the constitution, power, and procedure of such legislature; provided that such laws shall have been passed in such manner and form as may from time to time be required by any Act of Parliament, letters patent, Order in Council, or colonial law, for the time being in force in the said colony.

It is this section which dictated the decision in **Attorney General for New South Wales v Trethowan** (1932). The government of New South Wales was not free to introduce the 1932 Bill and attempt to enact it other than in conformity with the requirements of section 5. Section 5 required that the legislature complied with the 'manner and form' provisions in force. The specific 'manner and form' provisions were those laid down in the 1929 Constitution Act, and these requirements could not merely be ignored by the subordinate legislature.[30] In the High Court of Australia in the **Trethowan** case, Rich J denied the proposition that the New South Wales Parliament had unlimited sovereign power.

A similar constitutional arrangement can be seen demonstrated by the South African case of **Harris v The Minister of the Interior** (1952) and that of **Bribery Commissioner v Ranasinghe** (1965) from Sri Lanka (Ceylon, as it then was). These cases demonstrate one fundamental principle: that legislative bodies do not necessarily enjoy full sovereign power, and that some form of 'higher law' may control their powers. In each of these cases, the powers of the legislatures of New South Wales, South Africa and Ceylon (as it then was) had been established under an Act of the sovereign United Kingdom Parliament. That being so, the legislative bodies had to comply with the constitutional laws in force, and failure to do so would give the courts the jurisdiction to declare a legislative act void.

No one may question the validity of an Act of Parliament

> True it is, that what the Parliament doth, no authority on earth can undo.[31]

As has been seen, an Act will be accepted as valid by the courts provided that it has passed through the requisite legislative stages and received royal assent.[32] Regardless of the subject matter of the Act, it will be upheld by the judges.[33] In the time before the 1688 settlement, it was not uncommon for judges to proclaim that an Act of Parliament could be held to be invalid because it conflicted with some higher form of divine law.

In **Dr Bonham's Case** (1610), there is the often-cited *obiter dictum* of Coke CJ to the effect that:

> When an Act of Parliament is against common right and reason, or repugnant, or impossible to be performed, the common law will control it, and adjudge such act to be void.

---

30 The Australia Act 1986 (Commonwealth and UK), s 3(1), provides that the Colonial Laws Validity Act 1865 shall not apply 'to any law made after the commencement of this Act by the Parliament of a State'.
31 Blackstone's *Commentaries on the Laws of England* (1765–69), Vol I.
32 See **The Prince's Case** (1606).
33 But see further below and Chapter 8, on the complexity arising by virtue of membership of the European Union.

Such views, while appealing to the senses, were of doubtful validity when expressed and have no authority today. The opinion of Lord Reid expressed in **Pickin v British Railways Board** (1974) represents the correct contemporary judicial view on the authority of statute:

> In earlier times many learned lawyers seem to have believed that an Act of Parliament could be disregarded in so far as it was contrary to the law of God or the law of nature or natural justice, but since the supremacy of Parliament was finally demonstrated by the revolution of 1688 any such idea has become obsolete.[34]

Non-legal constraints on Parliament's powers

Political acceptability to the electorate represents the strongest external basis of restraint. All governments are accountable to the electorate, albeit in terms of a direct vote only periodically. But elections do not of themselves always provide the means of sanctioning governments, nor do they guarantee that government invariably acts in accordance with the electorate's wishes. Still less can the electorate be regarded as exercising any power to enact law. Whilst the electorate may be correctly regarded as politically sovereign, and can, at the end of the day, oust a government which violates its trust, on the exercise of the franchise the electorate conditionally transfers sovereign legislative power to Parliament. As Dicey puts it:

> The electors can in the long run always enforce their will. But the courts will take no notice of the will of the electors. The judges know nothing about any will of the people except in so far as that will is expressed by an Act of Parliament, and would never suffer the validity of a statute to be questioned on the ground of having been passed or being kept alive in opposition to the wishes of the electors. [1885, pp 73–74]

Whereas, therefore, the power of the electorate is great at the time of a general election, it is a more limited power during a government's term of office — most particularly where the government has a strong majority in Parliament. It is the task of Parliament as a whole, both Commons and Lords, to scrutinise government policy and legislative proposals, and a range of procedural devices exists which facilitate such inquiry. It is through Parliament that the will or wishes of the electorate for the most part find expression.[35] No government can afford to ignore Parliament and, ultimately, a government can be brought down if its policies are such that it loses the confidence of the House as a whole. If Parliament is truly the 'sounding board of the nation', Parliament must reflect the political morality within society.[36]

A further political restraint imposed on governments relates to international relations. No state today exists in isolation from its neighbours. The United Kingdom, as with most states, is bound by numerous treaties under international law which impose restrictions on the freedom of government action. Across virtually every aspect of government, such restraints are visible: environmental protection, protection of human rights, the protection of children from abduction, the regulation of currency exchanges, agreements on trade and tariffs and so on. In addition to such treaties, the United Kingdom is bound in practical terms by membership of the European Union and the United Nations. In theoretical terms, therefore, Parliament may remain free to enact laws violating any or all of the United Kingdom's international obligations; in practice, it would not and could not.

---

34 The case of **Jackson v Attorney General** (2005) represents a recent challenge to the validity of a statute – the Hunting Act 2004. The case is discussed in detail in Chapter 16.
35 See JS Mill, 1865, Chapter V.
36 See Allan, 1985b; and Lee, 1985.

Academic Arguments Against the Traditional Doctrine of Sovereignty

We have seen above that there are a number of sophisticated academic arguments concerning the traditional doctrine of sovereignty. In this brief section, the differing approaches are brought together for further consideration.

In **Bribery Commissioner v Ranasinghe** (1965), Lord Pearce had asserted that:

> The proposition which is not acceptable is that a legislature, once established, has some inherent power derived from the mere fact of establishment to make a valid law by the resolution of a bare majority which its own constituent instrument has said shall not be a valid law unless made by a different type of majority or by a different legislative process.

Geoffrey Marshall seizes upon this dictum and argues that Lord Pearce:

> . . . seemed to imply equally that both non-sovereign and sovereign legislatures may be made subject to procedural rules entrenching parts of the law from simple majority repeal.

Sir Ivor Jennings has also questioned the orthodox Diceyan view. In *The Law and the Constitution*, Jennings distinguishes two situations:

> If a prince has supreme power, and continues to have supreme power, he can do anything, even to the extent of undoing the things which he has previously done. If he grants a constitution, binding himself not to make laws except with the consent of an elected legislature, he has power immediately afterwards to abolish the legislature without its consent and to continue legislating by his personal decree.

> But if the prince has not supreme power, but the rule is that the courts accept as law that which is in the proper legal form, the result is different. For when the prince enacts that henceforth no rule shall be law unless it is enacted by him with the consent of the legislature, the law has been altered, and the courts will not admit as law any rule which is not made in that form. Consequently a rule subsequently made by the prince alone abolishing the legislature is not law, for the legislature has not consented to it, and the rule has not been enacted according to the manner and form required by the law for the time being.

> The difference is this. In the one case, there is sovereignty. In the other, the courts have no concern with sovereignty, but only with the established law. 'Legal sovereignty' is merely a name indicating that the legislature has for the time being power to make laws of any kind in the manner required by law. That is, a rule expressed to be made by the Queen, 'with the advice and consent of the Lords spiritual and temporal, and Commons in this present Parliament assembled, and by the authority of the same', will be recognised by the courts, including a rule which alters this law itself. If this is so, the 'legal sovereign' may impose legal limitations upon itself, because its power to change the law includes the power to change the law affecting itself. [p 152]

Sir Ivor Jennings then illustrates his thesis by reference to **Attorney General for New South Wales v Trethowan** (1932), **Ndlwana v Hofmeyer** (1937) and **Harris v The Minister of the Interior** (1952).

Jennings concedes that the decisions do not necessarily 'determine the law as it applies in the United Kingdom', and leaps from that proposition to one which claims that Dicey 'failed to prove that that law made the King in Parliament a sovereign law making body' (1959b, p 156). Such a view is unconvincing. The constitutional justification for the decisions examined lay precisely in the fact that the legislatures of both New South Wales and South Africa had legislative powers conferred upon them by a fully sovereign superior sovereign body – the United Kingdom Parliament. Only once such complete sovereignty was conferred would the legislative fetters be removed. No such controlling device pertains to the Parliament of the United Kingdom itself.

Arguing from the proposition that Parliament may redefine itself – as in the Parliament Act 1911[37] – and may alter its own composition – as in the Life Peerages Act 1958, Professor JDB Mitchell turns to 'the purported self-limitations of Parliament' (1968, p 78). On section 4 of the Statute of Westminster, Mitchell argues that there are two possible interpretations when looked at from the point of view of the United Kingdom judges. The first is that section 4 amounts to a rule of construction directed to the courts, which does not raise the problem of limitation on Parliament. If, however, section 4 is understood to mean that Parliament has forfeited its legislative capacity – by conferring that capacity on the recipient legislature – then there 'is quite clearly a purported limitation of the United Kingdom Parliament' (p 79). Parliament has redefined itself in a manner which excludes its power to legislate for the Dominion.

Mitchell cites in support of the argument the *dictum* of Lord Radcliffe in **Ibralebbe v The Queen** (1964) in which Lord Radcliffe argues that while the United Kingdom Parliament has the legal power to legislate for Ceylon (as it then was), to use such power would be 'wholly inconsistent' with the powers of legislation conferred on the legislature of Ceylon.

Further authorities could be offered in support of this view. As seen above, in **British Coal Corporation v The King** (1935), Lord Sankey LC said, in relation to section 4, that:

> . . . indeed, the Imperial Parliament could, as a matter of abstract law, repeal or disregard section 4 of the statute. But that is theory and has no relation to realities.
> [p 20]

Further, in **Ndlwana v Hofmeyer** (1937), Lord Denning asserted that 'freedom once given cannot be revoked'. How should such claims be evaluated? First, as Dicey made clear, the United Kingdom Parliament – in the exercise of its sovereign power – clearly has the power to abolish itself, or to surrender its sovereignty in favour of another legislature, as in grants of independence. In political terms, it is, of course, unthinkable that Parliament would attempt to revoke such independence. The more troublesome question is whether Parliament retains the capacity to revoke such grants of freedom in legal terms. On this, Dicey was very clear:

> 'Limited sovereignty', in short, is, in the case of a Parliamentary as of every other sovereign, a contradiction in terms. [1885, p 68]

Professor RVF Heuston has put forward a 'new view' of sovereignty. This view is summarised as follows:

(a) sovereignty is a legal concept: the rules which identify the sovereign and prescribe its composition and functions are logically prior to it;

---

37 The Parliament Act 1911 reduced the powers of the House of Lords with respect to legislation. See Chapter 16.

(b) there is a distinction between rules which govern, on the one hand, (i) the composition and (ii) the procedure, and, on the other hand, (iii) the area of power, of a sovereign legislature;

(c) the courts have jurisdiction to question the validity of an alleged Act of Parliament on grounds b(i) and b(ii), but not on ground b(iii); and

(d) this jurisdiction is exercisable either before or after the royal assent has been signified – in the former case by way of injunction, in the latter by way of declaratory judgment.[38]

To what extent is it correct to state that the judiciary may 'question the validity of an alleged Act of Parliament' on the grounds of the composition and the procedure adopted within Parliament? Clearly, as demonstrated by **Attorney General for New South Wales v Trethowan** (1932) and other comparable cases, under certain circumstances, it is within the jurisdiction of the courts to question whether or not an Act is valid. Those circumstances usually arise within jurisdictions having subordinate rather than supreme legislatures.

In this regard, it may be said that the judges are protecting the sovereignty of the United Kingdom Parliament by keeping subordinate legislatures within the powers conferred. In the United Kingdom, however, Parliament is distinguishable by the absence of any such controlling powers. The orthodox position is that expressed in **British Railways Board v Pickin** (1974), where the House of Lords, affirming its earlier decision,[39] endorsed the 'enrolled Bill rule'. Thus, once the Bill has proceeded through Parliament, either under the normal legislative process or under the Parliament Acts 1911 and 1949, and received royal assent, the Bill becomes a validly enacted Act of Parliament and will not be impugned by the courts. The courts have jurisdiction to determine what is an Act of Parliament. As has been seen earlier, the courts have held, by way of illustration, that mere resolutions of the House of Commons are incapable of having legal effect in the same manner as an Act: **Stockdale v Hansard** (1839) and **Bowles v Bank of England** (1913) are clear authorities for that view.

The central distinguishing feature between the jurisdictions concerned in the 'manner and form' cases and the United Kingdom lies in the existence of a higher legislative authority. In each case, it was the United Kingdom Parliament which defined and limited the powers of a subordinate legislative body. Only once a Parliament enjoys full sovereignty can it be free of such constraints. The United Kingdom Parliament, by contrast, is 'uncontrolled': there exists no higher source of legal authority than Parliament itself. For this reason, to draw an analogy between the legislatures of New South Wales or South Africa and the United Kingdom misses the vital dimension of unlimited power which is enjoyed by the United Kingdom Parliament.

The last words on the manner and form arguments shall be left to Professors Wade (1989) and Munro (1999). Professor Wade summarises his views on manner and form theorists as follows:

> But, in the end, what is the substance of their argument? It is simply their prediction, made with varying degrees of dogmatism, that the judges will, or should, enforce restrictions about manner and form and abandon their clear and settled rule that the traditional manner and form is what counts. But if it is vain for Parliament to command the judges to transfer their allegiance to some new system of legislation if the judges are resolved to remain loyal to the old one, it is still more vain for professors to assert that they should. The judicial loyalty is the foundation of the legal system and, at the same time, a political fact.

---

38 Heuston, 1964a, Chapter I. See also Munro, 1999, Chapter 4. Professor Heuston is supported in his approach by Jennings, 1959b, Chapter 4, Appendix III; Cowen, 1951; Marshall, 1957, Chapters 2–4.

39 **Edinburgh and Dalkeith Railway Co v Wauchope** (1842).

Professor Munro finds the arguments as to manner and form equally unconvincing, stating that 'the cases cited by the "manner and form" school do not, in the end, seem very helpful'.

Parliamentary Sovereignty and the European Union

In Chapters 7 and 8, the aims, organisation and law-making power of the institutions of the European Union are considered, and the relationship between the law of the United Kingdom and European law will become clearer after those chapters have been studied. Nonetheless, it is necessary to consider here, in outline, the impact of membership of the European Union (EU) on the doctrine of parliamentary supremacy.

See Chapters 7 and 8.

The United Kingdom became a member of the European Communities (now EU)[40] in 1973. The original Communities had their own constitutional structure as defined in the Treaties. The European Court of Justice has, since the 1960s, asserted the supremacy of EU law over the laws of any Member State.[41] As will be seen later, the Court of Justice has adopted the view that, by becoming signatories to the Treaties, Member States have limited their own legislative competence in EU matters, conferring the supreme power to legislate on these matters on the law-making institutions of the Union.[42]

The laws of the Union – the Treaties, laws enacted by the Council of Ministers and the European Parliament together with the judicial decisions of the European Court – are binding on all Member States. In the United Kingdom, the acceptance of EU law is under the European Communities Act 1972 – an Act of the United Kingdom Parliament. Accordingly, all EU law derives its force and authority under this Act, which, as with any Act, has no special legal status within the constitution. However, membership of the EU raises some unique questions for the sovereignty of Parliament.

The principal issue for consideration is the attitude of the judges – both domestic and European – towards EU law. It is clear that, from the perspective of the European Court, EU law prevails over domestic law, and that domestic legislatures have no power to enact binding legislation contrary to the requirements of EU law. From the domestic perspective, however, the issue is not so clear-cut. The issues which require explanation are:

(a) the extent to which the judges are prepared to accept and apply EU law;

(b) the manner in which, and extent to which, inadvertent or deliberate parliamentary Acts are reconciled with the requirements of EU law; and

(c) whether membership of the EU entails an irrevocable relinquishment of parliamentary supremacy.

The application of European Union (formerly Community) Law

Section 2 of the European Communities Act 1972 provides that Community (now EU) law shall have direct applicability in the United Kingdom:

> 1. All such rights, powers, liabilities, obligations and restrictions from time to time created or arising by or under the Treaties, and all such remedies and procedures

---

40 European Economic Community, European Coal and Steel Community, European Community for Atomic Energy.

41 See the early cases of **Costa v ENEL** (1964); **Van Gend en Loos** (1963); **Simmenthal** (1977); **Internationale Handelsgesellschaft** (1972). Note that under the Lisbon Treaty 2007 the Court is renamed the Court of Justice of the European Union and from 2009 the term Community law becomes European Union law.

42 Under the proposed Reform Treaty (Treaty of Lisbon) the Union shall 'replace and succeed the Community' – see further Chapter 7.

from time to time provided for by or under the Treaties, as in accordance with the Treaties are without further enactment to be given legal effect or used in the United Kingdom shall be recognised and available in law, and be enforced, allowed and followed accordingly; and the expression 'enforceable Community right' and similar expressions shall be read as referring to one to which this sub-section applies.

Section 2(4) provides for the primacy of Community (now EU) law, without expressly stating that the law of the European Union is supreme:

The provision that may be made under sub-section (2) above[43] includes, subject to Schedule 2 of this Act, any such provision (of any such extent) as might be made by Act of Parliament, and any enactment passed or to be passed, other than one contained in this part of this Act, shall be construed and have effect subject to the foregoing provisions of this section.

Accordingly, all the rights, powers, liabilities, obligations and restrictions provided for under section 2(1) are to be given effect by the courts, and section 2(4) operates as a rule of construction to the courts to interpret law in accordance with the requirements of EU law. The manner in which the courts have achieved the objectives expressed in the European Communities Act 1972 are considered in Chapters 7 and 8, as is the view of the European Court of Justice on the supremacy of EU law. However, it would be misleading to leave this chapter on the traditional Diceyan theory of sovereignty without giving some introductory overview of the challenge which EU law has posed. The European Court of Justice (the ECJ) adopts as its guiding principle the supremacy of the law of the European Union. In the ECJ's view, a new legal order has been founded, a sovereign legal order within its sphere of competence. The sovereignty of EU law must, according to the ECJ, be respected by Member States, because through accession to the European Union, Member States have 'surrendered' their sovereign power in relation to those matters now regulated by the Union.

The ECJ has adopted several means by which to expand the applicability of EU law and to assert its supremacy. First, the EU treaties impose a duty on all Member States to comply with EU law and not to impede the application of EU law. Second, the treaties provide that a regulation[44] made under the Treaty (in part) 'shall be binding in its entirety and directly applicable in all Member States'. This principle of 'direct effect' has been adapted and developed by the ECJ to ensure the harmonious application of EU law throughout the legal systems of all Member States. The doctrine of 'indirect effect' is also a concept developed and expanded by the ECJ, and, as will be seen, has far-reaching implications for the courts and legislatures of each Member State. Where provisions of EU law have direct or indirect effect, the individual citizen of that state has a right of redress against the Member State, or against bodies which the ECJ deems to be 'emanations of the state', and, under certain circumstances, the right to compensation from the state. Moreover, while the ECJ does not rule on the validity of domestic legislation, it does rule on the requirements of EU law as interpreted by the Court, and, once that interpretation is received by the domestic courts, that interpretation must be given effect – notwithstanding incompatible domestic law.

While it would be premature to reach firm judgement on the fate of conventional Diceyan theory before studying the structure, organisation and objectives of the European Union,

---

43 Which provides for implementation of Community obligations by secondary legislation.
44 A form of secondary legislation.

some tentative conclusions may be suggested. Without rehearsing the arguments set out above, there are two differing approaches which may be taken to this conundrum. First, it may be argued that unreconstructed Diceyan theory remains unimpaired, despite all appearances and arguments to the contrary, on the basis that the United Kingdom voluntarily acceded to the European Union, the force of EU law within domestic law deriving from the 1972 European Communities Act. That Act, as seen, is consistent with constitutional law and convention – not entrenched (nor could it be) – and remains, in legal theory, repealable. From this perspective, parliamentary sovereignty remains the fundamental rule of the common law, and the key to the source of sovereignty lies with the judges. While the judges continue to cling to the rationale that EU law is given effect – even to the point of setting aside legislation[45] – because of the rule of construction provided under section 2 of the European Communities Act 1972, judicial loyalty remains unaffected. The clearest evidence for this view is expressed by Lord Bridge in **R v Secretary of State for Transport ex parte Factortame (No 2)** (1991), when he states that:

> By virtue of section 2(4) of the Act of 1972, Part II of the [Merchant Shipping Act 1998] is to be construed and take effect subject to enforceable Community rights – this has precisely the same effect as if a section were incorporated in Part II of the Act 1988 . . .

Moreover, it will be seen from the cases of **Macarthys v Smith** (1979) and **Garland v British Rail Engineering Ltd** (1983) that both the Court of Appeal and House of Lords, respectively, endorsed the view that, while effect must, in accordance with section 2(4) of the European Communities Act 1972, be given to Community (now EU) law, if Parliament chose expressly to legislate contrary to Community law, that intention would be given effect by the judges. No more so would this be clearer than if Parliament, implausible though this hypothesis may seem, chose to repeal the 1972 Act.

Alternatively, it could possibly be argued, as HWR Wade has argued,[46] that, for the first time in constitutional history, Parliament succeeded in 'entrenching' a provision (section 2(4) of the 1972 Act), so as to bind future Parliaments. This position, Wade submits, is more than evolutionary: it represents more than a rule of construction to be applied by the courts, and is rather an illustration of the Parliament of 1972 imposing 'a restriction upon the Parliament of 1988' (p 570). If this argument had substance, there would indeed have been a 'revolution' in the constitution. However, the argument does not convince in light of the *dicta* of the judges, exemplified by that of Lord Bridge cited above, which confirms the conventional allegiance of the judiciary to the United Kingdom Parliament. Moreover, successive cases raising questions on EU law have come before the Court of Appeal and House of Lords in which the courts have found the requisite interpretative mechanism to accommodate the requirements of EU law as interpreted by the Court of Justice. Judicial interpretative techniques are the essence of the common law, and the essence of the common law is its capacity to evolve in accordance with the socio-political and legal domain within which it resides. In this light, the insistence on the part of the domestic courts that section 2(4) of the European Communities Act 1972 is a rule of construction to be applied to future legislation is hardly 'revolutionary' but rather more a recognition of the requirements of the European legal order and the overriding force of EU law for which the 1972 Act provided. However, as discussed below, there is evidence that some judges are prepared to recognise that certain statutes – including the 1972 Act – have a 'special' constitutional status.

---

45 This issue being central to the **Factortame** cases, discussed in Chapter 8.
46 See Wade, 1996, but see the counter-arguments put forward by Allan, 1997, responding to Wade's analysis.

The preoccupation with parliamentary sovereignty is understandable given that sovereignty has conventionally, in the absence of a written constitution, represented the 'cornerstone' or foundation of the British constitution. Membership of the European Union, and the insistence of the European Court of Justice on the supremacy of EU law, inevitably challenges traditional understandings of that concept, and raises hitherto unforeseen questions. While traditional Diceyan theory can accommodate membership of the Union, it can do so only by clearly demarcating, as did its author, the realms of the legal and political. Legal theory resides against the backcloth of the political. Political sovereignty, while the United Kingdom remains a member of the Union, may (arguably) lie in the Institutions and law-making processes of the Union, in which every Member State participates, and which is supported by the political will of the citizens of the Member States. That political sovereignty, while membership continues, has a profound impact on the extent to which the domestic legislature may legislate over areas within the ambit of the treaties establishing the Union. Thus, as Dicey himself argued, back in the nineteenth century under fundamentally different socio-economic and political conditions, the extra-legal may *de facto* limit the exercise of sovereign power. This *de facto* limitation on *legal sovereignty* remains ultimately conditional on the political commitment of the United Kingdom government and people to continued membership of that unique legal order which it voluntarily joined in 1972.

The Coalition government elected in May 2010 has undertaken not to transfer any further powers from the United Kingdom to the European Union in the Parliament running until May 2015, without holding a referendum seeking the approval of the people. This commitment is reflected in the European Union Act 2011 (on which see further Chapter 8). On the question of sovereignty, section 18 of the 2011 Act makes an unequivocal statement of constitutional principle, as follows:

> Directly applicable or directly effective EU law (that is, the rights, powers, liabilities, obligations, restrictions, remedies and procedures referred to in section 2(1) of the European Communities Act 1972) falls to be recognised and available in law in the United Kingdom **only by virtue of that Act** or where it is required to be recognised and available in law by virtue of any other Act.

Constitutional Reform and Parliamentary Sovereignty

See Chapter 11.

As noted above, the devolution of power to regional assemblies (in the case of Wales and Northern Ireland) and the Scottish Parliament and the Human Rights Act 1998, which 'incorporates' the European Convention on Human Rights into domestic law, both raise the issue of sovereignty. While full discussion of these matters is found in Chapters 11 and 18 respectively, it is useful here to consider the sovereignty issue.

Devolution

The Scotland Act, Government of Wales Act and Northern Ireland Act 1998 each establish a system of self-government, in differing degrees, for the nations of the United Kingdom other than England. In London, a new layer of government was introduced with the Greater London Authority and the office of Mayor of London. Since the powers devolved are the will of Parliament, the continued existence of such power remains dependent upon Parliament's will. This ultimate power to confer and rescind powers granted to subordinate bodies is nothing new: at a lower governmental level, there is the granting of limited autonomy, defined by Act of Parliament and controlled by the courts, whereby local authorities have long enjoyed a measure of self-governance. This statement, however, and the legal provisions which give it expression, disguise a fundamentally important factor in the devolution debate: the dependence of legal-theoretical sovereignty upon the political sovereignty of the people of the nations.

It is the devolution of legislative power to the Scottish Parliament which illustrates the complexity of the sovereignty issue most starkly. By contrast with Northern Ireland and Wales, Scotland has retained a strong sense of national identity since the Union with England in 1707, and has a memory of national independence and a distinctive identity expressed through its own legal system.

The Labour government of 1997–2010, while enthusiastic about devolution to the regions, was also intent on preserving the United Kingdom and the sovereignty of the United Kingdom Parliament. This was expressed strongly in the government's 1997 White Paper, *Scotland's Parliament*:[47] '. . . the United Kingdom Parliament is and will remain sovereign in all matters.' Section 28(7) of the Scotland Act gives clear expression to this intention: '. . . this section does not affect the power of the Parliament of the United Kingdom to make laws for Scotland.'

However, while Westminster retains the right to legislate over 'reserved matters', which are adjudged to be of United Kingdom-wide concern rather than national concern, the legislative powers devolved are considerable. The theoretical stance that Westminster remains free to legislate for Scotland over such matters must be in doubt. While Northern Ireland enjoyed devolved power, the convention developed that Westminster would not legislate over areas devolved and, moreover, that domestic affairs of Northern Ireland would not even be debated at Westminster. Were the United Kingdom Parliament to attempt to legislate over Scottish domestic affairs which have been devolved to Edinburgh, against Scottish wishes, real conflict would arise – and no assertions of the sterile sovereignty of Westminster would quell political dissent from north of the border.

This adds up to considerable legislative and political autonomy for Scotland and its people. What, then, is left of 'the sovereignty of the United Kingdom Parliament' in conventional Diceyan terms? Theoretically, two aspects of sovereignty remain. The first is the ability – notwithstanding the political unreality – to legislate for Scotland contrary to Scottish wishes. The second is the power to abolish the Scottish Parliament and to reclaim the powers devolved. Given that the government chose first to seek the endorsement of the people for devolution before devolving power, the likelihood of either theoretical power being exercised, *without the support and consent of the people of Scotland*, is negligible. It will be recalled that, in **MacCormick v Lord Advocate** (1953), Lord Cooper questioned the notion that the Treaty of Union resulted in the adoption of the 'distinctively English principle [of sovereignty] which has no counterpart in Scottish constitutional law'. Under Scottish constitutional law, it has always been the case that it is the people, and not a Parliament, which is sovereign: the Scottish people exercised their sovereignty in choosing to have their own Parliament. Whether the future entails an independent Scotland outside the United Kingdom, or Scotland within some form of quasi-federal relationship with the rest of the United Kingdom, must be a matter for the political judgment of the Scottish people. This issue may finally be resolved if, as discussed above, the referendum on Scottish independence scheduled for 2014 produces a 'yes' vote for independence.

See Chapters 8 and 12.

The use of referendums[48]

The use of referendums raises the question of whether or not Parliament redefines itself to include the people – in a direct expression of their views – for the purpose of legislating. The

---

47 Cm 3648, para 42.
48 See Butler and Ranney, 1994; Marshall, 1997; Munro, 1997.

referendum has been used in relation to constitutional matters in Northern Ireland in 1973 and 1998; in relation to devolution to Scotland and Wales in 1977 and 1997 and in Wales in 2011; in London in 1998 in relation to the re-establishment of a London-wide elected authority; and in the United Kingdom as a whole in 1975 in relation to the United Kingdom's continued membership of the European Communities. Under the UK constitution, referendums are regarded as morally binding on government, but do not affect Parliament's sovereignty.

The European Union Act 2011 introduces a complex system of 'control mechanisms' to be employed when further transfers of power are to be made from the United Kingdom to the European Union (EU). One of these is a UK-wide referendum. The system is designed to restrict the government's power to transfer further powers to the EU, and to reinforce the doctrine of parliamentary sovereignty in the EU context.

The Human Rights Act 1998

See Chapter 18.

As with the devolution of power to the nations, the manner in which the government chose to 'incorporate' the rights protected under the European Convention on Human Rights into domestic law is based on the premise of ensuring that Parliament retains its sovereignty over law making. Whereas under most constitutions which include fundamental guarantees protecting human rights, those rights are protected from encroachment by the legislature, and the legislature is thereby limited in what it may enact – and is subject to the rulings of a constitutional court – the Human Rights Act 1998 utilises a peculiarly British device which preserves Parliament's theoretical sovereignty. The Act provides that judges in the higher courts may issue 'declarations of incompatibility' between statute and the Convention rights incorporated under the Act. Where such a declaration is made, the matter is then referred to the executive, which may choose whether and how to amend the law to bring it into line with Convention rights. Further, where proposals for legislation are introduced into Parliament, the relevant minister must declare whether the Bill in question accords with Convention rights. If it does not, an explanation as to the necessity for the legislation must be given. While both of these measures undoubtedly improve the protection of rights and generate a more rights-conscious society, they fall far short of making individual rights and freedoms immune from legislative change.

However, the traditional theory of sovereignty, as applied to the Human Rights Act 1998, disguises the importance of the constitutional change which the Act represents. All aspects of policy and practices of public and quasi-public bodies now fall for scrutiny in accordance with Convention requirements. The Human Rights Act has quickly become established at the heart of the legal system, providing a yardstick against which all actions of government and other public bodies may be judged.

While the government adopted a constitutional mechanism which preserves Parliament's sovereignty, and maintains the conventional (and subordinate) role of the judiciary, the working of the Act is more subtle than the restatement of sovereignty implies. The judges are under a duty to interpret legislation in a manner which gives effect to Convention requirements, save where such an interpretation is impossible. Here, there is a significant shift in the process of judicial reasoning which traditionally focuses on interpreting the 'latest will of parliament' as expressed in legislation. The requirement that ministers must state that legislative proposals are in compliance with Convention requirements, coupled with the directive to judges to interpret in line with Convention rights, gives rights a special constitutional and moral status. That the ultimate decision to amend the law in line with a declaration of incompatibility rests with the executive and Parliament does not suggest a lessening in the importance of rights so much as an ingenious device by which to keep constitutional fundamentals – sovereignty and separation of powers – intact, rather than turning the constitution on its head by reversing the balance of power between judges and Parliament. Nevertheless, the Act does give to judges an unprecedented scope for statutory interpretation and development of the common law in line with Convention rights.

The emergence of the 'constitutional statute'

It has been seen above that – however significant the subject matter – no Act of Parliament has any formal special status. The effect of this is that no Act may be entrenched: there are no special mechanisms necessary for amendment or repeal of any Act; and that all Acts are subject to implied repeal. However, the courts have long recognised that the European Communities Act 1972, at least, has a special status and that the principle of implied repeal does not apply to the Act.[49]

The constitutional reform programme undertaken since 1997, and most particularly the Human Rights Act 1998, has revived the question whether implied repeal applies to all statutes, or whether some – because of their constitutional importance – may only be expressly repealed. Two cases illustrate this view: **R v Secretary of State for the Home Department ex parte Simms** (2000) and **Thoburn v Sunderland City Council** (2002).

The case of **ex parte Simms** concerned a prisoner's right (under Article 10 of the European Convention) to communicate with journalists with a view to challenging his conviction for a crime. On parliamentary supremacy and the status of the Human Rights Act, Lord Hoffmann was to state that:

> Parliamentary sovereignty means that Parliament can, if it chooses, legislate contrary to fundamental principles of human rights. The Human Rights Act 1998 will not detract from this power. The constraints upon its exercise by Parliament are ultimately political, not legal. But the principle of legality means that Parliament must squarely confront what it is doing and accept the political cost. Fundamental rights cannot be overridden by general or ambiguous words . . . In the absence of express language or necessary implication to the contrary, the courts therefore presume that even the most general words were intended to be subject to the basic rights of the individual. In this way the courts of the UK, through acknowledging the sovereignty of Parliament, apply principles of constitutionality little different from those which exist in countries where the power of the legislature is expressly limited by a constitutional document.

The case of **Thoburn v Sunderland City Council** (2002) concerned the Weights and Measures Act 1985, which authorised both metric and imperial measures for the purposes of trade, and subsequent regulations made under section 2(2) of the European Communities Act 1972, which prohibited dual use and gave priority to the metric system. It was argued that the regulations were inconsistent with the 1985 Act and that this later Act must be taken as having impliedly amended section 2(2) of the European Communities Act 1972. The court held that there was no inconsistency between the 1985 Act and the 1972 Act, so there was no need to discuss implied repeal. Laws LJ, however, chose to consider the issue:

> We should recognise a hierarchy of Acts of Parliament: as it were 'ordinary' statutes and 'constitutional' statutes. The two categories must be distinguished on a principled

---

49 See *Garland v British Rail Engineering Ltd* (1983); Lord Denning in *Macarthys Ltd v Smith* (1981).

basis. In my opinion a constitutional statute is one which (a) conditions the legal relationship between citizen and state in some general, overarching manner, or (b) enlarges or diminishes the scope of which we would now regard as fundamental constitutional rights. (a) and (b) are of necessity closely related: it is difficult to think of an instance of (a) that is not also an instance of (b). The special status of constitutional statutes follows the special status of constitutional rights. Examples are the Magna Carta, the Bill of Rights 1689, the Act of Union, the Reform Acts which distributed and enlarged the franchise, the Human Rights Act 1998, the Scotland Act 1998 and the Government of Wales Act 1998. The European Communities Act clearly belongs to this family . . .

Ordinary statutes may be impliedly repealed. Constitutional statutes may not. For the repeal of a constitutional Act or the abrogation of a fundamental right to be effected by statutes, the court would apply this test: is it shown that the legislature's actual – not imputed, constructive or presumed – intention was to effect the repeal or abrogation? I think that this could only be met by express words in the later statute, or by words so specific that the inference of an actual determination to effect the result contended for was irresistible. The ordinary rule of implied repeal does not satisfy this test. Accordingly, it has no application to constitutional statutes.[50]

Summary

In any state there must be an ultimate source of authority. Under a written constitution this will be the Constitution itself, as interpreted by the Supreme or Constitutional Court. Under an unwritten constitution such as the United Kingdom, this ultimate source of legal authority is parliamentary sovereignty, or legislative supremacy, which rests on the political sovereignty of the people.

The traditional doctrine, expounded by AV Dicey, states that Parliament may legislate on any subject-matter, that no Parliament may be bound by a previous Parliament or bind a further Parliament and that no one, including a court of law, may challenge the validity of an Act of Parliament. Each of these principles is subject to qualification by non-legal – economic or political – factors. The most significant contemporary challenge to Parliament's legal authority is membership of the European Union, which requires that domestic law complies with the requirements of European Union law. However, while this restricts what Parliament may in fact do, membership of the EU is voluntary and any restrictions have been accepted by Parliament under the European Communities Act 1972.

Further Reading

Bradley, A. (2011) 'The Sovereignty of Parliament – Form or Substance?' in J. Jowell and D. Oliver (eds) *The Changing Constitution* (7th edn), Oxford: OUP.
Craig, P. (2003) 'Constitutional Foundations, the Rule of Law and Supremacy', Public Law, 92.

---

50 See Campbell and Young 2002.

Gordon, M. (2009) 'The Conceptual Foundations of Parliamentary Sovereignty: Reconsidering Jennings and Wade', Public Law, 519.

Hart, H.L.A. (1961) *The Concept of Law*, Oxford: Clarendon.

Jowell, J. (2006) 'Parliamentary Supremacy under the New Constitutional Hypothesis', Public Law, 562.

Munro, C.R. (1999) *Studies in Constitutional Law* (2nd edn), London: Butterworths, Chapters 5, 6.

Wade, H.W.R. (1955) 'The Basis of Legal Sovereignty', Cambridge Law Journal, 172.

Wade, H.W.R. (1996) 'Sovereignty – Revolution or Evolution?', Law Quarterly Review, 112: 568.

Part 3

The European Union

Chapter 7

Structures and Institutions of the European Union

A day will come when all the nations of this continent, without losing their distinct qualities or their glorious individuality, will fuse together in a higher unity and form the European brotherhood. A day will come when there will be no other battlefields than those of the mind – open marketplaces for ideas. A day will come when bullets and bombs will be replaced by votes.

Victor Hugo, address to Parliament, 1849

Chapter Contents

Introduction

The European Union (EU) now comprises 28 Member States with a population of over 500 million people. As will be seen below, the original three Communities arose from the desire to put the raw materials of war beyond the control of the nation state once and for all and to unite previously warring nations within a community which would foster not only peace and security but also economic growth and raised standards of living for all its peoples. The European Union – of which the European Community was the largest and most developed part – is based on the rule of law, the protection of individual human rights and a common European Union citizenship. For over half a century, the European project has fostered political and economic integration, while retaining respect for the individuality and identity of its Member States. Economically nowadays the Union represents a major trading power – a position which could not be achieved by any of the Member States acting alone. A common currency – the euro – was introduced in 1999. The ambitions of the Union have extended far beyond the original objectives of a common market for goods and services and now include common foreign and security policy and extensive co-operation between the police and authorities of the Member States. Citizens of all Member States have EU citizenship. Freedom of movement and rights of establishment are a central feature of the European Union. The elimination of border controls between Member States further extends the freedom of movement for persons within the territorial boundaries of the European Union.[1] In addition to rights of residence, every citizen of the Union has the right to stand as a candidate and to vote in municipal elections in the Member State in which he or she resides, and to stand as a candidate and vote in elections for the European Parliament. Union citizens are entitled to protection from the diplomatic or consular authorities of any Member State. Citizens of the EU have the right to petition the European Parliament, and have the right also to apply to the European Union Ombudsman.[2]

To understand the origins of the Union, it is necessary to look back to 1945 and a Europe that had been devastated by war: economically, politically and socially. In the desire to attain some form of harmony in order to guarantee peace and to rebuild Europe, the movement towards the integration of European countries was started. The movement took several forms. In 1948, the Organisation for Economic Co-operation and Development (OECD) was established with financial aid from the United States of America in order to restructure the European economies. In 1949, the North Atlantic Treaty Organisation (NATO) was formed as a military alliance between the United States, Canada and Europe. In 1950, under the leadership of the French Foreign Minister, Robert Schuman, a plan was devised whereby the raw materials of war – coal and steel – would be placed under the control of a supra-national organisation and, thus, the European Coal and Steel Community (ECSC) was established under the Treaty of Paris, signed in 1951. The original Member States were Germany, France, Belgium, Italy, Luxembourg and the Netherlands. Initiatives were being introduced to provide supra-national regulation of the non-military use of atomic energy. At the same time, the move towards greater economic co-operation and the creation of a European trading area was under way. The results of these developments took the form of the Treaties of Rome signed in 1957, establishing the European Economic Community (EEC) and the European Atomic Energy Community (Euratom).

---

1 The United Kingdom, however, retains its border controls.
2 On which see further below.

The EEC had the broadest aims of the three communities, seeking to create a European common market and close co-operation between Member States. The common market (now called the internal market) is based on four basic freedoms: persons, goods, capital and services.

The law relating to the European Union is now a wide-ranging subject. European Union law intrudes upon, and affects, an ever increasing volume of domestic law and now represents an important source of law in the United Kingdom. The original Treaties establishing the three European Communities have been much amended. Moreover, in 1992, the Treaty on European Union was signed by the Member States. The 1992 Treaty brought into being the European Union, the aims of which go far beyond the original objectives of the European Economic Community and seek to provide the further integration of the laws and policies of Member States. The 1992 Treaty also extended the competence of the EU institutions.

The Treaty of Amsterdam 1997 confirmed the Union's 'attachment to the principles of liberty, democracy and respect for human rights and fundamental freedoms and of the rule of law'. The political objectives of the Union are extensive, seeking to achieve European economic and monetary union, the promotion of economic and social progress, 'taking into account the principle of sustainable development and within the context of the accomplishment of the internal market and of reinforced cohesion and environmental protection', common defence and foreign policy,[3] and the complete elimination of border controls within the Union.[4]

The United Kingdom stood aloof from the early development of the Community, rejecting the call of Sir Winston Churchill in 1949 for a 'United States of Europe'.[5] Instead, Britain formed the European Free Trade Area (EFTA) together with Austria, Denmark, Norway, Portugal, Sweden and Switzerland. In part, EFTA was formed as a defensive action to fend off the potentially adverse effects of the free trading area established under the EEC.

By 1961, the Conservative government of Harold Macmillan had decided to seek entry to the Community, an application which was initially blocked by France. It was not until 1972 that the United Kingdom (along with Ireland, Denmark and Norway) was admitted with effect from January 1973.[6]

The current membership of the Union, with dates of accession, is as follows: Austria (1995), Belgium (1957), Denmark (1972), Finland (1995), France (1957), Germany (1957), Greece (1981), Ireland (1972), Italy (1957), Luxembourg (1957), Netherlands (1957), Portugal (1985), Spain (1985), Sweden (1995), United Kingdom (1973). Further expansion of the Union took place in 2004 when the following states became members: Cyprus, the Czech Republic, Estonia, Hungary, Latvia, Lithuania, Malta, Poland, Slovakia, and Slovenia.[7] In 2007 Romania and Bulgaria became members. Croatia is due to become a member on 1 July 2013.

The European Community

Note that the Treaty of Lisbon 2007 provides that the European Union replaces and succeeds the Community. Further, all references to the European Community in the Treaties are to be removed and replaced by the term European Union.

---

3 Article 11 TEU.5.
4 Article 2 TEU.
5 Speech at University of Zurich, 19 September 1946.
6 The people of Norway rejected EC membership in a referendum.
7 See the European Union (Accessions) Act 2003.

Aims and objectives

Article 3 of the Treaty on European Union (TEU) provides that the activities of the Union include, *inter alia*:

- the establishment of an internal market free of all internal tariffs;
- the abolition of measures obstructing the free movement of goods, persons, services and capital;
- common policies relating to agriculture and fisheries, commerce and transport;
- environmental protection;
- strengthening consumer and health protection;
- forming associations with overseas countries to increase trade and jointly promote economic and social development;
- strengthening economic and social cohesion;
- the promotion of research and technological development.

A unique legal order

The European Union is the creation of the original EEC Treaty, as amended. European Union law, however, is not international law as normally understood in the sense of merely establishing mutual obligations between contracting states. In addition to creating mutual obligations between Member States, EU law also involves the transfer of sovereign rights to the institutions of that system and the creation of rights and obligations for their citizens which are enforceable in their local courts. The EU is, therefore, a unique constitutional entity, having its own institutions and law-making powers, capable of creating rights and duties within the legal systems of the Member States. The law-making powers of the EU Institutions, as will be seen below, are far-reaching. When duties are imposed on Member States, these may imply rights for individuals which may be enforced in the domestic courts and ultimately in the Court of Justice, the EU's judicial forum.

In constitutional terms, the European Union is not a 'state', neither is it a 'federation', rather it is a unique supranational organisation. When new Member States are admitted to the Union, they became automatically bound by the entire law of the Union – in European terminology, the *acquis communautaire*.[8] Under international law, when a state becomes a signatory to a treaty, it becomes bound by the provisions of that treaty, but not bound by any acts done under the treaty before that state's accession. It is different with the European Union, and new Member States become automatically committed to the Treaties, all secondary legislation, judicial and non-judicial decisions made by the Institutions of the Union, together with non-binding opinions and resolutions of Institutions.

The major constitutional issues

From the constitutional law perspective, the issues which require scrutiny are:

(a) the nature of the European Union (EU), the institutions and their law-making powers;
(b) the nature and sources of EU law;
(c) the effect of membership of the EU on the constitution of the United Kingdom;
(d) the relationship between EU law and domestic law.

---

8 Which, literally translated, means 'Community patrimony'. See TEU 1992, Articles 2 and 3.

The allocation of functions between the institutions and Member States

In any federal or quasi-federal state or organisation, the functions of the federal government and the regional governments must be allocated. As discussed in Chapter 1, the concept of federalism involves the allocation of powers which may reserve some powers to the exclusive competence of the federal government, some powers which will be concurrently held by the federal and regional governments, and some powers over which the regional government has exclusive competence. In the European Union, the manner in which powers are allocated and exercised is largely determined by the Treaty provisions.

The principle of subsidiarity[9]

Subsidiarity is a fundamental concept designed to achieve an appropriate balance between the Institutions of the EU and Member States. Designed to determine the appropriate level of action across the whole spectrum of public activity, international (in the widest sense), national, regional and local, it has been invoked in the European context to assist in determining the exercise of powers. In this context, it has been described, variously, as 'the principle of necessity, or proportionality, of effectiveness, an elementary principle of good government, or simply a principle of good sense'. It has been interpreted as meaning that the EU should act only:

(a) where the objective cannot be achieved by regulation at national level;

(b) where the objective can be better, or more effectively, achieved by action at EU level (the 'efficiency by better results' criterion); or

(c) where the matter in question can be more effectively regulated at EU level (the 'administrative efficiency' criterion).[10]

Article 5 of the Treaty on European Union (TEU) provides:

1. the limits of Union competences are governed by the principle of conferral (ie the specific Treaty provisions). The use of Union competences is governed by the principles of subsidiarity and proportionality.

2. under the principle of conferral, the Union shall act only within the limits of the competences conferred upon it by the Member States in the Treaties to attain the objectives set out therein. Competences not conferred upon the Union in the Treaties remain with the Member States.

3. under the principle of subsidiarity, in areas which do not fall within its exclusive competence, the Union shall act only if and insofar as the objectives of the proposed action cannot be sufficiently achieved by the Member States, either at central level or at regional and local level, but can rather, by reason of the scale or effects of the proposed action, be better achieved at Union level.

The institutions of the Union shall apply the principle of subsidiarity as laid down in the Protocol on the application of the principles of subsidiarity and proportionality. National Parliaments ensure compliance with the principle of subsidiarity in accordance with the procedure set out in that Protocol.

---

9 See Emiliou, 1991, and 'Subsidiarity: panacea or fig leaf?', in O'Keefe and Twomey, 1994, Chapter 5; Toth, 1992.

10 Steiner, 'Subsidiarity under the Maastricht Treaty', and references therein, in O'Keefe and Twomey, 1994.

The closely related principles of subsidiarity and proportionality are thus both provided for in theTreaties.The Protocol on theApplication of the Principles of Subsidiarity and Proportionality restates the principles, listing guidelines to be followed in reaching decisions as to whether action should be taken at European Union level or at national level. Now a legal concept, it will be for the European Court of Justice (ECJ) to adjudicate on its scope and application. The Protocol also makes clear that subsidiarity is a concept which is dynamic and flexible, allowing decisions on the appropriate level at which action should be taken to develop on a case by case basis.The doctrine of proportionality requires that measures taken must not be more extensive than is necessary to achieve the desired result.

Categories of competence

Exclusive competence

As the text of Article 5 TEU makes clear, where the EU has 'exclusive competence', the subsidiarity principle has no application.The EU has sole power of decision and therefore no question arises as to whether others share that power, or the extent to which they should be entitled to act.Article 3 TFEU now provides a catalogue of areas in which the EU has exclusive competence, which includes customs, monetary policy, rules necessary for the functioning of the internal market, aspects of common fisheries policy and common commercial policy.[11]

Shared concurrent powers

Where a Member State has a concurrent power, the power to act remains, so long as the EU has not exercised that power. Once the EU takes action itself, the power of the Member State is pre-empted, and the power to act – once pre-empted – remains with the EU.[12] Where the EU has exclusive power, the Member State has no power to act unless the legislation in question contains a specific authorisation by the EU in favour of the Member States.[13] However, the Court has ruled that, where the EU has exclusive competence to act but has not so acted and urgent action is needed, the Member States may act as 'trustees of the common interest'.[14]

Issues of subsidiarity inevitably fall for the Court to consider. For example, if the EU legislates on a particular area, a Member State may wish to resist that legislation by invoking subsidiarity, and thus the Court will be obliged to make a decision.

On subsidiarity the Treaty of Lisbon provides that:

- competences not conferred upon the Union in the Treaties remain with the Member States;[15]
- the use of Union competences is governed by the principles of subsidiarity and proportionality;[16]
- under the principle of subsidiarity, in areas which do not fall within its exclusive competence, the Union shall act only if and insofar as the objectives of the proposed action cannot be sufficiently achieved by the Member States, either at central level or at regional and local level;

---

11 See Communication to the Council and Parliament outlining proposals for the Subsidiarity Principle Bulletin EC 10-1992, Pt 2.2.1, cited in *op cit*, Steiner, fn 34.
12 See Weatherill, 'Beyond pre-emption', in O'Keefe andTwomey, 1994.
13 Article 2 TFEU; **Donckerwolcke v Procureur de la Republique** (1976).
14 **Commission v United Kingdom** (1981).
15 Inserting Article 5 TEU.
16 Article 5 TEU amending Article 5 EC Treaty.These principles are supported by a Protocol on Subsidiarity.

- under the principle of proportionality, the content and form of Union action shall not exceed what is necessary to achieve the objectives of the Treaties;
- the Protocol on Subsidiarity, Article 8, provides that the Court of Justice shall have jurisdiction to rule on allegation of infringement of the principle of subsidiarity by a legislative act.

Evolution of the European Union

Since the establishment of the European Union in 1992, the European Community has been the major, and legally distinctive, part of the European Union which has more wide-ranging objectives. These are considered in detail below, following discussion of the stages of evolution which have been undertaken to date. It should be noted, however, that the Treaty of Lisbon, signed in 2007, dismantles the pillar structure created under the Treaty on European Union 1992 and removes references to the European Community, replacing that term with the European Union. Accordingly, references to the European Community (EC) and European Community law will continue to be made in relation to matters occurring before December 2009 when the Lisbon Treaty took effect, and in relation to matters thereafter, the terms European Union (EU) and European Union law (EU law) will be used.

The major provisions of the Lisbon Treaty will be considered in this chapter. At this introductory stage, note that the Lisbon Treaty renamed the EC Treaty the Treaty on the Functioning of the European Union (TFEU), makes amendments to both the EC Treaty and the Treaty on European Union (TEU) and transfers some current EC Treaty articles to the TEU.

The European Community/European Union Treaties

European Coal and Steel Community	Treaty of Paris	1951
European Atomic Energy Community	Treaty of Rome	1957
European Economic Community	Treaty of Rome	1957
Merging the Institutions	Merger Treaties	1957 and 1965
Revising the Treaties	The Single European Act	1986
The European Union	Treaty on European Union	1992
Consolidation	Treaty of Amsterdam	1997
Preparing for enlargement	Treaty of Nice	2000
A European Constitution?	(The rejected Constitutional Treaty)	2004
Consolidation	Treaty of Lisbon	2007

The Treaty establishing the ECSC provided for four institutions which today form the nucleus of the institutional framework of the European Union (EU). These are the Commission, the executive body which (broadly speaking) serves the interests of the EU; the Council, the executive body representing the interests of the Member States; the Assembly Parliament[17] – (originally a non-elected supervisory body) representing the citizens of the EU, and the European Court of Justice (ECJ).

Having established the three Treaties with differing organs and differing powers, the next logical step was to merge the Institutions. The 1957 Merger Treaty established a common

---

17 The European Parliament became directly elected in 1979.

Assembly and Court. The Merger Treaty 1965 established a single Council and Commission of the EC. From 1957 to 1987, the EEC Treaty remained unchanged, although membership of the Community expanded from the original six Members to 12.[18]

The Single European Act 1986

The Single European Act:

- increased the powers of the European Parliament, making it an active participant in the adoption of EU legislation;
- increased the use of the 'qualified majority vote' in the Council of Ministers, thereby making it more difficult for a Member State to block EU legislation;
- extended EU competence into new areas such as environment and regional development policy.

The Treaty on European Union 1992 (Maastricht)

The Treaty on European Union (TEU) – the Maastricht Treaty – came into effect in 1993 and created the European Union.

The Treaty represented a compromise between the federalists (those who wanted to move towards a more integrated union with greater centralised power) and inter-governmentalists – those wishing to retain the powers of the Member States and limit the power transferred to the EC. It needs to be understood that, in the development of the Union, there has been exhibited a constant tension between those Member States who see the movement towards almost total political and economic union, whereby the Union would take on the characteristics of a federal state, and those Member States (particularly the United Kingdom) who have reservations about greater fusion in Europe and wish to retain a higher degree of autonomy from Europe than the federalists would wish to see.

As a result of these tensions, rather than drafting a treaty to supplement the existing Treaties and to provide a coherent working 'constitution' for Europe, the 1992 Treaty produced a structure in which the Union was 'founded on the European Community, supplemented by the policies and forms of co-operation'[19] laid down by the TEU. The TEU also provided a framework for co-operation on future developments. There were now three 'pillars' which represent the structure of the Union. The first pillar amended the EEC Treaty (and renamed it the EC Treaty). The second pillar introduced and regulated common foreign and security policy. The third pillar concerned Justice and Home Affairs (later relabelled Police and Judicial Co-operation in Criminal Matters). The Maastricht Treaty involved economic and monetary union as a central process towards further European integration. The Maastricht Treaty also introduced two new Institutions. The European Central Bank was given law-making and other powers and plays a pivotal role in economic and monetary union. The Court of Auditors, having responsibility for scrutinising administration, received formal recognition as an Institution of the EU, its members having a six-year renewable term of office and being under the same requirements of independence from governments as the Commission. The euro came into existence as a currency in 1999 with notes and coins coming into circulation in January 2002. The United Kingdom, while meeting the convergence criteria for joining, opted out of this scheme,[20] but

---

18 The United Kingdom, Ireland and Denmark joined in 1973, Greece in 1981, Spain and Portugal in 1986.
19 TEU 1997, Article 1; see Curtin, 1993 for a critical account.
20 Protocol annexed to the EC Treaty on certain provisions relating to the United Kingdom of Great Britain and Northern Ireland, 1997, para 1. Denmark and Sweden also remain outside the 'Euro-zone'.

remains free to opt in in the future. The Schengen Agreement, which provided for the aboli-tion of border controls between participating Member States, was also formally incorporated into law under the TEU 1992. Denmark, Ireland and the United Kingdom derogated from these measures, because of their special geographical boundaries.[21] The ECJ has examined the national legislation governing identity checks on citizens when crossing frontiers. It has ruled that until all Member States are required to abolish all controls at frontiers, they are entitled to require that the person seeking entry is able to establish that he or she has the nationality of the Member State.[22]

The second pillar of the Union structure established under the Maastricht Treaty 1992 was that of Common Foreign and Security Policy, which represents one of the most politically difficult areas of the Union. These provisions were superseded by the Treaty of Lisbon.

The Treaty of Amsterdam 1997[23]

The Treaty of Amsterdam 1997:

- amended the pillar structure of the EU;
- provided for greater flexibility in the working of the Union, under the guise of 'closer cooperation' between Member States;
- formally incorporated the Schengen Agreement which provides for the abolition of border controls between the participating Member States (note that Denmark, Ireland and the United Kingdom have an 'opt out' from this arrangement);
- introduced a new form of law, the 'framework decision', similar to a Directive in that it leaves a degree of discretion to Member States in achieving the objective of the measure;
- reaffirmed EU citizenship as complementary to national citizenship;
- provided a right of access to Commission and Council documentation;
- adopted a Protocol on the principle of subsidiarity, thereby giving it legal, rather than influential, force.

The Treaty of Nice 2001

The Treaty of Nice reformed the institutions in preparation for the accession of new Member States. It:

- reorganised the Commission;
- revised the weighted voting system in the Council, extending qualified majority voting;
- increased the power of co-decision of the European Parliament.

Expansion of the EU's membership

In 2004, membership of the European Union expanded from 15 Member States to 25 States. This major enlargement prompted a revision of the Treaties governing the Union with a view to adapting the institutions and procedures for the future. A draft Constitution of Europe was introduced, designed to repeal and replace all the existing Treaties with a single text. To come into effect the EU Constitutional Treaty had to be ratified by all Member States according to

---

21 With effect from December 2007, the Schengen area includes the nine new Eastern European Member States, bringing the total number of states within the free travel area to 24.
22 Case C-378/97, Wijsenbeck J: Press Release of the ECJ No 69/99.
23 See *European Union Consolidated Treaties*, 1997, Luxembourg: Office for Official Publications of the European Communities; Petite, 1998; Editorial (CML Rev), 1997.

their constitutional arrangements (either through parliamentary approval or referendums). In referendums held in France and The Netherlands the people voted against the Constitution, thereby preventing it from coming into effect.[24]

The Treaty of Lisbon 2007

In 2007, the Lisbon Treaty was signed. It was ratified in 2009.[25] The Treaty amends the EC Treaty, and the Treaty on European Union, but does not represent a consolidation of those Treaties.[26] The EC Treaty is renamed the Treaty on the Functioning of the European Union.[27] The Reform Treaty, with amendments, incorporates the majority of the provisions of the rejected 2004 Treaty. The 2007 Treaty aims to make Europe more 'democratic and transparent' by strengthening the role of the European Parliament, introducing 'greater involvement of the national Parliaments' and giving 'citizens a stronger voice'.[28]

The main provisions of the Lisbon Treaty, in outline, are as follows:

- The European Union replaces and succeeds the European Community, thereby eliminating their separate identities.[29] The EC Treaty is renamed the Treaty on the Functioning of the European Union, the TFEU.
- The European Council comprises Heads of State or Government, the Presidents of the European Council and President of the Commission. The High Representative for Common Foreign and Security Policy participates in the work of the European Council. The function of the European Council is to 'provide the Union with the necessary impetus for its development and . . . define the general political directions and priorities . . .'. The Council does not exercise legislative functions.[30]
- The European Council shall meet twice every six months. Decisions are taken by consensus unless provisions of the Treaties provide otherwise. The President of the Council shall not hold national office. The President is to report to the Parliament following meetings of the European Council.[31]
- The post of EU 'Foreign Minister' – formally the High Representative of the Union for Foreign Affairs and Security Policy – is created.[32]
- A common security and defence policy is an integral part of the EU's Foreign and Security Policy. The EU is to have an operational capacity, drawing on civilian and military assets of Member States. Their use is to be in relation to peace-keeping, conflict prevention and strengthening international security. Member States shall make their capabilities available to the Union. Decisions having military or defence implications are to be reached by unanimity. In relation to other proposals/policies, the Treaty provides conditions under which decisions may be reached by Qualified Majority Voting (see Article 31 TEU).

---

24 See Shaw, 2005.
25 On the background to the Treaty see the Commission's Communication to Council, *Reforming Europe for the 21st Century*: http://europa.eu/rapid/press-release_IP-07-1044_en.htm. The Republic of Ireland is the only Member State to submit the Treaty to a referendum of the people. In relation to the UK see the European Union (Amendment) Bill 2007.
26 Article 1 TEU.
27 Article 2. With one exception, throughout the Treaty, the words Community and European Community are to be replaced by Union.
28 www.europa.eu/lisbon_treaty/glance/index_en.htm.
29 Article 1 TEU. The Court of Justice of the European Communities is renamed the Court of Justice of the European Union. The Court of First Instance is renamed the General Court.
30 Article 15 TEU.
31 *Ibid.* The Court of Justice has jurisdiction over acts of the European Council: A230, 231.
32 The High Representative presides over the Foreign Affairs Council. The High Representative is also one of the Vice-Presidents of the Commission.

- In respect of terrorist attacks, natural or man-made disasters, the Union shall 'act jointly and in the spirit of solidarity', giving assistance and coordinating action in the Council.[33]
- From 2014 membership of the Commission will be revised. At any one time, two-thirds of Member States will have the right to nominate a member of the Commission who will hold office for five years.
- The European Parliament is to have no more than 750 Members plus its President.[34] No Member State may have more than 96 seats.
- The powers of the Court of Justice are enhanced with most restrictions on its jurisdiction to rule on Justice and Home Affairs removed.
- A new system of voting in Council (of Ministers) will be in place from 2014. A measure will also be passed if fewer than four Member States oppose it.
- The Council meets in public when it deliberates and votes on a draft legislative act.[35]
- The Treaty abolishes national vetoes in relation to 45 to 70 policy areas, including aspects of Justice and Home Affairs. Police and Judicial Cooperation in Criminal Matters now become, with limited exceptions where unanimity is figured, subject to majority voting.
- Co-decision between the Council and the Parliament is increased in approximately 50 areas, placing the Parliament on an equal footing with Council for the majority of legislation.
- The EU institutions must notify national Parliaments of proposed legislation and provide eight weeks for comments. National Parliaments are given an opportunity to challenge legislation. If one third of national Parliaments object, the Commission must consider whether to maintain, amend or withdraw the proposal.
- A 'Citizen's Initiative' is introduced whereby at least one million citizens from a significant number of Member States call for reform, the Commission may draft a proposal.
- The European Union is declared to have legal personality, thereby providing the legal basis for entering into legal relations with non-EU states and international organisations (Article 47 TEU).
- The Treaty gives legal effect to the EU Charter of Fundamental Rights.[36] The United Kingdom has negotiated a legally binding Protocol to the effect that no court can rule that UK laws, regulations or administrative practices are inconsistent with the Charter. Furthermore, the Protocol states that the Charter creates no new legally enforceable rights in the United Kingdom.[37]
- Article 6.2 provides that the Union 'shall accede' to the European Convention on Human Rights. ECHR rights and freedoms constitute the general principles of EU law.
- The right to withdraw from the EU is for the first time made explicit. Article 50 TEU provides that any Member State may decide to withdraw from the EU in accordance with its own constitutional requirements. A withdrawal agreement must be negotiated with the EU.

---

33 Title VII, Article 222 TFEU.
34 Article 14 TEU.
35 Article 16(8) TEU.
36 Article 6 TEU.
37 The same exemptions apply to Poland and the Czech Republic.

The Institutions of the European Union
The European Commission[38]

Originally called the High Authority, the Commission is centrally concerned with all aspects of decision making at all levels and on all fronts: the Commission is the very heart of the EU, exercising both powers of initiative and powers of enforcement. As envisaged by the authors of the original Treaties, the Commission, while acting independently of governments and in pursuit of the objectives of the Community, would help preserve the interests of individual Member States. The Commission was intended to be the engine which drives Europe forward.

Article 17 TEU provides (in part) that the Commission shall:

- promote the general interest of the Union and take appropriate initiatives to that end;
- ensure the application of the Treaties and of measures adopted by the institutions;
- oversee the application of Union law under the control of the Court of Justice of the European Union;
- execute the budget;
- exercise coordinating, executive and management functions as laid down in the Treaties;
- ensure the Union's external representation (with the exception of common foreign and security policy and other cases provided in the Treaties).

Commissioners are appointed by the European Council upon the consent of the European Parliament (Article 17(7) TEU). Commissioners must be nationals of one of the Member States.[39] Commissioners are appointed for a renewable five-year term of office, and cannot be dismissed during their term of office by governments.[40] Commissioners remain in office until replaced, or compulsorily retired.[41] Decisions in the Commission are reached by majority voting.

Once appointed, Commissioners must act independently of government: they are not representatives of government. Article 17(3) TEU provides that:

> . . . the Commission shall be completely independent . . . members of the Commission shall neither seek nor take instructions from any Government or other institution, body, office or entity. They shall refrain from any action incompatible with their duties or the performance of their tasks.

The Commission is headed by a President, appointed by the European Parliament (Article 17(7) TEU).

The European Parliament has the power to pass a motion of censure to remove the Commission en bloc. However, when, in 1999, allegations of waste and mismanagement in the Commission surfaced, the Parliament failed to pass a motion of sanction. In the event, the entire Commission, including the President, resigned.

Organisationally, the Commission is divided into Directorates General, each headed by a Director responsible to the relevant Commissioner. Each Commissioner holds one or more

---

38 See new Article 17 TEU and Articles 244–250 TFEU.
39 Note that under the Lisbon Treaty, there will be a reduction in the number of Commissioners.
40 Commissioners can, however, have their reappointment blocked by a government, as occurred in 1989 when the Prime Minister felt that Lord Cockfield had been over-zealous in his support of the Community.
41 Article 247 TFEU provides that, if a Commissioner no longer fulfils the conditions required for the performance of his duties, or if he has been guilty of serious misconduct, the ECJ may, on an application of the Council or the Commission, compulsorily retire him.

portfolios, that is to say, special responsibility for some area of Community policy, and is assisted by a Cabinet of six.

The broad and ill-defined power conferred under the Treaty and the role of the Commission can only be understood within the framework of the European Union as a whole. It is clear that it is the Commission which is charged with the duty to act in the interests of the objectives of the Union as expressed in the Treaties. It is the Commission which puts forward proposals for decision by the Council of the EU (see below), having negotiated widely with representatives of Member States' governments and with interest groups within the EU. The Council of the EU may, in some instances, request the Commission to draft proposals, and the European Parliament has always been given the right to request the Commission to submit a proposal for legislation. Where the Commission is under an obligation to submit legislative proposals within a certain time laid down in the Treaty, failure to act within that time will render the Commission liable to a challenge before the ECJ. When such proposals assume the force of law, it is again the Commission which is charged primarily with the task of law enforcement.

The Commission's broad powers of initiative should not be understood to mean that the Commission has total freedom of action. The working of the EU depends on a variety of factors, actors and forces. In the final analysis, the EU can only be effective in achieving the goals set out in the Treaties if its proposals can carry the support of the Member States. The effectiveness of EU law within the legal systems of all Member States is ultimately dependent upon the political acceptability of that law. It is for this reason that the role of the Commission is so important, for the Commission – having the sole power to formulate proposals for the implementation of Treaty objectives – is responsible for ensuring that proposals have the support of Member States before they are hardened into law. As originally envisaged by the drafters of the original Treaties, only a body acting with complete independence was competent to negotiate with Member States and formulate acceptable policies. The European Union comprises 28 states of vastly differing sizes and populations, and within these states there are regions with differing interests and needs. It is vital, therefore, that there is some guarantee that the interests of the smaller Member States, and regions in all Member States, are protected against the power of the larger states. Accordingly, in the process of formulating policies, one of the Commission's principal tasks is to reconcile the differing interests at stake and to make the resulting law acceptable to all.[42]

Where a Member State is in default of Treaty obligations, the Commission has the power to deal with the breach. If the Commission considers that a Member State has failed to fulfil an obligation under the Treaties, it shall deliver a reasoned opinion on the matter after giving the state concerned the opportunity to submit its observations. If the state concerned does not comply with the opinion within the period laid down by the Commission, the latter may bring the matter before the Court of Justice (Article 258 TFEU).

Most matters are settled at an early stage – infringements being due not to wilful disregard of the law, but rather arising from genuine differences of opinion as to the meaning of requirements, or from administrative delay. Where, however, a Member State fails to fulfil its EU obligations, the Commission may take the case to the ECJ. Where the Court rules that the Member State is in default of its obligations and the Member State fails to comply with its judgment, the Court, at the request of the Commission, may impose a financial penalty on the Member State.[43]

---

42 Temple-Lang, J, 'The European Commission: safeguard for Member States', European Law Lecture (Queen Mary, University of London, 5 June 1995).
43 See Article 258 TFEU.

In **Commission v United Kingdom** (2000), the Commission sought a declaration that the United Kingdom had failed fully to comply with a Directive[44] concerning the protection of waters against pollution caused by nitrates from agricultural sources. The United Kingdom authorities had identified only surface waters intended for extraction of drinking water, whereas the Directive also required the identification of surface freshwaters not intended for the abstraction of drinking water which contained excessive nitrate concentrations or could do so. The fact that the authorities were now taking action to remedy the failure did not exclude the state's liability for breach of its obligations under the Directive.[45] Failure to transpose a Directive into national law by the stipulated date will not be excused on the basis that transposition required revision of provisions of a Member State's constitution. The ECJ so held in **Commission v Kingdom of Belgium** (1998).

The Council

The Council (of Ministers) has legislative and executive powers and functions. It is the Council which defends the interests of Member States. The Council has no fixed membership and its composition varies depending upon the subject matter under discussion. Each Member State is represented in Council by a government minister. Accordingly, when the subject on the agenda is agriculture, the Council will consist of the Ministers of Agriculture from all Member States; when the subject is transport, the membership will be made up of the respective Ministers of Transport. Article 16 TEU now provides that the Council is to exercise 'legislative and budgetary functions'. It shall also carry out 'policy making and coding functions laid down in the Treaties'.

The voting system for decision making[46]

Central to EU development is the voting system used in the Council. The Treaty provides for three basic methods by which the Council can reach a decision: unanimously, by qualified majority vote or by a simple majority vote. Unanimity is normally required where a new policy is to be initiated or the existing policy framework is to be developed or modified. Unanimity is also required when the Council wishes to amend a Commission proposal against the wishes of the Commission. While the Union rests on consensus, and there is little point in adopting a procedure which will cause national Parliaments' resentment or reluctance on the part of state authorities to implement decisions, a balance is needed between respecting the interests of the Member States while not impeding EU development.

Article c4 TEU states that, unless otherwise provided in the Treaty, that is to say under specific articles, the Council shall act by qualified majority vote. In some specific cases the Council is required to act by a qualified majority, for which purpose the votes of Member States are weighted, the largest states having a weighting of ten, the remaining, according to size, eight, five, four, three or two. Where the Council adopts a matter on a proposal from the Commission, 62 votes are required. Where unanimity is required, the abstention of a Member State shall not prevent the Council adopting a matter. The voting system was designed in order to minimise the circumstances in which one state could block EU progress. It became clear in the 1960s, however, that this was unworkable – most notably when France refused to co-operate in any decisions and caused a constitutional crisis.

---

44 Council Directive 91/676/EC of 12 December 1991.
45 See also **Commission of the European Union v United Kingdom** (2002).
46 See Morner, 'The conflicts inherent in enlargement – is history catching up with the European Union?', in Butterworths, 1994.

The outcome of the crisis was an agreement contained in what is known as the *Luxembourg Accord* of 1966, which provided that:

> Where in the case of decisions which may be taken by majority vote on a proposal from the Commission, very important interests of one or more partners are at stake, the Members of the Council will endeavour, within a reasonable time, to reach solutions which can be adopted by all Members of the Council while respecting their mutual interests and those of the Community in accordance with Article 2 of the Treaty. [Bulletin of the European Community 3/66, p 5]

The French government insisted that where very important state interests are at stake, the discussion should continue until unanimous agreement is reached.

This *Accord* had no formal legal status. It was an informal agreement, and probably unlawful. However, the *Accord* profoundly affected decision making, and the French amendment has been interpreted to mean that any state has the right to exercise a veto on questions which affect its vital national interests, and it is for the states themselves to determine when such interests are at stake. Under the Treaty of Amsterdam the issue of important national interests was resurrected and formalised in the EC Treaty. It has been noted that 'predictions of the demise of the Luxembourg Compromise were thus distinctly premature: it has been given a new lease of life, no longer in the *demi-monde* of political deals but as part of the legal machinery of the EC Treaty.'[47]

The Treaty of Nice revised the requirements for qualified majority voting, requiring that:

- 255 of the 345 votes must be cast in favour of the proposal;
- 62 per cent of the population must be represented; and
- a majority of Member States must support the proposal.

Table 7.1: Votes in Council

Country	Votes	Country	Votes
Austria	10	Latvia	4
Belgium	12	Lithuania	7
Bulgaria	10	Luxembourg	4
Cyprus	4	Malta	3
Czech Republic	12	Netherlands	13
Denmark	7	Poland	27
Estonia	4	Portugal	12
Finland	7	Romania	14
France	29	Slovakia	7
Germany	29	Slovenia	4
Greece	12	Spain	27
Hungary	12	Sweden	10
Ireland	7	United Kingdom	29
Italy	29	**Total**	**345**

47 Editorial, Common Market Law Review, 1997, p 769.

Article 16 TEU provides that:

- with effect from 2014, a new system of qualified majority voting in Council (of Ministers) will be in place. The new system is based on a 'double majority of Member States and people' and provides that a vote is passed if:

    (a) 55 per cent of Member States are in favour (15 of 27 states); and
    (b) these Member States represent 65 per cent of the EU's population;[48]

- a measure will also be passed if fewer than four Member States oppose it.

Where a Member State's national interest is at stake, the Treaty of Lisbon provides that a transitional rule is in place[49] that allows a Member State to make a request for the application of the current Nice rules.

The Council, together with the European Parliament, represents a major law-making body within the EU. Because the Council has a fluctuating membership and is not permanently in session,[50] the Committee of Permanent Representatives (COREPER) acts as the permanent body engaged in Council work (Article 240 TFEU). The Committee is supported by more than 150 committees and working groups consisting of delegates from Member States. Many of these committees have a specific role of providing coordination and expertise in a particular area.

The European Parliament[51]

Members of the Parliament were initially delegates designated by the Parliaments of Member States. In constitutional terms, the delegates had a dual mandate: that of membership of both the domestic and European Parliaments. The Treaty, however, envisaged that the Parliament should be directly elected by the people. The first direct elections to the European Parliament took place in 1979. The European Parliament agreed to end the dual mandate for elected representatives with effect from 2004.

Seats in the European Parliament, the name formally adopted in 1962, are allocated according to the size of population of the Member States, although there is no absolute equality in voting powers. Under the Treaty of Lisbon the maximum number of seats in Parliament is 750, with no Member State having more than 96 seats. Representatives are elected for a term of five years. Under the European Parliamentary Elections Act 1999, the United Kingdom is divided into electoral regions. England is divided into nine; Scotland, Wales and Northern Ireland each constitute a single electoral region.[52] The Members of Parliament do not sit in groupings organised by nationality but rather by political party groupings.[53] The major political parties are the Socialists, European People's Party, European Democrats, Communists and Liberals. Unless otherwise provided for under the Treaties, the Parliament acts by an absolute majority of the votes cast.

---

48 See also the Protocol on Transitional Provisions, Article 3 which, *inter alia*, specifies the number of votes per country until 2014: Article 16 TEU.
49 From 1 November 2014 to 31 March 2017: Protocol 10 on Transitional Provisions, Article 3.
50 Some 80 Council meetings take place each year.
51 Articles 189–210 EC. See now Articles 11 and 14 TEU and Articles 223–236 TFEU.
52 The European Parliamentary and Local Elections (Pilots) Act 2004 permitted pilot elections for the European Parliament in 2004 by postal vote. Pilot elections were held in four English regions. In all four regions the number of votes more than doubled.
53 See Article 11 TEU and Article 224 TFEU.

The European Parliament is required to hold an annual session, and may meet in extraordinary session at the request of a majority of its Members or at the request of the Council or of the Commission. In practice, the Parliament meets approximately 12 to 14 times a year for a few days per session. Members of the Commission may attend all parliamentary meetings and are entitled to address the Parliament. The Parliament holds plenary sessions in Strasbourg, committee meetings and additional plenary sessions in Brussels and has its secretariat based in Luxembourg. Much of the work of Parliament is undertaken by committees on, for example, agriculture, legal affairs and so on. Before a matter goes before Parliament sitting in plenary session, it will normally be considered by the relevant standing committee.

The original intention in relation to Parliament's function was that it would be a 'supervisory and advisory' body, with no legal effect being attached to its deliberations. Under specific Treaty articles, the Council of the EU is obliged to seek the advice of the Parliament, and failure to consider Parliament's view would cause the Council to be in violation of an essential procedural requirement of Community law, and could cause the decision of the Council to be declared void by the ECJ.[54] As will be seen, the powers of the European Parliament have been increasing since 1986 (under the SEA 1986), but even now it remains a very different constitutional institution from that of domestic Parliaments.

The European Parliament can adopt its own ideas and try to persuade the Commission to adopt them. Usually this takes the form of an initiative report – around 100 a year are approved by the European Parliament. However, Parliament has no power to insist that the Commission adopt a proposal from Parliament – the right of initiative is firmly in the hands of the Commission itself, other than where the European Parliament or the Council requests a proposal from the Commission.

The European Parliament has decision-making powers regarding the annual budget. This power in relation to the EU budget has always been of significance. The revenue of the EU comes primarily from agricultural levies, customs duties on imports from outside the EU and value added tax (VAT) levied within the EU. When the draft budget is drawn up by the Council, after receiving proposals from the Commission, it is then submitted to Parliament which has power to accept, amend or reject the budget.

Parliament has the power to reject the EU budget in total if there are 'important reasons to do so': Article 314 TFEU. There must be a majority of votes in Parliament and also two-thirds of the votes cast. Rejection of the budget occurred in 1979, when a new budget was subsequently drawn up. The Treaty of Lisbon extends Parliament's powers over all categories of expenditure.

Parliament has the right to question the Commission and Council, and replies are given both orally and in writing, and published in the *Official Journal of the European Communities*. Parliament also has the power to dismiss the entire Commission on a vote of censure if the vote is carried by a two-thirds majority of the votes cast, a vote which must represent an overall majority of the votes in Parliament. If the vote is carried, the Commission resigns as a body. However, in one sense, the power is too great to be effective, for Parliament has no power to force the incoming Commission to adopt a different policy from that of its predecessor.

Extension of Parliament's powers

The powers of the European Parliament have been extended significantly. The legislative process is now more complex and, in specific instances, it is necessary to consult the substantive

---

54 *Roquettes Frères SA v Council* (1980); *Maizena GmbH v Council* (1980).

Articles of the Treaty in order to establish the precise procedure to be followed. Note, however, that after the Treaty of Lisbon the former co-decision procedure is the ordinary procedure to be followed.

The co-operation and co-decision procedures

The SEA 1986 provided for a new 'co-operation procedure', which applied to many, but not all, instances in which the Treaties require Parliament to be consulted. This procedure, which gave the Parliament the power to propose amendments to legislative proposals, has been largely superseded by the co-decision powers introduced at Maastricht. The co-operation procedure does continue to apply, however, to some issues relating to European monetary union. The TEU 1992 and the 1997 Treaty further extended Parliament's role in the legislative process.[55] The Treaty of Lisbon extends the Parliament's powers of co-decision with the Council to the extent that the majority of proposals are now subject to the ordinary decision-making procedure.

The ordinary decision-making procedure is as follows:[56]

- the Commission puts forward a proposal to Council;
- Council submits this to Parliament for its opinion (First Reading stage);
- Parliament submits its opinion to Council which adopts – by a qualified majority of votes – a 'common position';
- the common position is considered by Parliament (Second Reading stage) and:

    - if approved the measure is adopted by Council;
    - if Parliament rejects the measure or proposes amendments which the Council will not accept a Conciliation Committee comprising Council members and MEPs is established to draft an agreed text;
    - if a majority in Parliament and qualified majority in Council approve the text it is adopted;
    - if no agreement is reached, Council may reinstate its original common position by majority vote;
    - the measure may then be adopted unless vetoed by a majority in Parliament.

The TEU 1992 provided that Parliament shall appoint an ombudsman to inquire into allegations of maladministration within the EU. Parliament may also establish committees of inquiry to investigate allegations of maladministration. It was a committee of inquiry which led to the downfall of the Santer Commission in 1999. The SEA gave the Parliament power to agree or to veto special trade agreements. It also extended Parliament's role in the admission of new Member States, whose admission must be approved by a majority, thus giving the Parliament a power of veto.

The concept of institutional balance

Under any constitution there must be a separation of powers in order to ensure that power is dispersed among the major institutions of the state rather than concentrated in one institution. However, as has been seen above, the separation of powers among the EU Institutions differs

---

55 On Parliament's powers under the TEU, see Bradley, '"Better rusty than missing"? The institutional reforms of the Maastricht Treaty and the European Parliament', in O'Keefe and Twomey, 1994.
56 And is further extended under the 2007 Treaty of Lisbon.

markedly from conventional arrangements. In the first place, it may be noted that the principal Institutions – the Council, Commission and Parliament – represent different interests: the Council representing the interests of the Member States, the Commission representing the interests of the EU and the Parliament representing the interests of EU citizens through the political parties. Second, there is no 'government' in the normal sense of that word: rather executive powers are shared between the Council and Commission, and the law-making powers shared by the Commission, Council and Parliament. As a result, the arrangements are governed not so much by the concept of separation of powers but by the concept of 'institutional balance'. This is a dynamic concept which has changed over the years – most notably with the increase in power of the European Parliament, but also in the move away from unanimity in decision-making in Council and towards Qualified Majority Voting.[57]

The principle of institutional balance is both political and legal. The case of **Roquettes Frères SA v Commission** (1976) illustrates the principle, the Court of Justice ruling that the requirement of consultation laid down in the EC Treaty 'represents an essential factor in the institutional balance intended by the Treaty'. The failure to consult resulted in a distortion of balance which would be remedied by declaring the relevant measure void. Institutional balance was also central to the case of **Parliament v Council**, the **Chernobyl** case (1990). In that case, although the (former) EC Treaty did not provide that the European Parliament had the right to challenge acts adopted in breach of the Treaty before the Court of Justice, the Court nevertheless ruled that its duty to ensure that the law is observed entailed the duty to maintain the institutional balance. Accordingly, it ruled that the absence of a right to bring an action was a procedural gap which the Court would not allow to 'prevail over the fundamental interest in the maintenance and observance of the institutional balance laid down in the Treaties . . .'.

Under the Treaty of Lisbon, the institutional balance is altered:

- The European Council is to propose a candidate for election to the Presidency of the Commission. The Parliament elects the President.
- The Parliament acquires the right of co-decision with the Council over a majority of legislative proposals.
- The Parliament's powers over the annual Budget are enhanced.
- Parliament acquires the right to initiate Treaty revision.

The European Council[58]

The year 1974 saw the formalisation of an informal arrangement which had pertained from the 1960s, with a communiqué providing that Heads of Government and their Foreign Ministers would meet at least three times a year to further political co-operation in the development of the Community (now Union). The first official recognition of the communiqué is found in the SEA 1986, which specified the membership of the European Council and reduces the minimum number of annual meetings from three to two. The TEU confirms this arrangement and Article 15 TEU states that:

> The European Council shall provide the Union with the necessary impetus for its development and shall define the general political guidelines thereof . . .

---

57 Which in turn affects the ability of a Member State to obstruct developments. See further below.
58 Not to be confused with the Council of the EU, which comprises Ministers of national governments, or with the Council of Europe (ECHR).

The Heads of Government and Foreign Ministers accordingly meet at least twice a year, together with the President of the Commission, two Members of the Commission and officials. A primary purpose of the meetings is to review economic and social matters such as inflation, economic growth, unemployment, the European monetary system, international political issues, reform of the Common Agricultural Policy and constitutional issues such as applications for membership of the Union and political integration.

The Treaty of Lisbon provides for the election of a President of the European Council by a qualified majority, for a term of two-and-a-half years, renewable once. The President 'shall not' hold national office. The functions of the President of the European Council are defined as:

- chairing Council;
- ensuring the preparation and continuity of the work of the European Council;
- endeavouring to facilitate cohesion and consensus with the European Council;
- reporting to the Parliament after each meeting of the European Council;
- ensuring the representation of the Union on issues concerning its common foreign and security policy.

The Court of Auditors

The Court of Auditors comprises one member from each Member State, appointed under similar terms and conditions to judges of the ECJ. The term of years is six, and Members are under a duty to act completely independently in the performance of their duties and to act in the general interests of the EU. A President of the Court, appointed for a renewable term of three years, heads the Court of Auditors. It is the Court of Auditors which has responsibility for monitoring the expenditure of the EU. It carries out audits, examining the accounts of all revenue and expenditure of the EU. At the end of each financial year, the Court of Auditors is under a duty to draw up an Annual Report which is forwarded to the other institutions of the EU and published, with replies from these institutions, in the *Official Journal of the European Union*.

The Court of Auditors has the full range of legal remedies available to other institutions, thus reinforcing the safeguards which ensure that it is able to perform effectively. The Court of Auditors' task is to assist the European Parliament and the Council in exercising their powers of control over the implementation of the budget. The Court may also submit observations on specific questions and deliver opinions at the request of one of the European institutions.

The Court of Auditors is required to provide the Council and Parliament with a Statement of Assurance relating to the reliability of accounts and the legality of the underlying transactions. In its auditing function, the Court of Auditors may examine records in the European institutions and the Member States. The Court of Auditors examines the accounts of EU revenue and expenditure and considers whether these have been received and incurred in a lawful manner and whether the financial management has been sound. The Court of Auditors is independent and has the power to carry out its audits at any level. In addition to monitoring the internal revenues and expenditure of the Union, the Court of Auditors also monitors co-operation agreements between the European Union and many developing countries, and the system of EU aid to Central and Eastern Europe.

The Economic and Social Committee

The Economic and Social Committee is appointed by the Council, the number of members being based on the populations of Member States. The Member States submit lists of nominees for appointment, and are required to nominate twice as many persons as will be appointed. Members of the Committee are representative of different occupational and social groups. The

Committee has advisory status. The Committee comprises representatives of producers, farmers, carriers, workers, dealers, craftsmen, professional occupations and representatives of the general public.

The Committee provides a forum for representatives of Europe's socio-occupational groups to express their points of view, and thus play a role in the EU's decision-making process. Members of the Committee are nominated by national governments and appointed by the Council for a renewable five-year term of office. The Committee issues advisory documents and opinions. Opinions are forwarded to the Council, Commission and European Parliament and published in the EU's Official Journal.

The Committee of the Regions

The Committee of the Regions comprises representatives of regional and local bodies and has advisory status (Articles 305–307 TFEU). It advises the Council and Commission on education, culture and regional development. The Committee, headed by a Chairman, meets at the request of the Council or Commission, and may also meet on its own initiative. The Committee must be consulted by the Council or the Commission where the Treaty so provides.

The European Investment Bank

Established under the TEU 1992, the European Investment Bank is charged with the task of promoting the 'balanced and steady development of the common market in the interest of the Community (EU)'. The Bank operates on a non-profit making basis, and grants loans and can give guarantees which facilitate the financing of a number of projects, including projects for developing less developed regions, modernising or conversion projects and projects of common interest to several Member States.

The European Court of Justice (ECJ)[59]

The Treaty of Lisbon provides that:[60]

- the Court of Justice of the European Communities is renamed the Court of Justice of the European Union;
- the Court comprises the Court of Justice, the General Court and specialised courts;
- the Court consists of one judge from each Member State;
- the Court has jurisdiction to rule on actions brought by Member States, an institution or a natural or legal person;
- the Court has jurisdiction to give preliminary ruling on the interpretation of Union law or the validity of acts adopted by institutions;
- the Court has jurisdiction where otherwise provided for by the Treaties;
- the Court of Justice has no jurisdiction relating to common Foreign and Security Policy or in relation to operations of the police and other law-enforcement agencies.[61]

On penalties, the Treaty of Lisbon provides that:[62]

59 EC Treaty, Articles 19 TEU, Articles 251–255 TFEU.
60 Treaty of Lisbon, Article 9F.
61 Article 24 TEU.
62 Article 260 TFEU.

- if the Commission considers that a Member State has failed to comply with the judgment of the Court, it 'shall specify', after giving the Member State the opportunity to make observations, the penalty to be paid;
- where a Member State has failed to fulfil its obligations relating to the notification of domestic measures designed to implement a Directive to the Commission, the Commission may specify the penalty to be paid and the Court may impose a penalty not exceeding the amount specified by the Commission.

The judges in the ECJ are appointed by 'common accord of the governments of Member States'. Each state makes one nomination. Unlike superior judges in the United Kingdom, the qualification for appointment to judicial office in the ECJ is that candidates are 'persons whose independence is beyond doubt and who possess the qualifications required for appointment to the highest judicial offices in their respective countries or who are jurisconsults of recognised competence'. Under the Treaty of Lisbon, judges will henceforth be appointed following consultation with a panel responsible for giving an opinion on candidates' suitability. The panel comprises seven persons from among former members of the Court, members of national supreme courts and lawyers of recognised competence. Judges are appointed for a six-year term of office (Article 253 TFEU).

The Court is presided over by a President, who holds office for a three-year term. Assisting the judges are Advocates General. It is the Advocates General who will examine each case and present the legal arguments to the Court for its decision.

Pressure on the ECJ resulted in a Court of First Instance (now called the General Court) being introduced under the SEA 1986. The majority of cases are heard in Chambers comprising three or five judges. The General Court is not empowered to hear and determine questions referred for a preliminary ruling under Article 267 TFEU, on which see further, Chapter 8.

The role of the ECJ is provided for in the most general terms by Article 19 TEU: 'The Court of Justice shall ensure that in the interpretation and application of the Treaties, the law is observed.' At first sight, given that the jurisdiction of the Court is derived solely from the Treaties, this would seem to confine the ECJ to consideration of EU law, a point reinforced by the wording of Article 267 TFEU. In the early days, the Court adopted this narrow interpretation of its jurisdiction and rejected any invitation to draw on the law of Member States in the forming of decisions. From the 1970s at least, a change in attitude can be discerned in the reasoning of the Court. From that time, judges felt able, indeed compelled, to make recourse to domestic law of Member States in order to ensure both the effectiveness of EU law within a particular Member State and to produce harmony between the laws of all Member States. The Court accordingly draws particularly on fundamental concepts existing in the laws of Member States in order to enable common legal concepts to be incorporated into EU law.[63] However, the ECJ can only rule on the interpretation and legality of EU law: it has no power to rule on the domestic laws of Member States. It is the need for uniformity of the law within the legal systems of Member States which represents a major function of the Court. It must also be recognised, however, that in its interpretation of the treaties and pursuit of the uniform application of EU law, the ECJ has proved itself to be extremely creative – the concepts of direct effect, indirect effect, the supremacy of Community (now EU) law and state liability all being 'judge-made'.

63 See Mendelsen, 1981; Dauses, 1985.

Preliminary rulings: Article 267 TFEU[64]

The single most important jurisdiction in terms of ensuring that EU law is uniformly interpreted within national legal systems is that conferred on the Court to give preliminary rulings under Article 267 TFEU. The Court may rule on the interpretation of the Treaty, and on the validity and interpretation of acts of the Institutions of the EU. Article 267 provides that:

> The Court of Justice shall have jurisdiction to give preliminary rulings concerning:
>
> (a) the interpretation of this Treaty;
> (b) the validity and interpretation of acts of the institutions, bodies, offices or agencies of the Union;
>
> Where such a question is raised before any court or tribunal of a Member State that court or tribunal may, if it considers that a decision on the question is necessary to enable it to give judgment, request the Court to give a ruling thereon.
>
> Where any such question is raised in a case pending before a court or tribunal of a Member State against whose decision there is no judicial remedy under national law, that court or tribunal shall bring the matter before the Court.
>
> If such a question is raised in a case pending before a court or tribunal of a Member State with regard to a person in custody, the Court of Justice of the European Union shall act with the minimum of delay.

It is this Article which raises directly the nature of the legal system of the EU and the relationship between EU law, the ECJ and domestic law and the role of judges in national courts. The power to interpret the Treaty gives the ECJ a dynamic function and the ECJ has a role in the creation of law at least as important as the legislative powers of the Council and Parliament. This power, as utilised, is a matter of some controversy with the ECJ, being both criticised and praised for adopting a deliberate policy-making stance which goes beyond that of interpretation of the Treaty.[65]

Article 267 envisages a partnership approach between the domestic courts and the ECJ. It is important both as a matter of principle and as a practical matter that the domestic courts are actively involved in the application of EU law, and that a measure of discretion is left to domestic courts in the matter of referring a matter to the ECJ. It must also be recognised, however, that the discretion left to domestic courts carries with it the potential for a distortion of the meaning of EU law within the different legal systems. A particular difficulty faces the courts in the United Kingdom, whose traditional approach to the interpretation of statutes has been one very much constrained by the detailed wording of statutes and the pedantic literal, golden and mischief rules. By contrast, in civil law systems,[66] the judges are experienced in interpreting broadly phrased statutory provisions, using the teleological interpretative method which seeks the interpretation which most closely fits the objective sought by the legislature, if necessary departing from the literal interpretation.

---

64 See Arnull, 1988b, 1989 and 1990.
65 See Rasmussen, 1988; Slynn, 1984.
66 Defined as those deriving primarily from Roman law.

The Court of Justice considered the duty of a national court to refer a question under the discretionary second paragraph of Article 234 in **R (International Air Transport Association and European Low Fares Airline Association) v Department of Transport** (2006). Where a party had raised questions on the validity of an EU instrument which the court considered arguable and not unfounded, that court had a duty to stay proceedings and refer the matter to the Court of Justice for a preliminary ruling on validity.

Under EC law, both the common law and civil law systems must coexist in a manner which best promotes the harmony of the new legal system created by the Treaties. For harmony to be achieved, it is axiomatic that judges with very differing backgrounds and experience adopt a common approach both to interpretation and to the circumstances under which it is appropriate and necessary to refer a matter to the ECJ for interpretation. In **Kelly v National University of Ireland (University College, Dublin)** (2012), the European Court of Justice (ECJ) considered whether the obligation to make a reference to the ECJ, under Article 267 TFEU, differed in a Member State with an adversarial, rather than an inquisitorial, legal system. The ECJ explained that the preliminary ruling mechanism was one designed to avoid differences in the interpretation of European Union law and to eliminate difficulties in the application of EU law. The reference procedure represents 'direct co-operation' between the Court of Justice and the national courts. In the ECJ's view, it is for the national courts to decide whether an interpretation of EU law by the ECJ is necessary to enable it to reach a decision, and it is also for the national court to decide how to frame the question. In relation to differing legal systems within the EU, whether a system was adversarial or inquisitorial made no difference to the obligation to refer.

In order to understand the relationship between the ECJ and national courts, and the issue of the supremacy of EC (now EU) law, it is first necessary to examine the sources of EC/EU law, and the manner in which EU law comes into effect in domestic law. These issues are discussed in the next chapter.

Under Article 259 TFEU one Member State may bring a fellow Member State before the Court. Again, a procedure is specified which gives the Commission a quasi-judicial function. Before an action is brought before the Court the aggrieved Member State must bring the matter to the attention of the Commission. The Commission must give a reasoned opinion, the Member State having been given the opportunity to make oral and written submissions on the allegation. Once this procedure has been completed, the Member State has a discretion whether or not to bring the matter before the Court. If the Commission fails to deliver its opinion within three months from the date of the allegation, then the aggrieved state may proceed with the action before the Court.

Penalties for failure to comply with rulings of the European Court

Article 260 TFEU provides that, if the ECJ finds that a Member State has failed to fulfil its obligations, the state shall be required to take the necessary measures to comply with the judgment of the Court.

As with Article 259, the Commission plays a role:

If the Commission considers that the Member State concerned has not taken the necessary measures to comply with the judgment of the Court, it may bring the case before the Court after giving that State the opportunity to submit its observations. It shall specify the amount of the lump sum or penalty payment to be paid by the Member State concerned which it considers appropriate in the circumstances.

If the Court finds that the Member State concerned has not complied with its judgment it may impose a lump sum or penalty payment on it.

Actions against EU Institutions

Article 263 TFEU provides the ECJ's jurisdiction to review the legality of acts adopted 'jointly by the European Parliament and the Council, of acts of the Council [and] of the Commission . . .'. Actions may be brought by Member States, the Council, the Commission or the European Parliament on grounds of 'lack of competence, infringement of an essential procedural requirement, infringement of the Treaties or of any rule of law relating to its application, or misuse of powers'. If an action is well founded, the Court may declare the act concerned to be void.[67] It is by these means that the ECJ controls the exercise of powers by the Institutions of the EU.[68]

However, EU law did not impose any obligation on a Member State to bring, for the benefit of one of its citizens, an action against an EU Institution under Article 263 TFEU for annulment of an act adopted by the Institution, or under Article 265 TFEU for failure to act. That did not in principle preclude national law from providing for such an obligation. The Court of Justice so ruled in **Staat der Nederlanden (Ministerie van Landbouw, Natuurbeheer enVisseril) v Ten Kate Holding Musselkanaal BV** (2005).

An action for annulment was undertaken in **Othman v Council and Commission**[69] (2009).[70] The applicant Othman (otherwise known as Abu Qatada), a Jordanian citizen who had lived in the UK since 1993, was arrested and held for investigation under the Prevention of Terrorism (Temporary Provisions) Act 1989. The police seized a substantial sum of money in cash in pounds sterling, German marks, Spanish pesetas and US dollars and the applicant's bank accounts were frozen. Mr Othman was held from October 2002 to March 2005 under the Anti-terrorism, Crime and Security Act 2001, section 23, which authorised indefinite detention without trial of foreign nationals suspected of terrorist activities. In **Othman** the applicant advanced three grounds in support of his claim for annulment. The first alleged infringement of Articles 60 and 301 EC Treaty and misuse of powers; the second alleged breach of fundamental rights as guaranteed by Articles 3 and 8 of the ECHR and of the principles of proportionality and subsidiarity; and the third alleged infringement of the obligation to state reasons. The Court ruled that the Council had not informed the applicant of the evidence adduced against him, and therefore his rights of defence, in particular the right to be heard were not respected. Moreover his right to an effective legal remedy was infringed. The restrictive measures laid down in the contested Regulation constituted an 'unjustified restriction of his right to property'[71] and accordingly the contested Regulation, in so far as it concerned the applicant, must be annulled.

In **Kadi and Al Barakaat International Foundation v Council and Commission** (2008 Regulations relating to the seizure of terrorist funds, and their legality under EU law were challenged. The Court in **Kadi** ruled that respect for property was a general principle of EU law, and that for guidance the court had to take into account Article 1 of the European Convention on Human Rights Protocol which enshrines that right. The question to be asked was whether a freezing measure provided by contested Regulations amounted to 'disproportionate and intolerable interference impairing the very substance of the fundamental right to respect for . . . property'.[72] The Regulation would be annulled. In **Kadi v EU Council** (2011) the ECJ ruled that the Council's response to its former ruling again breached the rights of the defence and therefore the principle of effective judicial protection. The contested Regulation was annulled.

---

67 Article 264 TFEU.
68 See Steiner, 1995, and references therein. See **European Parliament v Council of the European Union** (1999); **Re Cosmetic Products Directive: France v European Parliament, Council** (2005).
69 Case T-318/01; Judgment of Court of First Instance, 11 June 2009.
70 An action for annulment of Regulations Nos 467/2001 and 2062/2001, and as amended No 881/2002, promulgated in response to UN Security Council resolutions.
71 At para 92.
72 At para 357.

A recent example of a challenge by the United Kingdom against a decision of the EU Council is seen in **UK v EU Council** (2011). Under the Schengen Agreement (discussed above at page 149), the United Kingdom participates in relation to police co-operation measures but not provisions relating to the abolition of border checks and movement of persons, including the common visa policy. The Visa Information System (VIS) is aimed at the exchange of visa information between Member States for the purpose of the common visa policy, internal security and combating terrorism. The Republic of Ireland and the United Kingdom wanted direct access to VIS. The Council, however, took the view that the UK was not a participant in relation to the visa provisions and therefore not entitled to access. The UK argued that the correct legal base for the decision was police co-operation rather than the development of a common visa policy. The Court of Justice ruled that Member States who had participated in the Schengen acquis were not obliged to provide adaptation measures for Member States who did not participate. Accordingly the Council did not act unlawfully in deciding to develop the Schengen acquis and exclude the United Kingdom.

Understanding Human Rights in Europe

See Chapter 18.

The Council of Europe was founded in 1949 with the express purpose of protecting individual rights and freedoms. The Council has a membership of some 47 states and is quite separate and distinct from the European Union. It was under the authority of the Council of Europe that the European Convention on Human Rights and Fundamental Freedoms (ECHR) was drafted and implemented. The rights are ultimately interpreted and enforced by the Court of Human Rights and the Committee of Ministers of the Council of Europe.

Accordingly, the European Convention on Human Rights is the principal treaty under which rights and freedoms are protected throughout Europe. However, as the European Community and Union have developed there has emerged a separate, parallel, mechanism for the protection of rights, enforced not by the European Court of Human Rights in Strasbourg, but by the European Court of Justice in Luxembourg. As a result, rights in Europe are protected under domestic law, the law of the ECHR and the law of the EU. This may be portrayed as follows:

The protection of rights and freedoms stems from:

- the domestic (or national) law of Member States;
- the European Convention on Human Rights and Fundamental Freedoms (ECHR);
- the law of the European Union, with specific Treaty articles stipulating rights (eg the right to equal pay etc);
- the EU's Charter of Fundamental Rights and Freedoms;
- the law of the European Union which regards the rights protected under the ECHR as part of the general principles of EU law, and accordingly enforceable by the Court of Justice of the EU (see Article 6(2) TEU).

In order to understand human rights law, therefore, it is necessary to understand the various sources of law and the relationship/interaction between them.

National Law

- All European States which are members of the European Union have written constitutions, with the exception of the United Kingdom. Human rights are a key feature of written constitutions, and all domestic laws must comply with the constitution, as interpreted by the Supreme (Constitutional) Court.

- In the United Kingdom, the protection of human rights and freedoms is effected by ordinary Act of Parliament (for example the Equality Act 2010 and Human Rights Act 1998) and by the common law (judicial decisions).
- With membership of the Council of Europe and the European Union, domestic laws must conform to the requirements of the European Convention on Human Rights and European Union law.

The Council of Europe

- All Member States of the EU are members (High Contracting Parties) of the Council of Europe, membership of which is a condition of membership of the EU.
- The European Convention on Human Rights, promulgated by the Council of Europe, sets out the civil and political rights which all European states are obliged to respect and protect.

The European Union

- The European Union is founded on respect for the rights set out in the European Convention on Human Rights (Article 6(2) Treaty on European Union 1992), which provides that:

  > The Union shall respect fundamental rights, as guaranteed by the European Convention for the Protection of Human Rights and Fundamental Freedoms signed in Rome on 4 November 1950 and as they result from the constitutional traditions common to the Member States, as general principles of Community law.

- Specific rights are provided for in the Treaties, for example the right to equal pay and equal treatment in employment (Article 157 TFEU).
- Under the Lisbon Treaty 2007, the Charter of Fundamental Rights and Freedoms, which covers civil and political and economic and social rights, comes into effect. Note that the United Kingdom has opted out of the Charter.
- The Court of Justice of the EU (ECJ) does not have jurisdiction to rule on rights protected by the national law of Member States or the ECHR. However the ECJ has – through its case law – incorporated into EU law those fundamental rights and freedoms which are common to Member States (see for example **Internationale Handelsgesellschaft** 1970; **Simmanthal** 1979; **Kadi** (2008); **FIAMM** (2008)).

It is inevitable that situations will arise where the relationship between the Charter and the ECHR falls for consideration, particularly since the Lisbon Treaty provides for the EU to become a signatory to the ECHR.[73]

The original Treaties made no explicit reference to the protection of individual rights in their entirety, although Treaty articles such as Article 141 EC provide for equal treatment of

---

73 An early example of a case concerning rights under EC law and the ECHR was **Bosphorus Hava Yollari Turizm ve Ticaret AS v Minister for Transport, Energy and Communications** (1996).

men and women in matters of employment. The manner in which the ECJ has developed the jurisprudence on rights is linked inextricably with its insistence on the supremacy of Community law over the domestic law of Member States. In 1969, the ECJ turned its attention specifically to the status of fundamental individual rights in relation to the principles of Community law. In **Stauder v City of Ulm** (1969), the ECJ stated that it had a duty to protect the rights of individuals as provided for by the constitution of the Member State, and that such provisions formed part of the general principles of Community law. **Internationale Handelsgesellschaft mbH v EVST** (1970) clarified the relationship between domestic constitutional law and Community law in the protection of rights. The ECJ expressed its opinion that respect for fundamental rights 'forms an integral part of the general principles of law protected by the Court of Justice. The protection of such rights, whilst inspired by the constitutional traditions common to the Member States, must be ensured within the framework of the structures and objectives of the Community'.[74] In **Nold v Commission** (1974), a case concerning a person's status as a wholesaler, the ECJ ruled that, consistent with its earlier judgment in **Internationale Handelsgesellschaft**, constitutional rights protected under Member States' constitutions must be respected, but also declared that 'international treaties for the protection of human rights' can 'supply guidelines which should be followed within the framework of Community law' (para 13). The German Constitutional Court has been reluctant to concede jurisdiction over fundamental rights to the ECJ.[75]

On a piecemeal, case-by-case basis, the ECJ has gradually and steadily incorporated the protection of individual rights into its case law. However, while all Member States of the Union are signatories to the ECHR, the Union is not a party to the ECHR, and the relationship between the Union and ECHR remains indistinct. The ECJ accepts the significance of the ECHR, and regards the ECHR provisions as part of the general principles of EU law. Once the EU accedes to the ECHR as envisaged by the Treaty of Lisbon, the ECHR will become a central, integral part of EU law.[76]

The Treaty of Amsterdam 1997, reiterating the fundamental commitment of the Union to human rights and fundamental freedoms, introduced the power to issue penalties to Member States who are in breach of rights. Aware of the potential problems entailed in the enlargement of the Union, the Treaty provides for a penalty falling short of expulsion from the Union, a penalty which itself could undermine the protection of rights of that Member State's citizens. The principle of respect for human rights is also binding on Member States when acting within the scope of EU law, namely when implementing a EU measure,[77] or seeking to derogate from a fundamental freedom.[78]

The Charter of Fundamental Rights

The European Union's Charter of Fundamental Rights originated in 2000. It was not enshrined in the Treaties, and its legal status was in doubt. The (failed) Constitutional Treaty of 2004 would have incorporated the Charter and thus given it legal effect. This has now been achieved under the Treaty of Lisbon, which declares that the Charter will have 'legally binding value'. The Charter does not replace either the human rights laws of Member States or the ECHR, but rather reinforces the EU's commitment to the protection of individual rights.

---

74 See also **Nold v Commission** (1974).
75 See, in particular, Sadurski, Wojciech, 'Solange, chapter 3: Constitutional Courts in Central Europe – Democracy – European Union' (2008) 14 European Law Journal 1.
76 On this see Schermers, 1990 and 1987 and Dremczewski, 1981.
77 **Wauchauf v Bundescourt für Ernährung und Fortwistschalt** (1989).
78 **ERT v Dimotiki** (1991).

The Charter contains civil, economic, political and social rights which must be respected by the institutions of the EU and by Member States when implementing EU law. Because of its potentially wide-ranging implications, the Czech Republic, Poland and the United Kingdom have negotiated exemptions from the Charter, creating uncertainty regarding the uniform application of EU law throughout the European Union.

The Treaty of Lisbon gives effect to the EU's Charter of Fundamental Rights. A Protocol to the Treaty provides that the Court of Justice has no power to find the laws, regulations or administration of Poland or the United Kingdom inconsistent with the Charter. Moreover, the Charter provides no new justiciable rights in Poland or the United Kingdom.[79]

Summary

The origins of the European Union lie in the treaties establishing the European Coal and Steel Community (the Treaty of Paris 1951), the Atomic Energy Community and the European Economic Community (the Treaty of Rome 1957). Originally having six Member States, the European Union how has a membership of 27 States.

Under the treaties there are now five principal institutions:[80]

- the European Council, headed by a President and having a High Representative for Foreign Affairs;
- the Council (formerly known as the Council of Ministers), representing the interests of Member States;
- the European Commission (independent of nominating governments and representing the interests of the EU);
- the European Parliament, directly elected and representing the interests of the citizens of Europe;
- the Court of Justice of the European Union, the highest court in the Union with the task of interpreting and applying European Union law.

The European Union (EU) came into being in 1993 with the Treaty on European Union (the Maastricht Treaty). With the expansion in membership, the organisation of the EU required adaptation. The Treaty of Lisbon 2007, ratified in 2009, effects this. The two principal Treaties are now the Treaty on European Union and the Treaty on the Functioning of the European Union, which replaces the EC Treaty.

Under the European Union Act 2011 any further transfer of law-making powers (competence) to the EU or revision of the EU Treaties must be approved by both an Act of Parliament and a referendum of the people. The Act also reaffirms the doctrine of parliamentary sovereignty in relation to the EU by making clear that directly applicable and directly effective EU law takes effect in the United Kingdom by virtue of an Act of Parliament (the European Communities Act 1972).

---

79 Protocol, Articles 1 and 2.
80 Other institutions include the Court of Auditors, the European Ombudsman, specialist institutions such as the Economic and Social Committee.

Further Reading

Birkinshaw, P. (2005) 'Constitutions, Constitutionalism and the State', 11 European Public Law, 31.

Craig, P. (2011) 'Britain in the European Union' in J. Jowell and D. Oliver (eds) *The Changing Constitution* (7th edn), Oxford: OUP.

Craig, P. (2008) 'The Treaty of Lisbon, Process, Architecture and Substance', 33 EL Rev 137.

Dougan, M. (2008) 'The Treaty of Lisbon 2007: Winning Minds, Not Hearts', 45 CML Rev 617.

Doukas, D. (2009) 'The Verdict of the German Federal Constitutional Court on the Lisbon Treaty: Not Guilty, but don't do it again', 34 EL Rev 866.

Harlow, C. (2003) 'European Governance and Accountability' in M. Bamforth and P. Leyland (eds) *Public Law in a Multi-Layered Constitution*, Oxford: Hart Publishing.

Harlow, C. and Rawlings, R. (2006) 'Accountability and law enforcement: the centralised EU infringement procedure', 31 EL Rev 447, 226 and 228 EC.

Lenaerts, K. (2007) 'The Rule of Law and the Coherence of the Judicial System of the EU', Common Market Law Review, 44.6: 1625.

Peers, S. (2008) 'Finally "Fit for Purpose"? The Treaty of Lisbon and the End of the Third Pillar Legal Order', 27 Yearbook European Law 47.

Rasmujssen, H. (2007) 'Present and future European Judicial Problems after Enlargement and the Post-2005 Ideological Revolt', Common Market Law Review, 44.6: 1661.

Sadurski, W. (2008) 'Solange, chapter 3: Constitutional Courts in Central Europe – Democracy – European Union', 14 European Law Journal 1.

Schutze, R. (2006) 'Cooperative federalism constitutionalised: the emergence of complementary competences in the EU legal order', 31 EL Rev 167.

Schutze, R. (2010) 'From Rome to Lisbon: "Executive Federalism" in the (new) European Union', 47 Common Market Law Review 1385.

Shaw, J. (2005) 'Europe's Constitutional Future', Public Law, 132.

Snyder F. (Editorial) (2005) 'Enhancing EU Democracy, Constituting the EU', 11(2) ELJ 131.

Somek, A. (2007) 'Postconstitutional Treaty', German Law Journal 8: 1121.

Walker N. (2005) 'European Constitutionalism and European Integration, Public Law, 266.

Chapter 8

European Union Law and National Law

Chapter Contents

Introduction

Having examined the structure, institutions and law-making process of the European Union, it is now necessary to turn attention to the forms of EU law and the interaction between EU law and domestic law.

With the membership of the European Union now at 28 Member States, the task of ensuring that the law is interpreted and applied in a uniform manner is complex. The differing forms of law – principally Treaty Articles, Regulations and Directives – have differing effects and leave to the Member States differing degrees of discretion relating to their implementation. For the law to be uniform it is essential that the domestic courts work in partnership with the European Court of Justice (ECJ) and that – where necessary – the domestic courts can seek the advice of the ECJ on the correct interpretation of the law. It will be seen that the ECJ has, since the 1960s, insisted on the supremacy of EU law over domestic law. From the Court's point of view, what has been created is nothing less than a new legal order: a *supranational* organisation which imposes legal duties on Member States and creates enforceable legal rights for citizens. In order to achieve this supremacy the Court insists that Member States have, in signing the Treaties, surrendered or transferred part of their sovereign law-making powers over matters governed by the Treaties to the Institutions of the EU. Furthermore the Court, in its role as 'guardian of the Treaties', has to ensure that EU law is given priority over domestic law.

Sources of EU Law

Primary and secondary sources

Every act and decision of the EU must have a basis in law, and if there is no such base a decision or provision will be annulled by the European Court of Justice.[1] The primary sources of EU law are the Treaties, as amended. Secondary legislation is law made by the EU Institutions, and includes the interpretation of both primary and secondary sources by the European Court of Justice (ECJ). Secondary legislation comprises regulations, directives and decisions. Article 288 of the Treaty on the Functioning of the European Union (TFEU) defines these terms as follows:

> To exercise the Union's competences, the institutions shall adopt regulations, directives, decisions, recommendations and opinions.
>
> - a regulation shall have general application. It shall be binding in its entirety and directly applicable in all Member States;
> - a directive shall be binding, as to the result to be achieved, upon each Member State to which it is addressed, but shall leave to the national authorities the choice of form or methods;
> - a decision shall be binding in its entirety. A decision which specifies those to whom it is addressed shall be binding only on them;
> - recommendations and opinions shall have no binding force.

It is clear from Article 288 TFEU that regulations and directives have 'binding effect' in all Member States, but, as discussed below, this takes different forms. Decisions and recommendations, on the other hand, have more limited effect, the former binding those to whom they are addressed, the latter having 'no binding force'. There are, however, other 'sources' which, while not having legally binding force, nevertheless have a significant impact on the working

---

1 See **European Commission v European Council** (2010).

of the Union. The Institutions of the Union, for example, formulate their own procedures for self-regulation. As will be seen below, the Council has the power to enter into international agreements between the Union and non-EU states on behalf of the Member States of the Union. In addition, there are measures which are labelled 'soft' (as opposed to 'hard') law. As well as recommendations and opinions under Article 288, Jo Shaw (2000) cites 'communications, conclusions, declarations, action programmes and communiqués' as examples of soft law. Joint actions taken by Member States in pursuit of Union objectives also fall within soft law.[2] While the principal concern in this chapter is with the 'hard law' of the EU, it must also be recognised that these disparate mechanisms exist in order to further European objectives across wide ranging fields of policy on which it may not be possible always to secure complete agreement between all Member States which would enable the translation of a soft law measure into hard law with binding legal effect.

Direct Applicability and Direct Effect[3,4]

> Direct applicability: an EU provision/measure is automatically legally effective from the relevant date, without any legislative action on the part of the Member State's legislature.
>
> Direct effect: an EU provision automatically confers legal rights on individuals which are enforceable against the Member State government and other bodies. Direct effect may be vertical or horizontal (see below). Where a provision does not have direct effect, it may be indirectly effective as a result of a national court's duty to interpret law in a manner which gives effect to EU law.

As can be seen from the text of Article 288 TFEU, a regulation is 'binding in its entirety' and has direct applicability. By 'direct applicability' it is meant that the measure leaves no discretion to the Member States but, rather, confers rights and duties within the Member States without further legislative participation. In other words, the provision is self-executing. On the other hand, a directive, whilst binding in its objective, leaves the Member State some leeway in its introduction and the manner in which a Member State implements and achieves the objectives set by the Council, Commission and European Parliament.

In order to understand the way in which EU law operates within Member States' legal systems, the principle of direct effect must be examined. The basic principle of direct effect of EU measures is that individuals may invoke certain provisions as conferring direct rights, which may be relied on in the national courts. While Article 288 TFEU states specifically that regulations are directly applicable, the Article is silent as to the legal *consequence* of this applicability, and as to whether a Treaty provision itself, or regulations or directives, can have direct legal effect on individuals.[5]

The principle of direct effect is linked to the principle of 'loyal cooperation' or 'fidelity' enshrined in Article 4.3 TEU (formerly Article 10 EC) which provides, in part, that:

---

2 The Court of Justice has ruled that the principle that national law must be interpreted in line with EU law applies as much to framework decisions as to other sources: **Criminal Proceedings against Pupino** (2005).

3 See, *inter alia*, Steiner, 1993; Ross, 1993.

4 The two terms are used synonymously by the ECJ. See Winter, 1972; Eleftheriadis, 1996.

5 See **Consorzio del Prosciutto di Parma v Asda Food Stores Ltd** (1999), in which the Court of Appeal ruled that a regulation did not have direct effect, *inter alia*, since it was not sufficiently clear and precise and itself indicated that it was not intended to have direct effect.

> Pursuant to the principle of sincere cooperation, the Union and the Member States shall, in full mutual respect, assist each other in carrying out tasks which flow from the Treaties.
>
> The Member States shall take any appropriate measure, general or particular, to ensure fulfilment of the obligations arising out of the Treaties or resulting from the acts of the institutions of the Union.
>
> The Member States shall facilitate the achievement of the Union's tasks and refrain from any measure which could jeopardise the attainment of the Union's objectives.

As can be seen from Article 4.3 TEU, Member States are under a legal duty both to take action to ensure compliance with EU law and to refrain from any action which might impede the application and effectiveness of EU law. Article 4.3 TEU forms the basis of much of the jurisprudence of the ECJ, and the foundation for the enforcement of individual rights against Member States.

Direct effect and Treaty (TFEU) provisions

In 1963, the ECJ articulated the theoretical basis for the principle of direct effect in **Van Gend en Loos** (1963), a case which involved a reference to the ECJ from the Dutch courts. From this case many significant later developments of EU law can be seen to originate. Under Article 25 of the EC Treaty (formerly Article 12 EEC Treaty; now Article 30 TFEU):

> Customs duties on imports and exports and charges having equivalent effect shall be prohibited between Member States. This prohibition shall also apply to customs duties of a fiscal nature.

Before 1958, and the coming into force of the EEC Treaty, the Dutch firm of Van Gend en Loos had been importing glue from Germany, applying a customs duty of 3 per cent. In 1959, the Dutch government ratified an agreement with other countries establishing an 8 per cent duty. The company protested to the Customs Court, relying on the direct effect of Article 12 of the EEC Treaty. The Court referred the matter to the ECJ. The principal question for the court was whether, as claimed, Article 12 had direct effect on the legal position of the company. The Treaty Article did not stipulate its legal effect, and Article 189 of the EEC Treaty (later Article 249, now Article 288 TFEU) refers only to regulations having direct applicability. The ECJ held that if a Treaty provision is to confer individual enforceable rights, it must:

(a)   indicate that it applies not just to Member States but also to individuals within the state;
(b)   be clear and precise;
(c)   be unconditional and unqualified and not subject to any further measures on the part of Member States;
(d)   be one which does not leave any substantial latitude or discretion to Member States.

Specifically in relation to Article 12, as it then was, the ECJ held that the text was clear and unconditional, that it required no legislative intervention by the Member State and that the Member State had no power to subordinate Article 12 to its own law. Thus, it can be seen that both provisions in the Treaty and regulations are capable of having direct effect if they satisfy the requirements laid down by the ECJ.

The principle of direct effect of Treaty provisions was examined by the House of Lords and the ECJ in **Henn and Darby v Director of Public Prosecutions** (1981). In that case, the accused defended a criminal prosecution on the basis that the subject matter of the charge offended against Treaty provisions. The accused were charged with conspiracy to import obscene materials contrary to the law of the United Kingdom. Article 28 of the EC Treaty (now Article 34 TFEU), however, prohibits quantitative restrictions on imports. The ECJ ruled that English law infringed Article 28 (now Article 34 TFEU) but that lawful restrictions on pornography could be imposed by a Member State under Article 30 of the EC Treaty (now Article 36 TFEU), which provides that restrictions on imports otherwise contrary to Article 30 are justified on the grounds of, *inter alia*, public morality, public policy or public security. Accordingly, the prosecution was able to proceed, but the point was established that the defendants could raise the direct effect of Article 28 (now Article 34 TFEU) in their defence.[6]

Regulations and direct effect

It was noted above that Article 288 TFEU provides, in part, that a Regulation shall 'be binding in its entirety' and 'directly applicable in all Member States'. The Regulation becomes directly applicable in domestic law from the date on which it is brought into force. Any domestic legislation which is needed to bring it into effect may not obstruct or change the Regulation. The clear wording of Article 288 suggests that Regulations should have direct effect and that individuals can rely on the Regulation and have it enforced in his or her domestic courts. In *Commission v Italy* (1973)[7] the Court of Justice confirmed this view: Regulations – provided that they are sufficiently precise, clear and unconditional – have direct effect, stating that:

> . . . it cannot be accepted that a Member State should apply in an incomplete or selective manner provisions of a Community (now EU) Regulation so as to render abortive certain aspects of Community (now EU) legislation which it has opposed or which it considers contrary to its national interests.

Directives and direct effect[8]

A further question which arises is whether directives are similarly capable of having direct effect. It has been seen from Article 288 TFEU that directives leave no discretion as to their objectives, but do leave some discretion as to manner of implementation. Nevertheless, the ECJ has found provisions of directives to be capable of having direct effect. The reasoning of the ECJ is revealed in **Van Duyn v Home Office** (1975). Article 45 TFEU provides (in part) that:

1. Freedom of movement for workers shall be secured within the Union.
2. Such freedom of movement shall entail the abolition of any discrimination based on nationality . . . as regards employment, remuneration and other conditions of work and employment.
3. It shall entail the right, subject to limitations justified on grounds of public policy, public security and public health to accept offers of employment . . .

Yvonne Van Duyn, a Dutch national, arrived in England in May 1973, having accepted a job as a secretary with the Church of Scientology. Immigration Officials refused Ms Van Duyn admission

---

6 See also **Erich Ciola v Land Vorarlberg** (1999).
7 For Index of Cases: Case 39/72, [1973] ECR 101.
8 See Craig, 1997.

to the United Kingdom on the basis that the Secretary of State considered employment with the Church undesirable. In an action against the Home Office, Ms Van Duyn sought to rely on Article 48 of the EEC Treaty (now Article 45 TFEU) and a reference was made to the ECJ.

The directive in question was that of the Council[9] which set out the objective of co-ordinating measures concerning movement and residence. The public policy issue, relied on by the Home Office, was then regulated by Article 3(1) of Directive 64/221, which stipulated that: '. . . measures taken on grounds of public policy and public security shall be based exclusively on the personal conduct of the individual concerned.' The ECJ held that since the directive laid down an obligation which was not subject to any exception or condition, and by its nature did not require intervention on the part of the Community or Member States, it followed that the directive was to be regarded as directly effective and conferred enforceable individual rights which national courts must protect.

Thus, it can be seen that, in some cases, directives, as well as regulations and Treaty provisions, may have direct effect – depending on their wording and clarity and whether or not Member State action is required as a prerequisite to implementation. The deadline for implementation of the directive must, however, have passed.[10] Where a directive is not precise, and a right insufficiently defined, it will not have direct effect.[11] Note that in the period allowed for the implementation of a directive, a Member State must not take any action which would frustrate or undermine the objective sought by the Directive: **Inter-Environnement Wallonie** (1997).

Vertical and horizontal effect of EU law

The concept of direct effect utilises the concepts of vertical and horizontal effect of legal provisions. In essence, the concept of vertical effect means that a measure – whether a Treaty provision, regulation or directive (depending on whether the qualifying criteria are met) – is directly enforceable by an individual against the Member State and its institutions. In other words, the rights conferred and obligations imposed are enforceable at the suit of an individual against his or her own Member State and its agents, which are responsible for giving effect to the provision. For example, in **Van Duyn v The Home Office** (above), the citizen was challenging the decision of a government minister: the action was thus vertical in nature and the directive could be invoked. Of greater difficulty is the question of whether an enforceable obligation exists which entitles an individual to pursue his or her rights, not directly against the Member State and its agencies but horizontally against private institutions, organisations or individuals other than the government of the state and public bodies.

With vertical effect, the law imposes a duty on the Member State to comply and confers an enforceable right on the citizen. The Member State is thus responsible to the citizen for the enforcement of his or her rights under EU law. Directives enjoy vertical, but not horizontal, effect and can only be invoked against the state and emanations of the state. The ECJ denies the possibility of horizontal direct effect of directives,[12] which would extend the liability for failure to comply with EU law requirements to non-state bodies or individuals. However, the concept of indirect effect (on which, see below) of directives complicates this theoretically straightforward position. Under the concept of indirect effect, the ECJ insists that national courts as public bodies have a duty to interpret national law in a manner consistent with EU directives so far as possible. This doctrine applies even in actions between two individuals, and

---

9 64/221/EEC, Article 3.
10 See **Pubblico Ministero v Ratti** (1979).
11 See **Gibson v East Riding of Yorkshire Council** (2000).
12 See **Marshall v Southampton and SW Hampshire AHA** (1986); **Faccini Dori** (1994).

regardless of whether the directive or national law is earlier in time. Where indirect effect applies, therefore, a directive appears to have been given horizontal effect.

In securing the uniformity of the application of EU law within Member States, the ECJ has utilised Article 10 EC (now Article 4.3 TEU) to great effect. National courts are required to interpret all national law in light of EU law, and that duty exists irrespective of whether a measure has direct effect.

In **Defrenne v SABENA** (1978), the ECJ confirmed the principle of horizontal direct effect of Treaty provisions. Gabrielle Defrenne, an air hostess with the Belgian airline SABENA, was required, under her contract of employment, to retire at the age of 40, whereas men did not have to retire at that age. Moreover, she was paid less than male employees, and would receive a smaller state pension than men. The state pension question went to the ECJ, which ruled that Article 119 of the EEC Treaty (now Article 157 TFEU) did not cover state pension rights.[13] Ms Defrenne then commenced actions against her employer, on the issue of equal pay and on the discriminatory retirement ages. In relation to the question of equal pay (but not retirement age), the action was successful.[14] The matter was referred to the ECJ, which ruled that Member States were obliged to implement Article 119 EEC by the end of a transitional period, and that the principle of direct effect of the Article entitled individuals to rely on Article 119 EEC, against both public and private sector employers, even where the provisions implementing the principle of equal pay had not been implemented by the state.

The question of whether a directive could be relied on by individuals against employers was tested in the English courts in **Marshall v Southampton and South West Hampshire Area Health Authority** (1986). The Sex Discrimination Act 1975 enabled differing retirement ages to be fixed for men and women. Mrs Marshall challenged the legality of the requirement for women to retire at the age of 60, alleging that the Act was contrary to the European Community's Equal Treatment Directive.[15] Two issues, therefore, fell for consideration by the court. First, were different retirement ages in breach of the directive and, second, if so, could an individual rely on the directive to challenge an Area Health Authority? In other words, the issue was whether the directive was directly effective against an employer in its contractual relationship with an employee or, alternatively, whether the Area Health Authority was an 'emanation of the state'. An Area Health Authority was deemed to be a public (as opposed to a private) body, and accordingly bound by EU law. The ECJ made clear that in principle a directive could not, of itself, create obligations for non-state actors.

In **Foster v British Gas plc** (1991), however, which also entailed differing retirement ages for employees, the Court of Appeal had held that British Gas, a statutory corporation, was not a public body against whom the directive could be enforced. The House of Lords sought clarification on this issue from the ECJ. The ECJ refused to accept British Gas's argument that there was a distinction between a nationalised undertaking and a state agency and ruled that a directive might be relied on against organisations or bodies which were 'subject to the authority or control of the state or had special powers beyond those which result from the normal relations between individuals'. The Court accordingly ruled that a directive might be invoked against 'a body, whatever its legal form, which has been made responsible, pursuant to a measure adopted by the state, for providing a public service under the control of the state and has for that purpose special powers beyond those which result from the normal rules applicable in relations between individuals'. Therefore, British Gas was a public body against which a directive might be enforced, a ruling which the House of Lords subsequently accepted. In

---

13 **Defrenne v Belgian State** (1971). See now State Social Security Directive 79/7/EEC.
14 **Defrenne v SABENA** (1978).
15 Directive 76/207/EEC.

Doughty v Rolls Royce plc (1992), however, the Court of Appeal distinguished *Foster* and held that Rolls-Royce plc, although 'under the control of the state', had not been 'made responsible pursuant to a measure adopted by the state for providing a public service'. Rolls-Royce was at the time a nationalised body, responsible for providing defence equipment. However, the court distinguished between services for the public and services provided to the state, and thereby ruled Rolls-Royce not to be a public body for the purposes of the effectiveness of directives. A different result was reached by the Court of Appeal in **National Union of Teachers v Governing Body of St Mary's Church of England (Aided) Junior School** (1997). The court ruled that the governors of a voluntary aided school who had chosen to enter it into the state system were a public body. The powers and duties the Secretary of State for Education and the local education authority amounted to control of the school while it remained in the state system.

The ECJ, in **Faccini Dori v Recreb srl** (1994), re-examined the principle of the horizontal effect of directives. An EC consumer directive,[16] which had not yet been implemented by the Italian authorities, founded a claim against a private undertaking. The Advocate General argued that the ECJ should extend the principle of direct effect of directives to claims against all parties (irrespective of their public or private nature). The ECJ declined to do this, and reasserted its view that directives could not be invoked directly against private bodies. However, the ECJ referred to the possibility that directives could be deemed to be indirectly effective and also that they might be enforceable via the principle of state liability to give effect to Community measures, as seen in **Francovich and Bonifaci v Italy** (1992) (on which, see below).

In relation to directives, the ECJ has ruled that these can, at best, have vertical effect against an emanation of the state – as laid down in **Marshall v Southampton Area Health Authority (No 1)** and subsequently confirmed, as in **Faccini Dori v Recreb srl** (1994) – and not horizontal effect. The role of directives in ensuring the harmonisation and approximation of laws within the legal systems of the Member States of the Union, and the manner in which direct effect ensures harmonisation, is illustrated by the case of **CIA Security International SA v Signalson SA and Securitel SPRL** (1996),[17] which also has significant implications on the direct effect of directives. Involved in this case was the interpretation of Article 28 of the EC Treaty (now Article 34 TFEU) (free movement of goods) and of Directive 83/189/EEC.

Articles 8 and 9 of Directive 83/189 lay down procedures for the provision of information in the field of technical standards and regulations. Under these provisions, Member States must notify the Commission of all draft technical regulations, and, except in particularly urgent cases, suspend their adoption and implementation for specified periods until the requirement of notification has been complied with. The provisions are unconditional and sufficiently precise in terms of their content to have direct effect and so enable an individual to rely on them before a national court, which must decline to apply a national technical regulation which has not been notified in advance in accordance with the directive. The purpose of making such regulations inapplicable is in order to ensure the effectiveness of EU control for which the directive is made. The ECJ ruled that:

It is settled law that, wherever provisions of a directive appear to be, from the point of view of their content, unconditional and sufficiently precise, they may be relied on against any national provision which is not in accordance with the directive. [judgment, para 42]

16 85/577/EC.
17 See Slot, 1996; Coppel, 1997.

This decision appears to undermine the clear rule against the horizontal effect of directives as expressed in **Faccini Dori**.[18]

The principle of indirect effect

Whereas the principle of direct effect entails rights which are directly enforceable against the Member State or an emanation of the state, indirect effect provides a more subtle mechanism for ensuring compliance with EU law. Indirect effect involves the application of the duty imposed on Member States, including courts of law under Article 4.3 TEU discussed above.

In **Von Colson v Land Nordrhein-Westfalen** (1984), Article 5 of the EEC Treaty (now Article 4.3 TEU) and the Equal Treatment Directive 76/207 fell for consideration by the ECJ. Ms Von Colson's application for employment in the prison service was rejected. The rejection was based on gender, and was justifiable according to the German court. Under German law, the only compensation payable to Ms Von Colson was her travelling expenses. The question arose as to whether such compensation gave effect to the requirements of Article 5, as it then was. On a reference, the ECJ examined Article 5 of EEC Treaty (now Article 4.3 TEU). The ECJ ruled that Article 5 imposed a duty not just on the governments of Member States, but on all national authorities, including the courts. It is therefore the duty of the domestic courts to interpret national law in such a way as to ensure that the obligations imposed by EC law are achieved. The result is that, although a provision is not directly effective, it may be applied indirectly as law by means of interpretation.[19]

The question of the relationship between domestic law and subsequently introduced EU law came before the ECJ in **Marleasing SA v La Comercial Internacional de Alimentacion SA** (1992).[20] The ECJ had ruled that, whereas a directive cannot of itself impose obligations on private parties, national courts must as far as possible interpret national law in order to achieve a result pursued by a directive, and that this must be done whether the national provisions in question were adopted before or after the directive. In **Marleasing**, no legislation had been passed to comply with the directive: the duty was nevertheless on the courts to give effect to the **Von Colson** principle, that is to say, the court must interpret domestic law in accordance with EU law. This principle enables directives to have horizontal effect 'by the back door'. A gap in protection, however, still remained. Where there was no domestic law on an EU matter and where, as a result, there was no domestic provision to construe in line with EU law, a problem would remain. The ECJ reaffirmed the interpretative duty in **Centrosteel Srl v Adipol GmbH** (2000), in which the Court stated that it was well settled that 'in the absence of proper transposition into national law, a directive cannot of itself impose obligations on individuals'. However, it went on to state that: '. . . when applying national law, whether adopted before or after the directive, the national court that has to interpret that law must do so, as far as possible, in the light of the wording and the purpose of the directive so as to achieve the result it has in view . . .'[21]

The liability of the state

As seen above, Article 4.3 TEU imposes an obligation on Member States to facilitate and not to impede the objectives of the European Union. Where a Member State has failed to undertake

---

18 See also **Unilever Italia v Central Food** (2000).
19 See Drake, 2005.
20 See also **Criminal Proceedings Against Arcaro** (1997); and **Perceval-Price v Department of Economic Development** (2000).
21 In **Aannemersbedrijf PK Kraaijeveld BV ea v Gedeputeerde Staten van Zuid-Holland** (1996) and **World Wildlife Fund (WWF) v Autonome Provinz Bozen** (2000) the ECJ considered the question of whether directives could be invoked by individuals in their national courts in the context of judicial review applications, and accepted that this could be the case, without enquiring into their capacity for direct effect. The implication of this is that directives may have an effect distinct from direct effect, which is labelled the 'public law effect'. See Scott, 1998, pp 123, 157.

its duty, the concept of state liability arises. In **Francovich and Bonifaci v Italy** (1991), employees were seeking compensation against Italy for failure to implement a directive which was designed to guarantee the payment of arrears of wages to employees in the event of their employer's insolvency. The time limit set down for implementation of the directive had expired and, as a result, Italy was held to be in breach of its EC obligations under Article 5 EEC Treaty (now Article 4.3 TEU).[22]

The ECJ held that, while the directive was not sufficiently clear to be directly effective against the state, as regards the identity of institutions responsible for payments, Italy was under an obligation to implement the directive under Article 5 of the EEC Treaty. Accordingly, since Italy had failed in its obligation, it was under a duty to compensate individuals for damage suffered as a result of its failure.[23] The ECJ laid down three conditions which applied to the issue of compensation for loss, namely that:

(a)   the directive confers individual rights;
(b)   the content of those rights can be identified on the basis of the provisions of the directive; and
(c)   there is a causal link between the state's failure and the damage suffered by individuals affected.[24]

Under such conditions, an individual may proceed directly against the state. Accordingly, the importance of the principle of direct effect diminishes, and liability falls not on the employer – whether public or private – but on the state, by virtue of its obligations under the Treaty.

However, many questions remained unanswered. Was the state liable only for failure to implement the directive? Was the state liable, irrespective of whether there was any fault involved on the part of the state? Furthermore, was the state liable for loss incurred prior to the ECJ finding the Member State in breach of its obligations? What form of compensation is recoverable? Does it include loss of profits? Is compensation confined to economic loss?

In **Brasserie du Pêcheur SA v Federal Republic of Germany** (1996)[25] and **R v Secretary of State for Transport ex parte Factortame Ltd (No 4)** (1996), the ECJ ruled on the principles which regulate the grant of compensation to bodies suffering damage as a result of Member States' breach of EU law. Member States are obliged to make good the loss suffered by individuals when:

●   the national legislature, executive or judiciary is responsible for the breach;
●   the rule of law breached is intended to confer rights on individuals;
●   the breach is sufficiently serious, defined as a manifest and grave disregard of the limits on the Member State's discretion; and
●   there is a direct causal link between the breach of the obligation and the damage suffered.

As to the degree of seriousness of the breach, the considerations to be taken into account by the court considering the issue of compensation, as stipulated by the ECJ, are:

> . . . the clarity and precision of the rule breached; the measure of discretion left by
> that rule . . .; whether the infringement and the damage caused was intentional or

---

22 See **Gibson v East Riding of Yorkshire DC** (1999).
23 Cf **Evans v Motor Insurers Bureau** (1999).
24 See also **Marks & Spencer plc v Customs and Excise Commissioners (No 1)** (2000); and **R v Durham County Council ex parte Huddleston** (2000).
25 For the development of this case, see **R v Secretary of State for Transport ex parte Factortame Ltd (No 1)** (1989); **(No 2)** (1991); **(No 3)** (1992); **(No 5)** (2000).

involuntary; whether any error of law was excusable or inexcusable; the fact that the position taken by a Community institution may have contributed towards the omission, and the adoption or retention of national measures or practices contrary to Community law.

On any view, a breach of Community law will clearly be sufficiently serious if it has persisted despite a judgment finding the infringement in question to be established, or a preliminary ruling or settled case law of the court on the matter from which it is clear that the conduct in question constituted an infringement. [*Ex parte Factortame (No 4)* (1996)]

Note that **Brasserie** and **Factortame** concerned loss suffered as a result of breaches of Treaty provisions that are directly effective. In other words, the scope of state liability is neither limited to the failure to implement directives nor to the absence of direct effect. Member States must compensate individuals at a level which is commensurate with the loss or damage suffered. Further, if damages could be awarded under English law to similar claims based on domestic law, it is possible to award exemplary damages for the breach of EU law.

The question of compensation was also considered by the ECJ in **R v HM Treasury ex parte British Telecommunications plc** (1996). The United Kingdom had incorrectly transposed a directive into domestic law. The ECJ ruled that compensation for loss caused was only payable under the circumstances laid down in **Factortame (No 4)** (above). In the instant case, no reparation was payable because the breach was not sufficiently serious. The directive was imprecisely worded and was reasonably capable of being interpreted in the manner adopted by the United Kingdom.[26]

In **Dillenkofer v Federal Republic of Germany** (1996), the ECJ ruled, once again, that if a Member State failed to take 'timeous' (timely) action to implement a Directive, individuals injured by that failure were entitled to seek reparation from the Member State. Member States had been required to bring a Directive[27] into effect before 31 December 1992. Germany brought the Directive into effect as from July 1994. Travellers adversely affected by this delay sought compensation for their loss. Reciting the precedents, the Court stated that individuals who had suffered damage were entitled to compensation where the three conditions set out above were met. Germany had argued in its defence that the time allowed for full implementation of the Directive was too short. This argument, however, did not succeed and the Court ruled clearly that failure to implement a Directive within the specified time period *per se* constituted a sufficiently serious breach of EC law.

In **Haim v Kassenzahnärztliche Vereinigung Nordrhein** (2000), the ECJ made it clear that a public body – as well as the state itself – could be liable for damages for breaches of EU law. Citing *Hedley Lomas*, the Court stated that the same principles applied when considering the liability of the public body as when considering the liability of the state. The question of whether a court of law could be liable to individuals for loss suffered as a result of an error in interpretation was considered by the ECJ in **Köbler v Republic of Austria** (2004). The Court ruled that a Member State's highest court was in principle liable, but only where the court had 'manifestly infringed the applicable law'. All state authorities – legislative, executive and judicial – incurred liability for breach of EU law.

---

26 By contrast see **R v Ministry of Agriculture, Fisheries and Food ex parte Hedley Lomas (Ireland) Ltd** (1996).
27 Council Directive 90/314/EEC of 13 June 1990, Article 9.

The concept of state liability was examined in **Traghetti del Metiterraneo SpA (in liq) v Italy** (2006). The Court stressed the exceptional nature of state liability:

> . . . state liability can be incurred only in the exceptional case where the national court adjudicating at last instance has manifestly infringed the applicable law.
>
> Manifest infringement is to be assessed, inter alia, in the light of a number of criteria, such as the degree of clarity and precision of the rule infringed, whether the infringe-ment was intentional, whether the error of law was excusable or inexcusable, and the non-compliance by the court in question with its obligation to make a reference for a preliminary ruling under the third paragraph of Article 234 EC.[28]

Fundamental principles

The application and enforcement of EU law has been extended by the ECJ enforcing the funda-mental principles of EU law. The starting point is the case of **Werner Mangold v Rudiger Helm** (2005). In this case a Directive (2000/78) laid down a

> . . . general framework for combating discrimination on the grounds of religion or belief, disability, age or sexual orientation as regards employment and occupa-tion, with a view to putting into effect in the Member States the principle of equal treatment.

Differences of treatment on grounds of age would not constitute discrimination if they were 'reasonably justified by a legitimate aim' and if the means of 'achieving that aim are appro-priate and necessary.' A German national law introduced a difference of treatment on the grounds directly of age.

As discussed above, Directives are not legally enforceable horizontally, and Directive 2000/78 could not therefore be relied on by Mr Mangold against Mr Helm. Furthermore, the date for implementing Directive 2000/78 had not yet expired. Notwithstanding these difficulties, the European Court of Justice ruled that any provision of national law which may conflict with EU law was to be set aside by the national court. It did so by resorting to the *source of the principle underlying the prohibition on forms of discrimination.* That source lay in various international instruments and in the constitutional traditions common to the Member States: 'the principle of non-discrimination on grounds of age must thus be regarded as a general principle of Community law' (see paras 74 and 75).

This controversial decision was followed in **Kukukdeveci v Swedex GmbH** (2009). This case involved a factual situation similar to **Mangold**, and the action involved two private parties. As in **Mangold**, the time for implementing the Directive had not yet expired. The ECJ once again stated that Directives could not have horizontal effect. Nevertheless, the Court ruled that national law conflicting with the fundamental principles of EU law should be disapplied.[29]

---

28 See also **TUSGAL v Administracion del Estado** (2011).
29 In **Dominguez v Centre informatique du Centre Ouest Atlantique** (2012) the ECJ was asked for a preliminary ruling in respect of a Directive (2003/88) relating to the right to annual paid leave. The ECJ did not follow the cases of **Mangold** and **Kucukdeveci** (above), but stated that if an individual was unable to rely on a Directive and if the party concerned was injured as a result of domestic law not being in conformity with European law, he or she could rely on **Francovich** (1991) in order to obtain compensation for the loss sustained.

Summarising direct and indirect effect

Table 8.1: Article 288 of the Treaty on the Functioning of the European Union (TFEU)

TREATY PROVISIONS	Direct effect if clear and unconditional: ***Van Gend en Loos*** (1963)	Vertical and horizontal effect
REGULATIONS	Direct effect if clear and unconditional: Article 288 and ***Commission v Italy*** (1972)	Vertical and horizontal effect
DIRECTIVES	Direct effect if: The date for implementation has passed: ***Marshall*** (1984); and the text is clear and unconditional: ***Van Duyn*** (1975)	Vertical effect only

Table 8.2: Exceptions to the rule that directives have only vertical effect

Indirect effect	TEU A 4(3) imposes a duty on Member States, including national courts, to apply EU law: ***Von Colson*** (1984)
State liability	(i) the Directive confers an individual right; (ii) the failure of the State causes damage/loss which is causally related to the failure: ***Francovich*** (1992)

The Interaction between National Courts and the European Court of Justice[30]

Article 267 TFEU represents a vital means by which the harmony of laws between Member States is achieved. The ECJ is insistent both that EU law has supremacy and that it be uniformly applied within Member States. And yet, the treaties establish a partnership between the judges within the national legal systems and the ECJ. It is not difficult to see that the task of uniformity is problematic as all nation states adopt and adapt to the requirements of EU law. For optimum effectiveness, a balance needs to be struck between making references to the ECJ where necessary and the domestic courts being able to apply EU law without undue delay or cost. The obligation to refer applies equally to adversarial and inquisitorial legal systems.[31]

The text of Article 267 is set out on page 163 and from this it can be seen that courts or tribunals may refer a question, provided that it is a question of EU law – and not national law – which requires interpretation, and provided also that a decision of the ECJ is necessary to enable the national court to reach a decision in the case.[32] A reference becomes mandatory

---

30 See Watson, 1986; Winter, 1972; Curtin, 1990; Pescatore, 1983.
31 See **Kelly v National University of Ireland** (2012).
32 The office of immigration adjudicator has been held to be within the meaning of 'court or tribunal' for the purposes of Article 234: **El-Yassini v Secretary of State for the Home Department** (1999).

when the question of law is before a court or tribunal of last resort, that is to say, a court or tribunal from which there is no further appeal. This does not always mean the Supreme Court: in many cases, the appeal structure will end lower in the hierarchy, or leave to appeal may be needed and be refused. Accordingly the court of last resort may effectively be at any level in the judicial hierarchy. If no appeal is possible and the other criteria of a question of EU law and the necessity for interpretation exist, a reference must be made. In **Costa v ENEL** (1964), the reference was from a magistrates' court and involved a claim of less than £2.00 in value: no right of appeal existed because the amount in issue was so small.

The English Court of Appeal, in **Bulmer v Bollinger** (1974), considered the question of when references to the ECJ should be made and Lord Denning laid down the following guidelines for English courts to apply when a reference was a matter of discretion:

(a) the decision must be necessary to enable the court to give judgment – a court must feel that it cannot reach a decision unless a reference is made;

(b) the decision of the question must be conclusive to the case – not just a peripheral issue;

(c) even if the court considers a reference to be necessary, regard must still be paid to the delay involved, the expense, the difficulty of the point of law, and the burden on the ECJ.

These 'guidelines' are questionable in so far as they may impede the willingness of a court to refer matters to the ECJ, and they represent a gloss on the wording of Article 267 TFEU. A further impediment to referral may arise from the doctrine of *acte clair* – the concept which states that if a matter is so obvious in its meaning to the domestic court, then no reference need be made. As with the **Bulmer v Bollinger** guidelines, the doctrine of *acte clair* can lead to distortions in interpretation within domestic legal systems. The ECJ has itself considered the circumstances under which courts should refer, and the doctrine of *acte clair*,[33] in the **CILFIT** case of 1983.[34] The Court was asked to consider the meaning of Article 177(3) (now 267) which relates to mandatory references from a court of last resort. The Court ruled that:

(a) there is no duty to refer where a question of Community law was irrelevant – that is, if the interpretation can have no effect on the outcome of the case;

(b) there is no duty to refer when the question is one substantially the same as one previously answered by the ECJ;[35]

(c) there is no need to refer where no real doubt about the law exists. The national court must, however, be satisfied that the matter is equally obvious to courts of other Member States and to the ECJ. To this limited extent, the doctrine of *acte clair* is endorsed.

In **CILFIT**, the ECJ emphasised that the purpose of Article 177 EEC Treaty (now Article 267 TFEU) in general, was to ensure the proper application and uniform interpretation of EC law in all Member States and to prevent divergencies occurring within Member States.[36] This objective, however, may be frustrated if domestic courts within any one or more of the now

---

33 The concept derives from French law.
34 See Rasmussen, 1984.
35 See *Da Costa en Schaake NV* (1963).
36 See *Grattan plc v Revenue and Customs Commissioners* (2011).

27 (and soon 28) Member States' legal systems misinterprets the meaning of EU law. In **Kobler v Republik Österreich**[37] the ECJ returned to the doctrine of *acte clair* and the duty imposed on national courts of last resort to refer questions to the ECJ. The Austrian Court held that a question arising under Article 39 EC (now Article 45 TFEU) had been settled by an earlier decision of the ECJ and decided it was *acte clair* and stopped the reference procedure. The applicant sought compensation from the Austrian government, arguing that he had suffered financial loss as a result of the national court's decision. The ECJ held that the Austrian Supreme Administrative Court had been wrong to hold that the matter was *acte clair*, in that the precedent case had not decided the issue in question and that where a national court incorrectly interpreted and applied EU law that could give rise to state liability which under certain circumstances (on which see above at pp 175–176) entitles the applicant to compensation.

The ECJ returned once more to *acte clair* in **Traghetti del Mediterraneo SpA v Italy**.[38] In this case concerning EU competition law, Traghetti brought an action for damages against the State based on the court of last instance's wrongful interpretation of EU law and its failure to refer to the ECJ. The ECJ ruled that failure to refer could be classified as an infringement of EU law which gives rise to state liability.

Whereas national courts have some discretion as to whether to refer a matter to the ECJ, the position is different in relation to matters of validity – as opposed to interpretation – of EU law. It is clear that the ECJ has the sole power to rule on whether a measure of EU law is invalid. It is not for national courts to rule on that question. National courts only have the power to uphold the validity of EC legislation.[39]

As seen from the text of Article 267 TFEU, the questions which may be referred are:

(a) interpretation of the Treaties;
(b) the validity and interpretation of acts of institutions of the Community: regulations, directives, etc.

Once the ECJ accepts jurisdiction – and a discretion is conferred on the ECJ over whether or not to accept jurisdiction – and gives a ruling, the matter is then returned to the domestic court for application, thus preserving the partnership ideal.

What is the legal position when a higher court establishes a precedent which is binding on a lower court, but which conflicts with a decision of the ECJ? In **Rheinmullen-Dusseldorf** (1973), the ECJ ruled that national procedures could not prevent a lower court from making further preliminary references to the ECJ to clarify the law. In **Elchinov v NZOK** (2009), the ECJ went further, ruling that a lower court was under a duty to depart from the precedent of a higher court where that precedent conflicted with EU law. This decision has profound implications for the common law system which has the doctrine of precedent at its heart, and directly raises the question of legal supremacy, discussed below.

The Question of Legal Supremacy

The question of legal supremacy can be examined both from the standpoint of the EU and from that of national law.

---

37 Case C-224/01, [2003] ECR I-239.
38 Case C-173/03, [2006] ECR I-5177.
39 See **Henn and Darby v Director of Public Prosecutions** (1981); **Foto-Frost v Hauptzollamt Lubeck Ost** (1987). See also Arnull, 1988a; and Bebr, 1988.

The European Court of Justice's view

The ECJ claims that EU law is supreme over national law. This claim carries the following implications:

(a) EU law confers rights on individuals to which national law must give effect;
(b) national law cannot prevail over EU law;
(c) the effectiveness of EU law must be the same in all Member States – it cannot vary in effect from one Member State to another;
(d) courts of Member States must follow the interpretation of laws given by the ECJ or, where there is no authority, and under certain conditions, must refer the matter to the ECJ under Article 267 of the Treaty;
(e) where the ECJ gives a ruling, Member States are under an obligation to amend their national laws so as to conform to EU law.

The ECJ has asserted the supremacy of EC/EU law on many occasions. The early cases lay the foundations for the current relationship between domestic law and EU law. The starting point is once again the case of *Van Gend en Loos v Nederlandse Tariefcommissie* (1963), in which the ECJ enunciated the view that, by signing the treaties, the Member States had created a new legal order, in which individual states had limited their sovereign rights. In **Costa v ENEL** (1964), this view was reaffirmed by the ECJ:

> The transfer by the states from their domestic legal system to the Community legal system of the rights and obligations arising under the Treaty carries with it a permanent limitation of their sovereign rights against which a subsequent unilateral act incompatible with the concept of Community law cannot prevail.

Internationale Handelsgesellschaft mbH v EVST (1970) took the principle of EC supremacy further. Under EC law, in order to export produce, the company was required to obtain a licence, for which a 'permanent deposit' had to be paid. If the goods were not exported within the licence period, the deposit was to be forfeited. The company paid the deposit, failed to complete the export, and forfeiture was made. The firm sued the agency involved for return of the deposit, arguing that the forfeiture was contrary to the Constitution of the Federal Republic of Germany. The matter was referred to the ECJ.

The ECJ declared that giving effect to rules or concepts of national law contained even within the constitution of a state, for the purposes of judging the validity of EC measures, would have an adverse effect on the uniformity and efficacy of EC law. The validity of EC measures could be judged only in the light of EC law and could not be affected by allegations that the measures ran counter to fundamental rights as formulated by the constitution of the Member State. Having made this unequivocal and controversial statement, the ECJ softened its tone, ruling that the respect for fundamental rights forms an integral part of the 'general principles of law' protected by the ECJ, and that the protection of such rights, inspired by traditions common to Member States, must be ensured within the framework of the structure and objectives of the EC.

The **Simmenthal** case (1979) further developed the jurisprudence of the ECJ in relation to supremacy. Simmenthal imported beef from France into Italy. Under Italian legislation of 1970, fees for veterinary and health checks had to be paid by the importer at the frontier. Simmenthal sued the Italian Minister of Finance for return of the money, arguing that the fee was equivalent to a customs duty and was contrary to Article 12 of the Treaty and Community regulations on the common organisation on beef imports. The national court ordered the Ministry to return the money. The minister pleaded that the domestic 1970 Act was binding unless and until set aside by the Italian Constitutional Court.

The Italian court was thus faced with a conflict between Article 12, as it then was, of the Treaty and a later Italian statute. A reference was made, the question at issue being whether directly applicable regulations required national courts to disregard subsequently passed domestic legislation, without waiting for the Constitutional Court to declare it invalid. The ECJ held that regulations take precedence over previous and subsequent domestic legislation and that a national court, whatever its position or role in the national judicial hierarchy, must set aside any provision which conflicts with EC law and apply EC law in its entirety, without waiting until the domestic legislation had been set aside by the Constitutional Court.

The **European Road Transport Agreement** (ERTA) case (**Commission v Council**) (1971) offers another perspective.[40] In 1962, several European states, five of which were EC Member States, others being Eastern European states, signed the European Road Transport Agreement, which sought to establish common rules concerning conditions of work of long-distance lorry drivers crossing several state boundaries. As such, the Agreement was not an EC agreement. In 1969, the EC had acted for the (then) six Member States by issuing a regulation covering the same issue. In 1970, the matter was further complicated by the Council meeting to attempt to find a common basis for a new transport agreement. The Commission attempted to have the proceedings of the Council annulled on the basis that the Council was not competent to reach agreements of this kind.[41]

At the heart of the matter lay the question as to who had the power – Member States, the Council or the Commission – to make such 'international' agreements. If Member States retained the power to enter into international agreements (and such a power is a basic attribute of sovereignty), then the Council proceedings were merely recommendatory; if the Council had power then the proceedings took on more of a law-making character, which deprived the Member States of competence to act either unilaterally or collectively. The Court held that, having regard to the legal personality of the Community (now EU) the sole power to enter into such agreements would, by implication, vest in the Community Institutions, thus depriving Member States of any capacity in this regard.[42]

In summary, the effect of these early cases is that, since 1962, the ECJ has declared the existence of a new legal order, one to which Member States have limited their sovereign rights by transferring these to the EU. These rights include even the protection of constitutionally guaranteed individual rights. Further, it matters not whether a domestic law in conflict with EU law was passed prior to accession to the Union or subsequently: neither can prevail over EU law. Third, where the EU has the power to act on behalf of Member States in the making of international agreements, Member States have lost that capacity.

Before examining the position of the English courts, it is necessary to consider the means by which EU law is received into English law.

The Reception of EU Law into the United Kingdom

The concepts of monism and dualism

At a conceptual level, the manner in which international law, of which EU law may be regarded as a *sui generis* (that is to say, unique) example, is dependent upon whether a particular state adopts a monist or dualist approach to international law. Monism is the doctrine whereby

---

40 See Mancini and Keeling, 1991.
41 (Article 217 TFEU). The power to enter treaties is conferred under Article 310 EC Treaty. In 2006 the Court of Justice reaffirmed the Community's exclusive competence to conclude treaties: see Press Release No 10/06 7 February 2006, Opinion 1/03.
42 See also **Commission v Finland** (2002).

international law and national law form a single whole, or part of the same conceptual structure, in which international law takes precedence. Under this doctrine, adhered to by, *inter alia*, France and Italy, the obligations of international law, once assumed, enter automatically into the legal system, needing no domestic legislative acts. Once entered, the obligations take precedence over national law.

Dualism, on the other hand, regards the systems of international law and national law as separate: in order for international law to enter into national law, some domestic legislation must be enacted by the national Parliament. This is the view adopted by the United Kingdom and is one consistent with the sovereignty of Parliament. Treaties are part of international law, and can have no effect in domestic law unless and until a statute of the sovereign United Kingdom Parliament is enacted to give them effect.

In 1972, Lord Denning MR confirmed this view in **Blackburn v Attorney General** (1971):

> Even if a Treaty is signed, it is elementary that these courts take no notice of treaties as such. We take no notice of treaties until they are embodied in laws enacted by Parliament, and then only to the extent that Parliament tells us. [p 1382]

Accordingly, the signing of the EC Treaties, without any further parliamentary action, had no effect in English law. In order to have effect, it was necessary for Parliament to pass the European Communities Act 1972.

The European Communities Act 1972

The most fundamental provisions of the Act can be found in sections 2 and 3(1). Here it is specified that rights and duties which are directly applicable or effective are to be given legal effect within the United Kingdom; that the executive has the power to give effect to EU obligations; that existing and future enactments are to be interpreted and have effect; and that the meaning or effect of Treaty provisions is to be decided according to EU law.

THE EUROPEAN COMMUNITIES ACT 1972	
Provision	Meaning
Section 2(1)	EU law automatically part of domestic law
Section 2(2)	Allows delegated legislation to implement EU law in domestic law
Section 2(4)	Directs the courts to interpret domestic law in line with EU law
Section 3(1)	EU law is not foreign law, but is part of UK law

The view of the United Kingdom courts

The manner in which, and extent to which, the United Kingdom courts have accommodated EU obligations requires consideration. First, it should be noted that nothing in the European Communities Act (ECA) 1972 represents an attempt to entrench its provisions, that is to say, to make them immune from amendment or repeal. There is no statement in the Act that EU law is a 'higher form of law', or that the Act cannot be repealed, or could be repealed but only by some specified 'manner and form'. As discussed in Chapter 6, however, it is clear that the doctrine of implied repeal does not operate in relation to the ECA 1972.

Two early challenges were made to the signing of the Treaty on the basis of the potential or actual loss of parliamentary sovereignty. In **Blackburn v Attorney General** in 1971, the plaintiff sought a declaration that the government, by signing the Treaty of Rome, would surrender part of Parliament's sovereignty which it could not lawfully do, as no Parliament could bind another. In **McWhirter v Attorney General** (1972), the plaintiff adduced that joining the EC (now EU) was contrary to the Bill of Rights 1689, which declared that all powers of government are vested in the Crown and Parliament could not, therefore, by means of a Treaty, transfer those rights. In both cases, the arguments were disposed of with speed. In **Blackburn**, Lord Denning MR stated that 'even if the Treaty is signed, it is elementary that the courts take no notice of [it] until embodied in an Act of Parliament'. Further, in **McWhirter**, Lord Denning stated that 'even though the Treaty of Rome has been signed, it has no effect as far as the courts are concerned until implemented by Act of Parliament. Until that day, we take no notice of it'.[43]

Conflicts between EC law and UK domestic law[44]

One area of law which has given rise to an instructive array of case law concerning the relationship between domestic law and EC law is that of sex discrimination. There are, of course, a variety of ways in which discrimination on the basis of sex may arise: in relation to equal pay or equal treatment in respect of access to employment, promotion, training, working conditions, social security and retirement ages.

In **Macarthys v Smith** (1981), Mrs Smith was employed by Macarthys as a stockroom manageress. The man who had previously held the position had been paid a higher wage than Mrs Smith. The applicable domestic legislation was the Equal Pay Act 1970, as amended by the Sex Discrimination Act 1975, which provided, inter alia, that men and women employed in the same job should be paid equal amounts. The Act was silent, however, as to whether employers were required to pay the same wage to a woman who came to the job after the man had left their employment. The relevant point for interpretation, therefore, was whether men and women, employed at differing times for the same job, were required to be paid equally.[45]

Article 141, now Article 157 TFEU (formerly Article 119) of the EC Treaty provides for equal pay for men and women. This Article is couched in far broader terms than those used by the Equal Pay Act 1970. The ECJ held that Article 119 required equal pay for men and women whether they were employed contemporaneously or in succession. On receiving the judgment of the ECJ, the Court of Appeal ruled in favour of Mrs Smith. Lord Denning's judgment is of particular significance:

In construing our statute, we are entitled to look to the Treaty as an aid in its construction: and even more, not only as an aid, but as an overriding force. If on close investigation it should appear that our legislation is deficient – or is inconsistent with Community law – by some oversight of our draftsmen – then it is our bounden duty to give priority to Community law. Such is the result of section 2(1) and (4) of the European Communities Act 1972.

Thus far, I have assumed that our Parliament, whenever it passes legislation, intends to fulfil its obligations under the Treaty. If the time should come when our Parliament deliberately passes an Act with the intention of repudiating the Treaty or

---

43 See also **R v Secretary of State for Foreign and Commonwealth Affairs ex parte Rees-Mogg** (1994).
44 See, inter alia, Szyszczack, 1990; de Búrca, 1992a and 1992b.
45 Where women whose work was of equal value to men when employed by a local authority were transferred to another employer by the local authority, the new employer was not obliged to pay the women the same rate as previously. There was no violation of Article 141(1) of the EC Treaty since there was no one body which was responsible for the irregularity and could bring about equal treatment: **Lawrence v Regent Office Care Ltd** (2000).

any provision in it – or intentionally of acting inconsistently with it – and says so in express terms – then I should have thought that it would be the duty of our courts to follow the statute of our Parliament.

Article 141 fell for further consideration in **Garland v British Rail Engineering Ltd** in 1983, this time by the House of Lords. British Rail made concessionary travel facilities available to the children of male employees reaching retirement, but not to the children of women reaching retirement. The question was whether this policy amounted to discrimination contrary to EC law and whether the courts in England should construe the Sex Discrimination Act 1975 in a manner so as to make it compatible with the requirements of EC law. The House of Lords referred the matter to the ECJ, which ruled that the policy amounted to discrimination contrary to EC law, and that EC law must prevail.

In **Duke v GEC Reliance Ltd** (1988), the House of Lords considered the construction of section 6(4) of the Sex Discrimination Act 1975. In the **Duke** case, the plaintiff's claim for damages based on unequal treatment was for a period prior to Parliament's amendment of the Sex Discrimination Act to bring English law into line with the requirements of European law. The House of Lords declined to give retrospective effect to the amendment in light of Parliament's express decision not to amend the Act retrospectively. One interpretation of **Duke** is that, being a pre-**Marleasing** case – which makes it clear that the Article 10 (now Article 4.3 TEU) duty is imposed on national courts – the House of Lords was in line with the ECJ's interpretation of the law at the time.

In **Litster v Forth Dry Dock Ltd** (1990), however, the House of Lords interpreted a domestic regulation contrary to its clear meaning in order to comply with a directive as interpreted by the ECJ. The domestic regulation had been introduced for the purpose of complying with the directive and, accordingly, the House of Lords was complying with its duty under section 2(4) of the ECA 1972 to give effect to Community law.[46]

Pickstone v Freemans plc (1989) illustrates the same approach. The applicants were female warehouse workers – operatives – who were paid the same as male operatives but claimed that their work was of equal value to that of warehouse checkers, who were paid more than they were. The Equal Pay Act 1970 did not encompass the concept of equal value, but had been amended in 1983, by statutory instrument under section 2(2) of the ECA 1972, following a ruling by the ECJ that the Equal Pay Act was in breach of a Directive. The 1983 amendment was intended to bring the Equal Pay Act protection in line with Article 119 and the Directive, but had been obscurely worded. The result was that the House of Lords was forced to strain to achieve an interpretation which could give effect to what Lord Oliver described as the 'compulsive provision of section 2(4)' of the ECA 1972. The required result was achieved by the House of Lords departing from the strict literal interpretation of the text and implying words to fill the legislative gap in order to reach conformity with European law.

In **Webb v EMO Cargo (UK) Ltd** (1992), the issue of dismissal on the basis of pregnancy was considered in relation to the Directive on Equal Treatment. The English Trades Union Reform and Employment Rights Act 1993 provides that dismissal on the grounds of pregnancy is unfair.[47] However, in **Webb v EMO Cargo (UK) Ltd** (1992), the Court of Appeal ruled, and the House of Lords affirmed, that a woman who was dismissed from employment because of her pregnancy was not unlawfully dismissed, since – comparing her to a man with a temporary

---

46 See further below on the 1972 Act. See also **Finnegan v Clowney Youth Training Programme Ltd** (1990).
47 Trades Union Reform and Employment Rights Act 1993, ss 23–25 and Scheds 2 and 3; EC Pregnancy Directive 92/85.

physical disability who would also have been unable to work – the man would also have been dismissed. The ECJ ruled that English law was inadequate and held, first, that pregnancy was not a pathological condition to be compared with illness and, secondly, that a pregnant woman's inability to work was temporary and not permanent. Accordingly, the dismissal had amounted to sex discrimination.[48] The Court ruled that the Article 'precludes dismissal of an employee who is recruited for an unlimited term with a view, initially, to replacing another employee during the latter's maternity leave and who cannot do so, because, shortly after recruitment, she is herself found to be pregnant'. The House of Lords, in **Webb v EMO Air Cargo (UK) Ltd (No 2)** (1995) ruled that sections 1(1)(a) and 5(3) of the 1975 Act were to be construed in accordance with the ECJ's ruling.[49]

In **Grant v South West Trains Ltd** (1998), the ECJ apparently reached the limits of its respect for equality. A Southampton employment tribunal had referred a question to the ECJ concerning whether the female partner of a lesbian woman was entitled to the same employment benefits enjoyed by married or cohabiting heterosexual couples. The ECJ ruled that there had been no violation of the Treaty on the basis of sexual inequality.[50]

A further exception to equality was shown in **Cadman v Health and Safety Executive, Equal Opportunities Commission, intervenor** (2006). The Health and Safety Executive operated a pay structure which reflected and rewarded both length of service and employees' individual performance. The applicant was paid less than four male employees who were in the same band of employment. The Court of Justice ruled that whenever there was evidence of discrimination, it was for the employer to prove that the practice was justified by objective factors unrelated to any discrimination based on sex. The justification given had to be based on a legitimate objective, and the means chosen to achieve that objective had to be appropriate and necessary for that purpose. Rewarding, in particular, experience acquired which enabled a worker to perform his duties better constituted a legitimate objective of pay policy. Experience and length of service went hand in hand. That was an objective requirement and in the instant case the disparity in pay was justified.[51]

The limits to formal equality were also apparent in **Rutherford v Secretary of State for Trade and Industry** (2006). The Employment Rights Act 1996 provides for a cut-off age beyond which protection from unfair dismissal is removed and redundancy payments become unavailable. The applicants claimed that the provisions were discriminatory in that more men than women worked over the age of 65. The House of Lords ruled that the purpose of Article 141 (Article 157 TFEU) was to provide for equal pay for men and women doing equal work: not to guarantee equality throughout working lives which ended at different ages.

Undoubtedly, the most constitutionally significant British case revealing the relationship between European law and domestic law is that of **R v Secretary of State for Transport ex parte Factortame** (1991). In 1970, the Council of Ministers passed a regulation relating to the common organisation of the market in fishery products. The basic principle employed was that, subject to certain exceptions, there should be equal access for the fishing vessels of all Member States to the fishing grounds of fellow Member States. In 1983, due to fears of over-fishing caused by such open access, the Council established, by way of regulation, a system for the conservation and management of resources. This entailed, in part, setting limits to

---

48 *Dekker v VJV Centrum* (1991).
49 In **Strathclyde Regional Council v Wallace** (1998), the House of Lords ruled that an objectively justifiable employment practice which was not 'tainted' by sexual discrimination, which resulted in unequal pay, did not contravene the Equal Pay Act 1970, relying on **Bilka-Kaufhaus GmbH v Weber von Hartz** (1987), EC Treaty, Article 119 (now Article 141).
50 Note that discrimination on the basis of sexual orientation is now unlawful. See **KB v National Health Service Pensions Agency** (2004).
51 See also **Palacios de la Villa v Cortfiel Servicios SA** (2007).

the amount of fish to be caught in certain periods by way of 'total allowable catches' – the allocation of total allowable catches being fairly distributed among the Member States by way of national quotas. The quotas were based on the number of ships flying the flag of a Member State or registered in a Member State.

Spain acceded to the EC in 1986. Before 1986, the extent to which Spanish vessels could ship in British waters was determined under agreements between the Spanish and United Kingdom governments. Under English law, the Merchant Shipping Act 1894 prohibited non-British nationals from owning British fishing vessels but did permit corporate ownership by British companies. Thus, directors/shareholders of Spanish vessels were able to register under the 1894 Act. Some 96 Spanish fishing boats were registered under the Act, and each of these vessels counted as part of the United Kingdom's quota under European law.

The United Kingdom government, understandably alarmed at the restrictions imposed on the domestic fishing industry and the ability of foreign companies to register and therefore take up part of the United Kingdom's quota, imposed additional conditions for registration which came into force in 1986. The three principal conditions for registration were to be that a proportion of the catch was to be sold in the United Kingdom; that 75 per cent of the crews were to be EC nationals ordinarily resident in the United Kingdom; and that all crew were to be required to contribute to the National Insurance Scheme.

In 1988, the United Kingdom Parliament passed the Merchant Shipping Act and enacted fresh merchant shipping regulations. The new system of registration[52] entailed qualification on the basis of a 'genuine and substantial connection with the United Kingdom'. The revised conditions required that not less than 75 per cent of vessels be owned by United Kingdom citizens resident in the United Kingdom; or wholly owned in the United Kingdom, with 75 per cent of shareholders and directors in the United Kingdom; or part owned, with 75 per cent of owners in the United Kingdom; and, further, that vessels be effectively operated from the United Kingdom. Registration would be lost with effect from 31 March 1989 until vessel owners could satisfy the government that they were eligible for registration.

As a result, Factortame, which did not comply with these more stringent requirements, challenged the domestic requirements as incompatible with European law, claiming discrimination on the grounds of nationality contrary to Article 14 of the Treaty and the rights of companies to establishment under Articles 43–48 (now Articles 49–52 TFEU). The Divisional Court, in 1990, granted an interim injunction against the government restraining it from applying the Merchant Shipping Act regulations until final judgment was made following a reference to the ECJ. The government appealed to the Court of Appeal, which ruled that the court had no jurisdiction to grant interim relief disapplying an Act of Parliament. On appeal to the House of Lords, the decision of the Court of Appeal was upheld: injunctive relief against the Crown was not within the court's jurisdiction.

Three constitutionally significant factors arose in **Factortame**. First, whether the court could protect alleged rather than established rights under European law; second, whether the English courts could grant injunctive relief against the Crown; and, third, the conditions under which such relief could be granted.

The ECJ, in its preliminary ruling on the first point (Case 213/89), held that the offending provisions of the Merchant Shipping Act should be suspended, pending a full determination of Factortame's claim, stating that:

---

52 SI 1988/1926.

The full effectiveness of Community [now EU] law would be impaired if a rule of national law could prevent a court seized of a dispute governed by Community law from granting interim relief in order to ensure the full effectiveness of the judicial decision to be given on the existence of rights claimed under Community law.

The ECJ reverted to its decision in **Simmenthal** (1979), reiterating that directly applicable rules were to be fully and uniformly applied in all Member States in accordance with the principle of precedence of European law over national law. Article 5 of the EEC Treaty (see now Article 4.3 TEU) imposes an obligation, as has been seen above, to ensure the legal protection which is provided for under the principle of direct effect. The House of Lords in **R v Secretary of State for Transport ex parte Factortame Ltd (No 2)** accepted the ECJ's ruling and granted interim relief.[53]

In **R v HM Treasury ex parte British Telecommunications plc** (1993) (the BT case), the applicant sought an interim injunction which would have had the effect – as in **Factortame** – of causing national legislation to be disapplied while the substantive issue was being considered by the ECJ. In **Factortame**, great weight was attached to the very strong prima facie case put forward by the applicants. In the **BT** case, the Court of Appeal cautioned against over-reliance on the likelihood of success in the ECJ as a basis for granting relief. In part, this caution was based on the fact that a reference had been made to the ECJ, and that to give great weight to the prognosis for success was to prejudge the interpretation to be given by the ECJ. The fact that a reference had been made meant that the English court was uncertain as to the question in issue. Accordingly it would be inappropriate to prejudge the issue by granting relief at an interim stage. The Court of Appeal also warned of the difficulties in disapplying domestic legislation. As the court stated, there should be a distinction drawn between a 'major piece of primary legislation' and a 'minor piece of subordinate legislation'. In relation to the former, the court ruled that it would be far more circumspect than in relation to secondary legislation. In the instant case, unlike **Factortame**, the issues were not clear-cut. The court, ruling that it would only grant an interim order 'in the most compelling circumstances', declined to grant the injunction.[54]

The question of the compatibility of domestic law with EU law arose once more in the case of **R v Secretary of State for Employment ex parte Equal Opportunities Commission** (1995) (the **EOC** case). There, the Equal Opportunities Commission had brought an action challenging allegedly discriminatory employment protection provisions in English law, arguing that these contravened European Community legislation. The House of Lords, in a bold decision, granted a declaration to the effect that national law was incompatible with European law. However, the House of Lords did not go so far as to rule that the English provisions were void; rather, it confined its ruling to the compatibility issue – thus avoiding any potential conflict with Parliament and the concept of sovereignty.[55]

---

53 On the duty to disapply domestic law in favour of Community law see also **Autologic Holdings plc v Inland Revenue Commissioners** (2005). **Re Nationality of Fishermen: EC Commission (Spain intervening) v United Kingdom (Ireland intervening)** (1991). In **R v Secretary of State for Transport ex parte Factortame Ltd (No 5)** (2000), the House of Lords ruled that the United Kingdom's breach of Community law was sufficiently serious as to warrant damages. For contrasting interpretations of the **Factortame** case, see Craig, 1991; Wade, 1996; Allan, 1997. See also Williams, 2000.

54 In a challenge to a directive, a company sought to restrain the United Kingdom government from laying before Parliament regulations to implement a Council directive. Proceedings were already before the ECJ which was not expected to give judgment until some four months after the time limit for implementation by Member States. The Court of Appeal declined to interfere, stating that interim relief could only be given in cases where there would be irreparable damage and that, in any case, the UK government should not be constrained from making regulations: **R v Secretary of State for Health ex parte Imperial Tobacco Ltd** (2001).

55 See also **Lawrence v Regent Office Care Ltd** (2003); **Armstrong v Newcastle upon Tyne NHS Hospital Trust** (2005).

Summary

The law of the European Union (EU) enters into the legal systems of the United Kingdom[56] via the European Communities Act 1972. The legal effect of EU law on domestic law depends on the type of law: whether it is a Treaty Article, Regulation, Directive, Recommendation or Opinion. While the Treaty stipulates that Regulations shall have 'direct effect', it has been the Court of Justice which has developed the concepts of vertical and horizontal direct effect and indirect effect of EC (now EU) provisions which determine their legal significance. In addition the Court has developed the concept of state liability which requires that Member States which fail in their duty to implement/apply EU law correctly, and by that failure directly cause loss, must compensate the party which has suffered loss.

The domestic courts of Member States are under a duty to apply and give effect to EU law to ensure that it has supremacy over domestic law. In doing so the courts act in a form of partnership with the Court of Justice of the European Union. In order that EU law is given priority over incompatible national law, the Treaty provides for references to be made to the Court of Justice requesting clarification of the meaning of EU law. Once the Court of Justice has ruled, it is for the domestic court to apply the correct interpretation of EU law to the case in question, thereby ensuring the supremacy of EU law.

Further Reading

Convery, J. (1997) 'State Liability in the United Kingdom after *Brasserie du Pecheur*', Common Market Law Review, 34: 603.

Craig, P. (1991) 'Sovereignty after Factortame', 11 YNEL 221.

Craig, P. (1997) 'Directives: Direct Effect, Indirect Effect and the Construction of National Legislation', European Law Review, 22: 519.

Craig, P. and de Búrca, G. (2011) *EU Law: Text Cases and Materials* (5th edn), Oxford: OUP.

Drake, S. (2005) 'Twenty Years after Von Colson: The Impact of "Indirect Effect" on the Protection of the Individual's Community Rights', European Law Review, 30: 329.

du Burca, G. (1992) 'Giving Effect to European Community Directives', Modern Law Review, 55: 215.

Hartley, T. (1996) 'The European Court, Judicial Objectivity and the Constitution of the European Union', Law Quarterly Review, 112: 411.

Murphy, C, (2011) 'An Effective Right to Cross-border Healthcare? . . . Comment on *Elchinov*', European Current Law Yearbook, cxv.

---

56 Note that Northern Ireland and Scotland have separate legal systems from England and Wales.

Part 4

Central, Regional and Local Government

Chapter 9

Central Government

Introduction

In this chapter, the structure and roles of the institutions of central government – the Crown, Privy Council, Prime Minister, Cabinet, ministers and government departments – are examined. If government is to be conducted under the law, and in line with the principles of democracy and constitutionalism, it is of the utmost importance that those holding power should be accountable to citizens through their elected legislature. The responsibility of ministers of the Crown is thus fundamental to the constitution, and the more so in the absence of an authoritative constitutional document which defines the scope and limits of ministerial power. Note that the procedural means by which Parliament scrutinises government action is considered in Chapter 15.

The Structure of Government

The Crown

> It is commonly hidden like a mystery, and sometimes paraded like a pageant, but in neither case is it contentious. The nation is divided into parties, but the Crown is of no party. Its apparent separation from business is that which removes it both from enmities and from desecration, which preserves its mystery, which enables it to combine the affection of conflicting parties – to be a visible symbol of unity to those still so imperfectly educated as to need a symbol.[1]

While the Monarch is titular head of the government and all government acts are carried out in the name of the Crown, the role of the Queen is largely, but not completely, formal and ceremonial. In the study of the government it is necessary to bear in mind that the United Kingdom remains a constitutional monarchy and that the Crown is the symbolic head of the executive, legislature and judiciary. The remaining prerogatives of the Crown have been discussed in Chapter 5, which should be referred to for discussion of the Crown's role in the appointment of the Prime Minister.

See Chapter 5.

Succession to the Crown

The Act of Settlement 1700 provides that succession to the throne is confined to members of the Protestant religion and specifically excludes Roman Catholics, or those married to Roman Catholics, from succession.[2] Succession to the Crown traditionally devolves according to the principles of *primogeniture*, that is to say that male heirs, and their children (irrespective of sex), take precedence over female heirs. In 2011 the Commonwealth Heads of Government agreed to alter the rules so that the line of succession would be based on date of birth, rather than gender, and that the prohibition against marrying a Roman Catholic be removed. The change in the line of succession will take effect with the birth of the first child of Prince Charles's eldest son William and his wife Catherine.

The Regency Acts

Should the Crown fall 'vacant', through death or (more rarely) abdication, or the Monarch becomes too ill to fulfil his or her constitutional duties,[3] and the successor has not yet reached

---

1 Bagehot, 1867, p 90.
2 For this reason, Prince Michael of Kent was excluded from the line of succession upon his marriage to a Catholic in 1978.
3 As occurred in the reigns of George III (in 1811) and George VI (in 1938).

the age of majority, there will be a need for the appointment of an adult with responsibility for the Crown's duties during the successor's minority. This situation is regulated under the Regency Acts 1937–53.

The Regency Act 1937 provides that the Sovereign may appoint Counsellors of State, charged with the responsibility of carrying out the Sovereign's duties whenever he or she is either absent from the United Kingdom, or suffering from temporary physical or mental illness. Those eligible to be appointed include the Monarch's spouse and the next four persons in line of succession.

Where there is the need to appoint a Regent, the Regency Act 1937 provides that, until the heir to the Throne reaches the age of 18, his or her duties will be carried out by a Regent.[4] The appointment of a Regent continues until it is declared to be no longer necessary by the wife or husband of the Monarch, the Lord Chancellor, the Speaker, the Lord Chief Justice and the Master of the Rolls.

The Royal Titles Act 1953

By statute, the Monarch may assume whatever title she thinks fit, with the assent of member governments of the Commonwealth. The Royal Titles Act provides the title:

> Elizabeth II by the Grace of God of the United Kingdom of Great Britain and Northern Ireland and of her other Realms and Territories Queen, Head of the Commonwealth, Defender of the Faith.

Within the Commonwealth, it was agreed in 1952 that the title of the Monarch within the Commonwealth was for each state to determine.[5] Accordingly, the only title of the Monarch which is uniform throughout the Commonwealth is that of 'Head of the Commonwealth'. Prince Charles has made it known that he would prefer, on succession, to be known as 'Defender of Faith', rather than Defender of the (Protestant) Faith.

The role of the Monarch in the United Kingdom's constitutional democracy

In Walter Bagehot's often-quoted phrase, the Monarch has the right to 'be consulted, the right to encourage, the right to warn' (1867). As such, the Queen must be fully informed of the actions of her government, and given adequate opportunity to express her views.

If the role of the Monarch is to remain respected by governments of all political persuasions, and the nation, it is axiomatic that the Queen be seen formally to be immune from party-political differences and to fulfil her duties in an even-handed manner. This is not to suggest that the Queen has no views on her government's policies or that she should not express them to the Prime Minister. What is required, however, is the absolute confidentiality of discussions between herself and the Prime Minister, and, should there be a disagreement over policy, it is required that, once the Monarch's views are made known, irrespective of her approval or otherwise, she follows the advice of her Prime Minister on policy matters.[6]

---

4   The 1953 Regency Act provided that if one of Queen Elizabeth II's minor children succeeded to the throne, the Queen and the Duke of Edinburgh would be appointed Regent.
5   At a meeting of Commonwealth Prime Ministers. See Cmd 8748, 1952, London: HMSO.
6   See the letter to *The Times*, by the Queen's Press Secretary, Sir William Heseltine, 29 July 1986.

Queen Elizabeth II, since her accession to the throne in 1952, has presided over 60 years of government and accumulated a wealth of experience in political matters unmatched by her individual Prime Ministers.

The State Opening of Parliament

At the start of each new parliamentary session, the Monarch formally opens Parliament. The Queen's Speech is formally delivered to the House of Lords with members of the House of Commons having been summoned to the Lords by Black Rod. The Speech outlines the government of the day's proposals for legislation in the forthcoming session. Thereafter, there is a four- or five-day debate on the Speech in the Commons.

The Channels of Communication between Crown and Government

Government papers

The Monarch receives copies of all significant government papers. She also receives copies of reports from ambassadors abroad and Commonwealth High Commissioners. All Cabinet papers and the minutes of Cabinet meetings are received by the Queen.

The weekly prime ministerial audience

Whatever the pressure of work, the Prime Minister attends a weekly half- to one-hour audience with the Queen. It is at this weekly meeting that issues will be discussed and the Queen's views made known to the Prime Minister.[7] Channels of communication are facilitated by the Queen's Private Secretary, whose appointment is the choice of the Queen, and who on appointment will become a Member of the Privy Council. The Private Secretary may not belong to any political party. Very rarely will the Queen's Private Secretary be drawn into public debate although, in 1986, the then Private Secretary, Sir William Heseltine, wrote to The Times (following public claims that the Queen and the Prime Minister – then Mrs Thatcher – disagreed on policy matters). In his letter, Sir William Heseltine spelled out three main points concerning the relationship between the Crown and the Prime Minister:

(a)   the Sovereign has the right and duty to counsel, encourage and warn her government. She is thus entitled to have opinions on government policy and to express them to the Prime Minister;

(b)   whatever the Queen's personal opinions may be, she is bound to accept and act on the advice of her Ministers;

(c)   the Sovereign is obliged to treat communications with the Prime Minister as entirely confidential.[8]

---

7   See further Brazier, 1990, Chapter 8 and 1999, Chapter 9.
8   The Times, 29 July 1986; see also Marshall, 1986b.

The Privy Council

Historical origins

The Privy Council is traceable to the thirteenth century. It was through the Privy Council that monarchs would rule without recourse to Parliament. With the Glorious Revolution of 1688 and the rise of parliamentary sovereignty, the role of the Council changed. Under William, the inner circle of the Council became known as the Cabinet Council. Through this Cabinet, the King could exercise all his powers, although he had to have recourse to the wider membership of the Privy Council in order to undertake acts which required Orders in Council, the formal means by which such prerogative acts came into effect. It was the Privy Council which determined the summoning and dissolution of Parliament, although it seems clear that the King would act through Orders in Council published after consultation with an inner circle of the Privy Council. The early origins of Cabinet government can be seen here.

With the Glorious Revolution of 1688 and the rise of parliamentary sovereignty, the role of the Council changed. Under William, the inner circle of the Council became known as the Cabinet Council. Through the Cabinet, the King could exercise all his powers, although he had to have recourse to the wider membership of the Privy Council in order to undertake acts which required Orders in Council, the formal means by which such prerogative acts came into effect. While King William and Queen Anne attended Council meetings regularly, a change of practice occurred with the reign of George I (1714–27) and George II (1727–60). Neither could speak English, and nor were they particularly concerned with English matters. Accordingly, the Cabinet began to meet without the King. Under George III (1760–1820), the same situation prevailed, the Cabinet meeting without the King and communicating its decision to the King. Again, we find the origins of today's Cabinet, with the three principles of Cabinet government becoming apparent: those of 'political unanimity, common responsibility to Parliament and a common leader'.[9] With the rise of the Cabinet system of government in the eighteenth century, the Privy Council gradually lost much of its power.[10]

Composition of the Privy Council

The Privy Council has around 600 members. There is no fixed number of members. Appointments are made by the Crown, on the advice of the Prime Minister. By convention, all present and past Cabinet members are appointed to the Privy Council. Also included in the membership are members of the Royal Family, senior judges, two Archbishops, British Ambassadors, the Speaker of the House of Commons, present and former leaders of the Opposition, and leading Commonwealth spokesmen and judges. On appointment, a new member of the Council takes the oath of allegiance, or affirms loyalty. The Privy Council oath binds the member to secrecy in relation to any matters discussed in the Council.[11]

Meetings of the Privy Council

The Privy Council may meet wherever the Queen so decides although, normally, the Council will meet at Buckingham Palace. The quorum is three.

---

9 Maitland, 1908, p 395.
10 See Mackintosh, 1977, Chapter 2. On the constitutional struggles between King, courts and Parliament, see Chapter 5.
11 Privy Councillors would in any event be prevented from disclosing confidential information by virtue of the Official Secrets Acts 1911–89.

Functions of the Privy Council

Proclamations and Orders in Council

Proclamations are used for the summoning of Parliament and declarations of war and peace. Orders in Council give effect to decisions reached under the royal prerogative and under statute. Orders in Council may be legislative, executive or judicial.

Committees of the Privy Council

The majority of Privy Council functions are undertaken in committees. Miscellaneous committees have been established. These include committees dealing with scientific research, universities and the granting of charters. The most important committee is the Judicial Committee.

The Judicial Committee was established under statute by the Judicial Committee Act 1833. The Judicial Committee Act 1844 provided that the Queen may, by Order in Council, admit appeals from courts of British colonies or overseas territories. In addition, under the Devolution Acts[12] the Judicial Committee has jurisdiction to determine disputes relating to devolved or reserved powers of the Scottish Parliament, the Northern Ireland Assembly and the Welsh Assembly.

The Constitutional Reform Act 2005 amends the composition and jurisdiction of the Judicial Committee of the Privy Council. In terms of composition, the Lord Chancellor and Lord President of the Council are no longer entitled to sit as members of the Privy Council which comprises Justices of the Supreme Court. In relation to jurisdiction, the power to determine devolution issues is transferred from the Privy Council to the Supreme Court.[13]

The Office of Prime Minister[14]

As with so much of the United Kingdom's constitution the office of Prime Minister is one which developed by convention rather than by law. The office dates from the early eighteenth century,[15] and had become firmly established as a necessary and inevitable post in the latter half of the nineteenth century, when the extension of the franchise combined with the growth of political parties to produce both a (reasonably) accountable government and an opposition party. The first official recognition of the post of Prime Minister derives from the Treaty of Berlin 1878, and statutory and other formal references to the office remain scant.[16]

In 1889, Lord Morley[17] stated that:

> . . . the Prime Minister is the keystone of the Cabinet arch. Although in Cabinet all its members stand on an equal footing, speak with an equal voice, and, on the rare occasions when a division is taken, are counted on the fraternal principle of one man, one vote, yet the head of the Cabinet is primus inter pares, and occupies a position which, so long as it lasts, is one of exceptional and peculiar authority.

---

12 Government of Wales Act 1998, Government of Wales Act 2006, Northern Ireland Act 1998, Scotland Act 1998.
13 See the Constitutional Reform Act 2005, ss 40, 138 and Sched 9.
14 See Blake, 1975. For a listing of prime ministers and their political parties, see the Companion Website.
15 Sir Robert Walpole, 1721–42.
16 Inter alia, the Chequers Estates Act 1917, Chevening Estate Act 1959, the Parliamentary and Other Pensions Act 1972, the House of Commons Disqualification Act 1975, Ministerial and Other Pensions and Salaries Act 1991.
17 Cited in Gwynn, 1932.

Little has changed over the intervening century and Lord Morley's view remains true today. Contemporary interest focuses on the power of the office, the relationship between the Prime Minister and the Cabinet and the occasional dominance of the Prime Minister over Cabinet colleagues.[18] One question which inevitably arises is whether government has changed from being parliamentary government, through to being best described as Cabinet government and now through to prime ministerial government.[19] The extent to which there exists prime ministerial dominance depends very much upon the individual personality of the incumbent Prime Minister: there can be no broad generalisations. It must also be recognised that, whatever the personal power of the Prime Minister, he or she is ultimately dependent upon the support of Cabinet, party and Parliament; and, in turn, that support is dependent upon the support of the electorate expressed not just through the vote at a general election, but continually expressed in that amorphous concept 'the mood of the people'. As the resignation of Mrs Margaret Thatcher in 1990 demonstrated,[20] even a seemingly invincible Prime Minister, who had enjoyed success at three general elections, can fall victim to the loss of the vital support of Cabinet and consequently the loss of office.

The powers of the Prime Minister

The role and powers of the Prime Minister are not set down in any Code or statute, but include the following:

- the Prime Minister holds office as Prime Minister and First Lord of the Treasury;[21]
- the Prime Minister as First Lord of the Treasury has responsibility for the Civil Service and assumes the title of Minister for the Civil Service;[22]
- by convention the Prime Minister must be a Member of the House of Commons; and is an elected constituency Member of Parliament;
- the Prime Minister has powers of appointment and dismissal of Ministers (formally this is undertaken by the Crown);
- the Prime Minister determines the size of Cabinet (on Cabinet see further below);
- the Prime Minister determines which Ministers sit in Cabinet;
- the Prime Minister controls the agenda for Cabinet;
- the Prime Minister controls the number and role of Cabinet Committees;
- the Prime Minister has special responsibility for national security and receives intelligence data from the security services;
- the Prime Minister has the power to declare war and peace and to send troops to war;
- the Prime Minister has a weekly audience with the Queen;
- the Prime Minister represents the Crown in foreign affairs;
- the Prime Minister, together with the Secretary of State for Foreign Affairs, participates in European Union Heads of State Summit (the European Council) Meetings;
- the Prime Minister is accountable to Parliament through weekly Prime Ministerial Question Time and the convention that the government must maintain the confidence of the House of Commons.

---

18 See Hennessy, 1986b, Chapter 3.
19 See Wolf-Phillips, 1984; Brazier, 1991. On this question and the role of Mrs Thatcher, see Doherty, 1988; Marshall, 1991.
20 See, inter alia, Alderman and Carter, 1991; Alderman and Smith, 1990; Marshall, 1991; Blackburn, 'Margaret Thatcher's resignation as Prime Minister', in 1992.
21 Ministerial and Other Salaries Act 1975. As First Lord of the Treasury the Prime Minister has responsibility for the Civil Service which is controlled by the Treasury.
22 See Mancini and Keeling, 1991.

The Prime Minister has significant powers and influence over the appointment of persons to senior positions. For example, it is the Prime Minister who is responsible for the appointment of a Commission to oversee the work of the Security Service, and his consent is required for the appointment of most senior civil servants. Prime Ministerial nomination leads to the appointment of, inter alia, bishops and the Parliamentary Commissioner for Administration. His advice is given to the Queen on honours and on appointments to the Privy Council.

The Prime Minister and membership of the House of Commons

Between 1837 and 1902, six Prime Ministers were peers.[23] However, as early as 1839, the Duke of Wellington expressed the view that:

> I have long entertained the opinion that the Prime Minister of this country, under existing circumstances, ought to have a seat in the other House of Parliament, and that he would have great advantage in carrying on the business of the Sovereign by being there.[24]

With the extension of the franchise in 1832, 1867 and 1884, the supremacy of the Commons over the Lords was firmly established and the role of the House of Lords in legislation was reduced significantly by the Parliament Acts of 1911 and 1949. There are good reasons – aside from the office of First Lord of the Treasury – for arguing that the Prime Minister must be a member of the House of Commons. First, he is today the elected leader of the parliamentary party and must lead that party into a general election for an affirmation – or denial – of the party's, and hence his own, mandate. Secondly, the doctrine of individual and collective ministerial responsibility applies to the Prime Minister as it does to all other holders of office. Above all, the doctrines require that a minister is accountable to the electorate through Parliament. For the Prime Minister not to be accountable to the democratically elected House of Commons would effectively defeat the concept of collective responsibility and would be an affront to democracy and the very idea of constitutionalism.

The choice of Prime Minister[25]

A change in Prime Minister will be brought about by either resignation or death or – rarely – dismissal of the office holder. Resignation from office may stem from electoral defeat at a general election, from conflict within the government, from losing the support of the party, from losing a vote of confidence in the House, from a challenge to the leadership of the party, from illness or old age, from death, from voluntary retirement or from loss of support of the Cabinet.[26]

Whatever the explanation for a change in Prime Minister, it is for the monarch to appoint the succeeding Prime Minister. It was seen in Chapter 5 that it is the prerogative right of the Crown to appoint whosoever she pleases, but that by convention rather than law the Queen appoints as Prime Minister the leader of the political party who can command a majority in the House of Commons. In the days before the major parties chose their leaders by some form

---

23 Lords Melbourne, John Russell, Derby, Aberdeen, Beaconsfield and Salisbury.
24 Parl Debs 3rd Ser Vol 47 Col 1016, cited in Jennings, 1959a, p 21.
25 See, inter alia, Jennings, 1959a, Chapter II; Mackintosh, 1977, Chapter 20; Brazier, 1982 and 1990, Chapter 4.
26 Defeat: 1945, 1951, 1964, 1970, 1974, 1979, 1997, 2010. Conflict: as in 1931. Loss of Cabinet support: Mrs Margaret Thatcher's resignation, 1990. Loss of confidence vote: 1895, 1923, 1979. Leadership challenge: Thatcher, 1990. Illness: Campbell-Bannerman, 1908, Bonar Law, 1923, Eden, 1957, Macmillan, 1963. Old age: Salisbury, 1902, MacDonald, 1935, Churchill, 1955. Voluntary retirement: Baldwin, 1937, Wilson, 1976, Blair, 2007.

of election, some discretion was left to the Queen as to the choice of Prime Minister. Nowadays, such discretion is all but dead, other than where a general election produces a situation where there is no overall majority party in the House of Commons (as occurred in 2010: see further below). The actual choice of Prime Minister will thus be dictated by the election process within the major political parties[27] and, where relevant, by the result of a general election.[28]

Formation of Cabinet[29]

Once in office, the first task of the Prime Minister is to form his Cabinet. Constitutionally, the appointment of all ministers is a decision for the monarch but, in practice, it is the Prime Minister who determines who shall be appointed. The Prime Minister decides which government departments should be represented in Cabinet although, by convention, certain Departments are always represented. Thus, the Chancellor of the Exchequer, the Secretary of State for Foreign and Commonwealth Affairs, the Home Secretary, the Secretary of State for Justice and Lord Chancellor, the Secretary of State for Defence, the Secretary of State for Scotland and the Leader of the House of Commons always hold a seat in Cabinet. Further constraints on membership exist. For example, under the Ministers of the Crown Act 1975, certain Cabinet positions are allocated to Members of the House of Lords. Further, under the House of Commons Disqualification Act 1975, the size of Cabinet is effectively controlled – if indirectly – by limiting the number of ministers who may draw a ministerial salary.

It is also for the Prime Minister to decide whether Cabinet Members should remain in office, and he has the right to require a member to resign and, if they refuse, to request the Queen to dismiss them. This form of control was most strikingly seen in 1962 when Harold Macmillan in 'the night of the long knives' removed seven ministers (from a Cabinet of 20) overnight. The Cabinet normally comprises approximately 20 senior members of the government of the day. The actual membership is not fixed, and is (subject to convention) for the Prime Minister to determine.

The role and functions of Cabinet[30]

A Cabinet is a combining committee – a hyphen which joins, a buckle which fastens the legislative part of the state to the executive part of the state. In its origins, it belongs to the one and in its functions, it belongs to the other.[31]

The Cabinet represents the nucleus of government. It is the Cabinet as a whole which, at least in theoretical terms, formulates, initiates and implements the policy of the government. *The Cabinet Manual: A guide to laws, conventions and rules on the operation of government*[32] is a guide to those working in government. The use and working of Cabinets will vary with different governments and the different style and personality of the Prime Minister of the day.

As the central decision-making body, the Cabinet has great power in relation to Parliament as a whole, in relation to the political party it represents and in relation to the Prime Minister.

---

27 See Brazier, 1990, Chapter 1.
28 As in 1906, 1918, 1922, 1931, 1935, 1950, 1955, 1959, 1966, October 1974, 1983, 1987, 1992 where the Government was returned with a clear majority in the House of Commons.
29 See Jennings, 1959a, Chapter III.
30 See, *inter alia*, Jennings, 1959a; Mackintosh, 1977; Hennessy, 1986b.
31 Bagehot, 1867, p 68; see also Jones, 'Cabinet government since Bagehot', in Blackburn, 1992.
32 First edition published in 2011.

While the Prime Minister may control the composition and working of Cabinet, no Prime Minister can ultimately survive in office without the support of Cabinet and party.[33] The style of leadership will depend upon the personality of the premier, and an evaluation of whether it is parliamentary government, Cabinet government or Prime Ministerial government will also depend upon the strength of the Prime Minister vis à vis his or her colleagues.

Cabinet committees

In order to facilitate efficiency, the Cabinet is supported by a system of committees which, again, is largely determined by the Prime Minister.[34] Some of these are standing committees which will exist for the life of the government. Ad hoc committees may be established to consider particular matters. In addition, a whole range of official committees staffed by civil servants exist to complement the work of Ministers.

While the use of committees is both necessary and inevitable, it raises important constitutional questions concerning the doctrine of collective responsibility. Collective responsibility requires that each member of Cabinet, and all government ministers and Parliamentary Private Secretaries, are bound by the decisions of the Cabinet. The extent to which the doctrine will in practice be binding will depend upon the extent government members are prepared to maintain confidentiality and unanimity over decisions in which they may have played no part.[35]

The Prime Minister's private office

While it has often been mooted, and its absence is an apparent anomaly in a sophisticated system of government, there has never been a 'Prime Minister's Department' dedicated to the task of organising, co-ordinating and liaising on behalf of the Prime Minister. Instead, a British Prime Minister's team comprises civil service support and non-civil service political support in the form of a specially appointed team of advisers. Heading the Prime Minister's support system is his Chief of Staff and Principal Private Secretary, who heads the Private Office and who has close relations with both the Cabinet Secretary and the Queen's Private Secretary. A civil servant, usually seconded from the Treasury for a three-year period, it is the Chief of Staff who coordinates the work of the Prime Minister. In addition there is the Director of Communications and Spokesman for the Prime Minister. The Prime Minister also has Special Advisers.[36]

The Cabinet Office[37]

The daily working of Cabinet is assisted by the Cabinet Office, established in 1917, headed by the Secretary to the Cabinet. It is the Secretary to the Cabinet who is responsible for the recording of Cabinet meetings and circulation of the agreed conclusions. Within the Cabinet Office there exist a number of secretariats, including the Economic and Domestic Affairs Secretariat; Defence and Overseas Secretariat; European Secretariat and Government Communication Network Unit and Strategy Unit.

---

33 See Brazier, 1999; Alderman and Carter, 1991; Alderman and Smith, 1990.
34 See Jennings, 1959a, Chapter IX; Mackintosh, 1977, Chapter 21; Hennessy, 1986b. See www.cabinetoffice.gov.uk.
35 On Cabinet committees under different Prime Ministers see Hennessy, 1986b, pp 100–01.
36 On Special Advisers see further below.
37 See Wilson, 1976, Chapter 4; Mosley, 1969; Jennings, 1959a, Chapter 9; Mackintosh, 1977, Chapter 21.

In 2011 the Prime Minister announced reform of the office of Cabinet Secretary. The role previously entailed three posts: Cabinet Secretary, Head of the Civil Service and Permanent Secretary at the Cabinet Office. That role is now divided into three: Cabinet Secretary, Permanent Secretary at Cabinet Office and Head of the Civil Service.

The 2010 Coalition Government

Where, as in 1974 and 2010, there is no political party which secures the required number of seats to form a clear majority in the House of Commons (326 seats), the incumbent Prime Minister, by convention, remains in post until a political agreement can be reached as to which party, or parties, should form a government. Also by convention, the incumbent Prime Minister is entitled to form an alliance with one or several other political parties in the attempt to form a stable government.

The fundamental requirement is that any prospective government can command the confidence of the House of Commons and so ensure stable government. Normally, but not invariably, this requires that a majority of the Members of Parliament will support the government so that it is not at risk of defeat on crucial issues in the Commons which could require the government to resign and trigger another general election. In the May 2010 election, the Conservative Party won more seats than any other party (306), but was twenty seats short of the necessary majority (326 seats).

Several options presented themselves. As the governing party immediately before the general election, the Labour Party could have sought an alliance with the Liberal Democrat Party and other minority parties in an attempt to create a majority. However, an alliance with the Liberal Democrats would leave the Labour Party without the requisite majority (258 + 57 = 315) and would require further parliamentary support from other minority parties to ensure a majority. Alternatively, the Conservative Party could seek an alliance with the Liberal Democrat Party which would give it a clear majority of seats (306 + 57 = 363). As a further alternative, had both the Labour Party and Conservative Party failed in their attempt to form an alliance with other parties the Conservative Party, having the largest number of seats, could have governed as a minority government. After five days of negotiations, the Leaders of the Conservative Party and Liberal Democrat Party reached agreement on a full Coalition government – a form of government unknown in the United Kingdom since the 1930s.

The Leader of the Conservative Party took office as Prime Minister with the Leader of the Liberal Democrat Party becoming Deputy Prime Minister. The Liberal Democrat Party has five Cabinet members. To promote stability, the two parties agreed that there would be a fixed-term five-year Parliament – an unprecedented constitutional development which provides certainty over the timing of the next general election.[38] Further constitutional reform was introduced, with the Parliamentary Voting System and Constituencies Act 2011 requiring a referendum on the introduction of the Alternative Vote system for general elections, and the reduction in the number of parliamentary constituencies from 650 to 600. The doctrine of collective Cabinet responsibility was adjusted in order to accommodate the policy differences between the two political parties without causing a constitutional crisis which could arise if one or both parties were unable to agree and support certain policies (see further Chapter 10).

---

38 Subject to the government being able to maintain the confidence of the House of Commons. Note that the Fixed-term Parliaments Act 2011 gives statutory effect to this development.

The Civil Service

A civil servant has been defined as: '. . . a servant of the Crown, other than holders of political or judicial offices, who is employed in a civil capacity and whose remuneration is paid wholly and directly out of monies voted by Parliament.'[39]

Some doubt exists as to the precise number of personnel in the Civil Service, doubts which arise from the difficulties concerning the appropriate classification of some occupations within the public service. For example, employees of the National Health Service are not technically employees of the Crown – and therefore not civil servants – although responsibility for the Health Service lies with the Secretary of State.

One further difficulty in evaluating the operation of the Civil Service arises from the disparity in size between government departments, with some departments having a staff of over 100,000, while others may have fewer than 10,000. The size of a department has a practical bearing on the extent to which ministers can realistically be said to be making decisions. Added to that difficulty is the preference of some governments for large departments of state. Moreover, recent changes to the structure of the Civil Service to enhance its efficiency have led to a proliferation of government agencies (see below).

When considering responsibility for the Civil Service and accountability to Parliament, a further feature of political life must be borne in mind: that of ministerial mobility. The average tenure of responsibility for a department is two years. The Department of Education and Science, between 1944 and 1986, had 21 ministerial heads. During the Thatcher administration (1979–90), Cabinet reshuffles were frequent with several ministers holding a number of portfolios during that government.

A final practical preliminary point to consider is the sheer volume of work entailed in government. An estimated[40] two-thirds of a minister's working week is taken up by non-departmental business: Cabinet meetings, Cabinet committees, parliamentary party meetings, debates and questions in the House, official visits, and constituency duties. The task of heading a major department of state in addition to all the other duties is a major one, and the practical impact of regular government 'reshuffles', the size of departments and non-departmental duties is great.

Improving efficiency in the Civil Service

Much of the work of government departments is carried out by Agencies.[41] The (Social Security) Benefits Agency is the largest. Others include the Child Support Agency, Driver and Vehicle Licensing Agency, Stationery Office, Land Registry, Ordnance Survey, Patent Office and United Kingdom Passport Agency. Issues of responsibility of ministers are also raised in respect of non-departmental public bodies – 'quangos' – whereby state enterprises are privatised.[42] A non-departmental public body is defined as a body 'which has a role in the processes of national government but is not a government department'.[43] The movement towards increased government involvement in commerce and industry stems from 1945, although public corporations had been established earlier.[44] More recently, the movement has been towards privatisation,

---

39 Report of the Royal Commission on the Civil Service, 1929–31, Cmd 3909, 1931, London: HMSO.

40 Headey, 1974.

41 Report to the Prime Minister, *Improving Management in Government: The Next Steps*, 1988, London: HMSO. See also the Agency Policy Review, *Better Government Services: Executive Agencies in the 21st Century*, 2002.

42 See, *inter alia*, Lewis, 'Regulating non-governmental bodies: privatization, accountability and the public-private divide', in Jowell and Oliver, 2000, Chapter 9.

43 *Non-Departmental Public Bodies: Guide for Departments*, 1986, Cabinet Office/MPO, London: HMSO.

44 Eg the Port of London Authority 1908; Central Electricity Board 1926; London Passenger Transport Board 1933; British Overseas Airways Corporation and British European Airways 1939.

with, among others, British Rail, British Gas, British Telecom, The Stationery Office and the Naval Dockyards being sold into private ownership. Accountability for such organisations, when publicly owned, was weak. Today the question is to what extent these organisations are truly private; to what extent ministers exert control over them, whether via financial power or the power to issue policy guidance; and, more importantly, the extent to which Parliament assures that ministers are accountable for the implementation of policies.

Appointment and management

The Constitutional Reform and Governance Act 2010, section 2, provides for the establishment of the Civil Service Commission with responsibility for the appointment of civil servant. Recruitment is based on 'merit on the basis of fair and open competition'.[45]

The management of the civil service (with the exception of the Northern Ireland civil service diplomatic service and the security services) lies with the Minister for the Civil Service.[46] The prerogative is retained in relation to the management of the diplomatic service and the security services.

Constitutional Principles and the Civil Service

The role of the Civil Service must be considered against the constitutional features of permanence, political neutrality and anonymity.

Permanence

In many countries, such as the United States of America, the Civil Service is a semi-permanent body, the most senior posts of which change hands with a change in government. A variation on this model, which is employed in Germany and France, involves incoming ministers bringing into the department a small body of hand-picked professional advisers. The constitutional significance of permanency lies in the development of expertise and the natural growth of a Civil Service 'ethos'. Most importantly, permanency ensures the availability of such expertise to governments of differing political persuasions. The Private Secretary is a minister's closest contact with a department, and his adviser.

Political neutrality

The Civil Service owes its loyalty to the government of the day, irrespective of political party, and it is imperative that the Civil Service avoids creating the impression of political bias.

The anonymity and political neutrality of civil servants is reinforced by the rules restricting political activity. If the Civil Service is to serve governments of all political persuasions, it is imperative that civil servants, whatever their private political views, should not be seen to be politically active in a manner which would inevitably compromise their neutrality under one political party or another.

The Civil Service is divided, for the purpose of control over political activity, into three groups:

---

45 Constitutional Reform and Governance Act 2010, section 10.
46 A role normally undertaken by the Prime Minister.

(a)   the 'politically free' category which comprises industrial staff and non-officer grades, who may freely engage in either national or local politics;

(b)   the 'politically restricted' category, comprising higher staff grades who are debarred from participating in national political activities, but may be permitted to engage in local politics;

(c)   an intermediate group which comprises those who are employed in neither the highest or lowest grades.

Political activities which are subject to restriction are divided into activities at both national and local level. Those activities subject to restriction at national level include standing as a candidate for election to the European Parliament; holding office in party political organisations which relate to party politics in relation to the United Kingdom or the European Parliament; and speaking on matters of national political controversy, or expressing such views to the press or in books, articles or leaflets. Canvassing on behalf of a candidate for election to the United Kingdom Parliament or the European Parliament, or on behalf of a political party in respect of such elections, is also prohibited. At local level, civil servants in the restricted category may not stand as candidates for local elections; hold office in party political organisations relating to local government; speak on local politically controversial matters or express such views in the media or other publications; and may not canvass on behalf of either a candidate or a political party in the course of local elections.[47]

Anonymity

In order that the minister be seen to be responsible and accountable for the working of his Department, the Civil Service has traditionally been shielded from the public gaze and protected from public inquiry. By protecting the Civil Service, its impartiality and integrity is enhanced. Further, if civil servants become public figures scrutinised in Parliament or the media, their capacity for maintaining the appearance of political impartiality, so important to the concept of permanence, would be damaged.

It has been seen that the minister in charge of a particular government department is absolutely responsible to Parliament for the conduct of civil servants, and that this responsibility in turn involves two aspects. The first of these is that the minister has an obligation to explain and answer for the work of his department to Parliament; the second is that the minister is responsible in constitutional terms for any failure of departmental policy and administration. As a corollary to ministerial responsibility, the Civil Service is not accountable to Parliament and is protected by the concept of anonymity. The *Departmental Evidence and Response to Select Committees* (the 'Osmotherley Rules'), states:

> Civil servants are accountable to Ministers and are subject to their instruction. . . . It is for this reason that when civil servants appear before Select Committees they do so on behalf of their Ministers and under their directions . . .

While, in theoretical constitutional terms, the anonymity of civil servants is important in buttressing the responsibility of ministers of the Crown, it is becoming an increasingly less notable feature of the Civil Service. The explanations for the decrease in anonymity are manifold: the vagaries of individual ministerial responsibility, the increasing strength of departmental select committees and the televising of those proceedings, and recent developments in the management of government departments.

---

47 *Pay and Conditions of Service Code.*

The Civil Service Code[48]

Civil servants working in England are governed by the Civil Service Code.[49] Civil Servants working in the Scottish Executive, the National Assembly for Wales and the Northern Ireland Civil Service have their own versions of the Code. As long ago as 1854, the Northcote-Trevelyan Report set out the key principles that underpin the role and governance of the civil service: integrity, honesty, impartiality and objectivity. The Constitutional Reform and Governance Act 2010, section 5, provides that the Minister for the Civil Service must publish a code of conduct for the civil service (excluding the diplomatic service) and that separate codes may be published for civil servants serving the Scottish Executive or the Welsh Assembly government.

Special advisers

The appointment of special advisers to ministers blurs the lines of responsibility between ministers and civil servants. The Committee on Standards in Public Life examined a whole tranche of issues in 1999, including the role of special advisers, lobbying, sponsorship and public appointments. The Committee accepted that there was no evidence that special advisers were 'politicising the civil service' but expressed the concern that 'the considerable increase in numbers, particularly at Number 10, where influential roles are played by special advisers, raises the question of whether their authority outweighs that of objective advisers' and that 'any future growth in numbers would raise questions about a move towards the establishment of a "cabinet system" within departments'.[50]

The Constitutional Reform and Governance Act 2010 now regulates the appointment of special advisers. Section 15 provides that special advisers are persons appointed to assist a Minister after being selected by that Minister personally and the appointment approved by the Prime Minister under terms and conditions approved by the Minister for the Civil Service. Appointments are to end either when the Minister who appointed the adviser ceases to be a Minister, or on the day after a general election following his or her appointment. Similar provisions apply to advisers serving the Scottish Executive and Welsh Assembly Government.

The Government and the Courts

Liability of the Crown[51]

The government, acting in the name of the Crown, has an historic right to privileges and immunities.[52] Before the Crown Proceedings Act 1947, two main principles governed the question of the legal liability of the Crown. The first principle was that 'the King could do no wrong' and, accordingly, could not be held liable for any actions which would be unlawful if committed by individuals. The second rule was that the King could not be sued in his own courts. Designed to protect the unique constitutional position of the Crown, as state regulation

---

48 HC 27-I (1993–94), London: HMSO; Nolan Report, *Standards in Public Life*, Cm 2850-I, 1995, London: HMSO. See the Civil Service Management Code issued under the Civil Service Order in Council 1995, as amended by the Civil Service (Amendment) Order 1995 and the Civil Service (Amendment) Order 1996.

49 See: www.civilservice.gov.uk/about/values.

50 See *Reinforcing Standards*, the Report of the Committee on Standards in Public Life, 2000.

51 The law is complex and outside the scope of this text. See Craig, 2003a; de Smith, Woolf and Jowell, 1995; Hogg and Monahan, 2000. See also Fairgrieve, 2002; Sunkin, 2003; Andenas and Fairgrieve, 2003.

52 An aspect of the royal prerogative. See Chapter 5.

increased, Crown privilege extended to a wide range of central government activities, thereby weakening the legal protection given to individuals aggrieved by government action. In 1947, the Crown Proceedings Act extended the liability of the Crown to areas of tort and contract. European Community law, the European Convention on Human Rights and the Human Rights Act have all had an impact on this area of law.

The Crown Proceedings Act 1947, section 17, provides that civil proceedings against the Crown must be instituted against the relevant government department, or, if there is no government department which has clear responsibility, the proceedings must be brought against the Attorney General. In Scotland, actions against United Kingdom departments may be instituted against the Advocate General for Scotland, and actions against Scottish devolved bodies instituted against the Lord Advocate.[53]

Section 21 relates to remedies, section 21(1) providing that the court may make such orders as could be made in proceedings between subjects. This is subject to the restriction that the court may not issue injunctions or order specific performance, but may instead grant a declaration. In **M v Home Office** (1994), the House of Lords ruled that an injunction could be granted in an action against a minister personally. Lord Woolf stated:

> There appears to be no reason in principle why, if a statute places a duty on a specified minister or other official which creates a cause of action, an action cannot be brought for breach of statutory duty claiming damages or for an injunction, in the limited circumstances where injunctive relief would be appropriate, against the specified minister personally by any person entitled to the benefit of the cause of action . . .
>
> . . . I do not believe there is any impediment to a court making such a finding [of contempt], when it is appropriate to do so, not against the Crown directly, but against a government department or a minister of the Crown in his official capacity.

The House of Lords also ruled in **M v Home Office** that applications for judicial review are not 'proceedings against the Crown' for the purposes of the Crown Proceedings Act 1947: accordingly injunctive relief against a minister or officer of the Crown is available in judicial review.

See Chapters 7 and 8.

European Union law requires that rights must be given effective protection, and that any domestic restriction on the grant of a remedy must give way to European Union law. As the European Court of Justice stated in **R v Secretary of State for Transport ex parte Factortame Ltd (No 2)** (1991):

> . . . a national court, which in a case before it concerning Community (now EU) law, considers that the sole obstacle which precludes it from granting interim relief is a rule of national law must set aside that rule.

The concept of state liability explained by the ECJ in **Francovich v Italy** (1991) is also relevant. Article 10 of the EC Treaty (now Article 4.3 TEU) provides that Member States must do all they can to facilitate the achievement of EU objectives and refrain from actions which obstruct the achievement of EU objectives. In **Francovich** and subsequent cases the ECJ has used Article 10 to impose liability on Member States.[54]

---

53 See the Scotland Act 1998, Sched 8.
54 See further Convery, 1997; Downes, 1997.

The European Convention on Human Rights, Article 13, requires that everyone whose rights have been violated 'shall have an effective remedy before a national authority notwithstanding that the violation has been committed by persons acting in an official capacity'. Moreover, Article 41 provides that where the Court finds a violation of a Convention right or Protocol and the internal law of a Member State allows only partial reparation to be made, the Court 'shall, if necessary, afford just satisfaction to the injured party'. Section 8 of the Human Rights Act 1998 reflects these provisions, requiring a court which has the power to award damages to make an award where this is necessary to achieve 'just satisfaction' and to have regard to the principles applied by the Court of Human Rights.

See Chapter 18.

Liability in tort

In relation to tortious liability, the Crown is placed in the same legal position as any other adult individual, and has the same liability for the tortious acts of its employees and agents as do private persons and organisations. Two important exceptions to liability remained: liability in respect of actions of members of the armed forces while on duty or on premises used for the purposes of the armed forces, and liability for tortious actions committed by the Post Office.[55] In relation to the armed forces exception, the Crown Proceedings (Armed Forces) Act 1987 abolished the immunity. The Act was not, however, retrospective and the immunity can be revived in times of war or national emergency. In **Matthews v Ministry of Defence** (2002), the Court of Appeal ruled that the immunity was not incompatible with Article 6 of the Convention. These exceptions aside, the Crown is placed in the same position as a private person.

Liability in contract

In principle the liability of the Crown under contract is the same as that of a private person. In practice, however, special considerations apply. The legal status of the Crown has been considered and explained by the judiciary. For example, in **BBC v Johns** (1965) Lord Diplock was to state that the Crown 'personifies the executive government of the country'. In **Town Investments Ltd v Department of the Environment** (1978) Lord Simon of Glaisdale described the Crown as a 'corporation aggregate': a corporation comprising many persons and offices. That description was echoed in part by Lord Woolf in **M v Home Office** (1994) when he said – citing Lord Diplock and Lord Simon of Glaisdale in **Town Investments** – that '... the Crown has a legal personality. It can be appropriately described as a corporation sole or a corporation aggregate ...The Crown can hold property and enter into contracts'.

One distinction between contracts between private parties and a contract involving the Crown lies in the sheer scale of government contracts for the procurement of goods and services and the use of standard conditions in government contracts. A further distinction lies in the responsibility of the Crown to act in the public interest. It has been held judicially that:

> ... the Crown cannot put itself in a position where it is prevented from performing its public duty ... If it seeks to make an agreement which has that consequence, that agreement is of no effect.[56]

---

55 The Post Office ceased to be a government department and became a public corporation in 1969. The restrictions on liability were nevertheless retained.

56 Woolf J in **R v IRC ex parte Preston** (1983), p 306.

Two cases illustrate this rule of 'executive necessity'. The first concerns exceptional wartime conditions.[57] A Swedish shipping company had obtained an undertaking by the British government[58] that its ship would be allowed – contrary to government policy – to leave a British port into which it had entered to deliver its cargo without being replaced by a ship of the same tonnage: the 'ship for ship' policy. In breach of this undertaking the ship *Amphitrite* was detained. The owners sold the ship to avoid further loss and claimed damages for breach of contract. The court ruled that, while the government could bind itself through a contract, and be liable for damages for breach of contract, the arrangement in question was not a commercial contract.[59] Rowlatt J stated:

> . . . it is not competent for the Government to fetter its future executive action, which must necessarily be determined by the needs of the community when the question arises. It cannot by contract hamper its freedom of action in matters which concern the welfare of the State.

The second case is that of **Crown Lands Commissioners v Page** (1960), in which the Court of Appeal ruled that the exercise of the Crown's discretionary powers in relation to land could not be fettered by an implied covenant in favour of the tenant. Devlin LJ stated the principle:

> When the Crown, in dealing with one of its subjects, is dealing as if it too were a private person, and is granting leases or buying and selling as ordinary persons do, it is absurd to suppose that it is making any promise about the way in which it will conduct the affairs of the nation.

Public interest immunity[60]

The phrase 'Crown privilege' has been superseded by the term 'public interest immunity'. One aspect of the immunity which is of contemporary and continuing concern is the extent to which governments – and agencies of government – may be required to disclose information to a court of law. While the immunity from disclosure of information relates principally to the government, it extends to other persons and organisations. The rules regulating the disclosure of documents in civil and criminal cases vary, but in each case there are common features. First, a document may or may not fall within a category of documents which prima facie must be disclosed. Second, disclosure may be denied on the basis that the contents of the documents fall within a particular category of disclosure or non-disclosure,[61] or that the documents fall within a class of documents which may or may not be disclosed.[62] Third, disclosure involves the evaluation of the relevance of the information or documents, which in some cases will be clear, but in other cases less clear until disclosed and evaluated by counsel and the court. Over and above these rules is the public interest immunity certificate. The certificate may be used to claim that it is contrary to the public interest for information or documents to be

---

57 *Rederiaktiebolaget Amphitrite v The King* (1921).
58 Sweden being neutral during the First World War.
59 Contrast this case with that of *Attorney General v De Keyser's Royal Hotel* (1920), discussed in Chapter 5, in which the liability of the Crown to award compensation arose out of statute, and not the royal prerogative.
60 See, *inter alia*, Jacob, 1993; Simon Brown, 1994; Zuckerman, 1994.
61 Eg, non-disclosure is in the public interest if the contents reveal the identity of a police informer, or the workings of the security services.
62 Eg, non-disclosure of Cabinet proceedings, or intergovernmental negotiations, or documents relating to military operations. See *Duncan v Cammell Laird* (1942); *Conway v Rimmer* (1968); *Burmah Oil v Bank of England* (1980); *Air Canada* (1983); *R v Chief Constable of West Midlands Police ex parte Wiley* (1995), discussed above.

disclosed irrespective of the first two rules, and may be claimed on the basis of either contents or class. Where the government would prefer not to disclose information, and the information falls into a 'grey area', there is a temptation to claim public interest immunity to protect the information.

Public interest immunity was raised, for example, in **D v NSPCC** (1978)[63] in order to protect the sources of information given to the National Society for the Prevention of Cruelty to Children.

The need for confidentiality was also accepted in **Bookbinder v Tebbit** (1992) in relation to sources of information given to the Audit Commission, which was investigating alleged irregularities in the financial dealings of a local authority. The court must, however, be satisfied that there is a real need to prevent the disclosure of an informant's identity.[64]

Under the Crown Proceedings Act 1947, a court may order the disclosure of documents in the interests of justice. Section 28, however, also provides that the power of the court in civil proceedings does not extend to disclosures which it would not be in the public interest to make.

There are two aspects of public interest entailed within this area of the law: the public interest in the administration of justice and the public interest in non-disclosure of damaging information. The questions which arise are: who has the power to decide whether disclosure would or would not be in the public interest, and on what basis is the 'public interest' to be evaluated?

In **Duncan v Cammell Laird** (1942), dependants of victims who died in the submarine *Thetis*, which sank during trials, sued the builders of the submarine. Disclosure was sought of documents relating to contracts between the Admiralty and the building contractors, and salvage reports on the submarine. The Admiralty refused to disclose the information, relying on national security, and the minister certified that disclosure was against the public interest. The House of Lords held that the minister's certificate was conclusive and could not be questioned. Accordingly, the rule emerged that a court of law could never question a claim of Crown privilege (or public interest immunity), irrespective of the type of documents being sought. The House of Lords ruled that public interest immunity could lie in respect of the contents of a particular document, or to a class of documents which ought to be withheld in the interests of the proper functioning of the public service. This decision altered the law and, in the words of Professor Wade, gave the Crown the right to withhold information and thereby 'to override the rights of litigants not only in cases of genuine necessity but in any case where a government department thought fit'.[65]

In 1956, the Lord Chancellor, Lord Kilmuir, issued a statement.[66] He drew a distinction between documents which were absolutely necessary to protect the 'proper functioning of the civil service', and documents which are relevant to litigation but which do not require 'the highest degree of confidentiality . . . in the public interest', and stated that privilege relating to medical and other documents relevant to the defence in criminal proceedings should not be routinely claimed.[67] The rule in **Duncan v Cammell Laird**, however, prevailed until 1967. In **Conway v Rimmer** (1968), the House of Lords took a more robust attitude to a claim of public interest immunity, reversing its own decision in **Duncan v Cammell Laird**. In an action for malicious prosecution against his former Superintendent of Police, the Home Secretary

63 And see **Alfred Crompton Amusement Machines Ltd v Customs and Excise Commissioners (No 2)** (1974).
64 See **Norwich Pharmaceutical Co Ltd v Customs and Excise Commissioners** (1974).
65 Wade and Forsyth, 2004.
66 HL Deb Col 741–48, 6 June 1956.
67 On guidelines issued by the Court of Appeal in relation to disclosure in criminal proceedings, see **R v Keane** (1994).

objected to the disclosure of reports made on the former police probationary officer. The court refused to follow the broad ruling in **Duncan v Cammell Laird** and ruled that it was for the court – and not the person seeking to prevent disclosure – to rule on the competing public interests in the administration of justice and confidential information. Accordingly, it is for the person seeking to withhold information to assert – through the use of a public interest immunity certificate – the right to non-disclosure, and for the court to determine whether or not non-disclosure is in the public interest. Lord Reid, in rejecting the claim that the power of decision lay solely with ministers of the Crown, stated that he did not doubt that:

> There were certain classes of documents[68] which ought not to be disclosed whatever their content may be . . . To my mind the most important reason is that such disclosure would create or fan ill informed or captious public or political criticism. The business of government is difficult enough as it is, and no government could contemplate with equanimity the inner workings of the government machine being exposed to the gaze of those ready to criticise without adequate knowledge of the background and perhaps with an axe to grind.

In **Burmah Oil Co v Bank of England** (1980), the oil company sought disclosure of information relating to the rescue of the company by the bank, in exchange for low-priced stock in the company. The Attorney General produced a public interest immunity certificate from the Chief Secretary to the Treasury, in which objection was made against producing documents sought on the basis that they related to government policy. The House of Lords inspected the documents, but felt that their disclosure was unnecessary.

A question relating to public interest immunity certificates which assumed particular importance in the Arms to Iraq affair, was whether the minister was under a duty to sign the certificate when advised to do so by the Attorney General. The notion of duty arose in **Air Canada v Secretary of State for Trade** (1983) in which Lord Scarman (in the minority) stated that, whilst it was for the court to accept or deny the claim, in claiming public interest immunity the Crown was not 'claiming a privilege but discharging a duty'. In the **Air Canada** case, the House of Lords ruled, by a majority, that the government was entitled to immunity. At issue were the circumstances under which, in judicial review proceedings, the court would examine documents for which immunity was claimed. No order for disclosure can be made unless the documents are inspected by the court. The majority in the House of Lords ruled that the party seeking disclosure of documents had to show that 'the documents are very likely to contain material which would give substantial support to his contention on an issue which arises in the case' (per Lord Fraser, p 917e). It was not sufficient that the documents might reveal information relevant to the case; it had to be established by the person seeking disclosure that it was 'very likely' that the information would assist his case.

The distinction between a right and a duty was also considered in **Makanjuola v Metropolitan Police Commissioner** (1992). In that case, Bingham LJ stated that:

> . . . where a litigant asserts that documents are immune from production or disclosure on public interest grounds he is not (if the claim is well founded) claiming a right but observing a duty . . .

Bingham LJ went on to state that:

---

68 Lord Reid refers here specifically to Cabinet minutes.

. . . it [the distinction between a right and a duty] does, I think, mean: (1) that public interest immunity cannot in any ordinary sense be waived, since, although one can waive rights, one cannot waive duties; (2) that, where a litigant holds documents in a class prima facie immune, he should (save perhaps in a very exceptional case) assert that the documents are immune and decline to disclose them, since the ultimate judge of where the balance of public interest lies is not him but the court; and (3) that, where a document is, or is held to be, in an immune class, it may not be used for any purpose whatever in the proceedings to which the immunity applies, and certainly cannot (for instance) be used for the purpose of cross-examination.

Woolf LJ, while endorsing much of this analysis, noted that **Makanjuola** did not involve a Department of State, represented by a Secretary of State. He stated that:

If a Secretary of State on behalf of his department, as opposed to any ordinary liti-gant, concludes that any public interest in the documents being withheld from production is outweighed by the public interest in the documents being available for purposes of litigation, it is difficult to conceive that, unless the documents do not relate to an area for which the Secretary of State was responsible, the court would feel it appropriate to come to any different conclusion from that of the Secretary of State. The position would be the same if the Attorney General was of the opinion that the documents should be disclosed.

However, that situation did not pertain to other bodies or persons, and it could not be left to individuals to decide that documents should be disclosed. The court retained the ultimate right to determine disclosure and would 'intervene to protect the public interest'. The decision in **Neilson v Laugharne** (1981), and those cases in which it had been applied, was wrong and could no longer be justified. It was not, Woolf LJ stated, that 'there had been a change in attitudes since the **Neilson** decision' but rather that 'establishing a class of public interest immunity of this nature was never justified'. In **Wiley**, the House of Lords ruled that in **Neilson** and the subsequent cases in which it had been applied, the law was incorrectly stated. The House of Lords did not, however, go so far as to say that material which came to light in investigations against the police could never be entitled to class immunity.

The House of Lords had the opportunity to re-examine the issue in **R v Chief Constable of West Midlands Police ex parteWiley; Chief Constable of Nottinghamshire Police ex parte Sunderland** (1995). In that case, the defendant, MrWiley, was charged with robbery, but at his trial the prosecution offered no evidence. He subsequently made formal complaints against the police and commenced a civil action against the Chief Constable. Mr Sunderland had been charged with assault but, again, no evidence was offered at trial by the prosecution. He also made a formal complaint against the police. He alleged assault by the police and indicated that he would institute civil proceedings against them. The problem faced by both complainants was that the police had documents which it was thought would attract public interest immunity on behalf of the police, thereby making them unavailable to the complainants. The Chief Constables concerned refused to give undertakings that the documents would not be used to the detri-ment of the complainants, and the complainants secured a declaration that the Chief Constables had acted unlawfully in refusing to give the undertakings. The Chief Constables appealed against the declarations to the House of Lords. In the earlier case of **Neilson v Laugharne** (1981),[69]

---

69 Applied in **Halford v Sharples** (1992) in proceedings alleging unlawful sexual discrimination; distinguished in **Peach v Metropolitan Police Commissioner** (1986) on the basis that the allegation is of a serious crime committed by the police, and **Ex parte Coventry Newspapers Ltd** (1993).

the House of Lords had ruled that public interest immunity attached to police complaints documents, on the basis that if it did not the complaints procedure would be damaged. However, the House of Lords ruled that, in principle, documents which are relevant to litigation should be disclosed, unless that disclosure would cause 'substantial harm'. In particular, Lord Templeman stated that 'a rubber stamp approach to public interest immunity by the holder of a document is neither necessary nor appropriate . . .'.[70]

On recent developments relating to the disclosure of evidence in court and national security see Chapter 22.

Summary

All acts of government are undertaken in the name of the Crown. Central government comprises the Prime Minister and Cabinet and non-Cabinet Ministers backed by the Civil Service. The office of Prime Minister is conventional and unregulated by statute. The respective powers and duties of government are set out in the *Cabinet Manual*, the first edition of which was published in 2011.

The Prime Minister, by convention, must be a member of the House of Commons and the majority of Ministers will also sit in the Commons, although a few will be Members of the House of Lords.

The Civil Service is largely administered under the Royal Prerogative (see Chapter 5). The Constitutional Reform and Governance Act places the Civil Service under the authority of Act of Parliament.

Further Reading

Blackburn, R. (2011), 'The 2010 General Election outcome and formation of the Conservative-Liberal Democrat Coalition Government', Public Law, 30.
Daintith, T. and Page, A. (1999) *The Executive in the Constitution*, Oxford: OUP, Chapters 1–6.
Drewry, G. (2011) 'The Executive: Towards Accountable Government and Effective Governance?' in J. Jowell and D. Oliver (eds) *The Changing Constitution* (7th edn), Oxford: OUP.
Hennessy, P. (1995) *The Hidden Wiring*, London: Gollancz, Chapters 3, 4, 5, 8.
Twomey, A. (2011), 'Changing the Rules of Succession to the Throne', Public Law, 378.

---

70 At p 281. In **Rowe v United Kingdom** (2000) the European Court of Human Rights has ruled that the use of Public Interest Immunity Certificates which prevent a judge from considering whether or not evidence should be disclosed in the court of a murder trial violates Article 6 of the Convention.

Chapter 10

Responsible Government

Introduction

The idea of responsible government is inextricably linked with the rule of law: government *under* or *subject* to the law. However, as has been seen, much of the United Kingdom's constitution is regulated not under formal legal rules but by non-legal, but obligatory, constitutional conventions. A key convention in relation to responsible government is that of ministerial responsibility.

The convention of ministerial responsibility is central to the constitution, and plays a fundamental role in the relationship between the executive and Parliament. For the doctrine of government under the law to be observed, it is essential that government is accountable to both Parliament and the electorate, and that government is conducted in a manner sufficiently open, subject to the requirements of the national interest, to inspire public confidence. The origins of ministerial responsibility are traced by FW Maitland to the principle that 'for every exercise of royal power some minister is answerable' (1908, p 203).

The doctrine has two limbs – individual and collective responsibility. As with so much of the constitution, there is vagueness on occasion as to the distinction between the two limbs which are both closely related and also complementary of one another. In order to facilitate analysis, the topic may be broken down into three aspects:

(a) the collective responsibility of the Cabinet to Parliament, and ultimately the electorate, for policy and administration;

(b) the individual responsibility of ministers for the policy and administration of his or her Department;

(c) the individual responsibility of ministers for their personal conduct.

Collective Cabinet Responsibility[1]

The convention of collective Cabinet responsibility emphasises the unanimity of government and its accountability to Parliament. The classic expression of collective responsibility remains that of Lord Salisbury:

See Chapter 2.

> For all that passes in Cabinet every member of it who does not resign is absolutely and irretrievably responsible and has no right afterwards to say that he agreed in one case to a compromise, while in another he was persuaded by his colleagues . . . It is only on the principle that absolute responsibility is undertaken by every member of the Cabinet, who, after a decision is arrived at, remains a member of it, that the joint responsibility of Ministers to Parliament can be upheld and one of the essential principles of parliamentary responsibility established. [Official Report, HC Cols 833–34, 8 April 1878]

The rationale for the convention lies in the need for government to present a united front to Parliament and the public in order to maintain confidence. A government which exhibits public disagreements over policy matters is one which will be regarded as weak, and will be subjected to challenges to its authority to continue in office.

---

1   See Mackintosh, 1977, Chapter 2; Marshall, 1984, Chapter IV.

Two principal sub-rules underlie collective responsibility. The first rule is that, once an agreement is reached in Cabinet, all members of Cabinet – and many outside Cabinet – are bound to speak in support of the decision. There should be no criticism or dissent from the decision in public – irrespective of whether or not the particular member of Cabinet was party to the discussion. Equally, if a decision is reached by the Prime Minister in Cabinet Committee or the Inner Cabinet when only a small handful of members are present, the decision binds all. The second supporting rule is that records of Cabinet discussions are absolutely secret. The knowledge that Cabinet records are protected by confidentiality enhances the opportunity for members of Cabinet to discuss matters freely, secure in the knowledge that their personal point of view, whatever the decision, will be protected from the public gaze.

These principles are expressed in the Ministerial Code in the following manner:

> Collective responsibility requires that ministers should be able to express their views frankly in the expectation that they can argue freely in private while maintaining a united front when decisions have been reached. This in turn requires that the privacy of opinions expressed in Cabinet and Ministerial Committees should be maintained. [Cabinet Office, 2010, para 2.1]

An example of a breakdown in collective responsibility is seen with the Westland Helicopter saga in 1986.[2] Westland, a helicopter manufacturing company, was threatened with closure. The government sought to promote a rescue bid for the company. Two alternative plans were put forward, one from an American consortium, the other from Europe. Mr Heseltine, Secretary of State for Trade and Industry, wanted the European option to be taken up. Mrs Thatcher, however, favoured the American plan. Mr Heseltine had been informed that he would be able to put his preferred plan to a Cabinet meeting. In the event, however, Mrs Thatcher cancelled that meeting. Mr Heseltine resigned.[3]

The Iraq War in 2003 resulted in two resignations from Cabinet. The Leader of the House of Commons and former Foreign Secretary, Robin Cook, resigned in March 2003 on the basis that he could not support the government's decision to go to war. The International Development Secretary, Clare Short, resigned in May 2003 on the basis that she could not accept the government's position on establishing a legitimate Iraqi government after the war.

As with the convention of individual responsibility, there is dispute about the status and scope of collective responsibility. So many exceptions to the classic doctrine can be discerned that it is possible to question whether it is a convention at all within the classical definition, or whether the term convention should be discarded and replaced by the words practice or usage. Alternatively, it may be argued that the variations which can be observed in the working of the convention merely illustrate one of the greatest strengths of conventional rules – their flexibility.

Agreements to differ

It is possible for the convention of collective responsibility to be waived when the circumstances are such that the political disagreements within Cabinet are of such magnitude that the

---

2 See Oliver and Austin, 1987; Hennessy, 1986a; Marshall, 1989, Chapter 18.
3 Leon Brittan also resigned from government for breaching the convention that the advice of Law Officers to the Crown should not be disclosed.

Prime Minister finds it more expedient to set aside the convention than to have the convention broken by members of Cabinet. In 1931–32, the National (coalition) government contained bitterly opposing views over economic policy; in particular, over the levy of tariff duties. Four members of Cabinet handed in their resignations, and withdrew them only after the Prime Minister, Ramsey MacDonald, decided to waive the convention and allow the dissident members to express their views publicly. In 1975, the Labour government of Harold Wilson was faced with an equally intransigent faction in Cabinet on the matter of the United Kingdom's continued membership of the European Community. Mr Wilson announced a limited waiver of the convention, in the guise of an 'agreement to differ'.[4] The waiver was limited to the single issue of continued membership of the European Community and did not extend to any other areas of government policy.

See Chapter 9.

In May 2010 the general election resulted in no political party having a sufficient number of seats in the House of Commons to enable it to form a government with a clear majority. The party with the largest number of seats, the Conservatives, formed a coalition with the Liberal Democrat Party which gave it a secure majority of seats. However, with marked political differences between the two parties over a range of issues, it was necessary for there to be a relaxation of the rules on collective responsibility on policy areas where disagreement is most pronounced, without which fundamental conflicts could arise and threaten to destabilise the government.

Cabinet papers[5]

The confidentiality of Cabinet discussion is protected by the prohibition against disclosure by members of Cabinet. In addition, the rules regarding the confidentiality of Cabinet papers include the rule that the government of the day may not release the papers of a previous government without the consent of the former Prime Minister.[6] Furthermore, the papers of the previous government may not be disclosed to a government of a different political persuasion. It may at first sight appear curious that an incoming government cannot gain access to the papers of the previous government, and it may be wondered how the government is supposed to act effectively in any policy area if denied so much data. Nevertheless, the rule is justified on the basis that an outgoing government might be tempted to remove politically sensitive documentation if it feared that a new government would make political capital out of it. Three categories of papers are excepted from the convention:[7]

(a) papers which, even if not publicly available, can be deemed to be in the public domain, for example letters sent by former ministers to trade associations, trade unions, etc, or to Members of Parliament about constituency cases, or to members of the public;

(b) papers, other than genuinely personal messages, dealing with matters which are known to foreign governments, for example, messages about intergovernmental negotiations;

(c) written opinions of the Law Officers, which are essentially legal rather than political documents.

---

4 HC Deb Col 1745, 23 January 1975; Col 351, 7 April 1975; Cmnd 6003, 1975; Wilson, 1976, pp 194–97.
5 On secrecy in government, see further below.
6 HC Deb Col 1039, 1 July 1982; Cols 468, 8 July 1982; 474; Hunt, 1982.
7 Hunt (Lord), 'Access to a previous government's papers', in Marshall, 1989.

Ministerial memoirs

The publication of a former minister's memoirs of his political life poses problems for the rules relating to Cabinet secrecy. In 1976, the Radcliffe Committee Report[8] stated that:

The author should be free to use his ministerial experience for the purpose of giving an account of his own work, subject to restrictions on three separate categories of information:

(a) he must not reveal anything that contravenes the requirements of national security operative at the time of his proposed publication;

(b) he must not make disclosures injurious to this country's relations with other nations;

(c) he must refrain from publishing information destructive of the confidential relationships on which our system of government is based.

The final restriction relates to opinions or attitudes of Cabinet colleagues, advice given to him by colleagues and criticism of those working for him in office.

The Ministerial Code prohibits the writing and publication of memoirs by a Minister still in office. In relation to former Ministers the Code requires that the draft manuscript is submitted to the Cabinet Secretary before publication.[9]

In *Attorney General v Jonathan Cape Ltd* (1976), the issue of the publication of the diaries of Richard Crossman, a former Labour Cabinet member, was considered. Executors of the estate of Richard Crossman sought to publish his *Diaries*; the government sought an injunction restraining publication. Recognising the convention of collective responsibility, Lord Widgery CJ stated:

I find overwhelming evidence that the doctrine of joint responsibility is generally understood and practised, and equally strong evidence that it is on occasion ignored.

Having given such ambivalent recognition to the convention, which in any event was not court-enforceable, the injunction was denied.

Individual Ministerial Responsibility[10]

The Ministerial Code provides that: the minister in charge of a Department is solely accountable to Parliament for the exercise of the powers on which the administration of the Department depends.

Ministerial responsibility for the department

Hierarchical structure of a typical Government Department:

---

8 *Report of the Committee of Privy Councillors*, Cmnd 6386, 1976, London: HMSO, Appendix 2.

9 Ministerial Code, 2010, paras 8.9 and 8.10.

10 See Turpin, 'Ministerial responsibility: myth or reality?', in Jowell and Oliver, 2000, Chapter 3.

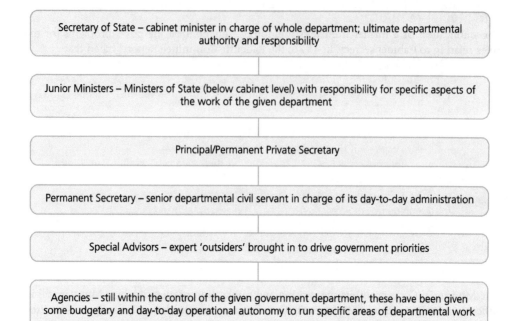

The classic doctrine of this limb of ministerial responsibility states that a minister is responsible for every action of his department. As AV Dicey expressed it, the responsibility of ministers means, where used in its strict sense, the legal responsibility of every minister for every act of the Crown in which he takes part.

Ministerial responsibility is governed by parliamentary Resolutions, the Codes of Conduct of both Houses of Parliament, the Seven Principles of Public Life and the Ministerial Code.[11] The general principle governing Ministers of the Crown is that:

> Ministers of the Crown are expected to behave in a way that upholds the highest standards of propriety.[12]

The Ministerial Code also provides, in part, that:

- Ministers must uphold the principle of collective responsibility;
- Ministers have a duty to Parliament to account, and be held to account, for the policies, decisions and actions of their departments and agencies;
- Ministers must give 'accurate and truthful information to Parliament' . . . Ministers who knowingly mislead Parliament will be expected to offer their resignation to the Prime Minister;
- Ministers must be as 'open as possible with Parliament and the public' . . . refusing to provide information only when disclosure would not be in the public interest;
- Ministers must ensure that no conflict arises, or appears to arise, between their public duties and their private interests.[13]

---

11 Cabinet Office, 2010.
12 *Ibid*, para 1.1.
13 Cabinet Office, 2010, para 4.6. See also *Civil Servants and Ministers: Duties and Responsibilities*, Cmnd 9841, 1986, London: HMSO, para 11.

The Code also makes clear the role and power of the Prime Minister in relation to Ministers:

> Ministers are personally responsible for deciding how to act and conduct themselves in the light of the Code and for justifying their actions and conduct to Parliament and the public. However, Ministers only remain in office for as long as they retain the confidence of the Prime Minister. He is the ultimate judge of the standards of behaviour expected of a Minister and the appropriate consequences of a breach of those standards.[14]

It is the Minister who represents the public face of the Department and who speaks for the department in Parliament. The doctrine is underpinned by Parliamentary Question Time and in debates in Parliament and in committees. During the passage of legislation relating to a particular department's responsibilities, it is the Minister who will introduce the Bill and who will defend the Bill throughout its passage through the House of Commons. The Minister thus stands as the link between the Civil Service and Parliament, assuming full responsibility for the Department. As seen in Chapter 9, the conventionally recognised characteristics of the Civil Service are permanence, political neutrality and anonymity. The civil servant owes his or her duty to the government of the day, and is directly accountable to his or her Secretary of State. The principle of ministerial responsibility to Parliament not only underpins the doctrine of democratic responsibility of ministers to the people through Parliament, but also facilitates the distinction between the responsibility of elected representatives and the civil servants who are responsible for the practical implementation of policy.

In practical terms nowadays, several factors diminish the extent to which a Minister can assume responsibility for every action of the Department. The size of departments, the usually short ministerial tenure of office in any one department and the complexity of modern government have long made the pure doctrine unworkable. As a former Home Secretary, Mr Reginald Maudling, stated in 1973, the classic doctrine of responsibility must be viewed in the light of modern conditions, with large departments of state. Furthermore, the complexity of defining the scope of ministerial responsibility must also be seen in light of the rapid and extensive administrative framework under the system of agencies which are designed to increase efficiency in administration by establishing specialist agencies, each with its own executive.

Crichel Down

The classic doctrine of individual ministerial responsibility was seen to operate most clearly in the Crichel Down affair in 1954.[15] Crichel Down, an area of some 725 acres in Dorset, had been compulsorily acquired by the Air Ministry in 1937 for use as a bombing range. After the Second World War, the land was no longer needed and it was transferred to the Ministry of Agriculture and administered by the Agriculture Land Commission. In 1950, the Commission decided that the best way of disposing of the land was to equip it as a single farm unit and lease it.

Three hundred and twenty eight acres of Crichel Down had been part of the Crichel Estates owned by a Mrs Marten. Her husband wanted to reclaim the land. In both 1950 and 1952 he asked the Commission whether he could buy back the land. The Commission wrongly thought that they had no power of sale and declined to investigate his request. Mr Marten raised the matter with his Member of Parliament, who referred the matter to the Parliamentary Secretary to the Minister of Agriculture, who requested a report from the Land Commission.

---

14 Cabinet Office, 2010, paras 1.1–1.5.
15 Cmnd 9220, 1954, London: HMSO.

The official in charge of making the report was instructed not to approach the previous owners or to inspect the land, and to treat the matter as one of great confidentiality. The resulting report was full of inaccuracies, and went unchecked by the Ministry, which decided to adhere to its original plan for the land.

Mr Marten was informed of the decision in 1953, and advised the Ministry that he would rent the whole of the land. Meanwhile, the Ministry had committed itself to another course of action. Mr Marten's letters to the authorities went unanswered and he pressed for a public inquiry. The inquiry found that there had been inaccuracies in the report on the land, muddle and inefficiency in handling the matter and hostility to Mr Marten. In July 1954, the minister Thomas Dugdale accepted responsibility and resigned.[16]

Ministerial responsibility after Crichel Down

It is notable that, between 1954 and 1982, there were no instances of ministerial resignation following allegations of and inquiries into serious defects in departmental administration. In 1959, 52 people were killed by security forces in Nyasaland but the Colonial Secretary Mr Lennox-Boyd did not resign. In 1964, due to a lack of co-ordination within the Ministry of Aviation, an overpayment of some £4 million was made to the Ferranti company, but the minister did not resign. In 1968, the Foreign Secretary, Mr George Brown, did not resign over the Sachsenhausen affair in which 12 former detainees in a Nazi prison camp were wrongly denied compensation under a scheme set up to compensate victims of Nazi persecution.[17]

In 1971, the Vehicle and General Insurance Company collapsed leaving over a million policyholders uninsured. The Department of Trade and Industry had supervisory responsibility for insurance companies. An inquiry report placed the blame on a civil servant, Mr Jardine, an Under Secretary in the Department, and the minister did not resign.[18] In 1982, the Home Secretary, Mr William Whitelaw, did not resign over a breach of security at Buckingham Palace which resulted in an intruder entering the Queen's bedroom, nor did Mr James Prior (as he then was), the Northern Ireland Minister, resign in 1984, following the escape of terrorists from the Maze Prison. The exchange in Parliament revealed divergent views about accountability. In debate, Mr Prior distinguished carefully between responsibility for policy – for which he accepted responsibility – and the failure of officials to follow the correct orders and procedures – for which he denied responsibility:

> However, I do not accept – and I do not think it right for the House to accept – that there is any constitutional or other principle that requires ministerial resignations in the face of failure, either by others to carry out orders or procedures or by their supervisors to ensure that staff carried out those orders . . .

In 1994, the Home Secretary, Michael Howard, faced several calls for his resignation over escapes from Whitemore prison and over the finding of escape equipment and weapons in prisons. Mr Howard refused to resign, citing in his support the precedent set by Mr James Prior (as he then was) over escapes from the Maze prison in Ulster, and the distinction between responsibility for operational matters and matters of policy.[19]

---

16 See, inter alia, Nicolson, 1986; Griffith, 1987.
17 Third Report of the Parliamentary Commissioner for Administration, HC 54 (1967–68), London: HMSO; Select Committee Report, HC 258 (1967–68); Fry, 1970.
18 HL Deb 80; HC Deb 133 (1971–72), para 344.
19 In 2006 the Home Secretary, Charles Clarke, refused to resign over the Home Office failure to deport foreign criminals on the expiry of their sentences. Mr Clarke was sacked by the Prime Minister.

The Falklands War in 1982 provided the scenario for three ministerial resignations. Lord Carrington, the Foreign Secretary, resigned following allegations, which he denied, over the lack of preparation of the British forces when the Argentineans attacked; Mr Luce and Mr Atkins also resigned from the Foreign Office.[20]

In 1989, Mrs Edwina Currie resigned over the furore caused by her claim that the majority of eggs in the United Kingdom were infected with salmonella and, in 1990, Mr Nicholas Ridley resigned from the Department of Trade and Industry, having accepted responsibility for making intemperate remarks about a fellow Member State of the European Community. In 2002, the Secretary of State for Transport, Stephen Byers, resigned. He had seemed unable to produce progress in transport revitalisation. He also, fatally, failed to dismiss his special adviser after a callous remark made on 11 September 2001. Also in 2002, the Secretary of State for Education resigned following sustained criticism over examinations. The Health Secretary, Alan Milburn, resigned office in 2003, not for any shortcomings in office, but on the basis that he wanted to have more time to spend with his family.

The Work and Pensions Secretary, David Blunkett, resigned office for the second time in November 2005. He had first resigned his post as Secretary of State for the Home Department in 2004, having had an affair with a married woman and allegedly having intervened to have her nanny's application to remain in Britain 'fast tracked' through the system. The reason given for the second resignation was a breach of the rule that former ministers should consult the Advisory Committee on Business Appointments about any business appointments they intend to take within two years of leaving office. The Ministerial Code now makes it clear that Ministers must seek advice from the Committee and are expected to abide by the advice received.[21]

In 2011 the Secretary of State for Defence, Dr Liam Fox, resigned office following disclosures that a close friend, Adam Werritty, had gained access to high-level meetings by representing himself as Dr Fox's adviser. A report by the Cabinet Secretary stated that Dr Fox had put the security of his staff at risk by disclosing details of his overseas visits and had risked causing confusion overseas about Britain's foreign policy by allowing the impression that Mr Werritty represented the British government. Furthermore, Mr Werritty had accepted donations from Conservative supporters, which could have given rise to the perception of a conflict of interest.

Evaluating the evidence

From the above evidence, how is the working of the doctrine of individual ministerial responsibility to be evaluated? First, it is arguable that the doctrine represents one of the most significant conventions of the constitution, enhancing the accountability of the government to Parliament and the electorate. However, as has been seen above, the existence and acceptance of responsibility does not inevitably lead to the consequence of the resignation of a minister for the failures within his or her department. No hard and fast rules exist which will determine whether and when a minister should resign, and accordingly it cannot clearly be said that resignation forms a part of the convention itself. On the question of the circumstances under which a minister will resign as a result of departmental mismanagement, Professor SE Finer (1956) considered that:

> . . . whether a minister is forced to resign depends on three factors: on himself, his Prime Minister and his party.

---

20 See Cmnd 8787, 1983, London: HMSO.
21 Ministerial Code, 2010, para 7.25.

For a resignation to occur, all three factors have to be just so: the minister compliant, the Prime Minister firm, the party clamorous. This conjuncture is rare, and is in fact fortuitous. Above all, it is indiscriminate – which ministers escape and which do not is decided neither by the circumstances of the offence nor by its gravity.

In recent years there have been considerable improvements in the system of monitoring the conduct of ministers and Members of Parliament through the Register of Members' Interests, the Advisory Committee on Business Appointments, the Committee on Standards in Public Life and the Parliamentary Commissioner for Standards and the Independent Parliamentary Standards Authority and Compliance Officer. However, there is no automatic sanction for breach of the rules by Ministers – the issue of resignation remains firmly in the political arena.

The Morality of Public Office

Qualification for ministerial office

Given the fundamental importance of ministerial responsibility, it is perhaps surprising that there are neither formal qualifications for office nor formal means by which the suitability for office is scrutinised in advance. Sir Ivor Jennings states that:

> . . . the most elementary qualification demanded of a Minister is honesty and incorruptibility. It is, however, necessary not only that he should possess this qualification but also that he should appear to possess it. [1959a, Chapter V, p 106]

Lord Hailsham expresses the same sentiment as follows:

> A politician must be trustworthy, and if he is found out telling a lie or if he is discovered in even a small financial dishonesty, he can only bow himself out of public life. [1975, p 199]

If a minister of the Crown or Member of Parliament conducts his personal or financial affairs in a manner that falls below an 'acceptable standard', the minister may be required to resign. Finer (1956) describes such conduct as being:

> . . . a personal misadventure of the minister which raises such doubt about his personal prudence or integrity as to cause him to resign.

Vetting of prospective ministers?

In the United States of America, appointment to Cabinet office is undertaken only after the 'advice and consent' of the Senate has been obtained.[22] By this means, it is intended to test the suitability of candidates prior to appointment and to avoid the inevitable embarrassment which occurs when resignation is forced through disclosure of some financial, sexual or other impropriety. In the United Kingdom, by contrast, appointment is entirely at the discretion of the Prime Minister and will be made on information which is publicly available and from the personal and political reputation of the candidate. As has been seen above, the standard of

---

22 Constitution, Article II, s 2.

conduct required for public life and the reality frequently part company. It is thus at least argu-able that some form of 'vetting' – such as occurs with prospective holders of senior Civil Service posts – should be introduced. Professor Rodney Brazier has advocated this course of action,[23] favouring some form of pre-appointment formal inquiry into fitness for office. Such an approach has not found favour with others who have considered it. In the inquiry following the Profumo scandal, Lord Denning stated that there should be no inquiry into politicians' private lives by the security services other than where state security was under threat, a view endorsed by the Security Commission in its report following the resignations of Lords Lambton and Jellicoe.[24] Lord Hailsham expressed the view that, in a democracy, there should be no such invasive advance inquiries into the private lives of public figures (1975), while recognising the real risks of corruption in public life which 'is hard to define ... harder to detect, and almost as catching as smallpox' (p 201). It must, however, be conceded that when the standard of conduct is lowered and the esteem of a government damaged by lack of integrity, then some action is needed.

Individual Responsibility for Personal Conduct

Personal conduct

While responsibility for the implementation and execution of policy of course entails 'personal conduct', one aspect of ministerial responsibility which has also given rise to particular concern is the conduct of ministers in relation to their private lives. The personal relationships of ministers are also matters which fall under intense public scrutiny. In 1963, the Minister of War, Mr John Profumo, was found to have been having a sexual relationship with a prostitute, Christine Keeler. Ms Keeler, it was discovered, also enjoyed a close personal relationship with a Russian Naval Attaché at the Soviet Embassy. When questioned in the House of Commons about the affair, Mr Profumo lied to the House. When the truth emerged, Mr Profumo resigned office. The cause of his resignation was not so much the sexual affair, but contempt of the House committed through lying. The potential security aspects of the affair led to a judicial inquiry headed by Lord Denning MR.[25]

In 1973, Lords Lambton and Jellicoe resigned office. Earl Jellicoe, Lord Privy Seal and Leader of the House of Lords, resigned after it had been revealed that he had been associating with prostitutes. Lord Lambton, Parliamentary Under Secretary of State for Defence for the Royal Air Force, resigned over allegations of involvement with illegal drugs. The government requested an inquiry by the Security Commission into any security aspects of the affairs, which resulted in the finding that no classified information had in fact been revealed either directly or indirectly to 'any potentially hostile power'.[26]

In 1983, Cecil Parkinson MP, the Secretary of State for Trade and Industry and Conservative Party Chairman, resigned following revelations about a long-standing relationship with his secretary, Sarah Keays, who became pregnant. For some time, the Prime Minister, Mrs Thatcher and the Party maintained their support for Mr Parkinson,[27] as did his wife throughout the public attention focused on the affair. When Sarah Keays published a series of articles in the

23 Brazier, 1998, Chapter 3, and 1994.
24 Lord Denning's Report, Cmnd 2152, 1963, London: HMSO, para 230; Report of the Security Commission, Cmnd 5367, 1973, London: HMSO, para 42.
25 Statement to the House 674 HC Deb 809–10, 21 March 1963; Lord Denning's Report, Cmnd 2152, 1963, London: HMSO; Macmillan, 1973, pp 436–41; Denning, 1980, Pt 2, Chapter II; Marshall, 1984, Chapter VI.
26 Report of the Security Commission, Cmnd 5367, 1973, London: HMSO, para 5; Marshall, 1984, Chapter VI. On the role of the Security Commission, see further Chapter 22.
27 Thatcher, 1993, pp 310–11; Tebbitt, 1988, pp 205, 208–11.

national press about the matter, and alleged that Mr Parkinson had said that he wanted to marry her, public and political support began to wane, and Mr Parkinson resigned.

In 1992, Alan Amos MP resigned after allegations of indecency with another man. Also in 1992, the Heritage Secretary David Mellor was forced to resign following revelations of a sexual relationship with an actress (and the receipt of gifts). The majority of the revelations had been brought about through the illicit bugging of an apartment used by Mr Mellor. While this affair alone may not have caused his downfall, the revelation that Mr Mellor and his family had enjoyed the hospitality, while on holiday, of the wife of a Palestinian Liberation Organisation official, sealed his fate. Despite his being regarded as an excellent Heritage Secretary, the intense and hostile coverage by the media ensured his resignation.[28] In January 1994, Tim Yeo MP, Minister of State for the Environment, resigned after admitting fathering a child out of wedlock, as did Alan Duncan MP after allegations that he had used the 'right to buy' legislation to make money in property deals with a neighbour. In February 1994, Hartley Booth MP resigned after a 'close relationship' with a research assistant; in May 1994, Michael Brown MP resigned following newspaper reports of a 'friendship' with a male civil servant. In 1998, Ron Davies, the Welsh Secretary, resigned immediately after being discovered in unexplained but curious circumstances on Clapham Common. In 2012 the Energy and Climate Change Secretary, Chris Huhne, resigned from Cabinet following criminal charges of perverting the course of justice. In 2012 the Conservative Chief Whip, Andrew Mitchell, resigned following a disputed argument with a police officer. At the time of writing, the matter is subject to investigation. The message is, if you are caught out, resign sooner rather than later in order to spare the government embarrassment and loss of public confidence.

Financial probity

The personal financial probity of ministers, their Parliamentary Private Secretaries and other Members of Parliament is regarded with seriousness. Under the law and custom of Parliament, Members must declare their financial interests in the Register of Members' Interests and make public declarations in debate or committee proceedings of any interests they hold which may affect their impartiality.[29] The holding of directorships, ownership of shares, consultancy positions and receipt of gifts all raise issues concerning integrity and fitness for office. The Ministerial Code states that 'Ministers must scrupulously avoid any danger of an actual or apparent conflict of interest between their Ministerial position and their private financial interests'. The general principle is that a Minister must either dispose of an interest or take steps to prevent any conflict.[30] Where a financial interest is retained, processes must be put in place to ensure that the Minister is not involved in any decision-making relating to that interest. The Ministerial Code also requires that ministers consult the Advisory Committee on Business Appointments about any business appointments they intend to take up within two years of leaving office – a requirement breached by David Blunkett in 2005 (above). There is an inherent vagueness in such criteria, yet relatively few ministers and other Members of Parliament have fallen from grace as a result of imprudent (or dishonest) financial dealings. In 1913, the issue of ministers holding shares was raised in debate following allegations of improper ministerial involvement in the Marconi Company.[31] It was rumoured that ministers[32] had used information

28 Statement of Resignation 212 HC Deb 139, 25 September 1992.
29 On alleged payments for parliamentary questions, see Chapter 17.
30 A full list of interests which might give rise to an appearance of conflict must be provided.
31 54 HC Deb 5 Ser 391–514, 543–664. See Donaldson, 1962.
32 Attorney General, Sir Rufus Isaacs, Chancellor of the Exchequer, D Lloyd George, and Postmaster General, Sir Herbert Samuel.

received as ministers for their own personal advantage. All three ministers involved denied any share dealings. A select committee inquiry exonerated the ministers of all charges of corruption and from charges that they had used their ministerial positions for personal gain.

In 1949, a Tribunal of Inquiry[33] was established to inquire into allegations of payments and other benefits being made to John Belcher MP, Parliamentary Secretary to the Board of Trade. Mr Belcher had received gifts offered with a view to securing favourable treatment in relation to licences granted by the Board of Trade. He resigned office and his parliamentary seat as a result.[34]

Ministerial resignations involving allegations of financial imprudence – although in each case there were additional factors involved in the resignations – include, as noted above, David Mellor, the Heritage Secretary, who resigned following a mixture of allegations, one of which involved the receipt of a free holiday from a woman with Palestinian Liberation Organisation associations.[35] In 1992, it was revealed that the Chancellor of the Exchequer, Norman Lamont, had received £4,700 of public money for legal fees involved in the eviction of a tenant from his apartment.[36] In June 1993, the Minister for Northern Ireland, Michael Mates MP, resigned office after it had been revealed that Mr Mates gave to the fugitive businessman Asil Nadir, who faced prosecution on charges of theft and fraud, an inexpensive watch, shortly before Mr Nadir fled the United Kingdom. A subsequent allegation was made that Mr Mates accepted the loan of a car from Mr Nadir for his ex-wife's use and he ultimately resigned despite claiming to have the full support of the Prime Minister.[37] Further embarrassment was caused to the government in 1994, when it was alleged that Jeffrey Archer, former Conservative Party Chairman, had been involved in share-dealing in Anglia Television, on whose Board of Directors his wife held a directorship. Also in 1994, allegations were made that Members of Parliament had accepted payment for asking parliamentary questions. This affair escalated into a full-scale judicial inquiry into 'standards in public life', and to a tightening of the rules regulating the financial interests of all members of the House of Commons.[38] In 1998 came the culmination of the long-running inquiry into the financial affairs of Geoffrey Robinson, the former Paymaster General, when in December both Robinson and Peter Mandelson, Secretary of State for Trade and Industry, resigned. Peter Mandelson had been a leading architect in making the 'New' Labour Party 'electable' and a pivotal figure in the general election campaign. However, it was revealed that Mandelson had accepted a personal loan from Robinson to finance the purchase of a London home, and that the loan had not been disclosed. While protesting that he had done nothing 'wrong', Mandelson resigned. He returned to ministerial office in 1999 as Secretary of State for Northern Ireland, only to resign again over allegations that he interfered in a passport application of a wealthy Indian businessman who had contributed money to the Millennium Dome, for which Mandelson had responsibility at the time.[39] In 2005 the resignation of the Work and Pensions Secretary, David Blunkett, discussed above, was in part prompted by allegations concerning shares in a company which was due to bid for a government contract.

See Chapter 17.

In 2009 it was disclosed that several government Ministers and numerous Members of Parliament had abused the system of parliamentary allowances and expenses, leading to many resignations. The matter is discussed in detail in Chapter 17. Perhaps the most high-profile

---

33 Under the Tribunals of Inquiry (Evidence) Act 1921.
34 *Report of the Tribunal*, Cmnd 2616, 1949, London: HMSO.
35 HC Deb Col 139, 25 September 1992.
36 See Brazier, 1992 and 1993.
37 Interview, BBC News, 22 June 1993.
38 On this see Chapter 17.
39 An Inquiry chaired by former Treasury Secretary Sir Anthony Hammond cleared Mandelson of any wrongdoing.

ministerial resignation caused by the affair was that of David Laws, appointed by the Coalition government formed in 2010 as Chief Secretary to the Treasury, to head its financial deficit-reduction programme. Mr Laws had broken the rules against leasing accommodation from partners, doing so to protect his private life.

Premature disclosure of confidential information

By convention the contents of the Chancellor of the Exchequer's Budget are kept secret until revealed in Parliament. Traditionally, the rule about secrecy was so strict that the details would not even be revealed to Cabinet before Parliament. Nowadays, however, the rule is much relaxed and it is not uncommon for the Chancellor to discuss proposals prior to formal disclosure.

The Nolan Committee

The continued and intensive media interest in ministerial conduct has caused a loss of public confidence in Members of Parliament as a whole, and in the conduct and probity of ministers. The Nolan Committee, appointed to inquire into standards in public life, examined in general the standards of conduct expected of ministers. More specifically, the Committee has investi-gated the question of the rules relating to ministers who retire from office and subsequently take up employment with organisations with whom they had dealings whilst in ministerial office. In addition, the Committee considered the organisation, regulation and personnel employed in non-departmental public bodies (NDPBs or 'quangos').[40]

The conduct of ministers of the Crown

The Nolan Committee endorsed the view that the 'public is entitled to expect very high stand-ards of behaviour from ministers, as they have profound influence over the daily lives of us all'.[42] The Committee distinguished between the need for clear enforceable rules regulating financial conduct and those regulating sexual conduct. In respect of the latter, the Committee, whilst recognising that sexual improprieties may on occasion be relevant to the performance of a minister's public duties, took the view that it was not possible to lay down hard and fast rules to regulate such private conduct. The Committee recommended that the Prime Minister should be given explicit power to determine whether ministers – who are responsible for complying with the standards of conduct – have in fact upheld the required standard (paragraph 13).

Matrix Churchill and arms to Iraq[42]

Between 1987 and 1989, the Matrix Churchill company exported machine tools to Iraq. It was alleged by Customs and Excise (which brought the prosecution against the directors of the company) that those exports breached the export regulations in place at the time. In defence, it was argued that the government knew about the exports and had in fact authorised them, and that MI6 (the Secret Intelligence Service) was aware of the exports. When the matter came

---

40 Quasi-autonomous non-governmental organisations, on which see further below and Chapter 23.
41 Nolan Report, *Standards in Public Life*, Cm 2850-I, 1995, London: HMSO, Chapter 3, para 4.
42 See Leigh, D, 1993; Norton-Taylor, 1995; Tomkins, 1998.

to trial, four government ministers[43] signed public interest immunity certificates (on which see further below) refusing disclosure of documents relating to, *inter alia*, records of meetings and communications between the Department of Trade and Industry and the Foreign and Commonwealth Office. The effect of the certificates was to deny to the court the evidence which might have led to the acquittal of the defendants, each of whom was facing a significant term of imprisonment if convicted. The trial of the directors of Matrix Churchill collapsed after a former government minister, Alan Clark, revealed to the court that the government had – as the defence claimed – in fact known of the exports. The Prime Minister established a judicial inquiry, chaired by Sir Richard Scott, the day after the collapse of the trial.[44] The decision to establish a judicial inquiry was brought about in large measure through the failure of select committee inquiries to unravel the full facts surrounding the issue.[45]

For further details see the Website.

In 'Ministerial accountability' (1996), Sir Richard Scott developed the themes analysed by Sir David Maxwell-Fyfe in his report on the Crichel Down affair (see above), and evidence given to the Scott Inquiry by Sir Robin Butler, the Cabinet Secretary. Referring to the distinction increasingly frequently made in recent years between ministerial constitutional responsibility and ministerial constitutional accountability, Sir Richard Scott cited Sir Robin's evidence as follows:

> I am using 'accountability' to mean that the Minister must always answer questions and give an account to Parliament for the action of his department, whether he is 'responsible' in the sense of attracting personal criticism himself, or not. So I am using 'accountability' to leave out, as it were, the blame element of it. The blame element is an open question. There are cases where he is accountable in which he may be personally blameworthy, and there will be occasions when he is not personally blameworthy.[46]

The 'divorce' between the acceptance of responsibility and the consequence of resignation was not, in Sir Richard's expressed view, the 'heart of an effective system of parliamentary accountability' as the Treasury and Civil Service Select Committee regarded it to be.[47] In Sir Richard's view, what does lie at the heart of the constitutional doctrine is rather the:

> . . . obligation of ministers to give, or to facilitate the giving, of information about the activities of their departments and about the actions and omission of their civil servants.[48]

In the Arms to Iraq affair, the obligation to provide information came into conflict with the government's insistence on following the practice of not disclosing to Parliament information concerning individual export licensing matters. The refusal to answer questions at all is but part of the problem of the duty to give information. A further cause for concern lay in the failure of ministers to give full answers to questions and, in relation to the Scott Inquiry, in the

---

43 Tristan Garel-Jones (Foreign and Commonwealth Office on behalf of Douglas Hurd, the Foreign Secretary); Malcolm Rifkind (Defence Secretary); Michael Heseltine (President of the Board of Trade); Kenneth Clarke (Home Secretary).

44 See *Report of the Inquiry into the Export of Defence Equipment and Dual-Use Goods to Iraq and Related Prosecution*, HC 115 (1995–96), 15 February 1996 (the Scott Report).

45 See the Trade and Industry Select Committee, *Second Report, Exports to Iraq: Project Babylon and Long Range Guns*, HC 86 (1991–92), London: HMSO; see also Tomkins, 1993; Bradley, 1992a.

46 Evidence given to the Inquiry on 9 February 1994: transcript, pp 22–23, cited in the Scott Report.

47 *Fifth Report of the Treasury and Civil Service Committee: The Role of the Civil Service*, HC 27-I (1993–94), London: HMSO, para 133; cited in the Scott Report, p 415.

48 Scott Report, p 415.

failure of witnesses to provide the full picture. 'Commercial confidentiality' is an accepted reason for the denial of information, but that, in Sir Richard's view, did not excuse the refusal of information or the provision of information about weapons supply. National security is another justified exception to the duty to make full disclosure. Nevertheless:

> ... setting those rare cases aside, the proposition that it is acceptable for a Minister to give an answer that is deliberately incomplete is one which, in my opinion, is inconsistent with the requirements of the constitutional principle of ministerial accountability. Half the picture can be true ... But the audience does not know that it is seeing only half the picture. If it did know, it would protest.[49]

A strong democracy can only be a legitimate label if the electors are able to express their view on the basis of adequate knowledge of government activities:

> A failure by Ministers to meet the obligations of ministerial accountability by providing information about the activities of their departments engenders cynicism about government and undermines, in my opinion, the democratic process.[50]

The Public Service Committee Report: ministerial accountability and responsibility[51]

Reviewing the doctrine of ministerial responsibility from the Crichel Down affair in 1954, the Committee produced 34 conclusions and recommendations. In the Committee's view, it was not possible to distinguish absolutely between areas in which a minister is personally responsible (and blameworthy) and areas in which the minister is constitutionally accountable.[52] Further, the Committee concluded that 'proper and rigorous scrutiny and accountability' is a more important feature of ministerial responsibility than Parliament's ability to force that minister's resignation.[53] The Public Service Committee had been critical of the fact that the definition and scope of ministerial responsibility was formulated by the government of the day, via *Question of Procedures for Ministers*, rather than by Parliament, which alone had the right to demand and enforce ministerial responsibility. As a result, and after much inter-Party debate, the House of Commons resolved in 1997 that:

> In the opinion of the House, the following principles should govern the conduct of ministers of the Crown in relation to Parliament:
>
> (1) Ministers have a duty to Parliament to account, and be held to account, for the policies, decisions and actions of their departments and next step agencies;
>
> (2) It is of paramount importance that ministers should give accurate and truthful information to Parliament, correcting any inadvertent error at the earliest opportunity. Ministers who knowingly mislead Parliament will be expected to offer their resignation to the Prime Minister;
>
> (3) Ministers should be as open as possible with Parliament, refusing to provide information only when disclosure would not be in the public interest;

---

49 *Scott Report*, p 422. See Tomkins, 1996.
50 Ibid, p 425.
51 *Second Report from the Public Service Committee*, HC 313 (1995–96), London: HMSO.
52 See HC Deb Vol 290 Col 273, 12 February 1997; and *Government Response to the Report of the Public Service Committee on Ministerial Accountability*, HC 67 (1996–97), London: HMSO, November 1996, p vi.
53 See *Government Response to the Report of the Public Service Committee on Ministerial Accountability*, HC 67 (1996–97), London: HMSO.

(4) Ministers should require civil servants who give evidence before parliamentary committees on their behalf and under their directions to be as helpful as possible in providing accurate, truthful and full information.[54]

The Hutton Inquiry[55]

The Iraq War in 2003 was to lead to two judicial inquiries. The first, the Hutton Inquiry, was prompted by the suicide of Dr David Kelly CMG, a senior government scientist who, inter alia, had been one of the chief weapons inspectors in Iraq on behalf of the United Nations' Special Commission.

Central to the circumstances surrounding Dr Kelly's death was the intelligence relating to weapons of mass destruction (WMD) set out in a government dossier published in September 2002. In May 2003 a journalist, who had met with Dr Kelly, alleged in a radio programme that the government's dossier was wrong in that it claimed that Iraq had WMD which were deployable within 45 minutes and that the government had exaggerated the intelligence to bolster its case to attack Iraq. Dr Kelly acted as an adviser to the Ministry of Defence, the Defence Intelligence Staff and the Secret Intelligence Service (MI6) and part of his role was to speak to the media and other institutions on Iraq issues. The government complained to the BBC about the broadcast. The identity of the journalist's source of information then became of central importance.

Among the several issues which Lord Hutton considered in relation to the government dossier was whether the Prime Minister or officials in 10 Downing Street were responsible for intelligence being set out in the dossier which they knew or suspected was incorrect or misleading. The Inquiry's conclusions regarding the dossier exonerated the government from any attempt to embellish the data relied on. The 45-minute claim at the heart of the controversy had been received by the SIS from a source in Iraq which was regarded as reliable. The allegation that the government 'knew' that the claim was wrong was unfounded. Further, the Inquiry found that Downing Street recognised that nothing should be stated in the dossier which was inconsistent with the intelligence received.

The Butler Inquiry

In February 2004 the Prime Minister decided to establish a committee of inquiry to review intelligence on weapons of mass destruction. The Inquiry was chaired by the Rt Hon Lord Butler, a former Cabinet Secretary.[56] The terms of reference of the Inquiry were to investigate the intelligence coverage available in respect of WMD programmes in countries of concern and on the global trade in WMD, taking into account what is now known about these programmes; as part of this work, to investigate the accuracy of intelligence on Iraqi WMD up to March 2003, and to examine any discrepancies between the intelligence gathered, evaluated and used by the government before the conflict, and between that intelligence and what has been discovered by the Iraq survey group since the end of the conflict; and to make recommendations to the Prime Minister for the future on the gathering, evaluation and use of intelligence on WMD, in the light of the difficulties of operating in countries of concern.

The Inquiry concluded that there had been no wrongdoing on the part of the government. On the '45-minute claim' the Inquiry found that the intelligence report itself was 'vague

---

54 These principles are reflected in the Ministerial Code 2010, para 1.2 b–e.
55 See Blom-Cooper and Munro, 2004.
56 See *Review of Intelligence on Weapons of Mass Destruction*, Report of a Committee of Privy Counsellors, London: The Stationery Office, HC 898, July 2004.

and ambiguous'.[57] On allegations that the government's motivation for going to war was a desire to control Iraq's oil supplies, the Inquiry found 'no evidence' to support such an allegation.

The Chilcot Inquiry

The Chilcot Inquiry was established to examine the United Kingdom's involvement in the Iraq War 2003, including the way in which decisions were made and actions taken. The Inquiry was chaired by Sir John Chilcot.[58] Public hearings began in November 2009.[59] The hearings were open to the public and televised. The hearings were not covered by parliamentary or other privilege, and witnesses were entitled to have a legal representative present during the hearing, although not to give evidence or ask questions. The Inquiry was not a court of law and questions of guilt or innocence were not in issue.[60] The Report of the Inquiry is expected in 2013–14.

Government Openness and Government Secrecy

The issue of the confidentiality of Cabinet papers has been discussed above. More generally, the issue of confidentiality of government papers gives rise to questions about the extent to which the government in the United Kingdom operates with an unnecessary degree of secrecy. Secrecy in government raises important questions for the individual citizen concerning the right of access to personal information stored by the government and also to the right of access of citizens more generally to documents concerning government of the state and of access to information about the policies and standards of service of public bodies. The issue of access to personal data held by government is discussed later in this chapter. A further question arises as to the disclosure of government documents to courts of law and the use of public interest immunity certificates by the government to conceal evidence.

Standards of Public Service and the Openness of Government

Access to information[61]

The balance to be struck between the right of authorities to maintain confidential records and the right of individuals to access to that information is increasingly a matter of concern. There is no general right of access to data stored by the state, for example records maintained by the Police, Inland Revenue, National Health Service and Department of Social Security. Under the Official Secrets Act 1989, categories of information can never be disclosed. A limited right of access to personal files is granted under the Data Protection Act 1984.[62] Citizens in the United Kingdom are entitled to access to official records in certain categories of cases.[63] The information which can be disclosed is currently confined to computerised records, in other

---

57 *Review of Intelligence on Weapons of Mass Destruction*, para 507.
58 A retired senior civil servant. All five members of the Committee are Privy Councillors.
59 For security reasons a number of hearings have been held in private.
60 http://www.iraqinquiry.org.uk.
61 See Savage and Edwards, 1985; Tapper, 1989; Reed, 1993.
62 As extended by the Data Protection (Subject Access Modifications) Health Order, SI 1987/1903.
63 On current proposals for greater access to information, see further below.

words excluding manually created files, although access to these will be introduced in the future.

In any heavily regulated state, government departments will have access to large amounts of personal data on its citizens. Tax authorities, social security offices, local authorities and driving licence authorities are but four major holders of personal information. The individual has two interests in personal records. The first is that information held about the individual should be accessible to him or her. The second is that the individual should be protected against disclosure of such personal data to third parties.

The protection of personal data

A range of statutes prohibit the unauthorised disclosure of personal data to third parties. Local authority records (relating to, *inter alia*, adoption, education, child support, housing, medical records and social security) are protected. Equally, in the finance industry, there is protection given to confidential information. In relation to such information, the government does not accept that there is a need to relax the restrictions on disclosure.

Access to personal data

The Data Protection Act 1984 provided that computer-held personal information should be made available to individuals, in order that the person concerned may check the accuracy of the data. The Data Protection Act 1998 replaced and repealed the 1984 Act. The Act applies only to personal data, defined in section 1(1), and confers the right to be informed of whether data is being held and to have that data communicated to the subject. The data covered by the Act is wider than under the 1984 Act and relates to both computer-held records and manual files. Disclosure may be refused where it would, *inter alia*, damage national security, or be counter to the interests of the prevention or detection of crime or the apprehension or prosecution of offenders (sections 28 and 29). The Information Commissioner supervises the operation of the Act, and may issue enforcement notices on any data controller who is not acting in accordance with the principles of the Act (see section 4 and Schedule 1). The Commissioner lays an annual report before Parliament. The Access to Personal Files Act 1987 provides that individuals have the right to inspect records relating to social services and housing tenancies. Medical records prepared for insurance or employment purposes are accessible under the Access to Medical Reports Act 1988. The Access to Health Records Act 1990 gives patients the right to see records held by general practitioners, health authorities or NHS trusts.

Access to public records

The Public Records Acts 1958 and 1967 provide for the inspection of public records at the Public Records Office after 30 years, unless there is justification for withholding them. The Lord Chancellor also has the power under the Act to order the release of documents at an earlier period if in the public interest. Under section 5 of the 1958 Act, records may be kept closed for a longer period.[64] The main classes of information not disclosed relate to population census returns, Ministry of Pensions First World War war pensions awards files and the Inland Revenue Stamps and Taxes Division registered files.

---

64 Only one to two per cent of records remain closed for longer periods.

The Freedom of Information Act 2000

In 1997, the incoming Labour government promised to inject greater openness into the machinery of government. Towards this end, a White Paper, *Your Right to Know: White Paper on Freedom of Information*, was published in December 1997.[65] The government intended that, for the first time, citizens should have a legal right to information and to the records in which that information is contained. In addition, an independent Information Commissioner would be appointed, who would be answerable not to Parliament, but to the courts. The new legal right applies throughout the public sector, as well as to some private organisations carrying out duties on behalf of government and privatised utilities. Citizens are entitled to information, subject to 'harm tests'. The Freedom of Information Act supersedes the Code of Practice on Access to Government Information and amends the Data Protection Act 1998 and the Public Records Act 1958. The Act was fully implemented in 2005, and applies to central government with effect from November 2002. The Act is the culmination of years of attempting to open up the processes of government. There are, however, a number of restrictions imposed on the right to information.

The Freedom of Information Act for the first time confers on citizens a general right of access to data held by public authorities (section 1), including local government, National Health Service bodies, schools and colleges, the police and others. Requests must be in writing, and the authority is under a duty to respond to the request within 20 working days of its receipt. A fee is payable and the duty to disclose does not arise until the fee is paid. The Act is regulated by a Commissioner to whom the public has a right of direct access (section 18; see further below). A public authority may decline to provide information where the cost exceeds the 'appropriate limit' (section 11; the limits are prescribed and may be changed). The Act also provides a list of exempted information, which considerably weakens the general principle of a 'right to know'.

Information which is exempt from disclosure falls into two categories: that which is absolutely exempt and other information which requires the balancing of the public interest in maintaining the exemption and the public interest in disclosure. The following categories of information are exempt from the duty of disclosure (Part II of the Act):

- information which is accessible by other means or which is to be published;
- information relating to the security services or the royal household;
- personal information or information provided to the authority in confidence;
- information to which professional privilege applies;
- information which might prejudice:

  - national security, defence or the effectiveness of the armed forces;
  - international relations or relations between administrations within the United Kingdom;
  - the country's economic interests;
  - criminal investigations or proceedings;
  - law enforcement;
  - the effective conduct of public affairs;
  - the physical or mental health of any person;
  - trade secrets or commercial interests.

Interpretation of the scope of exemptions ultimately falls to the courts (on appeals see below). For example in **British Broadcasting Corporation v Sugar (No 2)** (2012), the Supreme Court

---

65 Cm 3818, London: HMSO.

interpreted section 7(1) of and Part VI of Schedule 1 to the Act which provided that the BBC was under a duty to disclose information on request only if it was 'held for purposes other than those of journalism, art or literature'. The applicant had sought disclosure of an internal report on the quality of its coverage of a particular area of news reporting. The Supreme Court ruled that if material was held to 'any significant degree for the purposes of journalism' and was also held for some other purpose, there was no duty of disclosure. In **Kennedy v Information Commissioner** (2012), the Court of Appeal examined the exemption from disclosure relating to a statutory inquiry undertaken by the Charity Commission into a particular charity. Section 32(2) of the 2000 Act provides that information is exempt information 'if it is held only by virtue of being contained in (a) any document placed in the custody. . . . . .' or '(b) any document created by . . . . for the purposes of the inquiry'. The Court of Appeal ruled that the material remained exempt following the conclusion of the inquiry. Applying **BBC v Sugar** (2012), the exemption was absolute. Article 10 was not engaged where a public authority refused disclosure in accordance with domestic legislation.

The Act specifies the investigative and enforcement powers of the Commissioner. Where the Commissioner decides that a public authority has failed to communicate information, or to provide confirmation or denial, in a case where it is required to do so, the Commissioner may issue a decision notice specifying the steps which must be taken by the authority in order to comply (section 49(4)). The Commissioner may also issue enforcement notices requiring the authority to take, within a specified time, such steps as are required to comply. Where the Commissioner has issued a decision or enforcement notice in respect of the disclosure of information under section 13, a certificate may be issued by an 'accountable person' as defined in the Act, the effect of which is that a public authority need not comply with the Commissioner's notice (section 52). If an authority fails to comply with the Commissioner's notice, the Commissioner may so certify to the High Court or, in Scotland, the Court of Session, and the court may, having conducted a hearing, deal with the authority as if it had committed a contempt of court (section 53).

Appeals

Either the complainant or the pubic authority may appeal against a decision notice to the Tribunal under section 56. The Tribunal shall either allow the appeal or substitute such other notice as could have been served by the Commissioner, or in other cases must dismiss the appeal. Appeals from the decision of the Tribunal on a point of law lie to the High Court or to the Court of Session in relation to Scotland and to the High Court of Justice in Northern Ireland.

Amendments relating to public records

Part VI of the Act provides a statutory regime for access to public records, replacing the provisions of the Public Records Act 1958 relating to discretionary disclosure. It also provides for increased access to information contained in records more than 30 years old.

Amendments to the Data Protection Act 1998

Part VII extends the Data Protection Act 1998 in relation to subject access and data accuracy on information held by public authorities. Schedule 6 extends the 1998 Act to include relevant personal information processed by or on behalf of both Houses of Parliament. Personal data is, however, exempt if the exemption is required for the purpose of avoiding an infringement of the privileges of either House of Parliament.[66]

---

66 Freedom of Information Act 2000, Sched 6, inserting s 35A into the Data Protection Act 1998.

Summary

The accountability of government to Parliament and the people is essential in any democratic state. The constitutional conventions of collective and individual ministerial responsibility are central to ensuring this accountability. Collective responsibility refers to the requirements that decisions reached in Cabinet are binding on all Cabinet and non-Cabinet Ministers and that Cabinet discussions are confidential and may not be disclosed. Individual ministerial responsibility also has two aspects: the first being the responsibility of the Minister to account to Parliament for the operation of his or her Department; the second being responsibility for personal conduct.

Government must retain the confidence of the House of Commons, and failure to do so may result in a successful Motion of No Confidence which by convention forces the government to resign. Aspects of government policy may also give rise to serious questions which require a formal inquiry to examine and report. Examples of such inquiries include the inquiry into Arms to Iraq (the Scott Report), the inquiry into the death of Dr David Kelly and the soundness of intelligence relating to weapons of mass destruction in Iraq (the Hutton Report) and the further inquiry into weapons of mass destruction undertaken by Lord Butler in 2004. The most recent inquiry, in 2009–10, relates to the legality of the Iraq War, chaired by Lord Chilcot.

The openness of government is also a matter of constitutional importance. The Freedom of Information Act 2000 provides citizens with a right of access to data held by public authorities, subject to a number of exceptions and qualifications.

Further Reading

Benn, T. (1980), 'The Case for a Constitutional Premiership', Parliamentary Affairs, 33: 7.

Blackburn, R. (2008) *King and Country: Monarchy and the Future King Charles III*, London: Politico's.

Brazier, R. (1991), 'Reducing the Power of the Prime Minister', Parliamentary Affairs, 44: 453.

Brazier, R. (1999), *Constitutional Practice* (3rd edn), Oxford: OUP, Chapters 5–7.

Drewry, G. (2011) 'The Executive: Towards Accountable Government and Effective Governance?' in J. Jowell and D. Oliver (eds) *The Changing Constitution* (7th edn), Oxford: OUP.

Finders, M. (2000) 'The Enduring Centrality of Individual Ministerial Responsibility within the British Constitution', Journal of Legislative Studies, 6: 73.

Hough, B. (2003) 'Ministerial Responses to Parliamentary Questions: Some Recent Concerns', Public Law, 211.

Woodhouse, D. (1993) 'Ministerial Responsibility in the 1990s: when do Ministers Resign?', Parliamentary Affairs: 46: 277.

Woodhouse, D. (1997) 'Ministerial Responsibility: Something Old, Something New', Public Law, 262.

Chapter 11

Devolution and Local Government

Chapter Contents

Introduction

As discussed in Chapters 1 and 2, the constitution of the United Kingdom has traditionally been characterised by the unity of its several parts, with centralised government. The history of Ireland and the union of Northern Ireland with Britain is long and complex and is outlined below. Wales became united with England through being conquered in 1262, while the Acts of Union 1706 and 1707 marked the end of the separation of Scotland and England under two sovereign Parliaments. Despite the former attempt at devolution of power to both Wales and Scotland in 1978, the population of neither country then expressed – according to the terms of the referendum – the desire for greater separation from centralised government. Two decades later, however, the political position was much changed. A disenchantment with the extent to which the national Parliament reflected the views of the people of Scotland, in particular, and Wales, and a rising tide of nationalist regional sentiment, led to change and power being devolved from the centre to the nations. In addition, settlement reached in Northern Ireland under the 1998 Good Friday agreement facilitated the re-establishment of the Northern Ireland Assembly. The Scotland Act 1998 and the Government of Wales Acts 1998 gave effect to devolution of power with the establishment of a Scottish Parliament and the Welsh Assembly.[1]

In 2007 the Scottish Parliament and UK Government established the Commission on Scottish Devolution to review the working of Scottish devolution and to make recommendations. The Commission, chaired by Sir Kenneth Calman, reported in 2009.[2]

As discussed further below, the Calman Commission Report led to the passing of the Scotland Act 2012, which enhances Scottish devolution, particularly in relation to financial matters. In 2012 the Scottish First Minister announced his intention to hold a referendum in 2014, asking the Scottish people whether they wish to be independent of the United Kingdom and clearly raising the question of the future of the 'United' Kingdom.

One of the constitutional consequences of devolution is that Members of the United Kingdom Parliament in London (Westminster) who represent constituencies in Northern Ireland, Scotland and Wales vote on matters which relate solely to England, whereas English MPs do not have any say in matters which have been devolved to the national parliaments.[3] This issue is under consideration by the Commission on the Consequences of Devolution for the House of Commons (the McKay Commission), established in 2012.

Forms of local government – which reflect the needs and wishes of people living in local communities – have existed as long as communities have existed and pre-date central government by centuries. Local government represents both a form of decentralisation of power from central government and a basis for local democracy. The country is divided into local authorities – either county or district – each having law-making and administrative powers as delegated by Parliament. Local authorities nowadays are entirely creatures of statute: accordingly, the only powers which they have are those conferred by the sovereign United Kingdom Parliament. Increasingly, however, the law of the European Union also requires action at local authority level.

The combined effect of devolution to Northern Ireland, Scotland and Wales and local government is a constitution which is less 'unitary' and increasingly multilayered.

---

1 See also the Government of Wales Act 2006 and Scotland Act 2012.
2 See *Serving Scotland Better: Scotland and the United Kingdom in the 21st Century*, Final Report of the Commission on Devolution 2009.
3 The 'West Lothian Question': see below at page 250.

Northern Ireland

The early history

Ireland first came under the control of the English in the twelfth century. The province of Ulster – then the nine northern counties of Ireland – was largely unaffected by English rule until the sixteenth century. In the seventeenth century there was a considerable level of immigration into the north, principally from Scotland and Wales, resulting in a significant Protestant (non-Roman Catholic) population. Relations between Ireland (which adhered to the Roman Catholic faith) and England – fuelled by the issue of religion – worsened. In an attempt to quell unrest and reach a lasting settlement, negotiations took place which resulted in the Act of Union 1800. Intended to be a permanent union, it was not to survive the economic crises which led to famine and mass emigration from Ireland. The movement towards independence from England grew. In 1919 civil unrest escalated into war. In 1920 the United Kingdom Parliament passed the Government of Ireland Act under which the country was partitioned, with six of the original nine Ulster counties being separated from the remainder of Ireland. In the following year the Anglo-Irish Treaty gave to southern Ireland (the Irish Free State) self-governing dominion status. In 1937 the Irish Prime Minister published the Constitution of the Irish Free State, proclaiming independence from the United Kingdom: a situation not formally accepted by the United Kingdom until 1949.

From the time of partition until 1972, Northern Ireland enjoyed a measure of self-government represented by the assembly at Stormont. However, the turbulent legacy of the past continued to exert its influence with the Irish Republican Army (IRA) seeking to rid Northern Ireland of British rule and reunite the province with the Republic of Ireland. The terrorist campaign was to last for 30 years. In 1974 the Northern Ireland Act led to the restoration of direct rule of Northern Ireland by Westminster.

The election of the Labour government in 1997 led to renewed efforts to revitalise the peace talks. Success followed with the 'Good Friday Agreement' of 1998.[4] Uniquely the settlement required that former political opponents, the Ulster Unionist Party (now the Democratic Unionist Party) and Sinn Fein (the political wing of the republican movement) work together. In other words co-operation between representatives of both communities was a prerequisite for the devolution of power. In 1999 the re-devolution of power was complete, the Assembly elected and a power sharing executive in place. However, in 2002 power was recalled to Westminster.[5] The Northern Ireland (St Andrews Agreement) Act 2006, section 2, provided for the re-devolution of power to Northern Ireland, subject to three conditions being met before a specified date. These conditions were that:

- members of the Assembly would elect a First Minister and Deputy First Minister;[6]
- nominations would be made for other ministerial offices; and
- that those elected or nominated would affirm the pledge of office.

Once those conditions were met, the Secretary of State was obliged to make a restoration order under the 2000 Act, restoring devolution and ending direct rule.[7]

---

4   Cm 3883.
5   Under the Northern Ireland Act 2000.
6   Section 8 of the Northern Ireland (St Andrews Agreement) Act 2006 inserts new ss 16A–16C into the 1998 Act making detailed provision for the appointment of First and Deputy First Minister.
7   The 2000 Act was to be repealed automatically on the day after the restoration order took effect: Sched 2, para 3(1). The Northern Ireland (St Andrews Agreement) Act 2006 makes further provision relating to the restoration of devolved government.

The devolution of powers to the Northern Ireland Assembly under the 1998 Act excluded powers in relation to policing and justice in Northern Ireland – a contentious political matter over which no agreement could be reached. However, in March 2010 agreement between the parties in Northern Ireland was finally reached, enabling the transfer of powers and the establishment of a Department of Justice for Northern Ireland.

The status of Northern Ireland

Section 1 of the Northern Ireland Act 1998 reiterates earlier pledges regarding the status of Northern Ireland, stating that:

> . . . Northern Ireland in its entirety remains part of the United Kingdom and shall not cease to be so without the consent of a majority of the people of Northern Ireland voting in a poll held for the purposes of this section . . .

Giving recognition to long-held Republican ambitions for a united Ireland, section 1 commits the government of the United Kingdom to giving effect to the wishes of the people should a majority express the wish to cease to be part of the United Kingdom and form part of a united Ireland, following such agreement as may be made between the United Kingdom government and the government of Ireland.

The Northern Ireland Act 1998 regulates the Northern Ireland Assembly and Executive. The Act includes many significant distinguishing features unique to the situation pertaining in Northern Ireland. In particular, the Act provides for a power-sharing executive, with offices allocated between differing political parties according to their electoral support. The Assembly has statutory power to exclude a minister or junior minister, or a political party, from holding office for a 12-month period if the Assembly resolves that he, she or it no longer enjoys the confidence of the Assembly on the basis that he or she is not committed to non-violence and exclusively peaceful and democratic means. The Act also provides for the protection of all citizens of Northern Ireland from discrimination on the grounds of religious belief and introduces a Human Rights Commission and Equal Opportunities Commission.[8]

The executive

Part III of the Northern Ireland Act 1998 regulates the executive authorities. Within six weeks of the date of the first meeting of the Assembly, the Assembly elected the First Minister and Deputy First Minister. If either the First Minister or Deputy First Minister resigns or otherwise ceases to hold office, the other minister must also cease to hold office at that time, but may continue in office until a new election is held.[9]

Ministerial offices

The number of ministerial offices is determined by the First Minister and Deputy First Minister acting jointly, but may not exceed ten, or such greater number as is approved by the Secretary

---

8   The Act repeals, *inter alia*, in full, the Government of Ireland Act 1920, Northern Ireland (Temporary Provisions) Act 1972, Northern Ireland Assembly Act 1973, Northern Ireland Constitution (Amendment) Act 1973, Northern Ireland Act 1974, and, in part, the Northern Ireland Constitution Act 1973 and all of the Northern Ireland Act 1982 and the Northern Ireland (Elections) Act 1998.
9   Northern Ireland Act 1998, s 16 subs by Northern Ireland (St Andrews Agreement) Act 2006, s 8(1).

of State. The allocation of ministerial offices provided for under the Act is designed to achieve power sharing between the political parties, in proportion to the number of seats held in the Assembly. An Executive Committee is established, comprising the First Minister, the Deputy First Minister and the Northern Ireland Ministers. The First Minister and Deputy First Minister are chairmen of the Committee.[10] In addition to providing a forum for discussion of issues which cut across the responsibility of two or more Ministers, prioritising executive and legislative proposals and formulating an agreed position on various issues, the Northern Ireland (St Andrews Agreement) Act 2006 provides that the Committee is the forum for discussion and agreement on controversial matters which the First and Deputy First Minister have decided should be dealt with by the Committee.[11]

Ministers of Northern Ireland Departments have no power to make, confirm or approve any subordinate legislation, or do any act, so far as the legislation or act is incompatible with Convention rights or EU law, or discriminates against, or aids or incites another person to discriminate against, a person or class of person on the ground of religious belief or political opinion.[12]

Elections

Assembly elections are held every four years. Provision is made for extraordinary elections, whereby, if the Assembly passes a resolution that it should be dissolved, the Secretary of State must propose a date for the election of the next Assembly. Constituencies are the same as those for parliamentary elections and each constituency returns six members. Voting is by single transferable vote.

The Northern Ireland (Miscellaneous Provisions) Act 2006 amends section 84(1) of the Northern Ireland Act 1998 to enable the anonymous registration of voters in situations where the voter would be at risk if he or she were identified.

Control over donations to political parties are regulated under Political Parties, Elections and Referendums Act 2000. The prohibition in relation to foreign donors is moderated in relation to Northern Ireland to enable donations to be made from Irish citizens and other Irish bodies.[13] Special provision is also made to protect the identity of donors. The Electoral Commission is under a duty to verify information submitted in donation reports but is also placed under a duty of confidentiality.[14]

The Assembly

The Assembly consists of 108 elected members, six from each of the 18 Westminster constituencies. Proceedings of the Assembly are regulated under Standing Orders. The first task of the elected Assembly is to elect from among its members a Presiding Officer and deputies, positions analogous to the Speaker of the House of Commons and his or her deputy.[15] Consistent also with the Scotland Act 1998, there is established a corporate body, known as the Northern Ireland Assembly Commission, comprising the Presiding Officer and members of the Assembly, to perform the functions of providing property, staff and services, and other contractual functions.

---

10 Ibid, s 20 a/a Northern Ireland (St Andrews Agreement) Act 2006.
11 The 2006 Act, s 5 also makes provision for a statutory Ministerial Code, inserting s 28A into the 1998 Act.
12 Northern Ireland Act 1998, s 24.
13 Section 12 Northern Ireland (Miscellaneous Provisions) Act 2006, inserting new ss 71A–71C into the 2000 PPER Act.
14 Schedule 1 ibid, inserting new ss 71D and 71E into the 2000 PPER Act.
15 Northern Ireland Act 1998, s 39.

Legislation

Section 5 of the Northern Ireland Act 1998 provides for the making of Acts of the Assembly, but reserves to the United Kingdom Parliament the right to make laws for Northern Ireland, subject to the right of the Assembly to modify provisions made by Act of Parliament in so far as it is part of the law of Northern Ireland. The legislative competence of the Assembly is regulated by sections 6 and 7, and section 6(1) states that a provision of an Act is not law if it is outside the legislative competence of the Assembly. Schedule 10 defines and regulates proceedings in relation to disputes over the legislative competence of the Assembly.

Members' interests

A register of members' interests is provided for under section 43. Members having a financial or other interest must declare that interest before participating in Assembly proceedings, and standing orders may include a provision preventing or restricting participation in proceedings by a member with a registrable interest. It is an offence to advocate or initiate any cause, or urge another member to do so, in consideration of any payment or benefit in kind. A person guilty of an offence is liable to a fine not exceeding level five on the standard scale. Proceedings may only be brought with the consent of the Director of Public Prosecutions for Northern Ireland.

Privilege

For the purposes of the law of defamation, absolute privilege attaches to the making of a statement in Assembly proceedings, and to the publication of a statement under the Assembly's authority.[16]

Human Rights and Equal Opportunities

The Act establishes a Human Rights Commission,[17] consisting of a Chief Commissioner and other Commissioners appointed by the Secretary of State.[18] The functions of the Commission include ensuring the adequacy and effectiveness of law and practice in relation to the protection of human rights, and reporting to the Secretary of State such recommendations as are considered necessary to improve law and practice. The Commission has a duty to advise the Assembly on the compatibility of Bills with human rights. The Commission is also under a duty to promote understanding and awareness of the importance of human rights in Northern Ireland. The Justice and Security (Northern Ireland) Act 2007 Act amends the Northern Ireland Act 1998 by granting new powers to the Northern Ireland Human Rights Commission, including the power to institute judicial proceedings in its own right. This will enable the Commission to bring test cases without the involvement of an individual victim.

The Act also establishes an Equality Commission for Northern Ireland, consisting of between 14 and 20 Commissioners appointed by the Secretary of State. The Equality Commission replaces bodies formerly promoting equal opportunities.[19] A statutory duty is imposed on all public authorities to have due regard to the need to promote equality of opportunity between persons of different religious belief, political opinion, racial group, age, marital

---

16 Northern Ireland Act 1998, s 50.
17 See also ibid, Sched 7.
18 Northern Ireland Act 1998, s 68.
19 Ibid, s 74.

status or sexual orientation; between men and women generally; between persons with a disability and those without; and between those with dependants and those without. It is unlawful for a public authority to discriminate, or aid or incite another to discriminate, against a person or class of persons on the grounds of religious belief or political opinion.[20]

North–South Ministerial Council and British-Irish Council

The Belfast Agreement established two new bodies, designed to facilitate and promote co-operative relations between the United Kingdom and the Republic of Ireland. The North–South Ministerial Council comprises representatives of the Irish government and the Northern Ireland Executive with a view to fostering cross-community participation in the Council. The First Minister and Deputy First Minister acting jointly nominate ministers to the Council. Agreements reached by meetings of the North–South Ministerial Council are given effect by the Assembly, and no agreement entered into may come into effect without the approval of the Assembly.[21]

A British–Irish Council provides a forum for debate on matters of mutual interest between the British and Irish governments and representatives of the devolved institutions in Northern Ireland, Scotland and Wales, together with representatives from the Isle of Man and the Channel Islands.

Scotland

Scotland has a total area of some 30,000 square miles representing an area three-fifths the size of England, with a population of some ten per cent of the United Kingdom total.

The early history

The historical relationship between England and Scotland is one marked by conflict and war resulting from English attempts at seizing sovereignty over Scotland. Perhaps the original force uniting the two countries was the marriage, in 1503, of James IV of Scotland to Margaret, Henry VII's daughter. When Elizabeth I of England died in 1603, the heir to the throne was James VI of Scotland, Henry VII's great-great-grandson. The union under the Crown did not, however, secure peace. The long-term solution to the continuing conflicts of interest between the two countries was the full union of England and Scotland.

The Union with Scotland Act 1706 and Union with England Act 1707 'abolished' the respective sovereign Parliaments, which became united under the title of the Parliament of Great Britain. The Union was subject to strict conditions and terms. In particular the Act of Union protects the separate Scottish legal system and provided special protection for the Presbyterian Church. There was to be, however, a common Parliament, common taxation and coinage.

The referendum

The Referendums (Scotland and Wales) Act 1997 provided the mechanisms for testing the wishes of the people. The Scottish people were asked to vote both for or against a Scottish

---

20 Northern Ireland Act 1998, s 76.
21 Ibid, ss 52, 53.

Parliament, and for or against the proposition that the Scottish Parliament should have tax-varying powers. In favour of the establishment of a Scottish Parliament were 74.3 per cent of voters, and in favour of tax-varying powers, 63.5 per cent.

Devolution and the Treaty of Union

The Union with Scotland Act 1706 and Union with England Act 1707 remain in force and have effect subject to the provisions of the Scotland Act 1998.[22]

The Scottish Parliament

The Scottish Parliament was established under section 1 of the Scotland Act 1998. The 129-seat Parliament is based in Edinburgh. The Parliament's first task was to elect a Presiding Officer and two deputies.[23] The Scottish Parliament is unicameral and has a fixed four-year term of office, subject to provisions made for the holding of extraordinary general elections under section 3. A Clerk of the Parliament, and Assistant Clerks, are appointed by the Scottish Parliamentary Corporate Body, comprising the Presiding Officer and four Members of Parliament. Parliamentary proceedings are regulated by standing orders.[24] The Scottish Parliament has the power to call for witnesses and documents, and provides for criminal penalties in the event of failure to comply with Parliament's directions.

The electoral process

In the White Paper, *Scotland's Parliament*, the government recognised the need both for a strong constituency link and for greater proportionality between votes cast and seats won to be achieved through the election of additional members. Members of the Scottish Parliament (MSPs) are elected in two different ways. The majority are elected from individual constituencies. The remaining members – 'additional members' – are selected from party lists drawn up for each of the current European Parliament constituencies.

Members' interests

Section 39 of the Scotland Act 1998, as amended by section 7 of the Scotland Act 2012, regulates members' interests. It provides for a register of interests and requires members to register financial interests, including benefits in kind, and declare interests before taking part in any proceedings in Parliament relating to that matter. A Member of Parliament who fails to comply with or contravenes the prohibition is guilty of an offence.

Parliamentary privilege[25]

Section 41 provides that for the purposes of the law of defamation any statement made in proceedings of the Parliament and the publication of any statement under the authority of Parliament is absolutely privileged.

---

22 Scotland Act 1998, s 37. *Scotland's Parliament*, Cm 3658, 1997, London: HMSO, para 3.1.
23 Scotland Act 1998, s 19 as amended by section 4 of the Scotland Act 2012.
24 Ibid, s 22.
25 See Munro, 2000.

Maladministration

Section 91 of the Scotland Act makes provision for the investigation of complaints made to members in respect of the exercise of functions by the Scottish Executive.

Legislation

The Scottish Parliament has the power to make Acts of Parliament within the sphere of competence laid down in the Scotland Act. Any Act which is outside the legislative competence of the Parliament is not law.[26] Section 28(7) makes clear that the legislative competence of the Scottish Parliament does not affect the power of the Parliament of the United Kingdom to make laws for Scotland. The member of the Scottish Executive in charge of a Bill must state, on or before its introduction in Parliament, that the provisions of the Bill are within the legislative competence of Parliament,[27] and section 29 stipulates that an Act is not law if it is outside the Parliament's legislative competence.[28]

The Scotland Act 2012 extends the legislative competence of the Scottish Parliament. The Scotland Act 1998 conferred the power to vary the rate of taxation by 3 per cent. The Scotland Act 2012 removes that power but replaces it with the power to set the rate of income tax in Scotland, a power described by the UK Government as the 'biggest transfer of fiscal power to Scotland since the creation of the United Kingdom'.[29] In addition, powers relating to stamp duty on property and landfill tax have been transferred to Scotland. Non-fiscal powers being transferred include the running of elections,[30] the power to set national speed limits and the power to legislate on drink-driving and the control of airguns.

Schedule 5: reserved matters

Part I of Schedule 5 lays down five general categories of matters reserved to the United Kingdom Parliament: the constitution; the registration of political parties; foreign affairs; Civil Service, defence and treason. Part II lists specific reservations under 11 broad heads, namely: financial and economic matters; home affairs; trade and industry; energy; transport; social security; regulation of the professions; employment; health and medicines; media and culture; and miscellaneous. Matters reserved facilitate United Kingdom-wide uniformity, while devolving to the Scottish Parliament the power to regulate non-reserved matters according to national requirements.

The executive

The Scottish Executive, renamed the Scottish Government under section 12 of the Scotland Act 2012, comprises the First Minister, and such ministers as the First Minister appoints, the Lord Advocate, and the Solicitor General for Scotland. The First Minister is appointed by Her Majesty from among members of the Parliament, and holds office at Her Majesty's pleasure.[31] Members of the Executive are responsible to the Scottish Parliament.

---

26 Scotland Act 1998, ss 28, 29.
27 Ibid, s 31(1).
28 For a recent (unsuccessful) challenge over the competence of the Scottish Parliament see **Martin v HM's Advocate** (2010); [2010] UKSC 10; 2010 SLT 412.
29 Scotland Act 2012, section 25, inserting section 80 to the Scotland Act 1998.
30 See section 1 and Schedule 1 Scotland Act 2012 amending Schedule 1 to the Scotland Act 1998.
31 Ibid, ss 44 and 45 and also Scotland Act 2012, s 12(2)(a). 30 *Scotland's Parliament*, Cm 3658, 1997, London: HMSO, paras 4.8, 4.9.

In **Davidson v Scottish Ministers** (2005) the House of Lords ruled that the Scottish courts had jurisdiction to make coercive orders against ministers of the Scottish Government in judicial review proceedings. Section 21(1) of the Crown Proceedings Act 1947 should be interpreted so as to ensure that the protection Parliament intended they should have against government ministers was the same as that available in the English courts.

The continuing role of the Secretary of State for Scotland

The Secretary of State for Scotland is responsible for promoting communication between the Scottish Parliament and Government and between the United Kingdom Parliament and Government on matters of mutual interests, and on representing Scottish interests in reserved matters.[32] The Secretary of State and the Scottish Executive meet in order to monitor progress.

Law officers

The Law Officers of the Scottish Government are the Lord Advocate and the Solicitor General for Scotland. The United Kingdom government also needs advice on Scottish law, and the office of Scottish Law Officer to the United Kingdom government was created to meet this need.[33]

Scottish representation at Westminster

The problematic issue of continued Scottish representation at Westminster after devolution, particularly in relation to matters exclusively English (the 'West Lothian question'),[34] was addressed by initially continuing the same level of Scottish representation as before. However, section 86 of the Scotland Act 1998 amends Schedule 2 to the Parliamentary Constituencies Act 1986 and provides for Scottish representation to be based on the same electoral quota as for England, the effect of which is to reduce the number of constituencies to 59.

Continuing unease over the anomaly caused by the current representation at Westminster of Northern Ireland, Scotland and Wales following devolution prompted the establishment in 2012 of an independent Commission, the McKay Commission, to examine the consequences of devolution for the House of Commons. The Terms of Reference of the Commission are to consider how the House of Commons might deal with legislation which affects only part of the United Kingdom, following the devolution of certain legislative powers to the Scottish Parliament, the Northern Ireland Assembly and the National Assembly for Wales. The Commission is expected to report in 2013.

Financial arrangements[35]

Under the Scotland Act 1998 the Scottish Parliament had the power to increase or decrease the basic rate of income tax set by the United Kingdom Parliament by up to three pence in the pound. The Inland Revenue continues to administer tax variations. The Scotland Act 2012 removes this power, but transfers to the Scottish Parliament the power to set the basic and higher rate of income tax to be paid by Scottish taxpayers.

---

32 *Scotland's Parliament*, Cm 3658, 1997, London: HMSO, para 4.12.
33 Ibid.
34 On which see the 4th edition of this book, pp 381–84.
35 See the Scotland Act 1998, Pt III.

Since the 1970s, there has existed a 'block formula' system of funding Scotland's public expenditure programmes. The Scotland Act 2012 reduces the block grant to reflect the power to set income tax rates. The Scotland Act 1998, as amended by the Scotland Act 2012, confers power on the Scottish Ministers to borrow funds from the UK Treasury.[36]

Debating powers

The Scottish Parliament is able to examine devolved matters, and debate all matters irrespective of whether they are devolved or reserved.[37]

Scotland and the European Union

While relations with Europe are the responsibility of the United Kingdom Parliament and Government, the Scottish Parliament and Government play an important role in relation to those aspects of European Union affairs which affect devolved areas. The government has promised to ensure that Scottish Office ministers play a full role in European Union Councils. Scottish Office officials participate in discussions with the relevant Whitehall department. The Scottish Government and officials are directly involved in the government's decision making and formulation of policy in relation to European Union matters.

The Scottish Parliament scrutinises European Union legislative proposals 'to ensure that Scotland's interests are properly reflected'. Responsibility for ensuring the implementation of European Union obligations lies with the Scottish Government.

Wales

Wales covers an area of some 8,000 square miles, having a population approximately five per cent of that of the United Kingdom.

Wales was conquered by the English in 1282 and from 1284 Wales was subject to English law. As with Scotland there was an attempt at devolution in 1978, but this failed due to lack of popular support. Accordingly it was in 1998 that devolution was effected with the passage of the Government of Wales Act.

The Government of Wales Act 1998 devolved limited powers to a directly elected Welsh Assembly which assumed the responsibilities formerly exercised by the Secretary of State for Wales. The law-making powers of the Assembly were restricted to secondary legislation ('Assembly Orders'), and the United Kingdom Parliament continued to legislate for Wales. While the executive powers were formally exercised by the Assembly as a corporate body, in practice the powers were exercised on its behalf by Assembly Ministers. The result was a lack of separation of powers between the legislature and executive.

The Government of Wales Act 2006 addresses this issue and confers additional legislative power on the Assembly (on which see below).[38]

---

36 See section 66 Scotland Act 1998, as amended by section 32 Scotland Act 2012.
37 *Scotland's Parliament*, Cm 3658, 1997, London: HMSO, para 2.5.
38 See *The Report of the Commission on the Powers and Electoral Arrangements of the National Assembly for Wales* (the Richard Report), 2004 and *Better Governance for Wales*, Cm 6582, London: The Stationery Office, 2004.

The referendum

The result of the referendum held to determine the people's wishes in respect of devolved powers was less clear-cut than that of the Scottish referendum. Only 50 per cent of the electorate voted, as compared with 60 per cent in the Scottish referendum, and 50.3 per cent voted in favour of the establishment of an Assembly.

The executive

The 2006 Act establishes a Welsh Assembly Government as an entity separate from the National Assembly.[39] The First Minister and other Ministers and Deputy Ministers comprise the Government. The First Minister is nominated for appointment by the Assembly and the First Minister appoints Welsh Ministers from among the Assembly members.[40] Under section 51 there is a limit of 12 on the number of Ministers and Deputy Ministers. Ministers must resign if the Assembly resolves that the Ministers no longer enjoy the confidence of the Assembly.[41]

The office of Counsel General is established. The Counsel General (or the Attorney General) may refer a question relating to the statutory powers of the Assembly to the Supreme Court for decision.[42]

The Assembly

The Assembly has 60 members and sits for a fixed four-year term. However, the 2006 Act gives the Assembly the right to dissolve itself earlier, provided that a two-thirds majority of members approves the proposal. The Assembly elects committees the membership of which represents the political party composition of the Assembly as a whole.

The electoral system

The additional member electoral system is employed for elections.[43] There are 40 constituency members, elected on the simple majority system, and 20 additional members elected from the party list. Each voter has two votes – one for the constituency member and one for the additional member. The first elections took place in the spring of 1999. Thereafter, elections take place every four years, on the first Thursday in May.[44]

Welsh representation at Westminster

The Secretary of State for Wales and Welsh Members of Parliament play a full role at Westminster, but one which also involves a new partnership with the Assembly.[45] The number of Welsh MPs is 40. The Parliamentary Voting System and Constituencies Act 2011 provides for the reduction of the number of seats in the UK Parliament to be reduced from 650 to 600. This reduction, if it comes into effect, will see a reduction in the number of Welsh constituencies from 40 to 30.[46]

---

39 Government of Wales Act 2006, Pt 2 and Sched 3.
40 Ibid, ss 47 and 48. Appointments are subject to approval by Her Majesty the Queen.
41 Government of Wales Act 2006, s 48(5).
42 Ibid, s 96.
43 Ibid, s 4.
44 Ibid, s 3.
45 A Voice for Wales: The Government's Proposals for a Welsh Assembly, Cm 3718, 1997, London: HMSO, para 3.33.
46 See the Boundary Commission for Wales, The 2013 Review of Parliamentary Constituencies in Wales 2011, available at www.bcomm-wales. gov.uk.

The relationship between Westminster and the Assembly

Whereas under the 1998 Act, the Assembly had no power to make primary legislation, the Government of Wales Act 2006 conferred potentially more wide-ranging legislative power. The 2006 Act stipulates the matters on which the Assembly may legislate and no Acts or Measures which are outside its legislative competence will be law. The 2006 Act preserves the ultimate right of the United Kingdom Parliament to legislate for Wales.[47]

An Assembly Measure is a form of subordinate legislation. Section 94(1) provides that, subject to the restrictions laid down in the Act, an Assembly Measure may make any provision that could be made by an Act of Parliament.[48] Schedule 5, Part 1 specifies 20 'fields', ranging from Agriculture to the Welsh language, over which the Assembly has competence. Part 2 stipulates the general restrictions on competence and protects various Acts of the United Kingdom Parliament from amendment by the Assembly.[49] The general restrictions include amendment of ministerial functions, the creation of criminal offences carrying a stipulated level of punishment, legislation contradicting the Human Rights Act 1998 or legislation contrary to European Union law.

The power to pass primary legislation (an Assembly Act) was dependent upon a referendum being held in which the people approved the power.[50] A referendum was held in March 2011, with a majority voting in favour of increasing the Assembly's powers. Schedule 7 to the Government of Wales Act 2006 specifies the 'fields' over which the Assembly has competence which mirror those for Measures.[51] Disputes over competence will be resolved by the courts.[52]

The procedure for passing proposed Measures and Bills reflects the Westminster procedure. There is a general debate on the principles equivalent to Second Reading. There is then detailed consideration of the matter, equivalent to the Committee stage, and finally there is a vote on whether the matter should be passed, equivalent to the Third Reading. Bills then require the Royal Assent. There is to be a four-week time lapse between completion of Assembly deliberations on a Bill and the submission for the Royal Assent. This period is designed to enable the Counsel General (or Attorney General) to refer the matter to the Supreme Court in order to determine whether the matter is within the legislative competence of the Assembly. Furthermore, the Secretary of State for Wales may intervene to prevent the Royal Assent being granted where he or she has reasonable grounds to believe that the matter is contrary to international obligations or contrary to the interests of defence or national security, would have an adverse effect on water resources or supply or would adversely affect the operation of law in England or on non-devolved matters.

Members' interests

A register of interests is established, requiring any Assembly member who has a financial or other interest in any matter to be registered and requiring declarations of interests to be made before participating in Assembly proceedings. Under section 72, members are prohibited from

---

47 Government of Wales Act 2006, s 93.
48 The 2006 Act is amended by the Local Democracy, Economic Development and Construction Act 2009, s 33 which extends the legislative competence of the Assembly.
49 These include the European Communities Act 1972, Data Protection Act 1998, Government of Wales Act 1998, Human Rights Act 1998 and Civil Contingencies Act 2004.
50 Government of Wales Act 2006, s 105. See also the White Paper *Your Region, Your Choice, Revitalising the English Regions* Cm 5511, May 2002, Cabinet Office/DTLR.
51 Government of Wales Act 2006, s 103.
52 See for example *Attorney General v National Assembly for Wales Commission* (2012).

advocating any cause on behalf of any person in consideration of payments or benefits in kind. It is an offence to act in violation of the section 72 procedures, and a person found guilty of an offence is liable on summary conviction to a fine. Prosecutions may only be instituted by or with the consent of the Director of Public Prosecutions. Similar provisions to those in the Scotland Act relate to the attendance of witnesses, the giving of evidence and the production of documents.[53]

Privilege

The Government of Wales Act 2006, section 42 confers absolute privilege on any statement made in Assembly proceedings and on the publication of any statement made under the authority of the Assembly. Accordingly no actions for defamation may be taken in respect of such proceedings or publications.

Resolving disputes about devolution issues

Section 149 of the Government of Wales Act 2006 and Schedule 9 regulate devolution issues and make detailed provision concerning the courts with jurisdiction to resolve disputes.

The Welsh Assembly and the European Union

While the United Kingdom Government remains responsible for issues arising out of membership of the European Union, it is recognised that Wales needs a strong voice in Europe.[54] The Assembly is able to scrutinise legislative proposals and other European documents. The Assembly also has responsibility for ensuring that European Union obligations are implemented and enforced, and that any financial penalties which may arise out of failure to implement or enforce Union obligations are met. Within the framework of the Council of Ministers, the Secretary of State for Wales participates in meetings of the Council. The Wales European Centre in Brussels continues to act as a facilitator and source of advice on European matters. Members of the Assembly represent Wales on the Committee of the Regions. European Structural Funds are an important source of funding for the regeneration of the Welsh economy.

Regional Government for England?

It had been the Labour government's intention to introduce – as a complement to devolution – regional assemblies in England. Referendums were to be held where the government believed there was sufficient interest. The introduction of assemblies, however, was dependent upon the results of referendums.[55] In a referendum in the North-East of England in 2004, the electorate voted against the introduction of an assembly. In 2012 referendums were held in 11 English cities, asking voters whether or not they favoured the introduction of a Mayoral system of local government.

---

53 Government of Wales Act 2006, ss 74, 75.
54 *A Voice for Wales: The Government's Proposals for a Welsh Assembly*, Cm 3718, 1997, London: HMSO, para 3.46.
55 See the Regional Assemblies (Preparations) Act 2002.

London: The Greater London Authority and Mayor

In addition to the 1997 Labour government's firm commitment to devolution to Scotland and Wales, and the future consideration of devolution to the English regions, the government intended to introduce an elected 'strategic authority' for London. As noted below, the Greater London Council (GLC), which formerly represented a centralising focus for the capital city, was abolished in 1985. Many of the GLC's functions reverted to the individual London councils. London was unique in being a capital city without an elected Mayor and centralised area government. The government's White Paper, *A Mayor and Assembly for London*, proposed an elected Mayor and 25-seat Greater London Assembly. The Authority does not have direct tax-raising powers, but revenue is raised from congestion charging and parking fees. The Greater London Authority Act 1999 (as amended by the Greater London Authority Act 2007 and Localism Act 2011) establishes and regulates the Authority. The Authority comprises the Mayor and the London Assembly.

Elections

The first election was held in May 2000, electing an Assembly and Mayor for a four-year term of office.[56] Every eligible elector has one vote for the mayoral candidate, one vote for an Assembly member and one vote – a 'London vote' – for a registered political party.

The simple majority voting system is used for the mayoral election unless there are three or more candidates. Where three or more candidates stand, the Mayor is elected under the supplementary vote system, a vote which indicates the voter's first and second preferences from among the candidates.[57] The Assembly members are elected under the simple majority system.[58] 'London members' are elected on the party-list system. The qualifications for election to be Mayor or an Assembly member are that the person must be a Commonwealth citizen, citizen of the Republic of Ireland or citizen of the European Union and be over 21 years of age.[59] In addition, the candidate must have demonstrable links with Greater London, either by being a local government elector for Greater London, or through residency or principal employment in Greater London throughout the preceding 12 months.

The Greater London Authority

The general power of the Authority, as defined in Part II of the Act, is to 'do anything which it considers will further any one or more of its principal purposes', which are defined as:

(a) promoting economic development and wealth creation in Greater London;
(b) promoting social development in Greater London; and
(c) promoting the improvement of the environment in Greater London.

The Secretary of State may issue guidance to the Authority in relation to the above general power.[60]

The Authority is required to consult with London councils and representative voluntary bodies (section 32).

---

56 Greater London Authority Act 1999, s 3.
57 Ibid, s 4(2), (3) and Sched 2, Pt 1.
58 Ibid, s 4(4).
59 Greater London Authority Act 1999, s 20.
60 Ibid, s 30.

The Authority is regulated by Standing Orders defining its procedures, which are made in consultation with the Mayor. The offices of Chair and Deputy Chair of the London Assembly are created. The Local Government Act 1972, Part VA, regulating access to meetings and documents, applies to the Assembly and its committees, with the exception of confidential information and exempt information which may be withheld from the press and the public.

The Assembly is under a statutory duty to keep under review the Mayor's exercise of statutory functions, and has the power to investigate and report on any actions and decisions of the Mayor, actions and decisions of any member of staff of the Authority, matters relating to the principal purposes of the Authority and any other matters which the Assembly considers to be of importance to Greater London. The Assembly may submit proposals to the Mayor, but this function cannot be delegated to a committee or sub-committee.[61]

Bills in Parliament

The Authority may promote a local Bill in Parliament, or oppose any local Bill which affects the inhabitants of Greater London. The Mayor acts on behalf of the Authority, having consulted the Assembly. In addition, the Mayor on behalf of the Assembly, and following consultation with it, may request a London local authority to include provisions in local Bills. A local Bill promoted in Parliament by a London local authority may include provisions which affect the exercise of statutory functions by the Authority or any of the functional bodies, only if the Authority gives its written consent.[62]

The London Mayor

The Mayor is under a duty to prepare, keep under review and revise strategies relating to economic development, transport, spatial development (planning),[63] the London Biodiversity Action Plan, municipal waste management, air quality, ambient noise, and culture.[64] In preparing or revising strategies, the Mayor must consult the Assembly, the functional bodies, each London borough council, the Common Council of the City of London and any other 'appropriate person or body'. Adequate publicity must be given to the strategies, and copies provided to the Common Council and each London borough council. The Secretary of State may issue directions to the Mayor to prepare and publish any strategy which the Mayor has not prepared and to stipulate the period in which the strategy must be prepared.[65] The Greater London Authority Act 2007 extends the duties and powers of the Mayor.[66] The Mayor is now under a duty to prepare and publish a Health Inequalities Strategy and a Housing Strategy.[67] The Mayor is also given additional powers in relation to planning. He or she is entitled to intervene in a local planning authority's development schemes and is empowered to determine planning applications which are of 'potential strategic importance', taking over the role of the local planning authority.[68] In addition, under the Further Education and Training Act 2007 the Mayor is given a new role in adult skills and employment in London.

---

61 Greater London Authority Act 1999, ss 59, 60.
62 Ibid, ss 77–79.
63 Separate provision is made for revision of spatial development strategy under s 340.
64 Greater London Authority Act 1999, ss 41, 142; Regional Development Agencies Act 1998, s 7A(2); Greater London Authority Act 1999, Pt VIII; Greater London Authority Act 1999, ss 352, 353, 362, 370 and 376, respectively.
65 Greater London Authority Act 1999, ss 42–44.
66 The 2007 Act also makes detailed amendments to the Greater London Authority Act 1999.
67 Sections 22 and 28 Greater London Authority Act 2007 respectively.
68 Ibid, ss 30–34.

The Police Reform and Social Responsibility Act 2011 abolishes the Metropolitan Police Authority and confers greater powers on the Mayor of London in relation to the Metropolitan Police (see further below).

Accountability

The Mayor is under a duty to report to the Assembly, not less than five clear working days before each meeting of the Assembly (section 3 Greater London Authority Act 2007, amending section 45 of the 1999 Act), on significant decisions taken and the reasons for them, and his response to proposals submitted by the Assembly under section 60. The Mayor must attend every meeting of the Assembly and answer questions put to him about matters relating to his statutory functions.[69] Questions will be answered orally 'so far as practicable to do so', or in writing before the end of the third working day following the day on which the question was asked at the meeting. An Annual Report is to be prepared by the Mayor as soon as practicable after the end of each financial year, reporting on his mayoral activities during the year.

Once in each financial year the Mayor must hold and attend a 'State of London debate', open to all members of the public. In addition, twice in every financial year, a 'People's Question Time' is open to all members of the public, for the purpose of putting questions to the Mayor and Assembly members. People's Question Time must be held within one month of the State of London debate.[70]

The Metropolitan Police[71]

The Police Reform and Social Responsibility Act 2011, discussed further in Chapter 21, established the Mayor's Office for Policing and Crime (replacing the former Metropolitan Police Authority).[72] The principal functions of the Mayor's Office for Policing and Crime are to ensure the maintenance of the Metropolitan Police force and ensure that the force is 'efficient and effective' and to hold the Commissioner of Police to account.

The Metropolitan Police force is under the operational direction and control of the Commissioner of Police of the Metropolis,[73] appointed by Her Majesty on the recommendation of the Secretary of State following any recommendations made to him or her by the Mayor's Office for Policing and Crime.

London Fire and Emergency Planning Authority

The Fire and Emergency Planning Authority replaces the London Fire and Civil Defence Authority as established under the Local Government Act 1985.[74] The reconstituted Authority is responsible to the Mayor. The Fire and Emergency Planning Authority consists of 17 members, of whom nine are Assembly members appointed by the Mayor and the remainder members of London borough councils appointed by the Mayor on the nomination of the London borough councils acting jointly. Members are appointed for a renewable one-year term of office. The Mayor is also responsible for appointing a chairman from among the members of the Authority.

---

69 Should the Mayor be absent from six consecutive monthly Assembly meetings, he or she is disqualified from office: ibid, s 13.
70 Greater London Authority Act 1999, ss 45–48.
71 See further Chapter 21.
72 Police Reform and Social Responsibility Act 2011, section 3 and Sched 3.
73 Ibid, s 314.
74 Ibid, s 328.

Local Government: An Outline[75]

Introduction

Central government is ill equipped to deal with many matters which require special local knowledge and regulation on the basis of local needs. The devolution of power to directly elected local authorities enables those with local knowledge and expertise to regulate the provision of services, such as public housing, public sanitation, educational and recreational facilities. Local government, therefore, is justified on the basis of efficiency. Local government also represents the citizen's closest contact with a democratic institution and enables individuals to play a role in the administration of their geographical area. The merits of local government were summarised by the Widdicombe Committee as follows:

> The value of local government stems from its three attributes of:
>
> (a) pluralism, through which it contributes to the national political system;
> (b) participation, through which it contributes to local democracy;
> (c) responsiveness, through which it contributes to the provision of local needs through the delivery of services.[76]

Local government represents the democratic form of government closest to the people. Successive governments have introduced reforms to both the structure and powers of local government, with major structural reforms during the 1960s, 1970s, 1980s and 1990s, the effect of which is a complex body of legislation.

The structure and powers of local government are determined by central government, and all powers exercised by local government are derived from Acts of Parliament, or in the devolved administrations of Northern Ireland, Scotland and Wales, by Acts of the national assembly. Local authorities in the United Kingdom, therefore, do not have independence from central government. By contrast, Germany's Basic Law guarantees local authorities power to regulate all local affairs. Furthermore, the Council of Europe's European Charter of Local Self-Government commits Member States to guaranteeing the political, administrative and financial independence of local government.

The Local Government Act 2000, as amended, is currently the principal statute regulating local government in England. This Act has been substantially reformed by the Localism Act 2011, a key objective of which was to devolve further powers on local authorities and to give local communities greater control over local authority decisions. The 2011 Act also confers on local authorities in England a 'general power of competence'. This power gives local authorities the legal power to act in the same way as an individual may act, provided that the action does not contravene any existing statutory limitations or restrictions.

The structure of local government

England

In England there are over 400 local authorities, employing over two million people in the task of delivering, directly or indirectly, more than 700 different services. Under the Local

---

75 See, *inter alia*, Sharpe, 1970; Byrne, 2000; Stewart and Stoker, 1989; Newton and Karran, 1985; Leach *et al*, 1994; Jones, 1997. Note that local government in Scotland and Northern Ireland is differently arranged.

76 *The Conduct of Local Authority Business*, Cmnd 9797, 1986, London: HMSO, p 47, and see McAuslan, 1987. See also, *inter alia*, Keith-Lucas and Richards, 1979.

Government Act 1972 there were two levels of local government in England: a county council and a district council. The County Council provided key services such as education, social services and transportation. District Councils covered smaller areas and provided day-to-day services such as leisure facilities, rubbish and recycling.

This two-tier arrangement made it difficult for the individual to understand which authority was responsible for which service, and weakened the accountability of local government. Voters were also confused over which council they were voting for.[77] In order to improve clarity and accountability, two-tier authorities were replaced by unitary authorities that now operate in all metropolitan, and many other areas, in England. Unitary authorities are also established in Northern Ireland, Scotland and Wales.

The Conservative Government's intention in the 1990s was to introduce unitary authorities across most of non-metropolitan England. However, political difficulties with the reform resulted in a mix of single tier – unitary – local authorities and two-tier authorities. Local authorities may be 'unitary' or single-tier, or two-tier.

In England there are:

Single-tier councils:
33 London Boroughs
36 Metropolitan districts
55 unitary authorities
1 Isles of Scilly

Two-tier councils:
27 County Councils
201 District Councils

TOTAL: 353 Councils

Northern Ireland

In Northern Ireland there are 26 unitary District Councils. Elections are held every four years. Councils elect a chairman. In city and borough councils, the chairman is known as the Mayor. There have been attempts to reduce the number of councils in Northern Ireland, but failure to reach agreement over council boundaries caused these to be abandoned.

Northern Ireland is administered both by the UK Government and by the Northern Ireland Executive in Belfast. International relations, policing and justice are reserved to the UK Parliament, while the Northern Ireland Executive is responsible for health, education, industry, agriculture, environment and culture.

Scotland

In Scotland – which has its own directly elected Parliament with law-making powers – there are 32 unitary local authorities. Each local authority is governed by a council, made up of councillors directly elected by voters in council 'wards' (voting areas). Each ward will have three or four councillors. Elections are held every four years. The leader of the largest political party in the council will normally act as Leader of the Council. In addition local authorities elect a Provost or Convenor who chairs council meetings and acts as the ceremonial figurehead.

---

77 Electoral Commission, *The cycle of Local Government Elections in England*, London 2004, p 13.

Wales

In Wales – with its directly elected Assembly – there are 22 unitary local authorities. Elections are held every four years. Local authorities have a cabinet-style executive.

The functions of local government

Local government has no powers other than those conferred by Parliament. The powers conferred must be exercised according to law, and judicial review of local authority decisions may be made to ensure that the rule of law is respected.[78] Some discretion exists, however, as to the means by which local authorities achieve the goals set by central government.

Local authorities are required to put many services out to tender to the private sector, and may provide services themselves only if they can do so in a manner which is competitive with private companies and organisations. The provision of services is also undertaken in cooperation with private commercial organisations. In addition to taxation and the provision of services, local authorities have a regulatory and law-making role. Local councils have wide powers to regulate, for example, the granting of licences for taxis and market trading, and the approval of child care facilities and private welfare homes for the elderly, disabled or sick. In relation to law making, local authorities, acting under the authority of Acts of Parliament, have the power to make bylaws – local laws which regulate the area. For example, footpaths, parks and recreational facilities are controlled by local bylaws. In the exercise of all such power, the local authority is subject to control by the courts: all local authorities must act *intra vires* (within their powers), or their decisions will be declared null and void by the courts.

The Localism Act 2011

Section 1 of the Localism Act confers on local authorities in England (but not Northern Ireland, Wales or Scotland) a 'general power of competence'. This power confers on authorities the same competence to act as an individual may have. The power is subject to boundaries set out in section 2. In essence, the general power may only be exercised in accordance with any existing statutory limitations or restrictions. Where statutory restrictions are introduced subsequently, they will apply to the general power only where they are expressed to do so. Section 2(3) makes clear that the general power does not give local authorities the power to delegate or contract out of their functions, nor to alter their government structure. The Secretary of State is given power to remove or change statutory provisions that prevent or restrict the capacity of local authorities to use the general power. This power to amend legislation is subject to statutory limits (see sections 5 and 6). The exercise of this power is subject to parliamentary procedures to be followed in relation to orders made under section 5.[79]

The allocation of functions between authorities in England and Wales

Functions are allocated between local authorities principally on the basis of 'operational efficiency and cost-effectiveness'.[80] The provision of certain services, for example education, is clearly a matter for regulation on a large scale, whereas the provision of local libraries and refuse collection may be appropriate for smaller councils to administer. However, there can be no generalisations about the distribution of functions: there are variations throughout. From

---

78 See Chapters 3 and 23–25.
79 On procedure, see Chapter 14.
80 Byrne, 2000, p 80.

the point of view of local democracy, and the accountability and responsiveness of local councillors, however, the larger the local government unit, and the more diffuse the provision of services between differing levels of local government, the more difficult it becomes for the individual to apportion responsibility. In Byrne's analysis, the allocation of responsibilities is made the more complex by the sharing of responsibilities, which of itself takes several forms. Shared responsibilities in this analysis may include *concurrent provision*, whereby all local authorities provide the same service in their area; or *joint provision*, where two or more local authorities combine to provide a common service to all within their common area; or *shared but divided provision*, in which different levels of local authority provide differing aspects of the same service; *reserve powers*, under which larger authorities reserve the power to provide particular aspects of a service otherwise provided by smaller authorities; *claimed powers*, through which individual, small authorities assume responsibility for a service or function formally allocated to a larger authority and *agency powers*, whereby one authority will act as the agent of another authority in the provision of a service or exercise of certain functions.[81]

In addition to the complexity in the allocation of functions between local authorities must be considered the requirement that services be provided in line with the principle of 'best value'.[82] As a result, local authorities nowadays are far less the actual providers of services and more bodies which, through contract, enable services to be provided by those in the private sector. Moreover, no picture of local government can be complete without recognition of the increased, and increasing, functions formerly undertaken by local authorities, which are now undertaken by boards and trusts under provisions introduced by the Conservative government in relation to education and housing which further fragments local government, accountability and democracy.

The election process

Section 10 of the Representation of the People Act 2000 makes provision for greater flexibility in the voting arrangements for local government elections. A local authority may submit to the Secretary of State proposals for a scheme relating to when, where and how voting is to take place, how the votes cast are to be counted and the sending by candidates of election communications free of postage charges. The scheme may make provision for voting to take place on more than one day, and at places other than polling booths. The Secretary of State has power to approve the proposals either without modification or with such modifications as, after consulting the authority, he considers appropriate. Once elections under the scheme have taken place, the authority concerned must prepare a report on the scheme, detailing its provisions and assessing the scheme's success or otherwise in facilitating voting at the elections in question and, if relevant, the counting of votes, or in encouraging voting at the elections in question or enabling voters to make informed decisions at those elections.

A copy of the report must be sent to the Secretary of State, and published in the relevant area, by the end of a period of three months beginning with the date of the declaration of the result. If it appears to the Secretary of State that it would be desirable for provision to be made to apply generally and on a permanent basis to local government elections in England and Wales, he may by order make such provision as he considers appropriate. Such an order must be made by statutory instrument, and laid before and approved by a resolution of each House of Parliament.[83]

---

81 Byrne, 2000, pp 82–83.
82 Local Government Act 1999.
83 Representation of the People Act 2000, s 11.

The election of councillors

Councillors are elected for a four-year term of office and represent 'wards' within the local government area. In metropolitan districts, one third of councillors retire each year, other than in a year in which there will be county council elections. In other, non-metropolitan districts, councillors retire every four years, or may choose to adopt the metropolitan model. The electoral system reflects that used for general elections, being the simple majority or 'first past the post' system.

Detailed rules regulate election expenditure and, as with general elections, a number of corrupt and illegal practices are proscribed. An election challenge may be presented by way of a petition to the Queen's Bench Division of the High Court.[84] The petition is heard by the election court, which consists of a commissioner appointed by the judges who are nominated to try election petitions.

Qualification and disqualification for election

A candidate must – unlike candidates for Parliament – be able to demonstrate a close connection with the locality. Accordingly, he or she must either be on the local register of electors, or have been resident or have occupied property or have had his or her place of employment within the local authority area for a 12-month period preceding 'nomination day'.[85] Bankruptcy, conviction for corrupt or illegal practices, a conviction and sentence of three months' imprisonment within five years of the election or the imposition of a surcharge by the Audit Commission for unlawful local government expenditure will all disqualify a person from standing for election.

Standards of conduct

The conduct of local government came under review from the Committee of Standards in Public Life, chaired by Lord Nolan.[86] The inquiry examined the 'seven principles of public life' – selflessness, integrity, objectivity, accountability, openness, honesty and leadership – identified by the Committee in its inquiries into parliamentary standards. Lord Nolan's frame of reference included the issue of the manner in which, and extent to which, local government operates these principles.

Sections 27 and 28 of the Localism Act 2011 relate to standards of conduct in local government, and require all local authorities to adopt a code of conduct reflecting the Nolan principles, namely selflessness, integrity, objectivity, accountability, openness, honesty and leadership. Every local authority maintains a register of members' interests.[87]

Forms of local government[88]

Prior to the reforms introduced by the Local Government Act 2000, the majority of local authority decision making was undertaken by committees, with their decisions being ratified by a meeting of the full council.[89] Committees operated on subject lines: education, transport

---

84 Representation of the People Act 1983, ss 127–63, as amended.
85 Local Government Act 1972, s 79.
86 See Nolan (Lord), 'Lord Nolan's shopping list', in Jones, 1997, p 58.
87 Localism Act 2011, sections 29–34.
88 See Oliver, 2003, Chapter 16; Leach et al, 1994.
89 Local Government Act 1972, section 101.

and so forth, backed by departments staffed by Council officials. There were many criticisms of this system, not least that in reality most councils were dominated by one political party, and where the membership of committees reflected the party-political strengths of the council as a whole, opposition councillors had little impact. The Committee plus department model also encouraged specialisation, with councillors losing sight of the overall aims and objectives of the Council. To co-ordinate the work of the committees most councils established a Policy and Resources Committee. A further criticism was that the opportunities for holding the majority party to account were weak.

The Local Government Act 2000 aimed to end the perceived inefficiency and lack of transparency in local government and to provide for an identifiable figurehead. The 2000 Act, section 11, provided for new management structures in local government:

- an elected Mayor and Cabinet Executive;
- a Leader and Cabinet Executive; or
- a Mayor and Council Manager Executive.

The Localism Act 2011 reforms the 2000 Act and makes provision for three forms of local government. The permitted forms of local authority governance are executive arrangements, a committee system or 'prescribed arrangements'.

Executive arrangements

Executive arrangements must be either:

(a) a directly elected Mayor together with two or more councillors appointed to the executive by the mayor; or

(b) an executive Leader, elected by the full council from among the councillors, together with two or more councillors of the authority appointed to the executive by the Leader.

The Local Government Act 2000, new section 9H to 9HE, regulates elected Mayors. The Mayor is to be elected by local government electors in the local authority area. Elections are to take place on the same day as council elections. An elected Mayor's term of office is four years. The voting system to be used for electing a Mayor is the supplementary vote system, unless there are fewer than three candidates where the simple majority system will be used.[90]

Councils operating executive arrangements must establish overview and scrutiny committees to keep the work of the executive under scrutiny and to make reports and recommendations on any aspect of council business.[91]

The committee system

The committee system which had been the traditional form of local government for centuries was regulated under the Local Government Act 1972. As noted above, typically the committee form of local government operated on subject-based lines – for example, environment, children, family and education, housing, economy and business, social services and health. This system was abandoned under the Local Government Act 2000 which introduced the Executive style of governance.

The Coalition government's *Programme for Government* 2010 heralded a return to the Committee system, if local authorities chose to adopt it.

---

90 Section 9HC and Schedule 2 to the Local Government Act 2000.
91 Localism Act 2011, section 21 inserting new sections 9F–9FE to the Local Government Act 2000.

Prescribed arrangements

These relate to local authorities which do not wish to operate an Executive or Committee system of governance. The Secretary of State may make regulations providing for arrangements proposed by a local authority. The regulations must include provisions about how, and by whom, the functions of the local authority are to be discharged. The conditions which must be satisfied before making regulations are: (a) that the operation of the proposed arrangements would be an improvement on current arrangements; (b) that the operation of the new arrangements would be likely to ensure that decisions are taken in an efficient, transparent and accountable way; and (c) that the proposed arrangements would be appropriate for all other local authorities to consider.[92]

Changes in the form of governance

The Localism Act 2011[93] provides that a local authority may change its form of governance and must pass a resolution to do so. The proposed change may be subject to a local referendum. The Secretary of State has the power to require a referendum to be held on forms of government.

Local authority constitution

Each local authority is required to maintain a constitution which is open to the public.[94]

Local authority meetings

The Secretary of State may specify in regulations the circumstances in which meetings of the executive or its committees must be open to the public and which must be held in private. Where there are no regulations governing the issue the local authority executive may decide whether and which of its meetings are to be held in public or in private. Written records of meetings held in private must be kept and made available to the public[95] and must include reasons for the decisions to which they relate.

Standards of conduct

Section 26 of the Localism Act 2011 imposes a duty on local authorities to ensure that their members maintain high standards of conduct. The authority must adopt a Code of Conduct and establish a Register of Members' Interests.[96]

Central government and local government

Parliament is supreme and can control both the structure of local government and the extent of local government powers and functions. The major forms of control are through primary and delegated legislation. Local authorities have statutory power to make bylaws but these are subject to confirmation by the minister. Central government policy and standard-setting

---

92 Schedule 2 to the Localism Act 2011, inserting section 9BA to Local Government Act 2000.
93 Inserting new sections 9K and 9KA into the Local Government Act 2000.
94 Section 9P Local Government Act 2000.
95 Section 9G and 9GA Local Government Act 2000.
96 Localism Act 2011 sections 28 and 29.

control the manner in which local authorities may exercise their powers. Schemes for town planning, transport and education must have central approval and, in town planning, appeals will ultimately lie to the Secretary of State, and his approval will be needed in relation to compulsory purchase orders. In relation to fire, education and the police, regular inspections are made by central government inspectors.

Local government finance[97]

Some 50 per cent of local government revenue comes from or via central government; the remaining revenue coming from local taxes. In addition, local authorities may borrow money, subject to strict control by the Treasury.

The financial needs of local government are thus met by a mixture of local and central revenues. In terms of local revenue, from around 1600 until 1988, local domestic rates had been in existence. The rates, calculated according to the value of the property, were cheap and easy to collect, and the public were used to them. Rates applied to a property irrespective of the number of persons living in it.

By 1974, the Conservative Party was committed to abolishing local rates and introduced – under the Local Government Finance Act 1988 – the community charge, or poll tax. The same rate within a local authority area would apply to every person: it was a person-based rather than property-based tax. Accordingly, each resident in a local area would contribute to the costs of services which were enjoyed by all. In addition to that personal tax, the government was keen to reform business rates, and introduced the National Non-Domestic Rate, to be set by government and outside local authority control.

From 1993, the Council Tax is based on values of property within differing price bands and is payable irrespective of the number of people living within a house, although, to mitigate the perceived unfairness of the old rating system, a 25 per cent discount is allowable for single-person households.

Local authority expenditure is monitored by audit. The Coalition government, formed in 2010, was intent on conferring greater autonomy on local government. This in part is effected by enabling local government to retain a share of the Non-Domestic Rate (ie that of business, which formerly went to central government, which in turn redistributed it to local government), to encourage the local economy.[98] Local authorities also are able to determine the level of Council Tax payable. However, should this figure exceed the figure set by central government, a local authority is obliged to hold a referendum.[99]

In terms of expenditure, the majority goes to education. Other services include court services, housing, planning, parking, public transport and the police. In 2010–11 the total net current expenditure by local authorities in England was estimated to be £121.3 billion. Of this, 37.4 per cent was spent on education; 17.4 per cent on social care, 15.3 per cent on housing benefits; and 9.9 per cent on police. Of revenue expenditure, 55.5 per cent was funded by government grants, 25.2 per cent by council tax and 20.6 per cent by redistributed non-domestic rates.[100] Local authority expenditure is subject to audit. Transparency in spending is encouraged, with the government requiring councils to publish items of spending over £500. Audit is carried out by the Audit Commission. However, that requirement is to be abolished from 2013, and in the future local authorities will be free to appoint local auditors.

97 See Report of the Layfield Committee of Inquiry into Local Government Finance, Cmnd 6453, 1976, London: HMSO.
98 See the Local Government Finance Act 2012.
99 Localism Act 2011.
100 Department for Communities and Local Government, Statistical Release, April 2012.

Complaints about local government

Complaints against local government may be made to the authority itself and, if such a complaint does not receive satisfactory treatment, a complaint may be made to the Commissioner for Local Administration. The jurisdiction, role and powers of Commissioners for Administration are considered in Chapter 26.

Local government and Europe

While the role and function of local government is defined, controlled and restrained by central government, local government must also be seen within the wider context of the European Union. Since the United Kingdom acceded to the European Community in 1973, an increasing volume of European law not only affects the legislative sphere of competence of Parliament in relation to matters within the competence of the Union, but also affects both national and local policies and standards. The original Economic Community was founded on the four freedoms – persons, goods, capital and services – which affect all levels of government. In addition, the Union has expanded its sphere of competence over the years to include such diverse matters as environmental protection, health and hygiene standards and weights and measures. Many of the EU laws on these areas fall on local authorities to implement.

The European Union's relationship to local government is not limited to the imposition of regulations and directives imposing duties on local authorities, but extends to the provision of regional aid. The Committee of the Regions of the European Union[101] provides the means by which the views and interests of local authorities may be taken into account. Furthermore, the provision of financial aids and grants through the Social Fund, European Investment Bank and Regional Development Fund provides an additional source of finance for local authorities.

Local government and the courts

Local authorities, being bodies to whom powers are delegated by Parliament, may exercise their powers and spend money only for the purposes authorised by statute. In order to ensure that bodies with delegated law-making, administrative and/or judicial powers act within those powers (intra vires), the courts are seized with jurisdiction to review any action challenged by a person or body aggrieved by that action. Applications for judicial review proceed by way of an application for leave to apply for judicial review. Applicants must have sufficient interest (locus standi) in the matter to apply, and the matter challenged must be one falling under public law as opposed to private law. Furthermore, the matter must be one which is justiciable, that is to say, a matter in which the courts deem themselves to be the appropriate body to adjudicate on the matter.[102]

See Chapters 23–25.

Local government is a regular participant in judicial review proceedings. As seen earlier, all the powers exercised by them are powers delegated by statute; local authorities have no inherent jurisdiction. Accordingly, the courts may rule on the 'vires' of their activities. Judicial review is considered in Chapters 23 to 25 and those chapters should be consulted for discussion of the case law. In relation to control over the exercise of local government powers, the courts employ the concept of fiduciary duty. Local government is in a fiduciary position of trustee of resources to be exercised for the benefit of the consumers of those resources, Council Tax payers.[103]

---

101 Formerly, the Consultative Council of Regional and Local Authorities.
102 **Council of Civil Service Unions v Minister for Civil Service** (1985).
103 **Roberts v Hopwood** (1925); **Bromley London Borough Council v Greater London Council** (1982); **Hazell v Hammersmith London Borough Council** (1992).

Summary

The United Kingdom comprises the nations of England, Northern Ireland, Scotland and Wales, which have long been united under central government in London. The establishment of national assemblies with law-making powers has been on the political agenda for many years, and in the case of Northern Ireland, a high degree of legislative autonomy existed between 1922 and 1974. In 1998 powers were devolved by statute to the newly established Scottish Parliament and Welsh Assembly and re-devolved to the Northern Ireland Assembly. The powers of these national assemblies derive entirely from statute, and remain conditional upon the support of the people. In theory, the legislative sovereignty of the United Kingdom Parliament is unaffected by the Devolution Acts; in practice its powers are controlled by constitutional convention and politics.

A system of local government has existed for centuries and represents the most localised form of democracy. Local government is older than central government. The powers of directly elected local authorities are entirely statute-based, and may be altered as Parliament so decides.

Further Reading

Bogdanor, V. (2001) *Devolution in the United Kingdom*, Oxford: OUP.
Bogdanor, V. (2004) 'Our New Constitution', 120 LQR 242.
Brazier, R. (1998) 'The Scottish government', PL 212.
Byrne, A. (2000) *Local Government in Britain* (7th edn), Penguin: Harmondsworth.
Cornes, R. (2003) 'Devolution and England: What is on Offer?' in N. Bamforth and
    P. Leyland (eds) *Public Law in a Multi-Layered Constitution*, Oxford: Hart Publishing.
Hadfield, B. (1998) 'The Belfast Agreement', PL 599.
Hadfield, B. (1999) 'The Nature of Devolution in Scotland and Northern Ireland: Key
    Issues of Responsibility and Control', Edinburgh Law Review, 3.
Hadfield, B. (2005), 'Devolution, Westminster and the English Question', Public Law,
    286.
Hazell, R. (1999) 'Reinventing the Constitution: Can the State Survive?', Public Law, 84.
Hughes, M. (1994), *Ireland Divided: The Roots of the Modern Irish Problems*, Cardiff:
    Wales UP.
Jones, T. and Williams, J. (2005) 'The Legislative Future of Wales', 68 MLR 642.
Jones, T., Turnbull, J. and Williams, J. (2005) 'The Law of Wales or the Law of England
    and Wales?', Stat LR 135.
Jowell, J. and Oliver, D. (eds) (2011) *The Changing Constitution* (7th edn), Oxford: OUP,
    Chapters 7–9.
McCrudden, C. (2007) 'Northern Ireland and the British Constitution since the Belfast
    Agreement' in Jowell, J. and Oliver, D. (eds) *The Changing Constitution* (6th edn),
    Oxford: OUP.
Rawlings, R. (2005) 'Hastening Slowly: the Next Phase in Welsh Devolution', Public
    Law, 824.
Stanton, J. (2010) 'Local Democracy, Economic Development and Construction Act
    2009: a reinvigorated local democracy?', Public Law, 1.
Trench, A. (2006) 'The Government of Wales Act 2006: the Next Step in Devolution for
    Wales', Public Law, 687.

Walker, D. (2000) 'Beyond the Unitary Conception of the United Kingdom Constitution',
    Public Law, 384.
Walker, D. (2002) 'The Idea of Constitutional Pluralism', Modern Law Review, 65: 317.
Wicks, E. (2001) 'A New Constitution for a New State? The 1707 Union of England and
    Scotland', 117 LQR 109.

Part 5

Parliament

Chapter 12

The Electoral System

Chapter Contents

Introduction

In a democratic state, the electoral process determines who will hold political office. It is the electorate which confers the power to govern and calls government to account. If the electorate is to enjoy true equality in constitutional participation, it is of fundamental constitutional importance that the electoral system ensures four principles:

(a)   that there is a full franchise, subject to limited restrictions;

(b)   that the value of each vote cast is equal to that of every other vote;

(c)   that the conduct of election campaigns is regulated to ensure legality and fairness;

(d)   that the voting system is such as to produce both a legislative body representative of the electorate and a government with sufficient democratic support to be able to govern effectively.

It is against these four principal objectives that the law must be evaluated. However, it must be recognised that these elements are in large measure inseparable from each other. Each aspect of the electoral process combines to form a system:

> Any code of electoral law includes a number of essential sections of almost equal importance ... Each of these sections is meaningless in isolation from the others. A wide and equal suffrage loses its value if political bosses are able to gerrymander constituencies so as to suit their own interests; there is no point in having an elaborate system of proportional representation if the electors are all driven in one direction by a preponderance of bribes and threats; legal provisions mean nothing if enforcement is left wholly in the hands of those who profit by breaking it.
>
> That is why it is right to speak of the 'electoral system'. Procedure for elections is systematic in that its parts are interdependent; it is impossible to advance on one 'front' without regard to others.[1]

The Electoral Commission

The Political Parties, Elections and Referendums Act 2000 established an Electoral Commission, comprising not fewer than five but not more than nine Electoral Commissioners, appointed by the Crown. The Commission is an independent body which regulates political party and election finances and set the standards for running elections. Schedule 1 makes detailed provision for the terms of office. The Commission regulates its own procedure, and may appoint a chief executive and such other staff as the Commission considers necessary.

The Commission's functions include preparing and publishing reports relating to parliamentary general elections and elections to the European Parliament, Scottish Parliament, National Assembly for Wales and Northern Ireland Assembly.[2] The Commission must keep under review matters relating to elections and referendums, including the redistribution of seats at parliamentary elections, the registration of political parties[3] and the regulation of their

---

1   Mackenzie, 1967, p 19, cited in Rawlings, 1988, p 2.
2   Political Parties, Elections and Referendums Act 2000, s 5.
3   Introduced under the Registration of Political Parties Act 1998.

income and expenditure and political advertising.[4] No nomination may be made in relation to an election in the name of a party unless that party is registered, or the candidate is a person who does not propose to represent any party.[5]

The Commission may provide advice and assistance in relation to elections.[6] The Commission is under a duty to promote public awareness about electoral and democratic systems, including the institutions of the European Union.[7] The Act provided for 69 offences, with liability ranging from a fine at level five or six months' imprisonment on summary conviction to a fine or one year's imprisonment on conviction on indictment.

There is a Speaker's Committee, consisting of the Speaker and the Chairman of the Home Affairs Select Committee, the Secretary of State for the Home Department, the minister with responsibilities in relation to local government and five Members of the Commons who are not ministers.[8] The Speaker's Committee scrutinises the annual estimates of the Commission, and decides whether the estimated level of income and expenditure is consistent with the 'economical, efficient and effective discharge' by the Commission of their functions. If the Committee is not satisfied, it may modify the estimates. The estimates are laid before the House of Commons. The Commission also submits to the Speaker's Committee a five-year plan, setting out the aims and objectives for the period and estimated requirements for resources. The Speaker's Committee is assisted by the Comptroller and Auditor General, who each year carries out an examination into the economy, efficiency and effectiveness with which the Commission has used its resources in discharging its functions, and reports to the Speaker's Committee, including such recommendations as he considers appropriate.[9]

The Franchise[10]

Evolution of the franchise

Prior to the Reform Acts of 1832 and 1867, the right to vote was limited and based on rights in property. The 1832 Act – the Representation of the People Act – increased the franchise by 50 per cent, which still represented only seven per cent of the population. The Reform Act of 1867 doubled the number of people entitled to vote.

The extension of the franchise in 1867 to skilled and unskilled male labourers was not a matter greeted with universal approval. Walter Bagehot retorted that:

> . . . no one will contend that the ordinary working man who has no special skill, and who is only rated because he has a house, can judge much of intellectual matters. [(1867) 1993, p 273]

Bagehot feared the potential power of the working class: should they combine as a class, the 'higher orders' might have to consider whether to concede to their demands or 'risk the effect of the working men's combination' (p 278).

---

4 Political Parties, Elections and Referendums Act 2000, Pt II.
5 Ibid, s 22.
6 Ibid, s 10.
7 Ibid, s 13.
8 Political Parties, Elections and Referendums Act 2000, s 2.
9 For a critical assessment of the Electoral Commission see the Eleventh Report of the Committee of Standards and Privileges, January 2007.
10 For a full history of the franchise see, inter alia, Anson, 1933; Maitland, 1908, pp 352–64.

Women and the right to vote

Women were to remain disenfranchised until 1928, but the movement for women's right to vote pre-dates the 1867 Act.[11] In 1851, Harriet Taylor Mill had published 'The Enfranchisement of Women' in the *Westminster Review*. In 1886, John Stuart Mill[12] presented a petition to Parliament calling for the enfranchisement of women. The following year, the Manchester Women's Suffrage Committee was formed, soon to be united in a National Committee based in London. When the Reform Bill was before Parliament, Mill introduced an amendment – changing the word 'man' to 'person' – thereby entitling women to vote. The amendment was defeated.

A legal challenge to disenfranchisement came in **Chorlton v Lings** (1868). It was argued before the Court of Common Pleas that the Representation of the People Act 1867 had conferred on women a right to vote. The argument centred on the use of the word 'man' in the Act. It was contended that Lord Brougham's Act which stipulated that the word 'man' included 'women' applied to an interpretation of the Representation of the People Act. The court rejected such a view. Willis J declared himself opposed to any view that women were excluded from the franchise on the basis of 'fickleness of judgment and liability to influence', which would be quite inconsistent 'with one of the glories of our civilisation – the respect and honour in which women are held'. However, concerning the prohibition of voting – and the prohibition against peeresses in the House of Lords – Willis J declared that 'out of respect to women, and a sense of decorum, and not from their want of intellect, or their being for any other reason unfit to take part in the government of the country, they have been excused from taking any share in this department of public affairs'.

In 1869, JS Mill published *The Subjection of Women*. The right to vote was but one campaign. Women were also seeking equal rights in education, in politics and in the medical profession. In 1897, the differing suffrage movements were to be united under the National Union of Women's Suffrage Societies. By 1913, the number of affiliated societies had reached 400. The leadership of Emmeline and Christabel Pankhurst injected new energy into the campaign and the age of militancy in support of the right to vote began. The tide of public opinion started to turn in women's favour in 1909, when the authorities started to force feed hunger-striking suffragettes imprisoned as a result of their campaign. A Bill to give women the right to vote passed second reading in 1910, but was defeated by the Prime Minister, Asquith, acting in concert with Lloyd George, the Opposition Leader. The failure of a second Bill in 1911 sparked violent protest all over London: 217 women were arrested. A Bill of 1913 met with a similar fate and reaction. Fearful of the consequences of imprisonment and hunger strikes, the government passed the 'Cat and Mouse' Act,[13] which enabled the authorities to release hunger-striking prisoners who were in medical danger and re-arrest them on their physical recovery.

The persistence of the suffragettes, combined with the involvement of women in industry during the First World War, acted as catalysts for winning the right to vote. In 1916, an all-party conference on electoral reform was established under the chairmanship of the Speaker of the House of Commons.

The Representation of the People Act 1918, which implemented the conference's proposals, introduced a full franchise of all men in parliamentary elections and conferred

---

11 See Kent, 1987.
12 A Member of Parliament and radical reformer. See, *inter alia*, *Representative Government* (1865); see also *On Liberty* (1859) and *The Subjection of Women* (1869).
13 Prisoners (Temporary Discharge for Ill Health) Act 1913.

the right to vote in Parliament on all women over the age of 30 who were either local government electors or the wives of local government electors.[14] Full equality with men was delayed until 1928. A full franchise, on the basis of equality, and respecting the principle of 'one person, one vote', was finally achieved under the Representation of the People Act 1948.

The current franchise

The right to vote is defined in the Representation of the People Act 1983, as amended. Prior to enactment of the Representation of the People Act 2000, eligibility was based solely on residency in a constituency at a 'qualifying date'.[15] The 2000 Act introduced greater flexibility, allowing registration once resident in a constituency at any date, and supplements the residency requirement with registration on the register of parliamentary electors for that constituency. In addition to residency, a person is eligible to vote once they have made a 'declaration of local connection'.[16] A declaration of local connection must state the name of the declarant and either an address to which election correspondence can be delivered, or that he or she is willing to collect such correspondence periodically from the registration officer's office. The declaration must state the required address and also be dated, and, on the date of declaration, the declarant must also be otherwise qualified to vote by virtue of relevant citizenship and age. A declaration of local connection may be cancelled at any time by the declarant. The declaration is of no effect unless it is received by the relevant registration officer within the period of three months beginning with the date of the declaration.[17] The Electoral Administration Act 2006 amends the 1983 Act and allows for anonymous entries to the register. Section 9B(10) provides that a person is eligible for anonymous entry if his or her safety (or that of any other person of the same household) would be at risk if the register revealed his or her name and/or address.

The right to vote is linked to citizenship, residence and entry on the electoral register. Under section 1 of the Representation of the People Act 1983, as amended, a person is eligible to vote in parliamentary elections if he or she:

- is 18 years of age at the date of the election;
- is a British citizen; a Commonwealth citizen who has the right to remain in the United Kingdom indefinitely; a citizen of the Republic of Ireland;
- is resident in or has a local connection with (see below) a constituency and is registered on the electoral register for the constituency.

A person is not allowed to vote more than once in the same parliamentary constituency or vote in more than one constituency. A person may, however, be eligible to vote in more than one constituency but must choose in which to vote. In **Fox v Stirk** (1970), for example, it was held that a university student living in university halls of residence could register in that constituency provided that he or she was ordinarily resident there: there had to be a reasonable degree of permanence to the residency.

---

14 In addition, the Parliament (Qualification of Women) Act 1918 provided that: 'A woman shall not be disqualified by sex or marriage from being elected to or sitting or voting as a Member of the Commons House of Parliament.'
15 Representation of the People Act 1983, ss 1, 2.
16 2000 Act, s 6.
17 The Representation of the People Act 2000, Sched 2 extends the parliamentary franchise in relation to overseas voters, amending the Representation of the People Act 1985.

Persons who are not allowed to vote in General Elections and By-elections include the following:

- persons under the age of 18;
- aliens;
- Commonwealth citizens who do not have the right to remain in the United Kingdom indefinitely;
- non-British EU citizens;[18]
- members of the House of Lords (other than Bishops sitting *ex officio*). Former members of the House of Lords may now vote;[19]
- convicted prisoners in detention[20] (prisoners on remand may vote if they are on the electoral register);
- mental patients who are detained under statutory authority;[21]
- persons convicted of corrupt or illegal practices at elections.[22]

In **Hirst v United Kingdom** (2004) the European Court of Human Rights ruled that the blanket restriction which deprives all prisoners of the right to vote – irrespective of the length of their sentence or the seriousness of the offence committed – was unlawful.[23] In **R (Chester) v Secretary of State for Justice** (2011) the Court of Appeal ruled that it was for Parliament, not the courts, to amend the law. The issue, Laws LJ stated, was controversial and a matter of social policy. The Court of Human Rights returned to prisoner voting rights in **Scoppola v Italy (No 3)** (2012),[24] ruling that there was no violation of human rights provided that the removal of a prisoner's right to vote was not automatic and indiscriminate. The Court accepted that restricting a prisoner's right to vote pursued a legitimate aim of preventing crime, enhancing civic responsibility and respect for the rule of law and democracy. The issue was whether the restriction was proportionate to the offence. Here the applicant had been sentenced to life imprisonment for murder and if he displayed good conduct was entitled to apply for rehabilitation and recover the right to vote. There was no violation of Article 3 of Protocol 1.[25]

In November 2012 the government published the Voting Eligibility (Prisoners) Draft Bill for scrutiny by a Joint Committee.[26] Three options have been put forward for consideration:

- a ban for prisoners sentenced to four years or more;
- a ban for prisoners sentenced to more than six months;
- a ban for all convicted prisoners: a restatement of the existing ban.

The government will propose legislation once it has considered the Joint Committee's report.

---

18 EU citizens resident in Britain are entitled to vote in elections to the European Parliament and local government elections but not to elections to the United Kingdom Parliament.
19 House of Lords Act 1999, s 3.
20 Representation of the People Act 1983, s 3, as amended by the Representation of the People Act 1985, Sched 5. But see **Hirst v United Kingdom** (2004) and see HL Deb Vol 687, col WS203, 14 December 2006.
21 Representation of the People Act 1983, s 1.
22 Ibid, ss 51, 160. The disqualification is for a five-year period.
23 Article 3 of the First Protocol to the Convention provides for the holding of free elections under conditions ensuring 'the free expression of the opinion of the people in the choice of the legislature'. See also **Matthews v United Kingdom** (1999) and **Greens and MT v United Kingdom** (2010).
24 Application No 126/05; Times LR 12 June 2012. See also **Frodl v Austria** (2010).
25 An attempt to bring voting rights within the ambit of EU law failed in **George McGeoch v Lord President of the Council** (2012).
26 Cm 8499.

Postal voting and voting by proxy

The majority of votes are cast by individuals attending designated polling stations in their constituency. However, circumstances may require that a person's vote be cast by post or by someone on his or her behalf. The Representation of the People Act 2000[27] introduced greater flexibility in the rules in the hope of encouraging more people to vote, and in anticipation of the possible introduction of electronic voting.

Postal voting, however, carries risks and in the 2005 general election there was evidence of the misuse of postal votes. The Electoral Administration Act 2006 seeks to tighten the law and amends the Representation of the People Act 1983. Section 14 of the 2006 Act provides that applicants for proxy and postal votes must produce 'personal identifiers', namely their date of birth and a signature on their application forms. Furthermore, under section 37[28] postal voters are also required to provide their signature and date of birth on the postal voting statement which must be completed and returned with the postal ballot paper.

Section 62A of the 1983 Act provides that it is both a corrupt practice and criminal offence to apply for a postal or proxy vote with the intention of stealing another's vote or gaining a vote to which the applicant is not entitled. If found guilty by an election court a person can be disqualified, from standing for election or from being registered as a voter, for five years. If found guilty in criminal proceedings a person may be imprisoned for up to two years and fined. Section 13D of the 1983 Act is amended to make it an offence to provide false information for any purposes connected with registration.[29] The Political Parties, Elections and Referendums Act 2000 makes special provision for assistance with voting for persons with disabilities, whether by virtue of partial sight, blindness or other physical incapacity or inability to read.[30]

Reform

Concerns over electoral fraud – in part the lack of checks on the identity of those registering to vote – have led to proposals for reform. The Electoral Registration and Administration Act 2013 amends the Representation of the People Act 1983 and introduces a system of individual electoral registration (IER).[31] The current system relies on trust and there is evidence that there have been abuses of the system. The Individual Electoral Registration system provides that each elector must apply individually to be registered to vote. Regulations will provide that registration offices may require a person who is applying to register to provide evidence of his or her identity.

The European Convention on Human Rights: Protocol 1

The First Protocol to the European Convention on Human Rights, Article 3, guarantees the right to fair elections under conditions ensuring the free expression of the opinion of the people in the choice of the legislature. Those requirements were not breached by the existence of two unelected, but non-voting, members of the legislature of the Channel Island of Sark (on which see page 16). The Supreme Court so ruled in **R (Barclay) v The Lord Chancellor and Secretary of State for Justice** (2009). The Reform (Sark) Law 2008 provided for the replacement of

---

27 See Scheds 1 and 4.
28 And para 73 of Sched 1.
29 The more limited version of this section formerly applied only to Northern Ireland. It now applies to the whole of the United Kingdom.
30 Representation of the People Act 2000, s 13, amending the 1983 Act, Sched 1, the parliamentary elections rules. The Act also makes provision for the free delivery of election addresses by candidates at the first election for London Mayor: s 14 of the 2000 Act amending the Greater London Authority Act 1999, s 17, on which see Chapter 11.
31 For the background see the White Paper, *Individual Electoral Registration*, Cm 8108, 2011, London: TSO.

unelected landowners with 28 democratically elected conseillers. It also provided that the Seigneur (an ancient office first appointed in 1565) lost his right to vote in the legislature (Chief Pleas) but retained his right to sit as an unelected member and to speak, and temporarily to veto ordinances. The Seneschal (President of Chief Pleas) also lost his right to vote and speak in Chief Pleas but continued to sit as an unelected member. Reviewing the Strasbourg jurisprudence the Supreme Court ruled that it did not require that every member of a legislature should be elected, particularly where, as here, the unelected members did not have the right to vote. Even if Article 3 required non-voting members to be elected, it was well within the margin of appreciation allowed by Article 3 in light of the constitutional and political factors relevant to Sark.

See further Chapter 18.

Constituencies

The United Kingdom is divided for electoral purposes into 650 constituencies, or voting areas. Each constituency is represented in Parliament by just one member, who has secured a majority of votes in a general election or by-election.[32]

The Boundary Commissions

The task of regulating constituency boundaries falls to the Boundary Commissions for England, Northern Ireland, Scotland and Wales. Under the Parliamentary Voting System and Constituencies Act 2011, section 10, the Boundary Commissions are to report by October 2013, and thereafter every five years (rather than the former eight to ten years).

The constitutional principle of 'one man, one vote, one value' is given formal recognition in the rules regulating the work of the Boundary Commissions[33] contained in the Parliamentary Constituencies Act 1986, Schedule 2.[34] Equality is not, however, as will be seen below, the sole, or even dominant, criterion. By way of comparison, in the United States of America, the principle was judicially considered by the Supreme Court in **Baker v Carr**, in 1962. In that case, the principle was regarded as of such constitutional importance that the Supreme Court held that the Fourteenth Amendment of the Constitution – the 'equal protection' clause – required that electoral districts had to have an approximately equal number of electors to prevent over- or under-representation and inequality in voting power.

The target figure for constituency electorates is based on the simple division of the eligible voting population in the country divided by the number of constituencies. The Commission aims to achieve a result which brings the majority of constituencies within a narrow band of this target figure, bearing in mind the other criteria contained within the rules. Schedule 2 specifies the number of constituencies in Great Britain as a whole, and in Scotland, Wales and Northern Ireland. Parliamentary constituencies are required to respect – as far as possible – local authority boundaries. While constituencies must respect the electoral quota, this may be departed from where there are special geographical considerations which must be respected.

Under the Parliamentary Voting System and Constituencies Act 2011, the rules have been altered to give priority to numerical equality as a principle. There is now a uniform electoral

---

32 An election in a single constituency, conducted as a result of the seat falling vacant during the life of a Parliament.
33 Parliamentary Constituencies Act 1986, Sched 2.
34 As amended by the Boundary Commissions Act 1992.

quota for the United Kingdom (76,000), and (with limited exceptions) the number of voters must not vary more than five per cent from the quota.

Legal challenges to Boundary Commission reports

The political difficulties – generally the loss of a number of 'safe' seats by one party – caused by boundary changes have given rise to challenges in the courts. In **R v Home Secretary ex parte McWhirter** (1969), the Labour Party feared the loss of up to ten constituencies as a result of the Commission's recommendations. The Home Secretary laid the report before Parliament, without the draft Orders in Council which were necessary to implement the changes. The reason given for failure to produce the draft Orders was that it made little sense to implement changes, given that local government boundaries were under review at the time.

The Home Secretary introduced the House of Commons Redistribution of Seats Bill, implementing some of the recommendations regarding large urban areas, but not the remaining recommendations. The House of Lords introduced amendments, which the Home Secretary rejected. The Home Secretary then suggested compromise amendments, which the House of Lords rejected. Subsequently, the Home Secretary introduced the draft Orders in Council, leaving the Lords' amendments intact, but inviting the House of Commons to reject the Orders. The application for mandamus was withdrawn. In 1970, however, the incoming Conservative government reintroduced and passed the Orders.

In **R v Boundary Commission for England ex parte Foot** (1983), the Labour Party, having been aggrieved by the Boundary Commission's recommendations, sought an order of prohibition and injunctions to restrain the Commission from putting the recommendations to the Home Secretary, alleging that the Commission had misinterpreted the rules.[35] The court rejected the argument, relying on the considerable discretion built into the rules by the Parliamentary Constituencies Act. Sir John Donaldson MR, having referred to the constitutional role of judicial review, and accepted that jurisdiction lay to review the decision of the Boundary Commission, stated that unless there was sufficient evidence that the Commission had made recommendations which no reasonable body could make, the court should not intervene.

The reluctant attitude of the courts towards controlling the Boundary Commission's exercise of power is understandable, given the politically charged nature of the subject matter. Judicial inquiry in this matter comes very close to questioning a matter which is more appropriately dealt with in Parliament, and to thereby infringing the privileges of Parliament.[36] Nevertheless, such an attitude is thrown into sharp relief when compared with the position in the United States of America, where the constitutional guarantee of 'the equal protection of the law'[37] has been utilised to ensure real equality in voting power.

Initiating the Election Process

General elections

General elections must be held every five years, the maximum life of any Parliament.[38]

Until 2010 the Prime Minister had control over the timing of general elections although, in theory, the dissolution of Parliament lay within the prerogative of the Crown. While a

---

35 Parliamentary Constituencies Act 1986, Sched 2.
36 See Chapter 4 on separation of powers and Chapter 17 on privilege.
37 The Fourteenth Amendment to the Constitution.
38 Fixed-term Parliament Act 2011, s 1.

Parliament could run for a full five-year term, there were often political reasons against this, which resulted in Prime Ministers choosing a politically convenient date for his or her own party. Although there is a maximum time limit on the life of a Parliament, there was no **minimum** period which a government must serve before calling an election. In May 2010 the incoming Prime Minister announced that the Conservative/Liberal Democrat government would serve a fixed five-year term of office.

See Chapter 5.

The Fixed-term Parliaments Act 2011 gave effect to this proposal. The Act provides that the next general election will take place on 7 May 2015, and general elections thereafter are to take place on the first Thursday in May in the fifth calendar year following the 2015 election.[39] To provide flexibility in the event of short-term crises, provision is made for the Prime Minister, by statutory instrument, to vary the election date by no more than two months earlier or later than the prescribed date. An early general election may take place if the Speaker of the House of Commons issues a certificate certifying that the House of Commons has passed a motion of no confidence, and that a period of 14 days has ended without the House expressing confidence in the government. Where there is a vote on the motion, the number of Members voting in favour of the motion must be equal to or greater than two-thirds of the number of seats in the House. Section 3 of the Act provides that Parliament dissolves automatically 17 working days before the date of the general election.[40] This removes the power of the Queen to dissolve Parliament under the royal prerogative.

By-elections

By-elections take place following the death or retirement of a Member of Parliament. Any Member of Parliament may put down a motion to the House, which if successful, requires the Speaker to issue a writ commencing the election procedure. In practice, the Chief Whip of the party which held the seat of the Member moves the motion for a writ. There is no limit laid down by law as to the time period in which a by-election must be held. In 1973, a Speaker's Conference recommended that the motion initiating the by-election process should be moved within three months of the vacancy arising.

Eligibility of candidates

There is no statutory or other authority defining the qualifications for membership of the House of Commons. In order to promote a greater gender balance in Parliament, the Sex Discrimination (Election of Candidates) Act 2002 provides that the Sex Discrimination Act 1975 and Sex Discrimination (Northern Ireland) Order 1976 do not apply to the selection of candidates by political parties. The Equality Act 2010[41] replicates the provisions of the 2002 Act and extends its provisions until 2030.

Under the House of Commons Disqualification Act 1975, certain categories of persons are eligible for election and others are disqualified under the Act. Those disqualified include:

- members of the House of Lords;
- holders of judicial office specified in Part I of Schedule I;
- civil servants;
- members of the regular armed forces of the Crown or the Police Service of Northern Ireland;

---

39 The Act repeals the Septennial Act 1715.
40 The Electoral Registration and Administration Bill 2012–13, Clause 13, extends this period to 25 days.
41 Sections 104–105.

- members of the police forces;
- members of legislative bodies outside the Commonwealth (other than Ireland);
- Commonwealth citizens who do not have a right of abode or indefinite leave to remain in the United Kingdom;[42]
- members of Boards of nationalised industries, Commissions, Tribunals and other bodies specified in Part II or Part III of Schedule I.

In addition, a number of general restrictions on eligibility apply:

Persons under the age of 18

The Electoral Administration Act 2006, section 17, reduces the age of qualification for election to the House of Commons or a local authority, and election to Mayor, Mayor of London and Assembly Members of the Greater London Authority from 21 to 18.

Persons suffering from mental illness

Formerly, if an elected Member of Parliament was authorised to be detained on grounds of mental illness for more than six months, the Member's seat was declared vacant. The Mental Health (Discrimination) Act 2013 reforms the law, repealing section 141 of the Mental Health Act 1983 and any common law rule that has the same effect.

Peers

Members of the House of Lords, or persons succeeding to a peerage, are not eligible for office. Under the Peerage Act 1963, a person succeeding to a peerage has a limited right to disclaim his peerage. If a member of the House of Commons succeeds to a peerage, he has one month in which to disclaim his peerage or resign from the House of Commons.

Members of the clergy

Formerly, no person who had been ordained 'to the office of priest or deacon' or who was a Minister of the Church of Scotland could stand for election,[43] although a clergyman could relinquish his office and thereby become eligible to stand for election.[44] The House of Commons (Removal of Clergy Disqualification) Act 2001 removes the disqualification, other than for those who hold office as Lords Spiritual in the House of Lords.

Bankrupts

Persons declared bankrupt are ineligible for election to the House of Commons and, if already a Member, may not either sit or vote in Parliament until the bankruptcy is discharged by a court or the adjudication annulled.[45]

Treason

Persons convicted of treason are disqualified for election to the House and, if already a Member of the House, may not sit or vote until a pardon has been received or the sentence of the court has expired.[46]

---

42 Electoral Administration Act 2006, s 18.
43 House of Commons (Clergy Disqualification) Act 1801; Roman Catholic Relief Act 1929; Welsh Church Act 1914.
44 Clerical Disabilities Act 1870.
45 Insolvency Act 1986, s 427.
46 Forfeiture Act 1870, ss 2 and 7.

The Conduct of Election Campaigns

The Representation of the People Act 1983 governs the law relating to election campaigns, controlling both the amount of expenditure and the manner in which it can lawfully be spent, proscribing certain unlawful practices and providing for challenges to the legality of a campaign. Corrupt practices include exceeding the lawful expenditure limits, bribery, treating, and undue influence which includes making threats or attempts to intimidate electors.[47] A bribe is defined as 'any money, gift, loan or valuable consideration, office, place or employ-ment, in order to influence how an elector will cast his or her vote'.[48] 'Treating' occurs where a candidate offers or gives food, drink or entertainment with a view to influencing how the elector will vote.[49] A corrupt practice may be committed by any person, not just the candi-date or his or her election agent. While minor infringement of the strict rules may be excused by a court,[50] a finding of corrupt practices may cause the election of the candidate to be invalidated.[51]

On disputed elections, see below at pages 284–285.

Expenditure

Section 75 of the Representation of the People Act 1983 provides that no expenditure shall be made other than by the candidate or through his or her election agent. Each candidate is obliged to appoint an election agent.[52] The rationale for this rule lies in establishing and maintaining fairness between candidates and providing a mechanism for accountability as to election expenses. All accounts relating to election expenses must be reported, within 21 days of the election result, to the Returning Officer. Section 76 of the Act[53] permits the Secretary of State to set and raise the permitted amounts of expenditure, in line with inflation, by way of statutory instrument. The allowable amount comprises a fixed sum per constituency plus a sum calculated on the number of voters in a constituency. Any expenditure exceeding the prescribed limits amounts to a corrupt practice under section 75(1). Expenditure on national party election broadcasts is met by central party funds.

Several challenges to expenditure have been presented to the courts. In **R v Tronoh Mines Ltd** (1952), Tronoh Mines placed an advertisement in The Times newspaper urging voters not to vote socialist. The company and The Times were charged under the Act. The court held that the expenditure had been incurred with a view to promoting the interests of a Party generally, rather than an individual candidate; that any advantage incurred was incidental and not direct; and that accordingly the expenditure did not fall within section 75. Conversely, in **DPP v Luft** (1977), an anti-fascist group had distributed pamphlets in three constituencies urging voters not to vote for National Front (extreme right wing) candidates. The group was prosecuted under section 75 of the 1983 Act for incurring expenditure with a view to promoting the election of a candidate without the authority of an election agent. It was held that an offence had been committed, even though the promoters were seeking to prevent election of a candi-date, rather than directly promote the election of a preferred candidate. In **Walker v Unison** (1995), the court ruled that section 75(1) of the Representation of the People Act 1983 had

---

47 Originally, the Corrupt and Illegal Practices Prevention Act 1883. See now the Representation of the People Act 1983, ss 72–75,107, 109, 111, 115.
48 Ibid, s 113.
49 Representation of the People Act 1983, s 114. [2010] EWHC 2702; Times LR 16 November 2010.
50 Ibid, s 167.
51 Ibid, s 159.
52 Representation of the People Act 1983, s 67(2).
53 As amended by the Representation of the People Act 1985.

not been breached. During local elections in Scotland, Unison, a trade union, placed advertisements in national newspapers and on billboards, urging voters not to vote Conservative. The advertisements were placed without the authorisation of an election agent. Two Conservative candidates argued that there had been an illegal expenditure. The court ruled that the advertisements were a generalised attack on a political party, and not a direct attack on the candidates and, accordingly, the advertisements did not contravene the Act.[54]

In **Grieve v Douglas-Home** (1965), Alec Douglas-Home's election was alleged to be void on the basis that he had participated in a national Party Political Broadcast on behalf of the Conservative Party and had not declared the cost of this expenditure within his election expenses. The court held that no offence had been committed either by the candidate or by the broadcasters. The court accepted the contention that the intention behind the broadcast was not to promote the candidature of Douglas-Home in his own constituency but to provide general information about the Party to the general public. In **Finch v Richardson** (2008) the Court accepted that exceeding the permitted limits could be caused by an inadvertent ignorance of the law.

It may be noted that, before the Political Parties, Elections and Referendums Act 2000, while the law closely regulated the conduct of constituency campaigns, it virtually ignored regulation of the national political party campaigns. In an age of mass communication, and ever increasing personality politics in terms of political party leaders, the absence of regulation at national level – other than via broadcasting controls – was a matter for concern. On the 2000 Act, see below.

Broadcasting and Elections

Ofcom, the Office of communications, which oversees broadcasting, telecommunications and postal industries in the United Kingdom, was established under the Office of Communications Act 2002. In relation to political party broadcasts, section 333 of the Communications Act 2003 imposes a duty on Ofcom to ensure that Party Political Broadcasts and Party Election Broadcasts and Referendum Campaign Broadcasts are included in every licensed public service television channel and radio services. The Broadcasters' Liaison Group, formed in 1997 and comprising representatives of each of the broadcasters, works with the Electoral Commission to ensure a consistent approach to political broadcasts.

Broadcasts are allocated to the main parties, and to parties standing in at least one-sixth of seats in each of the four nations of the United Kingdom. Parties must be registered with the Electoral Commission to qualify for broadcasts. Broadcasts must comply with Ofcom's Broadcasting Code and the BBC Editorial Guidelines. All broadcasts must observe the law relating to libel, copyright, contempt, obscenity and incitement to racial hatred or violence.

Political advertisements and the European Convention on Human Rights

Political advertisements are banned under the Communications Act 2003, section 321. The law was considered in **R (Animal Defenders International) v Secretary of State for Culture, Media and Sport** (2008). Animal Defenders International (ADI) is a non-profit-making campaign organisation. It submitted an advertisement to the Broadcast Advertising Clearance Centre which refused to

See further Chapters 18 and 19.

---

54 On a challenge to the former £5 limit on expenditure not authorised by the candidate or his/her election agent, see **Bowman v United Kingdom** (1998). The limit operated as a restriction on freedom of expression and violated the Convention. The limit has been raised to £500: see the Representation of the People Act 1983, s 75(1ZA).

clear it for broadcasting as being in breach of the ban on political advertising. ADI challenged the decision, arguing that the ban violated its right to freedom of expression as protected by Article 10 of the European Convention on Human Rights and seeking a Declaration that section 321 was incompatible with Article 10. The Court refused: the government had not certified the Communications Bill as compatible with the Convention (see section 19 Human Rights Act 1998). The ban was justified and the Court had to give great weight to Parliament's view on the matter.

The issue of freedom of speech protected under the Human Rights Act 1998 was considered by the House of Lords in **R (ProLife Alliance) v British Broadcasting Corporation** (2003). At issue was the right of a registered political party, the ProLife Alliance, to insist that the BBC and other terrestrial broadcasters transmit its party election broadcast which contravened, in the BBC's opinion, the obligation to ensure that nothing in its programmes, inter alia, offended against good taste or decency.[55] In the Court of Appeal, Laws LJ had asserted that the court had a constitutional responsibility to protect political speech, and that while the film was 'graphic and disturbing' that could not justify any restriction. The House of Lords disagreed: the BBC and other terrestrial broadcasters had been entitled to refuse to televise the proposed election broadcast on the ground that it would be offensive to public feeling.

Disputed Elections

Any challenge to an election campaign must be made within three weeks of the result being declared. The complaint may be made by a registered elector, by unsuccessful candidates or by their nominees. Since 1868, such challenges go to the Election Court.

The Election Court has High Court status and comprises judges of the High Court.[56] The Election Court has jurisdiction to try parliamentary election petitions presented to the High Court in accordance with sections 120 and 121 of the 1983 Act. At the conclusion of the trial of a parliamentary election petition, the Election Court must certify its decision to the Speaker of the House of Commons, who will give directions as to the consequences.[57]

A decision of the Election Court can be subject to judicial review by the High Court: **R (Woolas) v Watkins** (2010). In that case it had been argued that there could be no judicial review of a decision of the Election Court on the basis that decisions of the High Court were not subject to review by the High Court. However, the Court ruled that High Court judges sitting as judges in the Election Court, although having the same powers as the judges of the High Court, exercised the more limited jurisdiction conferred under the Representation of the People Act 1983. Furthermore, the Court ruled that while Parliament intended that a lawful decision of the Election Court was to be final (and therefore not reviewable), Parliament could 'not have intended that a decision that had been made on a wrong interpretation of the law' could not be challenged.[58]

The court has the power to order a recount; declare corrupt or illegal practices; disqualify a candidate from membership of the House of Commons and declare the runner-up duly elected; or order a fresh election. In **Re Parliamentary Election for Bristol South East** (1964), Tony Benn MP, who had recently succeeded to a peerage as Viscount Stansgate, stood for re-election. The election was declared void and awarded to the runner-up. In **Ruffle v Rogers** (1982), the

---

55 Under para 5(1)(d) of the agreement between the BBC and Home Secretary, and in the case of independent broadcasters, the obligation is imposed by s 6(1)(a) of the Broadcasting Act 1990.

56 Established under section 123 of the Representation of the People Act 1983.

57 Ibid., section 144.

58 See para 47.

election papers were incorrectly counted and affected the outcome of the election. The election was declared void, but the court made clear that had the miscount not affected the result, the election would have been upheld. In **Gough v Local Sunday Newspapers (North) Ltd** (2003), the Court of Appeal ruled that informal counts of ballot papers should not take place under any circumstances. The solicitor to Bedford Borough Council had approved an informal count – in the absence of the candidates and their agents – of postal votes which were discovered after the election had been declared. The rules governing local elections under section 36(2) of the Representation of the People Act 1983 did not provide for a situation where the ballot papers had been overlooked. A fresh election was ordered in 1997, following allegations concerning the accuracy of the count of the vote which returned a Member of Parliament with a majority of just two votes. In **Knight v Nicholls** (2004) it was held that a returning officer had fulfilled his duty to issue ballot papers by delivering them to a carrier (Royal Mail) chosen and paid for the purpose in good time for them to be delivered and returned before the election. At the local election Nicholls was elected by a majority of 40 votes over Knight. The Royal Mail had failed to deliver 110 papers on time for the election. However, since the returning officer had discharged his duty, the election was not invalid.[59]

In **Watkins v Woolas** (2010), the petitioner contested the result of the parliamentary election on the basis that the respondent had lied in his election literature in order to sway the vote, and was guilty of an illegal practice contrary to section 106 of the RPA 1983. Section 106 provides that it is an offence to publish, '. . . for the purpose of affecting the return of any candidate at the election', '. . . any false statement of fact in relation to the candidate's personal character or conduct' unless they believed it was true and had 'reasonable grounds' to do so. The Election Court ruled that the respondent had been personally guilty of an illegal practice, declared the election void (under section 159 of the RPA) and ordered that the respondent be disqualified from standing for election to Parliament for a period of three years.

The Registration of Political Parties Act 1998

This Act introduced for the first time a register of political parties. A political party is entitled to be entered on the Register of Political Parties if that party intends to have one or more candidates at parliamentary elections, elections to the European Parliament, Scottish Parliament, National Assembly for Wales, the Northern Ireland Assembly or local government elections. Registration is intended to clarify the identity of bona fide political parties and thereby make regulation more certain. Under section 14, no party political broadcast may be made by broadcasters other than on behalf of a registered political party. The responsibility for the register lies with the Electoral Commission.

Political Party Funding[60]

In the United Kingdom, there is no provision for state aid for political parties for the conduct of election campaigns. Political parties do, however, receive public funds for their parliamentary work. In the House of Commons, under the system generally known as 'Short Money',[61]

---

59 In **R v Hussain** (2005) the Court of Appeal ruled that it was the duty of the courts to protect the UK's system of democracy and, therefore, those who committed electoral fraud could expect to receive sentences which were designed to deter others from such conduct.

60 See the Electoral Commission, *The Funding of Political Parties: Report and Recommendations* (2004); Rowbottom, J (2005).

61 After the Rt Hon Edward Short (later Lord Glenamara), the Leader of the House of Commons in 1975 when the system was introduced.

the money allocated is to be spent exclusively in relation to the party's parliamentary business, and not for election expenses. A similar scheme operates in the House of Lords. Introduced in 1996 by the then Leader of the House of Lords, Viscount Cranborne, 'Cranborne Money' is paid to the first two opposition parties. The Committee on Standards in Public Life has recommended that both the Commons and the Lords consider considerable increases of the amounts paid to opposition parties. In addition to financial support for parliamentary business, candidates at parliamentary elections or elections to the European Parliament are entitled to free postage for one election communication to every elector within the constituency. Candidates are also entitled to the free use of publicly funded premises for an election meeting. Indirect assistance is provided through party political broadcasts during election campaigns.

In addition, public funds in the form of Policy Development Grants (PDGs) are paid to political parties by the Electoral Commission.[62] There is a total grant of £2 million per year distributed to political parties on a formula based on performance at national and devolved legislature elections. In order to qualify for a PDG a political party must have two sitting MPs and have taken the Oath of Allegiance to the Crown. An application must be made by a political party to the Electoral Commission outlining their policy development plans for the forthcoming year.

For election purposes, parties are dependent upon the support of the membership and, more importantly, from companies and trades unions. Concerns over party political funding led to an examination of the matter by the Committee on Standards in Public Life. Recognising that 'political parties are essential to democracy', the Committee identified three of the seven 'principles of public life', namely integrity, accountability and openness, as particularly relevant to the funding of political parties. Increasing election spending by the two main parties, who between them spent some £54 million on the 1997 general election, and the issue of large donations to political parties by persons known or unknown, gave rise to the public perception that election results can be affected by spending and that wealthy organisations or individuals could effectively influence public policy. Undisclosed foreign donations to the Conservative Party also caused concern.

In the Committee's view, it was 'undesirable that a political party should be dependent for its financial survival on funds provided by a few well-endowed individuals, corporations or organisations', irrespective of 'whether or not the suspicion [that he who pays the piper calls the tune] is justified'. The problem of public confidence in the political system was compounded when such donations came from undisclosed sources.[63]

The Political Parties, Elections and Referendums Act 2000

Part IV of the Political Parties, Elections and Referendums Act 2000 provides for the control of donations to registered parties and their members, defining permissible donors and providing rules regulating the acceptance or return of donations, and providing for the forfeiture of donations by impermissible or unidentifiable donors, under a court order on an application by the Electoral Commission. It is an offence to knowingly enter into, or do any act in furtherance of any arrangement which facilitates or is likely to facilitate the making of donations by any person other than a permissible donor. The Act provides for a quarterly donations report to be made, and, in the period of general elections, for weekly reports.[64] Under section 69, the Commission is to maintain a register of donations. On the circumstances in which forfeiture

---

62 Under section 12 of the Political Parties, Elections and Referendums Act 2000.
63 See further below for the 2011 Report of the Committee on Standards in Public Life.
64 Political Parties, Elections and Referendums Act 2000, ss 62, 63, respectively.

should be ordered see **R (Electoral Commission) v City of Westminster Magistrates' Court** (2010). The Supreme Court ruled, by four to three, that the court had a discretionary power to order partial, rather than total, forfeiture of an impermissible donation. It was held that the object of the 2000 Act was primarily to prohibit the receipt of foreign funding by a political party and secondarily to provide a scheme which was easy to apply and police. Impermissible donors could be foreign or not (in the instant case the donor was eligible for entry on the electoral register, but was not so registered, and was therefore an impermissible donor). If the donor was not foreign, the circumstances of the donation might vary widely. Parliament intended that there should be a discretion with the intention that the court should discriminate between cases where full forfeiture was warranted and those where it was not. In some cases, total forfeiture would be disproportionate. The decision of the Court of Appeal was reversed.

Part V of the Act relates to campaign expenditure. No expenditure may be incurred by or on behalf of the registered party unless it is incurred with the authority of the treasurer or deputy treasurer of the party, or a person authorised by the treasurer or deputy treasurer. Section 74 and Schedule 8 impose limits on campaign expenditure in relation to parliamentary general elections and general elections to the European Parliament, Scottish Parliament, National Assembly for Wales and the Northern Ireland Assembly.[65]

In relation to a general election, Part V of the Political Parties, Elections and Referendums Act 2000 provides that a political party may spend a specified sum per constituency it contests. The overall effect is that a party fielding candidates in every constituency is entitled to spend some £20 million. This figure is quite separate from the allowable expenditure that may be incurred by individual candidates in their constituencies.

In addition to expenditure by political parties, Part VI of the 2000 Act also regulates expenditure by bodies such as companies, trades unions and pressure groups. Section 85 of the Act allows such bodies to incur a fixed sum of money in each of Northern Ireland, Scotland and Wales for the production of election material. Any proposed expenditure over these limits requires the body to register with the Electoral Commission as a 'recognised third party'. Once registered, the body may expend prescribed amounts in England, Northern Ireland, Scotland and Wales. Following the election, details of expenditure must be submitted to the Commission.

The Political Parties and Elections Act 2009 amends the law relating to the Electoral Commission and the law relating to elections. The Act (which applies to the whole of the United Kingdom) is intended to strengthen the regulatory role of the Electoral Commission. Section 2 provides powers to enable access to information relating to donations. These include the power, under warrant, to enter premises and inspect and copy documents. Section 3 inserts a new section 147 to the 2000 Act, imposing civil sanctions for breach of the Act.

On the composition of the Commission, section 5 provides for four Commissioners to be nominated by the largest political parties. In order to ensure that the nominated Commissioners are in a minority, the Act increases the minimum number of Commissioners from five to nine and the maximum number of Commissioners from nine to ten.

Section 9 of the 2009 Act requires donors to make a formal declaration of donations over £7,500 to either national or local parties. It is a criminal offence to make a false declaration (Section 9(5)). Section 10 prohibits donations over £7,500 from non-resident donors. Donors must be resident and domiciled in the United Kingdom for income tax purposes in the tax year in which the donation was made. The same provisions relate to loans and other financial benefits/transactions.

---

65 Part VII and Sched 13 regulate expenditure at referendums.

A further inquiry into political party finance was undertaken by the Committee on Standards in Public Life in 2011. In its Thirteenth Report, *Political Party Finance: Ending the big donor culture*[66] the Committee recommended that there should be a cap on donations set at £10,000. Recognising that this would represent a significant reduction in income for the major parties, the Committee recommended that there should be increased support for political parties from public funds. Estimated to cost £23 million per year, public funding would depend on the number of votes cast for a party in the previous election. The rate payable would be around £3.00 a vote in Westminster elections and £1.50 a vote in devolved and European elections. The Committee also recommended that the existing limits on campaign expenditure should be reduced by 'around 15 per cent'. As at November 2012 there was no cross-party agreement on the recommendations and the Prime Minister was reported to have withdrawn support for the proposals, preferring a cap of £50,000.[67]

Financial support and granting of honours

The link between financial donations to political parties and the granting of honours has been a matter of concern since the early twentieth century. In 2006 – in spite of the reforms effected under the Political Parties, Elections and Referendums Act 2000 – fresh allegations of political impropriety were made. The 2000 Act did not regulate the granting of loans to political parties, and accordingly these were not declared. The allegation that the Labour government has been granting peerages to those who had made donations and loans to the Party came to light when the independent Appointments Commission which scrutinises nominations for life peerages blocked three nominees who allegedly made loans to the Party.

The Metropolitan Police investigated allegations that offences may have been committed under the Honours (Prevention of Abuse) Act 1925, which makes the granting of honours in exchange for financial support unlawful. In July 2007 it was announced that no charges would be brought under the Act. However, fresh concerns arose in November 2007 when it was disclosed that a wealthy donor to the Labour Party had disguised his identity by making donations under the names of other individuals.

The Electoral Administration Act 2006, section 61, amends the Political Parties, Elections and Referendums Act 2000 and now brings loans and other transactions formally within statutory regulation. Sections 71F to 71W of the 2000 Act provide that the granting of a loan, or the provision of credit, or the offer of any form of security which supports a financial transaction are 'regulated transactions'. Section 71G stipulates how regulated transactions are to be valued and with whom such transactions may be concluded.[68] The Electoral Administration Act 2006 introduces reporting requirements in relation to regulated transactions to bring them into line with the making of donations and specifies the frequency of reporting.[69] During a general election period (between the dissolution of Parliament and polling day) weekly transaction reports must be made by political parties.

State funding of political parties?[70]

Any limitation on the rights of parties to accept funds, disclosed or undisclosed, increases the arguments in favour of state funding of political parties. State funding in Europe is an accepted

---

66 Cm 8208, November 2011.
67 See *The Independent*, 19 November 2012.
68 No transaction under £200 is a regulated transaction. See ss 71I–K.
69 Reporting is to the Electoral Commission.
70 See *Report of the Committee on Financial Aid to Political Parties*, Cmd 6601, 1976, London: HMSO (the Houghton Report); Hansard Society Commission, *The Financing of Political Parties*, 1981; Home Affairs Select Committee, *Funding of Political Parties*, HC 301 (1993–94), London: HMSO.

commonplace. Austria, Denmark, France, Germany, Greece, Italy, Portugal and Spain all have publicly funded political parties. This issue is, however, contentious in the United Kingdom on a number of grounds. First, it is argued that state funding potentially undermines the cohesiveness of the party, and introduces the possibility of politically inspired changes to the bases of funding. Moreover, it is argued that state funding would encourage the formation and growth of extremist parties. Opposition is also voiced on the constitutional basis that, to compel citizens to finance political parties, through taxation, especially those with which they have no sympathy, would cause dissent. Set against these objections, however, are the benefits which would accrue from public funding. First, depending on the method used to calculate entitlement, greater equality and fairness would be achieved among the political parties. Second, party political finances would become most clearly a matter of open public record. Third, the elimination of contributions from individuals and organisations would eradicate the public's suspicions about the integrity of party political finance and thus enhance confidence in the political process. Fourth, the ability of parties to conduct their official duties would be enhanced by improving the level of contributions made.

In 2007, following an enquiry chaired by Sir Hayden Phillips, the Party Funding Review Report[71] made a number of recommendations. These included:

- a cap on donations and loans of £50,000;
- spending controls with an overall single limit on expenditure of £150 million to be spread over the life of a Parliament[72] and to include a £20 million general election 'premium';
- existing controls under the Representation of the People Acts to remain.

On the issue of public funding the Report recommended that political parties should be entitled to receive an amount of public funding equivalent to the sum donated by an individual in any one year: thus for every £10 donated, the party would receive £10 state funding. The Report also recommended that the Electoral Commission should play a more investigative and tougher role in enforcing the law.[73]

Voting Systems[74]

The first and foremost object of reforming zeal ought, in my opinion, to be the system of parliamentary representation, or rather misrepresentation.[75]

The Labour government came to power in 1997 committed to major electoral reform, and to holding a referendum to ascertain the people's view. Substantial reform has taken place. The 1999 elections to the new Scottish Parliament employed the additional member system, as did election to the new National Assembly for Wales. The 1999 elections to the Northern Ireland Assembly employed the single transferable vote system, one already utilised for elections in Northern Ireland to the European Parliament and for local elections. The 1999 elections for the European Parliament in the rest of the United Kingdom saw the introduction

---

71 *Strengthening Democracy: Fair and Sustainable Funding of Political Parties*, March 2007.
72 On average a period of four years.
73 Inter-party talks on the Report broke down in October 2007.
74 See Finer, 1975; Bogdanor, 1981 and 1983; Bogdanor and Butler, 1983; Chandler, 1982; Oliver, 1983; Butler, 'Electoral reform', in Jowell and Oliver, 2000.
75 Wade, 1989.

of a new system of proportional representation based on party lists. Despite these reforms, no move has yet been made to reform the simple majority system employed for election to the United Kingdom Parliament. In this section, the merits and demerits of differing systems are considered.

Vernon Bogdanor categorises voting systems under three heads: plurality systems, majority systems and proportional systems. Under the heading of proportional systems, there exists a range of differing systems:

> 'Proportional representation' is in fact a generic term denoting a number of different systems sharing only the common aim of proportionality between seats and votes. This common aim, however, does not prevent the various proportional systems diverging considerably, one from another; and their political consequences, therefore, can be quite different. [Bogdanor and Butler, 1983, p 2]

Despite recent reforms, the United Kingdom is out of step with much of the rest of the world in terms of systems employed for electing its national Parliament. As a generalisation, it can be said that those countries influenced by English common law are the countries which retain the majority system of voting. The majority of states on the continent of Europe employ a list system; France by contrast employs a system which involves two ballots. In France, when no candidate wins an absolute majority of the vote in the first ballot, a second ballot is held to determine which of those candidates who have gained 12.5 per cent of the registered electorate in the first ballot are to be elected. In Australia, two electoral systems are employed. For election to the House of Representatives, a system of compulsory preferential voting is used. For election to the Senate, a proportional representation system is employed.

The Parliamentary Voting System and Constituencies Act 2011 provided, in part, for a referendum to be held in 2011 on whether the Alternative Voting system should be used for general elections. However, in a referendum held in May 2011 the proposal was rejected by a substantial majority.

The simple majority system

> If it is accepted that a democratic Parliament ought to represent so far as possible the preferences of the voters, this system is probably the worst that could be devised.[76]

For elections to the United Kingdom Parliament, the system of election remains the simple majority (first past the post) system. The origins of the voting system lie in tradition, and the voting system is not a matter of law, but of past political practice. One principal merit of the system lies in its simplicity. The candidate who gains the largest number of votes in the election wins the seat – irrespective of the proportion of votes cast for himself or his opponents. To illustrate, if the votes cast for individual candidates at an election are Smith 3,200, Jones 2,700, Brown 2,500 (total votes 7,400), Smith wins the election, even though 5,200 voters, or 70 per cent, have voted for the other candidates. This lack of representativeness – when viewed from the perspective of proportionality of votes cast to seats won – is reflected in the results nationwide.

---

76 Wade, 1989, p 9.

The 2010 general election

The result of the May 2010 general election was as follows:

Party	Number of seats	Percentage of vote	Percentage of seats
Conservative	306	36.0%	47.0%
Labour	258	29.0%	40.0%
Lib Dem	57	23.0%	9.0%
Other	28	12.0%	4.0%
Vacant seat	1	–	–
Total	**650**	**100.0%**	**100.0%**

The percentage of eligible voters voting (the 'turn-out') was 65.1 per cent.

In order to have a clear majority and the right to form a government, a political party needed to secure 326 parliamentary seats. However, as the figures above show, the May 2010 general election, for the first time since 1974, resulted in a 'hung Parliament' – one in which no political party had a clear majority of seats in Parliament. As a consequence, there was no political party leader who could claim the right to be appointed Prime Minister and form a government. The Electoral Reform Society calculated that if the Alternative Vote system had been used in the 2010 election the major political parties (Conservative, Labour and Liberal Democrat) would have won 281 seats, 262 seats and 79 seats respectively. Had the more proportionally representative Single Transferable Vote been used, the results would have been Conservative 245, Labour 207 and Liberal Democrat 162.

Reform of the Voting System

The alternative vote

This system retains individual constituencies, but introduces the notion of multiple votes in order of preference. As noted above, it is a majoritarian system, not a proportional representation system. The voter marks his ballot paper with preferences expressed in numerical order. The candidate who wins 50 per cent of the first preference vote is declared elected. Should no candidate achieve 50 per cent, the votes of the candidate who achieves the lowest number of first preference votes are redistributed in accordance with that candidate's supporters' second preferences. The process is continued until one candidate achieves an overall majority of votes compared with all other candidates. Where the system fails is from the point of view of proportional representation, since the overall result will bear little or no resemblance to proportionality. It would also potentially have the effect of returning to Parliament candidates who have achieved no clear support (or mandate) from the people. The system does, however, ensure that, within each constituency, the candidate with most support overall is returned to Parliament. The advantages of the alternative vote are, first, that the traditional one member, one constituency principle is retained and, secondly, that the elected candidate has a majority of votes, as compared with other candidates.

It is the Alternative Vote which was proposed for general elections under the Parliamentary Voting System and Constituencies Act 2011. However, as noted above, in a referendum held in May 2011 the proposal was rejected by a substantial majority.

The supplementary vote

This system is very similar to the alternative vote system, and is the system recommended by the working party on electoral systems set up by the Labour Party, under the chairmanship of Lord Plant, which reported in 1993.[77] The system allows voters to express a preference through voting for two candidates. If no candidate secures 50 per cent of the vote, the second preferences cast for all candidates other than the top two are redistributed between the two leading candidates until a clear winner emerges. Where there are only three candidates, this system would work smoothly. However, the system becomes more complex in constituencies where a greater number of candidates are standing for election, for the electorate would not be clear as to who the leading two candidates will be, and may therefore vote tactically in order to ensure, as far as possible, that a candidate who they did not want elected, would not be in either of the two top positions.

The additional member system (AMS)

This is the system adopted for elections to the Scottish Parliament and Welsh Assembly. The AMS seeks to combine the advantages of the single member constituency, with overall proportionality between votes and seats. The system is used in Germany. Under AMS, three quarters of the United Kingdom's Members of Parliament would be elected in single member constituencies, using the first past the post system. The remaining quarter would be 'additional members', elected from party lists on a regional party basis, employing a formula based on the largest average of votes cast between the parties. The additional Members thus top up the total for each party in order to give overall proportionality.

Under AMS, each voter would thus have two votes: one for the candidate of his choice in the constituency, one for the party of his choice on a regional basis. It has the advantage of remaining close to the system which is currently in place, while departing from it sufficiently to ensure proportionality. The system would necessitate a reduction of the number of constituency Members of Parliament in order to accommodate the regionally elected Members. If the division between constituency and regional Members is to be equal, this would necessitate doubling the size of current constituencies. However, the AMS also confers wide powers on political parties who would control who is to be included on the regional list, and in what order of priority. For this reason, the Hansard Society Commission on Electoral Reform, chaired by Lord Blake, concluded that the German model of AMS was not suitable for Britain.[78]

A variant of this system is employed in local elections in Germany which avoids the problem of party control. Under this version of AMS, all candidates stand directly as constituency candidates, but only three quarters, or some other proportion, are elected in single member constituencies. The remaining one quarter of seats are allocated to those who were runners up in the election contest, who would sit as additional members.

Single transferable vote (STV)

Employed in the Republic of Ireland and in Northern Ireland for the European Parliament elections and elections to the Northern Ireland Assembly, the STV offers both proportionality

---

77 Report of the Working Party on Electoral Systems, 1993, London: Labour Party.
78 Hansard Society, Report of the Commission on Electoral Reform, 1976, London: Hansard Society, para 93.

between votes and seats and a constituency-based, but multi-member, system of election. The STV was recommended for introduction in urban constituencies as long ago as 1917. It would involve a rearrangement of the current single member constituencies into far larger regional units, each returning several Members of Parliament. The method of calculation varies, but is based on a quota of the votes cast that is achieved either by first preference voting producing the required quota or the redistribution of votes cast for losing candidates. The STV offers both proportionality and the greatest range of choice to electors. The system used for local elections and elections to the European Parliament in Northern Ireland[79] requires that the total number of votes be divided by one more than the number of vacant seats, plus one. The current constituencies would require alteration in order to increase their size to accommodate three Members (or four or five, as favoured by the Liberal Democrats),[80] which would require a fresh look at the criteria for constituency boundaries. The current requirement to respect local authority boundaries is the most obvious criterion which would be compromised if such a system were to be adopted.

This is the most complex of alternative systems and, for that reason alone, is not favoured by many, although, despite the complexity, the system works well in Northern Ireland. The voter expresses his or her preferences for candidates in numerical order. A quota is predetermined. Thus, in a five-member constituency, the quota would be approximate to one sixth of the votes cast. Successful candidates are those reaching the quota, and those who on a redistribution of second, third and more remote preferences reach the quota. If fewer than the required number of candidates reach the quota figure, then redistribution of second preferences will take place until the required number of elected Members is reached. If, on the other hand, the required number of elected Members is not achieved by the redistribution of second preferences, then a third stage comes into play. The candidate who polls the lowest number of votes is eliminated, and the votes for that candidate distributed among the other remaining candidates in order of preferences expressed. This process of elimination continues until the quota is reached for all five required elected Members.

The party list system[81]

This system requires that a list of candidates be nominated by each political party. The votes for each party's list are calculated on a nationwide basis – rather than a constituency basis – and the parties obtain the number of seats in the legislature in direct proportion to the votes in the country. The party list system is not a serious contender for adoption in the United Kingdom. Two principal defects are perceived with the system: first, it destroys election on the basis of constituencies, and secondly, too much patronage is placed in the hands of party leaders. Within the two principal political parties in the United Kingdom – Conservative and Labour – there exists a broad spectrum of political opinion: from the political left to the political right in each party. To leave the power of nomination, and the positioning of candidates on the 'list', to political leaders would potentially exclude some of the best candidates – most likely, those whose views are incompatible with, or troublesome to, the leadership.

---

79 European Assembly Elections Act 1978, Sched 1, para 2(2)(b).
80 Liberal/SDP Alliance, 1982.
81 Employed in Belgium, Denmark, Greece, Netherlands, Portugal and Spain.

The Case For and Against Reforming the Simple Majority System

Simple Majority System

Advantages	Disadvantages
Quick result, local and national	No [direct] proportionality between votes cast and seats won in Commons
Simple to understand and use	Many votes (even an overall majority in a constituency) 'wasted', only the winner relative to the second placed candidate being elected
Close link between MP and constituency	Two-party dominance, little representation of smaller parties (eg in UK the 'third party', the Liberal Democrats)
Voting preference not watered down by transfer to different candidate	National result may effectively be determined by just a few 'marginal seats'
Usually clear result (a majority of seats in Commons to one political party), hence strong, stable government	Implements a mandate but not necessarily of the majority
Clear mandate, carried out without watering down by compromise derived from coalition	

Proportional Representation Systems

Advantages	Disadvantages
More votes count so greater, wider representation of views, especially where more than one candidate (with different politics) elected	Possibly less stable government
Better representation of minority interests and smaller parties	Small parties (in terms of voter support), perhaps of 'marginal' or 'extreme' stance, may hold disproportionate or even the balance of power
Coalition produces wider representation in government; encourages consensus and compromise	Majority mandate not implemented
Encourages voter participation by more votes counting	
Enables voter to express more than one (ranked) preference	Voter does not decide or know to whom his vote ultimately goes

Most of the arguments for reform of the electoral system centre on the alleged defects of the present system. Reformers argue that the status quo results in a government that does not represent the majority of the voters' wishes. Since the Second World War, no government has been elected with a majority of votes overall.

The case for reform therefore centres on the principle of democracy and equality in voting power. For democracy to have real meaning, it is argued that the government of the day, and the composition of the legislature as a whole, must reflect the wishes of the electors. Under such a system, it can be argued that the government would have enhanced authority to pursue its electoral mandate. In answer to the charge that proportional representation can result in weak government, reformers argue that less extreme, rather than weak, government would be the result. Such an outcome would force a 'rethink' in radical politics, with governments being keenly aware that with a slim majority in Parliament, and possibly the balance of power being held by a third party (both outcomes being common to proportional representation systems), certain radical policies would have to be modified. Thus many of the more politically contentious subjects, such as education and health, might be largely removed from party political conflict: consensus would become the only way in which to make legislative progress.

Reformers also point to the inequity of the distribution of the vote between the parties under the current system. The simple majority system invariably favours a two-party system, and leaves little room for the adequate representation of smaller parties. The Liberal Democrat Party regularly achieves approximately 20 per cent of the popular vote at general elections (and has a high success rate at by-elections), but that overall popularity does not translate into a proportionally related number of parliamentary seats. One explanation for this result is that votes for the Liberal Democrats are spread fairly evenly over the United Kingdom, and not concentrated in one geographic area (although the south-west of England is becoming a Liberal Democrat stronghold).

The case for the status quo is linked to the point made above. The simple majority system generally, although not invariably, produces a government with a strong parliamentary majority which is able to implement its electoral programme without undue hindrance. This argument requires careful evaluation. One of the often experienced effects of proportional representation systems is that governments are returned with either a very small majority of seats or a minority of seats overall in the legislature. As a result, minority parties with few seats and relatively small electoral support may hold a disproportionate amount of power, making governments dependent upon their wishes in order to implement their legislative programme. As a consequence of this dependence, governments are also subject to the risk of defeats on motions of no confidence, thus producing general political insecurity and the potential for frequent elections.

A further, related effect is that a government may be required to compromise substantially upon its electoral promises in order to govern. Under the current system, it is generally the case that the elected government – always depending upon its majority in Parliament – is relatively free to implement its electoral programme. In other words, the voter knows what he or she is getting in terms of policies and proposals for legislation. Under proportional representation, where less strong government is the frequent result, voters can be far less certain either that the policies for which they are voting will be implemented or of the policies which will be pursued after the election.

There also exist doubts as to the effects of a reformed system on the convention of collective ministerial responsibility. Under current constitutional arrangements, the convention of collective responsibility requires that the Cabinet 'speaks with one voice' in order to maintain parliamentary, and electoral, confidence. The rule accordingly requires that, where a decision has been made by the Cabinet, each member of Cabinet and non-Cabinet ministers and all their Parliamentary Private Secretaries, adhere to the decision and do not speak out against it. Such a show of unity would prove difficult to sustain in coalition or minority governments. The sister doctrine of individual ministerial responsibility might also prove more difficult to adhere to, particularly where a minister felt unable to support and pursue a policy with which he or she disagreed on political principle. One consequence, therefore, that could flow from the introduction of some form of proportional representation is that governments become less cohesive and, as a result, less commanding of the confidence of the people.

See Chapter 10.

A further argument is put for the status quo: that of the close links currently established between the constituency Member and his or her electorate. Irrespective of the proportion of votes won in an election, the Member of Parliament, once duly elected, and irrespective of political party, represents each and every one of his or her constituents in Parliament. Constituencies are relatively small and Members of Parliament are accessible – through surgeries and other contact – to the voters. A Member is thus able to gain a detailed knowledge of his or her constituency, its geography, industry and economy, environment and populace. With large constituencies, such a detailed working knowledge of an area becomes more difficult, with the attendant possibility that a Member is less effective in his representation of that constituency in Parliament.

As can be seen, the issue of electoral reform is by no means clear-cut, and real potential constitutional problems could be encountered as a result of its introduction. At the end of the day, the quest for an alternative system is rooted in the paramountcy of the principle of real democracy and equality of representation of the people in Parliament. Against that ideal must be set the constitutional implications of introducing reform.

As noted above, one of the manifesto pledges of the Labour Party before the 1997 election was a review of the electoral system for the Westminster Parliament and, once in office, the government appointed Liberal peer Lord Jenkins to review the system. The Jenkins Commission reported in October 1998, and recommended a novel, if complex, solution. The Commission, wanting to retain single-member constituencies but also inject a greater degree of proportionality into the system, opted for a 'mixed system' made up of the alternative vote and regional list systems. Constituency members would be elected on the alternative vote system, and comprise 80 to 85 per cent of members, with additional members, 15 to 20 per cent elected on the regional list basis. Greater proportionality would be achieved, while the traditional strong link between a member and his or her constituency would be retained. The system would also, the Commission claimed, avoid coalition governments and in its estimation would have produced a single-party majority government in three out of the four last general elections.[82]

The current position is that the United Kingdom now employs a number of systems: a system of proportional representation was used in May 1999 for elections to the European Parliament; for elections to the Scottish Parliament and National Assembly for Wales the additional member system has been used; and for elections to the Northern Ireland Assembly the single transferable vote system was used. In relation to elections to the United Kingdom Parliament, however, despite recommendations for reform, the voting system remains the simple majority system. Irrespective of constitutional arguments in favour of reform, the referendum result in May 2011 rejecting the Alternative Vote system for general elections makes reform in the foreseeable future very unlikely.

Summary

Electoral law comprises several aspects: the right to vote, the organisation of constituencies, the regulation of election campaigns, the voting system, and the regulation of political parties.

The electoral system aims to ensure equality in terms of the size of constituencies, individual voting power and as between candidates for election. The regulation of constituency

---

82 Cm 4090-I, para 161. This claim has been disputed by M Pinto-Duschinsk, who calculates that coalition would have been the outcome in nine of the last 14 elections: The Times, 29 October 1998.

sizes, however, fails to produce formal equality because other statutory considerations come into play.

It has been seen above that there is a near-complete franchise (right to vote) and that the law regulating election campaigns at local level is strict. Until recently, however, there has been regulation of political parties – their funding and expenditure – at national level. The Political Parties, Elections and Referendums Act 2000 remedies this defect, establishing the Electoral Commission and requiring political parties to be formally registered and permissible donations to be recorded. The Act also sets a ceiling on election expenditure by political parties. The Political Parties and Elections Act 2009 amends the law and strengthens the powers of the Electoral Commission.

In relation to voting systems, it has been seen that there are several systems employed in the United Kingdom for different elections. For general elections, however, the system remains the easy to understand and administer but much-criticised simple majority system.

Further Reading

Blackburn, R (2011) 'The 2010 General Election Outcome and Formation of the Conservative – Liberal Democrat Coalition Government', Public Law, 30.

Easton, S. (2006) 'Electing the Electorate: The Problem of Prisoner Disenfranchisement', 69(3) Modern Law Review 443.

Electoral Commission (2004) 'The Funding of Political Parties: Report and Recommendations'.

Ewing, K. (2007) The Cost of Democracy: Party Funding in Modern British Politics, Oxford: Hart Publishing.

Lardy, H. (2002) 'Prisoner Disenfranchisement: Constitutional Rights and Wrongs', Public Law, 524.

Report of the Independent Commission on the Voting System (Jenkins Report), 1998, Cm 4090, London: HMSO.

Rowbottom, J. (2005) 'The Electoral Commission's Proposals on the Funding of Political Parties', Public Law, 168.

The Party Funding Review Report: 'Strengthening Democracy: Fair and Sustainable Funding of Political Parties', March 2007.

Webb, P. (2001) 'Parties and Party Systems: Modernisation, Regulation and Diversity', 54 Parliamentary Affairs, 308.

Chapter 13

Introduction to the House of Commons

Introduction

Parliament is composed of the Crown, the House of Lords and the House of Commons. Its origins lie in the King's Council – the assembly of advisers summoned by the King – and the term 'parliament' can be traced to the thirteenth century.[1]

In order to evaluate Parliament, it is necessary to examine its composition and procedure. The former task may be accomplished by either looking at the actual membership of Parliament by party allegiance at a fixed point in time or by looking at it in a more sociological manner in order to analyse the class and educational background of Members and their employment status. The undertaking is complicated by the bicameral nature of Parliament and the fact that the House of Commons is elected and the House of Lords unelected. The importance of procedure, particularly in the House of Commons, cannot be overemphasised. Only by acquiring an understanding of the procedural rules can sense be made of the functions of Parliament and its importance, or otherwise, in the process of government. In the absence of a written constitution which clearly defines and allocates powers and functions, the manner in which the legislative proposals of government are examined, and the administration of the state scrutinised, assumes central importance to the notion of democratic control of the executive. The doctrine of constitutionalism can only be effective if the procedures adopted by Parliament are effective in controlling the government.

The Functions of Parliament

In *Representative Government* (1861), John Stuart Mill wrote of Parliament:

> Instead of the function of governing, for which it is radically unfit, the proper office of a representative assembly is to watch and control the government; to throw the light of publicity on its acts; to compel a full exposition and justification of all of them which anyone considers questionable; to censure them if found condemnable; and if the men who compose the government abuse their trust, or fulfil it in a manner which conflicts with the deliberate sense of the nation, to expel them from office, and either expressly or virtually appoint their successors.
>
> The House of Commons is the sounding board of the nation – an arena in which not only the general opinion of the nation, but that of every section of it can produce itself in full light and challenge discussion.

Very little has changed. Parliament is not there to govern: that is for the executive. Parliament exists to represent the views and opinions of the people and to influence, constrain and demand justification for the actions of government and to give them legitimacy.

Accordingly, the functions of Parliament may be summarised as being:[2]

(a) to provide the personnel of government;
(b) to legitimise government actions; and
(c) to subject matters of public policy to scrutiny and influence.

As discussed in Chapters 6 and 11, the devolution of legislative power to the Northern Ireland Assembly and Scottish Parliament and, to a lesser extent, the Welsh Assembly affects the scope

---

1   The role of the sovereign is discussed in Chapter 5. The House of Lords is discussed in Chapter 16.
2   Norton, 1985a and see 1993.

of the United Kingdom Parliament's role and functions. In terms of debating and scrutinising government policy and administration and the passage of legislation, while the United Kingdom Parliament (Westminster) remains the sovereign legislature in the United Kingdom, there is now a diffusion of power – differing in nature and scope – between Westminster and the devolved institutions.

The Life of a Parliament

See Chapters 5 and 9.

A Parliament is summoned by the sovereign to meet following a general election, and the life of the Parliament will run until the subsequent general election. Prior to 2010, the choice of date for a general election was at the Prime Minister's discretion (subject to the consent of the Crown). The incoming Coalition government of 2010 announced that the new Parliament would run until May 2015. The Fixed-term Parliaments Act 2011 gives five-year fixed-term Parliaments statutory effect.

The parliamentary session

A parliamentary session is the parliamentary year, which as a consequence of the Fixed-term Parliaments Act 2011 runs from Spring to Spring. At the end of the session, Parliament stands 'prorogued' until the new session begins. The significance of prorogation lies in the fact that all business is suspended until the new session. The number of sitting days per session varies from year to year. The average session length is 168 days.

Parliamentary sittings

The term 'parliamentary sitting' relates to the daily business of the House. The Commons meets daily from Monday to Friday but is adjourned for three weeks at Christmas, one week at Easter, for the whole of August and for most of September. In emergency situations, the House may be recalled for urgent debate during a recess or at a weekend, as occurred in 1982 for debate on the invasion of the Falkland Islands.[3]

Westminster Hall

In addition to proceedings in the chamber of the Commons, since 1999 Westminster Hall has been used for backbench debates and debates on select committee reports (see Chapter 15). Any member of Parliament may attend. In addition, Westminster Hall sittings are used for the questioning of junior ministers generally on matters which affect more than one government department. In the 2001–02 session, the number of sitting hours in Westminster Hall was 474 and in the short 2004–05 session, just 154 hours.

Summoning, Adjournment, Prorogation[4] and Dissolution

Summoning

The Fixed-term Parliaments Act 2011, section 3, provides that once Parliament has been dissolved under section 1, the Queen may issue a proclamation summoning the new Parliament.

---

3   3 April 1982.
4   From the Latin, *prorogare*, literally to ask publicly, from *pro* in public and *rogare* to ask.

Adjournment

During a parliamentary session, Parliament will be adjourned on many occasions. The adjournment is no more than an 'interruption in the course of one and the same session'.[5] Up to a quarter of the time in the House of Commons is spent debating the question: '... that this House do now adjourn.'[6] The effect of adjournment is to suspend the sitting of the House for a period but leave unaffected the business of the House. Adjournments take place for a number of reasons and to effect a number of consequences.

A motion for adjournment can be used in debate to interrupt proceedings. The motion will take the form 'that the debate be now adjourned'. The device may be used as an alternative to moving an amendment to the question before the House, and will be used to determine consideration of the matter in question. The Speaker has a discretion whether to decline to put the matter to the House. The business which has been interrupted can be brought before the House at the next sitting day, provided that notice is given.

Daily adjournment debates

There is a daily motion for adjournment which suspends the day's sitting. Once the motion for adjournment has been moved, the daily adjournment debate takes place.[7] The adjournment debate enables one Member to speak on a topic, previously notified, for 15 minutes, and receive a ministerial reply. Topics may include any matter other than a request for legislation. There is a weekly ballot at which successful Members are chosen for the adjournment debate, other than for the debate on Thursdays when the choice of Member is made by the Speaker.

Adjournment debates before holidays

Adjournment debates also take place before the House adjourns for holidays.[8] No ballot is held for participation: five backbenchers speak for half an hour each and the Leader of the House replies to the debate.

Adjournment debates following consideration of Consolidated Fund Bills

In any session, there will be three Consolidated Fund Bills before Parliament. Second reading consideration is purely formal, with no debate. When proceedings are finished, any Member of the government may move a motion 'that this House do now adjourn'.

Adjournments for emergency debates

Provision is made under Standing Orders for urgent matters to be brought to the attention of the House for early debate. A Member may, at the start of business of the day, propose that the House be adjourned for consideration of an urgent matter. It is within the discretion of the Speaker as to whether the matter should be discussed. If satisfied, it is then for the House to give leave for the debate. If refused, the support of not more than 40 Members of the House is required in order for leave to be granted.[9] The debate will take place at the start of business the following day.

---

5   Erskine May, 1997.
6   Silk and Walters, 1987, p 210.
7   See further Chapter 15.
8   Four times a year.
9   If fewer than 40 Members but not less than ten Members support the motion, the House will determine the matter by a vote.

Prorogation

Prorogation is effected under the prerogative, by the announcement of the Queen's command. The effect of prorogation is that all business before Parliament is suspended. Parliament will be prorogued until a specified date. The prorogation of Parliament has not been effected in person by the Crown since 1854. The period between prorogation and the summoning of a new Parliament is known as the 'recess'. The power to prorogue Parliament is unaffected by the Fixed-term Parliaments Act 2011 (see section 6).

Dissolution

Parliament is dissolved prior to a general election. The Fixed-term Parliaments Act 2011 provides for five-year fixed-term Parliaments, with limited power to amend the date, and provision made for an earlier general election where a vote of no confidence in the government is passed by two-thirds or more Members of the House of Commons.

See further
Chapter 6.

The Organisation of Business

The organisation of business in a typical parliamentary session is as follows. The session opens with the State Opening of Parliament and the Queen's Speech, which takes place in the Spring. The Queen's Speech outlines the government's proposals for legislation in the session. The following four to five days are spent in Debate on the Address, including two days on which the Opposition proposes – 'moves' – amendments to specific areas of policy. Following the summer recess (usually from mid-July to early September), and until Christmas, most of the time of the House will be spent on second reading debates of Government Bills. Between Christmas and Easter, the majority of the time of the House will be spent in second reading debates and the committee stage of Bills. Before the end of July, the remaining legislative stages of Bills take place, unless these are to be carried over to the next parliamentary year.[10]

Personnel of the House of Commons

The office of Speaker

The office of Speaker is traceable to 1377 and the appointment of Sir Thomas Hungerford, although from 1258 Parliaments had similar officers.[11] The Speaker of the House featured in the constitutional struggles between King and Parliament in the seventeenth century. When Charles I arrived in the Commons to arrest the Five Knights, the Speaker declared:

> May it please Your Majesty, I have neither eyes to see, nor tongue to speak in this place, but as the House is pleased to direct me, whose servant I am here, and I humbly beg Your Majesty's pardon that I cannot give any other answer than this to what Your Majesty is pleased to demand of me.

Henceforth, the independence of the Speaker from the Crown was established.

The Speaker regulates the proceedings of the House. The Speaker is a senior Member appointed by common agreement of all Members and is generally a Member of the Opposition

---

10 On this see Chapter 14.
11 Known as parlour or prolocutor.

Party. The election of the Speaker and Deputy Speakers is the first task undertaken by Parliament following a general election. The Speaker acts with political impartiality and controls the business of the House.[12]

The Speaker is the presiding officer of the House and ensures that the rules of conduct and order are observed. The Speaker is also the representative of the Commons in relations with the Crown – it is through the Speaker that the privilege of access to the Sovereign is effected – and the House of Lords and other bodies outside Parliament. When the House of Lords amends Commons' Bills, the Speaker checks the amendments to ensure that they do not infringe the financial privileges of the lower House. It is also the function of the Speaker to certify Bills under the Parliament Act 1911.

The Speaker has a discretion in relation to the granting of an application for an emergency debate, whether to allow urgent questions or grant requests for emergency debates, and whether a prima facie case of a breach of the privileges of the House has been established. It is also for the Speaker to rule on matters of procedure. Furthermore, the Speaker will decide whether a proposed amendment to a motion will be accepted.

Disciplinary powers of the Speaker

The control of debate lies with the Speaker, who chooses who is allowed to speak. Advance notice of the wish to participate in debate is given and the Speaker calls each side (Government and Opposition) alternately, and respects the rights of minority parties to participate. The Speaker has powers under Standing Orders to control the following:

See further Chapter 17.

(a)   irrelevance or tedious repetition;
(b)   minor breaches of order;
(c)   the use of disorderly or unparliamentary expressions;
(d)   grossly disorderly conduct;
(e)   grave disorder;
(f)   obstruction of the business of the House by other means.

Disorderly conduct – such as damaging the Mace[13] – may result in the Member, if a suitable apology is not given to the House, being suspended from the House for a period determined by the House on a motion. Suspension from the House in the first instance will be for five sitting days, on a second occasion for 20 days and in the event of a further repetition, for the remainder of the session. Any Member refusing to withdraw from the chamber of the House may be forcibly removed by the Serjeant at Arms.[14] In such an event, the Member will be suspended for the remainder of the parliamentary session. In 2003 the House agreed the proposal that a Member could have his or her salary withheld for a defined period, without suspension.

If a Member persists in a speech after being ordered to discontinue on the basis of irrelevance or tedious repetition, the Speaker may direct him or her to withdraw from the House for the remainder of the sitting, or 'name' him or her for disregarding the authority of the Speaker's Chair. The same penalty may befall a Member who uses unparliamentary language. Unparliamentary language includes:

---

12 On the forced resignation of the Speaker in 2009, see Chapter 17.
13 The ceremonial staff of office of the Commons.
14 An officer of the House responsible for order.

(a)   the imputation of false or unavowed motives;
(b)   the misrepresentation of the language of another and the accusation of misrepresentation;
(c)   charges of uttering a deliberate falsehood;
(d)   abusive and insulting language likely to create disorder.

The Leader of the House

The Leader of the House is responsible to the Prime Minister for the organisation of business in the Commons. It is the function of the Leader of the House to announce the parliamentary business for the following week. The Leader of the House is a Minister of the Crown.[15] When the Prime Minister is unavailable, it is the Leader of the House who represents the House of Commons.

The party whips

The party political control of Members of Parliament is in the hands of the party whips. On the government side, all whips receive salaries[16] and are Ministers of the Crown. The Chief Whip[17] is assisted by up to 12 other Members. The Chief Whip organises the details of business of the House. The Opposition has a Chief Whip, two salaried assistants and eight to ten non-salaried assistants. The task of the government Chief Whip is to act as contact between the Prime Minister, the Leader of the House (to both of whom he is responsible) and Members. The whips (of all parties) keep Members informed about the House's business, and inform Members when they are obliged to attend the House. The degree of coercion of Members will depend on the importance of the matter in hand. When attendance is required – and when political consequences will flow from non-attendance – a 'three-line whip' is announced. Where attendance is necessary, but not essential, a 'two-line whip' is applied. In order that Members are not unduly pressured by the need for attendance in Parliament, 'pairing' is permitted. Pairing is the arrangement whereby Members of government and opposition parties will be linked together: if one is absent the other may abstain from voting. Thus, the non-attendance of one Member will be offset – in the counting of votes – by the absence of the other. Pairing arrangements must be registered with the Party Whips. Pairing is not permitted in relation to divisions on the most important matters. It is this arrangement which is most frequently threatened when relationships between the Government and Opposition break down.

Much of the organisation of the business of the House is in the hands of the whips, including planning the parliamentary timetable and advising on practice and procedure. Whips of all parties are also responsible for recommending candidates for membership of parliamentary committees.

Members of Parliament

Front- and backbenchers

Business in the House is conducted on adversarial lines. The adversarial nature of the Commons is reflected in the layout of the House. The House is divided into two sections which face

---

15 House of Commons (Administration) Act 1978, s 1.
16 Ministerial and Other Salaries Act 1975, s 1(1)(a) and Sched 1.
17 Who holds office as Parliamentary or Patronage Secretary to the Treasury.

each other, separated by the Table of the House, behind which the Speaker sits. Each side has a front bench and several rows of back benches. On the side to the right of the Speaker sit Members of the Government party, Ministers of the Government occupying the front bench. Opposite, on the front bench, will sit the shadow ministers of the Opposition party. All other Members of both the Government and Opposition will sit on the backbenches: hence the term 'backbenchers'.

The representation of women in the Commons

The Parliament (Qualification of Women) Act 1918 made women eligible to stand for election to Parliament. Of 1,613 candidates at the 1918 election, only 17 were women. The first female candidate to take her seat in the House of Commons was Lady Astor, elected in 1919 in a by-election. The representation of women has always been poor in the Commons. In 1918, there was just one woman Member; in 1945, 24 women were elected to Parliament. The figures remained between 17 and 29 until 1987, when 41 women were elected. All the major political parties are committed to increasing the representation of women in the Commons. The 2010 general election resulted in a significantly improved proportion of women Members of Parliament. The total number elected was 142 (22 per cent of 650 seats).

The first woman to hold ministerial office was Margaret Bondfield. She became the first female Member of Cabinet in 1929. Only one woman has held the office of Speaker: Betty Boothroyd from 1992 to 2000. The first female Prime Minister was the Rt Hon Margaret Thatcher MP (as she then was), who held office from 1979 to 1990, the longest premiership in the twentieth century.

Salaries and allowances of Members of Parliament

As far back as the thirteenth century, representatives attending Parliament were paid – either in cash or in kind – and, in addition, could claim travelling expenses. Payment by electors had ceased by the end of the seventeenth century. In the eighteenth and nineteenth centuries, though unpaid, a seat in the House of Commons was valuable, and could attract large sums of money for its purchase. Members of Parliament remained formally unpaid until 1911, despite numerous previous attempts to introduce payment. Salaries are now the responsibility of the Independent Parliamentary Standards Authority (IPSA).[18]

Members also receive allowances for secretarial and research assistance, car mileage, and limited travel between the constituency and Parliament.

Members' Code of Conduct

Members of Parliament are governed by a Code of Conduct setting out general principles to guide members on the standards of conduct that the House and the public have a right to expect.[19]

See further
Chapter 17.

The size of the House of Commons

For the 2010 general election there were 650 seats in the House of Commons. If the number of parliamentary representatives is compared with the total population of the country, it can

---

18 See the Constitutional Reform and Governance Act 2010 amending the Parliamentary Standards Act 2009.
19 As recommended by the Committee on Standards and Privileges: *Third Report of the Committee on Standards and Privileges*, HC 604 (1995–96), London: HMSO; HC Deb Vol 282 Col 392, 24 July 1996. See further Chapter 15.

be seen that there is a wide discrepancy in the representativeness of differing legislatures. In Ireland, for example, there are 166 Members of Parliament, each representing 24,000 citizens. By contrast, in Australia, there are 147 Members, each representing 122,000 citizens. In the United Kingdom each Member of Parliament represents approximately 100,000 citizens.

The Coalition government established in 2010 decided to reduce the number of seats in the House of Commons to 600 with effect from 2015. The Parliamentary Voting System and Constituencies Act 2011 made provision for this reduction. The Liberal Democrats however, withdrew their support and the proposal has been withdrawn.

Resignation of Members of Parliament

A Member, once duly elected, cannot relinquish his seat.[20] However, provision is made whereby a Member may retire under differing procedures,[21] each of which involves accepting office under the Crown, which obliges the Member to relinquish his seat on the basis of disqualification from membership[22] and a writ to be issued for a by-election. Application for the office is normally granted,[23] although power remains for the application to be refused. The offices are nowadays purely nominal and retained as a device to avoid the absence of any resignation procedure.

The political parties

The major political parties have a similar organisational structure in Parliament. The Conservative, Labour and Liberal Democrat Parties have a system of election for the party leader, and are organised into front- and backbench Members. The normal arrangement is that the Commons comprises the government, elected on the basis of the simple majority vote, Her Majesty's Loyal Opposition, being the second largest party in the House, and minority parties – Liberal Democrat, Ulster Unionist, Scottish Nationalist, Plaid Cymru. However, since the general election in 2010 there has been a Coalition government, comprising the Conservative Party and Liberal Democrat Party.

Government and Opposition

It is the Government which controls the majority of Parliament's time. On 75 per cent of sitting days, Government business takes priority and it is the Government which determines the business to be undertaken (subject to established practices as to Opposition Days, days set aside for Private Members' Bills, etc). From scrutinising the work of Parliament, it may be tempting to underplay the importance of Parliament as a whole, and the Opposition in particular, in comparison with the power of the Government. Such a view is implicit in the pejorative labelling of government as an 'elective dictatorship'.[24] Such charges need to be viewed

---

20 *Commons' Journal* (1547–1628) 724.
21 Most usually accepting the office of steward or bailiff of Her Majesty's Three Chiltern Hundreds of Stoke, Desborough and Burnham or steward of the Manor of Northstead.
22 Under the House of Commons Disqualification Act 1975, s 4.
23 By the Chancellor of the Exchequer.
24 Hailsham, 1978, p 21.

with some caution. In 1947, Sir Ivor Jennings described the role of the Opposition as 'at once the alternative to the government and a focus for the discontent of the people. Its function is almost as important as that of the government'.[25]

In its constitutional role, the Opposition must constantly be questioning, probing and calling government to account. Viewed in this light, notwithstanding the Government's control over the timetable and business of the House, it can be said that all parliamentary time is as much 'Opposition time' as 'Government time'.

The constitutional importance of the official Opposition is reflected in the fact that the Leader of the Opposition draws a substantial salary in both the House of Commons and Lords, which is drawn on the Consolidated Fund.[26] In addition, since 1975, financial assistance has been provided to all opposition parties to enable them to carry out their role effectively. Each party is entitled to a fixed sum per annum per seat won by the party, plus an amount for every 200 votes cast in the previous election.

The Opposition is allocated 20 days per session in which it can determine the business of the day, representing in an average session 11.6 per cent of parliamentary time. The provision of Opposition Days ensures that the Government is obliged to debate matters which it might prefer not to address. Following the Queen's Speech at the opening of a new parliamentary session, the Opposition has the right to determine the subjects for debate on the second of the six days set aside for debate on the speech.

In addition to normal parliamentary procedure for debate, questions, etc, and opposition time, the Opposition has the weapon of the motion of censure – or vote of no confidence. The motion takes the form 'the House has no confidence in Her Majesty's Government'. The Fixed-term Parliaments Act 2011, section 2, places this on a statutory basis. See further Chapter 5 on the dissolution of Parliament.

Voting in the Commons

A 'division' is the name for the counting of votes on important issues where conflict is apparent. Not every debate will result in a division: divisions are reserved for instances when it is important to register formally the number of votes for and against a particularly important issue. In the 2008–09 session there were 248 divisions and in the short 2009–10 session, 135 divisions were ordered. For the observer, there is something archaic and humorous about the procedure. The Speaker orders 'Division: clear the lobbies'. Division bells sound throughout Parliament and in the division district immediately surrounding Parliament. Members will interrupt whatever they are doing in response to the bell and return to Parliament for the vote. Members crowd into the 'Aye' or 'Noe' lobby, and as they exit the lobby their attendance is checked. The Speaker then announces the result of the division. Votes are recorded by name in the Official *Journal* of the House of Commons.

---

25 Jennings, 1959a, Chapter XV.
26 See Chapter 14.

Parliamentary Publications and Papers

The House of Commons

- *The Commons' Journal*: contains the official record of the proceedings of the House. The Journal dates back to 1547 and is published annually. The *Journal* contains rulings from the Speaker on procedural matters.
- *The Commons' Official Report*: contains the records of speeches made in the House and written answers to Parliamentary Questions. It is a substantially verbatim report of the proceedings.
- *The Vote*: the collective name of a bundle of papers delivered to Members daily during a parliamentary session. It contains the record of the previous day's proceedings together with the Order Paper for the day which lists the business of the House.
- *The Order Book*: a daily publication setting out the future business of the House.

The House of Lords

- *Minutes of proceedings*: the record of the proceedings in the House of Lords together with details of forthcoming business.
- *The Lords' Journal*: since 1461, the Journals have been kept, providing details of attendance and voting.

Televised proceedings in Parliament

Radio broadcasting of Ministerial Question Time (see Chapter 15) began in 1978. Televised broadcasts of the House of Lords have been transmitted since 1985. In 1988, the House of Commons resolved:

> . . . this House approves in principle the holding of an experiment in the public broadcasting of its proceedings by television.[27]

The Select Committee on Televising of Proceedings was established to make recommendations as to the rules of coverage.[28] Broadcasting commenced in 1989. The *Journals* of the House of Commons and Lords remain the official record of proceedings in Parliament.

Public Petitions

The right of individual citizens to petition Parliament is a fundamental constitutional right. Recognised in Magna Carta 1215 and restated in the Bill of Rights 1689, '. . . it is the right of the subjects to petition the King, and all commitments and prosecutions for such petitioning are illegal'. Before the right to vote was extended to all citizens, petitioning was the only form of redress open to the vast majority of people: in the years 1837 to 1841 the average number of petitions presented annually was almost 17,600.

A Petition must be addressed to the House of Commons, include the name and address of the petitioner and contain a 'prayer' (request) to the Commons, using 'respectful, decorous

---

27 HC 141 (1988–89), London: HMSO, and *Votes and Proceedings* 1988–89, 12 June 1989. And see Norton, 1991.
28 *Votes and Proceedings* 1987–88, 7 February and 9 March 1988.

and temperate' language.[29] The Petition will be presented to the House by a Member of Parliament immediately before the half-hour adjournment debate at the end of each day's business. The usual practice is that Petitions will be sent to the relevant Government Department for investigation. The Department will formally reply to the House and both the Petition and government response will be recorded in *Hansard*, the Official Journal of the House.[30]

Summary

The House of Commons has 650 directly elected representatives of the people: Members of Parliament. The political party with the largest number of seats will generally be the governing party and the leader of that party will be appointed as Prime Minister. The second-largest political party will form Her Majesty's Loyal Opposition: a government in waiting should the government be forced out of office. The political party leaders are supported by a number of Whips who act as a channel of communication with ordinary Members and also have a role in ensuring attendance in the House as necessary.

Control of proceedings in the Chamber of the Commons is in the hands of the Speaker, an elected Member of Parliament who acts as the politically impartial Chair of proceedings. The House of Commons is self-regulating, its procedures being laid down in Standing Orders.

The three principal tasks of the House of Commons are to represent the people, to enact legislation and to scrutinise the administration of government.

Further Reading

Blackburn, R. and Kennon, A. (2003) *Parliament: Functions, Practice and Procedures* (2nd edn), London: Sweet & Maxwell.

Brazier, R., Finders, M. and McHugh, D. (2005) *New Politics, New Parliament? A Review of Parliamentary Modernisation Since 1997*, London: Hansard Society.

Cowley, P. and Stuart, M. (2001) 'Parliament: a Few Headaches and a Dose of Modernisation', Parliamentary Affairs, 54(3): 442.

Erskine May, T. (2011) *Parliamentary Practice* (24th edn), London: Butterworths.

Rogers, R. and Walters, R. (2004) *How Parliament Works* (5th edn), London: Pearson, Chapters 6–11 and 13.

Tomkins, A. (2003) 'What is Parliament For?' in M. Bamforth and P. Leyland (eds) *Public Law in a Multi-Layered Constitution*, Oxford: Hart Publishing.

---

29 The Petition may be signed by one or many persons (the greatest number of signatures was an estimated four and a half million in a Petition concerning an Ambulance Dispute presented in 1989).

30 Petitions and government responses are available on the *Hansard* homepage: www.parliament.uk/business/publications.

Chapter 14

The Legislative Process[1]

Chapter Contents

---

1   See Silk and Walters, 2006, Chapter 6; Griffith and Ryle, 2003, Chapter 8.

Introduction

Approximately two-thirds of the time of the House of Commons is devoted to the consideration of proposals for legislation. In order to effect changes in the law, any proposal must receive the authority of Parliament: Parliament legitimises policy objectives. A mere decision of Parliament, in the form of a Resolution of the Commons, cannot change the law of the land.[2] In order to become law, a legislative proposal must receive the consent of the three component parts of Parliament: the Commons, the Lords,[3] and the Crown through the giving of royal assent. In this chapter the process of scrutiny in the House of Commons is considered. Discussion of the legislative role of the House of Lords is to be found in Chapter 16.

Before examining the process of scrutiny in the Commons, the various types of legislation must be considered. Legislative proposals fall under two main categories: primary and delegated (or secondary) legislation. Primary legislation refers to Acts of Parliament. Delegated or secondary legislation refers to legislation drafted by authorised persons or bodies under the authority of a 'parent' statute.

The United Kingdom Parliament and Devolution

As seen in Chapter 11, devolution to the Northern Ireland Assembly, Scottish Parliament and Welsh Assembly represents a diminution in the United Kingdom Parliament's (Westminster's) legislative role. Under devolution, in practical terms, the United Kingdom Parliament retains power to enact primary legislation only to the extent to which this power has not passed to the regional legislature.

Primary Legislation[4]

The classification of Bills

The majority of Bills will be those put forward by the government to implement its policy. Bills fall into four categories: Public Bills, Private Bills, Hybrid Bills and Money Bills. The procedure for passing a Bill depends on its classification. Most attention is here devoted to the legislative procedure for Public Bills.

A Public Bill is one which has general application to all members of society, for example Road Traffic Acts, Environmental Protection Acts and National Health Service Acts. A Private Bill is one which affects only a particular locality or group or body of persons.

A Hybrid Bill is one of general application, that is to say a Public Bill, which also affects particular private interests in a manner different from the private interests of other persons or bodies of the same category or class. The Bill regulating the development of the Channel Tunnel is an example of a Hybrid Bill, since it affected the private rights of landowners whose land would be compulsorily purchased.[5]

A Money Bill is one which is certified by the Speaker as such, and contains nothing other than financial measures.

---

2 **Stockdale v Hansard** (1839).
3 Other than where the Parliament Act procedure is employed. See Chapter 16.
4 See Rose, 1986; Hansard Society, 1993.
5 See also London (Transport) Bill 1968–69; Norfolk and Suffolk Broads Bill 1986–87.

A Private Member's Bill is one promoted by an individual Member of Parliament, as opposed to the government[6] or, alternatively, a matter which the government has been unable to fit into its legislative programme but will subsequently adopt and provide time – and support – for the passage of the Bill. Most often, such Bills involve sensitive issues of particular interest to their promoters. The Abortion Act 1967, for example, originated from a Private Member's Bill. Private Members' Bills follow the same legislative process as government Bills, but the time available for their consideration is restricted. Normally, ten (although occasionally more) Fridays each session will be set aside for Private Members' Bills, and it is rare for a Bill to succeed unless the government is prepared to provide additional time for its consideration.

Consolidation Bills represent a re-enactment of legislation in a comprehensive manner and they enable previous legislation – which will generally exist in several statutes – to be repealed. Consolidation Bills do not, for the most part, represent any change in the law; rather, they represent the chance to 'consolidate' all the law on a particular matter within one statute. Consolidation Bills are normally introduced in the House of Lords and then scrutinised by a Joint Committee on Consolidation Bills, composed of Members of both the House of Commons and the House of Lords. Since there is no change being made in the substantive law, parliamentary time devoted to Consolidation Bills is short and it is rare for a Consolidation Bill to be debated more than briefly on the floor of the Commons. In 1994, the House of Commons agreed that, in order to save further time, Consolidated Bills would no longer require a committee stage. Finally, there are Consolidated Fund and Appropriation Bills which provide statutory authority for government expenditure and which are not debated in Parliament.

The legislative picture cannot be complete without consideration of delegated or subordinate legislation. In each parliamentary session an average of 62 Bills are enacted, while the average number of statutory instruments (see further below) amounts to 2,000 per session. In addition, administrative rules drafted by government departments must be considered. These include Codes of Practice, Circulars and Guidances and, while they do not have the force of law, they nevertheless have an impact on the manner in which laws are implemented.[7]

The origins of legislation

The majority of Bills considered by Parliament will be introduced by the government of the day. This does not necessarily mean that the source of the proposal is one emanating from government policy, still less from the party manifesto on which the election was fought.

Consideration of the origins of legislative proposals is important in evaluating the extent to which government and the House of Commons interacts with the society it is elected to serve. JAG Griffith and M Ryle observe:

> It is a central feature of Parliament, however, that it performs a responsive rather than initiating function within the constitution. The government – at different levels – initiates policy, formulates its policy on legislation and other proposals, exercises powers under the prerogative or granted by statute and, in all these aspects, performs the governing role in the state. Both Houses of Parliament spend most of their time responding, in a variety of ways, to these initiatives, proposals or executive actions. [2003, p 5]

---

6 See Griffith and Ryle, 2003.
7 Eg, Guidance to Local Authorities on the Provision of Sites for Gypsies under the Caravan Sites Act 1968; Guidance on Allocation of Local Authority Housing under the Housing Act 1985. See Baldwin and Houghton, 1986; Ganz, 1987.

The government, however, is not the only source of business for Parliament. Much business originates from the Opposition front bench, and from backbenchers on either side of the two Houses. The inspiration for their input is largely found in general public opinion, outside pressures or interest groups, newspapers, radio and television, and in the minds and attitudes of millions of citizens represented in the Commons by Members.

Parliament therefore finds itself the recipient of a wide range of external pressures and proposals, broadly divided in origin between the government of the day on the one hand and the outside world – the public – on the other.

Professor Finer (1958) labels the forces external to Parliament which have an impact on its working as the 'anonymous empire'. Finer is here referring to all those individuals and organisations, lobby groups and interest groups whose aim is to influence the content of legislation. Finer claims that the detailed programme of government legislation 'owes a great deal to sectional groups'. Amongst these groups we can include such organisations as the Confederation of British Industry, Trades Union Congress, National Farmers' Union, National Union of Teachers, British Medical Association and Law Society, each of which is engaged in promoting its own sectional interests. Other pressure groups pursue particular causes: for example, the Royal Society for the Prevention of Cruelty to Animals, JUSTICE (the International Commission of Jurists), Howard League for Penal Reform, Friends of the Earth (environmental issues), and Shelter (housing).

In addition to these and many other groups, the law reform bodies provide a source of legislation. The Law Commission, established under the Law Commissions Act 1965, is under a duty to keep the law under review with a view to its systematic development and reform, including codification of law, and simplification and modernisation of law. If we take, by way of example, the Law Commission's work on family law, the Commission has reviewed the law of legitimacy, custody, wardship, divorce, domestic violence and occupation of the matrimonial home. In conjunction with interdepartmental committees, the Law Commission has also been engaged in a comprehensive review of adoption law.

Commissions of inquiry may be established by the government to examine and report on particular issues, often culminating in a change in the law. For example, the Committee of Inquiry into Child Abuse in Cleveland resulted (in part) in changes implemented in the Children Act 1989, which represented a major overhaul of the law relating to children. The Criminal Law Revision Committee has examined the law relating, inter alia, to conspiracy, contempt, arrest and detention, and criminal deception.

Each of these sources may result in proposals for changes in the law. The success of these proposals in terms of becoming law is largely dependent upon the government of the day and its willingness to provide parliamentary time for the consideration of Bills. In any parliamentary session, approximately 50 to 60 Bills will be introduced, the vast majority of which will reach the statute book.

The preparation of a Bill

Once the government has decided to implement a particular measure, the aims of government must be translated effectively into language which will achieve those objectives. That task is entrusted to parliamentary draftsmen, or parliamentary counsel, attached to the Management and Personnel Office of the Treasury.[8] Drafting involves five stages: understanding, analysis,

---

8 SI 1981/1670.

design, composition and revision.[9] Once a draft Bill is in being, it is examined by the Cabinet Home Affairs Committee before being formally submitted to Parliament for scrutiny and enactment.

The structure of a Bill

Each Bill has a short title, for example, the Transport Bill, which indicates the general area of policy involved, together with a long title which summarises the main objectives of the Bill. The Bill is made up of Chapters or Parts which encompass groups of related clauses, and Schedules which contain details supplementary to the primary clauses. The Bill may grant powers to make delegated legislation to ministers or other specified bodies, such as local authorities. There is, necessarily, no uniformity as to the length of Bills, which may range from one clause (Abortion Amendment Bill 1988–89) to 27 Parts, 747 clauses and 25 Schedules (Companies Bill 1985).

Pre-legislative scrutiny

In order to improve the quality of legislation, governments increasingly publish draft Bills for consideration before the Bill is presented in its proposed final form. Since 1997 there has been an increasing use of select committees to scrutinise draft Bills before they are formally presented to Parliament. As will be seen from the discussion in Chapter 15, select committees (unlike Public Bill Committees which examine Bills) have the power to call witnesses and consider documentary evidence. This form of pre-legislative scrutiny enables specialist individuals and groups to contribute to the legislative process and thereby improve the quality of legislation.

Pre-legislative scrutiny may be undertaken by a departmental select committee, a specially convened Committee or a Joint Committee comprising members of both the House of Commons and House of Lords.

The Joint Committee on Human Rights

The Joint Committee on Human Rights comprises six members of the House of Commons and six members of the House of Lords. The Committee examines every Bill which is presented to Parliament with a view to ensuring that the Bill is compatible with human rights.[10] It also examines Draft Bills which have been published for consultation prior to being formally presented to Parliament. The Committee reports to both Houses of Parliament.

The legislative stages: Public Bills

First reading

A Bill which is to be introduced will appear on the Order Paper of the relevant day. The Bill will be presented in 'dummy form' and is deemed to be read a 'first time'. Alternatively, a Bill may be introduced on order of the House, or after having been sent to the Commons following its passage by the House of Lords. Following the purely formal introduction into Parliament, a date will be set for second reading and the Bill will be printed and published.

---

9 Thornton, 1987, pp 116–17.
10 As guaranteed under the European Convention on Human Rights, now enforceable in the domestic courts by virtue of the Human Rights Act 1998.

Second reading

It is at the second reading that a Bill will receive its first in-depth scrutiny. The scrutiny occurs in the form of a debate, generally on the floor of the House, and is confined to matters of principle rather than detail. Exceptionally, the second reading debate may be referred to a committee for consideration, but may only be so referred if 20 or more Members of Parliament do not object and, accordingly, the procedure is reserved for non-controversial matters and not measures 'involving large questions of policy nor likely to give rise to differences on party lines'.[11] Public Bills which are to give effect to proposals contained in a report by either of the Law Commissions, other than a Private Members' Bill or a Consolidation Bill, when set down for second reading will be committed to a second reading committee, unless the House orders otherwise, or the Bill is referred to the Northern Ireland, Scottish or Welsh Grand Committee. If a minister of the Crown moves a motion that a Bill not be referred to a second reading committee, the House will vote on the motion. Where a Bill has been committed to a second reading committee, the committee considers the principles of the Bill, but the vote on the Bill is taken on the floor of the House. It is at second reading stage that the minister in charge of the Bill must explain and defend the contents of the Bill. The Opposition's task is to probe and question and set out reasons for opposing the Bill. It should not be assumed that the Opposition invariably opposes Bills. In many instances the proposed legislation is uncontroversial and may even be welcomed by the Opposition. The Dangerous Dogs Bill and the Child Support Bill 1990 are illustrations of this phenomenon. If the Bill is opposed, a vote will take place which determines the fate of the Bill. If the vote is lost, the Bill is rejected and the proposed legislation must either be abandoned or the Bill must be reintroduced at a later date.

Once a Bill has successfully completed the second reading stage, it 'stands committed' to a Public Bill Committee[12] unless, exceptionally, the House orders otherwise.[13]

Committee stage

Once the second reading has taken place, Bills are sent to a committee for further and detailed consideration. Committee stage may be undertaken by:

- Public Bill Committee: this is the automatic procedure unless the Commons orders otherwise;
- Committee of the whole House: this is reserved for Bills of constitutional importance. The Human Rights Bill and Northern Ireland, Scotland and Wales devolution Bills were considered by the whole House;
- Committee of the whole House for some parts of the Bill with the remainder being sent to a Public Bill Committee. The Greater London Authority Bill was considered in this way;
- Select Committee;
- Joint Committee of both Houses.[14]

Public Bill Committees are designed to scrutinise Bills in detail. The committee will be established for the purpose of examining a particular Bill and will then stand down, a feature which, as will be seen, may have implications for the adequacy of scrutiny.

At any one time, there will be eight to ten Public Bill Committees in operation. Committees may comprise between 16 and 50 Members of Parliament, and normally between 18 and 25.[15]

---

11 *First Report Select Committee on Procedure*, HC 149 (1964–65), London: HMSO, para 3.
12 Until the start of the 2006–07 session known as Standing Committees.
13 In the 2000–01 session, six Bills were considered by a Committee of the Whole House.
14 See Griffith and Ryle, 2003, 6-128–6-129.
15 Complex Bills may warrant a larger committee membership, as with the Finance Bill 1992.

Membership is drawn from Members of Parliament from all political parties and is proportionate to the overall strength of the party in the House, thus the larger the government's majority in the House, the larger its majority in the committee. Appointments are made by a Committee of Selection who will take advice from party whips as to appropriate Members. The Speaker of the House appoints the Chairman of the committee, who may be a Member of either side of the House (Government or Opposition). Once selected, the Chairman is impartial and enjoys the same powers as the Speaker of the House in relation to selection of amendments for discussion and imposition of the Closure Motion (see further below).

The function of the committee is to examine the Bill clause by clause. The minister in charge of the Bill has the task of steering it successfully through committee, aided by his Parliamentary Private Secretary and civil servants. Amendments may be proposed by Members giving notice to the Public Bill Office of the House of Commons. These amendments may take the form of linguistic details, adding or subtracting a word here or there; alternatively, amendments may be of major substance. Once the clauses of the Bill have been considered, the committee moves to consider any proposed new clauses. Proposals for amendment may be ruled out of order if they are irrelevant, beyond the scope of the Bill, conflict with other proposed amendments, conflict with the principle of the Bill, or are unintelligible, ineffective, vague or spurious.[16]

The proceedings in Public Bill Committees are formal and ritualistic. A Member moves an amendment, the Minister responds, the Opposition speaks, other Members comment, and debate continues until a decision on a clause – 'that the clause do stand part of the Bill' – is reached. The minister's task is to ensure a smooth passage for the Bill in the fastest possible time. Richard Crossman, Minister of Housing and Local Government in the Labour government of 1974, commented that committee stage is tedious with the Minister 'being pinned to the wall' throughout the process.[17] For the most part, deliberations will follow party political lines, and it follows that, provided the government has a majority on the committee, the chances of successfully moving amendments are slight.

The low success rate of backbench proposals for amendment should not be given disproportionate weight. It has been seen above that Standing Orders set out a number of 'inadmissible' categories of proposed amendments. It must also be noted that Members may put forward amendments solely with a view to gaining a clearer picture of the Bill, or for more spurious reasons, such as delaying a Bill or embarrassing the government. Equally, it should be remembered that the composition of the committee reflects that of the House overall: governments with a firm majority will inevitably suffer fewer defeats in committee. Finally, recognition must be given to the fact that the government has gained a mandate in a general election and, whether or not a specific legislative proposal stems from that mandate, the government has a legitimate expectation of getting its legislative programme on the statute book. Equally, the principle of the Bill has been approved on second reading by the House. While Parliament as a whole, through its representative committee, has the equally legitimate expectation of being able to give adequate scrutiny to government proposals, that should not necessarily be understood to mean that Public Bill Committees should expect to be able to force their views on government.

At first sight, it appears anomalous that there is no committee system organised on specialist lines. There is a prima facie case for committees to be geared to particular subjects, or groups of subjects. On this reasoning, a Public Bill Committee could be devised with the remit to consider transport matters, another to consider science and technology Bills, another to

16 See Erskine May, 2004; Griffith and Ryle, 2003.
17 Crossman, 1977.

consider environmental issues, and so on. If such committees were appointed for the life of the Parliament, or for a parliamentary session with Members appointed on the basis of their expertise and interests, the potential for improved scrutiny would be enhanced. However, there is a counter-argument to this. A specialist semi-permanent committee, while having the benefit of expertise, would lose the quality of the assortment of interests which is currently brought to bear on proposals. Members of the committee might become too familiar with each others' attitudes, and ministers and the committee could suffer from becoming inward looking and overly concerned with one subject at the expense of others. Committees are open to the public and their proceedings are recorded in the Official Report of the House, *Hansard*. For debate to become too narrow and technical might disadvantage other Members and the public in their capacity to understand proceedings.

One recognised shortcoming in the procedure of Standing Committees – the former Bill scrutiny committees – was the lack of power to send for 'persons and papers', in other words, witnesses and documents. Public Bill Committees now have the power to take written and oral evidence from officials and experts outside of Parliament.

Report stage[18]

Once the Bill has been considered in Public Bill Committee, the Bill is reported back to the House of Commons as a whole. If amendments have been made in committee, the Bill will be reprinted. Further amendments may be introduced at this stage, but the Speaker will be careful to avoid repetition of the debate in standing committee, so any proposed amendments previously considered will be rejected. The Speaker will accept amendments proposed by the government, proposals representing a compromise and amendments relating to new developments. Generally, the debate at this stage will be brief but, again, this will depend on the importance of the Bill. The Police and Criminal Evidence Bill, for example, was debated for eighteen and a half hours at report stage. Approximately nine per cent of time on the floor of the House is taken up with report.

Third reading

Third reading represents the last chance for the House of Commons to examine a Bill before it is passed to the House of Lords. At this stage, the Bill cannot be amended, other than to correct small mistakes such as grammatical or printing errors. A Bill may pass through the report and third reading stages at the same time.

Fast-track Legislation

On occasion there is a need for legislation to be enacted with speed. The need may arise through an emergency of some sort – as in the case of the banking collapse in 2008 – or some phenomenon which is causing unusual public disquiet. Anti-terrorism legislation has been fast-tracked in response to some terrorist events.

When an emergency, or fast-track, Bill is required, the normal parliamentary procedures are followed, but the time allowed for scrutiny much reduced. The government will seek the agreement of the Opposition parties on the date by which the Royal Assent must be achieved, and the stages of the Bill will be tailored to achieve that objective.

While fast-track legislation is necessary on occasion, it gives rise to constitutional questions, not least the ability of Parliament as a whole to give adequate scrutiny to government

---

18 See Griffith and Ryle, 2003.

proposals. Linked to this is the difficulty caused by the government tabling late amendments without providing adequate time for their debate and scrutiny. It is argued that the quality of the legislation may be reduced by the speed with which it has been processed. The need for speed also precludes valuable contributions being made by specialist interest groups.[19] The House of Lords Select Committee on the Constitution recommended by the Minister responsible for a fast-tracked Bill should be required to make an oral statement to the House of Lords outlining the case for fast-tracking. It also recommended that there should be a presumption in favour of 'sunset clauses' – a clause imposing a time limit on the operation of the Act following which it would need to be renewed or replaced, and that there should be a presumption in favour of early post-legislative scrutiny of fast-tracked Bills.

Private Members' Bills[20]

Introducing a Private Member's Bill

In addition to Public (and Private and Hybrid) Bills, a number of legislative proposals will be introduced by individual Members of Parliament. In any one session, dozens of Private Members' Bills will be introduced, a minority of which will reach the statute book.

The success of a Private Member's Bill is largely dependent upon it receiving government support. As has been seen in Chapter 13, the government controls the parliamentary timetable, and dominates parliamentary business. Since only six Fridays per session are allocated for consideration of Private Members' Bills, it will be necessary for the government to make additional time for the completion of such a Bill's parliamentary stages. Whether or not the government is willing to do this will depend upon the political support which the Bill acquires. However, even if a Bill does not successfully pass all its legislative stages, it may have served the useful purpose of heightening parliamentary and public awareness of a particular issue. For example, the Rt Hon Tony Benn MP introduced Private Member's Bills, *inter alia*, on placing the royal prerogative on a statutory basis,[21] and for enacting a written constitution.[22] Neither of these succeeded, but they represent matters in which there is widespread interest.

A Private Member's Bill may be introduced in one of four ways. The first procedure is that of the ballot.

Introduction by ballot

The House will agree, early in the session, for days to be appointed for the purpose of the ballot. Members of Parliament may put their names on the ballot paper on that day. Over 400 Members normally enter the ballot, although many will have no specific proposed legislation in mind. Twenty Members will be successful at the ballot. If successful, the Member must then, within nine days, table the subject matter for his or her Bill. Six Fridays per session are allocated to Private Members' Bills, on which days the Bills take precedence over other parliamentary business.

Introduction under Standing Order Procedure

Any Member may present a Bill under this procedure by placing the long and short title of the Bill on the Order Paper of the House. The Bill will not be considered, but simply be deemed to have received a first reading and a date set for second reading.

---

19 See the 15th Report of Session 2008–09, *Fast-track Legislation: Constitutional Implications and Safeguards*, HL Paper 116-I, July 2009.
20 See Marsh and Read, 1988.
21 Crown Prerogatives (House of Commons Control) Bill 1988–89.
22 Commonwealth of Britain Bill.

Introduction under the 'Ten Minute Rule'

A Member may give notice of a motion for leave to introduce a Bill. The motions will be considered at specific times allotted by the House, which permits the Member to raise an issue after Question Time on Tuesdays and Wednesdays, thus guaranteeing media attention.[23] Several rules apply. The Member may give one notice at any one time. No notice may be given for leave to bring in a Bill which relates to taxation or expenditure, or to bring in a Bill which covers matters which are substantially the same as those contained in Bills on which the House has already reached a decision in that session.

'Ordinary presentation' of a Bill

Every Member is permitted to introduce a Bill after having given notice. These Bills, however, are not presented until after the Ballot Bills have been presented and put down for second reading. They therefore have little chance of success. Nor do they enjoy the publicity given to Bills introduced under the Ten Minute Rule.

Introduction of a Bill after consideration in the House of Lords

Most Private Members' Bills are introduced in the House of Commons, but a small number in each session may have started their parliamentary life in the Lords. If the Bill passes the Lords, it then comes to the Commons. However, Bills introduced in the Lords are considered only after Bills introduced in the Commons and, accordingly, given the severe time constraints, few are likely even to receive a second reading in the Commons.

'Carry-over' of Bills

It has been noted above that Bills which do not pass all legislative stages within one session will lapse and have to be reintroduced in the following session.[24] In order to avoid duplication of effort and time wastage, the House of Commons agreed[25] that government Bills could be carried over from one session to the next. In 2002 the Commons approved a recommendation that no Bill should be carried over more than once.[26]

Curtailing debate on legislative proposals

As a result of the pressure on parliamentary time, and the need for a Bill to pass through all its legislative stages in a single session, procedures exist to limit consideration of a Bill.

Closure motions

The Closure Motion, introduced in 1881, is a means of stopping debate, usually by agreement between Government and Opposition, in order to ensure that debates end at times agreed by the parties. The closure can be used in debate on the floor of the House or in Public Bill Committee. It is an instrument of control, and one which is used sparingly: rarely will it be used without agreement. In the 1987–88 session, however (a long session), it was used 20 times without inter-party agreement.

---

23 Usually, on Tuesdays or Wednesdays before the start of public business.
24 There are two exceptions to this rule: Bills passed under the Parliament Acts and Private Bills. These may be suspended in one session and revived in the next.
25 Following the recommendation of the Modernisation Committee: Third Report, *Carry-over of Public Bills*, HC 543 of 1997–98.
26 See Standing Order No 80A.

In terms of procedure, the motion for closure is put to the Speaker, who has discretion whether or not to accept the motion. In addition, at least 100 Members of Parliament must vote in favour of closure.

Selection of amendments

This device is confined to legislative proposals and enables the procedure to be streamlined by the selection of amendments for discussion.

The Allocation of Time Motion

The most extreme form of control is the Allocation of Time Motion, colloquially called the Guillotine Motion, introduced in its present form in 1887. Erskine May (1997) describes Guillotine Motions as representing:

> . . . the extreme limit to which procedure goes in affirming the rights of the majority at the expense of the minorities of the House, and it cannot be denied that they are capable of being used in such a way as to upset the balance, generally so carefully preserved, between the claims of business, and the rights of debate.

The device, if approved by the House, enables the government to set dates by which the various stages of scrutiny and debate must be completed. If the government puts forward a motion for an Allocation of Time, Standing Orders provide that a debate of up to three hours may take place (which may be extended), unless otherwise proposed in the motion or decided by the Business Committee of the House. Once agreed, the Business Committee of the House, or a business sub-committee of the Public Bill Committee will determine how many scrutiny sessions are to be held and the date by which the next procedural stage must be accomplished.

However, since the introduction of Programme Orders (see below) which have become a regular feature of the law-making process, Guillotine Motions are now reserved for the most difficult cases of delay through obstruction by the Opposition.[27]

Programming of Bills

In the 2000–01 session, Orders of the House provided that Programme Motions should be employed to facilitate efficiency in the legislative process. The Modernisation Committee stated that the basic requirements of the reformed system were to ensure that the government gets its legislation through in a reasonable time while allowing Members to have a full opportunity to debate and propose amendments. Further, it was essential that all parts of the Bill be properly considered, and that there should be an improvement in the preparation of Bills so as to reduce the need for amendments.[28]

A motion (request) for a Programme Order is moved directly after the second reading debate and sets out timetabling for further stages in the Commons.

Delegated Legislation

The picture of the law-making process would be incomplete without a consideration of delegated, or subordinate, legislation.

---

27 In the 2002–03 session a total of 71 Programming Orders were made, with only three Guillotine Motions.
28 See Standing Order No 83A.

In 1972, Parliament's Joint Committee on Delegated Legislation described subordinate legislation as covering 'every exercise of power to legislate conferred by or under an Act of Parliament'.[29] Some examples will make the scope of delegated legislation clearer. Delegated legislation may be made by:

(a)   *ministers*, in the form of rules and regulations which supplement the provisions of an Act of Parliament;

(b)   *local authorities*, in the form of bylaws to regulate their locality according to particular localised needs;

(c)   *public bodies*, in the form of rules and regulations. Such bodies include the British Airways Authority, the British Railways Board and the Nature Conservancy Council;

(d)   *judges*, in the form of rules of court made under the authority of section 75 of the Supreme Court Act 1981;

(e)   *government departments*, in the form of codes of practice, circulars and guidance. These do not contain legal rules, but have a substantive effect on the manner in which the legal rules operate;

(f)   *the House of Commons*, in the form of Resolutions of the House. The Provisional Collection of Taxes Act 1968 makes possible the lawful imposition and collection of taxation between the Budget speech and the enactment of the Finance Bill in July/August. Whereas normal Resolutions of the House do not have the force of law, Resolutions enabling the impositions and collections of taxation – being authorised by statute – have legal effect.

The volume of delegated legislation also reveals its importance as a source of law. In any parliamentary year, between 1,500 and 3,000 pieces of delegated legislation will be approved.

The use of delegated law-making power is not a purely modern phenomenon, arising from increasing legal regulation of all aspects of life. The power to make subordinate legislation was exercised as early as the sixteenth century.[30] The increase in the volume of delegated legislation derives from the early nineteenth century.

Delegated legislation raises questions about the supremacy of Parliament. In *The New Despotism* (1929), Hewart CJ argued that the increased use of delegated legislation, particularly during the First World War under the Defence of the Realm Act 1914, amounted to an effective usurpation of the sovereign law-making powers of Parliament. Such criticisms led to the appointment, in 1929, of a committee of inquiry[31] to consider the powers exercised by ministers by way of delegated legislation and to report on safeguards that were desirable or necessary to secure the constitutional principles of the sovereignty of Parliament and the supremacy of the law.

The committee's report,[32] while recognising the need for improved parliamentary scrutiny of delegated legislation, nevertheless emphasised its necessity in terms of legislative efficiency. It is efficiency which is the principal justification for the delegation of law-making power. Put simply, Parliament, as currently constituted, struggles to give adequate scrutiny to primary legislation. To burden Parliament with the task of scrutinising every detail of legislation would overload the parliamentary timetable to the extent that the system would break under the strain. A related justification for delegated power lies in the need to supplement

---

29 *Report of the Joint Committee on Delegated Legislation*, HL 184, HC 475, 1971–72, London: HMSO, para 6.
30 Statute of Proclamations 1539 (31 Hen 8 c 26); and see Allen, 1965.
31 The Donoughmore-Scott Committee.
32 *Report on Ministers' Powers*, Cmnd 4060, 1932, London: HMSO.

or amend the primary rules in light of new developments. Delegated legislation enables the fine tuning of the primary rules to take place, without encumbering Parliament as a whole. Further, it may be that the government is clear as to the broad policy to be pursued under an Act, and as to the primary legal rules necessary to achieve a particular goal. There may be less certainty as to the technical, detailed rules necessary: the delegation of law-making power enables such rules to be worked out, often in consultation with specialist interest groups outside Parliament.

The justifications for subordinate legislation can hold good only if the powers granted are sufficiently clear and precise as to be adjudicated upon by the courts by way of judicial review[33] and if the parliamentary scrutiny accorded to it is adequate.

Under the doctrine of parliamentary sovereignty, the validity of Acts of Parliament cannot be questioned.[34] Subordinate legislation, however, can be reviewed, provided that the jurisdiction of the courts has not been excluded – or 'ousted' – in order to determine its compatibility with the enabling Act. Such exclusion of review is rare and, to ensure immunity from review, the exclusion clause would have to be unambiguous on the face of the parent Act. Of equal importance to the possibility of successful challenge in the courts is the breadth of discretion conferred on the delegate by the Act. If a statute conferred powers on a minister to make regulations 'whenever the minister thinks fit' or (say) to award compensation for injury 'under circumstances to be determined by the minister', the grant of discretion is so wide as to be virtually unreviewable by the courts. Also important is that delegated legislation should not impose retrospective liability on citizens, or be so vague as to be unintelligible. Further, it is necessary that the power granted is conferred on an identifiable delegate in order that the exercise of power be challengeable. On this latter point, the Emergency Powers Act 1939 provided for differing levels of delegation. The Act provided that regulations might empower any authority on persons to make orders, rules and bylaws, for any of the purposes for which the Defence Regulations might themselves be made. Ministerial orders were issued under the regulations, directions issued under the regulations and licences issued under the directions. Such subdelegation breaches the rule that a person or body to whom powers are entrusted may not delegate them to another, '*delegatus non potest delegare*'.

The Statutory Instruments Act 1946

The vast majority of delegated legislation is in the form of statutory instruments governed by the Statutory Instruments Act 1946. Section 1 provides that where any Act confers power on His Majesty in Council or on any minister of the Crown, where that power is expressed as a power exercisable by Order in Council or by statutory instrument, the provisions of the Act apply.

Parliamentary scrutiny of delegated legislation[35]

The Statutory Instruments Act 1946 lays down the means by which an instrument may come into effect, but the method adopted will depend on that which is stipulated in the particular enabling Act. First, the parent Act may provide that the instrument be laid before parliament[36] but that no parliamentary action is needed. Second, the parent Act may provide that the instrument

---

33 See Chapters 23 to 25.
34 **Pickin v British Railways Board** (1974). See Chapter 6.
35 See Beith, 1981; Hayhurst, and Wallington, 1988; Hansard Society, 1993, Annex A.
36 Statutory Instruments Act 1946, s 4.

is subject to the 'negative resolution procedure'.[37] Under this procedure, the instrument can be laid before Parliament in its final form and come into immediate effect subject only to there being a successful move to annul the instrument. This move takes the form of a motion, known here as a 'prayer' for annulment of the instrument, which can be made within 40 days of the instrument being laid. Third, the enabling Act may stipulate that the instrument be laid in draft form and that it will come into effect only if a prayer for annulment is not moved successfully. The Statutory Instruments Act also provides for an 'affirmative resolution procedure'. If this is adopted, the instrument may either come into immediate effect, subject to subsequent approval by Parliament, or be laid in draft form to come into effect if approved by Parliament.

Statutory Instruments are scrutinised by the following Committees:

- Joint Committee on Statutory Instruments;
- the House of Commons' Regulatory Reform Committee;
- the House of Lords Delegated Powers and Regulatory Reform Committee;
- the House of Lords Merits of Statutory Instruments Committee.

The choice of the procedure to be adopted lies with the government. The problem posed for Parliament is again one of time and opportunity. The affirmative resolution procedure is rarely adopted by government; the negative resolution procedure requires that Members of Parliament must be vigilant and astute if they (usually the Opposition) are to be aware that a particular instrument has been laid and are to be able to move a prayer for annulment within the 40-day period. Instruments made under the European Communities Act 1972 to give effect to Community law may be subject to either the affirmative or negative procedure.

Since 1994–95, instruments subject to affirmative resolution are automatically referred to a Public Bill Committee, unless the House orders otherwise. Instruments subject to the negative resolution procedure, to which a prayer has been tabled, may be referred to a Public Bill Committee on a Motion by a minister of the Crown.

Supplementing the above scrutiny methods is the Joint Select Committee on Delegated Legislation. The Joint Committee comprises seven Members of the House of Commons and seven Members of the House of Lords, and is chaired by a member of the House of Commons. The committee is charged with examining all instruments laid before Parliament and those instruments for which there is no laying requirement. The grounds on which the committee will report to Parliament are:

(a) that the instrument imposes a tax or charge;
(b) that the parent Act excludes review by the courts;
(c) that the instrument is to operate retrospectively;
(d) that there has been unjustifiable delay in publication or laying;
(e) that the instrument has come into effect in contravention of the rules of notice to the House;
(f) that there is doubt as to whether the instrument is *intra vires*;
(g) that the instrument requires clarification;
(h) that the instrument's drafting is defective.

The committee examines over 1,000 instruments per session. Less than 1 per cent are reported to Parliament and few are debated. The strength of the committee's work lies not in its reports

---

37 Statutory Instruments Act 1946, s 5.

to Parliament and any consequent action but rather in its scrutiny of instruments and drawing the relevant government department's attention to defects in instruments.[38]

The Legislative and Regulatory Reform Act 2006 makes provision for a Minister to make amendments to primary or secondary legislation in order to remove or reduce burdens imposed on businesses or charities. A burden is defined as a financial cost, an administrative inconvenience, an obstacle to efficiency, productivity or profitability or a sanction which affects the carrying on of any lawful activity. The burden must arise – directly or indirectly – from legislation.[39] The grant of power to ministers to amend primary legislation is known as a 'Henry VIII power': the power to change the law without parliamentary action. These powers have become increasingly common and create concerns over the separation of powers and the reduction in parliamentary control. This problem has been addressed by the introduction of the 'super-affirmative procedure' which provides for greater parliamentary scrutiny.[40] Under this procedure, a proposal for a statutory instrument is laid in the form of a draft instrument, usually with an explanatory statement. A period of (usually) 60 days is then allowed for parliamentary scrutiny and report. Following the expiry of that period and consideration of any reports or representations made about the Draft, the Minister may amend the Draft, or if he or she wishes to proceed without making any amendments a statement must be made to that effect. The Minister may then make the order, but only if it is approved by a resolution of each House of Parliament.[41]

An example of a Henry VIII power is section 10(3) of the Human Rights Act 1998, which provides that a Minister may – subject to certain conditions and restrictions – 'by order make such amendments to the primary legislation as he considers necessary'.

Scrutiny of Legislation by the House of Lords

Some Bills will start their life in the House of Lords and, once successfully passed in the Lords, will pass to the Commons for debate and scrutiny. Law Reform Bills, in particular, are regularly introduced in the House of Lords, under the aegis of the Lord Chancellor. The majority of Bills, however, start their parliamentary life in the Commons. Detailed consideration will be given to the House of Lords' role in legislation in Chapter 16. Note, however, that unless the Parliament Act procedure is used (which limits the role of the House of Lords in relation to legislation), Bills which have completed their passage in the Commons are passed to the House of Lords which employs, with some notable differences, the same legislative stages as the House of Commons. The House of Lords may propose amendments to Bills, the acceptance or rejection of which will be a matter for negotiation between the two Houses. Note that by convention the House of Lords will not oppose a Bill which reflects government policy which has been endorsed by the people, 'mandated', in a general election.

See further Chapter 16.

The Royal Assent

Receiving the royal assent represents the final stage in the enactment of legislation. The royal assent is a prerogative act; for further discussion of this, see Chapter 5. The giving of

---

38 The House of Lords' Scrutiny Committee for delegated legislation is discussed in Chapter 16. On delegated legislation and the Human Rights Act 1998, see Chapter 18.

39 See for example the Regulatory Reform Order 2007, No 1889 which amends the Parliamentary Commissioner Act 1967, the Local Government Act 1974 and the Health Service Commissioner Act 1993 on which see Chapter 26.

40 Legislative and Regulatory Reform Act 2006, section 18. See also the Localism Act 2011, section 7.

41 See Erskine May, 2011, p 672.

the royal assent is not a matter which involves the monarch personally. No monarch since 1854 has given the royal assent, although the power to do so still remains. When royal assent is required, the Lord Chancellor submits a list of Bills ready for the Assent. In the House of Lords, attended by the Commons with the Speaker, the Clerk of the Parliaments reads the title of the Bills for assent and pronounces the assent in Norman French. Once assent has been given, it is notified to each House of Parliament by the Speaker of the House.[42] It is a constitutional convention that the Royal Assent is granted once a Bill has passed both Houses of Parliament, or, where the Parliament Act procedure has been employed, the Bill has been approved by the House of Commons.

See Chapter 5.

Parliament and European Union (EU) Legislation

The manner in which EU law is enacted and takes effect within the United Kingdom is considered in Chapters 7 and 8. Note here that some EU legislation becomes directly applicable within the United Kingdom without any enactment by Parliament. Accordingly, it is of particular importance that Parliament has the opportunity to scrutinise both proposals for European legislation and legislation which has been enacted.

See Chapter 8.

In addition to periodic debates on Europe, Parliament sets aside time at Question Time for European matters to be considered. Furthermore, ministers make regular statements to Parliament concerning decisions reached in the Council of Ministers.

The House of Commons has established a select committee on European Legislation. The House of Lords also has a select committee on the European Union. Both committees consider delegated legislation which is being introduced to give effect to European law and also scrutinise legislative proposals for future European law. In addition the Commons has established two committees for the consideration of European matters. The select committee may refer such documentation to the standing committees as it thinks fit. The committees, comprising 13 Members, report to the House on matters referred to them.

Finally, successive governments have undertaken not to agree to important European legislative proposals until these have been considered by the committees. However, the effectiveness of these undertakings must be put in doubt by the increasing use of majority voting in the Council of Ministers, which makes it difficult for individual Member States to 'block' any proposed legislation.

Summary

Parliament – the Crown, House of Commons and Lords – is the sovereign law-making body in the United Kingdom. It may make law on any subject matter, except where limited by obligations such as the European Union and other international agreements, and non-legal constraints such as economics and public opinion. The origins of law lie primarily in government policies, but are also supplemented by a vast number of reform and other public interest groups outside Parliament.

Bills may be Public, Private or Hybrid and in addition there are Private Members' Bills. In addition to Primary Bills there is secondary or delegated legislation which fills in the detailed rules and provisions of an Act of Parliament. Bills may be introduced into either House of

---

42 Royal Assent Act 1967.

Parliament, and the proceedings are similar in both Houses, with a formal First Reading, Second Reading which deals with the principles of a Bill, Committee stage where the details of the Bills are scrutinised and amendments proposed, Report stage and the formal Third Reading. The Royal Assent is required to make a Bill into an Act of Parliament.

As discussed in more detail in Chapter 16, the powers of the House of Lords are restricted by the Parliament Acts 1911 and 1949 which ensure that the elected House of Commons has priority (with limited exceptions) over the House of Lords.

In addition to enacting law, Parliament must also scrutinise and approve the financing of government. The procedures designed to approve finance are complex and designed more to ensure openness and publicity rather than real control over finance, which is largely under government control.

Further Reading

Blackburn, R. and Kennon, A. (2003) *Parliament: Functions, Practice and Procedures* (2nd edn), London: Sweet & Maxwell.

Brazier, A., Flinders, M., and McHugh, D. (2005) *New Politics, New Parliament? A Review of Parliamentary Modernisation since 1997*, London: Hansard Society.

Cowley, P. and Stuart, M. (2001) 'Parliament: A Few Headaches and a Dose of Modernisation', Parliamentary Affairs, 54(3): 442.

Oliver, D. (2006) 'Improving the Scrutiny of Bills: the Case for Standards and Checklists', Public Law, 219.

Oliver, D. (2011) 'Reforming the United Kingdom Parliament' in Jowell and Oliver (eds) *The Changing Constitution* (7th edn), Oxford: OUP.

Silk, P. and Walters, R. (2006) *How Parliament Works* (6th edn), London: Longman.

Chapter 15

Scrutiny of the Executive

Introduction

The structure of central government, the concept of ministerial responsibility and the composition of the House of Commons are considered in Chapters 9, 10 and 13 respectively. It will be recalled that the Commons comprises Her Majesty's Government, which is drawn from the political party winning the largest number of seats at a general election, government backbenchers, Her Majesty's Loyal Opposition, comprising the Leader of the Opposition and Opposition spokesmen, who comprise the shadow Cabinet, and Opposition backbenchers, and Members of other minority political parties.

In this chapter the procedures by which the House of Commons scrutinises government action are discussed. Consistent with the doctrine of responsible government, the accountability of government towards the democratic legislature is of fundamental importance in ensuring that the government acts under the law and in accordance with the principles of constitutionalism and democracy. In order to evaluate the role of Parliament in ensuring compliance with these constitutional doctrines, the procedural mechanisms of the House must be examined.

It should be noted that scrutiny of both legislation and government administration is also undertaken in the House of Lords. The House of Lords' procedures are discussed in the following chapter.

Question Time[1]

Question Time in the House of Commons is one of the most publicised features of Parliament and represents one of the principal means by which information is obtained from ministers by Members of Parliament and the public, and of underpinning individual ministerial responsibility.

Standing Orders provide that, on Mondays, Tuesdays and Thursdays, the period from 2.35 pm to 3.30 pm is set aside for Question Time.[2] On these days, ministers from several departments may answer questions, appearing on a rota, determined by the Government,[3] which ensures that most departments feature in Question Time at least once every three to four weeks.

The Speaker calls the first Member listed on the Order of Business. The minister then answers the question, and the Member is able to ask a supplementary question. When that has been answered, the Speaker may then call on other Members to ask their supplementary questions. The time allocated to supplementary questions is within the Speaker's discretion. Currently, about 15 to 20 questions are answered orally on each day. The effect of the supplementary is that a Member is able to pose a question for which no notice has been given.

Questions may be put to ministers for either oral or written answers.[4] Questions requiring written answers, which are to be printed in the *Official Journal*, are marked with a 'W' and are subdivided into those requesting a priority answer and those requesting a non-priority answer. Those questions tabled for oral answer are printed on the Order Paper of the day. Only a few

---

1 See Griffith and Ryle, 2003; Erskine May, 2004.
2 No question shall be taken after 3.30 pm, other than where the Speaker deems it to be a matter of urgency relating to matters of public importance or to the arrangement of business of the House.
3 HC Deb 898 (1975–76), London: HMSO. See Erskine May, 2004, Chapter 16.
4 Standing Order No 21.

of the many questions put will receive an oral reply. However, those that do not receive an oral reply will receive a written reply published in the Official Report of the House. The number of questions which an individual Member of Parliament may have pending at any one time is eight during a period of ten sitting days, and not more than two on any one day, of which not more than one may be addressed to any one minister.[5] Answers to questions may be refused on the basis of their disproportionate cost.[6]

Question Time is not a spontaneous affair, and it should not necessarily be criticised for not being so. Members wishing to ask questions are required to give up to three sitting days' notice.[7] This time span for notice is designed to ensure both that there is adequate opportunity for ministers to prepare answers and that the issue being raised is still fresh and relevant.

Changes to Question Time agreed by the Commons and implemented in the 2002–03 session include the following:

- a limit of five written questions which may be put by a Member on any one day;
- a reduction in the number of questions for oral answer printed on the Order Paper;
- electronic tabling by Members;
- oral questions being put to junior ministers in Westminster Hall.

From 2003 cross-cutting questions have been introduced. These take place in Westminster Hall and cover issues which are the responsibility of more than one government department. An example is Youth Policy, which falls under the responsibility of the Department of Culture Media and Sport, the Department of Education, the Department of Health and the Home Office.

On occasion – and particularly near the end of a parliamentary session – questions may be answered in the form of 'I will write to the Honourable Member . . .' rather than receiving an oral response. Such replies have not been published in *Hansard* in the past, but placed in the House of Commons' Library for Members' use. These 'Will Writes' have attracted criticism from the Select Committee on Public Administration as being used to avoid answering questions.[8]

Prime Ministerial Question Time

Prime Minister's Question Time has been moved from the conventional 15-minute sessions on Tuesdays and Thursdays, to Wednesdays, when the Prime Minister answers questions for 30 minutes.[9] It is felt that more meaningful and in-depth scrutiny is facilitated by the reform.

Questions put to the Prime Minister simply request that the Prime Minister list his engagements for the day. Over 100 such questions may appear on the Order Papers; on occasions, this number has risen to over 200. The open question also avoids the possibility – given the rules of notice for questions – that a subsequent question put to the Prime Minister

---

5   Erskine May, 2004.
6   In 2006 the average cost of a Written Question was £140; the average cost of an Oral Question £385. The Disproportionate Cost Threshold for a Written Question is £700; there is no limit for Oral Questions.
7   The period of notice for questions to the Northern Ireland, Scottish and Welsh Secretaries of State is four working days.
8   See the Committee on Public Administration Second Special Report, HC 853. The Committee also monitors responses to requests for information under the Freedom of Information Act 2000.
9   See HC Deb, Vol 295, Col 349, 4 June 1997.

will be politically stale. The open question, therefore, provides a neutral peg on which to hang a supplementary, and real, question. Only two supplementary questions per Member are allowed. Supplementary questions may concern any matter for which the Prime Minister carries responsibility or matters which do not fall within any individual minister's responsibility. For example, if a question is addressed to the Prime Minister which should be addressed to the Secretary of State for Social Security, the Prime Minister will decline to answer and suggest that the matter be referred to the responsible minister. Generally, however, the issue raised will be one of general government policy in relation to matters such as the economy, unemployment, European or other international affairs. The strength of Prime Ministerial Question Time lies in the lack of notice given and the need for the Prime Minister to demonstrate his competence across the full range of government policy.

The Leader of the Opposition does not table questions for oral answer to the Prime Minister. Instead, he is entitled to ask up to six questions to the Prime Minister and may raise virtually any aspect of government policy. For the observer, this is frequently Parliament at its best, providing the opportunity – for Question Time is televised – to witness the leaders of the two main political parties in oral combat. As Griffith and Ryle observe:

> . . . here is experienced the direct confrontation of the Prime Minister and the Leader of the Opposition in its most concentrated and highly charged form. It is an opportunity no Leader of the Opposition can afford to neglect. It is also the occasion when the Prime Minister can be most critically tested, and various commentators or experienced observers have testified to how carefully the Prime Minister has to prepare for this ordeal. Success or failure on these occasions can greatly strengthen or seriously weaken the political standing of the two protagonists. [2003, pp 501–02]

The role of the Speaker

See further
Chapter 13.

The rules concerning questions have been developed over time by the Speaker of the House, who is responsible for enforcing them. Only questions on matters which are directly within a minister's responsibility may be put and in addition, by convention, there exists a range of issues which may not form the subject of questions in the House. The following matters are not subject to Question Time:

(a) questions bringing the Sovereign directly before Parliament, or questions reflecting on the Sovereign;

(b) questions concerning issues on which the Prime Minister has given advice to the Crown in relation to the royal prerogative: the grant of honours, ecclesiastical patronage, appointment and dismissal of Privy Counsellors;

(c) questions not relating to the individual responsibility of the relevant minister. Accordingly, questions relating to organisations under the control of authorities other than Parliament (for example, the Stock Exchange, trade unions and nationalised industries) are not permitted.[10]

The following subjects are also excluded:

---

10 Erskine May, 2004, Chapter 16.

- local authorities and nationalised industries;
- personal powers of the Monarch;
- internal affairs of other countries;
- questions which have previously been put, or on which a minister has previously refused to answer, or to which the answer is a matter of public record;
- defence and national security;
- Cabinet business, and advice given to ministers by civil servants;
- questions seeking legal advice;
- questions which raise issues so broad as to be incapable of reply within the time constraints;
- trivial or irrelevant questions;
- questions aiming to criticise judges;
- questions on matters which are *sub judice*;
- questions posed in unparliamentary language.[11]

The volume of parliamentary questions

In the 2010 to 2012 parliamentary sessions a total of 110,752 questions were put down. Of these, 12,789 received oral replies and 97,963 received written replies. Figures such as these emphasise one of the most important functions of Question Time: the accountability of government. A superficial observation of Question Time may prompt scepticism about its value. The charge is frequently made that Question Time is no more than a theatrical occasion, with ministers fully briefed by the Civil Service giving prepared answers to questions posed within the rules relating to notice and substance. Questions are not limited to the Opposition parties and may, accordingly, come from the Government's own supporters. This feature leads to the comment that questions are planted by Government supporters in order to give a minister the opportunity to promote the Government's views or boast about its achievements. To exaggerate such claims would be to miss a point of prime importance about Question Time: the provision of information. Every answer given, oral or written, becomes a matter of public record, thus providing a wealth of data about the workings of government.

Urgent questions

An Urgent Question[12] is an oral question put to a minister without the need to observe the normal rules as to notice. Standing Orders define Urgent Questions as raising matters which are: '. . . in the Speaker's opinion, of an urgent character, and relate either to matters of public importance or to the arrangement of business.'

Such questions enable a matter of urgency to be raised for immediate discussion in the period following Question Time. Because Urgent Questions take priority over other parliamentary business, rules provide that a Member who wishes to put such a question must give notice to the Speaker before noon on the day he seeks to put the question, and the Speaker has absolute discretion as to whether to allow or disallow the question to be put.[13] Many applications for an Urgent Question are made, but few are granted.

---

11 Erskine May, 2004, Chapter 17.
12 Urgent Questions were previously termed Private Notice Questions.
13 See Erskine May, 2004.

Emergency Debates

Under Standing Orders,[14] any Member of Parliament may apply to the Speaker to raise an urgent matter for debate.[15] If granted, the matter will be raised immediately after Question Time and private notice questions, if any. At that time, the matter is briefly introduced and a substantive three-hour debate will be arranged for the following day. Because emergency debates disrupt the parliamentary timetable, they are confined to matters deemed to be of urgent national importance, and applications are sparingly granted (normally only one or two per session). In the 2010–12 session there were five applications for an emergency debate, three of which were granted.

Daily Adjournment Debates

At the close of the parliamentary day, under Standing Orders, the opportunity is provided for backbenchers to initiate a short debate on a matter of their choosing. Competition for a debate is keen and Members take part in a ballot held in the Speaker's Office for the opportunity. If successful, the Member may speak for 15 minutes on the chosen subject and the relevant minister is given 15 minutes for reply. The subject matter for debate is as varied as are Members' interests. The matter raised may be one of relevance solely to the Member's constituency or the matter may be related to a particular source of general concern.

Early Day Motions

Behind this curious colloquial term lies one of the least well-known or evaluated parliamentary processes. An Early Day Motion (EDM) is a written motion tabled in Parliament requesting a debate 'at an early day'. Any Member of Parliament may table an EDM, on any subject matter, subject to a few procedural rules.[16]

Early Day Motions originated in the mid-nineteenth century. Before that time, the parliamentary timetable was relaxed and Members had adequate opportunity to raise matters for subsequent debate in the House. As pressure for time in the House increased, the practice developed of Members giving notice that they intended to raise a particular matter for debate at some future, unspecified, date. These notices were formally recorded from 1865 in the daily papers of the House and today appear on the Motions Notice Paper, which forms part of the daily 'Vote Bundle' – the working papers of the House.

The purpose of tabling an EDM is not only to express a view and request a debate, but also to test the strength of feeling in the House over the matter involved. An EDM may be tabled by one Member or by several, and other Members may add their names in support. Some EDMs are tabled by the Leader of the Opposition: for example, EDM No 351 of 1978–79, supported by five other senior Conservative Members, led to a debate on 28 March 1979, which resulted in the resignation of the government and the subsequent general election.

Once tabled, an EDM remains current for the duration of the parliamentary session and may or may not attract considerable support within the House. Between 1948–49 and 1990–91, 29 EDMs attracted over 300 signatures.

---

14 Dating from 1967.
15 See Erskine May, 2004 Chapter 16(3).
16 See Griffith and Ryle, 2003, Chapters 6 and 10.

The rules and restrictions on EDMs are few, and are consistent with the general rules concerning motions. Thus, the motion must be worded in parliamentary language, must not relate to a matter which is *sub judice* and is limited to 250 words. Within these limits, a Member may table an EDM on any subject. Many EDMs are tabled by Members of all parties on a particular issue, and provide an important outlet for the expression of views across party lines.[17]

In terms of the number of debates which flow from EDMs, their success rate must be regarded as low. The EDM censuring the government tabled by the Rt Hon Mrs Thatcher in 1979 is a rarity, both in terms of securing a debate and in the dramatic effect of signalling the fall of a government. The occasional success of the EDM was again seen in 1988 in relation to the Education Reform Bill 1988. There, two senior Conservative front-bench Members, Norman Tebbit and Michael Heseltine, tabled a motion calling for the abolition of the Inner London Education Authority: a matter which was contrary to the then policy of the Secretary of State for Education, Kenneth Baker. The EDM was supported by 120 other Conservative backbenchers and caused the Secretary of State to amend the Bill.[18]

Notwithstanding such rare examples of EDMs having important political and legal effects, the overall significance of the EDM should not be underestimated. Depending on the volume of support a particular EDM attracts, it represents an expression of the mood of the House across a whole spectrum of issues which places pressure on the government to respond. Furthermore, where the rules of the House prevent a Member from expressing a view in debate, perhaps because he cannot catch the Speaker's eye, or by means of a question, perhaps because of ministerial responsibility or because the subject matter falls within one of the excluded categories, the EDM may represent the only vehicle for expression.

Select Committees of the House of Commons

Select committees in the House of Commons are of some antiquity, although the current structure of committees dates back only to 1979. They take several forms and fulfil a number of different functions.[19] Some select committees relate to the running of the House of Commons itself, others relate to the procedures employed by the House, while a third class – the departmentally related select committees – fulfil an investigative and reporting function. In addition there may at any time be ad hoc select committees established to investigate and report on a specific matter. At any one time there will be a number of Joint Committees in existence, comprising members from the House of Commons and House of Lords, which will examine specific topics, or give pre-legislative scrutiny to Bills. Two permanent Joint Committees exist: the Joint Committee on Human Rights and the Joint Committee on Statutory Instruments (delegated legislation).

The 'domestic' committees include the following: Accommodation and Works; Administration Committee; Broadcasting Committee; Catering Committee; and Finance and Services Committee. The committees relating to procedures include: Modernisation Committee; Procedure Committee; Liaison Committee; and the Information Committee. While the Procedure Committee keeps all Commons' procedures under review, the Modernisation Committee is specifically charged with examining and recommending changes to procedures. The Information Committee advises the Speaker on information technology. The Liaison

---

17 In the 2010–12 session, 3,024 EDMs were tabled.
18 EDM 563; Notices of Motions, 1987–88, p 3519.
19 For select committees in the House of Lords, see Chapter 16.

Committee is made up of the Chairpersons of all the select committees and works to ensure that there is an efficient distribution on the workload of departmentally-related Committees (on this committee see below).

Scrutinising the efficiency and effectiveness with which government Departments and other public bodies have used their resources is the Public Accounts Committee.[20] The Public Administration Committee has the task of examining the reports of the Parliamentary Commissioner for Administration and the Health Service Commissioners for England, Scotland and Wales, and the Parliamentary Ombudsman for Northern Ireland. Additionally the Public Administration Committee also considers matters relating to the Civil Service. Monitoring the privileges of Parliament and the conduct of Members of Parliament is the Committee on Standards and Privileges, discussed in Chapter 17. Examining delegated legislation is the task of the Select Committee on Statutory Instruments, which works closely with the Joint Committee on Statutory Instruments discussed in Chapter 14. There is a European Scrutiny Committee which scrutinises European Union documents, decides which issues require debate and monitors the activities of UK Ministers in the European Council. There is also an Environmental Audit Committee, which has the task of monitoring the contribution made by government departments and public bodies towards environmental protection and sustainable development.

The current system of departmentally related select committees was established in 1979 following recommendations made by the Select Committee on Procedure.[21] In debate, the Leader of the House[22] described the proposals as:

> . . . a necessary preliminary to the more effective scrutiny of government . . . and opportunity for closer examination of departmental policy . . . an important contribution to greater openness in government, of a kind that is in accord with our parliamentary arrangements and our constitutional tradition.

Powers and functions of select committees

The functions of departmentally related select committees are defined as being to examine matters within the Department and to report to the House. To fulfil their tasks Committees have the following powers:

(a) to send for persons, papers and records;
(b) to sit notwithstanding any adjournment of the House;
(c) to adjourn from place to place;
(d) to appoint specialist advisers, either to supply information which is not readily available or to elucidate matters of complexity within the committee's terms of reference.

Select Committees have eleven members. The scope of power granted to select committees is very broad. It is for the committee to determine, within the confines of the work of the department, what subject matter to examine and to determine what evidence the committee needs to assist in its examination. To facilitate the working of select committees, each has a permanent staff of some three to four, and some committees have the power, under Standing Orders, to establish sub-committees.

---

20 See further pp 342–343.
21 HC 588 (1977–78), London: HMSO. *First Report of the Select Committee on Procedure* (1977–78), London: HMSO.
22 The Rt Hon Norman St John-Stevas, MP (subsequently, Lord St John of Fawsley).

The Liaison Committee

The task of co-ordinating the work of select committees falls to the Liaison Committee, first established in 1967, the membership of which comprises all the Chairmen of the departmentally related select committees, and the Chairmen of the Public Accounts Committee and the European Legislation Select Committee. Its role is defined as being:

(a)   to consider general matters relating to the work of select committees; and
(b)   to give such advice relating to the work of select committees as may be sought by the House of Commons Commission.

In 2003 the Prime Minister agreed to meet twice a year with the Liaison Committee to discuss matters of mutual concern.

Membership of select committees

Membership of select committees, unlike that of standing committees, lasts for the life of a Parliament, thus providing stability of membership and the opportunity for Members to develop a degree of expertise in the subject matter. Membership is largely limited, by convention, to backbenchers. The only ministers who are Members are the Leader of the House,[23] the government Deputy Chief Whip[24] and the Financial Secretary to the Treasury.[25] Opposition front-bench spokesmen are not appointed to select committees.

Competition for membership of select committees is keen, particularly for the high-profile committees. With effect from 2010 members of select committees are elected by their political parties, using a secret ballot 'by whichever transparent and democratic method they choose'.[26]

Committee chairmanship

The Chairs of Select Committees may be from government or opposition parties. The House of Commons' Reform Committee recommended that Chairs should be directly elected by Members of Parliament, rather than chosen by the Party Whips as previously. The majority of Select Committee Chairs are now elected by fellow MPs. All departmental select committee chairs are elected, together with the Environmental Audit, Political and Constitutional Reform, Procedure, Public Administration and Public Accounts Committees. Candidates may be elected unopposed. If there is a contest, election is by secret ballot using the Alternative Vote system.

The significance of the sharing of chairs between government and opposition parties lies in the attempt to minimise party political conflict, in order to increase the effectiveness and efficiency of the scrutiny to be brought to bear on government departments. Once appointed, the chairman acts with complete impartiality. Select committees are designed to operate on the basis of broad consensus as to aims and objectives, and to produce a single authoritative report to Parliament as a whole. It is not usual for the committee to vote on party lines although, in highly controversial matters, this may occasionally be inevitable. If the committee intends to be critical of the government in its report, it is necessary for at least one Member of the government party to agree with the criticism(s).

---

23 Services Committee.
24 Ibid.
25 Public Accounts Committee.
26 House of Commons Resolution, HC Deb 4 March 2010 col 1095. See House of Commons Library Standard Note SN/PC/3719, *Nominations to Select Committees*, 2010.

The work of select committees illustrated

The inquiries undertaken by select committees are both broad ranging and in depth. It is entirely a matter for the committee to determine what subject to investigate and, accordingly, every aspect of government administration is potentially susceptible to inquiry. In the past, for example, select committees have inquired into the conduct of the Falklands War[27] and the banning of trade union membership at the Government Communication Headquarters (GCHQ).[28] The committees have investigated such matters as the Westland Helicopter affair; Arms to Iraq; salmonella in eggs; and the loss of the Maxwell pension funds, on which see further below. The wide-ranging nature of inquiries undertaken is illustrated in the subject matter chosen by the Home Affairs Committee in 2009:

Home Affairs Committee Inquiries (a sample):

- Work of the UK Border Agency
- Police and the media
- Human trafficking
- Knife crime
- Policing of the G20 protests
- Violent crime and drugs

The co-operation of government

It has been seen above that committees have the power to send for 'persons and papers'. The work of select committees would be much impaired if the committee was obstructed in its attempt to gain access to evidence. The Select Committee on Procedure had suggested, inter alia, that there should be power to compel ministers to attend and to give evidence. That recommendation was rejected by the government, on the basis that select committees should not have power to issue orders to ministers – such a power lay with the House alone. Accordingly, there is no formal requirement that the government co-operate with select committees. However, the Leader of the House has undertaken that:

> . . . every Minister, from the most senior Cabinet Minister to the most junior Under Secretary, will do all in his or her power to co-operate with the new system of committees and to make it a success.[29]

For the most part, governments do co-operate with the committees, but limits to this co-operation can be perceived through an examination of four instances.

The Westland affair

In the aftermath of the Westland Helicopter affair, during which both the Secretary of State for Defence, Michael Heseltine, and the Secretary of State for Trade and Industry, Leon Brittan, resigned,[30] three select committees inquired into the matter.[31] When the Select Committee on Defence announced its intention to inquire into the matter, the government refused to allow

---

27 HC 11 (1984–85), London: HMSO.
28 HC 238 (1983–84), London: HMSO.
29 HC Deb Col 45, 25 June 1979; Col 1677, 16 January 1981.
30 See the discussion in Chapter 8. See also Hennessy, 1986a; Oliver and Austin, 1987; Linklater et al, 1986, Chapter 11; Marshall, 1986a.
31 Defence Committee, HC 518, 519 (1985–86), London: HMSO; Trade and Industry Committee, HC 176 (1986–87), London: HMSO; Treasury and Civil Service Committee, HC 92 (1985–86), London: HMSO.

witnesses from the Department of Trade and Industry, in particular the Director of Information, to whom a leak of the Solicitor General's letter had been attributed, to give evidence to the committee. The government's justification for this refusal was that the giving of evidence by a senior civil servant to a parliamentary committee would have major implications for the conduct of government and for relations between ministers and their civil servants. This refusal had two implications. First, it meant that Parliament was unable to check the accuracy of statements made by the Prime Minister in the House, or those made by Leon Brittan in relation to the leaked letter. The second implication was that the civil servants concerned were neither able to explain nor defend their actions.

Salmonella in eggs

In 1988, a junior Health Minister, Edwina Currie, resigned office, subsequent to public comments made about alleged contamination of eggs. Her remarks that 'most eggs produced in the country' were infected with salmonella had an immediate impact on the sale and consumption of eggs, causing financial damage to egg producers. The Select Committee on Agriculture invited Mrs Currie to give evidence to the committee, but she declined. Following an exchange of letters which involved the select committee chairman insisting that it was for the committee, and not Mrs Currie, to decide whether or not she should give evidence, Mrs Currie grudgingly agreed to appear. In the event, her evidence proved, as she had indicated that it would, unhelpful.

The Maxwell pension fund

During the 1991–92 session, the Social Services Select Committee was enquiring into the mismanagement of pension funds by the Mirror Newspaper Group's recently deceased Chairman, Mr Robert Maxwell. Mr Maxwell's sons, both holding prominent positions in the Group before their father's death, and subsequently assuming control of the companies, were summoned to give evidence. The Maxwells refused, relying on a claimed right to silence in the light of imminent criminal charges and the risk of jeopardising their own fair trial. The committee chairman wanted the Maxwells to be charged with contempt of Parliament (see Chapter 17), but no action was taken.

Reform of parliamentary evidence rules

The problem of witnesses who attend but who give evidence which is either untruthful or which paints only half the picture – a problem faced by Parliament in its committee inquiries into the Arms to Iraq affair, about which Sir Richard Scott was particularly critical – was considered in Chapter 10. In a further attempt to strengthen Parliament's powers over its Members, and witnesses giving evidence to its committees, new rules have applied since January 1997. Persons giving evidence are now required to take a formal oath. Anyone found to have lied to Parliament may be reported to the Crown Prosecution Service with a view to prosecution for perjury, which, in the event of conviction, could lead to a maximum prison sentence of seven years. Where the person is a Member of Parliament, the committee will ask the Commons to vote to remove the Member's immunity from prosecution.

Select committee reports

At the conclusion of a select committee inquiry, a report will be drawn up. The committee aims to produce an authoritative, unanimous report which is presented to Parliament. The degree of consensus over a particular issue within the committee membership will dictate the extent to which unanimity can be achieved.

Approximately one-third of all reports published will be debated on the floor of the House. This fact is one which also gives rise to criticism of select committee effectiveness, although it must be conceded that the time given for debate on reports has increased in recent years. Parliamentary procedure does not make specific provision for debate on reports. The Procedure Committee has suggested that eight days per session should be devoted to such debates but this proposal has not been acted upon. Sufficient, but not too much, weight should be attached to this alleged defect, and four arguments may be advanced which limit its impact. The first relates to the commitment undertaken by successive governments to respond to select committee reports. Such an undertaking does not, of itself, ensure that the recommendations of the committee will be implemented but it does ensure that the government will react to any criticisms made and proposals put forward. Members of the committee and other interested Members of Parliament, particularly the Opposition, will be slow to let an opportunity to criticise government pass. The second argument centres on the information gained through the process of the inquiry. It has been seen that ministers may decline or refuse to answer questions fully, and that they can restrict the extent to which civil servants may give evidence. Where a minister refuses to co-operate with a select committee he will inevitably find media attention focused upon him and some cogent justification for his reticence will have to be forthcoming. For the most part, evidence suggests that there is a high degree of ministerial co-operation with committees; this need not be seen as being necessarily willing participation but, rather, a matter of political prudence.

Third, it must be recognised that the reports emanating from select committee inquiries are matters of public record, available both to Members of Parliament and to the interested press and public. The information gathered in the course of an inquiry becomes public information, information which, before the introduction of the new committee structure, was often hidden from the public gaze. Finally, the absence of debate on the floor of the House in many cases will be justified by the pressure on the parliamentary timetable. It may well be the case that debate on all reports is desirable in principle. However, on many matters, opening debate to all Members of the House may involve a duplication of effort, with non-specialist Members of Parliament inexpertly attempting to re-analyse the information examined by the more specialised select committee Members.

Evaluation

An evaluation of the work of select committees in relation to the fundamentally important question concerning the accountability of government must be approached with caution. The outcome of an appraisal is inevitably related to the expectations which the appraiser holds and, as a consequence, the evaluation of one commentator may not be the same as another's. Caution is also urged against the making of sweeping generalisations as to the effectiveness of select committees which are diverse in nature and operation. Many factors are involved in the analysis: the extent to which media, and hence public, attention is focused on a particular enquiry; the sensitivity of the subject matter; the degree of political consensus within the committee; the extent to which governments are prepared to make time on the floor of the House to debate select committee reports; the extent to which select committee inquiries result in improved efficiency in government; and the extent to which government and other witnesses co-operate with the committees in the provision of information. All of these factors, and more, must be put in the balance before any reasoned conclusions can be reached.

Griffith and Ryle state that:

> . . . there are clear indications that the existence of select committees has affected the way government business is conducted . . . [2003, 11–054]

General assessment of the relative success or failure of select committees ... depends on differing expectations. On one matter, however, opinion is almost unanimous: select committees since 1979 have increased the flow of information coming out of Whitehall [ie government departments] and this has resulted to some extent in debates being better informed both inside and outside Parliament. [2003, 11–056]

At the heart of any evaluation must lie the recognition of the inherent tension – already stressed in Chapter 14 in relation to the scrutiny of legislation – between the legitimate right of the government to govern and the equally legitimate right of Parliament as a whole to ensure the collective accountability of government and the individual responsibility of ministers.

As seen above, failures within government Departments may be examined by Select Committees. They may also be subject to investigation by the Parliamentary Commission for Administration, on whose role and powers see Chapter 26. Alternatively, the government may establish a formal statutory or non-statutory inquiry into a matter, on which see Chapter 27. Judicial scrutiny may be effected through proceeding for Judicial Review, discussed in Chapters 23, 24 and 25. The National Audit Office plays an important role in monitoring departmental finances as discussed below. Finally, a government Department may initiate an inquiry into a particular matter.

An illustration of the National Audit Office's role combining with a Departmental Inquiry is seen in the mismanagement of the competition for the franchise to be granted to railway companies bidding for the InterCity West Coast route. The Department of Transport had awarded the franchise to First Group in August 2012, in preference to the former operator Virgin. Virgin initiated judicial review proceedings of the Department's decision and in October 2012 the Department cancelled its decision to award the franchise to First Group, cancelled the franchise competition and paused three other competitions. The Department of Transport then commissioned two independent reviews, and the National Audit Office undertook its own inquiry. The Report by the independent inquiry, led by Sam Laidlaw, identified a lack of transparency, a failure to follow Departmental guidance, a lack of clarity, inadequate planning and preparation, unclear lines of responsibility, poor governance and inadequate quality assurance as key failures in the process.[32] The Report of the National Audit Office, *Lessons from cancelling the Intercity West Coast franchise competition*,[33] made it clear that the Department's handling of the matter was not 'value for money' and was likely to 'result in significant cost for the taxpayer.'

Scrutiny of National Finance[34]

Any evaluation of Parliament's effectiveness in scrutinising government must incorporate discussion of the extent to which, and means by which, Parliament controls national finance, in terms of both taxation and expenditure. From a constitutional standpoint, the control over expenditure may be viewed as control over the government of the day and its policies. As

---

32 Report of the Laidlaw Inquiry: *Inquiry into the lessons learned for the Department for Transport from the Intercity West Coast Competition*, HC 809, London: TSO, November 2012.

33 Report, HC 796, 7 December 2012.

34 Note that the Budget Responsibility and National Audit Act 2011 imposes a duty on the Treasury in relation to the formulation and implementation of fiscal policy, and establishes the Office for Budget Responsibility (OBR) to examine and report on the sustainability of public finances. It produces economic and fiscal forecasts, for which the Chancellor of the Exchequer was formerly responsible. The OBR is independent of government. The Act also modernises the governance of the National Audit Office.

WE Gladstone[35] remarked, 'expenditure flows from policy – to control expenditure one must control policy'. Constitutionally, therefore, Parliament's role in relation to spending is but one part of its wider role of scrutinising and calling the government to account. Hence, general debates, Question Time, and select committees are all germane to this matter. The responsibility for expenditure lies with the Chancellor of the Exchequer. The manner in which Parliament scrutinises public expenditure is through the Public Accounts Select Committee which examines reports of audits conducted by the Comptroller and Auditor General, who is head of the National Audit Office.[36]

Expenditure (supply)

Historically, the need to summon Parliament arose from the financial needs of the Crown.[37]

The authority of the House of Commons sprang from, and is based on, its power to approve both the raising of taxation and expenditure. The governing maxim was, and remains, that 'the Crown demands, the Commons grant and the Lords assent to the grant of monies'.[38] The Bill of Rights 1689, Article IV, declared that raising money for the use of the Crown without Parliament's consent was unlawful.

Nowadays, for the 'Crown', must be inserted 'Ministers of the Crown'. Two propositions flow from this situation. First, that all charges – that is, proposals for the expenditure of monies – must be demanded by the Crown before they can be considered by Parliament. The demand for approval of monies comes today from ministers, not backbenchers. Second, all charges must be considered by the House of Commons before they are approved. The proposals for charges come before the House in the form of resolutions which, once approved, must be embodied in legislation originating in the House of Commons but approved by both Houses.[39]

National revenue to cover the cost of government is derived from three main sources: taxation, borrowing and revenue from Crown lands. All revenue, of whatever kind, is credited to the Exchequer Account at the Bank of England in the form of the Consolidated Fund. All withdrawals must be authorised by statute. Under the Consolidated Fund Acts, approximately one-third of expenditure is authorised in permanent form and does not require annual parliamentary approval. Charges which are immune from this scrutiny are those payments for service which it is deemed should not be constantly drawn into the political arena for debate. For example, payment of interest on the national debt, salaries of judges of superior courts, the Speaker of the House of Commons, Leader of the Opposition, Comptroller and Auditor General and Parliamentary Commissioner for Administration, and payments to meet European Union obligations all fall under Consolidated Fund Services.

In contrast to Consolidated Fund Services are Supply Services. These cover the bulk of annual public expenditure and cover the needs of all government departments and the cost of the armed forces. Provision for Supply Services requires annual approval. The following requirements must be satisfied. The government must lay before the House of Commons each year its estimates for the forthcoming financial year, in the form of resolutions. Once approved, these are translated into Bills – the Consolidated Fund Bills and Appropriation Bills. Money must be appropriated for specific purposes in the same session as that in which it is required

35 Prime Minister 1868–74; 1880–85; 1886; 1892–94.
36 National Audit Act 1983.
37 See Chapters 5 and 6 on the historic struggles between Crown and Parliament.
38 Erskine May, 2004, and see Standing Order No 46.
39 Subject to the Parliament Acts 1911–49.

by the government: thus, monies voted for one financial year cannot be applied to a subsequent year.

The Voting of Supply is announced in the Queen's Speech at the opening of the parliamentary session: 'Members of the House of Commons, estimates for the Public Service will be laid before you.' The Chancellor's Statement is made to Parliament, preceded by preparation of estimates by each government department for the forthcoming financial year, and the Budget announced in the spring. The timing of the Budget is not, however, fixed and may be timetabled for spring or autumn.

Estimates

Government Departments assess the level of finance they require for the forthcoming financial year. The Treasury, however, will determine the sum a Department will receive.

Prior to estimates being settled, the Public Expenditure Survey Committee, under the responsibility of the Chief Secretary to the Treasury, will have reported on anticipated needs of departments, and settled any disagreements between departments. Its confidential report is sent to the Cabinet, which formalises expenditure plans.

Following parliamentary debate and approval, the Appropriation Bill will be drafted authorising withdrawal from the Exchequer Fund. In most parliamentary sessions, three regular Consolidated Fund and Appropriation Bills (and, where necessary, extra Consolidated Fund Bills) are put to Parliament for approval.

It will have been noticed that parliamentary approval for these financial Bills is 'without amendment or debate'. Thus far, there seems to be a virtual abandonment of Parliament's role in assenting to the 'demands of the Crown'.

Limited time for the scrutiny of expenditure estimates is provided under Standing Orders, which provide for five days per session to be allocated for the consideration of estimates. The estimates to be considered are selected by the Liaison Committee. The estimates selected for debate will generally be those into which the select committee has inquired and reported. Amendments may be tabled, including the reduction in the estimates.

Aside from this limited opportunity, any control which Parliament exercises is through the control of policy and the normal parliamentary mechanisms for the scrutiny of government policy and administration.

As the Public Accounts Committee Report to the House in 1987 admitted, 'Parliament's consideration of annual estimates – the key constitutional control – remains largely a formality'.[40] The Public Accounts Committee was established in 1861, for the purpose of examining accounts of departments following the submission of reports from the National Audit Office.

Taxation (ways and means)

In relation to taxation – ways and means – the role of parliamentary scrutiny is rather different. The initiative in tax policies lies with the Treasury, under the political direction of the Chancellor of the Exchequer.[41]

The starting point for the annual cycle is the Chancellor's Budget in the spring or autumn wherein, as Erskine May points out, 'the Chancellor develops his views of the resources of the country, communicates his calculations of probable income and expenditure and declares whether the burdens upon the people are to be increased or diminished'.

---

40 HC 98 (1986–87), London: HMSO, para 2, cited in Griffith and Ryle, 2003.
41 Nominally, the Prime Minister as First Lord of the Treasury.

The Budget[42]

The Budget is the annual statement of tax proposals for the forthcoming year, together with the government's expenditure plans for the following three years. At the end of the Budget speech, the ways and means resolutions are tabled. These resolutions form the basis for the main debate on the Budget, which lasts for between three and five days. The Finance Bill is then introduced and, within three to four weeks, will receive its second reading. The Bill then stands committed, in part, to a Committee of the Whole House and to a standing committee. The size of the standing committee for consideration of the Finance Bill is larger than the normal composition, and will have about 30 to 40 Members.

Income tax rates are effective only until the end of the tax year and require annual renewal under the Finance Act. The authority to collect taxes expires on 5 April each year. The Finance Act becomes law in July.

In **Bowles v Bank of England** (1913), the legality of taxation was considered. On 2 April 1912, the House of Commons passed a resolution approving the income tax rate for the year beginning 6 April 1912. The plaintiff had purchased stocks. The Bank deducted income tax from dividends due on 1 July at the new tax rate before the Consolidated Fund Act authorising the new rate had been passed by Parliament. The plaintiff sought a declaration that the Bank was not entitled to deduct the tax until approved by Parliament. The court ruled that a resolution could have no legal effect. **Bowles v Bank of England** led to the Provisional Collection of Taxes Act 1913,[43] which gives statutory authority to resolutions, as if imposed by Act of Parliament.

In **Attorney General v Wilts United Dairies Ltd** (1921), the Food Controller had, under a regulation of 1919, established a pricing structure for the issue of licences for milk purchase. The company claimed that the Food Controller had no power to impose conditions of payment in granting licences and that the condition amounted to a tax, which could not be imposed without clear and distinct legal authority. The court agreed, Lord Justice Atkin declaring that in view of the 'historic struggle' of the legislature to secure to itself the sole power to levy tax on its subjects, Parliament could not have intended to entrust a Minister with 'undefined and unlimited powers' of imposing charges upon the subject.

Note that the Finance Act is not usually a Money Bill for the purposes of the Parliament Act 1911, since it deals with wider matters than those listed in section 1(2) of the Act. Accordingly, unless certified by the Speaker to be a Money Bill, the Finance Bill will pass through the Lords in the usual manner. By convention, however, in relation to a Finance Bill, the House of Lords has relinquished any effective role in relation to taxation or expenditure.

The Public Accounts Committee (PAC)

This committee was first established in 1861. It has the power to examine the accounts 'showing the appropriation of the sums granted by Parliament to meet the public expenditure, and of such other accounts laid before Parliament, as the committee may think fit'.[44] The committee consists of not more than 15 Members, of whom four represent a quorum. While the composition of the committee represents (as does that of all select committees) the party-political strength of the House, the PAC functions in a non-partisan manner. By convention, the PAC's Chairman is a Member of the Opposition. The committee has the power

---

42 The name derives from French: the *bougette*, or little bag.
43 Now, Provisional Collection of Taxes Act 1968.
44 Standing Order No 122.

to 'send for persons, papers and records' and to report from time to time.[45] The PAC issues approximately 30 to 40 reports per session.[46]

The principal function of the committee is to ensure that money is spent for the purposes intended by Parliament, and that money is spent effectively and economically. The committee holds many meetings in public. One day per session is set aside for debate of its reports. By critically examining the expenditure of departments and assessing the extent to which expenditure produces value for money, the PAC exerts considerable influence on government.

The Comptroller and Auditor General (CAG) and National Audit Office (NAO)[47]

The CAG is an officer of the House of Commons, appointed by the Crown, and can be removed from office for misbehaviour only on the successful moving of an address to both Houses of Parliament. As head of the National Audit Office, the CAG's function is to examine the economy, efficiency and effectiveness with which bodies have used their resources in the pursuit of policy.[48] The CAG appoints his own staff, who are not civil servants. The reports of the National Audit Office[49] are recorded in the Weekly Information Bulletin of the House of Commons and are available to the public.

The CAG audits and certifies the accounts of government departments and bodies. Three significant areas of administration lie outside his jurisdiction: nationalised industries, local authorities and private bodies. The independence of the CAG from government, backed by the non-partisan PAC, provides a powerful watchdog over the administration of government and the expenditure of public money. National Audit Office reports are presented to Parliament and published. Most reports are considered by the Committee of Public Accounts in hearings at which senior officials are questioned. The Public Accounts Committee then publishes detailed recommendations to which the government formally responds. The National Audit Office then monitors the implementation of recommendations.

Summary

The scrutiny of government policy and administration is one of the key functions of Parliament, ensuring that government is accountable both to Parliament and the people. The principal forum for scrutiny is the House of Commons, although the House of Lords also plays a significant role.

Aside from the scrutiny of legislative proposals discussed in the previous chapter, the procedures for scrutiny are several, ranging from debates in the Chamber, Question Time, Opposition Days and Select Committees. In addition, on controversial matters an independent Committee of Inquiry may be established to investigate and report. Of the parliamentary procedures, the most in-depth scrutiny is effected by the Departmental Select Committees. Each Government Department has a related Select Committee which comprises backbench Members of Parliament. The party-political composition reflects that of the Commons overall. Select Committees may choose their own area of inquiry, and the Government is committed

---

45 Standing Order No 122, para 2.
46 In May 1995, the PAC issued a highly critical report concerning delays and overspending by the Ministry of Defence in relation to defence equipment.
47 See the Budget Responsibility and National Audit Act 2011, Part 2.
48 National Audit Act 1983, ss 6 and 7.
49 And the corresponding Office for Northern Ireland.

to cooperation with the Committees and also to responding to their Reports. Select Committees do not, however, have the power to compel the attendance of Ministers.

 **Further Reading**

Judge, D. (2004) 'Whatever Happened to Parliamentary Democracy in the United Kingdom?', Parliamentary Affairs, 57(3).

Leopold, P. (2011) 'Standards of Conduct in Public Life' in J. Jowell and D. Oliver (eds) *The Changing Constitution* (7th edn), Oxford: OUP.

Maer, L. and Sandford, M. (2004) *Select Committees under Scrutiny*, London: The Constitution Unit, UCL.

Oliver, D. (2001) 'The Challenge for Parliament', Public Law, 666.

Tomkins, A. (2003) 'What is Parliament For?' in M. Bamforth and P. Leyland (eds) *Public Law in a Multi-Layered Constitution*, Oxford: Hart Publishing.

Wright, T. (2013) *British Politics: A Very Short Introduction* (2nd edn), Oxford: OUP.

Chapter 16

The House of Lords

trial, and which was introduced in the Lords. The Parliament Act procedures do not apply to Bills introduced in the Lords, thus making it easier for the Lords to press home its objections to the Bill successfully. The Lords rejected the Bill, forcing the government to reintroduce the Bill in the Commons where at second reading the government secured a substantial majority. The House of Lords again rejected the Bill and it was withdrawn.

The House of Lords and delegated legislation

The House of Lords' Delegated Powers and Regulatory Reform Committee's principal concern is to scrutinise Bills with a view to establishing the extent of legislative powers which Parliament intends to delegate to government ministers. The role of the Committee is 'to report whether the provision of any Bill inappropriately delegates legislative power, or whether they subject the exercise of legislative power to an inappropriate degree of parliamentary scrutiny'. The committee reports to the House, which decides whether or not to accept the committee's recommendations. The committee has eight members and meets as needs require. The committee hears oral evidence in public, and takes evidence in writing on each Public Bill from the relevant government department.

The committee, in the examination of a Bill, considers four principal matters. First, it considers whether the power to make delegated, or secondary, legislation is appropriate, or whether the grant of power is so important that it should only be granted in primary legislation. Second, the committee pays special attention to 'Henry VIII powers'.[17] Third, the committee considers which form of parliamentary scrutiny of delegated legislation is appropriate, and in particular whether the power specifies the use of the affirmative or negative resolution procedure.[18] Fourth, the committee considers whether the legislation should provide for consultation in draft form before the regulation is laid before Parliament, and whether its operation should be governed by a Code of Conduct.

The Balance of Power between the House of Lords and the House of Commons

The Parliament Acts 1911 and 1949

Before the Parliament Act 1911, the House of Lords enjoyed equal power with the Commons over legislation, with the exception of financial measures which, by convention, the Lords recognised as falling under the authority of the elected Lower House. However, in 1909, the Finance Bill containing Lloyd George's Budget was rejected, in breach of convention, by the House of Lords. As a consequence, the House of Commons passed a Resolution declaring that there had been a breach of the constitution and a usurpation of the rights of the Commons, and calling for the power of the House of Lords to be restricted. King Edward VII was called upon to create sufficient new peers to guarantee the passage of the Finance Bill but refused to do so until the Budget was approved by the electorate. Parliament was dissolved and, in the election of January 1910, the government secured a majority of seats only with the help of minor parties. The House of Lords then passed the Finance Bill.

This conflict between the House of Commons and House of Lords resulted in the Parliament Act 1911, passed by both Houses of Parliament but with the House of Lords being threatened with the creation of more peers to ensure the Bill's safe passage. The Act abolished the Lords'

---

17 The power conferred on Ministers to amend primary legislation.
18 See further Chapter 14.

right to reject Money Bills,[19] and imposed a one-month time limit during which the Lords may consider such Bills and suggest amendments. If the Bill has not been approved without amendment within one month, provided it has been sent to the Lords within one month before the end of the session, the Bill will proceed to receive the royal assent without the approval of the Lords. Not all financial Bills are Money Bills. Where a Bill contains provisions dealing with other subjects it will not be a Money Bill. The Finance Bill is not automatically a Money Bill, and over half of the Finance Bills sent to the Lords since the 1911 Act have not been certified as Money Bills. While the purpose of the 1911 Act is to prevent amendment or delay in Money Bills, should the Lords propose amendments, these can be either accepted or rejected by the Commons.

Regarding non-Money Bills, the power of the House of Lords was curtailed, their right to reject legislation replaced by a power to delay Bills for a two-year period spread over three parliamentary sessions.

Conflict between the two Houses resurfaced over the Labour government's nationalisation programme following the Second World War. The Labour government, fearful that the Lords would reject the Iron and Steel Bill, introduced the Parliament Bill in 1947. In 1948, a conference between party leaders from both Houses met to attempt to reach agreement on the terms of the Parliament Bill. In the event, the conference broke down and the Parliament Bill was rejected by the House of Lords at second reading, only to be passed by the Commons under the Parliament Act 1911. The 1949 Act reduced the House of Lords' power of delay over non-Money Bills from two years over three sessions to one year over two sessions. No amendment was made to the provisions of the Parliament Act 1911 regarding Money Bills.

Exclusions from the Parliament Acts

The Parliament Acts do not apply to Private Bills, Bills originating in the House of Lords, Bills containing financial measures but not certified as Money Bills (because they contain other non-money provisions), statutory instruments or Bills purporting to extend the life of a Parliament beyond the five years laid down in the Septennial Act 1715, as amended by section 7 of the Parliament Act 1911.

The use of the Parliament Acts

It is notable that the Parliament Acts have been used infrequently. Aside from the Parliament Act 1949, which was passed under the 1911 Act, the Government of Ireland Act 1914, the Welsh Church Act 1914, the War Crimes Act 1991, the European Parliamentary Elections Act 1999, the Sexual Offences (Amendment) Act 2000 and the Hunting Act 2004 were passed under this procedure. The explanation for the usually low use of the procedure lies largely in conventional practices regulating the relationship between the two Houses. First, as has been seen above, the House of Commons accepts a great many Lords' amendments, for a variety of reasons. Second, the House of Lords exercises its delaying powers with some caution. In debate on the War Damage Bill 1965, Lord Salisbury stated that the House of Lords should insist on amendments under two circumstances:

(a)   if a matter raises issues important enough to justify such 'drastic' action;
(b)   if the issue is such that the electorate can understand it and express approval for the House of Lords' position. In this regard, the House of Lords acts as a 'watchdog of the people'.[20]

---

19 Bills certified by the Speaker as Money Bills, defined by the Parliament Act 1911, s 1(2).
20 See also HL Deb Vol 365 Col 1742, 11 November 1975 (Lord Carrington).

Third, if the House of Lords strongly disapproves of a measure but does not wish to defeat the Bill, it may move a resolution deploring parts of the Bill, as occurred in relation to the Immigration Bill 1971 and the British Nationality Act 1981. Fourth, many disagreements between the House of Commons and the House of Lords will be resolved by negotiations between the two Houses which generally will result in the avoidance of ultimate deadlock. Finally, the Parliament Act procedure may be avoided under the amendment procedure laid down in section 2(4) of the Parliament Act 1911. Under that section, the Acts may only be used if the House of Lords, over two successive sessions, rejects the same Bill. A Bill will be deemed to be the same Bill if it is identical with the former Bill 'or contains only such alterations as are certified by the Speaker to be necessary owing to the time which has elapsed since the date of the former Bill, or to represent any amendments which have been made by the House of Lords in the former Bill in the preceding session'.[21] If amendments have been made which are not agreed to by the Commons, the Bill is deemed to be rejected. This formulation facilitates agreements between the two Houses, yet preserves the ultimate possible use of the Parliament Act procedure.

The Parliament Act procedure and validity

As **Pickin v British Railways Board** (1974) illustrates, the courts are – mindful of Parliament's sovereign right to determine its own composition and procedure – reluctant to look at the procedure employed in enacting law. However, the case of **Jackson v Attorney General** (2005) provided an opportunity for the House of Lords to consider the validity of an Act which had been passed under the Parliament Act procedure. The claimants argued – unsuccessfully – that the Hunting Act 2004 was invalid because it had been passed under the Parliament Act 1949, which was also invalid. The reason for claiming that the 1949 Act was invalid was because it had been passed under the Parliament Act 1911 without the consent of the House of Lords, a position which contrasts with the 1911 Act, which could only be amended with the consent of the House of Lords.[22]

Central to the argument was whether the Parliament Act 1949 was primary legislation or delegated legislation. It was argued that legislation is not 'primary' where it depends for its validity on a prior enactment. If it was in fact delegated legislation, then the principle came into play that a body which had been delegated power could not, without there being express permission in the delegating (parent) Act, enlarge its own powers. Applying that argument to the Parliament Acts 1911 and 1949, it was argued that the 1911 Act delegated power to the Crown and Commons to enact legislation, under specified circumstances and subject to stated exceptions, without the consent of the House of Lords. It followed that when the Parliament Act 1949 was enacted without the consent of the Lords and reduced the time period during which the Lords could delay legislation, it increased the powers delegated to the Crown and Commons and thereby infringed the principle that a delegate cannot increase its powers. Lord Bingham rejected the view that the 1911 Act delegated legislative power to the House of Commons. The overall objective of the Act, he stated, 'was not to delegate power: it was to restrict, subject to compliance with the specified statutory conditions, the power of the Lords to defeat measures supported by the majority of the Commons . . .'[23]

The House of Lords also took the opportunity to consider the precise *scope* of the power delegated to the Crown and Commons and this in turn entailed two issues. Section 2 of the

---

21 Erskine May, 2004.
22 See also **R (Countryside Alliance) v Attorney General** (2007).
23 At p 745, 25.

1911 Act states two types of Bills which are expressly excluded from passage under the Parliament Act procedure: Money Bills or Bills extending the life of Parliament beyond five years. The first question was whether the procedure could be used to amend section 2 itself and thereby extend the life of a Parliament.

The Court of Appeal had concluded that there was power under the 1911 Act to make a 'relatively modest and straightforward amendment' to the Act, including the amendment made by the 1949 Act, but not to making 'changes of a fundamentally different nature to the relationship between the House of Lords and the Commons from those which the 1911 Act had made'. Lord Bingham of Cornhill stated in the Lords that that was a proposition which could not be supported in principle. He went on to state that it was unnecessary to resolve the issue whether the 1911 and 1949 Acts could be relied on to extend the maximum duration of Parliament beyond five years. However, he did accept that, however academic the point might be, the Attorney General was right in submitting that the 1911 Act and 1949 Act could be used to amend or delete the reference to the maximum duration of Parliament in section 2(1) and that a further measure could then be introduced to extend the maximum duration. The issue was also considered by Lord Nicholls of Birkenhead. He accepted that the express language of the Act prevented the prolonging of the duration of a Parliament beyond five years. On whether the Commons could succeed by a two-stage process as considered by Lord Bingham, Lord Nicholls took the view that it could not be done, stating that the 'express exclusion carried with it, by necessary implication, a like exclusion in respect of legislation aimed at achieving the same result by two steps rather than one. If this were not so the express legislative intention could readily be defeated'.

The second, and related, issue was whether the Parliament Act procedure could be used to effect other fundamental constitutional reform, given that section 2 only made two stipulated exclusions from the use of the procedure: Money Bills and Bills to extend the life of a Parliament. In other words, could other exclusions be implied into section 2? Lord Bingham rejected that suggestion. The House of Lords ruled that the purpose of the Parliament Act 1911 was not to enlarge the powers of the House of Commons or to delegate powers to it, but to restrict the powers of the House of Lords to defeat measures supported by the House of Commons. The 1911 Act stated that legislation made under it 'became an Act of Parliament on the Royal Assent being signified' and that there was nothing doubtful or ambiguous about that term.

On a proper interpretation of the 1911 Act, it created a parallel route by which, subject to certain exceptions, 'any' public bill introduced into the Commons could become an Act of Parliament. The term 'any' was to be construed according to its ordinary meaning. There were stated exceptions expressly stated in section 2(1) and there was no scope for introducing or implying further exclusions. Moreover there was no constitutional principle or principle of statutory construction which prohibited a legislature from altering its own constitution. Baroness Hale was forthright, rejecting the Court of Appeal's view that the 1911 procedure could not be used to effect fundamental constitutional change, stating that '. . . the 1911 Act procedure can be used to effect any constitutional change, with the one exception stated'.

More generally on the contemporary interpretation of parliamentary sovereignty, Lord Steyn, having alluded to the European Union and the European Convention on Human Rights, stated that:

> [T]he classic account given by Dicey of the doctrine of the supremacy of Parliament, pure and absolute as it was, can now be seen to be out of place in the modern United Kingdom. Nevertheless, the supremacy of Parliament is still the general principle of our constitution. It is a construct of the common law. The judges created this principle.

Suspension motions

The Suspension Motion is a device currently available in relation to Private Bills which facilitates their passage through Parliament. Where the Suspension Motion is agreed by the House of Commons, a Private Bill may be carried over from one session to another, without the loss of that Bill.

The House of Commons Procedure Committee and House of Lords Procedure Committee agreed to extend the procedure to Public Bills. Where a Bill is in the Commons at the end of one session, and a Suspension Motion is agreed, that Bill will be able to continue its life into the next session. However, the procedure is not designed to 'rescue' contentious Bills over which the two Houses disagree.[24] Rather, the procedure will apply to those Bills which the government notifies to the House of Commons as candidates for the 'carry-over' procedure.[25] It will be for the Commons to agree the motion to suspend the Bill, should the need arise.

Select Committees in the House of Lords

The House of Lords has no structured system of select committees as exists in the House of Commons. The House may establish ad hoc committees to consider a matter of public importance.[26] Domestic select committees exist to consider matters of procedure and privileges of the House. In addition, as has been seen, Bills may be committed to select committee for in-depth consideration and report.

A number of sessional committees exist. Significant among these are the European Union Committee, the Science and Technology Committee and the Economic Affairs Committee. The former was established in 1974 to consider Commission proposals for European legislation. The committee has acquired a reputation for authoritative scrutiny of the proposals. The committee has a salaried chairman and 18 permanent members, seven sub-committees, and a considerable staff of clerks and legal advisers. It has the right to appoint expert advisers as and when needed.

By a Resolution of the House of Lords[27] the government will not, except in special circumstances, agree to any proposal in the Council until it has been cleared by the Committee.

All of the committee's reports (unlike those of the House of Commons) are debated in the Chamber. The government undertakes to respond to the reports within two months of a report's publication.

In the 2000–01 session, three new sessional committees were established. The Select Committee on the Constitution has two main functions. First, it examines the constitutional implications of all Public Bills coming before the House: the scrutiny function. Second, it keeps under review the operation of the constitution: the investigative function. The Committee has 12 members and is assisted by a Legal Adviser. When examining Bills, the Committee considers whether the Bill raises issues of principle affecting the constitution. If it does, the Committee may request information or clarification from the Minister responsible for the Bill or seek other advice. The Committee reports its evidence to the House and publishes any conclusion it has reached. If a Bill is subject to pre-legislative scrutiny, the Constitution Committee may communicate its views on the draft Bill to the Committee. In exercising its investigative function, the Committee may engage specialist advisers, take oral evidence and

---

24 Eg, the Crime and Disorder Bill 1998, which provided for the lowering of the age of consent to sexual intercourse between men.
25 The Financial Services and Markets Bill 1999 was passed under the carry-over procedure.
26 For example, Unemployment (1979–82); Overseas Trade (1984–85), Murder and Life Imprisonment (1988–89).
27 6 December 1999.

receive written evidence. The Committee publishes a report and the government is obliged to respond to the report.

A Joint Committee on Human Rights was also established, having six members from the House of Lords and five from the House of Commons.[28] The Committee's terms of reference are wide. It has power to consider 'matters relating to human rights' (but not individual cases); to consider proposals for remedial orders, draft remedial orders and those laid before Parliament and to consider whether the attention of the House should be drawn to any aspect of them. The Committee has expressed a preference for law reform to be accomplished by primary legislation rather than remedial orders wherever possible in order to ensure adequate parliamentary scrutiny.[29]

The Economic Affairs Committee, having a membership of 13 and supported by a Clerk, a Secretary and a part-time Specialist Adviser, examines economic matters with which Parliament should be concerned. The Committee works through formal investigative enquiries hearing oral evidence and examining written evidence following which a report will be published, to which the government must formally respond.

Joint Committees, with members from both the House of Commons and House of Lords, have been established. There is a Joint Committee on House of Lords Reform and a Joint Committee on Human Rights. In addition, Joint Committees may be established to consider particular Bills. Examples include the Joint Committee on the Draft Corruption Bill and the Joint Committee on the Civil Contingencies Bill.

The Steering Committee

In order to co-ordinate better the work of committees in the Lords, there is a Steering Committee which serves functions similar to those of the Liaison Committee in the Commons – namely, deciding on subjects for investigation by ad hoc select committees, allocating resources between differing select committees and monitoring the work of the committees.

Members' Interests in the House of Lords

In November 1995, a Register of Members' Interests was established, in which a number of interests must be recorded. The requirements are that three categories of interests must be registered, namely:

(a)   consultancies or other similar arrangements involving payment or other incentive or reward for providing parliamentary advice or services. Registration under this category is mandatory;

(b)   financial interests in businesses involved in parliamentary lobbying on behalf of clients. This requirement is also mandatory;

(c)   other particulars relating to matters which the Lords consider may affect the public perception of the way in which they discharge their parliamentary duties. Registration under this category is discretionary.

Interests should be declared in debate whenever Members have a direct financial interest in a subject, along with any other interest which might affect the judgment of the House. The

---

28 See Feldman, 2002.
29 See HL 58/HC 473 of 2001–02.

Committee on Lords' Interests has power to investigate allegations of failure to comply with the requirements. The register is published annually.

The 2009 scandal over MPs' allowances and expenses is discussed in Chapter 17. Similar charges were levelled against some members of the House of Lords and some were under investigation by the police. The Independent Parliamentary Standards Authority, established under the Parliamentary Standards Act 2009 to investigate and regulate allowances and expenses in the House of Commons, does not extend to the House of Lords. However, in 2010 a new Code of Conduct for members of the House of Lords came into effect. Furthermore, a Lords Commissioner for Standards was appointed in 2010. The Commissioner will investigate alleged breaches of the new Code, including breaches of the rules relating to financial interests.

Reform of the House of Lords

Parliament Acts 1911 and 1949
– giving primacy to the Commons, limiting the power of the Lords to revision and (limited) delay instead of rejection of Bills, no veto of money Bills

Life Peerages Act 1958
– creating merit-based peerages, letting in 'the great and the good' from various backgrounds of expertise and experience and ending the exclusively hereditary (and male-dominated) composition

Peerage Act 1963
– entitling a peer to renounce title (and thus be eligible to stand for the Commons)

House of Lords Act 1999
– ending voting rights of hereditary peers (including 'Royals') and reducing their number to 92

Constitutional Reform Act 2005
– enhanced separation of powers by replacement of judicial House of Lords with a new Supreme Court sitting in separate, new building (yet to be implemented)

'Completion' of post-1997 reforms
– Royal Commission 2000 ('Wakeham Report'); agreement not reached; further all-party talks; Government Paper 2007

2010 Coalition Government reform proposals
Draft Bill 2011; House of Lords Reform Bill 2012–13
As a result of opposition from a considerable number of Conservative MPs, the Bill was withdrawn

With a perfect Lower House it is certain that an Upper House would be scarcely of any value ... But though beside an ideal House of Commons the Lords would be unnecessary, and therefore pernicious, beside the actual House a revising and leisured legislature is extremely useful . . .[30]

Both the Labour and Liberal Democrat Parties have long had proposals to reform the House of Lords. As seen above, the former Labour government proposed a phased reform, as a first step removing the right of the majority of hereditary peers to sit and vote. In the past, the Labour Party has advocated total abolition of the Upper House. Much of the antagonism to the Lords stems from basic principles of democracy, its opponents focusing on the fundamental paradox of a sophisticated democratic state having, as part of its legislative body, an unelected and democratically unaccountable institution. The preamble to the Parliament Act 1911 envisaged replacing the House of Lords with an elected House:

> And whereas it is intended to substitute for the House of Lords as it at present exists a Second Chamber constituted on a popular instead of hereditary basis, but such substitution cannot be immediately brought into operation . . .

This did not represent the first proposal to reform the House of Lords. As early as 1886 and 1888, debate took place in the House of Commons on the desirability or otherwise of a hereditary element in the legislature. As has been seen above, the constitutional conflict between the House of Lords and Commons in 1908–10 resulted in the restriction on the Lords' powers and the intention to replace the House of Lords.

In 1917, a conference comprising 15 Members of each House was established, under the chairmanship of Viscount Bryce, to consider the composition and powers of the Upper House. Reporting in 1918, the conference recommended that the Upper House should consist of 246 Members indirectly elected by Members of Parliament grouped into regional units, plus 81 Members chosen by a joint standing committee of both Houses of Parliament. The conference regarded the appropriate functions of this revised chamber to be the examination and revision of Commons Bills, the initiation of non-controversial Bills, the discussion of policy, and the 'interposition of so much delay (and no more) in the passing of a Bill into law as may be needed to enable the opinion of the nation to be adequately expressed upon it'. No action was taken on the recommendations.

In 1922, the government put forward proposals for a House of Lords made up of 350 Members. The majority of these were to be either directly or indirectly elected 'from the outside', with the remainder comprising some hereditary peers elected by peers, plus Members nominated by the Crown. In 1949 the Parliament Act, discussed above, was passed by the Labour government and remains the basis for the relationship between the Houses of Commons and Lords today.

The Life Peerage Act 1958

The Life Peerage Act 1958 reinvigorated the Lords. This Act enabled the Crown, on the advice of the Prime Minister, to confer peerages for life on men and women who have reached prominence in public life. The Act provided an increased resource of specialisation and experience. By convention, life peerages are conferred on Members of any political party, and on those who have no particular political affiliation. Towards this end, the leaders of the major political parties put forward nominations to the Prime Minister on an annual basis.

---

30 Bagehot, 1867, pp 133–34.

The Labour Party in the 1980s refused to make any nominations at all, basing their refusal on principled objection to the elitist nature of the House of Lords. This stance has proven to be something of an 'own goal' for the Labour Party, whose membership of the House of Lords is now smaller than it might otherwise have been. Note that since 2000 nominations for peerages are considered by the independent Appointments Commission (see further below).

The Peerage Act 1963

In 1963, a more limited, but nonetheless important, reform was implemented. The Peerage Act 1963 has its origins in the succession to a peerage by Anthony Wedgwood-Benn (as he then was), a Member of the House of Commons. As a result of succeeding to the title of Viscount Stansgate, Tony Benn, the Member for Bristol South East,[31] was barred from taking his seat in the Commons. A joint committee of the Houses of Commons and Lords reported on this matter in 1962 and recommended reform. As noted earlier, the Peerage Act 1963 provides that a person succeeding to a peerage may disclaim his peerage within one year of his succession,[32] and that a Member of the House of Commons may disclaim within a one-month period from succession. The disclaimer is irrevocable, but operates only for the lifetime of the peer disclaiming the title: the title will devolve to his heir upon his death. Section 6 of the the the Peerage Act 1963 provides for the first time that peeresses in their own right are entitled to sit and vote in the House of Lords.

The 1968 reform proposals

The Labour government of 1967–69 again turned its attention to reform of the composition of the House of Lords. The party manifesto of 1966 declared the intention to introduce reforms to safeguard measures approved by the House of Commons against delay or defeat in the House of Lords. An all-party conference took place in 1967–68, at which substantial cross-party agreement was reached on the proposals for reform. The resultant government White Paper of 1968[33] proposed that there should be a two-tier House. The first tier would consist of 230 voting peers who satisfied a test of attendance on a regular basis. The second tier would consist of peers who remained entitled to attend and to participate in debate, but would not be entitled to vote. The right to a seat in the House of Lords by virtue of succession to a peerage would be removed but existing peers (who did not satisfy the attendance criteria) would either become non-voting peers or might be conferred a life peerage with entitlement to vote. It was recommended that the government of the day should have a small, but not overall, majority of voting peers in the House. The White Paper also recommended that the power of delay by the House of Lords be reduced to a six-month period.

The government proceeded to introduce the Parliament (No 2) Bill 1968 to give effect to the White Paper, but after extensive consideration the government withdrew the Bill.

The 1997 Labour government's reform agenda

The first commitment made in relation to the House of Lords by the Labour Party before its election to office in 1997 was to abolish, as a first measure, the voting rights of hereditary

---

31 See **Re Parliamentary Election for Bristol South East** (1964).
32 Or on attaining the age of majority.
33 Cmnd 3799, 1968, London: HMSO.

peers. This was accomplished under the <u>House of Lords Act 1999</u>. A Royal Commission was established to consider the next phase in reform and to make recommendations. All reform of the House of Lords is problematic. The 1968 reforms failed to be implemented, not because of opposition in the House of Lords, but through opposition in the House of Commons, which crossed party lines. The opposition arose from the Commons' perception that removing the right of hereditary peers to vote would enhance the authority of the House of Lords, and would risk the Lords becoming more bold in its dealing with the House of Commons. One key question for the Royal Commission and the government, therefore, was how to move forward to the second reform stage in order to produce an effective and valuable second chamber without threatening the supremacy of the democratically elected House of Commons.

The problem of legitimacy remained after the removal of the hereditary peers' right to vote. Life peers have no more constitutional legitimacy than do hereditary peers. Thus, removing the hereditary peers from the House of Lords did not effect any constitutional change of real value, and certainly did not mark a move towards greater democratic legitimacy, but represented no more than a starting point for further, largely undefined, future reform.

The Royal Commission Report *A House for the Future* was published in January 2000. To the disappointment of those advocating radical reform, the Commission recommended that the Upper House, having around 550 members, comprise a majority of nominated members and a minority of selected or elected members representing regional interests. However, despite widespread consultation, the Commission reached no consensus on the most difficult issue: the number of selected or elected members and the method by which members would be selected.

In 2000, a non-statutory House of Lords Appointments Commission was established as an interim measure, which has the function of making recommendations for non-party-political peerages in the House of Lords.[34] In addition, the Committee vets all nominations for peerages from political parties with a view to assessing their propriety. The government signalled its acceptance in principle of the Report. However, the White Paper published in November 2001 made clear that only a minority of peers would be elected.[35] Once again, no further reform was achieved.

The Coalition government formed in 2010 proposed to introduce a wholly or mainly elected Upper House on the basis of proportional representation. The major provisions of the House of Lords Reform Bill 2010–12 were as follows:

- the reformed House should have 300 members, 240 elected and 60 appointed;
- the constitutional powers of the House would remain unchanged;
- members would serve a single non-renewable term of office of 15 years;
- the elected element would be phased in, with 80 members elected in the first period; a further 80 in the second period and the remaining 80 in the third period;
- the appointed element would also be phased in, 20 members being appointed at each stage;
- elections would take place at the same time as general elections;
- the Single Transferable Voting system would be used for elections to the House of Lords;
- constituencies would be considerably larger than for the House of Commons;
- members would be salaried;

---

34 HL Deb Vol 60 Col WA179, 25 January 2000.
35 *The House of Lords: Completing the Reform*, Cmd 5291, London: HMSO. See also the Labour government's White Paper, *The House of Lords: Reform*, published in 2007.

- nomination for appointment would be made by a statutory Appointments Commission and recommended by the Prime Minister for appointment by The Queen;
- there would be up to 12 places for Archbishops and Bishops of the Church of England.

The Bill was withdrawn in 2012 following opposition from a significant number of Conservative MPs, without whose support the Bill was unlikely to be passed. Yet another attempt to reform of the House of Lords has, therefore, failed.

Summary

The House of Lords is the unelected Second Chamber, or Upper House of Parliament. Its membership comprises a small number of hereditary peers, a majority of Life Peers appointed under the Life Peerage Act 1958, retired Law Lords or Supreme Court Justices (judges) and 26 Archbishops and Bishops.

The House of Lords scrutinises proposals for legislation. Legislative proposals (Bills) may be introduced in either House of Parliament and the procedure in each House is similar. The powers of the House of Lords are, however, limited by the Parliament Acts 1911 and 1949. The Constitutional Reform Act 2005 provided for reform of the office of Lord Chancellor, who formerly acted as speaker of the House of Lords. The Lord Speaker is now elected by the House of Lords. The 2005 Act also improved the separation of powers by removing the Appellate Committee of the House of Lords (the highest domestic court) from Parliament, establishing a Supreme Court now staffed by Justices of the Supreme Court, who may no longer participate in the legislative work of the House of Lords while sitting as judges in the Supreme Court.

Reform of the composition of the House of Lords has been on the agenda for over a century. The House of Lords Act 1999 removed the right of all but 92 hereditary peers to sit in the House of Lords. While successive governments declare their intention to reform the House of Lords, little progress has been made as a result of concerns over the balance of power between the two Houses following reform.

Further Reading

Bingham of Cornhill, Lord (2010) 'The House of Lords: its future?' Public Law, 261.
Bogdanor, V. (1999) 'Reforming the Lords: A Sceptical View', Political Quarterly, 70: 375.
Hansard Society (1999) *The Future of Parliament: Reform of the Second Chamber*, London: Hansard Society.
Russell, M. (2000) *Reforming the House of Lords: Lessons from Overseas*, Oxford: OUP.
Russell, M. and Cornes, R. (2000), 'The Royal Commission on the House of Lords: A House for the Future?', Modern Law Review, 64: 82.
Wakeham, Lord (2000) 'A House for the Future: Royal Commission on the House of Lords', Cm 4534, London: HMSO.

Chapter 17

Parliamentary Privilege

Chapter Contents

Introduction

For details of the history of privilege see the Website.

The privileges of Parliament are those rules of both Houses of Parliament which offer protection from outside interference – from whatever source – to the Houses collectively, and to individual members. Parliamentary privilege also entails the right of Parliament to regulate its own composition and procedure: it is an aspect of Parliament's sovereignty or supremacy. Parliamentary privilege has a long history, dominated before 1688 by conflicts between Crown and Parliament. The constitutional settlement of 1688 settled that conflict in Parliament's favour.

The parliamentary authority Erskine May defines privilege as being:

> . . . the sum of the peculiar rights enjoyed by each House collectively as a constituent part of the High Court of Parliament, and by Members of each House individually, without which they could not discharge their functions, and which exceed those possessed by other bodies or individuals. Thus, privilege, though part of the law of the land, is to a certain extent an exemption from the general law. [1997, p 69]

Parliamentary privilege provides protection for Members of Parliament against accusations of defamation from outside Parliament and also protects the individual member – in the exercise of his or her freedom of speech – from the executive.

Parliamentary privilege presents some intriguing constitutional issues. In some respects, privilege may be compared with the royal prerogative, in so far as both privilege and the prerogative represent a unique aspect of legal power reserved exclusively for a special class of persons. Moreover, parliamentary privilege is a legal power in respect of which the courts – mindful of the doctrine of separation of powers – will be cautious in accepting jurisdiction to regulate. By asserting special powers and immunities for Parliament as a whole, and for its members individually, Parliament throws around itself a cloak of protection which provides rights and immunities not accorded to individual citizens. The balance which is – and ought to be – struck between legitimate and necessary safeguards for Parliament and its members in the exercise of parliamentary duties and the rights of individuals to the protection of the general law is not always satisfactorily achieved.

The law and practice of privilege reveals the extent to which individual members and Parliament as a body are free from outside pressure – whether from interest groups, sponsoring bodies and institutions or the media – a freedom which is central to ensure an independent Parliament. However, as Marshall and Moodie point out:

> . . . the boundary lines between free comment, legitimate pressure, and improper interference are obviously not easy to formulate in principle. [1971, p 112]

The law and custom of Parliament

The privileges enjoyed form part of the 'law and custom of parliament' – *lex et consuetudo parliament* – and, as such, it is for Parliament to adjudicate on matters of privilege, not the courts.[1] Privileges are embodied in rules of the Houses of Parliament. The United Kingdom Parliament, however, is not free to extend existing privileges by a mere resolution of the House: only statute can create new privileges.[2] Privileges derive from practice and tradition;

---

1 Coke, 1 Inst 15.
2 **Stockdale v Hansard** (1839).

they are thus customary in origin. Nevertheless, they are recognised as having the status of law, being the 'law and custom of parliament'. Parliament itself can – in the exercise of its sovereign power – place privileges on a statutory basis. For example, in 1770, the Parliamentary Privilege Act withdrew the privilege of freedom from arrest from servants of Members of Parliament. Further, in 1689, Article IX of the Bill of Rights gave statutory recognition to the freedom of speech in Parliament. In 1868, Parliament ended its own jurisdiction to determine disputed elections, conferring jurisdiction on the courts by way of the Administration of Justice Act.

The role of the courts

The role of the courts in matters of privilege is confined to determining whether a privilege exists, and its scope. If the court rules that a disputed matter falls within parliamentary privilege the court will decline jurisdiction. This relationship between Parliament and the courts may be viewed in two ways. First, it could be viewed as the courts giving recognition to the supremacy – or sovereignty – of Parliament. Historically, Parliament was established as the High Court of Parliament, having legislative *and* judicial powers.[3] Accordingly, it was appropriate for the ordinary courts of law to defer to the highest court in the land. Nowadays, this justification is less well founded. It is unconvincing to portray Parliament, except when exercising its judicial function in enforcing and upholding privilege, as a judicial body.[4] The relationship between Parliament and the courts may also be explained by reference to the doctrine of the separation of powers. For the judiciary to rule on the legality of actions of Members of Parliament acting in their parliamentary capacity or on the actions of the House as a whole would, under current constitutional arrangements, place judges in a potentially dangerous position, exercising a controlling power over both the legislature and the executive within it.

Baron Mereworth v Ministry of Justice (2011) illustrates the approach of the courts. In this case, the Chancery Division ruled that the court does not have jurisdiction to determine whether a peer is entitled to receive a writ of summons which would entitle him to sit in the House of Lords. Such decisions are for Parliament alone to determine. Lord Mereworth succeeded to the title in 2002. In 2010 he requested Her Majesty to issue him a writ of summons which would entitle him to sit in the House of Lords. The Crown Office refused, stating that Lord Mereworth was not entitled to a writ as a result of section 1 of the House of Lords Act 1999. Making reference to the separation of powers and Article 9 of the Bill of Rights 1689, Lewison J stated that 'Existing in parallel with Article 9 is the principle of exclusive cognisance', a phrase explained by Lord Phillips of Worth Matravers PSC in **R v Chaytor** (2011) as follows:

> This phrase describes areas where the courts have ruled that any issues should be left to be resolved by Parliament rather than determined judicially. Exclusive cognisance refers not simply to Parliament, but to the exclusive right of each House to manage its own affairs without interference from the other or from outside Parliament.

The Principal Privileges

The principal individual privileges are freedom of speech in Parliament and freedom of members from arrest in civil matters. The collective privileges of Parliament include the

See Chapter 4.

---

3 See McIlwain, 1910.
4 See below for a discussion of recent criticism of the Committee of Privileges and the decision-making process of the House of Commons in disciplining members.

exclusive right to regulate composition and procedure, right of access to the Sovereign, and the right to the 'favourable construction' by the Sovereign in relation to its actions. These are formally claimed by the Speaker, in the form of a Speaker's Petition to Her Majesty, at the opening of each new parliamentary session.

The privileges are substantially the same for both Houses of Parliament (though see below on the 'privilege of peerage'). Each House has the sole right to regulate the privileges it enjoys – although neither House is free to extend its own privileges other than by statute – and, as a result, some minor differences may be discerned between the two Houses.

The Current Scope and Role of Privilege

Freedom from arrest

For Members of the House of Commons, the freedom extends for 40 days before the start of and 40 days after the end of the session. For peers, the privilege protects from arrest in civil matters at all times. The freedom from arrest does not extend to criminal charges or convictions.[5]

Where the criminal law is concerned, there is no immunity, and the re-arrest of a Member of the House of Commons who had escaped from prison, in the Chamber of the House, was not contrary to privilege.[6] In 1939, a Member of Parliament – Captain Ramsay – was detained under defence regulations. His detention did not amount to a breach of privilege, although it would have done so had he been detained for words spoken in Parliament.[7]

Where a member is arrested on a criminal charge, the Speaker of the House is notified and in turn will report to the House either orally or in writing. If a member is detained on grounds of mental illness under the Mental Health Act 1983 then – following specialists' reports to the Speaker confirming the member's illness and detention – his seat will be declared vacant.

Nowadays, the freedom relates only to civil matters and is generally of little significance, given that, with one important exception, imprisonment for debt has been abolished. The exception concerns the availability of imprisonment as a penalty for the non-payment of financial provision during marriage, upon divorce, and for children born outside marriage. In 1963, in the case of **Stourton v Stourton**, a Member of the House of Lords was able to escape the sanction of prison for maintenance default by pleading privilege. It is anomalous that Members of Parliament should be immune from the law in even this limited manner. The Committee on Parliamentary Privilege recommended, in 1967, that the freedom be abolished,[8] but no action was taken.

Freedom of speech and 'proceedings in parliament'

At present, it is more important to notice that this freedom of speech holds good not only against the Crown, but also against private individuals. A member speaking in either House is quite outside the law of defamation:

> He may accuse any person of the basest crimes, may do so knowing that his words are false, and yet that person will be unable to take any action against him.[9]

---

5   4 Rot Parl 357; 1 Hatsell 17–22, **Thorpe's Case** (1452), cited in Erskine May, 1997, p 75; **John Wilke's Case** (1760–64).
6   Lord Cochrane, 1815: CJ (1814–16) 186; Parl Deb (1814–15) 30, c 309, 336; Colchester ii, 534, 536, cited in Erskine May, 1997, p 95.
7   HC 164 (1939–40), London: HMSO.
8   HC 34 (1967–68), London: HMSO, p xxix.
9   Maitland, 1908, p 375. On the Defamation Act 1996 see further below, p 377.

The most important privilege claimed by Parliament is freedom of speech. Article IX of the Bill of Rights 1689 provides that 'freedom of speech and debates in proceedings in Parliament ought not to be impeached or questioned in any court or place outside of Parliament'. It has been seen above that, if a matter falls within the privileges of Parliament, the courts will have no jurisdiction over the matter, other than to determine whether or not a matter of alleged privilege falls within the ambit of privilege. If a positive determination is made, jurisdiction to rule on the matter falls to Parliament and not the courts. In order to make such a determination in relation to freedom of speech, the courts are obliged to interpret Article IX of the Bill of Rights, and the phrase 'proceedings in Parliament'.

Some matters are settled. The Bill of Rights makes clear that freedom of speech in debate is protected from legal action and redress under the law of defamation. Debates and questions on the floor of the House and in standing and select committees are therefore clearly protected. Other situations are, or have been, less straightforward. For example, what is the situation where a Member of Parliament is discussing parliamentary matters outside the precincts of Parliament, or where a Member of Parliament writes to a minister on such a matter? Moreover, what is the position where a member writes to the minister or another member with regard to a matter which he wishes to raise in Parliament, or which involves allegations made against bodies or persons outside Parliament, on which he requires further information before raising the issue in Parliament? Despite numerous suggestions for reform to inject greater clarity into the law, many matters remain unclear. The most recent consideration of the scope of proceedings in Parliament is discussed below. The case law is instructive.

- In **Rivlin v Bilainkin** (1953), the plaintiff in an action for defamation had been granted an interim injunction to restrain the defendant from repeating the alleged defamation. The defendant repeated the defamatory remarks in letters and took them to the House of Commons, giving one to a messenger to deliver to a Member of Parliament and posting the other four, addressed to other members, in the House of Commons' post office. In an action for an order committing the defendant for a breach of the injunction, the defendant argued that publication of the repetition of the libel was committed within the precincts of the House of Commons and was accordingly not actionable in a court of law. Mr Justice McNair declared himself:

  . . . satisfied that no question of privilege arises, for a variety of reasons, and particularly I rely on the fact that the publication was not connected in any way with any proceedings in that House . . .

- In **Duncan Sandys'** case, in 1938, Mr Duncan Sandys had sent to the Secretary of State for War the draft of a parliamentary question in which he drew attention to a shortage of military equipment. Within the draft, Mr Sandys quoted figures which, in the view of the War Office, could have been obtained only as a result of a breach of the Official Secrets Acts 1911–20. The Attorney General interviewed Mr Sandys, who later complained that he was being threatened with prosecution – in breach of privilege – for failing to disclose the source of his information. A select committee was established to consider the relevance of the Official Secrets Acts to members acting in their parliamentary capacity. The Committee Report considered Article IX of the Bill of Rights, and it observed that:

  . . . the privilege is not confined to words spoken in debate or to spoken words, but extends to all proceedings in Parliament. While the term 'proceedings in Parliament' has never been construed by the courts, it covers both the asking of a question and the giving written notice of such question, and includes everything said or done by a Member in the exercise of his functions as a Member in a committee of either House, as well as everything said or done in either House in the transaction of parliamentary business.

The Committee ruled that if it were necessary, in order to prove the charge alleged, to produce evidence of what the defendant had said in the House it was 'in the power of the House to protect him by withholding permission for the evidence to be given'.[10]

- The response of the House differed markedly in the case of **Strauss and the London Electricity Board** in 1958.[11] At issue was whether or not communication in written form between a Member of Parliament and a minister was protected by privilege. George Strauss MP had forwarded a letter from a constituent to the relevant minister, in which criticism was made of the manner in which the Board disposed of scrap metal. The minister passed the letter to the Board for comment, whereupon the Board threatened to sue Mr Strauss for libel. The member believed that this was a matter concerned with his parliamentary duties and that he should be covered by privilege. The Committee of Privileges concluded that the letter written was a proceeding in Parliament and that, accordingly, the Board had committed a breach of the privilege of the House. The committee was undecided as to whether the Parliamentary Privilege Act 1770 (which provides that legal action taken against members is in itself a breach of the privilege of the House) applied. It was recommended that the House seek a ruling from the Judicial Committee of the Privy Council on the matter. The Judicial Committee ruled that the Act referred only to legal action taken against a member in his private capacity, and not as a result of his conduct as a Member of Parliament. The committee so reported to the House which, following debate, surprisingly rejected the finding of the committee. The London Electricity Board subsequently withdrew its action for libel, and an independent inquiry set up by the minister exonerated the Board.[12]

Strauss raises two important questions for consideration. First, a great many important negotiations and communications take place through informal discussion between members outside the precincts of the House. Much of this business is as important as matters raised for formal debate in the House, yet it is not covered by parliamentary privilege unless so closely associated to actual or pending proceedings in Parliament as to be brought within that phrase.

Second, many of the matters dealt with by Members of Parliament involve, as did the **Strauss** case, alleged grievances reported by constituents against government departments and associated public bodies. Inevitably, such grievances may entail actual or potentially libellous statements, but they are not protected by privilege. Where such a matter falls within the jurisdiction of the Parliamentary Commissioner, protection is now afforded by section 10(5) of the Parliamentary Commissioner Act 1967, which provides that such communications are absolutely privileged.[13] Uncertainty remains, however, where it is unclear as to whether or not the matter falls within his jurisdiction. It is unsatisfactory that neither members of the public, nor of Parliament, are clear as to the potential scope of liability under the law of defamation.

Four further cases illustrate the scope of the privilege.

- **R v Rule** (1937) involved a letter written by a constituent to his Member of Parliament complaining about the conduct of a police officer and a magistrate. In an action for libel

---

10 Report from the Select Committee on the Official Secrets Act, HC 146 (1938–39), London: HMSO.
11 HC 305 (1956–57), HC 227 (1957–58), 591, HC Official Report, 5th Ser, Col 208, London: HMSO; Re Parliamentary Privilege Act 1770 (1958); Cmnd 431, 1958, London: HMSO; Denning, 1985.
12 Cmnd 605, 1958, London: HMSO.
13 On the jurisdiction of the Commissioner, see Chapter 26.

the court held that, where a communication was one made under a duty or common interest, the matter would attract qualified privilege: that is to say, it would be protected from liability unless malice were proven.

- A similar conclusion was reached in **Beach v Freeson** (1972), where a Member of Parliament was sued by a firm of solicitors, concerning whom the member had received complaints from a constituent and forwarded the letter, with a covering letter, to the Lord Chancellor and the Law Society. That the letters were defamatory was not contested, but the court nevertheless held that publication of the letters (to the Lord Chancellor and Law Society) was protected by qualified privilege on the basis of public interest.
- In **Buchanan v Jennings** (2004)[14] the Privy Council considered the protection from defamation under Article IX of the Bill of Rights 1689.[15] The defendant had made defamatory statements in debate in the New Zealand House of Representatives: these were absolutely privileged and therefore not actionable. Subsequently, however, the defendant was interviewed by a newspaper journalist and stated that he 'did not resile'[16] from the claims made in Parliament. The plaintiff sued: such words were not covered by privilege. Further, nothing in the law of privilege prevented the plaintiff from relying on a record of what was said in Parliament as evidence to support an action against the Member based on what he had said outside the House. At common law every republication of a libel was a new libel and a new cause of action. Accordingly, the Member of Parliament could be held liable in defamation if he later adopted or confirmed the original statement, without repeating it, outside Parliament.
- The protection of privilege does not attach to criminal activities of Members of Parliament. The Court of Appeal so ruled in **R v Chaytor, R v Morley, R v Devine and R v Hanningfield** (2010).[17] The appellants attempted, unsuccessfully, to use privilege to protect themselves from prosecution on charges of false accounting in respect of their claims for expenses.

The protection granted by privilege was considered by the European Court of Human Rights in **A v United Kingdom** (2002). The applicant argued that defamatory remarks made about her and her children in a debate about housing policy which had been reported in local and national newspapers, which she could not challenge in court because of Article IX, violated Article 6 (right to a fair trial), Article 8 (right to respect for private life) and Article 13 (the right to an effective remedy) of the European Convention on Human Rights. The Court of Human Rights found the statements unnecessary and reference to her home 'regrettable', but nevertheless ruled that there was no violation of Convention rights. The rules on privilege were necessary to protect free speech in Parliament. Moreover, the British rules were narrower than those operating in several other states.

Freedom of speech: its use and misuse

In the Committee of Privileges report of 1986–87,[18] the Committee had endorsed the view expressed by the Speaker[19] that:

---

14 See Geddis, 2005.
15 Note that decisions of the Privy Council are persuasive rather than binding on the domestic courts.
16 Meaning that he stood by what he had said previously.
17 Times LR 23 August 2010.
18 Third Report of the Committee of Privileges 1986–87, HC 604 (1995–96), London: HMSO.
19 HC 110, Official Report, Col 1084.

> We should use our freedom of speech . . . with the greatest care, particularly if we
> impute any motives or dishonourable conduct to those outside the House who have
> no right of reply.

The Committee recognised that there is 'no clear dividing line between statements which represent a legitimate exercise of freedom of speech, on the one hand, and those which constitute an abuse, on the other' and called on members to exercise self-restraint.

- In 1955, Kim Philby was named in the House as a Soviet spy, an allegation which surely would not have been made without the protection of privilege. In the 1960s, the Minister of War's association with Christine Keeler, who also had a relationship with a Soviet Attaché, was revealed under the cloak of privilege.
- Also in the 1960s, a London property racketeer, Peter Rachmann, was identified in the House.
- In 1980, Jeff Rooker MP made a number of false accusations against a Director of Rolls-Royce: the allegations were withdrawn only after the lapse of five weeks.
- In the 1985–86 session, ministers were accused in Parliament of improper involvement with the Johnson Matthey Bank following its collapse.
- In 1986, Geoffrey Dickens MP accused an Essex doctor of the sexual abuse of children, following a decision of the Director of Public Prosecutions not to prosecute the doctor on the basis that there was insufficient evidence to secure a conviction.
- In 2011, John Hemming MP disclosed in the Commons that a former Chief Executive of the Bank of Scotland had been granted a 'superinjunction' by the court. A superinjunction means that the media is not only prohibited from disclosing factual matters but is also prevented from reporting that the injunction exists. The disclosure in Parliament undermined the court order.[20]

Which of these exercises of freedom of speech represented a legitimate exercise of the freedom and which represented an abuse is a matter for individual judgment.

The House relies heavily on the notion of the self-restraint of its members, and is slow to use its disciplinary powers against offending members. The Committee on Procedure in its First Report urged members to exercise caution, and to avoid misusing their freedom. Where members insist on using privilege as a protective device and cause damage to the reputations and livelihoods of citizens, the advice of the Procedure Committee will give little comfort.[21] Individuals may try to rebut any allegations, may petition Parliament and may try to persuade a Member of Parliament to retract a damaging allegation, but such forms of redress are wholly unsatisfactory in comparison with the right to legal redress.

A Joint Committee on Parliamentary Privilege issued its First Report in 1999. In relation to members of the public, the Committee considered whether a 'right of reply' should be introduced but decided against it. A right of reply would do nothing to prove the truth or falsity of any allegation and no financial redress could be made, nor would a statement published in *Hansard* attract the same degree of publicity as the offending allegation.

The courts and privilege

More case law further illustrates the meaning of Article IX and the role of the courts in relation to matters of privilege. In **Rost v Edwards** (1990), a Member of Parliament sued *The Guardian*

---

20 See the *Report of the Committee on Super-Injunctions*, 2011.
21 Given that 'advice' is less compelling than binding rules.

newspaper for alleged libel.[22] The *Guardian* article had stated that the member, who was a member of the Energy Select Committee and a nominee for selection to the standing committee, considering an Energy Bill, had not registered his interests – as a consultant with two organisations concerned with energy. Subsequent to publication of the article, the member was informed that he was no longer being considered for membership of the standing committee and, further, that he had not been given the chair of the Energy Select Committee. The member instituted libel proceedings, which were adjourned by the court in order to determine the issue of parliamentary privilege. The member wished to adduce evidence before the court which comprised correspondence between himself and a clerk of the House and the Register of Members' Interests.

Mr Justice Popplewell ruled that the correspondence could not be submitted in evidence: that clearly fell within the exclusive domain of Parliament and not the court. As to the Register, the judge took the view that it was a public document and, accordingly, could be put in evidence. Mr Justice Popplewell, recognising the respective jurisdictions of Parliament and the courts, declared that the courts should nevertheless be slow to refuse to admit in evidence documents which could affect the outcome of legal proceedings and hence individual rights.

Rost v Edwards was doubted by the Privy Council in **Prebble v Television New Zealand Ltd** (1994). In **Prebble**, a member of the New Zealand House of Representatives sued the television company for libel for publishing an article alleging that state assets had been sold off, contrary to stated policy, and that the member had been involved in a conspiracy to effect the sale. In its defence, the company wished to introduce in evidence parliamentary papers which substantiated its claim. The member pleaded privilege. The House of Representatives ruled that it had no power to waive its own privileges and thereby allow the papers to be considered in court. The Privy Council ruled that to adduce such evidence – without the House's waiver of privilege – contravened privilege and the protection given to parliamentary proceedings under Article IX of the Bill of Rights 1689.

In **Pepper v Hart** (1993),[23] the question considered by the House of Lords was whether judges may refer to *Hansard* as an aid to the interpretation of statutes. This issue has long been one of some controversy, and the orthodox view has hitherto been that judges may not under any circumstances refer to *Hansard*. In **Davis v Johnson** (1979), Lord Denning MR stated openly that he privately referred to *Hansard* as an aid to interpretation, only to be criticised for so doing by the House of Lords. However, in **Black-Clawson International Ltd v Papierwerke AG** (1975), all five judges in the House of Lords had agreed that official reports could be consulted to discern the 'mischief' with which the legislation was intended to deal, although their Lordships differed over the extent to which they could be used. Further, in **Pickstone v Freeman** (1988), three members of the House of Lords made reference to a parliamentary speech of the Secretary of State (the other two judges were silent on this matter).

In **Pepper v Hart** (1993), six of the seven judges hearing the case ruled in favour of admitting parliamentary debates before the court in some circumstances (the Lord Chancellor dissented on this point). Arguments were advanced by the Attorney General against such a decision – not least that, by consulting parliamentary debates, the courts would be acting contrary to Article IX of the Bill of Rights 1689, which prohibits the courts from questioning proceedings in Parliament. The court rejected those views, concluding that there were no constitutional reasons which outweighed the merits of a 'limited modification' of the rule. Lord Browne-Wilkinson, giving the leading judgment of the court, stated that the rule should be relaxed where:

---

22 See Leopold, 1991.
23 See Oliver, 1993.

(a) legislation is ambiguous or obscure, or leads to an absurdity;

(b) the material relied on consists of one or more statements by a minister or other promoter of the Bill together, if necessary, with such other parliamentary material as is necessary to understand such statements and their effect; and

(c) the statements relied on are clear.

The House of Lords in **Pepper v Hart** revealed a marked change in attitude, although the right to refer to *Hansard* is not an unqualified right. The significance of this judgment from the point of view of parliamentary privilege lies in the court's consideration of the scope of Article IX of the Bill of Rights 1689. The Attorney General had argued strongly before the court that for judges to refer to *Hansard* infringed Article IX, amounting to an inquiry into the proceedings in Parliament. This submission was rejected by the court, Lord Templeman declaring that reference to *Hansard*, under limited circumstances, involved no questioning of Parliament, but merely clarification as to Parliament's intention.[24]

The case of **Prebble v Television New Zealand Ltd** (1995) was reconsidered in **Allason v Haines** (1995). Joe Haines, a political journalist, and Mr Richard Stott, editor of the newspaper *Today*, applied to have a libel action brought against them by the plaintiff, Mr Rupert Allason MP stayed. The court held that where, in order to defend a libel action, it was necessary to bring evidence of a Member of Parliament's behaviour in the House of Commons, and such a defence would be in breach of parliamentary privilege, the action would be stayed, for it would be unjust to deprive the defendants of their defence. The defendants had sought to show that Early Day Motions were inspired by improper motives. Such evidence would be in contravention of Article IX of the Bill of Rights 1689. To enforce parliamentary privilege in this case would be to cause injustice to the defendants. A stay was granted.

Rost v Edwards was also critically considered by the Joint Committee on Parliamentary Privilege which reported in 1999. The report stated baldly that 'we are in no doubt that if this decision is correct, the law should be changed'.[25] In the Committee's opinion, it is quite wrong for a court of law to be free to investigate and adjudicate upon matters relating to the Register. If there are allegations of wrongful failure to register, that matter should be 'a matter for Parliament alone'. The Committee recommended that legislation be introduced to make clear that the Register and matters relating thereto are 'proceedings in parliament'.

Reference to *Hansard* was again considered in **Wilson v First County Trust** (2003). In this case the Court of Appeal referred to *Hansard* not, as in **Pepper v Hart**, to identify the intention of Parliament in order to give effect to it, but rather to understand the reason which led Parliament to enact a particular provision in the form that it took and to identify whether the statute was compatible with Convention rights. Unusually, legal representation on behalf of the Speaker of the House of Commons and the Clerk of the Parliaments gave evidence concerning the use of *Hansard* by the courts. Lord Nicholls of Birkenhead addressed the constitutional issue in the following way:

> This House sitting in its judicial capacity is keenly aware, as indeed are all courts, of the importance of the legislature and the judiciary discharging their constitutional roles and not trespassing inadvertently into the other's province. [p 584]

---

24 In **Three Rivers District Council v Bank of England** (No 2) and (No 3) (1996), it was held that references to ministers' speeches in *Hansard* may be made not only to construe a particular statutory provision whose meaning was ambiguous or unclear, but also in a case where the purpose or object of the statute as a whole is in issue. See also **R v Deegan** (1998).

25 First Report of the Joint Committee on Parliamentary Privilege, 1999, para 123.

The House of Lords ruled that:

> . . . it is a cardinal constitutional principle that the will of Parliament is expressed in the language used by it in its enactments. The proportionality of legislation is to be judged on that basis. The courts are to have due regard to the legislation as an expression of the will of Parliament. The proportionality of a statutory measure is not to be judged by the quality of the reasons advanced in support of it in the course of parliamentary debate, or by the subjective state of mind of individual ministers or other members.

The Defamation Act 1996 and Article IX of the Bill of Rights

The Defamation Act 1996 came into being as a result of the Rupert Allason case and Neil Hamilton's intended libel suit against The Guardian newspaper over its allegations that he had accepted rewards in relation to his parliamentary duties.[26] Section 13 of the Defamation Act provides that a person may waive, for the purpose of defamation proceedings in which his conduct in relation to proceedings in Parliament is in issue, the protection of any enactment or rule of law which prevents proceedings in Parliament being impeached or questioned in any court or place outside Parliament. As a result, a Member of Parliament may bring an action for defamation to defend his or her actions, provided that he or she waives the Article IX protection and thereby enables the defence to adduce evidence which otherwise would be excluded on the basis of privilege. If, however, the Member of Parliament is not willing to waive the Article IX privilege, then, on the authority of **Prebble v Television New Zealand Ltd**, the defamation action may be stayed in order to enable the newspaper to adduce evidence which proves the truth of its allegation.

In **Hamilton v Fayed** the House of Lords ruled that the effect of section 13 was that the defendant's waiver of his parliamentary protection in relation to the parliamentary inquiry into his conduct overrode any privilege belonging to Parliament as a whole and thus allowed the parties in the libel proceedings to challenge the veracity of evidence given to the parliamentary committee.[27]

The composition and procedure of Parliament

The Houses of Parliament have an inherent right to regulate their own composition and procedure: 'exclusive cognisance'. The purpose of exclusive cognisance is to protect each House of Parliament from 'interference from any outside body'. This includes 'the conduct of its Members, and of other participants such as witnesses before Select Committees'.[28]

- In **Ashby v White** (1703), the plaintiff – a qualified voter – had been denied the right to exercise his vote by the Mayor of Aylesbury. The House of Lords awarded Ashby damages. The case gave rise to a significant constitutional conflict between Parliament and the courts. The House of Commons – which at the time had jurisdiction to hear matters on disputed elections – regarded the decision of the House of Lords as interfering with the exclusive right of the House of Commons to adjudicate on disputed elections. Other voters, similarly denied the right to vote, instigated legal proceedings and were committed

---

26 **Hamilton v Hencke; Greer v Hencke** (1995), on which see further below.
27 **Hamilton v Al Fayed (No 1)** (1999) and **(No 2)** (2000).
28 Parliamentary Privilege, Cm 8318, London: TSO 2012, p 8.

to prison by the House of Commons. They brought an application for habeas corpus to test the legality of their detention. In **Paty's Case** (1704) the court refused the writ of habeas corpus. Counsel for the applicants, intending to appeal to the House of Lords, was committed to prison. The majority of the court refused to grant the application, deferring to the Commons.

- In **Bradlaugh v Gosset** (1884), Bradlaugh had been duly elected as a Member of Parliament. On arriving to take his seat, Bradlaugh refused to swear the required oath on the Bible, offering instead to swear an oath of allegiance to the Crown. The House of Commons resolved to exclude Bradlaugh from the House. The plaintiff sought a declaration from the court that the resolution was invalid and an injunction to prevent the House of Commons from excluding him. The Court of Queen's Bench declared that it had no jurisdiction to interfere with a matter concerning the internal regulation of Parliament's procedures.

- The right of the House to regulate its own procedures is further demonstrated in the case of **British Railways Board v Pickin** (1974). There the court declined to inquire into the manner of the passage of a Bill even though the plaintiff alleged that he had been denied his right to make representations on a matter adversely affecting his rights in breach of convention. The Court of Appeal held that the procedure used in relation to a Private – but not Public – Bill could be examined. Lord Denning MR took a bold approach, arguing that it was for the court to ensure that 'the procedure of Parliament itself is not abused, and that undue advantage is not taken of it. In so doing, the court is not trespassing on the jurisdiction of Parliament itself. It is acting in aid of Parliament and, I might add, in aid of justice'. The House of Lords disagreed and adopted its traditional stance: the court will not look 'behind the Parliamentary Roll'.[29]

- On a lighter note, the exclusive rights of the Commons were tested in **R v Campbell ex parte Herbert** (1935). Three members of the Kitchen Committee of the House of Commons were accused of breaching the licensing laws. The action failed, the court holding that the House was not governed by the ordinary laws relating to licensing, which would only apply if it could be shown that they were expressly intended to apply to Westminster. It is for this reason that the House remains free to open its bars at any time of day or night. Sir AP Herbert once speculated whether the immunity conceded in **R v Campbell ex parte Herbert** could be extended by analogy to permit other licentious behaviour in the Commons.

An early conflict between Parliament and the courts

In **Stockdale v Hansard** (1839), a prison inspector made a written report to the Secretary of State alleging that 'improper books' were being circulated in Newgate prison. The report was subsequently published by Hansard, on order of the House of Commons. Stockdale, the publisher of the 'improper book', sued Hansard as publishers of the report, which he regarded as being libellous. In defence, Hansard argued that the publication had been by an order of the House of Commons and was, accordingly, covered by the privilege of the House. The Court of Queen's Bench ruled that such publication was not covered by privilege and, moreover, that the House of Commons could not by a resolution deprive the courts of jurisdiction to protect the rights of individuals. Stockdale was awarded damages. The Sheriff of Middlesex levied execution on Hansard's property to satisfy the award of damages to Stockdale and the House of Commons responded by passing a resolution to commit the Sheriff for breach of privilege and contempt

---

29 Following, inter alia, **Edinburgh and Dalkeith Rly Co v Wauchope** (1842); **Lee v Bude and Torrington Junction Rly Co** (1871).

of Parliament. The Sheriff applied for a writ of habeas corpus to test the legality of his detention.[30] The Serjeant at Arms produced a certificate from the Speaker stating simply that the Sheriff was 'guilty of a contempt and a breach of the privileges of this House'. The court refused to examine the lawfulness of the Sheriff's detention, stating that, since the Speaker's warrant did not specify the facts justifying the detention, it was not for the court to inquire into Parliament's business. Accordingly, the court conceded jurisdiction to the House of Commons and rendered itself powerless to provide a remedy for an individual who, acting as an agent for the courts in enforcing the court's order for damages, found himself incarcerated on the order of the Commons. While such an outcome hardly inspires confidence in the judicial system, it nevertheless illustrates clearly the judges' reluctance to cross the boundary into matters of privilege.

Breach of privilege and contempt of Parliament

A breach of privilege is conduct offending against one of the known privileges of Parliament. Contempt is a far wider concept than this and has been defined as:

> . . . any act or omission which obstructs or impedes either House of Parliament in the performance of its functions, or which obstructs or impedes any Member or Officer of the House in the discharge of his duty or which has a tendency, directly or indirectly, to produce such results. [Erskine May, 1997, Chapter 9]

The main types of contempts dealt with by the House of Commons, with illustrations, are listed by Erskine May as being:

(a) misconduct in the presence of the House or its committees;
(b) disobedience to rules or orders of the House or its committees;
(c) presenting a forged or falsified document to the House or its committees;
(d) misconduct by Members or officers as such;
(e) constructive contempts: such as speeches or writing reflecting on the House; wilful misrepresentation of debates; premature disclosure of committee proceedings of evidence; other 'indignities' offered to the House;
(f) obstructing Members in the discharge of their duty;
(g) obstructing officers of the House while in the execution of their duty;
(h) obstructing witnesses.

Members' Interests and Members' Independence

Freedom from interference in Parliament's work is a foundational principle of privilege. Accordingly, it is essential that all Members of Parliament are under no external pressure which could pose an actual or potential threat to their independence. However, from a constitutional standpoint, this issue represents one of the most troublesome aspects of privilege. It remains a topic of much contemporary significance and raises difficult questions. In 1994, this issue came to the fore and, as a result of a number of allegations concerning members' interests, an inquiry headed by Lord Justice Nolan was established by the Prime Minister to examine the issue.[31] The findings of the inquiry are discussed below.

---

30 *Sheriff of Middlesex's Case* (1840).
31 Committee of Inquiry on Standards in Public Life.

A majority of members of the House of Commons are in paid employment in addition to being salaried members of the House.[32] Many members are also sponsored by outside bodies who contribute to their election expenses and may contribute towards the cost of secretarial and/or research staff employed by a member.[33] It may be argued as a point of principle that Members of Parliament should not receive any financial or other assistance from any outside party, whether a company or a trade union, since the very fact of receipt of such support potentially undermines the independence and integrity of the recipient.[34] This is not, however, the view adopted by the House of Commons itself although, from time to time, the House is troubled by such issues. The traditionally accepted view is that such sponsorship or remuneration is perfectly proper, provided that it does not impede the member's independence in the actual exercise of his parliamentary duties.

However, there is a fine line to be drawn between legitimate payments to members and payments designed to impede a member's independence, which may amount to bribery and corruption.

Rules regulating members' interests

In 1695, by a resolution of the House, the 'offer of money or other advantage' to a Member of Parliament for the purpose of persuading him or her to promote any matter in Parliament was ruled to be 'a high crime and misdemeanour'. Further, in 1858, a resolution declared it to be 'improper for any member to promote any matter' in relation to which he or she had received a financial reward.[35] Specifically in relation to the asking of parliamentary questions, the Committee of Privileges in 1945 ruled that it was a breach of the privileges of the House to 'offer money or other advantage' to induce members to take up questions with ministers.[36] Members of Parliament found guilty of corruption may be expelled from the House.

When speaking in debate or in any proceedings in the House or its committees, or when communicating with other members or ministers, a resolution of 1974 requires that members shall disclose 'any relevant pecuniary interest or benefit . . . whether direct or indirect, that he may have had, may have or may be expecting to have'.[37]

In 1947, the Committee of Privileges had the opportunity to examine the issue of contracts made between members and outside bodies. Mr WJ Brown was elected the Member for Rugby in 1942. He had previously held the post of General Secretary of the Civil Service Clerical Association and, following his election, agreed to become its Parliamentary General Secretary. Following disagreements between Mr Brown and the Association, it was resolved that Mr Brown's appointment should be terminated. The matter was raised in the Commons, the argument being advanced that the Association's threat to terminate Mr Brown's contract was calculated to influence the member in the exercise of his parliamentary duties and, accordingly, amounted to a breach of privilege.

On the facts of the case, the Committee ruled that the making of such payments in itself did not involve any breach of privilege, and that:

---

32 Non-ministerial salaries have only been payable since 1911. For the background, see Erskine May, 1997, Chapter 1.
33 The trade unions have a statutory right to sponsor Members of Parliament from separate political funds (Trade Union and Labour Relations (Consolidation) Act 1992).
34 A view expressed by Dennis Skinner MP: 'One Member, one salary' (BBC Television News, 20 April 1995).
35 CJ (1857–58) 247.
36 *Henderson's Case*, HC 63 (1944–45), London: HMSO.
37 Adopting recommendations of the Select Committee on Members' Interests (Declaration), HC 57 (1969–70), London: HMSO.

> On the other hand, your committee regard it as an inevitable corollary that if an outside body may properly enter into contractual relationships with and make payments to a Member as such, it must in general be entitled to terminate that relationship if it lawfully can where it considers it necessary for the protection of its own interest so to do. What, on the other hand, an outside body is certainly not entitled to do is to use the agreement or the payment as an instrument by which it controls, or seeks to control the conduct of a Member or to punish him for what he has done as a Member.[38]

A further instance of alleged improper pressure being brought to bear on Members of Parliament occurred in 1975. The Yorkshire Area Council of the National Union of Mineworkers, who sponsored a number of Labour Members of Parliament, resolved that it would withdraw its sponsorship from any member who voted in the House in a manner which conflicted with Union policy. The Committee of Privileges found this threat to be a serious contempt of the House, amounting as it did to an attempt to force a member to vote in a particular way and thus threatening a member's freedom of speech.[39] In the event, the National Executive of the Union nullified the resolution and no action was taken against the Union.

The Register of Members' Interests

On the wider question of the financial interests of Members of Parliament, under the rules of the House, all members are required to declare their interests, these being recorded in the Register of Members' Interests. A resolution of the House of Commons provided that:

> . . . in any debate or proceeding of the House or its committees or transactions or communications which a Member may have with other Members or with Ministers or servants of the Crown, he shall disclose any relevant pecuniary interest or benefit of whatever nature, whether direct or indirect, that he may have had, may have or may be expecting to have. [22 May 1974]

The Register of Members' Interests is published annually. The following classes of interests are required to be registered:[40]

(1) remunerated directorships of companies, public or private;
(2) remunerated employments, trades, professions, offices or vocations;
(3) the names and details of clients in relation to which a Member plays a parliamentary role;
(4) sponsorships, donations/support;
(5) gifts, benefits or hospitality received;
(6) overseas visits;
(7) overseas benefits and gifts;
(8) land and property;
(9) shareholdings;
(10) controlled transactions within section 7A Political Parties Elections and Referendums Act 2000 (loans; credit arrangements);

---

38 See HC Deb 15 Col 284, July 1947; HC 118 (1946–47), London: HMSO.
39 See HC 634 (1974–75), London: HMSO.
40 With effect from June 2009.

(11)   miscellaneous;

(12)   family members employed and paid in respect of parliamentary duties.

Failure to register an interest may be regarded as a contempt of the House. The only member who consistently refused to enter any interests on the Register was Mr Enoch Powell. Mr Powell adopted the constitutional stance that, since only statute could impose legal duties on individuals, the House could not – through the use of resolutions – lawfully require him to register. The select committee, having tried persuasion and inviting the House to take action to enforce the duty to register, took no further action.

The rules relating to ministers are more strict than those relating to ordinary Members of Parliament. The 2005 Ministerial Code required that Ministers must resign any directorships they hold when they take up office.[41] This requirement, however, is absent from the Code published in 2010. In its place is a restatement of the general principle that Ministers must ensure that no conflict arises between their public duties and their private interests, and procedures designed to ensure that no actual or potential conflict arises.[42]

Cash for questions[43]

The cash for questions affair began in 1993, when political lobbyist Ian Greer advised Mohamed Al Fayed to bribe Members of Parliament to pursue his interests in Parliament. In 1994, Al Fayed publicly claimed that Tory MPs were paid to plant questions. The *Guardian* newspaper pursued the story, leading to a libel action by Mr Hamilton and Mr Greer. That action was dropped when it became apparent that the *Guardian* had damning evidence which would cause the action to fail.[44]

In 1994, a number of allegations were made against Members of Parliament in relation to accepting money for the tabling of parliamentary questions to ministers. Allegations were also made in relation to improper payments being accepted by members from outsiders, in the form of payment for hotel bills. Further allegations were made in respect of the failure of a number of Members of Parliament who allegedly failed to record benefits received and other relationships in which members received financial reward for services in the Register of Members' Interests. In 1994, two Parliamentary Private Secretaries resigned (from the government but not from parliament) following allegations that they had received money in exchange for tabling parliamentary questions. The matter was referred to the Committee of Privileges. The rapidly accelerating and intensifying atmosphere of suspected corruption – or 'sleaze' – in public life caused the Prime Minister to appoint a judicial inquiry to be carried out by the Committee on Standards in Public Life.

The Committee on Standards in Public Life: The Nolan Inquiry

The Committee on Standards in Public Life, chaired by Lord Nolan, was established as a standing body, with membership being held for three years. The Committee's terms of reference were:

> To examine current concerns about standards of conduct of all holders of public office, including arrangements relating to financial and commercial activities, and to make recommendations as to any changes in present arrangements which might be required to ensure the highest standards of probity in public life.

---

41 Paragraph 5.20.
42 *Ministerial Code*, 2010, Cabinet Office, section 7.
43 See also Chapter 10 on fitness for public office.
44 For an entertaining account, see Leigh and Vulliamy, 1997.

Individual allegations of impropriety do not fall within the committee's terms of reference.[45]

The First Report (the Nolan Report) of 1995 stated that while 'there is no evidence . . . of a growth in actual corruption' (paragraph 6), there was a widespread loss of public confidence in the probity of Members of Parliament.

The committee set out the general principles of conduct which apply to public life as being selflessness, integrity, objectivity, accountability, openness, honesty and leadership.

Members of Parliament

The Nolan Report recorded that the 1995 Register of Members' Interests suggested that almost 30 per cent of Members of Parliament held some form of consultancy agreement and that almost 70 per cent of Members of Parliament (excluding ministers and the Speaker) had some form of financial relationship with outside bodies.

Despite the evidence of witnesses and persons writing to the committee, the committee did not conclude from this evidence that such arrangements should be banned. Indeed, the involvement of Members of Parliament in outside work was regarded by the committee as a benefit to Parliament as a whole. As the committee viewed the matter:

> . . . a Parliament composed entirely of full time professional politicians would not serve the best interests of democracy. The House needs if possible to contain people with a wide range of current experience which can contribute to its expertise. [para 19]

The committee was also concerned that a ban on outside financial interests would act as a deterrent to people who would otherwise stand for election to Parliament. The committee recommended, therefore, that Members of Parliament should continue to have the right to engage in outside employment. The matter which remained was how best to protect the integrity of members and the House as a whole in light of such continuing outside employment.

Having reviewed the early resolutions of the House, and the later resolution of 1947, and the rules regulating the registration of members' interests, the committee found that the Register had worked unsatisfactorily. The committee invited the House of Commons to review the statement of principle which governed the registration of interests.

Paid consultancies

Three-fifths of all members of the House have arrangements with clients or sponsors. While appreciating that paid consultancies enable 'many entirely respectable, and in some cases highly deserving, organisations' to 'gain a voice in the nation's affairs',[46] the committee recognised that there was a fine − and difficult − line to be drawn between paid advice and paid advocacy, the latter of which is a matter of concern. To remove the right to engage in such arrangements would be 'impracticable' and was, accordingly, not recommended. There was, however, one area − the issue of 'general consultancies' − in which the committee wanted to see firm and immediate action.

General consultancies

Public relations and lobbying firms are engaged in acting as advisers and advocates to a wide range of clients, all of which pursue their own objectives in terms of exerting pressure on Parliament. The problem posed by such companies is that registration of an agreement with

45 See Doig, 2002. In this chapter, the findings relating to Members of Parliament are discussed. The conduct of ministers and civil servants is considered in Chapter 10.

46 Nolan Report, para 46.

the company does not necessarily disclose the actual client for whom, in fact, the member is acting in a parliamentary capacity. The committee recommended that there be an immediate ban introduced on such relationships; Parliament did not act specifically on this proposal but, rather, tightened the rules relating to registration and the declaration of interests.

Clarifying the Register of Members' Interests

Members are now required to deposit in full any contracts which involve the member acting in a parliamentary capacity on behalf of any organisation, and these contracts are available for public inspection. In addition, members are required to reveal their annual remuneration, and also estimated monetary benefits received of any kind. Furthermore, all agreements which do not involve the member acting in a parliamentary capacity for an organisation and, therefore, do not need to be deposited, should contain clear terms stating that the agreement does not involve the member acting for the organisation in a parliamentary capacity.[47]

The committee also emphasised the requirement that Members of Parliament disclose their interests on 'each and every occasion when a member approaches other members or ministers on a subject where a financial interest exists'.[48] The onus is on the members to disclose the interest, and he or she should not assume that the interest is one known about by the other party.

Gifts and hospitality

In relation to gifts and hospitality, the committee found that the rules set out in *Questions of Procedure for Ministers*[49] were sufficiently detailed and that no further elaboration was required. The committee endorsed the important principle set out in *Questions of Procedure*:

> It is a well established and recognised rule that no Minister or public servant should accept gifts, hospitality or services from anyone which would, or might appear to, place him or her under an obligation.[50]

Enforcing members' obligations

The committee proposed the appointment of an independent Parliamentary Commissioner for Standards, responsible for maintaining the Register of Members' Interests and for providing guidance on standards of 'conduct, propriety and ethics'. The Commissioner fulfils a similar function to that of the Comptroller and Auditor General and the Parliamentary Commissioner for Administration.[51] The Commissioner has power to receive and investigate complaints concerning members' conduct.[52]

In relation to ministers, the Nolan Report was critical of the position whereby ministers may leave government office and assume senior positions with – in particular – companies which have recently been privatised by the government.

In response to aspects of the Nolan Report, the House approved a Code of Conduct, incorporating the key principles of conduct in public life.[53] The House of Commons passed a

---

47 Nolan Report, para 70.
48 *Ibid*, para 63.
49 *Ibid*, paras 80–81. Now known as the Ministerial Code.
50 At paragraph 126. See Chapter 3, para 40 of the report.
51 See Chapters 15 and 26, respectively.
52 In *R v Commissioner for Standards and Privileges ex parte Al Fayed* (1998) the Court of Appeal ruled that the court had no jurisdiction to review decisions of the Commissioner, on the basis that the Commissioner was concerned with activities within Parliament, and the Commissioner was accountable to a select committee in the House of Commons, which alone had the power to perform supervisory functions over the Commissioner.
53 HC 688 (1995–96).

resolution, now incorporated in the Code of Conduct for MPs, making it clear that any payment for promoting any matter in Parliament is not allowed.[54] The House also resolved to clarify the rules on declaration of interests when participating in parliamentary proceedings.

MPs' expenses and allowances

In 2009 it was revealed that MPs had been abusing the system of allowances and expenses. The revelation came following a request under the Freedom of Information Act 2000 and a decision of the High Court ruling that MPs were not exempt from disclosures under the Act.[55]

Many of the wrongful claims had been approved by the Commons' Department of Resources, the 'Fees Office', fuelling the demand for parliamentary reform. An inquiry was undertaken by an independent auditor, Sir Thomas Legg. As a result of his inquiry many MPs were ordered to repay monies which were regarded as wrongly claimed. The scandal also led to the forced resignation of the Speaker of the House of Commons, Michael Martin, who had lost the confidence of MPs. The Speaker is chairman of the Members' Estimates Committee, which oversees the *Green Book* which sets out the principles to which MPs are to adhere when making claims against allowances. He became the first Speaker to be forced out of office since 1695, leaving office following unprecedented cross-party calls for his resignation.

The scandal led to the rapid introduction and passage of the Parliamentary Standards Act 2009, which had the support of all political parties. The Act created an Independent Parliamentary Standards Authority (IPSA) to regulate the system of pay and allowances, to formulate rules to deal with financial interests and to prepare a code of conduct on financial interests.

Section 1 of the Act ensures that parliamentary privilege is unaffected, providing that:

> Nothing in this Act shall be construed by any court in the United Kingdom as affecting Article IX of the Bill of Rights 1689.

The Bill received the Royal Assent in July 2009, having completed all its parliamentary stages in a month. Constitutionally the Parliamentary Standards Act raises a number of issues. The Act for the first time established a body outside Parliament to regulate Parliament's affairs. Questions relating to Parliament's sovereignty and privileges inevitably arise. The question of who will oversee the working of the Independent Parliamentary Standards Authority and whether it would be subject to judicial review, giving rise to a potential difficulty in the relationship between Parliament and the courts. Concerns over the working of the Act, so hastily drafted and passed by Parliament, led to the insertion of a 'sunset clause' – a provision stating that sections of the Act would cease to have effect at the end of a period of two years (see section 15).[56]

The Constitutional Reform and Governance Act 2010, Part 3, amended the Parliamentary Standards Act 2009. The Act imposes a general duty on IPSA to promote efficiency, cost-effectiveness and transparency in the discharge of its functions and provides that IPSA is to determine MPs' pay.

Section 3 of the Parliamentary Standards Act (as amended) provides for the establishment of a Compliance Officer for IPSA. The Compliance Officer may review decisions of IPSA to

---

54 HC 816, 1994–5.

55 *Corporate Officer of the House of Commons v The Information Commissioner* (2008).

56 A further inquiry into MPs expenses was undertaken in 2009 by Sir Christopher Kelly, Chair of the Committee on Standards in Public Life. The Report, *Report on MPs Expenses and Allowances: Supporting Parliament, Safeguarding the Taxpayer*, Committee on Standards in Public Life, Cm 7724, November 2009.

III THE COMMITTEE ON STANDARDS IN PUBLIC LIFE

The Committee:

- was established in 1994 by the House of Commons as an independent body;
- has ten members appointed for up to three years;
- advises government on ethical standards across the whole of public life in the United Kingdom;
- has reviewed MPs' expenses and allowances and the funding of political parties.

IV THE INDEPENDENT PARLIAMENTARY STANDARDS AUTHORITY (IPSA)

Established under the Parliamentary Standards Act 2009, amended by the Constitutional Reform and Governance Act 2010:

- IPSA has responsibility for MPs' salaries, pensions, allowances and expenses;
- the Compliance Officer of IPSA investigates and reports on complaints concerning alleged breaches of the rules relating to expenses and allowances.

V THE ELECTORAL COMMISSION

Established under the Political Parties, Elections and Referendums Act 2000, as amended by the Electoral Administration Act 2006 and the Political Parties and Elections Act 2009.

The Electoral Commission:

- is an independent body set up by statute;
- the Commission maintains the Register of Political Parties;
- maintains and monitors donations and loans to political parties;
- investigates alleged breaches of the rules relating to donations;
- draws on the Register of Members' Interests for data on donations;
- oversees the conduct of elections and referendums;

The Commission is accountable to Parliament through the Speakers' Committee, chaired by the Speaker of the House of Commons and having one member appointed by the Prime Minister and five Members appointed by the Speaker of the House.

See further
Chapter 12.

Publication of Parliamentary Proceedings

The publication of proceedings in Parliament is covered by the same rules as the reporting of proceedings in court. The underlying principle is that publication is in the public interest and generally outweighs any disadvantage to individuals.

On the extent to which the reporting and publication of parliamentary proceedings is protected, section 1 of the Parliamentary Papers Act 1840 provides that, where civil or criminal proceedings are commenced, the defendant may present to the court a certificate stating that the publication in question was made under the authority of the House of Lords or House of Commons, and that the 'judge or court shall thereupon immediately stay such civil or criminal proceeding'.

Section 2 provides that similar protection exists for correct copies of official reports and authorised papers. Section 3 provides that extracts or abstracts from such reports or papers, for example in newspapers, are protected provided that such extracts are published *bona fide* and without malice. Thus papers of the House, or papers ordered to be published by the House, plus fair and accurate, but unauthorised, reports of proceedings are covered by qualified privilege, and an action for damages for injury allegedly caused by their publication would only lie if malice could be proven.

The Parliamentary Papers Act was passed as a direct result of two cases in which the courts and Parliament came into conflict, namely **Stockdale v Hansard** (1839) and the **Sheriff of Middlesex's Case**. While the passing of the Parliamentary Papers Act 1840 gives statutory authority to publication of official papers and authorised reports, uncertainty still remains as to the scope of the protection.

Privilege and the media

Publications which reflect on the dignity of the House as a whole are classified as 'constructive contempts', as are reflections on individual members.[76] Illustrations of adverse comments published in the press include that of the **Sunday Express** which, in 1953, commented that two members were asleep during an all-night sitting of the House. Further, in 1956, the *Sunday Express* criticised Members of Parliament for exempting themselves from the petrol rationing which had been imposed as a result of the Suez crises. The report of the Committee of Privileges held that the editor had been:

> . . . guilty of a serious contempt in reflecting upon all Members of the House and so upon the House itself by alleging that Members of the House had been guilty of contemptible conduct in failing, owing to self interest, to protest at an unfair discrimination in their favour. Such an attack on Members is calculated to diminish the respect due to the House and so to lessen its authority.[77]

The issue of media pressure again fell for consideration by the Committee of Privileges in 1956. A Member of Parliament, Mr Arthur Lewis, gave notice of a forthcoming Prime Ministerial parliamentary question, which asked:

> . . . whether he will arrange for part of the money contributed by the government for relief in Hungary to be allocated to the relief of the several thousand Egyptian people who have been rendered homeless and destitute by British shelling and rocket fire in Egypt.

In a scathing editorial in the **Sunday Graphic**, readers were invited to telephone Mr Lewis and give him their views. To assist this task, the newspaper published the member's telephone

---

76 Erskine May, 1997, p 121.
77 *Second Report from the Committee of Privileges*, HC 38 (1956–57), London: HMSO.

number. As a consequence, the member received thousands of irate telephone calls before the Post Office was able to change his number. In both cases, the editors were called to the Bar of the House and apologised.

Unauthorised disclosure of parliamentary proceedings

The unauthorised disclosure of proceedings conducted in private and of draft reports of committees which have not been reported to the House is governed by a resolution of the House of 1837, as amended in 1980. The resolution makes such disclosure a contempt of the House.[78] The House resolved in 1978 that its penal jurisdiction should only be used where the action complained of was likely to cause a 'substantial interference' with a committee's work.[79] The Committee of Privileges recommended in its 1985 report that 'substantial interference' with regard to leaked documents should be confined to confidential or classified information or deliberate attempts to undermine the work of the committee.[80]

Where a newspaper reports parliamentary proceedings and goes beyond the mere publication of a Member of Parliament's speech and includes material of its own, in order to determine whether the whole article is protected by privilege it is necessary for the court to determine first what was said in debate, then decide whether any extraneous material added by the newspaper made the report unfair or inaccurate and thereby removed any privilege from the report.[81]

Privilege and interests in the House of Lords

Privilege in the House of Lords

The House of Lords enjoys the same privilege of freedom from arrest[82] and freedom of speech as the Commons. Freedom of access to the Sovereign is enjoyed by the House collectively and by each peer individually. This privilege of peerage extends to all peers, irrespective of whether they sit in the House of Lords. The House of Lords has the same right as the Commons to determine its own procedure. In the event of a disputed peerage, the House of Lords has jurisdiction to determine the matter.[83] The House of Lords has the power to commit persons for breach of privilege or contempt and also the power to impose fines. The House of Lords may also summon judges to attend in order to give advice on points of law.

Members' interests

In 1996, in response to increased concerns over members' interests, a Register of Members' Interests was established in the House of Lords. In addition, the House has approved a motion that Lords should always act on their personal honour and should never accept any financial inducement as an incentive or reward for exercising parliamentary influence. Members are regulated by a Code of Conduct.

Peers are no longer permitted to act as advocates for companies or organisations from whom they receive remuneration. They are, however, allowed to act as advisers to outside

---

78 See Leopold, 1980.
79 HC Deb Vol 943 Col 1198, 6 February 1978.
80 *Second Report from the Committee of Privileges: Premature Disclosure of Proceedings of Select Committee*, HC 555 (1984–85), London: HMSO, paras 51–55; see Griffith and Ryle, 2003.
81 **Curistan v Times Newspapers Ltd** (2007).
82 *The Sunday Times*, 16 July 1995.
83 See **Stourton v Stourton** (1963).

groups. Peers are no longer free to ask questions or to table amendments where their sponsoring organisation stands to gain benefit.

On members' interests, the House of Lords agreed in 2011 to include in the Register of Interests 'the precise source of each individual payment made in relation to any directorship and the nature of the work carried on in return for that payment'. Transitional rules are in place to enable Members to regulate their relationships with outside bodies in compliance with the amended Guide to the Code of Conduct. From March 2013, any Member unable or unwilling to comply with the revised Code must take leave of absence.[84]

Enforcing the rules

In 2010 the House of Lords appointed a Lords Commissioner for Standards to investigate alleged breaches of the Code of Conduct or rules regulating Members' financial interests. The Commissioner reports to the Sub-Committee on Lords' Conduct. The Sub-Committee, where appropriate, recommends a disciplinary sanction to the Committee for Privileges and Conduct. The Member concerned has a right of appeal to the Committee for Privileges and Conduct against the Commissioner's findings and any recommended sanction. The Committee reports its recommendations to the House, which has the final decision. Members are under a duty to cooperate with any investigation.

Reform of parliamentary privilege

There remains a need to clarify the definition given to the phrase 'proceedings in parliament' in Article IX of the Bill of Rights in order that both members and other individuals may better understand the scope of the protection given by privilege.

The Joint Committee on Parliamentary Privilege considered the question of the definition of parliamentary proceedings in its 1999 report. The Committee recommended that there should be enacted a Parliamentary Privileges Act to cover this and a number of other reforms.

In 2012 the Government's Green Paper, *Parliamentary Privilege*,[85] reviewed the operation of parliamentary privilege and set out questions on which consultation is to be based. These cover freedom of speech, exclusive cognizance, Select Committee powers, the reporting of parliamentary proceedings and miscellaneous issues such as freedom from arrest in civil matters. It is understood that a Joint Committee of both Houses will be established to consider the issues raised.

Summary

The purpose of parliamentary privilege (which is enjoyed by both Houses of Parliament), both collective and individual, is to protect the independence and integrity of Parliament from outside influence and interference. To protect the separation of powers between the judiciary and Parliament, the courts may rule on the existence and scope of privilege, but once a matter is deemed to be within parliamentary privilege, the matter is left to Parliament to determine.

The collective privileges include the right to determine its own composition and procedure, and to discipline its Members (but note the Parliamentary Standards Act 2009). Individual

---

84 See the Privileges and Conduct Committee, HL Paper 15, First Report, June 2012.
85 Cm 8318.

privileges include freedom from arrest for civil matters for forty days before and after a parliamentary session, and most importantly, freedom of speech in proceedings in Parliament which is protected under Article IX of the Bill of Rights 1689.

Members of Parliament have always been permitted to have employment outside Parliament and to enter into contracts for services with outside bodies. In recent years, the issue of the financial interests of both Members of Parliament and Members of the House of Lords has caused damage to the integrity of Parliament. Most recently with the abuse of MPs expenses and allowances, Parliament finally agreed to establish an independent body and Commissioner to regulate MPs' pay and expenses, under the Parliamentary Standards Act 2009, as amended by the Constitutional Reform and Governance Act 2010.

Further Reading

Denning, Lord (1985) 'The Strauss Case', Public Law, 80.
Doig, A. (2002) 'Sleaze fatigue: The House of Ill-Repute', Parliamentary Affairs 55: 389.
Geddis, A. (2005) 'Parliamentary Privilege: Quis Custodiet Ipsos Custodes?', Public Law, 696.
Leopold, P. (1991) 'Proceedings in Parliament: The Grey Area', Public Law, 475.
Leopold, P. (1995) 'Free Speech in Parliament and the Courts', Legal Studies 15: 204.
Leyland, P. (2009) 'Freedom of Information and the 2009 Parliamentary Expenses Scandal', Public Law, 675.
Parpworth, N. (2010) 'The Parliamentary Standards Act 2009: A Constitutional Dangerous Dogs Measure?' 73 MLR 262.

Part 6

The Individual and the State

Chapter 18

The Protection of Human Rights

Chapter Contents

Introduction

On the philosophy of rights see the Website and see Chapter 3 for an introduction to Social Contract theory.

The protection of the rights and freedoms of citizens and others within their jurisdiction is a fundamental duty of the state. In the majority of democratic states, fundamental rights are defined and protected by law under a written constitution. Under the United Kingdom's largely unwritten (or uncodified) constitution, rights and freedoms have traditionally been protected either by individual Acts of Parliament passed to meet a particular need[1] or by the judges in developing the common law.

One response to the ravages of the Second World War was the formation of the Council of Europe. Under its authority the European Convention on Human Rights and Fundamental Freedoms were designed to guarantee the protection of basic rights against the state. The majority of Member States (formally High Contracting Parties) – of whom there are now 47 – either had a written constitution which protected rights or they had incorporated the Convention rights into their law. For reasons discussed below, the British government remained reluctant, until 1997, to make Convention rights directly enforceable before the domestic courts. Accordingly, until the Human Rights Act 1998 Convention rights could only be enforced before the Court of Human Rights in Strasbourg.[2]

In this chapter we consider:

- the working and scope of the European Convention as enforced by the European Court of Human Rights; and
- the Human Rights Act 1998, its structure and case law.

The Emergence of the Constitutional Protection of Rights

The attempt to protect human rights on an international level began with the founding of the League of Nations after the First World War and the imposition of certain safeguards of human rights in peace treaties negotiated after the war for the protection of minorities. It was not, however, until after the Second World War that the international community became convinced of the real and pressing need to protect and promote human rights as an integral and essential element for the preservation of world peace and co-operation. The United Nations[3] provided the appropriate forum for international quasi-legislative activity. In 1948, the Universal Declaration on Human Rights was adopted, supplemented by two implementing international covenants in 1966: the International Covenant on Civil and Political Rights and the International Covenant on Economic, Social and Cultural Rights. Taken together, these documents represent an international Bill of Human Rights. Inspired by the United Nations Declaration and Covenants, many other regional conventions were drafted, for example the European Convention on Human Rights and Fundamental Freedoms 1950, the American Convention on Human Rights 1969 and the African Charter of 1987.[4]

Rights and Freedoms in Britain

It has long been a paradox that the United Kingdom – viewed as a liberal democratic state – should have no comprehensive written Bill of Rights.[5] This is especially so given that the

---

1 For example the Race Relations Acts prohibiting discrimination. See further Chapter 19.
2 The Human Rights Act 1998 came into effect in Northern Ireland and Scotland in 1998, in England and Wales in 2000.
3 Which superseded the League of Nations in 1945.
4 See also the Hong Kong Bill of Rights based on the UN Covenant on Civil and Political Rights.
5 The Bill of Rights 1689, it will be recalled, was concerned with constitutional arrangements between the Crown and Parliament, not with the rights of individuals.

United Kingdom has been responsible for restoring independence to many former colonies and dominions and, in so doing, has conferred upon those states both a written constitution and a Bill of Rights. The Human Rights Act 1998 marks a significant constitutional change in relation to citizens' awareness about rights, and their protection by judges in the domestic courts.[6] The Act and its implications are considered later in this chapter. Prior to incorporation of Convention rights, the judges used the Convention as an aid to interpretation to assist in resolving ambiguities in domestic law. However, given the supremacy of Parliament, the judges previously had no jurisdictional basis on which they could employ the Convention to protect rights. The Human Rights Act confers this jurisdiction, requiring the courts not only to protect Convention rights, but to make 'declarations of incompatibility' wherever domestic law is judicially seen to conflict with Convention rights. By this means, Parliament preserves its supremacy over changes in the law which may be required by judicial evaluation of domestic law against the provisions of the Convention. Before considering the Human Rights Act, however, it is necessary to understand the status and working of the European Convention and the scope and application of the Convention rights which the Act incorporates.

PART A: THE EUROPEAN CONVENTION ON HUMAN RIGHTS AND FUNDAMENTAL FREEDOMS AND THE HUMAN RIGHTS ACT 1998

The European Convention on Human Rights and Fundamental Freedoms

Introduction

Europe was one of the principal theatres of the Second World War, following which there was felt to be a great need for European political, social and economic unity. Those objectives were perceived to be promoted, in part, by the adoption of a uniform Convention designed to protect human rights and fundamental freedoms. In 1949, the Council of Europe was established and the Convention on Human Rights ratified by signatory states (formally High Contracting Parties) in 1951, coming into force in 1953.[7] Despite having been instrumental in the drafting of the text of the Convention, the British government had strong reservations about the Convention and its impact on British constitutional law. As a result of such reservations, it was not until 1965 that the government gave individuals the right to petition under the Convention.

The influence of the Convention before the Human Rights Act 1998[8]

The attitude of the United Kingdom courts towards the Convention was, in the past, the traditional one adopted in relation to treaties. Treaties form part of international law and have no place within the domestic legal order unless and until incorporated into law.[9] The courts

---

6　See the Consultation Paper, *Bringing Rights Home: Labour's Plans to Incorporate the European Convention on Human Rights into United Kingdom Law*, 1996, London: Labour Party. Note that technically the Human Rights Act 1998 does not incorporate the Convention, but rather makes Convention rights enforceable before the domestic courts.

7　For a succinct history of the Convention, see Lester (Lord), 'European human rights and the British constitution', in Jowell and Oliver, 2000.

8　See Browne-Wilkinson, 1992; Bingham, 1993; Laws, 1993.

9　See *Kaur v Lord Advocate* (1980).

regarded the Convention as an aid to interpretation but had no jurisdiction directly to enforce the rights and freedoms under the Convention.[10] This could, however, of itself be significant. For example, in *Waddington v Miah* (1974), Lord Reid stated – having referred to Article 7 of the Convention which prohibits retrospective legislation – that 'it is hardly credible that any government department would promote, or that Parliament would pass, retrospective criminal legislation'.[11]

R v Secretary of State for the Home Department ex parte Brind (1991) also illustrates the influence of the Convention. The Home Secretary had exercised his discretionary power under section 29(3) of the Broadcasting Act 1981 to issue a notice prohibiting the broadcasting on television or radio of the voices of any person speaking on behalf of an organisation proscribed under the Prevention of Terrorism (Temporary Provisions) Act 1974. The words used could be reported through the medium of an actor, provided that the voice of the spokesperson was not broadcast. The challenge to this prohibition was, in the House of Lords, based primarily on the argument that it was contrary to the United Kingdom's obligations under Article 10 of the Convention, guaranteeing freedom of expression. It was argued that the Home Secretary should have had regard to the Convention in exercising his discretion under the Broadcasting Act.

The House of Lords was prepared to accept that there was a presumption that Parliament would enact laws that were in conformity with the Convention. Accordingly, it was accepted that where a statute permits two interpretations, one in line with the Convention, the other contrary to it, the interpretation which fitted with the Convention should be preferred. In *Brind*, the court could find no ambiguity in section 29(3) of the Broadcasting Act.[12] The only basis for challenge therefore was that the Home Secretary's decision was unreasonable in the *Wednesbury*[13] sense: that the decision was so irrational or unreasonable that no rational or reasonable person could have reached the same decision.

A rather different approach to the Convention was adopted in **Derbyshire County Council v Times Newspapers Ltd** (1993), concerning the question of whether a local council could bring an action in libel against newspapers (see further below). In the Court of Appeal, Butler-Sloss LJ was forthright in declaring that 'where there is ambiguity, or the law is otherwise unclear as so far undeclared by an appellate court, the English court is not only entitled but . . . obliged to consider the implications of Article 10'. The House of Lords, however, while arriving at the result achieved in the Court of Appeal – namely that local authorities enjoyed no standing to sue in defamation – did so without relying on Article 10 of the Convention, but relying on the common law.

Accordingly, there existed (before the Human Rights Act 1998 came into force) no obligation on courts to rely on the Convention if a source of authority could be found within domestic law. Increasingly, however, it appeared that – within certain limits – the judiciary expressed willingness to protect individual liberties and, where a statute was ambiguous, or silent, to construe the statute strictly and in favour of the liberty of the citizen.

However, there were limits to the extent to which judges were able to protect rights, as the case of **R v Inland Revenue Commissioners ex parte Rossminster Ltd** (1980) revealed.[14] In **Rossminster**, the House of Lords ruled that, where the meaning of a statute is clear and unambiguous, the court possessed no jurisdiction to go against its unambiguous words, and was under a duty to uphold the will of Parliament by giving effect to its words.[15] In both **Attorney**

---

10 *Waddington v Miah* (1974).
11 See further below for the (retrospective) War Crimes Act 1991.
12 On the post Human Rights Act 1998 position and ambiguity, see Lord Irvine, 1998.
13 *Associated Provincial Picture Houses Ltd v Wednesbury Corporation* (1948). See further Chapter 24.
14 See also *R v Kelly, R v Sandford* (1998); and *R v Secretary of State for the Home Department ex parte Hussain Ahmed* (1998).
15 See also *R v DPP ex parte Kebeline* (1999).

General v BBC (1981) and *Attorney General v Guardian Newspapers* **(No 2)** (1990), however, the House of Lords confirmed that it was the duty of the courts to have regard to the international obligations assumed under the Convention, and to interpret the law in accordance with those obligations.

Institutions and procedure under the Convention

The Council of Europe, under which the Convention operates, is constitutionally distinct from the European Union. The Council was founded in 1949, inspired by the United Nations' Universal Declaration of Human Rights of 1948. The Committee of Ministers is the political body, consisting of one representative from each state government (Foreign Ministers). The Parliamentary Assembly of the Council of Europe (PACE) has 636 members representing the countries belonging to the Council of Europe. The Assembly has power to investigate human rights issues, to make recommendations and to advise. Its work is valuable and bodies such as the Parliament of the European Union and other European Union institutions refer to its work. The Assembly elects the Secretary General of the Council of Europe and the judges of the Court of Human Rights. The Court of Human Rights represents the judicial body. Judges are elected for a renewable six-year term of office, and need not be drawn exclusively from the judiciary. To qualify for appointment, a person must be 'of high moral character' and must either possess the qualifications required for appointment of high judicial office or be a jurisconsult of recognised competence.

The right of application

Applications may be brought by states or by individuals. The right of individual petition to a body outside the jurisdiction of states was a constitutional innovation. As noted above, the British government was exceedingly cautious about conceding such a right and only in 1965 did the right of individual application become available to citizens of the United Kingdom. Applications may come from individuals, groups of individuals or non-governmental organisations. The applicant(s) must be personally affected by the issue: complaints involving alleged conduct which does not personally affect the individual complainant are not admissible.[16]

With the Human Rights Act 1998 fully in force, individuals will only make an application to the Court of Human Rights if they fail to secure an effective remedy before the domestic courts.

The procedure

Exhaustion of domestic remedies

Any domestic remedies which are available must be exhausted.[17] Thus, if a remedy is available within domestic law, it must first be sought. Only where there exists no remedy in law, or where the pursuit of a remedy would be unequivocally certain to fail,[18] may an individual lodge a petition.

---

16 *X v Norway* (1960). See also *Vijayanathan v France* (1991).
17 ECHR, Article 35.
18 Eg, where there are strong precedents established.

The time limit
The application must be made within six months of the final decision of the highest court having jurisdiction within the domestic legal system.[19]

Admissibility
A number of hurdles face the applicant in having his application declared admissible:

(a)   a complaint must not constitute an 'abuse of right of complaint'. In essence, this means that the complainant should not be pursuing a remedy out of improper motives – such as political advantage. In short, the complaint must be brought for genuine reasons;

(b)   a complaint must not be anonymous;

(c)   a complaint must not relate to a matter which has been investigated and ruled upon previously;

(d)   a complaint must relate to a right which is protected under the Convention;

(e)   a complaint is inadmissible if, although the application relates to a protected right, the state against which the complaint is made has derogated from that provision, or lodged a reservation (see below for further discussion of derogations and reservations);

(f)   the application must relate to violation of the Convention by a state which is bound by the Convention, or to an organisation for which the state has responsibility;

(g)   the application must not be such that it represents an attack on another right protected by the Convention. Article 17 provides that there is no right to 'engage in any activity or perform any act' which is aimed at the destruction of protected rights;

(h)   a complaint must not be 'manifestly ill founded'. By this is meant that the application must be plausible – there must be prima facie evidence of a violation.

Once an application is declared admissible, the examination of the merits will commence. The complainant has a limited right to appear where the Court requires further evidence. The Court's decision must be reasoned and, if not unanimous, individual judges may give a separate opinion. Under Article 43(1) of the Convention, any party to the case may, within three months from the date of the judgment of a Chamber (effectively the 'court of first instance' hearing the case), request that the case be referred to the Grand Chamber. If it is not so referred, the judgment becomes final. Alternatively, if referred, the judgment of the Grand Chamber is final (Article 44) and states undertake to abide by the decision of the Court. Compensation can be awarded by the Court.

Enforcing the judgment
As noted above, under Article 46, states are under an obligation to comply with the judgment of the Court of Human Rights. The task of ensuring that the judgment is complied with lies with the Committee of Ministers: the matter is thus returned to the political arena. If a state refuses to comply with the judgment, its membership of the Council of Europe can be suspended or, ultimately, it may be expelled from the Council. Where exercised, this ultimate power has regrettable implications and would remove the protection of the Convention from individuals within the state and thus further damage the protection of rights. Greece withdrew from the Council of Europe following five allegations of persecution against it between 1967 and 1970. In 1974, a new Greek government ratified the Convention once more. However,

---

19 ECHR, Article 35.

failure to comply with a judgment will cause adverse publicity for the state and there is thus great political pressure to conform.[20]

The 'margin of appreciation'

In respect of almost all Articles of the Convention, there is an area of discretion as to the means by which they protect the substantive rights. This margin of appreciation is necessary in order that the Convention can apply in a workable fashion in very diverse societies. It also means, however, that application of the Convention will not be uniform throughout the legal systems and that states may be able to deviate from the protection given.

Whether the state has a margin of appreciation – and the scope of it – is a matter to be determined under the Convention. The doctrine is unpredictable in operation and has become, over the years, applicable to all Articles. Accordingly, it is a concept which is capable of significantly undermining the protection given by the Convention, and has been criticised for so doing.[21]

Derogation and reservation

Where a state finds it impossible or undesirable to comply with specific Articles, it is possible for the state to derogate, or enter a reservation as to the matter. No derogation is permitted in relation to Article 2 (the right to life), other than in war situations. Derogation is not allowed in respect of Articles 3 (freedom from torture), 4(1) (slavery or servitude), and 7 (freedom from retrospective criminal liability).[22] The right of derogation is limited. Article 15 provides that:

> In time of war or other public emergency threatening the life of the nation any High Contracting Party may take measures derogating from its obligations under this Convention to the extent strictly required by the exigencies of the situation, provided that such measures are not inconsistent with its other obligations under international law.

A challenge can be made to the lawfulness of derogation. Following the United Kingdom's derogation after the decision in **Brogan v United Kingdom** (1988), a challenge was lodged, but failed when it was held that the situation in Northern Ireland did amount to a public emergency[23] and was thus within the terms of Article 15.

Article 17: the prohibition of abuse of rights

Article 17 prohibits the state or any 'group or person' from engaging in any activity which is aimed at the destruction of rights and freedoms protected under the Convention, or from limiting the rights and freedoms to a greater extent than is provided for in the Convention.

The Convention protocols

In addition to the substantive Articles of the Convention, there exists a series of Protocols on matters ranging from the right to peaceful enjoyment of possessions (First Protocol,

---

20 On derogation from Convention right see below.
21 See Van Dijk and Van Hoof, 1990, p 604.
22 But see the War Crimes Act 1991, which provides for the prosecution of war crimes committed during World War II.
23 **Brannigan and McBride v United Kingdom** (1993).

Article 1),[24] education (First Protocol, Article 2),[25] the holding of regular free elections (First Protocol, Article 3), freedom of movement (Fourth Protocol), abolition of the death penalty (Sixth Protocol), appeals in criminal cases and sexual equality (Seventh Protocol), procedural matters under the Convention (Ninth Protocol) and minority rights (Tenth Protocol). The Eleventh Protocol abolished the Commission and provided new procedures for applying directly to the court. The United Kingdom is not a party to the Fourth, Sixth or Seventh Protocols. In relation to Article 2 of the First Protocol, the government has entered a reservation to the effect that the rights of parents to determine the education of their children are respected in the United Kingdom only to the extent that such respect is compatible with the requirements of the Education Acts.[26]

The Human Rights Act 1998

The incorporation of Convention rights into domestic law under the 1998 Act put an end, finally, to the debate over whether or not to incorporate, which had endured for decades. That long-running debate focused on three principal concerns, namely the criticism that the Convention was outdated and not tailored specifically to British conditions; that the judiciary was ill equipped to assume the mantle of guardian of individual rights in the face of executive power and the concept of parliamentary sovereignty;[27] and concerns over the manner in which 'incorporation' would affect the conventional balance of power between judges and Parliament. There was also the argument that the House of Commons, as the democratically elected representative of the people, was best equipped to respond to the better protection of rights.

The effect of the Act is such that three avenues for challenging public bodies arise:

- first, a failure to comply with Convention rights now forms the basis for legal action;
- second, a new ground for judicial review has been introduced, namely the alleged breach of human rights; and
- third, Convention rights may in some circumstances be used as a defence to actions brought by public bodies.

The Act provides a charter of rights now enforceable before the domestic courts. The effectiveness of the Human Rights Act 1998 rests on three foundations:

- the willingness of the judges robustly to defend rights and to interpret Convention rights in a manner favouring individual protection against governmental encroachment;
- Parliament's willingness to amend the law to ensure compliance with declarations of incompatibility with Convention rights; and
- the energy with which individual citizens are prepared to assert their rights in courts of law.

The manner in which the Act was drafted raises a number of questions:

- the meaning of 'public authorities' for the purposes of the Act;

---

24 See **Stretch v United Kingdom** (2003).
25 See **Belgian Linguistics Case (No 2)** (1968).
26 On 4 November 2000, Protocol 12 opened for signature. Protocol 12 introduces an independent right to equality, stating that the 'enjoyment of any right set forth by law shall be secured without discrimination, on any arbitrary ground'.
27 See Griffith, 1997; but cf Lester, 1994 and 1997.

- whether the Act has solely 'vertical' effect – binding only those bodies for which the state is accountable to Strasbourg – or is capable of also having 'horizontal' effect, and being enforceable against bodies for which the state is not accountable to Strasbourg;
- the extent to which judicial interpretative techniques relating to statutes will change, and the extent to which the judges will develop the common law to give effect to Convention rights.

As will be seen below, the case law is clarifying these issues.

The territorial reach of the Convention

Article 1 of the Convention provides that signatory states 'shall secure to everyone within their jurisdiction the rights and freedoms defined in . . . this convention'. The question which has arisen is the scope of the state's jurisdiction. It is clear that jurisdiction relates to the country itself, but it is less clear as to whether it extends to territory or property abroad but under the control of the signatory state.

The issue was considered by the House of Lords in **R (Al-Skeini and Others) v Secretary of State for Defence** (2007) in relation to acts of the armed forces overseas. The Court referred to the general rule that every statute was to be interpreted, 'so far as language permitted', so as not to be inconsistent with the established rules of international law and the comity of nations. Following the jurisprudence of the European Court of Human Rights,[28] the House of Lords ruled that the Convention reflected an essentially territorial notion of jurisdiction and that the extra-territorial exercise of jurisdiction was exceptional and required justification. The Court ruled that the Convention operates extra-territorially first in circumstances where the state has – as a consequence of military occupation or the consent of the government of that country – effective control of the relevant country. Secondly, the Convention operates in relation to diplomatic embassies/consulates and on board craft and vessels registered or flying the flag of that state.[29] It does not, however, operate in relation to armed forces serving overseas when they are not in premises which are under state control. In **R (Smith) v Secretary of State for Defence** (2010) the Supreme Court confirmed that the Convention did not operate in relation to armed forces serving overseas when not on premises which are under state control. However, in **Al-Skeini and Others v United Kingdom** (2011) the Court of Human Rights ruled that the European Convention on Human Rights applied in Southern Iraq at the time when Britain was the occupying power in that region. The European Court of Human Rights' interpretation of territorial reach is broader than either the House of Lords or its successor, the Supreme Court. Contracting states are now required to comply with the Convention 'whenever a State through its agents exercises control and authority over an individual'.

The case was brought by relatives of five Iraqis, four of whom were shot by British forces, one of whom drowned. In each case there should have been a full investigation into the circumstances surrounding the deaths by an expert and independent investigator. The Military Special Investigation Branch (SIB) was not independent and therefore was not an appropriate investigator: there was a violation of Article 2 of the Convention.

---

28 See **Bankovic v Belgium** (2001); **Drozd v France** (1992); **Issa v Turkey** (2004).
29 On territorial reach, see also **R (Al-Saadoon) v Secretary of State for Defence** (2009).

A further illustration of the scope of the Convention arose in **R (Al Rawi) v Secretary of State for Foreign and Commonwealth Affairs** (2006), in which the Court of Appeal considered allegations of discrimination on the part of the Foreign Office between British nationals and non-nationals; the scope of responsibility of the state for non-nationals and the justiciability of the conduct of foreign affairs. The claimants were imprisoned by the United States authorities at Guantanamo Bay and sought judicial review of the Secretary of State's refusal to make diplomatic representations requesting their release and return to Britain, alleging discrimination on grounds of nationality and a violation of their rights under the European Convention. The Court of Appeal ruled that the difference in treatment between the claimants and British citizens in the same position was that the claimants, as non-nationals, were not persons the United Kingdom was under a duty to protect. On the issue of the justiciability of foreign policy, the court reiterated the principle that matters of 'delicate policy' were for the executive and not the courts.

The status of the Human Rights Act

As discussed in Chapter 6, under the constitution of the United Kingdom, and consistent with the doctrine of parliamentary sovereignty, legislation cannot be entrenched. That is to say, it cannot be given a 'special' or 'higher' status than other Acts of Parliament. This traditional doctrine has been preserved in relation to the Human Rights Act. In its White Paper, the government announced that it did not intend to permit the courts to strike down Acts of Parliament, whether that legislation preceded the Act or was introduced subsequently. Thereby, Parliament's sovereignty and, to the extent possible, the separation of powers, are preserved. The Act, in the government's view, was 'intended to provide a new basis for judicial interpretation of all legislation, not a basis for striking down any part of it'.[30]

However, notwithstanding the careful drafting of the Human Rights Act in order to preserve sovereignty, the judges appear to be developing the concept of the 'constitutional statute',[31] one consequence of which is that the doctrine of implied repeal does not operate and only an express intention to amend or repeal the Act will have effect.

The meaning of public authorities[32]

The Human Rights Act 1998 provides that public authorities exercising executive powers must comply with the requirements of the Convention. The European Convention imposes responsibilities on signatory states to protect rights, and as such it is the state and its agencies which are the defendants in allegations of Convention violations before the Court of Human Rights. The emphasis on public bodies/authorities under the Human Rights Act reflects this now traditional form of state liability.[33] As will be seen, however, the impact of the Human Rights Act is extending beyond the sphere of public bodies for which the state is responsible.

Section 6(3)(b) of the Act provides that a public authority includes 'any person certain of whose functions are functions of a public nature'. The test, therefore, is not state ownership, funding or control *per se* but rather the functions which a body performs. The position is complicated by section 6(5), which provides that a person is not a public authority (applying the functions test) 'if the nature of the act is private'. Accordingly, the Act recognises that some authorities may, notwithstanding their ownership or control or funding by the state, be public

---

30   White Paper, *Rights Brought Home: The Human Rights Bill*, Cm 3782, 1997, London: HMSO, para 2.14. However, the courts are given power over delegated, or secondary, legislation.
31   See **R v Secretary of State for the Home Department ex parte Simms** (2000); **Thoburn v Sunderland City Council** (2002).
32   See Oliver, 2004; Sunkin, 2004.
33   See Oliver, 2000.

on the functions test, but will not be treated as public bodies in relation to some actions which are deemed to be private. An example given in debate was that of Network Rail, which is a public authority when exercising its function as a safety regulator, but acts privately in its role as property developer.[34]

The definition of 'public body' was considered by the Court of Appeal in **R (Heather) v Leonard Cheshire Foundation** (2002). The Foundation is a private charity which provides accommodation for the disabled, some of which is funded by the local authority pursuant to its statutory duty under the National Assistance Act 1948, as amended. The court made it clear that residents of the home funded by the local authority could rely on their Convention rights against the authority but not against the charity, since it was not exercising public functions. Aside from the funding being provided by the state, there was no other evidence 'of there being a public flavour to the functions of the foundation or the foundation itself. The foundation was not standing in the shoes of the local authorities'.[35] In **Aston Cantlow and Billesley Parochial Church Council v Wallbank** (2003), the House of Lords ruled that a Parochial Church Council which had statutory duties to enforce parish church repairs was not a public authority for the purposes of the Human Rights Act. The Court ruled that although the Church of England had special links with central government and performed certain public functions, it was not a core public authority.

The 'functions test' which is central to whether a body is a public body and therefore bound by the Human Rights Act was considered by the House of Lords in **YL v Birmingham City Council and Others** (2007).[36] The case involved the rights of a resident in a private care home who had been placed there by her local authority, which paid the fees[37] save for a small top-up fee paid by her relatives. The Court ruled, Lord Bingham of Cornhill dissenting, that the company acted as a private, profit-earning company. Lord Bingham in his dissent, however, stated that this situation was 'precisely the case which section 6(3)(b) was intended to embrace'.[38] The unsatisfactory outcome of this decision, which left an estimated 300,000 elderly people living in private care homes unprotected by the Human Rights Act, was essentially caused by the undefined dividing line between public and private functions. The law has now been reformed. The Health and Social Care Act 2008, section 145, states that those providing accommodation under the National Assistance Act 1948 or equivalent Scottish and Northern Ireland statutes are exercising functions of a public nature.

However, the classification of bodies (public or private) does not exhaust the potential for the Act to develop the protection of human rights, because according to section 6 the courts themselves are public authorities and are under a statutory duty to give effect to Convention rights. Accordingly, the courts may, in complying with their section 6 duty, enforce Convention rights against private – or non-state – bodies.[39]

Section 2: The European Court of Human Rights and domestic courts

Section 2 of the Human Rights Act 1998 requires the court to 'take into account the judgments, decisions, declarations or advisory opinions' of the European Court of Human Rights,

---

34 See HC Deb Vol 314 Cols 406–414, 17 June 1998, and Col 1231 16 November 1997. The Home Secretary in debate stated that the British Broadcasting Corporation is a public authority but that independent television companies are not, whilst the Independent Television Commission is: *Hansard* Col 778, 16 December 1998.

35 See also **Poplar Housing and Regeneration Community Association Ltd v Donoghue** (2001): a housing association performing functions analogous to the local authority was a public authority for the purposes of the Act.

36 The decision was reached by a majority of three to two.

37 Pursuant to its duty under section 21 of the National Assistance Act 1948 as amended by s 195 of and para 2 of Sched 23 to the Local Government Act 1989.

38 At p 118, para 20. Baroness Hale echoed this approach: see p 132, para 73.

39 See Wade, 2000, p 223; cf Hunt, 1998. There is an analogy here with Article 10 of the EC Treaty, which the Court of Justice has used to great effect in extending the liability of Member States. See further Chapter 8.

Commission and Committee of Ministers. This does not, however, mean that the courts are bound to follow slavishly such judgments. The issue was central to the case of **Kay v Lambeth LBC; Leeds City Council v Price** (2006), in which the House of Lords considered both sections 2 and 6 of the Human Rights Act 1998. In the **Leeds** case before the Court of Appeal, the court concluded that the decision of **Connors v United Kingdom** (2004) was inconsistent with the earlier decision of the House of Lords in **Harrow LBC v Qazi** (2004) and that they were bound to follow the House of Lords. Lord Bingham of Cornhill recognised that effective implementation of the Convention depended upon 'constructive collaboration' between the Court of Human Rights and national courts. He also, however, insisted that adherence to precedent was a 'cornerstone of the legal system' which ensured a degree of certainty. In **R v Horncastle, R v Marquis** (2009), the Supreme Court made an important statement of principle concerning the duty to follow the case law of the Court of Human Rights. In this case, the applicants argued that their right to fair trial had been violated, based on the decision of the Court of Human Rights in **Al-Khawaja and Tahery v United Kingdom** (2009). Rejecting that argument, Lord Phillips of Worth Matravers PSC stated that on rare occasions the domestic court might have concerns that the Court of Human Rights had not 'sufficiently appreciated or accommodated particular aspects of the domestic process'. In those circumstances the domestic court could decline to follow the Strasbourg decision, giving reasons for doing so. That could then lead to a 'valuable dialogue' between the domestic and Strasbourg courts.

Section 3: The interpretative duty[40]

Section 3 of the Human Rights Act 1998 requires that primary and secondary legislation, whenever enacted, must be interpreted and applied in a manner consistent with Convention rights. However, section 3(2) makes it clear that this requirement does not affect the validity, continuing operation or enforcement of any incompatible primary legislation, and does not affect the validity, continuing operation or enforcement of incompatible subordinate legislation, if the primary legislation prevents removal of the incompatibility.[41] The definition of primary legislation is provided in section 21 of the Act, which in part provides that primary legislation includes any 'public general Act, local and personal Act, private Act . . . and Order in Council made in exercise of Her Majesty's Royal Prerogative'. It was seen in Chapter 5 that Acts of Parliament have always been deemed to have superior force to acts of the prerogative,[42] and that where a claimed prerogative power is held to exist, if it is not expressly overruled by statute, it will be held to be 'in abeyance' and the statute will prevail. The Human Rights Act 1998, however, appears to elevate Orders in Council to the same status as Acts of Parliament, thereby making them immune from invalidation by the courts. Accordingly, whereas the courts may set aside secondary legislation which is incompatible with the Convention – unless the parent Act makes this impossible – Orders in Council regulating the exercise of the prerogative may not be so set aside.[43]

Declarations of incompatibility are regulated under section 4, which provides that if a court is satisfied that a provision of primary or subordinate legislation is incompatible with one or more Convention rights, it may make a declaration of incompatibility. The courts with the jurisdiction to make declarations of incompatibility are the House of Lords, the Judicial Committee of the Privy Council, the Courts-Martial Appeal Court; in Scotland, the High Court

---

40 See Lord Irvine, 2003.
41 See Feldman, 2002.
42 See *Attorney General v de Keyser's Royal Hotel Ltd* (1920); **R v Secretary of State for the Home Department ex parte Fire Brigades' Union** (1995).
43 See Allen and Sales, 2000.

of Justiciary, sitting as a court of criminal appeal, or the Court of Session; and, in England, Wales and Northern Ireland, the High Court or Court of Appeal. Section 4(6), however, contains a vital limitation, in that a declaration of incompatibility does not affect the validity, continuing operation or enforcement of the provision in question, and is not binding on the parties to the proceedings in which it is made. However, where the court finds a violation of a Convention right, it has the power under section 8 to grant a remedy to the victim. The power to amend the law has thereby been preserved for the government and Parliament.[44]

In **Wilson v First County Trust Ltd (No 2)** (2003), the House of Lords took the opportunity to examine the structure and workings of the Human Rights Act. The House of Lords ruled that there was no power to grant a declaration under section 4 of the Human Rights Act unless the interpretative duty under section 3 had been engaged. There was a powerful presumption against the retrospective application of the Act, and, in relation to transactions which had taken place prior to the coming into force of the Act, there could be no question of interpretation under section 3 and accordingly no power to grant a declaration under section 4.

Proportionality[45]

In the exercise of the interpretative duty under section 3 of the Human Rights Act 1998, the courts have rapidly adapted to the approach of the Court of Human Rights in employing the concepts of *proportionality* and *necessity*, which give greater scope for the protection of rights than the conventional concepts employed in judicial review under the umbrella of the **Wednesbury**[46] unreasonableness test. Even before the Human Rights Act 1998 came into effect, the courts were developing a more vigorous approach to the protection of rights. In **R v Ministry of Defence ex parte Smith** (1996), it was recognised that in judicial review proceedings, where human rights were in issue, the courts should 'anxiously scrutinise' executive decisions. That approach, however, did not satisfy the interpretative duty according to Lord Steyn in **R (Daly) v Secretary of State for the Home Department** (2001), where he stated that while there was an overlap between the traditional **Wednesbury** grounds for review and the proportionality approach, there was nevertheless 'a material difference between the **Wednesbury** and **Smith** grounds of review and the approach of proportionality applicable in respect of review where Convention rights are at stake'.

Lord Steyn cited Lord Clyde's approach in **de Freitas v Permanent Secretary of Ministry of Agriculture, Fisheries, Lands and Housing** (1999), namely that in considering whether a restriction on a right is 'arbitrary' or 'excessive', the court should ask itself:

. . . whether:

(i) the legislative objective is sufficiently important to justify limiting a fundamental right;

(ii) the measures designed to meet the legislative objective are rationally connected to it; and

(iii) the means used to impair the right or freedom are no more than is necessary to accomplish thte objective.'

In Lord Steyn's analysis there are three 'concrete differences' between the traditional grounds for judicial review and the proportionality test, namely:

---

44 See below on declarations made under the 1998 Act.
45 See also pp 616–619.
46 *Associated Provincial Picture Houses Ltd v Wednesbury Corporation* (1948).

First, the doctrine of proportionality may require the reviewing court to assess the balance which the decision maker has struck, not merely whether it is within the range of rational or reasonable decisions.

Secondly, the proportionality test may go further than the traditional grounds of review inasmuch as it may require attention to be directed to the relative weight accorded to interests and considerations.

Thirdly, even the heightened scrutiny test developed in *R v Ministry of Defence, ex p Smith* (1996) is not necessarily appropriate to the protection of human rights.

Convention rights, section 3 and statute[47]

Section 3 of the Human Rights Act requires the courts to interpret primary and subordinate legislation in a way which is compatible with Convention rights, 'so far as it is possible to do so'.[48] The House of Lords in **R v A (Complainant's Sexual History)** (2002)[49] gave guidance as to the correct approach. At issue was whether the statutory restrictions on the admissibility of evidence prejudiced the right to fair trial.[50] The Court ruled that it first had to consider whether a legislative provision interfered with a Convention right. If there was an interference, then the court had to look at the legislative purpose of the provision and employ the concept of proportionality. Three issues had to be considered:

- first, was the legislative objective sufficiently important to justify limiting a fundamental right?
- second, were the measures adopted to meet that objective rationally connected to it?
- third, the court must be satisfied that the means used to impair the right or freedom were no more than necessary to accomplish the objective (the proportionality test).

Section 3 of the Human Rights Act 'went further than requiring the court to take the Convention into account: the court had a duty to strive to find a possible interpretation compatible with Convention rights'. Lord Steyn stated that this might even require the courts 'to adopt an interpretation which may appear linguistically strained'.[51]

Section 3 provided the basis for the reinterpretation of a statutory provision to make it compatible with Convention rights in **Ghaidan v Godin-Mendoza** (2004). The Rent Act 1977[52] provided that on the death of a protected tenant his or her surviving spouse, if then living in the house 'as his or her wife or husband', became a statutory tenant by succession. The House of Lords in **Fitzpatrick v Sterling Housing Association Ltd** (2001) had ruled that this provision did not include same-sex relationships. In **Ghaidan**, however, the House of Lords used Article 3 as a remedial section and reinterpreted the provision to read 'as if they were his wife or husband' and thereby protected the tenancy. Lord Steyn stated that it was necessary ' . . . to emphasise that interpretation under section 3(1) is the prime remedial remedy and that resort to section 4 must always be an exceptional course'.

---

47 See Klug and Starmer, 2001.
48 See Bennion, 2000.
49 On the joinder of the Home Secretary under s 5 see **R v A** (2001).
50 Under consideration was the Youth Justice and Criminal Evidence Act 1999, s 41(3)(c), which precluded evidence and questioning about a complainant's sexual history in an attempt to redress the problems of low conviction rates and outmoded stereotypes of women.
51 See also **R v Ashworth Special Hospital Authority ex parte N** (2001) and **R v Secretary of State for the Home Department ex parte Mellor** (2001), discussed below.
52 Schedule 1, para 2(2).

The interpretative duty was clear in the case of **Principal Reporter v K (Scotland)** (2010). In that case an unmarried father had been denied the opportunity to participate in discussion concerning his natural child's future, on the grounds that he was not a 'relevant person' under section 93 of the Children (Scotland) Act 1995. The Supreme Court ruled that there was an incompatibility between section 93 and Article 8, but that the incompatibility could be 'cured' by reading in words to the statute to make the natural father a 'relevant person'.

The limits of interpretation

Strive as the judges may to interpret statutes compatibly, there are limits. First, it is clear that the 1998 Act is not retrospective. For example, in **R v Kensal (No 2)** (2001), the House of Lords ruled that it should follow its previous decision notwithstanding that a majority of the House now believed the precedent case to have been wrongly decided. Note, however, that this case involved a pre-Human Rights Act precedent. The court ruled that if Parliament had intended convictions valid before the Act came into force to be re-opened on the basis of rights conferred by the 1998 Act, it would have said so clearly.[53]

In **Pearce v Governing Body of Mayfield School** (2001), the Court of Appeal considered the issue of gender orientation in relation to discrimination under the Human Rights Act 1998. Disruptive pupils abused a lesbian teacher at the school in the early 1990s. Such conduct was not discriminatory under the Sex Discrimination Act 1975. Since the Human Rights Act was not in force at the time of the conduct in question, the applicant could not seek compensation under that Act. In **Secretary of State for the Home Department v Wainwright** (2002), the Court of Appeal affirmed that there was no tort of invasion of privacy at common law, and that because the conduct complained of occurred in 1997, before the Human Rights Act came into force, section 3(1) of the Act did not apply to introduce a right to privacy retrospectively. Mrs Wainwright and her son had been strip-searched by prison officers,[54] having been told that they were under suspicion of bringing drugs into the prison when visiting an inmate. They consented to the searches. The county court judge ruled that the tort of trespass to the person had been committed and awarded damages. The claimants relied on section 3 of the 1998 Act, arguing that once the Act was in force the court had the duty to comply with it even though the matters complained of took place before the Act came into force.[55] The Lord Chief Justice stated that the 1998 Act could not change substantive law by introducing a retrospective right to privacy which did not exist at common law.

The second limitation lies in the distinction between legitimate interpretation and the 'redrafting' of statutes. For example, in **In re W and B (Children: Care Plan)** (2002), the Court of Appeal considered the interpretive duty and held that the duties of local authorities under the Children Act 1989 should be subject to a system of 'starred milestones' which require authorities to implement care plans within time limits. No such provision had been made by Parliament in the Children Act. In the House of Lords Lord Nicholls ruled that section 3 of the 1998 Act maintained the constitutional boundary between interpretation by the courts and the enactment and amendment of statutes by Parliament, and that an interpretation of an Act which departed from an essential feature of an Act of Parliament was likely to have crossed the boundary. Here, Parliament had entrusted local authorities with responsibility for looking after children in care. The House of Lords ruled that the Court of Appeal's interpretation went

---

53 See also **R v Secretary of State for the Home Department ex parte Mahmood (Amjad)** (2001).
54 Under r 86(1) of the Prison Rules (SI 1964/388), made pursuant to the Prison Act 1952, s 47.
55 **R v Kensal (No 2)** (2001) did not decide this point.

beyond the boundary of interpretation and exceeded its judicial jurisdiction.[56] Although the line between legislating and interpreting may appear to be fine, it is nevertheless understood by the judges.

Convention rights, interpretation and common law

The Lord Chancellor in debate stated that:

> . . . it is right as a matter of principle for the courts to have the duty of acting compatibly with the Convention not only in cases involving other public authorities but also in developing the common law in deciding cases between individuals. Why should they not?[57]

While section 3 does not refer to common law, as seen above, the Act requires that the common law be developed consistently with Convention rights, and section 6, which includes courts and tribunals as public bodies, underpins the jurisdiction. Development of the common law has been seen most clearly in relation to privacy, which engages three issues. First, there is no common law right to privacy: as Glidewell LJ stated in **Kaye v Robertson** (1991), 'It is well-known that in English law there is no right to privacy.' Second, privacy rights under common law derive from a relationship of confidence and breach of that confidentiality. Thirdly, Article 8 protects privacy rights in relation to family life, the home and correspondence. In **Venables v News Group Newspapers Ltd** (2001), an injunction was granted which prevents, indefinitely, the media from revealing the identity and whereabouts of the applicant. Butler-Sloss LJ recognised that the defendant newspapers were not within the definition of public authorities, but nevertheless asserted that the court – as a public authority – must itself act compatibly with the Convention. Article 8 of the Convention thus prevailed over Article 10 (freedom of expression) and was applied against a private body, thereby giving horizontal effect to the right.[58]

The doctrines of proportionality and necessity, developed by the Court of Human Rights, have been accepted as judicial tools in the enforcement of Convention rights. In **R (Daly) v Secretary of State for the Home Department** (2001), for example, in the House of Lords, in declaring the prison policy of requiring prisoners to leave their cells for the purpose of searches, including searches of privileged legal correspondence, unlawful, Lord Bingham of Cornhill stated that his conclusions had been reached 'on an orthodox application of common law principles' but stated that the same result would yield by reliance on the Convention. However, he recognised that this coincidence between common law and Convention might not always occur. Lord Steyn was more explicit regarding the requirements of proportionality. Citing Lord Clyde in **De Freitas v Permanent Secretary of Ministry of Agriculture, Fisheries, Lands and Housing** (1999), Lord Steyn declared that the criteria to be applied are 'more precise and more sophisticated than the traditional grounds of review', and that under the proportionality approach 'the intensity of review is somewhat greater'. Where there has been an infringement of a right, it must be established that the limitation of the right 'was necessary in a democratic society, in the sense of meeting a pressing social need, and the question whether the interference was really proportionate to the legitimate aim being pursued'.

---

56 See **Poplar Housing and Regeneration Community Association Ltd and Secretary of State for the Environment v Donoghue** (2001).
57 *Hansard* 583 HL Deb 783, 24 November 1997. And see Lord Irvine, 1998, in which the Lord Chancellor stated that 'the Convention rights must pervade all law and all court systems' (at p 232).
58 See also **Campbell v MGN Ltd** (2002) and **Douglas v Hello! Ltd** (2002), and Chapter 20.

Section 5 of the Human Rights Act

Section 5 of the Human Rights Act 1998 confers on a minister the right to be heard. The purpose of section 5(2) is to ensure that the appropriate minister has an opportunity to address the court on the objects and purposes of the legislation in question and any other matters which might be relevant. In **R v A (Joinder of Appropriate Minister)** (2001), the House of Lords ruled that where an issue was raised in criminal proceedings which might lead to the House of Lords considering making a declaration of compatibility, it was appropriate to join the Crown in advance of the appeal hearing. Where the Crown was already represented by the Director of Public Prosecutions, his role as prosecutor was different from that of a government minister in the discharge of executive responsibilities. The House granted the application for joinder made by the Home Secretary, who bore responsibility for promotion of the legislation in question. See also **Wilson v First County Trust Ltd (No 2)** (2003) (discussed above) in which the Attorney General appeared on behalf of the Speaker of the House of Commons and the Clerk of the Parliament intervened.

Declarations of incompatibility

Where the superior courts[59] are unable to interpret statutes in a manner which makes them compatible with Convention rights, a declaration of incompatibility may be issued. This puts the government and Parliament 'on notice' that the statute requires amendment.[60] The Court of Appeal has ruled that a declaration should not be granted to a claimant who had not been, and could not be adversely affected by, impugned legislation in **Lancashire County Council v Taylor** (2005).

There are a number of explanations for the relatively low number of declarations which have been issued. First, as **Wilson v First County Trust Ltd** (2003) makes clear, the power to make a declaration only arises where the duty of interpretation is engaged, and that cannot be engaged where the facts occurred before the Human Rights Act came into force. Secondly, there have been several cases in which the High Court has issued a declaration but this has been overturned on appeal. Thirdly, where there are defects in procedures or administrative practices, the courts will generally hold that these are cured by the supervisory jurisdiction of the courts. Finally, there is emerging from the case law a 'doctrine of deference'.

The doctrine of deference[61]

It is apparent from the case law that the judges are very conscious of the invisible boundary line between those matters on which they regard themselves as competent to adjudicate and those matters which should be left for the democratically elected government. This is the doctrine of deference. The doctrine may be compared with that of justiciability under judicial review. The principal distinction lies in the fact that whereas courts will rule on justiciability in order to decide whether to review, with deference the courts conduct an examination and then decide that they should defer to the elected government and/or Parliament on the grounds of competence and/or democratic principle. The concept is also similar to the concept of margin of appreciation, which is used by the Court of Human Rights and which confers on

---

59 The High Court and above.
60 See **R (D) v Secretary of State for the Home Department** (2002).
61 See Jowell, 2003; Jowell, 'Judicial deference and human rights: a question of competence', in Craig and Rawlings, 2003; Edwards, 2002; Oliver, 2003, Chapter 6; Steyn, 2005.

states an area of discretion with which the Court will not interfere.[62] 'Deference' may also be expressed in the form of competence – in the form of the question: 'Is this matter within the competence of the courts to decide or for Parliament and/or the executive?' Underlying the concept is the desire to preserve the separation of powers between the judiciary, executive and legislature and to protect the judges from charges that they are interfering in another institution's legitimate sphere of power. Notwithstanding the legitimacy of the objective, there is a fine line to be drawn between deferring to another institution and failing adequately to protect human rights – the duty which has been conferred on the judges by the Human Rights Act.

The doctrine can be illustrated by reference to a number of cases. For example, in **R v Secretary of State for the Environment ex parte Holding and Barnes plc** (2001) (the **Alconbury** case) – in which it was argued that the Secretary of State's power to rule on planning matters contravened the requirements of a fair and independent tribunal – the House of Lords held that decisions relating to planning were best made by the executive. In **R v Lichniak** (2002) the House of Lords ruled that the imposition of a mandatory life sentence on all convicted murderers did not violate Articles 3 and/or 5 and was a matter of policy best determined by the democratically-elected Parliament. In **ProLife Alliance v BBC** (2003) the House of Lords overturned the decision of the Court of Appeal which had ruled that freedom of political expression overrode the duty of the BBC not to broadcast material which was offensive. Lord Hoffmann – in the course of criticising the term 'deference' – argued that the decision was one 'within the proper competence of the legislature' – not the courts. Furthermore, in **R v Lambert** (2001) Lord Woolf stated that the courts:

> . . . should as a matter of constitutional principle pay a degree of deference to the view of Parliament as to what is in the interest of the public generally when upholding the rights of the individual under the Convention.

Making an application under the Act

Section 7(3) of the Act provides that an individual may make an application to the courts if, and only if, he or she 'is, or would be, a victim of an unlawful act'.[63] A person claiming that a public authority has acted, or proposes to act, in a way made unlawful by section 6(1) may bring proceedings against the authority, or may rely on the Convention right concerned in any legal proceedings. In relation to judicial review proceedings, the victim test is also applied, giving a narrower meaning to 'sufficient interest' (or 'standing') than that applied under other judicial review proceedings.

The definition of standing follows the approach of the Court of Human Rights. A victim or potential victim has standing, as does a person who, while not the immediate victim of an alleged violation, is nevertheless affected. An example is a family member of a person deported or threatened with deportation where this violates the Article 8 right to family life. The position of third parties who are not directly affected is more complex and gives rise to differing tests to be applied depending on the type of proceedings being brought. The sufficient interest – or standing – requirements in judicial review proceedings allow 'public interest' organisations to bring proceedings. Help the Aged, the Child Poverty Action Group

---

62 The margin of appreciation is a concept derived from international law: it has no application within domestic law.
63 On the interpretation of victim see **Lancashire County Council v Taylor** (2005).

and the Joint Council for the Welfare of Immigrants have all been taken to have standing.[64] Standing for the purposes of the Human Rights Act, however, excludes interest groups unless they can establish that their members are actual or potential victims. Interest groups whose members are not victims, but who have special expertise in an area (for example, environmental groups such as Greenpeace or Friends of the Earth), will not have standing. They will, however, be permitted to make submissions to the court on matters within their expertise. In debate, the Lord Chancellor, referring the practice before the Court of Human Rights, stated that '. . . our courts will be ready to permit *amicus* written briefs from non-governmental organisations; that is to say briefs, but not to treat them as full parties', and further that '. . . I dare say that the courts will be equally hospitable to oral interventions, provided that they are brief'.[65]

Proceedings must be brought within one year of the date on which the act complained of took place, but this limit may be extended by the court if it considers it 'equitable', having regard to any stricter time limit imposed on the proceedings in question (section 7(5) of the Act). 'Legal proceedings' is defined to mean proceedings brought by a public authority and appeals against the decision of a court or tribunal (section 7(6)).

Remedies

Article 13 of the Convention, which provides that everyone shall have an effective remedy before a national authority, has not been incorporated. Instead, section 8 of the Human Rights Act regulates remedies. Section 8 provides that, where a court finds that a public authority has acted unlawfully, it may grant 'such relief or remedy, or make such order within its jurisdiction as it considers just and appropriate'. Accordingly, courts and tribunals may only award a remedy which is within their statutory powers.

Damages may only be awarded by a court which has power to award damages or to order the payment of compensation in civil proceedings, and no award of damages is to be made unless, taking into account all the circumstances of the case and any other relief or remedy available, the court is satisfied that the award is necessary to afford just satisfaction to the complainant. The court must take into account the principles applied by the Court of Human Rights in relation to the award of compensation under Article 41. In many instances, a finding of a violation may be deemed to be a sufficient remedy. However, the full range of remedies – declarations, injunctions and the prerogative orders (quashing orders, mandatory orders and prohibitory orders) – are also available to those courts and tribunals with the power to grant them.

One question which arises is the issue whether or not section 8 provides an adequate remedy according to the jurisprudence of the European Court of Human Rights.[66] The courts are under a duty, under section 2, to take into account the case law developed in Strasbourg. Accordingly, there is the potential for considerable case law on the relationship between section 8 of the Human Rights Act 1998 and Article 13 of the Convention.

Ensuring legislative conformity with Convention rights

Ensuring that domestic legislation conforms to Convention requirements involves two procedures. The first relates to the enactment of legislation generally, and the second relates to legislative action taken after a declaration of incompatibility has been issued by the courts.

---

64 See **R v Sefton Metropolitan Borough Council ex parte Help the Aged** (1997); **R v Secretary of State for Social Security ex parte Joint Council for the Welfare of Immigrants** (1997); and **R v Lord Chancellor ex parte Child Poverty Action Group** (1998).

65 *Hansard* HL Deb Col 834, 24 November 1997.

66 See **Chahal v United Kingdom** (1996).

In relation to legislative proposals, the Act provides for declarations to be made to Parliament that the proposed legislation conforms to Convention requirements. Section 19 requires that a minister in charge of a Bill in either House of Parliament must, before second reading, make a statement to the effect that either a Bill does comply with Convention rights or that, although such a statement cannot be made, the government nevertheless wishes to proceed with the Bill.

In relation to remedial legislation, the Act introduces a special legislative procedure for reform. While this mechanism preserves the principle that it is Parliament, as the democratically elected legislature, which is sovereign in making and reforming law, it also opens the door to the possibility that governments of differing political persuasions may react with greater or lesser enthusiasm to declarations of incompatibility. The extent to which successive governments respond to the ruling of the courts thus lies in the *moral* rather than *legal* authority of the Convention.

The fast-track legislative procedure

Where a higher court[67] makes a declaration of incompatibility, or where the Court of Human Rights in Strasbourg declares that the Convention has been violated, the relevant government minister will have power to enact amending legislation by Order in Council (a 'remedial order'). Other than where it is necessary for the Order to have immediate effect, the Order will be subject to the approval of both Houses of Parliament, and will only come into effect once approval has been secured. Section 10 and Schedule 2 regulate remedial action and remedial orders.

Two procedures are provided for. Under the standard procedure,[68] a draft of the order must be laid before Parliament for a 60-day period before it is approved by resolution of each House. When laying the draft instrument, the minister must also provide the 'required information', which entails an explanation of:

> . . . the incompatibility which the proposed order seeks to remove, including particulars of the court declaration, finding or order which caused the minister to propose a remedial order; and a statement of the reasons for proceeding under section 10 and for making an order in the terms proposed.[69]

During the period in which the draft is laid before Parliament, representations may be made to the minister, either by Parliament or by any other person. If representations are made, the draft must be accompanied by a statement containing a summary of the representations and details of any changes introduced into the proposed order as a result of the representations.[70] Section 10 and Schedule 2 also provide that, if a minister considers that there are 'compelling reasons', he may make such amendments to legislation as he considers necessary to remove the incompatibility, by means of a statutory instrument. The power applies to both primary and subordinate legislation, thus conferring on the executive potentially wide law-making power – subject ultimately to Parliament's approval. In debate on the Bill, the Lord Chancellor stated that 'if legislation has been declared to be incompatible, a prompt parliamentary remedy should be available'.[71]

---

67 As interpreted by the Human Rights Act 1998, s 6.
68 Ibid, Sched 2.
69 Human Rights Act 1998, Sched 2, para 3.
70 Ibid, Sched 2, para 2.
71 *Hansard* HL Col 1231, 3 November 1997.

Derogations and reservations

The Human Rights Act 1998 makes provision for derogations and reservations in sections 14 to 17. Derogations are discussed on page 403 above.

In relation to reservations, section 15 provides in part that:

(1) In this Act, 'designated reservation' means:

  (a) the United Kingdom's reservation to Article 2 of the first protocol to the Convention [the right to education in conformity with parents' religious and philosophical convictions]; and

  (b) any other reservation by the United Kingdom to an Article of the Convention or of any protocol to the Convention, which is designated for the purposes of this Act in an order made by the Secretary of State.

PART B: THE SUBSTANTIVE RIGHTS

Case Law

Article 1 provides that states will 'secure to everyone within jurisdiction the rights and freedoms defined in Section 1 of this Convention'.

Article 2: the right to life

Article 2 guarantees the right to life. There is no violation of Article 2 where loss of life is caused by reasonable self-defence against unlawful violence or use of necessary force to effect a lawful arrest or to quell civil unrest. The scope of this Article is broad but vague. It is, for example, unclear as to the duty, if any, which is imposed on states to sustain life by providing the economic and social conditions under which the right to life is meaningfully upheld. In **Simon-Herald v Austria** (1971), for instance, allegations that the state had failed to provide adequate medical care to prisoners was ruled admissible, although a friendly settlement was reached thus avoiding the need for a judicial analysis.[72] The Court of Human Rights ruled, in **Evans v United Kingdom** (2006) that an embryo has no right to life. English law which required the consent of both parties to fertility treatment and which could be withdrawn up to the point of implantation of an embryo did not violate Article 2.

The allowable exceptions to the protection of Article 2 are designed to excuse unintentional causes of death in violent situations. Thus the use of plastic bullets in a riot will not violate Article 2,[73] nor will measures taken to prevent possible future terrorist activities.[74] There are, however, limits to the lawful use of force. The killing of three Irish Republican Army members by members of the SAS in Gibraltar was challenged under the Convention. In **McGann, Farrell and Savage v United Kingdom** (1995), the Court ruled that, given the information which the security forces had received regarding the movements of the suspected terrorists, their shooting did not violate Article 2 of the Convention. Nevertheless, the Court ruled that there had been inadequate control over the security forces operation and that, as a result, the killing of the suspected terrorists was 'more than absolutely necessary' as provided within Article 2. Thus the action taken, to be lawful, must be proportionate to the circumstances of the case.[75] A violation of Article 2 was also found in **Andronicus v Cyprus** (1996), a case arising when the police, in a siege operation, fired at the hostage taker but killed the hostage. It was held that the number of bullets fired reflected a lack of caution in the operation.

In **Jordan v United Kingdom** (2001), the Court ruled that the authorities had failed to conduct a proper investigation into the circumstances of the persons killed in the fight against terrorism. The required investigation had to be independent and effective in the sense that it was capable of leading to a determination of whether the force used was or was not justified in the circumstances and to the identification and punishment of those responsible: there is thus a procedural aspect to Article 2.[76] The duty to conduct an independent and effective investigation applies in respect of deaths caused to civilians killed during security operations oversees.[77] See also **Edwards v United Kingdom** (2002), where the United Kingdom was found to have violated Article 2 through its failure to protect the life of a prisoner who was killed in his cell.

---

72 See Articles 38 and 39. Where a friendly settlement is reached the Court gives the case no further consideration.
73 *Stewart v United Kingdom* (1985).
74 **Kelly v United Kingdom** (1993).
75 Compare *Kelly v United Kingdom* (1993).
76 See also *McShane v United Kingdom* (2002) and *Brecknell v United Kingdom* (2007). See also **In re McCaughey** (2011) in which the Supreme Court ruled that the procedural duty applies to inquests held before the Human Rights Act came into effect.
77 See *Al-Skeini v United Kingdom* (2011).

The Substantive Rights

Absolute rights
Article 3, freedom from torture, degrading or inhuman punishment or treatment is an 'absolute' right; there are no restrictions – one cannot be subject to 'a bit of torture'

Qualified rights
Article 2, right to protection of life, is qualified in that the wording of this right expressly provides that a death at the hands of the State may be lawful in certain prescribed circumstances such as use for defence against unlawful violence or in use of necessary force to effect a lawful arrest (for example by the police) of reasonable self-defence

Limited rights
Some ECHR rights are expressly limited, for example, Article 8(1) provides the right to respect for private and family life, home and correspondence but 8(2) provides that one's enjoyment and manifestation of that right may lawfully be restricted (ie one's privacy may be invaded, one's correspondence read) on grounds such as national security or the protection of the rights and freedoms of others
Similarly, Article 10(1) grants the right to individual free expression but 10(2) allows that expression similarly to be curtailed
The common denominator is that for the State interference with the enjoyment of the right to be lawful, certain prerequisites have to be met: the restriction must be necessary in a democratic society in pursuit of a legitimate aim (tied to one or more of the grounds for restriction), proportionate to the achievement of that legitimate aim, and grounded upon some pressing social need

Under the Human Rights Act 1998, the following cases are illustrative of the courts' approach.

- A court making a declaration of lawful withdrawal of treatment in a case where a patient was in a permanent vegetative state does not infringe the right to life: **NHS Trust A v M; NHS Trust B v H** (2001). The court applied the principle established in **Airedale National Health Trust v Bland** (1993).
- In **R (Pretty) v Director of Public Prosecutions** (2001) the House of Lords ruled, inter alia, that Article 2 was directed towards protecting the sanctity of life and did not entail a right to terminate one's own life.[78]

---

78 **R (Pretty) v Director of Public Prosecutions** (2001). Mrs Pretty subsequently lost her appeal to the Court of Human Rights.

● Where there was a serious risk to life to former soldiers through their giving evidence before a tribunal enquiring into the shootings in Northern Ireland on 'Bloody Sunday', the Court of Appeal ruled that the evidence should be given elsewhere.[79]

● In **R (Amin) v Secretary of State for the Home Department** (2003) the House of Lords emphasised the requirement that the state fulfil its procedural duty to establish an independent public investigation into the death of a prisoner in prison.

● The failure of the police to protect a vulnerable prosecution witness from a third party was held not to be a violation of Article 2 in **Van Colle v Chief Constable of Hertfordshire Police** (2008). Applying **Osman v United Kingdom**[80] (1998) the Court ruled that the test for finding that a public authority had violated an individual's fundamental rights or freedoms was – in the circumstances – that the authority knew that there was 'a real and immediate risk to the life of the individual' from a third party and had failed to take measures which, judged reasonably, might have been expected to avoid that risk. The threshold test was high. On the facts, from the information available at the time, it could not reasonably have been anticipated that there was a real and immediate threat to the deceased's life.

● By contrast, in **Rabone v Pennine Care NHS Trust** (2012) the Supreme Court ruled that the state had an operational duty to protect against a real and immediate risk of suicide those who were under its control. Allowing a vulnerable voluntary psychiatric patient to have a home visit, when known to be suicidal, breached that operational duty.

● Article 2 was central to **R (Gentle) v Prime Minister** (2008). The claimants argued, unsuccessfully, that Article 2 imposed a substantive obligation on the government to take reasonable steps to ensure that it did not send servicemen to face the risk of death without ensuring that the action was lawful and that in failing to do so the government had a procedural obligation under Article 2 to initiate an effective public investigation into the deaths, which would entail an examination of the legality of the invasion. The House of Lords ruled that the procedural requirement implied in Article 2 was parasitic upon the substantive right. There was no violation of Article 2 in the deployment of troops. Furthermore, questions relating to war were resolved under the United Nations Charter, not the European Convention. The claimants could not establish an arguable substantive right under Article 2. Still less could they establish a right to a public inquiry.[81]

Article 3: freedom from torture, inhuman and degrading treatment

Article 3 states that 'no one shall be subjected to torture or to inhuman or degrading treatment or punishment'. In **Ireland v United Kingdom** (1978), the Republic of Ireland[82] alleged that the United Kingdom had, *inter alia*, violated Article 3 of the Convention, which proscribes 'inhuman or degrading treatment or punishment'. In 1966, the United Kingdom had declared that there was a state of emergency in Northern Ireland. In 1971, acting under the Civil Authorities (Special Powers) Act 1922,[83] the government introduced new powers of detention and internment of suspected Irish Republican Army terrorists. Fourteen suspects were subjected to such techniques as hooding, wall-standing for between 23 and 29 hours, noise intrusions and

---

79 In **R (A) v Lord Saville of Newdigate** (2000). And see **re Officer L** (2007). The correct test to be applied in determining whether anonymity should be preserved is whether the risk to an officer would be materially increased without anonymity.
80 See also **R (D) v Secretary of State for the Home Department** (2006) and **Butchart v Home Office** (2006).
81 Namely, 'an effective investigation by an independent official body'. See **R (Middleton) v West Somerset Coroner** [2004] 2 AC 182. On investigation of deaths in custody see also **R (JL) v Secretary of State for the Home Department** (2007), and **Brecknell v United Kingdom** (2007), **R (L) v Secretary of State for the Home Department** (2007). See also **R (P) v Secretary of State for Justice** (2009).
82 Under ECHR, Article 24, which provides for inter-state applications.
83 See now the Northern Ireland (Emergency Provisions) Act 1991, Pt IV and Sched 3.

deprivation of sleep, food and water. There was evidence that the men subjected to these practices suffered weight loss and pain.

The treatment fell within the meaning of inhuman treatment; it was also degrading, arousing feelings of fear, anguish and inferiority capable of humiliating and debasing the prisoners and breaking their physical or moral resistance. To amount to torture, however, comparison must be made with inhuman and degrading treatment. The distinction, ruled the Court, derives from the difference in the intensity of suffering inflicted. In this case it did not occasion suffering of a particular intensity and cruelty implied by the word torture as understood by the Court.[84]

In **Tyrer v United Kingdom** (1978), the Court ruled on the compatibility of birching as a judicial punishment in the Isle of Man with the requirements of Article 3. Tyrer, then aged 15, was given three strokes of the birch as punishment for an assault on a school prefect. The question raised was whether the punishment amounted to a violation of Article 3. The Court held that, while a conviction for a criminal offence itself could humiliate, for a finding to be sustained under Article 3, there needed to be found a humiliation deriving from the execution of punishment imposed. The mere fact that the punishment being inflicted was distasteful was not enough. Under the circumstances, with the victim having to undress, the treatment reached a level of degrading punishment.[85] Issues are also raised as to the lawfulness of the conditions under which a prisoner is detained.[86] In **Price v United Kingdom** (2001), the Court of Human Rights ruled that the detention of a severely disabled person in unsuitable conditions at a police station and subsequently detention in prison in similar conditions amounted to degrading treatment contrary to Article 3.[87]

Similar facts also led to a finding of a breach of Article 3 in **MS v United Kingdom** (2012). In this case the detainee was mentally ill. He had been arrested and the police had endeavoured to have him admitted to a clinic for treatment. That attempt failed, and although there was no intention to humiliate him, the Court held that the conditions he had had to endure had reached the threshold of degrading treatment.

The law relating to immigration, race and citizenship has also been tested under Article 3. In **East African Asians v United Kingdom** (1973), legislation restricted immigration of British passport holders in East Africa, preventing those who had neither a parent nor grandparent born or naturalised in the United Kingdom from entering the country. The Commission ruled that racial discrimination of this type constituted a form of affront to human dignity and amounted to degrading treatment. More recently, the treatment of asylum seekers by the state has given rise to allegations of violations of Article 3. This issue is further discussed in Chapter 23.[88]

To return a person to his or her country of nationality will raise Article 3 if the person is liable to suffer ill-treatment by state officials. This issue was tested in **Chahal v United Kingdom** (1997). Mr Chahal, a Sikh, had been politically active in Sikh affairs. In 1990, the Home Secretary decided to deport him from the United Kingdom on grounds of national security and the international fight against terrorism. The Court of Human Rights ruled, by a majority, that the United Kingdom violated Article 3 of the Convention and – unanimously – that there

---

84 There was no violation of Article 14 (the harsher treatment given to the IRA suspects was justified by their greater menace), and no violation of Article 1 (which cannot be a head for a separate breach of the ECHR).
85 See also **Costello-Roberts v United Kingdom** (1993); **A v United Kingdom** (1998).
86 See **Krocher and Moller v Switzerland** (1984).
87 See also **Z v United Kingdom** (2001): a violation of Article 3 through failure of the state to protect children from long-term neglect and abuse. See **X v Bedfordshire County Council** (1995). Compare **Hill v Chief Constable of West Yorkshire** (1988) and **Osman v United Kingdom** (2000). See also **E v United Kingdom** (2002). In **Z v United Kingdom**, the children were awarded, in total, £192,000 as pecuniary damage, £32,000 each for non-pecuniary damage and a total of £39,000 for costs and expenses.
88 See **Soering v United Kingdom** (1989); **Vilvarajah v United Kingdom** (1991).

had been a violation of Article 13 in conjunction with Article 3, in that effective remedies did not exist before the courts in England. Mr Chahal had been subjected to torture in India on a visit in 1984. The Court was apprised of substantiated allegations of torture by the authorities in India. In addition, there was a violation of Article 5(4), in that Mr Chahal had been denied the opportunity to have the lawfulness of his detention decided by a national court.[89]

The Iraq War in 2003 has given rise to questions over the territorial reach of the Convention as well as substantive allegations. In **Al-Saadoon and Mufdhi v United Kingdom** (2010), for example, the Court of Human Rights held, unanimously, that there had been a violation of Article 3. The applicants had been arrested and detained by British forces as security internees and later on suspicion of the murder of two British soldiers. In June 2004 the occupation of Iraq came to an end and the death penalty was reintroduced into the Iraqi Penal Code. In 2006 the Basra Criminal Court made an order authorising their continued detention by UK forces. In 2008 the UK authorities physically transferred the applicants to the custody of the Iraqi police and they were tried in 2009. The Court of Human Rights ruled that since 2006 the applicants had been subject to the fear of execution by the Iraqi authorities, causing psychological suffering of a nature and degree which constituted inhuman treatment under Article 3.

Extradition – the process whereby a person is returned to or sent to another jurisdiction to stand trial – has also been considered under Article 3. In **Babar Ahmed and Others v United Kingdom** (2012) the Court of Human Rights ruled unanimously that the extradition of terrorist suspects to stand trial in the United States would not violate Article 3. If convicted, the applicants faced imprisonment in a maximum security prison. One faced 269 life sentences without the possibility of parole, and others discretionary life sentences. The Court accepted that, while in principle matters of sentencing fell outside the scope of the Convention, a grossly disproportionate sentence could amount to ill-treatment contrary to Article 3. However, even mandatory life sentences without the possibility of parole would not be grossly disproportionate for terrorist offences.[90]

The following cases illustrate the approach of the domestic courts to Article 3.

- In **Napier v Scottish Ministers** (2001), the Court of Session ruled that Article 3 was violated by the conditions in prisons. The court ordered the executive to transfer the applicant to conditions of detention which complied with Article 3.
- In **N v Secretary of State for the Home Department** (2005) the House of Lords ruled that the removal of a seriously ill illegal immigrant to a country where it was alleged that her life expectancy would be reduced would violate Article 3 only in exceptional circumstances. The European Court of Human Rights' decision in **D v United Kingdom** should be 'very strictly confined' (*per* Laws LJ). In **R (Limbuela) v Secretary of State for the Home Department** (2005), the House of Lords ruled that Article 3 may be violated if the state denies the barest necessities of life for an asylum seeker.
- There was no infringement of Article 3 or 5 through the imposition of a life sentence on a mentally ill offender rather than the making of a hospital order. The Court of Appeal (following the approach taken in **R v Offen**, below) so held in **R v Drew** (2002), in which the offender presented a serious and continuing danger to the safety of the public and a hospital order would not have ensured adequate security.

---

89 See also **D v United Kingdom** (1997): a violation of Article 3 arose from the threat to remove the defendant from the UK to his country of origin when he was terminally ill and there was no one to care for him in his own country.

90 On extradition, see **R (Wellington) v Secretary of State for the Home Department** (2008). See also **Vinter and Others v United Kingdom** (2012), **Harkins and Edwards v United Kingdom** (2012) and **Balogun v United Kingdom** (2012).

- In **R (B) v Director of Public Prosecutions** (2009) the claimant had suffered a serious assault. However, the CPS decided not to continue with the prosecution of the accused on the basis that the claimant, who was disabled, would not be a reliable witness. The decision was held to be irrational. There was also a violation of Article 3 which imposed a 'positive duty on a state to provide protection through its legal system against a person suffering such ill-treatment at the hands of others'. That duty included the provision of a legal system for bringing to justice those who commit serious acts of violence against others.

- In **R (Mousa) v Secretary of State for Defence** (2011) the Court of Appeal ruled that the inquiry group – the Iraq Historic Allegations Team (IHAT) – established by the Secretary of State to investigate allegations of ill-treatment of detainees by British troops lacked the necessary independence to satisfy the procedural requirement of Article 3. The IHAT was staffed by members of the the Military Provost Staff, representatives of the Ministry of Defence and the Army.

Article 4: freedom from slavery and forced labour

Article 4 states that no one shall be held in slavery or servitude, and no one shall be required to perform forced or compulsory labour. The term 'forced or compulsory labour' does not include any work required to be done in the ordinary course of lawful detention or during conditional release from such detention; or military service recognised in states of emergency or which forms a part of normal 'civil obligations'. This provision has little relevance in the majority of Western democracies and has given rise to little case law. Challenges have been made relating to the requirement that German lawyers undertake compulsory legal aid work, but these have failed.[91]

Articles 5 and 6: the right to liberty and security

Article 5 provides that everyone has the right to liberty and security of person and that no one shall be deprived of his liberty other than in accordance with lawful arrest or detention. The right includes the right to be informed of reasons for an arrest and of any charges being brought. It also includes the right to be brought 'promptly' before a court to determine the lawfulness of the detention, and the right to a trial within a reasonable time or to release pending trial.

This long and intricate Article has provided the platform for many challenges on behalf of persons detained and is in many cases linked to Article 6. The first requirement to be met in relation to Article 5 is that, where a person is deprived of his liberty, the deprivation must be in consequence of a lawful detention. The following cases illustrate the protection given by Article 5.

- The arrest and detention of protesters violated Article 5(1) on the grounds that the protest was entirely peaceful and there had been no obstruction or provocation: **Steel v United Kingdom** (1998).[92]

- A two-year delay between reviews by the Parole Board of detention was unreasonable and made the continued detention unlawful: **Oldham v United Kingdom** (2001).[93]

---

91 *Van der Mussele v Belgium* (1983).
92 See also *Weeks v United Kingdom* (1987); *Johnson v United Kingdom* (1997).
93 See *Wemhoff v Federal Republic of Germany* (1979); *Neumeister v Austria* (1968); and *Stogmuller v Austria* (1969).

- Detention for up to seven days, at the Home Secretary's discretion, under the Prevention of Terrorism (Temporary Provisions) Act 1974 violated Article 5: **Brogan v United Kingdom** (1988).[94]

- The failure of the police to bring an arrested person before a judge promptly violated Article 5: **O'Hara v United Kingdom** (2001).[95]

- The power of a Mental Health Tribunal to review the detention of a patient but not to order his release – a power which lay with the executive – violated Article 5: **Benjamin v United Kingdom** (2002).

- The lack of formal rules regulating the admission and detention of compliant incapacity patients, notwithstanding the need for protective detention, violated Article 5(1) and the absence of procedures to determine the lawfulness of continued detention violated Article 5(4): **L v United Kingdom** (2004).[96]

- The internment of an Iraqi citizen by British forces in Iraq, for three years and without being charged with any offence, violated Article 5: **Al-Jedda v United Kingdom** (2011).

- In **James, Wells and Lee v United Kingdom** (2012), the Court of Human Rights ruled that the failure by the prison authorities to make training courses available to prisoners who had served the tariff period of their sentence rendered their continued detention unlawful and a violation of Article 5 of the European Convention. At issue was whether the state was under a duty to provide courses which would promote their rehabilitation and so make their continued detention (on the ground that they were a danger to the public) redundant. The failure of the state to provide the necessary courses made their detention arbitrary and unlawful.

The major cases under the Human Rights Act include the following.

- In **R v Offen** (2001) the Court of Appeal ruled that if the offender was a significant risk to the public the court could impose a life sentence without contravening the Convention.[97]

- In **Anderson v Scottish Ministers** (2001), the Privy Council ruled that the continued detention of mental patients on grounds of public safety did not infringe Article 5 of the Convention, even where there was no medical treatment for the condition. The House of Lords in **R v Leeds Crown Court ex parte Wardle** (2001) ruled that continued detention in custody where the accused was charged with a second offence while in custody on the first charge did not infringe the Convention. The fresh time limit was justified by the need to give the prosecutor sufficient time to prepare the evidence relating to each offence.

- In **R (C) v Mental Health Review Tribunal** (2001) the Court of Appeal ruled that the listing of all hearings by the Mental Health Review Tribunal in a uniform specified period after a request for review had been made was unlawful in that it did not ensure that individual applications were heard as soon as reasonably practicable. In **In re K (A Child) (Secure Accommodation Order: Right to Liberty)** (2000) the Court of Appeal ruled that a secure accommodation order, while a deprivation of liberty, was justified as 'being detention of a minor by lawful order for the purpose of educational supervision' under Article 5(1)(d).

---

94 See also **Brannigan and McBride v United Kingdom** (1994). The government in response issued a derogation notice and re-enacted the provisions. See also **Yagci and Sargin v Turkey** and **Mansur v Turkey** (1995).
95 See also **Murray v United Kingdom** (1996); **Benham v United Kingdom** (1996); **Hussain v United Kingdom** (1996); **Curley v United Kingdom** (2001); **Blackstock v United Kingdom** (2005); **Kolanis v United Kingdom** (2005).
96 See also **Blackstock v United Kingdom** (2005); **Kolanis v United Kingdom** (2005).
97 At issue was the Crime (Sentences) Act 1997, under which an automatic life sentence could be imposed on a defendant who had committed two serious offences.

- A declaration of incompatibility was made by the Court of Appeal in **R (H) v Mental Health Review Tribunal, North and East London Region** (2001). The applicant was detained under the Mental Health Act 1983, section 73 of which provides, *inter alia*, that in order to satisfy a mental health review tribunal that he was entitled to discharge, the burden of proof fell on the restricted person to show that he was no longer suffering from a mental disorder warranting detention. Section 73 could not be given an interpretation which was compatible with the Convention. The Secretary of State for Health then made a remedial order amending section 73 in order to make it compatible with Article 5.

- The House of Lords overturned a declaration of incompatibility in **R (MH) v Secretary of State for Health** (2005). The claimant was severely mentally disordered and had been admitted for assessment to hospital under section 2 of the Mental Health Act 1983. She was not competent to take legal proceedings. However, the scheme of the 1983 Act was such that even if judicial proceedings could not be undertaken for some reason, there was access to a tribunal which could be initiated by a representative of the patient. Alternatively, the Secretary of State had power to refer under section 67, and that decision was judicially reviewable. There was sufficient protection in the Act to make it compatible with Article 5(4).

- The requirements of Article 5.4 in relation to proceedings to test the legality of detention, in relation to prisoners, are met by the Parole Board. The Board has come under increasing pressure on the basis that it lacks the necessary independence from the executive to be regarded as 'a court'. In **R (Girling) v Parole Board** (2005) a challenge to the lawfulness of the Board's decision was made on the grounds that (a) the Parole Board could only consider a prisoner's application for release if the matter was referred to it by the Home Secretary,[98] and (b) that the Home Secretary issued directions to the Board as to the matters to be taken into account when considering the application for release.[99] The Court ruled that the Home Secretary was under a statutory duty to refer cases regularly to the Parole Board and his or her failure to do so could be corrected by judicial review, and in relation to the second issue, that the power to give directions should be interpreted to read as being confined to the Board's administrative, rather than judicial functions. Furthermore, while the Court recognised that there was some 'trespass on the Parole Board's independence' this was not so substantial as to deprive the Parole Board of its true character as a judicial body.[100]

- The most significant case to date on Article 5 is that of **A v Secretary of State for the Home Department** (2004). In this case the Appellate Committee of the House of Lords ruled that the indefinite detention of foreign terrorist suspects, who could neither be put on trial (because of evidence which could not be adduced in open court) nor deported because that could infringe their Article 3 rights, was unlawful. It violated Article 5 and also Article 14 (the prohibition against discrimination in the enjoyment of Convention rights) on the basis that British terrorist suspects could not be similarly detained. Lord Bingham stated that great weight had to be given to the judgment of the Home Secretary in relation to matters of national security which involved political judgment. However, he did not accept that the courts must always defer to the executive. Lord Bingham viewed the issue as one of separation of powers: the more purely political the question the more appropriate it was for political resolution. The greater the legal content of any issue, the greater 'the court's potential role because under our constitution and subject to the sovereign

---

98 Under s 28(6) of the Crime (Sentences) Act 1997.
99 Under s 32(6) of the Criminal Justice Act 1991.
100 See also **R (Hirst) v Secretary of State for the Home Department** (2006).

power of Parliament it was the function of the courts and not of political bodies to resolve legal questions'. His Lordship further recognised the different functions of the executive and the courts, stating that 'the function of independent judges charged to interpret and apply the law was universally recognised as a cardinal feature of the modern democratic state, a cornerstone of the rule of law itself'.

The right to liberty was a fundamental Convention right. Detaining foreign nationals without trial – but not nationals suspected of terrorist offences – was not justified and infringed both Article 5 and 14. The Derogation Order (Human Rights Act 1998 [Designated Derogation] Order SI 2001 No 3644) was disproportionate and could not be justified.[101]

Lord Hoffmann specifically addressed the question of whether there was a public emergency within the meaning of Article 15 of the Convention. He recognised 'the power of fanatical groups of terrorists to kill and destroy' but did not consider that they threatened 'the life of the nation'. Lord Walker, dissenting, stated that while detention without trial was a grave matter, it was for Parliament and the Secretary of State to judge the necessary measures, and the 2001 Act contained important safeguards. The Home Secretary's powers were subject to judicial review by the statutory commission (the Special Immigration Appeals Tribunal, which is chaired by a High Court judge); the legislation was temporary in nature and while in force there was detailed scrutiny of the operation of sections 21 to 23. In nearly three years no more than 17 individuals had been certified under section 21: the number of persons actually detailed was relevant to the issue of proportionality.[102]

Habeas Corpus

As discussed above, Article 5 provides, in part, that every person who is detained is entitled to take proceedings by which the lawfulness of the detention is decided speedily by a court and release ordered if the detention is not lawful. Article 5 supplements the ancient writ of habeas corpus which is available to test the legality of a person's detention.[103]

The writ can be issued either by the person imprisoned or by someone acting on his behalf. If it is established that there is a prima facie ground for believing the detention to be unlawful, the writ will be issued. Habeas corpus is used in several areas of law where acts of the executive result in detention. Its use can be seen in, for example, immigration and asylum law and mental health law. In **Nikonovs v Governor of Brixton Prison** (2005), the Court of Appeal stated that the right to habeas corpus could only be restricted by express statutory language and could not be implied into an Act.

Originally a common law power, the right to a writ was placed on a statutory basis under the Habeas Corpus Act 1679. The Act of 1679 relates to persons imprisoned on a criminal charge. The Habeas Corpus Act 1816 relates to persons detained other than on a criminal charge.[104] AV Dicey instructed that:

> . . . if, in short, any man, woman, or child is deprived of liberty, the court will always issue a writ of habeas corpus to any one who has the aggrieved person in his custody

---

101 See also **A v United Kingdom** (2009).

102 See also **A v Secretary of State for the Home Department (No 2)** (2005) in which the House of Lords ruled that evidence obtained by torture by foreign state officials was inadmissible in court.

103 The use of habeas corpus now needs to be considered in light of the development of the European arrest warrant. See van Sliedregt, E. 'The European Arrest Warrant: Between trust, democracy and the rule of law: Introduction. The European Arrest Warrant: Extradition in Transition' (2007) European Constitutional Law Review 3:244. And **re Hilali (respondent) (application for a writ of Habeas Corpus)** (2008).

104 The Habeas Corpus Act 1862 prohibits the courts from issuing writs in respect of colonies or dominions where those jurisdictions have power to issue the writ.

to have such person brought before the court, and if he is suffering restraint without lawful cause, set him free.[105]

In the case of **Wolfe Tone** (1798), Tone was tried and found guilty of high treason by a court-martial and sentenced to death. A writ was issued on the basis that, since Wolfe Tone was not under commission to the English army, but rather held a commission from the French Republic, there was no jurisdiction for his trial by court-martial in Ireland. The Lord Chief Justice instructed the sheriff to go immediately to the army barracks and demand that Tone not be executed. When the officers refused to comply with the order, the Lord Chief Justice ordered that Tone, and the detaining officers, be taken into the custody of the sheriff. On seeking to recover Tone from detention, it was found that he had cut his throat and could not be moved. On this case, Dicey wrote, seemingly without irony, that 'it will be admitted that no more splendid assertion of the supremacy of law can be found than the protection of Wolfe Tone by the Irish Bench'.[106]

The writ has also been used to test the legality of detention of slaves: **Sommersett's Case** (1771) and of students: **Ex parte Daisy Hopkins** (1891). In **Board of Control ex parte Rutty** (1956), a writ was issued to test the legality of the detention of a mentally defective patient who had been detained for eight years without an order of a court. Nowadays, the writ of habeas corpus is most often used to test the legality of the detention of immigrants. However, in **R v Home Secretary ex parte Mughal** (1974) and **R v Home Secretary ex parte Zamir** (1980), the court refused to allow habeas corpus to be used to question the decision to remove an illegal immigrant from the country. Conversely, in **R v Home Secretary ex parte Khawaja** (1984), the House of Lords ruled that the question as to whether a person was an illegal immigrant was not within the exclusive jurisdiction of the Home Secretary to decide. Rather it was a matter of fact, which the courts would decide. Before Khawaja could be removed from the country, the court had to be satisfied on the evidence that he was in fact an illegal immigrant. Only if he was an illegal immigrant would the court permit deportation.

In **Yunus Rahmatullah v Secretary of State for Foreign and Commonwealth Affairs; Secretary of State for Defence** (2011), the Court of Appeal granted a writ of habeas corpus against the respondents, requiring the government to secure the release of Mr Rahmatullah and produce him for trial before a British court within seven days, or release him without trial. The appellant had been captured by British forces in Iraq in 2004 and handed over to US forces. The Secretary of State for Defence claimed that Rahmatullah was a member of a proscribed organisation with links to Al-Qaeda. He was detained in Afghanistan from 2004 to 2011, in a detention centre, and without any charges being brought against him. The appellant claimed that his detention was unlawful, and applied (through a relative) for a writ of habeas corpus. The government resisted the application on the basis that it did not have sufficient control over the applicant (he being in the custody of US forces), and that the issue of a writ would require the UK Government making a request to the US Government for his release – thereby involving the law stepping into the area of foreign relations. The Court of Appeal, unanimously, agreed to the grant of the writ.

See Chapter 22.

See Chapters 7 and 8.

On appeal to the Supreme Court, the decision of the Court of Appeal on the issue of the writ was upheld: see **Rahmatullah v Secretary of State for Defence** (2012). The Court rejected the government's argument that the issue of the writ would represent an intrusion on foreign policy. It would not: the Court was merely requiring the Secretary of State to explain whether or not it had control over the applicant.

---

105 Dicey, 1885, p 219.
106 Dicey, 1885, p 294. See also Heuston, 1964, Chapter 2; **Stockdale v Hansard** (1839); and **Sheriff of Middlesex's case** (1840), discussed in Chapter 17.

There exists an overlap between habeas corpus and judicial review which causes uncertainty. In **R v Home Secretary ex parte Cheblak** (1991), the Court of Appeal held that habeas corpus is not a substitute for judicial review proceedings. However, where an application for judicial review is pending, a writ may be used to ensure that the applicant is not prematurely removed from the country.[107]

See also Chapter 23.

Article 6: the right to fair trial[108]

Article 6 provides for the right of fair trial before an independent and impartial tribunal, and for the presumption of innocence. In addition, Article 6 requires that those accused of a criminal offence are informed promptly of the charges, have adequate time to prepare a defence, have a right to be represented by a lawyer and have free legal assistance 'when the interests of justice so require'. The right to examine witnesses is also included. Article 6 is the most frequently cited Article. The protection given relates to the 'determination of . . . civil rights and obligations' and 'of any criminal charge'. The Court has had to determine the meaning and scope of these phrases. A 'criminal charge' has been interpreted to mean 'the official notification given to an individual by the competent authority of an allegation that he has committed a criminal offence'.[109]

The phrase 'civil rights and obligations' has given rise to extensive interpretation. As a general principle, where the consequence of an administrative decision is one which affects the civil rights of individuals, then Article 6 may be held to apply.[110] For example, in **Konig** (1980), Dr Konig's licence to practise as a doctor in his own clinic was withdrawn. The Court ruled that the decision affected Dr Konig's civil rights and that, therefore, the protection of Article 6 applied.[111] By contrast, the Court of Appeal ruled, in **R (Maftah) v Secretary of State for the Foreign and Commonwealth Office** (2011) that a government decision to place the applicant on a list of terrorist suspects did not engage Article 6.

Where a person's civil right is the subject of two sets of formal proceedings, the question arises whether or not Article 6 applies to both sets of proceedings. This was considered by the Supreme Court in **R (G) v Governors of X School** (2011). A teacher had been subject to disciplinary proceedings prior to a determination by a statutory body whether he should be placed on a 'children's barred list' which would end his right to teach. In judicial review proceedings, he argued that Article 6 entitled him to legal representation at both proceedings. The Supreme Court disagreed: the question to be asked was whether the first set of proceedings was 'determinative' or would have a 'substantial influence or effect' on the second set of proceedings. In the instant case, it would not.

Article 6 was also instrumental in **T and V v United Kingdom** (1999). The Court ruled that the setting of the tariff period to be served by juveniles convicted of murder for retribution and deterrence by the Home Secretary deprived the applicants of the opportunity to have their detention reviewed by a judicial body. Furthermore, being tried in an adult court violated the right to a fair trial.

Particular difficulties arise in disciplinary proceedings for criminal offences in the armed forces. The consequence of trying the matter under disciplinary regulations rather than a court of law is to remove the normal application of Article 6. The Court has ruled that whether an

---

107   *R v Home Secretary ex parte Muboyayi* (1991).
108   See Craig, 2003b.
109   *Eckle v Federal Republic of Germany* (1982), para 73.
110   *Konig v Federal Republic of Germany* (1980); *Ringeisen v Austria* (1971).
111   See also *Devlin v United Kingdom* (2002); and *Devenney v United Kingdom* (2002).

offence is classified as criminal or disciplinary is less important than the nature of the offence. Article 6.1 was violated where the applicant, an army officer, had been detained before trial on the instruction of his commanding officer who then played a role in hearing the case against the applicant: **Hood v United Kingdom** (1999).[112] Royal Navy courts martial violated Article 6 in that the judge advocates were serving naval officers appointed by a naval officer. Furthermore, where there was no independent, full-time, permanent president of the court Article 6 was violated: **Grieves v United Kingdom** (2004).[113]

In **Campbell and Fell v United Kingdom** (1984), following involvement in a prison riot, the applicants had been punished by the Board of Prison Visitors with loss of remission of sentence. The Court held that Article 6 applied to the decision-making process of the Board of Visitors.[114] Article 6 has also been used to protect the rights of prisoners. The determination of charges relating to breach of prison rules being decided by those who were appointed by the Home Office and who had investigated those charges could not be said to be independent. Furthermore, in **Whitfield v United Kingdom** (2005) Article 6 was violated by denying the applicants legal representation.

A 'fair and public hearing' includes the right to legal advice before the judicial hearing: **Golder v United Kingdom** (1975). The applicant, who was serving a prison sentence, wanted to sue a prison officer for defamation. His request to the Home Secretary to consult a solicitor was denied. The Court held that Article 6 had been violated. On the right to legal advice see further below.

Article 6(1) also requires that the hearing take place 'within a reasonable time'. The reasonableness of the length of the proceedings will depend upon their complexity.[115]

Being compelled to answer questions by the investigating authorities under threat of contempt of court violates the right not to incriminate oneself: **Saunders v United Kingdom** (1996).[116] The Court of Human Rights in **O'Halloran v United Kingdom** (2007) ruled that the right to fair trial is not violated by the statutory duty imposed on the registered keepers of motor vehicles to disclose to the police the identity of the person who was driving the vehicle on a particular occasion or face a fine and conviction for a criminal offence.[117] Although the measures were coercive, this was not a strict liability offence and there was the defence that the owner did not know and could not have known the identity of the driver. The essence of the right to silence and their privilege against self-incrimination had not been destroyed. Article 6 protects the right to legal advice. The right is not expressly stated and may be subject to restrictions for good cause. Being detained for over 48 hours without access to legal advice, which resulted in the applicant signing a confession statement, violated Article 6: **Magee v United Kingdom** (2000).[118] Where the conviction of the applicants had been upheld as safe by the Court of Appeal, the applicants having exercised their right to silence on the advice of their solicitor, and the trial judge had failed accurately to instruct the jury as to the inferences to be drawn from the right to silence, a violation of Article 6 occurred: **Condron v United Kingdom**

---

112 See also **Findlay v United Kingdom** (1997); **Jordan v United Kingdom** (2001). In **Coyne v United Kingdom** (1996), a court martial conducted before the Armed Forces Act 1996 came into force was not an independent and impartial tribunal. See now the Armed Forces Discipline Act 2000.
113 See also **Cooper v United Kingdom** (2004). Cf **R v Spear** (2001).
114 Cf **Engel et al v Netherlands** (1976).
115 See **Davies v United Kingdom** (2002); **Mitchell v United Kingdom** (2002).
116 See **IJL, GMR and AKP v United Kingdom** (2000): the Court of Human Rights in 2000 found a violation of Article 6(1) through the use of the applicants' statements at trial which they had been compelled under statute to give to inspectors appointed by the Department of Trade and Industry. See also **Averill v United Kingdom** (2000).
117 Section 172 of the Road Traffic Act 1988.
118 Cf **Murray (John) v United Kingdom** (1996), and see Munday, 1996.

(2000).[119] The presence of police officers within hearing during an accused's interview with his solicitor violated Article 6: **Brennan v United Kingdom** (2001). The denial of legal aid where the interests of justice required legal representation violates Article 6: **Granger v United Kingdom** (1990); **Benham v United Kingdom** (1996). The failure of the prosecution to lay Public Interest Immunity Certificates (which preclude evidence being given in court) before the judge violated Article 6. While there was no absolute right to disclosure it was for the judge to control the release or otherwise of material: **Rowe v United Kingdom** (2000).[120]

Judicial impartiality is central to Article 6. The requirement of judicial impartiality was tested before the Court of Human Rights, in a judgment which had implications for the role of Lord Chancellor. In **McGonnell v United Kingdom** (2000), a case relating to the position of the Deputy Bailiff of Guernsey as President of the States of Deliberation, Guernsey's legislative body, and subsequently as the sole judge of law in proceedings relating to the applicant's planning application which had been refused, the Court of Human Rights held that the Deputy Bailiff's position was 'capable of casting doubt' as to his 'impartiality' and, as a result, was in violation of Article 6(1) of the European Convention on Human Rights, which guarantees 'a fair and public hearing . . . by an independent and impartial tribunal established by law'.[121]

Article 6 has been held not to be violated where state immunity had prevented the applicants from pursuing cases in domestic court proceedings.[122] The three applicants each sought redress for the actions of British, Kuwaiti and United States' authorities for, respectively, an alleged assault, wrongful imprisonment and torture, and discrimination. The respondent governments pleaded state immunity. The Court ruled that in each case the doctrine of state immunity, designed to promote comity between nations, applied.

As expected, Article 6 has generated a wealth of case law under the Human Rights Act 1998. It is clear that the courts are following the approach of the Court of Human Rights in looking less at detailed irregularities in trial procedures and more to the overall fairness of the criminal process. In **R (Dudson) v Secretary of State for the Home Department** (2005) the House of Lords ruled that the requirement of a 'fair and public hearing' under Article 6 did not require that there always be an oral hearing at every stage in criminal proceedings.[123] Here the process of reviewing the claimant's tariff which he was required to serve for retribution and deterrence, undertaken by the Lord Chief Justice, disclosed all relevant material and there had been a sufficient opportunity to make representations in writing. It was not a situation where procedural fairness required there to be an oral hearing before a final decision could be made.[124] Where there are alleged defects in the process, the courts will only rule that a violation of Article 6 has occurred where the cumulative effect is to render the trial unfair. Furthermore, where there are defects identified, if these are remedied by the appeal process, or through judicial review proceedings, then the courts will be slow to find a violation of Convention rights.[125] Article 6 comprises a number of rights relating to differing aspects of judicial decision making. In **Michel v The Queen,** (2009), the Judicial Committee of the Privy Council ruled that the right to fair trial was violated where the judge repeatedly interrupted

---

119 See also **Beckles v United Kingdom** (2003); **Cuscani v United Kingdom** (2002).
120 In **CG v United Kingdom** (2002), the Court of Human Rights ruled that excessive and undesirable interruptions by a judge did not necessarily render a trial unfair.
121 See also **Sander v United Kingdom** (2001).
122 **McElhinney v Ireland** (2001), **Al-Adsani v United Kingdom** and **Fogarty v United Kingdom** (2000).
123 See also **R (Wright) v Secretary of State for Health** (2009), the denial of an opportunity to make representations before a care worker was provisionally listed as unsuitable to work with vulnerable adults breached Article 6.
124 However, in **R (Hammond) v Secretary of State for the Home Department** (2005) the House of Lords ruled that the right to a fair and public hearing under Article 6 may necessitate a judge exercising his discretion and deciding to conduct an oral hearing.
125 See **McKeown v United Kingdom** (2011): safeguards ensuring that material not disclosed to the defence on public interest grounds was scrutinised by a Disclosure Judge ensured the overall fairness of a trial.

the trial proceedings and had been 'variously sarcastic, mocking and patronising'. The sheer volume of the interventions compelled the conclusion that the applicant's conviction could not stand.

Substantive issues and Article 6 protection

Article 6 does not apply where a prisoner serving a mandatory life sentence is accused of breaching prison rules. That is not a criminal charge and therefore the guarantees of Article 6 do not apply.[126] Similarly, the House of Lords ruled that the giving of a warning to a 15-year-old boy did not involve the determination of a criminal charge. Accordingly no issue arose under Article 6.[127] An administrative decision to segregate prisoners is not a determination of an Article 6 right: the Court of Appeal so ruled in **R (King) and others v Secretary of State for Justice** (2012). In **Matthews v Ministry of Defence** (2003)[128] the House of Lords ruled that section 10 of the Crown Proceedings Act 1947, which exempted the Crown from liability in tort for injuries suffered by members of the armed forces, operated as a bar to litigation. The Secretary of State had substituted a no-fault system of compensation for a claim for damages in such cases. The combined effect of these two factors was that the claimant had no civil rights to which Article 6 might apply.

Article 6 does not apply to proceedings relating to an accused's fitness to plead. The applicants in **R v M, R v Kerr, R v H** (2001) had argued that Article 6 applied because it was unfair to try someone under a disability which prevented him from participating in proceedings because of a mental handicap. The Court of Appeal stated that the proceedings could not result in a conviction and therefore the argument failed.

Child law and the powers and duties of local authorities in relation to housing law have also given rise to challenges. The Court of Appeal has held that secure accommodation orders against children, although not criminal proceedings, attract rights to fair trial.[129]

In **R (Anderson) v Secretary of State for the Home Department** (2002), the House of Lords, convened as a panel of seven, removed the power of the Home Secretary to determine the tariff term to be served for punitive purposes by defendants convicted of murder and sentenced to life imprisonment. The House of Lords made a declaration under section 4 of the Human Rights Act 1998 that section 29 of the Crime (Sentences) Act 1997, which conferred on the Home Secretary control of the release of mandatory life sentence prisoners, was incompatible with the right under Article 6 to have a sentence imposed by an independent and impartial tribunal.

Lord Bingham of Cornhill stated that the court 'would not without good reason depart from the principles laid down in a carefully considered judgment of [the Court of Human Rights] sitting as a grand chamber'. Referring to **Stafford v United Kingdom** (2002),[130] the court accepted the view there expressed that 'the imposition of what was in effect a substantial term of imprisonment by the exercise of executive discretion ... lay uneasily with ordinary concepts of the rule of law'. The Court also considered **Benjamin and Wilson v United Kingdom** (2002), in which the Court of Human Rights ruled that the Home Secretary's role remained

---

126 **Matthewson v The Scottish Ministers** (2001); see also **R (Tangney) v Secretary of State for the Home Department** (2005).

127 **R (R) v Durham Constabulary** (2005).

128 See Hickman, 2004.

129 **In re M** (2001).

130 The Court of Human Rights ruled that the Home Secretary's powers relating to sentencing were incompatible with Article 6. **V v United Kingdom** (2000). *A Practice Statement: Life Sentences* (2002) replaces the term 'tariff' with 'minimum term'. The sentencing judge should indicate the appropriate determinate sentence suitable for punishment and retribution. He should then calculate the minimum term to be served before the prisoner's case should be referred to the Parole Board. Differing considerations apply to adult and juvenile cases.

objectionable despite his showing that he always acted in accordance with the recommenda-tions of the Mental Health Review Tribunal. In that case it had been observed that this impinged on the fundamental principle of separation of powers. The functional separation of the judi-ciary from the executive was 'fundamental' since the rule of law depended on it.

A claimant's civil rights under Article 6 does not include the determination of claims for social welfare benefits which are dependent upon evaluative judgments by the provider as to whether the statutory criteria for entitlement were met.[131] The Supreme Court so ruled in **Ali v Birmingham City Council** (2010).

Freedom from bias

The impartiality of the jury is central to the requirement of fairness. In **R v Abdroikov** (2007) the House of Lords considered the effect of the presence on the jury of an acting police officer and an employed Crown Prosecution Service prosecutor. The House of Lords ruled that there was no difference between the common law requirement of fairness and Article 6 and that justice would not be seen to be done if a 'fair minded and informed observer' would conclude that there would be a real possibility of jury bias.[132]

Disclosure of informants' identity

When considering whether to disclose whether a person was a police informer, the court had to balance the need to protect the informer and the requirements of fair trial. The court would not be constrained by precedent which identified possible exceptions to the rule of non-disclosure.[133]

Temporary judges

Article 6 was also invoked in **Millar v Dickson** (2002). There, the defendants were tried by temporary sheriffs. The decision follows that of **Starrs v Ruxton** (2000), where it was held that temporary sheriffs were not an independent and impartial tribunal within the meaning of Article 6 of the Convention. The right to fair trial was of the utmost importance to citizens. By continuing prosecution of the accused before temporary sheriffs, the Lord Advocate had violated the right of the accused to the protection of Article 6.[134]

Article 6 was examined by the High Court of Justiciary in **Hoekstra v Her Majesty's Advocate** (2001). In that case, the right to an impartial tribunal was violated by a judge sitting in a case of criminal appeal, who wrote a newspaper article strongly critical of the Convention. The article, which *inter alia* suggested that persons suspected of drug dealing should not have the right to privacy (under Article 8) against covert surveillance, would create in the mind of an informed observer 'an apprehension of bias' on the part of its author against the Convention and its rights. The court ordered that fresh appeal proceedings should be heard by three different judges.

Evidence and Article 6[135]

The question of admitting evidence of previous sexual relations at trial came before the Court of Appeal in **R v A (No 2)** (2001). In **R v Botmeh, R v Alami** (2001), the Court of Appeal ruled that there was nothing 'unlawful or unfair' in the court considering an *ex parte* application to

---

131 An issue which was left unresolved in **Runa Begum v Tower Hamlets LBC** (2003).
132 See also **Hanif v United Kingdom** (2011).
133 **D v National Society for the Prevention of Cruelty to Children** (1978) at 218.
134 See also **Scanfuture United Kingdom Ltd v Secretary of State for Trade and Industry; Link v Same** (2001).
135 On evidence and Article 8, see below.

withhold evidence on the ground of public interest immunity where that evidence had not been subject to a public interest immunity application to the trial judge. The court ruled that the defence had no absolute right to disclosure of relevant evidence and that 'strictly necessary measures restricting the rights of the defence were permissible, provided they were counter-balanced by procedures followed by the judicial authority'. In the case of **Al-Khawaja and Tahery v United Kingdom** (2011) the issue before the Grand Chamber of the Court of Human Rights was whether reliance on hearsay evidence violated Article 6. The Court made it clear that such reliance would not automatically result in a breach of Article 6, but that there had to be strong procedural safeguards to compensate for the difficulties caused to the defence in admitting such evidence. In Al-Khawaja's case, written evidence of a complainant, ST, who had committed suicide, was admitted. Her evidence was supported by another complainant, and evidence given by two friends in whom ST confided shortly after the alleged assault. There was no violation of Article 6. In Tahery's case, however, there was one sole witness to an alleged stabbing. That witness refused to give evidence and his witness statement was read to the Court. There was no means by which the evidence could be tested, and it was the sole evidence against him. It that circumstance, there was a violation of Article 6.[136]

The Court of Appeal in **R v Looseley** (2001) ruled that an accused's right to a fair trial was not prejudiced by admitting evidence obtained through the use of undercover police officers. At the start of his trial, the accused alleged that the police officers had incited him to commit the offence. The correct test was:

> . . . whether the officers did no more, whether than by active or passive means, than to afford the accused the opportunity to offend of which he freely took advantage in circumstances where it appeared that he would have behaved in a similar way if offered the opportunity by someone else; or whether, on the other hand, by means of unworthy or shameful conduct, they had persuaded him to commit an offence of a kind which otherwise he would not have committed.[137]

The fact that a trial had been found to be unfair by the Court of Human Rights did not, of itself, make the conviction unsafe. The Court of Appeal so ruled in **R v Lewis** (2005). The Court of Human Rights in **Edwards and Lewis v United Kingdom** (2003) had ruled that Article 6 had been violated, the appellant being deprived of a fair trial in that proceedings had not been stayed as an abuse of process on the ground of entrapment by police officers. The Court of Appeal found that there had been overwhelming incontrovertible evidence, and that the appellant – following legal advice – had pleaded guilty. To deport an individual to his country of origin where he would face trial in which evidence against him was likely to have been obtained by torture, violates Article 6. The Court of Human Rights so held in **Othman (Abu Qatada) v United Kingdom** (2012).

Remedial proceedings

In **Taylor v Lawrence** (2002), the Court of Appeal ruled that if it was established that a significant injustice had occurred, the court could re-open an appeal after its final judgment had been delivered and there was no alternative remedy. When the alternative remedy would be an appeal to the House of Lords, the Court of Appeal could only re-open a case where it was satisfied that no leave to appeal would be given by the House of Lords. Similarly, defects at trial

---

136 See also **HM Advocate v P** (2011).
137 See also **Al-Khawaja v United Kingdom; Tahery v United Kingdom** (2009).

which were capable of being reviewed by the Court of Appeal did not violate Article 6.[138] The Court of Appeal has also considered the procedures under the Housing Act 1996 in relation to decisions as to the suitability of accommodation for the homeless and declared that the right to appeal to the county court, which granted full jurisdiction to that court, satisfied the requirements of the 'developing domestic law of human rights'.[139] Article 6 was considered in tandem with Article 8 (the right to respect for private and family life) by the Court of Appeal in **St Brice v Southwark London BC** (2002). The court ruled that where a local authority, acting on a possession order granted by a county court, evicted a tenant without notice, it did not infringe the tenant's rights under the Convention. Those rights had already been protected by the hearing in the county court.

Time lapses in proceedings

On the reasonableness of time lapses between charge and trial, the Court of Appeal in **Dyer v Watson; HM Advocate v K** (2002) ruled that it would be a breach of Article 6 for a boy charged with serious sexual offences when aged 13 to be tried some 28 months later, when he would be a youth of 16. However, a delay of 20 months between charging police officers with perjury and the date of trial was not such a delay as to violate Article 6.[140]

The fixing of a penalty by tax commissioners in relation to a defaulting taxpayer amounted to the determination of a criminal offence and Article 6 of the Convention applied. The Chancery Division of the High Court so ruled in **King v Walden (Inspector of Taxes)** (2001). Accordingly, the taxpayer was entitled to have his case determined 'within a reasonable time'. Here there was a delay of five years, which the court stated was 'marginally, but only just' acceptable. Article 6 applies to the determination of civil penalties pursuant to criminal charges brought under the Value Added Tax Act 1994 and the Finance Act 1994.[141] In **Attorney General's Reference (No 2 of 2001)** (2001), the Court of Appeal ruled that, in considering whether a criminal charge had been determined within a reasonable time for the purposes of Article 6 of the Convention, the relevant time normally started to run when the defendant was charged by the police or served with a summons, rather than when he was first interviewed by the police.[142]

The right to legal representation

Legal representation is an essential feature of a fair trial. The Court of Human Rights has ruled that access to law must not be impeded (by the denial of legal advice or other means), but also that the state has a duty to ensure effective access to law.[143] The right of access to law is not absolute, but any restrictions which are imposed must not be such as to impair 'the very essence of the right'. Limitations will be incompatible with the Convention if they do not pursue a legitimate aim and are not proportional to the objective being sought.[144]

---

138 R v Smith (Joe) (2001); R v Craven (2000).
139 Runa Begum v Tower Hamlets LBC (2002).
140 On length of proceedings, see also Bullen v United Kingdom; Soneji v United Kingdom (2009).
141 Han and Yau t/a Murdishaw Supper Bar v Commissioners of Customs and Excise (2001).
142 See also HM Advocate v R (2003).
143 Airey v Ireland (1979). See also P, C and S v United Kingdom (2002). The Court of Appeal ruled that the equality of arms between prosecution and defence in criminal proceedings did not require representation of the defendant by Queen's Counsel merely because the Crown was so represented: R v Lee (Attorney-General's Reference No 82 of 2000) (2002). A doctor subject to disciplinary proceedings is entitled to legal representation, either as a question of natural justice under domestic law or under Article 6, see Kulkarni v Milton Keynes Hospital NHS Foundation Trust (2009). On representation at disciplinary proceedings see also R (G) v X School Governors (2009). See also Cadder v HM Advocate (2010).
144 Ashingdane v United Kingdom (1985). See also Ezeh and Connors v United Kingdom (2003).

In **Ambrose v Harris and Others** (2011) the Supreme Court ruled that a suspect's right to legal advice arose from the time he had been taken into police custody or his freedom of action curtailed, but generally not earlier. Accordingly, there was no rigid principle which required laying down a rule that a suspect must always have access to legal advice before any police questioning took place. However, once the need to protection against self-incrimination arises, the right to legal advice comes into play.

The presumption of innocence

The presumption of innocence has fared badly. Making the assumption that property or expenditure by a person convicted of a drug trafficking offence was the proceeds of drug trafficking was not incompatible with the presumption of innocence: **HM Advocate v McIntosh** (2001). Admitting, under statutory compulsion, to being the driver of a motor vehicle did not violate the right not to incriminate oneself, provided the overall fairness of trial was not compromised: **Brown v Stott** (2001). The reversal of the burden of proof in the Drug Trafficking Act 1994 did not contravene Article 6, given the powers of review held by the Court of Appeal: **R v Benjafield** (2002). See, however, **Sheldrake v Director of Public Prosecutions** (2003), in which the House of Lords ruled that the reversal of the burden of proof under the Road Traffic Act 1988 should be interpreted so as to reduce the burden of proof from a legal burden to an evidential burden.[145]

Article 7: the prohibition against retrospectivity

Article 7 prohibits retrospective criminal law. It is an accepted presumption of statutory interpretation under English law that Parliament does not intend – in the absence of clear words – to legislate with retrospective effect, and Article 7 reflects this approach.

A challenge lodged under the Convention, claiming a violation of Article 7, for a penalty imposed which could not have been foreseen occurred in **Harman and Hewitt v United Kingdom** (1989). Ms Harman showed confidential documents to a journalist after they had been read out in court, as a result of which she was found guilty of contempt. Previously, no liability had been imposed in such situations – the information had been regarded as having entered the 'public domain' through disclosure in court. Ms Harman's application was ruled admissible, but a friendly settlement was reached with the government.

The European Court of Human Rights has ruled on the compatibility of a conviction for marital rape with Article 7 of the Convention: **SW v United Kingdom; CR v United Kingdom** (1995). In **R v R** (1992), the House of Lords ruled that the exemption of husbands from the law of rape against their wives was obsolete. Two men were convicted of rape or attempted rape of their wives in 1989 and 1990, following the decision in **R v R**. The applicants alleged that their conviction amounted to a violation of Article 7 which prohibits a retrospective change in the criminal law. The Court ruled that the convictions did not violate the Convention: the judicial decisions had done no more than continue a line of reasoning which diminished a husband's immunity; the decisions had become a reasonably foreseeable development of the law and the decisions were not in contravention of the aims of Article 7.[146]

The following cases illustrate the approach of the courts under the Human Rights Act 1998.

• In **Gough v Chief Constable of Derbyshire** (2001), the Queen's Bench Division ruled that banning orders which prevented UK nationals from leaving the country in order to attend

---

145 See also **Davies v Health and Safety Executive** (2003). On the secrecy of jury deliberations see **R v Mirza; R v Connor and Pollock** (2004).
146 See also **Welch v United Kingdom** (1995).

regulated international football matches were lawful and a proportionate restriction on freedom of movement under EC law. Further, such an order imposed after a conviction of a public order offence was not a penalty and there was no violation of Article 7 of the Convention.

- In **R v C** (2004) the Court of Appeal dismissed an appeal against conviction for the rape of a wife in 1970. In 2002 the defendant had been convicted of a number of sexual and violent offences including the rape of his wife over 30 years previously. The defendant alleged a violation of Article 7. The Court applied the cases of **R v R** (1992) and **SW v United Kingdom** (1995). There was no abuse of process in prosecuting for an offence committed before the immunity from prosecution was lifted. Further, Article 7(2) provided 'ample justification' for trial and punishment 'according to the general principles recognised by civilised nations'.

Article 8: the right to respect for private and family life, home and correspondence

Article 8 provides the right to respect for private and family life, home and correspondence. The right is not absolute and may be restricted by law in the interests of national security, public safety or the economic well being of the country, for the prevention of disorder or crime, for the protection of health or morals, or for the protection of the rights and freedoms of others.

Article 8 has provided the legal means by which to challenge domestic law and practice in two principal areas – respect for privacy and non-intervention by the state (including the keeping of personal records), and respect for the individual's private life in terms of his or her own personal relationships. As can be seen from the following, Article 8 has been invoked in relation to unmarried couples,[147] mental patients, prisoners, the evidence of defendants in criminal proceedings, planning law and the making of possession orders over a home. It has also been raised in matters relating to deportation orders[148] and electoral law.[149]

The Convention right to privacy, discussed here, must also be considered in relation to freedom of expression, with which it may conflict. It will be seen from the case law on Article 10, discussed in Chapter 19, that the restrictions imposed on freedom of expression are having the effect of substantially promoting privacy, at least when considered within the context of protection from intrusion by the media. The right to respect for individual privacy and the media's right to freedom of expression was considered in **Author of a Blog v Times Newspapers Ltd** (2009). A police officer discussed issues relating to his work in a blog and sought to restrain the *Times* newspaper from revealing his identity. The Court ruled that it had first to ask the question whether A had a reasonable expectation of privacy, and secondly, if so, was the public interest in his identity such as to override that expectation. In this case, there was no quality of confidence involved, nor did A have a reasonable expectation of privacy.

Respect for individual privacy

The interception of communications has given rise to challenges under the Convention. In **Foxley v United Kingdom** (2001),[150] the Court of Human Rights ruled that Article 8 was violated

---

147 **M v Secretary of State for Work and Pensions** (2006).
148 See **Huang v Home Secretary** (2007).
149 A ban on smoking in hospital does not violate Article 8: **R (G) v Nottingham Healthcare Trust** (2008) and **R (E) v Nottinghamshire Healthcare NHS Trust, R (N) v Secretary of State for Health** (2009).
150 See also **PG and JH v United Kingdom** (2001).

by the interception of correspondence which included correspondence between the applicant and his solicitors. The legal basis for the interception was an Act of Parliament, under which a court ordered the redirection of the applicant's mail to a trustee in bankruptcy. However, the intercepts continued after the expiry of the court order: that was unjustified and violated Article 8.[151]

In **Malone v United Kingdom** (1984), the Court found that the law was unclear, and that, accordingly, 'the minimum degree of legal protection to which citizens are entitled under the rule of law in a democratic society is lacking' (paragraph 79). The government's response to the judgment was to introduce the Interception of Communications Act 1985 (see Chapter 22), which placed the granting of warrants for interception of communications on a statutory basis.[152]

The Court of Human Rights ruled in **Khan v United Kingdom** (2000) that covert surveillance by the police without statutory authority violated the right to respect for private and family life. As there was no statutory authority for the intercept, the interference could not be considered to be in accordance with law.[153] Allegations that Articles 6, 8 and 13 were violated by the intercept regime under the Regulations of Investigatory Powers Act 2000 (RIPA) failed in **Kennedy v United Kingdom** (2009). The Court of Human Rights ruled, in relation to Article 8, that the law provided sufficient safeguards in relation to the authorisation and processing of intercept warrants and mechanisms for complaints about and oversight of the system and insofar as the surveillance applied to the applicant, the measures were justified under Article 8.2. In **S and Marper v United Kingdom** (2010) the Court of Human Rights ruled that the retention of fingerprints and DNA samples from persons who have not been found guilty of any crime violated Article 8. In **R (GC) v Commissioner of Police of the Metropolis** (2011) the Supreme Court ruled that Guidelines issued by the Association of Chief Police Officers (ACPO), which conflicted with Convention requirements, were unlawful. The Protection of Freedoms Act 2012 reforms the law. In **Halford v United Kingdom** (1997), the European Court of Human Rights ruled that the interception of telephone calls at work violated Article 8. Ms Halford's (a former Assistant Chief Constable) telephone calls were intercepted by senior police officers. The Court also ruled that domestic law provided no avenue for a complaint such as this to be determined and awarded £10,000 compensation. This case raised, for the first time, the issue of the right to privacy of employees at work. Government lawyers had argued, unsuccessfully, that there was no protection under the Convention on the basis that the telephones which had been tapped were government property.

See further Chapter 19.

The Grand Chamber of the Court of Human Rights ruled, unanimously, that there had been a violation of Article 8 in **Roche v United Kingdom** (2005). The applicant had joined the Army in 1953 and had participated in mustard gas and nerve gas tests conducted under the auspices of the Army at Porton Down in 1962–63. He later suffered a number of health problems which he attributed to his participation in the tests. From 1987 he sought access to his service medical records with limited success. The Court ruled that the state had a positive

---

151 See also **R (P) v Secretary of State for the Home Department; R (Q) v Same** (2001); **R (S) v Chief Constable of South Yorkshire** (2002); **Wood v United Kingdom** (2004).

152 See also **McLeod v United Kingdom** (1999); **Armstrong v United Kingdom** (2002); **Taylor-Satori v United Kingdom** (2002, **R v Loveridge** (2001); **R v X,Y and Z** (2000). The refusal of a local authority to disclose its full secrets in relation to a person who had been in its care as a child amounted to a failure to fulfil the positive obligation to protect a person's private and family life: see **MG v United Kingdom** (2002). See also **Liberty v United Kingdom** (2008) regarding the legality of Ministry of Defence intercepts of Liberty's communication. The state had a wide discretion but arrangements had not been contained in legislation and were therefore not in accordance with law. See also **Szuluk v United Kingdom** (2009) in which the state's monitoring of medical correspondence between a detainee and his medical practitioners was disproportionate and a violation of Article 8.

153 The Police Act 1997 remedied the legal defect. On the admissibility of evidence gained through foreign intercepts and consideration of **Khan v United Kingdom**, see **R v X,Y and Z** (2000), Court of Appeal, Criminal Division. On the disclosure of CCTV footage to the media, see **Peck v United Kingdom** (2003).

obligation to provide an effective and accessible procedure enabling an applicant to have access to all records, and that an individual should not be required to litigate to obtain disclosure. In a high-profile case, the House of Lords considered the right to respect for private life within the context of clarity in the law. In **R (Purdy) v Director of Public Prosecutions** (2009), the Court held that the Director of Public Prosecutions should be required to publish his policy identifying the facts and circumstances that would be taken into account in considering whether to prosecute persons for aiding and abetting an assisted suicide[154] abroad.

In a significant case relating to the responsibility of the state towards citizens affected by industrial and manufacturing hazards, the Court of Human Rights ruled in **Guerra v Italy** (1998) that the failure of state authorities to advise citizens of the threat posed by environmental pollution violated their right of enjoyment of their homes in such a way as to affect their private and family life adversely.

The House of Lords considered both common law and Article 8 of the Convention in **R (Daly) v Secretary of State for the Home Department** (2001). It was Home Office policy that prisoners should be required to leave their cells during searches conducted by prison officers. The search included the scrutiny of privileged legal correspondence. The House of Lords ruled that the policy infringed the common law right to legal professional privilege in communications with legal advisers. The court ruled that the policy interfered with Article 8. Lord Bingham stated that:

> . . . the policy interfered with Mr Daly's exercise of his right under Article 8(1) to an extent much greater than necessity requires. In this instance, therefore, the common law and the Convention yield the same result . . .

In **R v Ashworth Special Hospital Authority ex parte N** (2001), the High Court ruled that the right to privacy was not violated through the random monitoring of telephone calls of mental patients classified as having dangerous, violent or criminal propensities. Provision had been made to gather information on escape plans, disturbances and arrangements to bring in illicit substances, threats to others and behaviour presenting security implications. There was evidence that patients were likely to abuse the use of telephones unless prevented from doing so. Random monitoring interfered with Article 8 no more than was necessary to achieve the permitted purpose.[155]

The police powers of stop and search under the Terrorism Act 2000 were tested in **R (Gillan and Quinton) v Commissioner of Police of the Metropolis** (2006). An authorisation – lasting 28 days and covering the whole of the London Metropolitan District – had been made allowing police officers to stop and search members of the public at random for articles that could be used in connection with terrorism.[156] There had been successive authorisations in place since 2001. In 2003, an arms fair was being held in Docklands, East London, which attracted opposition and a demonstration. The claimants – one a student, the other a journalist – were stopped and searched. Nothing incriminating was found. Their application for judicial review was unsuccessful and their appeal was considered by the House of Lords. The House of Lords ruled that the powers were subject to effective restraints and that there had been justification for the authorisations made since 2001 and that they were lawful. Moreover, there was no violation

---

154 Contrary to the Suicide Act 1961.
155 The compulsory detention and treatment of a dangerous mental patient who lacked capacity to consent does not violate Articles 3 or 8 of the Convention: **R (B) v S** (2006). On the standards of treatment expected of local authorities, see **R (McDonald) v Royal Borough of Kensington and Chelsea** (2011).
156 Under sections 44 and 45 of the Terrorism Act 2000. The authorisation had been confirmed by the Home Secretary pursuant to section 46.

of Article 5(1) of the Convention, in that they were merely kept from proceeding or kept waiting rather than deprived of their liberty.

In **Gillan and Quinton v United Kingdom** (2010), however, the Court of Human Rights found a violation of Article 8. Sections 44 to 47 of the Terrorism Act 2000 and the related Code of Practice did not comply with the requirements of legality. The wording of section 44, providing that a constable may stop and search a pedestrian in any area specified by him if he 'considers it expedient for the prevention of acts of terrorism' contained no requirement of necessity and therefore no requirement of any assessment of the proportionality of the measure. The breadth of discretion conferred on a police officer, which required him or her only to be looking for items which could be used in terrorism, without any requirement of having reasonable grounds for suspecting the presence of such articles, was unnecessarily and unlawfully wide. The Home Secretary made a Remedial Order under section 10 of the Human Rights act 1998 providing more 'targeted and proportionate' powers. Sections 44 to 47 of the Terrorism Act 2000 are repealed by section 59 of the Protection of Freedoms Act 2012. The 2012 Act brings the law on stop and search into line with Convention requirements.

See further Chapters 21 and 22.

The Supreme Court considered the right to respect for private life in **R (L) v Commissioner of Police of the Metropolis** (2009). The claimant was employed by an agency providing staff for schools and required to apply for an Enhanced Criminal Record Certificate. The claimant had no criminal record. However, the Certificate revealed that her son had been on the child protection register as a result of her care, and the agency dispensed with her services. The Supreme Court ruled that the information was capable of falling within Article 8, but that the information was relevant to her suitability for employment with children and that the risk to children outweighed the prejudicial effect on her employment prospects. In **R (F) and Thompson v Secretary of State for the Home Department** (2010) the Supreme Court upheld a Declaration of Incompatibility made by the High Court. In this case, the Sexual Offences Act 2003 required, in part, that some convicted sex offenders were subject to lifelong notification requirements. The requirements were not subject to any form of review and on this basis they constituted a disproportionate interference with Article 8 rights.[157]

The right of local authorities to seek possession orders in relation to public housing has been considered in relation to Article 8. The principal domestic case, about which there was continuing debate, was **Kay v Lambeth London Borough Council** (2006).[158] The Court of Human Rights, in **Kay v United Kingdom** (2010) has clarified the position. Where a local authority sought a possession order, the central question was whether the interference with a person's Article 8 right was proportionate to the aim pursued and thus 'necessary in a democratic society'. The issue of proportionality should be determined by an independent tribunal. If such an opportunity was not available there was a violation of Article 8.

Respect for private sexual life

In **Dudgeon v United Kingdom** (1982), the right to respect for privacy was examined against the claim that legislation in force in Northern Ireland prohibited homosexual conduct between adult males. As a result, the Homosexual Offences (Northern Ireland) Order 1982 was passed to bring domestic law into line with the requirements of the Convention. See also **Lustig-Praen and Beckett v United Kingdom** and **Smith and Grady v United Kingdom** (2000), in which the Court of Human Rights ruled that the ban on homosexuals in the armed forces violated Article 8 of the Convention.

---

157 See also **R (Wright) v Health Secretary** (2009): a Declaration of Incompatibility meant that section 82(4) of the Care Standards Act 2000 was incompatible with Articles 6 and 8.7.

158 See also **Doherty v Birmingham City Council** (2009); **McCann v United Kingdom** (2008); **Central Bedfordshire Council v Housing Action Zone Ltd** (2009).

The prosecution and conviction of a man, for engaging in non-violent homosexual acts in private with up to four other men, was a violation of Article 8. The Court of Human Rights so held in **ADT v United Kingdom** (2000). The Court ruled that the applicant was a victim of an interference with his right to respect for his private life, both as to the existence of legislation prohibiting consensual sexual acts between more than two men in private, and as to the conviction for gross indecency. The interference was not justified as being 'necessary in a democratic society' in the protection of morals and rights and freedoms of others.

Respect for family life

In **Hoffman v Austria** (1994), the Court ruled that Ms Hoffman had been discriminated against (contrary to Article 14) and her respect for family life violated (Article 8) by the Supreme Court of Austria, which had denied her the custody of her children on divorce, principally because she had become a Jehovah's Witness. In **Marckx v Belgium** (1979), a complaint was lodged on the basis that Articles 12 and 14 had been violated by discriminatory inheritance rules for illegitimate children.[159] English law relating to care proceedings and the powers of local authorities to control access of parents to children in local authority care have also been successfully challenged under the Convention, leading to changes to the rights of parents to access to a court of law in order to challenge a local authority's decision to terminate contact between children and their parents.[160]

In **G v United Kingdom (Minors: Right of Contact)** (2000), there was no violation of Article 8 with regard to the alleged failure of the English and Scottish courts to enforce access arrangements between the applicant and his children, following his wife's refusal to comply with court orders. Compare **TP and KM v United Kingdom** (2001), in which a violation of Articles 8 and 13 was held to have been committed by the authorities. A mother and daughter had been separated for nearly a year by the local authority as a result of allegations that the child had been sexually abused by the mother's partner. The local authority had withheld evidence from the mother and failed to submit the issue to court, and had thereby excluded the mother from the decision-making process.[161]

The rights of Gypsies to live on their own land without planning permission was considered by the Court of Human Rights in **Buckley v United Kingdom** (1997).[162] The Court ruled that the United Kingdom authorities had not violated Article 8 or Article 14 (enjoyment of substantive rights without discrimination) of the Convention. Mrs Buckley had purchased land, and had sought and been refused planning permission. The Court ruled, by a majority, that the protected right to a home may be limited 'in accordance with law' as 'necessary in a democratic society'. However, the Court ruled that the measures taken by national authorities must be proportionate to the legitimate aim pursued.[163] In **South Buckinghamshire District Council v Porter, Chichester District Council v Searle, Wrexham Borough Council v Berry** and **Hertsmere Borough Council v Harty** (2003), the power to issue injunctions to restrain the breach of planning control was in issue in relation to Gypsies. In an unusually sympathetic decision in relation to Gypsies, the Court of Appeal ruled that the power to grant the injunction should not be used to evict Gypsies from their mobile homes unless the need for such a remedy to protect the environment outweighed the Gypsies' rights under Article 8. The precedents, **Mole Valley DC v Smith** (1992), **Guildford BC v Smith** (1994) and **Hambleton DC v Bird** (1995), could not be considered

---

159 See the Family Law Reform Act 1987; see also the Inheritance (Provision for Family and Dependants) Act 1975 and the Fatal Accidents Act 1976, as amended, both of which place the illegitimate child in the same position as legitimate children.
160 **WRO v United Kingdom** (1988), which resulted in the Child Care Act 1980, s 12.
161 On care proceedings relating to children see also **K v United Kingdom** (2009) on medical treatment and Article 8 see **MAK and RK v United Kingdom** (2010).
162 See Barnett, 1996.
163 See also **Chapman v United Kingdom** (2001).

consistent with the court's duty under section 6(1) of the Human Rights Act 1998 to act compatibly with Convention rights. Proportionality required not only that the injunction be appropriate and necessary for the attainment of the public interest objective sought, but also that it did not impose an excessive burden on the individual whose private interests – here the Gypsy's private life and home and the retention of his ethnic identity – were at stake.[164] Gypsy rights were also at issue in **Clarke v Secretary of State for the Environment, Transport and the Regions** (2002). In this case, the Queen's Bench Division ruled that in deciding whether to grant planning permission to a Gypsy to station a caravan on land for his residential use it could be a breach of Articles 8 and 14 (the right to enjoyment of Convention rights without discrimination) to take into account the fact that he had refused the offer of alternative, conventional housing accommodation as being contrary to his culture as a Gypsy.[165]

The right to respect for family life has been raised in asylum cases. In **Omojudi v United Kingdom** (2009), the Court of Human Rights ruled that the deportation of a sex offender who had been granted indefinite leave to remain in the United Kingdom and had resided in the United Kingdom for 26 years was disproportionate and a violation of Article 8. The Court attached great weight to the solidity of family ties in the United Kingdom and the difficulties the family would experience if they were to return to Nigeria. In **Beoku-Betts v Secretary of State for the Home Department** (2008), the House of Lords ruled that 'family life' should be interpreted so as to include all members of a close family unit, rather than solely the right of the individual. As Baroness Hale put it:

> . . . the central point about family life . . . is that the whole is greater than the sum of its individual parts. The right to respect for the family life of one necessarily encompasses the right to respect for the family life of others, normally a spouse or minor children, with whom that family life is enjoyed.[166]

The interests of children in assessing whether the extradition of their parents was a proportionate interference with the right to respect for family life was considered by the Supreme Court in **HH v Deputy Prosecutor of the Italian Republic and others** (2012). Extradition is the process whereby individuals accused of committing crimes in other countries are returned to that country to stand trial. Extradition is governed by international treaty obligations and the Extradition Act 2003. The children's interests were a 'primary consideration'. However, there was the public interest in extradition which also carried great weight, and unless the consequences of interference with the Article 8 right were 'exceptionally severe', the public interest was likely to prevail. The test to be applied was whether the gravity of the interference was justified by the gravity of the public interest pursued (per Baroness Hale of Richmond).

Where there is no 'family life' capable of protection, Article 8 may protect an individual's right to private life. This occurred in **AA v United Kingdom** (2011). A deportation order had been made against a convicted rapist, on the basis that the Home Secretary deemed his deportation to be conducive to the public good.[167] The Court of Human Rights ruled that for settled migrants the community in which he lived constituted part of the concept of 'private life'. Furthermore his deportation would not be proportionate, given that the offence had been committed whilst a minor and that he had been allowed to remain for three and a half years.

---

164 See also **First Secretary of State v Chichester DC** (2004), in which Article 8 rights prevailed over any harm to the public interest which could be offset by imposing conditions.
165 See also **Poplar Housing and Regeneration Community Association Ltd v Donoghue** (2001).
166 At para 4. See also **AS (Somalia) v Secretary of State for the Home Department** (2009); **Khan AW v United Kingdom** (2010).
167 See section 3(5)(a) Immigration Act 1971 and rule 364 of the Immigration Rules.

Article 8 was invoked alongside Article 12 (the right to marry and found a family) in **R v Secretary of State for the Home Department ex parte Mellor** (2001). A prisoner, who was sentenced to life imprisonment, claimed that he was entitled to facilities to enable him and his wife to have a child through the use of artificial insemination. The Court of Appeal ruled that imprisonment was incompatible with the exercise of conjugal rights and that the restrictions in Article 8(2) applied. The restrictions were necessary for the maintenance of security in prison. Prisoners inevitably forfeited aspects of their rights. It did not follow, however, that prisoners would always be prevented from inseminating their wives artificially, or naturally.[168] The interference with the fundamental human rights in question involved an exercise in proportionality. Exceptional circumstances could require the restriction to yield. In this case, however, they did not.[169]

Cases involving Article 8 and Article 10 (freedom of expression) are considered in Chapter 19.

An overlap may also occur between Article 8 and Article 12, the right to marry. Two cases are of interest here. In **R (Baiai) v Secretary of State for the Home Department** (2008) procedural requirements imposed on those persons subject to immigration controls relating to marriages which are to be solemnised on the authority of a Superintendent Registrar's Certificate (but not those intending to marry under Church of England procedures) were held to be unlawful.[170] The Secretary of State's claim that these requirements prevented 'sham' marriages was unproven and the procedures were discriminatory. They violated the right to marry, Article 12. In **R (Quila) v Secretary of State for the Home Department** (2011) an immigration rule which was designed to deter forced marriages was held to be an unjustified interference with family life protected under Article 8. The scheme provided that the minimum age for a person to be granted a visa for the purposes of settling in the United Kingdom as a spouse, or to sponsor another, was raised from 18 to 21. The Secretary of State had failed to justify the restriction and it was unlawful.[171]

Article 9: freedom of thought, conscience and religion

This Article has founded the basis for few cases under the Convention. Applications which have been made under this Article relate primarily to the conditions under which an individual may exercise his rights. In the case of prisoners detained following a criminal conviction, the prison authorities are entitled to prescribe limits to the exercise of religious and other rights, simply because such restrictions represent 'an inherent feature of lawful imprisonment'. In **X v Austria** (1965), refusal by prison authorities to allow a Buddhist prisoner to grow a beard was held not to violate the Convention.[172]

Under the Human Rights Act 1998 the following cases illustrate the courts' approach.

- Article 9 was not violated by the prohibition in the Misuse of Drugs Act 1971 in relation to the supply of cannabis which it was claimed was for use in acts of religious worship (Rastafarianism). The Court of Appeal so held in **R v Taylor (Paul Simon)** (2001).[173]

---

168 There was no breach of Article 8 through the entry in the register of sex offenders of persons convicted of sexual offences: **Forbes v Secretary of State for the Home Department** (2006).

169 There was no breach of Article 12 as a result of the prison authorities' refusal to allow artificial insemination while in prison: **Dickson v United Kingdom** (2006).

170 Marriage Act 1949; Asylum and Immigration (Treatment of Claimants, etc) Act 2004, section 19.

171 Immigration Rules, paragraph 277.

172 Note that in **R (Shabina Begum) v Denbigh High School** (2006), the House of Lords ruled that a school's uniform policy did not violate Article 9.

173 See also **Connolly v Director of Public Prosecutions** (2007).

- In **R v Secretary of State for Education and Employment ex parte Williamson** (2005), the House of Lords held that a genuine belief in corporal punishment in schools was not a manifestation in practice or observance of a religion or belief. Nor was it a religious or philosophical conviction for the purposes of the right to education in Article 2 of the First Protocol.
- In **R (Shabina Begum) v Denbigh High School** (2006) the House of Lords ruled that there was no violation of Article 9 where a school adopted a policy relating to permissible uniforms which prohibited the wearing of a jilbab. The school was sensitive to the needs of its pupils and provided a choice of uniforms.[174]

Special considerations apply to the position of religion and the churches. Section 13 of the Act provides for freedom of thought, conscience and religion, and states:

> 13(1) If a court's determination of any question arising under this Act might affect the exercise by a religious organisation (itself or its members collectively) of the Convention right to freedom of thought, conscience and religion, it must have a particular regard to the importance of that right.

The section was included to protect the churches from liability under the Convention. Thus, for example, if a person alleges that he or she is the victim of a breach of the Convention right to marry (Article 12) or the right to respect for private and family life (Article 8) by the beliefs, rules and practices of a religious faith, the court, in determining the issue, must have special regard to the importance of those beliefs and practices.

Article 10: freedom of expression

NOTE that freedom of expression is discussed in detail in the next chapter (Chapter 19)
Freedom of expression includes freedom to hold opinions and to receive and impart information and ideas without interference by public authority and regardless of frontiers. The right is not absolute and may be restricted by law – to the extent necessary in a democratic society – in the interests of national security, territorial integrity or public safety, for the prevention of disorder or crime, for the protection of health or morals, for the protection of the reputation or rights of others, for preventing the disclosure of information received in confidence, or for maintaining the authority and impartiality of the judiciary.

When the Human Rights Bill was before Parliament, the government made it clear that it did not intend the Act to create a right to privacy under English law. However, in interpreting the law, English judges have been faced with conflicts between the right to respect for private and family life (Article 8) and Article 10 – the right to freedom of expression. In resolving this conflict, the courts have extended the law relating to breach of confidence in a manner which restricts freedom of expression and thereby enhances the protection of a person's privacy. This is an important development in the law, and the major cases which should be considered (each of which is discussed in Chapter 19) are the following:

See further Chapter 19.

- **Douglas v Hello Ltd!** (2001)
- **A v B** (2002)
- **Campbell v MGN** (2004)
- **McKennitt v Ash** (2007)

---

174 See also **R (Playfoot) v Millais School Governing Body** (2007).

- **HRH Prince of Wales v Associated Newspapers Ltd** (2007)
- **Lord Browne of Madingley v Associated Newspapers Ltd** (2007).[175]

Article 11: Freedom of peaceful assembly and association

In this chapter the Article 11 right relating to 'assembly and association' is considered.

NOTE that the English law relating to freedom of assembly and association is discussed in detail in Chapter 20

The right to freedom of peaceful assembly and to freedom of association with others includes the right to form and join trade unions. The rights are not absolute and may be restricted by law. The right to join a trade union has been interpreted to incorporate the right not to join a trade union. In **Young, James and Webster** (1981), the Court interpreted Article 11 to mean that there is a measure of choice left to individual workers whether or not to join a trade union.

Deprivation of the right to be a member of a trade union was considered by the Court in **Council of Civil Service Unions v United Kingdom** (the **GCHQ** case) (1985). The Minister for the Civil Service, the Prime Minister, had, following industrial unrest, by Order in Council ruled that workers at Government Communications Headquarters (GCHQ) would no longer be entitled to membership of a trade union. The ban was challenged by judicial review proceedings, which were ultimately unsuccessful in the House of Lords. The applicants argued that their rights under Article 11 had been infringed, and also rights under Article 13, which provides for an effective domestic remedy. In answer, the government argued that the order was justified, *inter alia*, under Article 11(2) on the basis of the protection of national security. The Commission found a clear violation of Article 11. However, the ban on union membership was justifiable under Article 11(2) and therefore there was no violation of the Convention.

See further Chapters 5 and 25.

In **Wilson v United Kingdom** (2002), the Court of Human Rights held that financial incentives offered by employers to employees in exchange for employees giving up trade union protection for collective bargaining purposes violated Article 11. The applicants had applied to employment tribunals, arguing that the requirement to sign contracts giving up their rights was contrary to the Employment Protection (Consolidation) Act 1978, section 23(1)(a). Those proceedings culminated in the House of Lords, which ruled against them. The Court of Human Rights ruled that while the state was not directly involved, the responsibility of the state was engaged where it failed to secure to the applicants the rights conferred under Article 11. On the case law relating to the right to assembly, see Chapter 20.

In **ASLEF v United Kingdom** (2007) the Court of Human Rights ruled that English law violated Article 11. Mr Lee was a member of the British National Party. As a result of his political activities, he was expelled from his trade union, ASLEF. Following legal proceedings, ASLEF was compelled to readmit Mr Lee or be liable to pay him compensation. It was ASLEF's argument that Mr Lee's political values and ideals clashed fundamentally with its own. The Court ruled that the union had the right to control its own membership. If it did not, the union could not effectively pursue its own political goals. The legal restriction which prevented the union from expelling Mr Lee violated the right of freedom of association (Article 11).

Article 11 was considered in **Royal Society for the Prevention of Cruelty to Animals v Attorney General** (2002). The Chancery Division ruled that the RSPCA had the right to exclude applicants whom the Society thought in good faith were likely to damage its objectives. In question was

---

175 See also **Max Mosley v News Group Newspapers** (2008).

the right of the Society to exclude current members and deny membership to applicants who sought to reverse the Society's policy against hunting with dogs. However, the court ruled that the Society should adopt a procedure through which any potentially excluded person should have the opportunity to make representations. Freedom of association in relation to demonstrations and police powers was considered by the Court of Appeal in **R (Laporte) v Chief Constable of Gloucestershire Constabulary** (2004). The case is discussed in Chapter 20.

Challenges to the Hunting Act 2004, based in part on human rights grounds, reached the House of Lords in **R (Countryside Alliance and others) v Her Majesty's Attorney General and others** (2007).[176] It was argued that the prohibition on hunting with dogs infringed Articles 8, 11, 14 and Article 1 of Protocol 1.[177] Rejecting all the arguments, the House of Lords ruled that Article 8 was not engaged: fox hunting was a very public activity. Nor was Article 11, which was designed to protect freedom of political association and free speech: here the gathering was purely for pleasure and sport. As neither of these Articles was infringed, there was no breach of Article 14. In relation to Protocol 1, the Court ruled, following the Court of Human Rights, that a potential loss of future income could not found an enforceable claim.

Article 12: the right to marry and found a family

Article 12 provides that 'men and women of marriageable age have the right to marry and to found a family, according to the national laws governing the exercise of this right'.

The right of transsexuals to marry was previously denied by the Court of Human Rights; see **Rees v United Kingdom** (1987) and **Cossey v United Kingdom** (1992). In 2002, however, in **Goodwin v United Kingdom**, the Court found that English law, which prohibits transsexuals from marrying on the basis that a person's sex determines gender identity for marriage purposes and cannot be changed, violated both Articles 8 (the right to privacy) and 12. The Court ruled that the law placed transsexuals in a position where they could 'experience feelings of vulnerability, humiliation and anxiety' and that the 'very essence of the Convention was respect for human dignity and human freedom'. On the right to marry, the Court held that the matter could not be left entirely within the state's margin of appreciation and there was no justification for denying transsexuals the right to marry. In the earlier case of **B v France** (1992), the Court had ruled that French law violated Article 8, in that official documentation could not be altered, thereby causing the applicant distress and humiliation.[178] Following the **Goodwin** case, the House of Lords ruled in **Bellinger v Bellinger** (2003) that English law which prevented transsexuals from entering a valid marriage was incompatible with the Convention. As a result of these two cases, the Gender Recognition Act 2004 provides transsexual people with legal recognition of their acquired gender. Once legal recognition has been granted, a new birth certificate can be granted and the person will be eligible to marry someone of the opposite sex.

The right to marry and found a family does not entail a right to a termination of marriage by divorce. In **Johnston v Ireland** (1987), the applicant claimed that his right under Article 12 was violated by the government through its failure to provide for divorce in Ireland which would enable him to marry and found a family with the woman with whom he was now living. The Court of Human Rights ruled, in **B and L v United Kingdom** (2005), that the ban on in-law marriages (Marriage Act 1949, as amended by the Marriage (Prohibited Degrees of

---

176 HL 52, 53 and 54 respectively.
177 It was also argued that Arts 28 and 49 of the EC Treaty were infringed by the Act.
178 See also **X,Y and Z v United Kingdom** (1997); **AV v United Kingdom** (1998); Leach, 1998.

Relationship) Act 1986) violated Article 12. There was an inconsistency between the legal impediment to such marriages and the possibility of removing the incapacity by a private Act of Parliament and that made the ban irrational, illogical and a violation of the right to marry.

In **R (Baiai) v Secretary of State for the Home Department** (2007) the Court of Appeal ruled that the statutory scheme (2007) requiring permission to marry from the Home Office for those subject to immigration control or those who had entered the United Kingdom illegally contravened Articles 12 and 14. In order to be compatible with the Convention it was necessary that there be adequate investigation into individual cases to establish that they very likely fell within the target category.[179]

Article 13: the right to an effective remedy

Article 13 imposes a duty on Member States to provide effective remedies for any violation of the substantive rights protected by the Convention. Article 13 has been interpreted to mean that an effective remedy before a national authority is guaranteed to 'everyone who claims that his rights and freedoms under the Convention have been violated'.[180]

Judicial review provides an effective means by which to ensure that government complies with the procedural requirements of the law.[181] However, judicial review may not give the degree of protection required under the Convention. As will be seen in Chapter 25, judicial review is concerned with the procedural correctness of a decision, not with the merits of that decision. The adequacy of judicial review as a remedy was considered by the Court of Human Rights in **Kingsley v United Kingdom** (2002). There, the Gaming Board had revoked the applicant's licence. The applicant claimed that the Board was biased against him. The Court of Appeal held that even if there had been some form of bias, the decision on the licence had to be taken by the Board because there was no other body with jurisdiction to make the decision, and that as efforts had been made to minimise the effect of any potential bias, the decision could not be impugned for bias. The Court of Human Rights ruled that the Gaming Board did not present the 'necessary appearance of impartiality' and that 'the subsequent judicial review was not sufficiently broad to remedy that defect'.[182]

The failure to provide abused children with a procedure whereby their allegations that the local authority had failed to protect them from serious ill-treatment or the possibility of obtaining an enforceable award of compensation for the damage suffered through abuse See Chapters amounted to a violation of Article 13. The Court of Human Rights so held in **DP and JC v United** 23–25. **Kingdom** (2002).

Article 14: the prohibition of discrimination in the enjoyment of Convention rights

Article 14 provides for non-discrimination in the enjoyment of the substantive rights and freedoms protected by the Convention. There is not, therefore, a right to non-discrimination *per se* but, rather, a right not to be discriminated against in relation to any of the other rights and freedoms. Thus, Article 14 enjoys no independent existence; it is tied to other Articles in the Convention.[183] However, it is possible that a violation of Article 14 is found even where a

179 See also **O'Donoghue v United Kingdom** (2011).
180 **Klass v Federal Republic of Germany** (1978); see also **Bubbins v United Kingdom**: the absence of a judicial determination over the liability of the police in damages violated Article 13.
181 **Vilvarajah and Four Others v United Kingdom** (1991); and see **Leander v Sweden** (1987).
182 See also **Tsfayo v United Kingdom** (2006).
183 **X v Federal Republic of Germany** (1970).

claim that a breach of another Article has occurred fails. For example, in **Abdulaziz, Cabales and Balkandali** (1985), three foreign wives residing in England complained that their husbands were not allowed to enter the country. The applicants alleged a violation of Articles 8 and 14. The Court rejected the complaint concerning Article 8, adopting the view that the right to family life does not entail the right to establish a home wheresoever people choose. However, there was a violation of Article 14, in so far as the rules provided easier conditions under which men could bring in their wives than those which existed for wives trying to bring their husbands into the country.[184] The Court of Human Rights ruled that differential treatment in relation to sentences served before release violated Article 5 in conjunction with Article 14 in **Clift v United Kingdom** (2010). Discrimination under Article 14, in conjunction with Article 1 of Protocol 1 (below) has been found by the European Court of Human Rights in respect of differing treatment in relation to welfare benefits: see **Booth v United Kingdom** (2009); **Blackgrove v United Kingdom** (2009); **Robert Murray v United Kingdom** (2009); **Turner v United Kingdom** (2009) and **Twomey v United Kingdom** (2009).

Article 15: derogation in times of public emergency

This has been discussed above, at page 403.

Article 16: aliens

Article 16 authorises restrictions on the political activity of aliens. This provision affects all Articles in the Convention in so far as they relate to the political activities of aliens. Article 16 does not mean that there can be no violation of other substantive Articles in respect of aliens.

Protocol 1

By a majority of ten votes to seven, the Grand Chamber of the Court of Human Rights overturned the judgment of a Chamber of the Court in **JA Pye (Oxford) Ltd v United Kingdom** (2007). The Court ruled that English law which allows squatters to obtain the right to title of land after 12 years of adverse possession did not violate Protocol 1, nor did the Limitation Acts which pursued a legitimate aim in the public interest. The company could have taken measures such as asking for rent or commencing legal action for recovery of the land to end the adverse possession.

The Court of Appeal in **Lindsay v Commissioners of Customs and Excise** (2002) ruled that the policy of seizing motor vehicles belonging to people who evaded duty on tobacco and alcohol, and refusal to restore the vehicle save in exceptional circumstances, fettered the discretion of officers. It failed to distinguish between commercial smuggling and importation for distribution among family and friends. Under Article 1 of Protocol 1, deprivation of possessions could only be justified if it was in the public interest.[185] There had to be a reasonable relationship of proportionality between the means employed and the aim pursued. Here there was not.[186]

A child's right to education under Article 2 of Protocol 1 to the Convention was not violated by enforcement of immigration control which involved the removal of a child settled in a school in England after her parents' application to remain in the United Kingdom had been

---

184 The Immigration Rules were amended in 1985 as a result of this case.
185 In **R (Malik) v Waltham Forest NHS Primary Care Trust** (2007) the Court of Appeal ruled that neither the prospect of a future loss of income nor the right to practise in the National Health Service could amount to a possession under Protocol 1.
186 See also **Wilson v First County Trust Ltd (No 2)** (2003), discussed above.

rejected. The Court of Appeal so held in **R v Secretary of State for the Home Department ex parte Holub** (2001). Article 2 did not confer a right to education in any particular country and was accordingly limited in scope. This restrictive approach was reiterated in **A v Head Teacher and Governors of Lord Grey School** (2006), in which the House of Lords, following the reasoning in the **Belgian Linguistics Case** (1968), denied that the exclusion of a pupil from school amounted to a denial of the right to education, in light of the fact that there were alternative schools available.

Towards a Bill of Rights?

In 2011 the Commission on a Bill of Rights, an independent Commission set up by the government, published a Discussion Paper designed to begin a period of public consultation on the question of whether the United Kingdom should have a Bill of Rights. The terms of reference were:

- to investigate the creation of a UK Bill of Rights that incorporates and builds on all our obligations under the European Convention on Human Rights, ensures that these rights continue to be enshrined in UK law, and protects and extends our liberties;
- to examine the operation and implementation of these obligations, and consider ways to promote a better understanding of the true scope of these obligations and liberties;
- to provide advice to the Government on the ongoing Interlaken process to reform the Strasbourg court ahead of and following the UK's Chairmanship of the Council of Europe;
- to consult, including with the public, judiciary and devolved administrations and legislatures, and aim to report no later than by the end of 2012.

In carrying out its inquiries, the Commission adopted four principles, namely:

- The Human Rights Act is essential for the protection of human rights in the United Kingdom and should be retained. Any Bill of Rights should build on the HRA. Any Bill of Rights that replaces the HRA should not be brought into force until and unless it contains at least the same levels of protection of rights and mechanisms under the HRA, and complies with obligations under international treaties.
- The government and any future government should ensure that the process of developing any Bill of Rights involves and includes all sectors of society, that the process and result creates a feeling of ownership in society as a whole, that the consultation is conducted by an independent body, and that it is adequately resourced.
- In any Bill of Rights process, the government should actively promote understanding of the Human Rights Act, European Convention on Human Rights and the rights and mechanisms they protect, as well as countering any misconceptions.
- The Commission will use the results and recommendations from its Human Rights Inquiry to inform its response to any Bill of Rights and further develop the current human rights framework.

A second period of consultation commenced in July 2012.

Summary

The European Convention on Human Rights has provided vital protection for citizens against the power of the state. As has been seen, the case law against the United Kingdom is substantial and, in many instances, has led to considerable reform of the law. The Convention has for the most part, and despite its limitations in scope, served individuals well in the protection of fundamental rights. Nevertheless, the right of individual petition, conferred in 1965, meant long delays and high costs for litigants. The incorporation of Convention rights into domestic law under the Human Rights Act 1998 was a logical step forward for a government seriously committed to individual rights and freedoms and represents a significant extension of the rule of law. Incorporation may also change the traditional public conception of individual freedoms in favour of rights, and bring a greater clarity to the law relating to both civil liberties and human rights. The Act preserves the traditional balance in the constitution – ensuring that Parliament alone can reform the law but enabling judges of the higher courts to grant a Declaration of Incompatibility where a violation of a right which cannot be remedied by interpretation of the relevant domestic law is found. The Declaration does not invalidate the offending law but puts government and Parliament on notice that reform is called for.

Further Reading

Amos, M. (2007) 'The Impact of the Human Rights Act on the UK's Performance Before the European Court of Human Rights', Public Law, 655.

Buxton, R. (2010) 'The Future of Declarations of Incompatibility', Public Law, 213.

Clayton, R. (2001) 'Regaining a Sense of Proportion: The Human Rights Act and the Proportionality Principle', EHRLR 504.

Craig, P. (2001) 'The Courts, the Human Rights Act and Judicial Review', Law Quarterly Review, 117: 589.

Edwards, R. (2002) 'Judicial Deference under the Human Rights Act', Modern Law Review, 65: 859.

Ewing, K. 'The Futility of the Human Rights Act', Public Law, 829.

Fenwick, H. (2009) 'Marginalising Human Rights: breach of the peace, "kettling", the Human Rights Act and Public Protest', Public Law, 737.

Fredman, S. (2006) 'Human Rights Transformed: Positive Duties and Positive Rights', Public Law, 498.

Gearty, C. (2002) 'Reconciling Parliamentary Democracy and Human Rights', Law Quarterly Review, 118: 248.

Gearty, C. (2006) Can Human Rights Survive?, Cambridge: CUP (Hamlyn Lectures).

Harris, D.J. (2004) 'Human Rights or Mythical Beasts', Law Quarterly Review, 120: 428.

Harvey, C. (2004) 'Talking about Human Rights', European Human Rights Law Review, 500.

Hickman, T.R. (2005) 'Between Human Rights and the Rule of Law', Modern Law Review, 655.

Hoffmann, Lord (2009) 'The Universality of Human Rights', Law Quarterly Review, 125: 416.

Irvine of Lairg, Lord (2003) 'The Impact of the Human Rights Act: Parliament, the Courts and the Executive', Public Law, 308.

Jowell, J. (2003) 'Judicial Deference and Human Rights: A Question of Competence' in P. Craig and R. Rawlings (eds) Law and Administration in Europe, Oxford: OUP.

Kavanagh, A. (2009) 'Judging the Judges under the Human Rights Act: deference, disillusionment and the "war on terror"', Public Law, 287.

Kavanagh, A (2010) 'Defending Deference', 126 LQR 222.

Klug, F. (2007) 'A Bill of Rights: Do We Need One or Do We Already Have One?', Public Law, 701.

Klug, F. and Starmer, K. (2005), 'Standing Back from the Human Rights Act: How Effective is it Five Years On?', Public Law, 716.

Lester, A. (2005) 'The Utility of the Human Rights Act: A Reply to Keith Ewing', Public Law, 249.

Malleson, K (2011), 'The Evolving Role of the UK Supreme Court', Public Law, 754.

Nicol, D. (2006) 'Law and Politics after the Human Rights Act', Public Law, 722.

Oliver, D. (2004), 'Functions of a Public Nature and the Human Rights Act', Public Law, 329.

Redmayne, M, (2012) 'Hearsay and Human Rights: *Al-Khawaja* in the Grand Chamber', Modern Law Review, 75: 865.

Responding to Human Rights Judgments: Government Response to the Joint Committee on Human Rights' Thirty-first Report of Session 2007–08. Cm 7524, 2009.

Steyn, Lord (2005) 'Deference: A Tangled Story', Public Law, 346.

Van Zyl Smith, J. (2007) 'The New Purposive Interpretation of Statutes: HRA section 3 after *Ghaidan v Godin-Mendoza*'.

Young, A.L. (2009) 'In Defence of Due Deference', 72 MLR 554.

Young, A. (2005) 'A Peculiarly British Protection of Human Rights', Modern Law Review, 68: 858.

Young, A.J. (2011) 'Is Dialogue Working under the Human Rights Act 1998?', Public Law, 773.

Chapter 19

Freedom of Expression and Privacy

Introduction

In this chapter we examine the scope of freedom of expression and the lawful restrictions which may be imposed upon it together with the law relating to breach of confidence and privacy.

Freedom of Expression

Freedom of expression entails many aspects: an individual's freedom to express any view he or she wishes, however offensive to others, in private or public; freedom of the press to express any view; freedom of authors to write and publish; and freedom of film makers to record and distribute films/videos for private and public consumption. From the standpoint of democracy, freedom of speech is crucial to the exchange of political ideas and to the formation of political opinions. The freedom of speech guaranteed to Members of Parliament under Article IX of the Bill of Rights 1689 reflects the constitutional importance of political debate, as does the right of newspapers and broadcasters to publish fair and accurate reports of parliamentary proceedings.[1] Freedom of expression is essential in a free and democratic society, and restrictions which inhibit criticism of public authorities, in particular, undermine the potential for scrutiny of official action. For this reason, in **Derbyshire County Council v Times Newspapers** (1993), the House of Lords ruled that neither local nor central government had standing to sue for defamation. Lord Keith stated that 'it is of the highest importance that a democratically elected governmental body . . . should be open to uninhibited public criticism'.[2]

Freedom of Expression and the Human Rights Act

In the United Kingdom, before the Human Rights Act 1998 there was no right to free speech but, in a negative way, there was a freedom of expression subject to the limitations imposed by law. Freedom of expression is now regulated under Article 10 of the European Convention on Human Rights, incorporated into domestic law under the Human Rights Act 1998. However, the right is limited by restrictions.

Freedom of expression under Article 10 includes the 'freedom to hold opinions and to receive and impart information and ideas without interference by public authority and regardless of frontiers'.[3] The right is subject to such legal restrictions as are 'necessary in a democratic society in the interests of national security or public safety, for the prevention of disorder or crime, for the protection of health or morals or for the protection of the rights and freedoms of others'.[4] Legal restrictions on the exercise of the right by members of the armed forces, police or administration of the state are permitted. The effect of Article 10 is that all restrictions on the right must be justified, in common with other restricted Articles, according to these criteria: they must be both *necessary* and *proportionate*.[5]

---

1 The Parliamentary Papers Act 1840. See Chapter 17.
2 Note that both the Freedom of Information Act 2000 and the Data Protection Act 1998, as amended, discussed in Chapter 10, are central both to the availability of information and to the protection of privacy of the individual.
3 Article 10 does not prevent state licensing of broadcasting, television or cinemas.
4 The issue of whether to order the postponement of reporting of a trial until after the conclusion of a second related trial came before the Court of Appeal in **R v Sherwood ex parte Telegraph Group plc** (2001). The court ruled that the ban was necessary in the interests of justice.
5 On the meaning of these terms, see Chapter 18.

The Article 10 right is also regulated by section 12 of the Human Rights Act 1998, which was drafted so as to prevent claims to privacy[6] restricting freedom of the press. Section 12(4) provides that:

> The court must have particular regard to the importance of the Convention right to freedom of expression and, where the proceedings relate to material which the respondent claims, or which appears to the court, to be journalistic, literary or artistic material (or to conduct connected with such material), to –
>
> (a) the extent to which –
>
> (i) the material is, or is about to, become available to the public;[7] or
> (ii) it is, or would be, in the public interest for the material to be published;
>
> (b) any relevant privacy code.[8]

The House of Lords upheld the right of prisoners to freedom of expression in **R v Secretary of State for the Home Department ex parte Simms** (1999). The court ruled that an indiscriminate ban on all visits to prisoners by journalists or authors in their professional capacity was unlawful. A prisoner had a right to seek, through oral interviews, to persuade a journalist to investigate his allegations of miscarriage of justice in the hope that his case might be re-opened. The applicants were serving life sentences for murder and, having had their renewed applications for leave to appeal against conviction turned down, continued to protest their innocence. The Home Office had adopted a blanket policy that no prisoners had a right to oral interviews with journalists. Lord Steyn stated that the applicants wished to challenge the safety of their convictions, and that, 'in principle, it was not easy to conceive of a more important function which free speech might fulfil'. His Lordship was satisfied that it was administratively workable, and consistent with prison order and discipline, to allow prisoners to be interviewed for the purpose here at stake. The Home Secretary's policy and the governor's administrative decisions pursuant to that policy were unlawful.

Freedom of expression was also at issue in **R (Nilsen) v Governor of Full Sutton Prison** (2004). The Court of Appeal ruled that a prison rule preventing a prisoner from publishing material about his offences did not violate the right to freedom of expression and its application was proportionate and justified on the facts. In 1983 Nilsen had been sentenced to six life sentences for six murders, the details of which were horrifying. He intended to publish details in an autobiography. The Home Secretary had exercised powers under the Prison Act 1952 to withhold the work. The restriction was a legitimate exercise of power: it could not be argued that a prisoner should be permitted to publish an article 'glorifying in the pleasure that his crime had caused him'. The restriction was not disproportionate and it was legitimate to have

---

6   Protected under Article 8.

7   In *Attorney General v Times Newspapers* (2001) the government lost its appeal to restrain publication of Richard Tomlinson's *The Big Breach: From Top Secret to Maximum Security*, which the government alleged would damage national security. The Court of Appeal ruled that if the material was already in the public domain, whether at home or abroad (the book had been published in Moscow), then there should be no restraint on freedom of expression.

8   See *R v Advertising Standards Authority Ltd ex parte Matthias Rath BV* (2001), in which adjudications published by the Advertising Standards Authority under its non-statutory code were held to be 'prescribed by law' within the meaning of Article 10. The Codes of Advertising and Sales Promotion had the 'underpinning' of subordinate legislation which gave recognition to the means of dealing with complaints. The Code of Practice was readily accessible and therefore prescribed by law, its provisions being sufficiently clear and precise to enable any person to know the acceptable limits of advertisements and the consequences of infringing the provisions. The rights of children to freedom of expression and participation in family life was recognised by the Court of Appeal in *Mabon v Mabon* (2005). The Court recognised that in the case of articulate teenagers, it must accept that their rights outweighed the paternalistic judgment of the welfare of the child. 'There was a growing acknowledgment of the autonomy and consequential rights of children.' See also *Ferdinand v MGN Ltd* (2011).

regard to the effect the exercise of freedom of expression would have in the world outside the prison. The right of the state to restrict the distribution of pornography was considered in **Belfast City Council v Miss Behavin' Ltd** (2007) in which the House of Lords ruled that the Council was entitled by statute to restrict the company's rights. The restrictions only prevented the company from using unlicensed premises: it did not prohibit the exercise of a right. The state had a wide margin of appreciation in relation to controlling pornography, and provided that a local authority exercised its powers rationally and in accordance with statute 'it would require very unusual facts for it to amount to a disproportionate restriction on Convention rights'.[9]

Freedom of expression does not necessarily include the right to access to information. In **R v Secretary of State for Health ex parte Wagstaff; R v Secretary of State for Health ex parte Associated Newspapers Ltd** (2001), the High Court ruled that the holding in private of the inquiry into the multiple murders committed by Dr Harold Shipman contravened Article 10. It constituted unjustified governmental interference with the reception of information that others wish or may be willing to impart. Compare **R (Persey) v Secretary of State for Environment, Food and Rural Affairs** (2002), in which the High Court distinguished **Wagstaff** and ruled that Article 10 did not impose a positive obligation on government to provide an 'open forum'. The applications related to the Secretary of State's decision to hold three separate, independent inquiries into the outbreak of foot and mouth disease with the evidence for the most part to be heard in private. The court distinguished between the right to freedom of expression and access to information: Article 10 prohibited interference with freedom of expression, it did not require its facilitation. Equally, the High Court ruled in **R (Hard) v Secretary of State for Health** (2002) that there was no presumption one way or the other as to whether an inquiry should be held in public. There was no right of access to information conferred by Article 10. However, in **Open Door Counselling and Dublin Well Woman v Ireland** (1992), the Court of Human Rights ruled that restrictions – an injunction – placed on the dissemination of any information regarding the availability of abortion advice and treatment represented an unlawful restriction and was therefore contrary to Article 10.

In **MGN Ltd v United Kingdom** (2011) the European Court of Human Rights ruled that a court order requiring the losing party to legal proceedings to pay legal costs amounting to over £1,000,000 in total and including success fees agreed between the successful party and her lawyers was disproportionate to the aim of the success fee system. That system was intended to facilitate access to law for those who would otherwise not be able to afford legal representation. Accordingly, there was a violation of Article 10.

Restrictions on Freedom of Expression

Defamation[10]

Defamation – slander or libel – may be defined as the publication, whether oral or written, of a falsehood which damages the reputation of the person concerned and lowers the victim's reputation in the eyes of 'right thinking members of society generally'.[11] Slander is defamation in the form of the spoken word; libel is defamation in some permanent form, such as publication in books or newspapers. Publication via radio or television broadcasting, or in the course of public theatre performances, is defined as libel rather than slander.[12] Technological developments such as electronic mail (email) and the internet raise new questions for the law.

---

9 See para 1426.
10 For details, see textbooks on the law of tort. Note that the common law offence of criminal libel has been abolished: Coroners and Justice Act 2009, section 73.
11 **Sim v Stretch** (1936), p 671.
12 Theatres Act 1968, s 4; Broadcasting Act 1990, s 166.

Defamation poses difficult questions concerning the extent to which freedom of expression is to be balanced against protection of the reputation of others – whether individuals or organisations.

The technological advances in communications have prompted further regulation. The European Community Directive on Electronic Commerce (the E-Commerce Directive)[13] makes internet defamation law broadly consistent with domestic law. Defamatory statements in newsgroup postings, emails or on web pages are regarded as libel.[14] Defamatory statements made in the course of internet relay chat, internet phone or video teleconferencing are regarded as slander.

The law relating to defamation has hitherto comprised common law, the Defamation Act 1952 and the Defamation Act 1996. The Defamation Act 2013 represents a major reform of aspects of the law of defamation.

In order to prevent frivolous cases, and reflecting the trend for the courts to require a 'threshold of seriousness',[15] section 1 of the Act provides that a statement is not defamatory unless its publication has caused or is likely to cause serious harm to the reputation of the claimant. In relation to commercial enterprises, the concept of serious harm relates to serious financial loss. The 2013 Act also aims at restricting the use of the English courts for actions in defamation brought against persons not resident in the United Kingdom. Section 9(2) provides that a court shall not have jurisdiction to hear an action unless it is satisfied that, of all the places in which an allegedly defamatory statement has been published, England and Wales is the most appropriate place to bring an action. The 2013 Act introduces the 'single publication rule'. Formerly, each publication of defamatory material gave rise to a separate cause of action. The single publication rule is designed to prevent an action being brought in respect of the same material being republished after the one-year limitation period has passed. It does not apply if the manner of the subsequent publication is materially different from the first.

Under section 69 of the Senior Courts Act 1981 and section 66 of the County Courts Act 1984 there is a right to trial by jury in defamation cases unless the court considers that trial requires the prolonged examination of evidence which cannot 'conveniently be made with a jury'. Section 11 of the 2013 Act removes this presumption in favour of trial by jury. Defamation cases will in future be held without a jury unless the court orders otherwise.

Defences to an action for defamation

Unintentional defamation

The Defamation Act 1996 provides that the unintentional, or innocent, publication of statements which are defamatory may be defended. It must be shown that the publisher of the defamation has genuinely tried to make amends either by way of an apology or by correcting the false statement.

---

13 Directive 2000/31/EC.
14 For libel to be established, there must be publication. However, in relation to articles on the internet there is no presumption of publication and the claimant in a libel action bears the burden of proving that the material in question has been accessed and downloaded: *Al Amoudi v Brisard and another* (2006).
15 *Thornton v Telegraph Media Group Ltd* [2010] EWHC 1414; [2011] 1 WLR 1985.

Absolute privilege

Some speech is absolutely privileged. That is to say, the words, however libellous, are protected from the law of defamation. An example of such protection is parliamentary privilege. As we have seen, Article IX of the Bill of Rights 1689 gives absolute protection to words spoken in proceedings in Parliament. Statements made in the course of judicial proceedings also attract absolute privilege; as do statements by the Parliamentary Commissioner for Administration.[16] In **Buckley v Dalziel** (2007) it was held that absolute privilege and immunity from suit were available to a person who provided information to the police to set in motion the process of an inquiry into possible illegality. The Court, following **Taylor v Director of the Serious Fraud Office** (1999) ruled that it was necessary to protect those who provided evidence to the police in the course of an inquiry and that public policy considerations relating to the legal process applied equally to whose who were witnesses and to those who were initial complainants.

See Chapter 17.

The defence of truth

Section 2(1) of the Defamation Act 2013 provides that it is a defence for the defendant to show that the imputation conveyed by the statement complained of is substantially true. The common law defence of justification is abolished, and section 5 of the Defamation Act 1952 (justification) is repealed.

Honest opinion

This defence is important in giving limited protection to the publication of comments about public figures whose actions are matters of public interest.[17] In **Spiller v Joseph** (2010) Lord Philips of Worth Matravers suggested that there should be a review of the law, and stated that the common law defence of 'fair comment' should in future be known as 'honest comment'. Section 3 of the 2013 Act adopts the phrase 'honest opinion'. Section 3(8) provides that the common law defence of fair comment is abolished, and that section 6 of the Defamation Act 1952 (fair comment) is repealed.

Publication on matter of public interest

Section 4 creates a new defence of publication on a matter of public interest. This is based on the defence of qualified privilege. Qualified privilege is a defence to an action for defamation in relation to statements on a matter of public interest made without malice. Qualified privilege arises under common law and statute. It has been held to attach to a communication between a Member of Parliament, who forwarded a constituent's complaint, and the Lord Chancellor and the Law Society where the matter was in the public interest.[18] Qualified privilege also applies to newspapers, radio and television broadcasts. The Defamation Act 2013, section 7 amends the Defamation Act 1996 which provides protection to fair and accurate reports of judicial proceedings and international organisations, legislatures or governments anywhere in the world and other public bodies. Section 7(9) of the 2013 Act extends the law to provide protection for fair and accurate reports of proceedings of scientific or academic conferences held anywhere in the world, and reports of its publications.

The common law defence of qualified privilege was considered in **Reynolds v Times Newspapers** (1999). In Reynolds the former Prime Minister of the Republic of Ireland brought

---

16 Parliamentary Commissioner Act 1967, s 10(5).
17 See **Silkin v Beaverbrook Newspapers Ltd** (1958); **Slim v Daily Telegraph Ltd** (1968).
18 **Beech v Freeson** (1972).

libel proceedings against *The Times* newspaper in relation to an article which, he alleged, suggested that he had lied to Parliament and to Cabinet colleagues. No account of the Prime Minister's explanation was given. The House of Lords ruled, *inter alia*, that the article had made serious allegations without giving the former Prime Minister's explanation, and the defence of qualified privilege was not made out and could not be relied on by the defendants. In **Jameel (Mohammed) v Wall Street Journal sprl** (2006) the House of Lords ruled that a trading corporation was entitled to sue in respect of defamatory matters which could damage its business. The Court also held that a 'necessary precondition' of reliance on qualified privilege is 'that the matter should be one of public interest'. Furthermore, it was important that the publisher had taken reasonable steps to verify the material to be published. Where a matter was in the public interest and the publisher had sought to verify its contents, then qualified privilege applied. The public interest was also central in **Flood v Times Newspapers Ltd** (2012). *The Times* had published an article in which it alleged that a police officer, who it named, had accepted bribes in exchange for confidential information. Was the newspaper entitled to the public interest defence? The Supreme Court ruled that it was. The story, if true, was of high public interest. There was no evidence that the police were conducting an investigation into the allegation and there was circumstantial evidence that the allegation was true. The public interest lay in the fact that the allegation had been made and the publishers did not have to verify the substance of the allegation.

Section 4(1) of the Defamation Act 2013 provides it is a defence to an action for defamation for the defendant to show that:

(a) the statement complained of was, or formed part of, a statement on a matter of public interest, and;
(b) the defendant reasonably believed that publishing the statement complained of was in the public interest.

In determining whether the defendant has established the matters set out above, the court must 'have regard to all the circumstances of the case'. The reform is intended to codify the common law defence, and accordingly section 4(6) provides that the common law defence known as the Reynolds defence is abolished. The case law will remain relevant as an aid to interpreting the statutory words.

Incitement to disaffection and treason[19]

Incitement to disaffection

The Incitement to Disaffection Act 1934 provides that it is an offence intentionally to attempt to dissuade a member of the armed forces from complying with his duty. It is also an offence to aid, counsel or procure commission of the principal offence. In **R v Arrowsmith** (1975), the defendant was accused and convicted for distributing leaflets to soldiers urging them not to serve in Northern Ireland, and the conviction was upheld by the Court of Appeal.[20] A similar offence exists in relation to causing disaffection within the police force.[21] There also remains on the statute book the Aliens Restriction (Amendment) Act 1919, as amended, section 3 of which prohibits aliens from causing sedition or disaffection among the population and the

---

19 The common law offence of sedition was abolished by the Coroners and Justice Act 2009, section 73.
20 An application under the European Convention on Human Rights failed: see **Arrowsmith v United Kingdom** (1978).
21 Police Act 1997, s 91.

armed forces, and makes it a summary offence to cause industrial unrest in an industry in which one has not been employed for two years.

Treason

The Treason Act 1351 made it a capital offence to give 'aid and comfort to the King's enemies'. In *Joyce v Director of Public Prosecutions* (1946), William Joyce was convicted of making propaganda broadcasts on behalf of the Nazis during the Second World War. The death penalty for treason and piracy with violence was abolished by the Crime and Disorder Act 1998, section 36. Section 21(5) of the Human Rights Act 1998 abolishes the death penalty for military offences.

Incitement to racial hatred

The first attempt at protecting persons from racial hatred was contained in the Race Relations Act 1965. The justification for restricting offensive racist speech – and hence freedom of expression – lies in the greater need to protect individual minority groups from demeaning and discriminatory speech. Incitement to racial hatred is now regulated under sections 17 to 23 of the Public Order Act 1986. Section 17 defines racial hatred as meaning 'hatred against any group of persons in Great Britain defined by reference to colour, race, nationality (including citizenship) or ethnic or national origins'.

There are two basic requirements which relate to the offences in the Act. First, that the words used, or behaviour, must be 'threatening, abusive or insulting'. Second, the words or behaviour must either have been intended to incite racial hatred or be likely to do so. Under the Act, it is an offence to use words or behaviour, or display written material, which have the above elements. Publication of or distributing such material is also an offence.[22] The performance of plays, showing of films or videos or playing of records or broadcasts intended to or likely to incite racial hatred is an offence.[23] The Act, in section 23, also creates the offence of possession of such materials. Prosecutions may only be commenced with the consent of the Attorney General.

Racial abuse at football matches is a criminal offence.[24] The Crime and Disorder Act 1998 extends the law to include racially aggravated offences,[25] a reform prompted by the findings of the inquiry into the death of Stephen Lawrence.[26] The offences of racially aggravated assault, criminal damage, public disorder and harassment are created. In addition, higher sentences may be imposed in relation to any other offences found to be racially motivated.

The Racial and Religious Hatred Act 2006[27]

The Racial and Religious Hatred Act 2006 amends the Public Order Act 1986. Part IIIA of the Public Order Act defines religious hatred as being 'hatred against a group of persons defined by reference to religious belief or lack of religious belief'. It is an offence to use threatening words or behaviour, or to display any written material which is threatening, if the person intends to stir up religious hatred. It is also an offence to publish or distribute written material which is threatening if the person intends to stir up religious hatred.[28] The 2006 Act also

---

22 Public Order Act 1986, s 19.
23 Ibid, ss 20–22 and also Broadcasting Act 1990, s 164(1).
24 Football (Offences) Act 1991, s 3 and also Football (Offences and Disorder) Act 1999, s 9.
25 Sections 28–32 and also Anti-terrorism Crime and Security Act 2001, s 39.
26 *The Macpherson Report*, Cmnd 4262.
27 The Act does not extend to Northern Ireland or Scotland.
28 Racial and Religious Hatred Act 2006, Schedule, inserting ss 29A, 29B and 29C respectively to the Public Order Act 1986.

makes it an offence to present or direct a play which involves the use of threatening words or behaviour if there is intent to stir up religious hatred. The distribution, showing or playing of a recording of visual images or sounds which are threatening is also an offence. It is also an offence to have such materials in one's possession if there is the intention to stir up religious hatred.[29] No proceedings may be brought without the consent of the Attorney General.

The concerns of those who opposed the Bill on the grounds that it would restrict freedom of expression by criminalising discussion or criticism or ridicule of religions or beliefs or practices were met with the insertion of section 29J to the Public Order Act 1986, which now provides that:

> Nothing in this Part shall be read or given effect in a way which prohibits or restricts discussion, criticism or expressions of antipathy, dislike, ridicule, insult or abuse of particular religions or the beliefs or practices of their adherents, or of any other belief system or the beliefs or practices of its adherents, or proselytising or urging adherents of a different religion or belief system to cease practising their religion or belief system.

Obscenity, indecency, censorship and pornography[30]

The Obscene Publications Act 1959

The Obscene Publications Act 1959 creates the offence of publication of an obscene article, whether or not for gain. Further, it is an offence to have such articles in ownership, possession or control for the purpose of publication for gain or with a view to publication.[31] An article[32] is 'obscene' if 'its effect . . . is . . . such as to tend to deprave and corrupt persons who are likely, having regard to all relevant circumstances, to read, see or hear the matter contained or embodied in it'.[33]

An article will be 'published', according to section 1(3), if a person:

(a) distributes, circulates, sells, lets on hire, gives or lends it, or who offers it for sale or for letting on hire; or

(b) in the case of an article containing or embodying matter to be looked at or a record, shows, plays or projects it.

The Criminal Justice and Public Order Act 1994 amends section 1(3) by adding the words 'or where the matter is stored electronically, transmits that data'.[34] The Court of Appeal, in **R v Smith (Gavin)** (2012) allowed an appeal by the prosecution against a ruling of a Crown Court that there was no case to answer to charges of publishing obscene material contrary to section 2(1) of the Obscene Publications Act 1959 on the basis that communication to only one person could not amount to publication. The defendant had sent an obscene comment in an internet relay chat with an unknown person. Richards LJ stated that section 1(3), as amended by the Criminal Justice and Public Order Act 1994,[35] provided that communication,

29 Racial and Religious Hatred Act 2006, inserting ss 29D, 29E and 29F to the 1986 Act.
30 See Robertson, 2001, Chapter 5. On feminist arguments against pornography, see Smart, 1989, especially Chapter 6; Itzin, 1992; Barnett, 1998, Chapter 12.
31 Obscene Publications Act 1959, s 2(1), as amended.
32 Which covers books, pictures, films, records, video cassettes, CDs, DVDs etc.
33 Obscene Publications Act 1959, s 1(1).
34 Criminal Justice and Public Order Act 1994, s 84. See *R v Fellows and Arnold* (1997).
35 Section 168(1) and paragraph 3 of Schedule 9 to the 1994 Act.

including the transmission of electronically stored data to only one person, sufficed to constitute publication.

The tendency to 'deprave and corrupt'

It is not sufficient that an article disgusts, or is 'filthy', 'loathsome' or 'lewd'.[36] What must be established is that the article will 'deprave or corrupt'.[37] Nor is it sufficient that the article is capable of depraving or corrupting just one person: the test is whether or not a significant proportion of persons likely to read or see the article would be depraved or corrupted by it.[38] The fact that the persons likely to read the article regularly read such materials is irrelevant to whether or not the material can deprave or corrupt,[39] although the same argument may not hold if the likely audience is police officers experienced with dealing with pornography.[40]

In **Handyside v United Kingdom** (1976),[41] in which a publication entitled The Little Red Schoolbook had been seized under the Obscene Publications Act 1959, the Court of Human Rights ruled that there was no violation of Article 10.[42] The publishers claimed that the Obscene Publications Act represented a violation of Article 10 in several respects. The Court ruled that there was no breach of the Convention. The 'protection of morals' clause in Article 10(2) entitled the government to impose restrictions on freedom of expression, provided that the restrictions were proportionate to the aim pursued. It was for the Court to decide whether the restrictions were necessary and sufficient. In this case, the book was aimed at under-18-year-olds and encouraged promiscuity.

There exists a defence of public good[43] but the defence is interpreted narrowly.[44] For example, in **Director of Public Prosecutions v Jordan** (1977),[45] where the defendant argued the psychotherapeutic benefit of 'soft porn' for the consumer, the judge rejected the defence, holding that what was for the public good was art, literature or science. It is an offence to send or attempt to send indecent or obscene materials through the post.[46] It is also an offence to import indecent or obscene materials. Such materials may be forfeited.[47]

Indecency and pornography

While offences relating to obscenity require proof relating to its tendency to 'deprave and corrupt', indecency requires no such proof and is of a lesser order. Lord Parker in **R v Stanley** (1965) stated that indecency was 'something that offends the ordinary modesty of the average man . . . offending against recognised standards of propriety at the lower end of the scale.'[48]

Pornography is not a legal concept. There is no legal prohibition against pornography as such – rather prosecutions will be brought under the headings of obscenity and/or indecency. Pornography does, however, raise a number of issues which are of particular

---

36 **R v Anderson** (1972).
37 **R v Martin Secker and Warburg** (1954).
38 **DPP v Whyte** (1972), per Lord Wilberforce.
39 **Shaw v DPP** (1962).
40 **R v Clayton and Halsey** (1963).
41 See also **Muller v Switzerland** (1991).
42 See also **Wingrove v United Kingdom** (1996) and **Otto-Preminger Institut v Austria** (1994) on the law of blasphemy. On public order, see **Steel v UK** (1998) and **Hashman and Harrup v UK** (2000).
43 Obscene Publications Act 1959, s 4.
44 See eg **R v Penguin Books Ltd** (1973).
45 And see **Attorney General's Reference (No 3 of 1977)** (1978).
46 Postal Services Act 2000, s 85(3),(4).
47 Customs Consolidation Act 1876, Customs and Excise Act 1952 and Customs and Excise Management Act 1979, s 49.
48 See Robertson, 1979, Chapter 7.

concern to feminists and the literature is now extensive. The pornography industry is both global and vast. Concerns about pornography include the protection of women who work in the industry, and the impact that pornographic representations of women has on the status of women in society. However, the attempt in the United States to outlaw pornography on the grounds – inter alia – that it undermines women's equality, failed: freedom of expression prevailed.[49]

Broadcasting, cinemas, theatres and video recordings

Section 2 of the Theatres Act 1968 prohibits obscenity in theatrical performances. The law relating to obscenity applies to live performances, subject to the defence of public good. Legal regulation of live performances also exists in the form of section 20 of the Public Order Act 1986, which prohibits the use of threatening, abusive or insulting words or behaviour intended or likely to stir up racial hatred. Section 6 of the Theatres Act prohibits words or behaviour likely to cause a breach of the peace. In order to avoid frivolous or censorious legal action, the consent of the Attorney General is required in relation to prosecutions under the Theatres Act, Public Order Act and Sexual Offences Act.

The Broadcasting Act 1990 and Video Recordings Act 1984 each prohibited obscenity on local radio services, television and video. In relation to broadcasting, the British Broadcasting Corporation (BBC), established under the royal prerogative,[50] is under a duty not to adopt its own political stance on current affairs, and may only broadcast party political programmes with the consent of the major political parties.

The Office of Communications (Ofcom)[51]

The Office of Communications Act 2002 established Ofcom in preparation for the transfer of regulatory functions from the former broadcasting regulators.[52] The Communications Act 2003 provided for the transfer of functions from five bodies or office holders to Ofcom. The relevant bodies and offices are:

- the Broadcasting Standards Commission;
- the Director General of Telecommunications, who had responsibilities for regulating Oftel, a non-ministerial government department which regulated the telecommunications operators in the United Kingdom;
- the Independent Television Commission;
- the Radio Authority, which had regulatory and licensing powers in relation to all non-BBC radio services broadcasting in the United Kingdom, whose powers derived from the Broadcasting Act 1990 and 1996;
- the Secretary of State with regulatory powers in respect of radio exercised through the Radiocommunications Agency, an executive agency of the Department of Trade and Industry.

With effect from 1 October 2011, Ofcom assumed responsibility for postal services.[53]

The general duties of Ofcom are set out in section 3 of the Communications Act 2003. Ofcom's principal duty is to further the interests of the public and to further consumer

---

49 See Dworkin, 1981.
50 The BBC was established by Royal Charter. Its chairman and governors are appointed by the Crown on the advice of the Prime Minister. The BBC operates under licence from the government issued under the Wireless Telegraphy Act 1904–67.
51 See Office of Communications (Ofcom), *Annual Report 2011–12*, HC 237, London: TSO.
52 See the White Paper, *A New Future For Communications* (Cm 5010).
53 Postal Services Act 2011.

interests where appropriate through promoting competition. OFCOM is required to act in accordance with European Union requirements as laid down in EU Communications Directives which were adopted in 2002 and which provide for a common regulatory framework for electronic communications networks and services. The 2003 Act is designed to ensure that EU requirements are met. Ofcom is required to ensure a wide availability of a range of television and radio services and maintain a sufficient plurality of providers. It is also required to protect members of the public from offensive and harmful material and to apply standards in television and radio services which protect people from unfair treatment and infringements of privacy. In exercising its functions, Ofcom is to have regard to the principles of transparency, accountability and proportionality.[54]

Ofcom is under a duty to publish a Broadcasting Code for television and radio, covering 'standards in programmes, sponsorship, product placement in television programmes, fairness and privacy.' The Code must be read in light of the European Convention on Human Rights.[55]

Film and video

The regulation of films falls to the British Board of Film Classification (BBFC), and their availability for viewing by the public controlled by local authorities. The BBFC operates a system of classification by age: 'U' for general circulation, 'PG' (parental guidance), 12, 12A (children under 12 accompanied by an adult), 15, and 18 certificate films, and R18 films which are for restricted viewing only on segregated premises. The BBFC may refuse a certificate if the film contravenes the Obscene Publications Act 1959, and may insist on cuts to a film before a certificate is granted. Local authorities exercise control through the granting of licences for a particular film to be shown in its area.[56]

The BBFC also classifies videos, DVDs and Blu-ray discs for private viewing. The Video Recordings Act 1984 requires that the BBFC should have 'special regard to the likelihood of video works being viewed in the home' (section 4). The BBFC must also pay 'special regard' to the harm caused to potential viewers by the depiction of criminal activity, illegal drugs, violence and sexual behaviour.[57] The growth of the internet led to the transmission of electronically stored data being included within the Obscene Publications Act 1959 definition of 'publication'.[58] In 2009 it became apparent that the 1984 Act was legally unenforceable, having been enacted in breach of an EC Technical Standards Directive which required draft legislation to be notified to the European Commission for consultation. The Video Recordings Act 2010 re-enacts the provisions and came into force on receiving the Royal Assent.

Conspiracy to corrupt public morals

Under the common law, publishers may be liable for the offence of conspiracy to corrupt public morals. In **Shaw v Director of Public Prosecutions** (1962), Shaw, the publisher of a directory giving the names and details of prostitutes, was prosecuted for conspiracy to corrupt public morals.[59] The House of Lords (Lord Reid dissenting) held that the courts have a 'residual power

---

54 The OFCOM board does not meet in public to reach decisions, in part to protect commercial confidentiality. According to Lord Currie of Marylebone, OFCOM's Chairman, the Board will be open and transparent in its consultation processes and in the giving of reasons for its decisions: see the Minutes of Evidence taken before the Select Committee on Culture, Media and Sport, 16 December 2003, HC 132-i.
55 See **R (Gaunt) v Office of Communications (Ofcom)** (2011).
56 Under the Cinemas Act 1985.
57 Under the Criminal Justice and Public Order Act 1994, s 90.
58 Ibid, s 168.
59 Shaw was also found guilty of an offence under the Obscene Publications Act 1959. See further above.

to enforce the supreme and fundamental purpose of the law, to conserve not only the safety and order but also the moral welfare of the state'.[60]

Shaw v Director of Public Prosecutions was upheld in **Knuller Ltd v Director of Public Prosecutions** (1973). The publishers had produced a magazine containing advertisements for male homosexuals. The House of Lords, upholding **Shaw**, rejected as a defence the fact that the Sexual Offences Act 1967 provided that homosexual acts between adult males, in private, were no longer an offence. The use of this common law offence is rare; nevertheless, it remains an available offence which enables the state to avoid statutory offences which provide defences such as that of the 'public good'.[61]

Blasphemy and blasphemous libel[62]

Blasphemy was a common law offence which prohibited words abusing Christ or denying or attacking the established Church which caused outrage to the feelings of a Christian. Long criticised as being discriminatory, the Law Commission recommended in 1985 that the offence be abolished. However, it was not until 2008 that the government acted and section 79 of the Criminal Justice and Immigration Act 2008 states that:

> The offences of blasphemy and blasphemous libel under the common law of England and Wales are abolished.

Contempt of court

The law relating to contempt of court developed in order to protect the judiciary and judicial proceedings from actions or words which impede or adversely affect the administration of justice, or 'tends to obstruct, prejudice or abuse the administration of justice'.[63] Contempt of court, under English but not Scottish law, may be criminal or civil. In relation to criminal contempt, which may be dealt with in both the civil and criminal courts, the action relates to conduct which is designed to interfere with the administration of justice, which may of itself involve a criminal offence. The court has the power to rule on the existence of a contempt and to punish the guilty party. Where the judge finds the person guilty of contempt, he may commit the person instantly to prison. Two principal forms of criminal contempt exist.

Scandalising the court

The need to maintain public confidence in the judiciary underpins this offence. Criticism of a judge, or a court's decision, may be a contempt if it suggests bias or unfairness on the part of the judge or court.[64]

In 2011 the former Northern Ireland Secretary, the Rt Hon Peter Hain MP, published his autobiography in which he criticised the way in which a Northern Ireland High Court judge had dealt with an application for judicial review of one of Mr Hain's decisions. The Northern Ireland Attorney General brought proceedings claiming that the comments were contempt of court (scandalising the judiciary). The charge was withdrawn in May 2012, the Attorney

---

60 Seaborne Davies, 1962.
61 Obscene Publications Act 1959, s 4.
62 See Kenny, 1992.
63 Report of the Phillimore Committee on Contempt of Court, Cmnd 5794, 1974, p 2. See Dhavan, 1976.
64 See *R v New Statesman (Editor) ex parte DPP* (1928); *Ambard v Attorney General for Trinidad and Tobago* (1936); *R v Metropolitan Police Commissioner ex parte Blackburn (No 2)* (1968).

General accepting that there was no risk of damage to public confidence in the administration of justice.[65]

The common law offence of scandalising the judiciary was abolished in England and Wales by section 33 of the Crime and Courts Act 2013.

Contempt in the face of the court

Conduct in court which impedes the judicial process may be a contempt. A demonstration which interrupts proceedings,[66] or insulting behaviour, or refusal of a witness to answer questions or give evidence or comply with a court order to disclose information, may amount to contempt.[67]

Publications prejudicing the course of justice

The balance to be struck between freedom of expression and the protection of judicial proceedings is a matter for debate. The Contempt of Court Act 1981, which reformed the common law of contempt, sought to achieve the appropriate balance. Before that Act, the law relating to contempt proved capable of inhibiting freedom of the press for an extensive period of time, where judicial proceedings became protracted. The leading case which presaged reform of the law is that of **Sunday Times v United Kingdom** (1979). In 1974, the House of Lords restored an injunction[68] prohibiting *The Sunday Times* from publishing articles relating to the drug Thalidomide, manufactured by Distillers Ltd, which, it was alleged, caused serious deformities in babies. The parents of the affected children intended to sue Distillers for compensation. The company entered into protracted negotiations with the families' solicitors. The injunction restrained any further publication on the matter by the newspaper. *The Sunday Times* made an application under Article 10 of the European Convention on Human Rights, which protects freedom of expression, alleging that the common law of contempt violated Article 10. The European Court of Human Rights held that there had been a violation of Article 10. As a result, the Contempt of Court Act 1981 was enacted, clarifying the law on pre-trial publicity.[69]

The Contempt of Court Act 1981

Section 1 of the Contempt of Court Act provides for the 'strict liability rule'. The rule is defined as 'the rule of law whereby conduct may be treated as a contempt of court as tending to interfere with the course of justice in particular legal proceedings *regardless of intent to do so*' (emphasis added). In order for the strict liability rule to be established, a number of issues need to be satisfied. First, the test relates only to publications falling within section 2 of the Act. Publications are defined in section 2(1) as including 'any speech, writing [programme included in a programme service][70] or other communication in whatever form, which is addressed to the public at large or any section of the public'. Second, the publication must be such that it 'creates a substantial risk that the course of justice in the proceedings in question will be seriously impeded or prejudiced'.[71] Third, the strict liability rule applies only if the proceedings in question are 'active', as defined by Schedule 1 to the Act. In relation to appellate proceedings, these are active from the time they are commenced, by an application for leave

---

65 See David Pannick QC, 'Judges must be open to criticism to help to expose injustice', The Times, 24 May 2012.
66 See Morris v Crown Office (1970).
67 See *Attorney General v Mulholland and Foster* (1970); **British Steel Corporation v Granada Television Ltd** (1963).
68 *Attorney General v Times Newspapers Ltd* (1974). The injunction had been discharged by the Court of Appeal.
69 See further Chapter 20 on Article 10 and rights of protest.
70 Added by the Broadcasting Act 1990, s 203.
71 See **Re Lonrho** (1990).

to appeal or apply for review, or by notice of appeal or of application to review or by other originating process, 'until disposed of or abandoned, discontinued or withdrawn'. In relation to criminal proceedings, the starting point is the issue of a warrant for arrest, arrest without warrant or the service of an indictment. The end point is acquittal, sentence, any other verdict or discontinuance of the trial. In relation to civil proceedings, the start point is when the case is set down for a hearing in the High Court. The end point is when the proceedings are disposed of, discontinued or withdrawn.[72]

In **Attorney General v MGN Ltd** (2012) an application for the committal of newspaper publishers for contempt of court was granted on the basis that articles which vilified a suspect in a murder case were a potential impediment to the course of justice within section 2(2) of the 1981 Act. This was held even though the suspect was subsequently released without charge and would therefore never face trial.

It is a defence to prove that, at the time of publication, or distribution of the publication, the defendant does not know, and has no reason to suspect, that relevant proceedings are active.[73] Fair and accurate reports of legal proceedings, held in public and published 'contemporaneously and in good faith' do not attract the strict liability rule.[74] In addition, if publication is made as, or as part of, a discussion in 'good faith of public affairs or other matters of general public interest', it is not to be treated as contempt of court, 'if the risk of impediment or prejudice to particular legal proceedings is merely incidental to the discussion'.[75]

Section 10 of the Contempt of Court Act regulates the disclosure of sources. The court may not require disclosure, and a person will not be guilty of contempt as a result of non-disclosure unless the court is satisfied that 'disclosure is necessary in the interests of justice or national security or for the prevention of disorder or crime'. The leading case is **X Ltd v Morgan Grampian** (1991), in which the House of Lords ruled on the decision-making process entailed in section 10. In that case, a confidential plan was stolen from the plaintiffs and information from the plan given to a journalist. The plaintiffs applied for an order requiring the journalist, William Goodwin, to disclose the source and sought discovery of his notes of the telephone conversation in order to discover the identity of the source. The House of Lords, in balancing the competing interests – the applicant's right to take legal action against the source and the journalist's interest in maintaining confidentiality with the source – held that the interests of the plaintiffs outweighed the interests of the journalist. This decision led to an application under Article 10 of the European Convention – the right to freedom of expression. In **Goodwin v United Kingdom** (1996), the Court ruled that the order against the journalist violated his right to freedom of expression which was central to a free press.[76]

It is for the court to determine whether a particular decision-making forum is a 'court' for the purposes of the law of contempt of court. In **General Medical Council v British Broadcasting Corporation** (1998), the Court of Appeal ruled that the Professional Conduct Committee (PCC) of the General Medical Council was not part of the judicial process of the state and accordingly was not subject to the Contempt of Court Act 1981. The PCC was a statutory committee under the Medical Act 1983, which exercised a sort of judicial power, but it was not the judicial

---

72 See **Attorney General v Hislop and Pressdram** (1991).
73 Contempt of Court Act 1981, s 3(1), (2).
74 Ibid, s 4.
75 See **Attorney General v English** (1983); **Attorney General v TVS Television**; **Attorney General v HW Southey & Sons** (1989); **Pickering v Liverpool Daily Post and Echo Newspapers plc** (1991). See also the Public Interest Disclosure Act 1998, which amends the Employment Rights Act 1996 and provides protection for employees who disclose wrongdoing by his or her employer.
76 See also **John v Express Newspapers** (2000) but cf **Camelot Group plc v Centaur** (1999). The public interest in the protection of journalists' sources was sufficient to outweigh any threat of damage through future dissemination of a company's confidential information or any possibility of obtaining damages for past breaches of confidence. The Court of Human Rights so held in **Financial Times Ltd v United Kingdom** (2006).

power of the state. It had a recognisable judicial function, but was not part of the judicial system of the state.

Contempt of court and Article 10 of the European Convention

The impact of the Human Rights Act 1998 is being felt in this area of law. In **Ashworth Security Hospital v MGN Ltd** (2002), the Mirror newspaper had published verbatim extracts from hospital medical records of information concerning a convicted murderer who was detained at the hospital. The information had been supplied to the newspaper, in breach of confidence and breach of contract, by a hospital employee through an intermediary. The Contempt of Court Act 1981, section 10, provided for orders of disclosure of sources of information only where it was established that 'disclosure is necessary in the interests of justice or national security or for the prevention of disorder or crime'. The hospital had failed to identify the informant and sought an order that MGN identify the intermediary as the only likely means of discovering the source's identity. MGN argued that such an order would contravene Article 10 of the Convention. The Court of Appeal ruled that unless the source was identified and dismissed, there was a significant risk that there would be further selling of confidential information, and that such disclosures amounted to an attack on confidentiality which should be safeguarded in any democratic society. Where a person against whom disclosure was sought – in this case the intermediary – had 'become mixed up in wrongful, albeit not tortious, conduct that infringed a claimant's legal rights', the court had jurisdiction to order disclosure. The decision was affirmed by the House of Lords. In **Interbrew SA v Financial Times** (2002), the court declared itself bound by the decision in **Ashworth**. A claimant was entitled to an order for delivery up of leaked and partly forged documents held by publishers in order to enable him to ascertain the proper defendant to a breach of confidence action. The 'public interest in protecting the source of a leak was not sufficient to withstand the countervailing public interest in letting Interbrew seek justice in the courts against the source'.[77]

However, the importance of protecting journalistic sources was recognised in **Mersey Care NHS Trust v Ackroyd** (2006), the sequel to **Ashworth Hospital Authority v MGN Ltd** (supra). The Hospital Trust had commenced an action against the journalist identified as a result of the order of disclosure, Mr Ackroyd, in an attempt to compel the journalist to reveal the source of his information. The High Court ruled that in balancing conflicting rights – the right to privacy and the right to freedom of expression – it was necessary to apply the guidelines set out in **Campbell v Mirror Group Newspapers plc** (2004).[78] Applying those guidelines, the court came to the opposite conclusion to that reached in the **Ashworth Hospital** case. Here an order for disclosure would not be proportionate to the hospital's legitimate aim to seek redress against the source, given 'the vital public interest in the protection of a journalist's source'.[79]

In **Attorney General v Punch Ltd** (2002), the former editor of Punch magazine, and the publishers, had been fined for being in contempt of court. At issue was the publication by Punch of an article by David Shayler, the former MI5 officer. The Attorney General had been granted injunctions on the basis that revelations by Shayler about matters relating to his employment would be contrary to national security. The question was, where a court ordered that specified material was not to be published, would a third party who, with the knowledge of the order, published the specified material automatically commit a contempt of court, or would contempt only occur if the third party thereby knowingly defeated the

---

77 The restriction on publication of information which would lead to the identification of an HIV healthcare worker (here a dentist) was justified under Article 10(2) according to the Court of Appeal in **H v N (A Health Authority); H v Associated Newspapers Ltd** (2002).

78 Discussed below at p 472.

79 See **Financial Times Ltd v United Kingdom** (2006).

purpose for which the order was made? The House of Lords ruled that the editor must have known that by publishing the article he was doing 'precisely what the court order was intended to prevent, namely, pre-empting the court's decision on the confidentiality issues relevant to trial'.

In **In re s (A Child) (Identification: Restrictions on Publication)** (2004), the House of Lords considered the basis of the courts' jurisdiction to restrain publicity to protect a child's private and family life by way of injunction. The Court ruled that jurisdiction derived from Convention rights rather than the inherent jurisdiction of the High Court. At issue here was the conflict between the child's right to private and family life under Article 8 and the right of freedom of expression (of the press) under Article 10.

The House of Lords stated that:

> . . . neither Article as such had precedence over the other, the correct approach being to focus on the comparative importance of the specific rights claimed in the individual case, with the justifications for interfering or restricting each right being taken into account and the proportionality test applied to each . . .

On the fact of this case, the Court declared that:

> . . . although the ordinary rule was that the press could report everything that took place in a criminal court, it was the duty of the court to examine with care each appli-cation for a departure from the rule by reason of Article 8, but in so doing the court was not . . . to create further exceptions by a process of analogy save in the most compelling circumstances . . .

The freedom of the press to report criminal proceedings would be inhibited by an extension of the protection of Article 8 and there should be no injunction granted.

The Law of Confidence

At common law, where information is received in a situation where the recipient knows or ought to know that the information is confidential and therefore not to be disclosed to others, that information is protected by law and any unauthorised disclosure of that information – by whatever means – will be actionable.

Originally, actions for breach of confidence were relevant mainly to trade secrets, unfair competition and industrial espionage. However, the law has expanded into many other areas, proceeding on a case by case basis. The disclosure of information may amount to breach of confidence if the relationship is based on marriage,[80] contracts of employment, consultancies and potentially any situation involving a 'confidential relationship'.

Where there is a breach of the common law duty of confidence, or an anticipated breach, an injunction may be granted by the court, prohibiting publication or further publication of the information.[81] An example of this is seen in **Schering Chemical v Falkman Ltd** (1981). In **Schering**, a Thames Television documentary about a pregnancy drug was scheduled for transmission. The programme revealed material obtained by the producer in his role as a

---

80 *Duke of Argyll v Duchess of Argyll* (1967).
81 Injunctions may be used for several different purposes. We are concerned here solely with injunctions as a remedy for breach of confidence.

consultant to the company. The court held that an enforceable duty of confidence existed. A further example is seen in the proposal, in 1987, by the BBC to transmit a documentary *My Country Right or Wrong* in which former security officers were interviewed. An injunction was granted on the basis that there had occurred a breach of confidence in the course of the interviews.[82] *Spycatcher*, a book written by a former member of the Security Services, was also restrained by way of an injunction based on breach of confidence.[83] One difficult aspect of the use of such prior restraint is that there exists no trial of the facts until a future date, when it may transpire that there has been an unjustified, and often lengthy, restriction on freedom of expression.

Defences to an action for breach of confidence

Staleness

In **Attorney General v Jonathan Cape Ltd** (1976) (the **Crossman Diaries** case) the information disclosed in breach of confidence was some ten years old and no harm would follow from its publication. Accordingly, the court held that, in the absence of a breach of national security, further restraint was not justified. However, in the **Spycatcher** case, **Attorney General v Guardian (No 2)** (1990), while the injunction was eventually lifted, the government claimed that the duty of former Security Service personnel is lifelong and that no publication of any matter concerning their employment may be disclosed. Section 1 of the Official Secrets Act 1989 now reflects this duty and imposes criminal sanctions on any unauthorised revelations made in relation to security matters.

The material is in the public domain

While there may be found to be a duty of confidence, this duty does not necessarily result in an injunction being permanently imposed to restrain publication. In addition to the material being 'stale', it may be that the material has already been published elsewhere, and is thus in the 'public domain'. In relation to the book *Spycatcher*, this matter weighed with the court. The book had been published in Australia and the United States of America and was, in fact, freely available anywhere outside the United Kingdom. In **Attorney General v Times Newspapers Ltd** (2001) the Court of Appeal ruled that it was the responsibility of the newspaper's editors to form a judgment about whether material had been brought sufficiently into the public domain. The editor was not required to seek confirmation from either the Attorney General or the court that this was the case. Such an approach, the court ruled, was 'consonant with Article 10 of the European Convention on Human Rights and section 12 of the [Human Rights] Act'.

Revealing true information to correct falsity

Irrespective of the existence of a duty of confidence, there may be situations where material has been published which is false and which justifies a breach of confidence in order to rectify the falsehood. In **Woodward v Hutchins** (1977), for example, a falsehood concerning a pop star had been published. Notwithstanding a duty of confidence, there was a justified and legitimate need for rebuttal of the untruths.

Iniquity: to reveal evidence of crime/fraud

Breach of confidence may be excused by the court if the defence of revealing criminal or fraudulent activities is made out.

---

82 *The Times*, 5 and 18 December 1987.
83 See further Chapter 22.

Public interest

The defence of public interest was considered in **Lion Laboratories v Evans and Express Newspapers** (1984). The *Express* newspaper revealed information concerning faulty intoximeters used to measure the extent of alcohol in an individual's bloodstream. Deficiencies in the breathalyser equipment could have resulted in wrongful convictions for driving under the influence of alcohol. The disclosure of confidential information was justified. There was no question of the manufacturer having been guilty of any 'iniquity' or wrongdoing. However, the matter was one of public interest which overrode any claim to confidentiality of the information. Public interest disclosures by employees are now protected under the Public Interest Disclosure Act 1998 which amends the Employment Rights Act 1996.

Privacy

The idea that individuals have a 'right to privacy' has a strong and intuitive hold on the popular imagination: the autonomous human being claims a protective personal and family sphere into which others may not intrude without permission. Privacy is inextricably linked to liberty: the freedom from restriction on lawful activities whether by the state, its agents, or private bodies or individuals. As John Stuart Mill wrote in *On Liberty*:

> . . . the sole end for which mankind are warranted, individually or collectively, in interfering with the liberty of action of any of their number, is self-protection. [That] the only purpose for which power can be rightfully exercised over any member of a civilised community, against his will, is to prevent harm to others. His own good, either physical or moral, is not a sufficient warrant.

However, there has never been either a common law or statutory right to privacy as such.[84] In place of a right to privacy there are numerous provisions which restrict individuals and state officials from intruding on areas of a person's privacy. However, there are equally numerous provisions which permit intrusions into privacy, provided they are carried out under lawful authority. The principal reason for this lies in the difficulties in defining the full scope of privacy and its relationship with competing concepts and interests. The privacy of the individual, for example, competes with the right to freedom of expression of the press.[85] The need for the state to keep official records also competes with individual privacy. Privacy may compete also with the powers of the police to investigate crime and the powers of the security forces to combat terrorism. Increasingly as criminal activities such as drug trafficking, trafficking in human beings and international money laundering are globalised, there is a need for the police and security agencies to co-operate with European and international forces.

Examples of the legal protection of aspects of privacy include the following:

- The right to personal safety and the enjoyment of personal possessions is reflected in the law relating to offences against the person and the law of theft.
- The right to exclude uninvited visitors from one's home is reflected in laws relating to trespass (see **Entick v Carrington** (1765)) and the requirements of lawful authority to enter private property.

---

84 See, for example, **Kaye v Robertson** (1991) discussed below at p 477.
85 On the regulation of the press see *Report of the Younger Committee*, Cmnd 5012, 1972; *Report of the Committee on Privacy and Related Matters*, Cmnd 1102, 1990; *Review of Press Self-Regulation*, Cmnd 2135, 1993.

- The right to protect one's reputation is provided by the law of defamation.
- Private information which is disclosed to another in a situation of confidence is protected by the law of breach of confidence.[86]
- The right to express one's sexual identity, in private, is recognised in the laws legalising homosexuality and in laws prohibiting discrimination on grounds of gender.
- Surveillance, investigations and interception of communications by the police and security forces require statutory authority.[87]
- The law regulating the storing of individual data by the state requires authorisation and provides safeguards.[88]

The European Convention on Human Rights and the Human Rights Act 1998

Prior to the Human Rights Act 1998, Article 8 of the European Convention protected privacy and provided the legal means by which to challenge domestic law. Article 8 provides:

Everyone has the right to respect for his private and family life, his home and his correspondence.

There shall be no interference by a public authority with the exercise of this right except such as is in accordance with the law and is necessary in a democratic society in the interests of national security, public safety or the economic well-being of the country, for the prevention of disorder or crime, for the protection of health or morals, or for the protection of the rights and freedoms of others.

A summary of illustrative case law from the European Court of Human Rights may be considered under the following headings:

- respect for individual privacy, including private sexual life; and
- privacy of the family.

NOTE that Article 8 is discussed in more detail in Chapter 18

Respect for individual privacy

- In **Malone v United Kingdom** (1984) the Court ruled that the absence of statutory authority for intercepting an individual's communications meant that the law was unclear and 'lacking the degree of protection to which citizens are entitled under the rule of law in a democratic society.'[89]
- In **Khan v United Kingdom** (2000) covert surveillance by the police without statutory authority violated Article 8.[90]

---

86 See the discussion above and the case law below.
87 Police and Criminal Evidence Act 1984, Regulation of Investigatory Powers Act 2000.
88 See, *inter alia*, the Data Protection Act 1984 and Freedom of Information Act 2000.
89 See also **McLeod v United Kingdom** (1999); **Armstrong v United Kingdom** (2002); **Taylor-Satori v United Kingdom** (2002); **MG v United Kingdom** (2002). The government's response to **Malone** was to introduce the Interception of Communications Act 1985: see further Chapter 22.
90 See now Police Act 1997. See also **Wood v United Kingdom** (2004).

- In **Halford v United Kingdom** (1997) the Court ruled that it was unlawful to intercept an employee's telephone calls at work.
- In **Dudgeon v United Kingdom** (1982) the prohibition on homosexual conduct between adult males was ruled unlawful.[91]

Respect for family life

- In **Hoffmann v Austria** (1994) the law denying a woman custody of her children on grounds of her religious belief was unlawful.
- In **TP and KM v United Kingdom** (2001), the separation of a mother and daughter for nearly a year violated Article 8.[92]
- In **Buckley v United Kingdom** (1997) the Court ruled that there was no violation of Article 8 by the authorities denying a Gypsy the right to live on her own land without planning permission: the legal restriction pursued a legitimate aim and was proportionate to the aim pursued.[93]

In the absence of a legal *right to privacy* under domestic law, the law of confidence, discussed above, – now interpreted in light of the Human Rights Act 1998 – has proven central to extending the legal protection of aspects of privacy. Key factors in recent developments include the following:

- Section 6 of the Human Rights Act, which requires the courts, as a public body, to comply with Convention rights and thereby enables the courts to give horizontal effect to Convention rights;[94]
- Article 8 of the Convention: the right to respect for private and family life, home and correspondence;
- Article 10 of the Convention: the right to freedom of expression which includes restrictions on that right expressed as follows:

The exercise of these freedoms, since it carries with it duties and responsibilities, may be subject to such formalities, conditions, restrictions or penalties as are prescribed by law and are necessary in a democratic society . . . **for preventing disclosure of information received in confidence. . .**

- Section 12 of the Human Rights Act, which provides that where there is an application to a court to restrain in advance the publication of information, or prevent further publication of information to which confidentiality applies:

(3) No relief [affecting the exercise of freedom of expression] is to be granted so as to restrain publication before trial unless the court is satisfied that the applicant is likely to establish that publication should not be allowed.

In order to assess the relationship between these differing aspects of the law, the following cases should be considered:

---

91 Leading to the Homosexual Offences (Northern Ireland) Order 1982 reforming the law. See also **Lustig-Prean v United Kingdom** and **Smith and Grady v United Kingdom** (2000): the ban on homosexuals in the armed forces violated Article 8. See also **ADT v United Kingdom** (2000): the ban on consensual sexual acts between more than two men in private was unlawful.
92 Compare **G v United Kingdom** (2000).
93 See also **Chapman v United Kingdom** (2001).
94 Meaning that private bodies are required to comply with the Convention: see further Chapter 18.

- *Douglas v Hello!* (2001)
- *Campbell v MGN* (2004)
- *A v B plc* (2002)
- *Cream Holdings v Banerjee* (2005)
- *McKennitt v Ash* (2007)
- *HRH Prince of Wales v Associated Newspapers Ltd* (2007)
- *Lord Browne of Madingley v Associated Newspapers Ltd* (2007).

The law relating to breach of confidence has been expanded to a degree which suggests that, while there is no right to privacy under common law, privacy claims are being given greater protection than was the case prior to the Human Rights Act 1998. In **Douglas v Hello! Ltd** (2001), the Court of Appeal ruled that individuals had a right of personal privacy which was grounded in the equitable doctrine of breach of confidence.[95] Michael Douglas and Catherine Zeta-Jones had granted *OK!* magazine exclusive rights to publish photographs of their wedding. *Hello!* magazine had obtained photographs of the wedding and had been subjected to an interim injunction restraining publication before the trial of the substantive issues.[96] In this case, the claimants had lessened the degree of privacy concerning their wedding by allowing *OK!* magazine to publish photographs, thereby affecting the balance between their rights (to privacy) and the rights of others to freedom of expression. The court discharged the injunction. However, in a strong statement of principle, Sedley LJ said that 'we have reached a point at which it can be said with confidence that the law recognises and will appropriately protect a right of personal privacy'.

In **Campbell v Mirror Group Newspapers (MGN) Ltd** (2004), the model Naomi Campbell was awarded damages, albeit minimal, by the High Court for the disclosure of information relating to her attending meetings for the treatment of drug addiction. By a majority of three to two, the House of Lords held that the 'broad test' to be applied was 'whether disclosure of the information ... would give substantial offence to a reasonable person of ordinary sensibilities assuming that the person was placed in similar circumstances'. Lord Hope stated that the right to privacy (which lies at the heart of an action for breach of confidence) had to be balanced against the right of the media to publish information. Conversely, the media's freedom of expression had to be balanced against the respect which had to be given to private life. In this case, Lord Hope said that had it not been for the publication of photographs of Ms Campbell leaving the place of treatment, the balance between the competing rights would have been 'about even'. However, the photographs 'added greatly' to the intrusion of the claimant's private life and their publication outweighed the defendants' right to freedom of expression.[97]

In the House of Lords, Lord Nicholls of Birkenhead stated that:

> The time has come to recognise that the values enshrined in Articles 8 and 10 are now part of the cause of action for breach of confidence ... [and] are as much applicable in disputes between individuals or between an individual and a non-governmental body such as a newspaper as they are in disputes between individuals and a public authority.[98]

---

95 See also **Earl Spencer v United Kingdom** (1998), in which the Court of Human Rights stated, inter alia, that the claim to breach of privacy could have been adequately protected under the common law of breach of confidence.
96 Breach of confidence, malicious falsehood and interference with contractual relations.
97 **Campbell** was considered in **Murray v Express Newspapers plc** (2007) in which it was held that celebrities enjoy no special right to privacy and that going about their ordinary daily activities such as walking down the street or shopping did not attract an expectation or right to privacy. Leave to appeal was granted. See **Murray v Big Pictures (UK) Ltd** (2008).
98 At para 17.

Campbell may be compared with **A v B plc** (2002). The Court of Appeal ruled that any interference with freedom of the press had to be justified, and could not be limited because there was no identifiable public interest in the material being published. The court distinguished between the confidentiality which attached to sexual relations within marriage 'or other stable relationships' and the confidentiality which attached to transient relationships. Here, a footballer, A, had had sexual relationships with C and D. He did not want his wife to find out. C and D, however, had no interest in maintaining confidentiality. The Lord Chief Justice recognised that the Convention provided 'new parameters within which the court would decide in an action for breach of confidence whether a person was entitled to have his privacy protected', or 'whether the intrusion into freedom of information which such protection involved could not be justified'. In this case, it was not obvious why an injunction should be granted: A's relationships were not in the categories of relationships which the court should be astute to protect when other parties did not want them to remain confidential. Freedom of the press should prevail, and regulation of reporting in the press should be a matter for the Press Council, not the courts.

The Court of Appeal extended the right to privacy – through its interpretation of the scope of confidence – in **McKennitt v Ash** (2006). Buxton LJ stated that the first question for the court to ask was whether the information was 'private in the sense that it was in principle protected by Article 8. If it was not, that was the end of the case'. However, if the answer was 'yes', then the court had to consider whether, in all the circumstances, the interests of the owner of the private information had to give way to the right of freedom of expression conferred by Article 10. It was the balance between these two Articles which was crucial. Applying **Von Hannover v Germany** (2005) the matters disclosed were of a private nature and Article 8 was engaged.[99]

In **HRH Prince of Wales v Associated Newspapers Ltd** (2007), a former member of the Prince's staff disclosed to the defendant copies of travel journals written by the Prince. These were intended to remain confidential and were not intended for publication. Lord Phillips of Worth Matravers CJ laid emphasis on section 3 of the Human Rights Act 1998, stating that:

> Section 3 . . . requires the court, so far as it is possible, to read and give effect to legislation in a manner which is compatible with the Convention rights. The English court has recognised that it should also, in so far as possible, develop the common law in such a way as to give effect to Convention rights. In this way horizontal effect is given to the Convention . . .

> . . . The English court has been concerned to develop a law of privacy that provides protection of the rights to 'private and family life, his home and his correspondence' recognised by Article 8 of the Convention. To this end the courts have extended the law of confidentiality so as to protect Article 8 rights in circumstances which do not involve a breach of a confidential relationship.[100]

This introduces artificiality into the law: the law of confidentiality now appears to have been extended to cover situations where the court considers that privacy should be protected without developing a substantive right to privacy.

---

99 The Court rejected the argument that it would be a defence to establish that the information disclosed was in fact untrue.
100 The Court ruled that Prince Charles had 'an unanswerable claim for breach of privacy. When the breach of a confidential relationship is added to the balance, the case is overwhelming': para 74.

In **Campbell v MGN** (2002), discussed above, Lord Nicholls of Birkenhead had recognised the difficulty in this way:

> the law imposes a 'duty of confidence' whenever a person receives information he knows or ought to know is fairly and reasonably to be regarded as confidential . . . The continuing use of the phrase 'duty of confidence' and the description of the information as 'confidential' is not altogether comfortable. Information about an individual's private life would not, in ordinary usage, be called 'confidential'. The more natural description today is that such information is private. **The essence of the tort is better encapsulated now as misuse of private information.**[101]

The result of these developments is that the law of confidentiality now encompasses not only pre-existing relationships but also situations where no previous relationship of confidence exists but the information has been improperly obtained and used (as in the **Prince of Wales case**).

The Court of Appeal returned to its analysis of breach of confidence and privacy in **Lord Browne of Madingley v Associated Newspapers Ltd** (2007). The claimant, the group chief executive of a major international company, had obtained an interim injunction restraining the defendant newspaper from publishing information concerning his private life and business activities. The Master of the Rolls stated that the Court should first decide whether Article 8 is engaged; then consider whether Article 10 is engaged and then proceed to decide whether the applicant '. . . has shown that he is likely to establish at a trial that publication should not be allowed within the meaning of section 12(3)'.[102]

In **Max Mosley v News Group Newspapers** (2008) the court considered the applicant's right to privacy (Article 8) and the newspaper's right to freedom of expression (Article 10). Mr Mosley is a public figure. The cause of action was breach of confidence and/or the unauthorised disclosure of personal information allegedly infringing the complainant's right to privacy. It was argued that the content of the material (the portrayal of sado-masochistic activities) was inherently private in nature and that there had been a pre-existing relationship of confidentiality between the complainant and the five participants. The material had been secretly video-recorded by one of the participants and published in the newspaper and on the internet.

The newspaper claimed that, even if there was an infringement of Article 8, there was a public interest in the disclosure of the material, one aspect of which was the allegation that the activities represented Nazi or concentration camp role-play (Mr Mosley is the son of Sir Oswald Mosley, the British wartime fascist leader).

The newspaper's public interest defence was rejected and it was held that there had been a violation of the complainant's right to privacy. In considering the question of damages, the court considered the extent to which the complainant's own conduct had contributed to his distress and loss of dignity and observed that his behaviour could be regarded as 'reckless and almost self-destructive'. A relatively modest sum in damages was awarded (see further below).

In **Mosley v United Kingdom** (2011), the European Court of Human Rights ruled – unanimously – that Article 8 of the Convention on Human Rights does not impose a legal duty

---

101 At para 14. Cited in the **Prince of Wales case** at para 26. Emphasis added.

102 The Court ruled that it should be slow to make interim orders where the claimant had not satisfied the court that he was more likely than not to succeed at trial.

on newspapers to notify the subjects of intended publications in advance so as to give them an opportunity to seek an injunction to prevent publication.

Mr Mosley argued that damages alone were not an adequate remedy for the breach of his rights, on the basis that damages could not restore his privacy. He accordingly argued that newspapers should be under a legal duty to notify those who were to be the subject of damaging articles in order to allow them to seek to prevent publication. The European Court of Human Rights accepted that there had been a 'flagrant and unjustified invasion' of Mr Mosley's private life. It also recognised that English law provided a number of measures to protect the right to private life, including the system of self-regulation of the press, the right to claim damages for breaches and the right to seek an injunction to restrain publication. However, the Court considered that to introduce a pre-notification requirement would affect political reporting and serious journalism (in addition to the sensationalist reporting at issue in Mr Mosley's case). Accordingly, such a proposed restriction on journalism 'required careful scrutiny'. The Court also noted that a pre-notification requirement would have to allow for an exception if the public interest was at stake. Further such a requirement would only be as effective as the sanctions which would be imposed for failing to comply with the duty.

In conclusion, the Court ruled that a pre-notification requirement risked having a 'chilling effect' on freedom of expression which was protected under Article 10 of the Convention. Furthermore, given the wide margin of appreciation afforded to the United Kingdom in relation to the right to privacy, Article 8 did not require a legally binding pre-notification requirement.

In **Cream Holdings Ltd v Banerjee** (2004) the claimants sought an interim injunction to restrain publication of confidential information supplied by a former employee of the claimants who had obtained the information without permission. This raised the issue of the freedom of the press in relation to section 12(3) of the Human Rights Act 1998, which, as noted above, provides that no injunctive relief should be granted so as to restrain publication unless the court is satisfied that the applicant is likely to establish that publication should not be allowed. The House of Lords ruled that the principal purpose for which section 12(3) was enacted was to protect freedom of speech by setting a higher threshold for the granting of interlocutory injunctions against the media.

The House of Lords ruled that to construe the word 'likely' as to mean 'more likely than not' in all situations would impose too high a test; that there could be no single rigid standard governing all applications and some flexibility was needed. All the circumstances of the case had to be taken into consideration. Generally, the court should not make an interim restraint order unless it was satisfied 'that the applicant's prospects of success at trial were sufficiently favourable to justify the order being made in the light of all the other circumstances of the case'. In the instant case, the disclosures were matters of serious public interest and the claimants' prospects of success at trial were not sufficiently high to justify making an interim order.[103]

The House of Lords reconsidered Articles 8 and 10 in **Attorney General's Reference No 3 of 1999** (2009).[104] Under Part 10 of the Criminal Justice Act 2003 it became possible, for the first time, to re-try persons acquitted on specific serious offences if the Court of Appeal was satisfied that there was 'new and compelling evidence' and that a retrial would be 'in the interests of justice'. The British Broadcasting Corporation (BBC) wished to include details of the case in a television programme, suggesting that the defendant had been wrongly acquitted and identifying him as the perpetrator of the crime. Unless the 2000 order was discharged the BBC

---

103 On prior restraint see also *Martha Greene v Association Newspapers Ltd* (2004).
104 *Application by the British Broadcasting Corporation to set aside or vary a Reporting Restriction Order* (2009)

could not lawfully disclose the defendant's identity. In addition to considering Article 8 and Article 10, section 12 of the Human Rights Act 1998 required that a court must, in relation to freedom of expression, have regard *inter alia* to the 'extent to which' publication of the material is 'in the public interest'.

The House of Lords ruled that the removal of the 'double jeopardy rule' was a matter of legitimate public interest, and that the BBC's belief that disclosure of the defendant's identity would add credibility to their programme was legitimate and came down in favour of the BBC's right to freedom of expression.

Article 8 came into conflict with Article 10 once more in **In re Guardian and Media News Ltd and Others** (2010). The Supreme Court ruled that the general public interest in publishing a report of legal proceedings in which individuals had been named overrode the claimants' Article 8 rights. The claimants were subject to asset-freezing orders on the ground of suspicion of actually or potentially facilitating terrorist acts[105] and anonymity orders had been granted to protect them from identification in the media. While lifting the anonymity orders would undoubtedly have a direct effect on the individual's private life, there was a 'powerful general public interest' in identifying parties to such proceedings which justified curtailing Article 8 rights.[106]

In **JIH v News Group Newspapers Ltd** (2011) the Court of Appeal recognised the difficulties in balancing the rights in Articles 8 and 10. Granting an anonymity order until trial or further order, the Court stated that in general where anonymity was ordered the nature of the information was to be disclosed, but conversely, if the claimant was identified the nature of the information should not be disclosed.

Increasingly, celebrities have sought injunctions from the courts to prevent the disclosure of personal information. A recent trend has been for 'super-injunctions' to be granted. This form of injunction not only prevents the disclosure of information relating to an individual but also prevents disclosure of the fact that an injunction exists. Public concern over this development led to the Culture, Media and Sport Select Committee inquiring into their use.[107] Following that report, a committee, chaired by Lord Neuberger, MR, was established to investigate and report. The Committee Report, 'Report of the Committee on Super-injunctions, 2011, concluded that the use of such injunctions had been reduced, and they were now being granted only for very short periods, and only where the level of secrecy they effect is 'necessary to ensure that the whole point of the order is not destroyed'.[108]

Press freedom and individual rights

Blackstone, in his *Commentaries*, said of freedom of the press that:

> . . . the liberty of the press is indeed essential to the nature of a free state. Every free man has an undoubted right to lay what sentiments he pleases before the public; to forbid this is to destroy the freedom of the press; but if he publishes what is improper, mischievous or illegal, he must take the consequences of his own temerity.

The invasion of privacy by the media has become a matter of rising concern. In 1953, the Press Council was established.[109] This self-regulatory body proved woefully inadequate at

---

105 Terrorism (United Nations Measures) Orders (SI 2006 Nos 2652 and 2957).

106 The Supreme Court quashed SI No 2657: see Chapter 23. See also **Independent News and Media Ltd v A** (2010).

107 Culture, Media and Sport Select Committee Report, 24 February 2010.

108 On freedom of speech in Parliament see Chapter 17.

109 The Broadcasting Complaints Commission plays a similar role in relation to broadcasting: Broadcasting Act 1990, s 142.

controlling the press, not least because it had no powers to fine newspapers. In 1972, the Younger Committee was established to consider reforms in relation to press freedom. The Committee recommended that a tort of disclosure of information unlawfully acquired and a tort and crime of unlawful surveillance by technical devices be introduced.[110] The proposed reforms were not implemented. Concern over intrusions into individual privacy increased with the media attention given to the Royal Family in recent years. The case of **Kaye v Robertson** (1991) heightened public interest in the respective right of an individual to privacy and the right of the public to information. In **Kaye**, journalists entered a hospital room in which the well-known actor, Gorden Kaye, was being treated for severe injuries sustained in a car accident. Kaye agreed neither to be photographed nor interviewed. An injunction was sought, and granted, to restrain the newspaper from publishing the 'interview' and photographs. On appeal, the Court of Appeal ruled that there was no right to privacy under English law which could found the basis for an injunction.

In 1990, the Committee on Privacy and Related Matters (the Calcutt Committee) was established, which led to the creation of another self-regulatory body in 1991, the Press Complaints Commission.[111] A review of the workings of the Commission by Sir David Calcutt[112] found the protection accorded to individuals to be inadequate. It was recommended, therefore, that a statutory body be established, but no action has been taken.

The Press Complaints Commission administers a Code of Practice, drafted by the industry, which regulates accuracy of reporting and personal privacy. In relation to the latter, the Code provides that:

> Everyone is entitled to respect for his or her private and family life, home, health and correspondence. A publication will be expected to justify intrusions into any individual's private life without consent.

> The use of long lens photography to take pictures of people in private places without their consent is unacceptable.

Revelations in recent years relating to press conduct – allegations concerning phone hacking, intrusions into privacy, concerns over the relations between the press and the police and the press and politicians – led to the appointment of Lord Justice Leveson to inquire into and make recommendations concerning the future regulation of the press. The key issue from a constitutional point of view is how the freedom of the press can be maintained while at the same time protecting the rights of individuals whose lives or reputations may be harmed by the press. Another key question is whether, and how, the law could or should be used to regulate the press.

Lord Justice Leveson recognized the importance of a free press, stating in his Report that:

> I know how vital the press is – all of it – as the guardian of the interests of the public, as a critical witness to events, as the standard bearer for those who have no one else to speak up for them . . . The press, operating properly and in the public interest is one of the true safeguards of our democracy.[113]

110 *Report of the Younger Committee*, Cmnd 5012, 1972; and see MacCormick, 1973.
111 *Report of the Committee on Privacy and Related Matters*, Cmnd 1102, 1990. See Munro, 1991.
112 *Review of Press Self-Regulation*, Cmnd 2135, 1993, London: HMSO.
113 The Leveson Report. *An Inquiry into the Culture, Practices and Ethics of the Press: Executive Summary*, HC 779, London: TSO November 2012. www.official-documents.gov.uk/document/hc1213/hc07/0779/0779.pdf.

Moreover:

> There are truly countless examples of great journalism, great investigations and great campaigns. The exposure of thalidomide, the campaign to bring the killers of Stephen Lawrence to justice, the exposure of abuse in the operation of MPs expenses are but the best known in a long list.[114]

The purpose of the Leveson Inquiry was to expose malpractices by the press, as revealed in evidence to the Inquiry, and to make recommendations for reform.[115] Key to the proposed new system of regulation is the establishment of a new independent regulator governed by an independent Board, with members being appointed in an open and transparent way without any influence from industry or government. There should be no serving editors of newspapers on the Board. The Board should have the power to investigate complaints against the press, to order 'appropriate remedial action' and to impose 'appropriate and proportionate sanctions'.

In order to ensure that the regulatory body fulfils its functions and ensure its independence (of the press, Parliament and Government), the Report recommends that legislation be introduced to underpin the new body. The law should also, Leveson recommends, impose a clear duty on the Government to uphold the freedom of the press.

On the Press Complaints Commission, the Leveson Report was extremely critical, stating that it was not a regulatory body, but rather a complaints handling body; that it lacked independence from the press, and in practice aligned itself with the interests of the press; that the powers it held were under-utilised and that remedies were 'woefully inadequate'.[116]

The Prime Minister was swift in his expressing his reservations about using legislation. The Deputy Prime Minister and Leader of the Opposition supported Leveson. At the time of writing, the outcome is unknown.

Summary

Freedom of expression, under English law, has traditionally been regarded as a freedom which could be exercised subject to any restrictions imposed by law (for example defamation, the prohibition of race hate speech, speech likely to cause a breach of the peace, the unauthorised disclosure of confidential information). It is therefore necessary to understand the legal restrictions before any evaluation of the scope of freedom of expression can be undertaken.

Freedom of expression is now also governed by Article 10 of the European Convention on Human Rights, Article 10.2 of which imposes a number of restrictions. With the incorporation of Article 10 into domestic law, the domestic courts have increasingly been faced with the apparent conflict between freedom of expression and the right to privacy protected under Article 8 of the European Convention. Privacy, however, has never been recognised as a distinct legal entity under domestic law. The emerging case law suggests that the courts are interpreting Article 8 to expand the law relating to breach of confidentiality in a manner which suggests extending an individual's right to privacy.

Freedom of expression must also be considered in conjunction with freedom of assembly and association discussed in the next chapter.

---

114 The Leveson Report, paragraph 8.
115 www.levesoninquiry.org.uk.
116 See Executive Summary, paragraphs 41–46.

 **Further Reading**

Bailey, Harris and Jones (2009) *Civil Liberties: Cases, Materials and Commentary*, Oxford: OUP.

Barendt, E. (2005) *Freedom of Speech* (2nd edn), Oxford: OUP.

Fenwick, H. (2011) *Civil Liberties and Human Rights* (5th edn), London: Routledge–Cavendish.

Morgan, J. (2004) 'Privacy in the House of Lords Again', Law Quarterly Review, 120: 563.

Chapter 20

Freedom of Association and Assembly

Introduction

While the detection and prosecution of crime and the preservation of public order are of first importance in any state, the extent to which police powers reflect a legitimate interference with the liberty and security of citizens is a problematic question which involves evaluating the balance struck between the rights of the individual and the powers of the police. In this chapter, the manner in which law regulates associations and assemblies – whether meetings or processions – is examined. In addition, it is necessary to consider the manner in which law regulates an individual's freedom to move around, and the conditions under which it is or is not lawful to enter into and remain on land, both private and public.

The law of association and assembly must now be evaluated against Article 11 of the European Convention on Human Rights, incorporated under the Human Rights Act 1998. Article 11 provides that 'everyone has the right to freedom of peaceful assembly and to freedom of association with others, including the right to form and to join trade unions for the protection of his interests'. Article 11, however, is subject to a number of lawful exceptions. The rights may be restricted on the basis that they are 'necessary in a democratic society in the interests of national security or public safety, for the prevention of disorder or crime, for the protection of health or morals or for the protection of the rights and freedoms of others'. In addition, Article 11 does not prevent lawful restrictions being imposed by the state on members of the armed forces, or the police or the civil service. Accordingly, while all domestic law must be compatible with Article 11, a great deal of discretion is accorded to the state.

Freedom of assembly and association, protected by Article 11, must also be viewed in relation to freedom of expression guaranteed by Article 10 of the Convention and considered in the previous chapter.

Freedom of Association

While citizens are generally free to join any club, society or trade union, two statutory restrictions exist. The first restriction relates to membership of military or quasi-military organisations. The Public Order Act 1936 provides, in part, that the wearing of uniforms in public with the intention of promoting a political objective is unlawful, and that membership of groups organised and trained for the purpose of displaying physical force is unlawful. To be a member of such a group, or to solicit or invite financial or other support for the group, is an offence.

See further Chapter 23.

In **R v Jordan and Tyndall** (1963), the defendants were members of a fascist group, Spearhead. They exercised in military fashion and were known to be storing chemicals capable of being used for the manufacture of bombs. They were convicted under section 2(1)(b) of the Public Order Act 1936. In **Director of Public Prosecutions v Whelan** (1975), the defendants were charged under section 1 of the 1936 Act. Participating in a Sinn Fein march in Northern Ireland, the defendants wore black berets, dark clothing and carried the Irish flag. It was held that the wearing of similar clothing could amount to a 'uniform'. Specific groups are proscribed under the Terrorism Acts.

As noted above, the right of peaceful assembly and association includes the right to belong to a trade union (**Young, James and Webster v United Kingdom** (1981)) or political party. The European Court of Human Rights reconsidered this right in **Redfearn v United Kingdom** (2012). In this case, the applicant was a member of the British National Party (BNP), a right-wing political party. As a result of his membership he was dismissed from his employment, on the basis that his employment would cause problems in an area in which there was a high concentration of non-white families. He was unable to claim unfair dismissal because he had not been in the post for the qualifying one-year period. His claim that he had been discriminated against on grounds of race contrary to the Race Relations Act 1976 were dismissed by the Court of Appeal. The Court ruled, by four votes to three, that the United Kingdom government was under a duty to take 'reasonable and appropriate measures' to protect employees from dismissal on grounds of political opinion or affiliation. The legislation was 'deficient' in providing no remedy and there was, accordingly, a violation of Article 11.

Freedom of Assembly

> . . . it can hardly be said that our constitution knows of such a thing as any specific right of public meeting.[1]

An individual is free to assemble peacefully with others to the extent that the law does not prohibit such assemblies or the assembly does not involve unlawful actions. In 1885, Dicey was to record that 'the police have with us no special authority to control open air assemblies'. Today much has changed. Under common law, a number of restraints were placed on this freedom, and the Public Order Acts 1936 and 1986 and the Criminal Justice and Public Order Act 1994 restrict rights of assembly. While there is a general freedom to assemble on private property or on public land, in the case of the former, it will be a trespass to do so without the consent of the landowner. In relation to land to which the public have a right of access, the right of assembly is controlled by local authority bylaws, and a criminal offence is committed if these are breached. Further, the right of assembly may be controlled by statute. By way of example, the right to assemble in Trafalgar Square is regulated under statute, under which permission must be granted by the Secretary of State for the Environment.[2] Hyde Park is equally regulated.[3]

The duty to facilitate meetings

The constitutional importance of freedom of expression and involvement in civic life is reflected in the right to use schools and other public rooms for meetings in local elections, by-elections and general elections.[4] In addition, under the Education (No 2) Act 1986, the governing bodies of universities and colleges are under a duty to 'take such steps as are reasonably practicable to ensure that freedom of speech within the law is secured for members, students and employees of the establishment and for visiting speakers'.[5] This requirement gave rise to a challenge in **R v University of Liverpool ex parte Caesar-Gordon** (1991). In that case, the university had refused permission for a meeting at which two diplomats from the South African Embassy were due to speak. The decision was based on the fear that the meeting would cause public unrest in the surrounding area. The Divisional Court ruled that the university had acted *ultra vires* its powers. The university authorities were not entitled to take into account threats of violence outside its precincts. Only where the risk of violence would relate to university precincts, would the university be justified in imposing restrictions.

---

1   Dicey, 1885, p 271.
2   SI 1952/776. See also the Metropolitan Police Act 1839, s 52, which provides for police enforcement of access to Parliament by its members.
3   Royal and Other Parks and Gardens Regulations 1988, SI 1988/217, and see **Bailey v Williamson** (1873).
4   Representation of the People Act 1983, as amended by the Representation of the People Act 1985 and Greater London Authority Act 1999, s 17.
5   Education (No 2) Act 1986, s 43.

The meaning of 'public meeting' was considered by the House of Lords in **McCartan (Turkington Breen) v Times Newspapers Ltd** (2000). At issue was whether a meeting, in this case a press conference, held on private premises, to which members of the press had been invited and others also attended without an invitation but without any restriction, was a 'public meeting'.[6] A meeting was public if those who arranged it opened it to the public, or by issuing a general invitation to the press showed an intention that the proceedings of the meeting should be communicated to a wider public.

Indirect Restrictions on Freedom of Assembly

A number of indirect means may be employed in order to restrain public meetings. Such means include breach of the peace, obstruction of police officers and obstruction of the highway.

Breach of the peace

In **Beatty v Gillbanks** (1882), the Salvation Army met knowing that there would be an opposing meeting being held. The magistrates' court issued an order preventing the Salvation Army meeting. When the meeting assembled in defiance of the order, the police ordered the meeting to disband and arrested one of the members. On the defendant's appeal against conviction, the Queen's Bench Division refused to accept the restriction on freedom of assembly based on the threatened unlawful acts of others. A person acting lawfully was not responsible for the unlawful reaction of others. Where, however, participants in a meeting engage in unlawful conduct which provokes others and results in a breach of the peace – or a reasonable apprehension of a breach of the peace – the meeting may be held to be unlawful. Further, if the meeting is conducted lawfully and yet provokes an actual breach of the peace, the police may order the meeting to disband. Failure to comply with an order to leave an assembly on the grounds of an officer's reasonable belief that it is necessary to avoid a breach of the peace is a criminal offence.[7]

Breach of the peace is a concept which traditionally has involved a degree of proximity and immediacy between the conduct of individuals and the anticipated breach of the peace. However, in **Moss v McLachlan** (1985), in the course of the miners' strike of 1984–85, the defendants were ordered to turn back on a journey to another colliery some four miles away. The police suspected that they were intending to join the picket line in support of fellow miners and that a breach of the peace might occur. When the miners refused to obey the order to turn back, they were arrested for obstruction. The judge conceded a wide discretion to the police and ruled that, provided a senior police officer 'honestly and reasonably formed the opinion' that there was a real risk of a breach of the peace, in an area proximate to the point of arrest, they could take whatever measures were reasonably necessary to prevent it. This decision, whilst understandable from the police's point of view, is regrettable for it introduces a dangerous breadth to the offence. Furthermore, uncertainty is created as to the precise scope of the police's power to interfere with freedom of movement.

---

6   For the purposes of a claim to privilege under the Defamation Act (Northern Ireland) 1955, s 7.
7   **Duncan v Jones** (1936): see below.

The **Beatty v Gillbanks** principle has been undermined in a number of cases. In **Jordan v Burgoyne** (1963), the court ruled that a person addressing an audience would be found guilty of a breach of the peace if his or her words were likely to inflame the audience and lead to violence. Equally, in **Percy v Director of Public Prosecutions** (1995), the court ruled that conduct which was not itself unlawful could amount to a breach of the peace if the words spoken were likely to cause disorder among those listening, even if members of the audience had attended with the express intention of causing trouble. Further, in **Morpeth Ward Justices ex parte Ward** (1992), the issue was not so much the conduct of the protesters but, rather, whether or not the conduct had the effect of provoking violent behaviour, even where the reaction to the protest was unreasonable. However, in **Nicol v Director of Public Prosecutions** (1996), the court adopted a more restrictive approach. The protest in question concerned an attempt to stop anglers from fishing. The protesters blew horns and provoked the anglers. It was held that, although there was nothing unlawful in the protesters' actions, the provocation of the anglers was likely to cause a breach of the peace because it was unreasonable action.

A more liberal approach was taken in **Redmond-Bate v Director of Public Prosecutions** (1999). Three women preachers, who were preaching on the steps of a cathedral, were approached by a police constable and warned not to stop people. Later, he returned to find that a crowd had gathered, some of whom were hostile to the speakers. The constable asked the women to stop preaching, and when they refused arrested them for a breach of the peace. They were convicted of obstructing a police officer in the execution of his duty. On appeal, it was held that there was no lawful basis for the arrest. Free speech, provided that it did not tend to provoke violence, irrespective of its content (unless contrary to law), was to be respected. There were no grounds on which the constable could apprehend a breach of the peace, much less one for which the preachers would be responsible.

The European Convention on Human Rights is making an impact on the law of protest, in terms of both the right to liberty (Article 5) and the right to freedom of expression (Article 10). In **Hashman and Harrup v United Kingdom** (2000), the issue was freedom of expression relating to hunt saboteurs. The applicants were bound over 'to be of good behaviour' for one year. The applicants claimed that the concept of behaviour *contra bona mores* was so broadly defined that it did not comply with Article 10(2) of the Convention, the requirement that any interference with freedom of expression be 'prescribed by law'. The Court of Human Rights ruled that the definition of *contra bona mores*, as behaviour which was 'wrong rather than right in the judgment of the majority of contemporary fellow citizens', was particularly imprecise and failed to give the applicants sufficiently clear guidance as to how they should behave in future. Accordingly, the interference with freedom of expression was not 'prescribed by law' and there had been a violation of Article 10.[8]

In **Appleby v United Kingdom** (2003), the Court of Human Rights ruled that campaigners against building on a playing field did not suffer a deprivation of their right to freedom of speech or assembly when the owners of a shopping centre prevented them from meeting on their premises to exchange information and ideas about the proposed building plans. While freedom of expression was an important right it was not unlimited. Nor was it the only Convention right at stake. Regard must also be given to the property rights of the owner of the shopping centre under Article 1 of Protocol No 1. In the present case the restriction on the applicants' ability to communicate their views was limited to the entrance areas and passageways of the shopping centre. It did not prevent them from expressing their views elsewhere, including the public access paths into the area.

The House of Lords considered police powers in respect of demonstrations in **R (Laporte) v Chief Constable of Gloucestershire** (2006). The claimant was a member of an activist group

---

8 See also **Steel v United Kingdom** (1998).

travelling in three coaches from London to an air force base at which a demonstration was planned. The Chief Constable considered that a breach of the peace would occur if the protesters were allowed to join the demonstration. He ordered the driver of the coach to return to London, escorted by police riders who prevented the coaches from stopping, in effect 'imprisoning' the passengers for two and a half hours.

In a powerful judgment, the House of Lords ruled that the actions of the police were unlawful, not being prescribed by law and disproportionate. Lord Brown of Eaton-under-Heywood stated that 'if any power to prevent entirely innocent citizens' from taking part in a demonstration exists then the 'power can only be conferred by Parliament. It is not to be found in the common law.'

The balance to be struck between the right to liberty and the power of the police to protect public order was reconsidered in the House of Lords in **Austin v Commissioner of Police of the Metropolis** (2009). Some 3,000 people had assembled in central London as part of a May Day demonstration. The police were aware that a demonstration was planned, but the organisers had refused to inform the police of their plans. The police imposed a cordon around the area with the effect that thousands were detained for several hours.[9] The stated intention of the police was to prevent a breach of the peace and to control the crowd in order to effect an orderly dispersal of the crowd. On the legality of the action by the police, the Court ruled, inter alia, that measures of crowd control must 'be resorted to in good faith and must be proportionate to the situation which has made the measures necessary'. Provided that these requirements are met, measures of crowd control that are undertaken in the interests of the community will not infringe the Article 5 rights of individual people in the crowd.[10] In **Austin v United Kingdom** (2012) the Grand Chamber of the European Court of Human Rights upheld the decision of the House of Lords (now Supreme Court). In a situation of potential violence and risk of injury and damage to property the 'kettling' by the police did not amount to a deprivation of liberty. Notwithstanding its conclusion, the Court emphasised that such measures should not be employed to stifle or discourage protest which was of fundamental importance to freedom of expression.

Freedom of expression and freedom of assembly and association were considered in **Tabernacle v Secretary of State for Defence** (2009). The Women's Peace Camp had been established at Aldermaston (the Atomic Weapons Establishment at which nuclear weapons were designed, tested and built) for some 23 years. A local by-law prohibited camping. In answer to the claim that the state had violated the right to freedom of expression, association and assembly, the Secretary of State submitted that the restriction was on the 'manner and form' in which the right could be exercised, not a restriction on the right itself. The Court of Appeal disagreed. The manner and form in which a right might be exercised might constitute the very nature and quality of the protest in question. Here the manner and form – the protest on the prohibited site – was the protest itself. Moreover the Secretary of State's arguments were weak: the camp represented no more than a nuisance rather than a threat. There was a violation of Articles 10 and 11.

Obstructing the police

Under the Police Act 1996,[11] it is a criminal offence to obstruct the police in the execution of their duty. Section 89 provides that:

1. Any person who assaults a constable in the execution of his duty, or a person assisting a constable in the execution of his duty, shall be guilty of an offence . . .

---

9 A practice known as 'kettling'.
10 See also **R (Moos and McClure) v Commissioner of Police of the Metropolis** (2012).
11 Formerly, Police Act 1964, s 51.

2. Any person who resists or wilfully obstructs a constable in the execution of his duty, or a person assisting a constable in the execution of his duty, shall be guilty of an offence . . .

In **Duncan v Jones** (1936), the defendant had intended to hold a public meeting at a place previously used for that purpose. The police, aware that a disturbance had previously occurred in that place, instructed Mrs Duncan to hold the meeting on an alternative site. Mrs Duncan refused and started the meeting on the highway. She was arrested and charged under section 51 of the Police Act. The defendant could have been charged with obstruction of the highway (see below) or with inciting a breach of the peace. However, in the alternative the police charged her with obstructing a police officer. The court held that, once the police officer reasonably considered that a breach of the peace could occur, any action which impeded him in the course of preventing such an occurrence amounted to an obstruction of the police. In **Piddington v Bates** (1960), in the course of an industrial dispute, the police directed that no more than two pickets should be allowed at each entrance to the factory. The defendant joined the picket line in defiance of the order, regarding the restriction as unreasonable, and was charged with obstruction. On appeal, the Divisional Court upheld his conviction.

See also
Chapter 21.

Obstructing the highway: the Highways Act 1980

A citizen is free to move along the highway. It is, however, a criminal offence to obstruct the highway. Obstructing the highway also represents a public nuisance, which may be prosecuted on indictment under common law.[12] Under section 137 of the Highways Act 1980, 'if a person, without lawful authority or excuse, in any way wilfully obstructs the free passage along a highway he is guilty of an offence'. In **Hirst v Chief Constable for West Yorkshire** (1986), animal rights demonstrators protesting outside a store selling animal fur products were charged with obstructing the highway. The magistrates' court convicted them of obstruction. However, on appeal, the Divisional Court held that the justices should have considered the reasonableness of the action and weighed in the balance the right to protest and demonstrate and the need for public order. The magistrates' court had failed to consider this and, accordingly, failed to respect the freedom to protest on matters of public concern. This approach was echoed in **Director of Public Prosecutions v Jones** (1999), in which the House of Lords ruled that – provided a highway was not in fact obstructed – it could be lawful to use it for protest.

The granting of a possession order and the removal of a protest camp was not an unjustified interference with the protesters' rights to freedom of expression and assembly under Articles 10 and 11 of the European Convention on Human Rights. The Queen's Bench Division so ruled in **The Mayor, Commonality and Citizens of the City of London v Samede and Others** (2012). The camp – consisting of up to 200 tents – occupied highway land and open land owned by the Church of England. The relief claimed was not disproportionate and was 'entirely lawful and justified', both at common law and under statute.

Public Order

The Public Order Act 1986 was passed after growing concern over demonstrations, industrial disputes, riots and football hooliganism.[13] The Act had two principal objectives. The first was

---

12 **R v Clark (No 2)** (1964).
13 See *Report on the Red Lion Square Disorders*, Cmnd 5919, 1975, London: HMSO; *Report on the Brixton Disorders*, Cmnd 8427, 1981, London: HMSO; *Criminal Law: Offences Relating to Public Order*, Law Com No 123, 1983, London: HMSO; *Review of Public Order Law*, Cmnd 9510, 1985, London: HMSO.

to provide a comprehensive code as to the organisation and control of processions and demonstrations. The second was to provide a code relating to disorderly conduct, which can range from behaviour which causes alarm or distress to riot. In addition, the Act created offences relating to football hooliganism and to control of persons unlawfully camping on private land.

The law relating to public order was further reformed substantially by the Criminal Justice and Public Order Act 1994.[14] This Act made major reforms across a wide spectrum of criminal justice matters and matters relating to sexual offences. New sentences for young offenders were introduced; the right to silence of defendants was curtailed; and the powers of police to take body samples increased. In relation to public order, the Act increased the powers of the police and local authorities in respect of trespass, 'rave parties', squatters and campers, and marked a significant shift away from individual liberties towards increasing state regulation in favour of maintaining public order. The Crime and Disorder Act 1998 introduces new criminal offences where conduct contrary to public order is racially aggravated.[15]

The regulation of processions

A procession is not defined in the Public Order Act. Processions were originally regulated under the Public Order Act 1936 and the powers were extended under the Public Order Act 1986. In **Flockhart v Robinson** (1950), a procession was said to be 'not a mere body of persons: it is a body of persons moving along a route'. Accordingly, a procession must involve more than one person. To be regulated by the Act, a procession must be public. A public place is defined in section 16 as being:

(a) any highway . . .; and
(b) any place to which at the material time the public or any section of the public has access, on payment or otherwise, as of right or by virtue of express or implied permission.

The requirement of notice

Under section 11, notice must be given to the police of a procession which is designed to express or oppose the views of another, to publicise or encourage support for a campaign, or to commemorate an event. Processions which are regularly held within a particular area need not be notified to the police. Where it is impracticable to give notice in advance, the requirement may be waived. This exception enables spontaneous demonstrations to take place.

Six clear days' notice must be given, except where it is impracticable to do so.[16] Failure to give notice, or organising a procession different from the one notified, is a summary offence. In Scotland, similar requirements exist. Where a ban is imposed on a particular march, a right of appeal exists.

Under section 11(2) of the Public Order Act 1986 there is no requirement to give notice of processions which are 'commonly or customarily held' in an area. Examples would include the annual Remembrance Day service and the judges' annual procession to the courts of law at the start of the new term. The House of Lords had an opportunity to examine section 11(2) in **R (Kay) v Commissioner of Police of the Metropolis** (2008). The Court ruled that monthly cycle rides

---

14 *Implementing the Report of the Royal Commission on Criminal Justice*, Cmnd 2263, 1993, London: HMSO.
15 The Anti-Social Behaviour Act 2003 amends both the 1986 and 1994 Acts.
16 Public Order Act 1986, s 11(6).

through London, which had no formal organisation, but started from the same point each time and on each occasion followed a different route, did not require notice to be given under section 11. The cycle rides had sufficient common features to amount to a 'procession' 'commonly or customarily held' and were therefore exempt from the notification requirement.

The power to impose conditions

Where notice has been given in accordance with section 11, then a senior police office (Chief Constable or Commissioner) may impose conditions, under section 12. If a procession is under way, then a senior officer on the scene may impose conditions. The basis on which conditions may be attached include situations where the senior police officer reasonably believes that a procession may result in serious public disorder, serious damage to property or serious disruption of the life of the community.[17] An alternative basis for conditions is where it is reasonably believed that the procession is taking place for an illegitimate purpose. Intimidation, for example, would be an 'illegitimate purpose'. Under section 14 of the Act, conditions may also – on the same grounds as those stated in section 12 – be imposed on assemblies.

If the requirements for the imposition of conditions are met, the senior officer has a wide discretion as to the conditions which may in fact be imposed. Section 12(1) merely states that he may impose conditions 'as appear to him necessary'. Under section 12, there is power to impose conditions as to the route to be followed, and to prohibit entry into particular public places. Failure to comply with the conditions, or to incite others not to comply, is an offence.[18] However, with the Human Rights Act 1998 in force, the powers of the police are now subject to the requirements of the European Convention on Human Rights. As seen in the case of **Austin v Commissioner of Police** (2009), discussed above, this superimposes the requirements of proportionality on to the exercise of police power, enabling the courts to evaluate the justification for police action against the necessity for such action in the particular circumstances. In other words, the court will assess whether the action taken by the police was a proportionate response to the circumstances.

The power to ban processions

Under section 13(2), the Chief Officer of Police[19] may issue a banning order, which may only be issued if the power to impose conditions is insufficient to prevent serious public disorder. In London, the banning order must have the consent of the Home Secretary, and elsewhere the consent of the local authority. The power to ban processions represents a power to ban all processions, rather than to ban a particular procession, and can cover all or part of a police area and last for up to three months.[20] Organising or participating in, or inciting participation in, a banned procession is a summary offence.[21]

The power to enter meetings on private premises

Where a private meeting is held, the police have power to enter and remain on the premises under certain circumstances. A meeting is defined as a private meeting if it is held in entirely

---

17 Public Order Act 1986, s 12(1).
18 Ibid, s 12(4), (5).
19 In London, the Commissioner for the City of London or Commissioner for the Metropolis.
20 The power to ban a procession is subject to judicial review: **Kent v Metropolitan Police Commissioners** (1981).
21 Public Order Act 1986, s 13(7), (8), (9).

enclosed premises. Thus, even if the meeting is held in publicly owned and managed premises, such as a school or town hall, it will be a private meeting. In **Thomas v Sawkins** (1935), a police officer entered a private meeting which was held to protest against the Incitement to Disaffection Bill. The organiser of the meeting brought an action based on trespass, and argued that, as a result of trespass by the police, he had the right to evict the officers. The meeting had not given rise to a breach of the peace. However, the court held that notwithstanding its peaceful nature, the police had grounds for reasonably suspecting that a breach of the peace might occur and were therefore entitled to enter and remain on the premises.

The regulation of public assemblies[22]

While there is power to regulate a public assembly, there was no power to issue a banning order under the 1986 Act. A public assembly is defined as 'an assembly of two or more persons in a public place which is wholly or partly open to the air'.[23] However, an individual who disobeys an order, even where he or she does not actually join the assembly, is liable under the Act.[24] The basis on which the conditions which may be attached[25] are the same as those for conditions imposed on processions. Intimidation, as a ground for imposing a condition, has been interpreted to mean more than 'causing discomfort'.[26]

Special rules apply to demonstrations in the vicinity of Parliament. The Police Reform and Social Responsibility Act 2011, sections 142–148, authorise the police to direct a person not to start, or to cease, doing a 'prohibited activity', defined as including the operation of amplified noise equipment or the erecting of a tent or other structure in the area of Parliament Square. Section 143 confers power to seize prohibited items. Under section 144 a direction may be given requiring a person to cease doing, or not to start doing, a prohibited activity. The direction may not be longer than 90 days.

Trespassory assemblies

Section 70 of the Criminal Justice and Public Order Act 1994 inserted section 14A into the 1986 Act, which provided a power to ban trespassory assemblies.

A Chief Officer of Police may apply for a banning order if he reasonably believes that an assembly is likely to involve trespass or might result in serious disruption to community life or cause damage to buildings and structures. This power must be seen within the context of section 14C of the Public Order Act 1986,[27] which confers power on the police to stop persons within a five-mile radius of the assembly, if the police reasonably believe that they are on their way to the assembly, and the assembly is subject to a section 14A order.

In **Director of Public Prosecutions v Jones** (1999), section 14 was considered. A section 14A order had been issued, which prohibited the holding of a trespassory assembly within a four-mile radius of Stonehenge. The assembly was heading for Stonehenge, and was within the four-mile radius, and on the public highway. The court held that the highway was for passing and repassing only, and that assembling on the highway was outside the purpose for which the implied licence to use the highway was granted. The respondents argued that they were both peaceful and not obstructive and were making 'reasonable use' of the highway. The House of

---

22 See Bonner and Stone, 1987.
23 Public Order Act 1986, s 16, as amended by the Anti-Social Behaviour Act 2003, s 57.
24 **Broadwith v Chief Constable of Thames Valley Police** (2000).
25 Public Order Act 1986, s 14(1).
26 **Police v Reid** (1987).
27 Inserted by the Criminal Justice and Public Order Act 1994, s 71.

Lords ruled, by a majority of three to two, that the public had the right to use the highway for such reasonable and usual activities, inter alia including peaceful assembly, as was consistent with the primary use for passage and repassage. It was a question of fact and degree in each case whether the user was reasonable and not inconsistent with that primary right.

The right to move freely along the highway, for a minority group such as Gypsies, entails the need for a lawful place to stop. While local authorities had been under a duty to provide sites under the Caravan Sites Act 1968,[28] that statutory duty has now been removed.[29] This is of particular concern, given that Gypsies – a recognised racial group protected under the Race Relations Act 1976 and under international law[30] – traditionally travel with caravans from area to area, usually in search of seasonal work.

The problems encountered in the 1970s and 1980s with groups of New Age Travellers meeting for the summer solstice at Stonehenge and the problems caused by 'rave parties' resulted in the criminalisation of trespass for the first time under English law. The Criminal Justice and Public Order Act 1994 provides that the police may remove from land persons who are in fact trespassing, irrespective of whether or not they entered the land lawfully or as trespassers.[31] The 1994 Act also provides that the power of removal applies in relation to persons having six vehicles on land, as opposed to twelve under the 1986 Public Order Act. Furthermore the 1994 Act extended the land to which the provisions apply. Common land[32] is now included, as are footpaths, bridleways, byways, public paths and cycletracks.[33] Section 62 of the 1994 Act gave the police new powers to remove 'vehicles and other property' on land. The police must be satisfied that there are alternative caravan sites available to the trespassers to move to.[34] The power to seize vehicles and property arises where the trespasser fails to comply with a direction to leave within a reasonable time. Reasonableness is an objective test and will depend on all the circumstances of the case, including the roadworthiness of vehicles.[35]

Rave parties

The Criminal Justice and Public Order Act 1994 introduced new police powers to order persons to leave gatherings, created a new criminal offence of failing to leave within a reasonable time and provided for arrest without warrant. The provisions govern open-air gatherings of 20 or more persons, where amplified music is played at night time.[36] Failure to comply with a police direction may result in the power to seize and remove vehicles and sound equipment.[37]

The Act gives the police power to regulate the movement of persons to a gathering. Where a direction has been made under section 63, the police may stop persons and order them not to proceed to the gathering. The exercise of this sweeping power is confined to an area within a five-mile radius of the gathering.

Other public order offences under the 1986 Act

The Act replaces a number of common law offences. The Law Commission considered, for example, that the offence of breach of the peace was too vague a concept and that it should be

---

28 Caravan Sites Act 1968, s 6.
29 Criminal Justice and Public Order Act 1994, s 80.
30 **Commission for Racial Equality v Dutton** (1989).
31 Criminal Justice and Public Order Act 1994, s 61(2).
32 As defined in the Commons Registration Act 1965, s 22.
33 Criminal Justice and Public Order Act 1994, s 61(9)(b)(i).
34 Ibid, s 62A, as amended by the Anti-Social Behaviour Act 2003, s 60.
35 See **Krumpa v Director of Public Prosecutions** (1989).
36 Criminal Justice and Public Order Act 1994, s 63, as amended by the Anti-Social Behaviour Act 2003, s 58.
37 Ibid, s 64.

replaced with more specific offences. In its place, the concept of unlawful violence is used, which encompasses a number of situations. Violent conduct is defined as meaning any violent conduct, whether or not intended to cause injury or damage.[38]

Riot

Riot is the most serious offence under the Act. 'Riot' is defined in section 1 as being where 12 or more persons who are present together use or threaten unlawful violence for a common purpose and the conduct of them (taken together) is such as would cause a person of 'reasonable firmness' present at the scene to fear for his personal safety; each of the persons using unlawful violence for the common purpose is guilty of riot.

Under section 1, a riot may be committed in private as well as public places. The common purpose may be inferred from the conduct, and does not need to be articulated. The purpose itself need not be unlawful − a perfectly legitimate demonstration may turn into a riot if the conditions for a riot are satisfied, namely the use of unlawful violence for a common purpose which is such as to cause persons of reasonable firmness present to fear for their personal safety, although it is not necessary that such persons actually be present at the scene. The mental element required for liability, under section 6(1), is that a person 'intends to use violence or is aware that his conduct may be violent'. The seriousness with which the offence is viewed is reflected in the requirement of trial on indictment (trial by jury) and liability on conviction to imprisonment for a term not exceeding ten years or a fine, or both.[39]

Violent disorder

Section 2 of the Public Order Act 1986 created a new statutory offence of violent disorder, which replaced the common law offence of unlawful assembly. The offence shares similarities with the offence of riot, but differs in several respects. First, for the offence to be committed, there need to be only three people, rather than 12 as required for a riot, involved in the violent conduct. Second, there needs to be no common purpose, as is required for the offence of riot. It is sufficient for an offence of violent disorder to be committed that the persons be involved in the use or threat of violent conduct. It is necessary that the conduct be such that it causes a person 'of reasonable firmness' to 'fear for his personal safety', although such persons need not actually be present.[40] The offence can be committed in private or in public.[41] The mental element required under section 6 is that the person intends to use or to threaten violence, or is aware that his conduct may be violent or threaten violence. Self-induced intoxication, other than through prescribed medication in a course of medical treatment, is not an excuse.

The requirement of three persons' involvement in the violent disorder has caused difficulties. In **R v Fleming** (1989), for example, four persons were charged, one was acquitted and the jury failed to reach a decision on a second. Accordingly, the conviction of the remaining two defendants was quashed.[42] The Court of Appeal in **Fleming** noted that it was possible for fewer than three persons to be convicted where, for example, there was sufficient evidence as to the involvement of more than three persons but some of the greater number evaded arrest or lacked the required mental element for the offence. The jury must be correctly directed on the matter, and failure to direct appropriately will cause a conviction to be quashed. This occurred

---

38 Public Order Act 1986, s 8.
39 Ibid, s 1(6).
40 Ibid, s 2(3).
41 Ibid, s 2(4).
42 See also **R v Abdul Mahroof** (1988).

in **R v Whorton** (1990), where there was evidence that eight to ten people were involved in the violence, but only four were charged and only two convicted. Their appeal against conviction was successful, on the basis that the judge had not directed the jury that they could only convict if there were either three defendants before them or, if a lesser number, a greater number had in fact been involved in the violent disorder.

The offence is triable on indictment (by the Crown Court) or summarily (by a magistrates' court), and carries a term of imprisonment of up to five years on indictment, a fine or both and, on summary conviction, imprisonment of up to six months or a fine, or both.[43]

Affray

A person is guilty of an affray if he uses or threatens unlawful violence towards another and his conduct is such as would cause a person of reasonable firmness present at the scene to fear for his personal safety.[44]

Two or more persons may be involved in the offence, in which case it is necessary that their conduct be considered together for the purpose of section 3. A verbal threat of unlawful violence is not sufficient for the offence to be committed. The offence may take place in private or in public and, again, the test for unlawful violence is whether a person of reasonable firmness, who need not in fact be present, is put in fear of his personal safety. The mental element is the same as that required for violent disorder. Police constables may arrest without warrant, and the offence is triable on indictment or summarily. On indictment, the offence carries a term of imprisonment not exceeding three years or a fine or both; on summary conviction, there is liability to imprisonment of up to six months or a fine or both.[45]

The definition of affray was considered by the Court of Appeal in **R v Sanchez** (1996). On the charge of affray, the trial judge directed the jury on the requirement for a 'person of reasonable firmness' and said that the victim was such a person and that he was to be believed when he said that he was frightened. The Court of Appeal held that there was a misdirection, in that the judge's directions overlooked the need to direct the jury to consider not only the victim but also the putative third person, the hypothetical bystander; affray was a public order offence and there were other offences for the protection of persons at whom the violence was aimed.

Fear or provocation of violence

Under section 4 of the Public Order Act 1986, a person is guilty of an offence if he:

(a) uses towards another person threatening, abusive or insulting words or behaviour; or

(b) distributes or displays to another person any writing, sign or other visible representation which is threatening, abusive or insulting, with the intent to cause that person to believe that immediate unlawful violence will be used against him or another by any person, or to provoke the immediate use of unlawful violence by that person or another, or whereby that person is likely to believe that such violence will be used or it is likely that such violence will be provoked.

The offence is one which may be committed by a single person. For a prosecution to succeed, it is necessary to establish that threatening, abusive or insulting words or behaviour have been

---

43 Public Order Act 1986, s 2(5).
44 Ibid, s 3.
45 Ibid, s 3(7).

directed towards a specific person. Rude or offensive words or behaviour may not necessarily be insulting, and swearing may not be abusive.[46] It is also necessary to establish that the person affected is caused to believe that immediate unlawful violence is about to be used against him. In **Horseferry Road Metropolitan Stipendiary Magistrate ex parte Siadatan** (1990), it was held that the violence feared must be both immediate and unlawful.[47] A threat of violence at some future time will not suffice for this offence to be proven. The mental element required under section 6 is that the person intends his words or behaviour (or signs, etc) to be threatening, abusive or insulting or that he is aware that it may be threatening, abusive or insulting.

Harassment, alarm or distress[48]

Under sections 4A[49] and 5 of the Act, a person is guilty of an offence if he:

(a) uses threatening, abusive or insulting words or behaviour, or disorderly behaviour; or

(b) displays any writing, sign or other visible representation which is threatening, abusive or insulting, thereby causing . . . harassment, alarm or distress or within the hearing or sight of a person likely to be caused harassment, alarm or distress thereby.

The introduction of these offences, and the use to which they are put by the police, raises controversy. The offence was designed to provide powers to deal with relatively minor acts of antisocial, unruly or disorderly conduct which, while of itself not serious, causes fear in others. In its White Paper, the government illustrated the sort of behaviour that was being targeted:[50]

(a) hooligans on housing estates causing disturbances in the common parts of blocks of flats . . .;

(b) groups of youths persistently shouting abuse and obscenities or pestering people waiting to catch public transport or to enter a hall or cinema; someone turning out the lights in a crowded dance hall, in a way likely to cause panic;

(c) rowdy behaviour in the streets late at night which alarms local residents.

For the offence to be proven, it is necessary that the words or behaviour, or signs etc, are uttered or displayed within the sight of a person who is likely to be harassed or alarmed or distressed – it is not necessary to prove actual harassment, alarm or distress. However, the mental element required is that the person using the words, behaviour or signs either intended his conduct to be threatening, abusive or insulting or was aware that it might be. Thus, words uttered in a public place (for example, by demonstrators or persons attending football matches) which might in fact be threatening or abusive, and might in fact cause alarm or distress to someone hearing the words, will not be sufficient for a prosecution to succeed.[51] No offence occurs if the prohibited conduct occurs inside a dwelling used as a person's home or at other living accommodation.[52] A person detained in a police cell does not occupy it as a home or other living accommodation: see **R v Francis** (2006).

In **Jordan v Burgoyne** (1963), the accused made an inflammatory racist speech in Trafalgar Square. He was prosecuted under the forerunner to section 4 of the Public Order Act

---

46 **R v Ambrose** (1973).
47 See further below. On the Racial and Religious Hatred Act 2006 see Chapter 19.
48 See *Criminal Law: Offences Relating to Public Order*, Law Com No 123, 1983, and Williams, 1984. See Geddis, 2004.
49 Introduced by s 154 of the Criminal Justice and Public Order Act 1994.
50 *Review of Public Order Law*, Cmnd 9510, 1985, London: HMSO, para 3.22. On Anti-Social Behaviour Orders see Chapter 21.
51 See **Director of Public Prosecutions v Clarke** (1992); **Harvey v DPP** (2011)C 81HC B1 (admin).
52 Public Order Act 1986, s 4A(2).

1986, section 5 of the Public Order Act 1936. It was held that the speech went beyond the limits of tolerance. The defendant could not argue that the words used were not likely to cause ordinary persons to commit breaches of the peace. The defendant had to 'take his audience as he found them'. If the words used were likely to provoke that audience, or part thereof, to commit a breach of the peace, the defendant was guilty of an offence.

Insulting words were the subject of judicial scrutiny in **Brutus v Cozens** (1973). In **Brutus**, the defendant and other anti-apartheid protesters interrupted play at a Wimbledon tennis match. The audience resented the interruption. Brutus was charged with insulting behaviour likely to cause a breach of the peace. In the Divisional Court, it was held that an offence occurred where the behaviour affronted other people, and reflected a contempt for their rights. The House of Lords, however, allowed Brutus's appeal. Not all speech or conduct fell within the meaning of the section. It must be conduct or speech which the ordinary person would recognise as insulting – a term which was deemed incapable of precise definition. The mere resentment of the crowd, as opposed to violence, did not suffice to make the actions insulting.

The issue of violent reaction to provocative words was considered in **R v Horseferry Road Magistrates ex parte Siadatan** (1991). The case concerned Salman Rushdie's novel, *The Satanic Verses*. In an application laid against the publishers and the author, it was argued that distribution of the book offended against section 4 of the 1986 Act, in so far as it contained abusive and insulting language which was likely to provoke violence amongst devout Muslims. The magistrates refused to issue a summons. The issue went to the Divisional Court for judicial review. It was there held that the violence which was apprehended by the words must be immediate violence, not some distant act of violence.

In **R v Stephen Miller** (1999), the defendant appealed against sentence for racially aggravated threatening words. The defendant had pleaded guilty to two offences: first, aggravated threatening words and behaviour contrary to section 4 of the Public Order Act 1986, as amended by section 31 of the Crime and Disorder Act 1998; and secondly, travelling on a railway without a ticket. He was sentenced to 18 months' imprisonment, and appealed. The Court of Appeal dismissed his appeal. His conduct towards the conductor on the train was particularly bad. The sentence was designed to reflect public concern about conduct which damaged good racial relations within the community.[53]

The mental element on the part of the accused must be satisfied. KA Ewing and CA Gearty provide illustrations of the uses to which section 5 has been put.[54] The Act has been used to curb the wearing of obscene T-shirts and hats; to suppress a satirical poster of the former Prime Minister Mrs Thatcher; and to prosecute protesters outside abortion clinics in Ireland.[55] In Gearty and Ewing's assessment, section 5 of the Act represents a 'mechanism for punishing non-violent non-conformity for the crime of being itself'.[56] It must be conceded that section 5 represents a serious, and hitherto uncontemplated, limitation of freedom of expression and an alteration of the balance between individual liberty and the legitimate expectations of citizens to be protected from the consequences of another person's words and actions.

However, Article 10 proved constructive in relation to section 5 of the Public Order Act 1986 in **Percy v Director of Public Prosecutions** (2002). In this case, Ms Percy had been convicted under section 5 in relation to her protest against American military policy at an American air base. In the course of her protest Ms Percy defaced and trampled on an American flag. On appeal, it was held that too much reliance had been placed by the trial judge on the fact that her

---

53 In **R v Rogers (Philip)** (2007), the House of Lords ruled that using the words 'bloody foreigners' was capable of amounting to the offence of using racially aggravated abusive or insulting words with the intent to cause fear or provoke violence.
54 Ewing and Gearty, 1990, Chapter 4.
55 **Director of Public Prosecutions v Fidler** (1992); **Director of Public Prosecutions v Clarke** (1992).
56 Ewing and Gearty, 1990, p 123.

behaviour towards the flag – which was insulting to Americans at the base – was avoidable, at the expense of the defendant's right to freedom of expression. Her conviction was incompatible with Article 10 and was quashed. See also **Ajit Singh Dehal v Crown Prosecution Service** (2005).

Harassment

The Protection from Harassment Act 1997 makes it a criminal offence to pursue a course of conduct which amounts to harassment of another and which that person knows amounts to harassment of the other.[57] Section 3 provides a civil remedy which enables an individual to seek an injunction against a person who is harassing them or may be likely to do so. In addition, damages may be awarded for any anxiety caused by the harassment and any financial loss resulting from the harassment.[58] In order to secure a conviction under section 2, the following requirements must be met:

- there must be a 'course of conduct';
- the conduct must take place on at least two occasions;[59]
- the course of conduct must take place against 'another person';
- the conduct must harass or alarm another or cause that person distress.

Section 1(3) provides exceptions to liability under section 1, which does not apply if the person accused of harassment can show that:

(a) the conduct in question was pursued for the purpose of preventing or detecting crime;
(b) the conduct in question was pursued under any enactment or rule of law or to comply with any condition or requirement imposed by any person under any enactment; or
(c) in the particular circumstances the pursuit of the course of conduct was reasonable.

Section 1(3)(a) was considered by the Court of Appeal in **Hayes v Willoughby** (2013). In this case, the defendant had waged a 'lengthy and persistent campaign of correspondence and investigation' into the affairs of the claimant. His defence was that the conduct fell within section 1(3)(a). The Supreme Court ruled that a purely subjective belief in the mind of the harasser that he was preventing or detecting crime was not enough, and that Parliament intended there should be limits to the conduct falling within the defence. In this case the defendant's conduct had become irrational and he could not rely on section 1(3)(a).

Where a course of conduct causes fear, on at least two occasions, that violence will be used against another a criminal offence is committed. On conviction the court may, in addition to sentencing the offender, issue a restraining order prohibiting the offender from doing anything which amounts to harassment or causes a fear of violence.[60] A similar power exists in relation to a person who is acquitted of an offence.[61] A restraining order may be made for a specified period or may have effect until further order. The date of expiry of the order is variable.[62]

---

57 Protection from Harassment Act 1997, s 2. The exercise by an individual of his right to freedom of expression and the instigation of secret surveillance of another person were capable of constituting a course of conduct amounting to harassment: **Howlett v Holding** (2006).
58 On this see **Jones v Ruth** (2011).
59 See **Banks v Ablex Ltd** (2005).
60 Protection from Harassment Act 1997, s 5.
61 Protection from Harassment Act 1997, s 5A.
62 See **Director of Public Prosecutions v Hall** (2005).

In **Daiichi UK Ltd v Stop Huntingdon Animal Cruelty** (2004), the High Court ruled that the Protection from Harassment Act 1997 was intended to protect individuals and not corporate victims of harassment. However, individuals who were non-corporate claimants were entitled to protection. Stop Huntingdon Animal Cruelty was an unincorporated association whose stated objective was the closure of laboratories run by Huntingdon Life Sciences, which conducted research using live animals. As a result of a campaign of harassment and intimidation, Huntingdon Life's insurance brokers had ceased to act for them. In addition, its auditors withdrew their services. The claimants, their directors and employees had 'unquestionably been subject to harassment of a very serious nature intended to intimidate and terrify'. Granting the injunctive relief, Owen J ruled that the 'balance of justice and convenience weighed heavily in favour of granting interlocutory injunctive relief' bearing in mind 'the rights to freedom of speech and of assembly and association'.[63]

The courts have interpreted the 1997 Act strictly, requiring that 'another person' be a specific individual. As a result, it was unclear whether protection could be given to the employees of an organisation who had not been personally harassed, even though another employee had been. The Serious Organised Crime and Police Act 2005 (SOCPA) amends the 1997 Act to cover this situation. Section 125 SOPCA amends section 1 of the 1997 Act. Section 1A of the 1997 Act provides (in part) that:

A person must not pursue a course of conduct –

(a) which involves harassment of two or more persons, and
(b) which he knows or ought to know involves harassment of those persons, and
(c) by which he intends to persuade any person –

   (i) not to do something that he is entitled to do, or
   (ii) to do something that he is not under any obligation to do.

The provision is not intended to criminalise peaceful protesting but will be engaged where there are threats and intimidation which seek to force others to do something or not to do something. Section 125(5) SOCPA inserts a new section 3A into the 1997 Act which allows for an injunction to be sought where there is an actual or apprehended breach of section 1(1A). Section 125(7) amends the definition of course of conduct in section 7(3) of the 1997 Act stating that in the case of conduct in relation to two or more persons, a course of conduct means conduct on at least one occasion in relation to each person.[64]

The Crime and Disorder Act 1998

Sections 28 to 32 of the Crime and Disorder Act 1998 extend the law to encompass racially aggravated offences. It is an offence under sections 4 and 5 of the Public Order Act 1986 (fear of provocation of violence, intentional harassment, alarm or distress) to engage in racially aggravated conduct. Section 32 makes it an offence to act in a racially aggravated manner in relation to sections 2 and 4 of the Protection from Harassment Act 1997. Under section 28(1), an offence is racially aggravated if:

---

63 See also **Hall v Save Newchurch Guinea Pigs (Campaign)** (2005). An employer can be vicariously liable under s 3 of the 1997 Act for breach of a statutory duty imposed only on his employee for harassment committed by one of its employees in the course of his or her employment. The Court of Appeal so ruled in **Majrowski v Guy's and St Thomas's NHS Trust** (2005).

64 On harassment of a person in his or her home see SOCPA 2005, s 126. On harassment in employment see also the Equality Act 2010.

(a) at the time of committing the offence, or immediately before or after doing so, the offender demonstrates towards the victim of the offence hostility based on the victim's membership (or presumed membership) of a racial group; or

(b) the offence is motivated (wholly or partly) by hostility towards members of a racial group based on their membership of that group.[65]

Section 28(3) provides that:

It is immaterial . . . whether or not the offender's hostility is also based, to any extent, on –

(a) the fact of presumption that any person or group of persons belongs to any religious group . . .

Under section 82, the court may impose a higher penalty for racially aggravated offences.

Summary

Under domestic law, the law relating to assembly and association encompasses a number of different situations: the right to peaceful protest through a gathering or procession and restrictions imposed by the law relating to breach of the peace, obstruction of the police and obstructing the highway. The law seeks to achieve a balance between the right of the individual and group to demonstrate and the right of other citizens to a secure and peaceful society through public order law which confers on the police the power to control assemblies and processions.

Domestic law must be measured against Article 11 of the European Convention on Human Rights, incorporated into domestic law under the Human Rights Act 1998. The domestic courts are required to evaluate the legality of reactions to public disorder according to the European concept of proportionality.

The public order offences such as riot, affray, provocation of violence and harassment must also be considered in relation to public order law.

 Further Reading

Fenwick, H. (2011) *Civil Liberties and Human Rights* (5th edn), London: Routledge-Cavendish.

Fenwick, H. (2009) 'Marginalising Human Rights: breach of the peace, "kettling", the Human Rights Act and Public Protest', Public Law, 737.

Nicolson, D. and Reid, K. (1996) 'Arrest for Breach of the Peace and the ECHR', Criminal Law Review, 764.

Williams, D.G.T. (1987) 'Processions, Assemblies and the Freedom of the Individual', Criminal Law Review, 167.

---

65 In **DPP v M** (2004), the High Court ruled that the use of the phrase 'bloody foreigners' was contrary to s 28(1)(a) in that the word 'foreigners' was capable of describing a racial group and the word 'bloody' was capable of demonstrating hostility.

Chapter 21

The Police and Police Powers

Introduction

The police forces of England and Wales, Scotland and Northern Ireland are central to the detection and investigation of crime, the maintenance of a peaceful society and protection of citizens from criminal activities. In this chapter we look first at the organisation of the police in England and Wales[1] and then turn to police powers.

The United Kingdom has no national police force.[2] Instead, the police are organised on a basis which links them to the locality. In England and Wales, there now exist 43 police forces: the City of London Police, the Metropolitan Police and 41 forces outside London. Scotland has eight forces and Northern Ireland one. The Police Act 1996 provides that the Home Secretary may alter police areas 'in the interest of efficiency or effectiveness'.[3] In 1962, a Royal Commission examined the question whether there should be a national police force under central government control, but concluded that the status quo should be maintained, subject to supervision by central government.

The organisation of the police has been reformed. The Police Reform and Social Responsibility Act 2011 provides for the election of Police and Crime Commissioners (PCCs) for each police area in England and Wales outside London. The Commissioners are politically independent and are accountable to local Police and Crime Panels. Operating on a national basis is the National Crime Agency, discussed below.

While the organisation of the police is based on locality, policing must increasingly be considered within the national, European and international contexts. Terrorist threats, drug and human trafficking and money laundering operations do not respect national or local boundaries. For this reason, police forces must co-operate with other agencies and be guided by central government's analysis of various threats and the policing resources needed to counter those threats. Police funding comes partly from government grants and from local council tax. The Home Office establishes the amount to be spent on policing annually. The efficiency of police forces is under the jurisdiction of Her Majesty's Inspectors of Constabulary appointed by the Home Secretary and accountable to him or her.

National (or state) security is discussed in Chapter 22.

The Home Office

The Home Office is one of the largest departments of state. It has national responsibility for the police service in England and Wales. It is also responsible for state security and counter-terrorism, for immigration and for the passport service. Smaller organisations such the Criminal Records Bureau and the Forensic Science Service are within the Home Office's remit, together with a number of non-departmental public bodies including the Criminal Injuries Compensation Authority and Youth Justice Board. The National Crime Agency is also within the Department's responsibility.

---

1 Policing is devolved to the administrations of Northern Ireland and Scotland.
2 See Uglow, 2002, Chapter 2; Newburn, 2003, Chapter 4.
3 Police Act 1996, s 32.

Police and Crime Commissioners (PCCs)

The Police Reform and Social Responsibility Act 2011, which extends to England and Wales, introduced elected Police and Crime Commissioners with responsibility for ensuring the maintenance of the police force for the individual police area and ensuring that the police force is 'efficient and effective'.[4] The PCC is paid a salary, which may vary by police area.[5]

The first elections were held in November 2012 and subsequent elections will be held every four years. The voting system for the election of PCCs is the Supplementary Vote (on which see Chapter 12).

Section 1 of the Police Reform and Social Responsibility Act 2011 sets out the duties of Police and Crime Commissioners (PCCs). A PCC must 'secure the maintenance of the police force' for his or her area and 'secure that the police force is efficient and effective'. The PCC must also hold the Chief Constable, who has operational control over the police force, accountable for the exercise of his or her duties. The PCC is to issue a 'police and crime plan', following consultation with the Chief Constable and having regard to any recommendations made by the Police and Crime Panel. The PCC will also publish an Annual Report.

The PCC must appoint a Chief Executive and Finance Officer.[6] He or she may also appoint a Deputy PCC[7] to whom he or she may delegate his or her functions. Controversially, the appointment of a Deputy PCC is not subject to a veto by the Police and Crime Panel. Instead, the PCC must notify the Panel of the proposed appointee and the Panel must make recommendations. These, however, are not binding on the PCC.

Police and Crime Panels

Each police area in England and Wales, other than the metropolitan police district, is to have a Police and Crime Panel.[8] Each local authority within the police force area must appoint at least one elected representative and two independent members. Each Panel must have at least ten elected members, and with the consent of the Home Secretary, may co-opt additional members up to a maximum Panel size of 20. In Wales, the Panels will not be local authority committees, but public bodies set up and maintained by the Secretary of State.

Police and Crime Panels will examine the actions and decisions of the Police and Crime Commissioner (PCC), and hold him or her to account. They do not scrutinise the performance of the police force itself: that is the responsibility of the PCC. The Panels will consider the PCC's Police and Crime Plan and his or her Annual Report. They will also question the PCC at Panel meetings, make reports and recommendations of the action or decision of the PCC and monitor complaints against the PCC.

Police and Crime Panels have the power to suspend the PCC if the Commissioner has been charged with an offence which carries a term of imprisonment exceeding two years.[9] The Police and Crime Panels are funded by the Home Office.

---

4 Police Reform and Social Responsibility Act 2011, s 1.
5 Ibid, Sched 1, Para 2(3).
6 Ibid, Sched 1, para 6.
7 Ibid, s 18 and Sched 1.
8 Ibid, s 28.
9 Police Reform and Social Responsibility Act 2011, s 30.

London: The Mayor's Office for Policing and Crime

Until 1999, the Home Secretary was the police authority for the Metropolitan Police. Under the Greater London Authority Act 1999 (on which see Chapter 11), there was established a Metropolitan Police Authority, which replaced the Home Secretary as police authority.[10] Under the Police Reform and Social Responsibility Act 2011, the Metropolitan Police Authority is replaced by the Mayor's Office for Policing and Crime (MOPAC).[11] The Mayor's Office is under a duty to 'secure the maintenance of the metropolitan police force, and secure that the metropolitan police force is efficient and effective'. The Mayor of London assumes the role of the Mayor's Office for Policing and Crime. MOPAC has the duty to hold the Commissioner of Police of the Metropolis to account.[12] The London Assembly has a police and crime panel which is under a duty to scrutinize the Mayor's Office for Policing and Crime.[13]

Crime and Policing Plans

The PCCs and the Mayor's Office for Policing and Crime are under a duty to set a Crime and Policing Plan for their local police force.[14] This must comply with the Home Office's Strategic Policing Requirement, and the Home Secretary has the power to give guidance as to matters covered in the Plan. The Plan sets out the local police force's police and crime objectives, including crime and disorder reduction. It also sets out financial implications and resources and explains the manner in which the Chief Constable will report to the Police and Crime Panel.

Chief Constables of Police

Outside the Metropolitan area, which is headed by the Commissioner of Police of the Metropolis, police forces are under the operational control of Chief Constables.[15] The appointment of senior police officers is now undertaken by a Senior Police Appointments panel.[16] The Chief Constable is responsible for recruitment and promotions to the ranks below that of Assistant Chief Constable, and exercises disciplinary powers over the police.

The status of police officers

A police officer is a servant of the state.[17] He or she is not employed under a contract of employment, but is a holder of public office.[18] Police officers are not servants of the Chief Constable.[19] Police officers hold office under statute, and are subject to the police disciplinary code. They are not allowed to belong to trade unions, or any other association concerned with

---

10 Greater London Authority Act 1999, ss 310, 312.
11 Police Reform and Social Responsibility Act 2011, s 3.
12 Ibid. Section 1(9) abolished police authorities, whose functions included responsibility for setting policy objectives and ensuring the maintenance of 'an efficient and effective police force for its area'.
13 Police Reform and Social Responsibility Act 2011, s 32.
14 Ibid, s 7.
15 Ibid, s 2.
16 See s 53B–D Police Act 1996 as amended by ss 2–4 Policing and Crime Act 2009.
17 Fisher v Oldham Corporation (1930).
18 See Attorney General for New South Wales v Perpetual Trustee Company Ltd (1955).
19 White v Chief Constable of South Yorkshire (1999).

levels of pay or conditions of employment. Police Federations represent police officers in matters relating to welfare, and have restricted powers in relation to police discipline.[20] Police officers are not permitted to take any active part in politics, nor participate in any other activity which could actually impede, or give the suggestion that it could impede, the officer's impartiality.[21]

Police civilians

The Police Reform Act 2002 enables chief officers of police to employ suitably skilled and trained civilians to exercise functions as Community Support Officers, investigating officers, detention officers and escort officers.[22] A civilian officer is entitled to use reasonable force in the exercise of his or her functions. In relation to authorised forced entry into property, a civilian officer must be accompanied by a constable, unless the entry is required to save life or prevent injury, or to prevent serious damage to property.

Community Support Officers (CSOs) have the power to issue fixed penalty notices for certain offences.[23] The Secretary of State may add to or remove from the list of offences for which Community Support Officers may not issue fixed penalty notices.

The Serious Organised Crime and Police Act 2005[24] conferred new powers on Community Support Officers. These powers include a power to direct traffic and place traffic signs on the road, power to deal with begging, power to search detained persons for items that could cause injury or assist escape, power to enforce certain licensing offences, power to enforce by-laws, power to search persons for alcohol and tobacco in certain circumstances and a power to deal with possession of controlled drugs. Chief officers of police are also given power to designate CSOs with the power to require a name and address. It is a criminal offence not to comply with the request for a name and address. Where the CSO has reasonable grounds for believing that the information is false or inaccurate the CSO may detain the person for up to 30 minutes pending the arrival of a constable.

National Crime Agency (NCA)[25]

The Serious Organised Crime and Police Act 2005 (SOCPA) established the Serious Organised Crime Agency (SOCA), which brought together the National Crime Squad (NCS), the National Criminal Intelligence Service (NCIS), the investigative and intelligence work of Her Majesty's Customs and Excise (HMCE) on serious drug trafficking and the Immigration Service's responsibilities in relation to organised immigration crime. Special arrangements are made for Scotland and Northern Ireland, in relation to which the Agency works in partnership with the Scottish Drug Enforcement Agency and the Police Service of Northern Ireland respectively.

The Crime and Courts Act 2013 abolishes the Serious Organised Crime Agency and establishes the National Crime Agency (NCA). Section 1 of the Crime and Courts Act provides

---

20 Police Act 1996, s 59.
21 Police Regulations 1995, SI 1995/215.
22 Police Reform Act, s 38 and Sched 4. Schedule 4 provides detailed rules relating to civilian officers. The Police and Justice Act 2006, ss 7–9 and Sched 5 amend the powers of CSOs and confer power to deal with truancy.
23 Including those listed in s 1(1) of the Criminal Justice and Police Act 2001.
24 Schedule 8, amending Sched 4 to the Police Reform Act 2002.
25 See Policing in the 21st Century, London: Home Office 2010 and The National Crime Agency, Cm 8097 2011.

that the NCA is to have a crime-reduction function and a criminal intelligence function. Its crime reduction function relates to 'efficient and effective activities' to combat organised crime and serious crime. The criminal intelligence function entails the gathering, storing, processing, analysing and disseminating information relating to organised crime or serious crime and any other kind of crime. The NCA has four principal 'commands': organised crime, border policing and customs, economic crime and child protection. The NCA is to become fully operational by October 2013.

Section 3 provides that the Secretary of State must determine the strategic priorities for the NCA, in consultation with the Director General and other relevant persons. The Secretary of State may also, under section 2, by order make provision about counter-terrorism functions to be carried out by the NCA. The order may amend or otherwise modify the Crime and Courts Act 2013 or any other enactment (a 'Henry VIII power'). In order to ensure adequate parliamentary scrutiny such orders are to be subject to the super-affirmative procedure.[26]

The NCA is headed by a Director General who has operational control over the NCA. He or she will decide which operations are to be undertaken, and how they are to be conducted. The Director General must issue an annual plan before the beginning of each financial year, stating the strategic and operational priorities for the NCA. The Director General may request the Chief Officer of a UK police force or a UK law enforcement agency to undertake specific tasks to assist the NCA. Where such a request is made, the person given the direction must comply with it (see section 5(7)).

The Director General may designate any NCA officer as a person having the powers and privileges of a police constable, Revenue and Customs officer or Immigration Officer.

Codes of practice, notes for guidance and Home Office circulars

Under the Police and Criminal Evidence Act 1984, a number of Codes of Practice have been issued. The Codes do not have the force of law, but represent an administrative means of regulating differing aspects of police powers. Breach of the Codes does not give rise to civil or criminal liability.[27] Under the 1984 Act, there are eight Codes of Practice, each of which is regularly updated. Code A relates to stop and search procedures; Code B to the search of premises; Code C to interviews and conditions of detention not related to terrorism; Code D regulates identification procedures; and Code E and F regulate the tape and visual recording of interviews. Code G regulates the exercise of statutory powers of arrest under section 24 of PACE 1984 as amended by section 110 of the Serious Organised Crime and Police Act 2005. Code H sets out the requirements for detention, treatment and questioning of suspects related to terrorism in police custody. The notes for guidance are not part of the Code, but represent interpretative guidelines. Home Office circulars are designed to supplement the provisions of the Police and Criminal Evidence Act and other statutes.

---

26 See section 58 and Schedule 23. Super-affirmative procedure is discussed in Chapter 14.
27 39 PACE 1984, s 67(10).

Complaints against the police

The Police Reform Act 2002 established a new system for handling complaints against the police and introduced a new body – the Independent Police Complaints Commission (IPCC) – to oversee the system.[28] The IPCC is a non-departmental public body.

The IPCC consists of a chairperson appointed by the Crown and not fewer than ten other members appointed by the Secretary of State. The functions of the Commission are set out in section 10 of the Police Reform Act 2002 as being:

(a) the handling of complaints made against the police;[29]
(b) recording police conduct which may constitute a criminal offence or behaviour justifying disciplinary proceedings.

Complaints against the police may be made by a member of the public who claims to be the person in relation to whom the conduct took place, or a person who, while not being the direct victim, claims to have been adversely affected by the conduct. A person who witnesses the conduct may complain, as may a person acting on behalf of one of the people within the above categories.[30] Police conduct which has not been the subject of a complaint, but which involves a criminal offence or behaviour justifying disciplinary proceedings, must be referred to the IPCC. Where the IPCC considers that a matter requires investigation, it may choose to conduct one of four types of investigation:

● a police investigation on behalf of the appropriate police authority;
● a police investigation supervised by the IPCC;
● a police investigation managed by the IPCC;
● an investigation by the IPCC independent of the police.[31]

The Act imposes a duty on all chief officers of police forces and the Serious Organised Crime Agency to co-operate and assist in investigations and to provide information.[32] Independent IPCC investigations will take place in relation to the most serious complaints or conduct matters and those of the highest public interest.[33] Once the investigation is complete, the results must be reported. If the report indicates that a criminal offence may have been committed by a police officer, the IPCC must notify the Director of Public Prosecutions to decide whether criminal proceedings are to be brought against the officer. The complainant and other interested persons[34] must be informed of the outcome of an investigation.

Shortcomings in the existing legislation led to the Police (Complaints and Conduct) Act 2012. The Act introduces a new power to require serving officers, special constables and police staff to attend a hearing as a witness, with sanctions attached for non-compliance. The second principal reform is that under existing legislation, the IPCC cannot investigate matters which have previously been investigated by the Parliament Commissioner for Administration. That restriction is now removed.

---

28 The Independent Police Complaints Commission (www.ipcc.gov.uk) replaced the Police Complaints Authority originally established under the Police and Criminal Evidence Act 1984. See *Complaints Against the Police: Framework for a New System*, available through the Home Office website at www.homeoffice.gov.uk.
29 The Police and Justice Act 2006, s 41 enables the Home Secretary to extend the power of the IPCC to the investigation of complaints regarding the exercise of immigration and asylum enforcement functions.
30 Police Reform Act 2002, s 12.
31 Ibid, Sched 3, para 15(4).
32 Ibid, ss 15, 17.
33 These investigations result from recommendations of the Home Affairs Committee and the Inquiry into the death of Stephen Lawrence: see the Macpherson Report, available through www.official-documents.co.uk.
34 As defined in s 21.

The liability of the police

Prior to the enactment of section 88 of the Police Act 1996, the liability of a police officer for wrongful actions was personal. Whilst a servant of the Crown, the Crown was not, at common law, vicariously liable for wrongful actions of officers because, being neither appointed nor paid by the Crown, the officer was not 'in the employment of the Crown'. Section 88 of the Police Act 1996 makes it clear that Chief Constables are liable for torts committed by constables under their direction and control. Where damages or costs are ordered in a legal action, these are awarded against the Chief Constable and paid out of the local police budget.

The police were formerly also exempt from the legislation regulating racial discrimination, the Race Relations Act 1976 previously only applying to employers and employees, not office holders. The Race Relations (Amendment) Act 2000 reformed the law, following the recommendation of the Report of Inquiry into the death of Stephen Lawrence (the Macpherson Report), which stated:

> . . . the full force of the Race Relations legislation should apply to all police officers, and Chief Officers of Police should be made vicariously liable for the acts and omissions of their officers relevant to that legislation.[35]

The police are liable in law in actions for assault, wrongful arrest,[36] false imprisonment, trespass, public misfeasance, negligence or an action for the return of property which has been wrongfully taken. An action for malicious prosecution is available where a person believes that the police have maliciously and without reasonable cause abused their powers in recommending prosecution to the Crown Prosecution Service. Further, the police are liable in law for the care of those in their custody.[37]

The Police Reform Act 2002 provides a legal basis for civil liabilities arising from operations of joint investigation teams involving police officers from different forces and from abroad. Under the 2000 Convention on Mutual Assistance in Criminal Matters between Member States of the European Union, there is a requirement to provide arrangements for civil claims against joint forces. Section 103(1) of the 2002 Act extends the liability of chief officers of police by providing that they are liable for any unlawful conduct of members of international joint investigation teams.

The European Convention on Human Rights and the police

The Human Rights Act 1998 incorporates Convention rights. The Convention had already had an impact on the liability of police. The European Court of Human Rights ruled, in **Osman v United Kingdom** (1998), that Article 6 had been violated in respect of the effect of the police's immunity from civil actions under the rule formulated in **Hill v Chief Constable of West Yorkshire Police** (1989). In **Hill**, the House of Lords ruled that – for reasons of public policy – no action could lie against the police for their negligence in the investigation and suppression of crime. In **Osman v United Kingdom** (1998) the Court of Human Rights ruled unanimously that this exclusionary rule constituted a disproportionate restriction on the applicant's right of access to a court and thereby violated Article 6 of the Convention.

Notwithstanding the critical stance of the Court of Human Rights, the decision of **Hill v Chief Constable of West Yorkshire** (1989) was applied by the House of Lords in **Brooks v Commissioner**

---

35 The Equality Act 2010 repeals the 1976 Act and applies to the police.
36 See eg *Wershof v Metropolitan Police Commissioner* (1978).
37 See **Kirkham v Chief Constable of Greater Manchester** (1990); **Treadaway v Chief Constable of West Midlands** (1994). See further Chapter 18.

of Police of the Metropolis (2005).[38] The House of Lords ruled that as a matter of public policy the police generally owed no duty of care to victims or witnesses in respect of their activities when investigating suspected crimes. Since the duties of care alleged by the claimant had been inextricably bound up with the investigation of a crime, his claim based on those duties should be struck out.

In **Price v United Kingdom** (2001), the Court of Human Rights ruled that the detention of a severely disabled person in unsuitable conditions at a police station and subsequent detention in prison in similar conditions amounted to degrading treatment contrary to Article 3. The authorities admitted that they were unable to cope with the applicant's special needs. There was no evidence of any positive intention to humiliate or debase the applicant. However, to detain a seriously disabled person in such conditions which risked her health constituted a violation of Article 3.[39]

The police powers of stop and search under the Terrorism Act 2000 were tested in **Gillan and Quinton v United Kingdom** (2010) in which the Court of Human Rights found a violation of Article 8. Sections 44 to 47 of the Terrorism Act 2000 and the related Code of Practice did not comply with the requirements of legality. The Protection of Freedoms Act 2012, section 59 repeals sections 44–47 of the 2000 Act (see further Chapter 22).

The courts and police policy

The exercise of police discretion is reviewable by the courts, although the courts confer a great deal of latitude in relation to that discretion. In **R v Commissioner of Police for the Metropolis ex parte Blackburn (No 1)** (1968), the Court of Appeal made it clear that an order of mandamus would lie against the Metropolitan Police Commissioner. The Commissioner had issued a policy statement in which he made it clear that supervision of gambling clubs would not take place, other than where there was a suspicion that the clubs were being frequented by criminals. The applicant, Blackburn, claimed that illegal gambling was taking place and applied to the courts for an order of mandamus to compel the Commissioner to reverse his policy. The court insisted that the Commissioner had a public duty to enforce the law, and that his discretion could be controlled by the courts. Nevertheless, since the Commissioner had undertaken to reverse his former policy, the order would not be granted. Neither was mandamus ordered in **R v Commissioner of Police for the Metropolis ex parte Blackburn (No 3)** (1973). In that case, the applicant sought to compel, by order of the court, enforcement of the Obscene Publications Act 1959. However, the Chief Officer had increased the numbers in the vice squad, and reorganised its working methods.

Police discretion returned for consideration in **R v Chief Constable of Sussex ex parte International Traders' Ferry Ltd** (1997). In that case, animal rights protesters, concerned about the welfare of live animal exports, blockaded ports in order to stop the exports. To assist the exporter, the police deployed 1,125 officers, a level of policing which was maintained for some ten days. In order to maintain the operation, seven other police forces assisted.[40] The cost of the operation amounted to £1.25 million. The Home Office refused to make a special grant to assist with the financial cost of the operation. In April, the Chief Constable indicated that new arrangements would have to be made, which would involve the company having to reduce its shipments. The

---

38 Also see **Van Colle v Chief Constable of the Hertfordshire Police** (2008) discussed in Chapter 18.

39 See also **Edwards v United Kingdom** (2002), in which the United Kingdom was found to have violated Article 2 through its failure to protect the life of a prisoner killed in his cell by a fellow inmate who had a history of violence and had been diagnosed schizophrenic.

40 Under the Police Act 1964 (now the Police Act 1996, s 24).

company sought judicial review of the Chief Constable's decision. The Court of Appeal upheld the Divisional Court's refusal to interfere with the decision of the Chief Constable. In light of the circumstances, the Chief Constable's decision could not be 'regarded as so unreasonable as to enable a court to interfere'. The court approved the statement of Neill LJ in **Harris v Sheffield United Football Club Ltd** (1987):

> I see the force of the argument that the court must be very slow before it interferes in any way with a decision of a chief constable about the disposition of his forces.

The House of Lords (now the Supreme Court) affirmed the decision of the Court of Appeal.[41]

Police Powers in Relation to the Detection and Investigation of Crime

Questioning by the police

It is a fundamental rule that the citizen is not obliged to answer police questions, unless there is lawful justification for official interference with the citizen's liberty. The rule was endorsed in **Rice v Connolly** (1966). There, the appellant was questioned by the police. He refused to answer questions and was, accordingly, arrested for obstructing a police officer in the execution of his duty contrary to section 51(3) of the Police Act 1964.[42] On appeal, Lord Parker CJ stated that a citizen has every right to refuse to answer questions; generally the citizen has a 'right to silence'.

In **Kenlin v Gardiner** (1967), the issue in question concerned whether a person could lawfully be stopped in the street by the police. Police officers attempted to question two boys. One of the boys tried to run away, whereupon a police constable tried physically to stop him and a scuffle broke out. The boys were charged with assaulting a police constable in the execution of his duty. There was no question that an assault on the police had occurred. The question for decision was whether the assault by the boys was justified. The Divisional Court held that the attempt to restrain the boy amounted to an assault by the police officer, and was, accordingly, an unlawful attempt to detain him. As such, the police officer was not acting in the course of his duty and, as a result, the boys were not guilty of assaulting a police officer 'in the execution of his duty'. A distinction must be made between a refusal to answer questions and conduct which amounts to obstruction of the police; see further below.

There are, however, situations in which a citizen is under a duty to answer questions. For example, under road traffic law,[43] there is a duty to give one's name and address, and a refusal to do so and to give up one's driving licence and other motoring documents is an offence. There is also a duty to provide police with the name of the person driving the car at a particular time. Other than under statutory authority, however, there is a right to silence.[44]

Power exists to stop motorists on any ground, and failure to stop is an offence.[45] A police officer is entitled to immobilise a car by removing the ignition keys. The vehicle owner may be detained in order to allow the officer sufficient time to determine whether an arrest is to be made, to effect arrest, and to give reasons for the arrest. Moreover, the police have the power

---

41 See also **R (Tucker) v Director General of the National Crime Squad** (2003).
42 Now, Police Act 1996, s 89.
43 See the Road Traffic Act 1988, s 163, as amended by the Serious Organised Crime and Police Act 2005.
44 **Lodwick v Sanders** (1985), but see below.
45 Road Traffic Act 1988, s 163.

to detain a motorist in order to administer a breathalyser test.[46] Powers also exist under the Official Secrets Act 1911 whereby the Home Secretary can grant the police permission to question suspects. Refusal to answer questions in respect of inquiries made in respect of investigations into fraud and drug trafficking can amount to a criminal offence, as can refusal to disclose information under the Terrorism Acts.[47]

Helping the police with inquiries[48]

In law, the police have no power to detain a person in order to make inquiries. Section 29 of the Police and Criminal Evidence Act clarifies this rule. A person is either free to leave a police station where he voluntarily attends to assist the police, or the police must arrest him. If a person is detained by the police, he must be informed immediately that he is under arrest and be given reasons for the arrest, the absence of which may render the arrest unlawful.

The identification of suspects

One of the principal causes of wrongful conviction lies in the wrongful identification of suspects.[49] Identification may take place by witnessing, or by fingerprinting and the taking of bodily samples. Code of Practice D governs the procedures to be followed. Identification by identity parade is the most reliable means of identification, and will be carried out if the defendant requests it or consents to it. If it is impracticable to hold an identity parade,[50] perhaps because there are a large number of suspects or because there are insufficient people with similar characteristics to the suspect,[51] the police may then turn to alternative means of identification. Identification by witness may be effected by arranging for the witness to see the suspect in a group, generally in a public place away from the police station. The consent of the suspect is required, but his or her failure to consent does not prohibit the use of group identification. Alternatively, video identification may be used. Face to face confrontation of the witness and accused may take place provided identification is not possible by any other means.

Stop and search powers

Under the Police and Criminal Evidence Act 1984, the police have been given the power to stop and search a person reasonably suspected of carrying prohibited articles such as offensive weapons and/or housebreaking equipment or stolen goods.[52] A record of the search must be made, either on the spot or as soon as practicable thereafter.[53] The police also have the power to set up road blocks if there are reasonable grounds for suspicion that a person in the area has committed an offence (see further below), or that an offence is about to be committed, or that a person is unlawfully 'at large'.[54] Section 60 of the Criminal Justice and Public Order Act 1994 provides that powers may be given to the police, by a police officer of the rank of superintendent or above, to stop and search persons and vehicles, where that officer reasonably

---

46 *Lodwick v Sanders* (1985).
47 See Chapter 22. See also the Official Secrets Act, s 6, which imposes a duty to provide information as to offences under the 1911 Act.
48 See Zander, 1997; Clarke and Feldman, 1979.
49 *Report of the Criminal Law Revision Committee*, Cmnd 4991, 1972, London: HMSO, para 196.
50 Cf *R v Ladlow, Moss, Green and Jackson* (1989) and *R v Penny* (1991).
51 See *Campbell* (1993).
52 PACE 1984, s 1, as amended by the Criminal Justice Act 2003.
53 *Ibid*, s 3, as amended by s 1 of the Crime and Security Act 2010.
54 Road Traffic Act 1988 and PACE 1984, s 4.

believes that incidents involving serious violence may take place in any locality in his area, and that it is expedient so to do to prevent their occurrence. The authorisation lasts for up to 24 hours. The Terrorism Acts also confer powers of stop and search: see further Chapter 22. The European Court of Human Rights has confirmed that the use of these powers to stop and search people without grounds for suspicion is unlawful. The Protection of Freedoms Act 2012 reforms the law: see Chapter 22.

Before 1984, there was considerable doubt about the breadth of power to search an arrested person. The police had a common law power to search a person if they reasonably believed that he was carrying a weapon or evidence relevant to the crime of which he was suspected. Resisting a lawful search would amount to obstruction of the police.[55]

See Chapter 22.

Under section 32 of the Police and Criminal Evidence Act 1984, where a person is arrested at a place other than a police station, a police constable may search the arrested person for anything which might assist him to escape from lawful custody or for anything which might be evidence relating to an offence, and to enter and search any premises in which he was when arrested or immediately before he was arrested for evidence relating to the offence for which he has been arrested.[56] The power is subject to the requirement that the 'constable has reasonable grounds for believing that the arrested person may present a danger to himself or others'.[57] The power to search is limited to what is 'reasonably required' for the purpose of discovery.[58] Search of the person is restricted: a person may not be required to remove any of his or her clothing in public, other than an outer coat, jacket or gloves, and the search may only be conducted if the constable 'has reasonable grounds for believing' that the person concerned has concealed on his or her person anything for which a search is permitted.[59] If the permitted search discloses anything which might be used to cause physical injury to the person or any other person, the officer may seize and retain anything found, other than an item subject to legal privilege, if there are reasonable grounds for believing that the item may be used to assist escape from lawful custody, or is evidence of an offence, or has been obtained in consequence of the commission of an offence.[60]

Intimate body searches are also permitted under the 1984 Act. The search must be carried out by a doctor, unless a senior officer believes that that is impracticable. The search may only be made for articles which may cause injury or for class 'A' drugs.[61] The powers to search the person and take personal samples were extended by the Criminal Justice and Public Order Act 1994, section 58, which defines both intimate and non-intimate samples.

The Criminal Justice Act 2003 extended police powers, authorising the police to take electronic fingerprints and a DNA sample. Electronic fingerprinting enables the police to confirm the identity of a suspect within minutes where that person's fingerprints are already held on the National Fingerprint Database. The DNA sample will be entered onto the National DNA Database. Both databases enabled speculative searches to be made to see whether a suspect is linked to any unsolved crime.

The Protection of Freedoms Act 2012, Part 1,[62] now regulates the retention and destruction of fingerprints, footwear impressions and DNA samples and profiles. Section 63D

---

55 See **Lindley v Rutter** (1980); **Brazil v Chief Constable of Surrey** (1983). In both cases search of the person was held to be unlawful.
56 PACE 1984, s 32(2).
57 Ibid, s 32(1).
58 Ibid, s 32(3).
59 Ibid, s 32(4), (5).
60 Ibid, s 32(8), (9).
61 The Criminal Justice Act 2003 extends the power to test for Class A drugs to persons aged 14 and over.
62 Amending the Police and Criminal Evidence Act 1964. The reform was prompted by the decision in **S and Marper v United Kingdom** (2008).

of the Police and Criminal Evidence Act 1984 provides that fingerprints and DNA profiles ('section 63D material') must be destroyed if they were taken unlawfully. If they were taken lawfully, they must be destroyed unless the Act provides the power to retain the section 63D material in new sections 63E to 63P.

The Act distinguishes between two principal classes of person. Material taken from persons arrested for or charged with a minor offence will be destroyed following either a decision not to charge or following acquittal by a court (section 63E). Fingerprints and DNA profiles of persons charged with, but not convicted of, a 'qualifying offence' offence may be retained for three years. A single two-year extension may be available on the application of the police to a District Judge. The Act also regulates material taken from persons convicted outside England and Wales, persons under the age of 18 convicted of a first minor offence and persons given a penalty notice. The Act also makes special provision for material given voluntarily and material retained with consent (s 63N, 63O). Where a chief officer of police determines that section 63D material needs to be retained for national security purposes, the determination must be in writing, and has effect for a maximum, renewable term of two years (s 63M PACE). The Act makes detailed provision relating to the destruction of section 63D material, and restrictions on the use of retained material.

Intercepts

Article 8 of the European Convention on Human Rights provides for respect for private and family life, home and correspondence. Surveillance operations and interception of communications are intrinsic aspects of policing. There being no common law or statutory right to privacy under domestic law, such techniques were not unlawful, as confirmed by Sir Robert Megarry VC in **Malone v Metropolitan Police Commissioner** (1979). However, in **Malone v United Kingdom** (1984) the Court of Human Rights ruled that there was insufficient protection given by law. The Interception of Communications Act 1985 was passed to remedy the defects in domestic law. The legal framework is now set out in the Regulation of Investigatory Powers Act 2000 (on which see Chapter 22). The Police Act 1997 placed the power of the police to interfere with property and plant surveillance devices on a statutory basis. Modelled on the Interception of Communications Act 1985,[63] the Act provides that authorisation for the bugging of property may be given on the basis that it would facilitate the 'prevention and detection of serious crime' which cannot 'reasonably be achieved by other means'.[64] No exemptions from the provisions are made: thus, solicitors' offices, doctors' surgeries and even Roman Catholic confessionals may fall victim to bugging by the police. Authorisation must be given by the Chief Officer of Police[65] or, if he is unavailable, by an officer of Chief Constable rank.[66] Written authorisations remain in effect for three months whereas, in cases of emergency, oral authorisation may be made which will remain in force for 72 hours. Following opposition to the Bill, the government accepted that independent commissioners[67] should review the authorisations. Such review does not, however, necessarily precede police action on the warrant. In cases where private dwellings, hotel bedrooms or offices are involved, a commissioner's prior approval for the authorisation is required. Prior approval is also required

---

63 See now the Regulation of Investigatory Powers Act 2000, discussed in Chapter 22.
64 Police Act 1997, s 93(2).
65 Police Act 1997, s 93(5).
66 Ibid, s 94.
67 Police Act 1997, s 91(1).

where the surveillance may result in the revealing of confidential personal information, confidential journalistic material or matters which are subject to legal privilege.[68]

Concern over technological advances in communications and the inability of law enforcement agencies to access some data led to the Draft Communications Data Bill 2012. The Bill would replace Part 1 Chapter 2 of the Regulation of Investigatory Powers Act 2000 and Part 11 of the Anti-Terrorism Crime and Security Act 2001. Criticism of the breadth of the powers conferred under the Bill by a Joint Committee, and political opposition to the Bill, have resulted in it being reconsidered by the government with a view to presenting a revised Bill in 2013.

Property searches

In **Semayne's Case** (1605), the principle that an 'Englishman's home is his castle' was judicially declared. Two early cases reveal judicial boldness in the protection from unlawful entry into property. In **Wilkes v Wood** (1763), an Under Secretary of State, accompanied by police, entered Wilkes's home, broke open his desk and seized papers. In an action for trespass against the Under Secretary, Lord Pratt CJ stated that the power claimed would affect 'the person and property of every man in this kingdom, and is totally subversive of the liberty of the subject'. Moreover, such action, being without justification and unlawful, was 'contrary to the fundamental principles of the constitution'.

In the seminal case of **Entick v Carrington** (1765), the Secretary of State, under a general warrant, authorised the entry into property and the seizure of property belonging to Entick, who was suspected of publishing seditious literature. In an action for trespass against Carrington, Lord Camden CJ declared:

> This power, so claimed by the Secretary of State, is not supported by a single citation from any law book extant . . .

> If it is law, it will be found in our books. If it is not to be found there, it is not law.

> By the laws of England, every invasion of private property, be it ever so minute, is a trespass. No man can set his foot upon my ground without my licence, but he is liable to an action, though the damages be nothing . . .

Every entry into the property of the citizen must be authorised by law. However, such freedom from arbitrary intrusion is – in the absence of a written guarantee of rights – subject always to the sovereignty of Parliament. The principle that 'a man's home is his castle' has many exceptions. For example, statutory rights of entry are conferred on employees of public authorities. In addition to rights of physical entry into property, the issue of warrants to intercept communications[69] authorises a non-physical but nevertheless real intrusion into a person's private property.

Rights of entry and search under common law

At common law, the police had no right to enter private property without a warrant. Accordingly, if they so entered and were asked to leave – even where reasonable force was used to evict

---

68 Ibid, s 97.
69 Under the Regulation of Investigatory Powers Act 2000. See further Chapter 22.

them – the police were not acting in the execution of their duty and an individual could not be convicted for assaulting a police officer executing his duty.[70] The common law responded to this problem with a series of complex conditions. With the exception of rights of entry relating to a breach of the peace or for preventing a breach of the peace,[71] common law rights of entry are abolished and now regulated under the Police and Criminal Evidence Act 1984.[72]

Rights of entry and search under statute

The Police and Criminal Evidence Act 1984 (PACE) and Code of Practice B on the Searching of Premises and Seizure of Property regulate the power of the police.

The grounds on which a warrant may be issued are specified in section 8 of PACE, which provides, in part, that a justice of the peace 'is satisfied' [from the application made by the police] that 'there are reasonable grounds for believing':

- that an indictable offence has been committed;
- that there is material likely to be of substantial value to the investigation of the offence;
- that material is likely to be relevant evidence;
- that it does not consist of or include items subject to legal privilege,[73] or excluded material or special procedure material;[74]
- that any of the conditions below applies.

The conditions include the fact that it is impracticable to communicate with any person entitled to grant entry to the premises or grant access to the evidence or that entry will be denied unless a warrant is produced or that the purpose of the search will be frustrated or seriously prejudiced unless an officer can secure immediate entry to them.[75] Once a search is authorised, a constable may seize and retain any evidence relating to the search.[76]

Problems are encountered by the police in the seizure of materials which might be legally privileged, namely correspondence between a client and his or her lawyer. Where the police seize such material and the owner claims that it is privileged, the position of the police has proved uncertain.[77] In order to remedy the difficulties, the Criminal Justice and Police Act 2001 provides statutory authority for the removal of property for examination elsewhere and authorises the removal of material which is intrinsically related (such as computer disks), where it is not reasonably practicable for the property to be separated from that which it would otherwise be unlawful to remove. Where property is found to be privileged, it must be returned as soon as is practicable.[78] Any person from whom property is seized may apply to the Crown Court for the return of the property.[79]

---

70 *Davis v Lisle* (1936). See also **Khazanchi v Faircharm Investments Ltd; McLeod v Butterwick** (1998).
71 Preserved by s 17 Police and Criminal Evidence Act 1984.
72 Note that the 1984 Act preserves all existing statutory powers to issue search warrants. On the previous law see **Thomas v Sawkins** (1935); **R v Inland Revenue Commissioners ex parte Rossminster Ltd** (1980); **Mcleod v United Kingdom** (1998); **Ghani v Jones** (1969); **McLorie v Oxford** (1982).
73 For example, communications between a legal adviser and client: PACE, s 10.
74 For example, confidential records, confidential medical records, journalistic material held in confidence: PACE, s 11.
75 Police and Criminal Evidence Act 1984, s 8(1), (3) as amended by SOCPA 2005, s 113.
76 Ibid, s 19. A record of material seized must be made: s 10.
77 See **R v Chesterfield Justices ex parte Bramley** (2000), in which police seized large amounts of material in order to search it elsewhere, not knowing whether or not any of the material was privileged.
78 Criminal Justice and Police Act 2001, s 54.
79 Ibid, s 59.

As noted above, the police have special powers of entry and search under the Police and Criminal Evidence Act 1984.[80] For the most part, entry is authorised under a warrant authorised by a magistrate.[81] Where a warrant is issued, any constable may execute it and any person authorised to accompany a constable has the same powers as that constable.[82] A warrant must be executed within one month and entry and search must be undertaken at a reasonable time, unless the purpose of the search would be frustrated by entry at a reasonable time. Over and above entry under warrant, however, there exists a class of cases under which the police may enter without warrant under sections 17 and 18 of the Act. Included in this class are entry to arrest for an indictable offence or for offences under the Public Order Act 1936, or Criminal Law Act 1977. Entry without warrant is also lawful if exercised to recover a prison, court or mental hospital detainee and to save life or prevent serious damage to property.

The Protection of Freedoms Act 2012, Part 3, confers powers on ministers to repeal, by order, unnecessary powers of entry to land or other premises. Each Cabinet Minister is under a duty to review existing powers of entry.

The conditions of interviews

The Code of Practice on the Detention, Treatment, and Questioning of Persons by Police Officers (Code C) provides that a suspect should be given eight hours in any 24 hours free of questioning. Breaks for refreshment should be given regularly (every two hours), unless such breaks would adversely affect the inquiries. Persons who are mentally disordered and children should be interviewed in the presence of a competent adult. The detention must be reviewed regularly, the first taking place after six hours from the time of lawful detention; subsequent reviews to be conducted at intervals of no more than nine hours.

Tape recording of interviews[83]

The tape recording of police interviews acts as protection for the person being questioned, and as protection for the police against accusations of oppression. Tape recording is regulated by a code of practice.[84] Both the defence and prosecution have the right to listen to tape recordings, although the police provide summaries of the recordings.[85] The police must maintain proper records of any interview, including the time of commencement and ending and any breaks in questioning. The person interviewed must be allowed to read the record.

The caution

The caution to be administered is set out in Code of Practice C, paragraph 10.5:

> You do not have to say anything. But it may harm your defence if you do not mention when questioned something which you later rely on in Court. Anything you do say may be given in evidence.

---

80 As amended by ss 10–12 and Sched 6 to the Police and Justice Act 2006. The 2006 Act confers greater stop and search powers at aerodromes.
81 PACE 1984, s 8 as amended by SOCPA 2005, s 113.
82 PACE 1984, s 16, as amended by the Criminal Justice Act 2003, s 2.
83 See Baldwin, 1985.
84 Code of Practice for the Detention, Treatment and Questioning of Persons by Police Officers, Code C.
85 See Baldwin and Bedward, 1991.

Arrest

A lawful arrest is an arrest for which there is legal authority. Three categories of lawful arrest exist: arrest under warrant, arrest without warrant under common law and arrest without a warrant under statute. Where a person has been wrongly arrested and detained under statute,[86] the person detained is entitled to damages: **Roberts v Chief Constable of Cheshire Constabulary** (1999); **Woodward v Chief Constable, Fife Constabulary** (1998).

Arrest under warrant

Section 1(1) of the Magistrates' Courts Act 1980 provides that a warrant for arrest may be made on the basis that a 'person has, or is suspected of having, committed an offence'. The warrant should not be issued unless the offence is indictable[87] or punishable by imprisonment.[88] The warrant is issued by a magistrate after a written application by a police officer has been substantiated on oath. The warrant may be executed even if the police officer does not have it in his or her possession at the time, but the warrant must be shown to the person arrested as soon as possible. When an arrest warrant has been issued, a constable may enter and search premises to make the arrest, using such reasonable force as is necessary. Where a constable executes a warrant in good faith believing it to be valid, he or she is protected from liability under the Constables' Protection Act 1750. The magistrate may endorse the warrant for bail.

Arrest without warrant: common law

The only common law power to arrest without warrant is where there are reasonable grounds for suspicion that a breach of the peace is about to occur, or has been committed and is likely to continue or to reoccur.[89] If violence has occurred or is about to occur to persons or property, a police officer may reasonably believe that a breach of the peace is about to occur. If a breach of the peace has occurred, but has ceased, the power to arrest ceases.

In **Trevor Foulkes v Chief Constable of Merseyside Police** (1998), the Court of Appeal considered the issue of reasonable grounds in law for the arrest and subsequent detention of a person in relation to an apprehended breach of the peace. The police officer had arrested the appellant in the course of a domestic incident, honestly believing that arrest was necessary to prevent a breach of the peace. The Court of Appeal ruled that, where there was no actual breach of the peace but only an apprehended breach, the power of arrest was only to be exercised in the clearest of circumstances where the officer was satisfied that a breach of the peace was imminent. The arresting officer in this case acted honestly but did not have reasonable grounds for the arrest. Arrest was an inappropriate management of a dispute between husband and wife in the family home.

An apprehended breach of the peace was also central to the decision in **Bibby v Chief Constable of Essex Police** (2000). A bailiff had gone to a debtor's premises for the purpose of seizing assets due under a liability order issued by a magistrates' court. The debtor threatened to call his friends to prevent the removal of goods. Fearing a breach of the peace, a police constable, who had been called to the premises, ordered the bailiff to leave. When the bailiff refused, he was arrested and led away to the police station in handcuffs. He was later released without charge. The bailiff sued the police for assault and wrongful imprisonment. The Court of Appeal ruled that the bailiff was acting lawfully but although the constable reasonably

---

86 PACE 1984, s 34; Criminal Justice (Scotland) Act 1980.
87 A serious offence triable by jury in the Crown Court.
88 Magistrates' Courts Act 1980, s 1.
89 See **R v Howell** (1982).

came to the conclusion that a breach of the peace was imminent he had failed to consider where the threat was coming from. Accordingly, neither the arrest nor the use of handcuffs was justified.[90]

Arrest without warrant under statute

The powers of arrest provided under the Police and Criminal Act 1984 (PACE) are based on the concept of the seriousness of the offence in question. Sections 110 and 111 of the Serious Organised Crime and Police Act 2005 (SOCPA) amend these powers. Section 110 provides a replacement section 24 of PACE. The power of arrest without warrant for an 'arrestable offence' is replaced with the power of arrest without warrant for an 'offence'. Under the new section 24(1), a constable has the power of arrest without a warrant in relation to:

(a) anyone who is about to commit an offence;
(b) anyone who is in the act of committing an offence;
(c) anyone whom he has reasonable grounds for suspecting to be about to commit an offence;
(d) anyone whom he has reasonable grounds for suspecting to be committing an offence.

Under section 24(2) a constable may arrest without a warrant anyone whom he has reasonable grounds to suspect is guilty of an offence which the constable has reasonable grounds to suspect has been committed. If an offence has been committed, a constable may arrest without warrant anyone who is guilty of the offence or anyone whom he has reasonable grounds for suspecting to be guilty of it (section 24(3)). However, the exercise of the power of arrest under subsections (1), (2) or (3) is exercisable only if the constable has reasonable grounds for believing that it is *necessary* to arrest the person in question for any of the reasons specified in subsection (5).[91] These are:

(a) to enable the name of the person in question to be ascertained (in the case where the constable does not know, and cannot readily ascertain, the person's name, or has reasonable grounds for doubting whether a name given by the person as his name is his real name);
(b) correspondingly as regards the person's address;
(c) to prevent the person in question –

(i) causing physical injury to himself or any other persons;
(ii) suffering physical injury;
(iii) causing loss of or damage to property;
(iv) committing an offence against public decency (subject to subsection (6)); or
(v) causing an unlawful obstruction of the highway;

(d) to protect a child or other vulnerable person from the person in question;
(e) to allow the prompt and effective investigation of the offence or of the conduct of the person in question;
(f) to prevent any prosecution for the offence from being hindered by the disappearance of the person in question.

---

90 See also **Redmond-Bate v Director of Public Prosecutions** (1999).
91 These provisions reflect the requirements of Article 5 of the European Convention on Human Rights. Code of Practice G to PACE states that a lawful arrest requires two elements: a person's involvement, suspected involvement or attempted involvement in the commission of a criminal offence; and reasonable grounds for believing that the person's arrest is necessary.

Section 24 was considered by the Court of Appeal in **Hayes v Chief Constable of Merseyside Police** (2011). The claimant had been arrested but not charged, and released. It was not in dispute that the constable had reasonable grounds for suspecting that an offence had been committed and that the claimant was guilty of it. As to section 24(4) and (5)(e), the claimant argued that the constable had to consider all alternatives to arrest. The Court of Appeal rejected that argument: it was sufficient for an arrest to be lawful that the officer believed the arrest to be necessary and that the belief was reasonable. Contrast that case with **Richardson v Chief Constable of West Midlands Police** (2011), in which the arrest and detention of the claimant was declared unlawful. The claimant had attended the police station voluntarily and the police had failed to consider the necessity of his arrest in light of that attendance. Section 24A of PACE[92] relates to the power of persons other than police constables to make an arrest without a warrant. That right is now limited to the power of arrest for indictable offences, and the power may only be exercised on the basis of *necessity*, and in the absence of a constable who could make the arrest. The reasons making an arrest necessary are stipulated as being to prevent the person in question:

(a) causing physical injury to himself or any other person;
(b) suffering physical injury;
(c) causing loss of or damage to property; or
(d) making off before a constable can assume responsibility for him.

Giving reasons for the arrest

A failure to give reasons for an arrest will cause the arrest to be unlawful. In **Christie v Leachinsky** (1947), the House of Lords ruled that a person must be told of the fact of his or her arrest and the grounds for arrest, although this need not be done if the circumstances are obvious or it is difficult to communicate with the arrested person. Section 28 of the Police and Criminal Evidence Act 1984 places the requirements on a statutory basis and makes them more stringent. Subject to a person escaping before the information can be communicated, section 28 requires that:

(a) the person making the arrest must inform the arrested person of the fact of, and reasons for, arrest, either immediately or as soon as is reasonably practicable afterwards;
(b) a police officer making an arrest must inform the person arrested of these matters even if they are obvious.

No particular form of words need be used, but they must be in sufficient detail to enable the arrested person to understand the issue and, if possible, to deny the allegation and be released. Where it is not possible to state reasons immediately, for example because the arrestee is reacting violently, reasons must be stated as soon as practicable. This requirement is illustrated in **Director of Public Prosecutions v Hawkins** (1988). In that case, a violent struggle prevented reasons being given immediately. However, when the arrestee was subdued, reasons for the arrest were still not given. The arrest became unlawful when the opportunity to give reasons arose, and reasons were not given. A sympathetic attitude to the arresting authorities was seen in **Lewis v Chief Constable of the South Wales Constabulary** (1991). There, two people were arrested and not immediately informed of the reasons for arrest. In an action for false imprisonment, the Court of Appeal upheld the decision of the circuit judge: that the arrests

---

92 Substituted SOCPA 2005, s 110(1)(4).

were unlawful until the reasons were given but, once the reasons were given, the arrests became lawful.[93]

The giving of reasons for arrest is also a requirement under the European Convention on Human Rights. In **Fox, Campbell and Hartley v United Kingdom** (1990), the applicants were arrested on suspected terrorist offences, but were not informed of the reason for the arrest, although they were told they were being arrested under a specified statutory provision. When later interviewed, they were asked about specific criminal offences. The Court of Human Rights held that paragraph 5(2) of Article 5 had not been satisfied at the time of the arrest, but that the defect was later rectified. In **Murray v United Kingdom** (1996), the Court again found no breach of Article 5. Although the applicant was denied reasons for some half an hour, she was eventually informed of the reason for arrest during interrogation.

Detention following arrest

Once a person has been arrested, he or she may be detained by the police for questioning before a charge is laid. There exists a fine balance to be achieved here between permitting the police to question a suspect in order to determine whether there exist sufficient grounds on which to make a charge, and the need to protect persons from unwarranted detention by the police. As a general rule, where a person has been charged with an offence he or she must be brought before a magistrates' court 'as soon as practicable'.[94] This provision gives effect to the requirements of the European Convention on Human Rights. The Police and Criminal Evidence Act 1984, as amended, provides that a person may be detained, under the authority of a superintendent, for a maximum of 36 hours for any indictable offence. The time runs from the time of the person's arrest or, in the case of a person's arrest outside the relevant police area, from the time he arrives in the police station.[95]

The period is extendable. The grounds on which extended detention may be authorised are as follows. For authorisation by a senior officer of police, there must be reasonable grounds for believing that the detention is necessary in order to secure or preserve evidence or obtain evidence by questioning; that the offence in question is indictable; and that the police investigation is being conducted 'diligently and expeditiously'.[96] A review of detention must be made after 24 hours.[97] The police may apply to a magistrates' court for a further period of detention which, if granted, may extend the period of detention to a possible maximum of 96 hours.[98]

Bail

The Criminal Justice Act 2003 amends the Bail Act 1976 in order to ensure that the law is compliant with Article 5 of the European Convention on Human Rights. Article 5(3) specifically provides for entitlement to trial within a reasonable time or to release pending trial.

Section 41(7) provides that, if a person has not been charged at the expiry of 36 hours, he shall, subject to sub-section 8, be released, either on bail or without bail.[99] The time limit does not apply to persons whose extended detention has been authorised by a senior officer[100] or where a successful application has been made to a magistrates' court by the police for

---

93 See also **Taylor v Chief Constable of Thames Valley Police** (2004): **Ghagar v Chief Constable of West Midlands Police** (2000).
94 PACE 1984, s 46.
95 Ibid, s 41(2)(a)(i), (ii).
96 Ibid, s 42(1)(a), (b), (c).
97 Ibid, s 42(4).
98 Ibid, s 43 as amended by the Serious Organised Crime and Police Act 2005, and s 44.
99 Bail Act 1976, as amended.
100 PACE 1984, s 42(1).

continued detention.[101] The maximum period a person may be detained is 96 hours. Any time spent on bail is not counted as part of the allowable detention period.[102]

Bail may be subject to conditions, such as reporting to a police station. Exceptionally – as in the case of a Class A drug user whose drug taking contributed to the offence or where he or she has been assessed and refuses to undergo treatment – bail may be denied.[103] The Criminal Justice Act 2003 enables the police to make an immediate grant of bail ('street bail') where there is no need to deal with the arrested person at a police station.[104] Sections 114–115 Coroners and Justice Act 2009 makes the granting of bail more difficult for those charged with imprisonable offences.[105]

Conditions of detention

The Codes of Practice detail the conditions under which persons may be held. These include no more than one person in a cell, access to toilet and washing facilities, the provision of adequate food and daily exercise. The police may not use more than 'reasonable force' in relation to detainees in preventing escape or causing damage to property. Appropriate medical treatment must be given where necessary. Article 3 of the European Convention on Human Rights, incorporated into domestic law under the Human Rights Act 1998, prohibits torture and inhuman or degrading treatment or punishment.[106]

In **R v Commissioner of Police of the Metropolis** (1999), the House of Lords ruled that authorities, such as the police or prison service, who were entrusted with holding prisoners in custody, had a duty to take reasonable care to prevent them from harming themselves or committing suicide. Where there was a breach of that duty and a suicide occurred, the authorities were not entitled to rely on the defences of *volenti non fit injuria* or *novus actus interveniens* in an action for negligence brought by the estate of the deceased.[107]

The right to legal advice[108]

Under section 58(1) of the Police and Criminal Evidence Act 1984, 'a person arrested and held in custody in a police station or other premises shall be entitled, if he so requests, to consult a solicitor privately at any time'. The right to legal advice is also protected under Article 6 of the European Convention on Human Rights.[109] The right to legal advice under Article 6 arises once suspicion begins to fall on a person being questioned, because that is the point at which the need for protection against self-incrimination comes into play: **Ambrose v Harris; HM Advocate v G; Same v M** (2011).[110] Delay in complying with a request to consult a lawyer is only permitted where the person is being held in connection with an indictable offence and where a senior officer has authorised the delay. The grounds on which delay may be authorised include

---

101 Ibid, s 43.
102 Police (Detention and Bail) Act 2011, s 1, amending s 34 and 47 PACE 1984 and passed as a result of the case of **R (Chief Constable of Greater Manchester) v Salford Magistrates, Court** (2011).
103 Criminal Justice Act 2003, s 19, amending the Bail Act 1976, s 3.
104 Ibid, Part 1, amending PACE 1984, s 30.
105 In murder cases the power of the magistrates to consider bail has now been removed and the decision can only be made by a Crown Court judge.
106 See **Price v United Kingdom** (2001), and **Napier v Scottish Ministers** (2001).
107 On the liability of police see above.
108 See Baldwin, 1993.
109 See the discussion of **Magee v United Kingdom** (2000), **Condron v United Kingdom** (2001) and **Murray v United Kingdom** (1996) in Chapter 18.
110 See also **HM Advocate v P (Scotland)** (2011) and **McGowan v B** (2011).

reasonable grounds for believing that there will be interference with or harm to evidence; that exercising the right would lead to alerting other suspects who have not yet been arrested; or that exercising the right would hinder the recovery of any property obtained as a result of the offence.[111]

Legal representation may be crucial to the protection of the suspect from oppressive questioning by the police. Where confessions are obtained by oppression, a guilty verdict may subsequently be set aside.[112]

The right of access to a legal advice is not confined to questioning while in police custody. The question of precisely when a person is entitled to access to a lawyer, and the related question concerning the admissibility of evidence gained through questioning prior to the presence of a lawyer, was considered by the Supreme Court in **Ambrose and Others v Harris (Procurator Fiscal, Oban) (Scotland)** (2011). Having reviewed domestic and Strasbourg jurisprudence, Lord Hope stated that:

> . . . in principle the line as to when access to legal advice must be provided before the person is questioned should be drawn as from the moment that he has been taken into police custody, or his freedom of action has been significantly curtailed . . . (at para 55)

When a person has been arrested and is being held in custody at a police station, he or she has the right to communicate with one other person 'as soon as practicable'.[113] A delay is only permitted where an officer of the rank of superintendent authorises it, on the basis that 'he has reasonable grounds to believe' that the communication will lead to interference with evidence connected with an indictable offence, or physical injury to other persons, or will lead to alerting of other suspects connected with the offence, and will hinder the recovery of property obtained as a result of the offence.[114] Section 58(1) also provides that a person who is in police detention 'shall be entitled, if he so requests, to consult a solicitor privately at any time'. Under PACE Code of Practice C, a detainee is to be informed of the right to legal advice,[115] and given the name of a duty solicitor if he or she requires it.[116] The detainee is also entitled to have a solicitor present during questioning.[117] However, where a person is arrested for an indictable offence, and an officer of the rank of superintendent or above so authorises, access to a solicitor may be delayed for up to 36 hours. Under section 56(5A) PACE such a delay may be authorised where the officer is concerned that there is a risk to witnesses or to evidence relating to the case, or where immediate access would hinder the recovery of any property obtained as a result of the offence. The Court of Appeal initially construed section 58(8) narrowly. In **R v Samuel** (1988), it was held that delay in access to legal advice can only be justified on specific grounds which must be substantiated to the satisfaction of the court. However, recent changes under the Proceeds of Crime Act 2002 do suggest that if the person has benefited from their criminal conduct then delay may be more defensible.

---

111 PACE 1984, s 58(8) and see Code C.
112 See **R v Paris, Abdullahi and Miller** (1992).
113 PACE 1984, s 56.
114 Ibid, s 56(5)(a), (b), (c).
115 Ibid, para 3.1(ii).
116 Ibid, Note 6B.
117 Ibid, para 6.5.

The right to inform someone of arrest and detention

A person held in a police station is entitled to inform a relative or friend 'or other person concerned with his welfare' of his arrest without delay, unless such notification would prejudice the investigation of crime or the arrest of other suspects.[118]

The right to silence[119]

In relation to the right to silence, the position of a person who has been arrested is different from that of a citizen before arrest. The reforms introduced under the Criminal Justice and Public Order Act 1994 were amongst the most controversial reforms to the protection of an accused for many years. Those who opposed a weakening of the right to silence based their arguments on the relative vulnerability of the accused, and the need to protect the accused from making statements which might falsely incriminate him or her.[120] Against this concern must be set the argument that when individuals are permitted to remain silent when questioned by the police, advantage of this right is taken by 'professional criminals' who are familiar with the process. The concern has been that such persons will conceal information under questioning and then 'ambush' the prosecution by revealing the information in court.[121]

Sections 34 to 38 of the Criminal Justice and Public Order Act 1994 effected the reforms. Under section 34, where an accused is being questioned under caution and fails to mention any fact later relied on in his evidence or, where the accused has been officially charged with an offence[122] or officially informed that he might be prosecuted for it,[123] he fails to mention any fact which in the circumstances existing at the time 'the accused could reasonably have been expected to mention' when questioned, charged or informed, then the court, in determining whether there is a case to answer,[124] and the court of jury, in determining whether the accused is guilty of the offence charged,[125] may 'draw such inferences from the failure as appear proper'. Following the case of **Murray v United Kingdom** (1996),[126] such inferences may only be drawn when the accused has consulted a lawyer before exercising the right to silence.[127]

Section 35 relates to the accused's silence at trial. If the accused then chooses not to give evidence, or without good cause refuses to answer questions, it is permissible for the court or jury to draw such inferences 'as appear proper from his failure to give evidence or his refusal, without good cause, to answer any question'.[128]

Section 37 relates to the accused's failure to account for his or her presence at a particular place. If a person arrested by a constable was found at a place where the offence was committed, and the officer reasonably believes that his presence was attributable to participation in the offence, and the constable requests him to account for his presence, then, if that person fails to do so, a court, or court or jury, in circumstances (a), (b) and (c) in relation to section 36, may draw 'such inferences from the failure or refusal as appear proper'.[129]

---

118 PACE 1984, s 56.
119 See McConville and Hodgson, 1993.
120 The reform was opposed by, inter alia, the Law Society, the Bar Council and the Magistrates' Association. Those in favour included the Police Service, the Crown Prosecution Service, HM Council of Circuit Judges and many senior judges.
121 See **R v Zuckerman** (1989).
122 Criminal Justice and Public Order Act 1994, s 34(1)(a). For judicial guidance see **R v Argent** (1997). See also **R v Cowan** (1996); **R v Friend** (1997); **R v Morgan** (2001).
123 Ibid, s 34(1)(b).
124 Ibid, s 34(2)(c).
125 Ibid, s 34(2)(d).
126 See also **Re Bowden** (1999); **Condron v UK** (2000).
127 Youth Justice and Criminal Evidence Act 1999, s 58.
128 Criminal Justice and Public Order Act 1994, s 35(2). Section 36 relates to unexplained 'objects, substances or marks'.
129 Criminal Justice and Public Order Act 1994, s 37(1), (2), (3). Note that different rules apply to serious fraud trials: see **Director of the Serious Fraud Office ex parte Smith** (1993); **R v Saunders** (1995).

The reliability of evidence[130]

It is central to the protection of the individual that evidence is obtained in a lawful manner. The question arises as to how the law can secure a balance between ensuring that the police operate within the law and the Codes of Practice which supplement the law, and allowing evidence to be used which may have been obtained in a manner not strictly in accordance with the rules but which does prove that a suspect committed a particular crime. If evidence is made inadmissible on the basis of a procedural irregularity, a guilty suspect may go free. On the other hand, if the evidence – however obtained – is admitted, and proves false, there is a danger of innocent suspects being wrongfully convicted. The use of telephone intercepts by the police is authorised under the Police Act 1997, which makes it clear that such intercepts are lawful provided they are authorised under the Act. In addition, the Regulation of Investigatory Powers Act 2000 provides statutory authority for interceptions by the security forces. On intercepts see Chapter 22.

Prior to the Police and Criminal Evidence Act 1984, the admissibility of evidence was regulated under the common law. A distinction was drawn between illegally obtained evidence which was admissible, and involuntary confessions which were inadmissible on the basis that they might be unreliable.[131] The Police and Criminal Evidence Act 1984 placed the admissibility of evidence on a statutory basis. In relation to confessions, there are four criteria to be employed in determining whether they should be admissible in court. Section 76 regulates confessions.[132] Confessions are admissible into court unless the confession has been obtained by (a) oppression[133] or (b) in consequence of anything said or done which was likely, in the circumstances existing at the time, to render unreliable any confession which might be made by him in consequence thereof.[134] In those circumstances, the court 'shall not allow the confession to be given in evidence against him except in so far as the prosecution proves to the court beyond reasonable doubt that the confession (notwithstanding that it may be true) was not obtained as aforesaid'.[135] Moreover, in any case where the prosecution proposes to give in evidence a confession, the court may, of its own motion, require the prosecution to prove that the confession has not been obtained in the circumstances above.[136] However, where a confession has been partly or wholly excluded on the grounds above, that fact does not affect the admissibility in evidence (a) of any facts discovered as a result of the confession, or (b) where the confession is relevant as showing that the accused speaks, writes or expresses himself in a particular way, of so much of the confession as is necessary to show that he does so.[137]

In relation to the exclusion of 'unfair evidence', section 78 of the Police and Criminal Evidence Act 1984 provides that:

In any proceedings, the court may refuse to allow evidence on which the prosecution proposes to rely to be given if it appears to the court that, having regard to all the circumstances, including the circumstances in which the evidence was obtained, the

---

130 The law of evidence is complex and outside the scope of this chapter other than by way of introduction.
131 See **R v Isequilla** (1975); **R v Ping Lin** (1976); **R v Sang** (1980).
132 Confessions are defined to include 'any statement wholly or partly adverse to the person who made it, whether made to a person in authority or not and whether made in words or otherwise': PACE 1984, s 82.
133 'Oppression' is defined to include torture, inhuman or degrading treatment, and the use or threat of violence (whether or not amounting to torture): PACE 1984, s 76(8).
134 PACE 1984, s 76(1)(a), (b).
135 Ibid, s 76(2).
136 Ibid, s 76(3).
137 PACE 1984, s 76(4).

admission of the evidence would have such an adverse effect on the fairness of
the proceedings that the court ought not to admit it.[138]

Section 78 of the Police and Criminal Evidence Act 1984 is far wider than section 76, and may
be relevant to confessions obtained which do not fall within the requirements of section 76.[139]
Thus, for example, if a confession is fabricated, the defence will argue that the accused did not
make a confession and, accordingly, that 'confession' could not fall under section 76. The
power to refuse to allow evidence is discretionary. Where there has been a breach of the rules
under the Police and Criminal Evidence Act, and that breach is substantiated to the satisfaction
of the court, the question to be determined is whether the breach is substantial or significant,[140] other than where the police have acted in bad faith.[141] Having established whether a
breach of the rules is substantial or significant, the court will then look to the nature of the
rule in question in relation to the circumstances of the case. Thus, for example, the right to
have a legal adviser present will be deemed the more important in relation to a vulnerable
suspect who could be easily confused by police questioning.

Alternatives to Prosecution

The identification of the offender and having sufficient evidence to instigate a prosecution
does not mean that a prosecution will inevitably follow. The police may decide to take no
further action or to give an informal warning. Alternatively they may administer a formal
caution which diverts the offender away from the criminal justice system.[142] A caution may
only be given where the offender admits the offence, there is sufficient evidence to prosecute
and the offender gives informed consent to the caution.[143] Once these conditions are satisfied,
consideration must also be given to the public interest, taking into account the nature of the
offence, the likely penalty if convicted, the age and health of the offender, previous criminal
history and the offender's attitude to the offence. The caution is formally recorded and
subsequently may be disclosed in court. There are potential difficulties with the caution: for
example in relation to sex offenders, who will be entered on to the register of sex offenders
and required by the police to fulfil certain requirements even though the offender has not
been formally convicted of the offence.

The Criminal Justice Act 2003 introduced the Conditional Caution, which is defined as 'a
caution which is given in respect of an offence committed by the offender and which has
conditions attached to it'. If an offender fails, without reasonable excuse, to comply with any
of the conditions the Caution will be cancelled and the offender prosecuted for the original
offence. In order for a Conditional Caution to be given, three criteria must be satisfied. First
the offender must be aged 18 or over. Second, the offender must admit the offence to an
'authorised person' and third, the prosecutor must consider that there is sufficient evidence to
charge the offender with the offence.[144]

---

138 Ibid, s 82(3), preserves the common law power to exclude evidence at the court's discretion.
139 R v Mason (1987). See R v Khan (1997); Khan v UK, discussed in Chapter 18. See also R v Chalkley (1998).
140 R v Keenan (1989).
141 R v Walsh (1989).
142 See The National Standards Home Office Circular 18/1994.
143 The Crime and Disorder Act 1998, s 65 introduces a statutory scheme of reprimands and final warnings which replace cautions
      for young offenders.
144 See www.cps.gov.uk/publications/docs/conditionalcautioningcode2004.pdf.

Conditions attached to a Caution fall into three main categories: rehabilitation, reparation and punishment.[145] Rehabilitation conditions may relate to treatment for drug or alcohol dependence, or anger management courses. They may also involve restorative justice processes whereby the offender and victim are brought together with a view to helping reduce the victim's fear of crime and overcome the trauma caused by the crime and also to reduce reoffending.[146] Reparation conditions may include making good any damage caused, restoring stolen goods, paying modest financial compensation or in some cases a simple apology to the victim. The involvement of the victim is entirely voluntary. Punishment conditions include a financial penalty and the requirement to attend at a specific place at a specified time. Failure to comply with caution conditions may result in arrest.[147]

Habeas corpus

The ancient writ of habeas corpus is available to test the legality of a person's detention. The writ can be issued either by the person imprisoned or by someone acting on his behalf.

NOTE: Habeas corpus is discussed in detail in Chapter 18.

Summary

There are 43 police forces in England and Wales and these forces are responsible for the detection of crime and the maintenance of public order. To undertake these tasks the police have a range of powers. These powers are subject to review by the courts, especially in light of the Human Rights Act 1998. These powers include stop and search, arrest and detention for questioning. The Police and Criminal Evidence Act 1984, as amended, regulates the use of police powers. This regulation is important in helping us to understand the parameters of the relationship between the individual and the state. Note that public order law is considered in Chapter 20 and police powers relating to state security and terrorism are discussed in Chapter 22.

Further Reading

Austin, R. (2007) 'The new powers of arrest: plus ça change: more of the same or major change?', Criminal Law Review, 459.
Colvin, M. and Cooper, J. (2009) *Human Rights in the Investigation and Prosecution of Crime*, Oxford: OUP.
English, J. and Card, R. (2013) *Police Law* (13th edn), Oxford: OUP.
Jason-Lloyd, L. (2005) *An Introduction to Policing and Police Powers* (2nd edn), Abingdon: Routledge-Cavendish.
Jason-Lloyd, L. (2003) *Quasi-Policing*, Abingdon: Routledge-Cavendish.
Owen, T., Bailin, A., Knowles, J., Macdonald, A., Ryder, M., Sayers., D. and Tomlinson, H. (2005) *Blackstone's Guide to the Serious Organised Crime and Police Act 2005*, Oxford: OUP.

---

145 Punishment was added by the Police and Justice Act 2006, s 17 amending s 22 of the Criminal Justice Act 2003.
146 See Conditional Cautioning: Criminal Justice Act 2003, ss 22–27. Code of Practice and associated annexes, London: Home Office.
147 Police and Justice Act 2006, s 18 inserting s 24A into the Criminal Justice Act 2003.

Ozin, P., Norton, H. and Spivey, P. (2010) *PACE. A Practical Guide to the Police and Criminal Evidence Act 1984* (2nd edn), Oxford: OUP.

Parpworth, N. (2011) 'Arrest Under PACE – Part 1', 175 Criminal Law and Justice Weekly JPN 528.

Parpworth, N. (2011) 'Arrest Under Pace – Part 2', 175 Criminal Law and Justice Weekly JPN 543.

Stone, R. (2013) *The Law of Entry, Search and Seizure* (5th edn), Oxford: OUP.

Williams, V. (2006) *Surveillance and Intelligence Law Handbook*, Oxford: OUP.

Zander, M. (2005) *The Police and Criminal Evidence Act 1984* (5th edn), London: Sweet and Maxwell.

Zander, M. (2006) *The Police and Criminal Evidence Act 1984. First Supplement to the Fifth Edition*, London: Sweet and Maxwell.

Chapter 22

State Security[1]

---

1   See, *inter alia*, Bulloch, 1963; Deacon, 1969 Pincher, 1981; West, 1981, 1983; Williams, 1965; Andrew, 1985; Lustgarten and Leigh, 1994; Garton Ash, 1997.

Introduction

The security of the state is of the utmost importance to the integrity and well-being of a nation and to individual citizens whose rights and freedoms are protected by the security of the state. On the other hand, the rights of citizens may be adversely affected by the exercise of such powers and there exists the potential for governments to hide behind the doctrine of national security in order to prevent scrutiny of executive action. Two principal constitutional questions arise from state security. The first concerns the extent to which arrangements secure some form of balance between the competing needs of state security and protection of the individual. The second issue relates to the manner in which – and extent to which – the government is held accountable for powers exercised in the name of state security, either through supervision of the courts or through the democratic process.

Legal regulation of state security matters is relatively recent. Although the original Official Secrets Act dates from 1911, it has only been since the mid-1980s that statute has regulated the interception of communications,[2] and the Security and Intelligence Services, MI5 and MI6, and the government's signals intelligence organisation, Government Communications Headquarters (GCHQ). Incorporation of Convention rights under the Human Rights Act 1998 necessitated further clarity in the law, provided by the Regulation of Investigatory Powers Act 2000, the main purpose of which is to ensure that relevant investigatory powers are used in accordance with human rights.

The threat to national security has changed dramatically over the past few decades. In the Coalition Government's words:

> Our predecessors grappled with the brutal certainties of the Cold War – with an existential danger that was clear and present, with Soviet armies arrayed across half of Europe and the constant threat of nuclear confrontation between the superpowers. Today, Britain faces a different and more complex range of threats from a myriad of sources. Terrorism, cyber attack, unconventional attacks using chemical, nuclear or biological weapons, as well as large scale accidents or natural hazards – any one could do grave damage to our country.[3]

In 2010 the government set up the National Security Council (NSC) and appointed a National Security Adviser.[4] The National Security Council comprises Ministers and military and intelligence chiefs. It meets weekly and is chaired by the Prime Minister. The NSC is responsible for developing a National Security Strategy (NSS), the first of which was published in 2010.[5] In addition, the government has published its Strategic Defence and Security Review which sets out how the Armed Forces, police and intelligence agencies are to be equipped to deal with current and future threats to national security. A parliamentary Joint Committee has been established to review the NSS and the work of the National Security Council and National Security Adviser.[6]

---

2 Interception of Communications Act 1985, Security Services Act 1989, Intelligence Services Act 1994, Regulation of Investigatory Powers Act 2000.
3 Foreword, *A Strong Britain in an Age of Uncertainty: The National Security Strategy*, Cm 7953, 2010. See also *Securing Britain in an Age of Uncertainty: The Strategic Defence and Security Review*, Cm 7948, 2010.
4 The first National Security Adviser was Sir Peter Ricketts, Permanent Under-Secretary at the Foreign and Commonwealth Office.
5 The next National Security Strategy is due to be published in 2015.
6 See the First Report of the Joint Committee, 2010–2012, HL Paper 265, HC 1384, March 2012.

In this chapter we consider first the role and powers of the security services and their regulation; then the law relating to official secrets, emergency powers and the law relating to terrorism.

The Security Services

The terminology

The United Kingdom's internal Security Service is known as MI5 (MI stands for Military Intelligence). The Security Service dealing with matters overseas is the Secret Intelligence Service, or MI6. The government's signals intelligence-gathering headquarters is Government Communications Headquarters, or GCHQ. Special Branch is part of the police forces and has special duties in relation to public order, the gathering of intelligence and combating subversion and terrorism. The operations of MI5 and MI6 are co-ordinated by the Intelligence Co-ordinator, based in the Cabinet Office. In addition, there is the armed forces wing of military intelligence which, nowadays, is operative overseas.

The Security Service (MI5)

Until 1989, MI5 was unknown to law. It was not regulated by statute and did not enjoy any special common law powers. MI5 was established in 1909[7] under the royal prerogative as part of the defence forces of the realm. The Service is headed by a Director General who is responsible to the Secretary of State for the Home Office. It is not, however, formally a part of the Home Office and thus occupies a curious constitutional status. The Director General has access to the Prime Minister on matters of importance. Since the ending of the Cold War, approximately 70 per cent of MI5's resources have been devoted to gathering intelligence about terrorism. Moreover, the Security Service Act 1996 now extends the role of MI5 in relation to investigations relating to 'serious crime', particularly the drugs trade.

Functions of the Service

In 1952, the then Home Secretary, Sir David Maxwell-Fyfe, issued a directive to the Director General outlining the functions of the Service:

> The Security Service is part of the defence forces of the country. Its task is the defence of the Realm as a whole, from external and internal dangers arising from attempts at espionage and sabotage, or from actions of persons and organisations whether directed from within or without the country, which may be judged to be subversive of the state.[8]

The Profumo affair[9]

In 1963 the Secretary of State for War, the Rt Hon John Profumo, resigned from office as a result of his lying to the House of Commons over press disclosures concerning an alleged affair with Christine Keeler, who had associations with a Russian Naval Attaché. The Prime Minister, Harold Macmillan, appointed Lord Denning to inquire into the security aspects of the affair. In his report, Lord Denning stressed that the function of the Security Service:

---

7 As part of the War Office. MI5 was originally known as MO5.
8 Reproduced in Lord Denning MR's judgment in **R v Home Secretary ex parte Hosenball** (1977).
9 See Denning, 1980, Chapter 3.

. . . is to defend the Realm from dangers which would threaten it as a whole, such as espionage on behalf of a foreign power, or internal organisations subversive of the state. For this purpose it must collect information about individuals and give it to those concerned. But it must not, even at the behest of a Minister or a government department, take part in investigating the private lives of individuals except in a matter bearing on the defence of the Realm as a whole.[10]

Further judicial expression of the role of MI5 is found in the judgment of Taylor J in **R v Secretary of State for the Home Department ex parte Ruddock** (1987).

The function of the Security Service is the defence of the realm as a whole from, *inter alia*, the actions of persons who and organisations which may be subversive of the state . . . A warrant to intercept should only issue where there is reasonable cause to believe that major subversive activity is already being carried on and is likely to injure the national interest. The material reasonably likely to be obtained by the interception must be of direct use to the Security Service in its functions . . .

Normal methods of investigation must either have failed or be unlikely to succeed. Interception must be strictly limited to what is necessary to the Security Service's defined functions and must not be used for party political purposes . . .

Despite such strictures, there have been many charges made against MI5 from journalists and from members of MI5 itself.[11]

Spycatcher[12]

The most celebrated exposure of MI5 came in the form of Peter Wright's book, *Spycatcher* (1987). Among many allegations made by Wright in *Spycatcher* was the claim that MI5 had 'bugged and burgled its way across London' without lawful authority.

As an electrical engineer with MI5, Peter Wright's expertise included bugging embassies, diplomatic residences and international conferences. In 1963, Wright was promoted to an interrogator and to the post of Chairman of an internal committee inquiring into Soviet infiltration of the Security Services. Wright believed that MI5's perceived poor performance in the Cold War years of the 1950s and 1960s was in part due to Soviet infiltration at the highest level of MI5. The defections of two security agents, Donald Maclean and Guy Burgess, in 1951, and the confession and defection of Kim Philby in 1963,[13] gave added weight to the security fears. Wright was further convinced that the then head of MI5, Roger Hollis, was a Soviet agent: a matter officially denied.[14] The revelation in 1979 that Anthony Blunt, surveyor of the Queen's art collection and knight of the realm, had been a KGB[15] spy since his recruitment by the

---

10 The *Report on the Security Aspects of the Circumstances Leading up to the Resignation of Mr JD Profumo*, Cmnd 2152, 1963, London: HMSO, caused disquiet. One outcome was the establishment of the Security Commission in 1964. See Leigh and Lustgarten, 1991.
11 See, *inter alia*, Pincher, 1981; West, 1983.
12 See Watt, 1988; Pannick, '*Spycatcher*: two years of legal indignation', in Kingsford-Smith and Oliver, 1990.
13 An MI6 officer, appointed to MI6 Head of Station in Washington. See Trevor-Roper, 1968; Philby, 1968.
14 See Pincher, 1981. Pincher relied heavily on information obtained from Wright. An official inquiry chaired by Lord Trend in 1974–75 failed to establish Hollis's innocence. See HC Deb Vol 1 Cols 1079–85, 26 March 1981. Hollis retired from MI5 in 1965. The Security Commission investigated the charges: its report was never published. Instead, a government statement was issued outlining measures taken as a result of the report: see Cmnd 8450, 1982, London: HMSO.
15 The Russian secret service.

Russians while a student at Cambridge University[16] revealed the extent to which the Security Services had become vulnerable to Russian infiltration.

In 1976, Wright retired and Lord Rothschild introduced him to the journalist Chapman Pincher. In collaboration with Pincher, *Spycatcher* was written: a book which launched one of the most farcical chapters in recent legal and political history, revealing as much about the secrecy of government as about the workings of MI5. In *Spycatcher*, Wright alleged that MI5 had, over the years, in addition to 'bugging and burglary', interrogated and hounded hundreds of individuals in an inquiry into the membership of the Communist Party rivalling that of the McCarthy Inquiry in the United States of America in the 1930s. The allegations made by Wright became a matter of intense political and legal interest.

The government, intent on stopping circulation of *Spycatcher*, sought an injunction to restrain publication.[17] The litigation against *Spycatcher* commenced in Australia in 1985, and ultimately failed.[18] In 1986 the Attorney General was granted injunctions to restrain publication – injunctions which were to endure for some four years.[19] In 1990, however, the House of Lords held that the wide availability of the information and the public interest in freedom of speech and the right to receive information outweighed the interests of the Crown in preserving government secrecy.[20] The issue of the temporary injunctions was taken to the European Court of Human Rights, wherein it was held that the injunctions granted violated Article 10 of the Convention.[21]

One outcome of the *Spycatcher* affair was the enactment of the Security Service Act 1989, which placed MI5 on a statutory basis. The Regulation of Investigatory Powers Act 2000 reformed the law relating to the Security Services and the interception of communications.

The Security Service Act 1989[22]

The Act defined the functions of MI5 and placed the issuing of warrants under statutory authority. Section 3 of the Act empowered the Home Secretary to issue warrants authorising 'entry on or interference with property'. This power is now contained in sections 5 and 6 of the Intelligence Services Act 1994. The Act also provided, for the first time, a complaints procedure for individuals who are aggrieved by actions of MI5 and a Commissioner charged with the task of reviewing the procedure by which the Home Secretary issues warrants. Section 1 defines the functions of MI5 as being:

> (2) . . . the protection of national security and, in particular, its protection against threats from espionage, terrorism and sabotage, from the activities of agents of foreign powers and from actions intended to overthrow or undermine Parliamentary democracy by political, industrial or violent means.

> (3) It shall also be the function of the Service to safeguard the economic well being of the United Kingdom against threats posed by the actions or intentions of persons outside the British Islands.

---

16 From 1926. Following Blunt's exposure, Blunt was stripped of his knighthood.
17 See Turnbull, 1988; on *Attorney-General v Jonathan Cape Ltd* (1976) see Young 1976, particularly Chapters 2 and 11.
18 (1987) 8 NSWLR 341; HC of Australia (1988) 165 CLR 30.
19 *Attorney General v Guardian Newspapers Ltd* (1987).
20 *Attorney General v Guardian Newspapers Ltd (No 2)* (1990).
21 *The Observer, The Guardian and The Sunday Times v United Kingdom* (1991). See Bindman, 1989. See further Chapter 18; and see Leigh, 1992. In *Attorney General v Blake* (1996), Sir Richard Scott VC ruled that the Crown was not entitled to the profits gained by Blake, a former Secret Intelligence Officer who became a Soviet Agent in 1951 through the publication of his autobiography. By 1989, when the autobiography was published, none of the information was any longer confidential and, therefore, there was no breach of the lifelong duty imposed on former security service officers not to disclose confidential information. Furthermore, it was ruled that to grant relief would entail an infringement of Blake's rights under ECHR, Article 10.
22 See Leigh and Lustgarten, 1989.

In 1992, MI5 assumed responsibility for terrorism related to Northern Ireland. This had previously been under the jurisdiction of Special Branch.

MI5 itself is not defined in the Act. The Secret Intelligence Service – MI6 – did not fall under the control of the Act. Other agencies, such as Special Branch, which carries out many of the functions of MI5 (see below), and GCHQ, are not mentioned in the Act.[23] National security is not defined in the Act. In debate on the Bill, the Home Secretary stated that the 'phrase refers – and can only refer – to matters relating to the survival or well being of the nation as a whole, and not to party-political or sectional or lesser interests'.[24]

The duties of the Director General of MI5 are set out in section 2. These are primarily the responsibility 'for the efficiency of the Service', and for ensuring that the Service collects only information necessary for the proper discharge of its functions, and that it does not take any action to further the interests of any political party. The Director General is required to report annually to the Prime Minister and the Secretary of State for the Home Department, and may otherwise report to them at any time the Director General so decides.

While the Director General is under a duty to report to the Prime Minister, there is no duty imposed on the Prime Minister to lay that report before Parliament. There is thus no parliamentary scrutiny of the Director General's exercise of power. Attempts in both the House of Commons and the House of Lords to introduce such scrutiny failed. However, the Intelligence Services Act 1994,[25] for the first time, introduced parliamentary scrutiny to the work of the Security Services – both MI5 and MI6 – and to GCHQ. Under the Act, a Parliamentary Intelligence and Security Committee is established. As discussed below, the Committee is not a select committee, and is not given the powers of a select committee. Furthermore, under the Act, information may be withheld from the Committee on the basis that 'the Secretary of State has determined that it should not be disclosed'.[26] On reform of the Committee, see below.

The 1989 Act also introduced a Security Services Commissioner to keep under review the procedure by which warrants were issued by the Home Secretary. The office of Security Services Commissioner was abolished by the Regulation of Investigatory Powers Act 2000. It has been replaced by the Intelligence Services Commissioner. See further below.

The Security Service Act 1996

The Security Service Act 1996 extended the function of MI5 to matters concerning 'serious crime'. The government's objective was to enable MI5 to investigate 'organised crime' and 'drug trafficking, money launderers and racketeers'. MI5 acts in a supportive role, and the principal responsibility lies with the conventional law enforcement agencies.[27] However, 'serious crime' is not itself defined in the Act. Nor is the scope of MI5's jurisdiction entirely clear. Moreover, it remains under the operation control of the Director General, and is not accountable to local police authorities, nor are its operations supervised by the Police Complaints Authority.

The Secret Intelligence Service (MI6)[28]

MI6 is the branch of the Security Services which deals with information gathering and operations outside the United Kingdom. Whereas a degree of openness has been established

---

23 This omission is remedied by the Intelligence Services Act 1994, on which see further below.
24 *Hansard*, HC Vol 143 Col 1113; see also Vol 145 Col 217, and see HL Vol 357 Col 947.
25 See Supperstone, 1994.
26 Intelligence Services Act 1994, Sched 3, para 3(1)(b)(ii).
27 See HL Deb Cols 398–99, 14 May 1996.
28 See West, 1981; Bloch and Fitzgerald, 1983.

concerning the work of MI5, the work of MI6 remains closely guarded. It was only in 1992 that the Prime Minister acknowledged publicly for the first time that MI6 existed. It is MI6 operations – together with military intelligence and the work of GCHQ – which gathers intelligence from around the world through espionage and covert action. In times of war – whether 'hot' or 'cold' – the Service is of inestimable value to the protection of the state against outside threats.[29] MI6 is under the control of the Foreign and Commonwealth Office, and requires its approval before launching operations. Any politically sensitive matters require the personal approval of the Foreign Secretary. While, in theory, MI6 is confined to operations outside the United Kingdom, and hands responsibility over to MI5 once a matter becomes 'internal', there have been doubts expressed as to whether the boundaries are, or indeed can be, so clearly drawn.

The functions of MI6

The Intelligence Services Act 1994 defined, for the first time, the statutory functions of MI6. Section 1 provides that its function is to obtain and provide information relating to the actions or intentions of persons outside the British Islands, and to perform other tasks relating to the actions or intentions of such persons. Such actions must be related to the objectives defined in the Act, namely in the interests of national security 'with particular reference to defence and foreign policies', in the interests of the nation's economic well being, and assisting in the 'prevention or detection of serious crime'.[30] The Intelligence Services Act 1994 provides for the issue of warrants. Authorisation given by the Secretary of State excludes criminal or civil liability for acts done under the authorisation. The Secretary of State may only grant an authorisation if he is satisfied that the operation is necessary for the 'proper discharge of a function of the Intelligence Service or GCHQ'. The authorisation may relate to particular acts or acts undertaken in the course of a specified operation. It may be limited to a particular person or persons and be subject to conditions. The authorisation must be signed by the Secretary of State or, in an urgent case, a senior official where the Secretary of State has expressly authorised it to be given. Where the authorisation is signed by the Home Secretary it will expire at the end of a six-month period, subject to renewal by the Home Secretary for a further six-month period. Any other authorisation ceases to have effect at the end of the second working day following the day on which it was given.

Operations are authorised by the Secretary of State for Foreign and Commonwealth Affairs, and agents' activities are regulated by administrative internal rules. Where action within the British Islands is required, MI5 may apply to the Home Secretary for a warrant to carry out operations on behalf of MI6. The Terrorism Act 2006 amends the 1994 Act to extend protection for action taken within the British Islands under a warrant authorising action in relation to property outside the British Islands where the property is believed to be outside the British Islands or where there is a mistaken belief as to whether it is within the British Islands and action is taken in respect of that property within five days from the day on which the presence of the property became known.[31]

---

29 It was with MI6 that Paul Henderson, Managing Director of Matrix Churchill worked during the Iran-Iraq War – a matter which led to a judicial inquiry. See further Chapter 10.

30 Intelligence Services Act 1994, s 2.

31 Terrorism Act 2006, s 31.

Government Communications Headquarters (GCHQ)[32]

GCHQ at Cheltenham[33] was established under the royal prerogative, as part of the Foreign and Commonwealth Office.[34] The principal tasks of GCHQ include the security of military and official communications and the provision of signals intelligence (SIGINT) for the government. GCHQ has an annual budget of about £500 million and a staff of some 4,500 personnel, making it the largest of the three intelligence services in the United Kingdom.

Legal authority for the interception of international communications was first provided under the Official Secrets Act 1920, section 4 of which provided for the interception of 'telegrams' under the warrant of the Home Secretary on the basis of the public interest. The Intelligence Services Act 1994 placed GCHQ on a statutory basis.[35] The statutory duty of MI6 and GCHQ is to exercise its functions 'in the interests of national security, with particular reference to the defence and foreign policies of Her Majesty's government in the United Kingdom; in the interests of the economic well being of the United Kingdom in relation to the actions or intentions of persons outside the British Islands; or in support of the prevention or detection of serious crime'.[36] The Director of GCHQ is responsible for the 'efficiency of the agency'[37] and has a right of access to the Prime Minister and Secretary of State for Foreign and Commonwealth Affairs. The Director is under a duty to report annually to the Prime Minister.

The Intelligence Services Act 1994, sections 5–7, provides statutory authority for warrants issued by the Secretary of State. No warrant may be issued for interference with individual communications within the United Kingdom, unless the interception is designed to uncover information relating to the prevention or detection of terrorism. GCHQ co-operates in signals intelligence matters with its counterparts in Australia, Canada, New Zealand and the United States.

From 1947 until 1984, employees at GCHQ were entitled to belong to trade unions. In January 1984, the Foreign Secretary announced, without warning, that this right was to be removed. GCHQ had experienced disruption for some two years, with a loss of 10,000 working days. In 1983, a GCHQ employee, Geoffrey Prime,[38] was arrested and convicted of spying for the Soviet Union. Both factors – and the government's general desire to curb the power of trade unions – contributed to the banning of unions at GCHQ.[39] The legal outcome of the exercise of the prerogative[40] in banning union membership at GCHQ led to **Council of Civil Service Unions v Minister for the Civil Service** (1984), in which the House of Lords ruled in favour of the government on the basis of national security.[41]

Special Branch[42]

Established in 1883 to deal with problems of security in relation to Ireland, Special Branch rapidly expanded to deal with many security matters. Originally, Special Branch was confined to the

---

32 See Andrew, 1985; West, 1986; Lustgarten and Leigh, 1994.
33 GCHQ has stations abroad including Cyprus.
34 Its original title was the Government Code and Cipher School.
35 The Australian and Canadian equivalents, the Defence Signals Directorate and Communication Security Executive respectively, remain regulated under the prerogative.
36 Intelligence Services Act 1994, ss 1(2)(a) and also Scotland Act 2012, s 12(4); and 3(2)(a).
37 Ibid, s 4.
38 See Report of the Security Commission: GA Prime, Cmnd 8876, 1981, London: HMSO.
39 See Young, 1989, Chapter 16.
40 Under the Civil Service Order in Council 1982, Article 4, which empowers the minister to make regulations and issue instructions regarding the conditions of service of civil service employees. See Forsyth, 1985; cf Wade, 1985.
41 See further on this case, Chapters 5 and 18. In 1995, the government amended the terms and conditions of employment of staff at GCHQ. Staff are to be restricted to membership of a body whose officers and representatives are appointed from, and answerable only to, GCHQ staff. The conditions of service continue to exclude any form of industrial action: HL Deb Vol 567 Col 147, 20 December 1995. Note that in 1997 the Labour government restored trade union rights to employees at GCHQ.
42 See Bunyan, 1977; Allason, 1983.

Metropolitan Police Force; from 1945, other police forces established Special Branches. Nowadays, each provincial force has its own Special Branch. Special Branch is staffed by ordinary police officers under the direction of the Chief Constable. Much of their work is related to Security Service matters. The principal task of Special Branch is to counter threats of terrorism. Other functions include jury vetting in cases involving national security or terrorism, providing personal protection and assisting with immigration matters, including keeping watch at airports and seaports.

Military intelligence and the armed forces

In 1940, the Special Operations Executive (SOE) was formed to supplement the work of MI5 and MI6, which were geared principally to work in peace time. Subsequently, the need for special units to operate under military command, and under cover, became perceived as imperative. Originally known as L Detachment, Special Air Service Brigade and, later, simply SAS, the service was introduced on the initiative of David Stirling of the Scots Guards, and approved by the Commander-in-Chief. Members of the SAS were recruited primarily from commandos. A parallel organisation, the Special Boat Service (SBS), was established to complement the work of the SAS.

The SAS has been involved in many operations overseas, in Northern Ireland and on the mainland, principally working against terrorism. It was, for example, the SAS which stormed the Iranian Embassy in London in 1980 to free hostages from terrorists who had occupied the Embassy and, as discussed below, it was the SAS which was dispatched to Gibraltar to arrest suspected IRA terrorists.

The SAS is controlled at both a political level and a practical, operational level. In relation to terrorism, a special committee, known as COBRA and chaired by the Home Secretary, meets with representatives from the Ministry of Defence, MI5, the Foreign and Commonwealth Office and the SAS to decide the appropriate political and military response. In relation to operational matters, a special unit within the Ministry of Defence, the Joint Operations Centre (JOC), comprising the Foreign Office, Home Office, intelligence services and the SAS, activates the SAS at home or overseas. Exceptionally, the Prime Minister may personally activate the SAS, as in the Iranian Embassy siege. When the SAS is operational, it exercises the powers of the police, although formal authority remains with the police, and the police resume their normal functions once the operation is complete.

Defence intelligence

The Ministry of Defence has its own Defence Intelligence Staff, DIS, which is the main provider of strategic defence intelligence to the Ministry of Defence and the armed forces. The Chief of DIS, a serving three-star officer drawn from any of the three services, reports to the Chief of the Defence Staff and the Permanent Secretary of the Ministry of Defence, and is a member of the Joint Intelligence Committee (on which see further below). DIS is divided into two main parts: the Defence Intelligence Analysis Staff (DIAS) and the Intelligence and Geographic Resources Staff (IGRS). DIAS is responsible for providing global defence intelligence assessments and strategic warning, and draws on classified information provided by GCHQ. IGRS has six discrete policy branches, including the Joint Air Reconnaissance Intelligence Centre, and the Defence and Security Centre and Military Survey.

DIS analyses GCHQ's signals intelligence with a view to assessing the strength of foreign armies and weaponry, including chemical weapons. Defence attachés at foreign embassies act as information gatherers in the field. During the Cold War, the role of DIS was principally intelligence analysis. In times of war, however, that function changes from intelligence gathering and analysis to the provision of information for use of troops on the ground.

The Joint Intelligence Committee[43]

The Joint Intelligence Committee (JIC) co-ordinates the work of MI6 and GCHQ, and agrees intelligence requirements. The head of the JIC reports to the Cabinet Secretary and, through him, to the Prime Minister. The JIC has around 30 members, drawn on secondment from the Foreign Office and Ministry of Defence. Membership of the JIC includes the Director of GCHQ, the Chief of MI6, Chief of Defence Intelligence Staff and the Director General of MI5. Divided into geographic areas and by functions, the JIC meets weekly to review assessments.

MI5 contributes intelligence to the JIC on national matters. The JIC also makes international assessments, drawing on intelligence from other agencies such as the United States' Central Intelligence Agency (CIA). The intelligence requirements are reviewed annually by the Intelligence Co-ordinator. Close links are maintained between the JIC and MI5, with its Director General being a member of JIC. MI5 and MI6 also co-operate to avoid duplication and their financial resources in some areas are shared. MI5 also contributes intelligence to the JIC Assessments Staff, and is a major customer for intelligence produced by SIS and GCHQ, particularly in relation to terrorism.

The Interception of Communications[44]

The government's response to the outcome of **Malone v United Kingdom** (1984), in which the absence of statutory authority for intercept warrants was held to have violated Article 8 of the Convention on Human Rights, was to pass the Interception of Communications Act 1985. The Interception of Communications Act 1985 made it a criminal offence to intentionally intercept a communication and provided statutory power to the Secretary of State to issue warrants 'in the interests of national security, or for the purpose of preventing or detecting serious crime or for the purpose of safeguarding the economic well-being of the United Kingdom'.

The provisions relating to interception of communications under the 1985 Act were repealed and replaced by the Regulation of Investigatory Powers Act 2000 (RIPA), which also amends the Police Act 1997 and the Intelligence Services Act 1994. The 2000 Act was prompted by two major concerns. The first was that the 1985 Act regulated intercepts of communications transmitted via mail and by a public telecommunications system, which at the time of the legislation covered most data transmissions. Technological advances since 1985, however, have expanded communications systems – through the internet and email and through telecommunication systems not provided by public telecommunications providers. Also falling outside the 1985 Act was data which was 'encrypted' and required a 'key' to unlock it. The second motivation for reform was the influence of the European Convention on Human Rights and the Human Rights Act 1998. As discussed in more detail in Chapter 18, cases such as **Halford v United Kingdom** (1997) and **Khan v United Kingdom** (2000) had successfully challenged domestic law.

The Act relates to powers concerning the interception of communications, intrusive surveillance on residential premises and in private vehicles, covert surveillance in the course of specific operations, the use of covert human intelligence sources (agents, informants, undercover officers), the acquisition of communications data and access to encrypted data.[45]

---

43 See Adams, 1994, and Urban, 1997.

44 See *Report of the Committee on the Interception of Communications* (the Birkett Report), Cmnd 283, 1957, London: HMSO; *The Interception of Communications in Great Britain*, Cmnd 7873, 1980, London: HMSO; *The Interception of Communications in Great Britain* (the Diplock Report), Cmnd 8191, 1981, London: HMSO; Williams, 1979; Lambert, 1980; *The Interception of Communications in the United Kingdom*, Cmnd 9438, 1985, London: HMSO; Leigh, 1986; *Interception of Communications in the United Kingdom*, Cm 4368, 1999, London: HMSO.

45 Section 15 of the Terrorism Act 2006 amends the penalties relating to encryption offences in s 53 of RIPA 2000.

The Act is intended to ensure that the law clearly states the purposes for which such powers may be used; which authorities may exercise the powers; who should authorise the use of power; the use that can be made of material gained; independent judicial oversight of the exercise of powers; and a means of redress for aggrieved individuals.

Section 1 of RIPA 2000 creates the offence of unlawful interception and a separate tort of unlawful interception. Unlawful interceptions relate to any communication in the course of its transmission by means of a public postal service or public telecommunications system. Intercepts are lawful only if authorised under the Act. Conduct which has lawful authority is lawful for all other purposes. A person having the right to control the operation or use of the system which is intercepted, or having the express or implied consent of such a person to make the interception, is excluded from criminal liability.[46]

An intercept will be lawful under section 3(1) if the person intercepting has the consent of the sender and recipient of the communication, or has reasonable grounds for believing that they have consented. Section 3(2) provides that an intercept will be lawful if the communication is one sent by or intended for a person who has consented to the intercept and surveillance conducted via the intercept has been authorised under Part II of the Act, which regulates surveillance and the use of undercover agents. Section 4 provides lawful authority for intercepts of communications between the United Kingdom and other countries, where the interceptor overseas is required by law to intercept the communication.

Section 5 regulates interceptions under warrant. The Secretary of State may issue a warrant authorising or requiring interceptions only where he believes that the warrant is necessary in the interests of national security, or for the purpose of preventing or detecting serious crime, or for the purpose of safeguarding the economic well-being of the United Kingdom. The warrant may be issued only if the Secretary of State also believes that the conduct authorised is *proportionate* to what is sought to be achieved by that conduct. In considering whether to issue a warrant, the Secretary of State must take into account whether the information which it is thought necessary to obtain could reasonably be obtained by other means.

Warrants may be issued only on the application of persons specified under the Act. The warrant must be issued under the hand of the Secretary of State or, in certain circumstances, by a senior official,[47] who must be expressly authorised by the Secretary of State to do so.[48]

Concern over technological advances in communications and the inability of law enforcement agencies to access some data led to the Draft Communications Data Bill 2012. The Bill will replace Part I Chapter 2 of the Regulation of Investigatory Powers Act 2000 and Part II of the Anti-Terrorism Crime and Security Act 2001. Criticism by a Joint Committee of the breadth of the powers conferred under the Bill, and political opposition to the Bill, has resulted in it being reconsidered by the government with a view to presenting a revised Bill in 2013.

Authorisation of surveillance and human intelligence sources

Part II of the Regulation of Investigatory Powers Act 2000 provides a statutory basis for the authorisation and use of covert surveillance agents, informants and undercover officers. It is intended to regulate the use of such techniques and 'safeguard the public from unnecessary invasions of their privacy'.

---

46 A person found guilty of an offence is liable on conviction on indictment to a term of imprisonment not exceeding two years, or to a fine, or to both. On summary conviction, there is liability to a fine not exceeding the statutory maximum. Proceedings may only be instituted with the consent of the Director of Public Prosecutions or, in Northern Ireland, with the consent of the Director of Public Prosecutions for Northern Ireland. See **R v Stanford** (2006).

47 RIPA 2000, s 7. The Terrorism Act 2006, s 32, amends RIPA 2000, s 9 in relation to warrants.

48 The claim that the issue of warrants under RIPA violates Article 8 of the European Convention failed in **Kennedy v United Kingdom** (2010).

The Intelligence Services Commissioner and the Tribunal[49]

The Intelligence Services Commissioner is appointed by the Prime Minister.[50] A person may only be appointed as Commissioner if he or she holds or has held a high judicial office. The Justice and Security Act 2013 extends the functions of the Commissioner. Section 5 of the Act inserts a new section 59A into RIPA, providing that the Prime Minister may issue directions to the Commissioner to keep under review certain aspects of the functions of the Agencies or any part of the armed forces or intelligence activities of the Ministry of Defence. This new provision is intended to provide a statutory basis for an extension of the work of the Commissioner; at present any extension is extra-statutory.

The Regulation of Investigatory Powers Act 2000 (RIPA), section 65, established the Investigatory Powers Tribunal (IPT). The Tribunal has a duty to investigate allegations against the Security Services and to hear and determine any proceedings brought. The Tribunal is not under a duty to hear or determine any complaint which is frivolous or vexatious. Complaints must be brought within one year after the taking place of the conduct to which it relates, but the Tribunal may, if it is equitable to do so, extend the time. The Tribunal has the power to make an award of compensation. In addition, the Tribunal may order the quashing or cancelling of any warrant or authorisation and/or the destruction of any records of information. The Commissioner assists the Tribunal in connection with the investigation of any matter by the Tribunal. The Tribunal is the only tribunal to which proceedings under section 7 of the Human Rights Act 1998 may be brought against any of the intelligence services, or any other person in relation to conduct by or on behalf of any of those services.[51] The conduct in question must have been conduct by or on behalf of a person holding any office, rank or position with any of the intelligence services, any of Her Majesty's forces, any police force, or the National Crime Agency. All persons employed by the Security and Intelligence Services and police are under a duty to disclose or provide to the Commissioner all documents and information as he or she may require for the purposes of an investigation. The Commissioner makes an annual report to the Prime Minister, which is to be laid before each House of Parliament. If it appears to the Prime Minister, after consultation with the Commissioner, that the publication of any matter in an annual report would be contrary to the public interest or prejudicial to national security, the prevention or detection of serious crime or the economic well being of the United Kingdom, the Prime Minister may exclude that matter from the report laid before each House.

The adequacy of the system of the authorisation of warrants and the complaints procedure before the IPT was considered by the European Court of Human Rights in **Kennedy v United Kingdom** (2010).[52] The Court ruled that the system provided sufficient safeguards against abuse, and that the IPT was an independent and impartial body whose members must hold or have held high judicial office or be experienced lawyers and its procedures could not be held to violate the right to fair trial (Article 6). The jurisdiction of the IPT was considered in judicial review proceedings in **R (A) v Director of Establishments of the Security Service** (2009). The Supreme Court ruled that section 65 of RIPA did not amount to an ouster of the jurisdiction of the courts, but rather an allocation of an exclusive jurisdiction by Parliament to the Tribunal.

See further
Chapter 24.

---

49 RIPA 2000 repeals s 5 of and Sched 1 to the Security Service Act 1989 which provided for a Tribunal to investigate complaints. Section 9 of and Scheds 1 and 2 to the Intelligence Services Act 1994, which also provided for a Tribunal, are repealed and replaced by RIPA 2000, Part IV.
50 Regulation of Investigatory Powers Act 2000, ss 59–60.
51 Section 7 proceedings relate to applications brought by victims of an alleged violation of Convention rights by a public authority.
52 On this case see also Chapter 18. See also **Knaggs v United Kingdom** (2009).

In the United States, by contrast, security matters are regarded as being within the competence of the courts. In **United States v United District Court** (1972), the Supreme Court, in a unanimous judgment, declared:

> We cannot accept the government's argument that internal security matters are too subtle and complex for judicial evaluation. There is no reason to believe that federal judges will be insensitive to or uncomprehending of the issues involved in domestic security cases . . . If the threat is too subtle or complex for our senior enforcement officers to convey its significance to a court, one may question whether there is probable cause for surveillance.

The Canadian Security Intelligence Service Act 1984 involves judges and the Solicitor General in the process of granting warrants.[53]

Parliamentary Scrutiny of the Security Services

National security and the work of the Security Services have traditionally been matters on which governments have declined to provide information to Parliament. Parliamentary Committees repeatedly have been denied the right to investigate MI5[54] although, since 1979, the Defence Committee has considered aspects of security. In 1994 the Intelligence and Security Committee (ISC) was established, under the Intelligence Services Act, with limited powers to investigate security matters. The ISC, which has a membership of nine, is established to 'examine the expenditure, administration and policy of the Security Service, the Intelligence Service and GCHQ'.[55] Membership is confined to non-ministerial Members of the House of Lords and House of Commons. Members are appointed by the Prime Minister, after consultation with the Leader of the Opposition.[56] The ISC makes an annual report to the Prime Minister, which must be laid before Parliament. A Government Response is published. The annual reports are debated in both Houses of Parliament.

The Committee determines its own procedure.[57] Where the Committee requests information from the Director General of MI5, the Chief of MI6 or the Director of GCHQ, that information must be supplied unless the relevant person informs the Committee that it cannot be disclosed on the basis of sensitivity, or where the Secretary of State has determined that it should not be disclosed.

The Justice and Security Act 2013 strengthens the powers of the Intelligence Security Committee. Its role is expanded to include overseeing aspects of security[58] beyond the remit of the three security services and it also has the power to scrutinise, retrospectively, operational activities of the Agencies. In addition, the Committee has the power to require information from the Agencies which can only be vetoed by the Secretary of State rather than, as at present, by the Heads of the Agencies.

As noted above, currently the ISC makes an annual report to the Prime Minister, who is under a duty to lay it before Parliament, but not to publish it. Under the Justice and Security Bill, the annual report will be made to Parliament, subject to the Prime Minister having the

---

53 See Burns, 1976; Hazell, 1989; Hutchinson and Petter, 1988.
54 See HC 773 (1979–80); HC 242 (1982–83); HC Deb Col 444, 12 May 1983.
55 Intelligence Services Act 1994, s 10.
56 Intelligence Services Act 1994, s 10(3).
57 Ibid, Sched 3, para 2.
58 Such as the Joint Intelligence Organisation, the Office for Security and Counter-Terrorism in the Home Office and Defence Intelligence in the Ministry of Defence.

power to exclude any matter which would be prejudicial to the functions of the Agencies or any other bodies with which the ISC is concerned.

Official Secrets[59]

The Official Secrets Acts 1911–89

The first Official Secrets Act arrived on the statute book in 1889. The latest Act is that of 1989. The 1911 Act – which survived virtually untouched until 1989 – was passed through Parliament with one hour's debate and within 24 hours. Motivation for the 1911 Act lay in alleged enemy agent activity in the country.[60] The motives behind the 1989 Act were formed largely from the failure of the earlier Act. As will be seen, section 2 of the 1911 Act provided for numerous offences based on vague criteria of disclosure of information and juries have on occasion refused to convict, even where it was clear from the facts and the law that a guilty verdict should have been returned.[61] Official inquiries into the working of the Act revealed deficiencies.[62]

The **Spycatcher** case also provided motivation for the government to reform the law. In the government's view, members and ex-members of the Security Services should be under a life-long duty of confidentiality in respect of their work. One defect in the 1911 Act lay in the duty of – and hence liability for – non-disclosure enduring only for the duration of employment.

Section 1 of the 1911 Act provides penalties for spying. It is an offence to enter into top-secret establishments or to collect, publish or communicate any official document (which includes official code words, passwords, sketches, plans, models, articles or notes) or informa-tion which might be useful to a potential enemy, if the actions are carried out 'for any purpose prejudicial to the safety or interest of the state'. The accused has no 'right to silence' and a trial may be held in secret, or partly in secret. Section 2 of the Act reversed the normal burden of proof from the prosecution to the defence. It was not necessary for the prosecution to prove that the accused was guilty of any particular act 'tending to show a purpose prejudicial to the safety or interest of the state'. Guilt could be established if 'from the circumstances of the case, or his conduct, or his known character as proved, it appears that his purpose was a purpose prejudicial to the safety or interest of the state'. Moreover, any information or document handed over to another person, without lawful authority, could 'be deemed to have been made, obtained, collected, recorded or communicated for a purpose prejudicial to the safety or interests of the state unless the contrary is proved'. Penalties for espionage are swingeing. George Blake, a former MI6 officer convicted of espionage, was sentenced to 42 years' impris-onment.[63] In 1985, Michael Bettany, a former MI5 officer, was convicted of attempting to pass official information to the Russians and sentenced to 23 years' imprisonment. Geoffrey Prime was sentenced to 35 years for disclosing material while employed at GCHQ.[64] Not all offences will lead to a prosecution. Neither Kim Philby nor Anthony Blunt was prosecuted. Instead, each was offered immunity from prosecution in return for a confession, an offer declined by Kim Philby, who fled to Moscow.

Section 2 of the 1911 Act (now reformed under the Official Secrets Act 1989) prohibited the disclosure of any official information without authorisation to anyone not authorised to

---

59 See Robertson and Merrills, 1993; Hooper, 1988; Ewing and Gearty, 1990.
60 See Andrew, 1985; French, 1978; Le Queux, 1915.
61 See **R v Ponting** (1985), discussed in Chapter 3, p 56.
62 See *Departmental Committee on Section 2 of the Official Secrets Act 1911*, Cmnd 5104, 1972, London: HMSO; White Paper, *Reform of Section 2 of the Official Secrets Act 1911*, Cmnd 7285, 1978, London: HMSO.
63 Blake subsequently escaped from prison after 25 years, with the help of friends.
64 **R v Prime** (1983).

receive it, and covered some one million public servants and a further one million government contractors. It also covered the retention of any document by a person not entitled to retain the same, failure to take reasonable care of a document, and receiving any document without authority. Section 2 was capable of generating over 2,000 different criminal offences, including the disclosure of the number of cups of tea consumed in the MI5 canteen.[65]

Reform of the Official Secrets Act 1911[66]

In 1971 a Committee of Inquiry, headed by Lord Franks, was established to review the working of section 2. Reporting in 1972, the Committee was highly critical of section 2 and recommended that it be reformed.[67] It was not, however, until 1989 that reform took place.[68]

The major provisions of the Official Secrets Act 1989

Section 2 of the Official Secrets Act 1911 was repealed and replaced by the 1989 Act. Rather than the catch-all section 2 of the 1911 Act, the 1989 Act created offences directed to specific groups of people and information. In relation to most areas, the prosecution must prove both that the information has been unlawfully transmitted and that the disclosure of the information is 'damaging'. The concept of 'damaging disclosure' has, however, not been incorporated into section 1, which relates to security and intelligence matters. With this exception, there is a presumption of harm built into the Act. A further exception relates to those who are not Crown servants or government contractors in relation to whom the prosecution will have to prove – in addition to the harm test – that the defendant knew or had good reason to know that the specific harm was likely to have been caused. In relation to such information, the disclosure in itself is an offence. There is no longer a defence of 'public good' which applied under section 2 of the 1911 Act.

Security and intelligence

Under section 1 of the 1989 Act, any person who is, or has been, a member of the Security and Intelligence Services, and any other person who is informed that the provision of the Act applies to him, is guilty of an offence if 'without lawful authority' he discloses 'any information, document or other article related to security or intelligence'. The offence is committed irrespective of whether or not the disclosure is damaging. A person who is, or has been, a Crown servant or government contractor will be guilty of an offence if he makes a 'damaging disclosure of any information, document or other article relating to security or intelligence'. In **R v Shayler** (2001), the House of Lords ruled that a former member of the Security Services was not entitled to rely on the defence that the disclosure was made in the public or national interest. There was no contravention of Article 10 of the European Convention through the restriction of members and former members of the security forces disclosing information.[69]

---

65 *Departmental Committee on Section 2 of the Official Secrets Act 1911*, Cmnd 5104, 1972, London: HMSO, para 16, and see Robertson and Merrills, 1993. See **Chandler v Director of Public Prosecutions** (1964); **R v Aitken** (1971). For an account, see Aitken, 1971.

66 See, inter alia, Hooper, 1988; White Paper, *Reform of Section 2 of the Official Secrets Act 1911*, Cm 408, 1988, London: HMSO. See also the White Paper, *Open Government*, Cm 2290, 1993, London: HMSO, discussed in Chapter 10.

67 *Departmental Committee on Section 2 of the Official Secrets Act 1911*, Cmnd 5104, 1972, London: HMSO.

68 See the White Paper, *Reform of Section 2 of the Official Secrets Act 1911*, Cmnd 7285, 1978, London: HMSO; Green Paper, *Freedom of Information*, Cmnd 7520, 1979, London: HMSO; White Paper, *Reform of Section 2 of the Official Secrets Act 1911*, Cm 408, 1988, London: HMSO.

69 In **R (A) v Director of Establishments of the Security Service** (2009), the Court of Appeal ruled that the Investigatory Powers Tribunal (IPT) was the 'only appropriate tribunal' for the purposes of proceedings under section 7(1)(a) of the Human Rights Act 1998 brought against one of the intelligence services (the claimant was a former member of the Security Service who had been refused permission to publish a book relating to his work).

Security and intelligence are defined as being the work of, or work in support of, the Security and Intelligence Services. A disclosure is defined as damaging if 'it causes damage to the work of, or of any part of, the Security or Intelligence Services' or if unauthorised disclosure would be likely to cause such damage. A charge may be defended if the person in question can prove that, at the time of the alleged offence, 'he did not know, and had no reasonable cause to believe' that the unauthorised disclosure related to security or intelligence or, in the case of an offence under sub-section (3), he did not know, or had no reasonable cause to believe, that the disclosure would be damaging.

Defence

Any unauthorised damaging disclosure of information, documents or other articles relating to defence is an offence.[70] A disclosure is damaging if 'it damages the capability of any part of the armed forces, or leads to loss of life or injury to the forces, or endangers the interests of the United Kingdom abroad, or obstructs the promotion or protection of those interests, or is likely to have any of these effects'. It is a defence to prove that the person did not know, and had no reasonable cause to believe, that such disclosure would be damaging.

Section 4 defines 'defence' as including the 'size, shape, organisation, logistics, order of battle, deployment, operations, state of readiness and training of the armed forces of the Crown; weapons, stores or other equipment of those forces; defence policy and strategy, and military planning and intelligence; and plans and measures for the maintenance of essential supplies and services that are, or would be, needed in time of war'.

International relations

Under section 3 of the 1989 Act, an unauthorised damaging disclosure, by a person who is or has been a Crown servant or government contractor, of any information, document or other article relating to international relations, or confidential information obtained from another state or international organisation is an offence. A disclosure is damaging if it 'endangers the interests of the United Kingdom abroad, or seriously obstructs the promotion or protection of those interests or endangers the safety of British citizens abroad', or 'is likely to have any of those effects'. It is a defence to prove that the accused did not know, and had no reasonable cause to believe, that the information fell within sub-section (1), or that its disclosure would be damaging.

In **R v Keogh** (2007) the Court of Appeal considered the burden of proof relating to unauthorised disclosures contrary to sections 2 and 3 of the Official Secrets Act 1989. The defendant, employed in the government communications centre, photocopied a letter which recorded discussions between the Prime Minister and the President of the United States relating to political, diplomatic and defence issues relating to Iraq, and showed it to his co-defendant who was a researcher for a Member of Parliament who opposed the Iraq war. The co-defendant placed the photocopy in the MP's papers. The section 2(3) defence, given its ordinary meaning, reverses the burden of proof. Lord Phillips of Worth Matravers CJ cited Lord Bingham in **R v Sheldrake** (2005):

> The task for the court is never to decide whether a reverse burden of proof should be placed on a defendant, but always to assess whether a burden enacted by Parliament unjustifiably infringes the presumption of innocence.

---

70 Official Secrets Act 1989, s 2.

The Court of Appeal concluded that the 1989 Act could operate effectively without the imposition of the reverse burden of proof which 'would be disproportionate and unjustifiable'. Those sections were incompatible with Article 6 of the Convention and should be 'read down' to make them compatible.

Crime and special investigation powers

Section 4 of the Act makes it an offence to disclose, without lawful authority, information, documents or other articles which result in the commission of an offence, or facilitate an escape from legal custody or impede the prevention or detection of offences or the apprehension or prosecution of suspected offenders, or disclosures which are likely to have those effects. It is a defence to a charge to prove that the person did not know, and had no reasonable cause to believe, that the disclosure related to prohibited materials or that disclosure would have any of the damaging effects mentioned.

Authorised disclosures under the Act

A disclosure by a Crown servant (or other notified person) is authorised if it is made with lawful authority and if (and only if) the disclosure is made in accordance with a person's official duty.[71] In relation to government contractors, a disclosure is lawful only if it is made with official authorisation or for the purposes of his functions relating to the contract and without contravening an official restriction. In relation to any other person, a disclosure is lawful only if it is made to a Crown servant for the purposes of his functions as such, or in accordance with official authorisation. It is a defence to a charge to prove that, at the time of disclosure, the person believed that he had lawful authority to make the disclosure in question.

The duty to safeguard information

Under section 8, Crown servants and government contractors are under a duty to protect any information, document or other article which it would be an offence to disclose under the Act. It is an offence for a Crown servant to retain an article contrary to his or her official duty, and for a government contractor to fail to comply with a request for the return or disposal of the information or document, or to fail to take such care of the information or document as 'a person in his position may be reasonably expected to take'. It is a defence for a Crown servant to prove that he believed he was acting in accordance with his official duty and 'had no reasonable cause to believe otherwise'.

Prosecutions

No prosecution may be instituted other than with the consent of the Attorney General.[72]

Penalties

A person convicted of an offence under the Act, other than under section 8(1), (4) or (5), shall, on indictment, be liable to imprisonment for a two-year term, or a fine, or both. On summary conviction, a person is liable to up to a six-month term of imprisonment, or a fine, or both. A person convicted under section 8(1), (4) or (5) is liable, on summary conviction, to a term of imprisonment of up to three months, or a fine, or both.

The catch-all nature of section 2 of the Official Secrets Act 1911 has thus been reformed. Whether, in fact, the 1989 Act is less swingeing in scope is another matter. Geoffrey Robertson

---

71 Official Secrets Act 1989, s 7.
72 Official Secrets Act 1989, s 9.

QC states that the scope of the 1989 legislation, 'while not the theoretical dragnet of the old section 2, is none the less considerable'.[73]

Restrictions on the media: defence advisory notices[74]

The Official Secrets Acts of course apply to information which might be revealed by the press, and the doctrine of breach of confidence also represents a fetter on freedom of information. A further restriction on press freedom is the 'DA' (Defence Advisory) Notice system. The basis for the system is entirely extralegal and voluntary. No formal sanction exists for failure to comply with a DA Notice. The system was established in 1912. A DA Notice Committee was established, chaired by a Permanent Under Secretary of the Ministry of Defence, which comprised both newspaper editors and civil servants.[75] At the request of a government department, the committee will draft a Notice, and advice as to its scope and meaning will be given to the press by the committee's secretary. Compliance with a DA Notice will not affect any right to bring legal action against a newspaper,[76] and neither will non-compliance. The system is vague and defective. It is also contrary to principle to have a non-statutory system which effectively fetters the freedom of the press. The system was reviewed in both 1962 and 1980, when retention of the system was recommended. The 1980 inquiry by the Defence Committee of the House of Commons nevertheless expressed reservations about retaining the system.[77] A further review was conducted in 2000. The current DA Notices cover Military Operations, Plans and Capabilities; Nuclear and Non-nuclear Weapons and Equipment; Ciphers and Secure Communications; Sensitive Installations and Addresses; and British Security and Intelligence Services and Special Forces.

Judicial attitudes to pleas of national security

Where national security is pleaded by the government in judicial review proceedings, the courts are exceedingly reluctant to challenge the executive. Whilst this is, *prima facie*, regrettable from the point of view of the aggrieved citizen, it is explained – although not necessarily justified – by the relationship between the executive, legislature and judiciary. As seen in Chapter 4, the doctrine of separation of powers, whilst not strictly adhered to under the United Kingdom's constitution, is respected by the courts. In no area of policy is this respect more clearly demonstrated than in matters of national security, which will frequently, but not inevitably, be linked to the exercise of the royal prerogative. In Chapter 5, the judiciary's cautious approach to review of the prerogative was examined, and it was there seen that the prerogative ensures for the executive a wide and inadequately defined area of power which is largely immune from judicial review. It will be recalled that in **Council of Civil Service Unions v Minister for Civil Service** (1985) (the **GCHQ** case) the House of Lords ruled that the courts have jurisdiction to review the exercise of executive power irrespective of whether the source of power was statutory, or under the common law prerogative.

---

73 Robertson and Merrills, 1993. See also Palmer, 1990.
74 See The 'D' Notice System, Cmnd 3312, 1967, London: HMSO; Report of the Committee of Privy Councillors Appointed to Inquire into 'D' Notice Matters, Cmnd 3309, 1967, London: HMSO; Third Report of the Defence Committee: The 'D' Notice System, HC 773 (1979–80), London: HMSO; Ministry of Defence: The Defence Advisory Notices: A Review of the 'D' Notice System, MOD Open Government Document 93/1993.
75 Then known as the Admiralty, War Office and Press Committee; now the Defence Press and Broadcasting Advisory Committee.
76 As occurred in 1970 when The Sunday Telegraph was prosecuted under the Official Secrets Act 1911 for disclosure of material supplied by Jonathan Aitken.
77 HC 773 (1979–80), London: HMSO, and see Jaconelli, 1982.

Notwithstanding that claim, the House of Lords conceded that matters of national security fell within the class of powers deemed 'non-justiciable' by the courts (by which is meant that the subject matter is one more appropriately controlled by the executive accountable to Parliament rather than the courts of law).[78] However, the incorporation of Convention rights under the Human Rights Act 1998 extends judicial protection. The Convention protects, *inter alia*, the right to liberty and the right to fair trial. In **A v Secretary of State for the Home Department** (2004) (discussed at p 545 below) the House of Lords took a robust approach to the power of the executive to detain non-British terrorist suspects, declaring that the relevant statutory provision was incompatible with the right to liberty protected under Article 5.

Detention in wartime

In **Liversidge v Anderson** (1942), the House of Lords refused[79] to review the Home Secretary's power of detention under the Defence of the Realm Acts. It will be recalled from Chapter 5 that the regulation provided that the minister had power to order the detention of persons whom he 'had reasonable cause to believe' to be of hostile origin or associations and 'in need of subjection to preventative control'.[80]

Emergency Powers

While, in peace time, the responsibility for maintaining order and detecting crime lies with the police forces, in times of emergency, further assistance will be needed if order is to be restored.

The Civil Contingencies Act 2004 confers on the executive wide-ranging powers to deal with emergency situations. The Act is separated into two main parts: Part 1 making provision for local arrangements for civil protection and Part 2 providing for emergency powers. An 'emergency' is broadly defined.[81] In relation to Part 1 of the Act, it is defined as 'an event or situation' which threatens serious damage to human welfare, serious damage to the environment of a place in the United Kingdom, or war or terrorism which threatens serious damage to the security of the United Kingdom. In relation to Part 2, an emergency is defined in the same way but relates to emergencies in the United Kingdom or in a part or region rather than a 'place'. In both Parts of the Act, an event or situation which threatens damage to human welfare only if it involves loss of human life; human illness or injury; homelessness; damage to property; disruption of a supply of money, food, water, energy or fuel; disruption of a system of communication; disruption of facilities for transport, or disruption of services relating to health. An event or situation threatening damage to the environment involves contamination of land, water or air with biological, chemical or radioactive matter, or disruption or destruction of plant life or animal life.

The Act confers on the executive the power to amend the definition of an emergency by amending, by order, the list of events or situations which may threaten damage to human welfare. Any such orders are subject to the affirmative resolution procedure. Under Part 2, section 20, emergency regulations may be made by Order in Council if the conditions in

---

78 On the definition of harm to national security see **Secretary of State for the Home Department v Rehman** (2001).
79 Lord Atkin dissenting. Note that Lord Atkin's dissent was accepted as a correct statement of common law in **R v Inland Revenue Commissioners ex parte Rossminster Ltd** (1980).
80 On deportation see further below. On extradition see Chapter 18.
81 Civil Contingencies Act 2004, ss 1 and 19.

section 21 are satisfied. Those conditions are that an emergency has occurred, is occurring or is about to occur; that it is necessary to make provision for the purpose of preventing, controlling or mitigating an aspect or effect of the emergency and that the need for such provision is urgent. Emergency regulations lapse 30 days after they are made unless an earlier date is specified. The regulations are renewable.[82] They must be laid before Parliament as soon as reasonably practicable and lapse at the end of seven days unless each House of Parliament passes a resolution approving them.

The Act imposes duties on public authorities to assess and make provision for emergencies, and to provide information and assistance to the public.

The use of the armed forces in times of unrest

The use of troops in 1911 in South Wales is the only occasion on which troops have been brought in to assist the police. During the miners' strike 1984–85, the troops were not called in. Instead, the police forces co-ordinated their operations in order to contain the situation successfully. Where troops are deemed necessary to aid the police, it is the Home Secretary, acting on the request of the Chief Officer of police, who has responsibility. As was seen in Chapter 5, the Home Secretary has the power to issue weapons to police forces for the quelling of civil disturbance.[83]

In time of war

The Defence of the Realm Act 1914–15 conferred wide powers on the Crown to make Regulations for ensuring public safety and defence of the realm. The courts have ruled that these broad powers include the power to detain a person without trial on the basis of his or her hostile associations.[84] The power to regulate supplies does not, however, include the power to impose a tax upon produce.[85] Specific power to impose charges in relation to matters regulated under Defence Regulations was conferred under the Emergency Powers (Defence) Act 1939. Under the regulations, the Home Secretary was given power to detain persons whom he had reasonable cause to believe came within certain categories. The power was regarded by the courts as reviewable.[86] Under the Emergency Powers (Defence) (No 2) Act 1940, powers were conferred compulsorily to direct labour in support of the war effort. Compulsory military service was introduced under National Service Acts.

Terrorism

The Terrorism Act 2000 reformed and extended existing terrorist legislation.[87] Whereas the Prevention of Terrorism (Temporary Provisions) Act 1989 required annual renewal, the Terrorism Act has permanent status.

---

82 Civil Contingencies Act 2004, s 26.
83 See **R v Secretary of State for the Home Department ex parte Northumbria Police Authority** (1988).
84 See **R v Halliday ex parte Zadig** (1917).
85 See **Attorney General v Wilts United Dairies Ltd** (1921) and the War Charges Validity Act 1925.
86 See **Liversidge v Anderson** (1942).
87 It repealed the Prevention of Terrorism (Temporary Provisions) Act 1989, the Prevention of Terrorism (Additional Powers) Act 1996, the Northern Ireland (Emergency Provisions) Act 1996 and the Northern Ireland (Emergency Provisions) Act 1998, and made minor amendments to other relevant Acts. See Inquiry into Legislation Against Terrorism, Cm 3420, 1996, London: Stationery Office; Legislation Against Terrorism, Cm 4178, 1998, London: Stationery Office.

The terrorist attacks on New York and Washington in September 2001 prompted a swift response from the British government. The Anti-Terrorism, Crime and Security Act 2001 built on existing legislation in order to ensure that the security forces have the necessary powers to combat terrorist threats to the United Kingdom. The 2001 Act aimed to cut off terrorist funding and to enable government departments and agencies to collect and share information in the attempt to avert threats. The Act also altered immigration procedures, and provided additional powers for the detention of suspected international terrorists who have been certified by the Secretary of State as a threat to national security. In *A v Secretary of State for the Home Department* (2004) a panel of nine Law Lords (Lord Walker dissenting) ruled that measures empowering the Home Secretary to detain indefinitely, without charge or trial, non-nationals whom he suspected of international terrorist activity, but whom he could not deport, were incompatible with the United Kingdom's European Convention obligations. The House of Lords made a declaration of incompatibility under section 4 of the Human Rights Act that section 23 of the Anti-terrorism, Crime and Security Act 2001 was incompatible with Articles 5 and 14 of the Convention.

The 2001 Act also enhanced the security of nuclear and aviation industries and aimed to improve the security of dangerous substances which may be used by terrorists. It extended police powers and facilitated greater co-operation between police forces. Controversially, the Act also provided for extended powers of disclosure of information by public authorities to the police and security agencies involved in criminal investigations.

See further Chapter 18.

The law relating to terrorism must be seen within the wider geographical context as the world seeks to counter the globalisation of terror. In 2001 the United Nations (UN) adopted Security Council Resolution 1373 on the fight against terrorism and there are 12 UN terrorism conventions setting standards for international action:

- to prevent and combat terrorist acts such as bombing, hijacking and hostage-taking;
- to prevent and combat terrorist financing, recruitment and supply of weapons; and
- to extradite or prosecute terrorists and deny them safe haven.

Within the European context, both the Council of Europe and the European Union have been active. In 2003 the Council of Europe set up the Committee of Experts on Terrorism (CODEXTER) with the responsibility of coordinating and monitoring terrorism. Under the auspices of the Committee of Experts two new Conventions against terrorism have been drafted and opened for signature by Member States: the *Council of Europe Convention on the Prevention of Terrorism* and the *Council of Europe Convention on the Laundering, Search, Seizure and Confiscation of the Proceeds from Crime and on the Financing of Terrorism*.[88] In 2002 the Council of the European Union adopted Council Framework Decision on Combating Terrorism.[89] Article 1 of the Framework Decision requires all Member States to take the necessary action to ensure that terrorist acts committed with the aim of seriously intimidating a population, or unduly compelling a government or international organisation to perform or abstain from performing any act, or seriously destabilising or destroying the fundamental political, constitutional, economic or social structures of a country or international organisation are defined as criminal offences under domestic law.

---

88 Council of Europe Treaty Series 196 and 198 respectively (2005).
89 2002/475/JHA.

Defining terrorism

Whereas under the Prevention of Terrorism (Temporary Provisions) Act 1989, terrorism was defined as the 'use of violence for political ends, and included the use of violence for the purpose of putting the public or any section of the public in fear',[90] section 1 of the Terrorism Act 2000[91] adopted a wider definition, namely:

(1) In this Act 'terrorism' means the use or threat of action where –

   (a) The action falls within subsection (2),
   (b) the use or threat is designed to influence the government or an international governmental organization or to intimidate the public or a section of the public, and
   (c) the use or threat is made for the purpose of advancing a political, religious, racial or ideological cause.

(2) Action falls within this subsection it if –

   (a) involves serious violence against a person,
   (b) involves serious damage to property,
   (c) endangers a person's life, other than that of the person committing the action,
   (d) creates a serious risk to the health or safety of the public, or a section of the public, or
   (e) is designed seriously to interfere with or seriously to disrupt an electronic system.

Action includes action outside the United Kingdom, and references to any person or to property mean any person or property wherever situated, and a reference to the public includes a reference to the public of a country other than the United Kingdom.[92] This definition is intended to cover not just terrorism for political ends but terrorism undertaken for religious or ideological motives, which, while not necessarily violent in themselves, are capable of having widespread adverse affects. Examples cited are of disruption to key computer systems or interference with the supply of water or power where life, health or safety may be put at risk. In **Secretary of State for the Home Department v Rehman** (2002), it was held that the promotion of terrorism against any state by an individual in the United Kingdom was capable of being a threat to the national security of the United Kingdom, and accordingly deportation in the interests of national security for terrorist activities which were not targeted against the United Kingdom or its citizens was lawful under the Immigration Act 1971. Lord Hoffmann expressed the view that judges should respect the decisions of Ministers of the Crown in relation to whether national security is threatened.[93]

In **R v Gul** (2012) the Court of Appeal ruled that the definition of terrorism included those who encouraged terrorism by glorifying attacks on the armed forces.

---

90 Prevention of Terrorism (Temporary Provisions) Act 1989, s 20.
91 As amended by s 34 of the Terrorism Act 2006 and s 75 of the Counter-Terrorism Act 2008.
92 Terrorism Act 2000, s 1(2).
93 In **R v F** (2007) the defendant, charged under section 1 of the 2000 Act, argued that activities proposed in documents in his possession did not amount to terrorism against a foreign government on the basis that the government in question, Libya, was a tyrannical undemocratic regime which fell outside the protective structure of the 2000 Act and that he had a defence under section 58(3) of 'reasonable excuse' for the possession of the document. The Court of Appeal dismissed his appeal. Had Parliament intended to limit the application of the Act only to democratic regimes the statute would have expressly addressed the problem of tyrannical regimes. On the interpretation of section 1 see also **R v Rowe** (2007).

Proscribed organisations

The Terrorism Act 2000 governs proscribed organisations, listed under Schedule 2. Part II of the Terrorism Act 2006 amends the 2000 Act to cover organisations which promote or encourage terrorism. The 2006 Act also provides that an organisation listed in Schedule 2 which is operating under a different name shall be treated as the listed organisation (section 22). The Secretary of State may add or remove an organisation from the list, but may only add an organisation if he believes that the organisation is concerned in terrorism.[94] An organisation is concerned in terrorism if it commits or participates in acts of terrorism, prepares for terrorism, promotes or encourages terrorism, or is otherwise concerned in terrorism.[95] The Act introduces a Proscribed Organisations Appeal Commission (POAC),[96] to which individuals or organisations may appeal, having first applied to the Secretary of State for de-proscription and been refused.[97]

The Commission must allow an appeal if it considers that the Secretary of State's decision was flawed when considered in the light of the principles applicable on an application for judicial review.[98] If the appeal is allowed, the Secretary of State must lay a draft order before Parliament or, in urgent cases, make an order removing the organisation from the list.[99] Appeals from the POAC, on a question of law, lie to the Court of Appeal, Court of Session or Court of Appeal in Northern Ireland. An appeal may only be brought with the consent of the Commission or, where the Commission refuses permission, with the permission of the relevant court.[100] If an appeal to the POAC is successful, and an order made de-proscribing the organisation, any individual convicted of an offence in relation to the organisation, provided the offence was committed after the date of the Secretary of State's refusal to de-proscribe, may appeal against his conviction to the Court or Appeal or Crown Court.[101] In order that individuals seeking de-proscription should not be deterred from pursuing an appeal or from instituting proceedings under section 7 of the Human Rights Act 1998, through a risk of prosecution for offences in relation to a proscribed organisation, section 10 of the Terrorism Act provides that evidence cannot be relied on in criminal proceedings for such an offence except as part of the defence case. In **R v Z (Attorney General for Northern Ireland's Reference)** (2005) the House of Lords considered the definition of a proscribed organisation under the 2000 Act. Z and others had been charged with belonging to a proscribed organisation, being an organisation listed in Schedule 2 or, by section 3(1)(b) one that operated 'under the same name as an organisation listed in that Schedule'. Z belonged not to the Irish Republican Army listed in the Schedule, but to the Real Irish Republican Army, a splinter group formed in 1997, and was convicted. The Court of Appeal dismissed Z's appeal, ruling that in the interpretation of a controversial provision in a statute, it had to be read in the context of the statute as a whole and the historical context of the situation which led to its enactment. Faced with rival claims as to who represented the IRA, a blanket description had been adopted to embrace all 'emanations, manifestations and representations of that organisation': accordingly the term IRA encompassed the Real Irish Republican Army.

---

94 Terrorism Act 2000, s 3.
95 Ibid, s 3(5).
96 Ibid, s 5, as amended by s 22 of the Terrorism Act 2006.
97 Ibid, s 4, as amended by s 22 of the Terrorism Act 2006.
98 See Chapter 23. See *Alton v Secretary of State for the Home Department* (2008).
99 Terrorism Act 2000, s 5.
100 Ibid, s 6.
101 Ibid, s 7, as amended by s 22 of the Terrorism Act 2006. Section 8 makes equivalent provision for Scotland and Northern Ireland. Section 9 makes provision for the Human Rights Act 1998, s 7, to apply to appeal proceedings brought before the POAC, in relation to s 5(4) and (5), ss 6 and 7 (appeals to a court of law from a decision of the POAC), and paras 4–8 of Sched 3 (relating to procedure before the POAC).

Sections 11 to 12 relate to offences concerning membership of and support for a proscribed organisation. A person guilty of an offence under these sections shall be liable, on conviction on indictment, to a term of imprisonment not exceeding ten years, to a fine or to both, and on summary conviction, to a term of imprisonment not exceeding six months, to a fine not exceeding the statutory maximum or to both. It is a defence for a person charged with an offence under section 11(1) to prove that the organisation was not proscribed on the last occasion on which he became a member or began to profess to be a member, and that he has not taken part in the activities of the organisation at any time while it was proscribed. Section 12 relates to the support for a proscribed organisation and makes it an offence to invite support and/or to arrange, manage or assist in arranging or managing a meeting and/or to address such a meeting. A 'meeting' means a meeting of three or more persons, whether or not the public are admitted.

The wearing of an item of clothing, or wearing, carrying or displaying an article in a public place, in such a way or in such circumstances as to arouse reasonable suspicion that that person is a member or supporter of a proscribed organisation is an offence. On summary conviction, a person guilty under section 13 is liable to six months' imprisonment, a fine not exceeding level five on the standard scale or both.

Terrorist property

Part III of the Terrorism Act 2000 relates to terrorist property, defined under section 14 to mean money or other property which is likely to be used for the purposes of terrorism (including the resources of a proscribed organisation) and proceeds of acts of terrorism. It is an offence to partake in fundraising for the purposes of terrorism. In relation to inviting support from others or receiving money or other property, there must be an intention that it should be used, or reasonable cause to suspect that it may be used, for terrorist purposes. Part III of the 2000 Act introduced powers for the police, customs officers and immigration officers to seize cash at borders and to seek forfeiture of cash in civil proceedings. The Anti-Terrorism, Crime and Security Act 2001 extended the law in order to prevent terrorists gaining access to their money.

The lawfulness of asset-freezing orders was considered by the Supreme Court in **Ahmed v HM Treasury** (2010). The Supreme Court ruled that the Orders were unlawful and would be quashed. The Terrorist Asset-Freezing Act 2010 now regulates asset-freezing. See further page 595.

Terrorist investigations

Part IV of the Terrorism Act 2000 regulates powers in relation to terrorist investigations, defined to include the commission, preparation or instigation of acts of terrorism, an act which appears to have been done for such purposes, the resources of a proscribed organisation, the possibility of making a proscription or de-proscription order under section 3(3), or the commission, preparation or instigation of an offence under the Act.[102] Sections 33 to 36 give power to the police to designate and demarcate a specified area by cordons for the purposes of a terrorist investigation. It is an offence to fail to comply with an order.

For further details on police powers in relation to terrorism see the Website.

Under section 39, it is an offence to disclose to another anything which is likely to prejudice a terrorist investigation or to interfere with material which is likely to be relevant to the investigation.[103]

---

102 Terrorism Act 2000, s 32.
103 Terrorism Act 2000, s 39(7). It is also an offence for a person to collect, make a record of, publish, communicate or attempt to elicit information which is useful to a person committing or preparing an act of terrorism, or to possess a document or record containing information which would be useful (ibid, s 103). The offence is confined to a person who is or has been a constable, a member of Her Majesty's Forces, the holder of a judicial office, an officer of any court or a full time employee of the prison service in Northern Ireland. It is a defence to prove that he had a reasonable excuse for his action or possession.

Terrorism overseas

The Terrorism Act 2000 also regulates terrorism overseas. Under section 59, it is an offence to incite another person to commit an act of terrorism wholly or partly outside the United Kingdom, if that act would constitute an offence listed in subsection (2) in England and Wales, namely, murder, wounding with intent, and offences involving poison, explosions and endangering life by damaging property. A person found guilty shall be liable to any penalty to which he would be liable on conviction of the relevant offence. Sections 60 and 61 make equivalent provision in relation to Scotland and Northern Ireland. Section 62 regulates acts of terrorism outside the United Kingdom involving causing explosions[104] and the use of biological or chemical weapons, and provides that a person committing such an act is guilty of an offence. Equally, it is an offence to do anything outside the United Kingdom which would amount to an offence under sections 15 to 18 if it had been done in the United Kingdom.

Port and border controls

Section 53 and Schedule 7 to the Terrorism Act 2000 regulate border controls. An 'examining officer', being a constable, immigration officer or customs officer designated for the purposes of Schedule 7 by the Secretary of State and Commissioners of Customs and Excise, has the power to stop, question and detain a person, at an airport, port or border area, for the purposes of determining whether he or she is a person suspected of being concerned in the commission, preparation or instigation of acts of terrorism.[105]

A person questioned is required to provide any information requested, and produce a valid passport or other document establishing his or her identity. A person may be removed from a ship, aircraft or vehicle for the purpose of detaining for questioning. A person detained for questioning must be released no later than the end of a nine-hour period beginning with the time when the questioning begins, unless otherwise detained under any other power.

Powers of search are granted to examining officers. The examining officer may 'for the purpose of satisfying himself whether there are any persons who he may wish to question' search a ship or aircraft, a person and/or his possessions.

The Prevention of Terrorism Act 2005

The Prevention of Terrorism Act 2005 was a response to the House of Lords' decision in **A v Secretary of State for the Home Department supra**. The 2005 Act provided for the making of 'control orders' over terrorist suspects. These were preventative in nature and imposed any conditions necessary to prevent or restrict an individual's further involvement in terrorist-related activities. Controversy over control orders led to reform.[106] In a Ministerial Statement in 2011,[107] the Home Secretary announced that legislation was to be introduced to provide for a less restrictive system than control orders, but that the control order system would continue to operate until replacement measures were in force.[108] The Terrorism Prevention and Investigation Measures Act 2011 reforms the law and abolishes the Prevention of Terrorism Act 2005. On the 2011 Act see further below.

---

104 An offence under the Explosive Substances Act 1883, s 2, 3 or 5; an offence under the Biological Weapons Act; 1974, s 1; an offence under the Chemical Weapons Act 1996, s 2.
105 Defined in the Terrorism Act 2000, s 40(1)(b) and 40(2), as including a person who has been, whether before or after the passing of the Act, concerned in the commission, preparation or instigation of acts of terrorism within the meaning given in s 1.
106 See Control Orders in 2011: Final Report of the Independent Reviewer on the Prevention of Terrorism Act 2005, London: TSO 2012.
107 Hansard, 17 March 2011, Col 27 WS.
108 See Sched 8 to the Terrorism Prevention and Investigation Measures Act 2011.

The Terrorism Act 2006

The Terrorism Act 2006 was introduced to tighten the law following two attacks on London in July 2005. The Act introduced new criminal offences in relation to terrorism, amended the definition of terrorism, increased the penalties available, extended the grounds for detention and extended the period of detention and made other miscellaneous changes to the law. Section 36 provides that the Secretary of State must appoint a person to review the operation of the Terrorism Act 2000 and Part I of the 2006 Act. The review must be carried out every 12 months and the report made to the Secretary of State must be laid before Parliament.

The definition of terrorism is extended to include actions and threats or using noxious substances or things to influence a government or to intimidate international governmental organisations.[109] Section 1 creates the offence of encouragement of terrorism, and applies to a statement 'that is likely to be understood by some or all of the members of the public to whom it is published as a direct or indirect encouragement or other inducement to them to the commission, preparation or instigation of acts of terrorism or Convention offences'. It is an offence to publish such a statement, or cause another to publish such a statement with the intention that members of the public 'be directly or indirectly encouraged to commit, prepare or instigate acts of terrorism or Convention offences'.[110] It is also an offence to be 'reckless as to whether members of the public will be directly or indirectly encouraged etc'. An indirect encouragement is defined as being a 'statement describing terrorism in such a way that the listener would infer that he should emulate it'. Section 2 creates the offence of disseminating a terrorism publication with the intention, or being reckless, of directly or indirectly encouraging or inducing the commission, preparation or instigation of acts of terrorism.[111] The criminal offences under sections 1 and 2 extend to internet activity.[112]

The Act extends the law to cover *any* conduct undertaken in preparation for committing, or assisting another to commit, acts of terrorism. Conviction carries a sentence of life imprisonment. Providing training or instruction for, or receiving instruction or training in, skills relating to terrorism is a criminal offence carrying a sentence on conviction on indictment to a term of imprisonment of up to ten years or a fine, or both. If tried summarily, the offences carry a term of imprisonment of up to 12 months, a fine not exceeding the statutory maximum, or both.[113] The same penalties apply to the offence of attendance at a place used for terrorist training.[114] The making and possession of radioactive material or devices, or the misuse of devices or material, or demands or threats relating to such items are criminal offences punishable with life imprisonment.[115] Conduct outside the United Kingdom is a criminal offence in the United Kingdom if it would amount to an offence listed in section 17(2). Prosecutions may be instituted in England and Wales only with the consent of the Director of Public Prosecutions and in Northern Ireland with the consent of the Director of Public Prosecutions for Northern Ireland.

The Terrorism Act 2006 extended the period in which a terrorist suspect may be held in detention without charge to 28 days. That period has been reduced to 14 days by section 57 of the Protection of Freedoms Act 2012.

---

109 Amending s 1(1)(b) of the Terrorism Act 2000 and s 113(1)(c) of the Anti-Terrorism, Crime and Security Act 2001.
110 Convention offences are those listed in Sched 1 to the Act.
111 The Terrorism Act 2006, s 28 provides for warrants to enter and search and seize terrorist publications and for forfeiture.
112 Terrorism Act 2006, s 3.
113 In Scotland or Northern Ireland, on summary conviction to imprisonment for a term not exceeding six months or a fine not exceeding the statutory maximum, or both.
114 Terrorism Act 2006, s 8.
115 Ibid, ss 9–11.

The Counter-terrorism Act 2008

The Counter-terrorism Act 2008 amended the definition of terrorism to make it clear that advancing a racial cause, in addition to a political, religious or ideological cause, is within the definition. The Act also made provision for the gathering and sharing of information for counter-terrorism purposes; and introduced a number of extensions to police powers in respect of entry, search and seizure.[116]

The Terrorism Prevention and Investigation Measures Act 2011

The Terrorism Prevention and Investigation Measures Act 2011 (TPIMA) repeals the Prevention of Terrorism Act 2005. Replacing control orders are Terrorism Prevention and Investigation Measures (TPIMs), defined as 'requirements, restrictions and other provisions' which may be imposed. Schedule 1 to the 2011 Act sets out the details, which include overnight residence requirements, travel restrictions and exclusions from specified areas or places, restrictions on financial services and property transfers, restrictions on possession or use of electronic communications devices, restrictions on employment or studies, and reporting and monitoring requirements.

A TPIM may be imposed on an individual if the conditions specified in section 3 are met. These conditions are as follows:

A   that the Secretary of State reasonably believes that the individual is, or has been, involved in terrorism-related activity (the 'relevant activity');

B   that some or all of the relevant activity is new terrorism-related activity;

C   that the Secretary of State reasonably considers that it is necessary, for purposes connected with protecting members of the public from a risk of terrorism, for TPIMs to be imposed on the individual;

D   that the Secretary of State reasonably considers that it is necessary for the specified TPIMs to be imposed;

E   that:

     (a)   the court gives the Secretary of State permission under section 6, or

     (b)   the Secretary of State reasonably considers that the urgency of the case requires TPIMs to be imposed without obtaining permission of the court.

Terrorism-related activity is defined under section 4(1) as including the commission, preparation or instigation of acts of terrorism, conduct which facilitates or encourages acts of terrorism, and conduct which gives support or assistance to individuals known or believed to be involved in terrorism.

A TPIM notice lasts for a period of one year, which may be extended once only and only if conditions A, C and D are met. During the period that a TPIM is in force, the Secretary of State must keep under review whether conditions C and D are met (section 11).

The Secretary of State may vary the measures specified in a TPIM notice, and the individual may apply for a variation of the notice (section 12). A TPIM may be revoked at any time and a notice may also be revived (section 13).

A TPIM may be quashed in 'TPIM proceedings'. The individual may appeal to the court in relation to the extension, variation or revival of measures. Further, if the individual has applied unsuccessfully to the Secretary of State for variation or revocation of measures, the individual

---

116 Section 1 of the 2008 Act is amended by s 56 of the Crime and Security Act 2010.

may appeal to the court. An appeal also lies against a decision by the Secretary of State in relation to matters requiring permission. The court only has the power to quash the extension or revival of the TPIM notice, quash measures in the notice or give direction to the Secretary of State for revocation or variation of measures, or give directions in relation to permissions (section 16). Section 17 makes clear that TPIM decisions are not to be questioned in any legal proceedings other than TPIM proceedings.

The Secretary of State is under a duty to report to Parliament, on a three-monthly basis, on the operation of the Act (section 19). In addition, the Secretary of State must appoint an independent reviewer to carry out an annual review of the working of the Act. The review must be laid before Parliament by the Secretary of State (section 20). The Secretary of State's TPIM powers expire at the end of five years from the date on which the Act was passed. However, the powers may be extended, by statutory instrument, for a further five-year period. Before making such an order the Secretary of State must consult the independent reviewer, the Intelligence Services Commission and the Director-General of the Security Service. An order may not be made unless a draft has been laid before Parliament and approved by a resolution of each House (section 21).

During the period when Parliament is dissolved,[117] the Secretary of State has the power to make a temporary enhanced TPIM order (section 26). These may only be made if the Secretary of State considers it is 'necessary to do so by reason of urgency' and is satisfied, on the balance of probabilities, that an individual is or has been involved in terrorism-related activity.

A 2011 review of counter-terrorism and security powers preceded the TPIM Act.[118] That review also concluded that there could be exceptional circumstances where additional restrictive measures were needed. The Draft Enhanced Terrorism Prevention and Investigation Measures Bill 2012–13 provides for these. The Bill was scrutinised by a Joint Committee. In its Report the Committee accepted the need for such stringent measures but stated that only the 'most extreme circumstances' could justify them and that their use must be 'strictly limited'.[119] The Committee criticised the government's failure to stipulate the circumstances in which such measures would be imposed and called for a full judicial review of the merits of each enhanced TPIM, rather than – as suggested by the government – judicial scrutiny on judicial review principles.

Discussion of control orders and related case law is on the Website.

The Protection of Freedoms Act 2012

The Protection of Freedoms Act (PFA) reduces the period for which a suspected terrorist may be detained from 28 to 14 days (section 57). In an emergency situation, section 58 permits a temporary extension of that period to 28 days. The stop and search powers in sections 44 to 47 of the Terrorism Act 2000 are repealed and the 2000 Act amended to provide a replacement regime (see section 60). Section 62 provides that the Secretary of State must publish a Code of Practice on stop, search and seizure powers. Section 1 of the Act sets out a replacement regime for the retention and destruction of fingerprints and DNA samples (on this see Chapter 21).

The Protection of Freedoms Act 2012 also provides for increased control over the use of surveillance devices operated by the police and local authorities. The PFA amends the Regulation of Investigatory Powers Act 2000 so as to require local authorities to obtain judicial approval for the use of covert investigatory techniques.

---

117 From the date of dissolution until the date of the Queen's Speech at the opening of a new Parliament.
118 See *Review of Counter-Terrorism and Security Powers*, Cm 8004, TSO 2011.
119 *Report on the Draft Enhanced Terrorism Prevention and Investigation Measures Bill*, HL Paper 70/HC 495, 27 November 2012.

National security and the public interest

The state has the right to expel non-British citizens, subject to international obligations,[120] on the grounds of national security, namely that their presence is 'contrary to the public interest' or 'not conducive to the public good'. Prior to 1997 there was no right of appeal to a court of law against the government's decision to deport a person where national security was pleaded.[121] Instead there was a right to a hearing before a panel of three advisers to the Home Secretary.[122]

In 1962, Dr Soblen, an American citizen who had been convicted of espionage in the United States, fled from the country before being sentenced. While on an aeroplane Dr Soblen cut his wrists and was landed in London for hospital treatment. The Home Secretary issued a deportation order on the basis that his continued presence was 'not conducive to the public good'. When Dr Soblen applied for habeas corpus, the Court of Appeal ruled that Dr Soblen had no right to make representations, and that deportation was an administrative matter for the Home Secretary.[123]

In **R v Home Secretary ex parte Hosenball** (1977), two American journalists, Philip Agee and Mark Hosenball, were detained with a view to deportation, on the basis that their work involved obtaining and publishing information prejudicial to national security. There was no appeal against the Home Secretary's decision where national security was pleaded. Instead, there was a right to a hearing before a panel of three advisers to the Home Secretary. When Hosenball tried to challenge the Home Secretary's decision in the courts, the Court of Appeal upheld the deportation order. While recognising that the rules of natural justice[124] had not been complied with in the decision to deport Hosenball, the Court of Appeal nevertheless ruled that the requirements of national security prevailed and that, in matters of national security, the Home Secretary was responsible to Parliament, and not to the courts.

The case of **R v Home Secretary ex parte Cheblak** (1991) also reveals the extensive powers of the Home Secretary to detain persons 'in the interests of national security'. During the Gulf War, 160 Iraqi and Palestinian citizens were detained with a view to deportation, on the basis that their presence was not 'conducive to the public good'. Abbas Cheblak and his family had been resident in the United Kingdom for 16 years. In an application for habeas corpus, the Court of Appeal accepted the Home Secretary's explanation that Cheblak had associations with an unspecified organisation which supported the Iraqi government, and refused to press the Home Secretary for further information.[125] The problem of trying to balance the need for judicial control over proposed deportations of those whose presence is deemed contrary to the public interest and the requirements of national security was met by the Special Immigration Appeals Commission Act 1997, establishing the Commission (SIAC) with jurisdiction to hear immigration appeals[126] where an order had been made on the ground that exclusion, departure or deportation on the basis that the person's removal was 'conducive to the public good' (on the Special Immigration Appeals Commission see below).

In **Rehman v Secretary of State for the Home Department** (2003), the House of Lords considered the Secretary of State's decision to refuse an application for indefinite leave to remain in the United Kingdom on the basis that the applicant represented a threat to national security, in that

---

120 These include the Geneva Convention on Refugees 1951; the European Convention on Human Rights; and EU law.
121 Immigration Act 1971, s 15(3).
122 A process which did not satisfy the requirements of Art 5 of the European Convention on Human Rights.
123 See R v Home Secretary ex parte Soblen (1963). See also Thornberry, 1963.
124 See Chapter 25. The rules of natural justice apply to immigration decisions: Re HK (1967).
125 Mr Cheblak was subsequently released from detention following a hearing before the Home Secretary's panel. See also R v Secretary of State for the Home Department ex parte Jahromi (1995) and Chahal v UK (1997).
126 Relating to refusals of leave to enter, refusal of admission, deportation etc: see s 2(1).

he was allegedly involved in an Islamist terrorist organisation. The Special Immigration Appeals Commission (SIAC) had ruled that the conduct relied on by the Secretary of State had to be conduct targeted at the United Kingdom or its citizens. The House of Lords upheld the Secretary of State's appeal: action against a foreign state could indirectly affect the security of the United Kingdom, and preventative or precautionary action might be justified. While there had to be material from which the Secretary of State could proportionately and reasonably conclude that there was a real possibility of actions harmful to national security, deciding whether deportation would be conducive to the public good was a matter of executive judgment.

In **RB (Algeria) v Secretary of State for the Home Department; U (Algeria) v Same; Othman v Same** (2009), the claimants appealed against the decision of the Secretary of State to deport them on the ground that their deportation would be conducive to the public good because they were a danger to national security. They argued that returning them to their country of origin would involve a real risk that they would be subjected to torture or to inhuman or degrading treatment or punishment, and that their right to fair trial would be breached.

The Special Immigration Appeals Commission (SIAC) had concluded that there were no substantial grounds for believing that the claimants would be exposed to treatment contrary to Article 3. It had considered closed as well as open material.[127] Section 7(1) of the Special Immigration Appeals Act 1997 limits review of SIAC's decisions to questions of law. SIAC's conclusions, therefore, could only be attacked on the grounds that it had failed to have due regard for some rule of law, had regard to irrelevant matters, failed to take into account relevant matters or that its procedures had failed to meet the requirements imposed by law, none of which were applicable in the instant case.

The Special Immigration Appeals Commission

The Special Immigration Appeals Commission (SIAC) (a superior court of record) was established to provide a forum for appeals in situations where the normal principle of open justice cannot operate without risking damage to the security of the state.[128] SIAC deals with appeals where the Secretary of State for the Home Department exercises his or her power to deport a person, or refuses to admit a person to the UK, on national security or other public interest grounds.[129]

The Commission comprises three persons, one of whom must have held high judicial office, one a present or former legally-qualified member of the Asylum and Immigration Tribunal (AIT), and a third member with experience of national security matters.

SIAC considers both 'open' and 'closed' material. Neither the applicants nor their legal advisers are entitled to see the closed material. Instead, the closed material is disclosed to one or more 'Special Advocates' appointed by the Solicitor General to act on behalf of each of the applicants. During closed sessions before SIAC, the Special Advocate can make submissions on behalf of the applicant. However, from the time at which the Special Advocate had sight of the closed material, he is not permitted any further contact with the applicant and his representatives, unless permission to do so is given by SIAC. Note that the closed material procedure cannot be used in ordinary civil claims for damages without statutory authority. The Supreme Court so held, by a majority, in **Al Rawi and others v Security Service** (2011). On reform proposals see below.

---

127 Closed material being material which the Secretary of State relies on but cannot disclose to the appellant for reasons of national security or public interest.
128 See the Special Immigration Appeals Act 1997.
129 SIAC also deals with appeals against decisions refusing a person citizenship under the British Nationality Act 1981 as amended.

The Special Advocate's role is to cross-examine witnesses, make written submissions and make submission at a hearing from which the appellant is excluded.[130] Appeals from SIAC lie to the Court of Appeal on points of law.

- The need to appoint a Special Advocate to assist a claimant was considered in **R (AHK and others) v Secretary of State for the Home Department** (2009). The Secretary of State had refused an application for British citizenship, on the ground that the applicant had failed to demonstrate good character.[131] The legal burden of establishing good character is on the claimant, as is the burden of showing that the decision of the Secretary of State is wrong in law. The Secretary of State was unwilling to disclose the relevant material on public interest grounds. The Court considered the case of **Malik** (2008), and Lord Bingham's opinion that the appointment of a Special Advocate must be necessary and will 'always be exceptional, never automatic; a course of last and never first resort'. In the instant case, the Court of Appeal ruled that a Special Advocate should be appointed 'where it is just, and therefore necessary, to do so in order for the issues to be determined fairly' (see paragraph 37).
- In **RB (Algeria) v Secretary of State for the Home Department; U (Algeria) v Same; Othman v Same** (2009) the House of Lords considered the grounds on which a decision of SIAC could be challenged. The claimants appealed against the decision of the Secretary of State to deport them on the ground that their deportation would be conducive to the public good because they were a danger to national security. The Special Immigration Appeals Commission (SIAC) had concluded that there were no substantial grounds for believing that the claimants would be exposed to treatment contrary to Article 3 or Article 6. It had considered closed as well as open material. Section 7(1) of the Special Immigration Appeals Act 1997 had limited review of SIAC's decisions which the Court of Appeal could undertake to questions of law. Accordingly, SIAC's conclusions could only be attacked on the grounds that it had failed to have due regard for some rule of law, had regard to irrelevant matters, failed to take into account relevant matters or that its procedures had failed to meet the requirements imposed by law.

The use of closed material was considered by the Court of Appeal in **AT v Secretary of State for the Home Department** (2012). AT was alleged to be a 'significant and influential member' of a terrorist group. The allegation was general and any determinative evidence was in closed material which had not been disclosed to AT. Accordingly he could not refute the allegation. The Court of Appeal allowed his appeal. Carnworth LJ, following the reasoning of the European Court of Human Rights in **A v United Kingdom** (2009), stated that:

> Where reliance is placed on closed material to determine an issue of significance, that needs to be made clear in the judgment, and the judge needs to satisfy himself that the subject has had adequate notice of the points against him. (at para 51)

Where a witness, subject to a deportation order, appeared before SIAC and feared reprisals, it is open to the Commission to make an irrevocable non-disclosure order, without prior notice to the Home Secretary, to protect the identity of that witness. Such orders should be exceptional. They had the effect of preventing the Home Secretary from examining the evidence and explaining or refuting it. They were justified, however, on the basis that SIAC needed as much

---

130 SIAC Procedure Rules 2003.
131 As required by the British Nationality Act 1981.

evidence as possible in order to reach the correct decision. The Supreme Court so ruled in *W (Algeria) and Others v Secretary of State for the Home Department* (2012).

Closed Material Proceedings (CMP)

The difficulties caused by the disclosure of sensitive evidence in open court are dealt with by the Justice and Security Act 2013. Public Interest Immunity (PII) is a claim that material should not be disclosed to the court. It is a common law principle, the use of which is controlled by the courts. PII operates in relation to national security, international relations and the prevention or detection of crime. Where a Minister claims PII, on the basis that the disclosure of evidence would cause harm to the public interest, there is no guarantee that a court will uphold that claim – despite the general willingness of the courts to defer to Ministers on matters of national interest. A clear, if rare, example of the court rejecting such a claim occurred in **R (Binyam Mohamed) v Secretary of State for Foreign and Commonwealth Affairs** (2010). In 2008 Binyam Mohamed brought judicial review proceedings against the Foreign Secretary. He sought disclosure of evidence to assist his defence before a US military commission. The Foreign Secretary argued that disclosure should not be ordered on the basis that it would harm the relationship between the US intelligence agencies and the UK. The Foreign Secretary claimed PII in relation to sensitive information contained in the judicial review proceedings. The Court of Appeal rejected the Foreign Secretary's claim for PII. In a civil action for damages against the UK government, alleging complicity in his rendition, detention and torture, the government, without admitting liability, agreed a settlement rather than risk the disclosure of intelligence damaging to national security.

This case highlights the difficulties faced by government in ensuring the maximum openness and transparency in the interests of the rule of law while simultaneously trying to protect state security. The Justice and Security Act 2013, broadens the scope of Closed Material Proceedings (CMP) to remedy the problem of a court refusing to uphold a claim for PII. The proposals are controversial and have attracted many criticisms. However, the government's stated intentions are to ensure that, rather than abandoning a case for fear of revealing sensitive information, CMP will enable all the evidence to be considered by a court of law without the risk of harm to national security.

Section 6 of the Act provides that the Secretary of State may apply to a court hearing a civil case for a declaration that the case is one in which CMP ('section 6 proceedings') may be used. Where it is used, non-government parties, who will be represented by special advocates, leave the court while sensitive material is heard. The use of CMP is to be confined to civil proceedings before the High Court, Court of Appeal, Court of Session or the Supreme Court. Where the court agrees to CMP it may require the person withholding the information to provide a summary of it to other parties to the proceedings and their legal representatives, providing that the summary would not damage national security.

In addition to CMP, the Justice and Security Act 2013, section 17, prevents a court from ordering the disclosure of sensitive information under its residual disclosure jurisdiction, generally referred to as the **Norwich Pharmacal** jurisdiction (derived from **Norwich Pharmacal Co v Customs and Excise Commissioners** (1974)). A Norwich Pharmacal order is one which requires a third party to release information if a party has been involved in an alleged wrongdoing: it assists the individual in bringing or defending proceedings overseas (as in the **Binyam Mohamed** case). The restriction on disclosure would relate to sensitive national security information held by the security services, the armed forces or Ministry of Defence intelligence activities.

The government considers that the provisions of the Justice and Security Act 2013 are compatible with the European Convention on Human Rights.

Summary

The law relating to state, or national, security spans a number of different issues.

For many years the role and powers of the security services were formally unrecognised and unregulated by statute. From 1989, however, Acts of Parliament have been passed to regulate the services: the Security Services Act 1989, Intelligence Services Act 1994 and Regulation of Investigatory Powers Act 2000. In addition to the security services, the related matter of the interception of communications and its regulation are central to the balance to be struck between the rights of individuals to be free from state interference and the requirements of national security.

The law relating to official secrets is also vital to state security. The Official Secrets Act 1911 provided an absolute prohibition on the unauthorised disclosure of official information and was reformed by the Official Secrets Act 1989 which introduces the concept of harmful disclosure in relation to many, but not all, confidential information.

The law relating to terrorism has become an increasingly important area of the law. Until recent years, the law was directed towards protecting against terrorism relating to the situation in Northern Ireland. With the resolution of that conflict, new threats to security have emerged from extremist groups outside and within the United Kingdom. Organised crime, national and international, also increasingly engages the security forces and requires cooperation with security forces both in Europe and world-wide.

Further Reading

Anderson, D, QC, (2012) 'Control Orders in 2011: Final Report of the Independent Reviewer on the Prevention of Terrorism Act 2005', London: TSO.

Arden, M. (2005) 'Human Rights in the Age of Terrorism', Law Quarterly Review, 121: 609.

Bonner, D. (2004) 'Terrorism, Human Rights and the Rule of Law: 120 Years of the UK's Response to Terrorism', Criminal Law Review, 981.

Dickson, B. (2005) 'Law versus Terror: Can Law Win?', European Human Rights Law Review, 12.

Feldman, D. (2005) 'Proportionality and Discrimination in Anti-Terror Legislation', Cambridge Law Journal, 271.

Feldman, D. (2006) 'Human Rights, Terrorism and Risk: The Roles of Politicians and Judges', Public Law, 364.

Gearty, C. (2005) 'Counter Terrorism and the Human Rights Act', Journal of Law and Society, 32(1): 18.

Gearty, C. (2005) 'Human Rights in an Age of Counter Terrorism: Injurious, Irrelevant or Indispensable?', Current Legal Issues, 58: 25.

Ip, J. (2012) 'Al Rawi, Tariq, and the Future of Closed Material Procedures', 75 MLR 606.

Kavanagh, A. (2009) 'Judging the Judges under the Human Rights Act: deference, disillusionment and the "war on terror" ', Public Law, 287.

Supperstone, M. (1994) 'The Intelligence Services Act 1994', Public Law, 329.

Tomkins, A. (2005) 'Readings of A v Secretary of State for the Home Department', Public Law, 259.

Walker, C. (2007) 'The Legal Definition of "Terrorism" in United Kingdom Law and Beyond', Public Law, 331.

Walker, C. (2010) 'The Threat of Terrorism and Fate of Control Orders', Public Law, 4.

White Paper (2004) Counter Terrorist Powers: Reconciling Security and Liberty in an Open Society, Cm 6147.

Zedner, L. (2005) 'Security Liberty in the Face of Terror: Reflections from Criminal Justice', Journal of Law and Society, 32(4): 507.

Part 7

Administrative Law

Chapter 23

Judicial Review: Introduction, Jurisdiction and Procedure[1]

Chapter Contents

---

1   See Craig, 2008; Wade and Forsyth, 2004.

Introduction

Judicial review represents the means by which the courts control the exercise of governmental power. Government departments, local authorities, tribunals, state agencies and agencies exercising powers which are governmental in nature must exercise their powers in a lawful manner. Judicial review has developed to ensure that public bodies which exercise law-making power or adjudicatory powers are kept within the confines of the power conferred. In one sense, therefore, judicial review is relevant to most aspects of the constitution. The Human Rights Act 1998 extends the scope of judicial review in that any failure on the part of a public body to respect human rights will be subject to review by the courts.

Judicial review is concerned with the legality of the decision made, not with the merits of the particular decision. Accordingly, the task of the judges is to ensure that the exercise of any power which has been delegated to ministers and administrative and adjudicatory bodies is lawful according to the power given to that body by Act of Parliament. As will be seen below, there is academic debate concerning the appropriate basis on which the courts exercise their supervisory jurisdiction. The traditional view has been that the judge's task is to ensure that public bodies act within their powers – or *intra vires* – and that, provided that the body has acted within its powers as defined by statute, and according to the common law based rules of natural justice, the body's decision will not be challengeable under the public law process of judicial review.[2]

From this traditional perspective, judicial review is principally concerned with questions of jurisdiction and natural justice. The primary question to be asked is whether a particular person or body with delegated law-making or adjudicatory powers had acted *intra vires* or *ultra vires*, and whether the decision-making process entailed the application of natural justice. If the person or body was acting within its jurisdiction, and respecting the demands of natural justice, the courts would not interfere with the decision – even if the decision was in some respect wrong. Nowadays, although the judges still express their role in the traditional language of 'vires', the approach taken is more robust than before. If a public body, as defined in law, makes an error of law, the courts – through the process of judicial review – will intervene to ensure that the body in question reconsiders a matter and acts in a procedurally correct manner.[3] Furthermore, the Human Rights Act 1998 now requires that all public bodies comply with the right protected by the European Convention on Human Rights and judicial review proceedings may be brought to enforce that legal duty.[4]

The uncertain and expanding role of judicial review causes controversy.[5] Simply expressed, in any society regulated by a complex administrative machinery, an essential feature of that society is that administrators have a sphere of power within which, in the interests of certainty and efficiency, they should be free to operate. The doctrine of ministerial responsibility ensures that accountability for policy and administration lies with the relevant Secretary of State, who is accountable to the electorate through Parliament. However, against that argument for non-interference with matters of administration must be set the demands of individual justice and fairness. If an individual, or a body of persons, is aggrieved by an administrative decision, and their rights adversely affected, there is a requirement that procedures exist whereby such decisions may be challenged in the courts. It is through judicial review that the requirements of legality of the exercise of powers by public bodies is tested. From this perspective, judicial

---

2   See Chapter 25 on natural justice.
3   See Chapter 24 for further discussion of the concept of *ultra vires*.
4   See Human Rights Act 1998, s 7.
5   See eg the differing views of Stephen Sedley J and Professor Ross Cranston expressed in Richardson and Genn, 1994, Chapters 2 and 3, respectively.

review exemplifies the application of the rule of law[6] in a democratic society.[7] This raises a further question of constitutional significance. To what extent is it legitimate for a non-elected judiciary to intervene to correct the administrative process which is controlled through powers granted by the democratically elected Parliament? One response to this question is that judicial review – with respect to the review of delegated law making and adjudicatory powers – ensures that Parliament's will is observed, and judicial review may thus be regarded as an aspect of parliamentary sovereignty.[8]

See Chapter 6.

The balance to be struck between these views is usefully understood using the traffic light analogy. There are those theorists who are generally suspicious of the executive and believe that the state should be controlled and prevented from interfering with individual rights. These theorists are 'red light' because they wish to ensure that the courts are effectively used to control the excesses of the state.[9] The opposing view to 'red light' theory is 'green light' theory. This emerged during the inter-war period.[10] It argues that administrative law should be used as a way of facilitating the operation of the state rather than controlling it. As society has become more complex so it argued that the courts should endeavour to take a less restrictive view of administrative action. The courts should be less interventionist, and although the result may compromise an individual's rights, this is defended on the basis it assists the functioning of the state, which necessarily has a wider commitment to society as a whole. Supporters of 'green light' theory believe that political and democratic forms of accountability are preferable to the courts.[11] In response to these two schools of thought a third way has been advocated:[12] the 'amber light' theory. It lies between the 'red' and 'green' extremes and takes the view that the approach to be used will be directed by an individual case. This suggests that solutions should be found inside and outside the courts and more flexibility in approach will support a more successful outcome.

See Chapter 10.

The role of judicial review

As a result of extensive regulation, powers have been conferred by Parliament upon various government departments, administrative bodies and tribunals – powers which must be exercised within the 'four corners' of the legislation. Traditionally, judicial review has been regarded as unconcerned with the merits of a particular case, or with the justice or injustice of the rules which are being applied, but rather as being concerned with the manner in which decisions have been taken: has this decision maker acted within the powers given? Most of the rules applied by administrators will be statutory, but the courts have also – under common law – developed rules which will apply to decision makers over and above the statutory rules. Thus, decision makers must not only exercise their powers in the correct manner as prescribed by the statute and in accordance with human rights, but must also comply with the rules of reasonableness, natural justice and fairness.

In essence – the courts seek, by judicial review, to ensure four principal objectives:

(a)   that Acts of Parliament have been correctly interpreted;
(b)   that discretion conferred by statute has been lawfully exercised;

---

6 For an early expression of this view, see Dicey, 1885, Appendix 2.
7 See Allan, 2001.
8 See also Craig, 1999, and Jowell, 1999.
9 Supporters of this view include Dicey and Hayek. Both wrote at different points in the history of constitutional law but both believed that any attempt to restrict access to the courts by the executive was pernicious and contrary to the rule of law.
10 Between 1918 and 1939.
11 Ganz discussed in Harlow and Rawlings (2009) p 41.
12 Harlow and Rawlings (2006), p 127.

(c)   that the decision maker has acted fairly;

(d)   that the exercise of power by a public body does not violate human rights.

Judicial Review and the Human Rights Act 1998

As will be seen from the discussion in this and the following chapters, the Human Rights Act 1998 has had a major impact on judicial review. By way of introduction, the impact of the Act can be summarised as follows:

- public bodies – as defined by the courts – have a legal duty to act in accordance with Convention rights and failure to do so may result in proceedings for judicial review;[13]
- consistent with the procedural requirements of the European Convention on Human Rights, only 'victims' of a public body's unlawful act may apply for judicial review in relation to human rights claims;[14]
- an application for judicial review on human rights grounds must be made within a period of one year from the date on which the act complained of took place (for other judicial review proceedings the normal period is three months).[15] The one-year period may be extended by the court;[16]
- the Act was intended to operate vertically (binding only state bodies). However, because section 6(3) of the Act includes courts and tribunals in the definition of public bodies, the courts have a duty to comply with Convention rights and have been able to extend the operation of the Act to private bodies;
- in addition to the remedies which a court may award in other proceedings, in judicial review proceedings based on human rights claims, the High Court and above may make a 'Declaration of Incompatibility' which – while having no effect on the parties to the case – may result in the law being reformed;[17]
- consistent with the interpretative method of the European Court of Human Rights, in addition to the usual techniques of interpretation, the courts now also employ the concept of 'proportionality';
- the Human Rights Act 1998 supplements the statutory and common law requirements of natural justice through incorporation of Article 6 of the Convention which stipulates the requirements of fair trial.

In **Secretary of State for the Home Department v Nasseri** (2009) the House of Lords explained the correct judicial approach to applications for judicial review based on an alleged infringement of a Convention right. Mr Nasseri, an Afghan national, had claimed asylum in Greece. That application was rejected and he travelled to the United Kingdom and again claimed asylum. Under an EC Regulation, where an asylum seeker enters a third country from another Member State, that Member State is solely responsible for determining the application. Accordingly, the Home Office notified the applicant that he would be returned to Greece on the basis that it was a safe country.[18] The applicant sought judicial review of the removal decision which was arguably incompatible with Article 3.

---

13   The definition of public bodies is linked to their function rather than formal legal status.
14   Section 7: this creates a different test of 'sufficient interest' or 'standing' from that required for other judicial review proceedings.
15   Part 54.5 Civil Procedure Rules 1998.
16   Section 7(5)(1),(b) Human Rights Act 1998.
17   Human Rights Act 1998, s 4.
18   Deemed to be a safe country under Sched 3 to the Asylum and Immigration (Treatment of Claimants, etc) Act 2004.

Lord Hoffmann stated that when a court is hearing an application for judicial review, its focus is on whether the decision maker reached a decision according to law: it is concerned with the decision-making process rather than the merits of the decision. However, when an application involves an alleged violation of a Convention right, the court's approach must differ. The focus is not on whether the decision-making process is defective, but on whether or not the applicant's Convention rights have been violated. Lord Hoffmann went on to state that:

> ... when breach of a Convention right is in issue, an impeccable decision-making process by the Secretary of State will be of no avail if she actually gets the answer wrong (at paragraph 14).

The European Court of Human Rights has welcomed the domestic courts' willingness to 'develop and expand conventional judicial review grounds' beyond the traditional **Wednesbury** *unreasonableness* ground (in this case in light of Article 8). In **Kay v United Kingdom** (2010) the European Court found a violation of Article 8 in respect of procedures for seeking the repossession of property under English law.[19] In particular, the applicants had been dispossessed of their homes without any opportunity to have the *proportionality* of the measure determined by an independent tribunal.

The Growth in Public Administration[20]

Judicial review derives from the historical power of the courts to keep inferior bodies within their legal powers. While 'public administration' may be traced back to Elizabethan times,[21] it *or earlier surely* was in the mid-nineteenth century that government expanded its legislative and administrative functions into areas hitherto untouched. The growth in the nineteenth century of industrialisation resulted in central regulation, for example of town and country planning, the provision of housing and housing improvement,[22] public health, regulation of the railways and factory management and schemes for compensation for injury.[23] One consequence of such regulation was the need for mechanisms for resolving disputes between individuals and the regulatory bodies. Statutory inquiries became the formal mechanism by which disputes were to be resolved.[24]

The early twentieth century laid the foundations for the Welfare State. The introduction of health insurance[25] and measures to combat unemployment[26] led to the establishment of tribunals of administration and adjudication. The major reform came with the publication of the Beveridge Report,[27] which set out radical proposals for extensive reforms in social welfare and led to the introduction of the National Health Service. The incoming Conservative government in 1979 embarked on a programme of privatisation of public authorities, including the denationalisation of major public bodies such as British Airways, British Coal, British Gas, British Rail and British Telecom. The further rolling back of state control came through the government divesting itself of its shares in such companies as Jaguar, Rolls-Royce and British

---

19 The case derives from **Kay v Lambeth LBC** (2006), and subsequent cases in which doubts over the correct interpretation of the law were expressed.
20 See, *inter alia*, Dynes and Walker, 1995.
21 Eg the Poor Relief Act 1601.
22 Artisans' and Labourers' Dwelling Improvement Act 1875; Housing of the Working Classes Act 1890.
23 Public Health Acts 1848, 1872, 1875; Factory Act 1833; Workmen's Compensation Acts 1897 and 1906, respectively.
24 Craig (2008), pp 283–301.
25 National Insurance Act 1911.
26 Labour Exchanges Act 1909 and National Insurance Act 1911.
27 *Social Insurance and Allied Services*, Cmnd 6404, 1942, London: HMSO.

Nuclear Fuels. However, while governments have continued to privatise, other bodies have been created to regulate certain bodies and others created as self-regulatory bodies. Examples in the former category include the Independent Television Commission, the Police Complaints Authority, Higher Education Funding Councils and the Financial Services Authority. Examples in the latter category include the Press Complaints Commission and City Panel on Take-Overs and Mergers.

To portray succinctly the administrative system existing nowadays is not an easy task. As with so much of the institutional framework of the state, developments have proceeded in a pragmatic, ad hoc fashion. In 1980, the *Report on Non-Departmental Public Bodies*[28] classified administrative bodies into executive bodies, advisory bodies and tribunals. Today, numerous different tribunals exist, with jurisdiction over such diverse subject matters as commerce, economic matters, education, employment, Foreign Compensation, housing, physical and mental health, immigration, the National Health Service, pensions and residential homes.

What is a 'public body' for the purposes of judicial review?

Judicial review is only available to test the lawfulness of decisions made by public bodies. If judicial review is applied for, and the court rules that the body whose decision is being challenged is a private body, then the remedy of the aggrieved individual will lie in private law, not public law, proceedings. In determining whether or not the body whose decision is being challenged on an application for judicial review is a public as opposed to private body, the court will look at its functions. The test is not whether or not the authority is a government body as such but, rather, whether it is a body exercising powers analogous to those of government bodies. National public agencies have been a feature of administration since the Reform Act of 1832. The Poor Law Commissioners established in 1834, for whom there was no responsible Minister in Parliament (until 1847) are an early example of such an agency. The post-Second World War nationalisation programmes of the Labour government between 1945 and 1951 and the expansion of welfare provision, both then and subsequently, resulted in numerous public bodies being established which were not government bodies, nor were they part of local government. Examples of such bodies include the British Broadcasting Authority, Legal Aid Board (now the Legal Services Commission), Atomic Energy Authority and British Airports Authority. It was estimated that by 1991 there were some 1,444 public bodies which were not related to government departments.[29] In 1979, the incoming Conservative government was firmly committed to privatisation. British Gas, British Airways, British Rail, British Telecom, the water supply industry and electricity industry were all privatised.[30] The drive towards privatisation and reduced state holdings in many other enterprises[31] has not, however, reduced the number of public bodies. Parallelling the privatisation movement has been the growth in standard setting and regulatory bodies designed to ensure appropriate accountability of providers to consumers. The Police Complaints Authority, Lord Chancellor's Advisory Committee on Legal Education and Conduct, Higher Education Funding Council, and Human Fertilisation and Embryology Authority are all examples of bodies created under statute.[32] Furthermore, there have been a number of regulatory bodies established on a voluntary basis.

---

28 Cmnd 7797, 1980, London: HMSO; see also *Report of the Committee on Administrative Tribunals and Enquiries*, Cmnd 218, 1957, London: HMSO.
29 *Public Bodies*, 1991, London: HMSO.
30 Gas Act 1986, Civil Aviation Act 1980, Water Act 1989, Electricity Act 1989.
31 Eg British Petroleum, British Nuclear Fuels Ltd, Cable and Wireless, Rolls-Royce, Jaguar.
32 Police and Criminal Evidence Act 1984, Courts and Legal Services Act 1990, Higher Education Act 1992, Human Fertilisation and Embryology Act 1990.

The Press Complaints Commission, City Panel on Takeovers and Mergers, Advertising Standards Authority, Jockey Club and Football Association are all examples of such bodies. One question which arises is how the courts determine whether a body – howsoever established – is a public body and thus amenable to judicial review of its decisions.

The Courts' Interpretation of Public Bodies

In **R v City Panel on Takeovers and Mergers ex parte Datafin Ltd** (1987), the Takeover Panel had dismissed a complaint made by a bidder of 'acting in concert' contrary to the rules on take-overs. The bidder applied for judicial review. The court declined to grant the application on the basis that there were no grounds for judicial review (on which, see below) but, nevertheless, rejected the claim made by the City Panel that the court had no jurisdiction to consider the application. The Panel was subject to judicial review, despite its lack of statutory or prerogative source of power, because it was a body exercising public functions analogous to those which could be, or could have been in the absence of the Panel, exercised by a government department. Lord Justice Lloyd stated that, for the most part, the source of the power will be decisive. Accordingly, if a body is set up under statute or by delegated legislation, then the source of the power brings the body within the scope of judicial review. However, Lloyd LJ also recognised that in some cases the matter would be unclear. Where that situation existed, it was necessary to look beyond the source of the power and consider the 'nature of the power' being exercised. In Lloyd LJ's view, '[i]f a body in question is exercising public law functions, or if the exercise of its functions have public law consequences, then that may be sufficient to bring the body within the reach of judicial review'.

By contrast with the **City Panel on Takeover and Mergers** case, in **R v Disciplinary Committee of the Jockey Club ex parte Aga Khan** (1993), the Aga Khan sought judicial review of the Jockey Club's decision to disqualify his winning horse from a race for failing a dope test. The court ruled that the relationship between racehorse owners and the Club, and the powers of the Club, derived from agreement between the parties and was a matter of private rather than public law.[33]

More recently, in **R (Julian West) v Lloyd's of London** (2004) the Court of Appeal ruled that decisions taken by Lloyd's of London were not amenable to judicial review either on the basis that it was performing a governmental function or because it was a public authority within the meaning of section 6(1) of the Human Rights Act 1998. The decisions were solely concerned with the commercial relationship between the applicant and Lloyd's and were governed by the contracts into which the applicant had entered. Accordingly the decisions were of a private and not a public nature. The same principle will be applied whenever a matter is regulated by contract between two private parties – the matter is one of private and not public law. There is a fine distinction to be drawn here. The regulation of a private school, for example, has been held to be a matter of private law, whereas the regulation of City Technical Colleges, non-fee-paying publicly funded institutions, is a matter of public law. However, where a pupil attends a private school under a publicly funded assisted places scheme, that school falls within the jurisdiction for judicial review in relation to the school's decision; in particular, the decision to expel a pupil.[34]

---

33 See also **R v Chief Rabbi ex parte Wachmann** (1993); and Barendt et al, 1993. See also **R (Mullins) v Appeal Board of the Jockey Club** (2004).
34 See **R v Governors of Haberdashers' Aske's Hatcham College Trust ex parte T** (1994), per Dyson J.

Under section 6 of the Human Rights Act 1998, public authorities are defined as including courts and tribunals and 'any person certain of whose functions are functions of a public nature'. In **Marcic v Thames Water** (2004), for example, a privatised water and sewerage company was held to be a public body for the purposes of the Act. The Act excludes both Houses of Parliament and those acting in connection with parliamentary proceedings. For the purposes of judicial review, section 7 provides that an applicant is only to have sufficient interest if he or she is a victim of the unlawful act. In relation to proceedings relating to judicial acts, these may be brought only by exercising a right of appeal or by an application for judicial review.[35]

The case law on the interpretation of public bodies for the purposes of the Human Rights Act 1998 is discussed in Chapter 18.

Review and appeal[36]

Judicial review must be distinguished from an appeal against a decision. The court and tribunal structure provides a more or less rational appeal structure for those aggrieved by a judicial decision. The appellate court will have the power to reconsider the case and to substitute its own decision for that of the lower court. An appeal may be made on both the law and the facts of the case, so that a full re-hearing may take place. Judicial review, by contrast, is concerned solely with the manner in which the decision maker has applied the relevant rules: it is thus procedural in nature. It is not for the court – in judicial review proceedings – to substitute its judgment for that of the decision-making body to which powers have been delegated but, rather, to ensure that the adjudicator has kept within the rules laid down by statute and the common law. In short, the role of the courts in judicial review is to exercise a supervisory, not an appellate, jurisdiction. Judicial review 'is not an appeal from a decision, but a review of the manner in which the decision was made'.[37]

The question of whether judicial review or the appeal mechanism was the appropriate method of challenging a judicial decision was considered by the Court of Appeal in **R (Sivasubramaniam) v Wandsworth County Court** (2003). The Court of Appeal ruled that the High Court ought not to entertain an application for permission to apply for judicial review of the decision of a judge in the county court where the applicant had failed to pursue the alternative available remedy of an appeal, or where a county court judge had refused permission to appeal against the decision of a district judge, save in the exceptional circumstances of clear want of jurisdiction, or procedural irregularity amounting to a denial of a fair hearing.

Two issues arose, according to the Master of the Rolls:

1. If an unsuccessful party to a decision by a county court judge sought judicial review of the decision, rather than pursuing the alternative remedy of appeal to the High Court, or in the case of a second appeal to the Court of Appeal, should that application be entertained?
2. Where an appeal court had refused permission to appeal against a decision of the lower court and the unsuccessful party then sought judicial review, should that application be entertained?

The Master of the Rolls recalled that 'authority showed that judicial review was customarily refused as an exercise of judicial discretion where an alternative remedy was available'. The

---

35 Human Rights Act 1998, s 9.
36 See **Chief Constable of the North Wales Police v Evans** (1982).
37 Per Lord Brightman in **Chief Constable of the North Wales Police v Evans** (1982), p 1174.

Access to Justice Act 1999 had introduced a new system of appeals in civil cases. The 1999 Act provided 'a coherent statutory scheme' governing appeals at all levels short of the House of Lords. To allow an applicant to pursue a claim for judicial review was to defeat the object of access to justice and should not be permitted unless there were exceptional circumstances.

Judicial review derives from the courts' inherent powers to keep decision-making bodies within the bounds of their powers, and to provide remedies for abuse of power, and its purpose is not to substitute a decision of the court for the decision of the administrative body.

It should be noted that seeking judicial review is not the only avenue for those complaining about public bodies. The case of **Marcic v Thames Water Utilities Ltd** (2004) illustrates the courts' approach. The appellant sought an injunction to restrain Thames Water from permitting the use of its sewerage system in such a way as to cause flooding to his property, and a mandatory order compelling Thames Water to improve the sewerage system, and damages. Thames Water operates its system under statutory powers and subject to statutory duties. The Water Industry Act 1991 provides for a Director General of Water Services with wide-ranging powers and duties, not least of which the power to make Enforcement Orders requiring providers to comply with the requirements of the Act. The House of Lords ruled that the appellant had chosen to side-step the statutory scheme by pursuing judicial review proceedings against the Secretary of State rather than seeking to enforce the statutory duty of the water authority. The House of Lords emphasised that the courts were ill-equipped to deal with statutory undertakings which involved large-scale capital expenditure: Parliament had entrusted that function to the Director.

The outcome of judicial review

Differences also exist in the respective outcomes of appeal and judicial review. In the case of appeals, where the appeal is successful, it will usually result in a new decision being substituted for the previous decision.[38] In the case of review, a successful case will usually result in the previous decision being nullified – or quashed – but no new decision will be put in its place. Instead, the body in relation to which a successful application for judicial review has been made will be directed to redetermine the case according to the correct rules and procedure, and it is by no means inevitable that the decision reached according to the lawful procedure will be more favourable to the individual than the original decision.

Furthermore, there is no automatic right to a remedy in judicial review proceedings: the remedy is discretionary. This matter is contentious.[39] In some cases, the court will decline to grant a remedy. The court may hold, for example, that while the decision-making process was defective, nevertheless the applicant has suffered no injustice, or that even if a remedy were granted, the decision maker would reach the same conclusion on the merits, or that the impact on administration would be too great if a remedy were granted.

The Basis for Judicial Review

The Senior Courts Act 1981[40]

The basis for review today lies in section 31 of the Senior Courts Act 1981 and the Civil Procedure Rules 1998.

---

38 In some instances, a new trial may have to be ordered in order for a fresh decision to be reached.
39 See Bingham, 1991.
40 The Supreme Court Act 1981 was renamed the Senior Courts Act under the Constitutional Reform Act 2005. See Sched 11, Part I.

Section 31 provides, in part, that:

(1) An application to the High Court for one or more of the following forms of relief, namely:

   (a) an order of mandamus, prohibition or *certiorari*;
   (b) a declaration or injunction under sub-section (2); or
   (c) an injunction under section 30 restraining a person not entitled to do so from acting in an office to which that section applies,

   shall be made in accordance with rules of court by a procedure to be known as an application for judicial review.

(2) A declaration may be made or an injunction granted under this subsection in any case where an application for judicial review, seeking that relief, has been made and the High Court considers that, having regard to:

   (a) the nature of the matters in respect of which relief may be granted by orders of mandamus, prohibition or *certiorari*;
   (b) the nature of the persons and bodies against whom relief may be granted by such orders; and
   (c) all the circumstances of the case,

   it would be just and convenient for the declaration to be made or for the injunction to be granted, as the case may be.

(3) No application for judicial review shall be made unless the leave of the High Court has been obtained in accordance with rules of court; and the court shall not grant leave to make such an application unless it considers that the applicant has a sufficient interest in the matter to which the application relates.

Under the Civil Procedure Rules 1998, an action must be brought within three months of the decision against which review is sought. However, shorter time periods may be specified in statute and these must be complied with.

Applying for leave for judicial review

It must be noted here that there is no unfettered right to judicial review. The aggrieved individual must seek leave to apply for judicial review, and a number of criteria, which are discussed below, govern the exercise of the discretion to grant or refuse the application for judicial review.

The requirement to seek leave for judicial review is controversial, and there are cogent arguments for its reform. For example, the JUSTICE-All Souls Report[41] argued for its repeal on the basis, first, that the leave requirement is discriminatory; second, that the justification for leave based on eliminating 'groundless, unmeritorious or tardy harassment' on the part of applicants can be dealt with in the same manner as in ordinary litigation;[42] and third, that the issue of standing is no longer finally determined at the stage at which the application for leave is considered; see further below. However, there is support for the view that, while the need to seek leave represents a procedural hurdle which does not exist in other areas of the law, there remains a need to filter out unmeritorious cases at an early stage. The Law Commission

---

41 *Administrative Law: Some Necessary Reforms*, 1988. See also Law Commission, *Administrative Law: Judicial Review and Statutory Appeals*, Consultation Paper No 226/HC 669.
42 As provided for by RSC Ord 18, r 19.

re-examined the question of application for leave and concluded that it remains 'essential to filter out hopeless applications for judicial review by a requirement such as leave'.[43]

When seeking leave to apply the application must be served on the defendant and unless the court orders otherwise, any person the claimant considers to be an interested party. Permission will be granted where an arguable case has been shown. If permission is refused, the claimant can request reconsideration at a hearing. Furthermore, a dissatisfied claimant may apply to the Court of Appeal for permission to appeal against the refusal of permission.[44]

Standing to Apply for Judicial Review

The 'sufficient interest' test[45]

Prior to 1977 the rules on standing were largely in the hands of judges and the way the rules operated largely depended on the remedy being sought.[46] The test was one of whether the person was 'aggrieved' and not a 'mere busybody'.[47] The 1977 Rules of the Supreme Court Order 53 r3(7) and the Senior Courts Act 1981 placed the test for standing on a statutory footing. The Senior Courts Act 1981 provides that the court must not grant leave for an application for judicial review 'unless it considers that the applicant has a sufficient interest [otherwise expressed as "standing" or *locus standi*] in the matter to which the application relates'. The justification for such a requirement lies in the need to limit challenges to administrative decision making to genuine cases of grievance and to avoid unnecessary interference in the administrative process by those whose objectives are not authentic. The applicant may be an individual whose personal rights and interests have been affected by a decision, or an individual concerned with official decisions which affect the interests of society as a whole. Alternatively, the application may be brought by an interest or pressure group desiring to challenge a decision which affects the rights and interests of members of that group or society at large. To limit access to the courts using a test for standing is controversial. On the one hand there are practical objections to opening the doors of the courts too wide for fear of vexatious litigants[48] but at the same time public bodies should be held accountable for the decisions they make.

The manner in which the test is applied

The test of 'sufficient interest' was provided in **R v Inland Revenue Commissioners ex parte National Federation of Self-Employed and Small Businesses** (1982). The House of Lords' approach was as follows. The question of whether there is standing should be examined in two stages. At the first instance, standing should be considered when leave to apply is sought. At that stage, the court is concerned, according to Lord Scarman, to ensure that 'it prevents abuse by busybodies, cranks and other mischief makers'. If leave is granted, the court may – at a second stage, when the merits of the case are known – revise its original decision and decide that after all the applicants do not have sufficient interest. The effect of this is to reduce the issue of sufficient interest and to elevate the question of the merits of the case.

---

43 Law Commission, *Administrative Law: Judicial Review and Statutory Appeals*, Consultation Paper No 226/HC 669.
44 See Bridges, Meszaros and Sunkin, 2000 and Cornford and Sunkin, 2001.
45 Senior Courts Act 1981, s 31(3).
46 See **Ware v Regents Canal Company** (1858); **Boyce v Paddington Borough Council** (1903); **R v Thames Magistrates Court ex parte Greenbaum** (1957); **Thorne v British Broadcasting Corporation** (1967); **Blackburn v Attorney General** (1971); **Attorney General (ex rel McWhirter) v Independent Broadcasting Authority** (1973).
47 **R v Liverpool Corporation ex parte Liverpool Taxi Fleet Owners Association** (1972).
48 A vexatious litigant is someone who has been prevented by the court from bringing an action due to a history of bringing superfluous and largely irrelevant cases before the court.

Individual standing: personal rights and interests

Given the breadth of administrative decision making in a heavily regulated society, individuals may have their rights or expectations affected in multifarious ways, as has been seen above. Further examples from the case law illustrate the concept of individual standing. In **Schmidt v Secretary of State for Home Affairs** (1969), students who had entered the country as 'students of scientology' challenged the decision of the Home Office not to allow them to remain once the permitted period of stay had expired. The students had 'sufficient interest' for leave to be granted.

In the case of **R v Secretary of State for the Environment ex parte Ward** (1984) a Gypsy living on a caravan site was held to have standing to apply for an order requiring that the Secretary of State should direct the local authority to fulfil its statutory duty to provide an adequate site. Standing was also granted to Mrs Gillick, the mother of several daughters, who wished to challenge a Health Authority over its policy relating to contraception for young girls,[49] and to a journalist acting in the public interest.[50] By contrast, in **Holmes v Checkland** (1987) an opponent of cigarette smoking was deemed not to have standing to seek to restrain the BBC from broadcasting a snooker championship sponsored by a tobacco company on the ground that he had no more interest than any other member of the public and accordingly could only proceed with the aid of the Attorney General.[51]

In **R v Secretary of State for Foreign and Commonwealth Affairs ex parte Rees-Mogg** (1994), the applicant sought judicial review of the government's ratification of the Treaty on European Union without parliamentary consent. Rees-Mogg was held to have sufficient standing, but the application was dismissed on the basis that the issue was non-justiciable.[52]

The Human Rights Act 1998 introduced a new basis for 'standing'. Section 7 of the Act provides that only a 'victim' of an act of a public body may make a claim.[53] That test – which is the same as the test applied under the European Convention on Human Rights – is narrower than standing in other judicial review proceedings. It also excludes representative bodies and interest groups taking action on behalf of their members.[54]

The standing of interest and pressure groups

Actions in defence of the group's own interests

A group may have its interests adversely affected by administrative decision making. By way of illustration, in **R v Liverpool Corporation ex parte Liverpool Taxi Fleet Operators' Association** (1972), Liverpool Corporation had the duty of licensing taxis and fixing the number of licences to be granted. When the Corporation announced that the number of licences was to be increased, without consulting the Operators' Association, leave to apply for judicial review was sought. The Association had sufficient standing. Equally, in **Royal College of Nursing v Department for Health and Social Security** (1981), the Royal College had standing to challenge a departmental circular concerning the role of nurses in abortions.

Both these cases involve organisations seeking to challenge decisions which affect their own members. Accordingly, the standing requirement is relatively easy to satisfy, since each of their members would have individual standing. The position is less straightforward where a group seeks to defend what it regards as the wider interests of society.

---

49 *Gillick v West Norfolk and Wisbech Area Health Authority* (1986).
50 *R v Felixstowe Judges ex parte Leigh* (1987).
51 Note that the Attorney General's decision whether to bring a relator action cannot be challenged in court: *Gouriet v Union of Post Office Workers* (1978).
52 For the meaning of 'justiciability', see above. See also *Blackburn v Attorney General* (1971), wherein a challenge to accession to the Treaty of Rome was unsuccessful.
53 See *Adams v Lord Advocate* (2003); *Lancashire City Council v Taylor* (2005).
54 See *R (Johnson) (Deceased) v SSHD & Cumbria County Council (Interested Party)* (2006).

The standing of interest and pressure groups acting in the public interest

Inland Revenue Commissioners v *National Federation of Self-Employed and Small Businesses* (1982) provided the test for standing. The facts, in brief, entailed the employment of casual labour on newspapers, where the workers frequently adopted false names and paid no income tax. The Inland Revenue Commissioners (IRC) entered into an agreement with the relevant trade unions, workers and employers to the effect that if the workers filled in tax returns for the previous two years, the IRC would not pursue tax due for previous years. The National Federation (an association of taxpayers) argued that the IRC had no power to enter into this agreement and sought judicial review. The IRC defended the action on the basis that the National Federation did not have sufficient interest – or standing (*locus standi*) – to apply for judicial review. The court upheld the IRC's claim. The House of Lords ruled that the court had been correct in granting leave at the first stage, but that on the facts – the second stage – the National Federation lacked sufficient interest to challenge the legality of the agreement. The House of Lords ruled that there was no standing to challenge the particular wrongdoing alleged but that, if the Revenue had in fact been acting with impropriety, there would have been standing in a taxpayer to challenge its unlawful acts. In *R* v *Her Majesty's Treasury ex parte Smedley* (1985), the applicant for review sought to challenge the decision of the Treasury to pay a sum of money from the Consolidated Fund, without express parliamentary approval, to meet European Community obligations. Smedley was thus applying in his own interest and in the interests of all British taxpayers and electors.[55] The court held that he had standing, although the challenge failed on its merits. A case to be distinguished from the *National Federation* case is that of *R* v *Attorney General ex parte ICI plc* (1986). The application was based on a complaint that four competitor companies had been assessed at too lenient a rate, contrary to the Oil Taxation Act 1975. The court held that the company had standing: it had a genuine and substantial complaint.

The judges are, however, not united in their approach to the 'sufficient interest' test, which confers on the courts a great deal of discretion. In *R* v *Secretary of State for the Environment ex parte Rose Theatre Trust Company Ltd* (1990), Schiemann J cited a number of propositions which he deduced from the *IRC* case. The *Rose Theatre* case concerned the question of whether a company which had been incorporated for the purpose of campaigning to save the historic Globe Theatre site in London had sufficient interest, or *locus standi*. Included in the guidelines were that the question of whether sufficient interest exists is not purely a matter within the discretion of the court; that sufficient interest did not necessarily entail a direct financial or legal interest; that the assertion of an interest by a person or a group does not mean that sufficient interest exists; and that, even where thousands of people joined together in a campaign, that was not conclusive that sufficient interest existed. The court ruled that the company did not have sufficient interest. However, in *R* v *Poole Borough Council ex parte BeeBee* (1991), the same judge ruled that two pressure groups, the World Wildlife Fund (WWF) and the British Herpetological Society (BHS), had sufficient interest to challenge a decision of the Council which had granted planning permission to itself for the development of a heathland with designated 'special scientific interest' status. The BHS had a financial interest in the site, and the WWF had undertaken to pay any legal costs if necessary.[56]

A liberal approach to sufficient interest was also taken in *R* v *Secretary of State for the Environment ex parte Greenpeace Ltd (No 2)* (1994). Greenpeace applied for judicial review to challenge the decision of the Inspectorate of Pollution to allow the siting of a nuclear reprocessing plant (THORP) at Sellafield in Cumbria. It was held that the Inspectorate had not

---

55 Per Sir John Donaldson MR.
56 But for another decision denying sufficient interest to interest groups see *R* v *Darlington Borough Council ex parte Association of Darlington Taxi Owners* (1994).

abused its powers in varying British Nuclear Fuel plc's licence. However, while Greenpeace lost the case, the court nevertheless ruled that Greenpeace did have standing to challenge the decision. It was in the interests of justice to allow Greenpeace – an organisation with over 400,000 supporters in the United Kingdom – to bring an action on behalf of all concerned with the project. The court declined to follow the **Rose Theatre** decision, but warned that it should not be assumed that Greenpeace or other pressure groups would automatically be held to have sufficient interest in any future case.

Further cases involving successful challenges by pressure groups include **R v Secretary of State for Foreign and Commonwealth Affairs ex parte World Development Movement Ltd** (1995), **R v Secretary of State for Employment ex parte Equal Opportunities Commission** (1995) (the **EOC** case) and **R v Secretary of State for the Environment ex parte the Royal Society for the Protection of Birds** (the **RSPB** case) (1995). In the first case, the World Development Movement (WDM) sought judicial review of the Foreign Secretary's decision to grant financial aid to Malaysia for the building of the Pergau dam. The WDM argued that the Secretary of State had exceeded his powers. The court held that the WDM had sufficient interest. The WDM played a prominent role in giving advice and assistance in relation to aid and had consultative status with the United Nation's bodies. Further, it was unlikely that there would be any other person or body with sufficient interest to challenge the decision. In the **EOC** case, the Equal Opportunities Commission (EOC) sought a declaration that the United Kingdom was in breach of European Community law (now EU law) obligations in relation to Article 119 (now Article 141) of the EC Treaty and the Equal Pay and Equal Treatment Directives of the Community. The alleged breach concerned the Employment Protection (Consolidation) Act 1978, which discriminated between full time and part time employees in relation to redundancy pay and compensation for unfair dismissal. The House of Lords confirmed that the EOC had sufficient interest and, moreover, that English law was incompatible with the requirements of European Community law. In the **RSPB** case, the Royal Society had sufficient interest to challenge the decision of the Secretary of State's affecting the development of land which had hitherto been a special site for the conservation of birds.

The Existence of Alternative Remedies

The availability of alternative remedies is a relevant factor in deciding whether leave will be granted for judicial review. In **R v Inland Revenue Commissioners ex parte Preston** (1985), Lord Templeman stated that leave for an application for judicial review should not be granted 'where an alternative remedy was available'. Thus, by way of example, where Parliament has set up under statute a comprehensive appeals structure, judicial review cannot be used as a means of circumventing this.[57] Moreover, the statutory rights of appeal must be exhausted.[58] If, however, there are exceptional circumstances – for example if inordinate delays are experienced in the proceedings – the court may grant leave to apply for judicial review.[59]

A Matter of Public – Not Private – Law

Judicial review is confined to matters of public – as opposed to private – law. The courts will not seize jurisdiction to review an administrative action or decision if the matter involved is

---

57 R v Secretary of State for Social Services ex parte Connolly (1986).
58 R v Secretary of State for the Home Department ex parte Swati (1986).
59 R v Chief Constable of Merseyside Police ex parte Calveley (1986).

one of private law. Accordingly, the respondent must be a public authority, and the right at issue must be a public right. If the matter is one of public law, the aggrieved person must apply by way of judicial review and not under any other procedure.

The 'exclusivity principle'

In **O'Reilly v Mackman** (1983), the applicants had taken part in a prison riot at Hull gaol and the Board of Visitors (who exercise disciplinary powers over prisoners) reduced the remission of sentence as punishment. The applicants tried to establish that the Board of Visitors had acted contrary to the rules of natural justice. This they attempted to do by means of an originating summons or writ.[60] It was not contested that the issue was a matter of public law and that they could have employed the judicial review procedure, provided that they applied for leave within the requisite three months. No leave from the court is needed in relation to private law proceedings. The issue for the court was whether it was an abuse of the process of the court to use the alternative basis to bring the action. Lord Diplock stated:

> If what should emerge is that his complaint is not of an infringement of any of his rights that are entitled to protection in public law, but may be an infringement of his rights in private law and this is not a proper subject for judicial review, the court has power under rule 9(5), instead of refusing the application, to order the proceedings to continue as if they had begun by writ . . . [pp 283–84]

Referring to the procedural disadvantages which had existed prior to the reforms introduced in 1977 by Order 53,[61] Lord Diplock went on to state:

> . . . now that those disadvantages to applicants have been removed and all remedies for infringement of rights protected by public law can be obtained upon an application for judicial review, as also can remedies for infringements of rights under private law if such infringement should also be involved, it would in my view as a general rule be contrary to public policy, and as such an abuse of the process of the court to permit a person seeking to establish that a decision of a public authority infringed rights to which he was entitled to protection under public law to proceed by way of an ordinary action and by this means evade the provisions of Order 53 for the protection of such authorities. [p 285]

The decision in **O'Reilly** has been trenchantly criticised by Professor HWR Wade.[62] The 'exclusivity principle' – keeping public and private law rigidly distinct – was introduced by Lord Diplock in **O'Reilly**, notwithstanding the Law Commission's intention that procedural reforms introduced in 1977 were not intended to create a rigid distinction between public and private law proceedings.[63] Before that time, although the distinction between public and private law was drawn, the system was not exclusive. Professor Wade regards the exclusivity principle, declared in **O'Reilly**, as amounting to a 'serious setback for administrative law'. He goes on to state that:

> . . . it has caused many cases, which on their merits might have succeeded, to fail merely because of choice of the wrong form of action . . . It has produced great

---

60 The means by which private law proceedings are initiated.
61 Now replaced by the Civil Procedure Rules 1998.
62 Wade and Forsyth, 2004.
63 Cmnd 6407, 1976, London: HMSO.

> uncertainty, which seems likely to continue, as to the boundary between public and private law, since these terms have no clear or settled meaning . . . [Wade and Forsyth, 1994, p 682]

Professor Wade regards this as an unnecessary restriction on access to the courts, a restriction which has been avoided in Scotland, Australia, New Zealand and Canada. His assessment of the House of Lords' decision in **O'Reilly** is that:

> . . . the House of Lords has expounded the new law as designed for the protection of public authorities rather than of the citizen. Such are the misfortunes which can flow from the best intentioned reforms.

Exceptions to the exclusivity principle

The harshness with which the exclusivity principle could operate led Lord Diplock in **O'Reilly** to state that exceptions to the rule would exist where the case involved both public and private law elements, particularly where the public law element was collateral (auxiliary or secondary) to the private law element. What is evident in this matter is that a balance needs to be struck between too rigid a rule, which denies individuals the protection of judicial review, and too lax an approach, which would enable individuals either to pursue a remedy in judicial review when other procedures are in fact more appropriate or, conversely, to pursue other remedies when judicial review would be appropriate, in order to evade the requirements of judicial review. It is also evident that the judges are struggling to find the correct balance.

A public law issue used in defence in private law proceedings

In **Wandsworth London Borough Council v Winder** (1985), the House of Lords allowed a matter of public law (the lawfulness of the council's decision) to be used as a defence to private law proceedings (possession proceedings). Winder was a tenant of the local authority, which gave notice that rents were to be raised. Winder claimed that the increase was unreasonable and contrary to law. The local authority brought an action for possession of the premises. Winder defended this action on the basis that the rent increase was outside the powers of the local authority and void for unreasonableness. On appeal to the House of Lords, the question for the court was whether Winder could challenge the local authority's action by way of a defence based on judicial review grounds, or whether he should have instigated separate judicial review proceedings by way of an application to the High Court. The local authority submitted that Winder should have used judicial review but that, since he was by then out of time to do so, he could not challenge their decision by way of a defence to the possession proceedings.

Lord Fraser of Tullybelton, citing **O'Reilly**, acknowledged that it was in the interests of good administration to protect authorities from unmeritorious or late challenges, but that this factor had to be weighed in the balance against the argument for preserving the ordinary rights of private citizens to defend themselves against unfounded claims. In his opinion, Winder's action could not be described as an abuse of the process of the court. Winder had not selected the procedure, he was merely seeking to defend himself. If the public interest required that people should not have the right to defend themselves, then that was a matter for Parliament, not the courts.

Cases involving both public and private law issues

In **Roy v Kensington and Chelsea and Westminster Family Practitioner Committee** (1992) a further exception to the exclusivity principle emerged, whereby the House of Lords ruled that the principle did not apply where the proceedings involved matters of both public and private law.

In **Roy**, a Family Practitioner Committee was responsible for making payments to general practitioners in respect of their National Health Service work.[64] Dr Roy's allowance was reduced by the committee on the basis that he had reduced the amount of his time spent on National Health Service work. Dr Roy litigated to recover the sum reduced. At first instance, the judge decided that the decision to reduce his payments was a matter of public law to be challenged under judicial review proceedings. On appeal to the House of Lords, it was held that, when a litigant had a private law right – in relation to a matter which involved an issue of public law – he was not precluded from pursuing his private law right. Accordingly, the fact that the public law issue could have been determined under judicial review proceedings was not held to deny him a remedy under private law. In **Andreou v Institute of Chartered Accountants in England and Wales** (1998), the applicant had been granted leave to bring judicial review to challenge the validity of a bylaw of the Chartered Institute, but failed to observe the time limit. He then commenced a private law action alleging breach of contractual duty to exercise its bylaw-making powers fairly and to act fairly in its disciplinary proceedings. The Court of Appeal ruled that the Institute was, in part, a public body. However, here it was appropriate to proceed under private law since there was a private law right at issue, even though there was also a public law issue involved.

In **R v Peter Edward Wicks** (1997), the House of Lords ruled that the validity of an enforcement notice under the Town and Country Planning Act 1990 could not be impugned in criminal proceedings, but only by the High Court on an application for judicial review. The defendant appealed against the Court of Appeal decision dismissing his appeal against conviction for failure to comply with the enforcement notice. So long as the enforcement notice was not a nullity or patently defective on its face, it was valid and would remain so until quashed. No criminal court had the power to quash, and it was not open to the defence to go behind the notice and seek to investigate its validity. The proper course to take was to apply for an adjournment of the criminal proceedings and apply to the High Court for judicial review in which the validity of the notice could be attacked.[65]

A challenge to the vires of subordinate legislation or an administrative act can be raised in criminal proceedings. The House of Lords so held in **Boddington v British Transport Police** (1998). The defendant, in criminal proceedings on charges of smoking a cigarette in a railway carriage where smoking was prohibited, sought to argue that the Network South Central's decision to post notices banning smoking was ultra vires its powers to bring the relevant bylaw into force. On appeal, the court had ruled that it was not open to the defendant to raise that public law defence in criminal proceedings against him. The House of Lords, however, stated that a defendant was so entitled, and that if the defendant managed to rebut the presumption in favour of the lawfulness of the subordinate legislation or administrative act, the legislation or act had no legal effect at all and could not found a prosecution. In the instant case, there was nothing in the bylaws or the relevant Act to rebut the presumption that the defendant was entitled to defend himself against a criminal charge on the basis of the validity of the decision to put no smoking notices in carriages. However, the manner in which the relevant bylaw had been brought into force was not ultra vires and accordingly the appeal was dismissed.

Broad versus restrictive approaches

O'Reilly and **Winder** were both considered extensively in **Roy v Kensington and Chelsea and Westminster Family Practitioner Committee** (above), in which Lord Lowry examined the 'broad' or

---

64 Under the National Health Service (General Medical and Pharmaceutical) Regulations 1974.
65 See also **Steed v Secretary of State for the Home Department** (2000); **R v Falmouth and Truro Port Health Authority ex parte Southwest Water Ltd** (2000); **Wandsworth LBC v A** (2001).

'liberal' approach to judicial review and the 'narrow' or 'restrictive' approach. A broad approach lessens the importance of the distinction between public and private law and would allow either the Order 53 procedure to be used or the pursuit of a private law remedy. A narrow approach, however, would dictate that if the matter is primarily a matter of private law then the judicial review procedure is inappropriate. While Lord Lowry 'disclaimed any intention of discussing the scope of the rule in *O'Reilly*', he nevertheless went on to make a case for a more liberal approach. Lord Lowry stated that:

> . . . the Law Commission, when recommending the new judicial review procedure, contemplated the continued co-existence of judicial review proceedings and actions for a declaration with regard to public law issues . . .

> . . . this House has expressly approved actions for a declaration of nullity as alternative to applications for *certiorari* to quash, where private law rights were concerned: **Wandsworth London Borough Council v Winder** (1992), p 655, per Robert Goff LJ.

Citing Goff LJ, Lord Lowry continued:

> The principle remains in fact that public authorities and public servants are, unless clearly exempted, answerable in the ordinary courts for wrongs done to individuals. But by an extension of remedies and a flexible procedure it can be said that something resembling a system of public law is being developed. Before the expression 'public law' can be used to deny a subject a right of action in the court of his choice it must be related to a positive prescription of law, by statute or by statutory rules. We have not yet reached the point at which mere characterisation of a claim as a claim in public law is sufficient to exclude it from consideration by the ordinary courts: to permit this would be to create a dual system of law with the rigidity and procedural hardship for plaintiffs which it was the purpose of the recent reforms to remove': **Davy v Spelthorn Borough Council** (1984), per Lord Wilberforce.

> In conclusion, my Lords, it seems to me that, unless the procedure adopted by the moving party is ill suited to dispose of the question at issue, there is much to be said in favour of the proposition that a court having jurisdiction ought to let a case be heard rather than entertain a debate concerning the form of the proceedings.

Lord Slynn advanced the argument for a more flexible approach to the choice of proceedings in **Mercury Communications Ltd v Director General of Telecommunications** (1996). In that case, the effect of **O'Reilly v Mackman** was further limited. A dispute arose between Mercury Communications and British Telecom (BT), both of which are public limited companies licensed by the Secretary of State under the Telecommunications Act 1984. Mercury Communications was dependent upon the rental of part of BT's network. The Director General, exercising powers under the 1984 Act, determined the dispute, and his decision affected the terms of the contract between Mercury and BT. Mercury initiated private proceedings in the Commercial Court by originating summons. At first instance, the Director General and BT failed to have the proceeding struck out, the court applying the **O'Reilly** principle. On appeal, however, it was argued, successfully, that this was an abuse of process. The case went to the House of Lords, which reversed the decision of the Court of Appeal. Lord Slynn emphasised that when determining the issue of the choice of private or public law proceedings, flexibility must be retained. It was recognised that the Director General had statutory functions and performed public duties. However, this did not eliminate the possibility of private law proceedings. Since the Director General's decision had been imposed as part of a contract, this could be regarded as a contractual dispute. Accordingly, the commencement of private law proceedings was equally well suited to determine the issue as judicial review proceedings. The issue of the appropriateness of proceedings was a matter to be determined by the courts on a case by case basis. Lord Slynn stated that:

> . . . when it comes to a question of striking out for abuse of process of the court the discretion exercised by the trial judge should stand unless the arguments are clearly and strongly in favour of a different result to that to which he has come. [p 59]

The House of Lords reconsidered the question of the appropriate form of proceedings once more in **O'Rourke v Camden London Borough Council** (1997). In this case, the plaintiff had applied to the local authority for accommodation, under the Housing Act 1985, on his release from prison. Section 63(1) of the Housing Act provides that a local authority is under a duty to provide accommodation in respect of those who are 'homeless and [have] a priority need', and that includes persons who are 'vulnerable as a result of . . . physical disability or other special reason'. Initially, the authority refused him accommodation, but subsequently provided accommodation for a 12-day period, after which the plaintiff was evicted and no alternative accommodation offered. The plaintiff brought a private action against the council for wrongful eviction without providing alternative accommodation, and claimed damages. The House of Lords ruled that the question of whether section 63 of the Housing Act gave rise to public or private law proceedings depended on the intention of Parliament. The duty to provide accommodation was a matter of public law and the Act 'was a scheme of social welfare, intended on grounds of public policy and public interest to confer benefits at the public expense not only for the private benefit of people who found themselves homeless but also for the benefit of society in general'. The provision of accommodation, and the type of accommodation, was 'largely dependent on the housing authority's judgment and discretion'. Accordingly, it was 'unlikely' that Parliament had intended section 63 to give rise to a private action.

The issue of the choice between public and private proceedings returned to the courts in **Trustees of the Dennis Rye Pension Fund v Sheffield City Council** (1997). The plaintiffs were required by the local council to carry out repairs to certain houses to make them fit for human habitation,[66] and applied for improvement grants from the council under the Local Government and Housing Act 1989. When the work was complete, the council refused to pay the grant, on the basis that, inter alia, the repairs had not been carried out to the required standard. The plaintiff then commenced private law proceedings for recovery of the money due. The council, however, argued that if there were any grounds for complaint, the appropriate process was an application for judicial review. Accordingly, the council sought to have the plaintiff's claim struck out, on the grounds that the private law proceedings were an abuse of process. The issue went to the Court of Appeal. Lord Woolf MR regretted that the 'tactical' issue of the choice of proceedings had inevitably led to very substantial costs being incurred 'to little or no purpose'. He further criticised the narrow approach taken by the House of Lords in **O'Rourke v Camden London Borough Council**.

The Court of Appeal considered the choice between judicial review proceedings and other legal action against a public authority. In determining that question, the court should not be overly concerned with the distinction between public and private rights, but look to the practical consequences of pursuing the alternative actions. The court accepted that when a council was performing its role in relation to the making of grants, it was performing a public

---

66 Under the Housing Act 1989, s 189.

function which did not give rise to private rights. If the choice made had 'no significant disadvantages' for the parties, the public or the courts, it should not normally be regarded as an abuse of process. The court applied **O'Reilly v Mackman** (1982) and **Roy v Kensington and Chelsea and Westminster Family Practitioner Committee** (1992). Lord Woolf MR, after a consideration of these and other cases, ruled that as a general rule it is contrary to public policy, and as a result an abuse of the process of the court:

> . . . to permit a person seeking to establish that a decision of a public authority infringed rights to which he was entitled to protection under public law to proceed by way of an ordinary action and by this means to evade the provisions of Order 53 for the protection of such authorities.

However, Lord Woolf made three 'pragmatic suggestions' and stated that it is to be remembered that:

> If it is not clear whether judicial review or an ordinary action is the correct procedure it will be safer to make an application for judicial review than commence an ordinary action since there then should be no question of being treated as abusing the process of the court by avoiding the protection provided by judicial review . . .

> If a case is brought by an ordinary action and there is an application to strike out the case, the court should, at least if it is unclear whether the case should have been brought by judicial review, ask itself whether, if the case had been brought by judicial review when the action was commenced, it is clear leave would have been granted. If it would, then that is at least an indication that there has been no harm to the interests judicial review is designed to protect . . .

> Finally, in cases where it is unclear whether proceedings have been correctly brought by an ordinary action, it should be remembered that, after consulting the Crown Office, a case can always be transferred to the Crown Office List as an alternative to being struck out.[67]

The more liberal approach to procedure was evident in **Clark v University of Lincolnshire and Humberside** (2000) in which a student sued her university for breach of contract after having been failed in her examination following unproven allegations of plagiarism. She was outside the three-month time limit for judicial review and the university argued that this would have been the appropriate form of proceeding. The Court of Appeal disagreed, stating that the distinction between judicial review and private actions was now limited and that a claim would not be struck out on the basis that the applicant had proceeded under contract rather than judicial review.

It must also be recognised that the courts are keen to ensure that the parties have made use of any alternative suitable remedies. In the case of **R (Cowl) v Plymouth City Council (Practice Note)** (2001) the Court of Appeal was critical of litigation which raised no point of legal principle but which the claimants nevertheless appealed against the decision of the Council. Lord Woolf CJ, having reviewed the facts and the alternative remedy of having the matter determined by a complaints panel, stated that:

---

67 **Trustees of the Dennis Rye Pension Fund v Sheffield City Council** (1997), p 755.

The courts should not permit, except for good reason, proceedings for judicial review to proceed if a significant part of the issues are limited. If subsequently it becomes apparent that there is a legal issue to be resolved, that can thereafter be examined by the courts which may be considerably assisted by the findings made by the complaints panel.

This case will have served some purpose if it makes clear that the lawyers acting on both sides of a dispute of this sort are under a heavy obligation to resort to litigation only if it is really unavoidable. If they cannot resolve the whole of the dispute by the use of the complaints procedure they should resolve the dispute so far as is practicable without involving litigation.[68]

Limitations on Judicial Review

Justiciability

Justiciability is a concept which defines the judges' view of the suitability of the subject matter to be judicially reviewed.[69] There are some matters in relation to which the courts – mindful of the doctrine of separation of powers – prove to be exceedingly reluctant to review. Matters such as the exercise of prerogative power and, most importantly, issues of national security, and matters of high policy, the courts may regard as non-justiciable. However, the courts will not decline to review a matter simply because the source of the power exercised is the royal prerogative. The House of Lords made it clear in **Council of Civil Service Unions v Minister for Civil Service** (1985) that the source of the power was not determinative of whether the courts would review, but rather whether the subject matter of the application was justiciable or not.[70]

Matters of public policy not for judicial review

Where a matter complained of involves issues of high policy, the courts will decline to exercise a supervisory function over such decisions. Matters of public policy are for determination by the executive, and not the judiciary, and any purported attempt to control the decision will be regarded as a violation of the separation of powers and an intrusion into the proper decision-making sphere of the executive. For example, in **Nottinghamshire County Council v Secretary of State for the Environment** (1986), it was held that the court should not intervene to quash guidance drafted by the Secretary of State, on the authority of Parliament, setting limits to public expenditure by local authorities. Lord Scarman ruled that:

> Unless and until a statute provides otherwise, or it is established that the Secretary of State has abused his power, these are matters of political judgment for him and for the House of Commons. They are not for the judges or your Lordships' House in its judicial capacity.

Similarly, in **Hammersmith and Fulham London Borough Council v Department of the Environment** (1991), concerning the lawfulness of 'charge capping' local authorities (penalising local

---

68 R (Cowl) v Plymouth City Council (Practice Note), paras 14 and 27.
69 See **Thorne v University of London** (1966); R v Bristol Corporation ex parte Hendy (1974).
70 See also **Attorney General v de Keyser's Royal Hotel Ltd** (1920); **Laker Airways v Department of Trade** (1977); R v Secretary of State for the Home Department ex parte Fire Brigades' Union (1995); M v Home Office (1993).

authorities for exceeding their budgets), the House of Lords ruled that the decision was not open to challenge on the grounds of irrationality 'short of the extremes of bad faith, improper motive or manifest absurdity'. Lord Bridge went on to rule that such decisions, relating to national economic policy, 'are matters depending essentially on political judgment' and that, in the absence of any evidence of bad faith or abuse of power, the courts would be 'exceeding their proper function if they presumed to condemn the policy as unreasonable'. In **R v Parliamentary Commissioner for Administration ex parte Dyer** (1994), Simon Brown LJ held that matters of national policy were not open to challenge before the courts other than on the basis of bad faith, improper motive or manifest absurdity. Matters of national economic policy were for political – not judicial – judgment.

Then in **R (Friends of the Earth) v Secretary of State for Business, Enterprise and Regulatory Reform; R (Help the Aged) v Secretary of State for Environment, Food and Rural Affairs** (2009) the Court of Appeal ruled that it was not unlawful for government ministers to consider 'reasonable practicability', at least to some extent by reference to departmental budgets, when taking steps to implement specific targets, including eliminating fuel poverty.[71]

Under the Warm Homes and Energy Conservation Act 2000 the government's strategy targets were set for ending fuel poverty for vulnerable households by 2010, 'as far as reasonably practicable'. The government argued that it had done all it could to achieve the targets, given the overall spending priorities of government and the budgets allowed for ending fuel poverty. The claimants argued that the statutory duty must be complied with, irrespective of budgets. The statute provided that Secretaries of State were only obliged to take such steps as 'in their opinion' are necessary to implement the strategy. The Court of Appeal accepted that opinions could differ as to how best to implement such a policy and it was not for the court to adjudicate on the merits of the opinions formed, in the absence of a challenge as to its rationality. This is another example of the courts being careful not to trespass on areas more appropriately decided by the democratically-accountable executive. As Maurice Kay LJ stated, if the position was otherwise 'the scene would be set for a wholly undesirable judicialisation of public spending priorities'.

The doctrine of deference

The doctrine of deference has been discussed in Chapter 18: see pages 413–414. Closely related to the courts' self-imposed restrictions on jurisdiction by excluding matters of public policy from judicial review, judicial deference to the executive government is a distinctive manifestation of the concept of justiciability (or non-justiciability).

Deference by the judges to the executive protects the courts from accusations that they have intruded on a sphere of decision-making which is more appropriately undertaken by the democratically-elected and accountable government, and is an important feature of the doctrine of separation of powers. The doctrine can be seen working in areas of law such as national security, particularly in relation to emergency situations such as war or terrorist threats. Foreign affairs (including Treaties), immigration and deportation decisions are also areas where the judges exercise restraint, leaving an area of discretion to the executive. Difficult situations arise where individual human rights are pitted against the principle of deference. For example in **R v Ministry of Defence ex parte Smith** (1996) the Court of Appeal upheld the

---

71 The claimants sought a declaration that the relevant Secretaries of State had unlawfully failed to perform their statutory duties under the Warm Homes and Energy Conservation Act 2000 and the UK Fuel Poverty Strategy, and a mandatory order that the defendants perform those duties.

government's policy of not allowing homosexuals to serve in the armed forces. The European Court of Human Rights, however, found a violation of the right to respect for the claimants' private lives (Article 8) which could not be justified as being 'necessary in a democratic society'.[72]

Time limits and exclusion clauses

It is a first principle of justice and the rule of law that public bodies are required to act within the scope of the powers allocated to them by Parliament and, accordingly, in principle, judicial review should lie wherever the *vires* of administrative action is in question. However, that principle must be set in the balance against the needs of certain administration, and the necessary restrictions which may be imposed on individuals or bodies seeking to disrupt the administrative process, without good cause. The balance to be struck between these often competing principles is a difficult matter. Where Parliament limits the availability of judicial review, the courts will adopt a restrictive interpretation to the statutory words, employing the presumption that Parliament did not intend – save in the most express manner – to exclude the jurisdiction of the courts. A number of different statutory means are employed in the attempt to limit the availability of judicial review. In summary, Parliament may adopt the following means:

(a) the general requirement that applications for judicial review are brought within three months of the challenged decision;
(b) clauses which are intended to prevent any challenge;
(c) clauses which are designed to limit review to a specified time period in relation to particular matters where delay needs to be avoided;
(d) 'conclusive evidence' clauses.

Time limits

In the attempt to protect decisions from challenges which may impede or otherwise affect their implementation, statute may provide that there should be no challenge by way of judicial review other than within a specified time period. **Smith v East Elloe Rural District Council** (1956) illustrates the attitude of the courts to such time limits. In **Smith**, a challenge to the validity of a compulsory purchase order was limited, under statute, to a six-week period following the date of confirmation of the order. If not challenged within that period the order 'shall not . . . be questioned in any legal proceedings whatsoever'. Mrs Smith did not challenge the order within the time limit but, some six years later, sought to challenge the order on the basis that the clerk to the council had acted in bad faith, and that bad faith was a ground on which – despite the clear wording of the time limit in the statute – the order's validity could be impugned. The House of Lords, by a majority, rejected this view. It was, however, unanimously agreed that Mrs Smith could proceed against the clerk to the council for damages, on the basis of bad faith in procuring the order. Viscount Simonds explained the attitude of the court:

My Lords, I think that anyone bred in the tradition of the law is likely to regard with little sympathy legislative provisions for ousting the jurisdiction of the court . . . But it is our plain duty to give the words of an Act their proper meaning, and . . . I find it quite impossible to qualify the words . . . in the manner suggested . . . What is abundantly

---

72 See **Smith and Grady v United Kingdom** (1999).

clear is that words are used which are wide enough to cover any kind of challenge which an aggrieved person may think fit to make. I cannot think of any wider words . . . I come, then to the conclusion that the court cannot entertain this action in so far as it impugns the validity of the compulsory purchase order . . . [pp 750–52]

The Court of Appeal in **R v Secretary of State for the Environment ex parte Ostler** (1976) followed the reasoning in **Smith**. In **Ostler**, the Highways Act 1959[73] provided that an aggrieved person had the right to challenge the validity of a compulsory purchase order – on the basis of *ultra vires* – within six weeks from the date of publication of the order. Subject to that right, the order 'shall not be questioned in any legal proceedings whatsoever'. The proposed road-building scheme had two stages. The first involved the acquisition of the land for the main road; the second related to the acquisition of land for the side roads which would give access to the main road. Two public inquiries were held, at the first of which there were allegations that an officer of the Department of the Environment had given assurances that vehicular access would be gained by a widening of the access road during the second phase of the development. Ostler's business would be affected by the widening of the access road, but he was unaware of the assurance allegedly given at the inquiry and did not challenge the decision. At the second inquiry, Ostler wished to object to the road widening, and wanted to give evidence that he would have objected at the first inquiry had he known of the secret undertaking. He was refused permission to give evidence on the basis that his objection related to the first stage of the development. Ostler subsequently learned of the undertakings and sought to challenge the compulsory order on the ground that natural justice had been denied and that the order had been made in bad faith amounting to fraud. The court accepted that, had Ostler challenged the order within six weeks, the court would have considered his complaint. The court was faced with the question of whether **Anisminic** (discussed below) applied, or whether the decision in **Smith v East Elloe** (1956) was the relevant precedent. Lord Denning MR considered the two precedent decisions and distinguished between them in three respects. First, the limitation in the **Smith** case amounted to a time limitation for review, as opposed to a purported total ouster of jurisdiction as in **Anisminic**. Second, the decision by the Foreign Compensation Board in **Anisminic** was a 'truly judicial' decision, whereas that in **Smith** was an administrative decision. Third, in **Anisminic**, the court was required to consider the 'actual determination of the tribunal', whereas in **Smith** the court was considering the process by which the decision was reached. Lord Denning concluded:

. . . the policy of the 1959 Act is that when a compulsory purchase order has been made, then if it has been wrongly obtained or made, a person aggrieved should have a remedy. But he must come promptly. He must come within six weeks. If he does so, the court can and will entertain his complaint. But if the six weeks expire without any application being made, the court cannot entertain it afterwards. The reason is because, as soon as that time has elapsed, the authority will take steps to acquire property, demolish it and so forth. The public interest demand that they should be safe in doing so. [pp 95–96]

Exclusion clauses

Any attempt to exclude judicial review goes to the heart of the argument regarding the respective freedom of government to act and the right of the individual to seek the protection

---

73 Sched 2, paras 2 and 3.

of his or her rights through the courts. In **R v Medical Appeal Tribunal ex parte Gilmore** (1957), the statute provided that 'the decision on any medical question by a medical appeal tribunal . . . is final'. Under an industrial injuries scheme, compensation for accidental industrial injuries was set under a tariff. Gilmore went blind in both eyes in two accidents and was assessed at a disablement of 20 per cent. The tariff provided that the loss of sight in both eyes entitled the applicant to a 100 per cent assessment. The tribunal had, accordingly, made an error of law. However, the opportunity for the court to redress the wrong turned on the exclusion of review in the statute. The Court of Appeal held that the jurisdiction of the court was not ousted by the statutory words, Denning LJ stating that:

> . . . the remedy of *certiorari* is never to be taken away by any statute except by the most clear and explicit words. The word 'final' is not enough. That only means 'without appeal'. It does not mean 'without recourse to *certiorari*'. It makes the decision final on the facts, but not final on the law. Notwithstanding that the decision is by a statute made 'final', *certiorari* can still issue for excess of jurisdiction or for error of law on the face of the record . . . [p 583]

However, in **South East Asia Firebricks v Non-Metallic Mineral Products Manufacturing Employees' Union** (1981), an 'ouster clause' succeeded. The Malaysian Industrial Court, in a successful legal challenge by trade unions, had ordered employers to take back employees after a strike. Statute[74] provided that an award of the court was 'final and conclusive' and that '. . . no award shall be challenged, appealed against, reviewed, quashed or called into question in any court of law'.

The Privy Council, citing **Gilmore** with approval, nevertheless distinguished between an error which affected the jurisdiction of the court to make a determination[75] and decisions which, whilst in error, were not of such a fundamental nature as to deprive the court of jurisdiction. In this case, the error was within the jurisdiction of the court and, accordingly, the ouster clause was effective. According to Lord Fraser of Tullybelton:

> . . . the Industrial Court applied its mind to the proper question for the purpose of making its award. The award was accordingly within the jurisdiction of that court, and neither party has contended to the contrary . . . the error or errors did not affect the jurisdiction of the Industrial Court and their Lordships are therefore of the opinion that section 29(3)(a) effectively ousted the jurisdiction of the High Court to quash the decision by *certiorari* proceedings . . . [pp 373–74]

The seminal case on ouster clauses is **Anisminic v Foreign Compensation Commission** (1969). In 1956, property in Egypt belonging to an English company was sequestrated by the Egyptian authorities and subsequently sold to an Egyptian organisation, TEDO. Anisminic then sold to TEDO its mining business. In 1959, a Treaty signed by the United Kingdom and the United Arab Republic provided for the return of sequestrated property, other than property sequestrated in a period during which Anisminic's property was taken over. The Foreign Compensation Commission (FCC), established to make awards of compensation to companies adversely affected by sequestration of property, ruled that Anisminic did not qualify for compensation. The Foreign Compensation Order 1962,[76] Article 4(1)(b)(ii), provided that both the applicant and the successor in title be British nationals. TEDO – the successor in

---

74 Industrial Relations Act 1967, s 29(3)(a).
75 Relying on **Anisminic v Foreign Compensation Commission** (1968).
76 Egypt: Determination and Registration of Claims. An Order in Council.

title – was not a British national and, accordingly, Anisminic's claim failed. The Foreign Compensation Act 1950 provided that the decisions of the FCC 'shall not be called in question in any court of law'.[77]

Anisminic sought judicial review of the FCC's decision. The question for the court was whether the phrase 'shall not be questioned' succeeded in ousting the jurisdiction of the courts, or whether, notwithstanding that section, the courts had the power to rule on the lawfulness of the FCC's decision. The House of Lords ruled that the jurisdiction of the courts was not ousted. Accordingly the court had power to review the FCC's decision, which it declared to be null and void. The FCC had acted outside its jurisdiction by misinterpreting the Order in Council and reached a decision based on a ground which it was not entitled to take into account, namely the nationality of the successor in title. The nationality of the successor in title, according to the House of Lords, was not a relevant consideration when the applicant was the original owner of the sequestered property. The House of Lords ruled unanimously that section 4(4) did not protect decisions which were taken outside of jurisdiction.

Anisminic was considered by the Supreme Court in **R (A) v Director of Establishments of the Security Service** (2009). In **A's case** section 65(2)(a) of the Regulation of Investigatory Powers Act 2000 (RIPA) provided that the Investigatory Powers Tribunal (IPT) was 'the only appropriate court or tribunal' in relation to proceedings under section 7(1)(a) of the Human Rights Act 1998 before which a claim by a member of the intelligence services could be made in relation to alleged abuses of human rights (in this case Article 10, freedom of expression). The Supreme Court ruled that section 65(2)(a) did not amount to an ouster of the jurisdiction of the courts, but rather the allocation, by Parliament, of an exclusive jurisdiction to the Tribunal.[78]

The **Anisminic** decision raises complex issues. The House of Lords appeared to destroy the distinction between errors of law within the jurisdiction of the decision-making body, which had previously been regarded as non-reviewable, and errors of law which took the decision-maker outside its jurisdiction and were therefore reviewable. In effect, clauses which attempted to oust the jurisdiction of the courts appeared to have been rendered meaningless. The problem which remains is whether **Anisminic** provides clear guidelines as to how to distinguish between those elements of a tribunal's decision which, if decided incorrectly, cause the tribunal to exceed its jurisdiction, and those aspects of a tribunal's decision which, although decided incorrectly, do not cause the tribunal to exceed its jurisdiction – in other words the error is 'within jurisdiction'. The decision also reveals judicial emphasis on the rule of law – even in the face of apparently clear words that Parliament does not intend review to take place. In the view of Wade and Forsyth (2004), the judges in **Anisminic** have ensured that the courts are 'the exclusive arbiters on all questions of law'.

In **Pearlman v Keepers and Governors of Harrow School** (1979), the Court of Appeal ruled that the misinterpretation of provisions in the Housing Act 1974 by the county court amounted to a 'jurisdictional error' which nullified the court's decision. Lord Denning MR stated that the distinction between errors which entail an excess of jurisdiction and an error made within jurisdiction should be abandoned.

The question of exactly which errors of law are 'jurisdictional' was considered in **Re Racal Communication Ltd** (1981). In **Racal**, the Director of Public Prosecutions (DPP) sought an order of the court[79] in order to obtain evidence relating to an alleged offence. The order was refused. Section 441(3) of the Companies Act provided that no appeal lay from a decision of the judge hearing the application. Nevertheless the DPP appealed, and the Court of Appeal allowed the

---

77 Foreign Compensation Act 1950, s 4(4).
78 The claim that the IPT's procedures violated the right to fair trial was also rejected.
79 Under the Companies Act 1948, s 411.

appeal, relying on **Anisminic** and **Pearlman**. Lord Denning ruled that the 'no appeal' clause was of no effect, for the judge had misconstrued the words in section 411 of the Act. The House of Lords overturned the Court of Appeal's decision, approving of Geoffrey Lane LJ's dissenting judgment in **Pearlman**, in which he had held that the judge had done nothing which was outside his scope of inquiry. A distinction was drawn between errors made by a tribunal or other administrative bodies, which would be reviewable, and errors made by a court of law. Lord Diplock, in *Racal*, supported the view expressed by Lord Denning MR in **Pearlman**, stating:

> The breakthrough made by *Anisminic* was that, as respects administrative tribunals and authorities, the old distinction between errors of law that went to jurisdiction and errors of law that did not was for practical purposes abolished. [p 383]

A further distinction, and limitation to the **Anisminic** principle, is to be seen in **R v Lord President of the Privy Council ex parte Page** (1992). There, the issue concerned a decision made by a university Visitor, and whether such a decision was reviewable on the basis of **Anisminic**. The House of Lords ruled that it was not. The powers of Visitors were established by the founder of the university, who had established a body of law and the office of Visitor to enforce that 'domestic' law. Accordingly, per Lord Browne-Wilkinson, the Visitor could not 'err in law in reaching his decision since the general law is not the applicable law'. Accordingly, the Visitor could not act *ultra vires* by applying his interpretation of the rules of the university. Jurisdiction to review did lie in cases where the Visitor acted outside his jurisdiction, or where he acted without regard to the rules of natural justice. However, there was no jurisdiction to review decisions taken within jurisdiction.

'Conclusive evidence clauses'

Parliament may effectively oust the jurisdiction of the courts by inserting a clause into statute which provides that a subordinate piece of legislation shall have effect 'as if enacted in this Act', or that confirmation of an order by a designated minister shall be 'conclusive evidence that the requirements of this Act have been complied with, and that the order has been duly made and is within the powers of this Act'. Such clauses were strongly criticised in 1932 by the Committee on Ministers' Powers[80] but, nevertheless, they continue to be used and have been effective in ousting judicial review. In **R v Registrar of Companies ex parte Central Bank of India** (1986), for example, a clause in the Companies Act 1985 effectively ousted the jurisdiction of the courts. Nevertheless, the potential for their use, and their effectiveness, provides the basis for a damaging exclusion of judicial review.

The Freedom of Information Act 2000 and judicial review

As discussed in Chapter 10, the Freedom of Information Act gave legislative force to the Labour government's commitment to more open government. An Information Commissioner was appointed, with jurisdiction to investigate allegations that public authorities and bodies have failed to provide information and documents requested. The Act, it will be recalled, introduced the principle that information and documents will be disclosed, subject to a test of harm which justifies official non-disclosure. The Commissioner's decisions are published and are subject to judicial review. The effect of the Freedom of Information Act on judicial review will,

---

80 Cmd 4060, 1932, London: HMSO.

however, arguably be to reduce the number of applications for judicial review, in particular on the basis of failure to give reasons.

Judicial review is concerned with the decision-making process rather than the merits of the decision, and provides a discretionary remedy, which requires the decision maker to reconsider the matter in accordance with the correct procedure. Provided that the decision-making process is in accordance with the requirements of law and the principles of natural justice, the decision will not be impugned. Under the Freedom of Information Act, however, where a public body – which is widely defined – fails to give reasons for its decision, recourse may be had to the Commissioner who has wide ranging powers to investigate, and has the power to order disclosure. Where a public body refuses to supply, for example, reasons for its decision, and the Commissioner orders it to disclose reasons, should the public body then continue to refuse to disclose, with no justification, that refusal may be deemed to be analogous to contempt of court. Furthermore, should the body concerned reveal to the Commissioner that it had no rational basis for its decision, that decision may then be impugned on the basis of irrationality. The citizen may, accordingly, find a more efficient and effective remedy under the jurisdiction of the Commissioner than the courts.[81]

See Chapter 10.

Protective costs orders

It has been seen above that access to judicial review is subject to considerable restrictions. One of these restrictions in real terms is cost. Normally in civil litigation an order for costs is not made until that litigation has been concluded. This is not just the costs associated with bringing the claim but also payment of the costs incurred by the other side. The cost of bringing an action in judicial review can be substantial and to promote greater access to justice the courts can use a protective costs order. A protective costs order can be sought to limit the claimant's exposure to the other side's costs. Protective costs orders are useful as they allow the issue of costs to be settled before the costs of preparing submissions for a substantive hearing of a judicial review is incurred. They also allow the claimant to assess their likely exposure to costs before deciding whether or not to proceed with the challenge. The test for the granting of these orders was in 'the most exceptional circumstances'.[82] The leading authority on the use of protective costs orders is currently **R (Corner House Research) v Secretary of State for Trade and Industry** (2005).[83] In this case guidance was provided as to when such an order can be granted. These are where:

- the issues raised are of public importance;
- the public interest requires that those issues should be resolved;
- the applicant has no private interest in the outcome of the case;
- having due regard to the applicants and respondent's financial resources it is fair and just in the circumstances to make the order; and
- if the order is not made the applicant is likely to discontinue proceedings and this would be reasonable in the circumstances.

Recently Lord Justice Jackson reviewed civil litigation costs[84] including the use of the protective costs order in judicial review cases. He concluded that although the courts have

---

81 See Pitt-Payne, T. & Kamm, R. (2009) 'Freedom of Information: the story so far', *Judicial Review*, 239.
82 **R v Lord Chancellor ex parte CPAG** (1999).
83 As confirmed in **R (Compton) v Wiltshire Primary Care Trust** (2008). See Chapter 4 for further discussion of **R (Corner House Research) v Secretary of State for Trade and Industry** (2005).
84 Lord Jackson (2010), *Review of Civil Litigation Costs: Final Report*, TSO.

demonstrated a willingness to grant these orders in judicial review cases the criteria are still seen to be unduly restrictive and they continue to impede access to justice.[85]

Remedies[86]

Introduction

The granting of a remedy in judicial review proceedings is at the discretion of the court. Even where the applicant establishes his or her case, the court may refuse a remedy if there has been a delay in commencing proceedings, or if the applicant has acted unreasonably, or where the public interest in efficient administration could be damaged by the granting of a remedy. The available remedies under public law are the 'prerogative remedies': quashing orders, prohibiting orders and mandatory orders. In addition, under private law there are the remedies of declaration and injunction, which may also be granted under judicial review proceedings. Historically claimants used to have to specify which of the remedies they required. Since 1978 the claimant now brings an action for judicial review and it is for the court to decide which remedy should be granted.

Quashing order (formerly *certiorari*)

This remedy overlaps with that of prohibition (below). A quashing order is one which 'quashes', or sets aside as a nullity, the original decision: accordingly it is both negative and retrospective in nature: **R v Criminal Injuries Compensation Board ex parte Lain** (1967); **O'Reilly v Mackman** (1983). The classic dictum is that of Lord Atkin:[87]

> . . . whenever any body of persons having legal authority to determine questions affecting the rights of subjects, and having the duty to act judicially, act in excess of their legal authority, they are subject to the controlling jurisdiction of the King's Bench Division exercised in these writs.

If only part of a decision is *ultra vires* that part may be severed from the good and the order of *certiorari* granted to quash the bad part of the decision. A quashing order is similar to a prohibiting order, the quashing order operating retrospectively, the prohibiting order operating prospectively.

Prohibiting order (formerly prohibition)

Prohibition is an order which prevents a body from making a decision which would be capable of being quashed by *certiorari*. It is thus protective in nature. Neither quashing orders nor prohibiting orders lie against decisions of the higher courts.

Lord Atkin explained the relationship between *certiorari* and prohibition in the **London Electricity** case:

> I see no difference in principle between *certiorari* and prohibition, except that the latter may be invoked at an earlier stage. If the proceedings establish that the body complained of is exceeding its jurisdiction by entertaining matters which would result

---

85 See **R (Garner) v Elmbridge BC** (2011); **R (Edwards) v Environment Agency** (2011).
86 The orders were renamed under the Civil Procedure Rules 1999, r 54.1. See Oliver, 2001.
87 **R v Electricity Commissioners ex parte London Electricity Joint Committee Company (1920) Ltd** (1924).

in its final decision being subject to being brought up and quashed on certiorari, I think that prohibition will lie to restrain it from exceeding its jurisdiction.

Prohibition will prevent a public body from acting unlawfully in the future. It may also be used to prevent a body from implementing a decision which has already been taken which was itself *ultra vires*. A failure to comply with an order amounts to a contempt of court.

Mandatory order (formerly *mandamus*)

This order is one which compels an authority to act. A mandatory order does not lie against an authority which has complete discretion to act. A failure to comply with the order amounts to a contempt of court. Mandatory orders do lie against the Crown, and may be used to enforce action by a minister or official, as for example in **Padfield v Minister of Agriculture Fisheries and Food** (1968) in which a minister was compelled to refer a complaint to a statutory committee.

Whereas prohibition prevents a future unlawful act, a mandatory order prevents an unlawful failure to act. Whenever a public body is under a duty to act, and fails to comply with that duty, a citizen with sufficient interest may seek an order which compels the authority to act. A mandatory order and a quashing order may work together. For example, if an authority has abused its power, a quashing order may be issued together with a mandatory order requiring the authority to act according to law. On the other hand, a mandatory order alone implies that the authority has acted *ultra vires* and therefore operates like a quashing order to nullify the defective decision.

Declarations

A declaration is a statement of the legal position of the parties, and is not accordingly a remedy *per se*. Although lacking coercive force, public bodies will respond to a declaration and comply with its terms by rectifying its actions.[88] Declarations are available against the Crown.

Injunctions

Injunctions may be interim or permanent, and positive or negative. Injunctions may be used to prevent a minister or administrative body from acting unlawfully. In **M v Home Office** (1993), the House of Lords held that injunctions could lie against ministers of the Crown, and that breach of an injunction could lead to a minister, in his official capacity as representative of the Crown, being held in contempt of court.

See further Chapters 5 and 10.

Damages

An applicant for judicial review may be awarded damages in conjunction with one of the other remedies. Damages will only be awarded if they would have been recoverable had the applicant begun an action by writ (that is, a private law action).

Habeas corpus

See Chapter 18.

The writ of habeas corpus has long been used to challenge the legality of a decision to detain an individual. Literally meaning 'you shall have the body', habeas corpus enjoys a treasured position in English legal history.[89]

---

88 See **Dyson v Attorney General** (1911); **Pyx Granite Co Ltd v Ministry of Housing and Local Government** (1958); **R v Secretary of State for the Home Department ex parte Salem** (1999).

89 See Sharpe, *The Law of Habeas Corpus* (1989).

Default Powers

Statute may provide that a minister has powers to act in order to oblige a decision-making body to comply with its statutory duty. For example, section 9 of the Caravan Sites Act 1968 provided that the Secretary of State had the power to give directions to local authorities to comply with their statutory duty to provide adequate sites for Gypsies residing in, or resorting to their area.[90] Other examples of similar powers are found in the Public Health Act 1936, the Education Act 1944, the National Health Service Act 1977, the Housing Act 1985, the Local Government Act 1985 and the Town and Country Planning Act 1990. In respect of the Housing Act provisions, in **R v Secretary of State for the Environment ex parte Norwich City Council** (1982), the Secretary of State had the power to act as he 'thinks necessary' to ensure that tenants are able to exercise their 'right to buy' from local authorities. His failure to enforce the local authorities' duty was itself subject to the control of the courts through judicial review. Default powers are a backstop, but an important weapon in ensuring that local authorities and other bodies comply with the requirements of statute.

Remedies and the Human Rights Act 1998

Section 8 of the Human Rights Act 1998 authorises a court to 'grant such relief or remedy, or make such order, within its powers as it considers just and appropriate'. Accordingly, any remedies which a particular court may award are available for breaches of Convention rights. Declarations, damages, injunctions or the prerogative orders are available. When awarding damages, the courts must take into account the principles applied by the European Court of Human Rights in relation to awards of compensation. Claims for damages do not lie against the decision of a court which has breached the Convention, even though courts are defined as public bodies under the Act. Section 9 of the 1998 Act requires that proceedings against a first instance court be brought by way of appeal or by judicial review. An exception to this is provided in section 9(3) and (4), which provide for awards of damages against the Crown where any judicial body has been guilty of a breach of Article 5 (the right to liberty). Where there has been a breach of a Convention right caused by an Act of Parliament, damages cannot be awarded. In this situation, the consequence will be the making of a declaration of incompatibility. Only the High Court and courts above have the power to issue declarations of incompatibility.

Summary

Judicial review of administrative action is the mechanism by which the judges ensure that those to whom powers are given by Parliament are kept within the scope of power granted. In judicial review proceedings the court is concerned with whether the decision maker reached the decision in accordance with the correct rules and principles, not with whether the decision was just or unjust, right or wrong. Accordingly, the judicial review process must be contrasted with that of a right of appeal, and the difference in outcome between an appeal and an application for judicial review.

An individual who is aggrieved by an administrative decision may apply for judicial review. The law relating to judicial review is both statutory and common law. In order to protect the administrative process from unmeritorious challenges, the law requires that applicants satisfy a number of criteria.

---

90 The duty to provide sites has been repealed: Criminal Justice and Public Order Act 1994, s 80.

The matter complained of must be a matter of public, not private law and be directed against a public, not private body. The aggrieved individual must apply within three months of knowledge of the impugned decision. He or she must also have a 'sufficient interest' in the matter to justify the intervention of the courts, and the application must (with exceptions) be through the stipulated public law procedure.

There are a number of restrictions on judicial review. In order to protect the administrative process Parliament may insert clauses in a statute which preclude judicial review, or which restrict applications for judicial review to a shorter time period. Furthermore, the judges impose their own restrictions on judicial review through the concepts of justiciability and non-justiciability, which ensure that the courts do not trespass on the executive's sphere of decision making.

The law of judicial review has expanded with the Human Rights Act 1998, which makes it unlawful for a public authority to act contrary to Convention rights, other than where an Act of Parliament prevents the authority from acting differently. An application for judicial review under the Human Rights Act may only be made by a victim, or potential victim, of an allegedly unlawful act.

Further Reading

Blom-Cooper, L. & Drabble, R. (2010) 'GCHQ Revisited', Public Law, 18.

Bondy, V. & Sunkin, M. (2009) 'Settlement in judicial review proceedings', Public Law, 237.

Cane, P. (2003) 'Accountability and the Public/Private Distinction' in N. Bamforth and P. Leyland (eds) Public Law in a Multi-Layered Constitution, Oxford: Hart Publishing.

Cane, P. (2011) Introduction to Administrative Law (5th edn), Oxford: Clarendon Press, Chapter 3.

Craig, P. (1999) 'Competing Models of Judicial Review', Public Law, 428.

Craig, P. (2004) 'The Common Law, Shared Power and Judicial Review', Oxford Journal of Legal Studies, 24: 129.

Craig, P. (2004) 'Judicial Review, Appeal and Factual Error', Public Law, 788.

Craig, P. (2012) Administrative Law (7th edn), London: Sweet and Maxwell.

Daly, P. (2010) 'Justiciability and the "political question" ', Public Law, 160.

Eliantoniom, M. (2010) 'Europeanisation of Administrative Justice? The Influence of the ECJ's case law in Italy, Germany and England', European Review of Public Law, 22.3: 681.

Jowell, J. (1999) 'Of vires and Vacuums: The Constitutional Context of Judicial Review', Public Law, 448.

Jowell, J. (2000) 'Beyond the Rule of Law: Towards Constitutional Judicial Review', Public Law, 671.

Lever, A. (2007) 'Is Judicial Review Undemocratic?', Public Law, 280.

Wade, W. and Forsyth, C. (2009) Administrative Law (10th edn), Oxford: OUP.

Chapter 24

Grounds for Judicial Review I: The Substantive Grounds for Judicial Review

Introduction

With the procedural aspects of judicial review proceedings in mind, attention can now be turned to the grounds on which judicial review may be sought. Two principal classes of action may be pursued: those which allege that there has been a breach of statutory requirements, and those alleging that a decision has been reached in an unreasonable manner or in disregard of the rules of natural justice. These broad headings have traditionally been divided into a number of subheadings. In **Council of Civil Service Unions v Minister of State for Civil Service** (1985) (the **GCHQ** case), the House of Lords took the opportunity to offer a rationalisation of the grounds for judicial review and ruled that the bases for judicial review could be subsumed under three principal heads, namely illegality, irrationality and procedural impropriety.[1] It was accepted that further grounds for review such as 'proportionality' might emerge. Lord Diplock elucidated the concepts:

> By 'illegality' as a ground for judicial review, I mean that the decision maker must understand correctly the law that regulates his decision making power and give effect to it. Whether he had or not is par excellence a justiciable question to be decided, in the event of dispute, by those persons, the judges, by whom the judicial power of the State is exercisable.

> By 'irrationality', I mean what can now be succinctly referred to as *Wednesbury* unreasonableness.[2] It applies to a decision which is so outrageous in its defiance of logic or of accepted moral standards that no sensible person who had applied his mind to the question to be decided could have arrived at it. Whether a decision falls within this category is a question that judges by their training and experience should be well equipped to answer . . .

> I have described the third head as 'procedural impropriety' rather than failure to observe basic rules of natural justice or failure to act with procedural fairness towards the person who will be affected by the decision. This is because suscepti-bility to judicial review under this head covers also failure by an administrative tribunal to observe the procedural rules that are expressly laid down in the legislative instrument by which its jurisdiction is conferred, even though such failure does not involve any denial of natural justice.

> That is not to say that further development on a case by case basis may not in course of time add further grounds. I have in mind particularly the possible adoption in the future of the principle of 'proportionality' which is recognised in the administrative law of several of our fellow members of the European [Economic] Community . . . [pp 410–11]

The Traditional Doctrine of *Ultra Vires*

Ultra vires refers to action which is outside – or in excess of – powers of decision-making bodies. While judges continue to use the term *ultra vires*, it is nowadays too limited a term to

---

1   Chapter 25 will consider procedural impropriety in more detail.
2   *Associated Provincial Picture Houses Ltd v Wednesbury Corporation* (1948). See further below.

encompass the whole ambit of judicial review. It may be preferable, therefore, to regard judicial review as the control of discretion and the regulation of the decision-making process by the courts. By way of example, in **R v Hull University Visitor ex parte Page** (1993), Lord Browne-Wilkinson adopted the traditional language of ultra vires:

> If the decision maker exercises his powers outside the jurisdiction conferred, in a manner which is procedurally irregular or is *Wednesbury* unreasonable, he is acting *ultra vires* his powers and therefore unlawfully.

In **R v Richmond upon Thames Council ex parte McCarthy and Stone Ltd** (1992), the local planning authority implemented a scheme of charging £25.00 for informal consultation between corporation officers and property developers. The House of Lords held that the imposition of the charge was unlawful. Such a charge was neither incidental to the planning function of the local authority, nor could a charge be levied on the public without statutory authority. The council had misconstrued its powers and, accordingly, acted ultra vires. Further, in **Hazell v Hammersmith and Fulham Council** (1992), the council attempted to increase its revenue through financial investments which, for success, were dependent upon the fluctuation in interest rates. The House of Lords ruled that the council had no power to enter into 'interest rate swaps' which were purely speculative in nature. Such speculation was inconsistent with the statutory borrowing powers conferred on local authorities and neither conducive to nor incidental to the exercise of those powers.[3]

More recently, in **A v HM Treasury** (2010), the Supreme Court ruled that Orders in Council were ultra vires and unlawful. The United Kingdom, as a member of the United Nations, was required to give effect to decisions of the UN Security Council. Security Council Resolutions were made to combat terrorism, in part by freezing financial assets and other economic resources of terrorists. The United Nations Act 1946, section 1, provided that in order to give effect to Security Council Resolutions, 'His Majesty may by Order in Council make such provision as appears to Him necessary or expedient for enabling those measures to be effectively applied . . .'. Unlike other forms of delegated legislation which are subjected to parliamentary proceedings, the Orders in Council came into effect following their laying before Parliament. The effect of this was to leave the content of the Orders entirely in the hands of the executive. Two Orders in Council were made, each of which laid down conditions which had to be satisfied before the Treasury could 'designate' a person and freeze his or her financial assets or economic resources. One condition was that the Treasury 'have reasonable grounds for suspicion that the person is or may be' involved in terrorism.

The four appellants in **A v HM Treasury** argued that the Orders were ultra vires the 1946 Act. The power conferred by section 1 was for measures which were 'necessary or expedient'. The Terrorism Order (TO) and the Al-Qaeda and Taliban Orders (AQO) were so widely drawn as to deprive the designated person of any resources whatsoever. Lord Hope of Craighead DPSC approved the dictum of Sedley SJ in the Court of Appeal that designated persons 'are effectively prisoners of the state'. In adopting the test of 'reasonable suspicion' the Orders went beyond what was 'necessary or expedient' to comply with the Security Council Resolutions and were accordingly beyond the scope of section 1 of the 1946 Act.

---

3   More recently in **EN (Serbia) v Secretary of State for the Home Department; KC (South Africa) v Same** (2009) the Court of Appeal ruled that the Secretary of State had misunderstood the extent and purpose of the statutory power when formulating subordinate legislation. As a result he had exceeded his powers and the order was ultra vires and unlawful. The Court of Appeal stated that a tribunal had no power to quash delegated legislation but should have adjourned proceedings, where it considered that the instrument was ultra vires, in order to give the party challenging its lawfulness an opportunity to issue judicial review proceedings.

Difficulties with the traditional *ultra vires* doctrine

The *ultra vires* principle is consistent with the doctrine of parliamentary sovereignty and, to some extent, with the concept of the rule of law. However, there are objections to the courts holding so tenaciously to a concept which, in some respects, is inappropriate to describe what the courts actually do in the control of administrative powers. The judges cling to the *ultra vires* doctrine as a means of protecting their constitutional position. As has been seen in Chapters 4 and 6, the judges are not entrusted with constitutional powers to invalidate Acts of Parliament, and judicial decisions are susceptible to being overruled by Acts of Parliament.[4] With the supremacy of Parliament in mind, the judges exercise care to maintain a sufficient separation of powers. It is for this reason that judges are cautious about reviewing the exercise of prerogative powers and limit their role in relation to parliamentary privileges to ruling on the existence and scope of privilege. Keen awareness of this constitutional position explains the hold which the traditional doctrine of *ultra vires* has for judges. *Ultra vires* is entirely consistent with the supremacy of Parliament and the rule of law. However, the doctrine of *ultra vires* cannot explain adequately the judges' power to rule, as they do, on certain aspects of decision making. While the judges declare that matters of 'high policy' are not for them to decide, when judges rule on 'unreasonableness' or, as Lord Diplock classifies the concept, 'irrationality', the judges come close to ruling on the merits of a particular decision. Furthermore, as will be seen below, the concept of 'error of law' fits uneasily with the concept of *ultra vires*.

For reasons such as these, the concept of *ultra vires* is nowadays regarded by many as an inadequate rationale for judicial review. The preferred view is that the courts need not resort to fictions such as the 'intention of Parliament' or the technicalities of 'jurisdictional facts' and 'errors of law' (on which, see below), but that rather the courts will intervene wherever there has been an unlawful exercise of power. As Professor Oliver expresses the matter, 'judicial review has moved on from the *ultra vires* rule to a concern for the protection of individuals, and for the control of power'.[5]

Traditional terminology and classificatory difficulties in judicial review

While Lord Diplock, in the **GCHQ** case, offered a rationalisation of the headings of review, the question of terminology and classification remains difficult and sometimes obscure. This problem should be recognised at the outset. It should also be borne in mind that the categories are by no means watertight and discrete: in many instances, there will appear overlaps between the headings. By way of illustration, a decision maker may act *ultra vires* by taking into account irrelevant considerations. Depending upon the magnitude of the irrelevant consideration, he or she may also be acting irrationally.

In **Boddington v British Transport Police** (1999)[6] Lord Irvine echoed Lord Diplock's concerns when he stated:

> Categorisation of types of challenge assists in an orderly exposition of the principles underlying our developing public law. But these are not watertight compartments because the various grounds for judicial review run together. The exercise of a power for an improper purpose may involve taking irrelevant considerations into account,

---

4   See eg **Burmah Oil v Lord Advocate** (1965) and the War Damage Act 1965.
5   Oliver, 1987.
6   At page 152.

or ignoring relevant considerations; and either may lead to an irrational result. The failure to grant a person affected by a decision to a hearing, in breach of principles of procedural fairness, may result in a failure to take into account relevant considerations. [p 152]

Recognising these difficulties in classification – and the overlapping of differing heads – the different grounds for judicial review may be portrayed as follows:

Illegality: acting *'ultra vires'*

- errors of law and/or fact;
- onerous conditions;
- using powers for the wrong purpose;
- taking irrelevant factors into account;
- failing to take relevant factors into account;
- acting in bad faith;
- fettering discretion;
- unauthorised delegation;
- failure to act; and
- failing to comply with Convention rights.

Irrationality

- *Wednesbury* unreasonableness;
- failing to act proportionately, especially under the Human Rights Act 1998.

Procedural impropriety

Procedural impropriety is considered in Chapter 25.

Illegality

Acting for improper motives, failing to take account of relevant considerations, failing to respect the requirements of natural justice and fettering a discretion by adopting a rigid policy will all amount to unreasonableness – and hence illegality – as understood by the courts.

While the terms 'unreasonableness' and 'illegality' are frequently and confusingly used interchangeably, illegality most accurately expresses the purpose of judicial review: to ensure that decision makers act according to the law.

Errors of law

The problem concerning the role of the courts and the extent to which it is appropriate for there to be judicial intervention in administration, discussed in Chapter 23, is clearly illustrated in relation to errors of law and errors of fact. The question for determination is whether, and to what extent, administrators enjoy a measure of discretion in decision making, which empowers them to make determinations of fact which are immune from judicial review. Before considering the courts' approach, it is necessary to define the terms error of law and error of fact.

An error of law may take several forms. An authority may wrongly interpret a word to which a legal meaning is attributed. For example, where an authority is under a duty to provide 'accommodation', the question arises as to whether the quality of what they have, in fact, provided amounts, in law, to accommodation. Does the accommodation have to be of a particular quality, or be particularly suited to what the applicant needs?[7] Questions may also arise as to whether there has been a legal exercise of power in relation to the objectives of relevant legislation, or whether a discretion has been properly exercised, or whether relevant considerations have been taken into account, or irrelevant considerations excluded from the decision-making process.

Historically, the judges have assumed the power to adjudicate on matters which are termed 'errors on the face of the record'. Errors on the face of the record – that is to say, evidence from the documentation that the decision maker has made a wrong decision in law – will cause the judges to rule that the decision was defective, even if the decision maker was acting inside jurisdiction (intra vires). Such a power does not sit easily alongside the concept of ultra vires, the very basis of which is to strike down decisions which have been taken ultra vires (outside jurisdiction).

As has been seen, if an authority is to act intra vires, it must conduct itself according to a correct interpretation of the law. However, what is of the essence in relation to error of law is that the authority misinterprets or misunderstands the powers which it has been granted and, accordingly, acts ultra vires whereas, when an authority uses powers for the wrong purpose, the authority has correctly interpreted its powers but used them towards the wrong objective. As has been said, an error of law may manifest itself in several ways. It may be that an authority misinterprets its legal powers, as in **Perilly v Tower Hamlets Borough Council** (1973), where the local authority believed – erroneously – that it was obliged to consider applications for stall licences in a street market in the order in which they were received. The effect of this was to deny a licence to Perilly even though his mother, by then deceased, had held a licence for some 30 years. The licence granted to an incoming applicant in preference to Perilly was set aside by the court.

See further Chapter 23.

The seminal case is that of **Anisminic Ltd v Foreign Compensation Commission** (1969), discussed in Chapter 23. It will be recalled that the House of Lords held the decision of the Commission to be ultra vires. The decision made by the Commission was so wrong that, in law, it did not amount to a decision at all. As a result, the section preventing the questioning of the Commission's decision in a court of law was not relevant or binding on the court, for the ruling of the Commission – being so wrong in law – resulted in the Commission acting outside its jurisdiction, and nothing in the Act prohibited a court of law from reviewing what was, in law and in effect, a nullity.

The House of Lords ruled that:

> If the inferior tribunal, as a result of its misconstruing the statutory description of the kind of case in which it has jurisdiction to inquire, makes a purported determination in a case of a kind into which it has no jurisdiction to inquire, its purported determination is a nullity.

Anisminic Ltd v Foreign Compensation Commission destroyed the distinction between errors of law which 'went to jurisdiction' (that is, deprived the decision-making body of power to determine the question) and errors of law within jurisdiction. In **Anisminic**, the House of Lords ruled that, in effect, the old distinctions were obsolete in relation to the decisions of administrative

---

7   See **R v Hillingdon London Borough Council ex parte Pulhofer** (1986).

and other bodies (but not necessarily inferior courts of law).[8] Lord Diplock reasserted his support for this view in **Re Racal Communications Ltd** (1981) and **O'Reilly v Mackman** (1983). In the former case, Lord Diplock confirmed the 'breakthrough' achieved in **Anisminic**. In **O'Reilly**, Lord Diplock went further and asserted that the distinction had been rendered obsolete in relation both to tribunals and inferior courts. This approach was confirmed by the House of Lords in **R v Hull University Visitor ex parte Page** (1993). Professor HWR Wade's evaluation of these cases is that 'it is clear now that they made an important extension of judicial review in English law . . .'.[9]

The House of Lords returned to the questions of jurisdictional errors in **R v Monopolies and Mergers Commission ex parte South Yorkshire Transport Ltd** (1993). Under section 64(1)(a) of the Fair Trading Act 1973, the Secretary of State has power to refer a merger of companies to the Monopolies and Mergers Commission (MMC). The jurisdiction of the MMC was to consider mergers which result in more than 25 per cent of services being supplied by one company 'in a substantial part of the United Kingdom'. Two merged bus companies sought judicial review of the MMC's investigation, on the basis that the land area did not amount to a 'substantial part of the United Kingdom'. The court ruled that the MMC had directed itself properly as to the meaning of 'substantial'. However, it was also recognised that what amounted to 'substantial' could be interpreted in different ways, and that persons might reasonably disagree about that interpretation. Lord Mustill ruled that, in such a situation, a decision would only be ruled unlawful if the decision 'is so aberrant that it cannot be classed as rational'. Thus, where the statute provides broad criteria, over the meaning of which reasonable persons might reasonably disagree, the court will be slow to step in and substitute its judgment, unless the decision maker's decision falls outside what the court regards as a reasonable interpretation of a word which is essentially imprecise.[10]

Errors of fact[11]

An error of law will be reviewed by the courts. An error of fact is an error which the courts will be more reluctant to review. Administrators are given powers to exercise in relation to their specialised area, and it is the decision maker who has all the factual information to hand on which to base a decision. For the courts to intervene in this matter, would – unless some caution is exercised – amount to the courts taking over the very role of the administrators. Nevertheless, there may be some errors of fact which are of such a fundamental nature that they cause a decision to be unlawful. Ian Yeats offers the following illustrative example of the role of fact in administrative decision making. He writes:

> In the simplest situations, the facts which have to be found and the law which has to be determined can be presented as a series of preconditions which have to exist before the duty can be performed or the power exercised. A board is empowered (or obliged) to take some action in respect of 'dilapidated dwelling houses in Greater London'. The ability (or duty) to act in respect of a particular building depends on establishing that it is (1) in Greater London, (2) a dwelling house and (3) dilapidated. If the board finds that the three conditions are satisfied, it may (or must) proceed. If it finds that any one of them is not satisfied, then it cannot.

---

8 See Diplock, 1974; Wade, 1969; Gould, 1970; Gordon, 1971.
9 Wade and Forsyth, 2004.
10 See also **R v Ministry of Defence ex parte Walker** (1999).
11 See Jones, 1990; Yeats, I, 'Errors of fact: the role of the courts law', in Richardson and Genn, 1994; Craig, 2004.

A disgruntled property owner invites a court to review the board's findings: the court has to decide whether, and how far, it should defer to the board's views. If the complaint is that the premises are not in Greater London, the court is likely to intervene. The question defines in the most literal way the area in which the board has competence, can easily be resolved by a court, and is unlikely to occur frequently. The question is not about the correctness of the decision on the building's fate, but about whether the board whose decision is under review had the function of determining it. If the complaint is that the house is not dilapidated, the court will be reluctant to intervene. That is a question involving elements of judgment which naturally appear to have been remitted to the board and which it, rather than the court, has the facilities and probably the specialised expertise to answer; if the court were to agree to answer it, every decision of the board would be potentially reviewable. If the complaint is that the premises do not constitute a dwelling house, the issue is less clear-cut. The court might think it proper to impose its view, partly because the problem might be posed in a narrowly legal form, that of identifying the correct sense in which the expression 'dwelling house' was used in the legislation. [pp 131–32]

When the court considers whether there has been an error of law, it is seeking to discover the correct definition of the legal words in the relevant statute. When the court is considering whether there has been an error of fact, the court is trying to determine whether the facts of the case 'fit' with the interpretation of the statute.

Errors of fact raise difficult questions. As has been seen, an error of law will be made when the decision maker acts contrary to the requirements of legality – or, in other words, he has broken one of the rules for lawful decision making. Errors of fact are more complex. If a decision maker bases his decision on a misunderstanding of the factual situation of the case, he will reach a decision which is wrong. The question which then arises is whether the courts will review such an error in judicial review proceedings. In general, the answer to that question is that the courts will be very cautious. After all, the courts will often not have the expertise to assess the factual situation, and may have great difficulty in deciding whether a factual error has resulted in the wrong decision. The courts have traditionally approached this matter by dividing errors of fact into two categories. The first relates to reviewable errors of facts, which are jurisdictional, and the other category is that of non-reviewable, non-jurisdictional facts.

Professor Wade illustrates a jurisdictional fact as follows:

A rent tribunal . . . may have power to reduce the rent of a dwelling house. If it mistakenly finds that the property is a dwelling house when in fact it is let for business purposes, and then purports to reduce the rent, its order will be ultra vires and void, for its jurisdiction depends upon the facts which must exist objectively before the tribunal has power to act. [Wade and Forsyth, 2004]

On the other hand, other mistakes will not have this effect. Professor Wade illustrates as follows:

Many facts on the other hand will not be jurisdictional, since they will have no bearing on the limits of the power. A rent tribunal's findings as to the state of repair of the property, the terms of the tenancy, and the defaults of landlord or tenant will probably not affect its jurisdiction in any way and will therefore be immune from jurisdictional challenge.

The question to be asked, therefore, is whether the mistake of fact is one which is central to the decision maker's power of decision. Only such crucial errors of fact will be reviewed by the court. In addition, if a decision is reached on the basis of facts for which there is no evidence, or based on essential facts which have been proven wrong, or been misunderstood or ignored, the court will quash the decision.

Two cases further illustrate the courts' approach to law and fact, and demonstrate that the judges will – depending upon the circumstances of the case – adopt either a strict approach or a more lenient approach to the matter. In **R v Secretary of State for the Home Department ex parte Khawaja** (1984), the House of Lords was required to rule on two questions. The first question was whether the phrase 'illegal immigrant' in the Immigration Act 1971 covered a person who had been granted permission to enter the country through fraud or deception as well as a person who secretly entered the country without any leave. On this point, the House of Lords held that it could. The second question concerned the standard of proof which the immigration officer had to apply. It was argued that the correct standard to be applied was whether the immigration officer had reasonable grounds for his decision. The House of Lords rejected that view, holding that, because the liberty of the person was involved, the standard of proof that deception had taken place was one of a high degree of probability.

In **R v Hillingdon London Borough Council ex parte Pulhofer** (1986), the House of Lords approached the matter rather differently. Under the Housing Act 1985,[12] local authorities are under a duty to provide accommodation for homeless persons as defined by the Act. For the purposes of their decision, the House of Lords had to interpret the meaning of 'accommodation'. The House of Lords adopted a very broad interpretation of the word, refusing to import a standard of reasonableness of accommodation which would protect the individual from being placed in unsuitable housing. Unlike the decision in **Khawaja**, where the House of Lords introduced a standard of proof which was protective of the individual against the administration, in **Pulhofer**, the court's ruling protected the administration – the housing authority – and not the individual. The Housing and Planning Act 1986 reverses the House of Lords' decision in **Pulhofer**, and requires that 'accommodation' be accommodation which it is reasonable for a person to continue to occupy. It can be seen from these two cases that the interpretation of the question of law can dictate a very different outcome, depending upon the judicial approach taken.

When the issue concerns individual rights, for example, the courts will be slow to adopt an approach which has the effect of delimiting those rights. **Tan Te Lam v Superintendent of Tai A Chau Detention Centre** (1996), decided by the Privy Council, illustrates the point well.[13] The applicants were detainees in Hong Kong, having arrived there by boat from Vietnam. They were detained in detention centres, pending decisions as to whether to grant or refuse permission to remain in Hong Kong, or, if a decision to refuse permission were made, pending their removal from Hong Kong and repatriation to Vietnam. They applied for writs of habeas corpus to test the legality of their detention. By the time the appeal reached the Privy Council, the applicants had been detained for long periods of time, the longest being 24 months, pending determination of refugee status, followed by a further 44 months. The Privy Council stated, first, that the power to detain could only be exercised during the period necessary, in all the circumstances, to effect removal; secondly, that, if it becomes clear that removal is not going to be possible within a reasonable time, further detention is not authorised; thirdly, that the person seeking to exercise the power of detention must take all reasonable steps to ensure removal within a reasonable time.

---

12 Originally, the Housing (Homeless Persons) Act 1977.
13 Following the transfer of sovereignty in 1997, appeals no longer lie to the Privy Council from the Hong Kong courts.

In **Khawaja v Secretary of State for the Home Department** (1984), discussed above, the House of Lords had earlier considered the legality of a detention order pending removal, as an illegal immigrant, from the United Kingdom.[14] There was a dispute of fact as to whether the applicant had obtained leave to enter as a result of fraud. The House of Lords ruled that the issue of whether the applicant was an illegal immigrant was a matter which had to be established before it could be determined whether there was any power to detain with a view to deportation. That question 'was a precedent or jurisdictional fact which, in the case of deprivation of liberty, had to be proved to exist before any power to detain was exercisable at all'.

E v Secretary of State for the Home Department (2004) provided the opportunity for the Court of Appeal to reconsider the review of fact. The applicants claimed that the Immigration Appeal Tribunal (IAT) which had refused leave to appeal to the Court of Appeal had erred in not taking account evidence which had become available since the hearing before the IAT but before making the decision whether to allow an appeal. The evidence supported the applicants' claims that they would be at risk if returned to their country of origin. The Court of Appeal ruled that the IAT should reconsider the decision to take account of the evidence where there was a serious risk of injustice because the evidence had not been considered.

Onerous conditions attached to decision

A decision by an authority may also be unreasonable and unlawful if conditions are attached to the decision which are difficult or impossible to perform. For example, in **Pyx Granite Co Ltd v Ministry of Housing and Local Government** (1958), Lord Denning MR in the Court of Appeal held that planning conditions '. . . must fairly and reasonably relate to the permitted development' and must not be so unreasonable that it can be said that Parliament clearly cannot have intended that they should be imposed.

Accordingly, in the **Pyx Granite** case, the condition that permission be conditional upon the company constructing a road ancillary to the development at its own expense when so required by the authority and to grant a public right of passage over it was ultra vires. **Pyx Granite** was followed in **Hall and Co Ltd v Shoreham-by-Sea Urban District Council** (1964). The defendant council granted planning permission for a development, subject to conditions, which included the requirement to construct an ancillary road over the entire frontage of the site and subject to the right of public passage. While the objective of the council was viewed as 'reasonable', the terms of the conditions requiring the plaintiffs to construct a road at their own expense, for public use and without compensation, were not reasonable. The ultra vires conditions were fundamental to the whole planning permission which was, accordingly, void. Equally, in **R v Hillingdon London Borough Council ex parte Royco Homes Ltd** (1974), planning permission was also tied to conditions. The conditions were that Royco Homes make properties constructed available for occupation by those on the council's housing waiting list and, further, that for ten years the houses be occupied by persons subject to security of tenure under the Rent Acts. The conditions were ultra vires.

According to Lord Widgery CJ, the conditions represented:

> . . . the equivalent of requiring the applicants to take on at their own expense a significant part of the duty of the council as housing authority. However well intentioned and however sensible such a desire on the part of the council may have been, it seems to me that it is unreasonable . . . [p 732]

---

14 The power to detain in **Khawaja** arose from the Immigration Act 1971, Sched 2, paras 9 and 16.

Where an authority makes a decision which is in part good, but in part bad – perhaps because of attaching onerous conditions to planning permission – the court may either invalidate the entire decision or sever the bad part of the decision from the good. The decision in **Agricultural Horticultural and Forestry Industry Training Board v Aylesbury Mushrooms Ltd** (1972) illustrates the principle. There, the Training Board was under a mandatory statutory duty to consult certain organisations and trade unions before reaching a decision. The Board failed to consult the Mushroom Growers Association. The court held that the decision was good, and could remain, in relation to those associations which had been consulted, but bad in relation to the Mushroom Growers Association, and that the Board had a duty to reconsider their decision after consultations with the Association.

In some cases, it will not be possible to sever a part of a decision from the whole decision, in which case the entire decision may be invalidated.[15] For example, in **Director of Public Prosecutions v Hutchinson** (1990), the local authority passed a bylaw which prohibited unauthorised access to Greenham Common air force base. The Act of Parliament, under which the authority purported to exercise its powers, provided that no bylaw should be passed which affected the rights of registered commoners in the area. In an action for trespass against anti-nuclear protesters, the defendants pleaded the invalidity of the bylaw. The House of Lords ruled that the bylaw was invalid and, as a result, the protesters escaped conviction for trespass. Conditions were held to be *ultra vires* in **Director of Public Prosecutions v Haw** (2007).[16] The police had imposed a number of conditions on Brian Haw's demonstration (which had been on-going since 2001) in Parliament Square. Haw challenged the conditions as being either *ultra vires* or incompatible with Articles 10 and 11 of the European Convention on the grounds that they were unreasonable or insufficiently clear.[17] The Court ruled that the objective behind the conditions – which in part were designed to ensure others did not use the demonstration as a cover for terrorist activities – provided 'a perfectly reasonable and proportionate justification for imposing appropriate conditions'. However, as the conditions were unworkable they were *ultra vires* for lack of clarity.

Using powers for the wrong purpose

Powers conferred must be used for the purpose for which they were granted. In **Attorney General v Fulham Corporation** (1921), the authority was empowered under statute to establish washhouses for the non-commercial use of local residents. The Corporation decided to open a laundry on a commercial basis. The Corporation was held to have acted *ultra vires* the statute. **Westminster Corporation v London and Northern Western Railway Company** (1905), however, represents a case where a charge of wrong purpose failed. The Corporation had power, under section 44 of the Public Health Act 1891, to provide public conveniences and had constructed them midway under the street with access gained by means of a subway. The Railway Company which owned stock in adjacent buildings claimed that the power had been used improperly. The House of Lords disagreed, stating that 'the primary object of the council was the construction of the conveniences with the requisite and proper means of approach thereto and exit therefrom'.

Thus, where a public authority uses a power for the purpose intended by Parliament and reasonably provides a facility incidental to – or complementary to – the power conferred, the

---

15 As in **Hall and Co Ltd v Shoreham-by-Sea Urban District Council** (1964) discussed above.

16 Also at issue was delegation of powers: it was held, following **Carltona v Works Commissioners** (1943) that the Commissioner of Police could not be expected personally to draft conditions and that delegation was not unlawful.

17 The conditions included restrictions on the size of the site, its supervision, ensuring that no items could be used to conceal other items, and requirements to report to the police if 20 or more persons were to be present.

authority is acting within its powers. It can of course be argued that the Corporation's prime objective was, in fact, the provision of a subway; nevertheless, that objective – if it was the primary objective – did not invalidate the action.

The **Westminster Corporation** case was further considered in **R v Inner London Education Authority ex parte Westminster City Council** (1986), which provided an opportunity for the Divisional Court to consider the issue of two purposes being pursued under one power. On the facts of the case, it was held that, in pursuing two purposes in relation to education funding, the Council had allowed an 'irrelevant consideration' to dominate its decision making and that, accordingly, it had acted *ultra vires*.

The test which Professor Evans prescribes is: 'What is the true purpose for which the power was exercised? If the actor has in truth used his power for the purposes for which it was conferred, it is immaterial that he was thus enabled to achieve a subsidiary object . . .'

Acting in a manner inconsistent with the purpose of an Act was seen in **Padfield v Minister for Agriculture, Fisheries and Food** (1968). Under the Agricultural Marketing Act 1958, a Committee of Investigation was established to make inquiries, if the minister 'so directed', into complaints made to the minister concerning the operation of, amongst other products, milk. South Eastern dairy farmers complained that the Milk Marketing Board had fixed prices in a manner prejudicial to farmers in the South Eastern region of the country. The minister refused to refer the matter to the Committee of Investigation. The farmers challenged the minister's decision. The House of Lords granted an order of mandamus, requiring the minister to consider properly whether he should exercise his discretion to refer. The House of Lords ruled by a majority[18] that, while the minister was not obliged to refer every complaint made, he did not have an unfettered discretion to refuse to refer a case. The result was something of a hollow victory for the farmers, since the incoming minister, having referred the matter to the committee, which upheld the complaint, rejected the committee's recommendations.

R v Brixton Prison Governor ex parte Soblen (1963) also illustrates the problem of distinguishing between proper and improper motives. The United States of America had requested the return of Soblen to face criminal charges. The offence with which he was charged was not a legal basis for extradition. In judicial review proceedings, the Home Secretary argued that his deportation was on the basis that his continued presence in Britain was not 'conducive to the public good'.[19] The Court of Appeal ruled that the Home Secretary's power to deport on that ground was not restricted by the fact that he was also responding to a request from the government of the United States.

In **R v Secretary of State for Foreign and Commonwealth Affairs ex parte World Development Movement** (1995), the government was held to have acted unlawfully in relation to aid money paid to Malaysia. In 1988,[20] the United Kingdom government signed an agreement with the Malaysian Prime Minister for the sale of arms valued at £1.3 billion.[21] In 1989, Britain offered £234 million towards the building of the Pergau Dam. In 1991,[22] the deal went ahead, despite warnings from officials that the project was uneconomic and a waste of public funds. The monies were paid out of the Overseas Development Administration (ODA) budget. Under international law, any linkage between aid monies and arms sales is prohibited. While the government denied any such link, a House of Commons Foreign Affairs Committee inquiry concluded that the government had, in effect, made such a link. Furthermore, under section 1

---

18 Lord Morris of Borth-y-Gest dissenting.
19 On this concept, see further Chapter 22.
20 When Baroness Thatcher was Prime Minister.
21 The agreement being signed by the then Secretary of State for Defence, George Younger.
22 Under the premiership of John Major.

of the Overseas Development and Co-operation Act 1980, the Foreign Secretary is empowered to authorise payments only 'for the purpose of promoting the development or maintaining the economy of a country or territory outside the United Kingdom or the welfare of its people'. The High Court ruled that the Foreign Secretary had acted unlawfully, in part because the project was 'economically unsound', and also because the aid did not promote the development of a country's economy as required by law. As a result, some £55 million already spent on the project had to be returned to the ODA.[23]

In **Porter v Magill** (2002), the House of Lords ruled that the power to sell property to tenants in the hope of gaining party political advantage at an election was unlawful. It was argued that provided some proper purpose was being pursued, the decision was not unlawful. The House of Lords disagreed: the power had to be used for its intended purpose – and that was not to secure an electoral advantage.

Relevant and irrelevant considerations in decision making

The following section considers relevant and irrelevant considerations which are taken into account in decision making. To a large extent, there is at best a fine line between using powers for the wrong purpose and the relevancy of considerations. Categorisation is a limited, although organisationally useful, device: the essential point to remember is that the heart of the matter lies in whether discretionary powers have been exercised lawfully or not, irrespective of the headings under which cases may be grouped. One case which straddles the boundaries of using powers for an improper purpose and taking irrelevant considerations into account is that of **R v Somerset County Council ex parte Fewings** (1995). The local authority decided to ban stag hunting on land owned by the council and designated for recreational purposes.[24] Laws J accepted that, in some circumstances, stag hunting could legitimately be banned – for example, where the hunt would damage rare flora, or if the animals themselves were rare. Here, however, the motivation behind the ban was the moral objection of the councillors to hunting. Laws J ruled that:

> If the activity in question is permissible under the general law, as is the practice of deer hunting, it is by no means to be prohibited on grounds only of the decision maker's distaste or ethical objection where the reach of his statutory function on its face requires no more than the making of objective judgments for the management of a particular regime. [p 530]

On appeal to the Court of Appeal, the decision was upheld, but on narrower grounds. The Court ruled that the Council's mind had not been directed to relevant statutory provisions, and it had not considered, as it was required to do, whether a ban of hunting would be for the general public benefit.

A case which illustrates the intermingling of grounds for review is that of **Wheeler v Leicester City Council** (1985). In **Wheeler**, the House of Lords thoroughly examined the concepts of unreasonableness and of fairness, and here the interaction between bad faith, unreasonableness and procedural impropriety can be discerned. In 1984, the Rugby Football Union announced a tour to South Africa, with a team including three members of the Leicester Football Club. At the time, the government was opposed to any sporting links with South Africa. Leicester City

---

23 See also **R v Secretary of State for the Environment ex parte Spath Holme Ltd** (2000).
24 Under the Local Government Act 1972, s 120.

Council – with a 25 per cent immigrant population – was virulently opposed to the proposed tour. The Leicester Club secretary attended a meeting with the leader of Leicester Council, at which he was asked to support the government's – and the council's – policy of opposition to the South African regime of apartheid. The club's response was to assert its opposition to apartheid but to stress that they were not constrained from playing in South Africa as a result of governmental opposition, which had neither made such tours illegal nor subject to sanctions on those who visited South Africa. As a result of the club's refusal to comply with the City Council's request that they withdraw from the tour, Leicester City Council resolved that the club would be suspended from using a local playing field for a 12-month period, the ban to be reviewed after a year and a new decision to be taken based on the club's attitude to South Africa at that time. The House of Lords ruled that a political policy – however morally justified – could not provide the lawful basis on which to deprive the club of engaging in its lawful activities.

As can be seen, the two purposes test involves the issue of irrelevant considerations. That is to say, a subsidiary or secondary purpose being pursued may – if it dictates the decision-making process – invalidate that process. Here, attention is turned to situations where an authority fails to take account of relevant considerations, or takes into account irrelevant considerations which materially affect the decision reached, and may be held to be acting *ultra vires*. Many of the cases involve the fiduciary duty which is owed by local authorities to their ratepayers. In **Roberts v Hopwood** (1925), for example, the local authority was empowered by statute to pay its workers 'as it thought fit'.[25] Nevertheless, when the council decided to pay wages which were higher than the national average and to pay men and women equally, it was held to have been acting beyond its powers. Its duty to its ratepayers overrode its desire to better the lot of its workers.[26] The court held that the council was pursuing a policy of 'philanthropic socialism' which was inconsistent with its duties to its ratepayers. Compare **Roberts v Hopwood** with **Pickwell v Camden London Borough Council** (1983), in which the council had paid additional monies to its manual workers in order to secure settlement of an industrial dispute. It was held that the payments were reasonable.

Similar considerations applied in **Bromley London Borough Council v Greater London Council** (1983). There, the Greater London Council, wishing to increase passenger numbers – and thereby reduce the traffic congestion on the roads – by decreasing fares on public transport, sought to pay for this by seeking a higher level of subsidy for London Transport by increasing the rates payable by ratepayers, the burden of which would fall on the residents of London boroughs. The House of Lords held the Greater London Council to be acting *ultra vires*. The House of Lords ruled that, whilst section 3 of the Transport (London) Act 1969 conferred a wide discretion on the authority, and that grants could be levied to supplement the income from transport fares, that discretion was limited by London Transport's basic obligation to run its operations on ordinary business principles, which their fare reduction policy contravened. As in **Roberts v Hopwood** (1925), the council could not use its grant-making powers to achieve a social policy which was inconsistent with those obligations: the Greater London Council (GLC) was using its powers for the wrong purpose. Moreover, the rate reduction was also invalid in so far as it involved a breach of fiduciary duty owed by the council to its ratepayers. The fact that the policy had been part of an election mandate was not sufficient justification for the policy. The members of the council were representatives of the people, not delegates thereof. Accordingly, they were not irrevocably bound to fulfil election promises but, rather,

---

25 Under the Metropolis Management Act 1855, s 62.
26 See also **Prescott v Birmingham Corporation** (1955); **Taylor v Munrow** (1960).

must act in the interests of all constituents – not just those constituents who were users of London Transport.

This view on the doctrine of mandate – or responsibility to electors – may be contrasted with the decision in **Secretary of State for Education v Tameside Metropolitan Borough Council** (1977). The Labour-controlled Council in March 1975 proposed a scheme of comprehensive education to come into effect in 1976. In 1976, a Conservative Council was elected. The Party had conducted its election campaign in large part on the education platform. On entering office, the council reversed the education policy of the previous administration. The Secretary of State issued a direction under section 68 of the Education Act 1944, ordering the council to implement the comprehensive schooling policy of the previous local council. The House of Lords laid much emphasis on the wishes of the electorate. Lord Wilberforce declared:

> . . . if he [the Secretary of State] had exercised his judgment on the basis of the factual situation in which this newly elected authority were placed – with a policy approved by the electorate, and massively supported by the parents – there was no ground, however much he might disagree with the new policy and regret such administrative dislocation as was brought about by the change, on which he could find that the authority were acting or proposing to act unreasonably . . .

Where an irrelevant consideration does not affect the outcome of a decision, the court may hold that the authority is acting *intra vires*. For example, in **R v Broadcasting Complaints Commission ex parte Owen** (1985), the Broadcasting Authority – with the statutory responsibility of ensuring fairness in the allocation of broadcasting time for political parties at election time – refused to consider a complaint that a political party had been given too little broadcasting time. That decision was challenged in the courts. However, while the Commission had some good reasons for not considering the complaint, it had also erred by giving weight to an irrelevant consideration, namely, that the task would be burdensome. The court nevertheless held that the Commission was acting within its lawful discretion.

Whether or not a local authority may take into account considerations relating to financial resources when assessing an individual's needs was considered by the Court of Appeal and House of Lords in **R v Gloucestershire County Council ex parte Barry; R v Lancashire County Council ex parte Royal Association for Disability and Rehabilitation** (1997).[27] Under the Chronically Sick and Disabled Persons Act 1970, a local authority is under the duty to identify the needs of disabled persons, and to meet such needs. The House of Lords ruled that the resources of the authority were a relevant consideration. Lord Nicholls of Birkenhead conceded that the argument put forward by Lord Lloyd, dissenting, that a person's needs were unaffected by local authority resources was an 'alluring argument', but one which he could not accept. The argument, he stated, was flawed by a 'failure to recognise that needs for services cannot sensibly be assessed without having some regard to the cost of providing them'.[28] The reasoning of the majority in the House of Lords in **Barry** was followed in **R v Sefton Metropolitan Borough Council ex parte Help the Aged** (1997). In that case, the needs of an elderly woman who was admitted to a nursing home, and the cost of meeting those needs, were in issue. Having considered the case of **Barry**, the Court of Appeal ruled that a local authority was entitled to have regard to its own limited financial resources. However, where a need existed, the authority was under a statutory duty to make arrangements to meet that need and lack of resources was no excuse. The authority

---

27 See also **R v Liverpool Crown Court ex parte Luxury Leisure Ltd** (1998).
28 Local authority resources were also significant in the case of **R (McDonald) v Kensington and Chelsea LBC** (2011). See Gordon, K, 'Counting the votes: a brief look at McDonald', 920110 14 CCLR 337.

could not, from the time that a person was assessed as being in need, fail to meet their statutory duty. Financial considerations were uppermost in the decision in **R v Cambridge Health Authority ex parte B** (1995), in which the Court of Appeal held that the courts could not make judgments about how health authorities decide to allocate a limited budget. The health authority had refused to fund further chemotherapy or a second bone marrow transplant for a ten-year-old girl with only a few weeks to live. Notwithstanding that decisions relating to human life had to treated with the greatest seriousness, the court could not substitute its judgment about the allocation of financial resources for that of the authority.[29]

The Home Secretary was held to have taken irrelevant considerations into account, and failed to give weight to relevant considerations, in **R v Secretary of State for the Home Department ex parte Venables** (1997). In this case, when the Home Secretary decided to impose a tariff (the minimum sentence to be served to reflect retribution and deterrence) on the teenage killers of a young child, he took into account public opinion demanding that they be detained for life and failed to consider the progress which the killers had made in detention.

Acting in bad faith

To some extent, any decision which is ultra vires may involve 'bad faith' whenever there has been a failure to decide a case in the manner required by law. Some decisions, however, may have inadvertently breached the requirements of legality, whereas others will reveal an improper motive and unreasonableness, and more clearly demonstrate that the decision maker acted in 'bad faith'. An early judicial explanation of the limits of powers conferred upon public bodies is provided by Lord Macnaghten in **Westminster Corporation v London & North West Railway** (1905):

> It is well settled that a public body invested with statutory powers . . . must take care not to exceed or abuse its powers. It must keep within the limits of the authority committed to it. It must act in good faith. And it must act reasonably. The last proposition is involved in the second, if not in the first. (at p 430)

While the courts regularly use the language of 'good' and 'bad' faith, this usually means no more than that a decision maker must act 'reasonably' and must pursue the true objective of a statute. It seldom implies any moral wrongdoing on the part of the decision maker.

Fettering discretion

An authority may act ultra vires if, in the exercise of its powers, it adopts a policy which effectively means that it is not truly exercising its discretion at all. This principle is explained in **R v Port of London Authority ex parte Kynoch** (1919), in which it was held that an authority could not adopt a rigid policy which had the effect of ensuring that applications of a certain category would invariably be refused. In **Kynoch**, the applicant sought judicial review of the decision of the Port of London Authority to refuse him permission to construct a wharf on land he owned adjoining the River Thames. Permission was refused on the basis that the Authority itself had a duty to provide the facilities. The challenge to the Authority's decision failed, on the basis that it appeared to the court that the Authority had given genuine consideration to the application on its merits.

---

29 See also **R v East Sussex County Council ex parte Tandy** (1998); **B v Harrow London Borough Council** (2000); **R v Camden and Islington Health Authority ex parte E** (2001).

Compare **Kynoch** with **British Oxygen Co v Board of Trade** (1971), in which **Kynoch** was judicially considered. In **BOC**, the House of Lords upheld the right of the Board of Trade to have a general policy, provided that the policy did not preclude the Board from considering individual cases. Lord Reid considered the scope of discretion, asserting that:

> There are two general grounds on which the exercise of an unqualified discretion can be attacked. It must not be exercised in bad faith, and it must not be so unreasonably exercised as to show that there cannot have been any real or genuine exercise of the discretion. But, apart from that, if the minister thinks that policy or good administration requires the operation of some limiting rule, I find nothing to stop him . . . What the authority must not do is to refuse to listen at all.

The application failed. The Board of Trade had not adopted a rigid and invariable policy which rendered the consideration of applications a mere sham exercise in which there was no possibility of a fair consideration of the merits because of the adoption of a rigid policy.

However, in **H Lavender & Sons Ltd v Minister of Housing and Local Government** (1970), a different conclusion was reached. Lavender had applied for planning permission to extract sand and gravel from high grade agricultural land. The local planning authority refused permission and Lavender appealed to the Minister of Housing and Local Government. The appeal was dismissed, the Minister of Housing and Local Government being persuaded by the Minister of Agriculture that such land should be preserved for agricultural purposes. Accordingly, the minister ruled that:

> It is the minister's present policy that land should not be released for mineral working unless the Minister of Agriculture is not opposed. In the present case, the agricultural objection has not been waived and the minister has therefore decided not to grant planning permission for the working of the site.

The decision was set aside. The minister was entitled to have a policy but, in reality, in this instance, the minister's decision had been based solely on another minister's objection. The minister, therefore, did not open his mind to Lavender's application and thereby fettered his discretion. In reality, the decision to refuse planning permission was that of the Minister of Agriculture, who had no power to determine such matters.

In **Stringer v Minister of Housing and Local Government** (1970), the court considered the legality of a minister's policy to restrict development of land which could interfere with the Jodrell Bank radio telescope. The court held that the minister's general policy was lawful, provided that the policy did not result in his failing to take into account relevant issues in each individual application for planning permission. In **Sagnata Investments v Norwich Corporation** (1971), the council had a policy never to grant permits for amusement arcades in Norwich. There was no objection to Sagnata Investments itself; rather, no application – whatever its merits – would have succeeded because of the council's policy. The court held that the council had paid no regard whatsoever to the merits of the application. The council's decision was therefore quashed.[30]

In **R v Chief Constable of North Wales Police ex parte AB** (1997),[31] the Court of Appeal ruled that the policy of the North Wales police to disclose information to members of the public

---

30 See also **R (Nicholds) v Security Industry Authority** (2007).
31 See **R (H) v Ashworth Hospital Authority; R (Ashworth Health Authority) v Mental Health Review Tribunal for West Midlands and North West Region** (2002).

concerning the presence of a former paedophile offender was not unlawful. The court recognised that, in general, good public administration involved not disclosing damaging information about individuals unless there was sound justification for so doing. The applicants for judicial review, who were married, had both been convicted of serious sexual offences against children, and had served long prison sentences. The Lord Chief Justice recognised the tension between the rights of former offenders and the interests of the community. The police had not adopted a policy of blanket disclosure, but had carefully considered the case on its merits, and accordingly had not fettered its discretion.[32]

The House of Lords' decision in **R v Secretary of State for the Home Department ex parte Simms** (1999) is also significant in demonstrating the courts' refusal to allow a strict policy to undermine individual rights. The decision in **Simms** was reached on common law principles and before the Human Rights Act 1998 came into force, but nevertheless the approach taken is consistent with post-Human Rights Act cases. It may be compared with the House of Lords' decision in **Daly**, discussed below, in which a prison policy was held to violate a Convention right.[33] In **Simms**, the applicants had been convicted of murder but continued to plead their innocence; they had been refused permission to appeal against their convictions. The prisoners wished to pursue their claim to justice through the press. The Home Secretary had adopted a policy which imposed a blanket ban on journalists interviewing prisoners with a view to publication, on the basis that such publicity could undermine prison control and discipline. Lord Steyn concluded – in the language of proportionality and human rights[34] – that 'these provisions are exorbitant in width in so far as they would undermine the fundamental rights invoked by the applicants in the present proceedings and are therefore ultra vires'.[35]

Unauthorised delegation

Where powers are conferred by statute, the general rule is that they may not be delegated unless that delegation is authorised by law. Not all delegations will be unlawful. The courts will not hold, for instance, that a minister must exercise each and every power personally. It is accepted that, where statute confers powers on ministers, the powers are, in fact, exercisable on his behalf by the personnel of his department. As explained in **Local Government Board v Arlidge** (1915), 'a minister cannot do everything himself'.[36] In **Arlidge** – an early and seminal case which ensured the conduct of government under the supervision of the courts – the court held that, whilst a minister could lawfully delegate his power of determination to a subordinate, he, nevertheless, remained constitutionally and personally accountable to Parliament for the conduct of his department.[37]

This principle was well illustrated in **Carltona v Works Commissioners** (1943). The Commissioners were given powers, under wartime regulations, to requisition property. Carltona's property was requisitioned, the order for requisition being signed, for and on behalf of the Commissioners, by a civil servant with the rank of assistant secretary. Lord Greene MR stated:

---

32 Reported as **R v Chief Constable of North Wales Police ex parte Thorpe** (1998). See also **R v Secretary of State for the Home Department ex parte Dinc** (1998); **R v North West Lancashire Health Authority ex parte A** (2000).

33 In **Daly**, the right in question was the right to privacy. In **Simms** – had it been heard after the Human Rights Act 1998 came into force – the issue would have been freedom of expression under Article 10.

34 On which see below.

35 See more recently a discussion of the scope of the rule against fettering in **R (on the application of Nicholds) v Security Industry Authority** (2007).

36 Note also that this case is an early authority for the proposition that the rules of natural justice do not necessarily require an oral hearing in every case: per Taylor LJ in **R v Army Board of the Defence Council ex parte Anderson** (1991).

37 See Dicey, 1885, Appendix 2.

It cannot be supposed that the particular statutory provision meant that in every case the minister in person should direct his mind to the matter. Constitutionally the decision of such an officer is the decision of the minister; the minister is responsible to Parliament. If the minister delegated to a junior official then he would have to answer to Parliament . . .

The decision in **Arlidge** may be compared with that of **Barnard v National Dock Labour Board** (1953). In **Barnard**, disciplinary powers delegated by statute to the London Dock Board were subdelegated to a port manager. That delegation was held to be ultra vires, on the basis that such a disciplinary function could not lawfully be delegated to another and must be exercised by the Board to whom the power was granted. Similarly, in **R v Talbot Borough Council ex parte Jones** (1988), where a local councillor applied for local authority housing. The housing tenancy committee resolved that the applicant should be given priority status and that her rehousing, subsequent to divorce, should be decided by the chairman and vice chairman of the committee, according to the Council's Standing Orders,[38] in consultation with the Borough Housing Officer. In 1986, the Housing Officer allocated her a house. In proceedings for judicial review, it was held that the decision to allocate housing could not lawfully be subdelegated from the chairman and vice chairman of the committee to the Housing Officer. The decision was also void on the grounds that irrelevant considerations had been taken into account and that relevant considerations – the needs of others on the waiting list – had been ignored.[39] Also in relation to housing, it was held in **Credit Suisse v Waltham Forest London Borough Council** (1997) that a local authority with a statutory duty to provide housing for the homeless could not lawfully set up a company (with finance guaranteed by the Council) to purchase homes, but over which the Council would have little control. The Council could not lawfully delegate its powers in this manner.

Failure to act

An authority may be under a statutory duty to take action and, depending upon the specificity of that duty, may be held to be acting unlawfully if it fails to act. This is a difficult area of law, in that some duties imposed by statute are clear and precise, and hence enforceable by the courts, whereas others may be of a general, non-specific nature and thus not court-enforceable: all will turn on the wording of the statute. Statute may stipulate the objective to be achieved but leave it to a local authority or other public body to determine the manner in which the objective should be achieved. Furthermore, in many cases, statute will provide that the Secretary of State shall have default powers, by the use of which he can compel a local authority to act should it fail so to do, in which case, the courts may be reluctant to permit the pursuit of an alternative remedy. In **R v Secretary of State for the Environment ex parte Norwich City Council** (1982), the authority had the duty to sell council housing to tenants[40] at a discounted rate. If a tenant exercised his or her right to buy, and the council did not respect that right, the minister could exercise his powers to ensure compliance with the legislation, if satisfied that a tenant's right had 'not effectively and expeditiously' been recognised. The council argued that

---

38 Under the Local Government Act 1972, s 101.
39 In **R v Home Secretary ex parte Oladehinde** (1991), the House of Lords ruled that the Immigration Act 1971 provided specific matters which could not be delegated by the minister, and the court would not infer further restrictions.
40 Housing Act 1980. The Housing Act 1985 confers default powers on the minister to act where a local council fails to comply with the policy of the Act.

this policy was reasonable. However, the Court of Appeal rejected that argument, since the council had no discretion in light of the statutory right to buy. The failure of the council to implement the 'right to buy' legislation was to be controlled by the minister. Should the minister, in the exercise of his powers, act *ultra vires*, the court will control the exercise of power by judicial review. However, the courts may not be willing to rule against the minister merely because the court takes a different view of the merits of the case (*per* Lord Denning).

Failure to comply with policy

The rule of law requires that there should be certainty and clarity in the law. However, in the administrative process, it is commonplace for there to be policies which supplement the legal rules. In relation to the powers of the police, for example, there exist Codes of Practice which guide the police in the exercise of their statutory duties. In relation to immigration law, there are Immigration Rules which similarly inform those applying the law. It is an established principle of public law that policy, while not law, must be adhered to unless there are justifiable reasons for departing from it.[41]

There are circumstances in which failure to comply with a published policy renders an otherwise lawful decision unlawful. An example of this is seen in **Shepherd Masimba Kambadzi v Secretary of State for the Home Department** (2011), a decision of the Supreme Court.[42] The appellant, a Zimbabwean national, had served a prison sentence at the end of which he was lawfully detained[43] pending deportation. The Home Secretary's published policy included the instruction that 'once detention has been authorised it must be kept under close review to ensure that it continues to be justified'. The system of review had not been complied with. Did this failure to comply with policy render the decision to detain unlawful? The Supreme Court ruled, by a majority of three to two, that it did. Lord Hope, while recognising that policy is not law, nevertheless endorsed the view expressed by Lord Phillips of Worth Matravers MR in **R (Saadi) v Secretary of State for the Home Department** (2002)[44] that the lawful exercise of statutory powers can be restricted, according to established principles of public law, by government policy and legitimate expectation to which such policy gives rise (at para 34E). Furthermore, Lord Hope stated that a 'failure by the executive to adhere to its published policy without good reason can amount to an abuse of power which renders the detention itself unlawful' (at para 41). Of particular importance in this case was the deprivation of liberty of the individual protected under Article 5 of the European Convention on Human Rights. This case may be contrasted with the Supreme Court's decision in **R (Munir) v Secretary of State for the Home Department; R (Rahman) v Same** (2012). In **Munir and Rahman** the key issue was whether the Secretary of State's policy (Deportation Policy 5/96) was a statement of practice which fell within the meaning of section 3(2) of the Immigration Act 1971, and therefore required laying before Parliament. The Supreme Court ruled that it did not: the statement did no more than state that a rule might be relaxed if certain conditions were satisfied, but that whether it would be relaxed would depend on all the circumstances. As such it was highly flexible and could not be regarded as a statement of practice. In **R (Alvi) v Home Secretary** (2012), however, the Supreme Court ruled that section 3(2) of the Immigration Act 1971 required that statements of the rules and any changes to the rules be laid before Parliament and that failure by the Home Secretary to comply with this duty had the consequence that he could not rely on the statements in

---

41 See **R (Hardial Singh) v Governor of Durham Prison** (1983) and **Nadarajah v Secretary of State for the Home Department** (2003).
42 Otherwise reported as **R (SK (Zimbabwe)) v Secretary of State for the Home Department** (2011).
43 Under the Immigration Act 1971.
44 At para 7.

reaching an immigration decision. In this case the statements formed a part of the Immigration Rules and were determinative of the claimant's case.

Questions of the legality of decisions are also raised where an executive policy exists but remains unpublished. In **Walumba Lumba v Secretary of State for the Home Department** (2011) the two claimants, who were foreign nationals, had committed serious offences and served prison sentences. The Home Secretary notified them that they were to be deported. The Home Office's published policy stated that there was a presumption in favour of release pending deportation. In 2006, however, the Home Office adopted a policy, which remained unpublished, which amounted to a near blanket ban on release. The Supreme Court ruled that an unpublished policy, which conflicted with previously published policy, rendered their detention unlawful. It was immaterial that they could have been detained lawfully pending deportation.

Irrationality: *Wednesbury* Unreasonableness

'Irrationality' is a concept which takes the courts further from reviewing the procedures by which a decision has been made and testing its legality, and closer to substituting the court's own view of the merits of the decision. The terms 'irrationality' and '**Wednesbury** unreasonableness' appear to be used at the judge's own preference.[45] Alternative expressions such as 'arbitrary and capricious', 'frivolous or vexatious' and 'capricious and vexatious' are also used on occasion to express the same concept.[46] 'Acting perversely' has also been used to judicially express the idea of unreasonableness.[47] The term 'unreasonableness' may thus be seen as an 'umbrella concept' which covers most of the major headings of review.

Early expression was given to the concept in two cases, **Rooke's Case** (1598) and **Keighley's Case** (1609). In **Rooke's Case**, Coke LJ proclaimed:

> . . . and notwithstanding the words of the commission give authority to the commissioners to do according to their discretions, yet their proceedings ought to be limited and bound with the rule of reason and law. For discretion is a science or understanding to discern between falsity and truth, between wrong and right, between shadows and substances, between equity and colourable glosses and pretences, and not to do according to their wills and private affections . . .

The classic case of more recent times is that of **Associated Provincial Picture Houses Ltd v Wednesbury Corporation** (1948). The local authority had the power to grant licences for the opening of cinemas subject to such conditions as the authority 'thought fit' to impose. The authority, when granting a Sunday licence, imposed a condition that no children under the age of 15 years should be admitted. The applicants argued that the imposition of the condition was unreasonable and *ultra vires* the corporation's powers. The authority argued that there were no limits on the conditions which could be imposed in the statute. Lord Greene MR alluded to the many grounds of attack which could be made against a decision, citing unreasonableness, bad faith, dishonesty, paying attention to irrelevant circumstances and disregard of the proper decision-making procedure, and held that each of these could be encompassed within the umbrella term 'unreasonableness'. The test propounded in that case was whether an authority

---

45 See eg Lord Donaldson MR in **R v Devon County Council ex parte G** (1989), p 577.
46 Per Wade and Forsyth, 2004 and references therein.
47 Per Lord Brightman in **R v Hillingdon London Borough Council ex parte Pulhofer** (1986). The test of **Wednesbury** unreasonableness is the foundation of the jurisdiction of University Visitors, who should only intervene in academic matters in exceptional circumstances: **Jhamat v Inns of Court School of Law (Visitors to the Inns of Court)** (1999).

had acted, or reached a decision, in a manner 'so unreasonable that no reasonable authority could ever have come to it':

> . . . a person entrusted with a discretion must, so to speak, direct himself properly in law. He must call his own attention to the matters which he is bound to consider. He must exclude from his consideration matters which are irrelevant to what he has to consider. If he does not obey those rules, he may truly be said, and often is said, to be acting 'unreasonably'. Similarly, there may be something so absurd that no sensible person could ever dream that it lay within the powers of the authority . . .

> The court is entitled to investigate the action of the local authority with a view to seeing whether they have taken into account matters which they ought not to take into account, or, conversely, have refused to take into account and once that question is answered in favour of the local authority, it may still be possible to say that, although the local authority have kept within the four corners of the matters which they ought to consider, they have nevertheless come to a conclusion so unreasonable that no reasonable authority could ever have come to it. In such a case, again, I think the court can interfere. [p 229]

'Unreasonableness' was employed to challenge a bylaw which prohibited singing 'in any public place or highway within fifty yards of any dwelling house' although, on the merits of the case, the challenge failed.[48] In **Roberts v Hopwood** (1925), the council, in adopting a policy of paying higher wages than the national average for its workers, was unreasonable, for the discretion of the council was limited by law – it was not free to pursue a socialist policy at the expense of its ratepayers. The House of Lords ruled that, irrespective of the wording of the statute, the council had a duty to act 'reasonably'; its discretion was limited by law.[49]

The standard of reasonableness imposed by the courts is high: to impose too low a standard would in effect mean the substitution of judicial discretion for administrative discretion. It is for this reason that Lord Greene, cited above, states that a decision is unreasonable if it is 'so absurd that no sensible person could ever dream that it lay within the powers of the authority', and Lord Diplock, in **Council of Civil Service Unions v Minister for the Civil Service** (1985), regarded unreasonableness as entailing a decision '. . . so outrageous in its defiance of logic or of accepted moral standards that no sensible person who had applied his mind to the question to be decided could have arrived at it'.

In **Secretary of State for Education and Science v Tameside Metropolitan Borough Council** (1977), the Secretary of State for Education directed a newly elected local authority to implement plans, devised by the predecessor council, to introduce comprehensive schooling and abolish grammar schools.[50] At the election, there had been a change in the political composition of the council, which resulted in the change of policy. The Secretary of State's power was to direct an authority as to the exercise of its powers if he was satisfied that the authority was acting unreasonably. The Secretary of State argued that the new council would not be able to organise the necessary system of selective entry required for grammar schools in time for the new academic year, and that the authority was therefore unreasonable.

The matter went to the House of Lords. The court had to determine the extent of the Secretary of State's discretion under section 68 of the Education Act. The wording of the section

---

48 **Kruse v Johnson** (1898).
49 See Lord Wrenbury's judgment (1925) at p 613.
50 Under powers conferred by the Education Act 1944, s 68.

was subjective: '. . . if the Secretary of State is satisfied'. It fell to the court to determine whether, in the circumstances of the case, the Secretary of State had acted lawfully according to the court's interpretation of whether the Secretary of State did in fact have reasonable grounds for believing that the authority had acted unreasonably. Applying the **Wednesbury** reasonableness test to the decision of the local authority to retain grammar schools, the House of Lords ruled that the authority had not been unreasonable and, as a result, the Secretary of State's directions were unlawful.

Where human rights are concerned, the courts will subject decisions to a higher level of scrutiny than otherwise. In **R v Ministry of Defence ex parte Smith** (1996) Sir Thomas Bingham MR adopted the following as the correct approach to irrationality where human rights were in issue:

> The court may not interfere with the exercise of an administrative discretion on substantive grounds save where the court is satisfied that the decision is unreasonable in the sense that it is beyond the range of responses open to a reasonable decision-maker. But in judging whether the decision-maker has exceeded this margin of appreciation the human rights context is important. The more substantial the interference with human rights, the more the court will be required by way of justification before it is satisfied that the decision is reasonable in the sense outlined above.[51]

Irrationality was also central to **R (Rogers) v Swindon NHS Primary Care Trust** (2006). The applicant had been denied Herceptin treatment for breast cancer. She fell within the eligibility criteria, and the Trust did not deny funding on grounds of financial considerations.[52] However, the Trust had developed a policy which denied funding for treatment to any patient who could not show 'exceptional personal or clinical circumstances'. The Court of Appeal ruled that since financial considerations were irrelevant and the Trust had the resources to fund any treatment prescribed, to adopt a policy based on individual 'exceptional' circumstances was irrational.

In **R v Secretary of State for the Home Department ex parte Brind** (1991), the House of Lords re-examined the reasonableness of the exercise of the Home Secretary's discretion to issue a notice banning the transmission of speech by representatives of the Irish Republican Army and its political party, Sinn Fein. Despite the issue involving a denial of freedom of expression, the Court ruled that the exercise of the Home Secretary's power[53] did not amount to an unreasonable exercise of discretion.[54]

The courts continue to consider judicial review cases on the basis of irrationality. In **R (Limbu) v Secretary of State for the Home Department** (2008) a discretionary immigration policy was said irrationally to exclude material which would provide evidence which was imperative for the decision making involved. In **R (Ahmad) v Newham LBC** (2009) it was confirmed that a new scheme for the allocation of housing which in certain circumstances favoured those who had waited longest on the local authority list was not irrational as it involved prioritisation which was standard in such circumstances. In **Fargia Petitioner** (2008) the Court went as far as to say that proportionality was not a ground of review, preferring the language of irrationality when considering a cut off date for the claiming of compensation.

---

51 At p 554.
52 See *R v Cambridge Health Authority ex parte B* (1995).
53 Under the Broadcasting Act 1981. See further Chapter 18.
54 *R v Radio Authority ex parte Bull* (1995).

The doctrine of proportionality[55]

The Human Rights Act provides an additional basis on which the legality of actions of public authorities will be tested. The Human Rights Act 1998 provides for judicial review to extend to the review of administrative action to determine its compatibility with Convention requirements. As has been seen above, a fundamental concept utilised in domestic judicial review cases has conventionally been that of 'reasonableness'.[56] At issue is whether a public body, in its exercise of administrative discretion, has acted within the bounds of reasonableness conferred by the legislation, under which are subsumed the concepts of illegality, irrationality and procedural impropriety. Both the European Court of Justice of the European Community and the European Court of Human Rights – which are separate institutions and operate under separate jurisdictions[57] – have long employed the concept of 'proportionality', and it is this concept – traditionally regarded with some suspicion by domestic judges – which has now become applicable.[58]

The doctrine of proportionality is one which confines the limits of the exercise of power to means which are proportional to the objective to be pursued. The doctrine has taken firm roots in the jurisprudence of, for example, the United States of America, Canada and the law of many continental European countries. Both the Court of Justice of the European Union (ECJ)[59] and the European Court of Human Rights[60] adopt proportionality as a test against which to measure the legality of actions of authorities.[61] In **R v Home Secretary ex parte Brind** (1991), the House of Lords was not yet prepared to accept that the concept represented a separate and distinct head of judicial review.

Where issues of European Union law or the European Convention on Human Rights are involved, the doctrine is one which must be considered if the English interpretation of European law is to be consistent with that of the European Court of Justice and the Court of Human Rights. In **Stoke-on-Trent City Council v B & Q plc** (1984), for example, Hoffmann J was prepared to adopt the ECJ's proportionality test when considering the compatibility of the Shops Act 1950 and the free trade provisions of the EC Treaty.

Consistent with the requirements of the Convention, any action which *prima facie* violates protected rights must be justified on the basis that the infringement is justifiable on the grounds set out in the Convention Articles: thus, the action taken must be judged according to whether or not that action was proportionate to the objective behind the action. The Convention is replete with state discretion – the 'margin of appreciation' – allied to criteria such as 'necessary in a democratic society in the interests of national security, public safety or the economic well being of the country, for the prevention of disorder or crime for the protection of health or morals, or for the protection of rights and freedoms of others'.[62]

The doctrine of proportionality has now been adopted in domestic courts of law. In Brind, Lord Ackner asked pithily whether the Secretary of State had 'used a sledgehammer to crack a nut'. In several pre-Human Rights Act cases, it is clear that the courts have been using the doctrine of proportionality but without making explicit references thereto. For example, in

---

55 See the discussion on proportionality in Chapter 18. See Jowell and Lester, 'Proportionality: neither novel nor dangerous', in Jowell and Oliver, 1988; Jowell, 2000. On the status of the Convention before the Human Rights Act came into force, see Chapter 18. See also *R v Secretary of State for the Home Department ex parte Hussain Ahmed* (1999).

56 See *Associated Provincial Picture Houses Ltd v Wednesbury Corporation* (1948).

57 See further Chapter 7.

58 Proportionality has, however, been recognised by the Court of Appeal in the past. See eg *R v Barnsley Metropolitan BC ex parte Hook* (1976); *Attorney General v Jonathan Cape Ltd* (1976).

59 See Chapters 7 and 8.

60 See Chapter 18.

61 See eg *Dudgeon v United Kingdom* (1982), discussed in Chapter 18.

62 ECHR, Article 8(2).

R v Barnsley Metropolitan Borough Council ex parte Hook (1976), a market stall holder had had his licence revoked for urinating in public. Lord Denning MR quashed the decision, partly on the basis that the penalty – the loss of the licence – was disproportionate to the 'offence'.[63]

Proportionality was also evident in **R v Chief Constable of Sussex ex parte International Trader's Ferry Ltd** (1999). In that case, judicial review had been sought regarding the Chief Constable's decision to restrict the deployment of police officers to assist the exporters, who were being obstructed by demonstrators. In the House of Lords, Lord Slynn stated that when answering the question of whether 'appropriate measures' had been taken, the correct approach was to ask 'whether the steps taken were proportionate', and that the Chief Constable had 'shown here that what he did in providing police assistance was proportionate to what was required'. In his judgment, Lord Cook took the opportunity to consider proportionality and the **Wednesbury** test of unreasonableness, stating that 'the European concepts of proportionality and margin of appreciation produce the same result as what are commonly called **Wednesbury** principles', and re-defined the reasonableness test to the more simple formula of 'whether the decision in question was one which a reasonable authority could reach'.

With the Human Rights Act 1998, proportionality moves centre stage. In interpreting the Act, section 2 requires that domestic courts and tribunals 'must take into account' the judgments and decisions of the Court of Human Rights. Under section 6, courts and tribunals are public authorities under the Act and are therefore under a duty not to violate Convention rights. Furthermore, most Convention rights are not absolute and unqualified, but allow states to impose limitations on specified grounds, commonly in the interests of 'public safety' or 'national security'. Restrictions on the exercise of rights – derogations – must also commonly be 'prescribed by law' and 'necessary in a democratic society'. The combined effect of these provisions necessitates that courts follow the reasoning of the Court of Human Rights, and that includes the doctrine of proportionality. The domestic courts have traditionally been wary of the doctrine, on the basis that it requires judges to go beyond an analysis of the legality of the decision-making process on the grounds of legality, rationality and procedural propriety, and to address two further questions. The first is, where a breach of a right is found to have occurred, was the offending action justified as being both necessary and proportionate to the objective being sought? This requires the courts not only to look at the processes involved in reaching decisions, but to evaluate whether on the facts the decision maker adopted the approach which least undermined the right in question. That exercise involves the judges looking to the merits of decisions, rather than the process of decision making – which has been the conventional concern of judicial review – and blurs the line between review and appeal. Constitutionally, that alters the position of the judges vis à vis the executive.

See Chapter 18.

The decision of the House of Lords in **R (Daly) v Secretary of State for the Home Department** (2001) is also important in demonstrating the movement away from the traditional test of **Wednesbury** unreasonableness towards the doctrines of necessity and proportionality. The House of Lords ruled that the policy of excluding prisoners from their cells while prison officers conducted searches – which included scrutinising privileged legal correspondence – was unlawful. Lord Bingham stated that the conclusion had been reached according to common law principles, but accepted that the same result could have been achieved if the analysis had proceeded on the basis of the European Convention.[64] Lord Cooke was explicit in recognising the limitations of the traditional **Wednesbury** approach, stating that before long it would be accepted that the **Wednesbury** case was an unfortunately retrogressive decision in English law.

---

63 Also consider **Wheeler v Leicester City Council** (1985), discussed above.
64 The relevant Convention right being the right to privacy under Article 8.

However, the question arises as to whether the doctrine of proportionality applies only where fundamental human rights are in issue, or whether it will come to pervade all aspects of judicial review. This issue was addressed by Lord Slynn in **R (Alconbury Developments Ltd) v Secretary of State for the Environment, Transport and the Regions** (2001), where he stated that:

> I consider that even without reference to the Human Rights Act the time has come to recognise that this principle [proportionality] is part of English law, not only when judges are dealing with [European] Community acts, but also when they are dealing with acts subject to domestic law. *Trying to keep the **Wednesbury** principle and proportionality in separate compartments seems to me to be unnecessary and confusing.* [emphasis added]

Whether proportionality will ultimately supersede the concept of reasonableness or rationality was also considered by Dyson LJ in **R (Association of British Civilian Internees (Far East Region) v Secretary of State for Defence** (2003) in which he stated that:

> . . . we have difficulty in seeing what justification there now is for retaining the **Wednesbury** test . . .

> But we consider that it is not for this court to perform its burial rites. The continuing existence of the Wednesbury test has been acknowledged by the House of Lords on more than one occasion.

On the other hand, Professor Jowell QC has stated that 'The new constitutional approach will not affect all our judicial review. There will no doubt remain areas where traditional techniques of reasoning and justification will suffice to ensure standards of legal, fair and reasonable administration based upon the practical morality familiar to our common law' (2000, p 682).

The former Lord Chancellor, moreover, has expressed constitutional objections to the introduction of proportionality:

> . . . it invites review of the merits of public decisions on the basis of a standard which is considerably lower than that of **Wednesbury** unreasonableness and would involve the court in a process of policy evaluation which goes far beyond its allotted constitutional role. [Irvine, 1996]

The difficulty with proportionality from the traditional approach to judicial review is that it comes close to ruling on the substance, or merits, of a case and thereby risks the judges becoming embroiled in the administrative process in a manner which might be seen as infringing on the separation of powers between the executive and the judiciary. It also, at a conceptual level, raises the question of whether – and under what circumstances – differing levels of judicial scrutiny are required. Unreasonableness and irrationality are terms imbued not only with familiarity but with the comfort of a degree of objectivity which can (generally) be applied without a deep analysis of the merits of the case in hand. Proportionality, on the other hand, is more sensitive to the context of the case and requires the court to consider whether the decision reached or action taken is restricted to what is strictly required (proportionate) to the objective being sought which it cannot do without considering both the policy and the means adopted to achieving it.

In **R (Daly) v Secretary of State for the Home Department** (2001) Lord Steyn examined the differences between reasonableness and proportionality, identifying the following differences:

- the doctrine of proportionality may require the reviewing court to assess the balance which the decision maker has struck, not merely whether it is in the range of rational or reasonable decisions;
- the proportionality test may go further than the traditional grounds of review in as much as it may require attention to be directed to the relative weight accorded to interests and considerations;
- even the heightened scrutiny test (the *Smith and Grady* test) is not necessarily appropriate to the protection of human rights.

What has become clear from the case law is that there are now differing levels of review being applied, depending on the nature of the case in hand, ranging from non-justiciable issues on which the courts will not adjudicate,[65] from areas of policy where the judges will defer to the executive,[66] the conventional reasonableness test,[67] human rights issues where the courts will give 'anxious scrutiny' to the matter[68] and finally the proportionality test.[69]

Summary

The traditional focus of the courts in judicial review proceedings is that of *vires* – and the question whether a decision maker has acted inside (*intra vires*), or outside (*ultra vires*) his or her powers. However, these phrases are but a blanket expression or umbrella term for a number of ways in which an administrative body can 'go wrong'. In the **GCHQ** case (1985), Lord Diplock identified the headings for judicial review as being: illegality, irrationality or procedural impropriety, recognising that a further head of proportionality might be added in the future. Illegality, irrationality and procedural impropriety again cover a number of different, but often overlapping grounds and these and the case law must be studied. Judicial review on human rights grounds is a fertile and rapidly expanding area of the law. Here the courts are increasingly adopting the concept of proportionality to evaluate the legality of administrative action. As discussed above, it must be appreciated that the approach of the courts in human rights applications differs from that of traditional judicial review. Procedual impropriety is discussed in Chapter 25.

 Further Reading

Allan, T.R.S., (2011) 'Judicial Deference and Judicial Review: Legal Doctrine and Legal Theory', Law Quarterly Review, 127: 96.

Hickman, T.R. (2004) 'The Reasonableness Principle: Reassessing its Place in the Public Sphere', Cambridge Law Journal, 63: 166.

Hickman, T.R. (2008) 'The substance and structure of proportionality', Public Law, 694.

Hilson, C. (2002) 'JudicialReview, Policies and the Fettering of Discretion', Public Law, 111.

Hunt, M. (2003) 'Sovereignty's Blight: Why Contemporary Public Law Needs the Concept of Due Deference' in N. Bamforth and P. Leyland (eds) *Public Law in a Multi-Layered Constitution*, Oxford: Hart Publishing.

---

65 As in *Council for Civil Service Unions v Minister for the Civil Service* (1985).
66 See, eg, *A v Secretary of State for the Home Department* (2004).
67 See *Associated Provincial Picture Houses Ltd v Wednesbury Corporation* (1948).
68 *R v Ministry of Defence ex parte Smith* (1995).
69 *R v Secretary of State for the Home Department ex parte Daly* (2001). See Le Sueur, 2005 and Olley, 2004.

Lord Irvine of Lairg (1996) 'Judges and decision makers: the theory and practice of *Wednesbury* review', Public Law, 59.

Jowell, J. (2000) 'Beyond the Rule of Law: Towards Constitutional Judicial Review', Public Law, 671.

Jowell, J. (2003) 'Judicial Deference: Servility, Civility or Institutional Capacity', Public Law, 592.

Leigh, I. (2002) 'Taking rights proportionately: judicial review, the Human Rights Act 1998 and Strasbourg', Public Law, 265.

Tomkins, A. (2003) *Public Law*, Oxford: Clarendon Press, Chapter 6.

Chapter 25

Grounds for Judicial Review II: Procedural Impropriety

Introduction

Having considered the substantive grounds for judicial review we now consider those grounds which are largely brought under the umbrella term of procedural impropriety. It is important to note that although this is labelled as 'procedural' there are some aspects of natural justice which are deep rooted in the common law tradition and have significant theoretical importance within administrative law.[1] At the present time procedural impropriety could be said to cover the following aspects of judicial review:

Procedural grounds: procedural impropriety

- failing to comply with mandatory procedures;
- breach of natural justice;

  - Article 6 of the European Convention on Human Rights;
  - the right to a fair hearing: *audi alteram partem*;
  - the rule against bias: *nemo iudex in causa sua*;
  - the duty to act fairly;
  - legitimate expectations; and
  - the failure to give reasons.

Procedural Impropriety under Statute

Failure to comply with procedures laid down by statute may invalidate a decision. The courts distinguish between those procedural requirements which are mandatory, the breach of which will render a decision void, and those which are directory, which may not invalidate the decision taken. In **London and Clydesdale Estates Ltd v Aberdeen District Council** (1979), the House of Lords emphasised the inherent vagueness in the distinction and stressed that the court would not draw a hard and fast line: it is all a matter of degree and the particular circumstances of the case must be examined.[2] However, in some cases, the requirement to adhere to procedural correctness is clear. For example, in **Bradbury v Enfield London Borough Council** (1967), the Education Act 1944 provided that, if a local education authority intends to establish new schools or cease to maintain existing schools, notice must be given to the minister, following which, public notice must be given in order to allow interested parties to comment.[3] The Council breached the requirement of public notice and the plaintiffs sought an injunction. The Council claimed that educational chaos would occur if they were required to comply with the procedural requirements. That plea met with little sympathy in court. Lord Denning stated that:

> . . . if a local authority does not fulfil the requirements of the law, this court will see that it does fulfil them. . . . I can well see that there may be a considerable upset for a number of people, but I think it far more important to uphold the rule of law. Parliament has laid down these requirements so as to ensure that the electors can make their objections and have them properly considered. We must see that their rights are upheld. [p 1324]

---

1 See Wade, W. and Forsyth, C. (2004) *Administrative Law*, 439.
2 See also *Wang v Commissioner of the Inland Revenue* (1994).
3 Education Act 1944, s 13.

Further, as has been seen earlier, in the **Aylesbury Mushroom** case,[4] the court ruled that the statutory requirements of consultation[5] with organisations or associations which represented substantial numbers of people could not be avoided by consultation with the largest representative body of all agricultural horticultural and forestry industry workers – the National Farmers' Union. For true consultation to take place in accordance with law, there must be communication with the representative organisations and the opportunity given of responding thereto, without which 'there can be no consultation'.

However, on occasion, although an authority is under a duty to act, and fails to act, the court may nevertheless uphold the decision made, provided that the decision-making process was otherwise fair and the failure to act does not affect the quality of the decision reached. This was the position in **Berkeley v Secretary of State for the Environment** (2000). In this case, in a planning application by Fulham Football Club to redevelop part of its land to provide apartments and a riverside walk, the Secretary of State was required[6] to consider the environmental impact of the proposed development, and to issue an 'environmental statement'. The Court of Appeal ruled that the Secretary of State's failure to act did not invalidate the decision. The planning application had been referred to the Secretary of State, who had appointed an inspector. A public hearing had been held, at which the applicant had been heard and at which the environmental impact of the proposed development had been fully considered. The court found that 'the procedures adopted, although flawed, had been thorough and effective [so as] to enable the inspector to make a comprehensive judgment on all the environmental issues'.[7] By contrast, in **R (Smith) v North Eastern Derbyshire Primary Care Trust** (2006) the Court of Appeal quashed a decision which had been taken without the consultation required by statute. If there had been proper consultation a different decision might have been reached. Accordingly the decision was unlawful.

When an individual is charged with an indictable offence[8] an indictment is drafted which contains a list of the charges that are being brought against the accused. The defendant then pleads either guilty or not guilty to that indictment. The jury can only try one indictment at a time. Once this indictment has been prepared it must be signed by an officer of the Crown Court in accordance with s 2(1) of the Administration of Justice (Miscellaneous Provisions) Act 1933. If there is no signature, any conviction flowing from the indictment will be nullified. In **R v Clarke and McDaid** (2008) the question for the House of Lords was whether the absence of a signed indictment at the outset of proceedings and during most of the trial had the legal effect of invalidating those proceedings. The Court also considered if that invalidity had been cured by the late signature of the indictment. The Court decided the proceedings were invalid and the convictions should be quashed.

However, despite the House of Lords' robust defence of the need for strict compliance with procedures in relation to criminal trials, the decision in **Clarke and McDaid** was in effect nullified by section 116 of the Coroners and Justice Act 2009.

Breach of Natural Justice

The rules of natural justice are common law rules – although, in many instances, their requirements may be made statutory. The fundamental dictate of justice is that those affected

---

4   *Agricultural, Horticultural and Forestry Industry Training Board v Aylesbury Mushroom Ltd* (1972).
5   Under the Industrial Training Act 1964, s 1(4).
6   Under the Town and Country Planning (Assessment of Environmental Effects) Regulations, SI 1988/1199, reg 4.
7   See also *R v Secretary of State for the Home Department ex parte Jeyeanthan; Ravichandran v Secretary of State for the Home Department* (1999).
8   Historically referred to as a serious arrestable offence.

by decision makers should be dealt with in a fair manner. In order for this to be achieved, there may be several requirements which must be fulfilled. As Lord Lane CJ stated in **R v Commission for Racial Equality ex parte Cottrell and Rothon** (1980):[9]

> As has frequently been said, and there is no harm in repeating it, all that the rules of natural justice mean is that the proceedings must be conducted in a way which is fair . . . fair in all the circumstances.

That the rules of natural justice are not rigid and determinate is emphasised by Lord Bridge in **Lloyd v McMahon** (1987):

> . . . the so-called rules of natural justice are not engraved on tablets of stone. To use the phrase which better expresses the underlying concept, what the requirements of fairness demand when any body, domestic, administrative or judicial, has to make a decision which will affect the rights of individuals depends on the character of the decision making body, the kind of question it has to make and the statutory or other framework in which it operates.

The requirements of fairness are reflected in Article 6 of the European Convention on Human Rights, now enforceable in the domestic courts under the Human Rights Act 1998. Article 6 requires a 'fair and public hearing within a reasonable time by an independent and impartial tribunal established by law'.

The rule against bias: *nemo iudex in causa sua*[10]

The essence of justice lies in a fair hearing. The rule against bias is strict: it is not necessary to show that actual bias existed, the merest appearance or possibility of bias will suffice: '. . . justice should not only be done but should manifestly and undoubtedly be seen to be done.' The suspicion of bias must, however, be a reasonable one. Both financial or personal interest in a case may disqualify a person from adjudicating.

Financial bias

A financial interest in the outcome of a case will automatically disqualify a judge from hearing a case. In **Dr Bonham's Case** (1609), Lord Coke held that members of a board which determined the level of physicians' fines could not both impose and receive the fines, thus giving early judicial expression for the requirement of freedom from bias. An early expression of the absolute requirement not only to be impartial in fact, but also to be demonstrably and clearly free from the merest suspicion of bias, is found in **Dimes v Grand Junction Canal Ltd** (1852). In **Dimes**, Lord Cottenham LC held shares in the canal company involved in litigation. The House of Lords set aside the decision in which he had adjudicated despite the fact that:

> No one can suppose that Lord Cottenham could be in the remotest degree influenced by the interest . . . It is of the last importance that the maxim that no man is to be judge in his own cause should be held sacred.

Thus, the mere existence of a financial interest, even where it does not, in fact, result in actual bias but may present the appearance of bias will be sufficient to disqualify a judge from adjudication.

---

9   At p 1586.
10 On the independence of the judiciary see Chapter 4.

In **R v Sussex Justices ex parte McCarthy** (1924), the applicant had been charged with dangerous driving and convicted. On discovering that the clerk to the magistrates' court was a solicitor who had represented the person suing McCarthy for damages, McCarthy applied for judicial review based on bias on the part of the clerk. The clerk had retired with the magistrates when they were considering their verdict. It was accepted that the magistrates neither sought advice nor were given advice by the clerk during their retirement. Nevertheless, McCarthy's conviction was invalidated on the basis of the possibility of bias.[11]

The question of financial bias again arose in **Metropolitan Properties Co v Lannon** (1969), where an application was lodged by a property company in order to challenge a decision of a rent assessment committee on the basis that Lannon, a member of the committee had, in his professional capacity as a solicitor, given advice to tenants of a close business associate of the property company. Lord Denning MR ruled that, while there was no actual bias:

> . . . the court looks at the impression which would be given to other people. Even if he was as impartial as could be, nevertheless, if right minded persons would think that, in the circumstances, there was a real likelihood of bias on his part, then he should not sit. And, if he does sit, his decision cannot stand . . .
>
> The court will not inquire whether he did, in fact, favour one side unfairly. Suffice it that reasonable people might think he did. The reason is plain enough. Justice must be rooted in confidence: and confidence is destroyed when right minded people go away thinking: 'The judge was biased.' [p 599]

A financial interest in a case which does not go beyond the financial interest of any citizen does not disqualify judges from sitting. Thus, for example, in **Bromley London Borough Council v Greater London Council** (1983), the fact that all the judges in the Court of Appeal were themselves both taxpayers and users of public transport in London did not disqualify them from hearing the case. The same position prevails in the United States of America[12] but there the issue of the financial interests of federal judges is expressly covered by statute. The Ethics in Government Act 1978 requires that Supreme Court and Federal judges must make a public declaration of 'income, gifts, shares, liabilities and transactions in securities and real estate'.[13]

Other bias

Judges – as with any other person – may exhibit bias by virtue of race, sex, politics, background, association and opinions.[14] When adjudicating, however, they must be demonstrably impartial. This impartiality involves:

> . . . the judge, listening to each side with equal attention, and coming to a decision on the argument, irrespective of his personal view about the litigants . . .

and, further, a requirement that:

> Whatever his personal beliefs, the judge should seek to give effect to the common values of the community, rather than any sectional system of values to which he may adhere.[15]

---

11 See also **Virdi v Law Society** (2010).
12 28 USC S455(b).
13 See Cranston, 1979.
14 See Griffith, 1997; Devlin, 1978.
15 Bell, 1983, pp 4 and 8.

Where a judge feels that he has a bias against one of the parties to litigation he may disqualify himself from sitting on the case, as did Lord Denning MR in **Ex parte Church of Scientology of California** (1978). There, counsel for the Church requested that he disqualify himself as a result of eight previous cases involving the Church on which he had sat. In **R v Bow Street Metropolitan and Stipendiary Magistrate ex parte Pinochet Ugarte** (1999), extradition proceedings against the former Chilean Head of State were challenged on the basis that one of the Law Lords, Lord Hoffmann, had links with Amnesty International, the charitable pressure group which works on behalf of political prisoners around the world, which had been allowed to present evidence to the court. It was accepted that there was no actual bias on the part of Lord Hoffmann, but there were concerns that the public perception might be that a senior judge was biased. As a result, the proceedings were abandoned and re-heard by a new bench of seven judges.

The Court of Appeal has jurisdiction to re-open proceedings if it is clearly established that a significant injustice has probably occurred and that there is no alternative effective remedy. Before exercising such a power, the court considers the effect of re-opening the appeal on others and the extent to which the complaining party is the author of his own misfortune. Where a remedy lies in an appeal to the House of Lords, the Court of Appeal will only give permission to re-open an appeal if it is satisfied that leave to appeal to the House of Lords will not be given.[16]

There has been uncertainty and inconsistency in the interpretation of 'bias'. In **R v Gough** (1993), opposing counsel presented two different tests for bias. The first suggested criterion was whether a reasonable and fair-minded person sitting in the court and knowing all the relevant facts would have had a reasonable suspicion that a fair trial of the defendant was not possible – the 'reasonable suspicion' test. The second suggested test was whether there was a real likelihood of bias. The question to be asked is whether there was a 'real danger' that a trial may not have been fair as a result of bias – the 'real likelihood' test.[17] The House of Lords declared that the correct test was whether there was a real likelihood, in the sense of a real possibility, of bias on the part of a justice or member of a tribunal. The **Gough** test must now be considered in light of **Porter v Magill** (2002, discussed below), which provides the definitive test.

The Court of Appeal reconsidered judicial bias in the **Locabail (UK) Ltd v Bayfield Properties Ltd** (2000) cases. The court distinguished the two rules relating to disqualification, the first being where the judge had an interest in a case which he decided, as in **Dimes v Grand Junction Canal** (1852), and where he would be automatically disqualified. The second rule was that based on examination of all the relevant circumstances, where there was a real danger or possibility of bias, as in **R v Gough** (1993). In relation to the circumstances surrounding **Timmins v Gormley**, one of the **Locabail** cases, which concerned the publication, by the Recorder who adjudicated in a personal injury case, of articles which were allegedly biased in favour of claimants and against insurers, the court ruled that, taking a broad common sense approach, a lay observer with knowledge of the facts could not have excluded the possibility that the Recorder was biased. While it was not inappropriate for a judge to publish in his area of expertise, and that such contributions could further rather than hinder the administration of justice, nevertheless, it was always inappropriate for a judge to use intemperate language about subjects on which he had adjudicated or would have to adjudicate. The appeal was allowed and a retrial ordered.[18]

---

16 See **Taylor v Lawrence** (2002).
17 At p 727; see also **R v Spencer** (1987).
18 See also **R v Local Commissioner for Administration ex parte Liverpool City Council** (1999).

In **Porter v Magill** (2002) the Leader of Westminster Council had allegedly adopted a policy of selling certain properties to tenants who would then be disposed to vote Conservative in a forthcoming election. The issue of bias arose through the role of the district auditor, Magill. There were allegations that the auditor had acted as investigator, prosecutor and judge. Moreover, it was alleged that he had prejudged the issue. The common law rule against bias came under fresh scrutiny. Uncertainty had arisen due to a divergence between the English and Scottish courts, the fact that some Commonwealth jurisdictions did not follow the **Gough** test, and that the test also diverged from the approach used by the Court of Human Rights in Strasbourg. Lord Hope stated that the question of bias should be phrased in the following manner:

> The question is whether the fair-minded and informed observer, having considered the facts, would conclude that there was a real possibility that the tribunal was biased.[19]

The House of Lords considered the issue of bias in **Gillies v Secretary of State for Work and Pensions** (2006). A Disability Appeal Tribunal consists of a legally qualified chairman and two other members, including a medical member. The medical member of the tribunal in question was a doctor who for a number of years had been providing reports for the Benefits Agency as an examining medical practitioner. The appellant, whose application for renewal of a disability living allowance had been refused, argued that there was a reasonable apprehension that the medical member had been biased. Referring to **Porter v Magill** (2002) the House of Lords ruled that a fair-minded observer would have had no reason to suppose that the doctor would not act impartially towards the claimant. Her experience in the preparation of reports was an asset and the bringing of experience to bear when examining evidence and reaching a decision had nothing to do with bias.[20] However, in **Smith v Kvaerner Cementation Foundations Ltd** (2006)[21] the Court of Appeal, following **Metropolitan Properties v Lannon**, ruled that a litigant had the right not to have his case adjudicated by a judge who knew one of the witnesses. The applicant's counsel had advised that the judge was unlikely to be biased. The Court ruled that such advice should not have been given as it influenced the applicant's decision. The decision would be set aside.

Where there is a 'significant public interest' in an issue, funding may be required. This issue was explored in **R (Main) v Minister for Legal Aid** (2007). M's mother and sister had been killed in a rail accident. The coroner considered that legal aid funding was necessary to assist M on the grounds that rail safety issues were of significant public interest. The Minister for Legal Aid refused funding, despite a recommendation from the Legal Services Commission that it be granted. The decision was held to be **Wednesbury** unreasonable: the Minister should have given reasons for departing from the Commission's recommendations and had failed to take into account the potential benefit of representation for a party representing the travelling public.

In **R v Abdroikov** (2007) the House of Lords considered whether the possibility of bias was apparent where an employed Crown prosecutor were to sit as a juror in a prosecution which was brought by his own Crown prosecution authority. They decided in the majority that a fair-minded and reasonable observer would not have seen the possibility of bias in this case. This problem was considered again in **R v Khan (Bakish Alla)** (2008) where this time the composition of the jury included a serving police officer. It was decided that such issues should be

---

19 See also **Secretary of State for Work and Pensions v Cunningham** (2004); **AWG Group Ltd v Morrison** (2006).
20 See also **Ansar v Lloyds TSB Bank** (2006); **R (Paul) v Deputy Coroner of Queen's Household** (2007); **Helow v Advocate General for Scotland** (2007).
21 See also **AWG Group v Morrison** (2006).

dealt with prior to trial and the presence of a police officer on a jury would not automatically render a conviction unsafe.

In **El Faragy v El Faragy** (2007) a judge was asked to recuse himself (stand down) from a trial when it transpired that during a pre-trial review hearing he had made discriminatory racial comments about the second respondent. The Court held that he should have withdrawn from the case due to the real possibility of bias.[22]

The issue of decisions being made with a 'closed mind' was considered in **R (Lewis) v Redcar and Cleveland BC** (2008). The case concerned the granting of a planning application. It was claimed that the members of the planning committee made their decisions with political rather than legal issues in mind. It was held that as members of the planning committee were not exercising a judicial or quasi-judicial function they could consider matters of policy when making their decisions.

The issue of presumed bias was considered in **Helow v Advocate General for Scotland** (2008). In this case the judge in an immigration case (concerning a Palestinian petitioner) was a member of a Jewish association whose members, via their publications, expressed extreme views against Palestinian causes. The House of Lords took the view that the judge's membership did not itself imply that the judge shared or endorsed the views of the association. If the judge had expressed support for these extreme views then she would not have been eligible to hear the case, but she did not.

The right to a fair hearing: *audi alteram partem*

See also
Chapter 18.

It is a fundamental requirement of justice that, when a person's interests are affected by a judicial or administrative decision, he or she has the opportunity both to know and to understand any allegations made, and to make representations to the decision maker to meet the allegations. As noted above, the right to fair trial is protected under Article 6 of the European Convention on Human Rights. The case law of the Court of Human Rights and the domestic courts is discussed in Chapter 18. By way of example, a fair determination of a case may involve one or more of the following:

(a)   the right to be given notification of a hearing;
(b)   the right to be given indications of any adverse evidence;
(c)   the right to be given an opportunity to respond to the evidence;
(d)   the right to an oral hearing;[23]
(e)   the right to legal representation at a hearing;
(f)   the right to question witnesses.

The basic requirement is that – irrespective of the decision-making body, whether 'judicial', 'quasi-judicial' or 'administrative' – the individual should be treated fairly in the decision-making process.

'Judicial', 'quasi-judicial' and 'administrative' functions: the distinctions

An early expression of the requirement of a hearing is to be found in **Cooper v Wandsworth Board of Works** (1893). There, Cooper had – without giving notice to the Board, as required by

---

22 See also *JSC BTA Bank v Mukhtar Ablyazov* (2012).
23 This is closely linked to the right to be heard as in **R (Wright) v Secretary of State for Health** (2007) and **R (O'Connell) v Parole Board** (2007).

law – started to erect a house. The Board had the power to demolish buildings built without the requisite permission, and exercised its power so to do. Cooper applied for – and recovered – damages from the Board for trespass to his property. Byles J held that the plaintiff should have been given a hearing before the Board exercised its powers, even though there was no express statutory requirement that it do so:

> . . . although there are no positive words in a statute requiring that the party shall be heard, yet the justice of the common law shall supply the omission of the legislature.[24]

Ridge v Baldwin (1964) represents a classic case which reveals judicial insistence on procedural fairness.[25] Ridge, the Chief Constable of Brighton, had been suspended from duty following charges of conspiracy to obstruct the course of justice. Despite Ridge having been cleared of any allegations against him, the judge made comments which were critical of Ridge's conduct. Subsequently, Ridge was dismissed from the force.[26] Ridge was not invited to attend the meeting at which the decision to dismiss him was reached, although he was later given an opportunity to appear before the committee which confirmed its earlier decision. Ridge appealed to the Home Secretary,[27] who dismissed his appeal. Ridge then sought a declaration that the dismissal was *ultra vires*, on the basis that the committee had violated the rules of natural justice. The following extract is taken from Lord Reid's judgment, in which the opportunity was taken to review the doctrine.

> The principle of *audi alteram partem* goes back many centuries in our law and appears in a multitude of judgments of judges of the highest authority. In modern times opinions have sometimes been expressed to the effect that natural justice is so vague as to be almost meaningless . . . It appears to me that one reason why the authorities on natural justice have been found difficult to reconcile is that insufficient attention has been paid to the great difference between various kinds of cases in which it has been sought to apply the principle. What a minister ought to do in considering objections to a scheme may be very different from what a watch committee ought to do in considering whether to dismiss a chief constable . . . [p 64]
>
> . . . I would think that the authority was wholly in favour of the appellant, but the respondent's argument was mainly based on what has been said in a number of fairly recent cases dealing with different subject matter. Those cases deal with the decisions of ministers, officials and bodies of various kinds which adversely affected property rights or privileges of persons who had no opportunity or no proper opportunity of presenting their cases before the decisions were given . . . [p 68]

There were echoes of **Ridge v Baldwin** in **R (Shoesmith) v OFSTED** (2011). The Director of a local authority's Children's Services was dismissed following the death of a child on the protection register. The Secretary of State made a direction appointing a new Director. The council

---

24 See **Steeple v Derbyshire County Council** (1984); but cf **R v Amber Valley District Council ex parte Jackson** (1984). See also **R v Hendon Rural District Council ex parte Chorley** (1933).

25 See, on this point, **R v Hillingdon Borough Council ex parte Royco Homes Ltd** (1974); **R v Commission for Racial Equality ex parte Cottrell and Rothon** (1980).

26 Under the Municipal Corporations Act 1882, s 191(4), which provides that a constable may be dismissed on the basis of either negligence in the discharge of his duty or being 'otherwise unfit' for duty.

27 Under the Police (Appeals) Act 1927.

dismissed Ms Shoesmith. No opportunity had been given to make representations. The Secretary of State's decision was unlawful, as was the dismissal which had been based on the Secretary of State's directions.

The right to a hearing founded a challenge in **Re Pergamon Press Ltd** (1971),[28] in which the directors of two companies refused to answer questions unless given a judicial-style hearing. The court ruled, however, that, although the inspectors appointed to investigate the companies were under a duty to act fairly, this must be weighed against the interests of good administration.

Impartiality was scrutinised by the European Court of Human Rights in **Kingsley v United Kingdom** (2001). The Court ruled that the applicant's right to fair trial, guaranteed by Article 6, had been violated. The applicant had been refused a certificate to hold a management position in the gaming industry by the Gaming Board of Great Britain. He sought judicial review, alleging bias on the part of a supervisory board. The Court examined the composition of the panel which decided that the applicant was not a fit and proper person to hold a certificate, and concluded that it did not present the necessary appearance of impartiality to amount to an independent and impartial tribunal. However, the Court went on to assert that even where an adjudicatory body did not comply with the requirements of Article 6, there would be no breach of the Article if the proceedings were subject to 'subsequent control by a judicial body that had full jurisdiction and did provide the guarantees of Article 6(1)'. The Court of Appeal accepted that the applicant had an arguable case, and that there was a real risk of bias, but had concluded that the decision had to stand, since the decision could only be made by the board and could not be delegated to an independent tribunal. The Court of Human Rights ruled that where a complaint was made about a lack of impartiality, the concept of full jurisdiction required that the 'reviewing court not only considered the complaint but had the ability to quash the impugned decision and to remit the case for a new decision by an impartial body'. In the present case, the domestic courts were unable to remit the case to an impartial tribunal; neither the High Court nor the Court of Appeal had 'full jurisdiction' within the meaning of Article 6 and there was a violation of the Convention.

However, the Court of Appeal in **R (Beeson) v Dorset County Council** (2003) affirmed the view that the availability of judicial review satisfied the requirements of Article 6 of the European Convention on Human Rights regarding an independent and impartial tribunal. Even where the first instance decision maker lacked the necessary element of impartiality (here the tribunal had two members who were local councillors in a dispute over the now-deceased's entitlements regarding residential care and the value of his property), the availability of judicial review would remedy that defect 'unless there was some special feature of the case to show the contrary'. In the instant case there was no special feature and there was no evidence that the panel had not arrived at a fair and reasonable recommendation.

The duty to act 'fairly' and concept of 'legitimate expectation'[29]

Irrespective of the labelling attached to the body in question, there exists a duty to 'act fairly'. The principles of fairness have not been given either universal or consistent interpretations. For example, in **McInnes v Onslow Fane** (1978), Megarry VC stated:

> . . . the further the situation is away from anything that resembles a judicial or quasi-judicial decision, and the further the question is removed from what may reasonably be called a justiciable question, the more appropriate it is to reject an expression

---

28 See also **Maxwell v Department of Trade** (1974).
29 See Sales and Steyn, 2004.

which includes the word justice and to use instead terms such as 'fairness' or the 'duty to act fairly'. [p 1530]

In **Council of Civil Service Unions v Minister for the Civil Service** (1985), the House of Lords once again turned to the apparent differences in the concepts, Lord Roskill seemingly rejecting the phrase 'natural justice' in favour of the duty to 'act fairly'. Lord Roskill asserted that:

> The phrase [natural justice] might now be allowed to find a permanent resting place and be better replaced by speaking of a duty to act fairly. But the latter phrase must not in its turn be misunderstood or misused. It is not for the courts to determine whether a particular policy or particular decisions taken in fulfilment of that policy are fair. They are only concerned with the manner in which those decisions have been taken and the extent of the duty to act fairly will vary greatly from case to case as indeed the decided cases since 1950 consistently show. [p 414]

The principle of fairness can be clearly seen in the case of **Re HK (An Infant)** (1967), wherein it was held that, whilst immigration officers were not obliged to hold a hearing before deciding an immigrant's status, they were nevertheless under an obligation to act fairly. The duty to give a hearing will be higher if a 'legitimate expectation' has been created in the mind of the complainant by the public body concerned.[30]

A legitimate expectation will arise in the mind of the complainant wherever he or she has been led to understand – by the words or actions of the decision maker – that certain procedures will be followed in reaching a decision. The complainant may have been led to believe, for example, that there would be an oral hearing, or that he would be able to make formal representations. Where such expectations have been created, the decision maker is not free simply to ignore the procedures which have been indicated. Two considerations apply to legitimate expectations. The first is where an individual or group has been led to believe that a certain procedure will apply. The second is where an individual or group relies upon a policy or guidelines which have previously governed an area of executive action.

The principle of the protection of legitimate expectations was recognised under English law in the 1970s in **R v Liverpool Corporation ex parte Liverpool Taxi Fleet Operators' Association** (1972) (discussed below),[31] and it is one of the major principles of European Community law.[32] The concept is one which has given rise to judicial disagreement. The central difficulty with legitimate expectation is whether an individual affected by an administrative decision has a legitimate expectation that the correct procedure will be followed, or whether the expectation to be protected can also be substantive. The debate as to whether legitimate expectations are confined to procedure and do not extend to substance was considered in **R v Ministry of Agriculture ex parte Hamble Fisheries** (1995) in which Sedley J stated that the applicants had a legitimate expectation on the basis of the Ministry's previous policy and accepted that substantive as well as procedure legitimate expectations could be protected. Conversely in **R v Secretary of State for the Home Department ex parte Hargreaves** (1996), in the Court of Appeal Hirst LJ rejected Sedley J's approach and stated that in relation to matters of substance the test was that of **Wednesbury** unreasonableness – not legitimate expectation.

---

30 The courts are also concerned to ensure that government proposals which will affect individual citizens are fairly presented in order to enable objectors to address the issue in question. In **R v Secretary of State for Transport ex parte Richmond upon Thames London Borough Council (No 4)** (1994), the Court of Appeal ruled that the government's proposals to restrict night flights at Heathrow, Gatwick and Stansted had been fairly set out in consultation documents. On this issue see further Chapter 18. See also **R v National Lottery Commission ex parte Camelot Group plc** (2001).

31 See also **Council for Civil Service Unions v Minister for Civil Service** (1984).

32 See Usher, 2005.

The Court of Appeal ruled in **R (Bibi) v Newham LBC** (2001) that a local authority which made promises which gave rise to legitimate expectations that the applicants would be provided with accommodation with security of tenure had to be honoured to the extent that the expectation was taken into account when allocating the applicants' position on the housing list. The applicants were refugees and accepted by the authority as homeless. The authority wrongly thought that it was under a duty to provide accommodation with security of tenure. However, the promise that such accommodation would be provided founded a legitimate expectation which had to be considered.[33]

However, while the concept of legitimate expectation has, according to the Court of Appeal, achieved an important place in developing the law of administrative fairness, whether such an expectation has been raised is dependent upon the circumstances in which statements are made, and whether in an instant case they could be taken as propounding a policy or merely statements applicable to particular cases. In **R v Secretary for the Home Department ex parte Behluli** (1998), the Home Secretary had ordered the removal of the applicant to Italy under section 2 of the Asylum and Immigration Act 1996. The applicant argued that he had a legitimate expectation that his case would be dealt with in accordance with the Dublin Convention.[34] The Court of Appeal ruled, however, that the statements relied on by the applicant fell short of the requirements necessary to establish to the requisite degree of clarity and certainty that the Secretary of State would deal with all applications for asylum in accordance with the Convention and not in accordance with the Asylum and Immigration Act 1996 and rules made thereunder.

Legitimate expectations were again considered by the Court of Appeal in **R (Nadarajah) v Secretary of State for the Home Department, R (Abdi) v Same** (2005). Lord Justice Laws stated that the theme running through the legitimate expectation cases was that 'where a public authority had issued a promise or adopted a practice which represented how it proposed to act in a given area, the law would require the promise or practice to be honoured unless there was good reason not to do so'. The principle underlying that requirement was one of good administration, which was a legal standard, which although not articulated in the Convention on Human Rights nevertheless took its place alongside such rights as the right to fair trial and no punishment without law. The principle of good administration would be undermined 'if the law did not insist that any failure or refusal to comply was objectively justified as a proportionate measure in the circumstances'. Moreover, that approach made 'no distinction between procedural and substantive expectations'.[35]

In **R (X) v Head Teacher and Governors of Y School** (2007) a claim was made for judicial review when a pupil was not allowed to wear the niqab (a form of Muslim dress). Her elder sisters had been allowed to wear the niqab when being taught by a male teacher but this policy had recently been changed. It was held there was no claim based on legitimate expectation as the school was entitled to make changes to its uniform policy.

In **R (Bapio Action Ltd) v Secretary of State for the Home Department** (2008) there had been a change in the rules for those wishing to get medical training in the United Kingdom and return to their own country. New guidance stated that offers of places (training posts) should only be made to international medical graduates if there were no suitable home candidates. It was deemed to be unlawful as it was not made in accordance with the Immigration Act 1971 and because it undermined legitimate expectations generated by Immigration Rules and the Home Office.[36]

---

33 See also **Henry Boot Homes Ltd v Bassetlaw DC** (2002).
34 Relating to the removal of persons to safe third countries.
35 See also **R (Greenpeace Ltd) v Secretary of State for Trade and Industry** (2007); **R(Bapio Action Ltd) v Secretary of State for the Home Department** (2008).
36 And see discussion of **R (Bancoult) v Secretary of State for Foreign and Commonwealth Affairs** (2008) as discussed in Chapter 5.

The giving of assurances

In **Attorney General for Hong Kong v Ng Yuen Shiu** (1983), the applicant had been an illegal immigrant for some years. He was eventually detained and an order was made for his deportation. The Director of Immigration had given a public undertaking that illegal immigrants such as Ng Yuen Shiu would not be deported without first being interviewed. The assurance was also given that 'each case would be treated on its merits'. Lord Fraser of Tullybelton in the Privy Council ruled that there was no general right in an alien to have a hearing in accordance with the rules of natural justice. Nevertheless, a 'legitimate expectation' had been created in the mind of the immigrant and, accordingly, breach of the requirement of fairness justified the order for his removal from Hong Kong to be quashed.[37] A public body cannot give undertakings which conflict with its statutory duty. In **R v Inland Revenue Commissioners ex parte Preston** (1985),[38] the House of Lords ruled that if it should do so, it was in principle entitled to go back on its undertaking. However, if the authority made an assurance and then exercised its statutory power in a manner which caused unfairness, that exercise could be viewed as an abuse of power and the undertaking upheld by the courts.

Fairness may involve the due consultation of interested parties before their rights are affected by decisions. For example, in **R v Liverpool Corporation ex parte Liverpool Taxi Fleet Operators Association** (1972), the corporation had given undertakings to the taxi drivers to the effect that their licences would not be revoked without prior consultation. When the corporation acted in breach of this undertaking, the court ruled that it had a duty to comply with its commitment to consultation.[39]

The Court of Appeal in **R v North and East Devon Health Authority ex parte Coughlan** (1999)[40] ruled that a decision by a health authority to close a home for the severely disabled at which the applicant resided, and to transfer her to the care of a local authority, was unlawful. The applicant had been assured by the predecessor to the health authority that the home was her home for life, thus creating a legitimate expectation which no public interest overrode. Furthermore, under Article 8 of the Convention on Human Rights, everyone had a right to respect for his home and the judge had been entitled to treat the case as one in which there would be an unjustifiable breach of Article 8. Lord Woolf MR explained the concept as follows:

> Where the court considers that a lawful promise or practice has induced a legitimate expectation of a *benefit which is substantive*, not simply procedural, authority now establishes that here too the court will in a proper case decide whether to frustrate the expectation is so unfair that to take a new and different course will amount to an abuse of power. Here, once the legitimacy of the expectation is established, the court will have the task of weighing the requirements of fairness against any overriding interest relied upon for the change in policy. (at para 57)

The **Coughlan** decision has significant implications for judicial review. The Court of Appeal moved beyond the traditional test of procedural impropriety, thereby developing the law

---

37 See also R (Zegiri) v Secretary of State for the Home Department relying on R v Secretary of State for the Home Department ex parte Besnik Gashi (1999).

38 See also R v Inland Revenue Commissioners ex parte MFK Underwriting Agencies Ltd (1990).

39 See also R v Ministry of Defence ex parte Walker (2000) in which the House of Lords ruled that a soldier injured in action in the former Yugoslavia was not entitled to compensation under the Criminal Injuries Compensation Scheme. A policy adopted in 1994 excluding compensation for death or injury resulting from war operations or military action in peacekeeping operations in Bosnia was not irrational. The applicant had been given no assurances and the only legitimate expectation he had was that the Ministry of Defence would apply the policy in force at the time of his injury.

40 See Craig and Schonberg, 2000; Roberts, 2001; Elliott, 2000; Hilson, 2002.

relating to legitimate expectations. The Court identified three differing situations which would give rise to differing approaches to review. The first related to a public body which had to consider previous policy or representations before changing that policy. Here, review on **Wednesbury** grounds was appropriate. The second class of case concerned the legitimate expectation of being consulted, in which case the court would look closely at the reasons for the change of policy and whether that decision was fair. The third class of case is where a promise by a public body had brought about a 'substantive legitimate expectation' on the part of the applicant. Here the court's approach would be more intensive. Accordingly, there are two standards of review, one where the decision was irrational in the **Wednesbury** sense, and one on the basis of abuse of power, which was for the court to determine. Policy changes on the part of public authorities are not unusual nor unlawful in the general case, nor should the courts, as the Court of Appeal recognised, jeopardise 'the important principle that the executive's policy making powers should not be trammelled'. Where, however, a substantive legitimate expectation has arisen – as in **Coughlan** – through the express promise made in precise terms, and was relied on by the applicant, the decision was unlawful.[41]

 Coughlan was reconsidered by the Privy Council in **Paponette v Attorney Genral of Trinidad and Tobago** (2010). The applicants were members of an association who owned and operated public service vehicles. They were persuaded to move the site of their taxi stand on reliance on government assurances that, inter alia, they would not be under the control or management of the owners of the new site, and that the management of the site would, within six months be transferred to the association. In breach of this undertaking the government introduced new regulations giving control over the site to the land owners. There was no doubt that the assurances had created a legitimate expectation of a substantive benefit. At issue was whether the government was entitled to frustrate the legitimate expectation. This it could only do if there was a sufficient public interest to override the legitimate expectation and in this case the government was unable to do so.

Acting in a manner so as to create an expectation

A public body may act in a manner which creates an expectation in the mind of a person or body. For example, in **R v Secretary of State for Health ex parte US Tobacco International Inc** (1992), the company had opened a factory in 1985, with a government grant, for the production of oral snuff. The government made the grant available notwithstanding its awareness of the health risks of the product. In 1988, however, the government – having received further advice from a committee – announced its intention to ban snuff. The company sought judicial review, relying on a legitimate expectation based on the government's action. The court ruled, however, that, even though the applicant had a legitimate expectation, that expectation could not override the public interest in banning a harmful substance.

The existence of policies and/or guidance

In **R v Secretary of State for the Home Department ex parte Asif Mahmood Khan** (1984), the Home Office had published a circular stating the criteria to be used for determining whether a child could enter the United Kingdom. When the applicant sought to bring his nephew into the United Kingdom from Pakistan, entry was refused. In judicial review proceedings, it was established that the immigration rules did not specify any particular criteria, but that the Home Department's circular did so specify. It was also established that the criteria used in

---

41 See cases post-**Coughlan**: R v Secretary of State for Education and Employment, ex parte Begbie (2000); Henry Boot Homes Ltd v Bassetlaw District Council (2003); Nadarajah v Secretary of State for the Home Department (2008); R (S) v Secretary of State for the Home Department (2007).

determining whether to allow the child into the country were different from that provided under the circular. The Home Secretary had acted *ultra vires*: he had created legitimate expectation and was not free to employ different criteria.[42]

A further challenge to the powers of the Home Secretary can be seen in **R v Secretary of State for the Home Department ex parte Ruddock** (1987). The Home Secretary had authorised the interception of telephone calls without statutory authority.[43] The basis on which the Home Secretary decided to intercept calls was provided in a circular. The applicant claimed that the Home Secretary had failed to follow the criteria laid down in the circular. The court held that the applicant had a legitimate expectation that the criteria would be followed but, nevertheless, the applicant lost the case because it was held that the minister could have come to the judgment that the criteria were applied and that he was not acting unreasonably. The decision, which appears to weaken the binding nature of legitimate expectations, is explainable in light of the alleged national security aspects of the case. The applicant had been a leading member of the Campaign for Nuclear Disarmament, which the government feared was being influenced by the Communist Party.

A change made to a policy which had been embedded in an agreement between prison inmates and prison authorities was considered by the Court of Appeal in **R v Secretary of State for the Home Department ex parte Hargreaves** (1996). The agreement stated that prisoners could apply for home leave after serving one third of their sentence, subject to good behaviour. The Secretary of State decided, however, that only prisoners who had served half their sentence could apply for home leave. Hargreaves and others unsuccessfully applied for judicial review. They subsequently appealed to the Court of Appeal.

The Court of Appeal held that the agreement between the prison inmates and the prison authorities did not give rise to a legitimate expectation which could be enforced by judicial review. Furthermore, the Home Secretary's decision to change the policy was not to be tested against the overall fairness of that decision, but rather whether the policy was unreasonable in the **Wednesbury** sense. On that test, the Home Secretary's decision was not unlawful. The Court of Appeal expressed regret, however, that the documents on which the prisoners relied were 'other than completely clear and unambiguous', and called for greater clarity in the future.

The right to make representations

Inevitably, the extent to which the individual is enabled to make representations to a decision-making body will be inextricably linked to the question of the right to a hearing. Where there exists no right to an oral hearing, the question becomes one of the extent to which – and means by which – the view of the individual can be put to the decision-making authority. It may well be the case that the opportunity to make written submissions will satisfy the requirements for justice and fairness. For example, in **Lloyd v McMahon** (1987), local government councillors were in breach of their statutory duty to set the level of local rates. When the district auditor came to determine the issue, the applicants claimed the right to an oral hearing, and that the absence of such a hearing amounted to a breach of the rules of natural justice and was, accordingly, *ultra vires*. The court disagreed, holding that, since the auditor had given notice of the case against them and had considered written representations from them, he had acted fairly and, accordingly, lawfully.

The requirements of fairness mean that where a body was exercising penal powers which involved the imposition of a penalty which was more severe than would normally be expected,

---

42 Cf **Re Findlay** (1985), wherein the doctrine was limited merely to an expectation that prisoners would have their cases individually considered according to whatever policy the minister chose to adopt.

43 The case was decided before the Interception of Communications Act 1985 was implemented.

it had to give the person affected the opportunity of making representations on the issue. The High Court so held in **R (Gutta) v General Medical Council** (2001). The Medical Council had found Dr Gutta guilty of serious professional misconduct and resolved to have her name erased from the register and that her suspension should take effect immediately, rather than after an appeal had been heard, as was normal. The Council was under a duty to give notice of its intention to make such an order, give the opportunity to make representations and give adequate reasons for reaching its conclusion.[44]

The right to question the 'other side'

It is not invariably the case that, where there is to be an oral hearing, it should be conducted according to the strict rules which would apply in a court of law. Accordingly, it should not be assumed that a party will be entitled to cross-examine the 'other side'. However, in **Errington v Wilson** (1995), it was made clear that Justices of the Peace must observe the rules of natural justice and, in particular, allow cross-examination under certain circumstances. A food authority had seized batches of cheese which it believed to be contaminated with listeria monocytogenes. The authority then sought a destruction order from the justice of the peace. The magistrate refused to allow cross-examination of witnesses called by the authority. The court held that, given the nature of the proceedings, the magistrate was required to allow cross-examination if the proceedings were to be fair; and that, given the difference of opinion between experts on crucial points, Errington had been denied natural justice.

The admissibility of evidence and attendance of witnesses

In **R v Board of Visitors of Hull Prison ex parte St Germain (No 2)** (1979), prisoners who had been involved in a prison riot were charged with breaches of the Prison Rules. In the course of the hearing, hearsay evidence was given to the court on behalf of a number of officers who were unable to attend the hearing. The decision of guilt on the charges was challenged by judicial review proceedings, on the basis that the Board of Visitors had breached the rules of natural justice. Lane LJ, while not ruling that hearsay evidence could never be admissible, nevertheless ruled that, in the particular circumstance of the case, the Board should have ruled the hearsay evidence inadmissible. The decision of the Board was quashed by order of *certiorari*. Similar issues were under scrutiny in **R v Commissioner for Racial Equality ex parte Cottrell and Rothon** (1980). The Commissioner had received a complaint of unlawful discrimination by Messrs Cottrell and Rothon, a firm of estate agents. The company had been given the opportunity to make representations – both written and oral – to the commissioners. No witnesses were available at the hearing. Nevertheless, the Commission issued a non-discrimination notice.[45] The company sought to have the decision quashed, relying in part on **R v Board of Visitors of Hull Prison ex parte St Germain (No 2)** (1979). Noting the absence of any statutory requirement to provide an opportunity to cross-examine witnesses in the course of a hearing, and distinguishing between the facts of **St Germain**, the Court of Appeal ruled that there was no breach in the rules relating to fairness.

In **R v Panel on Takeovers and Mergers ex parte Guinness plc** (1990), the Takeover Panel refused to grant an adjournment of the inquisitorial proceedings in order to allow witnesses to attend. The court expressed anxiety about this refusal, but declined to hold that the Panel had acted unlawfully.

A different conclusion was reached in **R v Army Board of the Defence Council ex parte Anderson** (1991). The applicant for judicial review had made allegations of racial discrimination[46] which

---

44 See also **R (D) v Bromley LBC** (2007).
45 Under the Race Relations Act 1976, s 58(5).
46 Race Relations Act 1976, s 58(5).

resulted in him taking absence without leave. Members of the Board considered his allegation of discrimination on the basis of circulated papers, and did not meet for the purpose of reaching its decision. The complainant had requested, but been refused, an oral hearing, and had also requested, but been refused, the disclosure of documents relating to his case. The Board decided that whilst there was some *prima facie* evidence of discrimination, it was insufficient to warrant either an apology or an award of compensation. Anderson sought judicial review of the Army Board's decision. Counsel for the Board reverted to the distinction between administrative and judicial functions. Taylor LJ, in the course of ruling that such a distinction was unnecessary, held that, should the distinction have been a necessary one, he would characterise the role of the Army Board, in connection with the complaint, as judicial rather than administrative. Applying the principles established in **Lloyd v McMahon** (1987), Taylor LJ ruled that four principles applied to the standard of fairness required in a hearing such as that of the Board:

1. There must be a proper hearing of the complaint in the sense that the board must consider . . . all the relevant evidence and contentions before reaching its conclusion. This means, in my view, that the members of the Board must meet . . .
2. The hearing does not necessarily have to be an oral hearing in all cases . . . Provided that they [the board] achieve the degree of fairness appropriate to their task it is for them to decide how they will proceed and there is no rule that fairness always requires an oral hearing . . . What it [the board] cannot do . . . is to have an inflexible policy not to hold oral hearings. The board fettered its discretion and failed to consider the requirements for an oral hearing in the present case on its own merits.
3. The opportunity to have the evidence tested by cross-examination is again within the Army Board's discretion. The decision whether to allow it will usually be inseparable from the decision whether to have an oral hearing. The object of the latter will usually be to enable witnesses to be tested in cross-examination, although it would be possible to have an oral hearing simply to hear submissions.
4. Whether oral or not, there must be what amounts to a hearing of any complaint under the 1976 Act. This means that the Army Board must have such a complaint investigated, consider all the material gathered in the investigation, give the complainant an opportunity to respond to it and consider his response.

On the duty of disclosure of documents, Taylor LJ ruled that:

> Because of the nature of the Army Board's function pursuant to the 1976 Act, . . . I consider that a soldier complainant under that Act should be shown all the material seen by the board, apart from any documents for which public interest immunity can properly be claimed.

The decision of the board was quashed.

The rights of prisoners have also been scrutinised in relation to the requirement that they have sufficient information in order to challenge a Home Secretary's decision as to their detention or release. Under the Criminal Justice Act 1991, the Home Secretary has a statutory duty to release, on the direction of the Parole Board, discretionary life prisoners after they have served a 'tariff period' (section 34). The period to be served is considered by the trial judge. In **R v Secretary of State for the Home Department ex parte Doody** (1993), the House of Lords ruled that the prisoner was entitled to know the length of the tariff period recommended by the trial judge, and other relevant factors, in order that he may make written representation to the Home Secretary concerning the date fixed for consideration by the Parole Board of his sentence.[47] The failure to respect the entitlement to know the period recommended in order to make written submissions led to the Home Secretary's decision being quashed.[48]

See Chapter 10 on public interest immunity.

The availability of legal representation

Whether or not legal representation is available as of right will also depend upon the nature of the hearing and the nature of the rights affected. There is no general right to legal representation and, in some cases, it may prove to be either unnecessary or counterproductive to the proceedings and, accordingly, the courts have been unwilling to concede a general right to representation.[49] Where the proceedings are before a tribunal, the right to be represented is at the discretion of the tribunal. The general principle, according to the Royal Commission on Legal Services, is that 'it is desirable that every applicant before any tribunal should be able to present his case in person or to obtain representation'.[50]

Whereas legal representation is rarely denied before tribunals,[51] such representation is inextricably linked to the financial means of the applicant or to the availability of Legal Aid (now referred to as Legal Help). It may be more appropriate, in many instances, for applicants to be represented by non-lawyers. A range of organisations offer representation. The Citizens Advice Bureaux, trade unions, social workers, specialist agencies,[52] the Free Representation Unit, friends or relatives may all be allowed to appear before tribunals. The essential criterion for representation is that the tribunal should not adopt a rigid policy, but rather should exercise a genuine discretion in relation to the availability of representation.[53]

In **Martin v Greater Glasgow Primary Care NHS Trust** (2009) the issue of legal representation was raised once more.[54] In this case the claimant argued that she had not had legal representation whilst the hospital trust, as respondent, had representation. The Court decided that in these circumstances the presence or not of legal representation would have made very little difference to the outcome of the case and the test continued to be whether the presentation of the case was unduly affected by the absence of legal representation.

In **Kulkarni v Milton Keynes Hospital NHS Trust** (2009) a hospital doctor who was subject to hospital disciplinary proceedings was denied legal representation as the published guidance on disciplinary proceedings did not permit it. The published guidance had been modified to indicate that legal representation was possible. However, it was held that he could require legal representation but that it could not be instructed independently and instead had to be nominated by his Union. The Court indicated that given the gravity of the proceedings Article 6 of the European Convention on Human Rights would have been engaged if this point had been raised before the court.

In **R(G) v X School Governors** (2009) a teaching assistant in a school had allegedly kissed a 15-year-old boy on work experience. No criminal charges were brought but following an

---

47 Where the trial judge does not make a recommendation, the Home Secretary may certify the length of the period of sentence which must be served: Criminal Justice Act 1991, Sched 12, para 9. See **R v Home Department ex parte McCartney** (1993).

48 See also **R v Secretary of State for the Environment ex parte Slot** (1997); **R v Secretary of State for the Home Department ex parte McAvoy** (1998).

49 See, inter alia, **R v Secretary of State for the Home Department ex parte Tarrant** (1985); **R v Board of Visitors of HM Prison, The Maze ex parte Hone** (1988).

50 Report of the Royal Commission, 1979, Vol I, para 15.11, p 169.

51 Proceedings before the Family Practitioner Committee is an exception; National Health Service (Service Committees and Tribunal) Regulations, SI 1974/455, reg 7.

52 Eg, the Child Poverty Action Group; the United Kingdom Immigration Advisory Service.

53 Per Lord Denning MR in **Pett v Greyhound Racing Association (No 2)** (1970).

54 Also see **R (Bhatt Murphy) v Independent Assessor** (2008).

internal investigation and a disciplinary hearing the teaching assistant (G) was dismissed on the basis of an abuse of trust. The governors reported their decision to the relevant authorities and the name of the teaching assistant was placed on a statutory register that prevented him from being allowed to work with children in the future. G applied for a judicial review of the decision by the governors on the basis they had decided not to allow him legal representation at the original disciplinary hearing or the appeal hearing. He claimed this violated his Article 6 rights. The Court of Appeal ruled that, given the severity of the case, G's right to a fair hearing under Article 6 included the right to legal representation.

Failure to give reasons

According to Lord Denning MR, the giving of reasons is 'one of the fundamentals of good administration'.[55] Unless a decision maker provides adequate information as to the basis on which a decision has been reached, any possible protection which could be given to an aggrieved person is adversely affected.

Under the Tribunals and Inquiries Act 1992, there exists a statutory duty to give reasons, on request, where decisions are reached by tribunals, public inquiries, or under specific statutes. Under common law, however, there is no such duty,[56] although the argument that there should be such a duty is strong. A decision-making body is under a 'general duty' to give reasons, and any departure from the requirement to give reasons will require sound justification. Where an authority fails to give reasons for a decision which is challenged subsequently by judicial review proceedings, the failure to give reasons may cause the court to consider that there were no good reasons whatsoever for the decision. Lord Keith expressed it thus:

> . . . if all other known facts and circumstances appear to point overwhelmingly in favour of a different decision, the decision maker who has given no reasons cannot complain if the court draws the inference that he has no rational reason for his decision.[57]

The courts have developed a number of exceptions to the general rule that no reasons need be given at common law. The courts may hold, for example, that a failure to give reasons will prejudice an applicant's chances of successfully applying for judicial review,[58] or that a failure to give reasons amounts to arbitrariness,[59] or that legitimate expectations have been created which demand that any departure from that expectation be explained or, more sweepingly, that in the interests of fairness, reasons must be given.

In *R v Civil Service Appeal Board ex parte Cunningham* (1991), for example, the Court of Appeal, while again stating that there was no general duty to give reasons, held that the Civil Service Appeal Board − which determined the applicant's compensation for unfair dismissal − was under a duty to give reasons, for its powers were analogous to the judicial powers of an industrial tribunal. Fairness demanded that the Board give reasons, in the same manner as required for tribunals.[60]

---

55 *Breen v AEU* (1971), p 191.
56 See *R v Secretary of State for the Home Department ex parte Doody* (1993).
57 *R v Trade Secretary ex parte Lonrho plc* (1989), p 620. See Bradley, 1986; and Herberg, 1991.
58 As in the *Doody* case (1993).
59 See *Padfield v Minister of Agriculture, Fisheries and Food* (1968).
60 See also *R v Parole Board ex parte Wilson* (1992); *Selvanathan v General Medical Council* (2001); *Baird v Thurrock Borough Council* (2005).

The duty to give reasons must now be evaluated in light of the House of Lords' decision in **R v Secretary of State for the Home Department ex parte Doody** (1993). As seen above, in **Doody**, the applicants, who were serving mandatory life sentences, sought information as to the basis on which the decision concerning the period for their mandatory detention had been reached. The House of Lords laid down two justifications for the requirement that information be given. First, if reasons were not given to the applicants, the possibility of their successfully applying for judicial review would be frustrated. Second, a failure to give reasons adversely affected the concept of fairness. Lord Mustill, while acknowledging that there remained no general duty to give reasons, stated that a duty would be implied under certain circumstances. Where, as in **Doody**, the applicant did not know the reasons for a decision, it was impossible to make any effective representations in support of his case. Without the knowledge of any case against him, the applicant was denied the very information which would found the basis of making representations in support of his case. The Home Secretary was, accordingly, under a duty to provide reasons both on the basis that the giving of reasons was a prerequisite to an application for judicial review, and on the basis of requirements of fairness.

In **R v Ministry of Defence ex parte Murray** (1998), the Divisional Court ruled that, although there was no general overriding principle of law which required decision makers to give reasons for their decisions, the duty of fairness required that reasons be given, where demanded by the circumstances of the case. The applicant had been convicted by court martial of wounding. The court martial reached its conclusion and passed sentence without giving reasons. The applicant's conduct, which was 'entirely out of character', and to which he pleaded guilty, was caused by ingestion of an anti-malarial drug. Where there was no explicit duty of fairness in statute, the courts would require that reasons be given where fairness demanded it. In this case, the applicant, his regiment and his family were entitled to reasons.

In **R v Criminal Injuries Compensation Authority ex parte Leatherland** (2000), the High Court ruled that the Criminal Injuries Compensation Authority was obliged as a matter of procedural fairness to provide proper reasons, together with at least the gist of any supporting evidence, for its decisions to reduce or refuse claims for compensation. A practice of withholding such material until the day of any appeal hearing was bad administration and unfair.

However, not all bodies will be under a duty to give reasons on the basis of fairness. In **R v Universities Funding Council ex parte Institute of Dental Surgery** (1994), for example, the Divisional Court ruled that the Higher Education Funding Council was not under a duty to give reasons as to why an academic institution was given a downgraded research grading which resulted in a loss to the Institute of research funds. Such matters were, in the court's opinion, matters of academic judgment, and a duty to give reasons for a decision could not, in this case, be founded on the requirements of fairness alone.[61] Sedley J stated that there were two classes of case emerging. The first class was exemplified in the **Doody case**, where the nature of the process requires, in the interests of fairness, reasons to be given. The second class is illustrated by **Ex parte Cunningham** (1991), in which the majority of the court held that there was something peculiar to the case which required reasons to be given in the interests of fairness. In the **Institute of Dental Surgery case**, provided the decision was based purely on academic judgment, and did not involve any irrelevant or improper factors being taken into account, the decision would not be impugned on the basis that reasons had not been given for the decision. TRS Allan is critical of the decision. In his view, 'if the requirement of reasons, where it exists,

---

61 See also **R v University College London ex parte Idriss** (1999), in which it was held that it was 'very doubtful' whether a university's refusal to admit an applicant for entry to a course was susceptible to judicial review and that there was no duty to give reasons either at common law or under the university's own statutes.

reflects the demands of fairness and reasonableness, its denial in the present case must cause one to doubt whether the Institute was treated either fairly or reasonably' (1994, p 210).

The duty of the Crown Prosecution Service to give reasons for its decisions was considered by the Divisional Court in **R v Director of Public Prosecutions ex parte Manning** (2000). The applicant's brother had died of asphyxia while being restrained by prison officers whilst on remand in prison. At a coroner's inquest, the jury returned a verdict of unlawful killing. However, the Crown Prosecution Service concluded that, while there was a *prima facie* case against a prison officer, there was no realistic prospect of a successful prosecution. The applicant then requested the reasons for the Crown Prosecution Service's decision, but was refused. He then sought judicial review. It was held that while there was no absolute obligation on the Service to give reasons for a decision not to prosecute, a violent death in custody gave rise to great concern. Further, since a jury had returned a verdict of unlawful killing implicating an identifiable person, there was an expectation of a plausible explanation for the decision and of solid grounds to support the decision.

In **R v Secretary of State for the Home Department ex parte Al Fayed** (1997), the Court of Appeal ruled that the Home Secretary had a duty to indicate to the applicant the area(s) of concern on which he was basing his refusal to grant naturalisation in order that the applicant may have an opportunity to allay the Home Secretary's concerns. The Home Secretary's decision was quashed. In **R v Secretary of State for the Home Department ex parte Moon** (1995), the court ruled that the Secretary of State's refusal to explain his reasons for concluding that the entry of the Reverend Sun Myung Moon would not be conducive to the public good was unfair and contrary to the rules of natural justice.

The duty of a professional judge to give reasons was upheld by the Court of Appeal in **Flanner v Halifax Estate Agencies Ltd** (2000). In general, it was the duty of a judge to give reasons; the extent of the duty would depend on the circumstances, but, where the dispute involved opposing reasons and analysis, the judge must explain why he preferred one case over the other.[62] In **Stefan v General Medical Council** (1999), the health committee of the General Medical Council had suspended the applicant indefinitely because of her medical condition. No reasons were given. The court stated that the common law rule against a general duty to give reasons was changing and might have to be reconsidered in light of the Human Rights Act 1998 (on which, see below). Although there was no general duty to give reasons, nevertheless, in light of the nature of the appeal and the importance for the practitioner, they ought to have done so.[63]

The giving of reasons, whether by courts or administrative bodies, assumes increased importance in light of the Human Rights Act 1998. Article 5 of the Convention (the right to liberty and security) expressly states that persons arrested shall be informed promptly, in a language which he or she understands, of the reasons for the arrest. Article 6 of the Convention protects the right to a fair trial in the determination of civil rights and obligations or of criminal charges. While the giving of reasons is not an explicit requirement in Article 6, it is implicit in facilitating the right of appeal.

In **South Buckinghamshire District Council v Porter (No 2)** (2004) the House of Lords gave guidance concerning the adequacy of reasons given in planning decisions. The applicant, a Gypsy, had purchased land in a Green Belt area in 1985 and stationed her mobile home on it. She applied for, but was refused, planning permission to remain on the site and enforcement notices were issued by the Council. In 2000 the applicant reapplied, but was refused, permission. On appeal the inspector ruled that there were material changes in the circumstances since the previous application. There was now no alternative council site available for her and her

---

62 See *Practice Direction* (1999).
63 See also **R (I) v Independent Appeal Panel for G** (2005).

health had deteriorated considerably. He concluded that these circumstances were sufficient to override Green Belt policies. He granted personal planning permission to the applicant, meaning that she could remain there as long as she wished, but that thereafter the permission would lapse. The Court of Appeal ruled that the inspector had failed to give adequate reasons for his decision and that he had failed to have regard to the fact that continued occupation of the site was unlawful and in persistent breach of planning control.

The House of Lords allowed the applicant's appeal. Summarising the law, Lord Brown of Eaton-under-Heywood stated that:

> The reasons for a decision must be intelligible and they must be adequate. They must enable the reader to understand why the matter was decided as it was and what conclusions were reached on the 'principal important controversial issues', disclosing how any issue of law or fact was resolved. Reasons can be briefly stated, the degree of particularity required depending entirely on the nature of the issues falling for decision. The reasoning must not give rise to a substantial doubt as to whether the decision-maker erred in law, for example by misunderstanding some relevant policy or some other important matter or by failing to reach a rational decision on relevant grounds. . . . A reasons challenge will only succeed if the party aggrieved can satisfy the court that he has genuinely been substantially prejudiced by the failure to provide an adequately reasoned decision.

Summary

Breach of natural justice, which includes an aspect of procedural impropriety, is an increasingly important concept in ensuring fairness in the administrative process. Originally a common law requirement, it is often, but not always, incorporated into statute. Natural justice covers a very broad range of issues including the right to a fair hearing, the rule against bias, legitimate expectations and the giving of reasons for decisions.

Further Reading

Clark, D. (1975) 'Natural justice: substance or shadow', Public Law, 27.

Craig, P. (1994) 'The common law, reasons and administrative justice', Cambridge Law Journal, 282.

Forsyth, C. (1988) 'The provenance and protection of legitimate expectations', Cambridge Law Journal, 238.

Ganz, G. (1986) 'Legitimate expectation: a confusion of concepts' in Harlow, C. (ed) Public Law and Politics, London: Sweet and Maxwell.

Malleson, K. (1999) 'Judicial bias and disqualification in the Pinochet Case', Public Law, 391.

Malleson, K. (2000) 'Judicial bias and disqualification after Pinochet (No 2)', Modern Law Review, 119.

Mullan, D. (1975) 'Fairness: the new natural justice', University of Toronto Law Journal, 280.

Olowofoyeku, A. (2000) 'The Nemo Judex Rule: The Case Against Automatic Disqualification', Public Law, 456.

Chapter 26

Commissioners for Administration: Ombudsmen

Introduction

In the United Kingdom, the past 50 years have seen a major expansion in mechanisms for citizens to complain against government departments and other public bodies. When a citizen has a complaint against the administration of government, that complaint could be pursued in courts or tribunals or through Parliament via the constituency Member of Parliament. However, these means for the redress of grievances have been proven inadequate and, as a result, alternative and additional mechanisms have been introduced.

The word 'ombudsman' is Swedish, and means a representative of the people. In Sweden, the office of *Justitieombudsman* was established in 1809. Finland introduced a similar office in 1919, as did Denmark in 1955. In 1963, Norway followed, with a parliamentary ombudsman, the model which had been adopted by New Zealand in 1962. During the 1970s, countries throughout the world adopted some form of office of ombudsman.

Commissioners for Administration in the United Kingdom

The existing scheme of Commissioners for Administration is given below. Note that, in addition, there exist a number of ombudsmen in the private sector, for example the Banking Commissioner, Building Societies Commissioner, Corporate Estate Agents Commissioner, Pensions Commissioner,[1] Personal Investment Authority Ombudsman, Prisons Ombudsman, Investment Commissioner, Insurance Commissioner, Commissioner for Trade Union Members and the press and media and telephone information services.

COMMISSIONERS FOR ADMINISTRATION	
	Date of introduction
Parliamentary Commissioner for Administration[2]	1967
Parliamentary Commissioner for Administration[3] and Commissioner for Complaints (Northern Ireland)[4]	1969
Health Service Commissioners: England, Wales and Scotland[5]	1972
Local Government Commissioners: England, Wales[6] and Scotland[7] (Scotland 1975)	1974
Legal Services Commissioner[8]	1990
European Union and Community Ombudsman[9]	1992

---

1 It has been held that the Pensions Ombudsman is required to observe the statutory procedure within the Pensions Schemes Act 1993 and the rules of natural justice: see **Seifert v Pensions Ombudsman**; **Lynch v Pensions Ombudsman** (1997). See also **Miller v Stapleton** (1996); **Hamar v Pensions Ombudsman** (1996).
2 Parliamentary Commissioner Act 1967. As amended by the Parliamentary and Health Service Commissioner Act 1987; Parliamentary Commissioner Act 1994.
3 Parliamentary Commissioner (Northern Ireland) Act 1969.
4 Commissioner for Complaints (Northern Ireland) Act 1969.
5 National Health Service (Scotland) Act 1972; National Health Service Reorganisation Act 1973; Parliamentary and Health Service Commissioners Act 1987; Health Service Commissioners Act 1993; Health Service Commissioners (Amendment) Act 2000.
6 Local Government Act 1974; Local Government and Housing Act 1989, s 23.
7 Local Government (Scotland) Act 1975.
8 Courts and Legal Services Act 1990.
9 EC Treaty, Article 195, introduced under the Treaty on European Union 1992.

Scottish Parliamentary Commissioner[10]	1998
Welsh Administration Ombudsman[11]	1998
Public Services Ombudsman for Wales[12]	2005

The Parliamentary Commissioner for Administration[13]

The movement towards establishing a Parliamentary Commissioner for Administration (or Ombudsman) began in 1959. In that year, the British section of the International Commission of Jurists, JUSTICE, established an inquiry into grievances against the administration. The resultant report[14] advocated setting up an additional avenue for the redress of grievances, the office being modelled on the same lines as those of the ombudsmen in Scandinavian jurisdictions. As the report stated, there appeared to be:

> . . . a continuous flow of relatively minor complaints, not sufficient in themselves to attract public interest, but nevertheless of great importance to the individuals concerned, which give rise to feelings of frustration and resentment because of the inadequacy of the existing means of seeking redress.[15]

The existing machinery was found wanting: parliamentary Question Time was inadequate to deal with the volume of problems arising; if a complaint was made directly to the government department, the department investigated the complaint; if a Member of Parliament attempted to investigate, he could not gain access to all departmental documentation. Accordingly, the report advocated establishing a permanent office, independent of the executive and accountable only to Parliament, removable from office only after a successful address had been moved to both Houses of Parliament. The report recommended that a select committee should be established to consider the Commissioner's reports and to give parliamentary authority to the work of the Commissioner. The report also recommended that the Parliamentary Commissioner for Administration's office should be one which supplemented, rather than undermined, existing procedures for complaint. Complaints, at least initially, concerning maladministration[16] should be routed through Members of the House of Commons, rather than directly addressed to the Parliamentary Commissioner. This would preserve to Members of Parliament the opportunity to resolve a matter of complaint but, failing their ability to do so, confer the right to refer the matter to the Parliamentary Commissioner for investigation and report.

The government's response to the report was cautious. Concern was expressed as to the interference in the running of government,[17] and that the Commissioner's role would be incompatible with the doctrine of ministerial responsibility. Furthermore, the government felt that:

> . . . there is already adequate provision under our constitution and Parliamentary practice for the redress of any genuine complaint of maladministration, in particular by means of the citizen's rights of access to Members of Parliament.[18]

---

10 Scotland Act 1998. See Scotland Act 1998 (Transitory and Transitional Provisions) (Complaints of Maladministration) Order 1999, SI 1999/1351.
11 Government of Wales Act 1998.
12 Public Services Ombudsman (Wales) Act 2005.
13 See Pugh, 1978. See also Clothier, 1984.
14 *The Citizen and the Administration* (the Whyatt Report), 1961.
15 Ibid, para 76.
16 On which, see below.
17 Lord Chancellor, HL Deb Vol 244 Cols 384–85.
18 Attorney General, 666 HC Col 1125.

The incoming Labour government, however, accepted the need for an office to complement the existing complaints machinery.[19] Thus, in 1967, the Parliamentary Commissioner Act was passed. Being a constitutional innovation, the provisions as to procedure, jurisdiction and powers of enforcement were restrictive.

Appointment

The Parliamentary Commissioner for Administration is appointed by the Crown on the advice of the government, following consultation with the Chairman of the House of Commons' Select Committee on the Parliamentary Commissioner for Administration. The post is held 'during good health and behaviour' and is effectively until retirement. The Office of Parliamentary Ombudsman and Health Service Ombudsman for England is held by the same person.

The constitutional position of the Commissioner

By 1983, the office of Parliamentary Commissioner for Administration had been operative for 15 years, and the Commissioner[20] took the opportunity to review the working of his office in his annual report. He described his office in the following manner:

> The office of Parliamentary Commissioner stands curiously poised between the legislature and the executive, while discharging an almost judicial function in the citizen's dispute with his government, and yet it forms no part of the judiciary. It is from the centre of that triangle that I have been able to appreciate the virtues of our unwritten and therefore flexible constitutional arrangements and still more the goodwill of those men and women, legislators and administrators who govern us.

Aims and objectives

The purpose of the Office of Parliamentary and Health Service Ombudsman (OPHSO) is:

(a) to consider and resolve complaints impartially and promptly and to achieve appropriate redress of grievances;
(b) to report the results to complainants, Members of Parliament and the bodies complained about; and
(c) to promote improvements in public services by feeding back the lessons learned from casework to policy makers and providers.[21]

The Complaints Procedure

Complaints must be in writing, and made to the constituency Member of Parliament (ie a member of the House of Commons).[22] The complaint must be made within 12 months of the day on which the person became aware of the matters alleged, unless the time period is extended by the Commissioner, on the basis that an investigation is necessary.[23] There is no change involved in making a complaint, or for any investigation which is undertaken. The complaint must relate to maladministration and not the merits of a decision or the policy being pursued. This restriction has led to some 43 per cent of complaints made being rejected by the Commissioner.

---

19 *The Parliamentary Commissioner for Administration*, Cmnd 2767, 1965, London: HMSO.
20 Sir Cecil Clothier, who held office from 1979 to 1985.
21 OPHSO, *Business Plan* 2003–04.
22 Parliamentary Commissioner Act 1967, s 5(1)(a).
23 *Ibid*, s 6(3).

The requirement that complaints be made initially to Members of Parliament reinforces the view that the Commissioner is a supplement to the parliamentary process rather than a substitute. This restricted right of access, however, causes difficulties for complainants, and is not a model adopted elsewhere.[24] In the majority of countries having some form of parliamentary ombudsman, complaints are made directly to the ombudsman. Moreover, this filter mechanism has not been adopted in relation to the Health Service Commissioner, the Commissioners for Local Government or the Complaints Commissioner for Northern Ireland.[25]

Jurisdiction

Section 5(1) of the Parliamentary Commissioner Act 1967 provides that a member of the public may make a complaint and the Commissioner may investigate that complaint where, subject to the rules on jurisdiction, the person 'claims to have sustained injustice in consequence of maladministration'.[26] Before examining that concept, it must be noted that there are a number of restrictions to the jurisdiction of the Parliamentary Commissioner, which result in a large number of complaints each year not being investigated.

Excluded matters

The work of the police,[27] of nationalised industries, the Cabinet Office, Prime Minister's Office, Parole Board, tribunals, Bank of England, Criminal Injuries Compensation Board and government commercial and contractual transactions are all excluded.[28] The Commissioner may not investigate any matter where the complainant has a right of 'appeal, reference or review' to a tribunal, or a remedy in any court of law, unless it would be unreasonable to expect the complainant to have resort to such a remedy.[29] The Commissioner thus has a discretion as to whether or not a complaint should be accepted. It has been indicated that, where the legal process would be too cumbersome, slow or expensive in relation to the objective to be gained, the complaint will be accepted.[30]

The interaction between legal proceedings and complaints to the Commissioner was well illustrated in 1975. The government decided to increase the licence fee for television sets. In advance of the fee increase, individuals renewed their licences at the existing rate. The Home Office then decided to revoke the 36,000 licences issued at the cheaper rate. A number of complaints were referred to the Commissioner, who found maladministration on the part of government, inter alia, for not giving sufficient warning of the increases and for inefficiency. The Commissioner, however, ruled that the government was acting on legal advice and therefore should not be sanctioned. Judicial review proceedings were commenced to determine the lawfulness of the Home Secretary's decision, as a result of which the complainants established a legal remedy.[31] It may be argued that the Commissioner was wrong in exercising his discretionary jurisdiction in this case, since it should have been foreseen that an action in judicial review would lie.

The departments and matters which the Commissioner is precluded from investigating are wide ranging. Schedule 3 to the Parliamentary Commissioner Act 1967 sets out the excluded matters, the most significant of which are:

---

24 See the JUSTICE Report, *Our Fettered Ombudsman*, 1977, and the Select Committee Report, *Parliamentary Commissioner for Administration (Review of Access and Jurisdiction)*, HC 615 (1978–79), London: HMSO.
25 There is, however, a 'filter' procedure for the Parliamentary Commissioner for Northern Ireland.
26 See below for the meaning of 'maladministration'.
27 Which has its own internal complaints procedures.
28 See HC 322 (1983–84), London: HMSO.
29 Parliamentary Commissioner Act 1967, s 5(2).
30 See McMurtie, 1997.
31 **Congreve v Home Office** (1976).

- action taken in matters certified by a Secretary of State or other Minister of the Crown to affect relations or dealings between the government of the United Kingdom and any other government or any international organisation of States or government;
- action taken in connection with the administration of the government of any country or territory outside the United Kingdom which forms part of Her Majesty's dominions or in which Her Majesty has jurisdiction;
- action taken by the Secretary of State under the Fugitive Offenders Act 1967 or the Extradition Act 1989;
- action taken by or with the authority of the Secretary of State for the purposes of investigating crime or of protecting the security of the State, including action so taken with respect to passports;
- the commencement or conduct of civil or criminal proceedings before any court of law in the United Kingdom;
- any exercise of the prerogative of mercy;
- action taken in matters relating to contractual or other commercial transactions . . . being transactions of a government department;
- action taken in respect of appointments or removals, pay, discipline, superannuation or other personnel matters, in relation to the armed forces, any office or employment under the Crown;[32]
- the grant of honours, awards or privileges within the gift of the Crown, including the grant of Royal Charters.

Departments and matters within the Commissioner's jurisdiction

Schedule 2 to the Act lays down those departments subject to the jurisdiction of the Commissioner. The Parliamentary and Health Service Commissioners Act 1987 extended the Commissioner's jurisdiction to cover some non-departmental bodies, and the complete list of departments and bodies within the Commissioner's jurisdiction is now found in Schedule 1 to the 1987 Act, as amended by the Parliamentary Commissioner Act 1994.

The Commissioner's discretion

Where a matter falls within the Commissioner's jurisdiction, the Commissioner has discretion as to whether to accept the complaint.[33] Section 5(5) provides that the Commissioner shall act 'in accordance with his own discretion'. Because of the breadth of discretion conferred on the Commissioner, both in relation to accepting complaints and in the conduct of investigations, judicial review of his or her decisions is unlikely to succeed. For example, in **Re Fletcher** (1970), the applicant sought an order of mandamus to force the Commissioner to investigate a complaint. The House of Lords refused, relying on the broad discretion conferred on the Commissioner by statute. In **R v Parliamentary Commissioner for Administration ex parte Dyer** (1994), the applicant sought judicial review of the Commissioner's investigation into her complaints against the Department of Social Security. The applicant was dissatisfied with a report of the Commissioner and sought judicial review on four grounds. The allegations were, first, that the Commissioner had not investigated all her complaints; second, that she had not been given the opportunity to comment on the draft reports; third, that the Commissioner, having heard her complaints, refused to reopen the investigations; and, fourth, that the Commissioner was wrong in holding

---

32 Commissioner for Complaints (Northern Ireland) Act 1969, s 5(1), provides that the Commissioner has jurisdiction over matters of employment in the public sector.
33 Parliamentary Commissioner Act 1967, s 5(1).

that he could not reopen the inquiry. The Queen's Bench Division held that it had jurisdiction to review the work of the Commissioner. Lord Justice Simon Brown declared that he could see nothing in the Commissioner's role or the statutory framework in which he operated which is 'so singular as to take him wholly outside the purview of judicial review'. Nevertheless, the court would be slow to review given the breadth of discretion conferred under the Act.[34]

The meaning of 'maladministration'

Maladministration is the key concept relating to the Commissioner's jurisdiction, but it is not defined in the Act. The concept derives from the Whyatt Report of 1961, where it was described as a term which 'was not of precise meaning'. The failure to define the concept in the Act was deliberate. The minister responsible for introducing the legislation, Mr Richard Crossman, felt that the Act was of such an innovatory nature that time would be needed to adjust to the Act's introduction and that no rigid criteria should be set. In the House of Commons, Mr Crossman described maladministration as including 'bias, neglect, inattention, delay, incompetence, ineptitude, perversity, turpitude, arbitrariness and so on'.[35]

The meaning of maladministration can best be understood when placed in the context of actual investigations undertaken by the Ombudsman. Among its many cases undertaken in one year, the *Annual Report 2004–2005: A Year of Progress* presents the following examples:

The Ombudsman found that a General Practitioner had failed to provide an adequate standard of care and treatment through delay and obstruction.

The Ombudsman upheld a complaint concerning informed consent to surgery. The patient required treatment for cancer of the oesophagus. The Ombudsman found that the brief 'mention' of the surgery procedure was unacceptable and meant that informed consent was not given. Poor documentation was also found. It was also unacceptable that the task of obtaining signed consent was given to a junior doctor.

Jobcentre Plus had incorrectly advised a couple over their eligibility to income support. The couple had moved in together and the man had reduced his working hours as a result of the advice. They then suffered a loss of income. They complained to Jobcentre Plus which admitted the mistake but refused to pay any compensation for their loss which was exacerbated by the man's deterioration in health as a result of stress.

The Ombudsman found maladministration on the part of the Legal Services Commission which had failed to provide an appropriate level of service; as a result of the mistakes interest had accrued on her statutory charge liability. The Commission apologised and arranged for her statutory charge account to be reimbursed and for an *ex gratia* payment to compensate for the distress suffered as a result of the Commission's failings.

The courts have examined the concept of maladministration in relation to the work of Local Government Commissioners. For example, in **R v Commissioners for Local Administration ex parte Bradford Metropolitan Borough Council** (1979), maladministration was described as 'faulty

---

34 Cf **R v Parliamentary Commissioner for Administration ex parte Balchin** (1998) and **Balchin (No 2)** (2000), in which judicial review was granted, and the Parliamentary Commissioner found to have fallen into error.
35 *Official Report* HC 734 Col 51.

administration' and 'bad administration', whereas, in 1980, Lord Donaldson MR explained that maladministration is primarily concerned with the manner in which authorities reach or implement decisions, and is not concerned with the quality of the decision itself.[36] In **R v Local Commissioner for Administration ex parte Liverpool City Council** (1999), the Court of Appeal ruled that the failure of local councillors to follow the National Code of Local Government Conduct, and failure to observe the requirement to declare financial interests when taking part in decisions relating to planning, was maladministration.

Maladministration is a more restrictive concept than is employed in other jurisdictions. In Denmark, for example, the ombudsman may examine 'mistakes' and 'unreasonable decisions' and, in Norway, the ombudsman can investigate decisions which are 'clearly unreasonable'. In the United Kingdom, being tied to the concept of maladministration, the Commissioner is not concerned with the merits of any decision taken, nor the fairness or otherwise of the rules governing any situation, but rather with the manner of the application of the rules.

The Commissioner's investigation and report

In the exercise of his or her jurisdiction, the Commissioner is vested with strong powers by the Parliamentary Commissioner Act 1967. The Commissioner has the same powers as a court in respect of requiring the attendance of witnesses and the right of examination, and the production of documents, subject to the protections of Cabinet proceedings and documents and such information as a person would not be compelled to disclose to a court of law (section 8). To obstruct the Commissioner in the performance of his duties under the Act, without lawful excuse, may be certified as a contempt.

Under section 10, where the Commissioner accepts jurisdiction and investigates a complaint, a report of the findings is sent to the complainant and the principal officer of the department concerned. If the matter has not been remedied, or is unlikely to be, he or she may lay a special report before each House of Parliament. The Commissioner's *Annual General Report* is laid before Parliament. The Commissioner has no power to grant a remedy or to grant compensation. He or she does, however, make recommendations as to the appropriate remedy, and as to levels of suitable compensation.

The volume of complaints[37]

There are three categories of complaint: those made to the Parliamentary Commissioner and referred by a Member of Parliament; those referred by a Member of Parliament relating to the withholding of information contrary to the Code of Practice on Access to Government Information (AOI complaints); and those made to the Health Service Commissioner (HSC complaints).

The evidence indicates that, whilst a high number of complaints are rejected (either because they relate to matters not within the Commissioner's jurisdiction, whether relating to an excluded department or relating to matters of policy, or because they reveal no *prima facie* case of maladministration), once a complaint is admitted for investigation, the prospect of a finding of maladministration – at least in part – is high.

The Annual Report of the Parliamentary and Health Service Commissioner 2011–12 reveals that the government departments with the most complaints accepted for formal investigation were the Ministry of Justice, the Home Office (including the UK Border Agency), the Department for Work and Pensions and HM Revenue and Customs. Of the various health bodies, the most complaints investigated were in relation to NHS hospitals. Over 4,700

---

36 R v Commissioners for Local Administration ex parte Eastleigh Borough Council (1980).
37 Source: Parliamentary and Health Service Ombudsman Business Plan 2003–2004.

inquiries were looked at, of which there was no case to answer in 3,552 cases and in 759 cases the matter was put right without formal investigation. Of the 410 formal investigations under-taken, 60 per cent were fully upheld, 20 per cent partly upheld and 20 per cent not upheld.

The Problem of Accessibility and Public Awareness

On accessibility, the Commissioner has questioned his own position.[38] As seen, prior to reform, discussed below, access to the Commissioner could only be gained through a Member of Parliament, and not directly. Of the 100 plus national ombudsmen around the world, the British Commissioner was unique in having no powers of initiative, being dependent upon references from the MP 'filter'. In the report for 1988, the Commissioner considered the diffi-culties in increasing public awareness about the Commissioner's role and powers,[39] despite regular press notices, press and radio and television interviews and the booklet available from Citizens Advice Bureaux and public libraries. In the Commissioner's report of 1990,[40] the problem of public awareness was again alluded to.

The Commissioner himself has noted that public awareness is most usually raised through some major issue or scandal. Two illustrations may be cited. The first major investigation arising out of a number of complaints was into the non-payment of compensation by the Foreign Office to 12 persons who had been prisoners of war in the Sachsenhausen camp.[41] Monies had been made available by the German government and distributed by the Foreign Office to former detainees. The Commissioner found there had been maladministration[42] and the government awarded compensation to the complainants.

The Barlow Clowes affair resulted in hundreds of complaints being made to the Commissioner concerning the collapse of the Barlow Clowes company.[43] In 1988, the group of companies collapsed, causing significant losses to shareholders. The Department of Trade and Industry has responsibility for licensing such investment companies.[44] Following the company's collapse, numerous shareholders complained to Members of Parliament, 159 of whom referred the complaints to the Parliamentary Commissioner. The Commissioner made five findings of maladministration on the part of the Department of Trade and Industry, including errors, lack of information before making decisions, delay in instigating a formal inquiry, a failure to appreciate that auditors would not find the relevant information and insuf-ficient rigour in exercising its regulatory role – all of which resulted in injustice.

The government initially rejected the Commissioner's findings and recommendations as to compensation, arguing both that no investment is free of risk and that those with larger amounts of money should accept a higher level of responsibility and therefore loss. The Commissioner expressed disappointment that the government did not unreservedly accept his report. His recommendation was that compensation should be payable to investors at a rate of 90 per cent for losses incurred under £50,000, and 85 per cent for losses under £100,000. The Secretary of State for Trade and Industry accepted the recommendations, but maintained that the government had no legal liability to compensate investors, and claimed that the

---

38 *Parliamentary Commissioner for Administration Annual Report for 1983* (1983–84), London: HMSO. And see *Report of the Select Committee on the Parliamentary Commissioner for Administration: The Powers, Work and Jurisdiction of the Ombudsman* (1992–93), London: HMSO.
39 *Parliamentary Commissioner for Administration Annual Report for 1988* (1988–89), London: HMSO.
40 *Parliamentary Commissioner for Administration Annual Report for 1990* (1990–91), London: HMSO.
41 See Bradley, 1992b.
42 *Third Report of the Parliamentary Commissioner for Administration*, HC 54 (1967–68), London: HMSO; and see Gregory and Drewry, Part I and Part II, 1991.
43 See Gregory and Drewry, Part I and Part II, 1991.
44 Under the Prevention of Fraud (Investment) Act 1958; now Financial Services Act 1986.

Department's handling of the case was 'within acceptable range of standards reasonably to be expected of regulators'. The Secretary of State went on to say that compensation was being made only because of the Parliamentary Commissioner's recommendations.[45]

The losses caused to egg manufacturers over allegations made by officials concerning salmonella infection resulted in charges of maladministration and compensation of £600,000 being paid by the Ministry of Agriculture, Fisheries and Food.[46] The Animal Health Act 1981[47] provided that, where the salmonella virus was found in flocks, the flock should be slaughtered and compensation paid for the loss of the healthy birds. No compensation was payable for the diseased birds. The Ministry fixed the level of compensation – irrespective of the proportion of the flock infected by the virus – at 60 per cent of the value of the healthy birds. On investigation, the Commissioner found that inadequate compensation had been paid.[48]

It has been seen above that the government is, in general, prepared to accept the findings of the Commissioner and to implement his or her recommendations. In December 1991, the Financial Secretary to the Treasury[49] stated that 'I am not aware of any circumstances in which [the Parliamentary Ombudsman's] recommendations have been ignored. This is the basis on which the government has tended to work – and has, as far as I am aware, always worked – in that we do accept and implement the recommendations that are made'.[50] This commitment was reiterated by the Chancellor of the Duchy of Lancaster[51] in 1993, when he stated that 'invariably, in the end, [the government] accepted the Commissioner's say-so'.[52] However, it has also been seen above that, in relation to the Barlow Clowes affair, the government deviated from this normally accepted practice and, while prepared to offer compensation, did so 'without admission of fault or liability'.[53] The government has proved to be more obdurate in relation to the 1995 report of the Commissioner, relating to financial damage caused by the prolonged plans to build the Channel Tunnel Rail Link.

The Channel Tunnel Rail Link (the CTRL) is a stretch of railway line designed to take high-speed cross-channel trains. The government's original intention was that the CTRL would be financed by the private sector. However, when private funding was not forthcoming, the project could not proceed. In 1990, the Secretary of State for Transport announced that the route was to be reconsidered. The project was thus kept alive, but uncertainty surrounded the area of south-east England in which it was to be built. As a result, thousands of properties were 'blighted' and owners were unable to sell their homes. The route was finally decided in 1994.

In February 1995, the Commissioner[54] laid a special report before the House.[55] The special report was only the second such report to be made in the history of the office of Commissioner.[56] The basis for the laying of a special report is that the Commission considers that injustice has been caused to persons as a result of maladministration and that the injustice has not been, or will not be, remedied. In the Commissioner's report on the CTRL project, the Commissioner considered that maladministration had occurred in the Department of Transport between June

---

45 In total, £150 million was paid in compensation.
46 HC 947 (1992–93), London: HMSO.
47 Animal Health Act 1981, Sched 3, para 5(2).
48 *Fourth Report: Compensation to Farmers for Slaughtered Poultry*, HC 519 (1992–93), London: HMSO.
49 Mr Francis Maude MP.
50 *Second Report from the Select Committee on the PCA: The Implications of the Citizen's Charter for the Work of the Parliamentary Commissioner for Administration*, HC 159 (1991–92), London: HMSO, Q 11.
51 Then the Rt Hon William Waldegrave MP.
52 *First Report from the Select Committee on the PCA: The Powers, Work and Jurisdiction of the Ombudsman*, HC 33 (1993–94), London: HMSO, Q 733.
53 Observations by the government to the *Report of the PCA on Barlow Clowes*, HC 99 (1989–90), London: HMSO, para 43.
54 Mr William Reid CB.
55 Pursuant to the Parliamentary Commissioner Act 1967, s 10(3).
56 The first was in 1977–78, which also involved the Department of Transport.

1990 and April 1994. The Commissioner's view was that the Department of Transport 'had a responsibility to consider the position of . . . persons suffering exceptional or extreme hardship and to provide for redress where appropriate'[57] and that the government had a duty to consider the position not just of all citizens, but also of individual citizens harmed by its action. The Commissioner found that 'no special consideration was given to that aspect of good administration and it is on that basis that I criticise the department'.[58] The Commissioner recommended that individuals who had suffered exceptional hardship should receive compensation from the government. The government's reaction was to state that it was not its policy to compensate those affected by generalised blight, and that, in relation to those individuals who had suffered exceptional hardship, it was too difficult to define criteria to identify such individuals. With this, the Commissioner disagreed. While he accepted that there were definitional difficulties, he did not 'accept at all that it is technically beyond a government department's capabilities' to establish the relevant criteria.[59]

The Commissioner's report and the government's response was considered by the Select Committee on the Parliamentary Commissioner for Administration (see further below). In its report,[60] the committee agreed with the Commissioner's assessment of the evidence. The committee stated that:

> The department failed to provide any material to contradict this finding when invited to do so by the committee. At no point was direct and comprehensive consideration given to the question of whether it was either desirable or possible to offer ex gratia compensation to those exceptionally afflicted by the generalised blight of the CTRL project.

The committee considered that at the heart of the matter lay the definition of maladministration. In his annual report for 1993, the Commissioner included in his definition 'failure to mitigate the effects of rigid adherence to the letter of the law where that produces manifestly inequitable treatment'.[61] Endorsing this definition, the committee stated that the definition implies:

> . . . an expectation that when an individual citizen is faced with extraordinary hardship as a result of strict application of law or policy, the executive must be prepared to look again and consider whether help can be given. That the department did not do. It never considered the possibility of distinguishing cases of extreme hardship from the mass of those affected adversely by blight.[62]

The committee concluded that:

> 1(i) . . . the Department of Transport should have considered whether any ex gratia payments were due when the CTRL project entered the period of uncertainty caused by problems of funding between June 1990 and April 1994;
>
> (ii) . . . it is desirable to grant redress to those affected to an extreme and exceptional degree by generalised blight, in line with the principle that maladministration includes a failure to mitigate the effects of rigid adherence to the letter of the law where that produces manifestly inequitable treatment;

---

57 Fifth Report of the PCA: The Channel Tunnel Rail Link and Blight, HC 193 (1994–95), London: HMSO, para 46.
58 Ibid, Q 1.
59 Ibid.
60 Sixth Report of the PCA: The Channel Tunnel Rail Link and Exceptional Hardship, HC 270 (1994–95), London: HMSO.
61 Report of the Parliamentary Commissioner for Administration: Annual Report for 1993, HC 345 (1993–94), London: HMSO, para 10.
62 Sixth Report, fn 58, para 20.

(iii) . . . it should be possible to distinguish a small number of cases of exceptional hardship.

This highly critical report on the actions of the Department of Transport and the government's failure to respond positively to the Commissioner's report represents a landmark case in the complex tri-partite constitutional relationship between the Commissioner, his select committee and Parliament, and the executive. In 1997, the government finally agreed to pay compensation of £5,000 to property owners whose property value had been adversely affected by the delay in reaching decisions over the routing of the CTRL.[63]

The select committee

The Parliamentary Commissioner is aided by a select committee, which considers the annual and special reports of the Parliamentary Commissioner and Health Service Commissioner and takes evidence from the Commissioners and others, including government departments and health authorities, on matters arising from reports in order to ensure that all reasonable efforts are made to tighten up procedures, prevent the repetition of faults and provide any appropriate remedies.

The select committee represents the formal link between the Commissioner and Parliament. The committee is able to exert pressure on government departments to comply with the recommendations of the Commissioner.

The Parliamentary Commissioner and ministerial responsibility

One aspect of the office of Commissioner which caused concern when the office was proposed was the relationship between the Commissioner and ministers, and the impact of the Commissioner's office on the doctrine of ministerial responsibility.

See further Chapters 1 and 10.

Ministerial responsibility is a fundamental constitutional principle. Separated into the collective responsibility of the Cabinet and the individual responsibility of Ministers for their conduct and that of their department, the concept underpins the idea of governmental accountability to Parliament and to the electorate. Accordingly, where a person has a grievance against a government department or other public body which is not resolved to the complainant's satisfaction, responsibility falls on the relevant Minister and it is for the Minister to account to Parliament for any wrongdoing by a body under his responsibility. The view of the government at the time was that ministerial responsibility and the office of the Commissioner were irreconcilable. As noted above, in the Attorney General's view, there already existed 'adequate provision' under the constitution for the redress of grievances.

JUSTICE replied:

The Commissioner would help to make ministerial responsibility more effective. He would penetrate the screen which Ministers interpose between Members of Parliament and government departments and he would keep Parliament informed about administrative practices which were open to criticism. The responsibility of the Minister would remain as it is – neither more nor less.

---

63 See James and Longley, 1996. The Child Support Agency also attracted a significant volume of complaints. The number of complaints was such that, in 1994, the Commissioner took the 'unprecedented step of declining to investigate fresh individual complaints' other than where they concerned aspects of the Agency's work which the Commissioner had not yet inquired into. In 1995, complaints against the Child Support Agency amounted to one quarter of all cases referred to the Commissioner. See *Sixth Report*, paras 17–18 and *Parliamentary Commissioner for Administration Annual Report* for 1995, Cm 296; and see HC 193 (1994–95), London: HMSO.

The government's policy of making administration more open and accessible has an impact on the work of the Parliamentary Commissioner. Three major developments reflected this commitment. The Citizen's Charter provided that public bodies must state their objectives, must publicise the standards of service to be expected by consumers and establish complaints procedures for dissatisfied customers. Specific services must publish their own individuated Charter. The establishment of 'Next Step Agencies',[64] the task of which is to achieve greater efficiency in the delivery of public services, also affects the role of the Commissioner. The setting up of Agencies, the head of which are responsible for operational matters and accountable to Parliament through select committee inquiries, has the effect of reducing the size of the central Civil Service and introducing greater management efficiency and accountability. The minister remains responsible to Parliament for policy matters. In relation to the Parliamentary Commissioner,[65] his powers of investigation, report and recommendation continue to extend to Agencies. However, complaints made by the public to Members of Parliament about operational matters are to be directed to the chairman of the board of the Agency. Complaints regarding matters of policy remain within the political domain and the responsibility of ministers.

See Chapter 5.

Reform of the Office of Parliamentary Commissioner

The office of Commissioner suffers from a number of drawbacks. Individuals have – unlike in most other jurisdictions – no right of direct access to the Parliamentary Commissioner. The concept of maladministration is relatively narrow and is linked to injustice suffered as a result of a decision. Furthermore, while the 1987 Act has extended the bodies into which the Commissioner has jurisdiction to investigate, there remain a significant number of matters outside his jurisdiction. Many of these relate to matters which fall under the royal prerogative, which, as has been seen, is subject to inadequate parliamentary scrutiny and to limited judicial review.

The question of direct access to the Commissioner was again considered by the select committee in 1993–94.[66] The committee conducted a survey of Members of Parliament in order to ascertain their views on the filter. Of the 333 Members who responded, the committee reported that 38.4 per cent were in favour of direct access to the Commissioners, whereas 58.0 per cent were against direct access. The committee commented that:

> It is clear that many Members value their role as champions of their constituents' complaints and are unwilling to see this constitutional function in any way bypassed or diminished.[67]

The Commissioner himself, however, argued forcibly that the filter was 'potentially disadvantageous to complainants', in part because individuals may feel that their Member of Parliament would be unwilling to help them and because of the administrative burden on Members of Parliament in transmitting material to the Commissioner. JUSTICE and the National Consumer

---

64 See *Improving Management in Government:The Next Steps*, 1988, London: HMSO.
65 And Commissioner for Local Administration.
66 HC 33 (1993–94), London: HMSO, paras 53–77.
67 HC 33 (1993–94), London: HMSO, para 58.

Council also argued for reform of the system. The Committee summarised the objections to the MP filter as follows:

(a)   the public should have direct access to the Commissioner as a matter of right;
(b)   the filter is an anomaly, almost unknown in other ombudsman systems.[68] No such requirement exists, for instance, in the case of the Health Service Commissioner;
(c)   individuals with complaints may be unwilling to approach an MP, while desiring the ombudsman's assistance;
(d)   the filter means that the likelihood of individuals' cases being referred to the Commissioner will largely depend on the views and practice of the particular constituency MP. Some look with more favour on the Office of the Commissioner than others;
(e)   the filter acts as an obstacle to the Commissioner effectively promoting his services;
(f)   the filter creates an unnecessary bureaucratic barrier between the complainant and the Commissioner, involving considerable paperwork for MPs and their offices.[69]

The Committee concluded, however, that the advantages of retaining the filter system outweighed these significant disadvantages. The Committee was particularly concerned to retain the role of the Member of Parliament in the investigation of complaints, and about the potentially vast increase in the number of complaints being received by the Commissioner if the filter was removed.

The question of the jurisdictional basis of maladministration has also been subject to consideration. The JUSTICE-All Souls Report of 1988[70] recommended no change to the definition. In 2000 a Cabinet review of Ombudsmen concluded that there should be major reform aimed at simplifying the arrangements for complaints and removing the 'MP filter'. The review recommended that the offices of Parliamentary, Local Government and Health Service Commissioners should be restructured into one single Public Service Commissioner able to receive complaints about any matter within jurisdiction.[71]

The Regulatory Reform Order 2007[72] empowers Commissioners to conduct joint investigations, to share information and to issue joint reports. It also provides power to appoint a mediator to assist in the resolution of a case. The purpose of the reform is to facilitate co-operation over complaints which affect the jurisdiction of more than one Commissioner. Such issues are most likely to be related to housing and welfare benefits, health and social care and planning and the environment.

Commissioners for Northern Ireland, Scotland and Wales

Northern Ireland, Scotland and Wales each have a Parliamentary Commissioner for Administration with similar powers and functions as the United Kingdom Parliamentary Commissioner. In Northern Ireland there is also a Police Ombudsman.[73]

---

68   Only Sri Lanka and France employ similar filters.
69   HC 33 (1993–94), London: HMSO, para 65.
70   JUSTICE-All Souls, *Administrative Law: Some Necessary Reforms*, 1988, London: HMSO.
71   Cabinet Office, *Review of Public Sector Ombudsmen in England*, 2000. In 2000 a Parliamentary Commissioner (Amendment) Bill, removing the MP filter, was passed by the House of Lords but rejected by the Commons.
72   No 1889. The Order amends the Parliamentary Commissioner Act 1967, the Local Government Act 1974 and the Health Service Commissioner Act 1993.
73   Respectively, Parliamentary Commissioner (Northern Ireland) Act; 1969; Scotland Act 1998; Government of Wales Act 1998; Police (Northern Ireland) Act 1997.

The Health Service Commissioners

The National Health Service (Scotland) Act 1972 and National Health Service Reorganisation Act 1973[74] introduced separate Health Service Commissioners for England, Wales and Scotland. The Parliamentary Commissioner for Administration undertakes the role of Health Service Commissioner. The Commissioner reports directly to the Secretary of State for Health, but his reports are laid before both Houses of Parliament and will be considered by the Parliamentary Commissioner Select Committee.

Jurisdiction

Section 109 of the Health Service Act 1977 provided that the following are subject to investigation by the Health Commissioner: regional, district and special health authorities; family health services authorities; Mental Health Act Commission; Dental Practice Board; and National Health Service Trusts.

The Commissioner may investigate any matter relating to an alleged failure to provide a service it is meant to provide, and any other action taken by or on behalf of the authority. The jurisdiction is thus much broader than 'maladministration'. However, the complaint must be one which involves injustice or hardship suffered as a result of failures under the two headings for complaint. Individuals have the right of direct access to the Commissioner. Originally excluded from investigation by the Commissioner, the Health Service Commissioners (Amendment) Act 1996 extended the jurisdiction of Commissioners to include clinical judgments of medical practitioners.

Local Government Commissioners[75]

The Local Government Act 1974 established Commissioners for Local Administration for England and Wales. England is divided into three areas, each represented by one or more Commissioners.[76] The Scottish system is established under Part II of the Local Government (Scotland) Act 1975. Commissioners are appointed by the Crown and hold office 'during good behaviour'.

Jurisdiction

The Commissioners have jurisdiction to investigate any complaint of maladministration or failure in service provision by council committees, their members and officers of the council. Police authorities, water boards, development corporations and those bodies with whom the council has partnership arrangements for the provision of services are also within the Commissioners' jurisdiction.[77]

Since 1989 the public has had the right of direct access to the Commissioner, a reform which led to a significant increase in complaints.

---

74 As amended by the National Health Service Act 1977, Pt V. See now the Health Service Commissioners Act 1993.
75 Recommended by the JUSTICE Report, *The Citizen and His Council: Ombudsmen for Local Government?*, 1969; and see the White Paper, *Reform of Local Government in England*, 1970, London: HMSO.
76 Local Government Act 1974, s 23.
77 Local Government and Public Involvement in Health Act 2007, s 172.

Maladministration causing injustice

The concept of maladministration used for the Parliamentary Commissioner is adopted for the Local Commissioners. Maladministration resulting in injustice has been found to include incomplete record keeping and the failure to give reasons for decisions, and a finding of maladministration may be made where an authority fails to have adequate complaints procedures. Inadequate school places, and unreasonable delays in processing applications for improvement grants have also been found to amount to maladministration. Shortages of staff and financial resources will not excuse a council from a finding of maladministration.

Section 31 of the Act provides that an authority need only consider a Commissioner's report if it has been found that the maladministration in question has resulted in injustice. Mere maladministration is not enough.

Remedies

Where a finding of maladministration resulting in injustice has been made, section 31 of the Local Government Act 1974 imposes a duty on authorities to consider the report and to advise the Commissioner of any action taken to comply with the findings, or proposed action. Section 31 of the 1974 Act has been amended to provide that authorities may make 'any payment' to the aggrieved person that it thinks appropriate.

Not every decision of the Commissioners will be accepted. In 1986, for example, the Select Committee on the Parliamentary Commissioner noted that 19 per cent of local authorities who had adverse reports made by the Commissioners had ignored the recommendations.[78] The Local Government and Housing Act 1989 provides that local authorities have three months in which to respond to the Commissioner's report and that they should notify the Commissioner of any action taken, or action which they are proposing to take in response to his report.[79] If the Commissioner is not satisfied with the response he may issue a further report. Where the local authority proposes not to act in response to the report, the matter must be referred to a full council meeting.

Excluded matters

Schedule 5 to the Local Government Act excludes matters relating to the internal regulation of schools, personnel matters, action taken concerning the commencement of legal proceedings and criminal investigations. The general exclusion of commercial and contractual matters has been replaced by a list of particular excluded matters.[80]

Complaints

A complaint may be made by a person who claims to have sustained injustice as a result of the local authority's failure, or a person authorised to act on behalf of that person.[81] Where a complaint is made to a public authority over whom the Commissioner has jurisdiction, a member of that authority may refer the complaint to the Commissioner.[82] Complaints must be in writing unless the Commissioner disapplies this requirement.[83] The permitted period for

---

78 *Third Report from the Select Committee on the Parliamentary Commissioner for Administration: Local Government Cases: Enforcement of Remedies*, HC 448 (1985–86), London: HMSO.
79 Local Government and Housing Act 1989, s 26(2)–(2)(c).
80 Local Government and Public Involvement in Health Act 2007, s 173.
81 Section 26A Local Government Act 1974, inserted by s 174 Local Government etc Act 2007.
82 Section 26C Local Government Act 1974, inserted by s 174 Local Government etc Act 2007.
83 Complaints may now be made electronically: Local Government etc Act 2007, s 178.

bringing a complaint is 12 months from the day the person affected or his or her personal representative had notice of the matter, although these requirements may be set aside by the Commissioner.[84]

The Commissioners have the power to initiate an investigation into possible maladministration or service failure affecting persons other than the original complainant where this emerges in the course of an investigation.[85]

Housing matters form the basis for approximately 40 per cent of complaints each year, with complaints about planning accounting for approximately 30 per cent of complaints. Education, social services, local taxation and environmental health each comprise approximately five per cent of complaints.

Judicial review and commissioners for administration

Judicial review of decisions of Commissioners is an available form of redress, although the breadth of discretion conferred on Commissioners often renders their decisions beyond challenge. In **Law Debenture Trust Group plc v Pensions Ombudsman** (1999), the Chancery Division allowed an appeal against a finding of maladministration by the Pensions Ombudsman. The complainant had applied to trustees of his pension scheme for early retirement following an injury. The trustees concluded that he was not incapacitated, having carried out video surveillance. The court ruled that the only basis available to the Ombudsman for overturning the decision of the trustees was on the ground of perversity, and that such a finding would have to be expressed in clear terms in the Ombudsman's decision, which had not been done. Further, a finding of perversity could only be made after consideration of the **Wednesbury** criteria with respect to unreasonableness. The Ombudsman was wrong to find that surveillance *per se* amounted to maladministration.

In **R v Parliamentary Commissioner for Administration ex parte Balchin** (1998), the Queen's Bench Division quashed a decision of the Parliamentary Commissioner. The Commissioner had found maladministration in relation to property blighted by a road scheme in Norfolk, but following judicial review his decision was quashed, whereupon a second ombudsman investigated the matter. The second decision included fresh findings based on new evidence. It was disputed whether the Commissioner had made a finding as to whether, if there had been any maladministration, that had caused any injustice to the applicants. The court held that the decision on maladministration was flawed since his reasoning was inadequate, and that there had been a failure to give reasons for findings on the principal controversial issues. The application was granted and *certiorari* ordered.

The Information Commissioner

The Freedom of Information Act 2000 represents a step in the direction of more open government by conferring on citizens a legal right, subject to limited exceptions, to access to information held by public bodies. An Information Commissioner has been appointed who is independent of Parliament and accountable to the courts. The Commissioner's jurisdiction comes into play after there has been a complaint made to a department or other public body, and that body has conducted an internal inquiry which produces no satisfactory outcome. Complaints are made by the public via a Member of Parliament. The Commissioner has wide

---

84 Section 26B Local Government Act 1974, inserted by s 174 Local Government etc Act 2007.
85 Section 26D Local Government Act 1974, inserted by s 174 Local Government etc Act 2007.

See further Chapter 10.

powers to investigate complaints, including the right of access, under warrant, to enter and search the records of public authorities and, where it is suspected that information is being, or will be, suppressed, to remove that information. There is no right of appeal from the Commissioner to the courts, but his or her decisions are amenable to judicial review. The Commissioner lays an annual report before Parliament, and issues reports on investigations undertaken.

The Legal Services Commissioner

The Legal Services Ombudsman was established under the Courts and Legal Services Act 1990. The Legal Services Act 2007 established the Office for Legal Complaints (OLC) which now regulates the Ombudsman scheme. The OLC is responsible for the appointment of the Chief Ombudsman and one or more others as Assistant Ombudsmen. The Chief Ombudsman must be a lay person. Complaints against members of the legal profession must first be directed to the relevant professional body. If that body fails to investigate the complaint adequately, a complaint may then be made to the Ombudsman.

European Union Ombudsman[86]

The Treaty on European Union 1992 introduced the office of ombudsman, appointed by the European Parliament. Under Article 195, the ombudsman is appointed for the life of a Parliament, and may be removed by the Court of Justice, at the request of the Parliament, on the basis that 'he no longer fulfils the conditions required for the performance of his duties or if he is guilty of serious misconduct'. The ombudsman is completely independent in the exercise of his duties, and may not seek or take instructions from any body.

Citizens of the European Union have the right of direct access to the ombudsman, and complaints may be referred by a Member of the European Parliament. The ombudsman has jurisdiction to hear complaints relating to institutions of the Union and to require national government bodies to provide information relating to complaints. Where a finding of maladministration is made, the matter is referred to the relevant institution, which has a period of three months in which to respond. The ombudsman submits an annual report to the European Parliament. The complaint must relate to maladministration on the part of institutions of the Union. The European Court of Justice and the Court of First Instance, acting in their judicial role, are excluded from the ombudsman's jurisdiction.[87]

Summary

It became recognised in the 1960s that there was inadequate provision for the investigation and resolution of citizens' complaints against government departments. Adopting the Ombudsmen concept from Scandinavian countries, Parliament enacted the Parliamentary Commissioners Act 1967. This established the office of Parliamentary Commissioner, a post independent of Parliament and the executive, with wide-ranging powers to investigate complaints based on 'maladministration'.

---

86 On the institutions of the Community, see Chapter 7.
87 See Lord Millett, 2002.

Complaints must be made to the citizen's Member of Parliament who may attempt to resolve the matter or refer it to the Commissioner. The Commissioner has a discretion whether to investigate a complaint. He or she makes an annual Report to Parliament and is supported by a Select Committee. The Commissioner makes recommendations but cannot grant a remedy.

Since the introduction of the Parliamentary Commissioner, there has been introduced a Health Services Commissioner (the office being held by the Parliamentary Commissioner), local government Commissioners, and numerous Commissioners in the private sector.

Further Reading

Abraham, A. (2007) 'The Ombudsman as Part of the UK Constitution: A Contested Role?', Parliamentary Affairs, 61.1: 601.

Gregory and Giddings (2002) The Ombudsman and Parliament, London: Politico's Publishing.

Kirkham, R. (2006) 'Challenging the Authority of the Ombudsman: The Parliamentary Commissioner's Special Report on Wartime Detainees', Modern Law Review, 69: 792.

McMurtie, S.N. (1997) 'The Waiting Game – The Parliamentary Commissioner's Response to Delay in Administrative Procedures', Public Law, 159.

Millett, Lord (2002) 'The Right to Good Administration in Europe', Public Law, 309.

Seneviratne, M. (2002) Public Service and Administrative Justice, Oxford: OUP.

Chapter 27

Tribunals and Inquiries

PART A: TRIBUNALS

Introduction

A tribunal, like a court of law, is a forum in which disputes are settled by an impartial adjudicator. A network, or system, of tribunals – each focusing on a particular area of law – forms part of the civil justice system and represents an important part of administrative law.

It was the twentieth century expansion of the role of the state and the growth in government departments – in relation to taxation, the provision of welfare benefits, the National Health Service, transport, planning and public housing, immigration and asylum – which explains the expansion of tribunals. Disputes between the individual and the day to day administration of government are inevitable, and mechanisms were needed to deal with such disputes. While access to courts of law is open, it is also costly, time-consuming and formal, with strict rules of procedure and evidence. What was needed was a less-formal, but nevertheless specialist and authoritative forum to deal with the large volume of complaints and/or appeals against departmental decisions.[1] Historically tribunals were operated by the government department which had undertaken the decision being challenged by the citizen. Government ministers appointed tribunal members and the department took responsibility for the administration of the process.

Tribunals not only span a wide range of specialist areas of law, but also differ in their degree of specialism and formality. Some, for example the Lands Tribunal,[2] operate in a formal manner, hardly distinguishable from a court of law. For the most part, however, tribunals are intended to offer a less formal atmosphere in which the issues can be resolved. These tribunals do not necessarily consist of lawyers although more recent developments have required tribunal chairmen/women to be legally qualified. Lay membership has long been a common feature of tribunals and where the subject matter requires it, specialists from other disciplines may be appointed.[3] The appointment and training of tribunal judiciary is undertaken by the Judicial Appointments Commission established under the Constitutional Reform Act 2005.

The earliest examples of tribunals can be said to date back to the early nineteenth century. These dealt with issues concerning income tax.[4] As the range of areas for adjudication by tribunals developed over the next century it became clear that reliance on tribunals was useful because of the advantages they posed over the normal court process. As government became more complex and the level of administration grew, tribunals could be used to dispense quick and effective justice outside the court system. With their *ad hoc* development, the number and types of tribunals expanded without being organised in any formalised system.

The common features of a tribunal (although not applicable to all) are that they:

- should be able to make final and legally enforceable decisions which are subject to review and appeal;
- should be independent of any department of government;
- should hold oral hearings in public;
- should have sufficient expertise to deal with specialist matters;
- should be under a duty to give reasons for decisions taken.[5]

---

1 See Genn, H. (1993) 'Tribunals and Informal Justice', 56 *Modern Law Review* 3.
2 Established under the Lands Tribunal Act 1949 to determine complex aspects of property law.
3 For example a medical doctor is required for a mental health review tribunal.
4 Richardson, G. & Genn, H. (2007), 'Tribunals in transition: resolution or adjudication?', *Public Law*, 116.
5 Farmer, J. (1974), *Tribunals and Government*, Weidenfeld & Nicolson, pp 185–87.

In addition an appeal on a point of law should be available to the courts of law and judicial review of tribunal decisions should be available.

The Range of Tribunals

There are over 70 tribunals in England and Wales, although few of these hear more than 500 cases a year.[6] All tribunals are established by statute under which their jurisdiction, membership and procedure is defined. Tribunals include Agriculture, Aviation, Data Protection, Education, Employment, Fair Trading, Financial Services, Foreign Compensation, Immigration, Land, Taxation, Misuse of Drugs, National Health Service, Pensions, and Rents. In addition to the above, the following sample illustrates the wide-ranging subject matter of Tribunals.

The Social Security and Child Support Tribunal

The most heavily used tribunal at the current time is the Social Security and Child Support Tribunal. This tribunal is responsible for the resolution of disputes concerning an assessment of the wide variety of social security benefits offered by the welfare state.[7] The objective of this tribunal is:

> To bring together the parties to the appeal, and the judiciary, with all appropriate resources for the fair and independent delivery of decisions. We will do this in a way that best meets the expectations of all parties to the appeal and the demands of the public purse. (Social Security and Child Support Tribunal, 2010)[8]

The Mental Health Tribunal

In contrast the Mental Health Review Tribunal has less than ten per cent of the case load of the Social Security and Child Support Tribunal. This tribunal makes decisions, *inter alia*, on whether an individual detained under the Mental Health Act 1983[9] should be released from hospital supervision.

The Investigatory Powers Tribunal

The Investigatory Powers Tribunal is equally specialist, its jurisdiction being confined to the investigation of complaints against the security services (MI5, MI6 and GCHQ)[10] and replacing the Interception of Communications Tribunal, the Security Service Tribunal, the Intelligence Services Tribunal and the complaints provision under the Police Act 1997 relating to police interference with property. The Tribunal only investigates complaints relating to interception,

---

6 *Tribunals for Users – One System One Service: Report of the Review of Tribunals*, 2001. See the Tribunals and Inquiries Act 1992, Sched 1.
7 At the present time it is responsible for resolving disputes concerning Job Seekers Allowance, Income Support, Incapacity Benefit, Employment Support Allowance, Disability Living Allowance, Attendance Allowance and Retirement Pensions. It is also responsible for dealing with disputes concerning Child Support, Tax Credits, Statutory Sick Pay, Statutory Maternity Pay, Compensation Recovery Scheme, Road Traffic (NHS) Charges, Vaccine Damage and decisions made concerning Housing Benefit and Council Tax allowance.
8 The working practices of this tribunal in its many guises throughout the years has been considered by Prosser, T. (1977), 'Poverty, Ideology and Legality: Supplementary Benefit Appeal Tribunals and their Predecessors', 4 British Journal of Law and Society, 59.
9 As amended by the Mental Health Act 2007.
10 The Tribunal is established under the Regulation of Investigatory Powers Act 2000, Part IV.

intrusive surveillance, entry onto or interference with property or wireless telegraphy, directed surveillance or the use of agents. The function of the Tribunal is to consider whether conduct authorised under the Act has been properly authorised and carried out in accordance with appropriate guidelines. The IPT is the only tribunal to investigate complaints against the Security Services. Information concerning the Tribunal is restricted: the Tribunal is not a 'public authority' for the purpose of the Freedom of Information Act 2000, and accordingly there is no right to information under the Act.

See also
Chapter 22.

Reforming the System

By the 1950s concerns had been raised over the lack of supervision of decisions made by tribunals. The Committee on Administrative Tribunals and Enquiries (the Franks Committee)[11] was set up to review the operation of tribunals. The Committee stated that:

> . . . statutory tribunals are an integral part of the machinery of justice in the state and not merely administrative devices for disposing of claims and arguments conveniently[12]

and that tribunals should be:

> . . . open, impartial and fair.[13]

A series of recommendations followed which commented on the values that tribunals should share, their constitutional make-up, and the procedure which should be devised and supervised by a newly created Council on Tribunals. There was no proposal for a unitary tribunals system. The Committee recommended that tribunal chairmen/women should usually be legally qualified. Chairpersons should be appointed by the Lord Chancellor and the Council of Tribunals should take responsibility for appointing other members. The Franks Committee also recommended changes to the procedure for setting up and supervising tribunals to be undertaken by the Council of Tribunals.

It was the Council of Tribunals' task to maintain the informality of the system and to ensure that, unless specific circumstances required, tribunal hearings should be public. Legal representation would be permitted for those attending the tribunal and decisions taken should be supported by full reasons. Appellate tribunals would also be encouraged to publish their decisions so that lower tribunals could follow current working practices. Finally the Franks Committee concerned itself with the appellate structure of tribunals and recommended that appeals on questions of fact, law and the merits of a decision should be available. Judicial review of decisions should also continue to operate.

Many of these recommendations were implemented in the Tribunals and Inquiries Act 1958.[14] The Council of Tribunals[15] was established to provide an advisory and supervisory function over existing tribunals. The Committee accepted that it was necessary for tribunals to

---

11 Report of the Committee on Administrative Tribunals and Enquiries, Cmnd 218 (1957).
12 As discussed by Wade, W. and Forsyth, C. (2004), *Administrative Law*, Oxford University Press, 906.
13 Report of the Committee on Administrative Tribunals and Enquiries, Cmnd 218 (1957) para 42.
14 See also the Tribunals and Inquiries Act 1992.
15 Having at least ten members and not more than 15.

be connected to government departments and executive decision making, but insisted that they should remain firmly committed to impartiality and independence.

Recent Reforms

By 2000 it had become clear that the practices of tribunals were still disparate and lacked cohesion. The Council of Tribunals had also been criticised. Initially it was thought that the Council would advise, supervise and champion the merits of tribunals but it became clear that it had failed to meet these expectations. As the Council was composed of part-time members they had insufficient time to devote to the envisaged activities of the Council. It also had no opportunity to evaluate its practices through research. As a result it was suggested that the Council of Tribunals' work was unable to provide effective supervision of the way that tribunals were operating.

The Legatt Report

A review of tribunals was commissioned by the Lord Chancellor in 2000,[16] chaired by Sir Andrew Legatt and reporting in 2001.[17] The Report, *Tribunals for Users – One System, One Service*, noted that:

> The present collection of tribunals has grown up in an almost entirely haphazard way. Individual tribunals were set up, and usually administered by departments, as they developed new statutory schemes and procedures. The result is a collection of tribunals, mostly administered by departments, with wide variations of practice and approach, and almost no coherence. The current arrangements seem to us to have been developed to meet the needs and convenience of the departments and other bodies which run tribunals, rather than the needs of the user.

There also existed a concern that although tribunals were serving a crucial function their working practices were often old-fashioned and daunting to users. Information technology resources and training practices were criticised and as cases had become more complex the required levels of expertise had not been matched by the necessary level of training and support. The most important criticism made of tribunals was that they were not independent of the departments that sponsored them. The Report therefore recommended that a system be put in place within a clearly organised Tribunal Service which was 'independent, coherent, professional, cost effective and user friendly'.[18]

The Legatt Report led to the White Paper, *Transforming Public Services: Complaints, Redress and Tribunals*.[19] The White Paper echoed many of the recommendations made by the Legatt Report but went further. It proposed that a newly created unified Tribunals system would become a new type of organisation which was not simply a 'federation of existing tribunals'.[20] It would stimulate improved decision making and the leadership of this system would be expected to innovate and to re-engineer existing processes as a way of eradicating poor decision making.

---

16 There had already been a reorganisation of social security appeals after the Social Security Act 1998.
17 Report of the Review of Tribunals, 16 August 2001.
18 *Tribunals for Users – One System, One Service*, p 16. For further discussion see Wade and Forsyth, 906.
19 Cm 624.
20 *Transforming Public Services: Complaints, Redress and Tribunals* para 6.1–4, also see www.justice.gov.uk/about/hmcts.

In addition the Council of Tribunals would be replaced by a new Administrative Justice Council which would not only have a supervisory role for tribunals but would also provide advisory services for the whole of the administrative justice sector.

The Tribunals, Courts and Enforcement Act 2007

The Tribunals, Courts and Enforcement Act 2007 brought some unity to tribunals which had thus far not existed.[21] The new Tribunals Service was created as an Executive Agency of the Ministry of Justice and is operated under the responsibility of the Secretary of State, who is accountable to Parliament. The Tribunal Service has responsibility for the management and allocation of tribunal resources. It shares resources with the existing Courts Service and is responsible for the administration of the system.

Section 3 of the Tribunals, Courts and Enforcement Act 2007 creates two new generic tribunals into which the existing tribunal jurisdictions are transferred. The first of these is the First-tier tribunal and the second is the Upper Tribunal. The Upper Tribunal is intended to be an appellate tribunal from the First-tier tribunal although it may have other functions.[22]

The Act establishes a series of 'chambers' to accommodate the wide-ranging subject matter dealt with by tribunals. The various jurisdictions can therefore be grouped together. By 2010 there existed six chambers. These are:

- the Social Entitlement Chamber;
- the Health, Education and Social Care Chamber;
- the War Pensions and Armed Forces Compensation Chamber;
- the Tax Chamber;
- the Immigration and Asylum Chamber;
- the General Regulatory Chamber.

Employment tribunals and Employment Appeal Tribunals,[23] despite making up at least one quarter of the existing workload of tribunals, have not yet been transferred into this new system. This is in part due to its existing arrangements satisfying much of the flavour of the First-tier and Upper Tribunal form. Furthermore these tribunals deal with disputes between employees and employers rather than dealing with disputes between individuals and the state and can arguably be left outside the current reorganisation.

The Administrative Justice and Tribunals Council (AJTC)

The Administrative Justice and Tribunals Council (AJTC) replaces the Council on Tribunals and is a non-departmental public body. The AJTC is designed to be a 'powerful ally in the reform programme, and an independent guardian of the objectives of the service'.[24] The AJTC is headed by a Chairman, and has a membership of 14 acting on a part-time basis. The Parliamentary Commissioner for Administration is also a member of the Council.[25] There is a Scottish and Welsh Committee of the Council.[26] The Council's role is to 'cover the

21 Endicott, T. (2009), *Administrative Law*, Oxford University Press, 435.
22 Ibid, 463.
23 Report of Senior President of Tribunals' Annual Report, February 2010, Ministry of Justice, p 10.
24 Sir Robert Carnwath quoted in Harlow, C. & Rawlings, R. (2009) 'Tribunals in transition', *Law and Administration*, Cambridge University Press, 508.
25 See ss 44 and 45 and Sched 7 to the Tribunals, Courts and Enforcement Act 2007.
26 Tribunals, Courts and Enforcement Act 2007, Sched 7.

whole process from initial decision until final resolution at whatever level'.[27] The AJTC has a statutory duty to:

- keep the overall administrative justice system[28] under review;
- keep under review the constitution and working of specified tribunals, including the First-tier and Upper Tribunals;
- keep under review the constitution and working of specified statutory inquiries.

The Senior President and membership of Tribunals

Section 2 of the Tribunals, Courts and Enforcement Act 2007 creates the office of Senior President of Tribunals, appointed by the Crown on the recommendation of the Lord Chancellor following consultation with senior judges or the Judicial Appointments Commission.[29] The Senior President holds office 'during good behaviour' and is removable from office subject only to an address to both Houses of Parliament. The Senior President reports to the Lord Chancellor, may make practice directions and has a duty to maintain arrangements for the welfare and training of Tribunal members. The Senior President of Tribunals gives tribunal judges the representation they previously lacked, being under a statutory duty to represent the view of Tribunal members to Parliament, the Lord Chancellor and ministers of the Crown in general.[30] The Senior President is required to report annually to the Lord Chancellor in relation to Tribunal cases.[31]

In carrying out his functions the Senior President is required to have regard to:

- the need for tribunals to be accessible;
- the need for proceedings before tribunals to be fair and to be handled quickly and efficiently;
- the need for members of tribunals to be experts in the subject matter of, or the law to be applied in, cases in which they decide matters, and
- the need to develop innovative methods of resolving disputes that are of a type that may be brought before tribunals.[32]

Tribunal members are now appointed by the Judicial Appointments Commission rather than the Lord Chancellor, and the appointments process has greater independence from the executive than previously. Under section 1 of the Tribunals, Courts and Enforcement Act 2007 there is a guarantee of continued judicial independence for all tribunal members, thereby emphasising the independence of tribunals from government departments.

Judges and members who sat under the former system have been transferred into the new structure. For example specialist surveyor members of the Lands Tribunal have transferred into the Lands Chamber and continue to sit as previously. In addition judges of the High Court in England and Wales, and of the Court of Session in Scotland and of the High Court in Northern Ireland may also sit as full-time or part-time judges in the Upper Tribunal. First-tier judges

27 The Senior President of Tribunals' Annual Report, February 2010, para 96.
28 Defined as 'the overall system by which decisions of an administrative or executive nature are made in relation to particular persons, including the procedures, the law, and systems for resolving disputes'. Ibid.
29 Tribunals, Courts and Enforcement Act 2007, Sched 1, Parts 1 and 2.
30 Tribunals, Courts and Enforcement Act 2007, Schedule 1, para 14.
31 Section 43 Tribunals, Courts and Enforcement Act 2007.
32 Section 2(3) Tribunals, Courts and Enforcement Act 2007.

require a legal qualification and five years' post-qualification experience, while Upper-tier judges must be legally qualified and have seven years' post-qualification experience.

Non-lawyer members are retained in the new tribunal structure. However, there is no purely lay category of members, but rather non-lawyer members are appointed and allocated to tribunals on the basis of their expertise. Judges have long felt that non-lawyer members are a crucial addition to any tribunal.[33] The role of non-legal members is to be kept under review to ensure that new members with the skills and experience necessary are appointed.[34]

Procedure

The Tribunals, Courts and Enforcement Act 2007 also revises the procedural rules for tribunals. Historically tribunals had their own procedural rules which were usually drafted by the Lord Chancellor or Secretary of State in consultation with the Council on Tribunals. The procedural rules concerned such matters as the right to know that an application to a tribunal is possible and the right to a hearing and the process that the hearing may adopt. Legal representation was possible and after the hearing some tribunals had to provide reasons for the decisions taken. Many of the rules were governed by the Tribunals and Inquiries Act 1992.

The 2007 Act creates the Tribunal Procedure Committee to make procedural rules for each Chamber. Procedure is now governed by section 22 of the Tribunals, Courts and Enforcement Act 2007 and secondary legislation with the view to providing a more consistent and coherent approach to the procedural rules operating in any given tribunal. There exists a statutory duty to ensure that these new arrangements are efficiently and effectively administered.[35]

The procedure rules for the First-tier General Regulatory Chamber, for example, provide that the Tribunal (with stipulated exceptions) must hold a hearing, unless each party consents to the matter being determined without a hearing and the Tribunal is satisfied that it can properly determine the issues without a hearing.[36] Each party is entitled to attend any hearing that is held and make written representations to the Tribunal and to the other party prior to the hearing. The Tribunal must give reasonable notice of the time and place of any hearing. All hearings must be held in public, unless the Tribunal directs that it is to be held in private.[37]

Hearings and mediation

In addition to the usual hearings, the rules provide for judicial mediation – a form of alternative dispute resolution which attempts to reach a settlement of a dispute without going to court – thereby giving the parties a key role in reaching a settlement.[38] Where mediation has been agreed between the parties the judges in the First-tier Tribunal and Upper Tribunal will act as mediators. The Senior President's Annual Report states that where mediation is offered, the success rates are in excess of 65 per cent and that those parties who have experienced mediation 'have generally been positive about it'.[39]

---

33 See Lord Hope in *Gillies v Work and Pension Secretary* (Scotland) (2006).
34 The Senior President's Annual Report recognises that it is difficult to recruit sufficient medical members. One factor in recruitment of non-legal members is the level of remuneration.
35 See s 22(4) of the Tribunals, Courts and Enforcement Act 2007.
36 Oral hearings are important and it has been suggested that complainants are more likely to be successful when they appear before the Tribunal as they tend to be more articulate in person than on paper.
37 Tribunal Procedure (First-tier) (General Regulatory Chamber) Rules 2009, 2009 No 1976 (L.20).
38 Section 24 Tribunals, Courts and Enforcement Act 2007.
39 Ibid, para 197.

Legal representation

In relation to legal representation, the government White Paper favoured its reduction in tribunal hearings.[40] The practice in recent years has been for participants in tribunals to partake of legal representation where the issues were potentially complex or there was a need for skilled advocacy. Legal representation is generally permitted, but with the exception of certain Tribunals[41] state-funded legal assistance is not available to meet the costs of representation. However, given that all public authorities (the definition of which includes courts and tribunals)[42] are required to comply with the Human Rights Act 1998, the right to representation – depending on the seriousness of the case – is an aspect of the right to fair trial which includes the right to a 'fair' hearing 'in the determination of his [or her] civil rights'.

Reasons

Tribunal practice has long supported the giving of reasons which are essential in order to enable the parties to understand the decision and also form the basis for any appeal which may be undertaken. The Procedure Rules regulating the General Regulatory Chamber, for example, provide that the Tribunal may give a decision orally at a hearing and subject to limited exceptions must provide each party 'as soon as practicable' with a decision notice stating the Tribunal's decision, the written reasons for the decision, and notification of any right of appeal, time limits for appeal, and the manner in which a right of appeal may be exercised.[43]

Review and appeal

The new system offers a range of mechanisms for checking the decisions made by the tribunals.[44] These include:

- *self review*: under sections 9 and 10 of the 2007 Act, both First-tier Tribunals and Upper Tribunals have the jurisdiction to review their own decisions. If the First-tier Tribunal does review and set its own decision aside then it can either re-decide the issue or refer it to the Upper Tribunal. If the Upper Tribunal decides to set aside its own decision then it has to re-decide that decision itself;
- *a right of appeal*: with limited exceptions[45] a right of appeal on a point of law from the First-tier Tribunal to the Upper Tribunal is permitted. If there has been an error of law then the Upper Tribunal may set aside the decision of the First-tier Tribunal, remit the case back to the First-tier Tribunal for decision or make its own decision on the case.[46]

An appeal on a point of law lies to the Court of Appeal. Leave (ie permission) to appeal is required. Section 13(6) of the Tribunals, Courts and Enforcement Act 2007 and Article 2 of the Appeals from the Upper Tribunal to the Court of Appeal Order 2008[47] provides that permission to appeal was not to be granted unless the Upper Tribunal or the Court of Appeal consider that (a) a proposed appeal would raise some important point of principle or practice; or (b) there is some other compelling reason for the Court of Appeal to hear the appeal'.

---

40 The White Paper, *Transforming Public Services: Complaints, Redress and Tribunals*, Secretary of State for Constitutional Affairs, July 2004 (Cm 6243).
41 Employment Appeals Tribunals, Mental Health Tribunals, the Lands Tribunal and Revenue Commissioners.
42 See section 6 Human Rights Act 1998 and Chapter 18.
43 Ibid, para 38.
44 See Craig, P. (2008) *Administrative Law*, Sweet and Maxwell, 266.
45 See section 13(8) Tribunals, Courts and Enforcement Act 2007.
46 Under section 13 the right of appeal can be exercised to the Court of Appeal from the Upper Tribunal if permission has been granted. There are time limits governing this process which can be found in the Civil Procedure Rules.
47 SI 2008 No 2834.

The Court of Appeal may remit the case to the Upper Tribunal for reconsideration[48] or it can make the decision itself.

The power of judicial review lies with the High Court. Section 15 of the Tribunals, Courts and Enforcement Act 2007 also grants the power of judicial review to the Upper Tribunal (on this see **R (Cart) v Upper Tribunal** (2011), discussed below. Now able to grant mandatory, prohibition and quashing orders along with declarations and injunctions, the Upper Tribunal takes on many of the existing powers of the High Court. The Upper Tribunal applies the principles currently governing judicial review by the High Court which means that permission is required and a sufficient interest will need to be demonstrated before judicial review will be made available. The powers granted to the Upper Tribunal are subject to four conditions.[49] These are:

See further Chapters 24 to 26.

- that the relief sought can be obtained from the Upper Tribunal;
- that the activities of the Crown Court are not called into question;
- that the action falls within a specified class under section 18(6) Tribunals, Courts and Enforcement Act 2007;
- that a High Court or Court of Appeal judge in England, Wales and Northern Ireland or Court of Session in Scotland is presiding.

The Supreme Court considered the 2007 Act and judicial review in **R (Cart) v Upper Tribunal; R (MR (Pakistan)) v Same** (2011). At issue was the question of whether, and if so according to what criteria, judicial review was available of the decision of the Upper Tribunal (UT) to refuse permission to appeal to itself, a decision from which there is no statutory right of appeal. In the High Court, the judge held that refusal of permission to appeal by the Upper Tribunal was not amenable to judicial review. It was accepted by the Supreme Court that the Tribunals, Courts and Enforcement Act 2007 (TCEA) did not contain clear words ousting or excluding judicial review. However, it was also accepted that the 2007 Act established a 'new and in many ways enhanced tribunal structure which deserves a more restrained approach to judicial review than has previously been the case' (per Lord Phillips at para 57). There was discussion of the rule of law and the need to ensure that decisions of Tribunals were made according to law. Baroness Hale stated that the real question at issue in this case was 'what level of independent scrutiny outside the tribunal structure is required by the rule of law,' and that in deciding that question there must be a 'principled but proportionate approach' (at para 55).

Three approaches to the issue were considered. The first was the government's own approach, that judicial review should be available only in 'exceptional circumstances'. Set against this was the argument for unrestricted judicial review. Neither of these approaches was accepted by the Supreme Court. The exceptional circumstances criteria would be too stringent, while the unrestricted right to judicial review would ignore the standing of the Upper Tribunal as a superior court of record and create undue pressure on the system. Furthermore, according to Lord Dyson JSC, 'unrestricted judicial review of unappealable decisions of the UT, is neither proportionate nor necessary for maintaining the rule of law' (at para 122).

What was required was criteria which fell between these two approaches, and that adopted in relation to second appeals before the ordinary courts,[50] namely that (a) the proposed

---

48 Section 14 Tribunals, Courts and Enforcement Act 2007.
49 Section 18 Tribunals, Courts and Enforcement Act 2007.
50 See section 55(1) Access to Justice Act 1999 and section 13(6) of the TCEA 2007.

appeal would raise some important point of principle or practice; or (b) there is some other compelling reason for the relevant appellate court to hear the appeal'.[51]

Summary

The changes to the organisation of tribunals since 2007 have been substantial in form. For the first time, there now exists a rational Tribunal *system* as opposed to miscellaneous tribunals, established under statute as necessary, each with its own rules and procedures. The creation of the First-tier and Upper Tier Tribunals and Chambers within which various tribunals are organised creates a coherent structure. The arrangements for the appointment of legally-qualified judges and lay members emphasises the judicial independence of tribunal members from the executive. While uniformity of rules and practice – in light of the disparate subject matter with which Tribunals deal – would not be desirable, the Administrative Justice and Tribunals Council, and the role of the Senior President of Tribunals should act as a powerful rationalising force directed to ensuring the highest standards of administrative justice.

Further Reading

Adler, M. (1999) 'Lay tribunal members and administrative justice', Public Law, 616.
Bradley, A.W. (1991) 'The Council on Tribunals: time for a broader role?', Public Law, 6.
Cane, P. (2011) Administrative Law (5th edn), Oxford: Clarendon Press.
Cane, P. (2009) Administrative Tribunals and Adjudication, Oxford: Hart Publishing.
Cane, P. (2009) 'Judicial review in the age of tribunals', Public Law, 479.
Craig, P. (2012) Administrative Law (7th edn), London: Sweet and Maxwell.
Elliott, M. (2011) 'Has the Common Law duty to give reasons come of age yet?', Public Law, 56.
Endicott, T. (2011), Administrative Law (2nd edn), Oxford: OUP.
Foulkes, D. (1994) 'The Council on Tribunals: visits policy and practice', Public Law, 564.
Genn, H. (1993) 'Tribunals and Informal Justice', 56 Modern Law Review, 3.
Harlow, C. and Rawlings, R. (2009) 'Tribunals in transition', Law and Administration, Cambridge: CUP.
Machin, D. and Richardson, G. (2000) 'Judicial review and tribunal decision making: a study of the mental health review tribunal', Public Law, 494.
Nason, S. (2009) 'Regionalisation of the Administrative Court and the tribunalisation of judicial review', Public Law, 440.
Richardson, G. and Genn, H. (2007) 'Tribunals in transition: resolution or adjudication?', Public Law, 116.
Wade, W. and Forsyth, C. (2009) Administrative Law (10th edn), Oxford: OUP.

---

51 On compelling reasons, see **PR (Sri Lanka) v Secretary of State for the Home Department** (2012); **JD (Congo) v Secretary of State for the Home Department** (2012).

PART B: INQUIRIES

Introduction

Formal public inquiries are established to examine and report on a disaster or situation giving rise to public concern and are an important feature of government.[52] The role and function of public inquiries have been summarised by Lord Howe as follows:

- to establish the facts;
- to learn from events and thereby help prevent their recurrence;
- to provide an opportunity for reconciliation and resolution;
- to rebuild public confidence;
- to hold people and organizations to account;
- political considerations: the need to demonstrate that action has been taken or providing the impetus for change.[53]

Inquiries may be statutory (established under specific Acts of Parliament or under the Inquiries Act 2005) or non-statutory. The essential function of inquiries is fact-finding and the making of recommendations with a view to avoiding a recurrence of a situation, or establishing improved procedures which would apply in the event of a recurrence. Inquiries also contribute to transparency and accountability and to public confidence in a particular body. Inquiries do not establish civil or criminal liability (section 2 Inquiries Act 2005) or impose penalties or award compensation. They are therefore distinguishable from courts and tribunals. Since 1990 there have been over 40 public inquiries.[54] Inquiries in recent years include the following:

- transport disasters such as the rail crash outside Paddington Station, London in 1999, the inquiry being chaired by the Rt Hon Lord Cullen PC; and the sinking of the Thames pleasure-boat *Marchioness*, also in 1999, the inquiry being chaired by Lord Justice Clarke;[55]
- allegations of wrongdoing or injustices caused by the armed forces gave rise to two inquiries into the shooting of civilians on Bloody Sunday in Northern Ireland 1972. The first was established immediately after the shooting and chaired by Lord Widgery, who reported within three months. The second Inquiry was established in 1998 under the 1921 Tribunals of Inquiry Act and chaired by Lord Saville of Newdigate. The Inquiry finally reported in 2010;[56]
- the circumstances surrounding the racist murder of Stephen Lawrence led to an Inquiry which reported in 1999;[57]
- failures in the national health system have given rise to several inquiries. The deaths of child patients at the Bristol Royal Infirmary were investigated,[58] and the removal of organs from deceased children without parental consent at the Royal Liverpool Children's Hospital was also subject to a formal inquiry;[59]

---

52 Inquiries are also established as part of the process of planning permission in respect of property or major developments. These do not fall within the Inquiries Act 2005.
53 Lord Howe, 'The Management of Public Inquiries', (1999) Political Quarterly, 294–304.
54 See www.publicinquiries.org.
55 The Thames Safety Report, 2000.
56 *Principal Conclusions and Overall Assessment of the Bloody Sunday Inquiry*, HC 30 2010–11: www.bloody-sunday-inquiry.org.
57 *The Stephen Lawrence Inquiry Report*, CM 4262-I, London: TSO 1999.
58 *Learning from Bristol: Report of the Public Inquiry into Children's Heart Surgery at the BRI 1984–95*, Cm 5207, 2001
59 See respectively, *Learning from Bristol: Report of the Public Inquiry into Children's Heart Surgery at the BRI 1984–95*, Cm 5207, 2001; *The Royal Liverpool Children's Hospital (Alder Hey) Inquiry*, HC 12 1998–99.

- the 'Arms to Iraq' Inquiry, reporting in 1996, examined allegations concerning the export of defence equipment to Iraq (the Scott Inquiry, on which see pages 232ff);
- the death of government scientist David Kelly (the Hutton Inquiry, on which see page 235);[60]
- intelligence data on weapons of mass destruction 2004 (the Butler Inquiry, on which see pages 235–236);
- government decision making prior to the Iraq War 2003 (the Chilcot Inquiry, on which see page 236);
- the inquiry into the death of Iraqi civilian Baha Mousa, who was detained and tortured and died in the custody of British troops. Chaired by Sir William Gage, the Report was published in 2011;[61]
- allegations of widespread 'phone hacking' by the media led to the Media Inquiry into the 'culture, practices and ethics of the press' chaired by Lord Justice Leveson, which reported in 2012;[62]
- the inquiry into deaths and injuries at Hillsborough Football ground in 1989. Established in 2010 and chaired by the Bishop of Liverpool, the Report revealed basic flaws in policing and the response of the emergency services.[63]

Non-statutory Inquiries

Non-statutory inquiries may be established to examine a particular issue, and may be preferred by the government on the basis that there can be greater flexibility in procedures. Examples include the BSE Inquiry which reported in 2000 and which examined the crisis in agriculture caused by the BSE (bovine spongiform encephalopathy, or 'mad cow disease') outbreak which led to the slaughter of some 200,000 cattle.[64] The Paddington Rail Crash Inquiry, chaired by Lord Cullen, was also non-statutory. The Scott inquiry into the export of equipment capable of being transformed into weaponry in Iraq, the Hutton inquiry into alleged Weapons of Mass Destruction in Iraq, the inquiry into the circumstances surrounding the death of government scientist Dr David Kelly chaired by Lord Hutton and the Chilcot inquiry, chaired by Sir John Chilcot, into the circumstances leading to the decision to go to war in Iraq were also examples of non-statutory inquiries. However, non-statutory inquiries have disadvantages. There is no power, for example, to compel witnesses to give evidence or to compel the disclosure of documents as is the case with inquiries under the 2005 Act.[65] On the other hand, where the subject matter is sensitive or controversial, witnesses may be more likely to cooperate with a non-statutory inquiry than an inquiry under the 2005 Act in which coercive powers are available. As noted above, if the government feels that a non-statutory inquiry would be more effective if undertaken under statute, it can be 'converted' into a statutory inquiry under section 15 of the 2005 Act.

The Coalition Government formed in 2010 has made good use of inquiries. The Leveson Inquiry, chaired by Lord Justice Leveson, into the culture, practices and ethics of the media was established in 2011 (see Chapter 19). In 2012 there was a Commission on a Bill of Rights, established in 2011, to consider whether the United Kingdom needs a Bill of Rights to

60 Report of the Inquiry into the Circumstances Surrounding the Death of Dr David Kelly, HC 247 2003–04.
61 The Baha Mousa Public Inquiry Report, HC 1452-1, London TSO, 2011.
62 The Leveson Report: An Inquiry into the Culture, Practices and Ethics of the Press, HC 779, London: TSO.
63 The Report of the Hillsborough Independent Panel, HC 581, 2012, London: TSO.
64 The BSE Inquiry was chaired by Lord Phillips, and cost £30 million.
65 Inquiry Act 2005, s 21; and see s 35 on penalties for non-compliance.

supplement the Human Rights Act 1998 (see Chapter 18). There was also the McKay Commission, established in 2012, to examine the consequences of devolution on the House of Commons (see Chapter 11). The privileges of Parliament have also been subject to extensive review, not through a formal inquiry, but via the publication of a consultation paper.[66]

Statutory Inquiries

Many Acts of Parliament confer the power to establish tribunals of inquiry. The most common form of inquiry is that into planning applications, where a public inquiry may be ordered under section 20 of the Town and Country Planning Act 1990. Outside of planning matters, other inquiries include that into the *Marchioness* disaster, in which a pleasure cruiser on the River Thames sank, causing many deaths: the inquiry was set up under the Merchant Shipping Act 1995. The inquiry into the circumstances surrounding the death of Stephen Lawrence which reported in 1999 was established under section 49 of the Police Act 1996.[67] The Health and Safety at Work Act 1974 and the National Health Service Act 1977 are further examples of legislation conferring power to establish inquiries. Inquiries into the conduct of the prisons may be set up under the Prisons Acts.

Prior to the Inquiries Act 2005, the principal Act for general statutory tribunals of inquiry was the Tribunals of Inquiry Act 1921. The 1921 Act, however, required a formal Resolution of both Houses of Parliament before an inquiry could be established. While this had the merit of ensuring a link between inquiries and Parliament, it restricted the scope of inquiries. The 1921 Act had other disadvantages. First, there was no provision for procedural rules. Second, there was no provision to control the cost of inquiries. The example set by the Bloody Sunday Inquiry, set up under the 1921 Act – 12 years and a cost of £192 million – was one not to be followed in the future.

The 2005 Act repeals the 1921 Act and confers on government ministers a great deal of discretion in establishing tribunals of inquiry, their terms of reference and procedure.

Common issues and concerns

Irrespective of the basis for the inquiry, there are a number of common issues which may be summarised as follows:

- the discretion which the government has in relation to whether to establish an inquiry;[68]
- whether the inquiry should be held in public or private;
- the independence of inquiries from government;
- the chairmanship of inquiries;
- the procedure to be followed;
- the anonymity of witnesses;
- the disclosure of evidence;
- the government's and Parliament's response to inquiries.

One of the most difficult issues lies in the choice between a public inquiry and an inquiry conducted in private. That is a decision for the government to take, but is one that may be

---

66 Cm 8318, London: TSO 2012.
67 See the *Stephen Lawrence Inquiry*, Report of an Inquiry by Sir William Macpherson of Cluny, Cm 4262, 1999.
68 There is no legal duty to establish an Inquiry. **See *Keyu v Secretary of State for Foreign and Commonwealth Affairs* (2012); R *(Mousa) v Secretary of State for Defence* (2011).**

challenged by proceedings for judicial review. Two examples of inquiries conducted in private – and challenges made to them – are the inquiry into the murder of elderly patients by Dr Harold Shipman and the inquiry into the 2001 outbreak of foot and mouth disease (FMD) in cattle.

In 2000 Dr Shipman was found guilty on 15 counts of murder. The Secretary of State decided to establish an inquiry under the National Health Service Act 1977 and that the hearings should be in private but that the inquiry would publish its findings and a final report. In his statement to Parliament the Minister stated that there would be an 'independent inquiry' that would be 'comprehensive and inclusive'. In judicial review proceedings challenging the legality of the Minister's decision, the decision was set aside on grounds of irrationality.[69] In September 2000 the Secretary of State announced that the Inquiry would be held in public under the terms of the Tribunals of Inquiry (Evidence) Act 1921. Explaining the basis for the finding of irrationality, Simon Brown LJ in **Persey v Secretary of State for Environment, Food and Rural Affairs** (2002) cited four principal reasons: that the Secretary of State had mistakenly thought that the families of victims did not want a public inquiry; that the terms of reference were exceedingly wide; that a misunderstanding had arisen as a result of the Minister's statement to the House of Commons; that there was no body of opinion in favour of closed hearings; and that there was no reason why a public inquiry should take longer than one conducted in private.

Nevertheless, this does not mean that there is a presumption in favour of public inquiries, still less that there is a 'right' to a public inquiry or to a particular form of inquiry. As Simon Brown LJ remarked in **Persey**:

> Inquiries, in short, come in all shapes and sizes and it would be wrong to suppose that a single model – a full-scale open public inquiry – should be seen as the invariable panacea for all ills. (at para 42)

Persey v Secretary of State for Environment, Food and Rural Affairs (2002) was a challenge to the government's decision to set up three separate independent inquiries to examine the circumstances surrounding and response to the outbreak of foot and mouth disease in cattle in 2001. The inquiries – the Lessons Learned Inquiry, the Scientific Inquiry and the Policy Commission – were to receive evidence, mostly in private. The claimants' challenges focused on the Lessons Learned Inquiry and their principal contention was that as a matter of law the inquiry should be held in public. The Court found that the main factors influencing the government's decision were (a) the need to learn lessons as rapidly as possible, (b) the expectation that witnesses would be more open and forthcoming in private, as opposed to public hearings, and (c) that there would be a saving in financial and human resources. After examining the several grounds of challenge, the Court found they lacked substance and the Minister's decision was lawful.

The Inquiries Act 2005

The Inquiries Act 2005 was passed to give effect to the [then] Department of Constitutional Affairs consultation paper, *Effective Inquiries*,[70] which had concluded that defects in the current

---

69 *R v Secretary of State for Health ex parte Wagstaff* (2000).
70 Following on from the House of Commons' Public Administration Select Committee investigation, *Government by Inquiry*, HC 51 2005.

law necessitated reform. As noted above, the 1921 Act made no provision for rules of procedure, nor was there any power to control the costs of an inquiry: the Bloody Sunday Inquiry had lasted twelve years and cost £192 million. In the words of the Ministry of Justice's Memorandum to the Justice Select Committee, *Post-Legislative Assessment of the Inquiries Act 2005*, the 2005 Act:

> . . . aimed to make inquiries swifter, more effective at finding facts and making practical recommendations, and less costly whilst still meeting the need to satisfy the public expectation for a thorough and wide ranging investigation. (para 6)

It also:

> . . . codified best practice from previous statutory and non-statutory inquiries such as the need to ensure that those conducting inquiries are impartial and have appropriate expertise.

The Act applies across the United Kingdom, providing a uniform structure. There is also provision for joint inquiries to be conducted across national administrations. Inquiries are not empowered to rule on any person's civil or criminal liability (section 2, 2005 Act): they are not courts of law. Also distinguishing inquiries from courts of law is the fact that while proceedings in courts are *adversarial*, a tribunal of inquiry acts in an *inquisitorial* manner.

Concerns over the inquisitorial process and in particular concerns over procedural aspects of one judicial Inquiry, that of Lord Denning into the Profumo affair,[71] led to a Royal Commission on Tribunals of Inquiry, chaired by Lord Justice Salmon. Reporting in 1966, the Salmon Report laid down six basic principles of fair procedure for tribunals of inquiry. These are:

- before any person becomes involved in an inquiry, the tribunal must be satisfied that there are circumstances which affect them and which the tribunal proposes to investigate;
- before any person who is involved in an inquiry is called as a witness, they should be informed of any allegations made against them and the substance of the evidence in support of them;
- they should be given an adequate opportunity to prepare their case and of being assisted by legal advisers and their legal expenses should normally be met out of public funds;
- they should have the opportunity of being examined by their own solicitor or counsel and of stating their case in public at the inquiry;
- any material witnesses they wish to call at the inquiry should, if reasonably practicable, be heard;
- they should have the opportunity of testing by cross-examination conducted by their own solicitor or counsel any evidence which may affect them.

These principles, when applied, bring the inquiry process closer to the adversarial model of legal proceedings, injecting a greater degree of formality. However, it is for the chairman of an individual inquiry to decide whether or not, and to what extent, the Salmon principles should apply.

---

71 See *Lord Denning's Report*, Cmnd 2152, London: TSO 1963.

Power to establish an inquiry

The power to establish an inquiry is conferred on a United Kingdom Minister, Scottish Ministers, or a Northern Ireland Minister. The power is conferred under section 1, where 'it appears to him that':

(a)   particular events have caused, or are capable of causing, public concern; or
(b)   there is public concern that particular events may have occurred.

The decision whether or not to establish an inquiry can prove controversial and may lead to a legal challenge. This occurred in relation to the death in custody of a young offender, Zahid Mubarek, who had been placed in a cell with a known violent and racist offender. The Home Secretary refused to establish an inquiry into his death. This refusal was challenged in judicial review proceedings, in which the House of Lords ruled that his refusal violated the duty under Article 2 of the European Convention on Human Rights not only to protect the life of those in custody of the state but also, where death occurred, to investigate that death.[72] A judicial inquiry was established and its findings were highly critical of the Prison Service.[73]

Power to suspend or terminate an inquiry

Under section 13 of the Inquiries Act 2005, ministers are given the power to suspend an inquiry, following consultation with the Chairman, on the grounds that it is necessary to allow for the completion of other investigations into any of the matters to which the inquiry relates, or the determination of any civil or criminal proceedings arising out of matters to which the inquiry relates. This was the situation in January 2012 when the Justice Secretary announced the suspension of the Detainee Inquiry chaired by Sir Peter Gibson. The Inquiry had been established to examine the alleged role of MI5 and MI6 in the torture and rendition of detainees after the September 2001 terrorist attacks.

The power to terminate an inquiry is conferred under section 14 of the 2005 Act. An inquiry will come to an end on the date on which the Chairman notifies the Minister that the inquiry has fulfilled its terms of reference unless an earlier date is specified to the Chairman by the Minister.

Converting other inquiries into a 2005 Act inquiry

The Inquiries Act 2005, sections 15 to 16 enable a Minister to convert a non-statutory or statutory inquiry into a 2005 Act inquiry provided that he or she is satisfied that the matter being investigated falls within the scope of a 2005 Act inquiry. This precludes other forms of inquiry, such as planning inquiries, from being converted into 2005 Act inquiries. Where a non-statutory inquiry has been established and there is found to be a need for a greater degree of formality or control over potential costs, that inquiry may be converted into a 2005 Act inquiry. The power to convert an inquiry into an inquiry under the 2005 Act arises only where the Minister considers that there is public concern over an issue. Before exercising the power under section 15 the Minister must consult the chairman of the original inquiry. The terms of reference of the converted inquiry may differ from those of the original inquiry.

---

72 See **R (Amin) v Secretary of State for the Home Department** (2003).
73 *Report of the Zahid Mubarek Inquiry*, HC 1082, 2005–06.

The terms of reference

Under section 5 of the 2005 Act, the Minister must set out the terms of reference of the Inquiry. The terms of reference are defined in section 5(6) as being:

- the matters to which the Inquiry relates;
- any particular matter as to which the Inquiry panel is to determine the facts;
- whether the Inquiry panel is to make recommendations;
- any other matters relating to the scope of the Inquiry that the Minister may specify.

The terms of reference may be amended if the Minister considers that the 'public interest so requires' (section 5(3)).

Chairing the inquiry

It is for the Minister to decide who should chair an inquiry. Most inquiries will be chaired by a senior judge, former senior civil servant or an academic with expertise in the matter to be considered. High-profile and controversial inquires chaired by judges include the Security Inquiry chaired by Lord Denning in 1963 and the inquiry into the riots in Central London in 1981, chaired by Lord Scarman. The Arms to Iraq Inquiry, the Inquiry into Weapons of Mass Destruction and the circumstances surrounding the death of Dr David Kelly were also chaired by judges, as was the Media Inquiry (Lord Leveson). The Inquiry into intelligence data relating to weaponry in Iraq was chaired by a former Cabinet Secretary, Lord Butler. The Iraq Inquiry established in 2009 was chaired by a former senior civil servant, Sir John Chilcot.

There are arguments for and against the use of judges as chairs of inquiries. On the one hand, by training and expertise, judges are well qualified both to ensure impartiality and to evaluate evidence. On the other hand, the higher the public profile, and the more political the subject matter under examination, the greater the danger of drawing judges into the political arena which they are so careful to avoid. It may also be argued that judges are not best qualified to make judgements on matters of policy.[74] Recognising the potential drawbacks, the 2005 Act provides that when a Minister proposes to appoint a senior judge as a member of an Inquiry panel, he or she must first consult, as relevant, the Lord Chief Justice of England and Wales, the Lord President of the Scottish Court of Session or the Lord Chief Justice of Northern Ireland.[75]

The inquiry panel

An inquiry may be undertaken by the chairman alone, or by a chairman with one or more other members (section 3, 2005 Act). Panel members are appointed by the Minister, in consultation with the person appointed, or to be appointed as chairman. In making appointments, the Minister is under a statutory duty to ensure that the panel has the necessary expertise to undertake the inquiry, and that the composition of the panel is balanced (section 8). The impartiality of panel members is a fundamental requirement. No one may be appointed who has a direct interest in the matters to which the inquiry relates or who has a close association with any interested party (section 9).

---

74 Note the care with which judges avoid issues of high policy in judicial review proceedings: see the concept of justiciability discussed in Chapter 23.
75 Section 10, Inquiries Act 2005.

In addition to the chair and panel members, assessors may be appointed to assist the inquiry (section 11).

Procedure

The procedure to be followed (subject to the 2005 Act and subordinate legislation) is for the Chairman of the Inquiry to establish (section 17). In particular the Chairman may decide whether or not to take evidence on oath: section 17(2). In exceptional circumstances, the Chairman may also admit evidence anonymously, if the evidence would otherwise not be available to the Inquiry. Section 17(3) imposes a statutory duty on the chairman to act 'with fairness and with regard also to the need to avoid any unnecessary cost'.

Hearings in public

There is a presumption that proceedings will be open to members of the public (section 18) and that the public will have access to the record of evidence and documents before the inquiry. This presumption is subject to a 'restriction notice' given by a Minister to the Chairman 'at any time before the end of the inquiry', or by the Chairman during the course of the inquiry (sections 19–20).

Evidence

While the hearings will be public, witnesses may be permitted to give evidence in private. This is generally the case where the material to be disclosed would cause harm to the public interest, often on the grounds of national security and international relations. Where evidence is given in private, that evidence may be published by the inquiry, subject to redactions or summarising where necessary in accordance with the Inquiry's Protocol for Witnesses. Evidence may also be published anonymously. Some evidence may consist of classified documents. In relation to the Iraq Inquiry, for example, there was established a Protocol between the Inquiry and Her Majesty's Government regarding documents and other written and electronic information detailing the arrangements for the giving of evidence. In relation to classified documents, the Inquiry has sought declassification by the government prior to publication of its report.

Anonymity of witnesses

The giving of evidence by some witnesses, particularly those from the military or security forces, may bring the principle of open justice into conflict with the duty of the State to protect life under Article 2 of the European Convention on Human Rights. This situation has given rise to legal challenges. In **Re Officer L (Respondent) (Northern Ireland)** (2007) the House of Lords stated that the correct test to be applied to a request for anonymity is to ask the question whether the risk to life would be materially increased if the potential witness were required to give evidence without anonymity. Anonymity was also challenged in relation to the Leveson Inquiry, where Lord Justice Leveson allowed journalists who feared for their jobs or reputations, if their evidence was attributed to them, to give evidence anonymously.[76]

---

76 See **R (Associated Newspapers Ltd) v Leveson** (2012).

Legal representation

The Inquiry Rules 2006[77] provide that 'core participants', defined in Rule 5 as a person who has played, or may have played a significant role in relation to the matter under investigation, or a person with a significant interest, or a person who may be subject to explicit or significant criticism during the inquiry or in its report(s), and witnesses, are entitled to legal representation.

Counsel to the Inquiry may be appointed to advise on the law and to question witnesses.

The report

The findings of the inquiry are to be reported to the Minister, together with recommendations of the panel (where the terms of reference require recommendations to be made): section 24. The report of the inquiry should be unanimous, but if there are disagreements within the panel, those disagreements must be made clear in the report. The Minister is under a duty to arrange for inquiry reports to be published, unless that duty has been conferred on the inquiry Chairman: section 25.

Material may be withheld from publication if disclosure is prevented by any rule of law or on the basis of public interest. In deciding whether to withhold material, the person concerned must consider the following matters:

(a) the extent to which withholding material might inhibit the allaying of public concern;
(b) any risk of harm or damage that could be avoided or reduced by withholding any material;
(c) any conditions as to confidentiality subject to which a person acquired information that he or she has given to the inquiry.

The report must be laid before Parliament or the relevant Assembly 'at the time of publication or as soon afterwards as is reasonably practicable': section 26 Inquiries Act 2005.

Where criminal proceedings are taken against any person in relation to matters covered by the inquiry, publication of the report into the inquiry will be postponed until those proceedings are concluded. This situation arose in respect of the Inquiry into the death of Robert Hamill, who was murdered in Northern Ireland in 1997, when charges of perverting the course of justice were made against officers serving in the Royal Ulster Constabulary.[78]

In its *Memorandum to the Justice Select Committee: Post-Legislative Assessment of the Inquiries Act 2005*,[79] the Ministry of Justice gave a favourable overall assessment of the 2005 Act, stating that it operates 'well in practice' although minor amendments may be needed. The *Memorandum* notes, however, that the Act can only work well in ensuring a timely conclusion and without excessive costs if the chairman and inquiry team have the necessary expertise. Particular features of the Act selected for favourable comment include the rules relating to disclosure of evidence, the ability to convert another inquiry into a 2005 Act inquiry and the duty imposed on the chairman to act with fairness and with regard to the need to avoid any unnecessary costs.[80]

Summary

Inquiries are an important feature of the democratic process, promoting transparency and accountability. The form they take may be statutory or non-statutory. Commissions may also be

---

77 SI No 1838 2006.
78 The Secretary of State for Northern Ireland announced the delay in publishing the report in a Ministerial Statement to the House of Commons on 31 January 2011.
79 Cm 7943, London: TSO 2010.
80 Paras 41–44.

established by government to consult and make recommendations on various aspects of governance: the McKay Commission on the impact of devolution on the House of Commons and the Commission on a UK Bill of Rights are examples of these.

 Further Reading

Beatson, J. (2005) 'Should Judges Chair Public Inquiries?', 121 Law Quarterly Review, 221.

Denning, Lord (1963) *Lord Denning's Report*, Cmnd 2152, London: TSO.

Drewry, G. (1996) 'Judicial Inquiries and Public Reassurance', Public Law, 368.

Howe, G. (1999) 'The Management of Public Inquiries', 70 Political Quarterly, 294.

Scott, R. (1995), 'Procedures at Inquiries: The Duty to be Fair', 111 Law Quarterly Review, 596.

Steele, I. (2004) 'Judging Judicial Inquiries', Public Law, 738.

Bibliography

Adams, J, *The New Spies: Exploring the Frontiers of Espionage*, 1994, London: Hutchinson

Aitken, J, *Officially Secret*, 1971, London: Weidenfeld & Nicolson

Alderman, RK and Carter, N, 'A very Tory coup: the ousting of Mrs Thatcher' (1991) 44 Parl Aff 125

Alderman, RK and Smith, MJ, 'Can prime ministers be pushed out?' (1990) 43 Parl Aff 260

Allan, TRS, 'Legislative supremacy and the rule of law: democracy and constitutionalism' [1985] CLJ 111 (1985a)

Allan, TRS, 'The limits of parliamentary sovereignty' [1985] PL 614 (1985b)

Allan, TRS, 'Law, convention, prerogative: reflections prompted by the Canadian constitutional case' [1986] CLJ 305

Allan, TRS, *Law, Liberty and Justice*, 1993, Oxford: Clarendon

Allan, TRS, 'Requiring reasons for reasons of fairness and reasonableness' [1994] CLJ 207

Allan, TRS, 'Parliamentary sovereignty: law, politics and revolution' (1997) 113 LQR 443

Allan, TRS, *Constitutional Justice: A Liberal Theory of the Rule of Law*, 2001, Oxford: OUP

Allan, TRS, 'Judicial Deference and Judicial Review: Legal Doctrine and Legal Theory', (2011) Law Quarterly Review 127:96

Allason, R, *The Branch: A History of the Metropolitan Police Special Branch 1883–1983*, 1983, London: Secker & Warburg

Allen, CK, *Law and Orders*, 3rd edn, 1965, London: Stevens

Allen, R and Sales, P, 'The impact of the Human Rights Act 1998 upon subordinate legislation promulgated before October 2, 2000' [2000] PL 358

Andenas, M and Fairgrieve, D, 'Reforming Crown immunity: the comparative law perspective' [2003] PL 730

Anderson, D, QC, *Control Orders in 2011: Final Report of the Independent Reviewer on the Prevention of Terrorism Act 2005*, 2012, London: TSO

Andrew, C, *Secret Service: The Making of the British Intelligence Community*, 1985, London: Heinemann

Anson, W (Sir), *Law and Custom of the Constitution*, 4th edn, 1933, Oxford: Clarendon

Archbold: Criminal Pleading, Evidence and Practice 2003, 2002, London: Sweet & Maxwell

Aristotle, *The Politics*, 1962, Sinclair, TA (trans), Harmondsworth: Penguin

Arnull, A, 'National courts and the validity of Community acts' (1988) 13 EL Rev 125 (1988a)

Arnull, A, 'The scope of Article 177' (1988) 13 EL Rev 40 (1988b)

Arnull, A, 'The uses and abuses of Article 177 EEC' (1989) 52 MLR 622

Arnull, A, 'References to the European Court' (1990) 15 EL Rev 375

Ashworth, A, 'Involuntary confessions and illegally obtained evidence in criminal cases – Part I' [1963] Crim LR 15 (1963a)

Ashworth, A, 'Involuntary confessions and illegally obtained evidence in criminal cases – Part II' [1963] Crim LR 77 (1963b)

Ashworth, A, 'Excluding evidence and protecting rights' [1977] Crim LR 723

Atkins, E and Hoggett, B, *Women and the Law*, 1984, Oxford: Basil Blackwell

Aubert, V, *In Search of Law*, 1983, Oxford: Martin Robertson

Austin, J, *The Province of Jurisprudence Determined* (1832), 1954, London: Weidenfeld & Nicolson

Bacon, F, *Advancement of Learning* (1605), 1951, Oxford: OUP

Bagehot, W, The English Constitution (1867), 1993, London: Fontana

Bailey, SH et al, Smith, Bailey and Gunn on The Modern English Legal System, 4th edn, 2002, London: Sweet & Maxwell

Baldwin, J and Bedward, J, 'Summarising tape recordings of police interviews' [1991] Crim LR 671

Baldwin, J, 'The police and tape recorders' [1985] Crim LR 659

Baldwin, J, The Role of Legal Representatives at the Police Station, RCCJ Research Study No 3, 1993, London: HMSO

Baldwin, R and Houghton, J, 'Circular arguments: the status and legitimacy of administrative rules' [1986] PL 239

Barber, NW, 'Privacy and the police: private right, public right or human right? R v Chief Constable of the North Wales Police ex parte AB' [1998] PL 19

Barendt, E, Baron, A, Herberg, JW and Jowell, J, 'Public law' (1993) 46 CLP Annual Review 101

Barker, R, Political Legitimacy and the State, 1990, Oxford: Clarendon

Barnett, H, 'A privileged position? Gypsies, land and planning law' [1994] Conveyancer 454

Barnett, H, 'Reflections on the Child Support Act' (1993) 5 J of Child Law 77

Barnett, H, 'The end of the road for Gypsies?' (1995) 24 Anglo-American L Rev 133

Barnett, H, 'Buckley v United Kingdom: landmark or signpost?' (1996) 146 NLJ 1628

Barnett, H, Introduction to Feminist Jurisprudence, 1998, London: Cavendish Publishing

Barron, A and Scott, C, 'The Citizen's Charter programme' (1992) 55 MLR 526

Bates, St JT, Devolution to Scotland: The Legal Aspects, 1997, Edinburgh: T & T Clark

Beatson, J, 'Should Judges Chair Public Inquiries?' (2005) 121 LQR 221

Beattie, K, 'Control orders and ASBOs: taking liberties?' (2005) Legal Action, April

Bebr, G, 'The reinforcement of the constitutional review of Community acts under Article 177 EEC Treaty' (1988) 25 CML Rev 667

Beith, A, 'Prayers unanswered: a jaundiced view of the parliamentary scrutiny of statutory instruments' (1981) 34 Parl Aff 165

Bell, J, Policy Arguments in Judicial Decisions, 1983, Oxford: Clarendon

Bell, JB, The Secret Army: The IRA 1916–79, 1979, Dublin: Academy

Bennion, F, 'What interpretation is "possible" under section 3(1) of the Human Rights Act 1998?' [2000] PL 77

Bindman, G, 'Spycatcher: judging the judges' (1989) 139 NLJ 94

Bingham of Cornhill, Lord, 'The House of Lords: its future?' (2010) Public Law 261

Bingham, TH (Sir), 'Should public law remedies be discretionary?' [1991] PL 64

Bingham, TH (Sir), 'The European Convention on Human Rights: time to incorporate' (1993) 109 LQR 390

Birch, D, 'Excluding evidence from entrapment: what is a "fair cop"?' (1994) 47 CLP 73

Birch, D, 'The pace hots up: confessions and confusions under the 1984 Act' [1989] Crim LR 95

Birkenhead (Lord), Points of View, Vol 1, 1922, London: Hodder & Stoughton

Bishop, P and Maillie, E, The Provisional IRA, 1987, London: Heinemann

Blackburn, R, 'Monarchy and the Personal Prerogatives' (2004) PL 546

Blackburn, R, 'The 2010 General Election outcome and formation of the Conservative-Liberal Democrat Coalition Government' (2011) Public Law 30

Blackburn, RW and Kennon, A, with Sir Michael Wheeler-Booth, Parliament: Functions, Practice and Procedures, 2nd edn, 2003, London: Sweet & Maxwell (referred to as Griffith and Ryle, 2003 in the text)

Blackburn, RW, Constitutional Studies, 1992, London: Mansell

Blackstone, W (Sir), Commentaries on the Laws of England (1765–69), 2001 edn, Morrison, W (ed), London: Cavendish Publishing

Blake (Lord), The Office of Prime Minister, 1975, Oxford: OUP

Bloch, J and Fitzgerald, P, British Intelligence and Covert Action, 1983, Dingle, Co Kerry: Brandon

Blom-Cooper, L and Drabble, R, 'GCHQ Revisited' (2010) PL 18

Blom-Cooper, L and Drewry, G, *Final Appeal*, 1972, Oxford: Clarendon

Blom-Cooper, L and Munro, C, 'The Hutton Report' (2004) PL 472

Bogdanor, V and Butler, D, *Democracy and Elections*, 1983, Cambridge: CUP

Bogdanor, V, *Devolution in the United Kingdom*, 2001, Oxford: OUP

Bogdanor, V, 'The forty per cent rule' (1980) 33 Parl Aff 249

Bogdanor, V, *The People and the Party System*, 1981, Cambridge: CUP

Bogdanor, V, *Multi-Party Politics and the Constitution*, 1983, Cambridge: CUP

Bogdanor, V (ed), *Constitutions in Democratic Politics*, 1988, London: Policy Studies Institute

Bogdanor, V, *Power and the People*, 1997, London: Gollancz

Bogdanor, V, *Devolution in the United Kingdom*, 1999, Oxford: OUP

Bolingbroke, H, *Remarks on the History of England*, 3rd edn, 1748, London: Franklin

Bonner, D and Stone, R, 'The Public Order Act 1986: steps in the wrong direction' [1987] PL 202

Bowen, CD, *The Lion and the Throne*, 1957, London: Hamish Hamilton

Boyle, K, Hadden, T and Hillyard, P, *Law and State*, 1975, Oxford: Martin Robertson

Boyron, S, 'Proportionality in English administrative law: a faulty translation?' (1992) 12 OJLS 237

Bracton, H, *The Laws and Customs of England* (1200–68), 1968–77, Thorne, SE (trans), Cambridge, Mass: Harvard UP

Bradley, AW and Ewing, KD, *Constitutional and Administrative Law*, 13th edn, 2003, Harlow: Longman

Bradley, AW, 'Openness, direction and judicial review' [1986] PL 508

Bradley, AW, 'Good government and public interest immunity' [1992] PL 514 (1992a)

Bradley, AW, 'Sachsenhausen, Barlow Clowes – and then' [1992] PL 353 (1992b)

Bradley, AW, 'Relations between Executive, Judiciary and Parliament: an evolving saga?' (2008) Public Law 470

Bradney, A, 'The judicial activity of the Lord Chancellor 1946–87' (1989) 16 JLS 360

Brazier, M, 'Judicial immunity and the independence of the judiciary' [1976] PL 397

Brazier, R, 'Choosing a prime minister' [1982] PL 395

Brazier, R, 'Government and the law' [1989] PL 64

Brazier, R, *Constitutional Texts*, 1990, Oxford: Clarendon

Brazier, R, 'The downfall of Margaret Thatcher' (1991) 54 MLR 471

Brazier, R, 'Regulating ministers' and ex-ministers' finances' (1992) 43 NILQ 19

Brazier, R, 'Ministers in court: the personal legal liability of ministers' (1993) 44 NILQ 317

Brazier, R, 'It is a constitutional issue: fitness for ministerial office in the 1990s' [1994] PL 431

Brazier, R, *Constitutional Reform*, 2nd edn, 1998, Oxford: Clarendon

Brazier, R, *Constitutional Practice*, 3rd edn, 1999, Oxford: Clarendon

Bridges, L, Meszaros, G and Sunkin, M, 'Regulating the Judicial Review Caseload' (2000) PL 651

Bromhead, PA, *The House of Lords and Contemporary Politics*, 1958, London: Routledge & Kegan Paul

Brookfield, FM, 'The courts, Kelsen, and the Rhodesian revolution' (1969) 19 Toronto ULJ 326

Browne-Wilkinson (Lord), 'The independence of the judiciary in the 1980s' [1988] PL 44

Browne-Wilkinson (Lord), 'The infiltration of a Bill of Rights' [1992] PL 405

Bulloch, J, *MI5: The Origin and History of the British Counter-Espionage Service*, 1963, London: Arthur Barker

Bunyan, T, *The History and Practice of the Political Police in Britain*, 1977, London: Quartet

Burns, P, 'The law and privacy: the Canadian experience' (1976) 54 Canadian Bar Rev 1

Butler, D and Ranney, A (eds), *Referendums around the World*, 1994, Basingstoke: Macmillan

Butler, D, 'The Australian crisis of 1975' (1976) 29 Parl Aff 201

Butler, D, *Governing Without a Majority: Dilemmas for Hung Parliaments in Britain*, 1983, London: Collins

Butler, D, *British General Elections since 1945*, 1989, Oxford: Blackwell

Butterworths European Information Services, *Butterworths' Annual European Review*, 1994, London: Butterworths

Buxton, R 'The Future of Declarations of Incompatibility' (2010) Public Law 213

Byrne, A, *Local Government in Britain*, 7th edn, 2000, Harmondsworth: Penguin

Cabinet Office, *An Independent Review of Government Communications* (The Phillis report), 2004, London: The Cabinet Office

Cain, M and Hunt, A, *Marx and Engels on Law*, 1979, London: Academic

Callaghan, J, *Time and Chance*, 1987, London: Collins

Calvert, H, *Constitutional Law in Northern Ireland*, 1968, London: Stevens

Campbell, D and Young, J, 'The metric martyrs and the entrenchment jurisprudence of Lord Justice Laws' [2002] PL 399

Chambers, G, *Equality and Inequality in Northern Ireland, Part 2:The Workplace*, 1987, London: Policy Studies Institute

Chandler, JA, 'The plurality vote: a reappraisal' (1982) 30 Political Studies 87

Chester, N and Bowring, N, *Questions in Parliament*, 1962, Oxford: OUP

Chitty, J, *Law of the Prerogatives of the Crown*, 1820, London: Butterworths

Clarke, DN and Feldman, D, 'Arrest by any other name' [1979] Crim LR 702

Clayton, R and Tomlinson, H, *Civil Actions against the Police*, 2nd edn, 1992, London: Sweet & Maxwell

Clothier, C (Sir), 'Legal problems of an ombudsman' (1984) 81 Law Soc Gazette 3108

Coke, E (Sir), *Institutes of the Laws of England; Concerning the Jurisdiction of the Courts*, 1644

Collins, H, *Marxism and Law*, 1982, Oxford: Clarendon

Connolly, M and Loughlin, J, 'Reflections on the Anglo-Irish Agreement' (1986) 21 Government and Opposition 146

Convery, J, 'State liability in the United Kingdom after Brasserie du Pêcheur' (1997) 34 CML Rev 603

Cooke, Lord, 'The Law Lords: An Endangered Heritage' (2003) Law Quarterly Review 119:49

Coppel, J, 'Horizontal effect of directives' [1997] Industrial LJ 69

Cornford, T and Sunkin, M, 'Bowman, Access and the Recent Reforms of Judicial Review Procedure' (2001) PL 11

Cotterrell, RBM, 'The impact of sex discrimination legislation' [1981] PL 469

Cowen, DV, *Parliamentary Sovereignty and the Entrenched Sections of the South Africa Act*, 1951, Cape Town: Juta

Craig, P and de Búrca, G, *European Community Law*, 5th edn, 2011, Oxford: OUP

Craig, P, 'Judicial Review, Appeal and Factual Error' (2004) PL 788

Craig, PP and Rawlings, R (eds), *Law and Administration in Europe*, 2003, Oxford: OUP

Craig, PP and Schonberg, S, 'Substitute legitimate expectations after Coughlan' [2000] PL 684

Craig, PP, 'Dicey: unitary, self-correcting democracy and public law' (1990) 106 LQR 105

Craig, PP, 'Sovereignty of the United Kingdom after Factortame' (1991) 11 YBEL 221

Craig, PP, 'The common law, reasons and administrative justice' [1994] CLJ 282

Craig, PP, 'Directives: direct effect, indirect effect and the construction of national legislation' (1997) 22 EL Rev 519

Craig, PP, 'Competing models of judicial review' [1999] PL 428

Craig, PP, 'The courts, the Human Rights Act and judicial review' (2001) 117 LQR 589

Craig, PP, *Administrative Law*, 7th edn, 2012, London: Sweet & Maxwell

Craig, PP, 'The Human Rights Act, Article 6 and procedural rights' [2003] PL 753

Cranston, R, 'Disqualification of judges for interest or opinion' [1979] PL 237

Crossman, R, *The Diaries of a Cabinet Minister*, 1977, London: Jonathan Cape

Crossman, R, *Introduction to the English Constitution*, 1993, London: Fontana

Curtin, D, 'The province of government: delimiting the direct effect of directives in the common law context' (1990) 15 EL Rev 195

Curtin, D, 'The constitutional structure of the Union: a Europe of bits and pieces' (1993) 30 CML Rev 17

d'Entrèves, AP, *Natural Law*, 2nd edn, 1970, London: Hutchinson

Dale, W, *The Modern Commonwealth*, 1983, London: Butterworths

Daly, P, 'Justiciability and the "Political Question" Doctrine' (2010) PL 160

Dauses, M, 'The protection of fundamental right in the Community legal order' (1985) 10 EL Rev 398

David, R and Brierley, JEC, *Major Legal Systems*, 3rd edn, 1985, London: Sweet & Maxwell

de Búrca, G and Scott, J (eds), *From Uniformity to Flexibility*, 2000, London: Hart

de Búrca, G, 'A community of interests? Making the most of European law' (1992) 55 MLR 346 (1992a)

de Búrca, G, 'Giving effect to European Community directives' (1992) 55 MLR 215 (1992b)

de Búrca, G, 'The principle of subsidiarity and the Court of Justice as an institutional actor' (1998) 36(2) JCMS 217

de Smith, SA, *The New Commonwealth and its Constitutions*, 1964, London: Stevens

de Smith, SA and Brazier, R, *Constitutional and Administrative Law*, 8th edn, 1998, Harmondsworth: Penguin

de Smith, SA, Woolf, H and Jowell, J, Judicial Review of Administrative Action, 5th edn, 1995, Harmondsworth: Penguin

Deacon, R, *A History of the British Secret Service*, 1969, London: Frederick Muller (updated, 1980, London: Panther)

Denning (Lord), *Lord Denning's Report*, Cmnd 2152, 1963, London: TSO

Denning (Lord), *The Discipline of Law*, 1979, London: Butterworths

Denning (Lord), *The Due Process of Law*, 1980, London: Butterworths

Denning (Lord), *What Next in the Law?*, 1982, London: Butterworths

Denning (Lord), 'The Strauss case' [1985] PL 80

Devlin (Lord), 'Judges, government and politics' (1978) 41 MLR 501

Dhavan, R, 'Contempt of court and the *Phillimore Committee Report*' (1976) 5 Anglo-American L Rev 186

Dias, RWM, 'Legal politics: norms behind the *grundnorm*' [1968] CLJ 233

Dicey, AV, *Introduction to the Study of the Law of the Constitution* (1885), 10th edn, 1959, London: Macmillan

Dickson, B, 'Northern Ireland's emergency legislation: the wrong medicine' [1993] PL 592

Diplock (Lord), 'Administrative law: judicial review reviewed' [1974] CLJ 223

Doherty, M, 'Prime ministerial power and ministerial responsibility in the Thatcher era' (1988) 41 Parl Aff 49

Doig, A, 'Sleaze fatigue: the House of Ill-Repute' (2002) 55 Parliamentary Affairs 389

Donaldson, F, *The Marconi Scandal*, 1962, London: R Hart-Davis

Dougan, M, 'Case comment' (2001) 38 CML Rev 1503

Downes, A, 'Trawling for a remedy: state liability under Community law' (1997) LS 286

Drake, S, 'Twenty Years after Von Colson: The Impact of "Indirect Effect" on the Protection of the Individual's Community Rights' (2005) 30 EL Rev 329

Dremczewski, A, 'The domestic application of the European Human Rights Convention as European Community law' (1981) 30 ICLQ 118

Drewry, G and Butcher, T, *The Civil Service Today*, 1988, Oxford: Blackwell

Drewry, G, 'The Lord Chancellor as judge' (1972) 122 NLJ 855

Drewry, G (ed), *The New Select Committees*, 1989, Oxford: OUP

Drewry, G, 'Judicial inquiries and public reassurance' [1996] PL 368

Dworkin, A, *Pornography: Men Possessing Women*, 1981, London: Women's Press

Dworkin, R, *Taking Rights Seriously*, 1977, London: Duckworth

Dworkin, R, *A Matter of Principle*, 1986, Oxford: OUP

Dynes, M and Walker, D, *The Times Guide to the New British State: The Government Machine in the 1990s*, 1995, London: Times Books

Dyrberg, P, 'Current issues in the debate on public access to documents' (1999) 24 European L Rev 157

Editorial, 'The Treaty of Amsterdam: neither a bang nor a whimper' (1997) 34 CML Rev 767

Edwards, R, 'Judicial deference under the Human Rights Act' (2002) 65 MLR 859

Electoral Commission: *The Funding of Political Parties: Report and Recommendations* (2004)

Eleftheriadis, P, 'The direct effect of Community law: conceptual issues' (1996) 16 YBEL 205

Eliantoniom M, 'Europeanisation of Administrative Justice? The Influence of the ECJ's case law in Italy, Germany and England' (2010) European Review of Public Law 22.3: 681

Elliott, M, 'Coughlan: substantive protection of legitimate expectations revisited' (2000) 5 JR 27; (2000) 59 CLJ 421

Elliott, M, 'Has the Common Law duty to give reasons come of age yet?' (2011) Public Law 56

Emiliou, N, 'Subsidiarity: an effective barrier against "the enterprises of ambition"?' (1991) 17 EL Rev 383

Erskine May, T, *Parliamentary Practice*, 24th edn, 2011, London: Butterworths

Esher, RBB, *The Influence of King Edward: and Essays on Other Subjects*, 1915, London: John Murray

European Commission, 'Report from the Commission on monitoring the application of Community law' (2003) 21st Annual Report Com (2004) 839

Evans, JM, *Immigration Law*, 2nd edn, 1983, London: Sweet & Maxwell

Ewing, KD and Gearty, CA, *Freedom Under Thatcher*, 1990, Oxford: Clarendon

Ewing, KD, *The Funding of Political Parties*, 1987, Cambridge: CUP

Ewing, KD, 'The Futility of the Human Rights Act' (2004) PL 829

Fairgrieve, D, 'Pushing back the boundaries of public authority liability: tort law enters the classroom' [2002] PL 288

Fawcett, J, *The Application of the European Convention on Human Rights*, 1987, Oxford: Clarendon

Feldman, D, 'Parliamentary Scrutiny of Legislation and Human Rights' (2002) PL 323

Fenwick, H, *Civil Liberties & Human Rights*, 5th edn, 2011, London: Routledge-Cavendish

Fine, R, *Democracy and the Rule of Law: Liberal Ideals and Marxist Critiques*, 1984, London: Pluto

Finer, SE, 'The individual responsibility of ministers' (1956) 34 Public Admin 377

Finer, SE, *Anonymous Empire*, 1958, London: Pall Mall

Finer, SE, *Adversary Politics and Electoral Reform*, 1975, London: Anthony Wigram

Finer, SE, *The Changing British Party System*, 1980, Washington: AEI Studies

Finnis, JM, *Natural Law and Natural Rights*, 1980, Oxford: Clarendon

Forsyth, C, 'Judicial review, the royal prerogative' (1985) 36 NILQ 25

Foster, RF (ed), *The Oxford History of Ireland*, 1989, Oxford: OUP (1989a)

Foster, RF, *Modern Ireland 1600–1972*, 1989, Harmondsworth: Penguin (1989b)

Franklin, M and Norton, P, *Parliamentary Questions*, 1993, Oxford: Clarendon

Fredman, S, *Women and the Law*, 1997, Oxford: Clarendon

French, D, 'Spy fever in Britain 1900–15' (1978) 21 Historical Journal 355

Fry, GK, 'The Sachsenhausen concentration camp case and the convention of ministerial responsibility?' [1970] PL 336

Fuller, L, 'Positivism and fidelity to law – a reply to Professor Hart' (1958) 11 Harv L Rev 630

Fuller, L, *The Morality of Law*, 1964, New Haven: Yale UP

Galligan, DJ, 'The nature and functions of policies within discretionary power' [1976] PL 332

Ganz, G, *Quasi-legislation: Some Recent Developments in Secondary Legislation*, 1987, London: Sweet & Maxwell

Garton Ash, T, *The File: A Personal History*, 1997, London: HarperCollins

Gearty, G, *Terror*, 1991, London: Faber & Faber

Geddis, A, 'Free Speech Martyrs on Unreasonable Threats to Social Peace' (2004) PL 853

Geddis, A, 'Parliamentary Privilege: *Quis custodiet ipsos custodes?*' (2005) PL 696

Gibb, F, 'The Law Lord who took the rap over Pinochet' (1999) The Times, 19 October, p 3

Gilvarry, E, 'Selection changes to be urged' (1991) 88 Law Soc Gazette 6

Goodhart, AL, '*Thomas v Sawkins*: a constitutional innovation' [1936–38] CLJ 22

Goodhart, AL, *Essays in Jurisprudence and the Common Law*, 1931, Cambridge: CUP

Gordon, DM, 'What did the Anisminic case decide?' (1971) 34 MLR 1

Gould, BC, 'Anisminic and judicial review' [1970] PL 358

Gregory, R and Drewry, G, 'Barlow Clowes and the ombudsman: Part I' [1991] PL 192 (1991a)

Gregory, R and Drewry, G, 'Barlow Clowes and the ombudsman: Part II' [1991] PL 408 (1991b)

Griffith, JAG and Ryle, M, Parliament: Functions, Practice and Procedures, 2nd edn, 2003, London: Sweet & Maxwell

Griffith, JAG, 'Crichel Down: the most famous farm in British constitutional history' (1987) 1 Contemporary Record 35

Griffith, JAG, The Politics of the Judiciary, 5th edn, 1997, London: Fontana

Guest, AG (ed), Oxford Essays in Jurisprudence, 1961, Oxford: OUP

Gwynn, SL, The Life of Walpole, 1932, London: Butterworths

Hadfield, B, 'The Anglo-Irish Agreement 1985 – blue print or green print' (1986) 37 NILQ 1

Hadfield, B, The Constitution of Northern Ireland, 1989, Belfast: SLS

Hailsham (Lord), The Door Wherein I Went, 1975, London: Collins

Hailsham (Lord), The Dilemma of Democracy, 1978, London: Collins

Hale (Baroness), 'The Quest for Equal Treatment' (2005) PL 571

Hale, B (Dame), 'Equality and the judiciary – why should we want more women judges?' [2001] PL 489

Hale, M (Sir), The History of the Pleas of the Crown, 1736, Emlyn, S (ed), London: E and R Nott and R Gosling

Hamilton, E and Cairns, H (eds), Plato's Collected Dialogues, 1989, Ewing, New Jersey: Princeton UP

Hanks, PJ, Constitutional Law in Australia, 2nd edn, 1996, Sydney: Butterworths

Hansard Society, Making the Law, 1993, London: Hansard

Harlow, C (ed), Public Law and Politics, 1986, London: Sweet & Maxwell

Harris, DJ, O'Boyle, M and Warbrick, C, Law of the Convention on Human Rights, 1995, Edinburgh: Butterworths

Harris, J, Legal Philosophies, 1980, London: Butterworths

Hart, HLA, 'Positivism and the separation of law and morals' (1958) 71 Harv L Rev 593

Hart, HLA, The Concept of Law, 1961, Oxford: Clarendon

Hartley, T, The Foundations of European Community Law, 4th edn, 1998, Oxford: Clarendon

Harvey Cox, W, 'The Anglo-Irish Agreement' (1987) 40 Parl Aff 80

Hayhurst, JD and Wallington, P, 'The parliamentary scrutiny of delegated legislation' [1988] PL 547

Hazell, R, 'Freedom of information in Australia, Canada and New Zealand' (1989) 67 Public Admin 189

Headey, BW, British Cabinet Ministers: The Roles of Politicians in Executive Office, 1974, London: Allen & Unwin

Hennessy, P, 'Helicopter crashes into Cabinet: Prime Minister and constitution hurt' (1986) 13 JLS 423 (1986a)

Hennessy, P, Cabinet, 1986, Oxford: Blackwell (1986b)

Hennessy, P, Whitehall, 1990, London: Fontana

Herberg, JW, 'The right to reasons – palm trees in retreat?' [1991] PL 340

Heuston, RFV, Essays in Constitutional Law, 2nd edn, 1964, London: Stevens (1964a)

Heuston, RFV, Lives of the Lord Chancellors, 1885–1940, 1964, Oxford: Clarendon (1964b)

Heuston, RFV, Lives of the Lord Chancellors, 1940–70, 1987, Oxford: Clarendon

Hewart, CJ, The New Despotism, 1929, London: Benn

Heydon, JD, 'Illegally obtained evidence' [1973] Crim LR 690

Hickman, TR, 'The uncertain shadow . . .' [2004] PL 122

Hickman, TR, 'Between Human Rights and the Rule of Law: Indefinite Detention and the Derogation Model of Constitutionalism' (2005) MLR 655

Hilson, C, 'Judicial review, policies and the fettering of discretion' [2002] PL 111

HMSO, *Review of Intelligence on Weapons of Mass Destruction: Report of a Committee of Privy Counsellors*, 2004, London: The Stationery Office, HC 898

HMSO, 'Your Region, Your Choice, Revitalising the English Regions' (2002), Cm 5511

Hobbes, T, *The Leviathan* (1651), 1973, London: JM Dent

Hogg, PW and Monahan, P, *Liability of the Crown*, 3rd edn, 2000, London: Carswell

Holdsworth, W, 'The treaty making power of the Crown' (1942) 58 LQR 177

Holt, J, *Magna Carta*, 1965, Cambridge: CUP

Hooper, D, *Official Secrets: The Use and Abuse of the Act*, 1988, Sevenoaks: Coronet

Hope of Craighead (Lord), 'Voices from the Past – The Law Lords' Contribution to the Legislative Process' (2007) Law Quarterly Review, 123: 547

Howe, G, 'The Management of Public Inquiries' (1999) 70 Political Quarterly 294

Hughes, M, *Ireland Divided: The Roots of the Modern Irish Problem*, 1994, Cardiff: Wales UP

Hume, D, *An Enquiry Concerning the Principles of Morals* (1751), 1957, Indianapolis: Bobbs-Merrill

Hume, D, *Political Discourses* (1752), 1769, Edinburgh: Kineald and Donaldson

Hunt, M, 'The "horizontal effect" of the Human Rights Act' [1998] PL 423

Hunt (Lord), 'Access to a previous government's papers' [1982] PL 514

Hutchinson, A and Petter, A, 'Private rights/public wrongs: the liberal lie of the Charter' (1988) 38 Toronto ULJ 278

Hutchinson, AP and Monahan, P (eds), *The Rule of Law: Ideal or Ideology*, 1987, Toronto: Carswell

Identity Cards: a Summary of Findings from the consultation on Entitlement Cards and Identity Fraud, The Stationery Office, 2003, Cm 6019

Identity Cards: the next steps, The Stationery Office, 2003, Cm 6020

Ip, J, 'Al Rawi, Tariq, and the Future of Closed Material Procedures' [2012] 75 MLR 606

Irvine of Lairg (Lord), 'Judges and Decision-Makers: The Theory and Practice of *Wednesbury* Review' (1996) PL 59

Irvine (Lord), 'The development of human rights under an incorporated Convention on Human Rights' [1998] PL 221

Irvine (Lord), 'The impact of the Human Rights Act: Parliament, the courts and the executive [2003] PL 308

Itzin, C (ed), *Pornography: Women, Violence and Civil Liberties*, 1992, Oxford: OUP

Iyer, TKK, 'Constitutional law in Pakistan: Kelsen in the courts' (1973) 21 AJCL 759

Jackson, P and Leonard, P, *Constitutional and Administrative Law*, 8th edn, 2001, London: Sweet & Maxwell

Jacob, JM, 'From privileged Crown to interested public' [1993] PL 121

Jacobs, FG and White, RCA, *The European Convention on Human Rights*, 2nd edn, 1996, Oxford: Clarendon

Jaconelli, J, 'The "D notice" system' [1982] PL 37

Jalland, P, *The Liberals and Ireland: The Ulster Question in British Politics to 1914*, 1980, Hemel Hempstead: Harvester

James, R and Longley, D, 'The Channel Tunnel Rail Link, the Ombudsman and the Select Committee' [1996] PL 38

Jennings, I (Sir), *Cabinet Government*, 3rd edn, 1959, Cambridge: CUP (1959a)

Jennings, I (Sir), *The Law and the Constitution*, 5th edn, 1959, London: Hodder & Stoughton (1959b)

Jennings, I (Sir), *Parliament*, 2nd edn, 1969, Cambridge: CUP

Joint Committee on Human Rights Draft Bill of Rights for the UK, HL Paper 165-I; HC 150-I, The Stationery Office 2008

Jones, G (ed), *The New Government Agenda*, 1997, Hemel Hempstead: ICSA

Jones, T, 'Mistake of Fact in Administrative Law' (1990) PL 507

Jowell, J and Oliver, D (eds), *New Directions in Judicial Review*, 1988, London: Stevens

Jowell, J and Oliver, D (eds), *The Changing Constitution*, 7th edn, 2011, Oxford: OUP

Jowell, J, 'Of vires and vacuums: the constitutional context of judicial review' [1999] PL 448

Jowell, J, 'Beyond the rule of law: towards constitutional judicial review' [2000] PL 671

Jowell, J, 'Judicial deference: servility; civility or institutional capacity?' [2003] PL 592

Kafka, F, *The Trial*, Muir, E and Muir, W (trans), 1956, London: Secker & Warburg

Kavanagh, A, 'Defending Deference' (2010) 126 LQR 222

Keedy, ER, 'R v Sinnisiak: a remarkable murder trial' (1951) 100 Pennsylvania UL Rev 48

Keith, B, *The King, the Constitution, the Empire and Foreign Affairs: Letters and Essays 1936–37*, 1936, London: Longmans, Green

Keith-Lucas, B and Richards, PG, *A History of Local Government in the Twentieth Century*, 1979, London: Allen & Unwin

Kelsen, H, *The General Theory of Law and State*, 1961, New York: Russell

Kelsen, H, *The Pure Theory of Law*, 1967, Berkeley: California UP

Kenny, CS, 'The evolution of the law of blasphemy' [1992] CLJ 127

Kent, SK, *Sex and Suffrage in Britain 1860–1914*, 1987, Ewing, New Jersey: Princeton UP (rep 1990, London: Routledge)

King, ML, *Why We Can't Wait*, 1963, New York: Signet

Kingsford-Smith, D and Oliver, D (eds), *Economic With the Truth: The Law and Media in a Democratic Society*, 1990, Oxford: OUP

Klug, F and Starmer, K, 'Incorporation through the "front door": the first year of the Human Rights Act' [2001] PL 654

Krämer, L, *The EEC Treaty and Environmental Protection*, 1992, London: Sweet & Maxwell

Lambert, J, 'Executive authority to tap telephones' (1980) 43 MLR 59

Laski, H, *Reflections on the Constitution*, 1951, Manchester: Manchester UP

Laslett, P (ed), *Philosophy, Politics and Society*, 1975, Oxford: Blackwell

Laws, J (Sir), 'Is the High Court the guardian of fundamental constitutional rights?' [1993] PL 60

Le Queux, W, *German Spies in England*, 1915, London: S Paul

Leach, P, 'Birth certificates, privacy and human rights' (1998) 142 SJ 628

Leach, S, Stewart, J and Walsh, K (eds), *The Changing Organisation and Management of Local Government*, 1994, Basingstoke: Macmillan

Lee, HP, 'Reforming the Australian Constitution – the frozen continent refuses to thaw' [1988] PL 535

Lee, JJ, *Ireland 1912–85: Politics and Society*, 1990, Cambridge: CUP

Lee, S, 'The limits of parliamentary sovereignty' [1985] PL 633

Lee, S, 'And so to school' (1987) 103 LQR 166

Lee, S, *Judging Judges*, 1989, London: Faber & Faber

Legg, T (Sir), 'Judges for the new century' [2001] PL 62

Leigh, D and Vulliamy, E, *Sleaze: The Corruption of Parliament*, 1997, London: Fourth Estate

Leigh, D, *Betrayed: The Real Story of the Matrix Churchill Trial*, 1993, London: Bloomsbury

Leigh, I and Lustgarten, L, 'The Security Services Act 1989' (1989) 52 MLR 801

Leigh, I and Lustgarten, L, 'The Security Commission: constitutional achievement or curiosity?' [1991] PL 215

Leigh, I, 'A tapper's charter?' [1986] PL 8

Leigh, I, 'Spycatcher in Strasbourg' [1992] PL 200

Leigh, I, 'Matrix Churchill, supergun and the Scott Inquiry' [1993] PL 630

Leigh, I, 'By Law Established? The Crown, Constitutional Reform and the Church of England' (2004) PL 266

Legal Studies Special Issue, 'Constitutional Innovation: The Creation of a Supreme Court for the United Kingdom; Domestic, Comparative and International Reflections, 2, 3, 5, 7, 8, 9, 10' (2004)

Leopold, P, 'Leaks and squeaks in the Palace of Westminster' [1980] PL 368

Leopold, P, 'Freedom of speech in Parliament: its misuse and proposals for reform' [1981] PL 30

Leopold, P, '"Proceedings in Parliament": the grey area' [1991] PL 475

Lester (Lord), 'Fundamental rights' [1994] PL 70

Lester (Lord), 'First steps towards a constitutional Bill of Rights' (1997) 2 EHRLR 124

Lester, A, 'The Utility of the Human Rights Act: a Reply to Keith Ewing' (2005) PL 249

Le Sueur, A, 'The Rise and Ruin of Unreasonableness' (2005) Judicial Review 32

Linklater, M, Leigh, D with Mather, I, Not Without Honour: The Inside Story of the Westland Scandal, 1986, London: Sphere

Locke, J, Two Treatises of Government (1690), 1977, London: JM Dent

Lockyer, R, Tudor and Stuart Britain 1471–1714, 2nd edn, 1985, Harlow: Longman

Lustgarten, L and Leigh, I, In From the Cold: National Security and Parliamentary Democracy, 1994, Oxford: Clarendon

Lustgarten, L, The Legal Control of Racial Discrimination, 1980, London: Macmillan

Lustgarten, L, 'Racial inequality and the limits of law' (1981) 44 MLR 68

Lustgarten, L, 'Socialism and the rule of law' (1988) 15 JLS 25

Lysaght, CE, 'Irish peers and the House of Lords' (1967) 18 NILQ 277

MacCormick, DN, 'A note on privacy' (1973) 84 LQR 23

MacCormick, N, 'Does the United Kingdom have a constitution? Reflections on MacCormick v Lord Advocate' (1978) 29 NILQ 1

MacCormick, N, Questioning Sovereignty, 2001, Oxford: OUP

Macdermott (Lord), 'Law and order in times of emergency' [1972] Juridical Review 1

Mackay (Lord), The Administration of Justice, 1994, London: Stevens

Mackenzie, R, Free Elections, 1967, London: Allen & Unwin

Mackintosh, JP, The British Cabinet, 3rd edn, 1977, London: Stevens

MacMillan, CA, 'Burying treasure trove' (1996) 146 NLJ 1346

Macmillan, H, At the End of the Day (1961–63), 1973, London: Macmillan

Maitland, FW, The Constitutional History of England, 1908, Cambridge: CUP

Malleson, K, 'The Evolving Role of the UK Supreme Court' (2011) Public Law 754

Mancini, G and Keeling, D, 'From CILFIT to ERTA: the constitutional challenge facing the European Court' (1991) 11 YBEL 1

Markesinis, BS, The Theory and Practice of Dissolution of Parliament, 1972, Cambridge: CUP

Marsh, D and Read, M, Private Members' Bills, 1988, Cambridge: CUP

Marsh, NS, 'The declaration of Delhi' (1959) 2 J of the International Commission of Jurists 7

Marshall, G and Moodie, G, Some Problems of the Constitution, 5th edn, 1971, London: Hutchinson

Marshall, G, Parliamentary Sovereignty and the Commonwealth, 1957, Oxford: Clarendon

Marshall, G, Constitutional Theory, 1971, Oxford: Clarendon

Marshall, G, Constitutional Conventions, 1984, Oxford: Clarendon

Marshall, G, 'Cabinet Government and the Westland affair' [1986] PL 181 (1986a)

Marshall, G, 'The Queen's press relations' [1986] PL 505 (1986b)

Marshall, G (ed), Ministerial Responsibility, 1989, Oxford: Clarendon

Marshall, G, 'The end of prime ministerial government?' [1991] PL 1

Marshall, G, 'The referendum: what? when? how?' (1997) 50 Parl Aff 307

Martin, FX (ed), Leaders and Men of the Easter Rising: Dublin 1916, 1967, London: Methuen

Mathijsen, PSRF, A Guide to European Union Law, 7th edn, 1999, London: Sweet & Maxwell

McAuslan, P and McEldowney, JF, Legitimacy and the Constitution: The Dissonance between Theory and Practice in Law, 1985, London: Sweet & Maxwell

McAuslan, P, 'The Widdicombe Report: local government business or politics?' [1987] PL 154

McConville, M and Baldwin, J, 'Confessions: the dubious fruit of police interrogation' (1980) 130 NLJ 993

McConville, M and Hodgson, J, *Custodial Legal Advice and the Right to Silence*, RCCJ Research Study No 16, 1993, London: HMSO

McGarry, J, 'The Anglo-Irish Agreement and the prospects for power sharing in Northern Ireland' (1988) 59 Political Quarterly 236

McIlwain, CH, *The High Court of Parliament and its Supremacy*, 1910, New Haven: Yale UP

McIlwain, CH, *Constitutionalism, Ancient and Modern*, 1958, Ithaca, New York: Great Seal

McMurtie, SN, 'The waiting game – the Parliamentary Commissioner's response to delay in administrative procedures' [1997] PL 159

Mendelsen, M, 'The European Court of Justice and human rights' (1981) 1 YBEL 126

Miers, DR and Page, AC, *Legislation*, 2nd edn, 1990, London: Sweet & Maxwell

Mill, JS, *On Liberty* (1859), 1989, Cambridge: CUP

Mill, JS, *Representative Government* (1861), 1958, Indianapolis: Bobbs-Merrill

Mill, JS, *The Subjection of Women* (1869), 1989, Cambridge: CUP

Millar, E and Phillips, P, 'Evaluating anti-discrimination legislation in the United Kingdom: some issues and approaches' (1983) 11 Int J Soc L 417

Millett (Lord), 'The right to good administration in Europe' [2002] PL 309

Ministry of Justice: An Elected Second Chamber: Further Reform of the House of Lords, The Stationery Office 2008, Cm 7438

Ministry of Justice. Election Day: Weekend Voting CO 13/08, The Stationery Office 2008

Mitchell, JDB, 'Sovereignty of Parliament – yet again' (1963) 79 LQR 196

Mitchell, JDB, *Constitutional Law*, 2nd edn, 1968, Edinburgh: Green

Montesquieu, C, *De l'Esprit des Lois* (1748), 1989, Cambridge: CUP

Morgan, JP, *The House of Lords and the Labour Government 1964–1970*, 1975, Oxford: OUP

Morrison (Lord), *Government and Parliament*, 3rd edn, 1964, Oxford: OUP

Morton, G, *Home Rule and the Irish Question*, 1980, Harlow: Longman

Mosley, RK, *The Story of the Cabinet Office*, 1969, London: Routledge & Kegan Paul

Mummery, DR, 'The privilege of freedom of speech in Parliament' (1978) 94 LQR 276

Munday, R, 'Inferences from silence and European human rights law' [1996] Crim LR 370

Munro, CR, 'Laws and conventions distinguished' (1975) 91 LQR 224

Munro, CR, 'Press freedom: how the beast was tamed' (1991) 54 MLR 104

Munro, CR, 'Power to the people' [1997] PL 579

Munro, CR, *Studies in Constitutional Law*, 2nd edn, 1999, London: Butterworths

Munro, CR, 'Privilege at Holyrood' [2000] PL 347

Murphy, C, 'An Effective Right to Cross-border Healthcare?. . . Comment on Elchinov' (2011) European Current Law Yearbook, cxv

Naffine, N, 'Windows on the legal mind: evocations of rape in legal writing' (1992) 18 Melbourne UL Rev 741

Naffine, N, 'Possession: erotic love in the law of rape' (1994) 57 MLR 10

Neumann, F, *The Rule of Law: Political Theory and the Legal System in Modern Society*, 1986, Leamington Spa: Berg

Newburn, T, *The Settlement of Claims at the Criminal Injuries Commission Compensation Board*, Home Office Research Study No 112, 1989, London: HMSO

Newburn, T, *Crime and Criminal Justice Policy*, 2003, Harlow: Longman

Newton, K and Karran, TJ (eds), *The Politics of Local Expenditure*, 1985, London: Macmillan

Nicolson, IF, *The Mystery of Crichel Down*, 1986, Oxford: Clarendon

Norton, P, *Parliament in the 1980s*, 1985, Oxford: Blackwell (1985a)

Norton, P, *The Commons in Perspective*, 2nd edn, 1985, Oxford: Blackwell (1985b)

Norton, P, 'Televising the House of Commons' (1991) 44 Parl Aff 185

Norton, P, *Does Parliament Matter?*, 1993, Hemel Hempstead: Harvester

Norton-Taylor, R, *Truth is a Difficult Concept: Inside the Scott Inquiry*, 1995, London: Fourth Estate

Nozick, R, *Anarchy, State and Utopia*, 1974, Oxford: Blackwell

O'Cinneide, C, 'The Race Relations (Amendment) Act 2000' [2001] PL 220

O'Connor, U, *The Troubles: The Struggle for Irish Freedom 1912–1922*, 1989, London: Mandarin

O'Halpin, E, *The Decline of the Union: British Government in Ireland 1892–1920*, 1987, Dublin: Gill and Macmillan

O'Keefe, D and Twomey, PM (eds), *Legal Issues of the Maastricht Treaty*, 1994, London: Chancery

Oliver, D and Austin, R, 'Political and constitutional aspects of the Westland affair' (1987) 40 Parl Aff 20

Oliver, D, 'Reform of the electoral system' [1983] PL 108

Oliver, D, 'Is the *ultra vires* rule the basis of judicial review?' [1987] PL 543

Oliver, D, '*Pepper v Hart*: a suitable case for reference to Hansard?' [1993] PL 5

Oliver, D, 'The frontiers of the state: public authorities and public functions under the Human Rights Act' [2000] PL 476

Oliver, D, 'Public law procedures and remedies – do we need them?' [2001] PL 91

Oliver, D, *Constitutional Reform in the United Kingdom*, 2003, Oxford: OUP

Oliver, D, 'Functions of a Public Nature under the Human Rights Act' (2004) PL 329

Olley, K, 'Proportionality at Common Law' (2004) 9 Judicial Review 197

Olowofoyeku, AA, 'The *nemo judex* rule: the case against automatic disqualification' [2000] PL 456

Owen Dixon, J, 'The law and the constitution' (1935) 51 LQR 611

Padfield, N, 'The Anti-social Behaviour Act 2003: the ultimate nanny-state Act?' (2004) Crim LR 712

Paine, T, *Rights of Man* (1791, Pt I), 1984, rep 1998, Collins, H (ed), New York: Penguin

Paine, T, *Rights of Man* (1792, Pt II), 1984, rep 1998, Collins, H (ed), New York: Penguin

Palley, C, 'The evolution, disintegration and possible reconstruction of the Northern Ireland Constitution' (1972) 1 Anglo-American L Rev 368

Palley, C, *The United Kingdom and Human Rights*, 1991, London: Sweet & Maxwell

Palmer, S, 'Tightening secrecy law' [1990] PL 243

Pannick, D, *Sex Discrimination Law*, 1985, Oxford: Clarendon

Parpworth, N, 'The Parliamentary Standards Act 2009: A Constitutional Dangerous Dogs Measure?' (2010) 73 MLR 262

Parpworth, N, 'Arrest Under PACE – Part 1 (2011) 175 Criminal Law and Justice Weekly JPN 528

Parpworth, N, 'Arrest Under PACE – Part 2 (2011) 175 Criminal Law and Justice Weekly JPN 543

Pennock, JR and Chapman, JW (eds), *Political and Legal Obligation*, 1970, New York: Atherton

Pescatore, P, 'The "doctrine of direct effect": an infant disease of Community law' (1983) 8 EL Rev 155

Petite, M, 'The Treaty of Amsterdam' (http://centers.law.nyu.edu/jeanmonnet/archive/papers/98/98-2-.html)

Philby, K, *My Silent War*, 1968, London: MacGibbon and Kee

Phythian, M and Little, W, 'Parliament and arms sales: lessons of the Matrix Churchill affair' (1993) 46 Parl Aff 293

Pincher, C, *Their Trade is Treachery*, 1981, London: Sidgwick and Jackson

Plamenatz, J, *Man and Society*, 1963, New York: Longman

Plucknett, TFT, 'Dr Bonham's Case and judicial review' (1926) 40 Harv L Rev 30

Poole, KP, 'The Northern Ireland Commissioner for Complaints' [1972] PL 131

Powell, E and Wallis, K, *The House of Lords in the Middle Ages*, 1968, London: Weidenfeld & Nicolson

Priestley, J, *An Essay on the First Principles of Government; and on the Nature of Political, Civil, and Religious Liberty, including remarks on Dr Brown's Code of Education, and on Dr Balguy's Sermon on Church Authority*, 2nd edn, 1771, London: J Johnson

Pugh, I (Sir), 'The ombudsman – jurisdiction, power and practice' (1978) 56 Public Admin 127

Ramsay, P, 'What is anti-social behaviour?' (2004) Crim LR 908

Ranelagh, J, *A Short History of Ireland*, 1983, Cambridge: CUP

Rasmussen, H, 'The European Court's acte clair strategy in CILFIT' (1984) 9 EL Rev 242

Rasmussen, H, 'Between self-restraint and activism; a judicial policy for the European Court' (1988) 13 EL Rev 28

Rawlings, HF, Law and the Electoral Process, 1988, London: Sweet & Maxwell

Rawls, J, A Theory of Justice, 1973, rev edn 1999, Oxford: OUP

Raz, J, The Authority of Law, 1979, Oxford: OUP

Redmayne, M, 'Hearsay and Human Rights: Al-Khawaja in the Grand Chamber' (2012) Modern Law Review 75: 865

Reed, C (ed), Computer Law, 2nd edn, 1993, London: Blackstone

Reid (Lord), 'The judge as lawmaker' [1972] JSPTL 22

Richardson, G and Genn, H (eds), Administrative Law and Government Action, 1994, Oxford: OUP

Riddell, P, 'Quality control deficiency that lets down the law' (1994) The Times, 16 December

Ridley, FF, 'There is no British Constitution: a dangerous case of the Emperor's clothes' (1988) 41 Parl Aff 340

Roberts, M, 'Public law representations and substantive legitimate expectations' (2001) 64 MLR 112

Roberts-Wray, K, Commonwealth and Colonial Law, 1966, London: Stevens

Robertson, AH and Merrills, JG, Human Rights in Europe, 3rd edn, 1993, Manchester: Manchester UP

Robertson, G, Obscenity, 1979, London: Weidenfeld

Robertson, G, Freedom, the Individual and the Law, 7th edn, 2001, Harmondsworth: Penguin

Robilliard, StJ, 'Offences against religion and public worship' (1981) 44 MLR 556

Rose, R, 'Law as a resource of public policy' (1986) 39 Parl Aff 297

Ross, M, 'Beyond Francovich' (1993) 56 MLR 55

Rousseau, J, The Social Contract and Discourses (1762), 1977, London: JM Dent

Rowbottom, J, 'The Electoral Commission's Proposals on the Funding of Political Parties' (2005) PL 468

Ryle, M and Richards, G (eds), The Commons Under Scrutiny, 3rd edn, 1988, London: Routledge & Kegan Paul

Sales, P and Steyn, K, 'Legitimate Expectations in English Public Law: An Analysis' (2004) PL 564

Sampford, CJG, ' "Recognize and declare": an Australian experiment in codifying constitutional conventions' (1987) 7 OJLS 369

Samuals, A, 'Anti-social Behaviour Orders: Their legal and jurisprudential significance' (2005) 69 J Crim L 223

Savage, N and Edwards, C, A Guide to the Data Protection Act 1985, 1985, London: Financial Training

Sawer, G, Australian Federalism in the Courts, 1967, Melbourne: Melbourne UP

Sawer, G, Federation Under Strain, 1977, Melbourne: Melbourne UP

Schermers, HG, Judicial Protection in the European Community, 4th edn, 1987, Dordrecht: Kluwer

Schermers, HG, 'The European Community bound by fundamental human rights' (1990) 27 CML Rev 249

Schutze, R, 'From Rome to Lisbon: "Executive Federalism" in the (new) European Union' (2010) 47 Common Market Law Review 1385

Schwarze, J, European Administrative Law, 1992, Luxembourg: Office for Official Publications of the European Communities

Scott, J, Development Dilemmas in the EC: Rethinking Regional Development Policy, 1995, Milton Keynes: OU Press

Scott, J, European Community Environmental Law, 1998, London: Longman

Scott, R, 'Procedures at Inquiries: The Duty to be Fair' (1995) 111 LQR 596

Scott, R (Sir), 'Ministerial accountability' [1996] PL 410

Seaborne Davies, D, 'The House of Lords and the criminal law' (1962) 6 JSPTL 104

Sharpe, LG, 'Theories and values of local government' (1970) 18 Political Studies 153

Shaw, J, Law of the European Union, 3rd edn, 2000, Basingstoke: Palgrave

Shaw, J, 'Europe's Constitutional Future' (2005) PL 132

Shell, D, 'The House of Lords and the Thatcher government' (1983) 38 Parl Aff 16

Shell, D, The House of Lords, 2nd edn, 1992, London: Harvester

Silk, P and Walters, R, How Parliament Works, 1987, London: Longman

Simmonds, KR, 'The British Islands and the Community: II Isle of Man' (1970) 7 CMLR 454

Simmonds, KR, 'The British Islands and the Community: III Guernsey' (1971) 8 CMLR 475

Simon Brown LJ, 'Public interest immunity' [1994] PL 579

Slapper, G and Kelly, D, The English Legal System, 8th edn, 2006, Abingdon: Routledge-Cavendish

Slot, PJ, 'Case C-194/94: CIA Security International SA v Signalson SA and Securitel SPRL' (1996) 33 CML Rev 1035

Slynn, G, 'The Court of Justice of the European Community' (1984) 33 ICLQ 409

Smart, C, Feminism and the Power of Law, 1989, London: Routledge

Smith, ATH, 'Dicey and civil liberties: comment' [1985] PL 608

Smith, DJ, 'Policy and research: employment discrimination in Northern Ireland' (1988) 9(1) Policy Studies 41

Spalin, E, 'Abortion, speech and the European Community' [1992] J of Social Welfare and Family Law 17

Spjut, RJ, 'Internment and detention without trial in Northern Ireland' (1986) 49 MLR 712

Stanton, J, 'Local Democracy, Economic Development and Construction Act 2009: a reinvigorated local democracy?' (2010) PL 1

Steele, I, 'Judging Judicial Inquiries' [2004] PL 738

Steiner, J and Woods, L, Textbook on EC Law, 8th edn, 2003, Oxford: OUP

Steiner, J, 'From direct effects to Francovich: shifting means of enforcement of Community law' (1993) 18(3) EL Rev 3

Steiner, J, Enforcing EC Law, 1995, London: Blackstone

Stephens, L, The Science of Ethics (1882), 1972, Newton Abbot: David and Charles

Stewart, J and Stoker, J (eds), The Future of Local Government, 1989, Basingstoke: Macmillan

Steyn (Lord), 'The Case for a Supreme Court' (2002) Law Quarterly Review 118: 382

Steyn (Lord), 'Deference: a Tangled Story' (2005) PL 346

Stubbs, W, The Constitutional History of England: In its Origin and Development, 1880, Oxford: Clarendon

Sunkin, M, 'Crown immunity from criminal liability in English law' [2003] PL 716

Sunkin, M, 'Pushing Forward the Frontiers of Human Rights Protection' (2004) PL 643

Supperstone, M and Cavanagh, J, Immigration, 3rd edn, 1994, London: Longman

Supperstone, M, 'The Intelligence Services Act 1994' [1994] PL 329

Szyszczack, E, 'Sovereignty: crisis, compliance, confusion, complacency?' (1990) 15(6) EL Rev 483

Tebbitt, N, Upwardly Mobile, 1988, London, Weidenfeld & Nicolson

Temple-Lang, J, 'Community constitutional law: Article 5 EC Treaty' (1990) 27 CML Rev 645

Thatcher, M, The Downing Street Years, 1993, London: HarperCollins

Thompson, WI, The Imagination of an Insurrection: Dublin, Easter 1916, 1967, Oxford: OUP

Thoreau, HD, Resistance to Civil Government (1848), 2nd edn, 1992, Rossi, W (ed), London: Norton

Thornberry, CHR, 'Dr Soblen and the alien law of the United Kingdom' (1963) 12 ICLQ 414

Thorne, SE, 'Dr Bonham's Case' (1938) 54 LQR 543

Thornton, GC, Legislative Drafting, 3rd edn, 1987, London: Butterworths

Tomkins, A, 'Public interest immunity after Matrix Churchill' [1993] PL 650

Tomkins, A, 'Government information and Parliament: misleading by design or by default?' [1996] PL 472

Tomkins, A, The Constitution after Scott: Government Unwrapped, 1998, Oxford: Clarendon

Tomkins, A, 'Readings of A v Secretary of State for the Home Department' (2005) PL 259

Toth, AG, 'The principle of subsidiarity in the Maastricht Treaty' (1992) CML Rev 1079

Trevor-Roper, H, *The Philby Affair: Espionage, Treason and Secret Service*, 1968, London: Kimber

Tur, R and Twining, W (eds), *Essays on Kelsen*, 1986, Oxford: Clarendon

Turnbull, M, *The Spycatcher Trial*, 1988, London: Heinemann

Twomey, A, 'Changing the Rules of Succession to the Throne' (2011) Public Law 378

Uglow, S, *Criminal Justice*, 2002, London: Sweet & Maxwell

Urban, M, *UK Eyes Alpha: The Inside Story of British Intelligence*, 1997, London: Faber & Faber

Usher, J, 'The Reception of General Principles of Community Law in the United Kingdom' (2005) 16 European Business Law Review 489

Van Dijk, P and Van Hoof, G, *Theory and Practice of the European Convention on Human Rights*, 2nd edn, 1990, Deventer, Netherlands: Kluwer

Vile, MJC, *Constitutionalism and the Separation of Powers*, 1967, Oxford: Clarendon

von Hayek, F, *The Road to Serfdom* (1944), 1994, London: Routledge & Kegan Paul

von Hayek, F, *The Constitution of Liberty*, 1960, London: Routledge & Kegan Paul

Wade, ECS, 'Act of State in English law' (1934) 15 BYIL 98

Wade, HWR and Forsyth, CF, *Administrative Law*, 10th edn, 2009, Oxford: OUP

Wade, HWR, 'The basis of legal sovereignty' [1955] CLJ 177

Wade, HWR, 'Constitutional and administrative aspects of the *Anisminic* case' (1969) 85 LQR 198

Wade, HWR, 'Procedure and prerogative in public law' (1985) 101 LQR 180

Wade, HWR, *Constitutional Fundamentals*, rev edn, 1989, London: Stevens

Wade, HWR, 'Sovereignty – revolution or evolution' (1996) 112 LQR 568

Wade, HWR, 'Horizons of horizontality' [2000] LQR 217

Wagner, A and Squibb, GD, 'Precedence and courtesy titles' (1973) 89 LQR 352

Walker, C, 'Review of the prerogative' [1987] PL 63

Walker, C, 'The Threat of Terrorism and Fate of Control Orders' (2010) Public Law 4

Wallington, P (ed), *Civil Liberties*, 1984, Oxford: Martin Robertson

Walsh, D, *The Use and Abuse of Emergency Legislation in Northern Ireland*, 1983, London: The Cobden Trust

Wasserstrom, R, 'The obligation to obey the law' (1963) California UL Rev 780

Watkins, A, *A Conservative Coup*, 1992, London: Duckworth

Watson, J, 'Experience and problems in applying Article 177 EEC' (1986) 23 CML Rev 207

Watt, D, 'Fallout from treachery: Peter Wright and the Spycatcher case' [1988] Political Quarterly 206

Weatherill, S and Beaumont, P, *EU Law*, 3rd edn, 1999, Harmondsworth: Penguin

West, N, *MI5: British Security Service Operations 1909–45*, 1981, London: Bodley Head

West, N, *A Matter of Trust: MI5 1945–72*, 1983, London: Hodder & Stoughton

West, N, *GCHQ: The Secret Wireless War 1900–86*, 1986, London: Weidenfeld & Nicolson

Wheare, KC, *The Constitutional Structure of the Commonwealth*, 1960, Oxford: Clarendon

Wheare, KC, *Federal Government*, 4th edn, 1963, Oxford: OUP

Wheare, KC, *Modern Constitutions*, 2nd edn, 1966, Oxford: OUP

White, F and Hollingsworth, K, 'Public finance reform: the Government Resources and Account Act 2000' [2001] PL 50

White paper: *A New Future for Communications*, The Stationery Office, 2000, Cm 5010

White paper: *Respect and Responsibility – taking a stand against anti-social behaviour*, The Stationery Office, 2003, Cm 5778

Williams, DGT, *Not in the Public Interest*, 1965, London: Hutchinson

Williams, DGT, 'Telephone tapping' [1979] CLJ 225

Williams, DGT, 'Public order and common law' [1984] PL 12

Williams, G, *Learning the Law*, ATH Smith (ed), 12th edn, 2002, London: Sweet & Maxwell

Williams, L, 'Defining a sufficiently serious breach of Community law: the House of Lords casts its net into the waters' (2000) 25(4) EL Rev 452

Wilson, H, *The Labour Government 1964–70: A Personal Record*, 1971, London: Weidenfeld & Nicolson

Wilson, H, *The Governance of Britain*, 1976, London: Weidenfeld & Nicolson

Wilson, R (Sir), 'The Civil Service in the New Millennium', unpublished speech, May 1999

Winter, T, 'Direct applicability and direct effect: two distinct and different concepts in Community law' (1972) 9 CML Rev 425

Wolf-Phillips, L, 'A long look at the British Constitution' (1984) 37 Parl Aff 385

Woodhouse, D, 'Ministerial responsibility in the 1990s: when do ministers resign?' (1993) 46 Parl Aff 277

Woodhouse, D, 'Ministerial responsibility: something old, something new' [1997] PL 262

Wormald, J, 'James VI and I: Two Kings or one?' (1983) 68 History 187

Wright, P, *Spycatcher: The Candid Autobiography of a Senior Intelligence Officer*, 1987, New York: Viking

Young, AL, 'In Defence of Due Deference' (2010) 72 MLR 554

Young, AJ, 'Is Dialogue Working under the Human Rights Act 1998?' (2011) Public Law 773

Young, H, *The Crossman Affair*, 1976, London: Hamish Hamilton

Young, H, *One of Us*, 1989, London: Macmillan

Zander, M, 'When is an arrest not an arrest?' (1997) 147 NLJ 379

Zander, M, *Cases and Materials on the English Legal System*, 9th edn, 2003, London: Butterworths

Zellick, GJ, 'Government beyond law' [1985] PL 283

Zuckerman, AAS, 'Public interest immunity – a matter of prime judicial responsibility' (1994) 57 MLR 703

WEBSITES

Government

www.cabinetoffice.gov.uk
www.cabinetoffice.gov.uk/news/coalition-documents
www.homeoffice.gov.uk

Case law

www.criminallawandjustice.co.uk
www.baillii.org

Devolution and Local government

www.bcomm-wales.gov.uk
http://www.niassembly.gov.uk
http://www.northernireland.gov.uk
http://www.scottish.parliament.uk
http://www.scotland.gov.uk
http://www.assemblywales.org
http://www.wales.gov.uk
http://www.lga.gov.uk
http://www.directgov.uk

Elections and referendums

www.electoralcommission.org.uk

Public Inquiries

http://www.the-shipman-inquiry.org.uk.
http://www.publicinquiries.org
http://www.the-hutton-inquiry.org.uk.
http://www.bloody-sunday-inquiry.org
http://www.iraqinquiry.org.uk
http://www.detainteeinquiry.org.uk
http://www.levesoninquiry.org.uk

European Union

www.europa.eu/index_en.htm

Index